THE CAMBRIDGE HISTORY OF ISLAM

IN TWO VOLUMES

Volume 2

THE CAMBRIDGE HISTORY OF ISLAM

Volume 2

THE FURTHER ISLAMIC LANDS, ISLAMIC SOCIETY AND CIVILIZATION

edited by

P. M. HOLT

Professor of Arab History in the University of London

ANN K. S. LAMBTON

Professor of Persian in the University of London

BERNARD LEWIS

Professor of the History of the Near and Middle East in the University of London

CAMBRIDGE

AT THE UNIVERSITY PRESS

1970

Published by the Syndics of the Cambridge University Press
Bentley House, 200 Euston Road, London N.W.1
American Branch: 32 East 57th Street, New York, N.Y. 10022

Library of Congress Catalogue Card Number: 73-77291

Standard Book Number: 521 07601 3

Printed in Great Britain
Spottiswoode, Ballantyne & Co. Ltd.
London and Colchester

CONTENTS

ACKNOWLEDGMENTS

The editors are grateful to the following for granting permission to reproduce these illustrations:

The Trustees of the British Museum for plates 12b and 18b.

Victoria and Albert Museum. Crown Copyright for plates 29a, 31b, 32a and 32b.

The Department of Eastern Art, The Ashmolean Museum for plates 6a, 6b, 17a, 17b, 17c and 17d.

Edinburgh University Library for plate 25a.

The Metropolitan Museum of Art, Bequest of Cora Timken Burnett, 1957 for plate 19a.

The Metropolitan Museum of Art, Bequest of Cora Timken Burnett, 1957 for plate 25b.

The Metropolitan Museum of Art, Rogers Fund, 1917 for plate 26.

Courtesy of the Smithsonian Institution, Freer Gallery of Art, Washington, D.C. for plates 6d and 22a.

A Survey of Persian Art, Oxford, 1939, Re-issue Asia Institute Shiraz, 1966 for plates 3b and 18a.

Dr Edmund de Unger for plates 6c, 8b, 12a, 28a and 31a.

Mr David Stronach for plates 10b and 13.

Paul Hamlyn Publishers Ltd., for plate 20a.

Dr J. Ellman for plate 23a.

Mr R. Hillenbrand for plates 24a and 24b.

Professor Oktay Aslanapa for plate 20b.

Mr Nuri Arlasez for plate 29b.

Mr R. Jairazbhoy for plate 10a.

Dr Abdul Aziz Hameed for plate 5a.

Dr G. Fehervari for plates 1a, 1b, 2a, 4a, 4b, 5c, 7a, 7b, 8a, 9b, 11, 14a, 14b, 15a, 15b, 16a, 16b, 21a, 21b, 22b, 23b, 27a, 28b, 30 and 27b.

LIST OF PLATES

LIST OF MAPS

PREFACE

The aim of these volumes is to present the history of Islam as a cultural whole. It is hoped that in a single concise work the reader will be able to follow all the main threads: political, theological, philosophical, economic, scientific, military, artistic. But *The Cambridge history of Islam* is not a repository of facts, names and dates; it is not intended primarily for reference, but as a book for continuous reading. The editors believe that, while it will not be despised by the expert orientalist, it will be useful to students in other fields of history, and particularly to university students of oriental subjects, and will also appeal to those who read history for intellectual pleasure.

A standardized system of translation has been employed for proper names and technical terms in the three principal Islamic languages—Arabic, Persian and Turkish. Some anomalies have, however, been inevitable, and place-names which have a widely accepted conventional spelling have been given in that form. Dates before the nineteenth century have normally been given according to both the Islamic (*Hijrī*) and Christian eras. Footnotes have been used sparingly; principally to give references for quotations or authority for conclusions in the text. The bibliographies are not intended as an exhaustive documentation of the subjects to which they refer, but as a guide to further reading. For this reason, and to avoid extensive repetition of titles, many of the bibliographies have been consolidated to cover two or more related contributions.

The editors are responsible for the planning and organisation of the work as a whole. They have tried to avoid gaps and overlaps, and have given general guidance to contributors, designed to secure some consistency of form and presentation. The individual authors are, of course, responsible for their own opinions and interpretations.

The editors wish to express their thanks to all who have assisted in the preparation of this work. They are particularly grateful to those who undertook the translation of contributions or gave advice and sub-editorial assistance, especially Mr J. G. Burton-Page, Professor C. D. Cowan, Dr J. F. P. Hopkins, Dr A. I. Sabra, Professor H. R. Tinker, Col. Geoffrey Wheeler and Dr D. T. Whiteside. They would also like to thank members of the staff of the Cambridge University Press for their invariable patience and helpfulness.

THE EDITORS

INTRODUCTION

P. M. Holt[1]

A reader taking up a work entitled *The Cambridge history of Islam* may reasonably ask, 'What is Islam? In what sense is Islam an appropriate field for historical enquiry?' Primarily, of course, Islam is, like Christianity, a religion, the antecedents, origin and development of which may, without prejudice to its transcendental aspects, be a legitimate concern of historians. Religious history in the narrow sense is not, however, the only, or even the main, concern of the contributors to these volumes. For the faith of Islam has, again like Christianity, been a great synthesizing agent. From its earliest days it displayed features of kinship with the earlier monotheisms of Judaism and Christianity. Implanted in the former provinces of the Byzantine and Sasanian empires, it was compelled to maintain and define its autonomy against older and more developed faiths. Like Judaism and Christianity before it, it met the challenge of Greek philosophy, and adopted the conceptual and logical tools of this opponent to expand, to deepen, and to render articulate its self-consciousness. In this connexion, the first three centuries of Islam, like the first three centuries of Christianity, were critical for establishing the norms of belief and practice, and for embodying them in a tradition which was, or which purported to be, historical.

The Islamic synthesis did not stop at this stage. The external frontier of Islam has continued to move until our own day. For the most part, this movement has been one of expansion—into Central Asia, into the Indian sub-continent and south-east Asia, and into trans-Saharan Africa—but there have also been phases of retreat and withdrawal, notably in Spain, and in central and south-eastern Europe. But besides this external frontier, which has largely been the creation of conquering armies, (although with important exceptions in Central and south-east Asia and Africa) there has also been throughout Islamic history an internal frontier—the invisible line of division between Muslim and non-Muslim. Here also over the centuries there has been an expansion of Islam, so that, for example, in the former Byzantine and Sasanian lands the Christian and Zoroastrian communities were reduced to numerical insignificance, and became minority-groups like the Jews. This twofold expansion has brought new elements into the Islamic synthesis,

[1] I should like to thank my co-editors, Professors Lambton and Lewis, for reading and commenting on this Introduction in draft.

some permanent and widely accepted, others more transient or local in their effects.

The process of synthesization has not gone forward in a political vacuum. Unlike the early Christian Church, the Islamic *Umma*, or community of believers, achieved political power from the outset, and was organized for mutual support in the maintenance of the faith. This concern of the community for the faith survived the break-up of the caliphate and the emergence of new and often transitory régimes. It has taken various forms. Two of the principal institutions of Islam, *Sharīʿa* and *Jihād*, the Holy Law and the Holy War, are expressions of the concern in its conservative and militant aspects respectively—aspects moreover which are not wholly distinct, since the Holy War is fought in defence of the Holy Law against its external and internal enemies. In political matters as in others, Islam adopted and incorporated contributions from many sources. The successors of the Prophet as heads of his community drew on the customs of Arab tribal leadership, as well as the usages of the Meccan trading oligarchy. They inherited the legacy of Byzantine administration, as well as the traditions of the Sasanian monarchy. Later rulers were influenced by other political concepts: those brought into the medieval Islamic world by Turkish and Mongol immigrants from the steppes, and in the latest age the constitutional and legal doctrines of liberal Europe, followed by the seductive panaceas of totalitarianism.

Islam, then, as it will be examined in the following chapters, is a complex cultural synthesis, centred in a distinctive religious faith, and necessarily set in the framework of a continuing political life. The religion, the culture, and the political structures alike present many features which seem familiar to an observer whose own background is that of Christian Europe. It could hardly be otherwise, since elements derived from Judaism and Hellenism are common to both the Islamic and the Christian syntheses; since, furthermore, the histories of the Islamic community and of Christendom have touched so often and at so many points. But consciousness of the similarities must always be balanced by an awareness of the characteristic and substantial differences. Like Christianity, Islam is a monotheism with an historical founder and a sacred book; although its theology in regard to both differs essentially from Christian theology. There is also a perceptible difference in the criteria of membership of the community. Whereas in Christianity acceptance of the catholic creeds has been the basic criterion, in Islam credal theology has been of less relative importance; adherence to the Holy Law is the characteristic manifestation of faith, and hence orthopraxy rather than orthodoxy has been the usual token of membership. Another difference is that Islam has no equivalent to the Christian sacraments (although certain practices, notably the Fast of Ramaḍān and the Pilgrimage, appear to have an unacknowledged quasi-sacramental character), and no priesthood, although the '*ulamā'*' (the religious scholars) and the leaders of the Ṣūfī orders (two groups at some times and in some places closely interconnected) have often played a part in Muslim societies analogous to that of the clergy amongst Christians. The absence of a sacerdotal hierarchy, or of any conciliar system, to define the faith, linked with the primacy ascribed to orthopraxy, has made Islam more tolerant of variations of belief than Christianity. It is in general true to say that heresy (to use a term not quite appropriate in Islam) has been repressed only when it has been manifested as political subversion: it is also true to say that, since Islam is both a religious and a political community, the distinction between religious and political dissent is not clearcut.

Another question which the reader of this work may ask is, 'What are the sources on which knowledge of the history of Islam is based?' The Islamic civilization of the first three centuries (in this as in other respects the seminal period) evolved two characteristic types of historical writing. The first of these was the chronicle, of which the outstanding classical example is that composed by al-Ṭabarī (d. 310/923). But behind the chronicle lay diverse historiographical elements—the sagas and genealogies of the pre-Islamic Arab tribes, the semi-legendary narratives of the Persian kings, and, serving as the central theme to which all others were subservient, the career of the Prophet and the vicissitudes of the *Umma* which he founded. The early historians were primarily religious scholars: the traditions which they recorded were in part Traditions in the technical Islamic sense, i.e. *Ḥadīth,* the memorials of the alleged acts and sayings of the Prophet, as transmitted by a chain of informants. There was no formal distinction between the historical *Ḥadīth* and the main body of Traditions which formed a principal element in the elaboration of the Holy Law; indeed it is clear that many items ostensibly of an historical nature had in fact legal and social purposes. There is also a fundamental problem of criticism; namely, the difficulty of establishing how much of this copious *Ḥadīth* material is a veritable record of Muḥammad's activities, and how much is of subsequent and extraneous origin, assimilated in this form into Islam. The early Muslim scholars were keenly aware of the problem, although the criteria they adopted for discriminating between the authentic and the feigned Traditions seem artificial and insufficiently rigorous by modern standards of historical investigation. The whole subject is highly controversial at the present day, with, on the whole, non-Muslim scholars adopting a more radical, and Muslim scholars a more conservative attitude in *Ḥadīth* criticism.

Thus the motive which led to the development of Islamic historiography was primarily religious. In nothing does Islam so clearly demonstrate its kinship with Judaism and Christianity as in its sense of, and attitude towards, history; its consciousness of the existence of the world under a divine dispensation, and its emphasis on the significance of human lives and acts. Muḥammad saw himself as the last in a sequence of prophets who were God's apostles to mankind. The Qur'ān abounds in references to sacred history. Hence Islamic historiography assumes as axiomatic the pattern already evolved in Judaeo-Christian thought: a succession of events in time, opening with the creation, culminating in a point of supreme divine revelation (when, in effect, there is a new creation of a holy community), and looking prospectively to a Last Day and the end of history. In this connexion, it is significant that, in spite of the contacts between Islamic and late Hellenistic civilization, and of the Muslim reception of much of the Graeco-Roman cultural heritage, the Islamic historians were almost totally uninterested in their Classical predecessors, whether as sources of information, or as models of historiography. The Roman Empire played no part in the *praeparatio evangelica* for Islam as it did for Christianity.

This conception of Islamic history as sacred history was a factor in the development of the second characteristic type of historical writing, a type original in Islam—the biographical dictionary. The earliest of these to survive is a collection of lives of Companions of the Prophet, and, in the words of Sir Hamilton Gibb:

> it is clear that the conception that underlies the oldest biographical dictionaries is that the history of the Islamic Community is essentially the contribution of individual men and women to the building up and transmission of its specific culture; that it is these persons (rather than the political governors) who represent or reflect the active forces in Muslim society in their respective spheres; and that their individual contributions are worthy of being recorded for future generations.[1]

[1] H. A. R. Gibb, 'Islamic biographical literature', in *Historians of the Middle East,* ed. B. Lewis and P. M. Holt (London, 1962), p. 54.

Although both the chronicle and the biographical dictionary changed and developed as, after the third Islamic century, historical writing ceased to be the special field of the religious scholars, as the caliphate was fragmented, and as new states and dynasties arose, the two persisted as the standard forms of historical writing until recent times. From Arabic they were carried over into the Persian and Turkish literatures, and from the heartlands of the Middle East to the fringes of Islam. Only during the last century, and partly at least in consequence of the reception of Western historical objectives and techniques by Muslim scholars, have they become moribund.

One important class of source-material, familiar to the student of Western history, is almost completely lacking for the history of Islam—namely, archives. Certain documents are to be found transcribed in chronicles, as well as in collections of model letters and the encyclopaedic handbooks written for the guidance of government officials, but these are at least at one remove from their originals, and as isolated pieces are of diminished evidential value. Climatic conditions in Egypt, and chancery practice in Europe, have preserved some documents, more or less at random, but only with the records of the Ottoman Empire does a rich and systematically maintained government archive become available. With the nineteenth century, archival material increases. As in other fields of historical study, important contributions have been made by the auxiliary sciences of archaeology, epigraphy, palaeography, diplomatic and numismatics.

The modern study of Islamic history goes back to developments in Europe during the sixteenth and seventeenth centuries. Throughout the previous millennium, the peoples in the lands of Western Christendom and Islam had remained in almost total ignorance of each other's history; but whereas the Muslims almost without exception chose to ignore events which seemed to them extraneous and irrelevant, the Christian writers elaborated what has rightly been called a 'deformed image' of Islam and its founder.[1] In the sixteenth and seventeenth centuries, this came to be challenged. The contacts of trade and diplomacy were increasing between Muslim and Christian states. The study of Arabic was established in European universities for a variety of reasons, not least that it was seen to be the key to the writings of the Muslim philosophers and scientists, hitherto known only in imperfect medieval Latin translations. A knowledge of Arabic was also important in the

[1] See N. Daniel, *Islam and the West: the making of an image* (Edinburgh, 1960).

study of the Hebrew Bible—a study which flourished in the age of the Renaissance and the Reformation. During the same period in Western Europe, the foundations of critical historical enquiry were being laid: ancient texts were being published, old documents were being brought out of neglected archives. The motive behind much of this activity was ardently polemic; nevertheless, controversialists both in Britain and on the Continent were fashioning the instruments and devising the methods of modern research.

A new approach to the study of Islam was one aspect of this 'historical revolution', as it has been called.[1] It was demonstrated in two principal respects. The first of these was the publication of texts. Here the initiative was taken by Dutch scholars, Erpenius and Golius, in the first half of the seventeenth century, to be followed shortly by the Englishman, Edward Pococke (1604–91). The greatness of Pococke, however, lies mainly in a second respect. He had for his time an unrivalled knowledge of Muslim history and Arab antiquities, of which he gave an exposition in a short but very influential work, *Specimen historiae Arabum* (1650). The book remained authoritative for a century and a half, during which time it served as a quarry for a succession of writers. Resting on an encyclopaedic range of Arabic sources, the *Specimen,* implicitly by its scholarship, as well as by the occasional explicit comment, prepared the way for a more accurate and dispassionate view of Islam than the 'deformed image', which was still commonly accepted—and indeed lingered for two centuries. A later generation of orientalists extended the new understanding of Islam, and, by writing in modern languages, conveyed it to a less academic readership. Three highly important works in this connexion were the *Bibliothèque orientale* (1697) of Bartholomé d'Herbelot, *The history of the Saracens* (1708, 1718) of Simon Ockley, and George Sale's Preliminary Discourse to his translation of the Qur'ān (1734). Besides the information thus made available on the Islamic (and especially the Arab) past, there was in the same period a growing body of literature on the contemporary Muslim powers, especially the Ottomans and the Safavids. Through such publications, as well as others which were works of controversy rather than of scholarship, Islamic history became more familiar to educated Europeans, and was established beside ancient and modern history as an accepted field of study. This expansion of the world-view of European historians is

[1] See F. S. Fussner, *The historical revolution: English historical writing and thought, 1580–1640* (London, 1962).

demonstrated by Edward Gibbon, who, in his *Decline and fall of the Roman Empire* (1776–88) devoted nine out of seventy-one chapters to Islamic history, ranging from Arabia in the time of the Prophet to the Mongol and Ottoman conquests, and viewed its course with the same ironical detachment as he did the establishment of Christianity and the barbarian invasions of the West.

In the space of nearly two hundred years that have elapsed since Gibbon wrote, the Renaissance, the Reformation and the Enlightenment have themselves passed into history, and new forces have emerged in the development of European society. Political, social and economic change, the new ideologies of liberalism, nationalism and Marxism, have contributed to form the outlook and to define the preoccupations of historians in the nineteenth and twentieth centuries. At the same time, the methods of historical study have continued to evolve. The source-materials available for research have immensely increased, and the range of techniques at the historian's disposal has been extended. The aims of the historian have changed in response to both of these factors. Where the pioneers in the field sought primarily to construct, from the best sources they could find, the essential framework of political history, and to chronicle as accurately as possible the acts of rulers, historians today are more conscious of the need to evaluate their materials—a critique all the more important in Islamic history since the control supplied by archives is so largely deficient. They seek to penetrate the dynastic screen, to trace the real sites and shifts of power in the capitals and the camps, and to identify, not merely the leaders and figure-heads, but the ethnic, religious, social or economic groups of anonymous individuals who supported constituted authority or promoted subversion. It is no longer possible, therefore, to segregate the political history of Islam from its social and economic history—although in the latter field especially materials are notably sparse over wide regions and long periods. As the study of Islamic history is now developing, many of the apparent certainties of the older Western historiography (often reflecting the assertions and interpretations of the Muslim traditional historians) have dissolved, and it is only gradually through detailed research that a truer understanding of the past may be attained. At the same time, the range of investigation has been extended from its older foci, the heyday of classical Islam, the great dynastic empires, and the areas of confrontation with Christendom, to other periods and regions, which as recently as ten or twenty years ago aroused little interest among serious historians.

The Cambridge history of Islam cannot therefore pretend to supply a definitive conspectus of its field: it seeks rather to offer an authoritative guide to the state of knowledge at the present day, and to provide a sound foundation on which to build. The majority of its chapters are devoted to political history—this is inevitable in view of the relative abundance of source-material, and of the comparatively large amount of work that has been done here. Similar reasons explain the generous proportion of space allotted to the Muslim lands of the Middle East—which were, moreover, the region in which the classical Islamic synthesis evolved. Yet the picture which the work as a whole seeks to present is of the great and diversified community of Islam, evolving and expanding throughout thirteen centuries, creating its characteristic religious, political and social institutions, and making through its philosophy, literature and art a notable contribution to civilizations outside its own household of faith.

PART V

THE INDIAN SUB-CONTINENT

CHAPTER I

MUSLIM INDIA BEFORE THE MUGHALS

THE GHAZNAVIDS AND GHURIDS

When Alptigin rebelled against the Samanids he established himself at Ghazna in 352/962, where his slave and son-in-law Sebüktigin succeeded him in 367/977 and started vigorously to expand his dominions. Jayapāla of Waihind saw danger in the consolidation of the kingdom of Ghazna and decided to destroy it. He therefore invaded Ghazna, but was defeated and agreed to pay an indemnity. He defaulted, took the field again and was once more defeated. This was the beginning of the struggle between the Ghaznavids and the Hindu Shāhīs.

Sebüktigin died in 387/997 and in the following year was succeeded by the famous Maḥmūd. The latter defeated Jayapāla (391/1001), who immolated himself by fire because his subjects thought that he had brought disaster and disgrace to the dynasty. Jayapāla's son Ānandapāla carried on the struggle, and in a few years succeeded in organizing a confederacy of the Hindu rulers of Ujjayn, Gwalior (Gwālyār), Kālinjar, Kannawj, Delhi (Dihlī) and Ajmēr. This powerful confederacy was defeated at Peshāwar in 399/1008, despite the fact that during the greater part of the battle Maḥmūd and his army were hard-pressed. The tide turned when Ānandapāla's elephant was hit by an arrow, took fright and ran away. On this the Hindu army broke and fled. The Hindu Shāhī dominions came into Maḥmūd's possession and a governor was appointed to reside at Lahore (Lāhawr). He decided to teach the Hindu rajas a lesson so that they should not venture to combine against him again. He soon discovered that they were incredibly rich, having vast hoards of treasures, and that the Hindu temples also were repositories of great wealth. This also must have whetted his appetite for expeditions. Nagarkōt, Thānesar, Kannawj and Kālinjar were all conquered and left in the hands of the Hindu vassals. His last expedition was against Somnāth, which he captured in 415/1024 after a trying march through the desert. He returned to Ghazna in 417/1026. Four years later, in 421/1030, he died.

It would have been impossible for Maḥmūd to control all the vanquished Hindu kingdoms because of his involvement in Central Asia.

Therefore, he contented himself with the annexation of the Panjāb only. He was neither a mere robber nor a bloodthirsty tyrant, as some modern writers have called him, and shed no blood except in the exigencies of war. He did despoil and destroy many Hindu temples, but in his dealings with his own Hindu subjects he was tolerant, as is evident by his employment of Hindus, some of whom lived in Ghazna and rose to high posts. Maḥmūd's reputation as a great patron of culture and literature has remained undiminished throughout the ages. It was under his patronage that the well-known epic *Shāh-nāma* was written by Firdawsī. The story that Firdawsī was shabbily treated and wrote a poem maligning the sultan has been contested. One of the greatest scholars at his court was Abū Rayḥān Muḥammad al-Bīrūnī.

Maḥmūd's successor, Mas'ūd, maintained control over Lahore, and when he heard that its governor Aḥmad Niyaltigin had rebellious intentions he sent a Hindu general, Tilak, against him. Niyaltigin was defeated and killed. Mas'ūd decided to retire to Lahore after his defeat at the hands of the Seljuks but he was deposed by his guards near the Marghīla Pass between Attock (Ātak) and Rāwalpindī in 432/1040. The dynasty, however, continued to rule until Mu'izz al-Dīn Muḥammad b. Sām ousted them from Lahore in 582/1186. One of the Ghaznavid rulers of Lahore, Ibrāhīm (451–92/1059–99) deserves special mention because he was able not only to secure peace by entering into a treaty with the Seljuks, but was also to make inroads into the Hindu kingdoms of the Gangetic plain. Under him and his son Mas'ūd III (492–508/1099–1115) Lahore rose to be a great centre of culture.

The Ghaznavid monarch Bahrām (512–47/1118–52) came into conflict with the rulers of Ghūr. After a protracted conflict 'Alā' al-Dīn Ḥusayn (known as *Jahānsūz*) destroyed the city of Ghazna (545/1150) which was reduced to ashes. Bahrām was able to reoccupy a dilapidated Ghazna after *Jahānsūz* had been defeated and imprisoned by Sultan Sanjar of the Seljuk dynasty. When Bahrām died, the Oghuz Turks occupied Ghazna, and the dynasty once again moved to Lahore. The power of the Ghūrīs revived and prospered under Ghiyās̱ al-Dīn Muḥammad. His brother, Muḥammad b. Sām (who had the title of Shihāb al-Dīn as a prince) was destined to extend Muslim rule over the greater part of northern India. He took Ghazna, Mūltān and Ucch in 570/1175 and then turned towards Gujarāt in 573/1178. This expedition resulted in failure, and he decided to consolidate his position in the Panjāb which he did by capturing Peshāwar in 574/1179, Siālkot in

576/1181, Lahore in 582/1186 and Bhatinda in 587/1191. At this the Hindu raja of Ajmēr and Delhi marched upon Bhatinda and when the sultan went to meet the danger he was wounded and had to be hastily moved to Ghazna. The sultan, however, was not daunted and he defeated Prithvīrāja in 588/1192 at Nardīn, near Tarā'orī. Delhi and Ajmēr then passed to the sultan. Two years later he turned his attention to Kannawj and Banāras, which were added to the Muslim empire. His general Muḥammad b. Bakhtyār Khaljī conquered Bihār and Bengal. The conquest of Bengal is one of the romances of history. It was with the incredibly small force of eighteen troopers that Muḥammad b. Bakhtyār captured the capital city of Nadiyā. Ghiyās̱ al-Dīn having died in 599/1203, Shihāb al-Dīn Muḥammad assumed the title of Mu'izz al-Dīn and was officially invested as sultan. The major conquests, however, had already been made. The last few years of his life were mostly spent in dealing with difficulties in Central Asia, where in 602/1205 he suffered defeat at the hands of the Kara-Khitay. On rumours of this defeat reaching the Khokars they rose in rebellion which the sultan crushed in person. However, on his way back to Ghazna he was assassinated by an Ismā'īlī *fidā'ī* at Damīk in 603/1206. Mu'izz al-Dīn Muḥammad was not as brilliant as Maḥmūd of Ghazna, but he left a lasting impact on the history of India. He was reputed to be a mild and benevolent man, a good general and a just ruler.

THE ESTABLISHMENT OF THE SULTANATE OF DELHI

Three months later the sultan's slave and general, Quṭb al-Dīn Aybak, was enthroned as sultan of Delhi, and thus was ushered into existence the sultanate which gradually brought the greater part of the sub-continent under its sway, and established Muslim rule on a firm foundation. After a short reign of five years he died and was succeeded by his son Ārām Shāh, who proved incompetent. In his place was elected Shams al-Dīn Iltutmish, who was Aybak's son-in-law. A struggle between the powerful slaves and generals of Mu'izz al-Dīn Muḥammad was inevitable, and Iletmish had first to deal with his rivals. He was still in the throes of this struggle when Jalāl al-Dīn Mengübirdi of Khwārazm entered his dominions, being pursued by the famous Mongol conqueror Chingiz Khān. It was with some difficulty that Iltutmish was able to get rid of Jalāl al-Dīn, who ultimately left for Persia. In 632/1234 the Ismā'īlīs organized a *coup d'état* to assassinate the monarch and to establish their rule. They entered the mosque one Friday when the sultan was praying, and had hewed their way almost up to him when he made his escape. The effort was frustrated.

Iltutmish was one of the greatest sultans of Delhi. To him goes the credit of consolidating the empire. He was able to avert an imminent Mongol invasion by cold-shouldering Jalāl al-Dīn. He was ably assisted by Niẓām al-Mulk Kamāl al-Dīn Muḥammad Junaydī, who had considerable administrative talent and insight. About this time the Ṣūfī orders became very active, and contributed considerably to the growth of Islam in the newly-conquered areas.

Iltutmish died in 633/1236. He had thought highly of his daughter Raḍiyya as a possible heir, because she was more capable than her brothers. After her brother Fīrūz had ruled ineffectively for six months she then succeeded, but found it difficult to manage 'the Forty', a group of powerful officers who had rendered meritorious service in the reign of Iltutmish. After his death, however, they robbed the throne of all power and raised one prince after another to the throne. Raḍiyya showed some spirit and fought for her throne, but she was defeated, and, while in flight, was killed by some Hindus (637/1240). Her half-brother Bahrām was raised to the throne on promising that authority would rest in the hands of a group of high officials. This proved too irksome for the young sultan, who tried to free himself from tutelage, and was therefore deposed in 639/1242. Yet another son, Mas'ūd, was now raised to the throne and was deposed in 644/1246 because he too tried to assert his authority. Then came to the throne Nāṣir al-Dīn Maḥmūd, a pious and kindly prince, who reigned till his death in 664/1266 with all power vested in the hands of Balban, a capable slave of Iletmish and one of the powerful Forty.

The power of such a military oligarchy could not last. A modern speculation that if the Forty had exercised this power wisely they might have succeeded in establishing some constitutional precedents is baseless, because there was no ground of traditions or social institutions into which constitutionalism could have roots. The Forty were united neither in their outlook nor in their interests, the only binding factor was their aversion, for selfish reasons, to a powerful monarchy. This negative factor also disappeared when the Mongol pressure increased to such an extent that the very existence of the sultanate was threatened. The Mongols had penetrated Sind, Mūltān and the west Panjāb and had sacked Lahore in 638/1241, and some nobles had even begun to look to them for patronage and support. The Forty were divided into several groups because of mutual jealousies, their time and resources wasted in domestic quarrels. Hindu chieftains were discovering that the authority of the sultanate was not all-pervading, and the fear instilled by the rapid spread of Muslim power was wearing off. Gwalior and Ranthambor were lost and Katehr was giving trouble. Even the suburbs of Delhi had become unsafe, through the depredations of highwaymen, and the gates of Delhi had to be closed before dusk. Communications with Bengal were all but disrupted by Hindu robbers in the Do'āb. Bengal was under Muslim rule but virtually independent. It must have been obvious to all but the most selfish and short-sighted that the sultanate could not last long without vigorous effort and the strengthening of the central authority.

Nāṣir al-Dīn Maḥmūd entrusted all authority to Balban, and did not interfere with the administration throughout his reign except for a brief period of two years (651–3/1253–5) when, as the result of a palace conspiracy, Balban was removed from office. Balban was too circumspect to use his power in a manner that would alienate any strong group which might try to oust him with the help of the monarch. When Maḥmūd died in 664/1266, Balban ascended the throne with the title Ghiyās̱ al-Dīn, and began to assert himself fully. He belonged to a noble family of Ilbārī Turks of Central Asia, but was carried away as a slave during a Mongol incursion to Baghdād. He was ultimately sold to Iletmish at Delhi. He showed capacity and steadily rose to a position of eminence.

After his accession, Balban's first concern was to instil a sense of discipline into the officers. He strengthened the central army by reorganizing the department of recruitment and salaries—the office of the *'āriẓ-i mamālik*. After having strengthened the central army, he turned to the Forty and reduced their power. Those who resisted were heavily punished, and others soon saw the advantage of conforming to the new discipline. Balban established an exacting court etiquette. He deported himself with great dignity, never permitting anyone to take any liberty with him. It is said that even his personal valet did not see him half-dressed, bare-headed, or without his socks and shoes. He strengthened his intelligence system, and kept himself informed of the doings of his officers to stop them from indulging in any rebellious activities.

He limited himself to the area that he had inherited and made no effort even to recover parts of Mālwā which had been conquered earlier and then lost. He turned his attention to the improvement of peace and order. The forest near Delhi was cleared, and nests of robbers were rooted out. Katehr was again reduced to submission. Balban spent about a year in the districts of Patiālī, Bhojpur and Kampil in the Do'āb to punish the robbers and to suppress rebellions. He built forts and established townships of Muslims so that they might look after the security of the region. He then turned his attention to the Mongols and reorganized the administration of Sind and the west Panjāb. The capable Shēr Khān Sunqar was given command of the area and, on his death, Balban's eldest son, Muḥammad Khān, was appointed governor. These preparations kept the Mongols in check, though their incursions, in one of which the prince was killed, did not stop completely.

Balban decided to bring Bengal under his control. The main reason seems to be that the sultans of Delhi were dependent on Bengal for their supply of elephants, and an unfriendly Bengal could cut off these supplies. Two expeditions sent against the rebellious governor, Ṭughril, were defeated. Then Balban took the field in person in 679/1280. Ṭughril fled and took shelter in the forest of Orissa, from where he was captured and executed with his main supporters. The governorship was entrusted to Balban's second son, Bughrā Khān.

In 684/1285, when the news of the death of his eldest son, Muḥammad Khān, reached Balban, he heard it with fortitude and conducted his business as if nothing had happened, but at night he was disconsolate. He sent for Bughrā Khān with the intention of keeping him near the throne, so that he might succeed him without difficulty, but the prince left Delhi without permission. Balban died in 686/1287. He was succeeded by his worthless grandson, Kay-Qubād, who had been brought up under strict control, but who, when he was no longer under the tutelage of his grandfather, completely lost control over himself, and gave himself up to pleasure. His father, Bughrā Khān, marched from Bengal, and reached the river Ghāgrā (Gogra) at the same time as Kay-Qubād; because of the intercession of some nobles there were no hostilities. Bughrā Khān gave fatherly advice to Kay-Qubād, who seems to have made an effort to reform himself, but, even before he reached Delhi, he had been enticed back to his old ways. When shortly afterwards he was struck by paralysis his infant son Kayūmars̱ displaced him, as a puppet in the hands of first the Turkish faction and then of the Afghān party; his Khaljī deputy, Fērōz, defeated his rivals, and ascended the throne in 689/1290 under the title of Jalāl al-Dīn Fērōz Khaljī.

THE KHALJĪ SULTANATE IN DELHI

The Khaljīs were Turks by origin, but had resided in Afghanistan so long that they were no longer regarded as Turks. Their rise, therefore, was disliked by the Turks. Gradually the animosity wore off; but not before Jalāl al-Dīn had suppressed the rebellion of Chhajjū Khān (690/1291), a scion of the house of Balban, and executed a *darwīsh*, Sīdī Mawlā, who had become a centre of rebellious conspiracies. Fērōz had distinguished himself as a general and administrator, but was more than seventy years old at the time of his enthronement. He was mild, and did not like to take stern measures even when they were necessary. Many of his followers were dissatisfied because they saw in his mildness a danger to their own position. Apart from his solitary action against Sīdī Mawlā, Fērōz's nature led him to abstain from executing even robbers and thugs, who were deported instead. He treated Chhajjū Khān with quixotic mildness to the consternation of his supporters. Towards the close of Fērōz's reign in 694/1294 his nephew and son-in-law, Muḥammad, set out from Karā, at the head of 8,000 horse, crossed the Vindhyās and after a march of two months through difficult terrain, appeared before Devagiri and captured it. A huge booty of gold, silver, pearls, jewels and silk fell into his hands. When he returned he was summoned to court, but he pretended that he was afraid of punishment, having undertaken the expedition without royal permission. Fērōz was persuaded to go to Karā and reassure Muḥammad. He was also motivated by the hope of obtaining some of the wealth that Muḥammad had brought with him. He was, however, assassinated and Muḥammad proclaimed himself sultan as 'Alā' al-Dīn Muḥammad Khaljī in 695/1296.

Despite the circumstances in which he came to the throne, 'Alā' al-Dīn made a great impact upon the history of India. He was efficient, imaginative and strong. His expedition against Devagiri is in itself one of the boldest military ventures in history. His murder of Fērōz is no doubt a blot on his character, but he was motivated in this as much by the desire to maintain the authority of the Khaljīs as by self-interest.

'Alā' al-Dīn was soon able to make a correct assessment of the political situation. He undertook the task of securing his dominions from Mongol inroads and to extend his sovereignty further afield. This needed considerable organization and great resources. He therefore tightened his control over his officers as well as over Hindu chiefs, raised large sums of money through additional taxation, and built up a large army through rigid economy and establishing successfully a system of price-control. He introduced great austerity, and frowned upon any laxity in morals or indulgence in loose talk and intrigue. He further improved the intelligence services, and made them so efficient that the possibility of treasonable talk and association was eliminated. To stop the officials from organizing themselves into groups, he prohibited intermarriage without royal permission. He stopped convivial and drinking parties, so that the officers would not become too familiar with one another and establish relationships injurious to the state. He raised the state levy of agricultural produce from twenty per cent to fifty per cent in many areas and, to reduce any ensuing hardship, he eliminated the perquisites which Hindu chiefs used to extract from the peasantry. He also stopped the commission which the state paid them on the realization of the revenue. He examined the titles of rent-free grants of land given in previous reigns for pious purposes, and resumed them wherever they were no longer justified. In the same way, he abolished all grants in money which were no longer deserved. For the purpose of increasing his army and equipping it properly, he fixed salaries at a level lower than previously. His grants to poets and scholars also were not lavish.

For the purpose of removing any difficulty which smaller salaries might entail to public servants and others, he fixed prices at a reasonably low level, and was able to maintain them successfully throughout his reign. The system adopted was scientific and sensible. By lowering salaries he reduced the circulation of money, which had been artificially stimulated by the treasure that poured into Delhi as a result of the conquest of rich Hindu kingdoms. By raising the state levy on agricultural produce, he induced the peasant to cultivate more land, to enable him to make up for the lost margin in his net income. He ensured a continuous supply of food by the purchase of all surplus grain from the peasants, and bringing it to the town to ensure a constant supply. The cultivator was encouraged to pay the state in grain, which was stored at numerous places, and if, through a natural disaster or some unforeseen circumstance, the normal supply failed, the state granaries were able to make up the deficiency. Storage seems to have been managed skilfully, because as late as Ibn Baṭṭūṭa's visit to Delhi (1334–42), when the city was in the grip of a famine, rice stored in the reign of 'Alā' al-Dīn Khaljī was given to the public. The prices of other articles were also fixed, and they could be sold only in the *Sarā-yi 'adl* where royal officials supervised the transactions. The measures succeeded extremely well, and there is complete unanimity amongst the authorities of the period that throughout the reign prices were maintained at the low level fixed by the sultan.

He fixed the salaries of his troopers at levels where they would not face any difficulty. The horses were regularly examined and branded so that a horse could not pass muster twice, nor could horses be changed for fraudulent purposes. The reforms introduced by him in his agrarian administration were also effective. He eliminated middlemen, and insisted that the area cultivated should be properly assessed through a system of measurement.

The sultan succeeded in creating sufficient resources to secure his dominions from Mongol invasions. The need had indeed become pressing. As early as 702/1303, the Mongols reached Delhi itself, and a large army laid siege to the city. However, they raised the siege after two months. The sultan was quick to see that it was necessary to take proper steps to deal with the menace. The fortifications built by Balban were repaired, new forts were built and the frontier province of Dīpālpur was put under the charge of Tughluq. Ultimately the Mongols developed a wholesome respect for the sultan's army.

In the south he was equally successful. His general, Malik Kāfūr, a slave of Hindu origin, defeated Rājā Rāmadeva of Devagiri who had withheld tribute. The raja had to come to Delhi to renew his allegiance. The sultan wisely treated him with marks of favour, bestowed upon him the title of *ra'i rāyān* (raja of rajas) and sent him back to his capital. In 709/1308 Malik Kāfūr conquered Warangal. In this expedition Rājā Ramadeva rendered much help, which showed that 'Alā' al-Dīn's policy of reconciliation had borne fruit. In 710/1310 Malik Kāfūr conquered Madura and Dvārasamudra, and thus extended the boundaries of the sultanate to the sea-coast in the extreme south. 'Alā' al-Din's treatment of the rulers of southern India was conciliatory: he permitted them to retain their former kingdoms as vassals. Bengal, Sind, Mālwā and Gujarāt also were brought under control.

The historian Baranī,[1] for whom the sultan was wicked although strong and successful, has recorded a somewhat dramatized story of 'Alā' al-Dīn's intention to set himself up as a prophet, and to undertake the conquest of the world like another Alexander. There can be little doubt that the sultan did have the ambition to be a great conqueror, an

[1] Żiyā' al-Dīn Baranī (of Baran, i.e. Bulandshahr), a historian and writer on government in the style of Mirrors for Princes, was probably born *c.* 680/1279 and died *c.* 758/1357.

ambition in which he was remarkably successful. It is quite possible that the scheme of conquests was discussed at a time when there were other dangers besetting the sultanate, and the sultan was wisely persuaded not to undertake them until he had properly organized the resources of the sultanate, and established full control over it. The story regarding the intention to be a prophet seems difficult to believe because no other authority mentions it, nor is it in keeping with the sultan's actions and policies. The idea may have crossed his mind in a moment of weakness, and perhaps have been mentioned to one or two officers, but it does not seem to have been entertained seriously, and was, therefore, discarded when the folly of such an intention was pointed out.

The sultan's rule made a good impression upon the people. His crime of assassinating his uncle seems to have been forgotten, and, after his death, the people remembered him with gratitude and affection. His tomb was visited by large numbers like the tomb of a saint. 'Alā' al-Dīn died in the year 716/1316 as the result of illness. A great name of the period is that of the Chishtī mystic Shaykh Niẓām al-Dīn, whose influence was responsible for a great upsurge in religious and moral fervour among the people. It is said that 'Alā' al-Dīn's achievements would have been impossible but for the moral stamina among the Muslims engendered by Niẓam al-Dīn. The prayers of Niẓām al-Dīn were popularly believed to have brought about the raising of the Mongol siege of Delhi in 702/1303.

On 'Alā' al-Dīn's death, Malik Kāfūr, whose relations with the heir-apparent, Khiżr Khān, and his mother, the queen, had been unfriendly, caused the prince and his brother to be blinded and his mother to be imprisoned. He then sent some soldiers to blind the third son, Mubārak Khān, as well. This prince, however, persuaded the soldiers, who were by now probably tired of Malik Kāfūr's excesses, to return and avenge the wrongs perpetrated on the family. Kāfūr was killed, and Mubārak Khān ascended the throne with the title of Quṭb al-Dīn Mubārak Shāh in 716/1316. He showed some firmness in dealing with disorders in Gujarāt and Devagiri. However, he soon surpassed the limit in severity, and had some high officials wantonly executed. He also indulged in gross licentiousness. One of his favourites was Khusraw Khān, a low-born slave, who at last murdered the sultan and assumed the royal title himself in 720/1320. Under him, a large number of his Hindu kinsmen gained ascendancy, and openly insulted and vilified Islam. At last Ghāzī Malik Tughluq, who was a veteran general and warden of the marches in the Panjāb, could tolerate such a state of affairs no longer and set out for Delhi to punish the usurper. The battle which was fought in the suburbs of Delhi in 720/1320 ended in a victory for Tughluq.

THE TUGHLUQ SULTANATE IN DELHI

Tughluq adopted the title of Ghiyās̲ al-Dīn Tughluq. He applied himself to putting the administration in order again. He restored public works of utility such as forts and canals. Order was re-established, and severe action was taken against robbers. He encouraged agriculture, planted gardens, and took steps to safeguard the cultivator from the exactions of middlemen and officers.

He had to turn his attention to the Deccan when the ruler of Warangal rebelled, and Tughluq's son, Jawnā Khān, was sent to bring him back to his allegiance. This expedition, however, failed because a mischievous rumour was spread to the effect that Tughluq had died, which was generally believed in the absence of contradiction from Delhi. The prince, therefore, returned to Delhi. In 723/1323 he was again sent to the Deccan and, after capturing Bīdar, he marched on Warangal, reduced it, and annexed the surrounding regions, Telingānā.

Bengal was still under the descendants of Balban. Civil war broke out on the death of Balban's grandson, Shams al-Dīn Fērōz Shāh, in 718/1318. One of the parties, Nāṣir al-Dīn, appealed to Tughluq, who considered this to be an excellent opportunity for intervention. He marched to Bengal and placed Nāṣir al-Dīn as a vassal monarch on the throne of west Bengal. East Bengal was annexed and administered as a province. Tughluq then returned to Delhi in 725/1325. Preparations were made, as was normal, to accord the sultan a warm reception. Jawnā Khān built a special pavilion to entertain the monarch. When he had just finished the meal, the prince suggested that the elephants brought from Bengal might be paraded. The pavilion collapsed, killing Tughluq. It has been suggested by some later historians that the pavilion was specially designed to cause the monarch's death, which, instead of being an accident, was really parricide on the part of Jawnā Khān. The authority for this story is Ibn Baṭṭūṭa, but it seems that there is not much truth in the allegation. Historians of the period mention it as an unexpected accident, and evidence to the contrary is not convincing. Baranī, who fiercely condemns Muḥammad b. Tughluq for very much of his policy, makes no suggestion of parricide and sees Tughluq's death as a 'thunderbolt and heavenly calamity'.[1]

Jawnā Khān ascended the throne with the title of Muḥammad Shāh and is generally known to historians as Muḥammad b. Tughluq, a style used in contemporary literature and inscriptions. He was well educated and was equally at home in Islamic law, philosophy, mathematics, logic and medicine. He had a sharp intellect, and few could win a point in arguing with him. He had brilliant ideas, but often was blind to difficulties in implementing them. He was impatient, and did not tolerate inefficiency. He looked upon every failure to carry out his orders as wanton disobedience, which he punished sternly. He confused the officials by a succession of orders which they found difficult to enforce, and were sometimes heavily punished for this failure. His punishments were notoriously severe, for he could not see that not every little failure or delinquency was an act of rebellion. The virtue of moderation was absolutely foreign to him. He was not unjust. He had a scrupulous regard for law and justice, yet he was ruthless in punishment, and, once an offence was proved to his satisfaction, he knew no mercy. So great was his regard for justice that he would appear personally in the court of the *qāẓī* whose orders he would carry out, even though they were against him. There are at least two occasions on record when he did so. He was liberal in making gifts, but he was unforgiving, and executed a large number of men. He was perhaps embittered by rebellions, and he thought that the only way of dealing with them was inordinate severity. Some of his measures were well conceived, but they failed for the lack of obvious precautions. It also seems that he was not ably assisted, which made him more furious.

As the result of the annexations in the south Muḥammad b. Tughluq was convinced that a new imperial centre was needed there. He selected Devagiri which he named Dawlatābād, and decided to establish a metropolis there in 727/1327. He built a beautiful city with well laid out streets and imposing buildings, and strengthened the rock-built citadel, the circumference of which, about 500 yards, had under the Hindu kings been scarped smoothly, so that scaling was impossible, with a deep ditch dug in the solid rock. This city was intended to be a second capital, or, as some historians assert, to replace Delhi completely as the capital of the empire. Many government officials, scholars and others went to Dawlat-

[1] For a full discussion, see Syed Moinul Haq, 'Was Mohammad bin Tughlak a parricide?' *Muslim University Journal*, Aligarh, v/2, (October, 1958), 17–48.

ābād to settle, and others whose livelihood depended upon the court followed. Anyone who voluntarily decided to settle at Dawlatābād was encouraged to do so. Efforts were made to facilitate the journey by providing food and rest at convenient distances, the two cities having first been connected by a good and shady road. It seems that the sultan was not satisfied with the results of the voluntary migration and, therefore, he used compulsion after two years. Even then the story that Delhi was reduced to utter desolation does not seem to be true.[1] The non-Muslim population was not forced to migrate, as this would have been pointless. The sultan's action proved to be extremely unpopular. There is little doubt, however, that, but for his foresight, Muslim influence in southern India would have received a serious setback when the sultanate of Delhi was involved in difficulties and the rise of independent provincial dynasties reduced the extent of its dominions. But for Dawlatābād, there would have been no Bahmanī kingdom to check the rising power of Vijayanagara. The sultan's compulsion, however, seems to have embittered his relations with his Muslim officials to such an extent that he was involved in a series of rebellions.

In 729/1329 the sultan raised the state demand on agricultural produce in the Ganges-Jamnā Do'āb. Here again it has been stated that the demand was increased tenfold and twentyfold, others have said that it was raised threefold and fourfold. The truth seems to be that the demand was increased by five to ten per cent.[2] This increase was resented by the population, who left their holdings and took to robbery. As the thick forests were impenetrable to cavalry it was customary for recalcitrant peasants to leave their hamlets and enter the forest with all their belongings. The sultan sent punitive expeditions, which made it more difficult to restore agriculture in this fertile province, and produced famine in the area right up to Delhi.

The sultan in 731–2/1130–2 introduced a 'forced' currency, replacing gold, silver and bullion coins by tokens of copper and brass. Intrinsically this was not unsound, but he forgot that craftsmen could forge the token coins: there was large-scale forgery, and the entire scheme failed. The sultan redeemed all the token coins at face value, which caused considerable loss to the treasury. It has been suggested that the sultan had grandiose ideas of conquest, and he thought that the introduction of

[1] A. Mahdī Ḥusain, *The rise and fall of Muḥammad bin Tughluq* (London, 1938), 116 ff.

[2] For fuller discussion, see I. H. Qureshi, *The administration of the sultanate of Dehlī* (Karachi, 1954), 115–17.

brass and copper coins would give him the means for carrying out his projects. This does not look plausible, because the sultan could not be so ignorant as to imagine that brass and copper could completely replace gold and silver. Another explanation, more credible, has been offered that there was scarcity of specie during this period, but the sultan's ability to redeem both genuine and forged token coins counters this argument.

The sultan had to march to the south from Delhi in 735/1335 because Sayyid Jalāl al-Dīn Aḥsan of Kaythal, who had been appointed governor of Ma'bar, had rebelled at Madura. When Muḥammad b. Tughluq reached Warangal, an epidemic of cholera spread in the army. The sultan himself was taken ill. The expedition was, therefore, abandoned, and Ma'bar was lost to the sultanate. The kingdom of Ma'bar or Madura lasted to 779/1378, when the dynasty came to an end. It had to fight constantly against its Hindu neighbours, and ultimately was destroyed by the forces of Vijayanagara.

Muḥammad b. Tughluq returned to Delhi and was, it seems, hard-pressed for funds, the treasury having been emptied by rebellions, lavish grants and unwise measures. He therefore started farming out revenues of large areas. Men of no substance, and with little experience of revenue matters, offered unrealistic sums of money, which they were unable to pay. Being afraid of the dire consequences, they rebelled. The resultant deterioration in agriculture was aggravated by the failure of the monsoons in the area around Delhi, where famine conditions prevailed. The sultan first introduced a daily ration of grain to the citizens, and tried to conciliate and encourage the peasants by making grants of money for bringing land back into cultivation. The scheme failed, mostly because of lack of rainfall, but also because by now the peasants were puzzled and had lost confidence. The sultan, therefore, went with his court and a large number of people of Delhi to the fertile province of Oudh (Awadh) which had prospered under the wise administrator, 'Ayn al-Mulk. The sultan established a camp on the west bank of the Ganges about 165 miles from Delhi, a city of straw sheds and walls, which he called Svargadvāra, 'the gate of Paradise'.

This gave the sultan some respite, but, despite all his difficulties, he had not given up the idea of further conquests. For a considerable time he had kept alive his ambition of conquering Transoxania and Khurāsān. When the situation in those areas did not warrant such an undertaking, he thought of bringing the mountain area of Kāngrā and beyond under his sway. He sent an army of 100,000 horse and a large number of foot into the mountains by way of Kāngrā. After the conquest of Kāngrā, the army marched into the mountains beyond and secured considerable success. However, when the rains came, the army was cut off. There was disease among men and horses and it decided to retreat. This was difficult, partly because of bad weather and landslides, and partly because the local population was hostile, and hurled stones when the army was marching through narrow passes and valleys. The army was almost completely annihilated. Some writers have thought that the sultan's intention was to invade China, but there seems to be little justification for this conclusion because the objective is clearly mentioned as Himāchal or Qarāchal, the Himālaya or 'black mountains'. The destruction of such a large army and the consequent dwindling of the sultan's prestige now made rebellion even easier.

From many sides came news of risings and rebellions. East Bengal became independent in 739/1338. In 740/1339 an officer 'Alī Shāh Kar rebelled and occupied Bīdar after having taken possession of the treasury at Gulbargā. This rebellion, however, was suppressed by Qutlugh Khān who had charge of Dawlatābād. It has been noted that the sultan had established a camp at Svargadvāra, where all arrangements were made by 'Ayn al-Mulk. A number of fugitives from the sultan's anger had taken shelter with the governor. The sultan's mind was poisoned, and he decided to transfer him from Oudh to the Deccan. This was unwise, as 'Ayn al-Mulk was popular because of his good administration, and was reluctant to go to the Deccan, which was in turmoil. But the sultan insisted and 'Ayn al-Mulk was advised to rebel. The sultan, despite his difficulties, gave battle and 'Ayn al-Mulk was defeated. He was carried before the sultan, who, instead of executing him, ordered his imprisonment. Later he was pardoned and reinstated in his government of Oudh. In 741/1340 Malik Shādū Lodī, governor of Mūltān, rebelled, and when the sultan marched against him he fled into Afghanistan. In 743/1343 there was a rebellion in the areas of Sunām, Sāmāna, Kaythal and Guhrām in the Panjāb. Before it could be properly suppressed there was a rebellion of the *amīrān-i ṣada*[1] in Gujarāt.

The sultan had come to think that the *amīrān-i ṣada* were responsible for all mischief. Eighty-nine of them were executed by 'Azīz Khammār,

[1] Sing. *amīr-i ṣada:* literally 'commander of a hundred', is often taken to mean commander of a hundred horse, and misleadingly translated 'centurion'. They commanded small contingents to maintain order in the countryside.

the governor of Mālwā, under the sultan's instructions. This spread horror among the *amīrān-i ṣada* of Gujarāt and the Deccan. The first to take up arms were those in Gujarāt. Muḥammad b. Tughluq appointed a council of regency at Delhi and marched towards Gujarāt. 'Azīz Khammār in the meanwhile had been defeated and put to death by rebels. The *amīrān-i ṣada* in Gujarāt were defeated with heavy losses. The sultan ordered the governor of Dawlatābād to send the *amīrān-i ṣada* of that province to Gujarāt. They were despatched, but at the end of the first day's march they decided to rebel. Then they imprisoned the governor, seized the fort and proclaimed Ismā'īl Mukh sultan of the Deccan under the title of Nāṣir al-Dīn Shāh. Those *amīrān-i ṣada* who were imprisoned in Gujarāt escaped, and joined Ismā'īl Mukh. The sultan marched against Dawlatābād, where the citadel held out. In the meanwhile there was another serious rebellion in Gujarāt under Ṭaghī, a cobbler, who had gathered around himself a considerable following. The sultan left Dawlatābād and marched against Ṭaghī.

Ṭaghī was a capable leader and the monarch was not able to corner him. In the meanwhile the situation in the Deccan deteriorated. Another *amīr-i ṣada*, Ḥasan, had shown greater initiative and Ismā'īl Mukh abdicated in his favour. This Ḥasan became sultan under the title of Abu'l-Muẓaffar 'Alā' al-Dīn Bahman Shāh. Muḥammad b. Tughluq abandoned the idea of recovering the Deccan, and decided to devote his entire energy to Ṭaghī, who escaped to Thatthā in Sind, where he joined the local rulers who were also in revolt. The sultan, having summoned reinforcements from Delhi and other places, marched to Sind, and was within a short distance from Thatthā when on 10 Muḥarram 752/9 March 1351 he was taken ill. Ten days later he died.

When Muḥammad b. Tughluq was worried because of his growing unpopularity amongst the Muslims, he thought that recognition from the caliph would strengthen his position. Therefore, after making diligent inquiries, he applied for recognition from the 'Abbasid shadow-caliph in Egypt. For three years the Friday prayers and the observance of the two *'Īds* were suspended and coin was issued in the name of the caliph. It was in 745/1344 that Ḥājjī Sa'īd Ṣarṣarī came from Egypt bearing a letter from the caliph. The envoy was received with the utmost respect and the Friday prayers and the *'Īds* were restored. Another important event of the reign was the visit of the well-known traveller Ibn Baṭṭūṭa, who was at the court from 734–43/1334–42.

Muḥammad b. Tughluq's reign was a complete failure. After initial success, in spite of his great ability and perseverence, his harshness and ill-advised measures ruined the sultanate, which in the early days of his reign had reached its climax. He was a man of great ability, but his genius was of a kind that takes no account of realities. A poor judge of men, he was unbalanced in his views, and knew no compromise.

When Muḥammad b. Tughluq's army found itself in difficulties in Sind, being left without a leader, it started retreating in disorder, and was harassed both by its Mongol allies and the local population. The sultan's cousin, Fērōz, was present in the camp, but he was unwilling to take up the responsibilities of the throne. Ultimately, because of the sad plight of the army, he was persuaded to ascend the throne under the title of Fērōz Shāh, on 24 Muḥarram 752/23 March 1351. The minister Khwāja Jahān had proclaimed at Delhi a child whom he called Muḥammad b. Tughluq's son, but whose claims are dismissed by the writers of the period. While still on his way he was joined by several important officials from Delhi. One of these was the able Malik Maqbūl, a converted Brahman of Telingānā, subsequently entitled Khān Jahān Maqbūl Telingānī. He was appointed *wazīr*. Khwāja Jahān was able to gather little support and came as a suppliant. He was received with kindness, but later was nevertheless killed. Five months after his succession Fērōz entered Delhi.

He was confronted with a colossal task. The general dissatisfaction engendered by Muḥammad b. Tughluq's policies had to be removed, and the people reconciled. In addition there was the difficulty of suppressing widespread rebellion. Fērōz Shāh recognized the futility of trying to reconquer all the lost provinces. This proved to be wise, because the sultan could use his forces in consolidating the areas that he controlled.

Fērōz Shāh made a good beginning by remitting outstanding debts to the state which had been mostly incurred by rash tax-farmers and government servants who had been given advances for the purposes of improvement of agriculture. He did not try to recover even the large sums of money which had been freely spent by Khwāja Jahān when seeking support for his nominee to the throne. Fērōz Shāh appointed Khwāja Ḥusām al-Dīn Junayd for the purpose of making a new assessment of the revenues of the sultanate. This had become necessary because Muḥammad b. Tughluq's measures had created chaos in the revenue records. However, with the help of local records, this task was completed in a period of six years, and many unjust cesses which had grown up as the result of the breakdown in administration were abolished. These measures were rewarded with success, agriculture was restored to its original condition, and a greater area was brought under cultivation. The townsfolk were not forgotten, and a number of small but vexatious taxes were abolished. With the increase in productivity prices came down, and maintained a steady level for the greater part of the reign. It is interesting to note that the level was almost the same as in the days of 'Alā' al-Dīn Muḥammad Khaljī, which shows that the Khaljī monarch's measures were economically sound. The difference was that Fērōz Shāh did not have to use any extraordinary administrative machinery for the purpose of maintaining prices. Further to improve cultivation, he dug a number of important canals and sank wells. The failure of monsoons during Muḥammad b. Tughluq's reign must have brought home to Fērōz Shāh the necessity of artificial irrigation. Canals had been constructed earlier, especially by Ghiyāṯ al-Dīn Tughluq, but Fērōz Shāh's canals were more important, and some of them have survived even until today.

Fērōz Shāh was a great builder. He restored a large number of old monuments which had fallen into disrepair, one of these being the famous Quṭb Mīnār at Delhi. He repaired a large number of towns and cities, which, because of rebellions and maladministration, had suffered during the last reign, and he founded several new cities, of which Ḥiṣār and Jawnpur are the most famous. The latter became the capital of the Sharqī kingdom, and developed into a great seat of learning. He built a new 'city of Delhi' called Fērōzābād, and created south of that Delhi a vast *madrasa* beside the large reservoir called Ḥawż Khāṣṣ. The imposing remains of pavilions and lecture halls are still intact. He is credited with the construction of three hundred towns, which perhaps is not an exaggeration if the restoration of townships which had suffered under Muḥammad b. Tughluq is taken into consideration. In addition, he built four large mosques, thirty palaces, and many other public works and buildings.

Fērōz Shāh displayed an interest in the past by removing two of Ashoka's pillars. One was re-erected inside the citadel of Fērōzābād, and the other set up near Kushk-i Shikār on the Ridge north of Delhi. Around the former was built a double-storeyed pavilion, and the monolithic pillar was mounted on a solid base so that it seemed to the casual observer that it stood on the vaulted roof of the building. It was gilded, and therefore came to be known as Mīnāra-i Zarrīn. It is interesting to note that the Brahmans in the reign of Fērōz Shāh were not able to read the inscriptions, and falsely told the sultan that they contained a prophecy about his coming to the throne, and promised him great success as a monarch.

In the process of conciliation, Fērōz Shāh had to secure the co-operation of the Muslim '*ulamā*' and religious leaders. Many of Muḥammad b. Tughluq's difficulties had arisen because of his alienation of this class, first by ordering many of them to migrate from Delhi to Dawlatābād and, later, by punishing some of them heavily because of their reluctance to identify themselves with his measures. Partly because of his own temperament, and partly because of need, Fērōz Shāh went out of his way to reconcile the religious leaders, and showed the utmost respect to them. Some of his intolerant actions can be ascribed to their influence. Though the sultan abolished discretionary capital punishment, a Brahman was burnt to death for insulting Islam and the Prophet. The accepted practice whereby priests, recluses and hermits of other religions are exempt from paying *jizya* had been liberally interpreted in India, and no Brahman, however wealthy, was asked to pay the tax. Fērōz Shāh imposed the tax, in all probability, on those Brahmans who were not engaged in religious work. This measure was unpopular, and a large number of Brahmans assembled in front of the palace, and threatened to burn themselves alive. The sultan did not relent, and ultimately other Hindus voluntarily undertook to pay the tax on behalf of the Brahmans. He also dealt severely with the Ismā'īlīs, who had become active once again. This animosity was as much due to their reputation for underground political work as to doctrinal differences.

Fērōz Shāh had no military ambitions, but for the purpose of the consolidation of his empire he had to undertake a number of campaigns. He had extricated Muḥammad b. Tughluq's army from a desperate situation with considerable success. He first turned his attention to Bengal, which had become independent. He would perhaps have left that kingdom alone but for the fact that its ruler, Ilyās, who had made himself master of west Bengal in 745/1345 and then annexed east Bengal in 752/1352, invaded Tirhut. Fērōz Shāh could not tolerate this invasion of his territories, and therefore marched from Delhi in 753/1353 and chased Ilyās away from Tirhut to his capital Pānduā, and from there into Ikdalā, which stood on an island in the Brahmaputra. As the monsoons would have cut his communications, Fērōz Shāh retreated and reached

Delhi in 755/1354. In 760/1359 he again invaded Bengal. Now the ruler was Sikandar Shāh, who had succeeded to the throne in 758/1357 and who, like his father Ilyās, had entrenched himself in Ikdalā. Fērōz Shāh, finding it impossible to reduce Ikdalā, ultimately agreed to negotiations which resulted in the recognition of Sikandar as a tributary on the annual payment of forty elephants. On his way back, Fērōz Shāh led an expedition from Jawnpur into Orissa, which he occupied. The raja of Orissa sued for peace, and was restored as a tributary on surrendering twenty elephants and promising to send the same number annually to Delhi. On the way back the sultan's army lost its bearings in the jungle, and reached Delhi only after considerable hardship.

Khān Jahān Maqbūl Telingānī died in 774/1372 and was succeeded by his son, who also received the title of Khān Jahān. Next year Fērōz's eldest son, Fatḥ Khān, died. After this Fērōz Shāh was gradually reduced to utter senility, and became incapable of exercising control or judgment. The minister now started on a career of intrigue which ultimately resulted in civil war. Fērōz Shāh died in 790/1388 at the age of eighty-three. As the result of a prolonged struggle between the nobles and the princes of the royal family, the dynasty sank into insignificance and all the good work done by Fērōz Shāh was destroyed. It was in this state of chaos that Tīmūr marched upon Delhi in 801/1398. The forces of the sultanate were decisively beaten in a battle near Delhi, although even in this decrepit state they gave a good account of themselves. Tīmūr won huge booty, not only from Delhi but from the entire area on his route. Internal dissensions had demolished the structure of a mighty empire within a period of less than two decades. The last monarch of the dynasty, Maḥmūd, earned the satire that 'the writ of the lord of the world runs from Delhi to Pālam', Pālam being about nine miles from the city.

THE SAYYID AND LODĪ DYNASTIES IN DELHI

A certain Khiżr Khān had been appointed governor of Mūltān by Fērōz Shāh. When Tīmūr invaded the sultanate, Khiżr Khān cast his lot with him and was appointed governor of the Panjāb and Upper Sind. He consolidated his power, and ultimately absorbed Delhi. Thus he laid the foundation of the Sayyid dynasty, so named because Khiżr claimed to be a *sayyid*, i.e. a descendant of the Prophet. The history of his reign is mostly a narrative of expeditions against recalcitrant chiefs for the collection of revenue and their reduction to allegiance. He died in 824/1421, and was succeeded by his son Mubārak Shāh who, by constant fighting, was able to keep his territories together. Mubārak was assassinated at the instigation of his minister, Sarwar al-Mulk, who was annoyed at the curtailment of his powers, and was succeeded in 837/1434 by his nephew Muḥammad Shāh who, through his folly, alienated the sympathies of the supporters of the dynasty. His son 'Alā' al-Dīn 'Ālam Shāh succeeded him in 847/1444. 'Ālam Shāh displayed little interest in his office, and lived in comparative obscurity enjoying the income of the area settled upon him by Buhlūl Lodī.

One of the contestants for power, the minister Ḥamīd Khān, invited an Afghan noble, Buhlūl, to Delhi. He seized power, and, after 'Ālam Shāh's abdication in 855/1451, enthroned himself. Bahlūl was successful in obtaining powerful Afghan support. He used tact and foresight, and treated the Afghan nobles with consideration and did not assume airs of superiority. Gradually he built up so much strength that he was able to defeat Ḥusayn Shāh of Jawnpur, and to absorb the Sharqī kingdom into the sultanate (see p. 24). He died in 894/1489 and was succeeded by Sikandar Lodī, who was a capable monarch. His brother Bārbak, appointed governor of Jawnpur by Buhlūl, refused to recognize Sikandar's authority, and was defeated at Kannawj; but he was treated with leniency and was permitted to rule Jawnpur as a vassal. Bārbak showed little capacity for administration and was twice unable to control rebellions. At last he was arrested and Sikandar took over the administration. Ḥusayn Sharqī, who had been ousted by Buhlūl and was in exile, tried to create trouble. At last he took the field, was defeated near Banāras, and fled to Bengal where he lived as a pensioner. Sikandar was able to bring Bihār under his complete control. The raja of Tirhut also submitted. Sikandar next led an expedition into Bengal, where Ḥusayn Shāh of Bengal sent his son Dāniyāl for negotiations. Sikandar wisely entered into a treaty by which the two rulers agreed to respect each other's frontiers. Sikandar conquered Dholpur, and, to extend his authority over Rājpūtānā, he established his capital at Āgrā in 910/1504.

The sultan took great interest in the welfare of his subjects. He put the administration on a sound foundation. His intelligence system was so good that the credulous believed that he had supernatural powers. He was firm and tactful, and, without weakening their support, he kept the Afghans under discipline. He displayed intolerance in suppressing some Hindu religious practices. He died in 923/1517 and was succeeded by Ibrāhīm Lodī who alienated the sympathies of the Afghan nobles. One of them called upon Bābur, who ousted the dynasty in 932/1526.

PROVINCIAL DYNASTIES DURING THE TIME OF THE DELHI SULTANATE

The Sharqī dynasty of Jawnpur was established (796/1394) by Malik Sarwar, who was given the titles of Khwāja Jahān and Malik al-Sharq, and appointed governor of the eastern provinces by Nāṣir al-Dīn Maḥmūd, whom Sarwar had put on the throne of Delhi (795/1392). When Tīmūr invaded Delhi, Sarwar found it convenient to become independent. At his death he left a kingdom extending from ʿAlīgarh in the west to Bihār and Tirhut in the east, which early received tribute from the Bengal sultans, for whom it was a convenient buffer-state between themselves and Delhi. Malik Sarwar was succeeded by his adopted son, Qaranful, who ascended the throne as Mubārak Shāh in 802/1399. His son Ibrāhīm Shāh, who came to the throne in 804/1402, was a cultured prince and a great patron of learning. His reign established the Sharqī sultanate as one of the major powers of north India. Because of the disturbed conditions in Delhi, a large number of scholars migrated and built up Jawnpur as a great seat of art, letters and religion as well as of a distinguished building activity. There were constant but always indecisive hostilities with Mālwā, which continued under Ibrāhīm's son Maḥmūd (844–61/1440–57); the latter even besieged Delhi in 856/1452 in an attempt to oust Buhlūl Lodī, and extended the kingdom to the south. The last sultan, Ḥusayn, whose army was possibly the strongest in India, and who had married the daughter of ʿĀlam Shāh, the last Sayyid king of Delhi, made several attempts on her behalf to capture Delhi until decisively beaten by Buhlūl in early 884/spring 1479. Delhi thereupon annexed the Sharqī territories, and Ḥusayn was thereafter capable of no more than fomenting dissensions between rival Lodī nobles after Buhlūl's death.

It has already been noticed that Balban's son, Bughrā Khān, established himself as an independent ruler of Bengal (see above, p. 8). On the death of Shams al-Dīn Fērōz there was a war of succession and Ghiyāṯ al-Dīn Tughluq installed Nāṣir al-Dīn on the Bengal throne at Lakhnawti and annexed the rest of the kingdom (see above, p. 13). During Muḥammad b. Tughluq's reign, Bahādur, who had been displaced by Ghiyāṯ al-Dīn Tughluq, was placed on the throne of Sonārgāon under the tutelage of an official. Bahādur rebelled and was executed. Once again, because

Muḥammad b. Tughluq's attention was diverted by rebellions elsewhere, there was civil war in Bengal, which lasted until Fērōz Shāh invaded Bengal to chastise Ilyās. We have seen (pp. 21–2) that Fērōz recognized the independence of Bengal under Sikandar Shāh, who was wounded when his son A'ẓam rebelled in 795/1393. Sikandar Shāh died in the arms of A'ẓam, who ascended the throne with the title of Ghiyās̱ al-Dīn A'ẓam Shāh. He was a patron of learning and is also known for his sense of justice. He died in 798/1396. A Hindu official, Rājā Ganēsh, became *de facto* ruler, and is said to have persecuted Islam; at any rate a well-known Muslim saint, Quṭb al-'Ālam, invited Ibrāhīm Shāh of Jawnpur to attack Bengal for this reason. When Ibrāhīm's forces invaded Bengal, Ganēsh gave his son Jādav to the saint for conversion to Islam, and this son was raised to the throne under the title of Jalāl al-Dīn Muḥammad after Ganēsh's death (818/1415). The saint now interceded with Ibrāhīm, who reluctantly retired. Jalāl al-Dīn's reign seems to have been a time of peace and prosperity: architecture is to some extent a political barometer, and the buildings of this period are renowned for their magnificence. There is also some evidence for the growth of maritime trade with China. Then follows a period when the history of Bengal offers little beyond a tale of constant internecine warfare and intrigue. The conflict between Delhi and Jawnpur removed the threat from the west, although the east was troubled by disturbances in the Arakan province. The Ilyās Shāhī dynasty, restored in 837/1433, was finally superseded by a succession of Ḥabshī rulers, descendants of a large colony of Abyssinian slaves imported by the Ilyās Shāhīs. Ultimately the nobles raised Sayyid Ḥusayn to the throne in 898/1493. It was in his reign that Ḥusayn Shāh of the Sharqī dynasty took refuge in Bengal. Sayyid Ḥusayn recovered several lost parts of his kingdom and extended its frontiers by annexing Assam; he died in 924/1518. Some of the sultans of Bengal were enlightened patrons of literature. They showed a liberal attitude towards their Hindu subjects, especially those belonging to the lower castes, who reciprocated by depicting them in literature as their liberators from the tyranny of the Brahmans.

Islam was introduced into Kashmir by Shāh Mīr or Mīrzā of Swāt in 713/1313. He entered the service of the Hindu ruler Sūhadeva, and eventually, in about 739/1339, became the ruler with the title of Shams al-Dīn Shāh. The rule of his third (?) son Shihāb al-Dīn (755–74/1354–73 ?) saw Kashmir victorious over most of her Hindu neighbours. The next important ruler was Sikandar (*c.* 791–815/1389–1413), commonly called

Butshikan (idol-breaker) because of his intolerance of Hinduism. He made Kashmir a predominantly Muslim state. Four years after his death came Zayn al-ʿĀbidīn (823–75/1420–70), who reversed Sikandar's policies of persecution by recalling the exiled Brahmans and permitting the observance of Hindu practices, which had been prohibited during the reign of Sikandar, subject to their conforming to the Hindu scriptures. He suspended the *jizya*, abolished illegal taxes, and besides extensive patronage of literature and music was distinguished in public works and buildings. He maintained friendly relations with other rulers both Muslim and Hindu. But after his death the royal power declined, and a succession of puppet kings was eventually displaced by one of the powerful tribes.

When the Ghaznavid hold in Sind weakened because of Masʿūd's difficulties, the local dynasty of Sūmrās who were Ismāʿīlīs by faith established themselves in Sind. They were succeeded by the Sammās, a Sunnī dynasty, about 736/1335. They were of local origin and used the indigenous title of *Jām*. In Fērōz Shāh's reign, Jām Banhbina and Jām Jūnān, who were joint rulers owing allegiance to Delhi, instigated some Mongols to raid the sultan's dominions, causing Fērōz's Sind expedition of 767/1366 in which the Mongols were defeated and the rulers brought captive to Delhi. They were later released, and Jūnān returned to rule in Sind. After the death of Fērōz Shāh the Sammas became independent of Delhi. Little is known of events in Sind after this, and the chronology is uncertain; but the later Sammā kings are known to have been connected by marriage to the royal house of Gujarāt, and received support from Gujarāt when rebels, mostly Mongols of the Arghūn tribe, rose against the *Jām*, and again when reports came of persecution of Muslims by local Hindus. The dynasty, however, continued to rule until 933/1527, when the Arghūns gained control of Sind.

In Gujarāt Muẓaffar Khān, who had been appointed governor in 793/1391, declared his independence after five years. He was imprisoned by his son Tātār Khān, who proclaimed himself sultan under the title of Muḥammad Shāh in 806/1403, but the latter was poisoned and Muẓaffar was released in 810/1407. Muẓaffar was succeeded (813/1410) by his grandson, Aḥmad Shāh, who ruled for a period of thirty-two years and spent a good deal of his time in consolidating and extending his kingdom and improving its administration, building his capital of Aḥmadābād, and establishing Islam throughout his dominions. The most famous ruler of this dynasty was Maḥmūd I (862–917/1458–1511). It was during his reign that Gujarāt made common cause with the Mamluks of Egypt and defeated the Portuguese fleet off Chaul in 913/1508. The Portuguese, however, appeared with a stronger force next year and defeated the Muslim navies near the island of Diu (Dīw). This defeat destroyed Muslim trade in the Arabian Sea. Bahādur Shāh, 932–43/1526–37, who was engaged in war against the Mughal Humāyūn as well as continually against the Portuguese, was the last great sultan of Gujarāt, for he was followed by more puppet kings supported by rival nobles. The local Ḥabshī community rose to much power, as did the minor Mughal princelings known as the Mīrzās; and there was virtual anarchy for a few years before Akbar's conquest of the province in 980–1/1572–3.

Malik Rājā, an able official appointed by Fērōz Shāh of Delhi to an *iqṭā'* near Thālnēr, in the Sātpura hills between the rivers Narbadā and Tāptī, established himself sufficiently to act independently of Delhi, after the death of Fērōz, from about 784/1382, and sought alliance with Mālwā through a royal marriage. On his death in 801/1399, his state of Khāndēsh was divided between his two sons, of whom the elder, Naṣīr Khān, receiving scant support from Mālwā against his younger brother, had to recognize the overlordship of Gujarāt in 820/1417—a necessity in the case also of some later rulers, for alliances by marriage with neighbouring states gave little guarantee of their support. The rulers of this house, the Fārūqīs, were not recognized as equals by their stronger neighbours, and bore only the title of khan; yet the state was not interfered with much by its neighbours, partly because of the strength of its fortress Asīrgarh, partly because it formed a natural buffer-state between the great powers, Mālwā/Gujarāt and Mālwā/Bahmanī (later, after the fragmentation of the Bahmanī sultanate, between Mālwā and Aḥmadnagar also). Gujarāt later became a powerful ally, especially in the time of Muḥammad Khān I (926–43/1520–37) whose uncle, Bahādur Shāh, designated him his heir. By 972/1564 Khāndēsh had to accept the Mughals as overlords, as Gujarāt was in anarchy; Mālwā had been annexed by the Mughals, Aḥmadnagar was more concerned with her southern neighbours, and the balance of power had so changed that Khāndēsh's position as a buffer state was no longer tenable. Khāndēsh at first connived at the Mughal manipulation of the Aḥmadnagar throne, but eventually was annexed by the Mughals in 1009/1601.

The sultanate of Mālwā was established in 794/1392 at Dhār by Dilāwar Khān Ghūrī, who had been appointed governor of Mālwā by Fērōz Shāh or his successor. He died in 808/1405, and was succeeded by his son, Alp Khān, who assumed the title of Hōshang Shāh and transferred the capital to Māndū. Hōshang was a capable monarch who extended his kingdom and brought considerable prosperity. He died in 838/1435 and was succeeded by his son Muḥammad Shāh, who alienated the sympathies of his nobles because of cruelty. At last Maḥmūd Khān, a general and counsellor of Hōshang and the son of the *wazīr*, poisoned the sultan and made himself monarch in 839/1436. During his long reign the Mālwā sultanate reached its greatest extent, and he attacked not only his neighbours but also Jawnpur, the Deccan, and even Delhi. He was a good Muslim and a patron of the arts. He was succeeded by Ghiyāṣ al-Dīn (873–905/1469–1500), a man of peaceful disposition, and several minor kings, under whom Mālwā fell in 937/1531 to Gujarāt, then to Humāyūn, next to Shēr Shāh, and finally to Akbar in 968/1561.

Muḥammad b. Tughluq's loss of hegemony over Dawlatābād and the rise of 'Alā' al-Dīn Bahman Shāh to independence in the Deccan has been mentioned above (p. 18). After extensive campaigns of conquest which brought the Deccan—roughly the boundaries of the old Ḥaydarābād state before the 1956 reorganization of Indian provinces—under his control, he established his permanent capital at Gulbargā, where it remained until *c.* 827/1424. The second sultan, the dignified Muḥammad I (759–76/1358–75), set the kingdom on a sound footing, bringing in careful and extensive administrative reforms, both civil and military. The sultanate, peaceful internally, was involved in continual skirmishing with the Hindu state of Vijayanagara to the south, the *do'ab* of the Rāychūr district being a constant bone of contention; but the introduction of gunpowder gave the Bahmanīs the advantage over the numerous but less organized Vijayanagara forces. The fifth sultan, Muḥammad II (780–99/1378–97), did for Bahmanī culture what Muḥammad I had done for its administration, attracting numerous Persian and Arab poets and theologians (even Ḥāfiẓ of Shīrāz was invited), foreign civil and military architects, tile-workers and calligraphers, and not neglecting certain elements of Hindu culture. On his death a Turkish slave seized power and installed a puppet ruler, but Fērōz, a grandson of the first sultan, restored the dignity of the royal house, and succeeded as sultan in 800/1397. with his brother Aḥmad as *amīr al-umarā'*. In a reorganization of the administration Fērōz employed Brahmans extensively, probably to balance the high proportion of influential 'foreigners' (Persians and 'Irāqīs). He took pains to maintain good relations with his Hindu neighbours, taking wives from several prominent Hindu houses, not excluding Vijayanagara (being persuaded, although a Sunnī, that he could contract *mut'a* alliances: Shī'ī doctrines were being popularized in the Deccan at this time), although he was involved in border struggles with Vijayanagara and the Gond kings. Some opposition to Fērōz at the end of his reign centred round the Chishtī saint, Gēsū Dārāz, who favoured his brother Aḥmad, to whom Fērōz assigned the throne in 825/1422. The Gulbargā period ended in an atmosphere of constant intrigue.

Aḥmad soon moved his capital to Bīdar; Gulbargā, besides being a centre of intrigue, was also too near to the Vijayanagara kingdom for comfort. He strengthened his northern frontiers in order to attack Mālwā, Gujarāt and Khāndēsh in pursuit of the Bahmanīs' putative sovereignty over those regions 'conferred' on Fērōz by Tīmūr in 803/1401 (not recorded by Tīmūr's historians, but apparently confirmed by the actions of the Bahmanīs' neighbours at the time); and there were indeed hostilities with Mālwā and Gujarāt, and matrimonial alliances with Khāndēsh. Aḥmad Shāh, pious enough to have been generally known as *walī*, was sufficiently strong to manage the rival factions; not so his son Aḥmad II (839–62/1436–58), under whom faction between local (Dakhnī) and foreign Muslims crippled the stability of the state. A third party of importance was formed by the Ḥabshīs, who as Sunnīs generally supported the Dakhnīs against the predominantly Shī'ī foreigners, but were not invariably so aligned. The next king, Humāyūn, tried to maintain a balance between Dakhnīs and foreigners and to consolidate the kingdom in his short reign. In the reign of two minors the regent, the brilliant Persian Maḥmūd Gāwān, was able to pursue a similar policy of conciliation at home, in spite of much military activity against Vijayanagara. Maḥmūd Gāwān was the real power in the state until his assassination in 886/1481 by a Dakhnī-Ḥabshī conspiracy, after which there was political chaos. The reign of Maḥmūd, from 887/1482, saw the gradual decline of the Bahmanī state, which had earlier been a much greater force, politically and culturally, than the Delhi sultanate. The king became completely subservient to a Sunnī Turkish *wazīr*, Qāsim Barīd, in Bīdar, The provincial governors Niẓām al-Mulk (Aḥmadnagar), 'Imād al-Mulk (Barār), and Yūsuf 'Ādil Khān (Gulbargā and Bījāpur), breaking away from the Barīdī ascendancy in about 895/1490, became autonomous in their own territories where they founded respectively the Niẓām Shāhī, 'Imād Shāhī and 'Ādil Shāhī dynasties. The governor of Telingānā at Golkondā, Sulṭān Qulī Quṭb al-Mulk, who became virtually independent of Bīdar after 924/1518, was similarly the founder of the Quṭb Shāhī dynasty. Bahmanī sultans held the throne as Barīdī puppets until 934/1528, when the Barīd family succeeded as the Barīd Shāhī dynasty of Bīdar.

ADMINISTRATION

In the beginning, the sultans of Delhi recognized the suzerainty of the caliphs of Baghdād. The first investiture took place under Iltutmish, when in 626/1229 the emissaries brought a diploma from the Caliph al-Mustanṣir. On al-Musta'ṣim's death in 656/1258, the sultans were confronted with a difficulty, because the office of the caliph was not filled. They continued al-Musta'ṣim's name on the coinage until Jalāl al-Dīn Fērōz Khaljī's death in 695/1296, nearly forty years later. It has been suggested that 'Alā' al-Dīn Khaljī claimed to be caliph within his own dominions, but the evidence is not conclusive. His son, Mubārak Shāh, definitely claimed to be caliph. After his death there was no revival of the claim. Muḥammad b. Tughluq was persuaded to believe that recognition from the caliph was absolutely essential. He therefore applied to the caliph in Cairo, and received a diploma in 745/1344. Fērōz Shāh also received a diploma. The historian Firishta says that the Bahmanī kingdom also received recognition from Cairo, but this is doubtful in view of a clear statement by Fērōz Shāh to the contrary. The Sayyids and the Lodīs made vague references to the caliph on their coins.

The sultans of Delhi adhered to the legal conception of the position of the sultan which was common throughout the Muslim world. They also adhered to the form of an election by the *élite*. After the nobles had formally elected a monarch, they swore allegiance and later, the oath was taken by the people in the mosques of the state. The election of a sultan was in fact often purely nominal, because the candidate had already decided the issue by conquest or by the possession of superior force. The sultan was virtually bound by the election to control the state, defend Islam and its territories, protect his subjects and settle disputes between them, collect taxes and rightly administer the public treasury, and enforce the criminal code. It follows that an elected sultan could also be deposed for breach of those conditions, and a number of sultans of Delhi were in fact so removed for incompetence; loss of the mental faculties, physical infirmity, or blindness, were also held to render a ruler liable to dethronement. There was no prescriptive hereditary right of succession, and not many sultans were succeeded by their sons; but the nobles frequently limited the choice of successor from among members of the ruling house. In the Bahmanī sultanate, however, primogeniture became normal after Aḥmad Shāh Walī. As in other Islamic states, the mention of the ruler's name in the *khuṭba* and the minting of coins in his name were considered the most important attributes of sovereignty.

The administration of the sultanate was based upon models which had already developed under the 'Abbasids and their successors. All matters relating to the royal household were in the hands of the *wakīl-i dār*, while court functions and audiences were in the hands of *ḥājibs* under an *amīr ḥājib* or *bārbak*. The imperial household required a large commissariat which was divided into departments called *kārkhānas*. Some of these manufactured articles of use, others maintained stables, of which the *pāygāh* (stud) and the *fīl-khāna* (elephant-stables) were more important. Possession of elephants in India was a royal prerogative, not confined to Muslim kings. The *fīl-khāna* was maintained in the capital; for no ruler would permit a concentration of elephants in a distant town, from where they might have been used against him. The slaves were at first an integral part of the royal household, and the Turkish slaves of the early rulers of Delhi were well treated, given minor household offices, and promoted to such high posts as their merit fitted them—no office in the state being beyond their reach. But their power could be dangerous to the state, as both Iltutmish and Balban found when they had to deal with powerful slave nobles of previous reigns. Yet monarchy had often to rely on its slaves to counter the high-handedness of nobles, and many a battle, besides more domestic conflicts, was won for a sultan by the large force of slaves under his command. In the time of Fērōz Shāh, when prisoners of war and captive rebels were also enslaved, a separate department was organized to deal with their vast numbers. Ibn Baṭṭūṭa notices Ḥabshī[1] slaves employed in large numbers all over India, including many employed at sea.

The civil administration was mostly in the hand of the *wazīr*, who was the finance minister and chief adviser of the monarch. The *wazīr* (later often known by the honorific *khwāja jahān*) was assisted by two officers of ministerial rank, the *mushrif-i mamālik* and the *mustawfī-i mamālik*. The former was the accountant-general and the latter the auditor-general.

[1] Nominally Abyssinian, certainly African. For an account of them in India, see *EI2*, s.v. ḤABSHĪ (J. Burton-Page).

All affairs relating to the recruitment and maintenance of the army were dealt with by the *'āriẓ-i mamālik*. The *dabīr-i khāṣṣ* was in charge of state correspondence in the *dīwān-i inshā'*. The *barīd-i mamālik* was the head of the state information agency, including intelligence. Religious affairs were under the *ṣadr al-ṣudūr*, who generally was also the *qāẓī-i mamālik*, the chief judge of the empire.

The main source of income was the state demand on agricultural produce, most of the area being treated as *kharājī* land. Lands granted for religious purposes were generally treated as *'ushrī*. Assessment was mostly made on the basis of schedules of average produce applied to the area cultivated, which was measured. In case of a dispute, the peasant could demand crop-sharing. The demand was levied mostly in kind, and varied from area to area, depending upon local tradition. The level was generally one-fifth of the gross produce, which was raised by 'Alā' al-Dīn Khaljī to a half. It was again lowered to a fifth by Ghiyāṯ al-Dīn Tughluq. When Muḥammad b. Tughluq tried to enhance the demand in the Do'āb, there was disaffection and even rebellion. An important part was played by Hindu chiefs who acted in many areas as intermediaries between the government and the peasants. They, however, had their functions strictly defined, and care was taken that the peasant, who was recognized as the owner of the land, did not have to pay more than the prescribed demand.

The sultans maintained an excellent standing army, in which cavalry played the central role. Descriptive rolls of soldiers and their mounts were maintained, horses were branded, and annual reviews held to prevent fraud. Elephants were considered to be a great asset. There was infantry as well, recruited mainly from Hindus and others who could not afford a horse, and frequently not maintained as a permanent cadre except for the body-guards. The army was organized on a decimal basis.

The departments of justice, *ḥisba* (public morals) and police functioned in accordance with the general pattern that had developed elsewhere in the Muslim world. Justice was dispensed through *maẓālim* (governmental and administrative), *qaẓā* (civil), and *siyāsa* (martial law and cases of rebellion) courts. The chief of the police in the city was known by a term of Hindu origin—*kotwāl*.

The provincial government was under governors known as *wālīs* or *muqṭi's*. The provinces were divided into *shiqqs*, the *shiqqs* into *parganas*, and *parganas* into collections of *dihs* or villages. A *dih* was not only the residential part of a village but also included the agricultural land attached to it. The *pargana* was the main unit of local administration. Later the *shiqqs* came to be known as *sarkārs*. The pattern of the central government was repeated at the provincial level and the provincial departments corresponded directly with their counterparts at the centre. The head of the *pargana* administration was a *mutaṣarrif* who was also called an *'āmil*.

For most of the period the administration worked smoothly and a change of dynasty did not seriously affect its efficiency. However, it broke down under Muḥammad b. Tughluq with disastrous consequences. This system prevailed with only minor alterations in the provincial kingdoms as well when they became independent.

ASPECTS OF CULTURE

Among the great names associated with the Ghaznavids at Lahore are those of Abu'l-Faraj Rūnī, whose *dīwān* has been published in Persia. Mas'ūd Sa'd Salmān (441–515/1048–1121) was born and educated at Lahore and wrote in Persian, Arabic and the local dialect, but only his Persian poetry has been preserved and published. The famous author of *Kashf al-maḥjūb*, Sayyid 'Alī Hujwīrī, also belongs to this period. He died in 463/1071 and was buried at Lahore. *Imām* Ḥasan al-Saghānī, born at Lahore in 576/1181 and educated there, was a well-known lexicographer and jurist, and his *Mashāriq al-anwār* is a standard book on *Ḥadīth*. The greatest writer associated with Delhi is Amīr Khusraw (651–725/1253–1325), who wrote voluminous works in poetry and prose on historical subjects. His friend Ḥasan Sijzī is also famous as a poet, though not so prolific as Amīr Khusraw. Muḥammad b. Tughluq's court was also adorned by Badr-i Chāch, who has left a number of *qaṣīdas* in his praise which contain some historical information. And no account of Muḥammad b. Tughluq's court would be complete without mention of that acute observer, the Moorish traveller Ibn Baṭṭūṭa, whose *Riḥla* presents an invaluable view of fourteenth-century India through independent eyes. A good amount of historical writing was also produced in this period.[1]

The contribution to music made by Muslims in India is considerable. They certainly brought to India a number of Persian, Central Asian and Arab instruments, and introduced new musical modes and forms. In the absence of exact evidence of the period the Muslim contribution can

[1] For a detailed study of historians of this period, see P. Hardy, *Historians of medieval India* (London, 1960).

perhaps be appreciated only by the expert, who can evolve some sort of calculus from the evidence of the ancient Sanskrit texts on the original Indian music, and the divergences from this standard of modern north Indian music; with the proviso, however, that ancient, *folk*-music, not specifically dealt with in the old texts, may have persisted into the Muslim period.[1]

This period saw a great effort on the part of the Ṣūfīs to reconvert the Ismāʿīlīs in Sind to Sunnī Islam and to spread Islam amongst non-Muslims as well. Ismāʿīlī effort did not come to an end and there are many communities, some Hindu in origin, who still retain their Ismāʿīlī beliefs. The four main Ṣūfī orders in the sub-continent were the Chishtiyya, the Qādiriyya, the Suhrawardiyya and the Naqshbandiyya. It was through the efforts of these orders that a Muslim community grew up. This community did not consist only of converts, as is often imagined, but included a fair element of descendants of migrants from various regions, especially Central Asia and Persia. The school of jurisprudence which found favour was the Ḥanafiyya. Islam, especially some aspects of Sufism, had some impact upon the thought of some Hindu religious reformers from the fifteenth century.

[1] For a discussion on the nature of the Muslim contribution to music in India, see now N. A. Jairazbhoy, article 'Music', in *EI2*, s.v. HIND.

CHAPTER 2

INDIA UNDER THE MUGHALS

THE MUGHAL EMPERORS

Bābur

A Timurid prince, 'Umar Shaykh Mīrzā, ruler of Farghānā, died in 899/1494, leaving little more than a title to his principality for his son Bābur, then eleven years old. Bābur had to fight not only to defend Farghānā but also to fulfil his ambition of possessing Samarqand because of its prestige as the main city of Central Asia. His adventures described in his excellent memoirs read like a romance. He did succeed in occupying Samarqand, only to lose it again. His lasting possession proved to be Kābul which he occupied in 910/1504, and which became his headquarters. All else, including Farghānā, he lost in the struggle.

The rise of the Özbegs and the Safavids affected Bābur's career deeply. The Özbegs were able to extinguish the power of the Timurids because they proved incapable of serious and joint effort. The Safavids came into conflict with the Özbegs and defeated them. Bābur was restored to the kingdom of Samarqand as a vassal of Shāh Ismā'īl I after the defeat and death of Muḥammad Shaybānī Khān Özbeg (917/1511). The Safavids were defeated in the battle of Ghujduwān, and Bābur lost all hope of ruling Samarqand, and returned to Kābul (918/1512). When Bābur felt secure, his mind turned towards India. Ibrāhīm Lodī, the sultan of Delhi, had alienated his nobles. Dawlat Khān, the governor of Lahore, sent messengers to Kābul offering allegiance in return for help. Ibrāhīm's uncle, 'Ālam Khān, also went to Kābul seeking assistance to capture the throne of Delhi. Bābur, who had made some incursions into the Panjāb before, now marched, ostensibly to help Dawlat Khān, and captured Lahore. Dawlat Khān, finding that Bābur had no intention of handing over Lahore to him, turned hostile. In the meanwhile 'Ālam Khān attacked Delhi with the help of some Mughal troops without success. Bābur, whose attention had been diverted because of the siege of Balkh by the Özbegs, returned and heard at Siālkot of 'Ālam Khān's failure. Dawlāt Khān surrendered and died soon after, Ibrāhīm marched from Delhi, while Bābur occupied Pānīpat and waited for Ibrāhīm.

The first battle of Pānīpat (932/1526) is remarkable because Bābur succeeded in defeating an army of 100,000 men and 1,000 elephants with a small force of about 25,000. Bābur entered Delhi and his eldest son, Humāyūn, was sent to Āgrā. Bābur's name was read in the *khuṭba* as the emperor of Hindustan. Thus was established the Mughal empire.

Bābur had still to contend with formidable forces. The remnant of the Afghan nobles elected Ibrāhīm's brother, Maḥmūd, as sultan. Rānā Sāngā of Chitor, the head of a strong Rajput confederacy, saw in the débâcle of the Lodīs the opportunity of gaining vast territories; but Bābur defeated him at Khānua in 933/1527.

Bābur then turned his attention to Maḥmūd Lodī. The decisive battle was fought in 936/1529 near the confluence of the Gogra (Ghāgrā) with the Ganges, where Bābur was once again victorious. He was also able to conclude a treaty of peace with Nuṣrat Shāh, the king of Bengal. A year afterwards Bābur was taken ill, and died in 937/1530, nominating Humāyūn as his successor.

Bābur was not only a valiant soldier and a capable general but also an accomplished writer and a poet of merit. His memoirs are famous. Because of his preoccupations, some entries are sketchy as if made in a diary, but in other places the reader is fully compensated by Bābur's excellent pen-pictures of important contemporaries. He has also recorded a considerable amount of natural data of which he seemed to be a keen observer. In addition there are his essays in criticism of literary works and paintings, buildings and institutions. Outstanding is his great sincerity, which prevents him from indulging in self-praise or hiding his shortcomings. He emerges as a lovable, generous, capable and brave man, who wins the admiration and sympathy of the discerning reader by telling all about himself, whether creditable or otherwise.

Humāyūn

Humāyūn succeeded to the throne without any trouble, but later his younger brothers, Kāmrān, 'Askarī and Hindāl, created difficulties. After his defeat at the hands of Bābur, Maḥmūd Lodī had fled to Bengal. Now he invaded the Mughal territories and took Jawnpur. Humāyūn marched against him and gained a decisive victory.

The sultan of Gujarāt, Bahādur Shāh, thought it opportune to send three columns against various points in Mughal territories, all of which were defeated. Bahādur Shāh, who had been besieging Chitor, turned after its fall towards Humāyūn, who had reached Mandasor, only sixty miles away, in pursuit of one of the Gujarāt columns. Bahādur Shāh, instead of attacking Humāyūn, entrenched himself in a camp. The Mughals cut off all supplies, and ultimately Bahādur Shāh had to escape to Māndū (941/1535).

Humāyūn followed him. The fort fell, and Bahādur once again escaped with the Mughals in pursuit. He succeeded in reaching Diu (Dīw). Humāyūn, leaving 'Askarī at Aḥmadābād, returned to Māndū to organize the administration of Mālwā. 'Askarī did nothing to oust Bahādur Shāh from Diu, nor did he organize the administration. Bahādur Shāh was soon able to collect a force, and marched upon Aḥmadābād. 'Askarī retreated in the direction of Āgrā. Thus Gujarāt was won and lost in a little over one year. It was reported to Humāyūn that 'Askarī's followers had treasonable designs, so Humāyūn left Mālwā and marched towards Āgrā, meeting 'Askarī's forces on the way, but did not punish 'Askarī because, in addition to the loss of Gujarāt, there had come news of difficulties with the Afghans in the east. After Humāyūn's march from Māndū, Mālwā was seized by Mallū Khān who had been governor before the Mughal occupation.

At this juncture Humāyūn encountered a formidable rival in the Afghan, Shēr Khān, the son of Ḥasan Khān who held the *parganas* of Sahsarām, Ḥājīpur and Khawāṣpur Tāndā. Farīd, as Shēr Khān was originally called, fled from Sahsarām to Jawnpur because of his father's coldness, as Ḥasan was completely under the influence of Farīd's step-mother. At Jawnpur he devoted himself to his studies, and, when his father once visited Jawnpur, he was so struck with Farīd's capacity that he invited him back and put him in charge of his *parganas*. Here he showed his great talent for good administration.

This further excited his step-mother's jealousy, and he was soon forced to leave again, and seek service in Āgrā at the court of Ibrāhīm Lodī. After the sultan's defeat at Pānīpat, Farīd attached himself to the self-appointed Sultan Muḥammad of Bihār. It was in his service that, one day, while accompanying the monarch in a hunt, Farīd slew a tiger with a sword, and received the title of Shēr Khān. He was also appointed tutor to the sultan's young son, Jalāl Khān. After an interval in the service of Bābur, he returned to the court of Sultan Muḥammad, where he was restored to his former position. The sultan died shortly after; his son, Jalāl Khān, being a minor, his mother became the regent and appointed Shēr Khān as her agent. Thus he became the ruler of Bihār. When the queen died he was virtually king.

Sultan Muḥammad of Bengal sent a force against Bihār which was defeated with heavy losses. He sent another army, and this time the nobles persuaded Jalāl Khān to dismiss Shēr Khān. He retired to Sahsārām, and Jalāl Khān joined forces with Bengal. At this Shēr Khān enlisted more troops, advanced against the Bengal army, and defeated it. Jalāl Khān escaped into Bengal, and Shēr Khān's power became absolute. The treasures, animals and equipment left by the two Bengal armies had enriched and strengthened him. He then acquired the strong fort of Chunār on the Ganges through marriage with the widow of its commandant. Maḥmūd Lodī now took possession of Bihār, leaving only his *parganas* to Shēr Khān, who reluctantly joined him, but refrained from actively supporting the sultan against the Mughals. Maḥmūd Lodī was defeated and, being unable to raise a new army, retired to Orissa, where he died in 949/1542.

During all this time Shēr Khān had been quietly building up his power. He accumulated arms and devised a plan to seize the hoarded treasures of the rulers of Bengal. When reports of Shēr Khān's activities reached Humāyūn, he marched against Chunār, which was captured after a difficult siege in 944/1537. While Humāyūn was busy besieging Chunār, Shēr Khān marched into Bengal and took Gawr. Shēr Khān, knowing full well that Humāyūn would follow him into Bengal, lost no time. He removed his booty to the hills of southern Bihār, which he intended to use as a base against the Mughals. He also gained by a strategem the fort of Rohtās, where he put his family and his newly acquired treasures. Humāyūn marched into Bengal and, delighted with its verdure, prolonged his stay. He posted Hindāl on the north bank of the Ganges to guard his line of communication. Southern Bihār is hilly, and, being covered with thick jungle, is impenetrable by cavalry. The sole means of communication was through the Teliyāgahrī pass. Shēr Khān, who knew the terrain well, harassed the Mughal communications, so that Hindāl deserted his post; he retired to Āgrā with rebellious intentions. Shēr Khān took all the area between Banāras and Teliyāgarhī. Bengal was thus turned into a prison for Humāyūn by the superior strategy of Shēr Khān. At last Humāyūn realized his danger, marched out and reached Chawsa, where he halted, unaware of Shēr Khān's position.

Shēr Khān's forces soon appeared, and, instead of attacking them when they were tired, the Mughals waited. After resting his troops, Shēr Khān attacked Humāyūn, who was taken by surprise. The Mughal army was thoroughly beaten (946/1539). After the battle, Shēr Khān proclaimed himself sultan, with the title of Shēr Shāh.

While Humāyūn was in difficulties in Bengal, Hindāl had failed to help him, and had indulged in treasonable activities at Āgrā. Kāmrān also moved from Lahore, and established himself in Āgrā. Humāyūn and 'Askarī were able to reach Āgrā with difficulty, and Shēr Shāh occupied Bengal. Kāmrān left Humāyūn in this desperate situation and retired to the Panjāb. Shēr Shāh after having consolidated his position in Bengal, marched against the Mughals. Humāyūn advanced from Āgrā and stopped near Kannawj, with Shēr Shāh on the other bank of the Ganges. Defections forced Humāyūn into crossing the river. The Mughals fought a half-hearted battle, and Shēr Shāh's 10,000 troops put a Mughal force of 40,000 to flight (947/1540).

After this defeat Humāyūn reached Āgrā, but there was no chance of taking a stand. He evacuated Āgrā and, after a halt at Delhi, hurried on to Lahore, followed in close pursuit by the Afghans. Lahore was abandoned. His progress towards Afghanistan being barred by Kāmrān, Humāyūn turned towards Sind, where he had no success. He received an invitation from Rājā Māldeva of Mārwār, and faced grave difficulties in reaching there, only to discover that the raja had turned against him. He returned facing even greater hardships. Ultimately he reached 'Umarkōt, where the ruler gave him shelter. It was here that Akbar was born in 949/1542. Humāyūn could not stay long at 'Umarkōt and decided to go to Qandahār. 'Askarī, who was the governor of Qandahār on behalf of Kāmrān, strengthened his defences, and instigated some Balūch chiefs to arrest Humāyūn, who escaped, but Akbar fell into their hands and was sent to 'Askarī. Humāyūn entered Persia as a refugee, and, after many humiliations and difficulties, secured small reinforcements in 952/1545 from Shāh Ṭahmāsp to fight against Kāmrān. A protracted struggle ensued, until Humāyūn succeeded in ousting Kāmrān. 'Askarī, who had remained faithful to Kāmrān, was captured and was sent to Mecca, where he died in 965/1558. Hindāl was killed in a night attack by an Afghan (959/1551). Kāmrān joined, for a while, the court of Shēr Shāh's son, Islām Shāh, but disappointed with his contemptuous reception he ran away, and finally fell into Humāyūn's hands. In spite of pressure from the courtiers, Kāmrān was not executed, but was blinded and sent to Mecca, where he died in 964/1557.

After Humāyūn's departure from Lahore, Shēr Shāh occupied the Panjāb, Mālwā and Ranthambhor. He punished Pūranmal of Rāysēn for having massacred the Muslim inhabitants of Chānderī and enslaving Muslim and Hindu women. He brought Mārwār and Mēwār under his control. Then he marched against Kālinjar, which he besieged. A rocket, rebounding from the gate of the fort, fell into a heap of ammunition in proximity to the sultan. He was severely burnt, and was carried to his tent. The officers were summoned and commanded to take the fort, and before sunset he received the news of its capture by storm. Then he died (952/1545).

Shēr Shāh was a good general and a great strategist, as the way he trapped and defeated Humāyūn shows. He has been highly praised for his efficient administration. The lessons learnt in his youth in administering the *parganas* of his father were never forgotten, and he stands out as one of the greatest administrators who ever sat on the throne of Delhi. He was just, tolerant and benevolent. He took an interest in the welfare of his subjects, improved communications, built and repaired caravanserais, and took steps to maintain peace and order. He rose from being a student in exile to be first the ruler of Bihār, and then the sultan of Delhi. Afghan writers, who naturally wrote with considerable nostalgia in the days of Akbar, exaggerated his originality, though not his capacity as an administrator. Shēr Shāh had very little time at his disposal to create new institutions. He was, however, a keen student of history, and succeeded in putting into action the administrative machinery, which had been considerably damaged by disturbed conditions.

He was succeeded by his son, Islām Shāh, who was brave and determined, but suspicious by nature, and harsh in his dealings. Because of his harshness, his brother 'Ādil Khān was favoured by some nobles, which set Islām Shāh against him. 'Ādil Khān was defeated, and fled towards Patnā where he disappeared, but Islām Shāh's campaign against the nobles continued, and there is little else to narrate about the reign. On his death (961/1554) his son Fērōz was raised to the throne. His brother-in-law, Mubāriz Khān, marched at the head of a strong force towards Gwalior, where he forced his way into the presence of the young king and, despite the entreaties of the mother, murdered the boy and ascended the throne under the title of 'Ādil Shāh. He displayed little tact and even less capacity. Relations between the nobles and the sultan were embittered because of his harshness. A cousin of the sultan, Ibrāhīm Khān Sūr, came to know that an attempt was to be made on his life. He fled from Gwalior, occupied Delhi and assumed the royal title. 'Ādil Shāh then grew suspicious of another cousin, Aḥmad Khān, whom he intended to remove, but who was warned by his wife, the sultan's younger sister. He left Gwalior and escaped to Delhi. There he quarrelled with Ibrāhīm, and, having defeated him near Āgrā, occupied Delhi, and proclaimed himself sultan as Sikandar Shāh in 962/1555. There were now three sultans: 'Ādil Shāh, whose authority extended over Āgrā, Mālwā and Jawnpur; Sikandar Shāh, who was supreme from Delhi to Rohtās in the Panjāb; and Ibrāhīm Shāh, who ruled the foothills of the Himalayas in the Panjāb. A fourth contender for position was a petty shopkeeper of Rewārī called Hēmū who had gathered all local power into his hands.

The power of the Sūrs being thus divided, Humāyūn decided to try his luck again. He captured Lahore, Jullundar (Jālandhar), Sarhind, Ḥiṣār and Dīpālpur. Sikandar marched with an army of thirty thousand, was defeated at Māchiwārā, and retired into the hills. Sāmānā fell soon after, and from there Humāyūn marched upon Delhi, which he occupied. Forces were sent into the Do'āb. However, before much could be achieved, he fell from the stairs of his library, and died two days later in 963/1556.

Akbar

Akbar was little more than thirteen years old when he succeeded to the throne. Bayram Khān, a tried officer and friend of Humāyūn, was appointed his guardian. The reign began with difficulties. Apart from the three Sūr contestants, there was the ambitious Hēmū. He advanced from Gwalior to Āgrā, which was lost. Hēmū then marched upon Delhi, from which the Mughal governor, Tardī Beg, fled. Such areas in the Do'āb as had been occupied were evacuated. Bayram marched against Hēmū, at the second battle of Pānīpat. The Mughals were greatly outnumbered, but after an archer succeeded in piercing Hēmū's eye with an arrow, he was captured and executed. Āgrā and Delhi were recovered. 'Ādil Shāh was still in Chunār when he was attacked by his cousin Jalāl al-Dīn Bahādur Shāh of Bengal, and was slain. Sikandar surrendered in 964/1557, and the Do'āb was soon brought back under control.

When Akbar was eighteen years old, a number of his foster-relatives and others persuaded him to break with his guardian. Akbar left Āgrā and went to Delhi, from where he informed Bayram Khān that he was no longer needed as a regent and tutor. Bayram, rejecting all advice to rebel, announced his intention of going on Pilgrimage to Mecca. However, he wanted to dispose of his property in the Panjāb. Akbar showed impatience, and sent a former servant and personal enemy of Bayram Khān to hasten him. This goaded Bayram Khān into rebellion; he was defeated, and took refuge in Tilwārā, a hill fortress, from where he sent a messenger to Akbar expressing repentance. Bayram appeared before Akbar at Ḥājjīpur. He then departed for Mecca, and was killed by some Afghans near Pātan in 967/1560. Bayram deserved better treatment because of his services to Humāyūn and Akbar. He was an able, sincere and wise servant.

Mālwā had acted independently of its Mughal governor since 954/1547. In 968/1561 Akbar sent an expedition under Adham Khān, his foster-brother and the son of his chief nurse, Māham Anāga, who, along with other foster-relatives, had come to wield great influence in matters of state. Mālwā was under Bāz Bahādur, the enthroned son of a Khaljī noble, who is still remembered as an accomplished musician and for the famous romance between him and a beautiful Hindu girl, Rūpmatī. He was easily defeated and sought safety in flight. Rūpmatī took poison to save herself from Adham Khān, whose misbehaviour brought Akbar to Mālwā, but Adham Khān was permitted to continue as governor.

In the meanwhile ʿĀdil Shāh's son, Shēr Khān, marched on Jawnpur and was defeated. Āṣaf Khān was sent against Chunār, which surrendered. The eastern provinces were now relieved of any serious danger. Adham Khān continued to misbehave in Mālwā, and had to be recalled. His lieutenant, left in charge of the province, was even worse, and Bāz Bahādur recovered Mālwā. Akbar then sent ʿAbd Allāh Khān Özbeg, who reorganized the province.

Akbar invited Atga Khān from Kābul to take up the duties of chief minister, to the disappointment of the harem party. When Adham Khān reached the court he murdered Atga Khān (969/1562). Akbar executed Adham immediately, and Māham died of grief forty days later. This brought Akbar complete emancipation from the harem influence. Henceforth, Akbar, who had already shown considerable initiative, mostly followed his own counsel.

Āṣaf Khān was ordered to conquer the Hindu kingdom of Gondwānā, which was annexed (971/1564). Khān Zamān, along with several other Özbegs, was posted in the east, and extended the frontiers of the empire to the borders of Bengal. Because of their absence from the court, the interests of the Özbegs were neglected. This created disaffection, and ultimately revolt broke out in 973/1565. The rebellion was quelled when Khān Zamān was trampled to death by an elephant in a hard-fought battle near Karā (975/1567).

In the same year Akbar marched against the *rānā* of Chitor. Bihārī Mall of Ambēr had already allied himself with the Mughals by marrying his daughter to the emperor, which was the beginning of the intimate relationship between the Mughal dynasty and the Rājpūts. Uday Singh, the *rānā* of Chitor, however, had not offered submission, hence the campaign against Chitor. The fortress was considered impregnable, and the defence was left by the *rānā* to one Jay Mal, who put up a spirited fight. Akbar, however, succeeded in shooting Jay Mal with his musket when he was out on a round of the defences. The Rājpūts then committed the terrible rite of *jawhar*, in which they burnt their women, donned saffron robes, and rushed upon the enemy to be killed. Chitor thus fell into Akbar's hands. Ranthambor and Kālinjar were also taken, and Gujarāt, which had fallen into a state of anarchy, as mentioned above (p. 27), was conquered in 981/1573.

Akbar next turned his attention to Bengal. Sulaymān Karārānī had been the governor under Shēr Shāh, and, after the decline of the Sūrs, had become independent. He died in 980/1572. His son Dā'ūd invaded the Mughal dominions. This resulted in war, ending only when Dā'ūd was captured in battle and executed (984/1576).

Akbar's strictness in the enforcement of regulations regarding the maintenance of troops by local officers resulted in a rebellion in the eastern provinces. It was aggravated by Akbar's attitude towards orthodox Islam, which will be discussed later. Simultaneously his younger brother, Muḥammad Ḥakīm, marched into the Panjāb, and reached Lahore. He did not receive much support, and when he heard that Akbar was marching against him, he retreated. Akbar followed him to Kābul, where Ḥakīm was forgiven. He died four years later. The area around the Khyber pass was occupied by the fanatic sect of Rūshanā' īs. The campaign against them proved difficult, but they were ultimately defeated in 996/1586.

Akbar was disturbed by the rise of 'Abd Allāh Khān Özbeg in Central Asia. The province of Badakhshān was torn with internal dissensions. The tribal area, as has been mentioned, was in a state of unrest, and Kābul itself was badly administered by Ḥakīm. Akbar therefore moved to Lahore to be closer to the scenes of trouble and to plan the control of Kashmir as well. 'Abd Allāh Khān, to whom one of the contestants in

Badakhshān had appealed for help, took hold of that province. Shortly afterwards Muḥammad Ḥakīm died, and Kābul was occupied for Akbar (993/1585). Another Mughal force marched into Kashmir, where it received the homage of its ruler, Yūsuf Shāh, in 994/1586; subsequently Kashmir was formally annexed and Yūsuf was detained as a state prisoner. Sind was annexed in 999/1590 and the ruler, Jānī Beg, appeared at court in 1002/1593. There he won Akbar's favour by becoming his disciple, and was appointed governor of Sind.

Having secured the whole of northern India, Akbar started taking definite steps to bring the Deccan under his control. (An account of the Deccan sultanate is given later in the Appendix.) Missions were sent to different rulers who had sent gifts, these were treated as tribute and gave the Mughals a pretext to interfere in the affairs of the Deccan whenever it suited them. After a protracted war the imperial troops succeeded in occupying Aḥmadnagar (1009/1600), and then annexing the small principality of Khāndēsh. The fall of the Niẓām Shāhī sultanate of Aḥmadnagar demonstrated to the other rulers of the Deccan that it would be difficult for them to resist the might of the Mughal empire.

Salīm, Akbar's eldest son, later the Emperor Jahāngīr, was dissatisfied because his position as heir-apparent had not been recognized. His behaviour at Allahabad, where he was governor, caused some anxiety and in the view of some historians amounted to rebellion. He was reconciled with Akbar and forgiven in 1012/1603. Two years later, in 1014/1605, Akbar died.

By all standards Akbar was personally brave, a good general and an excellent administrator. He was responsible for converting a small kingdom into a resplendent and mighty empire. His name passed into legend and folklore as the embodiment of the qualities associated with great monarchs. However, a good deal of what Akbar did contributed to bringing about the destruction of the fabric that he had built. His patronage of architecture and literature will be discussed elsewhere, as also his peculiarities as a religious thinker.

Jahāngīr

Salīm succeeded to the throne as Nūr al-Dīn Muḥammad Jahāngīr Ghāzī. His son, Khusraw, had also been a claimant. Khusraw was influential, and had the quality of attracting devoted friends. Mān Singh, Khusraw's uncle, was his main supporter. When Jahāngīr ascended the throne, he tried to conciliate Mān Singh and Khusraw. However, Khusraw escaped to the Panjāb, where he attracted some support. An incident of far-reaching consequences was that the Sikh *gurū* Arjun gave his blessings to Khusraw; this embittered the relations between Jahāngīr and the Sikhs, and Sikh-Mughal animosity developed. Khusraw laid siege to Lahore. Jahāngīr marched in pursuit of Khusraw who, leaving a contingent in front of Lahore, turned to fight, and was defeated at Bhairowāl. He was captured in an attempt to cross the Jhelum. Jahāngīr imprisoned the prince, but his followers were punished severely. While in confinement Khusraw hatched a plot, which was revealed, and the ringleaders were executed. Jahāngīr refused to read the entire correspondence for humane reasons. The leading officials thought it unfair that whereas the supporters were punished heavily, nothing happened to the prince who was the root of the trouble. They, therefore, put pressure upon Jahāngīr, and induced him to blind Khusraw to stop him from any further mischief. Soon, however, Jahāngīr relented, and asked physicians to treat the prince whose eyesight was partially restored, but he was not released.

Jahāngīr's queen, Nūr Jahān, was the daughter of Mīrzā Ghiyāṯ Beg, a well-born man of talent, who migrated to India, and rose steadily in the imperial service. She was lady-in-waiting to Akbar's senior widow. Jahāngīr saw her for the first time in 1020/1611, fell in love with her, and married her. Nūr Jahān, beautiful and capable, proved to be a devoted wife. When Jahāngīr's health declined because of asthma, he came to rely more and more upon her. She was supported by her father who was given the title of I'timād al-Dawla. He would have risen anyhow, but his promotion was more rapid because of Nūr Jahān's influence. Her brother Āṣaf Khān was learned, a good administrator, and an expert financier. Her group included Prince Khurram, later the Emperor Shāh Jahān, the most capable of Jahāngīr's sons, and the one obviously marked out for succession. He was Āṣaf Khān's son-in-law.

Jahāngīr's reign can be divided into two parts. The first extends from 1020–32/1611–22 when Jahāngīr still had complete control over affairs. I'timād al-Dawla was alive and exercised a moderating influence, and Nūr Jahān and Khurram were in agreement. During the second period, from 1032/1622 to 1037/1627, Jahāngīr began to lose his hold on the administration because of his ill-health. I'timād al-Dawla was dead, while Khurram and Nūr Jahān became hostile to one another.

In 1021/1612 an Afghan revolt in Bengal gave considerable trouble until a young officer, Islām Khān, was made governor, and succeeded in defeating the rebels. After this the Afghans never gave trouble. Disturbances also broke out in Mēwār where the *rānā*, Amar Singh, had gradually increased his power. The Rājpūts waged guerrilla warfare in the hills. After some time in 1022/1614 Khurram was appointed to Mēwār, to whom Amar Singh submitted and promised not to occupy Chitor again. He was excused from attendance at the court because of his old age, but his son was sent as a hostage for his father's loyalty.

In 1024/1616 Jahāngīr received Sir Thomas Roe. The English had been trying to secure some concessions from the Mughals, and William Hawkins had visited the court eight years earlier. The Mughals had a poor opinion of the English, who were considered to be uncouth and unruly. Roe was unable to obtain any concession, but did succeed in securing permission to carry on trade from Khurram, who was the viceroy of the Deccan.

The situation in the Deccan had taken a turn for the worse, as far as the Mughals were concerned, because of the rise of a Ḥabshī officer, Malik ʻAnbar, to power in Aḥmadnagar. He recruited Marāthās and organized them into guerilla troops, and recovered a good deal of the territory lost to the Mughals. After initial difficulties, the command was given to Prince Khurram. Malik ʻAnbar thought it wise to cede the territory that he had captured. Khurram visited his father after this successful campaign, and was awarded the unprecedented rank of 30,000 (see below, p. 55) and given the title of Shāh Jahān.

By 1033/1623 all power had passed into the hands of Nūr Jahān. She could foresee that Shāh Jahān was not likely to remain under her influence and, therefore, she thought of advancing the incapable Shahryār, Jahangīr's youngest son, as her candidate. With this in view, she married her daughter by her first husband to him in 1030/1620. Iʻtimād al-Dawla died in 1032/1621 and, as Āṣaf Khān was Shāh Jahān's father-in-law, he was not likely to turn against him. Thus Nūr Jahān was isolated. Shāh Jahān's position was strengthened by Khusraw's death in 1031/1622.

In 1016/1606 Shāh ʻAbbās I of Persia instigated his officers to besiege Qandahār, but it was ably defended, and the Persians retired when Mughal reinforcements arrived. Shāh ʻAbbās disowned the campaign. In 1031/1622 Shāh Jahān was asked to march to its relief, but, being afraid of Nūr Jahān's intrigues in his absence, he laid down conditions which were rejected by Jahāngīr. When Shāh Jahān felt that he was likely to be punished, he rebelled. After a tedious campaign he was defeated. He had to send his sons, Dārā Shikōh and Awrangzēb, to court and was demoted to the governorship of Bālāghāt.

The general Mahābat Khān, who had been instrumental in defeating Shāh Jahān, was alienated by Nūr Jahān, and, while Jahāngīr was marching towards Kābul in 1036/1626, Mahābat Khān brought off a *coup* and captured the person of the emperor. Nūr Jahān's attempt to rescue him failed, and Mahābat Khān became the dictator though all appearances of Jahāngīr being at the helm of affairs were kept up. Nūr Jahān, however, was busy throughout, and finally succeeded in getting Mahābat Khān dismissed.

Shāh Jahān made another attempt when he heard that his father had fallen into Nūr Jahān's hands. He received no support, and his progress was stopped at Thatthā. Nūr Jahān, however, administered a strict warning, reminding him that Mahābat Khān's power had been broken. Shāh Jahān was sick, and was carried in a litter through Gujarāt, where Mahābat Khān joined him with a force of two thousand. Thus the two most capable and brilliant generals of the empire were united, but both of them were without resources. They waited for an opportunity. Jahāngīr died in 1037/1627 on his way back from Kashmīr, and his body was carried to Lahore, where he was buried.

Jahāngīr was a sensible, benevolent and generous man. In his beliefs he was a conforming Muslim, although he had in later life a weakness for alcohol. He was responsible for a number of minor reforms. He was a great patron of painting, of which he was a connoisseur, and his coinage is the most distinguished of all Indian issues. He was a simple and straightforward man with no cunning. He retained his affection for Khusraw despite his repeated rebellions, was a devoted husband to Nūr Jahān, was fond of sports, a great lover of nature and desirous of proving a benefactor to his people.

Shāh Jahān

Shāh Jahān was the elder surviving, and the more capable, son and his succession would have been without trouble but for Nūr Jahān's opposition. Āṣaf Khān, however, was in his favour and acted with great circumspection. He put Nūr Jahān under guard, removed Shāh Jahān's son from her charge, and put Khusraw's son on the throne as a stopgap. Shahryār, who proclaimed himself emperor at Lahore, was easily defeated. In the meanwhile Shāh Jahān marched through Gujarāt and reached Āgrā, where he was proclaimed emperor in 1038/1628. Nūr Jahān was given a good pension and lived near Lahore, building Jahāngīr's tomb and engaging in charitable works.

In the Deccan Mahābat Khān had captured Aḥmadnagar, which passed under Mughal rule in 1041/1631. The imperialists had already been encroaching upon Golkondā territory and by 1040/1630 about one third of it had passed into their hands. As Golkondā and Bījāpur were both creating trouble for the Mughals in Aḥmadnagar, Shāh Jahān decided to punish them. In 1047/1636 Golkondā agreed under pressure to remove the name of the shah of Persia from the *khuṭba* and to insert Shāh Jahān's name instead; to abolish the Shīʿī formula on the coins, because the association of a Shīʿī formula with Shāh Jahān's name might have created difficulties for the emperor within his own dominions; to pay an annual tribute, and to help the Mughal troops against Bījāpur.

In 1047/1636 Shāh Jahān demanded that Bījāpur should clearly recognize Mughal sovereignty, pay regular tribute, and cede the territories that had belonged to Aḥmadnagar. As Bījāpur took no action, Shāh Jahān decided on an invasion. Bījāpur sued for peace, which was granted on its acceptance of the demands. After the death of Muḥammad ʿĀdil Shāh in 1067/1656, when his son ʿAlī ʿĀdil Shāh found himself too young to control the factions at the court or suppress rebellion in the kingdom, Shāh Jahān decided to intervene. One of his sons, Awrangzēb, led a successful campaign but at the intervention of Dārā Shikōh, Shāh Jahān's eldest son, much to the chagrin of Awrangzēb, peace was granted on the surrender of some territory.

The Portuguese had established themselves at Huglī in Bengal and, with the help of a large number of converts and half-castes, carried on piracy and kidnapping children to sell them into slavery. In 1049/1639 an expedition freed a large number of slaves, and the Portuguese were forced to pay a large indemnity and evacuate the settlement.

Qandahār was restored to the Mughals through its Persian governor, who came over to them (1048/1638). The Mughals had never given up their dream of recovering their ancestral territories in Transoxania, where internal difficulties encouraged Shāh Jahān to send an expedition. His second son, Murād Bakhsh, was able to occupy Balkh, but because he disliked the climate he was replaced by Awrangzēb, who was able to defeat an Özbeg force in a pitched battle. In 1058/1648, however, Shāh ʿAbbās II intervened openly, and demanded the evacuation of Qandahār and the restoration of Balkh to the Özbegs. Shāh 'Abbās took Qandahār: it was lost to the Mughals, and the Central Asian adventure also came to an end.

In 1068/1657 Shāh Jahān fell ill and was not able to hold public audience. There were wild rumours, and the princes thought that they should make a bid for the throne. Murād Bakhsh proclaimed himself emperor in Gujarāt; Shāh Shujā', a capable administrator and then governor of Bengal, advanced towards the capital; Awrangzēb, with imperial troops under his command, was in correspondence with both, and Dārā Shikōh tried to reduce his power by recalling those troops. One army was sent against Shāh Shujā', another against Murād, and a third was despatched to keep Awrangzēb in check. Shāh Shujā' was defeated and fled to Bengal. Awrangzēb completed his preparations, and marched from Awrangābād in 1069/1658. Murād came and joined him and the two marched on Āgrā. A Rājpūt commander sent to stop Awrangzēb's progress was defeated at Dharmat. Then Dārā had to take the field himself at Sāmūgarh, ten miles east of Āgrā. Awrangzēb won the battle despite his inferior resources, and then marched on Āgrā and took the city. Shāh Jahān tried to lay a trap for him, but an intercepted letter addressed to Dārā Shikōh revealed the plot to Awrangzēb. Murād Bakhsh was arrested and confined, and Awrangzēb ascended the throne with the title of 'Ālamgīr. Shāh Jahān was deposed and confined in Āgrā at his son's order.

'Ālamgīr I (Awrangzēb)

Dārā Shikōh was pursued into Kachh. He crossed into Gujarāt, mustered sufficient resources, and marched northwards. He was captured, tried for heresy, and beheaded, Murād Bakhsh also was executed. Shāh Shujā' marched from Bengal, was defeated in pitched battle near Karā, and was pursued into Bengal. After continuous warfare he escaped into the Arakān, where he was killed in 1072/1661.

In 1072/1662 Mīr Jumlā, the governor of Bengal, led a campaign into Assam because the raja had taken hold of some Mughal territory. In spite of the difficulties of the terrain the raja was defeated.

In 1078/1667 the Yūsufzāy, a Pathān tribe, rose in rebellion. They were defeated near Ātak and were brought under control. Then in 1083/1672 the Afrīdīs revolted. They were inspired by the famous poet Khushḥāl Khān Khatak, who had served Shāh Jahān faithfully, but was disappointed with Awrangzēb when he extended imperial patronage to another tribe. Awrangzēb established himself at Ḥasan Abdāl and systematically brought the tribes under control. In 1086/1675 he left the campaign in the hands of Amīr Khān, who completed the work of pacifying the tribes.

Jaswant Singh, maharaja of Mārwār, had tried to plunder the imperial camp at night on the eve of the battle of Karā when Shāh Shujā' was defeated. He was forgiven and posted at Jamrūd. After his death without heirs in 1089/1678 Awrangzēb brought Mārwār under direct administrative control, and on a posthumous heir being born soon afterwards seized the infant, Ajīt Singh, and his mother. The child was rescued and conveyed to a place of hiding, while the Rājpūt national leader in Mārwār, Durgā Dās, after unsuccessfully opposing the Mughals openly, carried on guerrilla warfare from the hills. The neighbouring Mēwār, which tried to stand by the Mārwār Rājpūts, was no match for the imperial army with its European artillery. Awrangzēb's third son, Akbar, was left in command of Mēwar while Awrangzēb returned to the Mārwār campaign. Akbar ultimately joined forces with the Rājpūt contingents, and marched against his father who was almost defenceless at Ajmēr. However, Prince Mu'aẓẓam managed to join the emperor, who took up a position at Dorāhā to give battle. Through the familiar stratagem of addressing a letter to the prince, commending him for laying a trap for the Rājpūts, and taking care to see it fall into the hands of the enemy, he isolated Akbar who, deserted by his troops, wandered from one place to another until he made his way to the Deccan and joined the Marāthās. Later he made his way to Persia. The war against Mēwār was pursued until the *rānā* secured peace on surrendering three *parganas* in lieu of *jizya*. The campaign against Mārwār went on a little longer until ultimately Durgā Dās was reconciled.

It has been mentioned (p. 46) that Malik 'Anbar organized Marāthā guerillas to harass the Mughals. Even earlier the Marāthās had sought service in Muslim armies, and were prized for their hardihood. Shāhjī Bhonsle had risen to the position of king-maker in Aḥmadnagar. When Shāh Jahān captured that sultanate, Shāhjī migrated to Bījāpur, where also he became powerful. His son, Shivājī, was born in 1037/1627. After the death of Muḥammad 'Ādil Shāh in 1067/1656 Bījāpur declined rapidly, and its control over the mountainous areas so relaxed that Shivājī was able to take many forts, mostly by stratagem. His power went on increasing. In 1075/1664 he sacked Sūrat, two-thirds of the city being destroyed by fire or plunder. In 1076/1665 Awrangzēb sent

Rājā Jay Singh of Ambēr, who forced Shivājī to yield four-fifths of his territory and to acknowledge the sovereignty of the emperor. In 1077/1666 he visited Āgrā and was given command of 5,000 (see below, p. 55). He considered this inadequate, created a scene, and was confined but escaped. After three years of preparation he resumed his activities, occupied large areas, and crowned himself king in 1085/1674. He continued to harass the Mughals until he was attacked by an imperial force, and was forced to fight. The Marāthās suffered heavy losses, though Shivājī escaped. Soon afterwards he died in 1091/1680, and was succeeded by his son, Shambhūjī.

The rapid decline of the Deccan sultanates (see Appendix) and the creation of anarchic conditions, which contributed to the growth of the Marāthā power, could no longer be ignored by Awrangzēb. Bījāpur and Golkondā had not only encouraged the Marāthās, but had actually entered into secret alliances with them. The emperor, therefore, decided to conquer the sultanates so that the Marāthās should not thrive upon their decadence, and moved camp to the Deccan. In 1100/1689 Shambhūjī was defeated, captured and brought before Awrangzēb, when he abused the emperor and the Prophet. He was executed. His family was kept at court, and properly maintained.

The Mughals besieged Bījāpur in 1097/1686, and the ruler, unable to put up a long defence, waited on the emperor, was received kindly and enrolled as a *manṣabdār* with a large pension. All Bījāpurī officers were enrolled in the imperial service.

In 1083/1672 Abu'l-Ḥasan had come to the throne of Golkondā. The power was in the hands of a Brahman minister, Madanna, who entered into a secret alliance with Bījāpur and Shivājī. In 1097/1685 a secret letter to Bījāpur was intercepted in which all help was promised against the Mughals. At this Prince Muʿaẓẓam, now styled Shāh ʿĀlam, was sent against Golkondā. He took Ḥaydarābād and Abu'l-Ḥasan fled to Golkondā. Abu'l-Ḥasan, however, made his peace by the payment of an indemnity and a cession of territory. He promised to dismiss Madanna, but, because the dismissal was put off, the Muslim nobles, who were tired of his tyranny, brought about his assassination. Conditions in Golkondā did not improve, and ultimately Awrangzēb decided to put an end to the dynasty. He therefore annexed the kingdom by proclamation. Despite the fact that a mine under the fort misfired, and killed many of the assailants, the emperor stood firm and saved the situation. The fort was captured. Abu'l-Ḥasan was sent to Dawlatābād with a handsome pension. Awrangzēb was now free to devote his entire attention to the Marāthās. Rājā Rām, who had succeeded Shambhūjī, retired to Jinjī on the east coast, which became the centre of Marāthā activities. It was captured by the Mughals in 1110/1698.

In 1112/1700 Rājā Rām died, and Shivājī III was put on the throne. Between 1110/1689 and 1112/1700 the Mughals conquered the whole of the north Konkan from the Marāthās. Awrangzēb himself patiently went on conquering one fort after another between 1111/1699 and 1117/1705 but he fell ill and died in 1118/1707. The Marāthā snake had been scotched but not killed, and was to give considerable trouble to the Mughals (and to the British) in subsequent years.

Awrangzēb was a pious Muslim. He was an excellent general and possessed the qualities of determination and perseverance to a remarkable degree. The last great monarch of the dynasty, he took his responsibilities as an orthodox Muslim ruler seriously, and endeavoured to make Islam once again the dominant force in the realm. After the policies of the three previous reigns, this brought him into conflict with the forces arrayed against such a revival.

ADMINISTRATION

The Mughal emperors claimed to be fully independent monarchs, and to be caliphs within their dominions. After the abolition of the ʿAbbasid caliphate in Baghdād, some jurists had already come to believe that a universal caliphate was no longer necessary, and that every independent monarch should discharge the duties of a caliph inside his realm. However, the rulings of the jurists regarding the functions of the caliph were applicable to independent monarchs as well. The monarch was the chief executive of his realm, and the commander of its forces. His power was limited by the *Sharīʿa*.

Akbar, however, made a correct analysis of the situation and decided that if he allied himself with the non-Muslims and the heterodox elements in the Muslim population, he could reduce orthodoxy to helplessness. He succeeded, and became virtually a temporal sovereign outside the practice of Islamic kingship. Orthodoxy, however, rallied towards the end of his reign, and gradually built up a power which could not be ignored. Jahāngīr, therefore, had to restore such institutions of orthodox Islam as had been put in abeyance, the only exception being the *jizya*. The orthodox reaction did not subside, and ultimately resulted in the policies of Awrangzēb, who was not only personally orthodox like Shāh Jahān, but also relied heavily upon orthodox support.

The Mughal emperor was in a very real sense the head of the government. He had all authority centered in his hands. Next to the

Map 10a. The Indian sub-continent in 1525.

monarch was the *wakīl al-salṭana*, who was theoretically the lieutenant of the monarch in all civil and military matters. During the period of Akbar's minority, this office possessed real authority. Later, because of the active role played by the emperors themselves, the post became an empty honour. The *wazīr* or *dīwān*, as he came to be called, was the head

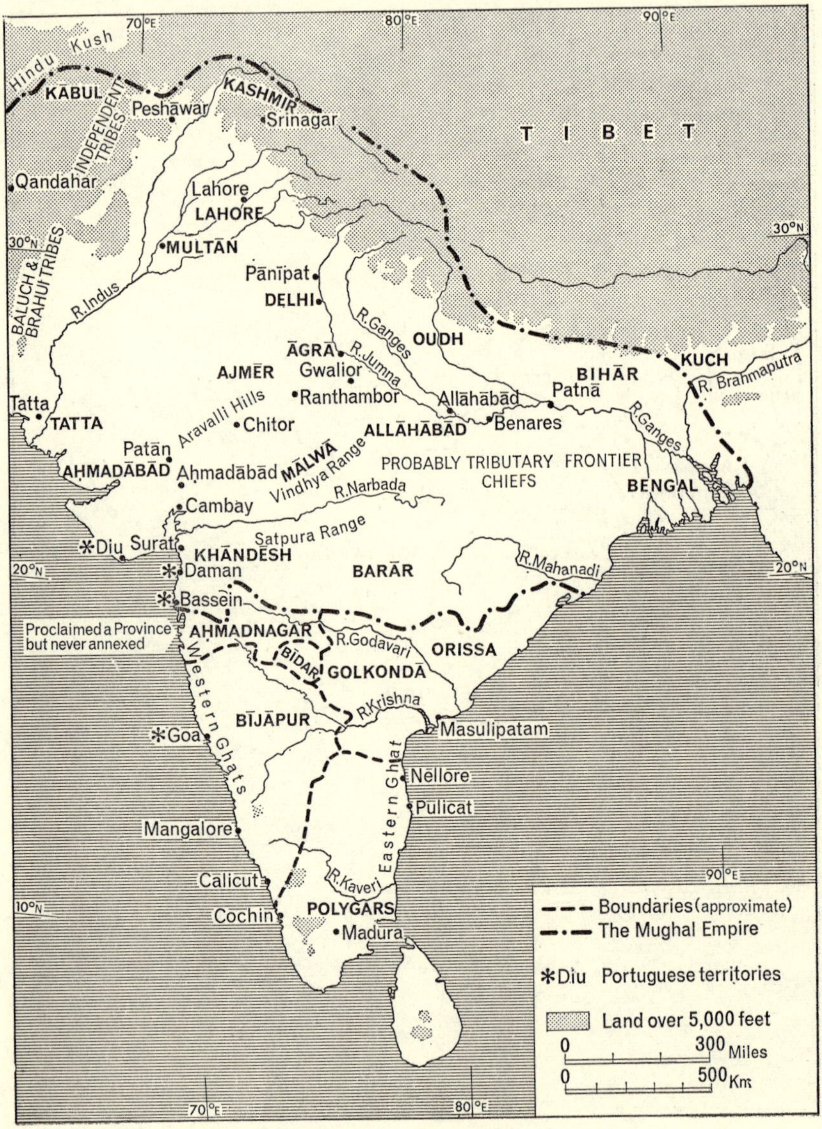

Map 10b. The Indian sub-continent in 1605.

of the fiscal administration. He was assisted by a *dīwān-i khāliṣa*, who looked after the unassigned lands and cash salaries; a *dīwān-i tan*, who was responsible for all assignments in land, called *jāgīrs*. The *mīr bakhshī* was responsible for the proper organization of the army, and was the chief recruiting officer and paymaster. He also controlled the various agencies that kept the central government informed of the happenings in the provinces. He was assisted by three assistants: the second, third, and fourth *bakhshīs*. The *ṣadr al-ṣudūr* was responsible for religious affairs, pious foundations, grants to scholars and men of merit. He was also the chief judge with the dual function of *qāẓī al-quẓāt*.

The public services were organized under a unified system called *manṣabdārī*. An official's rank was fixed within a complex cadre by his *manṣab*. In the beginning, officers were grouped into ranks ranging from commanders of ten (*dah bāshī*) to commanders of 5,000 (*panj hazārī*). Later the *manṣabs* were increased and commands of 7,000 (*haft hazārī*) were created. Sometimes very large *manṣabs* were conferred, for instance, Jahāngīr bestowed the unprecedented rank of 30,000 upon Khurram when he was awarded the title of Shāh Jahān. Within the same rank, however, were variations based upon the additional rank of *sawār* (troops). Thus a commander of 5,000 might have the rank of 5,000 *ẓāt* (personal) and 5,000 *sawār*. The *sawār* rank could vary from nil to the figure of the *manṣab*. Those officers whose *sawār* rank corresponded to the *ẓāt* rank belonged to the first class; those whose *sawār* rank was less than the *ẓāt* rank but half or more than half of the *ẓāt* rank to the second class; and the rest to the third. A further complication was introduced by the number of horses in the contingent. Thus, for instance, an officer could be 5,000 *ẓāt*, 5,000 *sawār*, 3,000 *dō aspa sih aspa*. The *dō aspa sih aspa* rank meant that a certain proportion of the contingent assigned to the officer contained, in a prescribed proportion, troopers with two horses and three horses each. The *dō aspa sih aspa* rank determined the number of months in the year for which the *manṣabdār* drew his salary. The system was further complicated by the fact that none of the figures denoted the actual number of troopers maintained by the *manṣabdār*. In Shāh Jahān's reign, for instance, many *manṣabdārs* were expected to maintain only a fifth of the *sawār* contingent. Another complication was created by the fact that sometimes all the ranks were purely fictitious and a *manṣabdār* was not expected to maintain any soldiers at all; this was merely a convenient device to fix the position of civilian officers in the cadre. So long as the emperors were vigilant, the *manṣabdārī* system, despite its cumbersome nature, served them well, because all appointments and promotions were made on merit.

The finances were provided mainly by the state demand upon agricultural produce. Other sources of revenue, such as the customs, were not so important. *Jizya*, never a great source of revenue, was abolished by Akbar and reimposed by Awrangzēb.

The agrarian administration of the Mughals was scientific and benevolent. Although Akbar's *dīwān* Todar Mall is given much credit for bringing the Mughal provinces within a unified system of administration, his principles were in fact those first applied in the extensive reforms of Shēr Shāh. Apart from the old systems of crop-sharing by division of the harvested yield, the division of the standing crops, or by appraisement of the estimated yield after harvesting, the system mainly in use was that of measuring the area cultivated and calculating the yield on the basis of schedules of produce. These were kept up to date through the maintenance of a record of the 'medium' produce of an area and taking a fresh decennial average of it every year. Sample cuttings were made of good, middling and poor crops, by which the figure of 'medium' produce was determined for the entire area which formed the basis of the schedule. Akbar raised the state demand from a fourth to a third of the gross produce, though in certain provinces, because of long-standing traditions, it varied from one-tenth to a half. Payments to public servants were made in cash or through *jāgīrs*, i.e. grants of land. The assignee collected the state demand, but maintained the same machinery of assessment and collection for the assigned area. The *jāgīrs* were not the property of the assignee; they were transferred, resumed or awarded to new assignees. The *manṣabdārs* were servants of the state, the salaries were fixed in cash and the assignment was only a method of payment.

All disputes between citizens were within the jurisdiction of the *qāẓī*. All complaints against servants of the government came within the purview of *maẓālim* courts. The *maẓālim* court at the centre was presided over by the monarch himself and was attended by the *qāẓī al-quẓāt* to tender advice on legal matters. The monarch acted as a *siyāsa* (summary) court in dealing with rebels and prisoners of war. No death-penalty could be enforced without the previous consent of the emperor.

The provincial government was organized on the pattern of the central government. Every department dealt with the corresponding department at the centre and was under its control. The head of the provincial government was the *ṣūbadār*. The provincial *maẓālim* courts consisted of the *ṣūbadār*, the *dīwān*, the provincial *bakhshī* and the provincial *qāẓī*. The provinces (sing., *ṣūba*) were divided into *sarkārs*, and the *sarkārs* into *parganas*. The units of administration were the village and the *pargana*.

ASPECTS OF CULTURE

Literature

Literary activities flourished under the patronage of the emperor as well as the nobles, some of whom were *littérateurs* themselves. Akbar's court poet was Fayżī. Other important poets were 'Urfī, Naẓīrī and Ẓuhūrī, all of whom hold a high position in the history of Persian poetry. Ṭālib Āmulī was the poet laureate in Jahāngīr's reign. Ṣā'ib came into prominence under Shāh Jahān. Under Awrangzēb, Bēdil's philosophical fancies and insight earned him great popularity amongst intellectuals. The poetry of this period is characterized by its polished and elegant diction and its remarkable insight into psychology, a complexity of thought, combined also with a concern for the philosophy of life. A Hindu poet of great eminence who wrote in Persian was Brahman, whose poems enjoy popularity even today. Translations were also made into Persian of the sacred writings of the Hindus.

The Mughal courts saw also a great development in the literatures of Indian languages: Mughal rulers and nobles were active patrons of Indian literature, especially Hindī, and there is a small but important corpus of Hindī works by Muslim writers. In addition, the toleration shown to Hindus by some Mughal courts, especially under Akbar and Jahāngīr, led to the production of fine devotional poetry by Hindus. The Ṣūfīs' allegorical poems in Hindī, known from the late eighth/fourteenth century, continued into Mughal times, and Malik Muḥammad Jāyasī's *Padmāvāt* of 947/1540, an allegory of the search of man's soul for wisdom cast in a delightful love-story, is the finest such epic of the period, of the calibre of Spenser's *Faerie Queene*. This and similar allegories are of a form resembling the Persian *maṣnavī*, but in Indian metres. A very different *genre* of poetry was in favour at the courts, a deliberately cultivated display of the poetic art, as originally formulated in Sanskrit court-poetry, on erotic themes. At Akbar's court the cultivated general and minister 'Abd al-Raḥīm, the Khān-i Khānān, was a leading Hindī poet under the pen-name Raḥīm, and popularized a new metre.

Other languages similarly produced fine literatures in the courts of the Deccan. At Bījāpur, especially under Ibrāhīm II, Kannada and Dakhnī poetry were as esteemed as Persian; while at Golkondā, besides some cultivation of Telugu verse, excellent Dakhnī poetry was written by members of the royal house.

Historiography was well represented, and except for the later part of Awrangzēb's reign there are reliable histories for every reign. The *Akbar-nāma* and *Ā'īn-i Akbarī* of Abu'l-Fażl, in spite of their difficult and rhetorical style, constitute the greatest historical works of Akbar's period, coloured throughout by excessive adulation of the emperor. In addition, a number of religious and literary biographies throw considerable light upon the period. Two autobiographies are famous: Bābur's memoirs are considered to be one of the most revealing and sincere autobiographies ever written; different in nature and style, Jahāngīr's memoirs are an excellent record of the period.

Awrangzēb himself was a master of style, and various collections have been made of his letters. The letters of Shaykh Aḥmad of Sirhind collected in *Maktūbāt-i imām-i rabbānī* form source-material for writing on his mission. A remarkable book is the *Dabistān-i maẕāhib*, which is almost an encyclopaedia of the various religions and sects found in the sub-continent during the period. The author, Muḥsin Fānī, was a Zoroastrian.

Painting

There is some evidence to show that painting was practised under the sultans of Delhi, and a well-defined school of miniature painting grew up in Gujarāt. Painting, however, received great impetus under the Mughals. Bābur was a critic and has relevant observations on the artists of his period. His son Humāyūn found time during his exile in Persia to go to Tabrīz and meet some of the leading artists of the city. He was able to attract Mīr Sayyid 'Alī and Khwāja 'Abd al-Ṣamad to his court after Shāh Ṭahmāsp's loss of interest in the arts, and these two artists joined him in Delhi after his return. They were entrusted with the task of illustrating the epic of Amīr Ḥamza. Some of these paintings on cloth are still extant though unfortunately many have been mutilated. Under Akbar the school was developed further. A large number of artists were employed to work under the direction of Mīr Sayyid 'Alī and later of Khwāja 'Abd al-Ṣamad, and a large number of books were illustrated, using new techniques and materials, under the emperor's personal interest. Because of the employment of a number of Hindu artists a new spirit entered the pictures. The growth of new trends soon freed the Mughal school from purely Persian conventions. Under

Jahāngīr, who while still a prince maintained his own *atelier*, the school developed further. It achieved maturity and distinctiveness. It retained its vigour but it was softened with grace and aesthetic sensitiveness. As Jahāngīr was fond of birds and flowers, more of the local environment entered into the paintings, especially in the background. Western influence also began to make itself felt through Jahāngīr's interest in the paintings brought from Europe by the Jesuit missions. It showed itself in the adoption, in some paintings, of linear and aerial perspective called *dūrnumā*. One typical Mughal canon of perspective was of one plane superimposed on the other with a plurality of vanishing-points, so that all details were shown equally clearly; but European unitary perspective was also introduced.

Under Shāh Jahān, though the excellence of the pictures was unaffected, there was a ripeness that felt baffled in seeking new avenues of excellence. It expressed itself in the richness of materials and especially in elaborately ornate margins. It is wrongly believed that painting languished under Awrangzēb. The ripeness of Shāh Jahān's reign, however, turned into decay and, though some excellent pictures were painted, art lost its vigour; certainly there was less patronage, and the status of the artist was much degraded.

The Mughal school of miniature painting reached an excellence which has seldom been surpassed. In spite of the handicaps of the conventions which admitted only profiles or three-quarter faces, and mostly stiff postures, the Mughal portrait painter was somehow able to depict the very soul of the subject. Even in large groups, this quality is maintained in drawing the individuals. The pictures were drawn in three styles: *rangīn qalam* (full colours), *nīm rang* (one prevailing colour, mostly sepia), and *siyāhī qalam* (black and white). The figures have the rhythmic beauty of the calligraphic curve, and the composition of groups, as well as the distribution of colours, is excellent. It was not uncommon for the outlines to be done by one artist and the colourings by another. Copies on vellum (*charba*) were taken of the linework of portraits and groups, from which further paintings might be made in later years. It is a remarkable testimony to the realism of the school that Awrangzēb, feeling concerned about his son Mu'aẓẓam, when he was placed in confinement in 1098/1687, asked the painters to send him regularly pictures of the prince so that the emperor could see himself that the prince's health had not suffered. Mughal art was entirely secular, and concerned itself mainly with the court, though sometimes pictures relating to the life of the people were also painted. Jahāngīr had the habit of having painted a new bird or a new flower that he came across, and his favourite painter, Manṣūr, has been acclaimed as one of the greatest nature painters of the world. The influence from Muslim countries was kept alive by the employment of painters from outside. One of the most outstanding of these was Farrukh Beg, who arrived in the last years of Akbar's reign.

The Rājpūt schools of painting, which grew up under the inspiration of the Mughal school, also deserve mention. Their themes were strikingly different: Hindu epics and religious themes, and also symbolic representations of the sentiment of musical modes (*rāgas*).

Calligraphy was looked upon as an allied art and received generous patronage. It was practised on a much wider scale and the period produced some outstanding calligraphists.

Music

The difficulties of the interpretation of the evidence concerning Indian music mentioned in the previous chapter are no less in the Mughal period. The greatest name, perhaps, of this period is that of Tānsēn, a converted Hindu who became a disciple of the saint Muḥammad Ghaws̱ of Gwalior, near whom he is buried. Everyone knows of him and pays lip-service to him; yet it is now almost completely impossible to form any idea of why he was so highly praised or of what contributions to music he made.

RELIGION

The first millennium of the Hijra came to a close in the sixteenth century. Many Muslim minds were attracted to the idea of the advent of the *mahdī*, a leader who would breathe new life into Islam. This idea had become common and was accepted even in orthodox circles. Sayyid Muḥammad, a pious and learned professor in the university town of Jawnpur, came to believe that he was the *mahdī* and proclaimed his mission. His teachings were not heretical. He demanded greater conformity with the *Sharī'a*. His claim, however, was rejected by the orthodox *'ulamā'*, and he met with such opposition that he had to emigrate from the sub-continent. He died in exile in 911/1505. Two of his disciples carried on his mission. The first was Shaykh 'Abd Allāh Niyāzī who settled near Bayānā. A young scholar, Shaykh 'Alā'ī, became his disciple, and gathered a large following, who did not limit themselves to preaching, but tried to enforce the *Sharī'a* through coercion. This brought conflict with the officials. Makhdūm al-Mulk, the *ṣadr al-ṣudūr*, asked for a trial of Shaykh 'Alā'ī. The ruling sultan, Islām Shāh, despite his strictness, did not want to push matters to extremes, but on Makhdūm al-Mulk's insistence, Shaykh 'Alā'ī was flogged. Already weak and emaciated through austerity and wandering, Shaykh 'Alā'ī collapsed and died at the very first stroke. 'Abd Allāh Niyāzī also was flogged, and was removed by his followers, who nursed him back to health. Later a message was received from Sayyid Muḥammad that he had repented at the time of his death and seen his error. 'Abd Allāh gave it credence and recanted. Many others, however, refused to believe the message. The followers of the sect are still found in the Deccan and in Gujarāt, though their numbers are small. The orthodox hostility to these Mahdawīs led to systematic persecution which made the theologians in power unpopular.

There was some impact of Islam on Indian religious thought at this time. Certainly some Ṣūfī teachers, especially those of the Chishtī order, had made a popular front for their own views through their allegorical romances in Indian vernaculars; probably with some acceptance, for Ṣūfī mysticism often has much in common with the pantheistic mysticism of the Indian *Vedānta*. To their influence, both from their teachings and on account of the popular respect they commanded as saints and thaumaturges, may be attributed the partial conversions amongst the lower strata of Indian society—communities with more or less of Muslim belief on particular points of doctrine but generally faithful also to the godlings of popular Hinduism, its rites, festivals, social implications and prescriptions. On a higher level of influence comes the strictly monotheistic thought of such teachers as Kabīr—who in spite of his Muslim name preached strongly against what he considered to be the fallacies of both Hinduism and Islam—and Nānak, who added to Kabīr's monotheism a discipline of religion which he so much admired in Islam. But his Sikhs later developed an antagonism to the Mughal rulers, and Sikhism became the implacable adversary of Islam in north India.

Akbar, who was tired of subservience to the leaders of orthodox Islam, sought political support from non-Muslims and heterodox sectors of Islam. They gradually led him away from orthodoxy. Akbar instituted discussions on religious topics, to which in the beginning only Muslims were invited, but later men of all faiths participated, and discussions took place regarding the very fundamentals of Islam.

Amongst those who participated were Hindu pandits, Jain anchorites, Zoroastrian *mūbids* and Catholic priests. Akbar was persuaded to believe in his own spiritual attainments and he began to enrol members of different faiths as his disciples. His views were certainly not those of orthodox Islam, though the charge that he denounced Islam and ceased consciously to be a Muslim is not proved. Too much importance has been attached to the reports of the Catholic fathers by some modern writers and errors have crept into the translations of Badā'ūnī's cryptic and ambiguous statements.[1] Akbar built up a superstructure of eclectic pantheism upon the heretical views of some heterodox Ṣūfīs and others, which he perhaps only partially understood. The system he promulgated is generally called *Dīn-i Ilāhī* (Divine Faith), which attracted a little support in his court. Towards the end of his life, Akbar's enthusiasm for religious innovation considerably cooled down and we do not find any exercise in religious speculation after the assassination of Abu'l-Fażl who, along with his brother Fayżī the poet, has been credited by some for turning Akbar away from orthodox Islam. There were so many complex influences at work that even Akbar was more the recipient of ideas than a thinker.

The political repercussions of Akbar's religious thought have been mentioned earlier. At the instigation of Abu'l-Fażl's father, Shaykh Mubārak, a manifesto was drawn up to which the leading *'ulamā'* of the court were forced to affix their signatures saying that Akbar was a just ruler (*imām-i 'ādil*), and as such empowered to choose any interpretation which was in accordance with the Qur'ān and good for the realm if the *mujtahids* disagreed. This has been wrongly termed a decree of infallibility, but it was intended to weaken the position of orthodox Islam. Akbar could not be termed *imām-i 'ādil*, because he was not equipped to adjudicate between the differences of opinion of learned lawyers. However, the decree was never utilized, and Akbar relied upon the political device of appointing to high religious and legal offices his own nominees, men with pliant consciences who would carry out his wishes.

At the time of Jahāngīr's accession the orthodox party had gained sufficient influence to defeat the machinations of their rivals, and extracted from him a promise that he would restore the institutions of Islam. The movement gained momentum under the leadership of Shaykh Aḥmad of Sirhind, who is known as the *mujaddid* (renewer of the faith)

[1] For a fuller discussion, see I. H. Qureshi, *The Muslim community of the Indo-Pakistan subcontinent* (The Hague, 1962).

of the second millennium. He was a practising Ṣūfī of the Naqshbandī order, but he was able to see the harm that was being done by the views of the monists of the Shaṭṭārī and Qādirī orders. He relied upon his mystic experience to state categorically that the sensation of monism (i.e. union with the godhead) was not the highest expression of mystic progress because it was experienced in a state of ecstasy which he called *sukr* (intoxication). The higher stage was when a person was able to have this experience without losing his own sense of identity. This doctrine was reinforced with philosophical arguments. The philosophy of *waḥdat al-shuhūd* (feeling of monism through mystic experience) as opposed to *waḥdat al-wūjūd* (monism as a reality) was used for the purpose of eliminating heterodox doctrines (mainly based upon monism) from Sufism. The shaykh's influence was considerable, and we find that gradually orthodoxy was able to recapture the minds of the people as well as the leaders and this expresses itself in its growing strength until it culminated in the orthodox measures of Awrangzēb. This was no doubt partly political: his popular elder brother, Dārā Shikōh, was a disciple of a Ṣūfī of the Qādiriyya, had studied Hindu philosophy and mysticism, and in his *Majma' al-baḥrayn* sees a 'mingling of the two seas' of Hindu pantheism and Muslim mysticism, of a type similar to Ibn al-'Arabī's. Shaykh Aḥmad's influence was not limited to the sub-continent: through the Mujaddidiyya branch of the Naqshbandīyya order it spread as far as Turkey in the west and Indonesia in the east. It was through his efforts that Sufism gradually turned away from heterodoxy, and became one of the main supporters of orthodoxy.

APPENDIX

THE SULTANATES OF THE DECCAN, SIXTEENTH TO EIGHTEENTH CENTURIES

The rise of the five Deccan sultanates from the chaos of the Bahmanī empire, through the assertion of autonomy by the provincial governors, has been mentioned in the previous chapter. Their subsequent political history is largely a record of continuous strife between them, with occasional and variously aligned alliances but only on one significant occasion a community of interest. Internally, however, in spite of their border troubles, they developed major literary, religious and cultural centres.

To some extent all the sultanates inherited the factionalism of local and foreign elements which had led to the disruption of the Bahmanī empire; although the religious tensions implicit in this faction were less prominent, as the influential Shī'a tended to be concentrated in the Shī'ī sultanates, Bījāpur and Golkondā. The Barīd Shāhīs in Bīdar and the 'Imād Shāhīs in Barār were Sunnī, as were the Niẓām Shāhīs of Aḥmadnagar until Burhān I adopted Shi'ism in 944/1537. The sultanate of the Barīd Shāhīs was gradually encroached upon in the north and west by Bījāpur, against which Bīdar made occasional alliances with the other sultanates; Bījāpur was subject to continual pressure on the south from the Vijayanagara kingdom, and the only occasion on which all the sultanates, except the northern Barār, acted jointly was when their confederation defeated Vijayanagara at the battle of Tālīkota in 972/1564–5. Bīdar was finally annexed by the 'Ādil Shāhīs of Bījāpur in 1028/1619.

The 'Imād Shāhīs were remote enough in Barār to avoid most of the Deccan inter-sultanate conflicts, although there were occasional clashes with the Niẓām Shāhīs. Eventually, after the battle of Tālīkota, when Bījāpur was able to enlarge its dominions by the annexation of former Vijayanagara possessions, Aḥmadnagar was anxious to achieve a similar increase of strength. She therefore invaded Barār in 981–2/1574–5, and extinguished and absorbed the 'Imād Shāhī power.

The Niẓām Shāhīs were generally in a state of dispute with the two large sultanates, Bījāpur and Golkondā; one sultanate was always eventually compelled to intervene in a war between any two others lest one should become victorious, and so upset the balance of power to the disadvantage of the original non-belligerent. It was indeed in this way that these three sultanates were able to remain in existence where the single Bahmanī sultanate had failed. Part of the Aḥmadnagar-Bījāpur dispute arose from a royal marriage in 927/1521 when the Bījāpur princess's dowry was stipulated as the border fort of Sholāpur, which Bījāpur consistently failed to cede. In 937/1531 Burhān I of Aḥmadnagar, alarmed by the growth of the power of Bahādur Shāh of Gujarāt, who had just annexed Mālwā and with whom Khāndēsh was now closely allied, offered him his allegiance. The aim of Bahādur was to enlist Aḥmadnagar's support against the Mughals, but Burhān secretly suggested to Humāyūn that he attack Gujarāt. A compact between Aḥmadnagar and Bījāpur to annex Barār and Golkondā respectively in 941/1534 was pursued, but abandoned on the death of the Bījāpur sultan, Ismā'īl. His successor, Ibrāhīm, instituted Sunnism as the official faith, dismissed most of the 'foreign' element, and by substituting Marāthī and Kannada for Persian allowed the free employment of Brahmans in his administration. Shortly afterwards Bījāpur-Aḥmadnagar relations worsened when the Niẓām Shāhī ruler embraced Shi'ism. Bījāpur was faced also with rebellion in its Konkan provinces, fomented by the Portuguese at Goa which they had taken from Bījāpur in 915/1510. From the 960s/1550s the 'Ādil Shāhīs actually turned to Vijayanagara for assistance against their rivals; but Vijayanagara soon became the dominant partner in the Bījāpur/Golkondā/Vijayanagara confederacy, offended allies and enemy alike by the insults it offered Islam, and made arrogant demands on the sultanates as the price of its assistance in arms, and their excesses led to the battle of Tālīkota already mentioned.

Aḥmadnagar, constantly at war with Bījāpur and weakened by wars of succession, had further trouble from a Mahdawī faction in 999/1591. On the death of the ruler some four years later, four contending factions were leading towards anarchy when an appeal was made to the Mughals for help. They were in fact preparing for an invasion of the Deccan when the appeal arrived, and Aḥmadnagar was soon under siege from them. The dowager queen, Chānd Bībī, purchased its liberty by the cession of Barār; but Mughal ambition was not to be denied, and the city fell to them in 1009/1600. Within ten years the Ḥabshī minister, Malik 'Anbar, had ousted the Mughals and restored a nominal Niẓām Shāhī dynasty, but the state was still under heavy Mughal pressure and Bījāpur was able to acquire much of the southern Aḥmadnagar lands. The defection of a Mughal nobleman to Aḥmadnagar led to a renewed Mughal attack in 1039/1630, and the kingdom finally fell to the Mughals three years later.

In Bījāpur a Mughal force had in 1046/1636 forced a peace compelling the acknowledgment of Mughal suzerainty, and the land remained peaceful for some twenty years thereafter until the Marāthās under Shivājī commenced a series of depredations on the north and west. This did not prevent Bījāpur from retaining its position as a great cultural centre; but politically it was almost a spent force when it finally fell to Awrangzēb in 1097/1686.

The Quṭb Shāhī kingdom of Golkondā was less disturbed than its neighbours, and knew less internal party and religious faction. The city of Hyderabad (Ḥaydarābād), built with much magnificence at the end of the tenth/sixteenth century, had for six years a Persian embassy from Shāh 'Abbās, and was a leading centre of Shī'ī scholarship. The Dutch established themselves at Masulipatam, on the Madras coast, in 1024/1615, and the English seven years later. In the 1040s/1630s the Golkondā possessions to the south were extended, but the Mughals were pressing on the north and in 1045/1635–6 Shāh Jahān forced the payment of tribute. The Golkondā minister Mīr Jumlā having aggrandized himself in the east, the sultan appealed to Awrangzēb for aid; this led to the Mughal siege of Golkondā in 1066/1656, which was bought off. But the later rise of two Brahman ministers provoked Awrangzēb to renewed attack, and Golkondā finally fell in 1098/1687.

CHAPTER 3

THE BREAKDOWN OF TRADITIONAL SOCIETY

By the beginning of the eighteenth century, Muslim society in India was composed of descendants of Turkic, Afghan, Persian and Arab immigrants, and of Indian Muslims who had embraced Islam in different regions and circumstances, and under varied pressures. The immigrants, who themselves belonged to distinct culture groups, brought with them the characteristic features of their ethnic and non-Islamic religious backgrounds. In the course of time, the interaction of their various ideas and values contributed to the rise of cultural traditions which were radically different from those of their birthplaces; Muslims, while retaining the broad basic framework of their religion, evolved healthy traditions of toleration, and of peaceful coexistence with the indigenous population. A great deal of similarity developed in the dress and ornaments of Hindus and Muslims. Though the eating habits of the members of the two religious groups differed in important respects, especially in the eating of meat, these difficulties did not undermine their social relations. They appreciated each other's religions and social taboos and adjusted their lives in an atmosphere of social amity and mutual understanding. Hindu and Muslim peasants, artisans, craftsmen and merchants worked in close co-operation with each other. Hindu bankers, merchants and money-lenders controlled trade and commerce and exercised considerable influence over the finances of the government. They were the backbone of society.

The use of Persian served as a strong unifying bond between the Hindu and Muslim upper classes. Translations of some Hindu religious works into Persian widened the outlook of those Hindus who were linked with the Mughal administrative machinery; and an atmosphere of sympathetic understanding of the spiritual problems of the two major religions of India was thus created. The verses of Sa'dī, Rūmī and Ḥāfiẓ regulated the patterns of social behaviour of Hindus and Muslims alike. The educational policy and the translation scheme undermined Brahmanical superiority in the interpretation of Hinduism. The obscurantism and bigotry of Awrangzēb disturbed the Hindu and Muslim nobility alike. The control of the Hindus over the revenue and the financial policies and administration of the Mughals had made even the Muslim theologians and other religious functionaries dependent upon them for the verification of their land grants. The occasional outbursts of the theologians and the Ṣūfīs against the Hindu administrative officers of the Mughals should be ascribed to their failure to make the administrative machinery subservient to their demands.

The system of state employment evolved by Akbar, known as the *manṣabdārī* system, absorbed all types of landed interests such as Rājpūts, Bundēlās, hill rajas, Jāts, Marāthās, and the Muslim tribes and ethnic groups, into the same graded hierarchy, with definite salaries either in the form of a *jāgīr* (assignment of land) or partly in cash and partly in *jāgīr*, for each *manṣab* (rank) and for the number of horsemen maintained. They constituted the upper crust of society. Their tribal, racial, or ethnic interests conditioned their alliances and enmities; religion played hardly any significant role in political and official dealings. The secular laws of the government exercised an overriding control over the administration.

The *zamīndārs* were those who held various types of hereditary land rights. From the highest Rājpūt chieftains down to the petty 'intermediaries' at village level, all were known as *zamīndārs*. They were ambitious, restless and given to intrigue. Akbar assimilated them to the Mughal administrative machinery by offering them *manṣabs* commensurate with their status and ability. The emperor's paramount authority to appoint, depose, or reduce rank kept them under proper control and various other restrictions ensured their loyalty to the emperor. They collected the revenue from the cultivators and credited the state's share to the imperial treasury through the official revenue collectors. They maintained law and order in their jurisdiction, protected the roads and other means of communication and were required to promote cultivation. Their rights and privileges were superior to those of the other cultivators in the village. The dispossessed Afghan nobles among the Muslims enjoyed large and compact *zamīndārī* interests. Under them, a considerable number of other Afghans and their retainers controlled many villages. The *zamīndārs* of other caste groups also held compact areas under their control. This enabled them to rebel without much inconvenience and on the slightest provocation. Religious and racial questions added to the confusion. The system itself was responsible for the frequent Jāt, Sikh and Afghan revolts in the north and those of the Marāthās and the Deccan Muslims in the south.

Grants were also made for religious and charitable purposes to scholars, theologians, and members of respectable families who had no other means of livelihood. The descendants of the Muslim saints, and of the Prophet, were the greatest beneficiaries under this system. Subsequently they also came to hold compact *zamīndārī* interests in different villages. These grants were liable to be resumed at the death of the assignee, though some grants were hereditary. The conditions under which grants were made were not always complied with by grantees; and any interference on the part of the administrators to curtail the privileges of the beneficiaries met with strong resistance.

The peculiar features of the Mughal administrative system produced three types of villages. There were villages consisting exclusively of a Hindu or Muslim population, and there were others with a mixed population. The exclusively or predominantly Muslim villages had their mosques with *imāms*, *mullās* and other religious functionaries, who played a vital role in directing village life into healthy channels, and exhibited restraint, understanding and sympathy in the celebration of religious festivals and other communal functions. The tomb of a genuine or legendary saint or a martyr was an object of veneration to Hindus and Muslims alike. Revivalistic and puritanical movements could not eradicate all syncretic tendencies.

The pressure on the supply of *jāgīrs*, the demand for which increased at the end of the seventeenth century because of the costly military campaigns of Awrangzēb ('Ālamgīr I) in the impoverished Deccan, and the need to reconcile Deccani nobles, unbalanced the Mughal administrative machinery. Awrangzēb's policy of breaking the *zamīndār* cliques by encouraging them to embrace Islam, and thus driving a wedge into their ranks, strengthened their parochial and separatist tendencies. Those *zamīndārs* who did not pay revenue unless military force was applied against them, were a perpetual source of trouble to the Mughal administration. At the end of the seventeenth century, in combination with other recalcitrants, such people rose in rebellion in several places. Some of them used religious slogans to rally support for their cause, and ambitious religious leaders lent a willing ear to them. In the eighteenth century these *zamīndārs* assumed the role of autonomous chiefs.

The war of succession after the death of Awrangzēb dealt a heavy blow to the straitened resources of the empire; and the prodigality of Shāh 'Ālam Bahādur Shāh (1119–24/1707–12) shattered the basis of the *jagīr*-

dārī system. Subsequently, to the detriment of the interests of the central government, encroachments were made on crown land which began to be assigned as *jāgīrs*. An attempt to replenish the treasury by introducing a revenue-farming system aggravated the crisis. The powerful factions at the court began to bid for the profitable and most easily manageable *jāgīrs*, and the leading aspirants for power embarked upon a scramble for the key positions of the empire. Gradually some *manṣabdārs* also acquired permanent *zamīndārī* rights.

Formerly the Mughal nobles had intrigued to gain the favour of their masters; now they assumed the position of king-makers. The leading Muslim factions unhesitatingly set out to seek the protection of the Marāthās, the Rājpūts and the Jāts whenever it suited their purpose. Ẕu'l-Faqār Khān, the all-powerful *wazīr*, obtained the abolition of the *jizya* through Jahāndār Shāh, whom he raised to the throne in 1124/1712. Even the reversal of the policy of Awrangzēb did not save the Mughal empire from dissolution. Failure to keep pace with technological developments in other parts of the world and to introduce much-needed administrative reforms precipitated its downfall. Nādir Shāh's invasion of 1152/1739 left the imperial capital, Delhi, bleeding and prostrate. The surrender of Sind, Kābul and the western parts of the Panjāb to the invader made the Mughal frontiers vulnerable to successive invasions by the Afghan chief, Aḥmad Shāh Durrānī (1160–87/1747–73). His rise contributed to the encouragement of the Indian Afghans, who began to make a fresh bid for supremacy over the ruins of the Mughal empire. The Afghan chief Najīb al-Dawla assumed the role of a fifth columnist. A headlong collision between the rising Marāthā power and the ambitious Afghans, both of whom were making a bid for political supremacy in northern India, became inevitable. On 14 January 1761, a fierce battle was fought between Aḥmad Shāh Durrānī and the Marāthās at Pānīpat in which the Marāthā power was worsted. The Durrānī invasion drained the impoverished Mughal empire of its entire resources; Najīb al-Dawla suppressed the Jāt incursions, but the Sikhs, who had gradually consolidated their power, obtained supreme control of the whole of the Panjāb. In less than ten years the Marāthās reappeared before Delhi; but neither they nor the Mughals could withstand the gradual penetration of the British into India. The battle of Pānīpat exposed the weakness of the Indian powers.

On the decline of the central authority at Delhi, there arose along with the Hindu states a number of Muslim principalities which pretended to owe nominal allegiance to the Mughal emperors, but to all intents and purposes were independent. Of these the most important in the north were Bengal, Oudh (Awadh) and the trans-Gangetic powers, and in the south, the Āṣaf Jāhī state of Ḥaydarābād (Deccan). They tried to reorganize their administrations on traditional lines, and their courts became the rendezvous of unemployed artists, craftsmen, musicians and poets, mainly Muslims.

RELIGIOUS CHALLENGES

Except for the Mujaddidī Naqshbandīs, all the mystic orders in India followed the principles of *waḥdat al-wujūd*. At the end of the eleventh/seventeenth century, Shāh Kalīm Allāh Jahānābādī (d. 1142/1729) revived the past glories of the Chishtīs at Delhi. He tactfully but firmly opposed the religious outlook of Awrangzēb, denounced him as presumptuous, and sought to stimulate the interest of all sections of Indians in his own preachings. His disciple, Shaykh Niẓām al-Dīn Awrangābādī (d. 1142/1730), preached the humanitarian teachings of the Chishtīs in the Deccan. His activities in Awrangzēb's camp in the Deccan stifled the Naqshbandī influence. About 1160/1747, his son, Shāh Fakhr al-Dīn, moved to Delhi, and plunged himself into the teaching of *Ḥadith* and Sufism. The Mughal emperor, a large number of important nobles, princes and princesses vied with one another in exhibiting their devotion to him. Till his death in 1199/1785, his teachings inspired many of the Sunnīs of Delhi, and were acceptable to Shīʿīs, as well as to many Hindus. The influence of his disciples extended from Delhi to the Panjāb in the west and to Ruhīlkhand in the east.

The most eminent Ṣūfī and the theologian of the twelfth/eighteenth century was Shāh Walī Allāh of Delhi. He was born on 4 Shawwāl 1114/3 March 1703, and received his early education from his father, whom he succeeded in 1131/1719 as the head of the *madrasa* which he had founded in Delhi. In 1143/1731 he visited Mecca on Pilgrimage, and studied *Ḥadīth* under some eminent scholars at Medina; he came back to Delhi on 14 Rajab 1145/31 December 1732. His studies in Arabia and contacts with other scholars of the Islamic world sharpened his intellectual faculties and extended his outlook. He began to feel a mystical confidence which enabled him to discard *taqlīd* (acceptance of religious authority) without compromising his belief in the innate perfection of the *Sharīʿa*: he asserted that the pursuit of Islamic ordinances conferred far-reaching social and individual benefits upon Muslims. His *magnum opus*, *Ḥujjat Allāh al-bāligha*, draws extensively upon the works of Ibn Miskawayh, al-Fārābī and al-Ghazālī; it reflects a deep understanding of the importance of the process of historical change and socio-economic challenges. His *Sharī'a*-state, which he sought to reorganize on the model of the government of the first four caliphs, was the *sine qua non* of a peaceful and prosperous life for all ages and times. *'Adl* (justice) was the golden mean which preserved the framework of all political and social organizations. *Tawāzun* (equilibrium) in economic life ensured the proper development of a healthy society. An excessive burden of taxation on the revenue-producing classes—peasants, merchants and artisans—undermined the health of the body politic.

In a letter addressed to the Mughal emperor, the *wazīr* and the nobles, he gave practical suggestions for the remedying of the defects in society and the administration. His letter to Aḥmad Shāh Durrānī details the chaotic condition of the imperial court, and includes a brief account of non-Muslim powers such as the Jāts, the Marāthās and the Sikhs. It was written mainly to seek the goodwill of the conqueror; and it would not be realistic to interpret it as an invitation to that adventurer to invade the country and restore the glory of Islam. Aḥmad Shāh Durrānī, who had already invaded India on four earlier occasions, hardly needed any invitation for the invasion of 1174/1761, or briefing about the state of affairs of the non-Muslim powers. Mīrzā Maẓhar Jān-i Jānān, another eminent saint of the times, had no respect for the Durrānī army and for him it was a scourge of God.

Shāh Walī Allāh was wholly sincere in his devotion to the cause of Islam, and had a firm faith in its power. 'If it so happens', he wrote, 'that the Hindus are able to obtain complete domination over India, the Divine Mystery would force their leaders to embrace Islam in the same manner as the Turks formerly did.'[1] Though his ancestors had migrated to India in the seventh/thirteenth century, he considered himself an alien, and exhorted his followers to abandon 'the customs of 'Ajam and the habits of the Hindus'.[2] His Arabic works subsequently found considerable popularity in Egypt and other Arabic-speaking countries which were experiencing an increasing tension because of the conflicts between eclecticism and revivalistic movements. His disciple, Sayyid Murtaḍā of Bilgrām (near Lucknow), achieved immense celebrity in Egypt. He

[1] Walī Allāh, *Tafhīmāt-i Ilāhiyya* (Delhi, 1936), I, 215–16.
[2] Walī Allāh, *Waṣiyat Nāma* (Lucknow, n.d.), 7.

wrote commentaries on al-Ghazālī's *Iḥyā' 'ulūm al-dīn* and other works on *Ḥadīth* and *fiqh*. Shāh Walī Allāh died in 1176/1762.

His son, Shāh 'Abd al-'Azīz (1159–1239/1746–1824), vigorously followed the traditions of his father. He wrote a detailed refutation of the beliefs of the Twelver Shī'a, which aroused considerable sectarian bickering. Mawlānā Sayyid Dildār 'Alī, the contemporary Shī'ī *mujtahid* of Lucknow, and his disciples, published several polemical works in refutation. His younger brothers, Shāh Rafī' al-Dīn, Shāh 'Abd al-Qādir and Shāh 'Abd al-Ghanī, co-operated with him in strengthening the cause of Sunnī orthodoxy. The first two translated the Qur'ān into Urdu. Students from Western Islamic countries also attended their seminaries.

The *fatwā* which he wrote after the Emperor Shāh 'Ālam was taken under the protection of the East India Company (1803) is regarded as a very revolutionary document, but it hardly solved any of the problems of the contemporary Muslims. In the *fatwā* he addressed the puppet Mughal emperor as the *imām* of the Muslims, and accused the British of wantonly demolishing the mosques and restricting the freedom of *dhimmīs* and Muslims alike. Their non-interference with practices such as the Friday and *'Īd* prayers, the call to prayer, and cow-slaughter, did not according to him merit any respect, because they felt no obligation to show such tolerance. He therefore declared that India was now *dār al-ḥarb* (the abode of war, i.e. outside the Islamic oecumene). The fact that he did not take the same view of the domination of the Marāthās, who had previously exercised supreme control over the emperor, cannot be defended on theological grounds. It seems that he examined the situation historically. Instances of Hindus exercising absolute control over the Muslim powers were not wanting in Indian history; but the supremacy of a foreign power was unprecedented. Neither Shāh Walī Allāh nor Shāh 'Abd al-'Azīz realized the strength of the challenge of the West, and they left Muslim society in a backward condition, torn with sectarian strife and groping in the dark.

Shāh 'Abd al-'Azīz's nephew, Ismā'īl Shahīd, and his disciple Sayyid Aḥmad Barēlwī (1201–46/1786–1831) made further contributions to the practical and theoretical aspects of the *jihād*. Sayyid Aḥmad was born at Rāe Barēlī, in the Shī'ī state of the nawabs of Oudh. He was not interested in literary education. In about 1804, he travelled to Delhi, and studied there under Shāh 'Abd al-Qādir, one of the sons of Shāh Walī Allāh. After approximately two years' stay he left for his native land.

In 1810 he joined the Pathān chief, Amīr Khān, and obtained considerable training and experience in guerrilla warfare. When Amīr Khān surrendered and was recognized as the ruler of Tōnk (November 1817), Sayyid Aḥmad came back to Delhi. His experience as a soldier and his achievements as a mystic elicited the immeasurable admiration of Shāh 'Abd al-'Azīz. Shāh Ismā'īl, son of Shāh 'Abd al-Ghanī, and Shāh 'Abd al-'Azīz's son-in-law, 'Abd al-Ḥayy, both became Sayyid Aḥmad's disciples. Like a roving missionary, accompanied by his disciples, he visited a number of towns in modern Uttar Pradesh, Bihār and Bengal, where they militantly sought to suppress popular religious practices, and combated the prejudice against the re-marriage of widows.

In 1821 Sayyid Aḥmad came to Calcutta, and set off for Mecca. A study of the Wahhābī movement there seems to have strengthened his zeal for militant Muslim revivalism; and in 1824 he returned to India with his mind full of ideas of *jihād*. A large number of disbanded sepoys of the East India Company, unemployed Pathān followers of Amīr Khān, Ruhillās and the supporters of the rulers of Sind warmly responded to his declaration of *jihād* against the Sikhs, whom he imagined he would be able to overthrow easily. In 1826 he left for the North West Frontier; patched up alliances with some tribal chiefs; and obtained considerable success in early skirmishes against the Sikhs. On 11 January 1827 he assumed the title of *imām*; he then wrote to the rulers of Bukhārā and Herat, explaining the differences between an *imām* and a sultan, and urging them to help him without any fear for their own thrones. Shāh Ismā'īl also wrote a treatise on the subject. Their arguments did not convince the Central Asian rulers, and their activities aroused considerable suspicion among the neighbouring Islamic powers and tribal chiefs. Yār Muḥammad Khān, the chief of Pēshāwar, strongly opposed Sayyid Aḥmad, whose followers defeated him heavily in 1830. The Sayyid formed a government in accordance with his ideas of a pious Islamic state. His attempts to stamp out the practice of giving daughters to the highest bidders, the enforcement of Islamic taxes on the poor tribes who had joined him in the lust for gold, and other rigorist judicial and economic laws, estranged the tribes from his followers, who were known as the *mujāhids* or 'fighters in the *jihād*'. His decree permitting his Indian disciples to take the young girls of the tribes as wives, provoked a violent storm of hostility against the *mujāhids*, and the tribes began to desert them. In the beginning of 1831 the Sayyid made a dash as far as Muẓaffarābād in Kashmir, was defeated, and returned to Bālākot, where he fell fighting against a strong force of Sikhs in May 1831. The claims of Sayyid Aḥmad to the imamate, his assumption of a status akin to that of the Rightly-guided Caliphs, his schemes for puritanical reforms, and the indiscreet interference of his followers with the lives of the tribes, brought rapid disaster to his plans of conquest and of founding an ideal Islamic empire extending from Pēshāwar to Calcutta. His schemes were too narrowly based to fit into the framework of contemporary Islamic society. The British authorities actively welcomed unrest on the frontiers with the Sikhs, and connived at the flow of arms, money and men from their Indian possessions to the Sayyid. The movement of Sayyid Aḥmad, though known as a Wahhābī movement, had no organic connexion with Muḥammad b. ʿAbd al-Wahhāb's movement, and was called by its followers the *Ṭarīqa i-Muḥammadīyya*. His followers were divided into several branches; some even went to the extent of calling him a messiah.

THE IMPACT OF THE BRITISH ADMINISTRATION

Political distintegration and social degeneration after the death of Shāh ʿĀlam Bahādur Shāh I brought little economic dislocation, and was not a corollary of intellectual or moral decay. The traditional seminaries of Delhi, and the *dars i-niẓāmī*, or the curriculum of the oriental learning evolved at Lucknow in the eleventh/seventeenth century, produced some eminent scholars in several branches of the traditional learning, and regional literatures were also greatly enriched. The development of Urdu was a singular contribution of the period. Scholars like Tafaḍḍul Ḥusayn Kāshmīrī who flourished in the reign of Āṣaf al-Dawla (1188–1212/1775–97) in Oudh, learnt English and Latin, and compiled some valuable mathematical works. Mīrzā Abū Ṭālib Khān, also called Abū Ṭālib Landanī ('the Londoner'), who was born at Lucknow in 1166/1752–3, served the court of Oudh and the East India Company in various capacities. In the years 1798–1803 he travelled to Europe and wrote a detailed account of his experiences in the *Masīr-i ṭālibī fī bilād-i Afranjī*, which he completed in 1804. He took a keen interest in British social, political and economic institutions, and assessed them in his work with a remarkable degree of comprehension.

The Rājpūts, Jāts, Marāthās and Sikhs who carved out independent principalities followed the broad pattern of the Mughal administration and welcomed the presence of talented Muslims at their courts; thus the general economic equilibrium of the Muslims remained undisturbed.

The battles of Plassey (Palāsī) in 1170/1757 and Buxar (Baksar) in 1178/1764 put an end to the independence of Bengal. The series of revenue legislative measures passed between 1772 and 1790 culminating in the permanent settlement (1793) of Lord Cornwallis replaced the old class of *zamīndārs*, mainly Muslims, with speculators comprising Calcutta *banians* (bankers), moneylenders and subordinate employees of the East India Company. The Muslim aristocracy, which took pride in its extravagance, had not the ready cash to profit by the new regulations as did the Hindus. The high-handedness of the Company's agents undermined the monopoly of the Muslim weavers, who possessed hereditary looms and adhered to the traditional system of manufacture. Subsequently the unfair competition of the manufacturers in England and the unwillingness of the Company either to protect the Bengal cotton industry from the repercussions of the Industrial Revolution, or to share with the Indians the widened horizon of their industrial experience, reduced the region to a plantation for the production of raw materials and a dumping-ground for cheap manufactured goods from the West.

A large section of the Muslim artisan class fell back upon the land for its livelihood. The Company's increasing interest in commercial crops such as jute, indigo, tea and opium, and the rapid development of a money economy undermined, especially in Bengal, the basis of Indian cultivation. A considerable number of Muslim agriculturists disposed of their land to Hindu bankers, and were soon reduced to the position of landless labourers. Suspicion of the British, their indifference towards the lot of the Muslims, and the high-handedness of the newly emerged landed aristocracy, prepared a breeding ground for several militant Muslim revivalist movements, which were regarded as offshoots of the Wahhābī movement.

The movement which Ḥājjī Sharī'at Allāh (1781–1840) started in East Bengal after his return from Mecca in 1818 was popularly known as the Farā'iżī movement, because of the emphasis which the adherents of the movement laid on the observance of *farā'iż* or obligatory religious duties. Sharī'at Allāh's long stay in the Ḥijāz (1799–1818) had imbued him with the spirit of the Wahhābī reforms, and driven him away from the mainstream of Bengali life. He set himself the task of restoring the puritanical customs of early Islam in rural Bengal. His followers emphasized that India under British rule was *dār al-ḥarb*, and therefore it was not lawful to perform Friday prayers or those of the two *'Īds*. A section of the Muslim peasantry became hostile to their uncompromising and fanatical attitude, and Hindu landlords helped the recalcitrants. In 1831 a major clash between the parties dealt a severe blow to the plans of Ḥājjī Sharī'at Allāh and he retired into seclusion. His son Ḥājjī Muḥsin, alias Dūdū Miān (1819–62), who after 1838 led the movement started by his father, divided most of East Bengal into districts and appointed a *khalīfa* (agent) to each. He took a determined stand against the levying of illegal cesses by landlords and indigo planters. Copying the Arabs, who ate locusts, he insisted that his disciples should eat grasshoppers. The cultivators and the village artisans responded enthusiastically to his preaching. The Hindu *zamīndārs* and his Muslim opponents, whom he forcibly tried to convert to his mission, implicated him in a number of criminal suits; he served several terms of imprisonment and died on 24 September 1862.

A similar revivalist movement based on socio-economic grievances was started in West Bengal by Mīr Nithār 'Alī, popularly known as Tītū Mīr, a well-known Calcutta wrestler who in 1821 had come under the influence of Sayyid Aḥmad of Rāe Barēlī. His followers wore a distinctive dress and would only eat with members of their own brotherhood. The landlords imposed a tax which was quite heavy for a poor peasant on each of them, which came to be known as the Beard Tax, for all of them wore beards. This gave rise to a number of minor riots and ultimately Tītū Mīr fell fighting against a military contingent sent to crush his uprising on 19 November 1831. The revivalists had little success in eradicating superstitions and backwardness in rural Bengal, and made themselves a target of attack by British officials and Hindu *zamīndārs*. Their zeal for reforms was praiseworthy, but they were antiquated and short-sighted.

The changes introduced into the revenue and judicial administration by Hastings and Cornwallis between 1772 and 1793 deprived the Muslims of all the higher posts that they had so far retained. By the end of the 1820s, the anglicization of Indian institutions, and the increased opportunities for the British to obtain home comforts, including the presence of their families in India, tended to set British administrators apart from Indian life. They became increasingly authoritarian and race-conscious, and the need to read and understand Persian or Hindustani was hardly felt. They regarded the use of native languages as a necessary aid to administration; few, indeed, took any cultivated interest in them.

Muslim scholars in India, who during the previous centuries had depended entirely on state patronage, suffered from its disappearance.

Until the end of the eighteenth century, the Muslims took a considerable interest in the service of the East India Company. Some of them wrote historical works of singular importance under the patronage of their English masters. Between 1800 and 1804, the encouragement of John Gilchrist of the Fort William College, Calcutta, contributed to the publication of works of outstanding value. Scholars from all over northern India applied to the authorities of the College for appointment. Even Mīr Taqī Mīr, the distinguished Urdu poet, applied for a position, but did not succeed because of his advanced age.

In 1835 the 'anglicizers' defeated the 'orientalists' and all the funds appropriated to education were directed to English education alone. In 1826 an English-language class was started in the Calcutta *madrasa*, which had been established in 1781; but already the Bengali Hindus had made considerable headway in learning English. The potential control by missionaries of the English education made the Muslims suspicious of the intentions of the government. They protested in vain against English being made an official language. Gradually there emerged in Bengal a class of uncovenanted government servants, medical practitioners, lawyers and their clerks, printers and publishers, who had acquired English as a commercial investment, and came to possess an outlook and ideology vitally different from that of previous generations. The Persian poets no longer stimulated the interest of the Bengali Hindus—in fact, Persian and Arabic words were deliberately purged from Bengali and a Sanskritized dialect was evolved for literary purposes. This effectively disqualified Muslim Bengalis from acquiring even minor posts in the government.

Bombay and Madras, the two other Presidency towns, did not witness the same process of economic distress. The influential and well-to-do Muslims in these towns, particularly in Bombay, were mostly descendants of Arab merchants. The Khōjās and Bohrās, who for centuries past had controlled trade in Gujarāt and Bombay, maintained an independent organisation for the betterment of their own communities. They also spent a portion of their obligatory religious taxes for the advancement of the Muslims in general. They kept their solidarity intact, and responded to the need to acquire an English education as far as it promoted their commercial interests. The Muslim landed nobility of the North-Western Provinces (created in 1843) and other parts of India that subsequently came under the control of the British, were not, as in Bengal, supplanted by a new class of Hindu *zamīndārs*; but they long remained suspicious of the government's intentions in spreading English. James Thomason, the lieutenant-governor of the North-Western Provinces[1] (1843–53) realized the potential dangers of the predominance in the public service of Bengalis educated in English. He designed a scheme of vernacular education which helped the Muslims to maintain their position in the lower ranks of government service. To all intents and purposes, the vernacular in that province meant Urdu, the language of Muslim intellectuals and Hindus who served Muslim chiefs.

Delhi College, founded in 1824, where English was also taught as a subject, stimulated considerable interest among Muslims; some of its pupils obtained commanding importance in the last years of the nineteenth century. It was primarily an institution of oriental learning, and used Urdu as the medium of instruction. The teaching of physics and chemistry and the experiments in laboratories stimulated considerable interest among the pupils. A body of scholars under its auspices translated a number of books from English and Persian into Urdu, which were published in Delhi, Āgrā and Lucknow. The College produced a galaxy of outstanding scholars who made singular contributions to the healthy development of the social and intellectual life of the second half of the nineteenth century.

RESISTANCE TO BRITISH IMPERIALISM

The most formidable resistance to British imperialistic designs was made by the Marāthās and the court of Mysore. The latter owed its glory to Ḥaydar ʿAlī, a man of humble origin, who with resourcefulness and admirable courage took control of the Hindu state of Mysore, overthrew his rivals, and in a very short time reorganised the administration on sound lines. After his death on 7 December 1782, his son, Tīpū Sulṭān, succeeded him. He introduced military reforms of far-reaching importance, created a navy, established armament factories, promoted trade and industries and reorganized the civil administration. His efforts to make alliances with the Ottomans, Persia and Kābul were in vain. The French did not respond to his overtures, and the *niẓām* of Ḥaydarābād and Marāthās found his power a challenge to their own existence. Yet he effectively resisted the British, and died defending his independence on 4 May 1799.

[1] The former name of the old province of Āgrā, later incorporated in the United Provinces (*sc.* of Āgrā and Oudh), and not to be confused with the North-West Frontier Province.

Oppressive revenue policies, the recklessness of unimaginative and inexperienced British settlement officers, the hardships of the artisans, economic distress, annoying delays in judicial proceedings, indiscreet evangelical preaching by Christian missionaries after their admission to the Company's territories in 1813, and the insular habits and prejudices of many British officers, all made the British power detestable in the mind of a large number of Indians, particularly the emotional and economically backward Muslims. The annexation of a number of states by Lord Dalhousie (1848–56) in pursuance of his policy of the 'Doctrine of Lapse', and the annexation of Oudh on the grounds of inefficient administration, precipitated a crisis. The introduction of Enfield rifles and greased cartridges sparked off the revolt. The rising began on 10 May 1857, when the sepoys at Meerut in the North-Western Provinces mutinied. Soon the leadership and initiative passed into the hands of dispossessed chiefs, *zamīndārs*, priests, civil servants and their supporters. Among the principal leaders were Khān Bahādur Khān in Rohīlkhand, Bēgam Ḥażrat Maḥall and Mawlawī Aḥmad Allāh Shāh in Oudh, Bēnī Mādhō Singh to the east of Lucknow, Kunwar Singh in Bihār, Nānā Ṣāḥib in Kanpur, Tatyā Tōpē and the *rānī* of Jhānsi in Bundēlkhand, and Bahādur Shāh II at Delhi. This concerted action cut across all barriers of caste and creed and of linguistic and regional prejudices. British officers, despite their active efforts, failed to stir up communal frenzy. The Muslims gave up cow-sacrifice in Delhi and other places to demonstrate their goodwill towards Hindus, and the latter exhibited due consideration towards the religious sentiments and prejudices of the Muslims. At many places in the North-Western Provinces, Oudh, Bihār and the Central Provinces, the entire population rose in a body against British domination. In Delhi, Barēlī and Lucknow, constitutions were hurriedly drafted, designed to ensure a sort of democratic government. The attempt to fight with antiquated weapons against forces trained on modern lines and using the hated Enfield rifles, lack of control over the means of communication and a want of proper organising capacity among the leaders shattered their hopes of expelling the British from India.

The failure of the revolt saw a complete liquidation of the old classes of *zamīndārs* throughout the British territories wherever they had been active in the rising. They were replaced by those who had loyally served the British. A horror of rebellion and its ruthless suppression made the new class of the *zamīndārs* and their supporters timid, suspicious, and dependent on the local British officers. Control of the Indian government was finally assumed by the British crown, and the perpetuation of the princely order under British paramountcy was ensured. The *taʿalluqdārī* order of big landlords was retained in Oudh; a number of influential *taʿalluqdārs* were Muslims. Some Muslim states, such as Rāmpur and Bhōpāl in northern India, and Ḥaydarābād in southern India, extended considerable patronage to talented Muslims from British India, and became centres of Islamic learning, art and literature. They retained Urdu as the court language. A considerable number of Muslims found important posts in the Hindu states too. The *taʿalluqdārs* of Oudh and the *zamīndārs* also offered minor posts to the Muslims, who gradually adjusted themselves to the changed circumstances and the new order.

A large number of Muslim sepoys escaped to the North West Frontier, joined the Indian *mujāhids* who lived round about Pēshāwar, and organized raids against the British. After a number of skirmishes they were badly crushed in 1863. Trial proceedings between 1864 and 1870 established the presence of close links between some Indian followers of Sayyid Aḥmad Barēlwī in India and the Frontier rebels, and dozens of them were sentenced to capital punishment. The publication of W. W. Hunter's *The Indian Mussalmans* in 1871 greatly alarmed many British officials but the lieutenant-governor of the North-Western Provinces denounced it as 'not only exaggerated but misguiding' and 'calculated to do much mischief, and create panic and alienation on both sides'.[1]

MUSLIMS AND ENGLISH EDUCATION

Before the outbreak of the revolt of 1857, some enlightened Muslims in Calcutta had realized the importance of English education for their community. The National Mohammedan Association, established in Calcutta in 1856, with Nawwāb Amīr ʿAlī (1817–79) as president, and the Mohammedan Literary Society founded by Nawwāb ʿAbd al-Laṭīf (1828–93) in April 1863, tried to overcome the difficulties that hindered the spread of English education among the Muslims. Karāmat ʿAlī of Jawnpur (d. 1873) advocated the study of European languages in order to acquire a knowledge of the sciences. Throughout the greater part of his life he preached in eastern Bengal.

In 1806 Ḥājjī Muḥammad Muḥsin, a prominent Persian philanthropist,

[1] Mayo Papers, Cambridge University, Add. 7490 (56).

had established an endowment yielding an annual income of Rs. 45,000 for religious purposes. For some time the trustees mismanaged the income, and subsequently the government used it for other purposes. As a result of the efforts of Nawwāb 'Abd al-Laṭīf and some others, the income of the fund was directed in 1873 towards the establishment of *madrasas* in Dacca, Chittagong and Rājshāhī. A substantial portion of the fund was assigned to the payment of fees of Muslim students in the modern schools and colleges of Bengal. Scholarships for education in England were also granted out of the fund.

The Anjuman-i Islām of Bombay played an active role in the promotion of English education in Bombay. Badr al-Dīn Ṭayyibjī (1844–1906), a leader of the Khōjā community, worked for many years as its secretary and for about sixteen years was its president. He ardently advocated the higher education of Indian women, particularly Muslims. His own daughters graduated from Bombay University with distinction, and one of them trained as a teacher in England on a government scholarship.

The increasing interest taken by the British in the Middle East after the completion of the Suez Canal (1869) made them conscious of the need to win the hearts of the Muslims. The viceroy, the earl of Mayo (1869–72), observed 'There is no doubt that, as regards the Mohammedan population, our present system of education is, to a great extent, a failure. We have not only failed to attract or attach the sympathies and confidence of a large and important section of the community, but we may even fear that we have caused positive disaffection, as is suggested by Mr O'Kinealy and others'.[1]

The benefits of this change were adequately reaped by Sayyid Aḥmad Khān (1817–98) whose loyal and fearless services to the cause of the British in 1857 had won him their favour. He had already written several works of outstanding merit. After the restoration of peace and order, he plunged into the task of removing misunderstandings between the British and the Muslims, and of promoting education and Western thought. He started schools at Murādābād and Ghāzīpur in the North-Western Provinces, and tried to bring English works within the reach of his fellow-countrymen through translations into Urdu. He also urged patronage of vernacular education. The translations of the Scientific Society, founded by him in 1864, were warmly welcomed by the govern-

[1] Note by H.E. the Viceroy, Simla, 26 June 1871; Mayo Papers, Cambridge University, Add. 7490 (12).

ment. He strove for the establishment of a vernacular department in Calcutta University, or alternatively the creation of a vernacular university in the North-Western Provinces. Lord Mayo also supported the demand for patronage of the vernacular.[1]

The Bengalis, however, strongly opposed the movement, and asked what was really meant by 'the vernacular.' With Sayyid Aḥmad, it amounted to the introduction of Urdu. His Hindu associates, particularly Rājā Jaikishan Dās Chaubē of Murādābād, belonged to western United Provinces, where Urdu was spoken by Hindus and Muslims alike. Sayyid Aḥmad had insufficient experience of the sentiments of the Hindus of eastern United Provinces and Bihār, though he had served at Ghāzīpur and Banāras for about five years. He failed to realize that the new educated Hindu middle class rapidly emerging there was resilient and vitally different from the landed nobility of medieval days. The emphasis on vernacular education on the part of the government coincided with a movement for the introduction of Hindi, written in *Devanāgarī* characters, as the official language of the courts. In 1867, Hindi written in *Kaithī* characters (a running hand for keeping accounts in Bihār somewhat similar to *Devanāgarī*) was approved by the lieutenant-governor of Bengal as the official vernacular of Bihār. This change encouraged the protagonists of Hindi in Banāras. Sayyid Aḥmad came into headlong conflict with them. Both Urdu and Hindi prose were in a preliminary stage at that time. Sayyid Aḥmad was himself a founder of simple modern Urdu prose writing. The main controversy revolved around the question of a script. The use of both the scripts, or of Roman script, was suggested to him but he maintained a rigid attitude on the subject and transformed the *Scientific Society's 'Alīgarh Gazette* into a forum for the defence of Urdu. His successor, Nawwāb Muhṣin al-Mulk (1837–1907), suggested that he should also publish the translations of the Scientific Society in Hindi, as a compromise; but the Sayyid scornfully rejected the proposal.

During his visit to England (1869–70) he came in close contact with the conservative section of the country; studied the educational system of Cambridge; and was deeply impressed by the cultural and material progress of the West. In 1870 he started an Urdu journal entitled *Tahdhīb al-akhlāq* to educate the Muslims for modernism, and to prepare the ground for the establishment of the Mohammedan Anglo-Oriental

[1] Letter of Lord Mayo to Sir E. Perry, India Office, July 1870, Cambridge University, Add. 7490 (40).

College at 'Alīgarh, which he started in the form of a school in 1875. Separate arrangements were made for teaching Sunnī and Shī'ī theology on traditional lines. Opposition to his religious views impelled Sayyid Aḥmad to keep himself aloof from the management of the teaching of theology in the College. The foundation-stone was laid by Lord Lytton in 1877, and it started functioning in 1879 on the lines of the colleges of Cambridge. In 1877 Sayyid Aḥmad supported the cause of simultaneous examinations for the Indian Civil Service in England and India. In a speech delivered during his tour of the Panjāb in 1884 he referred to India as one nation. Yet he was devoted to the cause of the education of Muslims, mainly of the upper classes, throughout the rest of his life. He was strongly opposed to the system of representation by election and was 'convinced that the introduction of the principle of election, pure and simple, for representation of various interests on the local boards and district councils, would be attended with evils of greater significance than purely economic considerations'.[1]

The establishment of the Indian National Congress alarmed some landlords of the North-Western Provinces. Its lieutenant-governor, Sir Auckland Colvin, was strongly opposed to A. O. Hume, the moving spirit behind the Congress movement. Sayyid Aḥmad was alarmed. He thought that political agitation was likely to take a violent turn, and that if Muslims joined Congress the second phase of their ruin would begin; he imagined that the success of Congress would bring the domination of the Bengali Hindus throughout India. In speeches delivered at Lucknow in 1887, and at Meerut in March 1888, he strongly opposed the policies and programmes of Congress and advocated the strengthening of the hand of the British government. He advised the Muslims to concentrate their energies upon the acquisition of higher English education, and to rely upon the good sense of the government to safeguard their rights. He earnestly desired that 'The Crescent and the Cross being united should shed their light over India'.[2] He formed the Indian Patriotic Association and later on the United Indian Patriotic Association to mobilize the opinion of the landlords and influential sections of Indian society against Congress. He issued circular letters to Muslim associations all over the country urging opposition to the National Congress. His appeal did not receive a satisfactory response,

[1] C. H. Philips, *The Evolution of India and Pakistan* (London, 1962), 188–9.

[2] Sir Sayyid's address to Sir Auckland Colvin, 10 March 1888. *'Alīgarh Institute Gazette*, 15 March 1888.

and he soon decided to found a separate Mohammedan Anglo-Oriental Defence Association of Upper India to mobilize Muslim public opinion there in support of his point of view.

The contradictory and irreconcilable aims and objectives of his new association failed, like all his political preachings, to arouse the interest of the Muslims. The Muslim *ta'alluqdārs* of Oudh did not sympathize with the educational movement of 'Alīgarh, which was generally dominated by the *zamīndārs* of the North-Western Provinces, Delhi and the Panjāb. The raja of Maḥmūdābād was planning to establish a separate Shī'ī College, which his son founded in 1919. Several Urdu periodicals were pitted against his activities. His Mohammedan Educational Congress, founded in December 1886, which was renamed the Mohammedan Educational Conference in 1890, held its sessions mainly in the North-Western Provinces and the Panjāb. His *'Alīgarh Institute Gazette* had a circulation of no more than four hundred. During the last years of his life, it was virtually controlled by the principal, Theodore Beck (1885–99), who regarded the Indian universities as centres of native rebels and a political evil of the first magnitude, and had a particular aversion to Bengalis. The strings of the student organizations in the College were always in the hands of Beck or some other English professor who never let slip any opportunity of instilling the benefits of loyalty to the British government into the minds of Muslim youth, and of injecting them with anti-Hindu communal views. The European staff considered themselves more in the capacity of residents accredited to the native states than as members of the teaching profession. In collaboration with the district officers, they played a leading role in the establishment of the Board of Trustees and in the selection of Sir Sayyid's successor. The private life of Sir Sayyid was embittered by the resignation in 1892 of his own son, Sayyid Maḥmūd, from the Allahabad High Court Bench because of his disagreements with the chief justice of Allahabad. Sir Sayyid Aḥmad died broken-hearted on 27 March 1898.

Modern Muslim scholars in India, drawing upon the thesis of Mawlānā Muḥammad 'Alī and other nationalists, tend to depict him as a great nationalist and a well-wisher of all Indians, while the Pakistani scholars find in him one of the fathers of their nation. In fact he did not advocate separatism but tried to seek safeguards for the Muslims under indefinitely continued British rule.

As long as Britain remained friendly to the Ottoman empire, the claims of Sultan 'Abd ül-Ḥamīd II (1876–1909) to be the caliph of the

Islamic world did not disturb him and his followers. Indeed, he popularized the use of the Turkish fez in India, and extolled the Ottoman Tanẓīmāt. But the change in British policy after 1880 alarmed him; and he very strongly denounced the claims of Sultan ʻAbd ül-Ḥamīd, and urged that the sultan's sovereignty or caliphate should be confined to his own territories.

The rise of Muḥammad Aḥmad b. ʻAbd Allāh, who claimed to be the Expected Mahdi in the Egyptian Sudan (1881), caused considerable panic among European officials in India. The religious significance of the movement was closely examined, and the intelligence service was alerted to discover where the sympathies of Indian Muslims lay. Sir Sayyid and Muḥsin al-Mulk wrote articles theorizing on the rise of *mahdīs* in Islam, and convinced the European officials that Indian Muslims had no sympathy for the Mahdi of the Sudan. Pan-Islamic ideas were reinforced, mainly among the younger generation, by the successive visits of reformers such as Jamāl al-Dīn al-Afghānī to India, and by the sufferings and misfortunes to which the Muslims of the Middle East were thought to be exposed. Sir Sayyid was too much concerned with the present to pay attention to the future. He therefore fought incessantly against all ideologies which tended to arouse British suspicion about the loyalty of the Muslims. He advocated the cause of Muslim landowners, and had little sympathy with the common Muslims, though he occasionally shed tears of sympathy for them. He clung to the antiquated policy of the East India Company that education would 'filter down' to the lower classes from their 'leaders'. He drew inspiration from the political ideals of John Stuart Mill, and did not sufficiently realize the importance of contemporary political and economic forces.

His far-fetched interpretations of Qur'anic verses to prove his thesis that *waḥy* (revelation) and 'natural law' or 'reason' were not conflicting and irreconcilable, failed to convince many of his closest associates. But his plea for a close examination of the Traditions ascribed to the Prophet Muḥammad, even if they were embodied in the classical collections of *Ḥadīth*, stimulated great interest amongst members of his own generation and among his successors too. They, like him, applied the theory to suit their interpretations of such institutions as polygamy and slavery, which were becoming more and more distasteful to Western opinion. One of his close associates, Chirāgh ʻAlī, who had studied the reform movements of the contemporary Middle East, and had come in contact with Jamāl al-Dīn al-Afghānī, elaborated Sir Sayyid's thesis with great confidence. He powerfully advocated the view that all the wars of Muḥammad were defensive, and that aggressive wars or forced conversion was not allowed in the Qur'ān. The *Spirit of Islam* by Sayyid Amīr 'Alī (1849–1928) is not defensive in tone but uses the findings of contemporary Western scholarship and a powerful mode of expression to establish the contributions made by Islam to the betterment of mankind. Such works equipped Muslims to carry out a dialogue with the critics of Islam.

Among the galaxy of scholars that supported Sayyid Aḥmad Khān in his educational programme but who pulled in different directions so far as his apologetics were concerned were Ḥālī, Shiblī and Nadhīr Aḥmad. Shiblī (1857–1914) wrote a large number of works in Urdu, including a detailed biography of the Prophet Muḥammad, in which for the first time he applied Western methods of research to historical writings in Urdu, and tried to demonstrate that Islam strongly protected the rights of non-Muslims. He passionately justified the levy of *jizya* on non-Muslims, and sought to prove that it was not a discriminatory tax, and did not seek to humiliate the *dhimmīs*. In 1879 Ḥālī (1837–1914) published his celebrated *Musaddas,* presenting in very appealing verse an account of the rise and fall of the Muslims. This work had a singular success and filled the Indian Muslims with pride in the past, and lamentations for the present. The work was intended to prepare them for the battle for life with understanding and confidence. Nadhīr Aḥmad (1831–1911) strongly defended the position of women in Islam, and urged their education on traditional lines. He endeavoured to reconcile the *Sharī'a* with the everyday needs of Muslims, and urged that the laws of the British government, being the source of peace and prosperity for Muslims, deserved the same implicit obedience as the *Sharī'a*. He did not hesitate to lend money on interest, and glossed over the injunctions concerning its illegality. He was a very good orator, and his subtle humour exercised great influence over his audience.

The traditional theologians strongly opposed the modernism of Sir Sayyid and his associates. They also were deeply concerned with the challenges that the Christian missionaries and the Arya Samāj movements offered to Islam, but they found the pseudo-intellectual fads of the westernized Muslims unsound and risky. The theologians trained at Deōband faced the above challenges on traditional lines. *Dār al-'Ulūm*, a seminary of traditional Islamic learning at Deōband in the North-Western Provinces, was established by a famous theologian, Mawlānā Muḥammad Qāsim Nānawtawī in 1867, and gradually attracted students from Afghanistan, Turkey and other Islamic countries. Since government rules did not permit assistance to theological institutions, *Dār al-'Ulūm* depended on donations from Muslims. Mawlānā Muḥammad Qāsim himself took an active interest in defending the traditional Muslim position in all polemical discussions. After his death on 14 April 1880, he was succeeded by Mawlānā Rashīd Aḥmad Gangōhī who passionately believed that the study of philosophy undermined theological beliefs. He urged the Muslims to co-operate with the Hindus in wordly matters, and to participate in the activities of the Indian National Congress as long as the basic principles of Islam were not violated. On his death in 1905, Mawlānā Maḥmūd Ḥasan (1851–1921) a man of courage and great organizing capacity, succeeded him. He organized former students of Deōband from India, Afghanistan and Turkey into a body known as the *Jam'iyyat al-Anṣār*. The theologians of this school made important contributions to the idea of Islamic brotherhood and the unity of Islamic countries.

The Barēlwīs, or the followers of Mawlāwī Aḥmad Riḍā Khān (b. 1855) of Barēlī, strictly adhered to the orthodox practices enjoined by the traditional theologians and the Ṣūfīs, and made a very strong impact upon the religious beliefs of the Muslim masses in the United Provinces and the Panjāb. *Nadwat al-'Ulama'* was started at Lucknow in 1894, with the avowed objectives of bridging the gulf between the old and the new ideals of Islamic learning, and of rousing the *'ulamā'*, as custodians of the interpretation of the *Sharī'a*, to the need for facing the challenges of the times effectively. The Shī'ī theologians also copied the example of *Nadwat al-'Ulamā'*, and organized a similar body at Lucknow.

Early in his career, Mīrzā Ghulām Aḥmad (1839–1908) of Qādiyān in the eastern Panjāb, took an active interest in the polemics directed against the Arya Samajists and the Christian missionaries. In 1889, he experienced a mystical urge which led him to declare himself to be the promised Mahdi or Messiah. His followers, who are known as the Aḥmadiyya or the Qādiyānīs, developed an organized and trained community in Qādiyān, which was upset after the partition of 1947. There they tried to restore the pristine purity of Islam, and endeavoured to solve economic and social problems within the framework of their brotherhood. They are keen missionaries, and actively propagate Islam in Europe, Africa and America.

Expanding facilities for higher education in the third quarter of the nineteenth century contributed to the rapid multiplication of Muslim graduates everywhere in India, but most of the native Muslim princes and richer *zamīndārs* sent their children to ʿAlīgarh for higher education. The mere fact that a man's son was at ʿAlīgarh enhanced his social prestige; many students there did not devote themselves seriously to studies but lived in idle elegance, willingly supported by their families. Some of them enthusiastically emulated English ways of life, etiquette and social behaviour. Most of them detested the compulsory theology classes and prayers; only a negligible number took an interest in them. This horrified the conservative Muslims, and a wide gap opened between them and the English-educated youths. The verses of Akbar of Allahabad (1846–1921) reflect the cultural tensions of the period. He bitterly mourned the fate of Muslims who acquired an English education in order to obtain higher government posts, but who were ultimately frustrated and disillusioned because of the want of adequate patronage from the British. He mercilessly criticized the growing indiscipline and neglect of parental authority among those who were educated in English. Unfortunately for him, his own son whom he sent (with most careful instructions about his behaviour) to London for higher education, threw his teachings overboard and married an English woman.

From the last decades of the nineteenth century, the Western style began to infiltrate systematically into the life of the English-educated Muslim aristocracy. Their village homes conformed to the traditional style of the eighteenth century, but those who possessed means tended to build bungalows of bastard Baroque or mock Gothic in Simla and other places where the European community retreated during the summer. There they found adequate opportunities for winning the favour of influential British officers. They were more than satisfied if their efforts won them the petty titles which, they imagined, established their superiority over the rest of the aristocracy, and certainly enabled them to obtain minor posts for their dependents.

Those who possessed resources sent their sons to England for higher education, where most preferred to seek admission to the bar, rather than to qualify as doctors, scientists or engineers. Those who did not possess adequate wealth or talents to read law in London, qualified themselves to practise in the district courts. Their strong links with the villages, most of them being themselves of *zamīndār* families, enabled them to earn a comfortable living and sufficient prestige in their own society. Soon these legal practitioners acquired more proprietary rights in the villages because of the ease with which they could learn about and profit from the financial difficulties of others. Thus, in 1901, of the seventeen barristers practising at Patna, twelve were Muslims. Of the eighteen advocates of the Allahabad High Court in 1901, ten were Europeans or Anglo-Indians, six Muslims, one Hindu, and there was one other.[1]

Since a literary education provided adequate opportunities for such ambitions as the Muslim youth then possessed, hardly any one in those days evinced any interest in technical education. So it was but natural that they should oppose the introduction of competitive examinations for services, and demand special privileges on the basis of their loyalty to the British government as a class, or of their links with the Muslim aristocracy.

THE MUSLIM POLITICAL AWAKENING

The political upheaval in the country, plague, famine, communal riots, movements relating to the protection of the cow, the Arya Samāj movement, and militant Marāthī and Bengali nationalism were all factors which drove the Muslims closer to the British government. The language question, however, shook the faith of a large section of the 'Alīgarh youth on the advisability of blind reliance on British protection. In 1900 Hindi was accorded the status of the court language in the North-Western Provinces and Oudh. The Muslims were naturally agitated; but the militant attitude of the lieutenant-governor silenced them.

Muhṣin al-Mulk infused considerable life into the activities of the Mohammedan Educational Conference. Its Bombay session, held in December 1904, was presided over by Badr al-Dīn Ṭayyibjī, who did not fail to criticize the policy of the Muslims of 'Alīgarh and their College. He also tried to mobilize the support of Muslim theologians in favour of the 'Alīgarh educational movement. The *Anjuman-i Ḥimāyat-i Islām* of Lahore also made considerable efforts to invigorate the lives of the Muslims on the lines suggested by Sayyid Aḥmad Khān. These efforts, however, did not go far towards satisfying Muslim youths not belonging to the landed nobility. Muslim graduates of other universities were intolerant of the preferential treatment accorded to the products of 'Alīgarh and the need for political awakening and political education was increasingly felt.

[1] B. B. Misra, *The Indian middle classes* (London, 1961), 329–30.

Lord Curzon's partition of Bengal (October 1905) which created a separate Muslim province of Eastern Bengal and Assam, promised fresh avenues to success, chances for higher education, and increased rank and responsibility to the Muslims of Eastern Bengal, particularly to those of Dacca, the capital. Nawwāb Salīm Allāh of Dacca, who, according to Sir Bampfylde Fuller (the lieutenant-governor of the new province and a most enthusiastic supporter of Curzon), was 'not a wise man' but 'exhibited courage and loyalty in the attitude he maintained' on partition,[1] became the leader of the Muslims overnight. The popular agitation that followed in the wake of the partition made the Muslims of other provinces restive. The Swadeshī movement, which among other aspects promoted the use of the handlooms and spindles of the Muslims of Bengal, was a significant challenge to the ideology of 'Alīgarh. Realizing its importance, Muḥsin al-Mulk urged Muslims to develop their handicrafts on the lines suggested by the agitators with a view to saving themselves from being left behind in the handicraft race as they had been left behind in others.

On 3 August 1906, Fuller offered his resignation in the hope of impressing the central government with the urgency of an unimportant matter. To his surprise, it was at once accepted; and as he had publicly stood forth as a champion of the Muslims, some turbulence seemed likely. The sensation was shortlived, however, and according to the viceroy was not 'so acute as to necessitate heroic measures'.[2] The excitement died down more quickly than was expected. However, the partition was accepted as a *fait accompli*. Lord Minto urged, 'in fact the Mohammedan community, when roused, would be a much stronger and more dangerous factor to deal with than the Bengalis'.[3]

The budget speech of the secretary of state for India, Lord Morley, (August 1906) embodying broad outlines of the introduction of reforms, evoked considerable interest on the part of Muḥsin al-Mulk who was finding it exceedingly difficult to pursue the policy of Sir Sayyid any longer. The factors leading to the presentation of an address embodying Muslim demands by a deputation to the viceroy on 1 October 1906, the formation of the Muslim League in December 1906, and the acceptance

[1] Letter of Fuller to Curzon, 18 October 1905, Curzon Papers, Mss. Eur. F. III (212); India Office, London.

[2] Reply to the letter of Archbold, principal of the Mohammedan Anglo-Oriental College 'Alīgarh; Dunlop Smith to L. Hare, 24 August 1906, Minto Papers, National Library of Scotland, Edinburgh.

[3] Letter of Minto to Arthur Godley, 17 October 1906, Minto Papers.

of the principle of a separate Muslim electorate have recently been examined at some length on the basis of the Minto and Morley papers by Wāsṭī and Das[1] from their respective points of view. An evaluation of the entire correspondence and the contemporary literature shows that the importance which the viceroy attached to Muḥsin al-Mulk's letter (which led to the deputation) and the manner in which the suggestions for the deputation were worked out indicate that such an opportunity was eagerly awaited. Certainly, no time was lost in exploiting the situation to the full.

The battle for reforms was fought mainly in London by Amīr 'Alī, the Aga Khan (Āghā Khān) and 'Alī Imām, who subsequently appeared on the scene, though Theodore Morison, the former principal of 'Alīgarh, played a leading part. The newly formed Muslim League was dominated mainly by members of the Mohammedan Educational Conference, and thus embodied the landed nobility and its protégés. Its permanent president, the Aga Khan (the *imām* of the Ismā'īlīs) was born in 1877 and had come in contact with Sir Sayyid Aḥmad Khān and Muḥsin al-Mulk as early as 1896. His appointment to the Legislative Council of Lord Curzon at the end of 1902 immensely enhanced his prestige among the Muslims, though he was warned by the governor of Bombay, with the approval of the viceroy, 'of the adverse effects of his lack of orthodoxy, his being over-anglicized and his fondness for European women'.[2] Of the younger generation, closely in touch with the youth of 'Alīgarh, was Muḥammad 'Alī (1878–1931). At the suggestion of the lieutenant-governor of the province, the Aga Khan transferred the League's headquarters from 'Alīgarh to Lucknow: the lieutenant-governor was frightened, 'lest the lawyer party, consisting of young and irresponsible persons, would attain a predominant position in the League, and that they might at some time coalesce with the advanced Hindu politicians against the Government on one or more questions, and later on rue the fact that they have done so'.[3]

The achievements of the Muslim League did not satisfy the educated Muslim youth. They were increasingly imbued with those pan-Islamic sentiments which had been so carefully controlled by Sir Sayyid Aḥmad and his followers. Faḍl al-Ḥasan Ḥasrat Muhānī, one of the most

[1] S. R. Wāsṭī, *Lord Minto and the Indian Nationalist movement 1905 to 1910* (Oxford, 1964); M. N. Das, *India under Morley and Minto* (London, 1964).

[2] Letter of Curzon to Lemington, 4 January 1904, Curzon Papers, India Office Library, London, F. 111 (209).

[3] Letter of Hewett to Minto, 3 February 1910, Minto Papers.

influential students of the period at 'Alīgarh, who edited a literary journal, was imbued with the revolutionary doctrines of Tilak, preached them fearlessly, and was convicted of sedition in 1908. Muḥammad 'Alī, although in the service of Baroda, frequently visited 'Alīgarh after his return from Oxford in 1902, and aroused political consciousness among the students.

The transfer of the headquarters of the Muslim League from 'Alīgarh to Lucknow (1 March 1910) brought it under the greater control of leaders from Oudh, eastern United Provinces and Bihār. The Aga Khan and his associates in their efforts to retain their leadership hurriedly launched a scheme for raising the College at 'Alīgarh to the status of a university, with a view to diverting the attention of Muslims from politics to educational progress. The funds collected exceeded two million rupees. The younger generation did not favour government control over the proposed university. They wanted to make it a central institution with power to affiliate Muslim institutions all over India. The Muslims of Eastern Bengal were also lukewarm in their support. The secretary of state refused to grant the power of affiliation and the scheme petered out. These events would not have proved more than short-lived ripples on the waters of Muslim politics, if the situation had not been aggravated by the successive misfortunes befalling the Ottoman empire, Persia and Morocco in 1911, 1912 and 1913.

Shiblī, who had come to believe that an oligarchy of the '*ulamā*' under his own leadership might control Indian Muslim politics, was bitterly opposed to the policies and programmes of the Muslim League. On the basis of first-hand knowledge of the affairs of the Middle East, he aroused the sympathies of Indian Muslims for their co-religionists. His disciple Muḥammad 'Alī, who had left the Baroda service towards the end of 1910, took up a journalistic career and in January 1911 started the publication in Calcutta of the *Comrade* with the motto, 'the comrade of all and partisan of none'. The paper was financed mainly by the Aga Khan and 'Alī Imām, and shifted to Delhi with the transfer there of the seat of government. *Hamdard*, its Urdu 'stable-companion' as Muḥammad 'Alī called it, was started at the close of 1913.

Mawlānā Abu'l-Kalām Āzād (1888–1958), who had obtained considerable journalistic experience under Shiblī, also travelled through Cairo and Turkey in 1908, and came in contact with the leaders of the Young Turk movement and other revolutionaries. He commenced a scheme for revitalizing Indian Muslims through his journal *al-Hilāl* which began in June 1912, marked a turning-point in Indian journalism, and soon reached a circulation of 26,000. Āzād utilized pan-Islamic feelings to whip up religious frenzy and arouse political consciousness among the Muslim masses. He strongly supported the need for a universal caliph and entertained the ambition of himself assuming the status of *imām* of all Indian Muslims. His immense learning, and mastery of the contemporary reform movements of the Middle East, endeared him even to the theologians, though most of them were envious of his increasing success and prestige. The Mawlānā himself regarded them as conservative and backward, but he could not ignore them if he was to realise his own dreams. He was in close touch with a number of Indian revolutionaries. Indeed, *jihād* and armed revolution to overthrow foreign domination were, in his opinion, identical in all respects. *Al-Hilāl* and its sister-journal *al-Balāgh* preached the notion of the Qur'anic state, which the Mawlānā's spiritual radicalism gradually transformed into a highly potent living force. He ridiculed the modernism of 'Alīgarh, as well as the backwardness of the traditional theologians, and denounced them both as blind copyists. He emphasized that the development of the sciences in the West did not necessarily undermine religious beliefs. What was needed by the Muslims was a resilient attitude towards the true Islamic values.

Intellectually much inferior but even more popular was the *Zamīndār* of Ẓafar 'Alī Khān, who never let slip a single opportunity to make capital of even the pettiest Muslim grievance. A number of other Urdu journals and newspapers in the United Provinces and Bihār also aroused political awakening among the Muslims. Dr (later Sir) Muḥammad Iqbāl (1876–1938), who formerly strove to worship in a *naya shiwālā* (new temple) of Hindu-Muslim amity and concord, set a new tone for their thinking by preaching 'that Islam as a spiritual force would one day dominate the world, and with its simple nationalism purge it of the dross of superstitions as well as of Godless materialism'.[1] His occasional verses were quoted *ad infinitum* by public speakers and whipped up the sentiments and emotions of the simple, intensely religious and sincere Muslim masses.

Amīr 'Alī, the founder of the London branch of the Muslim League and an uncompromising fighter for a separate electorate, was disillusioned after the reversal of the partition of Bengal (December 1911). He regarded it as a conspiracy between the Aga Khan, the nawab of

[1] Afzal Iqbal (ed.), *Select Writings and Speeches of Maulana Mohammed Ali* (Lahore, 1944), 51.

Dacca and the British government. He wrote to Lord Curzon on 4 January 1912, 'A telegram, copy of which I beg to enclose, reached the London League yesterday from the Honorable Syed Nawab Ally Choudhry for the East Bengal Provincial League. It was a very clever move to attempt to muzzle Salimollah with a G.C.I.E. and Aga Khan with a G.C.S.I. and it has partially achieved its objects'.[1] His proposals for closer cooperation between the Hindus and the Muslims because of the Italian aggression upon Tripoli, and Russian moves against Persia, evoked a sharp rebuff from Muḥammad 'Alī. An appeal to religion to arouse Muslim sentiments against foreign domination, became a convenient weapon in the hands of an important group of Muslim politicians in India, and retarded political awakening on a rational basis.

The Balkan War of 1912 inflamed Muslim feelings in India against the Western powers to the highest intensity. Funds were raised, and a medical mission was despatched. After the Russian bombardment of Mashhad, in 1912 and an absurd Italian threat to attack the Ka'ba from the air, all the holy places were conceived to be in danger. Their protection made a stronger appeal to the Indian Muslims than the difficulties of the Ottoman empire and Persia. Shawkat 'Alī, the elder brother of Muḥammad 'Alī, in collaboration with Mawlānā 'Abd al-Bārī, the head of the theologians of the Firangī Maḥall in Lucknow, founded the *Anjuman-i Khuddām-i Ka'ba* (Society of the Servants of the Ka'ba) with a view to uniting 'Mussalmans of every sect in maintaining inviolate the sanctity of the three *ḥarams* of Islam at Mecca, Medina and Jerusalem'.[2] Theologians of the Firangī Maḥall, who had hitherto kept themselves aloof from modern politics, became increasingly important; Muḥammad 'Alī and Shawkat 'Alī did not respond to Mahatma Gandhi's programme until 'Mawlānā 'Abd al-Barī of Firangī Maḥal had meditated and sought divine grace'.[3]

The demolition of a corridor of a mosque in Kanpur, on 1 July 1913, in order to improve the alignment of a road, named after the lieutenant-governor, stirred the resentment of the Indian Muslims very strongly. Several Muslim papers wrote passionately about the high-handedness of the government. Sir James Meston, the lieutenant-governor in question, conveniently laid the entire blame on the rising generation of the Muslims who according to him found 'a remunerative employment in agitation'.

[1] Curzon Papers, Eur. F. 111 (434). India Office Library, London.
[2] *My life: a fragment*, 67.
[3] A. K. Āzād, *India wins freedom* (Calcutta, 1959), 9.

Indeed, the incident was 'the first internal pretext',[1] but the resentment was not confined to one particular section.

After the Ottoman declaration of war against Britain, the Indian Muslim press was intensely agitated. The confiscation of the papers and presses of Muḥammad 'Alī, Abu'l-Kalām Āzād and Ẓafar 'Alī Khān, and their internment along with Shawkat 'Alī, suppressed the expression of pan-Islamic feelings for the time being. The Aga Khan, who could not accept the policies and programmes of the pan-Islamists, left the League after 1912, and it had to depend mainly on the raja of Maḥmūdābād for its finances. A Congress-League *rapprochement* was exceedingly helpful for satisfactory recruitment and the prosecution of the war. No one was better suited to achieve this than the raja of Maḥmūdābād and Sayyid Wazīr Ḥasan (later knighted), the secretary of the League from 1912 to 1919, who sincerely treasured the values of traditional Hindu-Muṣlim amity which the court of the nawabs of Oudh had fostered. Muḥammad 'Alī Jinnah (1876–1948), a leading Bombay barrister who was invited to join the Muslim League by Muḥammad 'Alī and Wazīr Ḥasan in London in 1913, became a trusted leader of the Congress and the League.

In 1915 Congress and the League held their sessions simultaneously at Bombay. The Congress-League scheme of 1916, whereby Congress agreed to a scheme for separate Muslim electorates (which it hitherto had strongly condemned) was the outcome of the co-operation and amity that developed in the wake of rising pan-Islamic feelings. The League and Congress worked in close co-operation for six more years. Congress, though dominated by Tilak's Hinduism and his Home Rule movement, did not arouse a sense of danger to Islam in the minds of the Muslim Leaguers of those days. Both Hindus and Muslims expressed their dissatisfaction with the Montagu-Chelmsford Report, published in July 1918. The establishment at Delhi by 'Ubayd Allāh Sindī, a student of Deōband, of an institution named *Niẓārat al-Ma'ārif al-Qur'āniyya*, to train the Muslim youth of 'Alīgarh, educated on Western lines, in the Qur'anic ideology of Shāh Walī Allāh, lent a romantic colour to the union of Deōband and 'Alīgarh. The Silk Letter conspiracy of 1915, in which the students, teachers and the principal of Deōband took an active part, adequately reflect revolutionary trends in the Deōband theologians.

[1] Minute by Sir James Meston, Lt. Governor of the U.P., 21 August 1913, Home Department, Political Proceedings No. 100/118, October 1913, Paras. 30–31, National Archives, New Delhi.

CHAPTER 4

INDIA AND PAKISTAN

Soon after the First World War, Muslim India was involved in a mass political convulsion of a composite nature. Its components were two parallel and mutually linked agitations: a tense and explosive pan-Islamic emotionalism apprehensive of the fate of the defeated Ottoman empire, of the Arab lands (especially the Ḥijāz), and of the institution of the caliphate; and an alliance with the Hindus in the nationalist and anti-imperialist mass-movement led by the Indian National Congress. These two elements of the agitation were directed against linked objectives: pressure on the government in Britain for a more sympathetic approach in deciding the fate of the vanquished Ottoman empire; and pressure on the British government in India for greater concessions towards self-determination.

The way for a working alliance with Congress had been prepared since 1911 by a series of national and international developments. The annulment of the partition of Bengal (1911), which deprived the Muslims of that province of the political and economic advantage conceded to them earlier, had convinced the Muslim leadership of the instability of British patronage. British action, inaction, or indifference on such developments as the Italian occupation of Libya, or the extension of French control over Morocco, the Balkan War, the suspected designs of a partition of Persia (and possibly Turkey) between Russia and Great Britain, had built up the image of British imperialism as an ally of all European imperialist thrusts directed against the Muslim lands. The annulment of the partition of Bengal had also taught the Muslim political leaders the lesson that the policy of loyalism, initiated by Sayyid Aḥmad Khān and followed ever since, did not pay as rich political dividends as the organised movement of political opposition conducted by Congress, or even the terrorism of extremist Hindus. The Muslim League's overtures for an alliance with Congress had begun in 1911, and had matured in the so-called 'Lucknow Pact' (1916) drafted by Muḥammad 'Ali Jinnah (Jināḥ) and approved by the Congress leaders including Tilak, whose policies had so far been unsympathetic, and occasionally actually hostile, to the Muslims. From 1917 to 1921 Congress and the Muslim League held their annual sessions simultaneously and in the same cities. Most Muslim leaders belonged to both these organizations, and naturally co-ordinated their policies.

As early as 1913 the *'ulamā'* had shown their concern over the possible fate of the Ḥijāz in the event of the dismemberment of the Ottoman empire, and Mawlānā 'Abd al-Bārī of Farangī Maḥall had founded the *Anjuman-i Khuddām-i Ka'ba*. After the war he and some other *'ulamā'* entered the political scene openly. In 1919 Muḥammad 'Alī, formerly editor of the *Comrade*, who had been imprisoned during the war for having written a fiery editorial supporting the Ottoman decision to enter the war against the Allies, was set free. In that highly tense atmosphere of Muslim political frustration, he soon emerged as the most eloquent and most influential leader of Muslim India. The Muslim League, which, despite its alliance with Congress, had followed a policy of caution when it came to open defiance of British rule in India, receded into the background. Its place in Muslim political life came to be taken by the Khilāfat Conference founded by Muḥammad 'Alī in 1919 with the objective of organizing Muslim mass-agitation to exercise pressure on the British government, to restore to the Ottoman empire its former frontiers. It was especially concerned with the independence of what it called *Jazīrat al-'Arab* (Arabia, including Iraq, Syria, Transjordan, Palestine, and especially the Ḥijāz) from non-Muslim domination, control or influence. The Khilāfat Conference was essentially a party of pan-Islam rather than of Indian Islam. The Ottoman Caliphate was its political symbol. In these policies the Khilafat Conference was supported by an organization of the *'ulamā'*, the *Jam'iyyat al-'ulamā'-yi Hind*, dominated by the theologians of Dēoband, who had a long tradition of resistance to British rule. Its leader, Maḥmūd al-Ḥasan, had contacted Enver and other Ottoman leaders in the Ḥijaz during the war, and agreed to work as an agent of the Turkish cause in India. He was arrested by the *Sharīf* Ḥusayn of Mecca, handed over to the British, and imprisoned in Malta, but released and allowed to return to India after the war.

The political philosophy of the Indian Khilāfat movement was formulated by Abu'l-Kalām Āzād, editor of the influential religious and cultural weekly, *al-Hilāl*, and a liberal theologian, who had come deeply under the influence of the pan-Islamic ideas generally attributed to Jamāl al-Dīn al-Afghānī. Āzād considered the concept of the Muslim *jamā'a* as a cohesive and monolithic social organism, the antithesis of which was *jāhiliyya*, a state of social chaos and confusion. The powers of the effective direction of the *jamā'a* had to be invested in the hands of a central authority, the caliph. Though after the four Patriarchal Caliphs the institution of the caliphate became monarchical, nevertheless under the Umayyads, the 'Abbasids and the Ottomans, the caliph still remained the rallying-point of the whole of the Sunnī Muslim community. The foundation of pan-Islamic society rested on this and on four other pillars: the rallying of the community to the call of the caliph, its obedience to the caliph, *hijra* or the migration of Muslims from a land conquered by non-Muslims to *dār al-Islām*, and *jihād* which in the modern context could be violent or non-violent according to the exigencies of the situation. For the Indo-Muslim section of the *jamā'a*, he favoured a regional *imām* or *qā'id*, a kind of a religious viceroy of the Ottoman caliph, and tried to persuade Maḥmūd al-Ḥasan of Dēoband to accept that responsibility. His concept of the Ottoman caliphate was that of a political sovereignty, and not a religious one like that of the pope; but still the monarchical caliph remained the only political symbol of the unity and coherence in the Muslim community. He commanded its obedience, which could be denied to him only if he acted in a way contrary to the Qur'ān and the *Sunna*.

But it was Muḥammad 'Alī who developed the Khilāfat movement of the Muslim masses, the first political agitation which carried almost the entire Muslim Indian population with it. From 1919 to 1922 the Khilāfat Conference and the Indian National Congress worked as twin organizations with a common leadership. Never before, and never afterwards, was Congress able to mobilize Muslim public opinion in its favour on any considerable scale.

In 1919, Mohandas Karamchand Gandhi, a London-trained barrister lately returned from South Africa, was effectively assuming the leadership of Congress, and replacing Tilak. Just then Indian nationalists were bitterly incensed against a repressive statute, the Rowlatt Act, which sought to perpetuate war-time restrictions on civil liberties. Tactless and unimaginative measures by local civil and military authorities in the Panjāb further exacerbated the situation. General Dyer, a military commander at Amritsar, had ordered firing at a public meeting held in defiance of the law, killing nearly four hundred people. Others were later made to crawl out of the area on all fours. This episode made the name of its venue, the Jaliānwāla Bāgh, the symbol of a sense of injustice and humiliation. Finally the Government of India Act of 1919, which had introduced some political reforms, modelled to some extent on the Congress-League 'Lucknow Pact' of 1916, had not come up to Indian expectations of a greater share in government and administration.

Gandhi developed at that stage the shrewd and incomparable technique of non-violent non-cooperation, a peaceful but revolutionary weapon which the vast millions of India could wield against the world's mightiest commercial empire. He took full advantage of the Muslim support which was available to him in the form of the Khilāfat unrest; lent it his full and unqualified support; used it as a testing-ground for his new technique of non-cooperation; and was able to create for a few years a monolithic structure of Hindu-Muslim solidarity, of which he was the first and undisputed leader. He pledged himself in support of the caliphate, and the territorial integrity of the Ottoman Empire. He swayed the Hindu masses towards the same political alliance and towards the mystique of the Khilāfat, a word which they considered to be derived from *khilāf*, meaning in Urdu 'opposition' and therefore implying 'opposed to the government'.

It was a Hindu-Muslim rather than an Indian nationalism. Jawaharlal Nehru describes it as 'a strange mixture of nationalism and politics and religion and mysticism and fanaticism'[1] in which the Hindu and the Muslim strains were clearly distinguishable. Gandhi's spiritualism, as described by a Hindu historian, was 'grounded in the theology of Hinduism and the ethics of Jainism'.[2] Muḥammad 'Alī was quite frank about the pull of his mind in opposite directions: 'I belong to two circles of equal size, but which are not concentric. One is India and the other is the Muslim world'.[3]

In its international role the Khilāfat movement achieved little. A deputation led by Muḥammad 'Alī visited London early in 1920, and laid before Lloyd George and H. A. L. Fisher the demands that Turkey might be allowed to retain her pre-war frontiers, and especially should not lose her control of the Ḥijāz. On 10 August 1920, the Allies sought to impose upon Turkey the treaty of Sèvres, which, if implemented, would have left her mutilated and shorn of her sovereignty. Some moves of the Khilāfat Conference in India were not only unsuccessful but disastrous in the larger interests of the Indian Muslims. The *hijra* from the British-occupied Indian *dār al-ḥarb* to the land of Islam in Afghanistan, counselled by Āzād, uprooted 18,000 Muslims, who were turned back

[1] Jawaharlal Nehru, *An autobiography* (London, 1942), 75.
[2] Beni Prasad, *The Hindu-Muslim questions* (Allahabad, 1941), 49.
[3] Afzal Iqbal (ed.), *Select Writings and Speeches of Maulana Mohammed Ali, passim.*

at the frontier by the Afghan government. From 1919 to 1924 Muḥammad 'Alī consistently expressed the view that in the event of an Afghan invasion of India, Indian Muslims should support it, even if it turned against the Hindus; a view from which Āzād dissociated himself at an early stage, signalling a parting of the ways between the separatist and nationalist trends in Indian Muslim politics. These statements, encouraging, or at least expressing, wishful thinking in favour of an Afghan invasion were resented by Tagore and Gandhi. In the case of extreme Hindu communalists like Lala Har Dayal, they led to utopian polemics, envisaging a purely Hindu India, and the total conversion of all Indian Muslims and Afghans. The political confusion in the mind of the *élite* soon came to be reflected among the Hindu and Muslim masses in the form of communal riots. The sanguinary riots of Chauri Chaura in 1921 depressed Gandhi to such an extent that he called off the civil disobedience movement, which could have been very troublesome to the government. Lack of organized guidance by the Khilāfat workers in the south resulted in the ugliest and most violent of the series of riots, when, in 1922, Moplah Muslims started an anti-British agitation. This got out of control, and was turned violently against the Hindus. Hindu reaction to Islam and the Muslims stiffened soon to bitter hostility in the vigorous province of the Panjāb, where the revivalist organization Arya Samāj resumed with a reinforced fury the task of converting Muslims to Hinduism. Counter-conversion organizations of the Muslims sprang up in the same province with the propagation of Islam as their objective. Another violently anti-Muslim organization, the Hindu Sanghatan, was started by a former member of Congress, Moonje. Finally the extremist Hindu political organization the Hindu Mahasabha upheld a triple ideal consisting of the complementary concepts: Hinduism or the Hindu faith, *Hindutva* or 'Hindu-ness', being the linguistic, cultural and political aspects of Hinduism, and 'Hindudom' a novel concept of the unity and solidarity of the whole Hindu (including the Buddhist) world corresponding to the Muslim *dār al-Islām*.

By 1924 the communal atmosphere had become so poisonous with polemic, abuse and riot that Gandhi fasted for twenty-one days to enforce some moral restraint over the movements of conversion and reconversion. But the communal poison had by now reinfected the Indian National Congress itself. During the last decade of the nineteenth century and the first of the twentieth, two rival factions, under the leadership of Tilak and Gokhale, represented the anti-Muslim and pro-Muslim trends within the Congress leadership, of which the former had been the more powerful, and had alienated the Muslims from that organization during those decades. Between 1919 and 1924, under the undisputed leadership of Gandhi the two factions had merged, and the Muslims had been won over through support of the Khilāfat movement. By 1924, Hindu exclusivists, Madan Mohan Malviya and Lala Lajpat Rai, revived the anti-Muslim faction under the name of the Nationalist Party within Congress, and were more than a match for the liberal and pro-Muslim wing of Congress led by Motilal Nehru and C. R. Das. The overall moderate leadership of Gandhi, though in firm control of Congress policies relating to political resistance against the British, on the Muslim question barely held the two rival factions from falling apart. On the whole the inner pattern of Congress's attitude towards the Muslims had already in 1924 taken a polarized form, which it continued to retain, with adjustments and reorientations, until 1947.

The failure of the Congress-Khilāfat alliance almost synchronized with the collapse of the Khilāfat movement itself. Muṣṭafā Kemāl's successful revolution had put Turkey back on the map of the world; but it was a Turkey different from the one to which the Khilāfat Conference was emotionally attached. Turkish secularism, even in its earlier stages, was quite unpalatable to the Indian *'ulamā'*. The image of the Turkish hero which appealed to the Indian Muslim mind was that of Enver Pasha and not Muṣṭafā Kemāl. However, the Turkish Grand National Assembly's decision to appoint 'Abd ül-Mejīd as a caliph shorn of the Ottoman monarchy was reluctantly accepted. Supreme humiliation came with the abolition of the caliphate by the Turks on 3 March 1924, leaving the Indian Khilāfat Conference without a *raison d'être*. It had lost by now its national as well as international platform, though it continued to exist nominally for a few more years and showed some fervour in its denunciation of the caliphal claims of King Ḥusayn of the Ḥijāz, who was suspected of being a British tool. It was intellectually too unsure of itself and too disorganized to participate in the Caliphate Conference held in Cairo in 1926. It did participate in a conference of Islamic countries held in Mecca under the auspices of Ibn Su'ūd in the same year, but the question of the caliphate was not even on its agenda. In 1933 the Khilāfat Conference, now a shadow of its former self, ceased to exist. The theory of caliphate received a decent burial in the political philosophy of Sir Muḥammad Iqbāl (1876–1938), who, endorsing the approach of Żiyā Gökalp, added that though the concept of a universal Muslim caliphate was a commendable ideal, each Muslim nation should first try to put its own house in order, striving in due course for an Islamic multi-national free association.

With the collapse of the Khilāfat movement and the growing distrust of Congress, Muslim politics in India entered the phase of its *Wanderjahre* from 1924 to 1937. Separatist trends born in the 1880s now re-emerged as the predominant political impulse. This separatism was voiced in the mass orations of Muḥammad 'Alī, and Jinnah gave it a constitutional formulation. In this journey of resentment and apprehension into the political unknown, the Muslim leaders were concerned primarily with setting up safeguards for their community, to preserve its distinct religious, cultural and economic identity. As time elapsed, the focus came to be fixed more and more on securing for the Muslims a position of predominant political power in the provinces of Bengal and the Panjāb where they were numerically in a majority. With this was linked a demand for the creation or development of other Muslim regions as full provinces. In short, rather vaguely, Muslim separatism in the sub-continent was already taking a territorial form.

The next landmark in these developments was formed by the controversy over the recommendations of the committee appointed by Congress in 1928 to determine the principles of a future constitution for India (popularly known as the Nehru Report). It presented the constitutional image of a secular state as a solvent for inter-communal tensions, and in doing so, it rejected the method of separate electorates for the Muslims in favour of joint electorates.[1] To Muslims, it appeared as a repudiation of the 'Lucknow Pact' of 1916, by which Congress had accepted the principle of separate electorates. Muslim political reaction to the Nehru Report was rather confused in the beginning, but in the wake of an All-Parties Muslim Conference held under the chairmanship of the Aga Khan, Muslim counter-proposals were formulated by Jinnah in fourteen points and remained the sheet-anchor of Muslim demands for a share in political power until 1937. These envisaged a federal structure for the future India with residuary, almost autonomous, powers vested in the provinces; effective representation of minorities in the provinces 'without reducing the majority in any province to a minority or even equality' (to safeguard the chances of Muslim predominance in Bengal and the Panjāb); separate electorates, with a

[1] For this and other documents referred to in the next few pages see C. H. Philips (ed.), *The evolution of India and Pakistan 1858–1947* (London, 1962), 228–52, 290–334, 337–407.

proviso for the revision of this provision; and safeguards for the protection and promotion of Muslim institutions and personal law.

In 1930 the British Labour government invited Indian leaders to the first of a series of Round Table Conferences. Congress participated in the second Round Table Conference (1931) with Gandhi as its sole representative. Its Minorities Committee came to a dead end, as Gandhi's proposal that the problem of the relative representation of minorities should be postponed until after the framing of a constitution for India, and then referred to a judicial tribunal, was rejected alike by Muslims, Christians, Anglo-Indians and Hindus of lower castes.

The situation was summed up in the Report of the Joint Committee on Indian Constitutional Reforms (1934) in these words:

> Parliamentary government, as it is understood in the United Kingdom, works by the interaction of four essential factors: the principle of majority rule; the willingness of the minority for the time being to accept the decisions of the majority; the existence of great political parties divided by broad issues of policy, rather than by sectional interests; and finally the existence of a mobile body of political opinion, owing no permanent allegiance to any party and therefore able, by its instinctive reaction against extravagant movements on one side or the other, to keep the vessel on an even keel. In India none of these factors can be said to exist today. There are no parties as we understand them, and there is no considerable body of political opinion which can be described as mobile. In their place we are confronted with the age-old antagonism of Hindu and Muhammedan,...representative not only of two religions but of two civilizations.

The government's proposed solution for this situation was 'to translate the customs of the British constitution into statutory safeguards'.

In 1932 a British White Paper had upheld separate electorates. But the game of weightage cut both ways; depriving the Muslims of their parliamentary majority in the legislatures of Bengal and the Panjāb; and conceding them weightage in the provinces where they were, and, despite the weightage, still remained an insignificant minority. The Conservatives were in office in Britain when the Government of India Act of 1935 was passed. It invested the governor-general of the future Indian Federation, and the (British) governors of Indian provinces, with the special responsibility of safeguarding the legitimate interests of minorities. This provision, implying the perpetuation of the British presence as a third party, led to further recrimination between Congress and the Muslims. The former accused the latter of serving the cause of imperialism by their intransigence; the latter accused the former of a lack of generosity and fairness; both accused the British of a policy of 'divide and rule'.

In 1937 elections were held under the Government of India Act to implement its provincial sections. The Muslim League was revived by a new group of leaders; some of them, like Liyāqat 'Alī Khān, were members of the landed gentry, others, like Fażl al-Ḥaqq, were professional men. Jinnah was persuaded by them to return from his self-imposed retirement in Britain, and to assume the supreme leadership. The campaign and pledges of the Muslim League during these elections were not very different from those of Congress. Both stood for political independence. Both accepted, though with difference in emphasis, the principles of a diluted socialism. Both emphasized the need for industrial development and rural uplift. During the election campaign they worked, not in rivalry, but with arrangements that were co-operative. It was generally assumed that after the elections the provincial cabinets formed by Congress would include League members. Congress decided to reject the association of the Muslim League in its governments, and insisted as a pre-condition for a Muslim to be appointed as a minister, that he should resign from the League and sign the Congress pledge of membership. No similar condition required the would-be Hindu ministers to resign from the extremist Hindu Mahasabha. The Congress argument for refusing to share power with the Muslim League was that it could redeem its election pledges only by a programme of political and social reforms, which a homogeneous cabinet alone could implement by presenting a monolithic front to possible obstruction from a British governor. League members would introduce a divisible, if not a divisive factor. Against this position it is interesting to read the views of Beni Prasad: 'Orthodox parliamentarism led the Congress leaders to forget that the one-party theory, even if true of political agitation, was not, in the absence of an accomplished revolution, applicable to ministerial office.'[1]

In rejecting the Muslim League as an associate, Congress drove it in opposition to become its most fundamental adversary. By refusing to concede a minor political issue, Congress created between itself and the Muslim consensus an ever-widening political gulf. Had the Congress governments acted with restraint and foresight, and kept Hindu revivalist trends in control, this gulf could yet have been bridged. But a Hindu ideological and terminological shape was chosen for new educa-

[1] Beni Prasad, *The Hindu-Muslim questions*, 60.

tional and cultural schemes in some provinces. Hindi in the *Devanāgarī* (Sanskrit) script was given official encouragement by several Congress ministers at the expense of Urdu. In short, to the Muslims the pattern of the Congress's cultural policies seemed a substitution and a supersession of the British by Hindu institutions—a situation in which they feared the annihilation of their religio-cultural identity. The Muslim League, as the spokesman of Muslim separatism, marched from strength to strength, until it was able to justify its claim to be the sole representative of Muslim political opinion in India. Attempts by Congress to win over the Muslims by mass contact, or by creation and encouragement of mushroom anti-League parties proved quite ineffective except in the North-West Frontier Province, where the Muslim Red Shirt movement sided consistently with Congress. When the Congress governments resigned at the advent of the Second World War in 1939 (after the rejection by the British government of their ultimatum for immediate transfer of power as a prerequisite for their participation in the war effort), the political atmosphere in India as described by Sir Reginald Coupland was such that 'Indian observers agreed with the British officials that Hindu-Muslim relations had never in their experience been so bad'.[1]

During the crucial years between 1937 and 1939 the Indian Muslims in several provinces became for the first time familiar with the implications of the transfer of power from British hands into those of Congress, which had a predominantly Hindu membership. Under this impact, their political outlook underwent a final change. They ceased to regard themselves a minority community within a single, composite Indian nation. They claimed to be a nation by themselves, and, as such, felt their way towards accepting a doctrine of a separate national status, and a demand for a separate national homeland.

Though vague references to the possibility or feasibility of a separate Muslim state in India had been made from time to time since the 1920s, the first clear statement of this occurs in Sir Muḥammad Iqbāl's presidential address to the annual session of the Muslim League in 1930. He rejected the geographical, racial and linguistic criteria of nationhood in favour of Renan's definition that a nation is a spiritual principle, possessing a common and indivisible heritage of the past, which it consciously wills to hold together through the present for the future. Iqbāl argued that the Indian people as an ethnic conglomeration did not possess an indivisible heritage of the past. Hindus and Muslims

[1] Sir Reginald Coupland, *The Indian problem* (London, 1942–43), II, 132.

were in fact aiming at different, and more often than not, conflicting concepts of the future. 'Muslim demand for the creation of a Muslim India within India, was therefore perfectly justified.' Iqbāl further added 'I would like to see the Punjab, North Western Frontier, Sind and Baluchistan amalgamated into a single state'. This, he said, appeared to him as the final destiny of the Muslims.[1] Iqbāl did not specifically mention Bengal, but in all subsequent political thinking in Muslim India the same principle of separatist self-determination came to be applied to it. In 1937, the crucial year of the final parting of the ways between Congress and the League, Iqbāl wrote a number of letters to Jinnah, who observed:

His views were substantially in consonance with my own and had finally led me to the same conclusions as a result of careful examination and study of the constitutional problems facing India, and finally found expression in due course in the united will of Muslim India as adumbrated in the Lahore resolution of All-India Muslim League (1940), popularly known as the 'Pakistan Resolution'.[2]

The name 'Pakistan', which fatefully captured the imagination of the Muslim masses because of its messianic connotations, was a contribution of Chawdharī Raḥmat 'Alī and a group of Indian Muslim students at Cambridge. It was explained that it did not represent its literal meaning 'the land of the pure', but was a mnemonic formation from the names of north-western Muslim regions. Panjāb, Afghania (for North-West Frontier), Kashmir, Sind and Baluchistan.

Iqbāl's concept of a separate Muslim state was still nebulous. The Muslim League resolution of 1940 sought to define it more precisely: '...that geographically contiguous units are demarcated into regions which should be so constituted with such territorial readjustments as may be necessary that the areas in which the Muslims are numerically in a majority, as in the north-western and eastern zones of India, should be grouped to constitute "independent States"'.[3]

From 1940 to 1947 the partition of the sub-continent on these lines remained an explosively controversial issue of Indian politics; and overshadowed all subsequent negotiations between Britain, Congress and the League. The principle of the secession of Muslim India as a separate

[1] Sir Muḥammad Iqbāl, 'The Presidential Address to the Annual Session of the Muslim League in 1930,' reprinted in *The struggle for independence* (Karachi, 1958), 16–17.

[2] M. A. Jinnah, Introduction to *The letters of Iqbal to Jinnah* (Lahore, n.d.), 4–5.

[3] Philips, *Evolution of India and Pakistan*, 353–4.

dominion was envisaged in the British Cabinet's proposals of transfer of power after the war, brought to India and discussed with the Indian leaders by Sir Stafford Cripps in March 1942, when a Japanese invasion of India seemed imminent.

Soon the concept of Pakistan as a solution of the problem of political deadlock came to be studied thoroughly by Muslims as well as non-Muslims. The case for Pakistan was perhaps argued much more convincingly by the Hindu Scheduled Castes leader, B. R. Ambedkar, and by the theorists of the Communist party of India, than by Muslim writers. A number of books were also written against the concept of Pakistan by non-Muslims, and by some nationalist Muslims; most significant of these is *India divided*, by Rajendra Prasad, who later became president of the Republic of India. The frustration which followed the failure of the Cripps Mission led a senior leader of Congress, C. Rajagopalchariyya, to introduce a resolution before the Congress Working Committee, in 1942, recommending the concession of an autonomous, if not independent, Muslim state, confined to the areas of Muslim majority, and with a confederal link with India. The Congress Working Committee rejected the resolution, but two years later it formed the basis of discussions between Gandhi and Jinnah which ended in failure. From 1942 onwards, however, Congress accepted in principle that it could not compel the people of any territorial unit to remain in a future Indian Union against 'its declared and established will'.

Elections to the legislatures, held at the end of the war in 1945, confirmed the Muslim League in its claim to be the sole representative of the Muslim consensus, as it captured all the Muslim seats in the Central Assembly, and 446 out of 495 Muslim seats in provincial legislatures.

The Labour government in the United Kingdom, which came into power at the end of the Second World War, applied itself sincerely to the problem of disengagement from India, and the transfer of power into the hands of the Indians. In 1946 a British Cabinet Mission was sent to India, which, in lieu of conceding a sovereign Pakistan, presented an alternative formula of a three-tier governmental structure consisting of a weak centre, the provinces, and between them a middle tier of provincial federal groupings. It envisaged three such groups: Group A was composed of the provinces with the Hindu majority in the middle and southern regions, and consisted of by far the greater part of India; Group B consisted of the provinces in the north-west with a large Muslim majority; and Group C consisted of the eastern provinces of Bengal and

Assam with a marginal Muslim majority. Against the feeling of the rank-and-file of the Muslim League which was now strongly in favour of a sovereign Muslim state, Jinnah accepted the Cabinet Mission's proposals. Congress also accepted them; but certain statements made, and certain stands taken by its leaders (such as Jawaharlal Nehru's proviso that the plan, including its scheme of groupings, could be subjected to future changes; and the general sympathy of the Congress leadership with the stand taken by Bordoloi, its chief leader in Assam, that the predominantly non-Hindu province of Assam should be a part of the Hindu Group A rather than the marginally Muslim Group C) filled the political atmosphere with uncertainty in so far as the Muslims were concerned. According to Abu'l-Kalām Āzād, this ambivalence in the attitude of Congress led Jinnah finally to believe that absolute separatism was the only alternative left for the Muslims, in view of the threat of revision by the Congress majority to any plan for a united India inherited from the British. The Muslim League revised its decision and rejected the Cabinet Mission plan. It reiterated its demand for a sovereign Pakistan, and launched upon a programme of direct action in an atmosphere which was already explosive with widespread communal riots.

British efforts for the transfer of power continued and a government was formed by Lord Wavell, the viceroy, with Jawaharlal Nehru as his deputy, and with Congress leaders for the first time in office at the centre. After an initial refusal the Muslim League also joined in, with the purpose of a divisive policy and an obstructionism which might serve as a pressure for the inevitable partition of the sub-continent. It was in this atmosphere that Earl Mountbatten succeeded Lord Wavell; and, as the head of a government divided against itself, it was possible for him to persuade first the anti-Muslim Patel, then the liberal Nehru and finally Gandhi himself of the inevitability of partition as the only solution.

On this basis the British government's proposal for the immediate transfer of power was announced by Earl Mountbatten on 3 June 1947, and accepted by the Indian National Congress and the Muslim League. The proposal envisaged the emergence of India and Pakistan as sovereign self-governing dominions of the British Commonwealth. The line of partition between them was to follow district boundaries (and later, according to the decisions of a Boundary Commission, sub-district boundaries) in the provinces of Bengal, the Panjāb and Assam, separating Muslim from non-Muslim areas.

British disengagement from India was largely a decision dictated by

Realpolitik and enlightened self-interest. During a debate in the House of Commons on 5 March 1947, Sir Stafford Cripps had pointed out that:

The exigencies of the war situation were such that it was not possible for the British Government to continue with the recruitment of Europeans, for the Secretary of State's Services [the higher cadres of the Indian Civil Service], while, at the same time, there was, of course, a great increase in the Indian Forces, accompanied by a rapid indianization of their officer cadre. This meant that, side by side with the growing demand for an acceleration of the transfer of power on the part of all parties in India, there was an obvious and inevitable weakening of the machinery of British control through the Secretary of State's Services.[1]

The British Parliament passed the Indian Independence Act on 18 July 1947. On 14 August 1947 the independent state of Pakistan came into existence as a dominion of the British Commonwealth with Muḥammad 'Alī Jinnah as its governor-general. India chose 15 August as the day of its independence, with Earl Mountbatten as its governor-general. The twin states were born in an atmosphere of the most sanguinary communal strife the sub-continent has known in historical times, this meant in the north-west the transfer of population involving millions in the regions on both sides of the frontier.

Hardly another state, except perhaps Algeria, was born to face from the very outset such overwhelming problems as did Pakistan. Whereas India had inherited the habitat and the smooth-geared machinery of the British administration, in the central government of Pakistan administrative institutions and offices had to start from the foundations. The two-way migration of refugees affected Pakistan adversely both ways. The exodus of non-Muslims from West Pakistan

included all the merchants, bankers and traders, most of the doctors and technical personnel, and a good proportion of teachers of higher education. In their place there arrived from East Punjab a flood of poor peasants, together with artisans and small shopkeepers from Delhi and other towns. On balance, there was an increase of almost a million out of this forced exchange. But those who came could not contribute anything vital to the economy, while those who were gone represented the whole network of commerce and exchange; the nerves and sinews of the economic system of West Pakistan...East Pakistan was crippled in a different way. The West was a viable economic unit, with a complete railroad system, a fully developed port, and an international airport: even if it entirely lacked an industrial base. The East had formed part

[1] *Parliamentary debates, House of Commons,* Vol. 434 (1946–7), cols. 497–508.

of the hinterland of Calcutta; its principal product, jute, was processed and exported from the Hooghley industrial nexus. Now, Calcutta with its mills was in another country. East Pakistan had no means of processing its staple crop, and only a second-rate port (Chittagong) through which to squeeze its exports.[1]

In 1949 neither East nor West Pakistan had any industries to speak of. This was partly due to the paucity of mineral deposits in these areas and partly to the British defence strategy of developing industrial centres at a safe distance from the frontiers. The economy of East and West Pakistan was to a certain extent complementary; but the distance of over a thousand miles between these two outlying territories made integrated economic planning very difficult from the very outset.

This geographical division of Pakistan in two far-flung units has been that country's most bewildering problem in several other ways. Situated at the opposite ends of the sub-continent, the two regions have only two elements of nationhood in common: Islam, and a dread of Indian aggression. These two elements of cohesion have to cope with a multiplicity of divisive factors. Fast air communication between these two regions has been possible only because of the courtesy of otherwise hostile India. The diet, the mode of living, the agricultural problems, the industrial requirements of the people of East and West Pakistan are different. West Pakistan is alive to the cultural pull of Shīrāz and Iṣfahān; East Pakistan to that of Calcutta. Urdu and the languages of West Pakistan are Persian-orientated; Bengali, on the other hand shares its cultural heritage with the Hindus of West Bengal, and is written in a Sanskritic script. West Pakistan itself is the home of a number of minor cultural communities, each with its own language, literature and traditions: the Pathāns, the Panjābīs, the Balūchīs and the Sindhīs who are only now beginning to merge into a single geographical and economic unity. Thus when Pakistan came into being it was a conglomeration of regional groups of peoples; it had yet to evolve into a nation.

Considering all these problems the emergence, survival and development of Pakistan has been a fairly creditable achievement. Into the vacuum created by the outgoing professional refugees entered fresh talent recruited from among the incoming middle class of Muslim evacuees. The civil service of Pakistan, though far less efficient than that of India—for under the British régime Muslim candidates who did not do so well in the competitive civil service examinations were selected to

[1] Hugh Tinker, *India and Pakistan. A political analysis* (London, 1962), 69, 71.

complete the Muslim quota—served as the steel frame which supported the superstructure of a hastily improvised administrative system. A Pakistan navy and an air force were built up *ab initio.* The army was reconstituted in the tradition of the British Indian army, which was taught to be loyal to the regimental flag, and to hold aloof from politics. In this process civil as well as defence officers received accelerated promotion, a development which to a certain extent weakened the calibre of government services. A foreign service was also created, which came to be regarded as the prize service, and therefore processes of selection to it reflected provincial rivalries and personal favouritism. Being of mediocre quality, it was less than a match for the highly professional Indian foreign service, which projected abroad a very favourable image of India in its disputes with Pakistan. Stabilizing factors in Pakistan were the vast masses of people, especially the refugees who had come in millions, and a new class of adventurous tradesmen and small-scale industrialists. The conservative religious lower middle class remained, in the years that followed, passionately loyal to the concept of Pakistan as an Islamic state. The Western-educated intelligensia, which was the real architect of Pakistan, presented a front of loyal patriotism to outside observers and in relation to all disputes with India; but within itself it had its frustrations in the way the things were going in the new state, the dangerous growth of religious fanaticism, which it used as a political instrument, and more especially in the chronic impact of provincial rivalries on the everyday life of the demoralized citizens.

In August 1948 Muḥammad ʿAlī Jinnah died. With him, Pakistan lost the only great leader it ever had. As long as he was alive, divisive trends, whether provincial or factional, were held firmly in control. Though theoretically a constitutional governor-general, he was given the title *Qā'id Aʿẓam* (the Greatest Leader) and as such in practice, the prime minister, Liyāqat ʿAlī Khān, recognized him unofficially as a sovereign authority, and was directed by him on larger issues of policy.

On the death of Jinnah, the prime minister assumed in practice as in theory his rightful position as head of the government and administration, in accordance with democratic theory and practice; and the new governor-general (selected from East Pakistan in the interests of provincial balance), Khwāja Nāẓim al-Dīn, assumed his appointment as the constitutional head of the state with a mainly ceremonial role. Liyāqat ʿAlī Khān's Cabinet was responsible to the Constituent Assembly of Pakistan, which also acted as the national legislature. This government stabilized the country's civil, financial and economic life to some extent, with considerable emphasis on law and order. It evolved a foreign policy which envisaged close friendship with Islamic countries, especially Persia, and which, after some hesitation, moved in the direction of a closer approach towards the U.S.A. On the debit side there was a weakness on the part of Liyāqat 'Alī Khān in his sacrifice of competitive criteria of selection for the administrative services to provincial political pressure for quotas by provinces; in delay in the framing of a constitution and the holding of general elections; and in undue emphasis on the tightening of security measures. Liyāqat 'Alī Khan's assassination in 1951 was a national disaster for Pakistan, which has not since been able to produce a prime minister of his calibre. Between 1951 and 1956 the principle of a balance of power between the Panjāb and East Pakistan at the top determined the choice of the governors and the prime ministers. In itself not an unsound principle, within two years it degenerated into a manoeuvring for power, first provincial, then blatantly personal. The rivalries between the governors-general and the prime ministers sharpened the basically provincial nature of Pakistani politics, and dwarfed the chances of the growth of a healthy political life.

The economy of East and West Pakistan is essentially agricultural. Its two fundamental problems are to grow enough food for its teeming millions, and to produce cash crops for the much-needed foreign exchange, to strike a balance between the country's agricultural and industrial growth. The two main food crops of the country are rice, the staple diet of East Pakistan, which has a population of over fifty millions, and wheat, the staple diet of West Pakistan with a population of nearly forty-three millions. Its two cash crops are jute, of which East Pakistan has almost a world monopoly as raw producer; and cotton, grown mainly in West Pakistan. Acute food shortages have occurred since 1953, owing to a multiplicity of causes: steep rise in population, lack of modern fertilizers, land erosion, general encroachment of the desert on the sown land, salinity and waterlogging over vast stretches, as well as the restrictions imposed from time to time by India on the timing and supply of irrigation waters to the canals in West Pakistan.

This last problem, known generally as the Canal Waters Dispute, arose in 1948 with India's claim of proprietary rights over the waters of the eastern tributaries of the Indus that flow from India into Pakistan. India's case was that it was constructing vast irrigation headworks on the upper reaches of the rivers Rāvi and Satlaj to bring the deserts of

Rājāsthān, further south, under cultivation, and could ill afford to spare large supplies of water to its neighbour. Half of West Pakistan's irrigation depended on the waters of these rivers; it was therefore a life-and-death challenge to its agricultural economy. After three and a half years of acrimonious negotiation, a break-through was made in 1951 towards a solution sponsored by the World Bank, on the basis of a complicated and very extensive engineering project to construct dams and link canals running from west to east contrary to the natural drainage system of the Indus basin. The project was based on the political formula that the waters of the three western rivers of the basin would be used exclusively by Pakistan, and those of the three eastern rivers by India. Under the sponsorship of the World Bank, and after prolonged negotiations, a treaty was signed between India and Pakistan in 1960, with the provision that the enormous cost of the project would be met by a vast contribution from India, and financial assistance from the West.

On the general scale of the growth of industrialization in under-developed countries, Pakistan's industrial growth has been creditable, considering its political instability. The volume of industrialization has so far been weighted heavily in favour of West Pakistan. The government's policy has been to offer a lead through official or semi-official agencies, such as a Development Board set up in 1947, a Planning Commission founded in 1950, and chiefly through the Pakistan Industrial Development Corporation, which has set up a number of industrial units covering the production of jute manufactures, paper, heavy engineering and ship-building. The policy of the Corporation is to 'create' industries and then to sell them as going concerns to private enterprise—an industrial policy which almost reverses the process of nationalization. As in other under-developed countries, Pakistan's economic planning has had to lean heavily on foreign aid, received from the U.S.A., under the Colombo Plan, from the British Commonwealth, other countries of the West, and Japan. Since the establishment of Pakistan, several hydro-electric and irrigation projects have been completed, a cotton industry has been built up almost from scratch to meet the bulk of the consumer demand, and a number of other projects have contributed to some extent to the ultimate goal of economic self-sufficiency.

The partition of the sub-continent into the successor-states of India and Pakistan was confined specifically to British India. Interspersed in the British Indian Empire, there were also some 560 large or small princely states, ruled over by feudal chiefs or princelings under the suzerainty of the British Imperial Crown. The constitutional position taken by the British government, in the context of the transfer of power in 1947, was that the British suzerainty over the princely states would lapse, and they would be free to accede either to India or to Pakistan, or to remain independent. They were advised, however, to accede to the contiguous dominion, bearing in mind geographical and ethnic considerations. All the states followed this British advice with the exception of three: Jūnāgarh with a Muslim ruler and a Hindu majority acceded to Pakistan; it was soon overrun by the Indian army; Hyderabad (Ḥaydarābād) with a Muslim ruler, but an overwhelming majority of Hindu subjects, and landlocked between Indian provinces, chose independence, but was blockaded, invaded and occupied by the Indians; Kashmir, with a Hindu ruler but an overwhelmingly Muslim majority of population signed a 'standstill agreement' with Pakistan, wavered for a while, but under political pressure from India and faced with militant tribal uprising and infiltration signed an instrument of accession with India. This was accepted by India provisionally, pending a free and impartial plebiscite.

The state of Hyderabad, which was occupied by India in 1948 and later partitioned among three linguistic provinces, was the largest principality in India, and was ruled by the *niẓāms*, the descendants of the Mughal governor, Niẓām al-Mulk. Since the early eighteenth century it had preserved something of the splendour of Mughal culture; its rulers had been patrons of Islamic institutions, of intellectual *émigrés* from northern India, of Urdu literature, and promoters of Islamic studies. The most brilliant product of the Muslim culture of Hyderabad was the Osmania University which made a bold and successful departure from the traditions of the British Indian educational system in using Urdu as the medium of instruction for modern sciences at a high academic level.

Kashmir proved to be a very explosive problem. The Hindu ruler of Kashmir had disarmed the Muslim elements of his police and army in July 1947. The vast communal disturbances of the neighbouring provinces of India and Pakistan were soon reflected in southern Kashmir, where, according to a report in *The Times* (10 October 1947), '237,000 Muslims were systematically exterminated, unless they escaped to Pakistan along the border, by his Hindu troops'. In reaction the martial Muslims of the Poonch province of the state rose against the Hindu maharaja, and were soon joined by their kinsmen and associates across the Jhelum and the Indus, from the frontier and tribal territories of Pakistan. The advancing tribesmen reached the outskirts of the capital Srinagar, and could have taken it but for their proverbial preoccupation with loot, and the lack of the presence or guidance of any elements of the Pakistan army with them at that stage. Under Indian persuasion the maharaja of Kashmir acceded to India; Indian troops were flown across the Himalayas and drove the tribesmen outside the Vale of Kashmir. The front became stabilized in May 1948 when units of the Pakistan army took up certain defensive positions using artillery but no air cover.

While negotiations were in progress between India and Pakistan for a joint reference to the United Nations to create conditions for a fair plebiscite, India decided to avail itself of the technical legal advantage of the maharaja's accession, and submitted a complaint to the Security Council against what it described as Pakistan's aggression. The position was exactly the reverse of India's action in the case of Jūnāgarh and Hyderabad. From May to December 1948 the two dominions remained locked in an undeclared localized war. On 1 January 1949 a ceasefire was effected through the good offices of the United Nations' Commission for India and Pakistan; and a cease-fire line was demarcated which has since then been patrolled by U.N. officers. It leaves two-thirds of the state including the contested Vale of Kashmir to India, while frontier areas of northern Kashmir and a south-western strip are in Pakistani hands. The Commission's proposals for a truce, maximum military disengagement in the areas occupied by either party, and a fair and impartial plebiscite under the auspices of the United Nations were accepted by both parties, but with different interpretations. Since 1949 India policy has been to delay fulfilment of its commitments to a U.N.-controlled plebiscite. Successive proposals of compromise since 1949 have been accepted by Pakistan, and rejected by India. Direct negotiations have been equally ineffective, narrowing down to the question of the destiny of the Vale of Kashmir, and breaking down at that stage. Because of Pakistan's association with the Western defence alliances, several proposals in the U.N. Security Council were vetoed by the U.S.S.R.

Finally one comes to the position of Islam and Muslims in the Republic of India itself. The transfer of population which followed the partition of the sub-continent led to the migration of millions of Muslims to Pakistan. Millions who were left felt their lives, honour and property insecure in several Indian provinces. Delhi, the federal capital, a great seat of Islamic culture and containing a large percentage of Muslim population, was one of the worst victims of anti-Muslim violence. Hundreds of thousands were killed or driven away, 117 mosques in the city were occupied by Hindus and Sikhs, some of them converted into temples; and though under pressure from Gandhi the minister for Home Affairs took strong action to stop the genocide of Muslims, the great Mahatma paid with his life for the stand he had taken for humanity. He was assassinated during a syncretic peace prayer meeting by a Hindu fanatic, Godse, in 1948.

It was under these circumstances that a new pattern of Muslim political life in India emerged. Leadership of Muslim India passed, quite naturally, to those who were closest to Congress, especially Abu'l-Kalām Āzād. He and the *Jamiyyat al-'ulamā'* had evolved a theory of composite nationalism in the 1930s which in 1947 became the manifesto of Muslim Indian nationalism. This theory was based on the analogy of the Prophet's covenant with the non-Muslims of Medina, who were regarded as a single community (*umma*) with the Muslims. Not as leaders of the Muslim masses, but as prestige symbols for the Muslim community, there also emerged a coterie of intellectuals and civil servants. The Muslim University of 'Alīgarh was placed under Ẕākir Ḥusayn, to be diverted psychologically from Islamic separatism to Indian nationalism. Later there was an official move to change its name and its Muslim personality.

The separatist opposition, the Muslim League, remained very quiet in the years after the partition, but asserted itself on such points of economic survival as the falling ratio of Muslims in the new recruitment to the government services, or of static but popular conservatism as opposition to the reforms in personal law.

The first prime minister of India, Jawaharlal Nehru, from a family of persianized Kashmiri Brahmans, whose mother-tongue was Urdu, and whose education was English, was for a decade and a half the chief champion of the concept of the evolution of India as a secular state. The challenges he had to face were so overwhelming that a leader of lower calibre would have succumbed to them. These included Hindu communalist organisations like the Hindu Mahasabha, which in 1952 declared it would tolerate Muslims in India only if they adopted Hindu names, manner of dress and personal law; the Hindu orthodox wing in Congress itself, which frustrated a number of Nehru's policies in matters relating to a fair treatment of the cultural and linguistic interests of the Muslims; and especially certain state (provincial) governments which failed under the pressure of Hindu electorates to use their control over law and order to guarantee security to the Muslim minority.

Finally Indian secularism has been facing the problem of Muslim conservatism, as represented not only by the intransigent Muslim League, but also the Indian establishment's chief Muslim ally, the *Jam'iyyat al-'ulamā'-yi Hind,* on such matters as the extension of personal law reforms to the Muslim community. Muslimmarriage and divorce laws which have been modernized in Pakistan, still remain traditionally medieval in India, permitting polygamy and other inequalities for women. The traditionalist *Jam'iyyat al-'ulamā'*, opposed to any reforms in the Muslim personal law, regards India as a case distinct from Turkey. In Turkey the secularization of Muslim law, however repugnant to the *'ulamā'*, was done by the Muslims themselves. Any such action in India, where the law-making elements have a non-Muslim majority, would be regarded by them as a breach of the covenant of composite nationalism. The Muslims in India therefore run the risk of pitiable stagnation.

If legal and social stagnation are largely the responsibility of the Indian religio-political leadership, the responsibility for their cultural decline falls almost entirely on the predominant Hindu orthodox wing of Congress, and the policies of the state governments. Reversing all the pre-independence pledges of the Indian National Congress, the constitution of free India stated that Hindi in the *Devanāgarī* script alone would be the official language of the country; Urdu was reduced to a minor place among the fourteen languages of the country; and even in this category its position is very insecure. In the states of northern India it was eliminated as a medium of instruction. Various representations made by Urdu organizations and influential Muslim leaders, and finally the redistribution of states on a linguistic basis, elicited some response in theory which remained largely untranslated into practice. The position has been well summed up by W. Cantwell Smith: 'The [Muslim] community is in danger of being deprived of its language, than which only religious faith is a deeper possession. Nine years of gradual adjustment in other fields have brought no improvement in this, and little prospect of improvement.'[1]

The problem of employment, despite all the theoretical secular legislation, has progressively haunted the Muslim middle classes in India. On the top rungs of the federal government in India, in certain key ambassadorial positions there is a small constellation of civil servants

[1] W. Cantwell Smith, *Islam in modern history* (London, 1956), 266–7.

drawn from the Muslim *élite*. At the lower levels of public services, the Muslim percentage has considerably dwindled considering the ratio of their population. In the Indian parliament, Muslims, who make up ten per cent of the total population of the country, have only a four per cent representation. The flow of Muslim middle class *émigrés* has continued through these years not only to Pakistan, but to the United Kingdom and North America, showing signs of the beginning of an Indo-Muslim diaspora in the West.

PART VI

SOUTH-EAST ASIA

CHAPTER I

SOUTH-EAST ASIAN ISLAM TO THE EIGHTEENTH CENTURY

THE COMING OF ISLAM

On the whole, accounts of conversion to Islam in Malay and Indonesian literature and tradition are not very reliable, however numerous they may be. There is a kind of uniformity about them which does not ring true. Often the ruler, destined to be the first among his people to pronounce the 'Two Words' (the profession of faith), the mere utterance of which will make him a member of the Muslim community, has already received notification of this in a dream or vision, even before the apostle of Islam drops anchor off his shores. Generally his conversion is immediate, with his subjects following soon after. There is no lack of wonders and miracles: opponents are easily persuaded or overawed by magic.

Yet the historian cannot afford to ignore such accounts. They shed a great deal of light on the nature of these societies and their organization, as well as providing clues as to the way Islam was in fact introduced amongst them.

An analysis of these stories suggests that Islam was propagated in South-East Asia by three methods; that is by Muslim traders in the course of peaceful trade, by preachers and holy men who set out from India and Arabia specifically to convert unbelievers and increase the knowledge of the faithful, and lastly by force and the waging of war against heathen states.

The importance of the role of the trader, especially in the early years, arose naturally from the situation of Malaya and the Archipelago along the main trade-route between western Asia and the Far East and the spice islands of the Moluccas. In the ports of the Archipelago, already part of this trading system, the Muslim merchant and his goods were as welcome as other traders from India had always been. The conversion of Gujarāt and other Indian trading centres to Islam increased the numbers and wealth of the Muslim merchants, so that they came more and more into prominence as the commercial partners and political allies of local rulers, and the Hindus vanished from the seas.

The way was thus open for the preachers, teachers of religion, and holy men to establish themselves. They were known in South-East Asia by a variety of names: *kiyayi*, *'ulamā'*, *datu*, *maqdūm*, *mawlānā*, *walī*, and we find them moving untiringly from place to place. One moment they would be in the service of the great, acting as both spiritual and political advisers; the next founding a school in opposition to local secular authority. Their teaching was often noted for its element of Sufism. This had a strong appeal to a people whose pantheistic traditions offered it very fertile ground in which to grow. The scribes and preachers, some of whom had visited Mecca, put the local populations in touch with a wider world community than they had known until then. For even the circle limiting the world of Majapahit, the last great Hindu empire (1292–1527), hardly extended beyond the Archipelago, and during the ninth/fifteenth century it steadily crumbled away. Before these holy men from the West the waning glory of the last god-kings of Majapahit paled.

Finally, when the Muslim communities in South-East Asia had grown in cohesion and confidence, they had recourse to war on several occasions in order to spread the true faith among the *kāfirs*. The remnant of the state of Majapahit, for instance, was conquered and subdued by this means. In many cases, however, it is difficult to distinguish between the true *jihād*, or Holy War, and the efforts of a recently converted ruler to extend his realm by the new faith.

These three methods of conversion cannot always be clearly distinguished. It appears that scribes sometimes had strong commercial links, and had begun their careers as merchants. Or, if circumstances favoured it, they might emerge as statesmen or warriors in the Holy War against the unbelievers. So far as the chronology and geographical pattern of the spread of Islam is concerned, however, it is clear that the trading element was the most important in determining events. In this sense Islam followed trade. North Sumatra, where the trade-route from India and the West reaches the Archipelago, was where Islam first obtained a firm footing. Malacca, the main trading centre of the area in the ninth/fifteenth century, was the great stronghold of the faith, from which it was disseminated along the trade-routes, north-east to Brunei and Sulu, south-east to the north Java ports and the Moluccas.

SAMUDRA (PASAI)

Marco Polo, on his return from China to Persia in 1292, visited six of the eight 'kingdoms', into which he divided the island of Sumatra, and only one of them did he consider to be converted to Islam. This was Ferlec, now known as Perlak. Muslim merchants had islamized the urban population, but outside the heathen continued to live like beasts, eating human flesh and all sorts of unclean food and worshipping all day long whatever they set eyes on first thing in the morning. So here Islam was still very immature.

And yet its influence does not appear to have been as limited as Marco Polo thought. As early as 1282, according to Chinese sources, the small kingdom of Sa-mu-ta-la (Samudra) sent ambassadors, called by the Muslim names of Ḥusayn and Sulaymān, to the Chinese emperor, and the extant tomb of Sultan al-Malik al-Ṣāliḥ, who is reported to have been the first ruler of this kingdom, dates from 697/1297. So although tradition confirms that Perlak was the first to be converted to Islam, Samudra, though later than Perlak, certainly received the faith before 1282, even though this was not yet observed in 1292 by Marco Polo.

The kingdom of Samudra, before long to be known as Pasai, soon grew into an important state which was to have a powerful Muslim influence on its surroundings. In 746/1345–6 it was visited by the famous traveller Ibn Baṭṭūṭa. An orderly situation prevailed at the time; the inhabitants offered fruit and fish, a deputy harbourmaster appeared and granted permission to land. As an ambassador passing through from Delhi to China, the traveller was led by a deputation to the devout ruler al-Malik al-Ẓāhir. There was a great deal of pomp and circumstance with processions on horseback accompanied by a band, but further inland fighting continued against the unbelievers. These were made to pay tribute. This kingdom was to remain in existence till 1521. Then it was conquered by the Portuguese, who occupied it for three years. After that the Achehnese took possession.

Magnificent tombs of the rulers in Gujarātī style still bear witness to earlier greatness and point to the country of origin of Sumatran Islam.

MALACCA

From North Sumatra, Islam spread along the trade route to Malacca. The founder of this relatively new town (*c.* 1400) was Parameswara, a name which in no way indicates his Muslim convictions. We meet him also, however, as Muḥammad Iskandar Shāh, after his marriage to a daughter of the ruler of Pasai. His successors too, Muḥammad Shāh and Abū Saʿīd, or Rājā Ibrāhīm (1424–44 and 1444–5 respectively), are also better known by non-Muslim names, as Sri Maharaja and Sri Parameswara Dewa Shāh, so that one suspects a heathen reaction, or at least sees that the conversion of Malacca was at best incomplete.

Not until a palace revolution led by Indian Muslims had brought Sultan Muẓaffar Shāh (1445–59) to the throne did true Islam prevail, although a partisan legend attributes Malacca's conversion to the earlier Muḥammad Shāh. He is supposed to have been taught the profession of faith by the Prophet himself in a dream and been given the name of Muḥammad, and in the same dream the arrival of a ship from Jedda was foretold. When he awoke the ruler smelled of nard and found to his amazement that he had been circumcized. He continually repeated the 'Two Words' aloud, terrifying his wives. And true enough the next evening Sayyid 'Abd al-'Azīz's ship arrived while the crew was saying evening prayer. The ruler, mounted on an elephant, made his way to the ship and invited the faithful to climb on his mount and ride to his palace. It was then that everyone was supposedly converted to Islam. That Pasai long continued to be looked upon as Malacca's spiritual home is borne out by the account, be it historical or not, in the book that was ceremoniously presented and studied during Sultan Manṣūr Shāh's reign (*c.* 1457–77). The sultan had the work taken to Pasai, so that Tuan Pamatakan could write a commentary.

Just as Malacca owed a great deal to Pasai for its Islamic faith, so in its turn Malacca passed on the faith to its own dependencies. The first Muslim ruler of Pahang was a son of the sultan of Malacca. Trengganu adopted Islam on becoming a vassal of Malacca, as did Kedah. Patani was converted from Malacca, and Kelantan as Patani's vassal. On the western side of the Straits, in Sumatra, Rokan, Kampar, Siak, and Indragiri, all accepted Islam as clients or dependencies of Malacca during the fifteenth century.

The Portuguese conquest of Malacca in 1511 of course put an end to its role as a centre of Islam. The wandering descendants of the princes of Malacca no longer had much influence to wield, and from their changing capitals on the Johore River and in the Riau Islands only with difficulty held their own between Achehnese, Portuguese and Dutch, until the latter captured Malacca in their turn in 1641. Meantime Acheh had replaced Malacca as a centre of Islamic trade and a stronghold of the faith.

ACHEH

It is remarkable that in Acheh, which considers itself so resoundingly Muslim, no accounts of conversions have been handed down. It is certain that it received its Islam from Pasai which is now part of Acheh, and the conversion can be dated near the middle of the fourteenth century.

When, early in the tenth/sixteenth century, two small states, the very ancient Lamri and the Acheh Dār al-Kamāl, had agreed to unite, Acheh entered upon a period of great prosperity. This was furthered by the fact that Malacca had lost much of its attraction for the Muslim merchants now that the bastion of La Famosa flew the Portuguese flag. Moreover they could now fill their holds with pepper, a commodity produced in Acheh.

The first great ruler, 'Alī Mughāyat Shāh, captured Pasai from the Portuguese in 930/1524, and thereby laid the foundations of Acheh's power. His son 'Alā' al-Dīn, who reigned from 1548–71, having conquered Aru and Johore, ventured to lay siege to Portuguese Malacca. In this he was encouraged by his possession of heavy guns from the Ottoman Empire, where he had sent envoys in 971/1562. However, this Muslim attack, like all the others, was repelled.

Acheh experienced its greatest prosperity under Sultan Iskandar Muda (1608–37). His power extended along the east and west coasts of Sumatra, controlling the export of pepper. His fleet and army, however, suffered a crushing defeat by Malacca, a final triumph for the Portuguese. Even the Achehnese admiral, Laksamana Malēm Dagang, fell into their hands and only death saved him from transportation to Lisbon (1629).

In Acheh itself, Iskandar Muda ruled with a firm, severe, sometimes cruel hand. His palace, glittering with gold, aroused the admiration of the West, as did the great five-storey mosque. From Acheh the bordering Gayo-lands were islamized, and also Minangkabau. Only the heathen Bataks managed to repel the oncoming Islamic forces, even going so far as to call in Portuguese help.

Under Iskandar Muda's son-in-law and successor, the liberal Iskandar Thānī, Acheh continued to flourish for another few years. Mild and just, he encouraged religion and prohibited trials by ordeal. Religious learning also throve in this period.

His premature death, however, was followed by disastrous times, as a series of females occupied the throne (1641–99); conquered territories were lost, the state disintegrated. After this, the reinstatement of the sultans was of no avail, so that by the end of the eighteenth century the Acheh empire was a mere shadow of its former self, leaderless and disrupted.

MINANGKABAU

The Padang hills only received Islam fairly late. As recently as 1511 a heathen delegation from that area offered its credentials to the conqueror of Malacca, Affonso d'Albuquerque.

It is true that there is a tradition which ascribes the advent of Islam to a Minangkabau, Shaykh Ibrāhīm, who is supposed to have become familiar with Islam on Java, and they still point out the stone where this preacher used to sit when he attempted to convert the bathers to the new religion. But it is more plausible that they received Islam from Acheh, from Pidjië via Priaman. This is moreover the normal route along which new Muslim ideas reached Minangkabau during the nineteenth century. The statement that the popular Shaykh Burhān al-Dīn, pupil of Shaykh 'Abd al-Ra'ūf of Singkel, brought Islam to Minangkabau, is entirely incorrect, since the latter mystic belongs to the eleventh/seventeenth century.

A more likely connexion is provided by the accounts of wars between Acheh and the rulers of Minangkabau. One such ruler is said to have been married to the daughter of Acheh's prince and to have become unfaithful. This had caused a quarrel with his father-in-law, as a result of which he had to concede a large portion of coastal territory. Acheh's subsequent possession of this coast area must have advanced the Islamic cause.

NORTH-WEST BORNEO, SULU ARCHIPELAGO, MINDANAO

North-west Borneo, the Sulu Islands and the southern Philippines are all situated along a trade-route which connected Malacca with the Philippines. It is therefore mostly Arabs, calling in at Malacca or Johore on their merchant travels, who are reputed to have been the bearers of Islam to these three regions.

In 1514 the Portuguese de Brito reported that Brunei's king was still a heathen, but that the traders were Muslims. In 1567 the Spaniards encountered Muslims in the Philippine Islands. During this half century a certain amount of proselytizing must have taken place.

When Magellan's ship the *Vittoria* called at the coast of Brunei in 1521, the pilot Pigafetta found a town of pile-dwellings whose population he assessed at 25,000 families, probably an over-estimate. The sultan lived in a fortified residence on the shore. He gave the visitors a royal reception. Although they were supposed to be Muslims, it was apparent from the simplicity of their attire that the conversion could only have been very recent. Local tradition mentions various names: a Sultan Muḥammad, originally named al-Akbar Tata, and supposedly converted in Johore, was succeeded by his brother Aḥmad, who had become acquainted with Islam through an Arab from Ṭā'if. As a result this Arab had been allowed to marry the king's daughter.

The sultan referred to by Pigafetta was probably Bulkiah, though his earlier name seems to have been Nakoda Ragam. Under his rule Brunei, profiting like Acheh and Bantam from Malacca's fall (in 1511), came to great prosperity, and even sent out military expeditions. When the Portuguese visited its capital, it seemed to have grown and it had been surrounded by a stone wall. Islam, however, was restricted to the coast; it had made little or no headway among the Dayaks inland.

Spreading along the trade-route beyond Brunei, Islam reached the Sulu Islands. The first proselytizer is held to have been the Arab Sharīf Karīm al-Makhdūm, who supposedly devoted himself to magic and medicine, kindred crafts at the time. He is said to have settled in the old capital, Bwansa, where the people built a mosque for him of their own free will. Many flocked to the mosque and one or two chiefs were converted. He visited other islands too and his grave is reputed to be at Sibutu.

The next preacher of Islam is said to have been the Arab Abū Bakr, who can hardly have been the same man who taught in Malacca under Sultan Manṣūr Shāh (1458-77). He is supposed to have reached the Sulu archipelago via Palembang and Brunei. He married the daughter of the prince of Bwansa, Rājā Baginda, already a Muslim and probably a usurper from Minangkabau. His father-in-law appointed him his heir. With great self-assurance he then reigned over his subjects, calling himself sultan. He administered the government and legislation in an orthodox manner, though with due observance of the ancient customary law (*adat*; Arabic *'āda*).

Finally Islam reached the southern Philippines, in Mindanao. Here we meet Sharīf Kabungsuwan, originating from Johore, son of an Arab father, claiming descent from Muḥammad, and a Malay mother. The later *datu* of Mindanao claim to be descended from him. He is said to have been willing to land only after the people had become converted to Islam. Many embraced the faith, after having first washed. He married Putri Tunîna, who was found in a hollow bamboo, which could be a mythical allusion to his taking possession of the land.

Armed Spaniards under Legaspi, however, certainly put a stop to further penetration by Islam *c.* 1570 at Manila. There followed centuries of fighting against the unremitting and bellicose 'Moros'.

JAVA

Java's first Muslim community is referred to by the Chinese Muslim Ma Huan, who noted three kinds of people in East Java between 1415 and 1432: Muslims who had settled there from the West; Chinese, many of whom had already become Muslims; and natives, about whom he could say nothing good. They were ugly and dirty, they ate and slept with their dogs and believed in devils. So there was indeed a Muslim community, but very few members indeed belonged to the indigenous population. And it was Chinese Muslims who were to leave their mark on Islam in East Java for a long time to come; according to eye-witnesses, their descendants, Javanese-Chinese mestizos, can to this day be distinguished by their appearance from Muslims of unmixed Javanese blood.

The magnificent Gujarātī tomb of Mālik Ibrāhīm also dates from this first period (822/1419). Tradition has it that he was a preacher of Islam, but this is not borne out by reports from reliable sources; he was probably just a prominent Persian merchant.

Of equal fame is the tomb of the so-called *putri Tjempa* (princess of Champa), traditionally the wife of the last Majapahit ruler Bra-Wijaya. Her husband is supposed to have had her buried in the royal grounds according to Muslim custom. The grave attributed to her still bears the Javanese date 1370 (A.D. 1448), and she is popularly believed to have been an aunt of Raden Raḥmat of Ngampel-Denta, the foreign quarter of Surabaya. In the third quarter of the ninth/fifteenth century this scribe had been appointed *imām* of the Muslim community by a Majapahit authority. His numerous pupils spread Islam further across Java. By nature sensible and peaceable he attempted only pacific penetration, and in this he and his followers were to some extent successful. Several of the 'coastal lords' (rulers of regions along Java's north coast), who had grown tired of the yoke of the Majapahit god-prince, broke their ties with him by becoming Muslim converts.

It is about this time that the conversion of Java enters upon a new phase with the emergence of the so-called Islamic preachers. They were often outsiders, who tried to seek out a circle of devout sympathizers.

They were extremely active and very mobile but were scarcely noted

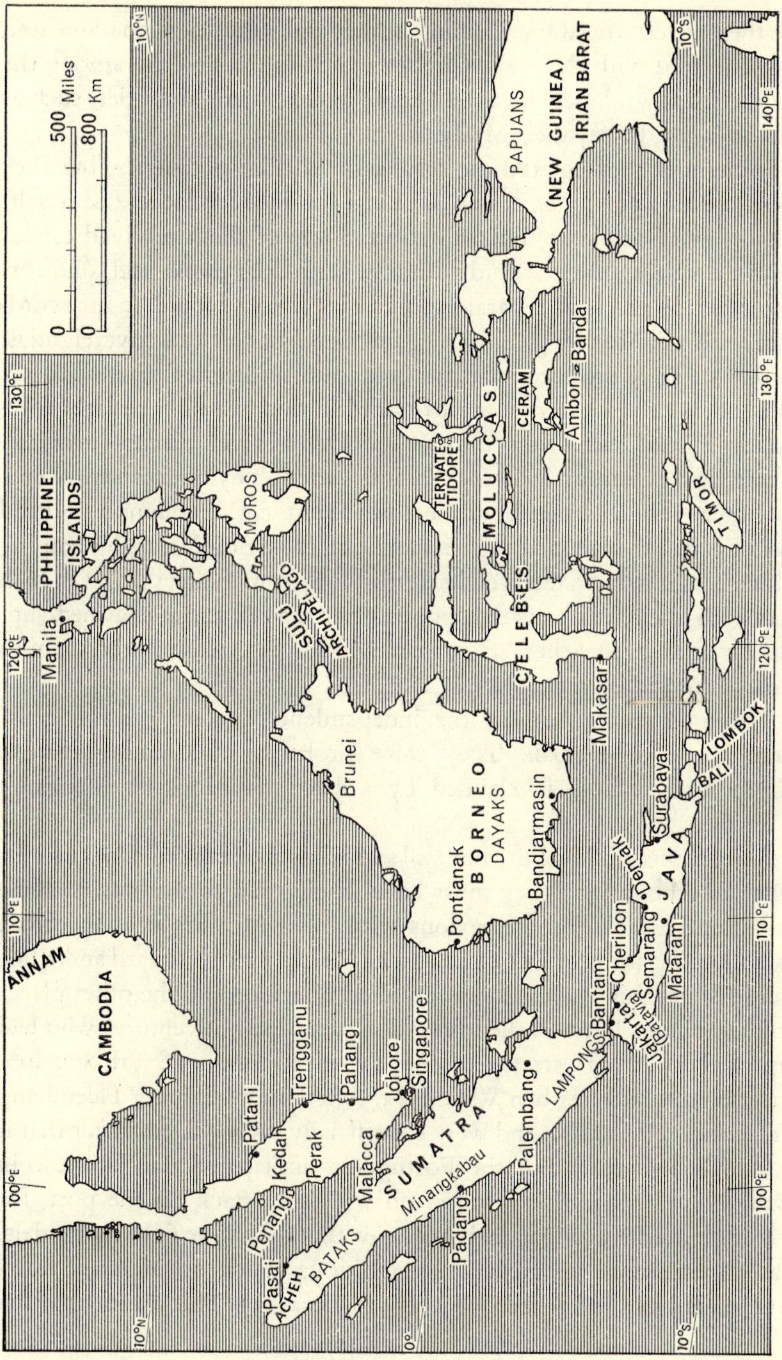

Map 11. South-East Asia

for their strict orthodoxy. Coming as they did from India, via Sumatra, they brought with them a mysticism which found an echo among the pantheistically-minded Javanese. Some Malay words and titles, such as *tuan* and *datu*, betray their Malay origin.

Sometimes they entered the service of Muslim potentates, but they were more often to be found looking for independence and a self-reliant, even obstinate, line of action. Some of them received estates from the rulers, others would withdraw with their pupils and followers into solitude and start separate communities. This would be in accordance with pre-Muslim traditions of independent spiritual sovereignties. Today we have the successors to these foundations in the *perdikan-desa* and the *pesantren*.[1] According to tradition they would regularly foregather in the sacrosanct mosque of Demak and discuss mystical-theological questions. It seems possible – though by no means proven – that there was a certain bond between them, e.g. a common political front against the languishing heathendom, the dying Majapahit empire, which is said to have received its death-blow from them (1527). On such occasions their followers and pupils often served them as armed supporters and the preachers' fanaticism and magic often inspired them to remarkable achievements.

The most prominent of the independent Muslim 'coastal lords' were those of Demak. They were probably of Chinese-Javanese origin and not, as is claimed by a later tradition, of Majapahit extraction.

At first, though Muslim, they still served the supreme ruler as customs officials. About 1475 they must have disengaged themselves to some extent and established connexions with other Muslim 'coastal lords'. Initially these lords of Demak extended their power westward and while still in Majapahit service they conquered Cheribon and the other places on their route. Then, at the instigation of a Malay adventurer who had captured Japara by a stratagem, they set out to conquer South Sumatra, ignoring the still heathen West Java. After heavy fighting Palembang and Jambi fell to them and were superficially proselytized. After that it was Malacca's turn, but the Portuguese anticipated the Javanese in 1511. Nevertheless they pressed on with the attack on the port, for according to the *mawlānā* the battle, now that they were fighting infidels, was all the more justified. This ambitious attack on Malacca, however, ended in a wretched débâcle (918/1512–13). This meant that the

[1] See below, pp. 152-54.

Javanese were powerless at sea, and it seemed as if the Portuguese were about to direct their offensive against the rising tide of Islam in Java.

In fact the Portuguese turned their attention to the Spice Islands, leaving Java in peace. This gave the Muslim Javanese a chance to recover from their defeat. The war against the infidels was resumed, but on land this time, against the heathen interior. In this campaign the holy men undoubtedly played an important role if they did not actually take the initiative.

After 927/1521 there appears to have been a sustained Muslim initiative throughout Java, and in our sources the figure of Shaykh Ibn Mawlānā, from Pasai, is conspicuous. When his native town had been captured by the Portuguese in 1521 he had made his pilgrimage to Mecca and on his return had settled in Japara and Demak. There he attracted so many pupils and won such esteem that the Demak ruler offered him his sister for a wife, and commissioned him to take Islam to the still unconverted West Java. In this he succeeded fairly rapidly.

He first gained possession of Bantam, and in 933/1526, perhaps on 12 Rabī II/17 December, he took the port of Sunda Kalapa and renamed it Djaja-Karta. Portuguese attempts to reopen communications with the Sunda state in the interior were thus completely foiled.

Cut off from the sea this empire succumbed to the Muslim forces fifty years later (1579). A small remnant of adherents to the ancient Sunda faith still hold their own as *Badui* in the Bantam interior.

In the meantime Demak had begun a long series of wars of conquest, to which the court and capital of Majapahit finally fell victim in 1527. In extensive areas of East Java, however, Javanese Hinduism held its own and fighting continued. When in 1546 a large-scale attack was made against the last important bulwark of Hinduism at Panarukan, it resulted in an utter failure. The Demak ruler Trengganu was murdered and his realm became the scene of endless confusion. The result was a temporary revival of East Javanese heathendom, from which it was never completely purged. The Tengger mountains still shelter worshippers of the mountain-god Brama, who have their own priests (*dukun*). Elsewhere Islam triumphed by force of arms.

In the south of Central Java the story is very different. Islam's peaceful penetration into this territory is the subject of the legend of Ki geḍé Panḍan-Arang. This erstwhile mundane and greedy ruler of Samarang was suddenly converted through the intervention of a holy man (the legend, probably wrongly, identifies him as the 'last of the *walīs'*, Sunan Kali-Jaga). Having given away all his treasures he set off in a southerly direction. According to the legend, he had many adventures and performed many miracles, until the hour of his calling came and he ascended Mount Jabalkat. There he built a mosque. He held long discussions with the holy men he found there and competed with them in the art of sorcery, always emerging as the victor. Now he rests on Mount Tembayat in a mausoleum, at the summit of a long flight of steps with magnificent archways. Each year thousands of pilgrims, chiefly from among the small tradespeople, come to worship this apostle of the southern part of Central Java, and invoke his assistance.

Likewise on a hill-top was the throne of Prabu Satmata, the first so-called priest-king of Giri (near Gresik). Tradition has it that he was the son of Mawlānā Iskak and a Balambangan princess from the most easterly part of Java. Mawlānā Iskak had cured her of a fatal disease. Since her father, the prince, refused to become a Muslim, Mawlānā Iskak left his bride and went to Malacca. When his son was born the cruel grandfather had him thrown into the sea in an iron box. He was hauled out of the sea by a fisherman and received tuition from Raden Raḥmat of Ngampel-Denta, together with the latter's own son. The teacher became aware of the boy's remarkable destiny because of the light emanating from him. After this course of instruction the young man, accompanied by his teacher's son, set out for Mecca, but he only got as far as Malacca, where he met his father. The latter advised him against the Pilgrimage, and finished his education. On his return to Java he entered commerce for a time and then applied himself to asceticism for forty days inside the corpse of a buffalo. When as a result he felt the need of a bath, his staff miraculously caused a spring to rise (an ancient sacred motif known too in Western Europe). His time had then come, and he ascended the Giri mountain. To this place, too, holy men flocked, but a punitive Majapahit column was also approaching. The attackers were miraculously hewn down by his pen, which had turned into a revolving *keris*. This *keris* became a sacred heirloom, and he himself now also rests in a sumptuous mausoleum on Mount Giri, the objective of many pilgrims.

During the reign of his successor, Sunan Dalem, the Hindu Javanese are said to have attempted another attack on Giri, so that the inhabitants fled in confusion. Only two watchmen remained loyally on guard at the tomb of the first saint. The attackers did not spare it and tried to exhume the body, but a huge swarm of bees burst out of the grave, driving the desecrators away, pursuing and killing them. Only the leader was spared because of his timely conversion to Islam. The reputation of Giri as a shrine of great sanctity is widespread throughout the Archipelago.

THE SPICE ISLANDS

Continuing eastwards along the trade-route, Islam reached the Spice Islands, now called the Moluccas, in the latter half of the ninth/fifteenth century.

According to local tradition there had been traces of Muslim influence a century before that. Ternate's twelfth ruler, Molomateya (1350–7) is said to have been very friendly with an Arab who instructed him in the art of ship-building, but seemingly not in the faith. And yet two Arabic names occur in the lists of rulers at this period; even on Tidor there was a ruler by the name of Ḥasan Shāh. Was it a passing fashion?

Not until the reign of Marḥūm (which is not really a name at all but the fragment of a title denoting a deceased ruler) did things really begin in earnest. His court was attended by the Javanese *datu*, Mawlānā Ḥusayn. His writings on the Qur'ān appealed to the inquisitive, who were fascinated by the mysterious letters and vainly attempted to imitate them. At their request the artful Javanese instructed them not only in Arabic script but also in the profession of faith. Only those who accepted this were allowed to learn the sacred letters. In this way he won many souls for Islam.

After Marḥūm's death religious fervour flagged, particularly when the Javanese Mawlānā also disappeared. Apparently Marḥūm himself never undertook the decisive step. The story is typical of a primitive society.

The first truly Muslim ruler was Zayn al-'Ābidīn (1486–1500). There was such an increasing flow of Muslim merchants that the ruler succumbed to their pressure and decided to study Islam at the source, which meant at the *madrasa* of Giri, probably with Prabu Satmata, whom we have already mentioned. He was known in Giri as Raja Bulawa, or king of the cloves, which he may have brought with him as an offering. On his return from Java the ruler brought with him Tuhubahahul, said to have become the main propagator of Islam.

In view of Islam's tender age on Ternate, the Portuguese, who had settled there in 1522, were hoping to replace it with Christianity. This proved an idle hope. Only very few were baptized, though it is true that some were members of the royal family. Eventually a Ternatan prince, Tabariji, was baptized, and he would have ascended the throne as Dom Manuel if he had not died suddenly (1545). Even the great apostle of Asia, Francis Xavier, who was in the Moluccas from 1546 until 1547, was unable to loosen Islam's hold there – all he could do was to strengthen the weak communities of Christians on Ambon. The Ternatans did adopt Portuguese culture and customs, their attire, armament, housing, and so on, but they would not be baptized.

Turning now to Ambon – the only Ambonese historian Rijali recounts how the Perdana Jamīlu, from Hitu (one of Ambon's two peninsulas), accompanied the ruler of Ternate, Zayn al-'Ābidīn, on his journey to Giri.[1] This account, however, implies too close a Ternate-Hitu co-operation for it to merit much credence. More plausible is the account of the arrival of a *Qāḍī* Ibrāhīm, who became judge of Ambon and from whom all the teachers of this island received instruction. Ambon even built a seven-storeyed mosque, reminiscent of Giri where a similar edifice was erected.

Local tradition also names Java as the source of Hitu Islam, although Pasai is named too, and even Mecca, with Banda as a half-way house. This is why the bearer of Islam to Rohomoni was called Pandita Pasai; he had been converted in Mecca. The founder of a village of Kailolo, by the name of 'Us̲mān, had acquired Islam from a Pandita Mahu (Java), who had travelled from Mecca to Gresik and who had there come into contact with Sunan Giri and other holy men. He had then gone to Banda and finally to Kailolo and Tèngah-Tèngah. The people of Kailolo still point out his grave and pay homage to it. What is more, his descendants receive *pitrah* (religious tribute). This 'Us̲mān is possibly the same as the Pangeran kalipah haji Ngusman, husband of the ascetic, later called Nyai ageng Moloko (Moluccas), who returned to Java after her husband's death.

At any rate communications between the Moluccas and Giri were maintained right up to the seventeenth century. Letters from the Giri priest-king to Hitu were welcomed with splendour; Giri fezzes showing magic formulae were much appreciated in Hitu and exchanged for spices (cloves), and for a long time the sons of prominent citizens continued to receive instruction in the *madrasa* of Giri.

Political and economic ties between the Moluccas and Java also survived. Demak and Japara were Hitu's allies in their fierce battle

[1] Rijali, *Hakajat Tanah Hitoe*. Malay MS. Leyden University Library, No. 3011.

against the Portuguese, when the latter had established themselves in Ambon's still heathen peninsula, Leitimor, and had introduced Christianity there.

SOUTH BORNEO

Borneo, too extensive to be under a single authority, has only in parts been converted to Islam; first the north-west, from Malaya, the south from Demak, the east from Makasar, and last of all the west, by an Arab adventurer. Since Brunei has been discussed earlier, we now turn to South Borneo, the state of Bandjarmasin. A. A. Cense's version of the chronicles, although not an early record, is probably the best account of the essential facts here.

South Borneo's accessibility from Java all through the year (the prevailing easterly or westerly winds do not seriously interfere with the north-south passage) encouraged Islamic expansion from there, and it also explains the presence in Bandjarmasin of many elements of Javanese culture.

The chronicle records a conflict between two pretenders, the *Pangerans* Samudra and Tumenggung, in which the former enlisted the help of Demak's ruler. This was promised on condition that he embraced Islam. He accepted and the Demak ruler dispatched 1,000 armed men under a *penghulu* (subordinate chief), which meant a considerable reinforcement for Samudra's 40,000 warriors. It was therefore decided to settle the dispute by a duel between the pretenders, but before they came to blows the two became reconciled. Amidst great festivities Samudra was made king.

The actual outcome was perhaps not quite so peaceful. In any event, 1,000 Demak fighters stayed behind while the *penghulu* converted all the inhabitants to Islam. An Arab gave Samudra the title *Surian Allāh*. After this the Demak contingent and the *penghulu* went home, laden with gifts (or perhaps booty). Subsequently all the rulers of Bandjarmasin boast Arab names.

SOUTH-WEST CELEBES

There is more information about the conversion of Gowa in South-west Celebes than about any other conversion in Indonesia. There are two reasons for this: firstly, the late date, the early eleventh/seventeenth century and secondly, the remarkably accurate accounts of the Makasar historians, who have kept countless diaries and chronicles. For instance, we know the exact date at which the prince of Tallo embraced Islam: 9 Jumādā I 1014/22 September 1605.[1] This was preceded by a long-established contact with Muslim merchants, so that Islam was not entirely unknown in Makasar.

In about 1591 the prince had already consulted the ruler of a neighbouring state on the subject of Islam, but since the latter was not a Muslim, this consultation had not been much help.

Then, just at the right moment, Dato'ri Bandang appeared on the scene. He was a Minangkabau, who had also received instruction in Giri. Conversion to Islam therefore was no mere gesture, but an action undertaken with full conviction. On the day mentioned the prince publicly made his profession of faith so that he could attend the Friday Prayer in the mosque of the Malay colony the next day. From then on he regularly read the holy books, and only illness would prevent him attending the Friday Prayer every week.

On 19 Rajab 1016/19 November 1607, two years after his conversion, the first Friday Prayer was held at Tallo, intended for a large number of inhabitants who had not previously made up their minds. Foreigners became aware of the conversion because of the shortage of pork which had been plentiful until then.

The very next year saw the start of religious wars against neighbouring states; Bone, Soppeng, Wajo'—one after the other they were forced to embrace Islam, though not without fierce opposition. One ruler, for instance, was dispossessed of all his offices by his lords for embracing Islam before the battle had been decided; he could have held out longer.

From then on the people of Makasar became the champions of Islam in East Indonesia. They played an important part in the battle between the Dutch and the Muslims in the Moluccas, which was not merely a religious conflict, but also a struggle for the monopoly of the spice trade. Muslim refugees from Ambon could be assured of a safe refuge in Makasar. This is how, in 1057/1647, it acquired the scholar Imām Rijali, who wrote the only Ambonese historical work, the *Hikayat Tanah Hitu,* while he was in exile in Makasar, on the advice of the studious prince Patingallowang.

Makasar's tough opposition to the Netherlands East India Company, which continued until 1656, was only the prelude to a war which the company began after another ten years against its troublesome rival.

[1] J. Noorduyn, *De Islamisering van Makassar*. B.K.I. CXII, 1956, 247–66.

Led by Admiral Cornelis Speelman this bitter struggle ended provisionally with the signing of the so-called Bongaais Treaty (1 Jumādā II 1078/18 November 1667). This put an end to the dominating position of Makasar in the trade and politics of East Indonesia.

EAST BORNEO

The conversion of Kutei in East Borneo followed hard on that of South Celebes, but would appear to have been at first somewhat superficial.

According to the Kutei chronicle,[1] two Muslim preachers arrived at Kutei during the reign of Rājā Makota. One of them was Tuan di Bandang, easily recognizable as the Dato'ri Bandang from Makasar; the other was Tuan Tunggang Parangan. Though they had already converted the people of Makasar, there is said to have been a relapse to heathendom, necessitating Tuan di Bandang's return to Celebes, but Tuan di Parangan remained in Borneo. He had been given this name after arriving in Kutei riding a swordfish (*jukut parang*). He buttressed his case for Islam by miracles: by becoming invisible, by making fire through sheer auto-suggestion, by bringing about the appearance of a *jukut parang*. After these three miracles Rājā Makota submitted to the new faith, stipulating only that the pork already on hand should first be eaten. In the meantime a mosque was erected so that their religious instruction could begin at once. Rājā Makota was first, then the princes, ministers, commanders and lords, and finally the common people.

From then on Rājā Makota did his best to propagate Islam by the sword, as a result of which the affairs of the state prospered. After some time Rājā Makota married, the marriage contract being concluded by Tuan di Parangan after a threefold votive offering to the Prophet. Yet all further games and festivities were arranged in accordance with the existing *adat*. The ruler's marriage too was solemnized by the Islamic preacher in the mosque. After this there is no more mention of Islam in the chronicle. There are no rulers with Arabic names prior to the eighteenth century.

RELIGIOUS JURISDICTION

The *Sharī'a* was in fact supposed to cover all aspects of life, but for practical reasons other rules of law were evolved, in many walks of life. The *Sharī'a* was confined to matters touching upon the intimate and

[1] Edited by C. A. Mees (Santpoort, 1935).

religious lives of the faithful, i.e. to questions of family and inheritance, as well as those related to *waqf*. This was the situation in South-East Asia as wherever there were Muslims.

There were, of course, local differences. In Minangkabau (Central Sumatra), where hereditary rights were decided by matriarchy, religious jurisdiction had to content itself with even less. The same applies to the Negri Sembilan in Malaya, where scattered Minangkabau had settled, taking their institutions with them.

In Bantam, on the other hand, during the eleventh/seventeenth and twelfth/eighteenth centuries, much more fell under the jurisdiction of the religious magistrate than was customary elsewhere. The *qāḍī* is said to have been in sole charge of juridical matters and the ruler intervened only in special cases.

In the principalities in Java and elsewhere in the Archipelago there existed, apart from the religious codes, statute books which, in parts, date back to pre-Muslim law and which included only very few Muslim elements. One of these is the *Pepakem Cheribon* (Handbook of Cheribon). Then there is the *Surja Alam* in Central Java, dating back to the time of the first Muslim Demak empire (tenth/sixteenth century) and perhaps even earlier. These manuals of jurisprudence were not used by the *qāḍī* or their deputies, but by secular magistrates, the *jaksa* (Sanskrit, *adhyaksa*). It is possible that during the ninth/fifteenth and tenth/sixteenth centuries in areas under spiritual authority, as in Kudus and Giri on Java's north coast, attempts were made to pass sentence according to Muslim law, but the sources leave us guessing on this matter.

THE RELIGIOUS TEACHERS

A quite remarkable part was played by the independent teachers, who appear under various names in the Archipelago: *'ulamā'*, *kiyayi*, *mawlānā*, *maqdūm*, *sunan*, *walī*. As a rule they did not belong to the mosque staff, yet they generally maintained their independence of the rulers. Many of them attracted pupils and became heads of schools. Their learning and piety assured them of the approval of the people who honoured them even after their death. To doubt their pronouncements was sometimes tantamount to unbelief. Some were mystics, others were conspicuous for their strict interpretation of the law. At times they caused trouble not only to Western but also to Muslim authorities because they became the rallying points of opposition. But this does not mean that there were no cautious and peaceful people among them.

Either way they certainly constituted the dynamic element in Indonesian Islam. The unattached scribes would inspire a fossilized religiosity with new life, thereby discrediting the institutions of the mosque. Their international contacts furthered co-operation between Muslims of different countries. They certainly deserve credit for their outspoken attitude towards the rulers, and in the fields of theology and law they made a very useful contribution.

After a brief consideration of the work of the Sumatran scribes, a fuller account will be given of the difficulties of the scribes on the island of Java. More detail is possible here because of the fullness of the historic sources, and the unique character of the relationship between ruler and *kiyayi* in Java deserves special attention.

SUMATRAN SCRIBES

Acheh, 'Forecourt of the Holy Land', was the field of activity of one or two theologians whose influence was felt far beyond the borders of the state. All were to some extent mystics and the names of several are honoured still.

Although Java can boast of countless anonymous mystics and of many others who concealed their identity behind famous pseudonyms, Sumatra's mystics were known by name, could be dated fairly accurately and were quite sharply defined personalities. The prosperity of the sultanate of Acheh during the late tenth/sixteenth and early eleventh/seventeenth centuries formed the background for their activities. We shall confine ourselves to the most important of these.

A few theologians from the Near East, tempted by the flourishing port of Acheh, had already brought their light to these parts when Ḥamza Fanṣūrī arrived there towards the end of the tenth/sixteenth century. He was a fervent supporter of the *wujūdiyya* doctrine, a doctrine of emanation, popularly known as *martabat tujuh*, or doctrine of the seven degrees. He was wise enough to wrap his dissenting views in a cloak of orthodoxy. For, while he declared that prayers and fasting were unnecessary, he wanted to maintain the *ṣalāt* (ritual prayer) as a pedagogic expedient to achieve unification with God. The power of his persuasive verses procured him many followers, and many enemies. His pupil and successor, Shams al-Dīn of Pasai, who died in 1630, was a contemporary of Sultan Iskandar Muda and he was in high favour with this powerful ruler. Various works of his have been preserved.

During the reign of Iskandar Thānī (1637–41) and his widow and successor ʻInāyat (1641–75) the tide turned. At that time Nūr al-Dīn al-Rānīrī, a native of Rander in Gujarāt, was residing at the court. In 1620 he made the Pilgrimage to Mecca, whence he returned to his native town, a declining trading-centre. In 1637 he travelled to Acheh, where he stayed until 1644. For unknown reasons he then returned to Rander, where he died in 1658.

During his stay in Acheh, al-Rānīrī, as he is generally known, displayed a fabulous industry. A stalwart of orthodoxy, he attempted to disseminate a fundamentalist faith by emphasizing such aspects as Hell and the Last Judgment; hence his popular book on eschatology. He fiercely contested the heretical mystics of the Shams al-Dīn school, committing their works and even their disciples mercilessly to the flames. And yet he he was not averse to mysticism: he believed in an orthodox doctrine of emanation. The number of his writings is vast, in Arabic as well as in Malay. One of his many works is the *Bustān al-salāṭīn* ('Garden of kings'), a voluminous mirror of princes in seven volumes.

The last of the great mystics and the most famous was ʻAbd al-Ra'ūf of Singkel. He was probably born soon after 1024/1615 and died after 1105/1693. In 1643 he left for Arabia, where he studied for nineteen years in different places. When his teacher died in 1661, his successor gave him permission to do teaching duties himself. He then returned to Acheh where he remained active for many years. At the request of the sultan he wrote a legal work, for the purpose of which he first had to take lessons in Pasai-Malay from the sultan's private secretary. He wrote altogether twenty-one works. He was no follower of the excessive mysticism of Ḥamza Fanṣūrī but gave an orthodox reinterpretation of the *Wujūdiyya* doctrine. His fame was not confined to his native country and spread as far as Java. After his death the people venerated him as a national hero, so that later he came to be regarded as the first Muslim preacher in Acheh. Thousands still visit his grave, from which he derives his name, Teunku di Kuala.

The fame of these Achehnese scribes spread the more rapidly beyond Acheh and Sumatra because, prior to the era of steam-navigation, many pilgrims or student-pilgrims would spend some time in Acheh on their way to and from Arabia. In this way they became acquainted with the prevailing religious trends there. So it is clear that the wild excesses of Sumatra's heterodox mysticism were curbed by al-Rānīrī's energetic action, and that from then on the mystics thought along more orthodox lines.

The Javanese mystics, on the other hand, came up against resistance of quite a different kind, namely the strong arm of worldly authority. This would explain their frequently manifested contempt of this authority, on which subject many references have come down to us. This antithesis led to prolonged and bloody wars. In the end the Mataram ruler emerged as victor in this issue. This struggle deserves to be looked at rather more closely.

THE PRINCES AND ISLAM ON JAVA—SECULARIZED SPIRITUAL LORDS

When Prince Trengganu of Demak was killed in the battle of Panarukan in East Java in 1546, his empire fell apart, and some spiritual lords thought that the moment had come to achieve their own independence.

Shaykh Ibn Mawlānā, who, having married the prince of Demak's sister, ruled over Bantam on his behalf, made himself not only virtually independent of central authority, but also managed to lay hands on Cheribon, whence he is said to have moved *c.* 957/1550. His son Ḥasan al-Dīn took his place in Bantam and tradition regards him as the first genuine prince of this territory. His grave, situated near the great mosque in the ancient, now deserted, town of Banten, is, however, honoured primarily as the resting place of a saint. He is the patriarch of the Bantam princes, who remained in power till 1813.

The father, who had settled in Cheribon, ruled this province till 1570 and his remains are now in an impressive mausoleum, which is one of the most frequented places of pilgrimage in West Java. His successors also became temporal rulers, although perhaps not to the same extent as the Bantam branch of the family. Having, since 1091/1680, branched out in three directions, Kasepuhan, Kanoman and Kacherbonan, the descendants of the great saint retained their high standing locally till well into the twentieth century.

In general, West Javanese Islam has a more orthodox character than elsewhere in Java. This may be due in the first place to the fact that Hinduism had much shallower roots in West Java, but it could also be because Islam was initially introduced here by men who had come to know the faith in Arabia. The spiritual lords travelled a great deal in those days. Whereas the lords of Cheribon had little share in the propagation of Islam by force – they inspired devotion rather than awe– Bantam contributed a great deal.

In 1579 Pangeran Yūsuf, the second prince of Bantam (1570–80), using subterfuge as well as force, secured for himself Pajajaran, the heathen state in the Sunda lands, and Islam came to stay. In 1596 his son, the young Pangeran Muḥammad, attacked Palembang, which was still considered heathen. The prince was killed in the battle however, and was deeply mourned. Palembang remained independent, but the Lampongs (South Sumatra) were conquered and had to accept Islam.

In the meantime Bantam had become a station on the main traffic route, since Malacca, taken by the Portuguese in 1511, lost much of its importance as a trade centre for the Asians. Portuguese from Malacca now came to Bantam to do business and in 1596 the Dutch also appeared, followed by other Westerners. They found a strong Muslim state, a large mosque and much trade in the local crop, pepper.

The Muslim character of the Bantam rulers is further borne out by their acquiring the title of sultan in 1638, and by the Pilgrimage made by one of them, who, being a ruling prince, earned the title of *Sulṭān Ḥājjī* (1682–7). It was during his reign, however, that the state first came under Dutch influence.

Bantam, on the main trade-route and until 1682 frequented by foreigners, was more exposed to external orthodox influences than Central and East Java, and as a result traces of puritanical Islam are found here quite early. During the eighteenth century the Arabs were particularly influential, and none more than the renowned Ratu Sharīfa, wife of the mentally deranged Sultan Zayn al-ʿĀrifīn (1733–47) and daughter of an Arab father and a Bantam mother. She managed everything in her own way for so long that an Arab dynasty seemed inevitable. The intervention of the Dutch East India Company, however, precipitated a bloody war of succession, which at times was more like a religious war. It ended in 1753 with the restoration of the old dynasty, and its recognition of Dutch overlordship. Not until 1813, however, during the British interim government of Java, did Bantam disappear as a separate state. Nevertheless Bantam always remained true to Islam, and the colonial authorities considered it wise not to admit Christian missionaries.

During the period 1550–1625 Surabaya was probably ruled by the descendants of the holy Raden Raḥmat of Ngampel-Denta. The son of the last of the princes, Pangeran Pekik, who spent his last years as a revered exile in Mataram, was, according to Javanese historical tradition, descended from a *walī* and his descendants have always paid homage to the holy man's grave at the harbour mouth at Surabaya. At that time Islam in Surabaya was by no means as orthodox as West Java's and in Mataram Pangeran Pekik was reputed to have introduced non-Muslim cultural elements too. This civilized nobleman, murdered in 1659 at the instigation of his son-in-law, Sunan Mangku-Rat I, formed a link between the cultures of the coast and the interior of Central Java.

THEOCRACIES

The spiritual lords who came to the fore on the disintegration of the Demak state in 1546 maintained a truer Muslim character in their state government than elsewhere.

Traditionally the first of these is the fifth *imām* of Demak's holy mosque, who left the ancient, perhaps ruined, residency for a nearby place, since named Kudus. This is one of the few Javanese towns with an Arab name and this holy man is associated with it in his name, Sunan Kudus. There is no doubt that the word is derived from al-Quds, Jerusalem, and it must surely have been the *imām*'s intention to establish this settlement as a theocracy in a holy city. Like the mosque on the site of the Temple in Jerusalem, the mosque in Kudus is called al-Aqṣā and it differs from most Indonesian mosques in having a minaret. This was built in Hindu-Javanese style, but of course without any images of living creatures.

Possibly as early as 1549, this spiritual lord bore the title of *qāḍī*. Temporal lords paid him the utmost respect. Tradition has it that princes sat at his feet. His spiritual and political influence extended far beyond Kudus, as far, on one side, as West Madura. He also pursued a policy of his own, directed against the nascent state of Mataram in the interior of Central Java, and his choice of candidate to rule over the whole of Java was Pangeran arya Panangsang of Jipang, who was opposed by Sunan Kali-Jaga. The downfall and death of his protégé damaged his reputation as well as his authority, and, when Kudus finally fell, it was supposedly by the prince of Mataram, Panembahan Sénapati, *c.* 996/1588, that it was taken. Sunan Kudus's descendants then fled eastwards and led somewhat obscure lives until a female member of the family married Sunan Mangku-Rat IV (1719–27) of Mataram and had a son, Sunan Paku-Buwana II (1727–49), whereby the family regained its prestige. It was included in the right wing (*panengen*) of the official

Mataram family tree, the *Sajarah Dalem*. The Hindu princes of Majapahit belong to the left wing (*pangiwa*).

The line of rulers (commonly called priest-kings) of Giri (near Gresik) remained longer in power. We have already seen how their high reputation dates from Prabu Satmata, who established himself on Mount Giri, built a seven-storeyed mosque there and was finally buried in state on that spot. To this day thousands of pilgrims visit his richly ornamented mausoleum every year.

The family reached the height of its power under Sunan Parapen (1546–1605). His influence extended far beyond Java, due no doubt also to his prolonged rule. It was not only the Dutch who knew him as 'the Mohammedans' pope'; his fame as a seer and prophet travelled as far as China. His independence, which he achieved after the fall of the Demak empire in 1546, is well expressed in the magnificence of the regal residence he built.

He showed a surprising concern for the other islands of the Archipelago. According to historical tradition he was responsible for Lombok's conversion to Islam. Bali, on the other hand, would not accept Islam and all attempts to introduce it were emphatically rejected. But the Minangkabau, Dato'ri Bandang, who achieved Makasar's conversion to Islam, is said to have started as a pupil at Giri. Tradition has it that there were matrimonial ties with Pasir (Borneo), and that they had close contacts with the Hituese on Ambon (Moluccas), who were fighting the Portuguese. The master at Giri sent them Javanese auxiliaries, who stayed for three years at a place later named *kota Jawa* (Javanese town).

Like the lord of Kudus, Sunan Giri was treated with the utmost respect. As his subjects, the temporal rulers came and offered him their respects. The story goes that even the prince of Pajang in the interior visited Giri to obtain recognition of his sovereignty of Java. For it is a fact that these spiritual lords, until well into the eleventh/seventeenth century, arrogated to themselves the right to consecrate and accredit local princes. When, finally, the powers temporal allied themselves with the Dutch unbelievers, the divines had to submit to secular authority. In 1680, at the instigation of Sunan Mangku-Rat II of Kartasura (1677–1703), and with the assistance of the Dutch, Giri was conquered, and the last of these kings was killed.

The third and the most extraordinary was Sunan Kali-Jaga. Tradition credits him with a distinguished descent, a dissolute early life and a miraculous conversion. He is said to have devoted himself to asceticism in Cheribon. The prince of Demak sent for him and presented him with Adi-Langu, an estate adjacent to the residency, where he instructed countless distinguished pupils. It is possible that he replaced Sunan Kudus as *imām* or *qāḍī* of Demak, for those two spiritual lords disliked each other intensely. After the catastrophe at Demak in 1546 he seems to have travelled about, pursuing a policy opposed to Sunan Kudus. In fact he became the spiritual father and patron of the rising Mataram house of princes in the interior, and for some time after close ties were maintained between this house and Sunan Kali-Jaga's descendants. The princes looked after their graves with great care and visited them at times. Culturally, too, Mataram is greatly indebted to these lords of Adi-Langu, specifically for the important contribution which they are said to have made to the Mataram chronicle of princes, known as *Babad Tanah Jawi*. And by their inclusion in these annals of references to their forebear's glorious deeds, they ensured his abiding fame.

JAVA'S INTERIOR AND ISLAM

Sunan Bayat of Tembayat is known as the apostle of South Central Java, and this area regards many of the lesser saints as his disciples. And yet it is strange that there is nowhere any reference to a remarkable conversion of the rulers, as is so often reported in the Malay countries. It might be concluded from this that the lukewarm reaction to Muslim affairs, a commonplace in Java's interior today, is no new or recent phenomenon. Even in the official chronicle of princes there is no mention of Sunan Bayat's activities.

South Central Java was never subjected to Muslim Demak. An attempt by *Sunan* Kudus to lay his hands on the small state of Pengging (to the west of Surakarta) failed dismally. To this day the time-honoured grave of Ki Ageng of Pengging can be found, near an ancient-looking cemetery, still containing Hindu-Javanese remains. Of his two sons Ki Kebo Kanigara was then an unbeliever; Ki Kebo Kenanga lived according to Muslim precepts and even attended the Friday Prayer. But his teacher, Pangeran Siti-Jenar, was known to be a heretic, and he would not dream of paying his respects in Demak. These stories do not give the impression of a very orthodox Islam. And it is precisely in this area that Sunan Kali-Jaga became so politically active.

He is believed first to have connived at the preferment of Jaka-Tingkir, later prince of Pajang, and still a legendary figure in popular belief; then he appears to have favoured the founder of the Mataram dynasty. He seems to have been forever on the move, encouraging, advising, intriguing, and always, being himself a man of the coast, opposing the policies of the coastal spiritual lords. At last a soldier of fortune, his protégé Panembahan Sénapati of Mataram (1584–1601), was triumphant, and laid the foundation of a dynasty which was one day to rule over virtually the whole of Java.

Panembahan Sénapati, a *Realpolitiker*, showed little evidence of a true Muslim mentality. His thoughts and emotions were guided by the worship of mountains and sea, and in particular by his communion with the mysterious Goddess of the South Sea. Apparently he did pray to Allāh in moments of crisis, but on the whole Islam took second place in his life. The teaching that Sénapati gave to his younger friend and ally, Pangeran Benawa of Pajang, reveals the character of his religion. His disciple, he considered, ought to have three different categories of people at his disposal: teachers of religion for putting his realm in order; seers for predicting the future; and ascetics to give guidance on magic powers. What he appreciated in the Muslim spiritual leaders was in the first place their political gifts. Marriages between his own Mataram family and members of these other families indicate that he did really value contacts with them. Doubtless both parties hoped to profit by these contacts. And yet there was a mosque near Sénapati's residence. In 1601, after what was on the whole a prosperous reign, he was buried on the south side of the mosque.

SULTAN AGUNG, SPIRITUAL AND TEMPORAL RULER

The Mataram empire reached its zenith during the reign of Sénapati's grandson, generally known as Sultan Agung (1613–46). He conquered nearly the whole of Java, with the exception of Batavia, founded in 1619 by the Dutch governor-general Jan Pietersz, Coen, and Bantam, which managed to shelter behind Batavia. Thus the north coast, where Islam had been proclaimed for two centuries, came under Mataram rule – a significant development for heterodox Mataram. For now the prince had to deal with countless Muslim subjects in the districts along the north coast, whose spiritual leaders were able to fortify the ranks of the *kiyayi* further inland.

It must be assumed that Sultan Agung wanted to pursue a positively religious policy, and that, unlike his predecessors, he adopted a strict

Muslim attitude. Hence he offered his Dutch prisoners the choice of circumcision or death. One of them, Antonie Paulo, died a martyr to his Christian faith in 1642.

The prince also strove to enhance his wordly reputation, and in view of the fact that his family had no background at all, this was energy well spent. To this end he had only to follow the admirable example set by the erstwhile spiritual lords. In 1624 therefore, after the hard-won conquest of Madura, he conferred upon himself the title of *susuhunan*, which until then appears to have been reserved for a deceased *walī*. And like the spiritual lords who sat enthroned on mountain tops, he had a raised terrace built in front of his residency, on which he and his retinue appeared in glorious array. Finally he began the construction of a mountain tomb for himself and his successors, with his own grave nearest the top, again in imitation of the holy men. On the other hand he openly prided himself on a collection of objects with magical power, the *pusaka*, which (in a slightly different category) included the large guns which he sported at his palace.

After two unsuccessful sieges of Batavia (1628–9) he was faced with a serious crisis. There were threats of rebellion and fanatics were roaming the country. He warded off the dangers, not only by despotic force but also by a sensible approach to Islam. The Islamic calendar was now officially introduced in the realm, although he retained the ancient Shaka era, which began in A.D. 78. In 1633 he also visited the holy grave of Tembayat, which he embellished with magnificent monuments. Was he paying his respects at Canossa?

Following Bantam's example he managed in the end to acquire the title of sultan, thanks to the co-operation of the English, who provided transport to Mecca for his envoys. After 1641 he called himself Sultan 'Abd Allāh Muḥammad Mawlānā Mataranī (i.e. of Mataram). It is, however, as Sultan Agung that he is generally known. So this ruler not only managed to preserve his authority, but by his wise policy of courting the spiritual lords with their time-honoured traditions and great influence among the people, he actually added to it. He even went so far as to humiliate one of them, the ruler of Giri, who refused to bow to him. In doing so, he used his brother-in-law, the Pangeran Pekik, son of the last of the Surabaya rulers. After a fierce battle the refractory ruler was forced to leave his holy mountain and settle in Mataram for a time. This was a great triumph for the Mataram ruler, who now combined temporal and spiritual power in his residency.

THE DOWNFALL OF THE SPIRITUAL LORDS

Sultan Agung's son and successor, known as Susuhunan Mangku-Rat I Tegal-Wangi, did not follow his father's footsteps. He refused the title of sultan and preferred to be just *susuhunan*, as his father had been from 1624 until 1641, and as his successors were after him. Since he suspected the spiritual lords of conspiring with his brother in a rebellion, he carefully planned a mass-murder of the divines, hoping in this way to settle with them for good. But enough of them survived to preserve an aftermath of hostility against him. Nor did this prevent him from appealing to them for spiritual ministrations in times of crisis, illness and so on. It was not by prudent statesmanship, but by terror and force that this ruler, with his deranged mind, sought to maintain his waning authority. It was the north coast in particular that he is believed to have alienated by his policies.

It is not surprising, therefore, that the spiritual lords, in league with his rebellious son, the crown-prince, conspired against him. One religious family in particular, under the grey-haired *Pangeran* of Kajoran, nicknamed Ambalik (the turn-coat), laid the foundation for a general conspiracy. The revolt broke out in 1675 and it was seven years before peace was restored. In 1677 the Susuhunan had to find refuge with the Dutch. He died on the way and was buried in a 'fragrant field' (*tegal-wangi*), whence his nickname. His grave is another miniature imitation of a mountain.

His son, Mangku-Rat II (1677–1703), followed his father's policies and allied himself to the Dutch, also on the advice of the lord of Adi-Langu. And so his power was restored with the help of the Dutch East India Company. The leader of the rebels, Raden Truna-Jaya from Madura, and several of the spiritual lords had to pay for their revolt with their lives. Now that the prince could boast of having allies who were insensitive to the hidden powers of the *kiyayi*, he did not want to miss his chance of settling with these rebels. The Dutch commander, Jan Albert Sloot, was able to capture Ambalik of Kajoran, but none of the Javanese allies dared to kill the holy man. The wild Buginese from South-west Celebes had to be invited to perform this task. The Susuhunan next provoked a clash between the Dutch and the grey-haired ruler of Giri. After a fierce battle, the fiercest of the entire seven years' war, the old man was wounded and taken prisoner, and was later beheaded by order of the prince (27 Rabīʿ I 1091/27 April 1680).

Even after Sunan Mangku-Rat II had moved into his new palace Karta-Sura, in 1680—the old one having been desecrated by the rebels—fanatics continued to cause disturbances. This time it was Kiyayi Wana-Kasuma, related to Ambalik, who predicted that the end of the dynasty was near. According to this prediction, the succession would now, after seven generations, fall to another house. For years the battle raged to and fro, and more than once the Dutch troops had to intervene to save Karta-Sura. Peace was restored in the end, but a Dutch garrison was necessary to protect the Sunan (or ensure his adherence to the Dutch alliance). Again in 1719, Sunan Mangku-Rat IV (1719–27) took advantage of a new war of succession to wipe out the priestly line of the lords of Tembayat, and only after this does the political role of the *kiyayi* seem to have come to an end.

THE ESCHATOLOGY

That the *kiyayi* party, though beaten, never completely lost heart, is borne out by a story that was current in South Central Java until recently. Pangeran Puger, who later became Sunan Paku-Buwana I (1703–19), is said to have been a suppositious child, and in fact Ambalik's son. When the latter, even before his revolt, was asked to remove the caul of a child born to Sunan Mangku-Rat I Tegal-Wangi, the future rebel did so, at the same time, however, exchanging this child with his own of the same age. Thus the state was still ruled by a descendant of the *kiyayi*.

Nevertheless, as the chances of political success faded, there must have been among the devout, somewhere near the turn of the seventeenth century, a growing belief in the coming of a messianic *ratu adil*, 'just (*ādil*) ruler'. To some extent this belief originated in Islamic eschatology. Hinduism contributed to it with the doctrine of the four world eras, which were to be followed by the end of all things. And it is quite feasible that ancient pre-Hindu native beliefs influenced the Javanese *ratu adil* complex too.

The Javanese eschatological speculations are attributed to a pre-Muslim ruler of Kaḍiri, Jaya-Baya, who lived in the twelfth century. Possibly the memory of his name was kept alive by the fact that he was mentioned in the ancient epic *Brata-Yuda* (1157) which is an episode of the Indian epic *Mahabharata*.

The first written records of such 'predictions of Jaya-Baya' date from 1719, and they have never failed to impress the Javanese people. Again and again someone would emerge who claimed to be the coming *mahdī*. Some of them acted in good faith, others were deceivers whose main concern was the sale of amulets and the collection of money. After a short while the police and the law usually put an end to their messianic careers. Some were indeed of high birth and were pretenders to the throne. Among them we can certainly place even the great rebel Pangeran Dipa-Negara who, at any rate during some stage in his career, was considered by himself and his followers as a *ratu adil*.

As far as the contents of the predictions are concerned, these mainly contain a compound of Muslim eschatology and Hindu-Javanese elements. They usually cover the complete history of Java, past, present and future. They have a strange knack of adapting themselves to the most recent events, so that the unprepared reader or listener is amazed at the completely correct description of the present by a so-called teacher from antiquity. This makes his predictions ring doubly true, and one forgets that earlier predictions of this kind sometimes did not come true at all, such as those published by Raffles.[1]

The fact is that these prophecies were coupled with dates which the world has survived completely unscathed.

SURVIVAL OF THE HOLY MEN

Kiyayi, with their miraculous gifts and secret teachings, have survived to the present, even though their numbers have gradually decreased. There were one or two very ancient institutions and customs which strengthened their social position.

In pre-Muslim times there had been religious villages whose inhabitants kept to certain strict rules. Later they became largely Muslim, and so they became Islamic holy villages, whose inhabitants kept strictly to Muslim precepts and to those of their *kiyayi*. The Muslim princes granted these villages privileges, thereby in fact merely extending or confirming privileges dating from pre-Muslim times. In later centuries these villages were called *pamutihan*, villages of the 'whites', or, since they were exempt from taxation, *perdikan-desa*. Colonial governments, with little concern for the religious ideals of these communities, tried to reduce them in number and size with an eye to a higher tax yield and the promotion of peace and order.

[1] *History of Java* (London, 1817) II, 40.

There were also *kiyayi* who established themselves outside the village communities in small settlements, accompanied by their relatives and their pupils. There they eked out a simple living from the produce of their fields. Where the *kiyayi* shed an odour of sanctity, others would join the settlement so as to receive instruction. In this way schools came into being, to this day known as *pesantren*, derived from *santri*, a *kiyayi* disciple. Life was lived according to earlier customs. The unmarried *santri* lived in small huts, the floor of which, according to ancient practice, was raised off the ground. It can be safely assumed that this type of teaching-establishment was to some extent a continuation of similar institutions in pre-Muslim times. They have also much in common with Indian ashrams.

Other relics from the distant past were retained in the ancient pre-Muslim dances and performances at the *pesantren*. Some of the members took instruction in magic, juggling and self-torture without shedding blood, in order to demonstrate their progress in Muslim mysticism. Music and dancing were effective in inducing an individual or communal trance. Some of these features may have originated in other parts of the Muslim world; the instruments of self-injury that are kept near the ancient mosque of Bantam, for instance, resemble similar implements in use among the mystics in Bosnia and Cape Town. From the *pesantren* these displays spread through the outside world, where they are still to be seen here and there.

The actual teaching in the *pesantren* was far from systematic. It consisted largely of reading and writing, and the memorizing of the Qur'ān, theological and legal texts, mystical proverbs and prayers, litanies and hymns in a corrupt form of Arabic. These things were written down in note-books which provide us with a glimpse into the spiritual life of these devout communities. Snouck Hurgronje was one of the first to draw attention to these particular writings.

The teaching is largely concerned with the unity of Lord and servant. To know oneself is to know the Lord. Unity of microcosm and macrocosm is taught along the same lines. All that exists can be summed up in the one word, *Ingsun*. This doctrine of the all-embracing self is the keystone of Javanese metaphysical speculations. Gradually this sometimes very tendentious heterodox mysticism was supplemented by the orthodox mysticism of some *ṭarīqas*, such as the Shaṭṭāriyya, and Naqshbandiyya. Various tracts stemming from these schools were put into Javanese. As time went on, even diehard *kiyayi* either became members of such *ṭarīqas*, or imitated them, in this way gradually adapting themselves to their pattern and causing less offence to the orthodox. Despite this adjustment, however, the steady decline of the *pesantren* could not be halted. The princes resisted them because of their attitude of bold independence, while the colonial authorities, fearing their tendency to create factions, sought to suppress them. The orthodox shunned their heretical teaching and finally educational institutions on the European model deprived them of many of their pupils.

CHAPTER 2

SOUTH-EAST ASIAN ISLAM IN THE NINETEENTH CENTURY

Centuries, calendrically precise, are seldom as meaningful historiographically as historians are apt to make them seem. The nineteenth century in Islamic South-East Asia is no exception, and yet, with the need to see a pattern in a period of years, patterns do emerge. The Java and Acheh Wars stand like tombstones at either end of a series of violent and often bloody conflicts fought to renovate or defend Islam and the *ummat* (Arabic, *umma*) against the vitiating syncretism of local tradition and increasing colonial encroachment. The early years of the century saw the beginnings of a redefinition of the relationship of the West with the Archipelago which was to culminate before the beginning of the next in the complete subjection of Indonesian and Malay political and administrative authority to alien rule. And finally, the opening of island and peninsular South-East Asian societies to the west meant, in the literal sense, not merely the consolidation of European power and influence, but a considerable increase in the flow of communications with the heartland of Islam which did much to determine the nature and intensity of the conflicts which characterize these years.

The Java War of 1825–30, though from one point of view the first in a series of manifestations of social unrest in Java in which protest at socio-economic change brought about by the West played a determining role, must also be seen as yet another in the succession of conflicts which had punctuated the previous hundred years, arising in large part out of social tensions present within Javanese society itself. The eighteenth century in central Java had been marked by an efflorescence of specifically Javanese culture, and of Javanism, prompted in part, it has been suggested, by the severance of Mataram from the coast and from the vitalizing trade contacts which (among other things) had helped to bring and sustain Islam. The partition of the empire in the mid-century, followed as it was by a turning in upon the courts of Jogjakarta and Surakarta, led to an intensification of the hierarchical qualities already present in the Javanese social order, and set the pattern for an aristocratic and bureaucratic, *priyayi* civilization which found little time for the relative austerities of the 'Arab religion'. Doctrinally, the Javanese form of Islam, which had always been characterized by an idiosyncratic blend of indigenous, Hindu-Buddhist, and rather florid (mainly Shaṭṭāriyya) Ṣūfī mysticism, tended to move even further away from its 'orthodox' sources towards traditional religious beliefs. Organizationally, the ruling class relied for the administration of Islam upon what came to be an appointed hierarchy of officials who functioned more or less as adjuncts of secular rule, staffing mosques, prayer-houses and religious courts—the 'priesthood' of contemporary European observers. Below or beyond this, in the interstices of village society—where the *abangan* variant of Javanese religion, compounded largely of pre-Hindu mysticism with Muslim accretions in varying degree, held sway over peasant life—stood the rural *kiyayi* and *'ulamā'*. As teachers and propagators of the faith, as the nucleus of the pious *santri* civilization of the earnestly Muslim, they derived their authority not from the fiat of a secular power but from their knowledge of Islam and the Holy Word, their esotericism as initiates in Ṣūfī *ṭarīqas*, and their espousal of an outwardly as well as inwardly Islamic mode of life. The *'ulamā'* constituted a distinct if unorganized element in Javanese society, standing aloof from, and at times fiercely critical of, Islamically imperfect secular governments, much in the manner of similar groups in other times and places. For the most part of and from the rural community to which they ministered, they formed a powerful focus for peasant discontents with the harshness of the world in general, and with the exactions of the ruling class (and its symbiotic relationship with the *kāfir* Dutch) in particular, as had already been amply demonstrated. The dichotomy this points to, between the syncretic and compromising *priyayi élite* and their official religious establishment on the one hand, and the independent *'ulamā'* on the other, each competing for the allegiance of the *abangan* peasant majority, formed the dynamic for much that was now to take place in Java. The direct and forceful entry of the Dutch on the side of the *priyayi*, the increasing islamization of the peasantry, and the growth during the century of new, and especially urban, groups with interests served by a more individualistic Islamic ethic, served only to strengthen and deepen these tendencies.

With the demise of the Dutch East India Company in the last days of the old century, Java entered upon two brief periods of administrative experiment at the hands successively of the Dutch-Napoleonic Herman Daendels and Thomas Stamford Raffles, which set in motion new processes of Western penetration into Indonesian society and the indigenous economy. In the complex political history of these years, the wars, revolutions and alliances of Europe played a larger part than any consideration of Eastern affairs. What is of relevance here is the character and effect of the Daendels and Raffles régimes and of the restored Dutch system which succeeded them.

Whereas the Company, bent on trade and not dominion, had for the most part retained Javanese traditional authority intact as a means of exacting forced deliveries of agricultural products from a peasantry heavily obligated to their traditional chiefs, Daendels set out to break this system, at least partially in the interests of the ordinary Javanese, by instituting direct payments for produce and by declaring the Javanese regents (local rulers) to be Dutch government officials, with military rank and a fixed income. In the semi-autonomous states of Central Java, Daendels reduced the status and authority of the princely rulers by appointing ministers rather than residents to the courts of Jogjakarta and Surakarta and entitling these officials to royal insignia, and he divided the remainder of the island into administrative divisions directly controlled from Batavia, and linked where possible by improved communications. Many of these reforms, especially the economic ones, were only partially carried out, if at all; but the patterns of indirect Company control had been broken, and for the first time all Java was fused into something approaching a colonial system of rule.

When the British took Java in 1811, the policies instituted by Raffles followed similar lines, with a number of important additional innovations which affected even further the position of traditional authority. Daendels's attempts to curtail the powers of the regents had been limited by his inability to run the economy of Java without recourse to the taxation functions of the ruling class, even if revised, and to a variety of other expedients (including the lease of villages and the sale of large tracts of land to private individuals, Chinese and European) which meant that the burdens on the peasantry were if anything increased. Of liberal economic views, and anxious to continue the 'defeudalization' of Javanese society, Raffles instituted a land-rent system which brought the peasant cultivator into direct contact with the government, and removed the regents and other traditional authorities from the revenue-producing machinery in return for certain sorts of compensation. One consequence of this system, which did not, it may be said, work very well economically during the brief period of Raffles's administration, was to intensify the degree of interaction between Javanese village society and a centralized and increasingly European civil service. At the same time, though the privileges of the ruling class were in many areas scarcely touched, there was a general and irksome undermining of their position and (at least as important) an increase in their dependence for favour upon a foreign administration. Open conflict in the princely states, where Raffles put down a movement to throw the British out, and deposed the sultan of Jogjakarta in favour of his son, further fragmenting the state in the process, did nothing to improve this situation and left resentment which before long was to bear fruit.

When the Dutch returned to Java in 1816, under orders from the revived monarchy 'to establish a colonial system based upon principles of free trade and free cultivation', Raffles's economic and social policies were continued for the time being, despite the parlous financial situation in which the administration now found itself, and growing evidence of Javanese restlessness. The unsettling effects of two decades of experiment and uncertainty were widespread. In the principalities in particular, discontent with changing times affected all classes of society. The nobility and aristocracy, chafing under reduced incomes and shrunken territory which made it difficult to meet traditional obligations to kin and clients, turned more and more to the leasing of their lands (and the labour upon them) to foreign cultivators. When this process was stopped by the government in 1823, with the requirement that all lands be returned together with large financial indemnities for improvements made in the interim, this was for many *priyayi* the last turn of the screw. Secondly, from 1817 onwards, the sale of customary taxes and tolls to the Dutch government, promptly farmed out to Chinese entrepreneurs, may have helped to raise additional income for aristocracy and government alike, but resulted in an inhuman exploitation of the peasantry which provided much of the fuel for the risings that followed. And finally, Muslims of all degrees, but particularly the *kiyayi* and '*ulamā*', felt a special hatred for the increasing manifestations of infidel rule and desired to see both it and its Javanese allies put down, sentiments which linked them with irredentist sections of the nobility seeking to see Mataram reunited and restored to its former greatness.

Dipa-Negara, the 'Hamlet prince' of Java (as he has been called), and chief progenitor of the war that now ensued, is in many ways a strange and enigmatic, and certainly a tragic figure. Son of Sultan Hamengku Buwana III of Jogjakarta by a morganatic marriage, he was close to the throne but had been passed over in the succession (or had himself declined it) on two separate occasions. Of markedly religious temper and mystical leanings, he had been a frequent and sombre critic of the laxity of the court and its increasingly European ways, and also, it would seem, of the miseries inflicted on the peasantry by the current dispensation. He himself retired largely from court life and was accustomed to wander the countryside dressed in black, Arab-style clothing and (in an older tradition than that of Islam) to seek solitude for prayer and meditation in sacred tombs and cave-shrines, where he was vouchsafed visions and heard voices that taught him of his own eschatological mission as leader of a great movement to purify Islam and its practices among his people. Sayings and prophesies associated with the prince achieved wide currency and attached themselves to characteristically Javanese messianic expectations concerning the coming of the *ratu adil*, or 'just king', who would save the land from oppression, and lead it to plenty and peace.

The occasion for the outbreak of hostilities in July 1825 was relatively trivial—little more than a dispute concerning the building of a road across Dipa-Negara's property at Tegalreja and the high-handed behaviour of a Dutch official. In the confusion that followed, Dipa-Negara and those around him prepared for rebellion by retreating to a strategically situated village and issuing a call to arms. The word spread like fire in stubble and within the next few weeks supporters came to his side by the hundred. Messages sent by Dipa-Negara to the outlying districts in the north and east appealed to the people 'to take up arms to fight for the country and for the restoration of the true Islam'. Of those who came immediately to his side, one Indonesian account says, the greater number were *'ulamā'* and *santri*. Chief among several leading *'ulamā'* who appeared was Kiyayi Maja, a forceful figure of great popular reputation, who besides playing an important part in arousing the peasantry acquired before long considerable influence over Dipa-Negara himself. Urging the prince to assume the titles of sultan and *panatagama* (head of religion) through all Java, Kiyayi Maja gave the insurrection increasingly the character of a *jihād*, and swore not to cease fighting until every last *kāfir* (European) had been killed.

In the early stages of the war, many of the Javanese nobility and aristocracy loyal to the Dutch or inclined to stand behind the court party were also put to the sword, though increasingly the older pattern of '*ulamā*'-led, peasant-fortified conflict with a compromising and oppressive *priyayi élite* gave way to a holy alliance of Islam and the aristocracy against the infidels, as traditional chiefs came over to Dipa-Negara's side. The Dutch, caught on the wrong foot, with little in the way of military reserves, were able for a time, despite reverses, to exploit factions within the ruling class and levy armed assistance from within the state of Jogjakarta itself and especially from rival Surakarta, but they were forced eventually to recruit troops in Madura, the Celebes and elsewhere, and to call for reinforcements from Europe. As the struggle developed and the Dutch gradually gained the upper hand in the principalities, the guerrilla character of the warfare became more marked, and seeking to avoid a long drawn out campaign the Dutch sought directly to negotiate a settlement and later encouraged approaches from among the insurgents themselves. Almost all these attempts, which took place during the latter part of 1827 and in 1828, seem to have failed on one basic ground, the refusal of the Dutch to recognize Dipa-Negara's claims to be head of the Islamic religion. Though there is evidence that the authorities might have been prepared to accept the prince as ruler of Jogjakarta and perhaps make other concessions as well, they were adamant in holding that 'fanatical' Islam, upon which with some justice they blamed the fireiness of the present dispute, must be taken out of the hands of the prince and his advisers. And so the war dragged on for a further two years, causing great loss of life, as much from disease as from the fighting, and bringing untold distress to a harried peasantry disturbed in its usual occupations by the coming and going of government troops and insurgent bands alike. Ultimate Dutch victory was assured, and as the end neared Dipa-Negara was deserted one by one by his principal supporters (including Kiyayi Maja, who was captured while suing for a separate peace), until he himself was forced to accept an invitation to discuss, under safe conduct, terms of surrender. Treacherously taken prisoner during the talks that followed, his final request that he be permitted to make the Pilgrimage to Mecca was refused and he spent the remainder of his days in exile in the Celebes, dying only in 1855.

Full understanding of the Java War and its meaning for Javanese society and Islam must await proper monographic research, for though, fortunately, many of the materials still exist, there has as yet been no detailed study in any language of the crowded and complex events of these years. Certain things, however, seem clear. The paramount role played by Islam in providing the ideology for the revolt associated purified Islamic belief and practice once and for all with defence against alien rule. One result of this, it seems likely, was that the position of the '*ulamā*' in Javanese society among the peasantry was considerably strengthened—a tendency assisted by the growing countervailing identification of the *priyayi élite* with Dutch authority in subsequent years. Together these circumstances help to explain the marked increase in islamization of the peasantry which took place even before the mid-century. For the Dutch themselves, whose understanding of Islam was for some time to remain at best superficial, the Java War drove home the danger of permitting any alliance between the secular chiefs and the forces of Islam. Though this lesson had to be re-learnt towards the close of the century, in the context of the Acheh War, it formed for the next twenty or thirty years a cardinal element in, on the one hand, the exercise of severely repressive policies towards independent Islam, and on the other, the return to supportive, indirect rule policies towards the traditional ruling class.

In the period following the war in Java, the Dutch, with local treasuries exhausted to the point of large-scale indebtedness, the ruins of an ill-understood and ill-applied economic liberalism lying at their feet, and pressing financial problems at home as a result of the Belgian revolt, began afresh the task of making the Indies pay. The system devised to achieve this end—the lifebelt, it has been said, that was to keep the Netherlands afloat—came to be known as the Culture (or Cultivation) System. Under it, the peasant was required, in lieu of tax, to cultivate on one-fifth of his land designated export crops for surrender to the government, or alternatively to provide a proportionate amount of labour for government-owned estates and other projects. To ensure the success of the system, and at the same time to reassert a measure of custom-sanctioned control over a still unsettled populace, it was necessary for the Dutch to re-establish, under allegiance to themselves, the position and authority of the traditional aristocracy. Accordingly the next two decades saw not only the conversion of large areas of Java into something like a state-owned plantation system, but a restoration of the recently undermined status of the regents and the *priyayi élite*, and their gradual transformation into an hereditary class of officials functioning as the executive arm of the colonial power. The nature of the mutually advantageous association thus formed between traditional authority and colonial exploitation was not lost on the Javanese people, and widened further the gulf between rulers and ruled.

Alongside the bureaucratic *élite*, and under the combined surveillance of this *élite* and their Dutch overlords, there developed a parallel class of religious officials, hierarchically organized and fitting neatly into regional administrative patterns. Regency *penghulu*, appointed by and responsible to the regent (as were all other mosque officials, according to customary law), functioned mainly as *qāḍīs*, though their independent jurisdiction was limited to family law and *waqf*, and part of their time was spent sitting as advisers in the secular courts, where, however, it has been said, their tasks tended to be limited to the administering of oaths. District *penghulu* performed similar roles at the district administrative level, and at the village level lesser *penghulu* and their assistants carried out tasks related mainly to the supervision of marriage contracts and the upkeep of mosques. The incorporation of this class of religious officials (regarded by the Dutch as 'priests') into the general administrative framework of the state resulted in the emasculation of the *'ulamā'* taking part, subject as they were to a *priyayi élite* who to some extent shared the prevailing Dutch fear of religious fanaticism, and who in any case had no interest in maintaining anything like a separate Islamic authority.

In the circumstances, it is scarcely surprising that the independent *kiyayi* and *'ulamā'* should as a rule have held religious officialdom in disrepute, nor that most of the Islamic life of the community (and the prestige associated with its leadership) should rest in their hands—from the multitude of small-scale religious activities and occasions attendant upon the incidents of everyday life to the running of religious schools (*pesantren*) and the setting up and regulation of the Ṣūfī *ṭarīqas* which still shaped much of Javanese religious thought. This independent focus for peasant loyalties was feared by the Dutch, who, in the belief that the principle sources of 'unrest' among the peasantry were returned pilgrims and itinerant Arabs, placed, or attempted to place, restrictions upon the Pilgrimage and upon the movement of Arabs out of the urban areas. Nevertheless, unrest persisted. Though the Java War, marking the onset of intensive Western interference in Javanese life, was the last of the great conflagrations in the island, the thirties, forties and subsequent years continued to be disturbed by spasmodic peasant risings, invariably under the banner of Islam.

Elsewhere in South-East Asia, Islamic communities were left much more to themselves in the early nineteenth century than in Java. The absence of an external threat from Western expansion was not in all instances, however, accompanied by internal tranquillity. In Sumatra in particular, parts of which had long been amongst the most intensely islamized in the region, there occurred in Minangkabau at the start of the century an inner convulsion generated by powerful reform influences which derived their initial impetus, it is true, from outside the state, but were for nearly two decades to be fought out strictly within the society itself.

This conflict has usually been seen as a struggle between more or less clearly defined *adat* (custom-centred) and *agama* (Islamic-centred) parties; but the complexities of the Minangkabau social and political systems are so considerable that anything like a simplified account of their working is bound to be defective in one respect or another. The most that can be done here is to try to clarify a little of the background to the events of the early nineteenth century, and look at some of their consequences for Islam.

Minangkabau society at the close of the eighteenth century manifested several sets of oppositions which, though always potentially and sometimes actually in conflict, found more or less precarious resolution in a variety of integrative concepts and institutions. In the first place, the social structure presented two separate faces, that of the royal family of the old Minangkabau kingdom, which had a patrilineal descent system, and that of the independent commonality, which was matrilineal. Both, however, were inseparable parts of one whole, with a shared as well as a divided view of life. Kingship seems never to have functioned as an instrument of government in Minangkabau proper—that is to say, in the inland central highlands known as the *darat*—but despite implicit conflict between the two social systems, acceptance of the institution served to maintain equilibrium among the separate *nagari* (or 'village republics', as they have been called), the basic political units into which the state divided. Among the *nagari* themselves a further divisive principle existed, between two conflicting political systems based on separate *adat* traditions, which differed little in fundamentals but the balance between which was vital for the well-being of the society as a whole. Territorially, Minangkabau presented yet another complex dichotomy—between the *darat*, identified as the source of *adat* or the corpus of 'custom', where royalty had its seat but did not rule, and what was known as the *rantau*, the peripheral areas in general but particularly the coastal plain, which, though directly governed by representatives of the royal family, was historically and traditionally the source of Islam. Here again, potential strife between the two, sometimes realized, was lessened by a recognition of economic interdependence, and by an encapsulation of *adat* and Islam in a common system of coexisting principles, together necessary for the persistence of the society.

Within this continuum of actual and incipient conflict (and the list is by no means exhaustive) the key to understanding is perhaps provided by the notion of *adat* itself, which in Minangkabau society, it has been argued, contains important ambiguities. On the one hand, the *adat* may be taken to refer to the complex of local customary rules, derived from 'ancient times', which regulate relationships and behaviour within the society. On the other, *adat* in a larger sense may refer to the whole structural system of society, to its inner world view, of which local custom and institutionalized conflict between variants of local custom are themselves component parts. Provided the system as a whole, and its bases, are not seriously challenged, conflict can be contained by the expression of conflict, and the idealized pattern of life continue undisrupted, even if subject to change as element jostles with element. Thus the original penetration into Minangkabau society of an Islam which, as elsewhere in Indonesia, was accommodating and syncretic, and more influenced by *ṭarīqa* practices than by strict adherence to either doctrine or 'orthodox' ritual, had not greatly shaken the existing social order. Though the growth of Islamic influence, and of more Islamically oriented groups (especially the religious teachers) within Minangkabau society, challenged by their nature certain other elements in the society, they did so more in the way of contributing another dimension to existing conflict, the result of which seems to have been the restructuring of the larger *adat* in order to domesticate and contain the foreign body while permitting continuation of the dynamic opposition which its presence constituted. This somewhat hypothetical discussion may be given some content by pointing, for example, to the organization of the ruling institution of the *nagari*, the *balai* or council, which, though it was 'owned' by the secular leadership of the community (just as the mosque was 'owned' by the religious) had as members not only the *penghulu* (in Sumatra, *adat* chief) and his staff, but some of the '*ulamā*', with a neutral group of elders to hold the middle. Most importantly, perhaps, the Islam involved in this situation, though staking a claim to a share in the determination of idealized patterns of behaviour for the society, and though at odds with the matrilineality (most obviously) of the commoners, and with the rival 'great tradition' represented by the king, was not in general militantly concerned to subvert the existing order.

Towards the end of the eighteenth century, symptoms of social disintegration and an accompanying social demoralization appear to have begun to make themselves evident in Minangkabau, perhaps associated with the decline in the power of the king (politically on the coast and sacrally elsewhere), and with the rise of new centres of religion in the interior under the leadership of *tuanku* (the title given to leading '*ulamā*') independent of the traditional structure of authority. None of this, however, seriously threatened the existing order, despite an increase in detached elements of social and political discontent, until the return of the famous three pilgrims from Mecca in 1803 unleashed the first wave of the puritanical reform movement known to the Dutch as the *Padri* movement, from the Portuguese *lingua franca* term for cleric.

The *padri*, like the Wahhābīs in Arabia, whose example may to some extent have been fortuitous but was certainly influential, directed their energies in the first place to the extirpation of moral laxity and an insistence upon strict adherence to the duties imposed by the faith. They proscribed the popular pastimes of cock-fighting, smoking, taking intoxicants or stimulants, and the like, and enjoined strict observance of the ritual prayers at the appointed times (upon pain of death for the unrepentent apostate), requiring also that women should go veiled and men wear white, Arab-style clothing (from which derived the name by which the *padri* were known locally—*kaum puteh*, 'the white ones'). Despite this apparent absorption, however, with what may be regarded as externals, the real importance and disruptive effect of the *padri*, whose campaign was waged relentlessly, and frequently with violence, lay less in their scourging of a ritually and doctrinally lax community than in the threat they offered to the socio-political *status quo*, demanding for Islam the right not merely to correct from within but to coerce from without, and to seize the largest share in the determination of the principles by which the community was to live. Their attacks upon *adat* in its more restricted sense, embodied in specific, locally hallowed custom seen to be in conflict with Islam, constituted at the same time a more serious attack on *adat* in the larger sense, as the structural system of society, embodied in its custodians, the *adat* chiefs, and in the institutionalized balance achieved between them and other contending elements. It is no accident that the first act of violence in the *padri* explosion was the burning of a *balai*, the integrative institution par excellence of the *nagari*, by followers of Ḥājjī Miskīn (Haji Miskin), one of the three returned pilgrims.

Thus, though the *padri* conflict may readily be seen in terms of opposition between religion and custom, and though it must to some degree have represented frustration on the part of the independent '*ulamā*' as a group within a social system which did not accord them a satisfactory place in the structure of authority, the familiar dichotomy is not wholly satisfactory. The reality was certainly more complex, and allegiances perhaps fell more clearly along the lines of those for or against change of a variety of kinds. Ḥājjī Miskīn's chief supporter in the affair mentioned was a *penghulu* from the same area. When Tuanku nan Rentjeh, the leading figure in the *padri* movement in the central district of Agam, turned for assistance to his own teacher, Tuanku Kota Tua, the latter, while agreeing with the general aims of the movement, refused to countenance its abrupt, violent, and intolerant abrogation of past accommodations. Conversely, the first prominent adherent of the *padri* when the movement spread into the northern valley of Alahan Panjang (later famed as the stronghold of Tuanku Imām Bonjol) was a leading traditional chief, Dato' Bendahara, accompanied by several of his fellows. In more general terms, accounts of this prolonged disturbance, which speak even of families divided against themselves, make it plain that it must have answered or become attached to many other sorts of conflict.

As the agents of change, the *padri* pursued for fifteen years their campaign of reformation, taking over, by force, intimidation or persuasion, one village after another, installing their own functionaries (usually an *imām* who laid down the law and a *qāḍī* who saw it observed) and expelling or killing *adat* chiefs and others who opposed them. Opposition was, indeed, not lacking, but progressively much of the interior came under *padri* control, and in 1818 a group of *penghulu*, led by two members of the royal family, appealed to the British on the coast at Padang for military aid. Though Raffles established only one armed post in the interior, probably in the hope of obtaining influence there before the impending return of the Dutch, the Dutch themselves assumed wider responsibilities a year or so later and before long were thoroughly implicated on the side of the opponents of the *padri* in what now became known as the *Padri* War.

The guerilla fighting that ensued was to last for some sixteen years before ending in 1837 with the reduction of the stronghold of the last *padri* leader, the redoubtable Tuanku Imām Bonjol. During the final years of this struggle its nature changed. Already in the 1820s the fires of dispute between the *padri* and their opponents had died down, partly as a result of a lessening of the extremes of religious fervour (in consequence, to some extent, of continued contact with the Ḥijāz, where Wahhabism itself waned after the political defeat of the Su'ūdīs in 1818) and partly because much had in fact been gained. The increased involvement of the Dutch, and a recognition of the threat to independence that this implied, led to a closing of the ranks and the formation of a common Muslim front against the *kāfirs* under *padri* leadership. The royal ruler of Minangkabau was exiled to Java in 1833, thus destroying the last vestiges of the old kingdom, never to be restored, and eventual Dutch victory was achieved by superior force of arms and the gradual isolation and dismemberment of final pockets of resistance.[1]

The long course of the *padri* movement had as its principal result a marked increase in the penetration of Islam into the fabric of Minangkabau society, with consequent long-term implications of importance for related peoples elsewhere in Sumatra and in the Malay peninsula. In Minangkabau itself, religious doctrine acquired a redefined and larger acceptance within the *adat*, as the basic referent for idealised patterns of life, even though the social schism between defenders of *adat* and innovators, buried briefly during the anti-Dutch years, reappeared before long. The leading practitioners of religion, the teachers and '*ulamā*,' emerged from the struggle with much enhanced prestige, despite subsequent Dutch attempts to curb their influence in favour of that of the *adat* chiefs in the interests of law and order and economic exploitation. Politically, the conclusion of the war, which was followed by occupation of the central highlands, opened the way for further extension of Dutch authority in this potentially most valuable of the 'Outer Possessions'. Though the resulting forward movement was pursued somewhat hesitantly in the face of British hostility, it resulted in substantial Dutch control over all Sumatra south of Acheh by shortly after the mid-century.

During the second half of the nineteenth century, and particularly in

[1] See Taufik Abdullah, 'Adat and Islam: an Examination of Conflict in Minangkabau', *Indonesia* (Ithaca), 2 (Oct. 1966), 1-24.

the final quarter, Islamic South-East Asia underwent a religious revival—perhaps more properly an intensification of religious life—of large proportions. Some of the many causes for this have already been suggested or discussed. In more than one area, long-standing conflicts for peasant allegiance between traditional secular *élites* and independent '*ulamā*,' which had helped retard the reception of Islam, were resolved in favour of the '*ulamā*'. The power and influence of rural Islamic leadership had been augmented by the onset of alien (and *kāfir*) rule which, at the same time as it added to the complexities and burdens of people's lives, came to be identified more and more with an increasingly discredited ruling class turned colonial bureaucracy. The spread of the faith in many parts of Java previously only nominally Muslim, for example, was greatly assisted by the readiness with which Islam became the standard-bearer of protest against changing times and consolation amidst the ills of the world. The growth in numbers of village Qur'anic schools and *pesantren* throughout Java in the latter part of the century represents, it is perhaps fair to say, more a hopeful turning away from the harshnesses of everyday life than a means of remedying them. The Dutch themselves, though going in fear of Muslim 'fanaticism', did much to hasten the islamization of the Archipelago. As the new administration tightened its grip on Java, it was accompanied by improved communications which broke down isolation and rendered previously closed communities open to outside influence. In the outer islands, the spread of Dutch authority was attended by hosts of subordinate Muslim officials who acted as witting or unwitting proselytizers, as in some of the Batak areas north of Minangkabau and in parts of Borneo. And though, as we shall see, there continued to be sporadic outbursts of village unrest, the *Pax Neerlandica* in the settled areas, while contributing, for example, to the quadrupling of population in Java from seven to twenty-eight millions between 1830 and 1900, helped to create conditions favourable to the peaceful growth of religion.

In addition to this fairly general and widespread dissemination of Islam during the latter part of the century, other processes were at work, especially in Java, enlarging the pious *santri* nucleus of the community and intensifying its attachment to Islamic ideas and values. For the most part these processes relate to fundamental socio-economic changes at work in Indonesian society, and to the growth of direct contact with the Middle East. After the abolition of the Culture System (progressively from about 1870) and the substitution of 'liberal' economic policies aiming at a shift from state to private European capital enterprise, the Javanese peasant economy ceased to be governed by 'remote control' contracts between the government and village heads, and was drawn increasingly into a more direct relationship with export markets and with Western economic life. Though this change of policy failed to have the successful demonstration effect believed likely by many liberal theorists, some stimulus did seep through to the village level. Individuals were enabled to grow and sell commercial crops, to lease and to aggregate land, and to participate in small-scale trade. Opportunities were by no means unlimited, and were frequently subject to cramping restrictions, not to mention better organized and more highly capitalized competition, but some advantage at least was provided for those able to respond to it. Though the increasing monetization of the village economy meant for many simply a new form of servitude, others found in thrift, frugality and individual effort a liberating sense of personal fulfilment and a means of rising in the world. For these energetic and industrious people, Islam supplied a system of values which validated economic behaviour differing from that of their fellows, and a status system which gave expression to these values. Of paramount importance in the latter was the Pilgrimage to Mecca which, fulfilled as the last religious duty, at one and the same time set the seal on accumulated wealth and gave enhanced prestige in village society to the returned *ḥājjī*, who in general became revivified exemplars and propagators of the faith. In addition to thus strengthening the *santri* element in rural religious life, the Pilgrimage, by its very nature involving travel and detachment from the *desa* (village), helped to link urban (or port town) and rural Islam in a shared complex of social and economic attitudes which were to be of great importance in mediating further social change.

Though the increase in the Pilgrimage was by far the most significant element in the furtherance of large-scale movement between Middle Eastern Islam and South-East Asia (and will be discussed in greater detail shortly), it was not the only one. In the course of the mid-century, migrant Arabs also came to play a larger part than in the past in Indonesian religious life. Itinerant Arabs, mainly traders but including some divines, had of course been a feature of the port societies of the Archipelago for centuries, and some had formed settled communities. In more recent times, individuals were often found in advisory religious capacities at the courts of local rulers, and in some cases, usually by marriage, had acquired actual political power. During the Java and *Padri* Wars Arabs had been used as armistice negotiators by both sides, but principally by the traditional *élite* and the colonial power, in whose service they tended to be. In the mid-century, however, and especially after 1870, what had been a relatively casual movement turned into a steadily increasing flow, in response to new economic opportunities on the periphery of colonial rule. Between 1859 and 1885, when the first important study of the community was undertaken, numbers rose from perhaps 7,000 in the Dutch possessions to more than 20,000, with another 1,500 in the Straits Settlements. Though interpretation of these figures (which, apart from other confusions, include non-immigrant women, children, and part-Arabs) presents some problems, it is clear that a major movement was under way. By far the greater proportion of the Arabs in the region came from the Ḥaḍramawt, with which regular communication was maintained by all able to afford it. Though there was among them an important minority of *sayyids* and shaykhs belonging to ancient Ḥaḍramī traditions of learning, most were common folk from the towns with a primary interest in small-scale trade. With few exceptions, however, all were earnest and orthoprax adherents of the faith, and this together with the respect paid almost automatically to any Arab, kinsman of the Prophet or not, gave them considerable authority in the eyes of their co-religionists. Dutch restrictions upon Arab movement outside the urban areas (for fear of their presumed deleterious economic influence and probable agitatory effect) were not entirely successful, but, together with a propensity for urban living and trading, probably did limit their impact on rural society. In the growing towns, however, the nodal points for much that was new in South-East Asian Islam, they became and remained an influential section of the community, active agents for an austere if often rather conservative version of the faith.

Where contact with the Middle East was concerned however, and indeed in most other terms, the real shaping influence on the Islam of the late nineteenth century came from the Pilgrimage to Mecca. Dutch mistrust of, and hostility towards, the *Ḥajj*, based on the belief (by no means always erroneous) that returned pilgrims were the chief troublemakers in rural village society, has already been referred to. Until late in the century, however, this fear was founded almost solely on the observable fact that leadership for village unrest was frequently exercised by the 'native priests', the independent '*ulamā*' (many of whom, of course, had made the Pilgrimage), and not on any understanding of the nature of the Pilgrimage, the sort of religious and social experience it constituted for participants, or the ideas with which they might be imbued. In short, the official attitude towards the Pilgrimage was determined by the almost complete ignorance with which the Dutch approached Islam in general. As a result, regulations passed in the early part of the century went as far in hindering the Pilgrimage as was possible without adopting the recognizably more dangerous alternative (if indeed this had been practicable) of suppressing it altogether. Thus by resolutions of 1825 and 1831 it was made obligatory in Java and Madura for intending pilgrims to obtain at enormous expense a special passport, failure to do so being visited by an even larger fine. At the same time, Dutch and higher Javanese officials were instructed to discourage passport applications, in the interests of reducing the dangerously idle and discontented class which returned pilgrims were believed to form. Nevertheless, numbers continued to rise; at least in part in consequence of the ready evasion of the regulations made possible by taking passage from Sumatra or Singapore. It was perhaps recognition of this evasion that led to the removal of the more draconian provisions in 1852, when the passport tax (though not the passport) was abolished, a step accompanied by fresh attempts to exercise surveillance over those making the Pilgrimage, and over their behaviour on return.

In 1859, after a brief period of liberalization, a further set of regulations was introduced in the Dutch territories, and remained in force till beyond the end of the century. The reasons for the change in policy at this time are not clear, but seem to have been related to anxiety over the manner in which the prestigious symbols of Pilgrimage-fulfilment (especially the title *ḥājjī* and the Arab-style dress assumed with it) were being used or abused, and presumably concern about the economics of the Pilgrimage for those remaining behind as well as those travelling. Under the new system the intending pilgrim had to prove that he possessed sufficient means both to complete the journey and to maintain his dependants in his absence, and on his return he had to undergo a special examination designed to show whether or not he had in fact been to Mecca. In passing it may be noted that the British in the peninsula were much less nervous, and consequently less restrictive, concerning the Pilgrimage, levying only a nominal fee for documents of identity provided to residents of their own directly controlled territories (until 1895, when even this charge was abolished), and imposing no hindrance at all on transit passengers from outside the 'protected states' and the Straits Settlements. One important consequence of this was the rapid growth of Singapore in the mid-century as the focal point of the Pilgrimage for the region as a whole.

During the 1850s, some 2,000 pilgrims were counted annually as leaving the Dutch possessions for Mecca, together with a smaller but unknown number from the Malay peninsula. After the opening of the Suez Canal in 1869, and the consequent increase and improvement in steamship services through the Red Sea area, the number grew steadily each year, until by the late 1890s the figure was fluctuating from more than 11,000 in 1895 (a 'Great Pilgrimage' year) to 7,000 in 1900, together with many hundreds more from the Malay peninsula, Acheh and elsewhere, comprising in all about twenty per cent of the total number of pilgrims from overseas. The great majority of pilgrims spent no longer out of South-East Asia than it took to make the voyage to the Ḥijāz, spend a month or so in and around the Holy Places at the time of the Pilgrimage, purchase a little religious literature, some Zamzam water, and a few locally-manufactured souvenirs, and take ship back again. Only a handful stayed on to study under a teacher, enter fully into the *ṭarīqas*, and become conversant with politically anti-colonial, pan-Islamic ideas. The distinction was important and hitherto unrecognized, if fairly obvious, as Snouck Hurgronje went to some pains to point out after 1889, and certainly fundamental to a proper appreciation of the influences exerted by Mecca. Nevertheless, the effect of even brief exposure to a wholly Muslim environment, in which all authority was subject to the law of God, and in which the universality of the faith was demonstrated by a congregation of pilgrims of all races, all levels of society, visibly joined in a levelling, if also exalting, religious experience, was by no means negligible. Even sojourners could hardly fail to be impressed by talk of the greatness of the Islamic peoples, or escape sharing in the common knowledge of the manner in which so much of Islam had become politically subordinate to the West and to Christendom. Returning to the Indies, to the towns and villages, the mosques and religious schools, they took with them not only a renewed zeal for purification of action and belief (and for the correction of their fellows), but a certain readiness to reject the colonial *status quo* if the occasion should present itself.

The effect on their own society of the *muqīm*, the permanent or semi-permanent residents from the Malay peninsula or the Archipelago, known collectively in Mecca as the *Jāwa*, was, however, certainly more profound and penetrating. Snouck Hurgronje remarked of the colony that it 'represents in essence the future of the peoples out of whom it is composed and increased', and his own detailed portayal of the community in the mid-1880s gives an invaluable account of the process at work. The core of the *Jāwa* was formed by the great teachers, of whom several commanded scholarly respect among the Meccans themselves. As instructors of their fellow-countrymen, as writers of formative and sometimes controversial religious works published in Arabic and Malay, which found their way in great quantity to the Indies, they fed a constant stream of revivified Islamic thought into the homeland. Lesser figures played a similar if less distinguished role, and themselves frequently moved back and forth between the Archipelago and the Ḥijāz, lecturing in the mosques, selling books and rosaries, gathering pilgrims, and in general inspiring their fellow Muslims.

Nowhere, perhaps, was the influence of the *Jāwa* more marked than in connection with the Ṣūfī *ṭarīqas* which flourished in Mecca. Countless hundreds of pilgrims and temporary settlers were inducted over the years into the Naqshbandiyya, Qādiriyya, and other orders, and on return home became active participants in *ṭarīqa* activity, and in some cases organizers of branches. In two areas in particular, though doubtless elsewhere as well, the consequences of this were considerable. In Minangkabau, 'orthodox' Naqshbandī influence originating with *Jāwa* shaykhs from the area, was responsible for reactivating *adat*-Islam conflicts within the society, by attacking the entrenched and somewhat decadent Shaṭṭāriyya *ṭarīqa*, closely associated with the *adat* religious officials and with old-style practices generally. Though the conflict acquired towards the end of the century other and modernist overtones, these also sprang from Meccan influence, by way of, amongst others, Shaykh Aḥmad Khaṭīb, who became the teacher of a whole generation of Minangkabau and Malayan reformers. In Banten, in West Java, the *ṭarīqas* (mainly Qādiriyya, and stemming largely from the great Bornean shaykh of the order, Khaṭīb Sambas, and his pupils) became the organizational framework for the revolutionary protest movement against the Dutch which resulted in the so-called Tjilegon risings of 1888. Though it may be argued that differences among the *ṭarīqas* helped to divide the community against itself quite as much as direct it against colonial rule, there can be no question that the appeal they exercised was a powerful force in raising and channelling popular feeling, especially in the rural areas.

So far in this account the Malay peninsula has received little more than incidental attention, as is perhaps appropriate to the relatively small proportion of the Islamic community it comprised. The increasing importance of Singapore after the mid-century, however, and the effects of British colonial control over the western states from the 1870s (which ratified the political cleavage of the Malay world foreshadowed in the 1824 treaty between the English and the Dutch, and for the first time began seriously to isolate Malayan experience from that of its neighbours) require more detailed discussion. As is well known, the British had established themselves on the periphery of the peninsula at the end of the eighteenth century, when Light occupied Penang, and had further consolidated this position by the acquisition of Singapore in 1819 and the receipt of Malacca from the Dutch a few years later. The three Straits Settlements thus formed were to mark the extent of British territorial control, though not of her political and commercial interest, for the next half-century. During this period, the Muslim states of the peninsula remained largely free from Western interference, though the northernmost (in particular Patani and Kedah) were brought under Siamese control in the early period, and experienced in consequence a largely Muslim-led reaction, the nature of which, however, has not so far been explored by historians.

Unlike the Muslim communities in Java and parts of Sumatra, the Malay states of the peninsula possessed little or nothing in the way of structured Islamic authority. It is true that the sacral powers of the rulers included responsibility for the defence and good governance of the faith, but in the realm of religion as of political organization these sparsely settled riverine states lacked either the resources or the stimulus for centralization of control. Though the theoretical association between the traditional secular *élite* (whether represented by the rulers or by the aristocracy) and the religious life of the people was never seriously questioned, it was seldom seriously tested either. From time to time individual rulers or chiefs did, from pious or other motives, appoint religious officials of a variety of kinds beyond those attached to their own mosques, but there was a marked absence of anything approaching hierarchical organization or systematic control. In these circumstances, religious authority tended to dwell in those members of village society who from piety, some pretence to learning, and perhaps through having made the Pilgrimage, were accepted as fit to exercise it—as *imāms* of mosques and religious teachers, as functionaries at Islamic occasions of one sort or another, and, increasingly in the nineteenth century, as *guru tarekat* (*ṭarīqa* teachers). The rural *'ulamā'* thus described constituted in no important sense a separate social class, and in the absence of anything more than a vestigial religious officialdom, the Malay states were markedly without the tradition of institutionalized opposition between independent *'ulamā'* and religious bureaucrats which formed such a persistent pattern elsewhere.

Though the use of the term 'protectorate' to describe the relationship contracted between the British and the Malay rulers during the forward movement of the 1870s carried in the long run a certain irony where the generality of Malay interests was concerned, it must in fairness be said that the expression was less inapt in relation both to the traditional ruling class (whose authority within Malay society was sustained), and to Islam. The Pangkor Engagement signed by the Perak chiefs in 1874, which became the model for all subsequent instruments of the sort, provided for the appointment to the state of a British resident, whose advice it was to be incumbent upon the ruler to ask for and act upon, in all matters 'other than those touching Malay Religion and Custom'. The bracketing together of religious and customary secular authority in the phrasing of this careful exclusion was not accidental, for to British observers and Malays alike the two were ultimately, at least on earth, inseparable. For the British in particular, they represented, in however ill-defined a way (and it is clear that by 'custom' they understood 'customs', as applied mainly to those ceremonial aspects of Malay life least likely to get in the way of colonial rule) the twin and associated areas in which direct interference was most likely to arouse discontent, and hence unrest. At the same time, the formal surrender to the ruling class of this joint authority seemed to the British, and doubtless to Malay observers as well, no more than testamentary recognition of an ideally as well as an actually existing state of affairs.

The extremely rapid growth of the export economy of the Malay states during the early years of protectorate rule, and the expansion of alien administration which accompanied and fostered this, did little to disrupt the patterns of peasant Malay economic and social life, conducted as most of the developmental activity was by means of Chinese and Indian immigrant labour. In the process, however, the Malay ruling class, its bases of authority within the society confirmed, found itself increasingly deprived of any real say in the running of affairs in general or in the direction of policy, and not unnaturally turned for compensation to the exercise of its sole remaining powers, those relating to religion and custom. British undertakings not to interfere in matters relating to religion were on the whole scrupulously observed, but the bureaucratic and legal apparatus of the colonial administration provided a model for organizational change, and administrators themselves were not averse to encouraging the systematization of Islamic law and practice. The last two decades of the century, therefore, saw the creation, piecemeal and largely at the instance of the traditional Malay *élite*, of a complex religio-legal bureaucracy, appointed by and dependent on the traditional *élite* itself. Restrictive Islamic legislation was enacted in the state councils, courts and legal procedures were established, and hierarchies of *qāḍīs* and other officials were brought into being, staffed for the most part from among the existing rural '*ulamā*'. Few of the measures were wholly innovatory in themselves; what was new was their systematic application, and the centralized organization that lay behind it.

The processes just described constitute the most striking developments in the Islam of the Malay states during the latter part of the century, and the movement they represent towards the growth of a series of doctrinally rather narrowly-based religious establishments, closely associated with the maintenance of the authority of the traditional secular *élite*, was to have considerable implications for the future. At the same time, however, other and perhaps less readily apparent changes were beginning to take place within the peninsular community, in response to those stimuli at work elsewhere in the region. In Malaya, as in the Archipelago at large, the Pilgrimage, with its feed-back of unpredictable energy, increased markedly in the last decades of the century, and the *ṭarīqas* (especially the Naqshbandiyya and Qādiriyya) made great advances in village society. As in other areas, some of the most obvious effects of ideas emanating from the Middle East (sometimes mediated by way of Acheh or Java) related to resistance to the advance of alien and infidel rule. It may be remarked that when, in 1875, the first British resident of Perak had been assassinated in the course of an attempt by a group of traditional chiefs to reject British control, Islam seems to have played no part whatsoever in the affair itself, or in the response to the subsequent punitive expedition. Less than twenty years later the disturbances which accompanied the extension of British rule to Pahang took much of their popular force from a rumoured document, said to have been signed by both the ruler and the principal rebel, appealing to the 'Sultan of Turkey' to help to throw the British out of southern and western Malaya, and also from religious appeals made by a famous Trengganu teacher and mystic, Ungku Sayyid Paloh, when the rebels sought refuge across the border in that state.

No influence on the peninsula was more important in the long run than that emanating from the remarkably heterogeneous Muslim community of the Straits Settlements, and especially from Singapore, which acted as the extremely dynamic metropolis for the region as a whole. As a result of a combination of circumstances—principally its strategic position on the sea-routes of South-East Asia and consequent focal role in the trade of both the British and the Dutch commercial empires, but also its labour-exchange functions for Java, Sumatra, and the peninsular and Borneo states, its lack of restriction on the movements of individuals and ideas, and its liberal (indeed commercial) attitude to the Pilgrimage—Singapore brought together a cross-section of the Muslim peoples of South-East and South Asia and the Middle East. Its reputation as a centre of Islamic life and learning rested primarily on its position in relation to the Pilgrimage and Arab migration, but was greatly contributed to by its role as a publication and distribution centre for religious writings and a gathering place for teachers. Students from all over the Archipelago wishing to further their studies in law or doctrine came, if not to Mecca, to Singapore, where they could meet and sit at the feet of itinerant scholars from the Ḥaḍramawt and the Ḥijāz, from Patani, Acheh, Palembang and Java—most of whom had themselves studied in Mecca. The city thus stood at the heart of that network of communications which, as we have seen, fed a constant stream of revitalized and revolutionary thought into the peninsula and Archipelago. It was the archetype of urban, mercantile society, piety and economic enterprise going hand in hand, which had for long—indeed, since the beginning—been important to Indonesian-Malaysian Islam. Markedly different in its way of life and thought from either its peasant or its aristocratic neighbours, by virtue of its insistence on fundamental Islamic values uncontaminated by excesses of innovation or impurities of customary belief, it offered an implied criticism of the syncretism which otherwise informed so much of its surroundings.

Not least in importance among the functions performed by Singapore in the late nineteenth century was that of providing a base for a variety of political activities associated with attempts to stave off the advance of European hegemony in the area. It was a place of frequent recourse for rulers and chiefs from the peninsula, seeking legal assistance, borrowing money, raising a following, or escaping from factional feuds, during the extension of British control over the western states and Pahang. As early as the mid-1860s the Dutch complained that there were too many malcontents and adventurers in the settlement, plotting against Netherlands interests in the Archipelago (especially in Sumatra), and organizing appeals to outside powers. Worse was to come, for after the onset in 1873 of the final large-scale and protracted conflict of the century, the Dutch subjugation of Acheh, Singapore (together with Penang) became the centre of opposition-in-exile for nearly thirty years.

The once great sultanate of Acheh, traditionally the most vigorously Islamic of Indonesian powers, had for much of the nineteenth century been in a state of suspended political decline, beset from within by periodic feuds surrounding the throne, and caught up in the commercial struggle being waged by the Western powers for control over the pepper trade of northern Sumatra. Under the political and administrative system which had obtained since at least the end of the seventeenth century, the sultanate itself, based on the port-capital of Kota Raja at the mouth of the Acheh river together with a small area of land surrounding this, did not represent any great concentration of power. Dependent almost for its existence upon the three largely autonomous confederacies of *hulubalang* (hereditary chiefs) which shared with it territorial control over Acheh proper (the northern coastal plain and the valley of the Acheh river, striking back up into the highlands), the sultanate derived what separate authority it had largely from residual tributary rights exercised over coastal dependencies on the eastern and western sides of the island. Within the confederacies, known in Acheh as the three *sagi*, or 'angles', of the state, there existed social and political structures resembling those already encountered in other parts of the Archipelago, with customary secular and religious authority concentrated in the hands of the *hulubalang* and their religious officials, and a countervailing power potentially of great strength present among the independent *'ulamā'*, in most of Acheh distinguished by the honorific *teungku*. Several of the more forceful and prestigious of the latter were either Arabs or, more specifically, of Ḥaḍramī *sayyid* descent, and in general the *'ulamā'*, highly receptive to the currents of the time, constituted a force to be reckoned with, as both the Dutch and the traditional chiefs were in due course to discover.

Under an arrangement made immediately subsequent to the 1824

Treaty of London (by which Britain and Holland staked out their respective areas of influence in the Straits) the Dutch had undertaken to secure the safety of trade with Acheh, while guaranteeing the continued independence of the state. This arrangement became in the course of time extremely irksome to the Dutch, as they were brought increasingly into conflict with Acheh by their own territorial expansion up the west and especially the east coasts, and as standards of international conduct deteriorated with the scramble for profits which took place around the riverine states in the northern part of the island. Matters were not helped when Acheh, after renewing in 1850 its ancient relations with the Ottoman empire, sought aid from the Sublime Porte (and other powers) in the 1860s, against Dutch interference in its affairs. Finally, in 1871, a fresh Anglo-Dutch treaty was concluded which gave the Netherlands a free hand in dealing with this unruly and recalcitrant state. Attempts at a negotiated settlement of points at issue having failed, the Dutch launched an armed invasion of Kota Raja in April 1873, and the Acheh War began.

From an early stage, Achehnese resistance to Dutch aggression assumed the character of a *jihād*, the prosecution of which came more and more to rest in the hands of those best fitted to organize and lead a Holy War, the independent *'ulama'*—who were, it may be observed, strengthened thereby in their own institutional conflict with the traditional chiefs, increasing in turn the strength of the appeals made by Islam. It is not of moment here to discuss the complex stages through which this long, tedious and often brutal conflict passed, but it is worth looking in a little more detail at the part played during the first few years of the war by specifically political pan-Islamic ideas. The unsuccessful appeal made in 1868 to Constantinople, which had been organized by a remarkable and dominant figure in Achenese politics during these years, the Ḥaḍramī Sayyid Ḥabīb 'Abd al-Raḥmān al-Ẓāhir, was followed by renewed attempts in 1873 to gain active support from the same quarter. Though these too failed, the belief that help would be forthcoming from the Ottomans gained ground in Acheh itself, in the Straits Settlements and throughout the Archipelago. Emissaries were sent from Singapore to Java and elsewhere to organize support for the Holy War, and rumours abounded that a general rising was imminent. Though in later years these hopes subsided, as a result of non-fulfilment, they played an important part in sustaining Achehnese resistance, and unrest elsewhere (in Banten, for instance), and millenarian expectations that a union of the Islamic peoples would shortly arise and defeat the West continued to manifest themselves at intervals in response to such events as the Russo-Turkish War of 1877–8, the Mahdist rising in the Sudan, and the passage through Singapore in 1890 of a Turkish warship on a courtesy visit to Japan.

Dutch fears of pan-Islam, which had in any case been gaining ground, were greatly stimulated by affairs in Acheh, where the course of the struggle continued to go against them until late in the century despite various attempts at holding actions and pacification, and long pauses in the fighting. Acheh was, of course, in one sense, merely the most recent (if also the most bitter) in a long series of colonial conflicts, in which the driving force of resistance had been supplied by Islam, and which together indicated to the Netherlands government a serious failure to elaborate a satisfactory Islamic policy, capable of assuring the peaceful continuance of Dutch rule. As the end of the century approached, the need to remedy this situation became increasingly imperative, partly as a means of ending the disturbance in Acheh, and partly to permit the diversion of Dutch energies to other social and economic tasks in what was now, effectively, the Netherlands Indies. It was in these circumstances, then, that a decision was made to appoint an Islamist to the newly created post of adviser on Arabian and Native Affairs.

C. Snouck Hurgronje (1857–1936) came to this office in 1889 possessed of a unique familiarity with certain aspects of Indonesian Islam, derived during a six-month stay in disguise (a pretence never really forgiven him by many Muslims) with the *Jāwa* community of Mecca a few years earlier. Despite a certain Christian superciliousness towards Islam, and an often disparaging attitude towards the Achehnese in particular, as displayed in his otherwise brilliant study of Achehnese life—both of which failings may, however, have been of the time as much as of the man—Snouck was a sensitive and highly intelligent observer of Indonesian society, equipped with insights into the religious life of the community which were far in advance of any owned by his contemporaries. In addition, he was a good nineteenth-century liberal, and an advocate not only of tolerance towards other systems of belief, but of a more positive and generous vision of a peaceful associative relationship between the Dutch and Indonesian peoples in the future.

Snouck's Islamic policy, as it came to be developed during the last decade of the century, was based on the replacement of the blindly restrictive and at times punitive measures of the past by a more discriminating analysis of the manner in which Islam worked in Indonesian society, and of the means necessary to control it. Arguing that in the absence of a professional religious hierarchy in Islam it was no more legitimate to see 'priests' in the '*ulamā*' than to find a 'pope' in Constantinople, he advocated that, though a proper and strict surveillance should be kept over ideological appeals to pan-Islam, it was not necessary to suppose all pious and enthusiatic Muslims, far less all returned pilgrims, to be sworn enemies of Dutch rule and unamenable to reason. He proposed, therefore, the removal of irritating restrictions upon the Pilgrimage together with increased but intelligent vigilance over and prohibitions upon any form of political activity directly connected with it. A policy of sympathetic religious neutrality would, it was believed, come to reassure Indonesian Muslims that they had nothing to fear from the colonial government, provided they forswore political propaganda, while at the same time it improved Holland's reputation in the Muslim world at large. Combined with these measures, Snouck proposed a more purposive return to the policy which had, indeed, been pursued by the Dutch at intervals since the days of the East India Company, the support of those elements in Indonesian society least zealously Islamic, the traditional *adat*-chiefs and the *priyayi élite*.

Even before the end of the decade, the last of these stratagems, combined with a newly organized military offensive against the independent '*ulamā*', was bringing the war in Acheh nearer its inevitable if long-delayed close, and though in general the effects of Snouck Hurgronje's policies were to be felt in the new century not in the old, another era had begun. The nineteenth century, with its dual set of conflicts for Islam—one within, between the forces of renewal and the traditional order; and one without, against the relentless political encroachment of the West—was over. In the process much had changed, often with violence, but other battles remained to be fought—in a sense had barely been joined.

CHAPTER 3

SOUTH-EAST ASIAN ISLAM IN THE TWENTIETH CENTURY

The nineteenth century had witnessed repeated and powerful commotion among the major Muslim communities in island South East Asia, especially in the Netherlands possessions. At considerable human and financial cost, the Dutch succeeded in defeating Muslim rebelliousness in the field. Pacification was followed by the implementation, at the end of the century, of a circumspect Islamic policy. Though Wahhābi-inspired Muslim 'puritanism' was to leave lasting marks in many parts of Indonesia—most notably, perhaps, in the gradual gains of orthodoxy at the expense of the mystical *ṭarīqas*—Islamic militancy in Indonesia had to all intents and purposes given way to relative stability and tranquillity in the opening years of the new century. But this tranquillity was short-lived and soon gave way to a virtual religious, social and political renaissance embracing many parts of the area. The impetus for this Islamic renaissance came, as so often before, from abroad; what lent it viability and a measure of cohesion were social changes resulting from accelerated modernization under colonial rule.

The sources as well as the development of South-East Asia's Islamic renaissance were varied. For one thing, the Pilgrimage continued to attract increasing numbers of South-East Asians. Thus in 1911, Dutch statistics recorded over 24,000 Indonesians, comprising almost thirty per cent of all overseas pilgrims in the Holy City. Ibn Su'ūd's conquest of Mecca in 1924 and the subsequent *Pax Wahhabica*—coinciding with temporary prosperity in the Indies—led to a dramatic augmentation in the number of pilgrims, culminating in over 52,000 Indonesians (over forty per cent of the overseas total) in 1926–7. During the same year over 12,000 pilgrims left Malaysia for the Holy City. These quantitative increments were obviously not the most significant aspect of Wahhābī rule. Heightened orthodoxy in Mecca could not but affect, more or less profoundly, the *Jāwa* colony in Mecca, the reservoir of Indonesian (and Malayan) Muslims who remained in the city for years, and whose returning members so often played an important role in South-East Asian Muslim affairs.

Of more far-reaching importance to the Islamic renaissance was

Muslim reformism and modernism, emanating from Shaykh Muḥammad 'Abduh in Egypt at the close of the nineteenth century. Reformism did not merely reinforce the trend toward greater Muslim self-awareness and orthodox militancy engendered by Wahhābī thought. It supplemented the negative onslaught on South-East Asian syncretism and Sufism by a positive appeal to adjust Islam to the requirements of the modern world, and in so doing it infused in the Islamic communities a new vitality and momentum, a clear orientation and a programme for action. Thus, side by side with pilgrims returning after years of study with Meccan shaykhs, Islam had found new and dynamic spokesmen from among Indonesian and Malayan youths returning from Cairo; by the mid-1920s, al-Azhar may have counted between two and three hundred students from the two countries, about two-thirds of them Indonesians. In addition to the traditional Middle Eastern religious literature, South-East Asian Muslims increasingly became acquainted with, and were influenced by, 'Abduh's writings, by *al-Manār* and a host of other periodicals and newspapers carrying the message of modernism.

Yet a third foreign influence, that of Indian reformism, came to exert a less spectacular, though intellectually perhaps not negligible, influence. The writings of Amīr 'Alī and Mawlānā Muḥammad 'Alī, if not those of Muḥammad Iqbāl, though rarely explicitly acknowledged as spiritual sources by Indonesian or Malay reformists, did not go unnoticed. Again, though the missionary enterprises of the Indian Aḥmadiyya movement—especially of its Lahore branch, brought to Java by Mīrzā Walī Beg in 1924—were, numerically speaking, far from successful, the Aḥmadiyya translation of the Qur'ān acted as a source of inspiration and even imitation to some outstanding Indonesian Muslims.

I

Both in origin and orientation, twentieth-century Islamic activities bore an intrinsically pan-Malaysian character largely transcending the political boundaries separating British from Dutch colonial possessions. Subjects of both powers freely intermingled in Mecca, in Cairo, and not least in the Straits Settlements. These contacts had some political significance in creating pan-Malaysian sentiments from the 1930s onward. But these common factors must not obscure the very real differences between Islamic developments in British Malaya and the Dutch East Indies. In part these differences were determined by divergences in social and political patterns and historical developments, in part also by the kind and degree of colonial rule. The Dutch colonial empire in the Indies comprised a far wider variety of peoples and cultures than did British Malaya. Again, Dutch rule in many parts of Indonesia antedated the British in Malaya by several decades, and in the case of Java by centuries. Western economic and administrative interference had thus been far more prolonged and thorough in the Dutch than the British colonial realm, with far-reaching consequences for Indonesian, and especially also Islamic, developments. Of at least equal importance, finally, were colonial policies regarding Islam, that of the Netherlands being elaborated and executed with a paternalistic sophistication altogether unparalleled in British Malaya.

In the opening years of the twentieth century, it was the small but important Muslim communities in the Straits Settlements, in Singapore at first, Penang later, that formed the intellectual nerve-centres of the Islamic renaissance; a role dictated by their rather unusual cosmopolitan composition, relative wealth and dynamism, by their location athwart the Pilgrimage route, and not least, by the freedom they enjoyed under direct British rule. At the opening of the century, Straits Muslims included some 1,500 Ḥaḍramawt Arabs, including several outstanding shaykhs and *sayyids*; though for the greater part locally born, they constituted a distinct, Arab-oriented minority of considerable affluence and prestige. Another economically influential group were the so-called *Jawi Peranakan,* Indo-Malays descended from Indian (largely Malabari) Muslims, who had pioneered Malay journalism in the mid-nineteenth century. To these groups must be added the constant flow of peninsular Malays, as well as the many Indonesians—primarily Sumatrans, but later on also Javanese—who made the Straits Settlements their temporary or permanent abode.

The most notable influence exerted by these pious mercantile communities in constant touch with the centres of Islamic life in the Middle East and with most parts of the Archipelago lay in the field of writing, especially in journalism. The first newspaper to carry the message of reformism to the Malayo-Indonesian world was *al-Imām*, founded in 1907, and closely modelled on Cairo's *al-Manār*. Its founder, Shaykh Muḥammad Ṭāhir b. Jalāl al-Dīn al-Azharī (1869–1957), a student of 'Abduh's and one of the most respected and influential reformers, was a Minangkabau. In fact, few peninsular Malays served on the paper's editorial and managerial staff, which reflected the ethnic variety—and the strong Indonesian component—among the Straits Muslim activists. They also pioneered in one other important field, that of education, by establishing, in 1908, an Egyptian-staffed *madrasa* in the city. It was soon followed by hundreds of such new schools throughout the Archipelago.

The outstanding role of Singapore and Penang, then, was that of cultural brokers, translating the new purity, rationalism, and vitality of Islam into the Malay language—the Archipelago's *lingua franca*—and also into terms relevant to a local, Malayo-Indonesian frame of reference. Great as this contribution was, the Straits Settlements provided too narrow a base for organizational experiment on a significant scale. Their vigorous and cosmopolitan Muslim groups were exceptional: small groups living in the shadow of thriving Western and Chinese mercantile communities that could afford to ignore Islamic activism, not being in the least challenged by it. But it was otherwise when this activism started, almost immediately, to radiate to the various parts of insular South-East Asia. Even though reformist spokesmen originally limited themselves to religious reform as such—especially to the purification of worship and ritual and the modernization of religious education—their teachings were bound to engender far-reaching social and political repercussions. These found expression in the fact that the appellations *Kaum Muda* ('The Young Group') and *Kaum Tua* ('The Old Group'), originally specifically used to designate Muslim religious reformers and their traditionally inclined religious opponents, before long came to stand for innovators and conservatives in a far wider sense.

On the religious plane, reformism's broad attack on traditional South-East Asian Islam posed a threat to old-fashioned *'ulamā'* and their practices. On the social plane, its target was—though selectively and thus by no means always consistently—customary social and legal usages as embodied in the *adat*, and hence also the upholders of the traditional order. Cautiously at first, but here and there with increasing vehemence, reformers finally and inevitably also came to criticize and challenge the political, colonial order. It was seen as the preserver of traditional indigenous, social systems, but also as the creator of plural societies in which foreigners, Western as well as Asian, had come to wield predominant commercial and economic power. No less invidious in Muslim eyes was the subtle penetration of Western values, carried into South-East Asia both by Christian missionaries and secular educators under the European overlords. Finally, intensified Muslim sentiment could not but look askance at *kāfir* overlordship.

In spite of the geographic proximity of the Straits Settlements, reformism was organizationally least successful in Malaya. Its failure to score noticeable successes in the Malay states was primarily due to the relatively slow pace of social change among the peninsular Muslim communities. Though economic modernization under the British aegis had been swift and impressive, its major impact fell on mostly non-Muslim immigrant groups, especially Chinese, rather than on the autochthonous, still predominantly rural Malays. Malay society therefore did not as yet provide adequate anchorages for innovation and reform. But the spread of reformism was also seriously inhibited by British colonial policy, the same policy which paradoxically did so little to inhibit Muslim activities in the Malayan areas under direct British rule. British policy towards Islam displays fairly consistent non-interference, implicitly as a matter of course in the Straits Settlements, and as a matter of explicit stipulation in the treaties concluded with Malay rulers. The pattern was established in the first such treaty, the Pangkor Engagement concluded with (in fact, forced upon) the sultanate of Perak (January, 1874); it stipulated that the only matters specifically to be withheld from the powers of the British resident were to be 'those touching Malay Religion and Custom'. When the Federated Malay States (Perak, Pahang, Selangor, and Negri Sembilan) were founded in 1895, reference to Malay customs was deleted from the terms of the formal agreement, but the 'Muhammadan religion' remained specifically outside the purview of the protecting power. Under the protective umbrella of an allegedly indirect rule the Malay sultans, endowed with unprecedented political stature and authority, embarked on institutional innovation by creating well-organized and salaried hierarchies of Muslim officials in charge of religious administration and law. The process was in similar fashion repeated in the Unfederated States (Johore, Kedah, Trengganu, Kelantan, and Perlis), where the rulers' authority was in any case far less fettered by British 'advisers'.

While the religious hierarchies and a good many of the regulatory and supervisory tasks entrusted to them were new, their personnel was almost exclusively recruited from among the vestigial, unorganized and poorly equipped religious dignitaries of earlier days, augmented by rural '*ulamā*'. The new establishments thus came to be staffed by proponents of traditional, syncretic, heterodox and often Ṣūfī-tinged Islam, solidly entrenched in positions of authority by their secular superiors. It was this combination of Muslim traditionalism with Malay secular power that placed such obstacles in the way of Islamic reformism in the peninsula. Moreover Malaya, unlike Java and Sumatra, was barely encumbered by a tradition of *'ulamā'* opposition to secular authorities, let alone by the legacy of Wahhābī radicalism that had elsewhere led to the sharpening of such opposition in the nineteenth century. The *Kaum Muda*, agitating from their sanctuaries in directly ruled territories, thus appeared as radical innovators threatening both the religious and the secular *status quo*. If individual reformers of stature, such as Ṭāhir, occasionally gained favour as advisers and companions to a Malay ruler, the posts of religious officialdom, such as *muftī* (*shaykh al-Islām*) or *kathi* (*qāḍī*), or membership in the newly created Councils of Religious and Malay Custom, almost without exception remained beyond their reach. By the same token, the *Kaum Tua*, from their positions of authority, not infrequently banned reformist literature and newspapers from the Malay states.

Thus, though reformism was by no means without its lasting effects on Malayan Islam (e.g., the adoption of the *madrasa*, the modern Islamic school, though more often as an institutional rather than an intrinsic innovation) it was prevented from growing into an organizational force led by a peninsular *élite*. These inhibitions also precluded the development of the stunted Islamic renaissance into a more clearly political, proto-nationalist movement as in other parts of the Malayo-Indonesian world. This relative tardiness of religious and political modernization to a large extent reflected the slow rate of social change in a still predominantly rural society.

Since the divergent course of the Islamic renaissance in colonial Indonesia was so closely affected by Dutch policies, they must be briefly dealt with. The architect of Netherlands Islamic policy in the Indies, Christiaan Snouck Hurgronje (1857–1936), left his stamp on Dutch dealings with Islamic problems for over half-a-century. His Islamic policy postulated toleration of the Muslim faith, combined with repressive vigilance towards Islamic, especially pan-Islamic, political activities. This divorce of religion and politics, however problematical in theory and later often also in practice, did at the outset reconcile the vast bulk of Indonesian believers, and indeed even a substantial number of *'ulamā'*, to the foreign overlord. Snouck Hurgronje's principles had been laid down before the onset of the Islamic renaissance in Indonesia; Snouck himself actually left his post in 1906, never to return to the islands. His successors, and Dutch administrators in general, continued to adhere to his principles after the appearance of reformism, not even abandoning them as major guidelines when the rapid growth of Muslim activism increasingly threatened to blur the thin and artificial dividing line between the religiously tolerable and the politically intolerable. Confronted by new Islamic challenges, Dutch practice at times perforce came to deviate quite markedly from non-interference. But the impressive gains which reformism was to score in twentieth-century Indonesia are undeniably in no small measure traceable to a *Pax Neerlandica* that kept the door ajar—even if neither always nor consistently wide open—to religious innovators.

The contrast between British Malaya and the Netherlands Indies stems, then, in part at least from differences in colonial policies and practices. We have seen that British non-interference in matters religious, while allowing free play to the vigorous, but politically insignificant, Muslim minorities in the Straits Settlements, had at the same time encouraged alliances of secular and religious traditionalists able to stem the tide of reformism in the Malay states. Dutch non-interference, by contrast, introduced the European-derived principle of religious toleration into the Indies and superimposed it, so to speak, upon the Indonesian *cuius regio eius religio*. This was of especial significance in the areas under direct Dutch control, most notably in Java. The difference between the two colonial realms is the more striking since resistance to the *Kaum Muda* was not necessarily weaker in many parts of Indonesia than in the Malay peninsula, and since, moreover, Dutch colonial policy in general tended to favour and support the social, political, and legal *status quo*. Yet social evolution, incomparably more far-reaching here than in the Malay states, combined with direct rule, had in the course of time eroded the authority and the independence of the erstwhile bearers of political power in Java to a point where in the twentieth century they lacked the ability to build a viable alliance between religious and secular conservatives. In the areas outside Java under indirect colonial rule, Indonesian chiefs and Muslim *Kaum Tua* often enough attempted to forge such alliances; but the Dutch guardians of religious freedom, at times unwittingly if not unwillingly, inhibited the consummation of their 'Counter-Reformation'.

In the early years of the twentieth century, reformism rapidly spread to most parts of the Archipelago. Intellectually, especially in the realm of journalism and literature, the Straits Muslim community served as a model that found ready Indonesian imitators. The first modernist journal, *al-Munīr*, was established in early 1911 on the west coast of Sumatra by Ḥājjī 'Abd Allāh Aḥmad (Haji Abdullah Ahmad 1878–1933) and Ḥājjī 'Abd al-Karīm 'Amr Allāh (Haji Abdul Karim Amrullah 1879–1945), who became one of the most impressive and influential representatives of Indonesian reformism. During its five years of life, *al-Munīr* in turn served as a model for the burgeoning Islamic press, particularly in Java, which almost from the outset developed into Indonesia's centre of the new Islamic activities. It was there that reformism was given organizational forms which spread out to the other islands, unhampered by the barriers which it encountered on the Malay peninsula. But since Java, the most populous and most modernized island, also acted as a magnet which attracted large numbers of Indonesians from other parts of the Archipelago, reformism was not exclusively led by Javanese Muslims, but before long by an all-Indonesian core of leaders. Even then, Indonesia's Islamic renaissance proper was by no means uniform. To survive, it had to find local leaders able to adapt, modify and domesticate—and also to defend—it in each particular social setting.

In fact, Islam in Java was in at least two major respects unique: it had been profoundly affected by Indian religious, cultural and social influences; and it had similarly experienced the longest and deepest impact of Western economic penetration and colonial rule. Indian influences had caused the process of islamization to be retarded and partly deflected. A specifically Hindu-Javanese culture thus survived, epitomized by an at best nominally Muslim nobility and aristocracy—the *priyayi*—at one end of the social spectrum. and by a highly syncretic, and in many parts likewise nominally Islamic, folk religion at the other. It was only on the periphery of indianization—on the north coast and in the westernmost part of the island—that Islam had struck deep roots before the twentieth century. Dutch influences, for their part, had considerably weakened the political authority of Javanese rulers and of the *priyayi* aristocracy, many members of the latter having become salaried civil servants of the colonial régime. Increasingly intensive administrative and economic penetration into the countryside, commencing in the late eighteenth century, had made progressive inroads into the social fabric of the peasantry. In the twentieth century, a whole host of Dutch-inspired innovations—most notably in the field of welfare and education—made their appearance under the so-called Ethical Policy, inaugurated by the Netherlands in 1901. These manifold changes, accompanied by a very rapid increase in population, created an increasingly volatile social setting. If the partial monetization of the native economy and increasing governmental interference in village life led to considerable rural *malaise*, new economic as well as educational opportunities brought into existence *élite* groups. Given the indianized matrix of Javanese traditional society, the Western nature of social and educational innovation, and finally the manifold repercussions from the political and intellectual stirrings elsewhere in Asia, the Islamic renaissance was bound to be only one, albeit an important, facet of Java's response to a rapidly changing situation. Often Islamic and non-Islamic developments tended to interact and overlap, since Islamic innovation from the very beginning touched not only the religious and social, but also the political, spheres.

These complexities are well exemplified by the two major organizations born in the princely states of Central Java in the year 1912, *Muhammadiyah* and *Sarekat Islam* ('Islamic League'). Though they had been preceded by earlier and smaller Islamic associations, the modern era may be said to commence with these two. Unlike other religious groups of modernist tendencies, both in the course of time developed into island-wide, and ultimately nation-wide, movements involving hundreds of thousands of Indonesians.

Muhammadiyah was founded by Kiyayi Ḥājjī Aḥmad Dachlan (1869–1923), a pious businessman from the *kauman* (the predominantly Muslim urban quarters adjacent to the principal mosque) of Jogjakarta, who had twice made the Pilgrimage and studied with renowned shaykhs in the Holy City. *Muhammadiyah* shunned organized political activities, concentrating on a bold programme of religious innovation directed towards the purification of Javanese Islam, the reformulation of Islamic doctrine in the light of modern knowledge, the reform of Muslim education, and the defence of the faith against external influences and attacks. From slow beginnings, *Muhammadiyah* soon grew to a membership of over 4,000 in 1925, to count 852 branches with a total membership of a quarter of a million thirteen years later. From the early 1920s, through intensive missionary work it found acceptance in parts of the Outer Islands. In 1938, well over 800 mosques and smaller houses of worship and—more important still—more than 1,700 schools (including secondary schools and teachers' colleges) testified to *Muhammadiyah*'s pioneering part in modern Indonesian Islam. If 'Abduh's *Tafsīr* and *Risālat al-tawḥīd* provided the guideposts for reformist education, it was Western organizational and institutional models—not least those successfully copied from Christian missions—that turned reformism into a new social force.

Muhammadiyah and its smaller sister organizations relied for their major support on the island's petty bourgeoisie, mostly urban (and including the small but influential group of Indo-Arabs) but also rural. In its formative years, these groups also played a leading role in *Sarekat Islam*, which in fact had originated in the *Sarekat Dagang Islam* ('Islamic Trade League'), founded in Surakarta (Solo) in 1911 by a Muslim merchant, Ḥājjī Samanhudi. The economic impetus behind these organizational activities stemmed from Chinese commercial competition, recently unfettered from restrictive controls by the colonial government. Religious activism was, for its part, spurred by Christian missionary activities, accelerated since 1910. But where *Muhammadiyah* remained firmly rooted in the specifically Muslim culture of the *kauman* and of the pious landowning *ḥājjī*, *Sarekat Islam* before long reached out beyond these geographic and social confines. Within less than a decade, *Sarekat Islam* expanded from its Central Javanese base into a heterogeneous mass-movement, losing in the process its merchant progenitors who, appalled at the increasing radicalization of the movement, sought affiliation with *Muhammadiyah* and similarly non-political, religious groupings.

This startling metamorphosis was accomplished, almost unwittingly it would seem, by a group of younger leaders, none of them reared in the *kauman's* mercantile piety. What distinguished them as a group from the *Muhammadiyah* leadership was greater social and ethnic variety, but above all Western education. Raden 'Umar Sayyid Tjokroaminoto (1882–1934), the movement's charismatic and forensically brilliant leader, was a *priyayi* by birth who, like his less prominent lieutenant, 'Abd al-Mu'izz (Abdul Muis 1878–1959) had been trained for government service. These two Javanese were soon joined by Ḥājjī Agus Salīm (1884–1954), scion of a prominent Minangkabau family, who as a young man had served the colonial government in various capacities and became an ardent convert to modernist Islam while working in the Netherlands consulate at Jedda. But Salīm's was the only specifically Islamic voice in the upper councils of *Sarekat Islam*, whose increasingly vehement agitation bore a decidedly political, even secular, ring. For some time, the movement's leadership was heavily infiltrated by Marxist youths, who in the early 1920s threatened to gain supreme control over it. *Sarekat Islam*, that is to say, attracted an urban audience by no means limited to those in search of religious innovation. Hence its major significance did not lie in its peripheral contribution to the Islamic renaissance in Java, but rather in the organizational experimentation which it brought to the younger generation of Indonesians. Undeniably, the *Sarekat*'s meteoric rise—it claimed over half a million members in 1919—owed a good deal to the religious mass-appeal conveyed by its very name. But this appeal was not of the leaders' conscious making. It stemmed, rather, from the spontaneous rural support mobilized by hundreds of local *kiyayi* and *'ulamā*,' purveyors of a syncretic, Javanese folk-Islam which saw in Tjokoraminoto not the harbinger of organized modernity but the messianic redeemer from the burdens of earthly existence. For a few years, *Sarekat Islam* thus served as a social barometer registering the mounting disaffection prevalent among the island's rural population as a result of economic and administrative change.

From the mid-1920s on *Sarekat Islam* started to decline as rapidly as it had risen. Lack of a viable programme of concerted action, disunity in its leadership, and increased governmental vigilance combined to bring about the gradual demise of colonial Indonesia's first and last political mass-movement. The Marxist element, unsuccessful in its bid for the domination of the organization, was expelled, and for a few years endeavoured to supplant the *Sarekat* leadership as the main spokesman for social unrest in towns and countryside, its efforts culminating in a series of strikes and peasant uprisings between 1925 and 1927. With the suppression of these outbreaks by the colonial government, social turmoil and the young Communist party virtually ceased to exist. Salīm, who had steered the *Sarekat* away from both its messianic associations and Marxist affiliations, now tried to imprint a distinctly Islamic orientation on the movement. But the desired prestigious connexion with revived pan-Islam evaporated after the collapse of the short-lived Caliphate movement in Egypt and Sa'udi Arabia. Attempts to forge close links with the modernist Aḥmadiyya led to estrangement from the doctrinally more cautious *Muhammadiyah* reformists. Thus deprived of its mass base and kept at bay by Muslim leaders, *Sarekat Islam*, continually torn by internal dissensions, dwindled to insignificance from the late 1920s.

If the movement's initiative in religious matters was lost, so was its leading political role. Leadership in Indonesian political life passed from *Sarekat Islam* to the proponents of a strictly secular nationalism, most of them—like Sukarno, Muḥammad Hatta, and Sutan Sjahrir—recipients of higher modern education in the colony or abroad.

The centre of gravity thus shifted from the *kauman* to the modern capital, Batavia, where the pulse of Muslim life beat but weakly in spite of a considerable semi-proletarian Muslim community. This did not indeed inhibit the steady growth of *Muhammadiyah* and other groups. In fact, they benefited from the selective repression practiced by the colonial authorities in the years after 1927, which placed far greater obstacles in the way of political than religious movements. Yet Muslims, reared outside the political climate of the capital city, for very many years failed to adapt themselves to Indonesia's political modernization. It was Agus Salīm who first recognized the dangers of this situation. In late 1925, he founded the *Jong Islamieten Bond* ('Young Muslims' League'), designed—as its Dutch name and its domicile, Batavia, suggest—to provide Western-educated Indonesians with a religiously based political organization at the centre of the colony's political life. The *Bond* became one of the important recruiting grounds for the political consummation of the Islamic renaissance. Other politically conscious Muslims, who for some years had moved in and out of *Sarekat Islam*, finally founded in 1938 the *Partai Islam Indonesia*, which through participation in elective bodies strove to provide an adequate political base for Indonesian Islam. By then, however, non-Islamic movements and parties had come to predominate in the organized political life and in the various institutions created by the colonial government.

Limited and belated as was the political role of reformism in twentieth century Indonesian political history, its impressive educational and religious achievements had far-reaching social and ultimately also political consequences, not least in some of the Outer Islands. To the extent that *Muhammadiyah* succeeded in educating a new generation of self-reliant Muslims, it gave birth to an increasingly sophisticated political public. And to the extent that reformist spokesmen found themselves at odds with the colonial government's intrusions in matters affecting the Muslim community in the 1930s—such as the jurisdiction of religious judges and the attempted reform of Muslim matrimonial law—they fanned a growing restiveness to *kāfir* overlordship. Nor was this all. The very vigour of the reformers' onslaught elicited spirited responses which before long resulted in the crystallization of distinct social and, implicitly at least, political attitudes dividing Indonesian society, especially in Java.

Not unexpectedly, the most vehement reaction to reformist inroads came from the *Kaum Tua*, the thousands of rural *kiyayi* and *'ulamā'*, for centuries the sole and undisputed spokesmen of Javanese Islam. Their opposition to the religious innovators was shared by the religious officialdom entrusted with the supervision of Islamic worship and the administration of the *Sharī'a*, but above all by the *priyayi* hierarchy which constituted the native segment of the Dutch administrative system on the island. For the greater part descendants of the royal office-holders of Mataram, the *priyayi* continued to hold a distinctly Hindu-Javanese world-view, barely tinged by Islam. Judging by Malayan developments, such dual opposition to religious innovation could have constituted a wellnigh insuperable barrier to Indonesian reformism, had not Dutch policy to a considerable extent neutralized administrative interference. The traditional religious leaders were thus forced to meet the *Kaum Muda* on their own ground, and in the process to accept a modicum of modernization. In January, 1926, several *kiyayi* from Central and East Java founded the *Nahdatul Ulama* ('The Awakening of the *'Ulamā'*'), their first and foremost modern-style organization which attracted some outstanding and venerable men, such as its later chairman, K. H. Hasjim Asj'ari (1871–1947), head of the famous religious school (*pesantren*) at Tebu Ireng in east Java. *Nahdatul Ulama*, though not as spectacularly successful as its reformist counterpart, copied some of its innovations and before long also emulated its missionary drive beyond the island. Opposition to increasing governmental interference in Muslim affairs in the 1930s, no less than growing apprehensions concerning the spreading appeal of Indonesian secular nationalism, were instrumental in bringing modernists and traditionalists together in a federative body, the *Majlisul Islamil A'laa Indonesia* ('Higher Islamic Council of Indonesia'), better known as *M.I.A.I.*, founded in Surabaya in September, 1937.

But this loose alliance could by no means bridge the profound gulf that came to divide Javanese Islam. Differences outwardly centred, as elsewhere, on the controversy between *ijtihād* and *taqlīd*, between the traditional *pesantren* and the modern *madrasa*, and hence between two contenders for the leadership of the Muslim community. Doctrinal controversy was reinforced by a more far-reaching social and cultural polarization between urban and rural Islam, or rather, between a sterner, more recognizably Middle Eastern, Islam on one hand, and the syncretic heterodox Javanese Islam, on the other. Though the organizational balance was decidedly in favour of the reformers, and though foreign overlordship allowed them relatively free rein, traditional Islam could count on a vast following not only among *'ulamā'* clinging to a stubborn individualism outside *Nahdatul Ulama* and its smaller, local, imitators, but also among millions of peasants whose religious allegiances ran the gamut from pre-Islamic *abangan* orientations to the specifically Javanese forms of Muslim orthodoxy.

This internal Islamic controversy constituted only one, and that by no means the most important, aspect of a wider confrontation. The fact that the two wings of the Islamic movement could—however tenuously and temporarily—agree to make common cause reflected a measure of basic unity in the face of outside threats to Islamic interests in general. But Muslim claims to the contrary notwithstanding, twentieth-century Javanese society was not coterminous with the Muslim community: *abangan* beliefs and especially *priyayi* culture not only retained their identities, but these pre-Islamic, if not inherently anti-Islamic, traditions provided secular nationalism with its specifically Javanese roots. These were already evident in the *Budi Utomo* ('Noble Vision') of 1908, but more importantly in the *Taman Siswo* ('Garden of Pupils') school system, founded in 1922 by Soewardi Soerianingrat (better known by his adopted name, Ki Hadjar Dewantoro), of the princely family of Paku Alam in the realm of Jogjakarta in Central Java. Dewantoro's was perhaps the most successful endeavour to translate *priyayi* culture into a modern milieu, attempting to do for Javanese culture what *Muhammadiyah* did for Islamic reformism.

The polarization between Islam and Javanese culture—a polarization going back to at least the sixteenth century—thus received reinforcement and modern expression through the leaders of Islamic reformism and the intellectuals who, whether trained in *Taman Siswo* or government schools, became the standard bearers of Indonesian nationalism. Joint opposition to colonial rule, it is true, could at times mute the discord between Muslims and secular nationalists. Indeed, the only significant concession that Indonesians were jointly able to wrest from the colonial government was the withdrawal of an ordinance seriously threatening the functioning of native private schools in 1933. But the gulf separating them was too wide to be more permanently bridged by such brief interludes of harmony and unity of purpose. What separated Western-trained intellectuals and Muslim spokesmen was not only differences concerning the outward goal—the modern secular state as against the *Dār al-Islām*—but the identification of nationalists with the legendary grandeur of pre-Islamic Majapahit, of Muslims with an intrinsically non-Indonesian culture. The cleavage was deepened by the political imbalance between nationalists and Muslims, the former having, since the eclipse of *Sarekat Islam*, gained predominance in organized political activities and in the representative institutions—such as the *Volksraad* (People's Council) and the Regency Councils—created by the colonial power in the twentieth century.

For both geographic and cultural reasons, the growing cleavage between Islam and modern nationalism was far more pronounced in Java than in the other islands. The institutions of higher learning, as well as the instrumentalities for modern political life, were almost exclusively concentrated in Java. It was there that the secular intelligentsia, and hence Indonesian nationalism, found their main abode. It is true, of course, that that intelligentsia was no more exclusively restricted to Javanese (and Sundanese) than was the leadership of Islamic reformism on the island. But such ethnic diversity, however important it was for the development of a truly all-Indonesian nationalism, was nonetheless counterbalanced by a peculiar blending of Javanese and Western values which permeated many among the intelligentsia, regardless of their ethnic origin, and which set them apart from most of their Muslim counterparts. The splendour and refinement of Javanese culture, still powerful in spite of the political impotence of the central Javanese principalities, thus exercised a far from negligible influence on Indonesian nationalism.

No comparable, viable cultural traditions existed in most of the other islands, many of whose most enterprising and dynamic youths moreover tended to be drawn to Java. More than that, even, the destruction of some ruling houses (the most notable examples being the Minangkabau during the *Padri* War and the Achehnese sultanate in the course of the Acheh War) had created social and political vacuums which neither territorial nor kinship units could adequately fill. Indeed, Sumatran royalty had never enjoyed either the substance or the aura of Javanese kingship. Equally important, unlike the Javanese *priyayi*, the Minangkabau *penghulu* and the Achehnese *ulèebalang* (secular territorial chiefs) merely represented local and parochial traditions. The pattern of Dutch rule in the Outer Islands in fact strengthened this innate parochialism of petty chiefs and village heads, thus precluding their gradual modernization along lines similar to those in Java. The absence of central secular authority, and the relative weakness of indigenous royal tradition, significantly determined the course of modern Islamic history in Sumatra and elsewhere. In none of the more sparsely populated Outer Islands was there, in fact, a politically and culturally dominant ethnic group comparable to the Javanese. Wahhabism had, as we saw, struck deep roots among both Achehnese and Minangkabaus in the nineteenth century. Though the militant *'ulamā'* had been subdued by the colonial power, Muslim sentiment only needed the impetus of modern activism to be rekindled to new vitality. But whereas in Java the Islamic renaissance encountered competition from both pre-Islamic Javanese tradition and modern nationalism, in Sumatra (and not only there) it was for some decades virtually the only modern, supra-local, and indeed proto-nationalist force. As such, it evoked a strong reaction among both traditionalist *'ulamā'* and secular chiefs. Even though the challenge of the *Kaum Muda* effected a rapprochement between these two historically antagonistic groups, their joint opposition to reformism was not nearly as effective in the Netherlands Indies as it was in British Malaya. This was in part due to the fact that Sumatran petty chiefs did not possess the authority and prestige enjoyed by Malayan sultans, in part to the modicum of protection extended to religious movements under Dutch Islamic policy, circumscribed and modified as it was in Sumatra by a general inclination—born of the experiences of the nineteenth century—to rely on the traditional representatives of the social order.

Modern trends in Sumatran Islam made their first appearance in the Minangkabau region on the island's West Coast, where reformists had taken the initiative in the fields of journalism, modelled on Straits publications, in the early years of the century. In 1918, Amrullah, together with Shaykh Muḥammad Jamīl Djambek (1860–1947) and others, founded the *Thawalib*, a reformist association catering for *madrasa* students, which before long spread to other parts of the island. In the mid-1920s, *Muhammadiyah* entered the region, whence Minangkabau emissaries—among them Amrullah's subsequently famous son, the prolific writer and publicist Ḥājjī 'Abd al-Malik (Haji Abdul Malik), better known under his pen-name Hamka—carried it to other parts of the island, and even to Borneo and Celebes. Though their organizational models derived from Java, both associations found themselves inextricably drawn into radical political channels to a far greater extent than their counterparts there. This was due to the fact that in an area already in the grips of accelerated economic and social change, reformist-educated youths became the prime leaders of political, gradually more pronouncedly nationalist-tinged, protest. In early 1927, the west coast of Sumatra experienced a widespread rural rebellion in which—as in Java a few months earlier—young Communists, allied with both traditional *'ulamā'* and some *Thawalib* graduates, played a leading role. Suppressed by the colonial government, radicalism nonetheless continued to smoulder until the end of Dutch rule in Indonesia. In the mid-1930s, the place of the proscribed *Thawalib* was taken by another local organization, *Permi* (*Persatuan Muslimin Indonesia*, 'Union of Indonesian Muslims'), but it, too, was disbanded, leaving only *Muhammadiyah* in the field. Yet in spite of increased governmental vigilance exercised through *adat* chiefs, and in spite also of the insistence of the movement's executive in Java that its unruly Minangkabau branches desist from political involvements, the stubborn restiveness of West Sumatran reformism proved difficult to contain. This was clearly demonstrated when, shortly before the outbreak of the Pacific war, Amrullah was banished to Java.

Achehnese society had not undergone a similar degree of social innovation in the twentieth century, and its response to outside influences thus differed from the Minangkabau pattern. *Muhammadiyah* branches had, it is true, been established in parts of Acheh, too, but their founders—as well as most of their members—were outsiders, so that the organization did not establish proper roots among the local population at large. To become effective, Islamic activism had to find a suitable indigenous organizational mould. It was only in 1939 that such a mould was found in the establishment of the *Persatuan Ulama-Ulama Seluruh Atjeh* ('All-Acheh Union of *'Ulama'*') or *PUSA*, under the energetic and brilliant leadership of Teungku Muḥammad Dā'ūd Beureu'eh. *PUSA* raised the banner of modernism, combining it with the peculiar, Muslim-tinged patriotism of Acheh in its successful efforts to undercut the equally modernist, but 'alien' *Muhammadiyah*. In spite of its reformist tendencies, the new organization in fact attracted some *Kaum Tua* elements to its fold; Achehnese Islam was so all-pervasive and so much identified with regional patriotism that the rift between *Kaum Tua* and *Kaum Muda*, quite unlike in Java and on Sumatra's west coast, never assumed important proportions in Acheh. Indeed, even the opposition between *'ulama'* and *ulèebalang* was primarily a social and political, not a religious phenomenon. Through its leader's skill, *PUSA* avoided a head-on collision with the *ulèebalang* and their Dutch patrons as long as Western colonial rule lasted, but it was preparing itself for an ultimate confrontation with its *kāfir* overlords, a confrontation that would erase from Achehnese memories the lost Acheh War.

II

Cataclysm and catalyst, the Japanese occupation of South-East Asia during the Second World War was for all its brevity of vast significance to the peoples of the area. Harsh military rule, accompanied by brutal requisitioning of food supplies and human labour, the virtual destruction of the area's modern economy, and progressive inflation, wrought abrupt and often painful social changes. At the same time, adroit Japanese propaganda and the creation of mass-movements, especially among the youth, did much to detach these South-East Asian societies from traditional moorings still precariously preserved by Western rule. Within this general upheaval, a crude yet often effective Japanese Islamic policy propelled the Islamic renaissance far beyond its confines in colonial times. The Japanese interregnum thus accelerated both its local consummation in some areas, and the confrontation with its opponents in others.

In the Malaysian world, Japanese administrative changes temporarily at least destroyed the arbitrary boundaries drawn by Europeans in the nineteenth century. Thus Malaya's four northern principalities were ceded to Thailand while Malaya's British-created threefold division gave way to administrative unity. Sumatra was for well over a year united with Malaya, but subsequently placed under a separate army command. The area was, finally, administratively divided between the army and navy, the army controlling Java, Sumatra, and Malaya, the navy, Borneo, Celebes and the smaller islands in the east. The jealously guarded existence of separate military administrations for each major island truncated Malaysian developments until almost the end of the war, when the Japanese hurriedly sought to replace separateness by unification, not only among the islands, but—unsuccessfully—even between Indonesia as a whole and Malaya.

The Japanese envisaged the permanent incorporation of both Indonesia and Malaya, as vital raw-material suppliers in the Co-Prosperity Sphere. They foresaw outright colonial status for large parts of the area, while others, most notably Java, were to attain an increasing measure of political co-determination, if not ultimate autonomy. Though the invader loudly proclaimed himself the liberator of South-East Asia from the yoke of alien overlordship, adherence to these basic policies placed serious obstacles in the way of indigenous political activities. Western-style political institutions disappeared, and nationalist organizational life as such was forced to a standstill. The Japanese, it is true, allowed and even encouraged individual nationalist spokesmen to play sometimes prominent public roles, but almost to the end their activities remained closely controlled. In pursuit of their short-term goals, Japanese administrators wittingly and unwittingly laid the groundwork for far-reaching social revolutions whose roots were in part at least embedded in the recent colonial past. Inevitably, the fate of the Muslim communities became crucially involved in this partial re-ordering of the Malaysian societies. To a large extent this was due to the lack of emphasis on politics inherent in early Japanese policies, coupled as it was with a pronounced interest in, and concern for, religion as a major social and ideological force in rural Malaysia. Japanese preoccupation with Islam thus spelt the end of the non-interference practiced by both their British and Dutch colonial predecessors, but without necessarily reversing, in fact here and there accelerating, the trends of the past decades.

In spite of the rather radical redrawing of the administrative map of Malaya by Japan, the effects of military occupation upon the Malay people and their institutions, and hence upon Malayan Islam, remained relatively slight. Thanks to the early abandonment by the military government of original plans which called for the abolition of the Malay sultanates, no violent changes occurred in the country's social and political structure. Thus the intrinsically evolutionary character of Malayan developments was affected but little by the change of sovereign. This was especially true of the position of Islam, entrenched, as we have seen, in a solid and viable alliance of religious *Kaum Tua* and secular rulers. The Japanese in fact indirectly strengthened the intimate tie between religious and secular traditionalism through the abolition of the State Councils which, in British days, had endowed the rulers with at least nominal, symbolic prestige in the Federated States. The sultans' considerably more substantial powers in the Unfederated States suffered an even more serious eclipse. The waning of political authority heightened the importance of the rulers' religious position, in effect the sole remaining attribute of their sovereign status. With the reconstitution and reorganization of the Religious Councils towards the end of 1944, the Japanese gave further proof of the significance they attached to matters Islamic. Japanese support, however grudging, for the pre-war social *status quo* on one hand, and the absence of a viable, modern Muslim organizational base, on the other, combined to leave the Malayan Islamic renaissance in its pre-war retarded state. When the Japanese, in the face of imminent defeat, embarked on political experiment, they chose members of the small, Indonesia-oriented and radical Malay intelligentsia, rather than Muslim leaders, to become the standard bearers of a still-born independent Malaya within a Greater Indonesia of Japanese make.

Of far greater and more far-reaching importance was the Japanese interregnum in Java, where Muslim organizational strength, as we noted, had been considerably augmented in the course of the twentieth century. Apparently quite cognizant of this strength, the Japanese from the very outset took vigorous measures to bring Islam on the island under their direct control, using as part of their tactics the services of several Japanese Muslims (or in any case, of Japanese with experience and some training in the Middle East). A Religious Affairs Bureau was among the first administrative offices opened after the invasion (March 1942), and it was through it that the military government's Islamic policies were to be channelled until the end of the war. An interesting counterpoint to Dutch Islamic policy, that of Japan nonetheless operated within a strikingly similar frame of reference. While in contrast to the Dutch the Japanese actively sought to intervene in religious affairs, and to lend a large measure of governmental—especially organizational and financial—support to the Muslims in Java, this conditional support—partly welcome, partly embarrassing as it proved to be to the Islamic leaders—was apparently based on the tacit assumption that it would undergird a religious, rather than a potentially or incipiently political, force on the island. Yet Japanese policies not only stimulated the further growth of the Islamic renaissance, they also—indirectly if not inadvertently—strengthened its precarious political stature. Much of this enhancement occurred in the early period, when autonomous political action by non-religious nationalists was in enforced abeyance in accordance with Japanese planning. When in late 1944 the ban was lifted and Indonesian nationalism allowed increasingly free rein, Islamic organizational strength had become a *fait accompli*.

The initial Japanese moves regarding Islam showed clearly that the new rulers wished to draw the line of demarcation between religion and politics even more consistently than had the Dutch. They immediately proscribed Muslim political parties, the *Partai Sarekat Islam Indonesia* (*Sarekat Islam's* name since 1929) and the modernist *Partai Islam Indonesia*, founded in 1938. At the same time, they set out to reassure religious leaders of their benevolence towards, and support for, the Islamic faith as such. Their initial organizational contacts were channelled through the prewar Islamic federation, *M.I.A.I.*, but in late 1943, it was replaced by a new federative body, the *Masjumi* (*Madjlisul Sjuro Muslimin Indonesia*, 'Consultative Council of Indonesian Muslims'). The new federation constituted a Japanese-decreed collaborative union of the two major pre-war Islamic religious associations, *Muhammadiyah* and *Nahdatul Ulama*, which had, unlike political parties, in fact never been banned by the occupying power; two smaller, local, traditionalist groups were subsequently added. Apart from these corporate members, individual *'ulamā'* were urged to join *Masjumi*. While the Japanese kept many Muslim politicians, such as the intellectuals from the *Jong Islamieten Bond*, beyond the pale of the only officially sanctioned Islamic organization, they brought—or forced—the thousands of hitherto unaffiliated *kiyayi* and *'ulamā'* out of their traditional isolation, in part through special training courses in the capital city.

Masjumi was directly linked with the Religious Affairs Bureau, and in early 1944 was entrusted with some of its executive functions, progressively vacated by Japanese personnel; soon the Bureau set about establishing a network of regional branch offices. For the first time in the modern history of Javanese Islam, an official, administrative structure had been created charged with the supervision and direction of Muslim life, and staffed by members of Muslim movements. This administrative innovation greatly diminished the supervisory powers hitherto vested in the *priyayi* and the religious officialdom subordinate to it; it thus constituted a significant redressing of the age-old balance between secular authorities and the proponents of both traditionalist and reformist Islam on the island.

Until mid-1944, *Masjumi* had no true organizational counterpart among nationalist groupings. The Japanese at first permitted, but subsequently disallowed, a small nationalist-led movement, replacing it by a multi-racial mass movement—the so-called *Djawa Hōkōkai* (Java Service Association)—in which all leading functions were in effect performed by Japanese, relegating the Indonesian leadership, including Sukarno and Hatta, to nominal and subordinate status. Even the various advisory bodies created by the military government in 1943 provided little scope for nationalist agitation; strictly controlled and narrowly circumscribed as to their limited competence, the pale Japanese imitations fell far short of the more representative bodies of the Dutch colonial era.

By the autumn of 1944, Japan's situation had deteriorated to the point where an Allied counter offensive in the Malaysian waters appeared likely. The Japanese home government therefore decided on a reversal of its policies *vis-à-vis* the political status of Indonesia and Malaya. After the Tokyo announcement (7 September 1944) that Indonesia would be granted independence 'in the future', the local military authorities started to reorient their policies. Before long, the balance between religious and secular factions started to change. Nationalist leaders, hitherto restricted to public prominence virtually devoid of organizational substance, gradually moved into commanding positions of political strength, in particular gaining control over funds and over the *Hōkōkai*. Even though several key groups created by the Japanese in the preceding three years—notably the Volunteer Defence Corps, various youth groups and guerilla units, as well as the personnel of the mass media—for quite some time remained outside the control of the nationalist leadership, the overall redressing of the balance benefited the secular nationalists at the expense of the Muslims. Nationalists, unlike their Muslim competitors, had actually for some months already been allowed access to top-level advisory positions in the executive departments of the military administration; they had even formed a 'shadow cabinet'. Islamic leaders now bent all efforts towards persuading their Japanese sponsors to retain as much of their hitherto privileged position as possible in the face of increasingly loud demands for the abolition of *Masjumi*'s organizational autonomy. With the sudden demise of Japanese rule and the proclamation of Indonesian independence (August 1945), the controversy between nationalism and Islam—accompanied by other conflicts—moved into the limelight of the new-born Republic's political arena.

In other parts of Indonesia, Islam had also gained significant advances under Japanese aegis, and here and there even more significant ones than in Java. This was due to the virtual absence of modern non-religious political leaders in most of the Outer Islands, as well as to the Archipelago's enforced dismemberment during the war, which obviated contacts with Java. The area most profoundly affected by the interregnum was Acheh, where the *PUSA* had taken the initiative in the organization of a pro-Japanese fifth column on the eve of the invasion; it subsequently continued to support the new régime. Even though the Japanese were far from throwing their entire support to *PUSA*—in fact they consciously played a divide-and-rule tactic in the area—they did much to endow the *'ulamā'* with increasing positions of influence. At the war's end, *PUSA* had thus gained considerable momentum and it was only continued foreign overlordship that barred it from the consummation of its prominence if not dominance. Without adequate organization, the *ulèebalang*, who for decades had been forfeiting popular support on account of their political and economic opportunism *vis-à-vis* both Dutch and Japanese rulers, fell prey to a concentrated *PUSA* attack with wide popular backing (December 1945–February 1946) in which well over half of the *ulèebalang* families were exterminated. Under the banner of a distinctly Islamic local and ethnic patriotism, Acheh thus entered independent Indonesia as a virtually autonomous *imperium in imperio.*

Less far-reaching in its effects on Sumatra's west coast, the interregnum nonetheless considerably strengthened Minangkabau Islam too. *Muhammadiyah* and *Permi* continued to function, albeit under manifold restrictions. In addition, the Japanese took the initiative in creating a consultative body, called *Madjelis Islam Tinggi* (Supreme Islamic Council), which not only comprised Muslim organizations but also, like *Masjumi* in Java, individual *'ulamā'* of both traditionalist and reformist leanings. This prestigious federation in which leading *'ulamā'* occupied prominent positions laid the foundations for Muslim political strength, precariously kept at bay by Dutch rule for many decades. Its existence forced the secular *penghulu* into an increasingly defensive position; but the Minangkabau *adat* chiefs, who not only enjoyed greater popular support than the Achehnese *ulèebalang*, but who had also started to organize themselves since before the war, were not subjected to frontal attack when Japanese rule collapsed.

III

The kaleidoscopic course of South-East Asian history since the Second World War has been both too turbulent and too recent to allow proper historical perspective for the assessment of the place of Islam in the postwar Malaysian-Indonesian world. Yet it is safe to say that decolonization forms a very real watershed between old and new, and nowhere with greater significance than in the political sphere. At long last released from alien direction and restraints, South-East Asian societies have, with greater or lesser vehemence, erupted into dynamic action which has put the stamp of politics on a multitude of social forces. It is equally obvious that the area's Islamic communities were similarly forced into the political arena, not only to a far greater extent than before and during the war, but also in a very different setting.

The slow modernization of Malaya under both British and Japanese rule and the country's peculiar ethnic composition were together responsible for the limited role Islam was to play in post-war Malayan history. The Japanese interregnum had, as we saw, not seriously affected the *status quo* within Malay society; if anything, it had deepened the close alliance between the Malay rulers and the intrinsically tradition-oriented religious leadership in the peninsula. By contrast, the occupation had wrought considerable changes among the numerically and economically very strong Chinese community. It was from among that community that organized armed resistance to the Japanese régime had arisen, ably led by the Malayan Communist party, and supported by the Allies. Japan's sudden surrender coincided with an open bid for power by the young Chinese Communist leadership. Thwarted in their attempt by the reimposition of firm British control, the Communists thereafter continued guerilla warfare in the jungles until their virtual defeat a decade later. The radicalization of part of the Chinese population, and the portent it bore for the deepening of communal cleavages, was one important determinant of the postwar Malayan scene. Another was British plans envisaging a centralized Malayan Union which would have abolished the sovereignty of the Malay sultans and provided far-reaching political concessions to non-Malays.

Reaction to this apparent twofold threat mobilized in a very short time hitherto dormant Malay national sentiment. Yet, though provoked by communal fears and colonial policy, post-war Malay nationalism followed neither a racially exclusivist nor a politically and economically radical course. Its intrinsically conservative orientation was charted by a leadership largely recruited from among the Malay aristocracy especially its Western-educated members. Combining traditional prestige with modern skills, members of this group founded the United Malays' National Organization (UMNO) in March, 1946. Before long, UMNO established close political links with the equally conservative leadership of the Chinese mercantile community, organized in the Malayan Chinese Association, and with the leaders of the smaller Indian minority organized in the Malayan Indian Congress. The Alliance party, formed of these three constituent groups, became the predominant political force in the Federation of Malaya, founded in 1948, and granted independence by Britain in 1957. The Federation originally comprised only peninsular Malaya (including Penang and Malacca, hitherto parts of the Straits Settlements), Singapore becoming a separate colony enjoying a large measure of internal autonomy. Six years later, a new political entity, the Federation of Malaysia, came into being, which in addition to Singapore (until mid-1965) extended to North Borneo (Sabah) and Sarawak.

In spite of an agonizing guerilla war, Malayan constitutional and political evolution towards a parliamentary democracy had proceeded swiftly yet smoothly. Yet given the plural nature of Malaysia, and the constitutional recognition of at least temporary separateness among the diverse ethnic groups coupled with preferential treatment of Malays, the new state's political leaders have had to steer a careful course between national and sectional interests. In the case of the Malay sectional interest, the Islamic factor has, especially since independence, gained in significance, if for no other reason than that Islam—almost by default—became one of the major marks of Malay identity, if not indeed the only one. The modern Malay political *élite*, it is true, is not only predominantly Western-educated and secularly oriented, it has also sought to fashion a multi-racial and multi-religious nation. But it has encountered—and not infrequently yielded to—Muslim pressures.

In Indonesia, the Japanese surrender set in motion a series of complex developments unparalled in neighbouring Malaya. In a matter of days after the Japanese surrender, an Indonesian Republic was proclaimed in Djakarta (Batavia), able to exercise loose control over parts of Java and Sumatra. Several months elapsed before the Netherlands returned in strength to their former colonial domain, after an interlude of British occupation. Though in 1945 no viable Communist movement existed in Indonesia comparable to that of Malaya, resistance to the reimposition of Dutch rule in Republican-held territories was widespread. Protracted Indonesian-Dutch negotiations were twice interrupted by Dutch military action (1947 and 1948–9) against the republic. In some of the areas outside republican control, the Dutch had succeeded in re-establishing their administration in cooperation with the traditional political *élites*. But stubborn Indonesian opposition, including widespread guerilla warfare, combined with outside diplomatic pressure exerted upon the Netherlands, finally led to the transfer of sovereignty to an Indonesian federal state in December, 1949, excluding West New Guinea (Irian Barat); only in 1962 was this hotly disputed area placed under Indonesian administration, through the intermediary of the United Nations.

Chaotic as the road to Indonesia's independence was, its attainment did not inaugurate an era of tranquility. The Japanese interregnum and, worse still, the subsequent years of bitter fighting had, moreover, taken a high toll in terms of human misery, social disorganization and economic deterioration which left their marks on subsequent developments. Unlike Malaya, post-war Indonesia has been in the grips of a truly revolutionary readjustment of which the separation from the former colonial overlord was only one, albeit a centrally significant, facet. The political fortunes of Indonesia were, moreover, in the hands of a revolutionary intelligentsia headed by President Sukarno, and not, as in Malaya, of a well-entrenched aristocracy. Indeed, a string of social revolutions—among them the Achehnese events briefly referred to above—took place within the larger Indonesian Revolution of 1945–9, resulting *inter alia* in the large-scale elimination of traditional ruling houses in many areas, and in a greatly diminished role for the *priyayi* aristocracy in Java, all of them tainted by alleged or real pro-Dutch and more often also pro-Japanese, orientations, before and immediately after the war. Quite apart from these social upheavals, the new state was almost from its birth plagued by serious factional cleavages within the political *élite* which weakened the position and the prestige of successive Cabinets and of the political parties that provided their personnel. The smooth functioning of parliamentary government was thus rendered increasingly difficult, if not wellnigh impossible. These bitter political conflicts, based on serious ideological and often also personal cleavages, were further aggravated by hardening opposition between politicians and the leaders of the republic's armed forces, which, created during the Japanese occupation, had played a key role in the struggle for independence. Shortly after the transfer of sovereignty, this opposition was reinforced by tensions between the central government and regional interests in some of the Outer Islands, a reaction to the attempted centralization that was the concomitant of the liquidation of the artificial federal structure in 1950. For some years, the very survival of the national state was jeopardized by regional revolts, usually spearheaded by local military commanders in close co-operation with dissident political leaders.

PART VII

AFRICA AND THE MUSLIM WEST

CHAPTER I

NORTH AFRICA TO THE SIXTEENTH CENTURY

According to the tradition of the chroniclers, it was in 26/647 that the Muslims first came into contact with North Africa. The Caliph ʿUmar had in fact forbidden his conquering generals to proceed westwards beyond Tripoli, but his successor ʿUthmān authorized the military commander ʿAbd Allāh b. Saʿd to lead an expedition into Ifrīqiya to obtain plunder. This ended in victory for the Muslims over the Byzantine troops of the Patrician Gregory on the plain of Sbeitla.

The new conquerors found a complex country. It is true that they found a Byzantine power that they were beginning to know well, since they had already conquered the Byzantine provinces of Syria and Egypt. But Byzantine authority did not by any means extend throughout the whole of North Africa: it stopped at the meridian of the Chott el-Hodna (Shaṭṭ al-Ḥaḍna) in the west and did not begin again until Ceuta, (Sabta) where a Byzantine governor held on for better or worse until 92/711. The rest of the country was controlled by the Berbers. Some of them had come under Carthaginian, and later under Roman influence: this was the case with the Berbers of the present-day Tunisia and of the region of Constantine. Others had come under Roman influence only—those of the present-day Algeria and of northern Morocco; but many of them had no direct contact with either Carthaginians or Romans: this was the case with the majority of the Berbers of Morocco and those of the high western plains of Algeria.

The former remained part of an age-old civilization which was patriarchal, rural and pastoral, knowing nothing of the big urban centres, and divided into a myriad of small political entities, tribes or villages. The earliest known facts about this civilization are provided by Sallust in his *Bellum Jugurthinum* and include a number of details which were still applicable to Berber society at the beginning of the twentieth century. But it is questionable whether the Berbers who had lived for four or five centuries in direct and permanent contact with the Romans or the Carthaginians led a life which was very different. It would seem that the Roman ruins which are scattered throughout North Africa have led to an exaggerated idea of the extent to which the Romans influenced the

Berbers. It is true that they influenced an urban *élite* which had adopted the language, the ideas and the customs of the conquerors; but this *élite* was never very numerous, for the towns were not in general large[1] and were in any case inhabited largely by Romans. Furthermore, certainly after the Vandal conquest and perhaps well before this,[2] over the greater part of Africa Roman influence had ceased, and the ancient Berber civilization had gradually reasserted itself. In any case, in the rural districts the impact of the civilization of Rome was probably never as great as its economic influence. In short it can be said that first/seventh century North Africa was much more Berber than Byzantine, or even Roman.

Very little information is available on the Muslim conquest from the chroniclers, who are in any case rather late, the earliest of them dating from the second half of the third/ninth century, and are eastern writers little acquainted with North African affairs, and only indirectly interested in them; and from traditions, which diverge on many points, and which, with no means of control, merely create uncertainty. There is still uncertainty over the dates[3] since we are concerned with early events which were not recorded until a century and a half later. It is more surprising that there is so little information on a phenomenon so important from all points of view as the islamization of the Berber population; the chroniclers contribute practically nothing about this, particularly about the actions of the governor Mūsā b. Nuṣayr, who seems to have played a decisive role in the stabilization of the conquest and the dissemination of Muslim doctrine. We shall limit ourselves here to pointing out the main features of this conquest, at least so far as they can be traced from the existing documentation.

The spearhead of the Byzantine army in Africa was destroyed at the battle of Sbeitla, and was never formed again, for Africa was very far from Byzantium and the rulers there had seceded just before the Muslims overran it. Nevertheless the *Rūm*, as the Arabs called the Byzantines, remained in Africa for a further fifty years, entrenched behind the natural barrier of the Tunisian dorsal, and based on the fortified town and port of Carthage, whence they formed alliances with the Berbers, or some of them at least, against the invader from the east.

Moreover the Muslims did not return immediately: after Sbeitla they

[1] Christian Courtois, *Les Vandales et l'Afrique* (Paris, 1955), 107 f. G. Charles Picard, *La Civilisation de l'Afrique Romaine* (Paris, 1959), 171 f., presents a completely different view.

[2] C. Courtois, *ibid.*, 79 f.

[3] E. Lévi-Provençal, 'Un nouveau récit de la conquête de l'Afrique du Nord par les Arabes', *Arabica*, I (1954), 17–43.

had evacuated Ifrīqiya loaded with booty, and did not reappear there until long afterwards. With the exception of one or two raids which affected only the south of the country, they did not think seriously of occupying it until after the Umayyad dynasty was firmly established in the east.

It was then that there appeared the first real Muslim conqueror of North Africa, 'Uqba b. Nāfi' al-Fihrī, and it is a pity that more is not known of him. Was he in fact a propagator of the new faith, or a re-morseless swordsman, or an intransigent and brutal governor? The information about him is so legendary that one hesitates to describe him. He was certainly a man of character and boldness. It was he who founded about 43/663–4,[1] on a plain which was almost entirely steppe, the first permanent Muslim settlement in the Maghrib, the military encampment Qayrawān (Kairouan) which later became for several centuries the capital of the Muslim West. It was he too who later made an extraordinary ride on horseback across the Maghrib which is said to have taken him through the territory of the Berber tribes as far as the western High Atlas and to the Atlantic coast.[2] The first Muslim impression on the Maghrib certainly came from him.

But he had to deal with considerable opposition, for several powerful Berber groups, at the instigation or at least with the help of the Byzantines of Carthage, resisted the invader with fierce energy. Of 'Uqba's chief adversary, the Berber Kusayla, even less is known than of the Muslim conqueror himself. The little that is known shows that his pride was wounded by the Arab leader, so that he made up his mind to wage a pitiless struggle against him. In fact he was able to take him by surprise in 63/682–3 to the south-west of the Aurès massif: the Muslims were outnumbered and suffered a crushing defeat near the oasis of Sīdī 'Uqba where today the tomb of the fighter for the faith is a venerated place of pilgrimage.

As a result of this battle the Muslims were driven out of Ifrīqiya for several years. They seem however to have left there the seeds of their faith and, in any case, the Umayyads did not accept this defeat as final. A new Muslim leader, Ḥassān b. al-Nu'mān was sent to reconquer the lost

[1] The traditional date for the founding of Qayrawān is 50/670. But E. Lévi-Provençal has shown (*art. cit.*, 26, 38) that there existed at least one other Arab tradition, an early and more probable one, according to which it was founded several years earlier.

[2] This exploit has been questioned by R. Brunschvig ('Ibn 'Abdalh'akam et la conquête de l'Afrique du Nord par les Arabes', *Annales de l'Institut d'Etudes Orientales de la Faculté des Lettres d'Alger*, Vol. VI (1942–7), 138). The text published by Lévi-Provençal (cf. note 3, p. 212) seems on the contrary to confirm it.

province. He encountered there a new Berber adversary, no less legendary than Kusayla, in the person of an old woman known as *al-Kāhina* ('the Soothsayer'), who for years made his life difficult and prevented him from progressing beyond the present frontiers of Tunisia. However, with the help of reinforcements and by persistent effort, he succeeded in eliminating the last Byzantines by taking Carthage (79/698) and finally got the better of al-Kāhina.

It was at this point that there took place the great mystery of the Muslim conquest of the Maghrib: suddenly the Berber resistance crumbled, and Muslim political domination and the propagation of Islam spread with extraordinary rapidity. This reversal of the situation is linked with the name of Mūsā b. Nuṣayr, and there is a temptation to see him as the true conqueror of North Africa. But even less is known of him than of his predecessors, and it is not clear how he achieved such a result. It is indeed surprising that the Arab chroniclers provide so little information about him, but the reason may be that the contemporary chroniclers judged it imprudent to expatiate on his exploits.

The fact remains that in 91/710, Mūsā judged that he had the Maghrib sufficiently under control to consider launching an attack on its neighbour, Spain, with an army which was composed chiefly of Berber contingents levied from the northern tribes of what today is Morocco. It is an obvious exaggeration to imply, as do most of the chroniclers, that this Maghrib was entirely Muslim. It is known in fact that it contained numerous Jewish communities, probably consisting mainly of Berber converts. A passage of Ibn Khaldūn even suggests that al-Kāhina belonged to the Jewish faith, and it is likely that Jews played a part in the resistance to the Muslim conquerors. There is no indication that the Christians of Africa, as Christians, did the same; this phenomenon is not peculiar to the Maghrib, since neither in the Fertile Crescent nor in Egypt did the Christians resist the Muslims in defence of their faith. But there are many indications that Christian communities continued to exist in North Africa until the seventh/twelfth century. They were certainly still important, although docile, even after Mūsā b. Nuṣayr's policy of islamization. Finally, there were many Berbers who had not been materially affected by the propagators of the new faith and there is no doubt that numerous groups of them remained pagan, particularly in Morocco.

Arabic certainly at once became the official language and was spoken, sometimes well and sometimes not, by all who came into contact with the conquerors; that is by the inhabitants of the main towns and a certain number of local chiefs, perhaps also by the peasants in the areas where the conquerors carved out domains for themselves, but not elsewhere. It can be said that Arabic quickly took the place of Latin, but made very little inroad on the Berber dialects.

Very little is known of the policy adopted by the new conquerors in relation to the local peoples. Such information as there is, however, indicates that they did not behave in the Maghrib with the moderation which they had shown elsewhere, and which they were soon to show in Spain. This was probably because in the Maghrib they were not surrounded by ancient societies which were coherent and organized, but by disparate primitive tribes, peoples in fact which they did not consider as civilized. This led to the attitude of arrogance and despotism which is apparent in some of the details related by the chroniclers, and explains the terrible Berber reaction which was to take place from 122/740 onwards.

The revolt began at Tangier (Ṭanja) under the leadership of a man of the people called Maysara, and from there it spread throughout North Africa like a train of gunpowder. The Umayyads sent reinforcements, but they were submerged by the Berber flood, and some of them had no alternative but to return to Spain. Within a few years, Muslim power was swept from almost the whole of North Africa. It was able to hold on—and there not without setbacks—only in the region of Qayrawān, which often gave the impression of a ship surrounded by waves, when powerful tribes attacked its walls.

However, all was not submerged in this tempest: on the contrary, Islam itself emerged from it with renewed vigour. This was because the revolt had been inspired by the Kharijite Muslim doctrine. It is not known how this doctrine penetrated to the Maghrib and spread there, but there is no doubt that its egalitarian character and its opposition to Umayyad rule reflected the aspirations of the Berber peoples. It can be said that in about 132/750 almost the whole of North Africa was Kharijite. This seems to have been a matter of expediency, since the Kharijite tide quickly ebbed, and in the middle of the fourth/tenth century there no longer remained many of its adherents, but it had important consequences, since it resulted in Islam becoming much more firmly rooted in North Africa, and being carried into areas which until then had been very little touched by it. Kharijism not only spread Islam but led to a deeper knowledge of it, producing a vast number of Berber theologians, particularly on the Jabal Nafūsa and in the region of Tāhart, the present-day Tiaret. It is from the Kharijite movement that the islamization of the Berbers really dates.

This islamization was still no more than superficial, if we are to judge it by the various Berber beliefs and practices of that time (of which little is known), such as those of the Barghawāṭa, but in certain places it was sound, for on the strictly doctrinal level Kharijism differed little from orthodoxy. Furthermore, the presence of Kharijism acted as a spur to orthodox theology, and probably contributed indirectly to the formation of the famous school of Qayrawān which shone so brilliantly in the third/ninth century. Thus from the point of view of the development of Islam, the Berber and Kharijite revolt must be considered on balance to have produced positive results. It is also possible that Kharijism, added to the natural self-restraint of the Berbers, has given North African Islam a touch of puritanism and rigour which is still conspicuous.

It is curious that the Kharijite egalitarianism existed side by side during this period with a particular veneration for the Muslims of the east, and especially for the descendants of the Prophet. It was thus that several of the ʿAlids (for whom life in the east under the ʿAbbasids, as under the Umayyads, was becoming impossible) not only found refuge in the Maghrib but succeeded there in directing political groups of greater or less importance. The best known of them is Idrīs b. ʿAbd Allāh, who came and settled in Morocco at the end of the second/eighth century, became chief of the Berber tribe of the Awrāba and founded the town of Fez (Fās), which was to be developed by his son, Idrīs b. Idrīs.

From this time onwards for a century a certain political equilibrium was established in the Maghrib. The Arab family of the Aghlabids had had its authority recognized by the ʿAbbasid caliph in 184/800, and ruled in Ifrīqiya. A Kharijite state, that of the Rustamids, had been founded in the neighbourhood of Tāhart by a Persian emigrant, and maintained itself there, though not without doctrinal and dynastic crises. Finally the Sharīfī state of Idrīs formed in Morocco a centre of orthodox Islam and of arabization among Berber tribes who remained very particularist. Around these three relatively important political centres there revolved a number of principalities and tribes who sought to avoid all political domination, and continued to lead the centuries-old life of the Berbers, scarcely tinged now with Islamic beliefs and practices. The least obscure and certainly one of the most important of these Berber groups was that of the Barghawāṭa. Friction existed among all these groups, but at no time during the century did it degenerate into outright wars.

The centre of this still precarious civilization was Qayrawān. The Aghlabids very soon made it into a city worthy of this name; it was there that Maghribī architecture was born, with a strong oriental influence in the general arrangement as well as in the decoration of the buildings. The great mosque dates from this period, as do the ramparts, Raqqāda, the residential town of the sovereigns not far from Qayrawān, and some large reservoirs, which served to irrigate the gardens and to supply water for the town, as well as being used for court entertainments.

But Qayrawān was not only the model for Muslim city life in North Africa; it was also an important cultural centre. The Aghlabid rulers, so much to be criticized from certain points of view, had the great merit of fostering the intellectual life of their capital: theology, jurisprudence, and Maghribī poetry began and first flourished there. It can even be said that towards the end of the third/ninth century, the school of Qayrawān could bear comparison with the other centres of Muslim culture of that time. It was there that jurists such as Saḥnūn worked out the Maghribī system of jurisprudence, the influence of which is still felt today. It was based on the Mālikī *madhhab*, the most formalist of the orthodox *madhhabs*, and offered a strict interpretation which was in harmony with the Berber inclination towards austerity and punctiliousness.

The Arabic language naturally spread: it was the official language of the three principal states of the Maghrib, and was spoken in towns of any importance, of which there were still few at that time, as also in some rural areas, particularly in the north-east of the country, where great numbers of Arabic-speaking colonists had settled and exerted a linguistic influence on the Berber peasants in the surrounding districts. Thus it was during the third/ninth century that the Arabo-Islamic Maghrib took shape and gave birth to an original type of civilization which still remains alive. This was the period in which the new civilization took root.

From the beginning of the fourth/tenth century, the Maghrib suffered serious upheavals which were to continue almost without ceasing until the middle of the fifth/eleventh century. They began with the installation in Ifrīqiya of the Fatimid dynasty. Already some descendants of the

Prophet, such as Idrīs, had found in Africa the possibility of playing a political role which the 'Abbasid dynasty forbade them in the east; but they had come there as individuals and without any preconceived plan. The Fatimids on the other hand had long been preparing for their arrival in the Maghrib. They sent there at the end of the third/ninth century a specially trained propagandist, Abū 'Abd Allāh al-Shī'ī, who found support among the Berber confederation of the Kutāma in the mountainous coastal region which extends from Bougie (Bijāya) to Djidjelli. After a slow and thorough preparation, he launched the Kutāma on an assault on the Aghlabid kingdom. The enthusiasm and religious zeal of the Berbers triumphed over the black mercenaries of the Aghlabids, and Qayrawān fell into the hands of the insurgents on 2 Rajab 296/27 March 909. Meanwhile the Fatimid claimant, 'Ubayd Allāh al-Mahdī, had reached North Africa by devious routes, and had gone, it is not known why, as far as Sijilmāsa, where he was held prisoner by the local prince. His precursor arrived to release him on 6 Dhu'l-Ḥijja 296/26 August 909, destroying as he passed the Kharijite kingdom of Tāhart. 'Ubayd Allāh made his triumphal entry into Qayrawān on 29 Rabī' II 297/15 January 910, and there proclaimed himself caliph.

The new dynasty was not interested in the Maghrib in itself: its ambition was to obtain recognition of its right to rule the whole of the Muslim world. It had settled in North Africa because this was a relatively easy thing to do, but saw it only as a springboard from which to embark on the conquest of the Near East: thus in the winter of 301/913–14, 'Ubayd Allāh launched an attack against Egypt, but it was a failure. After other unsuccessful attempts he realized that he needed time and meticulous preparations in order to achieve his aim: he made his capital in Mahdiyya, a new city built on the eastern coast of Ifrīqiya, then instituted a system of taxation which seems to have proved successful in raising the funds necessary for the maintenance of a powerful army.

As in addition to this the Shī'ī rulers behaved with intolerance towards the orthodox Mālikīs, there arose, in the towns as well as in the country districts, a sullen discontent which rapidly became concentrated around a Kharijite Berber, Abū Yazīd, nicknamed 'the man on the donkey'. Within a few weeks this extraordinary old man, at the head of enormous masses, hurled himself into the conquest of Ifrīqiya: by 333/944 all that remained of the Fatimid kingdom was Mahdiyya, which defended itself as best it could. However, the Fatimid rulers, al-Qā'im, the successor of 'Ubayd Allāh, and his son, Ismā'īl al-Manṣūr, managed to hold on, turned the tide, and ended by defeating the rebel in Muḥarram 336/August 947. This was the end of Kharijism in North Africa, and of all organized resistance until the time when, his army having conquered Egypt, the Fatimid al-Mu'izz moved to his new capital in Cairo (Ramaḍān 362/June 973).

Before achieving this, the Fatimids had had to face another adversary, the caliph in Spain. For a long time the two antagonists fought each other indirectly by setting one against the other the main tribal groups of the central and western Maghrib, the Ṣanhāja for the Fatimids, the Zanāta for the Umayyads of Spain; and it was only in 344–5/955–6 that their two fleets came into conflict, but without decisive results. The most important consequence of this sterile struggle was that it disturbed a large number of Berber tribes, and provoked migrations, the details of which are unknown. On the other hand it led the Muslims in Spain to interest themselves in the Maghrib, and to introduce a leaven of their brilliant civilization into the northern part of Morocco, which they occupied for about forty years (360–400/971–1010). At the same time the Fatimids strengthened eastern influence in Ifrīqiya as is proved by the sadly few monuments of this period which have survived.

When they moved to Egypt, the Fatimids did not intend to abandon North Africa to its fate; they entrusted the administration of it to the Ṣanhāja Zirids who had served them faithfully. Thus, after an oriental interlude of sixty years, North Africa came once again under the political control of the Berbers. But as regards civilization the oriental cause had triumphed: under the Zirids the Arabic language and Islamic culture progressed still further, at least in the towns and in the regions surrounding the royal residences.

The political situation soon deteriorated: the Spanish Muslims, oppressed by serious civil strife, abandoned Morocco in 400/1010, after which tribal rule once again became the norm. The Zirid state split into two; a strictly Zirid kingdom in the region of Qayrawān, and another ruled by a family, the Hammadids, which was related to the Zirids, but which threw off their authority by force of arms. The Hammadid kingdom established its capital at Qal'at Banī Ḥammād on the southern slope of the Hodna mountains. Thus gradually a return was made to the Berber political formula of relatively narrow groupings, made up of coherent ethnic groups. Such was the situation in the middle of the fifth/eleventh century, when a precarious equilibrium, which nevertheless seemed to be well on the way to establishing itself, was overturned by two nomad invasions.

Although they enjoyed a large measure of autonomy, the Zirid princes remained under the nominal suzerainty of the Fatimids, and retained Shiʿism as a state religion. Probably in 439 or 440/1047 or 1049,[1] the Zirid ruler, al-Muʿizz, repudiated the suzerainty of the Fatimids and placed himself under that of the ʿAbbasids, the worst enemies of the Cairo dynasty. This action was not prompted by strictly political motives, for at that time Fatimid control was as light as it had been at the beginning of the century, but it satisfied Mālikī public opinion as guided by the orthodox *ʿulamāʾ* of Qayrawān: the Maghribīs had never voluntarily subscribed to a doctrine which was prepared to denigrate and even to ridicule the Companions and the Successors of the Prophet with the exception of ʿAlī and his descendants.

The Fatimid state was no longer powerful enough to deal with this by resorting to arms, but it was nonetheless determined to avenge itself on its disloyal vassals. The *wazīr* al-Yāzūrī found a means of vengeance: he encouraged a number of bedouin tribes, whose encampments were close to the Nile valley, and who were making raids on the peasants there, to emigrate towards North Africa. By this means he rid himself of a troublesome people, and was certain that the bedouin would make life difficult for the Zirid rulers. In 442/1050–1 these bedouin, led by the Banū Hilāl, were in Cyrenaica; the next year they penetrated Ifrīqiya proper, and defeated the Zirids decisively on 11 Dhūʾl-Ḥijja 443/14 April 1052, at Jabal Ḥaydarān, a place which has not been identified.

From this time on the Arabs gradually spread like an irresistible tide throughout the country, where they found good pasture for their animals. Its fame spread through the tribes of Egypt and Arabia, to such effect that for three centuries there was a more or less continuous flow of immigration, bringing into North Africa an ever-increasing number of bedouin Arabs. There has been much controversy on this phenomenon, which became known as the Hilālī invasion. The majority of historians, chief among them Ibn Khaldūn, have seen it as a calamity which suddenly struck the Maghrib, devastating it in a flash. Recently, however, some historians have considered that the scope, the political, and still

[1] For a detailed study of the different dates put forward by the chroniclers, see H. R. Idris, *La Berbérie orientale sous les Zirides (Xe–XIIe siècles)* (Paris, 1962), I, 172–203.

more the economic, consequences of this migration have been greatly exaggerated, and that the Banū Hilāl and other tribes had arrived in a country which was already disintegrating rapidly.[1]

If the existing information is carefully analysed, it becomes apparent that the consequences of the Hilālī invasion became manifest only slowly: in about 462/1070, the geographer al-Bakrī describes a North Africa which, except for the region of Qayrawān, was still prosperous. Only the political system of the Zirids was disturbed, having broken up into several small principalities, but the economy had suffered hardly at all. Gradually however the demands of their pastoral economy caused the bedouin to encroach on the area of cultivated land, to disrupt the flow of trade, and to strangle the towns of the interior, and this was felt more and more the further the bedouin spread towards the west. The description of the Maghrib by the geographer al-Idrīsī (mid-sixth/mid-twelfth century) no longer paints such a cheerful picture as that of al-Bakrī. It now seems impossible to deny that the Hilālī invasion produced in the long run very serious political, economic and social consequences, and notably a fall in the level of civilization which had hitherto been attained by Ifrīqiya.

On the other hand, the Arabic language made great progress outside the towns where it had, so to speak, been confined until this time. It is to the bedouin that this arabization of the Maghrib is to be attributed; the exceptions were some mountainous massifs, where groups of Berbers had entrenched themselves, preserving their language and their customs almost intact. But many Berbers, both nomadic and settled, intermarried with the new arrivals, a phenomenon which does not appear to have occurred in the time of the earlier conquerors. The reason may be that the civilization which the bedouin Arabs brought to the Maghrib was as simple as that of the Berber cultivators or pastoralists. Thus there disappeared the barrier which was inevitably created by excessively unequal levels of civilization; as in addition the Arabs and the Berbers had the common religion of Islam, they found no difficulty in living together and in intermarrying. In this way there was gradually formed the Arabo-Berber population which today inhabits the greater part of North Africa.

[1] See especially the articles of Jean Poncet: 'L'évolution des genres de vie en Tunisie (autour d'une phrase d'Ibn Khaldoun)', *Les Cahiers de Tunisie,* no. 7–8 (1954), 315–23; 'Prospérité et décadence ifrikiyennes,' *ibid.,* no. 33–34–35 (1961), 221–43; 'Pays subdésertiques et exemple tunisien,' in *Annales (Economies-Sociétés-Civilisations),* Jan.–Feb. 1961. 104–6.

Some years later, North Africa suffered a second invasion by nomads which was to produce very different results from the earlier one. At first sight, however, there were many similarities between the two invasions. The second was that of a group of nomadic Berber tribes who for hundreds, if not thousands, of years had inhabited the western Sahara, subsisting entirely on their flocks and, according to al-Bakrī, ignorant even of how to grow cereals. The men had their heads veiled, as the Tuareg nowadays, and for this reason the people of the north gave them the general name of 'the veiled ones' (*al-mulaththamūn*). It was much later that, for reasons which are not well understood, they came to be called 'the people of the monastery-fortress' (*al-Murābiṭūn*), the Almoravids. The causes of their migration are obscure: almost all the chroniclers attribute it to religious zeal. In about 437/1045 one of the chiefs of the 'veiled ones' is said to have performed the Pilgrimage to Mecca, and there realized the state of religious ignorance in which his fellow-Berbers lived. He finally arranged, though not without difficulty, that a man of religion from southern Morocco, ʿAbd Allāh b. Yāsīn, should accompany him on his return to teach the 'veiled ones' what they did not know. After some disappointments, ʿAbd Allāh is said to have ended by inflaming his new adherents with reforming zeal, and to have led them against the masters of the oases of Darʿa and of Sijilmāsa who were leading a dissolute life. Without entirely rejecting these religious motives, it is possible to consider that there were others—perhaps a series of particularly dry years in the desert, certainly also the fact that ʿAbd Allāh, who seems to have been both energetic and skilful, was able to give the 'veiled ones' a sense of unity and a confidence in themselves which they had formerly lacked, and which now needed an outlet.

After conquering the Saharan regions of Morocco, the 'veiled ones' crossed the High Atlas during the summer of 450/1058, under the command of one of their great chiefs, Abū Bakr b. ʿUmar al-Lamtūnī. For many years they conducted wars in southern and central Morocco, fighting especially the Barghawāṭa whom they regarded as heretics. ʿAbd Allāh b. Yāsīn was killed in this fighting at the beginning of 451/1059, and from then on Abū Bakr was in complete power. Gradually this sort of sultanate grew, so that in 461/1069, Abū Bakr considered that the village of Aghmāt, where he had settled at first, was becoming much too small and decided to found a new township on the plain which extends to the north of the High Atlas. This was Marrakesh (Marrākush), the building of which seems to have begun in 462/1070.[1] Soon after this, Abū Bakr was summoned back to the Sahara by grave internal quarrels and left the power in Morocco in the hands of his cousin, Yūsuf b. Tāshufīn (1 Rabīʿ II 463/6 January 1071). The latter took his charge so seriously that he soon came to consider Morocco as his own, so that when Abū Bakr returned from the Sahara in Rabīʿ I 465/November 1072, he saw that he must abandon Morocco to Yūsuf, and himself resume command of the tribes remaining in the Sahara.

After this, Yūsuf b. Tāshufīn could give free reign to his genius for conquest, and took successively Fez in 467/1075, then Tlemcen (Tilimsān), and gradually extended his power to beyond Algiers, refraining from attacking the natural fortress of the mountain of the Kabyles. Soon the Muslims of Spain appealed to him to help them to put an end to the offensive of King Alfonso VI of Castile. He crossed the Straits and inflicted a severe defeat on the Castilians at Zallāqa on 11 Rajab 479/23 October 1086; but he soon grew tired of the incessant quarrels of the petty kings of Muslim Spain and annexed their territories one after another. This marks the turning point of the history of the Almoravids. Until this time these obstinate nomads had behaved purely and simply as conquerors. The vigorous impetus arising from their hardy life had overcome all opponents in Spain as elsewhere. But in Spain they found themselves surrounded by an ancient and refined civilization, and they found this pleasant. Gradually the luxury, the softness and the varied charms of life in Spain seduced them. Yūsuf had continued to belong to the Sahara; but his son ʿAlī, a child born to him late in life by a Christian concubine, was completely different. The result was that these magnificently wild 'veiled ones' were soon transformed into propagators of the Andalusian civilization, unlike the Hilālīs who remained shepherds, both physically and spiritually.

It was at this time that Marrakesh began to grow into a town, that Fez suddenly developed, and that monuments of a Spanish character appeared on the primitive soil of Morocco: the charming Qubbat al-Barūdiyyīn at Marrakesh, and the great mosque of al-Qarawiyyīn at Fez, are almost the only traces which now remain of a gracious and subtle architecture. At the same time, the first Moroccan chroniclers began to write. If it had not been for the still barbaric soldiery which

[1] On the controversial question of the date of the founding of Marrakesh, see E. Lévi-Provençal, 'La fondation de Marrakech (462–1070)', in *Mélanges d'art et d'archéologie de l'Occident musulman*, II (Algiers, 1957), 117–20 and G. Deverdun, *Marrakech des origines à 1912*, I, (Rabat, 1959), 59–64.

occupied Spain, the Almoravids could have been taken for a settled people who had long been civilized.

The Maghrib was thus cut into two: on one side the bedouin Arabs imposed their customs and their pastoral economy on a region where the Arabo-Islamic civilization had for long been implanted; on the other the Berber nomads appeared as harbingers of Andalusian civilization in the extreme western Maghrib. It is difficult to imagine a more complete reversal of the situation.

But in losing their former energy in the delights of Seville or elsewhere, the Almoravids lost their basic *raison d'être*. They soon became incapable of continuing their military exploits, and, on another plane, quickly became sunk in bigotry and narrowness of spirit, going so far as to burn in the public square in Cordova the masterpiece of the eastern theologian and mystic, al-Ghazālī, because they considered it to be heterodox.

They needed all their forces however to fight against the movement of the Almohads, which was growing up in a remote valley of the High Atlas. About 512/1118–19, Muḥammad b. ʿAbd Allāh b. Tūmart returned from the east where he had been studying for some years. He was a Berber from Sūs, who, like many others of his period had been travelling 'in search of learning'. He returned to his country as a reformer of morals, convinced that the Maghribīs were not behaving as they ought, and went about acting on this conviction, smashing musical instruments and jars of wine, and giving to whoever wished to hear it teaching which must have been of high quality, for he was a man of eminence. He seems to have thought that the Almoravids would recognize their errors, and would reform as soon as they heard him speak. Realizing that he had been mistaken, he became a political opponent of the Almoravid ruler, ʿAlī b. Yūsuf, and in 518/1124, founded in the upper valley of the Nafīs, in the heart of the High Atlas, a community in accordance with his ideas, which soon took the name of 'those who proclaim the unity of God' (*al-Muwaḥḥidūn*), the Almohads. The reason that Ibn Tūmart proclaimed so loudly the unity and the immanence of God was that he considered the Almoravids to be anthropomorphists who divided the godhead up into little pieces. He also stressed the necessity for moral reform, condemning the luxury of Marrakesh, and finally insisted so strongly on the idea of the *mahdī*, who was to come at the end of time to restore order in the world that at the end of 515/1121 he was himself recognized as *mahdī* by his disciples.

For a long time the Almohad community remained confined within a few valleys of the High Atlas, and when, in the spring of 524/1130, the Mahdi decided to attack Marrakesh, his troops suffered a resounding defeat. He died soon afterwards, and his successor, ʿAbd al-Mu'min, a Berber from the region of Tlemcen, was more prudent: in the space of several years he conquered numerous territories, but only in the mountains and in the Saharan regions of Morocco. It was not until 540/1145 that he decided to meet the Almoravid army in open country, gaining a complete victory. He was soon master of the whole of the Almoravid Maghrib, penetrated into Spain, then conquered the central Maghrib in 547/1152–3, and Ifrīqiya in 555/1160.

His son and successor, Abū Yaʿqūb Yūsuf, added still more to this huge empire by annexing the areas of Muslim Spain which had not been subjected from the outset to the Almohad rule. But above all, the Almohad caliphs favoured the development of a vigorous civilization. According to the accounts of the geographers of the period, notably al-Idrīsī, it would seem that in this empire prosperity and order reigned. Marrakesh was considerably enlarged and endowed with monuments which still exist, such as the famous al-Kutubiyya mosque. Fez, Tunis, Algiers and many other less important towns also expanded under the Almohads; the little fortress of Rabat (Ribāṭ al-Fatḥ), founded by ʿAbd al-Mu'min, became under his grandson, Abū Yūsuf Yaʿqūb al-Manṣūr, a huge fortified camp surrounded by a continuous wall, with monumental gates and a mosque which, if it had been completed, would have been one of the largest of the whole Muslim world. The little locality of Tinmāl in the upper valley of the Nafīs, which had served as a capital for Ibn Tūmart, was endowed with a fine mosque, surprising in such a remote place.

Nor were intellectual works behind those of architecture; it suffices to recall that two of the great Arabian philosphers, Ibn Ṭufayl and Ibn Rushd (Averroes) were welcomed and encouraged by the court at Marrakesh. In addition, the poets, historians and theologians were numerous and often notable. This can certainly be called the golden age of Maghribī civilization. Islamic civilization brought to it centuries of achievement, and the Arabic language with its remarkable means of expression, Spain added its delicate charm, and Berber austerity gave to the whole an original note of proud reserve and of indisputable grandeur. When the Arab East broke up after the death of Saladin, the Almohad West was ready to pick up and to carry the torch.

But not for long—for the Almohad empire crumbled in its turn, almost as quickly as it had grown up: within forty years all had vanished. As though exhausted by such an effort, the Maghrib once again split into fragments and its brilliance was lost. This decline can be attributed to the enormousness of the enterprise: like the ʿAbbasid empire or that of Charlemagne, the Almohad empire was on too large a scale for the resources of its time, although it seems to have been provided with an efficient administration. Furthermore the conquerors had not been able to associate those whom they had conquered in their political affairs, and perhaps not in economic matters either. The Maṣmūda of the High Atlas, who had been the founders of the empire, kept everything in their own hands, leaving to the Berbers and the Spaniards whom they had subjugated only subordinate positions and modest profits. The Almohad discipline was imposed and submitted to, rather than accepted, with the result that the ruling group, on which were focused all the rancour and envy, gradually became worn out in subduing the revolts which broke out on every side. As soon as it showed signs of weakness, the bolder ethnic groups, such as the Marinids, endeavoured to shake off the yoke, and gradually succeeded.

It must also be remembered that the Almohad group in its strict sense suffered from a serious lack of balance between the *élite* and the masses. The ruling classes quickly became powerful and opulent men of culture, for whom Arabic was the most normal means of expression; they adapted themselves with ease to their new life at court, or at least in the cities. But the common people of the Almohads did not enjoy the same amenities: the Maṣmūda who had become soldiers had remained rough mountain Berbers. Being perpetually engaged in campaigns, they had scarcely had time to accustom themselves to city life, and still less to acquire even the elements of education. We may imagine, although the chroniclers do not mention this, that the former warriors hardly ever returned to their mountains, having forgotten the way of life they had led there, but congregated in towns, where they formed a proletariat living in wretched conditions. In any case there was a wide difference between the great families and the common people: the latter were hardly changed from what they had been before the establishment of the Almohad régime, while the great families had obtained access to a civilization and a culture which separated them more and more from fighting men. Any attempt to understand the decline of the Almohads must certainly take account of this social division.

The Maṣmūda were not only at the end of their strength; they had rapidly lost the spirit which had inspired them. 'Abd al-Mu'min had perhaps thought he was doing well in changing the community movement of Ibn Tūmart into an hereditary monarchy. Certainly he had taken the precaution, followed by his successors, of leaving much of the authority and the profits in the hands of the principal leaders of the movement, in particular of the first companions of the Mahdi and of their descendants. Nevertheless the real power belonged henceforward to the clan of 'Abd al-Mu'min to the exclusion of the others: the members of a community had become the subjects of a prince.

Still more serious, the Almohad faith, which had been so vigorous in the time of Ibn Tūmart, had rapidly become moribund: the homilies of 'Abd al-Mu'min, to judge by those which have survived, had lost the vigour of the exhortations of the Mahdi, and become mere conventional sermons; faith had been replaced by ritual. The Almohad belief had ceased to be a driving force, and had become pure conservatism. Certain caliphs moreover went so far as to repudiate the doctrine of the Mahdi; among them was Ya'qūb al-Manṣūr (580–95/1184–99), whose secret belief was not revealed until later, and al-Ma'mūn (625–9/1128–32), who did not hesitate to make his position publicly known. In short, for dynastic and doctrinal reasons, the unity of the Almohads, which had been the cause of the success of the Maṣmūda, was soon shaken, to the very great detriment of the empire.

To this can be added the defeats inflicted on the Muslims by the Christians of Spain, beginning with the battle of Las Navas de Tolosa (Ṣafar 609/July 1212), and the political instability of the bedouin Arab tribes, who had been transported by 'Abd al-Mu'min, and then by Ya'qūb al-Manṣūr, into the very heart of their empire, not far from the capital. But Christians and Arabs would have carried little weight had the Almohad empire been as solid as it had been in the time of Ya'qūb al-Manṣūr.

Finally, the dynasty itself declined. After the first three rulers, who had shown exceptional qualities, the power descended to ordinary men who were not of a stature to undertake such responsibilities, sometimes even gay and careless youths, such as the fifth ruler, Yūsuf al-Mustanṣir (610–23/1213–26), who hardly left Marrakesh, or even his palace, during the thirteen years of his reign. Soon, moreover, the successor was not chosen from among the many claimants by the head of the family, as in the time of the first rulers, but raised to power, often with the aid of great violence, by various factions, which nearly always included some leaders of the régime, some military figures, and one or more Arab tribes.

With this régime, the local leaders ended by ceasing to obey such an unstable power. Thus, almost simultaneously, the Hafsid chief was in command in Ifrīqiya, and the chief of the Banū ʿAbd al-Wād, who held the power in the region of Tlemcen, ceased to obey the orders of the Almohad caliph; this happened in about 633/1235–6. All was still not lost however when in 646/1248, the Almohad Caliph al-Saʿīd at the head of a powerful army set out to reconquer the empire of his ancestors. He was about to besiege Tlemcen when he was killed in an ambush, the victim of his own boldness. The panic-stricken army then disbanded, and this was the end of the empire which ʿAbd al-Mu'min had founded. Al-Saʿīd's successor, al-Murtaḍā (646–64/1248–66), had to content himself with reigning over a territory bounded by the High Atlas, the river Umm al-Rabīʿa and the Atlantic Ocean, until the time when the Marinids conquered Marrakesh (667/1269) and forced the last Almohads to seek refuge in Tinmāl, the very place where Ibn Tūmart had founded the first community. They were annihilated there in 674/1275.

With the Almohad empire, the Maghrib saw its most brilliant period until the present day; never before had this immense territory been unified, even in the time of the Romans. Never, above all, had an autochthonous people succeeded in building up such a state by their own efforts, and in creating such a brilliant civilization. Although this enormous structure soon crumbled, it left behind it important influences in the life of North Africa.

The first paradox is that the Berber conquest led to an exceptional development of Arabic culture. There is of course no doubt that the bedouin Arabs, who by this time were dispersed throughout the whole of the Maghrib, helped to spread the Arabic language in the country districts, but this is not the point. Never until this time had there been such a flowering in the thought expressed in classical Arabic: theologians, jurists, chroniclers, poets, writers of memoirs, philosophers, all appeared in greater numbers even than when the school of Qayrawān was at its zenith, and many of them enjoyed the patronage of the sovereigns and the great families. During this period there was established a vigorous Maghribī literary tradition.

The second paradox is that the Almohad doctrine, which began as a reaction against the Malikism of the Almoravids, resulted in the victory of Malikism which then held undisputed sway for many centuries—a Malikism which was perhaps more rigorous and austere than in the time of the 'veiled ones', but Malikism nevertheless. Even more paradoxical is the success of popular Sufism. It was in fact towards the end of the Almohad period that there often began to appear in the country districts holy men who, in imitation of the oriental mystics, spread the observance of divine love and of asceticism. It would seem as though the dry intellectualism of the Almohad doctrine had produced this popular fervour as an antidote.

Even after its political decline, the Almohad movement must be considered as an essential factor in the history of North Africa, if only in having shown what the Berbers were capable of when stimulated and supported by Arabic and Islamic civilization.

The Almohad decline led to the division of North Africa into three kingdoms, a system which, within variable territorial frontiers, has remained until the present day. The Hafsids in Ifrīqiya, and the Banū 'Abd al-Wād in the region of Tlemcen had severed their ties with the threatened empire. The Marinids had to carve out their kingdom by force of arms. Like the Hafsids and the Banū 'Abd al-Wād, they were still Berbers—a nomadic tribe of minor importance which alternated according to the seasons between the central valley of the Mulūya and the region of Figuig. When the empire began to weaken, they infiltrated into eastern Morocco, searching for better pasture. There they they inflicted several successive defeats on the troops who had been commissioned to drive them out, and succeeded in remaining, without however seizing any town of importance or, it seems, harbouring any definite political ambitions. Nevertheless, when faced with the vigorous retaliation of the Caliph al-Sa'īd, they yielded, and were meekly returning to their former territory when their leadership was taken by a man of energy who certainly did have political ideas—Abū Yaḥyā Abū Bakr (642–56/1244–58). Impelled by him, they returned to northern Morocco, took Meknès, which at that time was no more than an agglomeration of villages (642/1244), and in particular took advantage of the Almohad disorder to seize Fez and form a state. After twenty-five years of fighting, they succeeded in eliminating the Almohads completely, and in gaining control of the whole of Morocco.

Such were the three kingdoms which took the place of the empire of 'Abd al-Mu'min, but not one of them was resigned to the division which had taken place. Each of them was to endeavour to restore the unity of

North Africa to its own advantage; the Hafsids because they considered themselves as the legitimate heirs of the lost caliphs, the ʿAbd al-Wadids because they found the region of Tlemcen too small for them, the Marinids because, having conquered Morocco by force, they expected to be able to do the same in the rest of North Africa. None of these power-groups succeeded in realizing its ambition with any lasting results, and we shall examine the reasons for this separately for each of them.

The Hafsids, who were the first to attempt it, seemed near to achieving it. The rulers Abū Zakariyya (633–47/1236–49) and his son al-Mustanṣir (647–75/1249–77), using alternatively diplomacy and arms, forced both the Banū ʿAbd al-Wād and the Marinids to recognize their sovereignty. Furthermore their fame spread far beyond the Maghrib: ambassadors flocked to Tunis from almost all the western Mediterranean states, but also even from countries as distant as Norway and Bornu. And, as the ʿAbbasid caliphate had disappeared in 656/1258 under the Mongol attacks, the Hafsid al-Mustanṣir was recognized as caliph by the *Sharīf* of Mecca, then by the Mamluk sultan of Egypt, until an ʿAbbasid who had escaped from the Mongol massacres was proclaimed caliph in Cairo in 659/1261.

With or without the caliphate, the power of the Hafsids was of short duration. The crusade organized by King Louis IX of France in 668/1270 gave a first savage blow to the prestige of the masters of Tunis; then, after the death of al-Mustanṣir, incessant dynastic rivalries plunged the kingdom into serious disorder, so that in 683/1284 it split into two parts and remained thus for a long time. The upheavals spread still further as the bedouin played an important part in them, always ready to embrace the cause of the side which offered them the most, and then to betray it when offered still more. In addition, the various claimants endeavoured to bring in on their side either the Zayyanids (the name of the reigning family of the Banū ʿAbd al-Wād), or the Marinids, and paid very heavily for these unstable alliances. It came to the point that the Marinids twice made themselves masters of Tunis for several months in 748/1347–8, then in 758/1357.

The Hafsid state did not collapse under so much misfortune however. The *Amīr* Abu'l- ʿAbbās (758–96/1357–94) succeeded in restoring its unity; his successors Abū Fāris (796–837/1394–1434) and Abū ʿAmr ʿUthmān (838–93/1435–88), owing in part to the length of their reigns, but also to their outstanding personal qualities, restored the greatness of their kingdom, to which once again ambassadors flocked to offer advantageous commercial treaties, or simply to bring the homage of distant countries. After this long and brilliant interval there broke out new dynastic quarrels which allowed the Spaniards and the Ottomans in the tenth/sixteenth century to gain a foothold in the country without difficulty.

If only because of its duration, the Hafsid dynasty left its mark deeply on the eastern section of the Maghrib. It maintained and accentuated the tradition of centralization which had already been introduced by the preceding dynasties; but while formerly the capital had alternated between Qayrawān and Mahdiyya, the Hafsids gave to Tunis a priority which it has retained until the present day; there concentrating the scholars in the district of the mosque of al-Zaytūna, the administration around the *Qaṣba*, the administrative and fortified quarter, and a large part of the army, including the sultan's Aragonese guard; while creating in the suburbs pleasant estates, supplied with fresh water by the Roman aqueduct leading from Jabal Zaghwān which was restored for this purpose. Tunis became also an economic capital, since it was separated from the sea only by a lake, which was fairly shallow but navigable by flat-bottomed boats. Thus there were united power, prosperity and learning.

Until the Zayyanids settled there, Tlemcen had occupied only a secondary position. With the advent of Yaghmurasān b. Zayyān (633–82/1236–83), it became a capital city and an important economic centre. Indeed, situated as it was close to the port of Ḥunayn and to the islet of Rashgūn at the mouth of the Tafna, which were frequented by Christian ships, it was able to serve as a terminus for the Sahara caravans. But although in its early days the Zayyanid kingdom benefited from the fact that the Hafsids and the Marinids had still to consolidate their power, it was soon caught between these two stronger powers, and spent its time in desperate battles to survive. It went through fairly long periods of occupation by the Marinids in the eighth/fourteenth century, and by the Hafsids in the ninth/fifteenth century, and had in addition to reckon with the bedouin, who were particularly numerous in the high plains in the region of Oran (Wahrān). It is almost a miracle that the dynasty which began with Yaghmurasān was able to last until the middle of the tenth/sixteenth century, when it was finally overthrown by the Turks.

It was to this dynasty and to the Marinids that Tlemcen owed its very real greatness and its relative prosperity; most of the monuments of which this town can boast date from the Banū 'Abd al-Wād or from the period of Marinid occupation, for the masters of Fez did a great deal to win the favour of the inhabitants of Tlemcen.

The rise of the Marinids was a difficult one. They were masters of the whole of Morocco only in 667/1269, after the capture of Marrakesh, and immediately made vain efforts to arrest, if not to drive back, the Christian reconquest in Spain; and they were also troubled for more than a quarter of a century by the Zayyanids who were impatient to extend their power. It was only in the eighth/fourteenth century that their dynasty really flourished under two important rulers, Abu'l-Ḥasan 'Alī (731–52/1331–51) and his son Abū 'Inān (749–59/1348–58). Each of them thought he had realized the dream of all the heirs of the Almohads—to restore the unity of the Maghrib, but this dream lasted barely a few months, because the bedouin Arabs were strong enough to oppose it, and the Marinid troops too few to impose it. Nevertheless during the thirty years that these two sovereigns reigned, the prosperity of their kingdom was reflected in the monuments which were built there—less well-constructed than those of the Almohads, more profusely decorated, and with a greater affectation of style, but still charming, and the witnesses of a superior civilization.

After the tragic death of Abū 'Inān, who was strangled by one of his *wazīrs* because he was taking too long to die of an illness, the kingdom became entangled in the intrigues of the great families and of the bedouin Arab tribes, and in the foreign intervention of the Muslim rulers of Granada, of the kings of Castile and of Aragon, of the Zayyanids and Hafsids, and even of the Christian militia employed by the rulers at Fez. In theory the Marinids reigned until 869/1465, but in fact from 823/1420 the power fell into the hands of a family which was related to them, the Banū Waṭṭās (Wattasids), who for more than forty years were content actually to wield the power without having the title of ruler. But they could do no more than hold together with great difficulty a kingdom which was split up into several parts, and exposed to attacks by the Christians. Ceuta was captured by the Portuguese as early as 818/1415, and at the beginning of the tenth/sixteenth century the Atlantic coast of Morocco was occupied by a chain of Portuguese factories from Tangier to Agadir, while the Spaniards settled at Melilla in 902/1497. As with the Zayyanids, this was a slow decline which ended in the installation of the Sa'did dynasty in Fez in 596/1549.

Nevertheless the Marinid period was an important one in the history of Morocco. During these three centuries the country assumed the religious character, and its towns the aspect, which lasted until the establishment of the French protectorate. The Marinids were neither religious reformers nor descendants of the Prophet, and were anxious to compensate for these inferiorities by serving as well as they could the interests of Islam. They built mosques, but even more *madrasas*, where the young men of the town and from the country came to study the religious sciences from the point of view of the Mālikī *madhhab*. The importance and fame of the university of Fez dates from the Marinid period, as does that of the *madrasas* of Salé, Meknes and Marrakesh, among others. By thus developing orthodox scholarship, the Marinids were endeavouring to counteract the spread of the Ṣūfī movements which had taken root in Morocco, particularly in the country districts, towards the end of the Almohad period. As they had only moderate success in this, they resigned themselves to a compromise with the emotionalism of the masses by giving official sanction to the festival of the birth of the Prophet, and, later, by organizing the cult of Mawlāy Idrīs, the founder of Fez. Thus was formed Moroccan Islam, which was a blend of the scrupulous intellectualism of the *'ulamā'* of Fez and the sometimes frenzied emotionalism of the ordinary masses.

From the Marinids date also the towns of Morocco as they existed until the establishment of the French protectorate, the most typical of them being Fez. They had no written institutions, but a lively tradition which preserved a flexible social hierarchy, and an economic organization which was at the same time strict and liberal, in which competition played a major part, and in which the common people were hardly protected at all against its hazards. The town consisted of an agglomeration of buildings surrounded by ramparts and threaded by a maze of streets, divided into districts which at night were separated from each other, the whole clustered round its principal mosques and its central market. The development of towns had already been the policy of the Almoravids and the Almohads, and the Marinids concentrated on it still further, to the point that until the beginning of the twentieth century, no new town was added to those of the tenth/sixteenth century, apart from the Andalusian section of Rabat, and the town of Mogador (al-Ṣuwayra); the one built at the beginning of the seventeenth, the other in the second half of the eighteenth century.

Rather than cover in detail three centuries which were full of petty and complicated events, we shall examine the period as a whole, and trace in it the broad lines of the development of the Maghrib. None of the three powers which had for so long been on the scene had a very strong ethnic basis. The great strength of Ibn Tūmart and of ʿAbd al-Muʾmin arose from the fact that they had won over to their cause a large number of Berber tribes of the High Atlas, among which there had formerly existed ethnic links and common customs. The Banū ʿAbd al-Wād and the Marinids on the other hand were tribes of only minor importance numerically, and the Hafsids were simply a family and its dependents. This was not enough to restore the Almohad empire, and they all exhausted themselves in a vain effort to do so.

On the other hand, the full importance of the bedouin phenomenon became apparent; it had already appeared at the end of the Almohad period, but then in the middle of a period of decadence. The three Maghribī kingdoms on the other hand, even at the height of their power had had to rely on the unstable support of the bedouin tribes: these tribes were spread out over a large part of the territory, and did not form compact groups in the same way as the groups of mountain Berbers, such as the Rīfīs, the Kabyles or the Maṣmūda of the High Atlas. Consequently each of them tended to act independently according to its immediate interests, and this gave a decided feature of uncertainty to the politics of the period.

The bedouin tribes did however help to arabize the areas in which they spread. As the Berber governments had on their side also adopted Arabic, following the example of the Almoravids and the Almohads, the use of this language expanded considerably during the period. This does not mean however that Arabic became the only means of communication among the inhabitants of the Maghrib. There remained a considerable proportion of Berber speakers, particularly in Morocco, where the Arabs had arrived late and lived only in restricted areas. Even in Ifrīqiya, where the Arabs were numerous, and where they had been settled since their first arrival in the Maghrib, there was still a considerable number of Berber speakers. All the same, the three centuries with which we are dealing were certainly the essential period in the arabization of the country.

There was also a certain stabilization of social conditions. Since the time of the invasion of the Hilālīs and of the Almoravids, in the course of barely two centuries, the ruling classes had several times completely changed. But once the Hafsid, Zayyanid or Marinid aristocracies were in power, that is from the middle of the seventh/thirteenth century, Maghribī society was to have three centuries relatively without change, with leaders taken from among the groups in power and the chiefs of the Arab tribes; the middle classes in the towns were themselves firmly established, except in the case of Marrakesh, where, even during the Almoravid and Almohad periods, there does not seem to have developed a local and firmly rooted bourgeoisie as was the case everywhere else. The only modification to be mentioned is the reinforcement of the local bourgeoisies by the arrival of Andalusian town-dwellers fleeing from the Christian reconquest.

In the cultural field also stabilization took place. If we except the genius Ibn Khaldūn (eighth/fourteenth century), it can be said that the intellectual works no longer possessed the fire of the Almohad period. There were many worthy chroniclers, poets, geographers or writers of travel accounts, as well as jurists, theologians and hagiographers; but among all their works there was nothing which had the feeling of novelty and discovery which characterized the preceding period. Similarly, Marinid art, the most successful among the Marinid achievements, was, as we have already said, only a sort of insipid version of Almohad art. Even the attractive *madrasas* of Fez cannot eclipse the monuments erected by ʿAbd al-Mu'min or Yaʿqūb al-Manṣūr. What they gained in charm, they lost in vigour and in majesty. It was, in short, a period when artists and intellectuals lived on the attainments which they had inherited, but showed no sign of any creativity.

Lastly, perhaps the most important phenomenon which characterized this period in the Maghrib was the European, or rather the Christian, invasion. Not until the end of the fifth/eleventh century did there appear in Muslim North Africa some Christian merchants, Italians for the most part. In the following century, the Normans of Sicily made, with Roger II, a first attempt to gain a foothold in Africa in an economic, military and even political form: an abortive attempt, since it encountered the decisive opposition of the Almohads. But no sooner had the latter become masters of Ifrīqiya than they authorized Christian merchants to settle there. At the beginning of the seventh/thirteenth century the last Almohad caliphs recruited Christian mercenaries, especially Spaniards, while Franciscan and Dominican missionaries penetrated into the Maghrib to preach Christianity. From the end of the same century, the Almohad empire having disappeared, this phenomenon grew in scale, for, in addition to the merchants, the mercenaries and the missionaries, several European powers sent military expeditions to seize various points on the coast of the Maghrib. None of these attempts achieved a permanent result until the capture of Ceuta by the Portuguese, but there were many of them and they constituted an almost continuous threat to the country.

The attempts of the missionaries resulted only in individual success, and these very few in number, and on several occasions ended in the violent death of the proselytizers. The part played by the mercenaries had hardly any effect. The commercial enterprises on the other hand achieved so great a success that it can be said that in the ninth/fifteenth century all the maritime commerce of the Maghrib was in the hands of the Europeans, mainly Italians and Catalans, also, to a lesser degree, Portuguese and natives of Provence. In the absence of any statistics we have to be content with vague and general impressions, but it seems reasonable to affirm that the Europeans were taking an increasing part in the commercial affairs of the Maghrib, not only as importers and exporters, but also in the impetus which they gave to the trans-Saharan trade. They traded in fact in a large part of the gold dust, ivory, ostrich feathers, and even the slaves which reached the Maghribī coast via the Sahara. This reappearance in force of the representatives of Christian Europe, which since the Muslim conquest had practically disappeared from the Maghrib, forms one of the essential elements of this period.

At the end of the ninth/fifteenth century therefore, the Maghrib appears as a territory completely islamized, except for the relatively few Jewish communities, and thoroughly arabized, in spite of the presence of compact Berber-speaking groups. But beneath this basic unity there existed great disparities. It was not only that the Maghrib itself, far from forming a political unity, consisted of three different powers which were often at war with each other; but that within each of the three kingdoms the superficial unity was maintained only with difficulty. The authorities in each case, often themselves unstable, had great difficulty in controlling a collection of very individualistic tribes, little inclined to obey the central power unless it showed itself to be strong and vigilant. On the other hand, the Maghrib was no longer merely a distant and autonomous part of the Muslim empire, but, since the return of the Europeans in the fifth/eleventh century, must be reckoned as one of the countries of the western Mediterranean. In short, after breaking away for several centuries from its natural geographical milieu, the western Mediterranean, it was drawn back into it by the spirit of enterprise of the Christian peoples; and was not to leave it again until the present day.

This short account, however incomplete, indicates the development of the peoples of the Maghrib from the time of the Muslim conquest. Once again they submitted to the domination of a civilization which was imported from outside, and which was at its zenith. But instead of remaining on the whole outside the country, as the preceding civilizations had done, the Arabo-Islamic contribution became an integral part of the life of the Maghrib. It is possible to consider that an affinity already existed, especially if one accepts the view that the majority of the Berbers came from the shores of the Red Sea. But the part played by Islam in this phenomenon cannot be denied. This religion gained adherents with much more vigour than Christianity, even when the latter had Saint Augustine as its spokesman. Simple and meticulous at the same time, Islam drew the Berbers to itself, and held them. Finally the Hilālī invasion had a great influence on the fate of the Maghrib; it was responsible for the amalgamation of the Berbers and the immigrants, and from it dates the present-day Arabo-Berber population. At any earlier time the Arab influence could have been swept away as the Roman influence had been; but two centuries after the advent of the first Hilālīs, Arabic civilization, culture and language had taken firm root in the country. Thus those who were really responsible for this phenomenon with its considerable consequences were less ‘Uqba b. Nāfi‘, Mūsā b. Nuṣayr or Idrīs b. ‘Abd Allāh than the poor and proud camel-drivers sent by a Fatimid *wazīr* to punish disloyal vassals.

CHAPTER 2

NORTH AFRICA IN THE SIXTEENTH AND SEVENTEENTH CENTURIES

GENERAL CHARACTERISTICS OF THE PERIOD

Before the end of the ninth/fifteenth century, the three great dynasties then in power in North Africa—the Marinids in Morocco, the 'Abd al-Wadids in the central Maghrib and the Hafsids in Ifrīqiya—were either being displaced by a new dynasty or suffered the decline of their authority and the dividing up of their lands; so that at the beginning of the tenth/sixteenth century the Maghrib was in complete political decay. This situation allowed the penetration of Africa by the Portuguese and the Spanish on the one hand, and by Ottoman Turks on the other. The Portuguese and the Spanish were unable to remain in Morocco, where the Sa'did dynasty succeeded in forming an indigenous government which lasted for a century before being supplanted by the 'Alawid dynasty. On the other hand, in the central and eastern Maghrib the Turkish corsairs, after conquering the rival Spanish forces, introduced governments of military occupation. These transformed themselves into local powers which were recognized by the Ottoman sultan, but their existence was troubled by many palace revolutions.

One of the principal activities of these states was privateering, from the ports of Salé, Algiers, Tunis and Tripoli, which provided resources for the rulers, but resulted in difficulties with the European maritime powers. Nevertheless, foreign merchants settled in Algiers, in Tunis, and in some other places; political relations were established between the North African states and England, France and Holland. The Mediterranean, in spite of the discovery of new sea routes and new countries, continued to play an important part in world politics, especially as the Ottoman empire, which until then had held only the eastern shores, was henceforward established along the greater part of its African coast, from the Nile Delta to Mulūya. Even although the Ottoman domination of Algeria, Tunisia and Tripolitania was only nominal, it is nevertheless true that this domination created a new political situation against which the Western powers struggled for three centuries.

MOROCCO

The Wattasids, the Portuguese invasion and the appearance of the Sa'dids

The seizure of power by the Wattasid *wazīr* Muḥammad al-Shaykh from the last Marinid ruler and the Idrīsī *Sharīfs*, took place at a difficult juncture. Within Morocco he was able to impose his authority only on the region of Fez, for the Berbers of the Atlas and the religious fraternities of the south refused to recognize his authority. Furthermore, the Portuguese who, taking advantage of the upheavals, had seized Arzila in 876/1471 and had forced the Castilians to recognize their rights on the African coast (treaty of 1479), proceeded to Morocco and settled firmly at Ceuta, al-Qaṣr al-Ṣaghīr, Tangier and Arzila. Spain, however, was uneasy that Portugal should be the only country to obtain the advantages of settlement in Morocco, particularly after the Reconquista was completed; for this reason, with the agreement of Portugal, they seized in 902/1497 the Mediterranean port of Melilla which provided them with a base for further operations.

The Portuguese, in the reign of Dom Manuel, continuing methodically their occupation of the Atlantic seaboard, and thus depriving Morocco of all possibility of maritime relations, settled in Agadir (909/1504), Safi (914/1508) and Azemmour (919/1513), all outlets from Marrakesh on to the Atlantic. In 921/1515 a Portuguese expedition, supported by some local contingents, after having subdued the greater part of the Ḥawḍ, got as far as the gates of Marrakesh but was unable to take it. However, although they spread their domination fairly widely throughout the central coastal plains, they limited themselves elsewhere to a restricted area surrounding their strongholds, from which they carried out incursions towards the interior. From these they returned with booty of cereals, flocks, and also men, whom they either sold as slaves or released against the payment of a ransom. Of more importance is the fact that, being in control of all the seaboard, they secured for themselves the monopoly of the maritime trade, reducing Moroccan navigation to nothing, and depriving the Moroccan rulers of hitherto assured revenues, notably those derived from the export of sugar. This Portuguese pressure was not without its consequences for the Wattasid rulers, Muḥammad al-Burtughālī (910–31/1505–24) and Abu'l-'Abbās Aḥmad (931–55/1524–49); being occupied in keeping in check so far as they could the Portuguese incursions, they could not face effectively the attempts at expansion being made by the *Sharīfs* of the south.

As early as the ninth/fifteenth century, a religious and, to a certain extent, a national movement had arisen in different regions of Morocco, and had manifested itself in the spreading of more or less mystical doctrines and in the increase in the numbers of marabouts.[1] This movement, in which the Ṣūfīs and the shaykhs played an important part, drew part of its strength from the hatred of Christianity and of the Europeans, and was particularly powerful in the south. Being, however, unable to achieve any successful action against the Portuguese, it directed its efforts against the Wattasids, who were accused of having done nothing to hinder the progress of the Europeans.

At the beginning of the tenth/sixteenth century, southern Morocco, and in particular Sūs, found itself under the authority of the tribe of the Banū Sa'd who claimed descent from the Prophet through a grandson of Fāṭima and 'Alī. Supported by the nomads of the south, and with the help of gold sent from the western *Bilād al-Sūdān*, which enabled him to obtain weapons, the chief of the Banū Sa'd—or Sa'dīs—fought against the Portuguese of the Agadir region, and proclaimed himself in 915/1509 independent ruler of Sūs, supported by the marabout of that country, Sīdī 'Abd Allāh b. al-Mubārak. Bearing the impressive title of *Sharīfs*, the Sa'dīs rallied to their cause a fair number of the southern tribes, made Taroudant into a formidable stronghold, then, having secured their rear, occupied Tafilelt and all the southern fringe of the High Atlas. On the second stage of their progress the Sa'dīs encountered the sultan of the south, their former ally, who was assassinated in 932/1525. They then set up their capital at Marrakesh, and commenced a decisive struggle against both the Wattasids and the Portuguese simultaneously.

The Wattasid ruler, Abu'l-'Abbās Aḥmad, attempted to conclude an agreement with the Sa'dīs, and conceded to them the complete possession of southern Morocco; but they ignored his proposals. In order to protect his own domain he gave battle to them, was conquered, and had to yield to them the greater part of central Morocco (942/1536). The prestige of the Sa'dīs was increased still further by their campaigns against the Portuguese settlements: after the Cape of Aguer (Agadir) which fell into their hands in 947/1541, Safi and Azemmour succumbed in 948/1542, al-Qaṣr al-Ṣaghīr and Arzila in 955/1549. The Portuguese domination of the Atlantic coast came to an end, and from that time Moroccan privateering was resumed from the ports of Salé and Larache, while the

[1] Marabout (Arabic, *murābiṭ*) signifies a popular religious leader, regarded as a saint. Many marabouts were connected with the Ṣūfī orders.

export of the sugar of Sūs and the gold of the *Bilād al-Sūdān* to France and England enabled Moroccan navigation to make a beginning again, with renewed vigour.

Strengthened as he was by these successes, nothing hindered the Sa'dī *Sharīf*, Muḥammad al-Mahdī, from turning his attention to the Wattasid Bā Ḥassūn, the brother of Muḥammad al-Burtughālī, and driving him out of Fez (955/1549). Unable to obtain help from the Spaniards, Bā Ḥassūn turned to the Turks of Tlemcen and of Algiers. Ṣāliḥ Re'īs, at the head of a strong armed contingent, succeeded in retaking Fez in the name of Bā Ḥassūn (960/1553), and sent his fleet to occupy the Peñon de Velez. But Bā Ḥassūn was killed soon afterwards during a battle against the Sa'dīs (14 Shawwāl 960/23 September 1553), which put to an end to the Wattasid dynasty, and completed the success of Muḥammad al-Mahdī and the installation of the new Sa'did dynasty as rulers of the whole of Morocco. Muḥammad al-Mahdī, wishing to avenge himself on the Turks, attempted to seize Tlemcen, but an army sent from Algiers succeeded in pushing him back towards Morocco. Nevertheless the conflict between Sa'dīs and Turks was not finished.

Thus after nearly a century the Wattasid dynasty disappeared, having achieved distinction only with its first ruler. Occupied with the struggle against the *Sharīfs*, the marabouts, the religious fraternities and the Christians, it undertook nothing constructive and was able to remain on the throne of Fez only thanks to the dissipation of the various forces then existing in Morocco. During this same period, the Portuguese, hesitating between Africa and America, were unable to gain a solid foothold in Morocco for lack of military resources, but also through lack of understanding of the surrounding Muslim milieu. In short, this was a period if not of anarchy, at least of characterless government from which there stands out, from 1525 onwards, only the tenacious effort of the Sa'dīs to seize power and to drive out the Portuguese.

The Sa'dids (960–1065/1553–1654)

With the Sa'did dynasty there began what has been called the Sharifian empire, so-called because the Sa'dīs, like their successors the 'Alawīs, claimed descent from the Prophet and thus had the right to the title of *sharīf*. With one exception, the Arabic sources on the Sa'dī period are of only mediocre value, consisting of biased works glorifying the sultans in excessive panegyrics; the facts themselves are presented uncritically and are often distorted; the hagiographies written during this period are of very little historical interest. The European sources, on the other hand, begin with the Sa'did dynasty to show a certain degree of consistency, including documents from the Spanish, Portuguese, French and other archives, as well as travellers' accounts, the number of which increases gradually through the eleventh/seventeenth century. With the help of these sources it is possible to follow fairly accurately the events which took place, as well as the Sa'dī system of government, economic life and commercial intercourse—of all which little is known under the preceding dynasties.

Muḥammad al-Mahdī, the real founder of the dynasty, is revealed as a great ruler, possessing a high conception of his title and his duty. Firmly resolved to impose his power on the whole of Morocco, he eliminated all political opposition, but had nevertheless to face a religious opposition led by the religious fraternities and the marabouts. Against these opponents, who did not hesitate to seek the aid of the Turks, he used violent methods of repression, intended to reduce the influence of the marabouts to nothing: a number of them were banished or executed and some *zāwiyas* (i.e. convents of Ṣūfīs) were destroyed. This action of Muḥammad al-Mahdī was not due solely to religious motives; it was prompted also by the fact that the marabouts and the *zāwiyas* had opposed the financial measures which he had promulgated. He wanted in fact to oblige those who lived in the mountains, as well as those who lived in the plains, to pay the *kharāj* or land tax; he was unable to enforce this without disturbances, of which the religious movements tried to take advantage. As these movements were particularly powerful in the region of Fez, the Sa'dī ruler set up his capital at Marrakesh, where the population was loyal to him.

In external politics, in order to be better able to oppose the Portuguese, he adopted a conciliatory policy towards the Spaniards, who could have become dangerous neighbours, as they were settled at Melilla, Oran and Mers el-Kebir. This rapprochement with the Spaniards was also connected with Muḥammad al-Mahdī's struggle against the Turks of Tlemcen. He wished in fact to avenge himself on the Turks who had given help to Bā Ḥassūn; taking the offensive, he succeeded in capturing Tlemcen but not its citadel, and finally had to return to Morocco. The Turks avenged themselves in their turn, and had Muḥammad al-Mahdī assassinated in 964/1557.

His son and successor, al-Ghālib (964–82/1557–74), encountered the same adversaries: against the Turks, he formed an alliance with the

Spaniards and the French; against the supporters of the marabouts he too used violence, and ordered the massacre of the members of the fraternity of the Yūsufiyya. The rest of his reign proceeded without incident. Finding himself master of a kingdom which was apparently pacified, well under control and well administered, al-Ghālib devoted himself to the planning and adornment of Marrakesh, where he built a mosque and a *madrasa*, and transformed the palace and the *qaṣba*. The reigns of Muḥammad al-Mahdī and of al-Ghālib, by eliminating the elements of opposition and providing a solid foundation for Sa'did rule, made possible the brilliant reign of Aḥmad al-Manṣūr. During the early years of the dynasty the Portuguese had undertaken no measures against it because of the alliance concluded between the Sa'dīs and the Spaniards, and above all because of the policy of John III (1521–57) which was directed entirely towards Brazil, to the extent that the Portuguese at that time evacuated Ceuta, Tangier and Mazagan, and, no longer possessing the necessary bases in Morocco, ceased to be a serious threat to the Sa'dīs. But this policy received little support in Lisbon, where the idea of a war against Islam, and especially against Morocco, had still some fanatical adherents: these prevailed in the reign of King Sebastian (1557–78) who, filled with an exalted mysticism, and anxious to revive the former spirit of the Crusades, abandoned the Brazilian and Indian policy of John III, and resolved to bring Morocco under the banner of Christianity.

He was encouraged in this attitude by the events which followed the death of al-Ghālib. In fact the latter's successor, Muḥammad al-Mutawakkil, had from the time of his accession (982/1574) to face strong opposition from two of his uncles. Internal quarrels reappeared, fostered and reinforced by the religious fraternities who saw in them a possibility of renewing their influence, by the interventions of the Turks of Algiers, and by the intrigues of the European powers, who hoped to weaken the Sa'did dynasty. One of the uncles of the sultan, 'Abd al-Malik, with the co-operation of the Turks and the Spaniards, succeeded in defeating him, and he fled to Portugal. But al-Mutawakkil did not admit himself irrevocably defeated, especially as he had made great plans of reconstruction for Morocco. He found ready co-operation from King Sebastian; for intervention in Morocco favoured the Portuguese king's plans for conquest, though he took part in the campaign against the advice of his army leaders, and even against that of Philip II of Spain—who had just lost in Tunisia his last bases in eastern

North Africa—against the advice also of all those who had been able to judge at first hand of the progress of the Sa'dīs. Moreover Sebastian mustered only a very small army, ill-prepared and ill-equipped, and, even more serious, he wanted to command it himself, although he was almost incapable of directing its advance or its operations. One section of this army was left at Tangier and the rest disembarked at Arzila on 7 Jumādā I 986/12 July 1578. The Portuguese troops then advanced towards Fez and arrived at Wādi'l-Makhāzin where they encountered the troops of 'Abd al-Malik near al-Qaṣr al-Kabīr. 'Abd al-Malik had gathered round him not only the southern tribes, who were traditionally faithful to the Sa'dīs, but also the other tribes who had formerly been more or less hostile, but whom he had rallied in the name of the struggle against Christianity and the Portuguese. In the battle which ensued on 30 Jumādā I 986/4 August 1578, the Portuguese troops, outnumbered and badly deployed, suffered a crushing defeat by the Moroccans. Sebastian was killed in the battle, al-Mutawakkil was drowned and the greater part of the Portuguese nobility were taken prisoner: Portugal was never again to be a dangerous enemy to the Moroccans, especially as Spain, taking advantage of the circumstances, hastened to put Portugal under its domination.

The battle of al-Qaṣr al-Kabīr was fatal also for 'Abd al-Malik, who died there, not from wounds, but probably from a heart attack. His brother Aḥmad was immediately proclaimed sultan without the slightest opposition, and the victory which was won over the Portuguese gained him the name of *al-Manṣūr* ('the Victorious'). In addition, a considerable booty was taken, and the ransoms paid for the deliverance of the Portuguese prisoners swelled considerably the treasury of the new sultan. Spain, France and England were impressed by the Moroccan victory and made efforts to enter into good political and economic relations with Aḥmad al-Manṣūr, who because of the difficulties and the upheavals then taking place in Algeria and Tunisia, was considered the greatest of the North African rulers.

It was in fact during his reign (986–1012/1578–1603) that the Sa'did dynasty reached its zenith in political as well as in economic affairs. In addition, Aḥmad al-Manṣūr had the distinction of instituting an administrative system which lasted practically until the beginning of the twentieth century. It was he who created the administrative system called the *Makhzen* (*Makhzan*), a central organization which was placed under the authority of the sultan, and which included the *wazīrs*, the officers, the governors, the palace personnel, and the military tribes or *gish* (*jaysh*), who were exempted from dues and taxes and provided with land. This organization administered the land, which was subject to land-tax and occupied by the tribes grouped in federations forming the *bled el-makhzen* (*bilād al-makhzan*). The unsubdued part of Morocco constituted the *bled el-siba* (*bilād al-sība*), which remained outside the sultan's authority. This centralized rule was directed energetically by Aḥmad al-Manṣūr, who, at the beginning of his reign, had had to face military insurrections and the opposition of the *zāwiyas* and the Berber tribes: all of them were vigorously suppressed. The sultan took advantage of the period of peace which followed to develop agriculture and the sugar industry, and then to increase the taxes, which were sometimes violently levied by his war-bands. This provoked in 1004/1595–6 the revolt of the Barānis Berbers, which was mercilessly crushed. At the end of the reign, however, the chiefs of some of the tribes began to free themselves from the sultan's tutelage, and, taking advantage of the growing discontent against the number of Christian renegades and of Jews in the sultan's entourage, found support among the religious fraternities and all the anti-Christian elements. They created again a mood of anarchy and of latent crisis, which came to a head on the very morrow of the death of Aḥmad al-Manṣūr.

Wishing to restore to his capital, Marrakesh, its former splendour, al-Manṣūr had built there palaces and various monuments, and for their construction brought workmen and artists from every land, among them being Europeans. He also built the palace of Badī', later to be destroyed by Mawlāy Ismā'īl, on which he spent considerable sums of money, and the eastern section of the mausoleum of the Sa'did sultans. His court was one of the most brilliant of the period: magnificent feasts were held there, and the sultan was followed, surrounded and protected by a numerous entourage and guards of honour in sumptuous uniforms, while around him thronged the foreign ambassadors, the Christian merchants, and the important figures of the administration, not all of Moroccan origin. The personality of Aḥmad al-Manṣūr made a striking impression on contemporary European rulers, but his prestige is explained also by the boldness of his foreign policy.

Having formed an army on the Ottoman model, incorporating a number of Spanish renegades, Andalusians, Turks and negroes, he sent it against the western *Bilād al-Sūdan*. This land, islamized in the time of the Almoravids, had since then maintained peaceful relations with Morocco, which exercised there a great intellectual and religious influence, especially during the period when the dynasty of the Askiyas of Gao was in power (898–999/1493–1591). But Aḥmad al-Manṣūr wanted to appropriate the salt-mines themselves, at least the trade-routes of the Sudanese gold. After the failure of a first expedition, a second, under the command of the Spanish renegade Jawdhar, reached the banks of the Niger, and was enabled by its musketry to rout the army of the Askiya ruler and to seize Gao (Jumādā I 999/March 1591), and then Timbuktu (1 Rajab 999/25 April 1591), where Jawdhar, who had received the title of pasha, made his residence. His successor, Maḥmūd Zarghūn, attempted to form an independent state, which he ruled by violence, massacre and terror. From 1021/1612 onwards, the sultans of Morocco lost interest in the pashalic of Timbuktu, which sank into anarchy, bringing with it the ruin of Sudanese trade, and the impoverishment and political decline of the country. Nevertheless Aḥmad al-Manṣūr had been able to gain from the Sudan enormous profits, in particular such a supply of gold as to enable him to pay his officials in pure gold, to give the Moroccan ducat supremacy on the money market, to maintain a large army and to undertake much building work, especially at Marrakesh. But he was the only Saʿdī who was able to do this, for his successors were unable to impose their authority on the pashas of Timbuktu.

Al-Manṣūr's power and wealth were a source of anxiety not only to his new Turkish neighbours but also to the Ottoman sultan, who saw him as a possible rival in the Mediterranean. For his part, the *beylerbeyi* of Algiers, Kılıj ʿAlī, would have liked to bring the Moroccan ports under his domination in order to extend the range of Algerian privateering. He prepared to invade Morocco, but al-Manṣūr, by diplomatic intervention at Istanbul and the offer of magnificent presents to the sultan, put a stop to this attempt, which was not repeated. With the departure of Kılıj ʿAlī in 996/1587 and the ensuing period of anarchy in Algiers, Aḥmad al-Manṣūr was freed from any threat from the Turks and even in his turn considered invading Algeria, but he soon gave up this idea.

He maintained close relations with the English, who, taking advantage of the decline in the fortunes of the Portuguese, had in 1511 begun a commerce of exchange with Morocco: the barter of cloth for gold, sugar and leather. There was also an attempt to organize merchants in a

Barbary Company (1585), but this lasted only twelve years. In addition the sultan formed a non-aggression pact with Philip II of Spain, who handed over Arzila to him (997/1589). But the Spanish king's projects in Africa alarmed al-Manṣūr, who approached the English. Queen Elizabeth I and the Moroccan sultan planned to conquer Spain, but this came to nothing, because in 1603 both rulers died.

The question of the succession to Aḥmad al-Manṣūr gave rise to terrible strife between his three sons. Finally one of them, Mawlāy Zaydān, gained the throne, but he was never firmly in power, and in fact was unable to gain authority over the region of Fez; even at Marrakesh he was three times obliged to abandon his throne. During the civil war, the Spanish had occupied Larache (1610) and then al-Maʿmūra. The progress made by the Christians had set in motion a national and religious movement of which a marabout of the south, Abū Maḥallī, took advantage to seize Tafilelt, drive out the Saʿdīs, and occupy Marrakesh. Zaydān was able to overcome him only with difficulty. In addition to this, at Salé the marabout al-ʿAyāshī organized privateer ing against the Spaniards, and received help from the Moors who had been driven out of Spain, and from the English corsairs. He succeeded in recapturing al-Maʿmūra and extended his authority over the hinterland as far as Tāzā. Zaydān was powerless against him and against Shaykh Abū Ḥassūn, who held Sūs and Tafilelt: all that remained to him were Marrakesh and Safi.

After the death of Zaydān (1036/1627), Morocco was in fact shared between the leaders of the fraternities, among which that of Dilā' was active in the region of Fez. Little by little it increased its territory, and finally succeeded in gaining power in central and northern Morocco, Sultan Muḥammad al-Shaykh al-Aṣghar being powerless to prevent this. But the Dilā'īs did not last long. When Muḥammad al-Aṣghar died (1064/1654), his son was unable to have himself proclaimed sultan, and was assassinated by the tribe of the Shabāna, who appointed its own shaykh as sultan. The Saʿdid dynasty thus came to an inglorious end. There followed in Morocco a period of more than ten years of anarchy, from which there finally emerged the Filālī or ʿAlawī *Sharīf* Mawlāy al-Rashīd who founded the ʿAlawī dynasty: having eliminated one after another the various little local rulers, he was able to assert his rule throughout Morocco.

During the final period of the Saʿdid dynasty, French influence increased, and a peace treaty was concluded between Morocco and

France in 1040/1631 and confirmed by Salé in 1045/1635. There had been established at Salé the independent republic of Bu Regreg, which became the principal privateering port of Morocco and, consequently an important centre of commerce. But the incursions which the Salé corsairs made into European waters brought them difficulties with the French (1038/1629) and later with the Dutch (1061–64/1651–54). The capture of Salé by the 'Alawīs certainly did not reduce the privateering, but from the end of the seventeenth century the Europeans began vigorous counter-measures and European privateering became a factor which impeded the progress of Morocco.

TURKISH ALGERIA AND TUNISIA

The rivalry between Spain and Turkey (914–82/1508–74).

In the same period as Morocco, there took place in Algeria and in Tunisia the weakening of the reigning dynasties and the intervention of foreign powers. At the end of the ninth/fifteenth century in Ifrīqiya the Hafsid rulers were no longer able to impose their authority either in Ifrīqiya proper or in eastern Algeria: with the exception of Tunis and its immediate suburbs, all their territory lay open to the nomadic Arab tribes who levied tribute on the coastal and inland towns. In Algeria, the 'Abd al-Wadids had lost control over the central Maghrib, and could exercise their authority only over Tlemcen and the western part of the country. Everywhere else there had arisen small autonomous states. The ports had also made themselves independent, and local governments had turned them into bases for corsairs who raided merchant ships and at the same time carried on the war against the infidels. This privateering, moreover, gained a new impetus at the end of the century when the Moors who had been driven out of Spain joined forces with the local corsairs. The central and eastern Maghrib was thus completely fragmented, and although it was not reduced to complete anarchy, it had no powerful rulers to control it. It was so weakened by its divisions as to be unable effectively to oppose the Spaniards, who at that time, under the pretext of a religious crusade, were trying to establish, as the Portuguese had done in Morocco, *presidios* (i.e. garrisons) in the main coastal towns; but the Spanish enterprise was soon to encounter, not so much local resistance as the simultaneous opposition of the Turkish corsairs, and then of the Ottoman government itself, which looked on Spain as its chief enemy in the Mediterranean.

Although the initial pretext for the Spanish crusade was the struggle of Christianity against Islam, particularly after the insurrection which flared up among the Moors of Granada in 906/1501, this soon became subordinate to the political and material considerations aroused by the breaking up of the Maghrib. The insurrection of Granada was used as a motive by the advocates of Spanish intervention in Africa, the most ardent of whom was Cardinal Ximenez de Cisneros. Ferdinand II decided to take action after an attack by the corsairs of Mers el-Kebir on south-eastern Spanish ports, and in October 1505 a fleet of considerable size captured Mers el-Kebir. Next the Spanish corsair, Pedro Navarro, occupied the Peñon de Velez (914/1508), Oran (915/1509), Bougie (Shawwāl 915/January 1510) and Tripoli (Rabīʿ II 916/July 1510), but was defeated off Djerba (917/1511). The success of the Spaniards led to the other Algerian ports paying them tribute, and the Algerians even surrendered to Navarro an islet on which he built the fortress of the Peñon commanding the entry to the port. Thus in a very short time the Spaniards had made themselves masters of the whole of the Algerian coast: it only remained for them to conquer the interior of the country, but it does not seem that such a project was ever launched. In fact Ferdinand was unable to divert a large proportion of his military force from his European, and especially his Italian, commitments, and he contented himself with a limited occupation in Africa. Garrisons were established in the conquered ports, and their defences considerably strengthened. The authority of these garrisons often did not extend beyond the walls which surrounded them, and some of them led a difficult existence with the risk of famine ever present. This was very different from the religious crusade and the Christian reconquest of Africa which had been envisaged.

The situation of the *presidios* became worse with the intervention of the Turks, whom the Algerians called to their aid. Algiers was at this time a town of about 20,000 inhabitants, governed by a bourgeois minority dependent on the support of the powerful Arab tribe of the Thaʿāliba. From the eighth/fourteenth century, one of its main activities was privateering and piracy, so that the threat of the Spanish fortress of the Peñon looking down on the town was not likely to please the corsairs and the merchants of Algiers. To rid themselves of the Spanish, they asked for the co-operation of the Turkish corsair ʿOruj, more often called ʿArūj. He, with his three brothers Ilyās, Khayr al-Dīn and Isḥāq (to all of whom has been attributed the nickname Barbarossa, which should in fact be given only to Khayr al-Dīn), had at first displayed his talents as a corsair in the Greek Archipelago, and then, after various adventures, transferred his attentions to the western and central Mediterranean, fighting especially against the Spaniards, and helping to establish many Moors from Spain in the central and eastern Maghrib. ʻArūj had gained great prestige, and he obtained permission from the Hafsid sultan to use the island of Djerba as a base for his activities. After failing twice to take Bougie, in 918/1512 and 920/1514, he succeeded in capturing Djidjelli in 920/1514. At the request of the inhabitants of Algiers, ʻArūj first occupied Cherchel, then entered Algiers (921/1515); but as he delayed in attacking the Peñon, the dissatisfied inhabitants tried to get rid of him. ʻArūj was warned of this, and exposed the conspirators, executed a number of them, and made himself completely master of Algiers (922/1516). Alarmed at this, the Spaniards attempted an attack on the town but were severely defeated (Shaʻbān 922/September 1516). Continuing his progress, ʻArūj gained control of Miliana, Medea and Tenes. Soon after this, at the invitation of the inhabitants of Tlemcen, he occupied this town also. But the Spaniards reacted to this growing menace: Isḥāq was captured and killed in a battle, and ʻArūj himself besieged for six months in Tlemcen; when he attempted to flee, he was overtaken and slain (924/1518). By this time he had succeeded in extending his authority throughout the north-west of Algeria.

After his death, his work was carried on by his brother Khayr al-Dīn, who at that time was in command of Algiers. Khayr al-Dīn was to become the founder of the *ojak* of Algiers, or, as it was called in the West, the Regency of Algiers. In order to combat the attempts to break up his embryo state, Khayr al-Dīn placed himself under the direct authority of the Ottoman sultan Selīm I who appointed him *beylerbeyi* (commander-in-chief of the *ojak*), conferred on him the title of pasha, and sent him reinforcements of men and supplies. But his situation remained difficult. Attacked by the Spaniards, betrayed by the inhabitants of Algiers, and abandoned by the local troops, he was defeated, withdrew from Algiers, and established himself at Djidjelli (926/1520) where he prepared his revenge. This was rapid and severe: in turn Collo, Bône and Constantine fell into his hands (927–928/1521–22), then Algiers was taken (931/1525) and the Mitidja reoccupied; the Arabs and the Kabyles who had betrayed him or who tried to revolt were mercilessly massacred. Algiers had for long not known such a master. To complete his domination, Khayr al-Dīn seized the Peñon of Algiers (19 Ramaḍān

935/27 May 1529), demolished the fortress, and, having joined to the town the islets which were situated very close to the shore, he created the port of Algiers which, in spite of the bad anchorage, he made the headquarters of Turkish privateering in the western Mediterranean—a base which was unrivalled in the Maghrib as long as the Spaniards held Oran and Bougie.

But between eastern Algeria and Djerba, Ifrīqiya still remained outside Turkish possession. Fearing perhaps that this part of the Maghrib would provide the Spaniards with a base for eventual action against the Ottomans (the antagonism between Süleymān the Magnificent and the Emperor Charles V was then at its height), and taking advantage of the anarchy among the Hafsids, Khayr al-Dīn decided to seize Ifrīqiya. He occupied Bizerta without difficulty, then La Goulette, and finally Tunis after a brief battle (7 Ṣafar 941/18 August 1534). From there he sent a body of troops to occupy Qayrawān, and obtained the support of the ports of the eastern coast. It was the turn of the Spaniards to be alarmed by this extension of Turkish dominion, and particularly by the Ottoman possession of numerous bases along the coast of the Maghrib. So Charles V, who found in Algeria no local elements on which he could rely, lost no time in responding to the request for help from the former Hafsid sultan, Mawlāy Ḥasan, and a Spanish expedition seized La Goulette; and shortly afterwards, Tunis (19 Muḥarram 942/20 July 1535). The Spaniards were particularly interested in the position of Tunis, for it allowed them to control the Sicilian Channel, and seriously hampered communications between Istanbul and Algiers. But the Emperor Charles V, like Ferdinand the Catholic too much occupied with fighting in Europe against the French and the Turks, did not wish to divert troops to conquer Ifrīqiya. He limited himself to establishing a garrison at La Goulette, the fortress of which was restored and strengthened, while Mawlāy Ḥasan was re-established on his former throne, though without much power. Moreover the fate of Ifrīqiya, like that of the central Maghrib, no longer depended on the local people, but on the results of the rivalry between Spain and the Ottomans.

Because of the Spanish attack, Khayr al-Dīn had withdrawn to Bône; but he was recalled to Istanbul by the sultan, who appointed him *kapudan pasha* (admiral-in-chief) of the Ottoman fleet in 943/1536. He left the direction of operations in North Africa to his second-in-command, Ḥasan Agha (943–50/1536–43), whose main task was to repel a powerful Spanish attack on Algiers (Rajab 949/October 1541). This victory gained him the support of the ruler of Tlemcen, in spite of Spanish efforts to prevent this. In western Algeria, however, Turkish authority was not yet firmly established, especially as the Spaniards and the Moroccans were each trying to create there a following for themselves. It took several years for the *beylerbeyi* Ḥasan Pasha the son of Khayr al-Dīn and the successor of Ḥasan Agha (951–9/1544–52), to eliminate his opponents and make Tlemcen into a military and administrative centre, controlled and commanded directly by the Turks, without the intervention or the intermediary of the former local rulers. The next *beylerbeyi*, Ṣāliḥ Re'īs, extended Turkish domination towards the south. An expedition in the Sahara achieved the submission of the chiefs of Tougourt and of Wargla, while a permanent Turkish garrison was established at Biskra. He also intervened in Morocco in support of the Wattasid Bā Ḥassūn, took Fez (960/1553) but was unable to hold it, and in the east, in spite of being defeated in Kabylia, took Bougie (962/1555), which until then the Spaniards had been able to hold. Ṣāliḥ Re'īs died in 963/1556 while attacking Oran. His death gave rise to a serious conflict in Algiers between the militia of the Janissaries and the corsairs, the former wishing to instal their leader Ḥasan Corso as *beylerbeyi* instead of the pasha nominated by Istanbul. The sultan was then obliged to send Ḥasan Pasha again to Algiers to restore order (Sha'bān 964/June 1557). The situation was grave also in the west, where the Sa'dī ruler, Muḥammad al-Mahdī was besieging Tlemcen, and where the Spanish governor of Oran was besieging Mostaganem: but the former was assassinated (964/1557) and the latter defeated and killed (August 1558). The Spaniards had to be satisfied with Oran and with Mers el-Kebir, which Ḥasan Pasha besieged in vain for three months (Ramaḍān-Shawwāl 970/April–June 1563). He was recalled to Constantinople in 974/1567 and replaced by the son of Ṣāliḥ Re'īs, Muḥammad, who endeavoured to restore calm to Algiers where the enmity between corsairs and Janissaries had gone on almost continuously: in particular he allowed the Janissaries to take part in privateering. In March 1568, he was replaced by another *beylerbeyi*, 'Ulūj 'Alī, better known under the name of Kılıj 'Alī,[1] who was to remain there for nearly twenty years and ensure the triumph of Turkish domination in Algeria and in Tunisia (975–95/1568–87).

[1] Kılıj 'Alī eventually became the official name of 'Ulūj 'Alī. The name of *Kılıj* (sword) was more suited to this warlike man than that of *'Ulūj* (rough, rustic, non-Muslim barbarian) which came from his Calabrian origins. It is he who is called by the western sources Euldj Ali or Ochialy.

In Ifrīqiya or Tunisia, Mawlāy Ḥasan, after being reinstated by the Spaniards, had found opposed to him his son, Mawlāy Ḥamīda (also called Aḥmad Sulṭān) and a large section of the population. Although, thanks to the Veneto-Spanish fleet of Admiral Doria, he was able to gain authority over several towns on the eastern coast, he was less fortunate in the interior, where he was defeated outside Qayrawān by the Shābbiyya Arabs, who had formed themselves into an independent state surrounding the town (Rajab 947/November 1540). Having obtained military reinforcements from the Spaniards, he launched a new campaign, this time against his son, but he was defeated, taken prisoner, blinded and deposed in favour of Aḥmad Sultān (950/1543). For twenty-five years, the latter vacillated between the Spaniards and the Turks in order to maintain power. Thus, he formed an alliance with the Turkish corsair, Ṭurghut (called Dragut in the Western sources), who held Djerba and Mahdiyya. But Ṭurghut was forced to yield Mahdiyya to the Spaniards (Ramaḍān 957/September 1550) and escaped defeat at Djerba only by a skilful stratagem (Rabīʿ II 958/April 1551).

Ṭurghut was recalled to the east until 960/1553, when he returned to the central Mediterranean as governor of Tripoli, and recommenced his activity against the Spaniards and against the Tunisians who had at that time allied themselves with them. He first recaptured Djerba, then occupied Gafsa in southern Tunisia, defeated the Shābbiyya and seized Qayrawān (Rabīʿ I 964/January 1558). Philip II then attempted to cut Ṭurghut off from his bases, and sent a Malto-Neapolitan fleet against Djerba, which was quickly occupied, and from which the Spaniards planned to undertake an expedition against Tripoli (Jumāda II 967/March 1560). But soon afterwards the Spanish fleet was defeated by the Ottoman fleet commanded by Ṭurghut and by Piyale Pasha, and, in spite of a stubborn resistance, the Spanish garrison at Djerba was reduced to famine and exterminated (Shawwāl 967/July 1560). From this time on the Spaniards, like the Shābbiyya, ceased to play any role in southern and central Tunisia, particularly as most of the ports on the eastern coast were reoccupied by the Turks.

There remained northern Tunisia, and Tunis in particular. Before attacking the latter, Kılıj ʿAlī Pasha and Ṭurghut made a vain attempt to besiege Malta, during which Ṭurghut was killed (973/1565). Kılıj ʿAlī Pasha then directed the action against Tunis from Algeria, and, in 976/1569, he occupied the Hafsid capital and expelled Aḥmad Sulṭān, who took refuge with the Spaniards. Kılıj ʿAlī had not, however, been able to capture the port of La Goulette (Ḥalq al-Wād), which remained in Spanish hands. The Spaniards seemed, moreover, to emerge victorious from their conflict with the Turks, when, after the victory of Lepanto (19 Jumādā I 979/9 October 1571), Don John of Austria, the brother of Philip II, seized Tunis and installed there a new Hafsid sultan. But these successes were short-lived, for in 981/1574, the Turkish forces, commanded by Kılıj ʻAlī Pasha and Sinān Pasha, took La Goulette and Tunis, definitively putting an end to the Hafsid régime and to the presence of the Spaniards. Henceforward Tunisia became a Turkish province, governed by a *beylerbeyi*. Philip II, overwhelmed by serious troubles in Europe, finally resigned himself to concluding with the Ottoman sultan a truce which in fact was the equivalent of a peace-treaty (989/1581). The Spaniards retained in North Africa only Melilla, Mers el-Kebir and Oran, while Algeria, Tunisia and Tripolitania, having become Turkish provinces, constituted the '*ojaks* of the West', and Morocco maintained its independence.

Turkish Algeria until 1123/1711

In spite of their foreign origin, and in spite of serious internal unrest, especially at the beginning of their occupation, the Turks created a characteristic and organized state, and a geographical and political entity, which became Algeria. Nevertheless, from its inception the *ojak* of Algiers was not without its difficulties, caused by the struggle for power which rapidly developed between the militia of the Janissaries and the corporation of the corsair-captains (*ṭāʼifat al-ruʼasā*ʼ).

It was the Janissaries, i.e. the infantry troops of the *ojak*, on whom Khayr al-Dīn Barbarossa and his successors depended to impose their authority on the country. These soldiers were recruited in Anatolia and sent to Algeria as ordinary Janissaries (sing., *yoldash*), but they could hope for promotion to any rank. The *ojak* had its own jurisdiction: Janissaries who had committed a breach of the law or an offence did not have to appear before the ordinary tribunals but before the tribunal of the militia. The *ojak* had a governing organization, the *Dīvān* which, originally formed to protect the interests of the Janissaries themselves, came later to take a greater and greater part in the direction of the affairs of the *ojak*. Following the success of the Algerian privateers, the Janissaries claimed—and obtained—a part of the booty, and even the right of themselves participating in the privateering. They were a corps which was formidable in its violence and its cohesion, but outstanding in battle.

The other dominant element was that of the corsairs who, in contrast to the Janissaries, included only a small number of Turks. The majority of them were renegades, natives of Sicily, Calabria, Corsica, and even of more distant countries, who, having been taken prisoner, had allied themselves with their conquerors, considering, often rightly, that they had nothing to lose by so doing.

So long as the *ojak* of Algiers was governed by *beylerbeyis* of worth and courage, both Janissaries and corsairs submitted to their authority, especially as the essential task at that time was to establish Turkish power firmly in the country, and, by privateering, to provide it with the men, supplies and money which were indispensable for the life of the *ojak*. The *beylerbeyis*, who held the honorific title of pasha, were appointed directly by the Ottoman sultan, of whom they were the official representatives in the *ojak*, both as governors and as military chiefs. The first *beylerbeyis*, from Khayr al-Dīn to Kılıj ʿAlī, had authority even over Tunisia and Tripolitania, but after 1574 each of the three countries had its own *beylerbeyi*, an arrangement which accentuated the political separation between them.

The first *beylerbeyis* of Algiers devoted themselves to establishing their authority over the interior of Algeria by placing garrisons in the principal towns, organizing the distribution and the collection of the taxes among the city-dwellers, the peasants and the tribes, and by greatly increasing privateering activity. Although they encountered only limited opposition from the Algerian population, they quickly realized that the difficulties created by the Janissaries and, to a lesser degree, by the corsairs, constituted a serious threat to the stability and the continuance of their power. This threat showed itself particularly during the absence of Kılıj ʿAlī, when the *ṭāʾifa* of the corsair-captains, at one moment directed by the renegade Ḥasan Veneziano (990–6/1582–8), was practically in control in Algeria until the end of the tenth/sixteenth century. It had, however, to reckon both with the Janissaries and with the presence of a pasha, who was generally appointed for three years and was in theory governor of the province. These pashas, who after Kılıj ʿAlī were in fact deprived of all authority, contented themselves with limiting, when they could, the conflicts between the militia and the corsairs, and concentrated their main efforts on becoming rich during their stay in Algeria. One alone among them, Ḥaydar Pasha, tried to establish strong personal power by relying on the Kouloughlis (*Kul oghlu*, the offspring of Turks and local women) and on the Kabyles (1004/1596). He was unable to maintain himself in power for long, and during the whole of the first half of the eleventh/seventeenth century the power belonged in effect to the *Dīvān* of the Janissaries, whose decisions, ratified without opposition by the pashas, had the force of law. Soon after the middle of the eleventh/seventeenth century, the intention of Ibrāhīm Pasha to deduct a tithe from the gratuities given to the corsair-captains caused a revolt of the militia, and the *Dīvān* suppressed the last remaining prerogatives of the pasha. The effective power in Algeria was then held by the *agha* of the militia, assisted by the *Dīvān* (1069/1659). But this new régime could not command sufficient authority. Riots and assassinations became usual in Algiers; furthermore, the captains who had been excluded from power, took their revenge. In 1082/1671 they put an end to the rule of the *aghas* and of the *Dīvān* and entrusted the command of the *ojak* to one of their number, Ḥājj Muḥammad, who was provided with the title of dey (*dayı*). The first four deys were elected by them; the later ones, from 1100/1689, by the officers of the militia. At the beginning of the twelfth/eighteenth century, the tenth dey, ʿAlī Chavush (Shāwūsh), drove out the pasha sent by the sultan, and forced the Ottoman ruler to acknowledge him as pasha himself, thus amalgamating the titles and the power (1123/1711), and inaugurating a new régime, which nevertheless still owed allegiance to Istanbul.

Although the rulers of Algiers did not much concern themselves with Algeria itself, they concentrated all their efforts on the development of privateering. Because of the weakness of the European navies in the Mediterranean, this was a period of great prosperity for privateering which enriched the inhabitants of Algiers, and enabled them to adorn the town by building many mosques, palaces and private residences. Above all, it brought to Algiers gold, commodities and slaves. The latter were the object of an active trade, as much for their use in many professions, as for the ransom which could be hoped for from some of them; a certain number were also used as galley-slaves. The majority of the slaves were housed in bagnios where their fate was not an enviable one, though it was no worse than that of contemporary galley-slaves in Europe. The prisoners could continue to practise their religion, but some of them had no hesitation in apostatizing, hoping thus to obtain a better situation in Algerian society. Such apostasy was not, however, regarded favourably by their masters, as it deprived them of the hope of obtaining ransom for them. Certain religious orders, such as those of the Trinitarians and of Notre Dame de la Merci were devoted to ransoming these slaves. In the middle of the seventeenth century, St Vincent de Paul—who, whatever he may have said, was probably never a prisoner at Tunis—and the Lazarists founded a charity intended for the moral and physical succour on the spot of the slaves in the bagnios of Barbary.

This privateering, however, resulted in the opening of hostilities with Holland, England and France, but never simultaneously. The English bombarded Algiers in 1031/1622, in 1065/1655, and in 1083/1672; the French in 1071/1661, 1075/1665, 1093/1682, and 1094/1683. An attempt by the French to occupy Djidjelli failed lamentably. The French had tried, in the years 1640–70, to launch a crusade against Barbary, at first with a religious basis, but later with a purely political aim. This was a failure, and in 1100/1689 a treaty was signed between France and Algiers which established cordial relations and allowed the development of commerce between the two countries. As early as 967/1560, Thomas Lenche, a native of Marseilles, had obtained a monopoly of the coral-fishing between Cape Roux and Bougie, and the right to establish a factory at the Bastion de France, to the west of La Calle; but the inhabitants of Algiers seized it in 1568. Recaptured soon afterwards, the Bastion de France was again lost in 1604. A Corsican from Marseilles, Sanson Napollon, succeeded in 1037/1628 in concluding with the Algerians the Agreement of the Bastion which gave him the coral-fishing concession; he made use of the Bastion in particular to carry out an illegal trade in wheat. His death in 1042/1633 was followed by the destruction of the Bastion. A new agreement concluded in 1050/1640 allowed the repair of the Bastion and the establishment of warehouses at Bône and at Collo. After this, the Bastion Company had more difficulties with the merchants of Marseilles than with the Algerians. Finally, at the beginning of the eighteenth century the French companies of eastern Algeria and of Tunisia were combined into the *Compagnie d'Afrique*.

Elsewhere the Spaniards carried on commerce on a reduced scale from Oran. In Algiers, the intermittent hostilities with the Europeans hindered commerce; but some European merchants had established themselves there, and French, English and Dutch, either directly, or through the intermediary of the Jews of Algiers and of Leghorn, carried on there an exchange of commodities, which remained, however, on a rather limited scale.

Turkish Tunisia

When Tunisia became an Ottoman province, the administration was entrusted by Sinān Pasha to a *beylerbeyi*, Ḥaydar Pasha, who had to assist him a militia of Janissaries some 3,000 to 4,000 strong and commanded by an *agha*; as in Algiers, this militia was divided into *ortas* and *odas*. From 982/1574 to 999/1591, nine *beylerbeyis* succeeded one another; like his counterpart in Algiers, the *beylerbeyi* of Tunis had to reckon with the militia of the Janissaries, and hence there was instituted the *Dīvān*, formed by the senior officers of the militia. It is possible that, after the death of Ḥaydar Pasha at the end of his second term as governor, the *beylerbeyi* was nominated by the officers of the *ojak*, and that this nomination was later ratified by the sultan. Tunisia was then a province subjected to a military régime. There were Turkish garrisons in the principal towns of the country, and fresh Janissaries were sent regularly from Anatolia. This régime lasted until 1002/1594, but as early as 999/1591 there had been unrest in Tunis, stirred up by the militia and the local population. Finally it was the subaltern officers of the Janissaries who seized power and formed a new *Dīvān* at the head of which they put one of themselves, elected by them and with the title of dey. This dey became the real ruler of the province; not that the *beylerbeyi-pasha* ceased to exist, but he had now merely a representative role. Nevertheless the continuance of the office of *beylerbeyi* maintained the links between Tunis and Istanbul. To a greater extent than in Algiers, the Tunisian militia included non-Turkish elements, Levantines, *Kul oghlus* and renegades, and some of them even rose to the office of dey.

The first dey, ʿUthmān (1002–19/1594–1610), pacified the interior of Tunisia and created two important offices: that of bey, or commander of the land-troops, charged particularly with the collection of the taxes during tours made for this purpose (*maḥalla*), and that of *kapudan*, commander of the fleet. Yūsuf Dey (1019–46/1610–37), the son-in-law of ʿUthmān, also wielded great authority. He effectively curbed the unrest of the Arab tribes, repelled an Algerian invasion, gave a vigorous impetus to privateering, and erected many buildings. After him Ustā Murād (1046–50/1637–40), a Genoese renegade appointed by the militia, was to yield the direction of the affairs of the province for all practical purposes to the Bey Ḥammūda b. Murād. The latter's father had already succeeded in getting his office of bey made hereditary, and in addition had received the title of pasha. Henceforward it was the Muradid beys who ruled Tunisia, although the offices of dey and of *beylerbeyi-pasha* were not suppressed. Ḥammūda (1040–70/1631–59) was an energetic ruler: he was responsible for the attachment to Tunisia of Djerba, claimed by the Tripolitanians, and for the complete pacification of the country. He was also a great builder, and under his rule Tunisia, enriched by privateering, led a relatively peaceful existence. Ḥammūda maintained fairly close relations with the sultans, and Tunisian ships took part in the war waged by the Ottomans against the Venetians in Crete. His son Murād (1070–86/1659–75) behaved like an actual monarch, dismissing when necessary those deys who displeased him, and installed himself in the palace of the Bardo. One of the most important buildings for which he was responsible is the mosque of Sidi Mahrez at Tunis, in which the influence of Turkish architecture is clearly seen. But after his death the succession was disputed by his son and his brother, resulting in twenty years of civil war in which the Algerians intervened. By means of a military plot, the *agha* of the *sipahis* (cavalry), Ibrāhīm al-Sharīf, seized power after having assassinated all the Muradids (1114/1702). Having become bey, he had himself given the title of dey and was recognized as *beylerbeyi-pasha* by Istanbul, thus gathering all the powers into his own hands and giving to the régime a new character of unity and of monarchy. But Ibrāhīm was defeated and taken prisoner by the Algerians in 1705. His successor, Ḥusayn b. ʿAlī (1117/1705), also an *agha* of the *sipahis*, received from the sultan the title of *beylerbeyi-pasha*, but suppressed from his titles that of dey: from then on the office of dey became a minor one. With Ḥusayn b. ʿAlī there began a new hereditary dynasty, which was to rule in Tunisia for more than two centuries.

Throughout the twelfth/seventeenth century, Tunisia had a less anarchic and troubled political life than Algeria. It had the advantage of being governed by leaders who were capable, energetic, and conscious of their responsibilities and duties. In general the army was kept under control, and although its leaders had seized power, they had not allowed it to take advantage of this to create disorder. It may be that this more authoritarian and more orderly aspect reflected a quite distinct influence of the elements originating from Anatolia, who played a leading part in the army and in the administration; it was certainly a factor which helped to create a growing differentiation between Tunisia and Algeria. In addition, the peace which prevailed in the country, and especially in the northern part, attracted the Moors, driven out of Spain in 1609. Some of them settled along the whole length of the Medjerda valley, which they helped to develop, and others in Tunis itself, where they created new industries or revived the old, such as the manufacture and weaving of silk and woollen materials, the manufacture of tarbushes, faïence, and so forth.

The authority of the deys, then of the beys, was imposed in the province through the garrisons spread throughout the country and by the *qā'ids*; the collection of taxes, levied during the two annual expeditions, does not seem to have given rise to many or serious incidents. Tunisia was a prosperous country, made more so by privateering (though it was of less importance here than in Algeria), and there took place, especially in the towns of Tunis and Qayrawān, tremendous activity in the building of religious monuments (mosques and *madrasas*), palaces and works of a utilitarian character such as bridges over the Medjerda, and the repair of the aqueduct of Carthage.

There was much privateering, and many European renegades took part in it; one of them, the Englishman, Ward, was responsible for the renewal of the Tunisian navy at the beginning of the seventeenth century. The slaves were consigned to bagnios as in Algiers, but their treatment there was perhaps less harsh. They probably had more opportunities of being appointed to some office if they apostatized; in any case the slaves and the renegades held a real position in the life of the country. Opportunities for ransom were not infrequent because of the activities of religious missions, that of the Lazarists in particular after the vigorous propaganda of St Vincent de Paul. Such men as Père Le Vacher, for example, acquired a great reputation among both Christians and Muslims.

In addition to the immediate neighbours—Sicilians, Maltese, Neapolitans and Calabrians—who often called in at Tunis, foreign merchants settled permanently there: English, Dutch, and above all French—chiefly Marseillais—who had a consul (originally, as at Algiers, a cleric, although subsequently officials were appointed by the French government) and a *funduq*, built in 1069/1659. This was the centre of French commercial life in Tunis, where French nationals took refuge if there were any incidents in the capital. The French also formed a company for coral-fishing, and in addition for trade, illegal as well as legal; this company was installed at Cap Nègre, near to the island of Ṭabarqa, which itself belonged to the Genoese. They had received it as the price of the ransom of the Turkish corsair, Ṭurghut, and had later handed it over to the Lomellini family, who made it into an active centre of commerce with Algeria and Tunisia and a centre for the work of coral. Sanson Napollon tried several times to seize Ṭabarqa, which was an extremely advantageous position, and competed successfully with the French factories of the Bastion and of Cap Nègre; on his third attempt he was captured by the Genoese and executed (May 1633). The Cap Nègre factory suffered a number of vicissitudes. It passed into the control of the Marseillais in 1040/1631, was taken by the Tunisians in 1047/1637, and given up again to the Marseillais soon after, but it was not until 1077/1666 that the latter obtained formal authority to trade in cereals and in coral, with no territorial concession. At the end of the eleventh/seventeenth century, the English endeavoured to take the place of the French in Tunis, but without success. At the beginning of the eighteenth century, the new *Compagnie d'Afrique* took the factory of Cap Nègre under its control, as it had done the Bastion de France.

TRIPOLITANIA

At the end of the ninth/fifteenth century, the inhabitants of Tripoli had freed themselves from the tutelage of the Hafsids and had formed a government the direction of which was entrusted to a dignitary of the town. This peaceful régime, essentially preoccupied with maintaining close commercial relations with the Mediterranean states, lasted until the beginning of the tenth/sixteenth century. It was then that the Spaniards, led by Pedro Navarro, seized Tripoli in Rabīʿ II 916/July 1510, thus completing the campaign which they had begun in Algeria and Tunisia, but the following month they suffered a crushing defeat during an attempt to land on the island of Djerba. As in Algeria, the Spaniards did not try to extend their occupation, and limited themselves to fortifying Tripoli. But the town, being far from Sicily and further still from Spain, was difficult to defend, so in 1530 the Emperor Charles V handed over Tripoli, at the same time as the islands of Malta and Gozzo, to the Knights of St John of Jerusalem (the Knights Hospitallers), who shortly before had been driven out of Rhodes by Süleymān the Magnificent.

In Rajab 957/August 1551, the inadequately defended town was captured by Ṭurghut. In 961/1554, Ṭurghut was appointed *beylerbeyi* of Tripolitania and immediately set about submitting the interior of the country to Turkish rule. He occupied the island of Djerba, and made

Tripoli an active centre of privateering against the Spaniards. The latter, having decided to take action against Ṭurghut, seized Djerba (Jumādā II 967/March 1560) and prepared an expedition against Tripoli, but their fleet was defeated by the Ottoman fleet, and Djerba was reconquered by Ṭurghut and Piyale Pasha (Shawwāl 967/July 1560). After his death (973/1565), Ṭurghut was succeeded at Tripoli by a pasha called Yaḥyā, who was unable to maintain discipline among the Janissaries. Their excesses led to a revolt, and the sultan then sent Kılıj 'Alī to restore order and peace (974–6/1566–8). The next *beylerbeyi*, Ja'far, was responsible for the conquest of the Fezzan in 985/1577. After him, Tripolitania was shaken by revolts of the Janissaries and the rebellion of the Arab population led finally by the marabout Niyāl, who succeeded for a brief time in becoming master of Tripoli (997/1589), but reinforcements sent from Istanbul enabled the Turks to get the situation under control again. The *beylerbeyis* of Tripoli made several attempts, particularly in 1006 and 1007/1598 and 1599, to gain control of the island of Djerba. This was contested by the deys of Tunis, who sent help to the inhabitants of the island, enabling them to repel the Tripolitanian attacks.

Until 1018/1609, Tripolitania was governed by *beylerbeyis* who were appointed directly by the Ottoman sultan, and who, as at Algiers and Tunis, were assisted in their task by the *Dīvān* of the Janissaries. Also as in these two towns, it was a revolt of the Janissaries which led to a change in the local régime. In 1609 the soldiers of the militia revolted against their superior officers and against the *beylerbeyi*, Aḥmad Pasha, and proclaimed as leader of the *ojak* one of their junior officers, Sulaymān, who thus inaugurated the régime of the deys, which lasted until 1123/1711. The sultan however continued to send pashas to Tripoli, their role being purely representational. To make more certain of his power, Sulaymān executed a number of senior officers, then re-established Turkish authority, which for a brief time had been shaken, over Jabal Nafūsa and the Fezzan. It was perhaps he also who about this time gave a fresh impetus to Tripolitanian privateering with the help of a Greek renegade. His authoritarian government, however, earned him enmity, echoes of which reached as far as Istanbul; perhaps also he tried too openly to free himself from Ottoman tutelage. In any case he was arrested at Tripoli by envoys of the sultan and put to death (1023/1614).

Little is recorded of the next years: it is known that in 1029/1620 one Muṣṭafā, who claimed to be a *sharīf*, succeeded in obtaining the confidence of the Janissaries, and was proclaimed dey. He was responsible for the pacification of the Arab tribes, and it was during his period of government that the first French consul was appointed in Tripoli, in 1630. Muṣṭafā Sharīf also met a violent death, in 1041/1631. After a year of unrest, it was one of the corsair leaders, Muḥammad Sakızlı, a renegade native of Chios, who seized power and, in return for certain concessions, obtained the support of the militia. Sakızlı formed a corps of cavalry, intended to maintain order among the Arab tribes who inhabited the hinterland of Tripoli; the command of this corps was entrusted to another renegade from Chios, ʿUthmān, who received the title of bey. But it was Sakızlı's wise administration, particularly in the assessment and collection of taxes, which did even more to ensure peace in the country. In addition he gave a new impetus to privateering, and his corsairs, not content with attacking Christian vessels, made incursions on the European coasts, from Spain to Italy, which provoked reactions, especially from the French, whose consul had been expelled in 1632. About the same time, ʿUthmān Bey had to suppress a revolt in the Fezzan, and obtained the submission of the inhabitants of Murzuk. Nevertheless there was a permanent state of insecurity in this region, and the caravans from the Sudan, which until then had travelled to Tripoli via the Fezzan, changed their route towards the towns of Benghazi and Derna in Cyrenaica, which at the end of the eighth/fifteenth and the beginning of the ninth/sixteenth century, were occupied by Andalusian emigrants and Tripolitanian refugees. In 1049/1639 Sakızlı, attacking by land and by sea, occupied without difficulty Benghazi, then Cyrenaica, and his lieutenant ʿUthmān extended Turkish domination to the south, as far as Awjila. From then on a permanent garrison was established at Benghazi.

During the period of Sakızlı's government, some French merchants came and settled at Tripoli; one of them, Bayon, performed there the function of consul and gained permission for two French clerics to succour the prisoners in the bagnio. Sakızlı died, probably poisoned, in Ramaḍān 1059/September 1649. He had surrounded himself by a large number of renegades who held the principal offices of the *ojak*. ʿUthmān Bey succeeded him. He had no difficulty in obtaining recognition from the sultan, who asked him for the co-operation of the Tripolitanian fleet (as he had already asked for that of the Tunisian and Algerian fleets) for the Cretan expedition. In 1068/1658 the English admiral John Stoakes came to Tripoli to sign a peace treaty with 'Uthmān, and from then on an English consul was established in the town. This treaty was renewed in 1072/1662 in the name of Charles II. During the years which followed, the corsairs of Tripoli distinguished themselves on several occasions, especially against Italian ships, and took part in the final assaults against the Venetian positions in Crete.

However, the inhabitants of Tripoli, the Janissaries, and the corsairs did not find it easy to endure the authoritarian rule of 'Uthmān, and in particular the stringency of his financial measures: he had increased the taxes, and increased his own personal share of the booty taken by the corsairs. He was overthrown by a revolution in November 1672. With this event there began a period of anarchy during which corsairs and Janissaries struggled for power, and the Tunisians attempted to intervene.

As the corsairs of Tripoli continued their ravages in the Mediterranean, the English sent a fleet which for several months blockaded the port of Tripoli (1086/1675–6), and destroyed part of the corsair fleet. Finally a treaty was signed in Dhu'l-Ḥijja 1086/March 1676. In 1092/1681, the Tripoli corsairs attacked the French ships, and even went so far as to ill-treat the French consul at Larnaca in Cyprus during one of their expeditions in the eastern Mediterranean; and then took refuge in the roads of Chios. At this the French fleet, under the command of Admiral Duquesne, destroyed the corsairs' ships and bombarded Chios. This incident caused lively repercussions in Istanbul, where the grand *vezīr*, Kara Muṣṭafā Pasha, remonstrated with the French ambassador. Finally peace was concluded between the French and the Tripolitanians, the latter undertaking to attack no more French ships and to free all the French slaves imprisoned in their bagnios, and allowing the appointment of a new consul at Tripoli (Ṣafar 1093/February 1682). But the Tripolitanians did not keep to their agreement, and imprisoned the delegates who came to arrange for the liberation of the slaves, so a French fleet was sent to bombard Tripoli, after which a new treaty was signed (27 Rajab 1096/June 1685). A similar peace treaty had been concluded earlier with the Dutch (Jumādā II 1094/June 1683).

There followed in Tripoli continual changes of government; the Janissaries or the corsairs, according to circumstances, put their own candidate in power, generally for only a short time. These incidents had their repercussions on the economic life of the country, and in the interior there was unrest among the Arab tribes. Tripoli was at this time, according to the description of Pétis de la Croix, a town of nearly 40,000 inhabitants, 3,500 of them Turks and Kouloughis, 35,000 Arabs and 2,000 Christians (including slaves). Although the deys were elected, or imposed, by the militia or the corsairs, the sultan continued to send a pasha as his representative; these pashas took no part in the affairs of the country and the Tripolitanians sometimes even refused to recognize them as such. One of them, Khalīl, did nevertheless intervene directly in governmental affairs in 1687, and helped to reinforce the powers of the Dey Muḥammad al-Imām in imposing discipline on the corsairs and in the clarification of the situation.

The Tripoli corsairs having in 1102 and 1103/1691 and 1692 resumed their activity against the French ships, and the dey having arrested the French consul, Tripoli was bombarded in Shawwāl 1103/July 1692 and a new treaty was signed in Ramaḍān 1104/May 1693. In 1704 there were clashes between Tripolitanians and Tunisians, who laid waste the oases around Tripoli, then besieged the town itself, but finally retreated without having achieved anything. The situation in Tripolitania was at this time a difficult one, both politically and economically; in addition the population of the capital was decimated by an epidemic of plague. It was then, after fresh palace revolutions which continued from 1117 to 1123/1706 to 1711, that a cavalry officer, Aḥmad Qaramānlī (the descendant of a Turkish corsair who had settled in Tripoli during the period of Ṭurghut), was put into power by the native population and, later supported by the *Dīvān*, was proclaimed dey and pasha (11 Jumādā II 1123/27 July 1711). With him began the Qaramānlī dynasty which was to rule Tripolitania for more than 120 years.

Thus, at the very beginning of the twelfth/eighteenth century, there arose in Algeria, and to a greater extent in Tunisia and Tripolitania, locally formed governments, created by the military classes which were all-powerful in these countries, but still preserving fairly close relations with the sultan's government, which regarded Algeria, Tunisia and Tripolitania as provinces of the Ottoman empire, distant provinces perhaps, but ones whose legal links with Istanbul had not been severed. In actual fact these provinces behaved like autonomous states, and this autonomy was made easier on the one hand by their remoteness and on the other by the increasing weakness of the Ottoman government. Nevertheless the fiction of Turkish suzerainty remained, and it was to remain until the nineteenth century.

CHAPTER 3

NORTH AFRICA IN THE PRE-COLONIAL PERIOD

In the last years of the eleventh/seventeenth and the first years of the twelfth/eighteenth century, the three countries of the Maghrib began almost simultaneously a new phase in their history. In 1076/1666, in Morocco, the 'Alawī dynasty established itself on the ruins of the Sa'did state; in 1082/1671, in Algeria, the authority of the deys replaced that of the pashas; and in 1117/1705, in Tunisia, the Husaynid dynasty was born in the midst of the unrest provoked by the defeat and capture of the Bey Ibrāhīm al-Sharīf by the Algerians.

The three states, whose modern history was really beginning at this time, had to face the same problems until the middle of the nineteenth century, when they were confronted with the impact of European expansion: the problems of their development as coherent national entities, of the building up of efficient institutions, and of economic and social progress. These problems were only imperfectly solved. Morocco, comparatively protected by its geographical isolation, developed slowly, leaving open the Berber question and the question of the modernization of the *Makhzan*. In the meantime, each of the two neighbouring states, starting with the same status as Ottoman provinces, developed in a different way: whereas in Tunisia, for reasons both of geography and of early and recent history, there arose a national monarchy within clearly defined territorial frontiers, Algeria remained, both as a nation and in its institutions, immature.

MOROCCO

Morocco under the first 'Alawīs to 1822

The 'Alawī dynasty which, about 1660, succeeded the Sa'did dynasty, emerged, in the middle of the Tafilelt, from the rise of a family of *sharīfs* which had come from Yanbu' in the time of the Marinids. At the time when, in the anarchy which was overwhelming Morocco, separate little states were arising—principalities formed around *zāwiyas*, like that of Dilā', or a republic of corsairs as at Salé—these *sharīfs* brought Tafilelt beneath their authority under Mawlāy al-Sharīf (1041–5/1631–5).

They then, under Mawlāy Muḥammad (1045–75/1635–64), spread towards eastern and northern Morocco where they encountered the Dilā'īs, who seemed to be in the best position to recover the Sa'did heritage in the north of the country. It was finally with Mawlāy al-Rashīd (1075–83/1664–72), the real founder of the dynasty, that the 'Alawīs imposed their authority on the whole of Morocco. In 1076/1666 this ruler seized Fez, and assumed the title of sultan; two years later he made himself master of the *zāwiya* of Dilā'; in 1079/1669 he occupied Marrakesh.

With the very long reign of Mawlāy Ismā'īl (1083–1139/1672–1727) the dynasty almost immediately reached its zenith. This intelligent and ostentatious sultan, whose temperament was full of contrasts, devoted his untiring energy to the subduing of his kingdom: he is said to have spent twenty-four years in his tent. The difficulties which he encountered at the beginning of his reign (it took him fifteen years to put an end completely to revolts among the tribes, and to movements instigated by his brothers) had proved to him the necessity of forming a strong army: he developed the Sa'did organization of the *Makhzan* tribes (the *gīsh*), incorporating into it in particular the tribe of the Udāya. Then from the Negro troops of Aḥmad al-Manṣūr, Mawlāy Ismā'īl organized his corps of slaves, the '*Abīd*: 150,000 Negroes, grouped together at Mashra' al-Ramal and at Meknes, and duly registered, formed the reserve from which each year he drew the future fighting soldiers. The sultan thus had at his disposal about 20,000 loyal and reliable men. *Qaṣbas* (fortified posts) allowed him to exercise control over the territories which were not entirely subdued, and to watch over the principal roads. By these methods, and by repeated campaigns against the Berbers of the Atlas, Mawlāy Ismā'īl was able to maintain internal order during the greater part of his reign. During the later years, however, the habit which the ruler formed of entrusting the government of the provinces to his sons provoked numerous revolts, and in 1130/1717–18 he had to make up his mind to deprive all except one of them of their commands.

The power of Mawlāy Ismā'īl was particularly brilliantly displayed in his relations with other countries. The sultan's attempted incursions into Algeria were thrice repulsed by the *ojak* but he met with more success in his effort to reconquer the coastal regions which were still in the hands of the Europeans: al-Ma'mūra (1681), Tangier (1684), Larache (1689) and Arzila (1691) were all regained by Morocco. The Portuguese retained only Mazagan, and the Spaniards their four small fortified towns near the Straits of Gibraltar. The sultan entered into continuous negotiations with the great powers, concluded treaties with Great Britain and France, and even conceived great diplomatic projects aimed against Spain, which met with little comprehension at Versailles. The development of commercial relations with which the sultan concerned himself, and the profits from which were to replace the gains from privateering, tended towards the establishment of more normal relations between Morocco and Europe. At the end of his reign, Mawlāy Ismāʿīl left a Morocco which was respected from without, and unified and pacified within: however, the crisis which followed his death showed that this success was due chiefly to the outstanding personality of a sultan whose love of power found its permanent embodiment in the magnificent buildings of Meknes.

The causes of the thirty years of anarchy which followed in Morocco (1139–70/1727–57) can be found in a lack of balance in the structure of the country. This was due to the incompleteness of the political institutions, and problems set by the Berbers, who began again their drive towards the north after 1139/1727, to which was added the insubordination of the ʿ*Abīd* and the *gīsh* of the Udāya, and finally the mediocrity of Ismāʿīl's successors. Between 1139/1727 and 1170/1757 there were no fewer than twelve proclamations of sultans; Mawlāy ʿAbd Allāh for instance, who reigned intermittently from 1141/1729 to 1170/1757, was proclaimed six times, and five times forced to abandon the throne. In a country ravaged by disorder, one of the few stabilizing factors was loyalty to the ʿAlawī dynasty, to which all the claimants to the throne belonged, and around which unity was restored after 1170/1757.

Morocco found once again a relative stability under Muḥammad b. ʿAbd Allāh (1170–1204/1757–90) and Mawlāy Sulaymān (1206–38/1792–1822) with a brief interval of disturbances under Mawlāy Yazīd (1204–6/1790–2). Muḥammad took advantage of the general desire for peace to achieve the reorganization and pacification of the country: he had to undertake numerous expeditions, however, in order to stem the revolts of the Berbers of the Middle Atlas. Master of the plains of the north and of the south, the sultan had to resign himself to the cutting of the direct route from Fez to Marrakesh by the Tādlā. It was as much to weaken southern Morocco, by concentrating its economic activity in a place easy to control, as to develop commerce, that the sultan founded in 1179/1765 the new town of Mogador (al-Suwayra). After having, it may be, envisaged the return to a policy of a Holy War (he attempted at the beginning of his reign to re-establish privateering, without much success), the sultan contented himself with retaking in 1182/1769 the port of Mazagan, an attempt next to take Melilla meeting with no success. Muḥammad, on the whole, attempted rather to normalize his relations with Europe: he concluded in 1775 a peace of *status quo* with Spain, and took measures to encourage trade, capable of furnishing new resources for the treasury, and to attract foreign merchants, such as the commercial treaty with France in 1767, the foundation of Mogador, and buildings at Casablanca in 1770.

After the crisis of 1204–6/1790–2, Mawlāy Sulaymān had some difficulty in establishing his authority, and in eliminating his rivals, who were other sons of Muḥammad. Although his reign was remarkably peaceful so far as relations between Morocco and Europe were concerned, within Morocco the sultan had to carry out continual police operations, particularly against the Berbers of the Middle Atlas, and his last years were shadowed by serious difficulties. The reason for this was largely the policy which the sultan followed concerning the religious fraternities. Himself a strictly orthodox Muslim, Mawlāy Sulaymān was influenced after 1810 by Wahhabism, which led him take a firm stand against maraboutism, at the very time when both the recently-founded order of the Darqāwa and the earlier order of the Wāzzāniyya were undergoing a great expansion in Morocco. The insurrection in which, from 1818 to 1820, the town of Fez (Fās) and the Darqāwa and Wazzānī Berbers revolted against the sultan, had therefore the threefold character of an outburst of Ṣūfī reaction, and of a Berber and a Fāsī movement. The sultan died in 1238/1822 without having entirely succeeded in re-establishing his authority.

Within a century and a half, the ʿAlawī dynasty had established itself firmly and incontestably, but it had been unable to solve the problem of Moroccan institutions or the Berber question. At the beginning of the nineteenth century the situation concerning the latter had even deteriorated in comparison with what it had been under Mawlāy Ismāʿīl. The alternation of powerful rulers capable of imposing order and weak successors, which was to continue to be characteristic of the dynasty, was to a large extent responsible for this stagnation and ineffectualness.

European penetration in Morocco

The history of Morocco in the nineteenth century was dominated by the phenomenon of European penetration, the effects of which were felt in all aspects of the country's life. Faced with this new problem, the sultans hesitated between two courses of action: to increase the isolation of Morocco, closing it to outside influences—a solution which the strength of European pressure and the lack of unity within the country made difficult to apply; or to take the opposite course, of attempting to modernize the empire by a policy of reform, to which the archaic structure of the country presented obstacles, and the consequences of which the European powers were not really prepared to accept. Incapable of resolving this dilemma, the sultans clung to an impossible *status quo*, and Morocco drifted towards the crisis in which it was to lose its independence.

Under Mawlāy 'Abd al-Raḥmān (1822–59), who inherited a difficult situation, operations were carried out against the Berbers in the plains, but the mountains and the south (where the *Sharīfs* of the Tazerwalt constituted a veritable small state of their own) evaded the action of the *Makhzan* almost entirely. While, for economic reasons, Morocco opened itself about 1830 to European trade, the occupation of Algeria revived European interest in this part of the Maghrib. Almost immediately serious problems faced the sultan. After having attempted to seize Tlemcen and the west of Algeria (1830–2), he became involved in a conflict with France over the help given to 'Abd al-Qādir al-Jazā'irī in Morocco. The Moroccan defeat at Isly (1844) had no immediate consequences, but it made clear how weak Morocco really was. After having initiated an effort to limit the development of the European enterprises, or at least to place a more rigid control on foreign trade by a system of monopolies and privileges, the sultan was finally forced to resign himself to the opening of Morocco to European penetration. A treaty signed with Great Britain in 1856 established free trade and abolished monopolies. In the long run the result was that the *Makhzan* abandoned part of its jurisdiction.

The reign of Muḥammad b. 'Abd al-Raḥmān (1859–73) began with a war with Spain (1859–60), from which Morocco emerged defeated and obliged to pay a heavy indemnity which forced it to borrow, and to place a part of its customs revenue under foreign control. Soon afterwards, the Béclard Convention, signed with France, by consolidating the privilege of the protection of Moroccans by the consular authorities, caused Morocco to go one step further on the way to becoming dependent (1863). While the *Makhzan* divided itself into a progressive and a reactionary party, the sultan considered encouraging the evolution of Morocco towards modernization by means of public works, agricultural and industrial enterprises, and some administrative and fiscal reforms. This modest and desultory effort came to nothing, but after 1870, thanks to the decline of French and Spanish influence in Morocco (leaving the field clear for the British consul, Hay), and also to the accession of Mawlāy al-Ḥasan, the question of reforms seemed to present itself in a more favourable light.

A worthy, active and experienced ruler who was conscious of his responsibilities, Mawlāy al-Ḥasan (1873–94) fought ceaselessly to preserve the internal unity of his country and its sovereignty abroad. Although he did not succeed completely in this task, at least he postponed the arrival of the crisis. He spent a large part of his reign in travelling through the country in order to quell the forces of disorder. Some of these expeditions were particularly spectacular, although probably not very decisive: among them were the two great raids of 1882 and 1886 in Sūs, where the efforts at penetration by the British at Cape Juby, and the Spanish at Ifni and in the Rio de Oro, increased the habitual difficulties which the sultan had in imposing his authority. The same was true of the campaign in the Tafilelt in 1893. Mawlāy al-Ḥasan's policy of reform took the form chiefly of an attempt to modernize the army. The permanent troops were put under European instructors and equipped with European-type arms; future Moroccan officers were sent abroad for training, and an arsenal was created at Fez. The fairly modest results obtained were out of proportion to the cost to the government. To this were added, in other fields, the monetary reform of 1881, various industrial and agricultural projects, and some improvements in the functioning of the *Makhzan*. The sultan lacked the technical and financial resources to go any further. Morever, had he tried, he would have exposed himself to strong internal opposition, public opinion in general, and particularly among the religious fraternities, being hostile to the reforms, which appeared to be an effect of foreign penetration. The ruler's caution can also be explained by the fear of arousing further European interference and of seeing the number of the *protégés* increase in proportion with the development of the foreign enterprises.

The abuses of the protection had become for the *Makhzan* one of the most irritating problems in relations with Europe, and constituted in the long term one of the most serious threats to Morocco's sovereignty. Mawlāy al-Ḥasan persevered in negotiating to put an end to them, or at least to limit them. But the results of the international conference at

Madrid (1880) fulfilled Moroccan hopes only very imperfectly; furthermore the procedure chosen for the discussion of the problem was evidently dangerous, for it opened the way for the internationalization of the Moroccan Question. The reappearance on the scene of France about 1880, the entry of Germany, and Spain's attempts at peaceful penetration marked the beginning of intense European competition, in which Great Britain, which until then had adhered firmly to the principle of preserving the *status quo*, seemed at one moment in 1892 tempted to take an active part. All the great powers developed in Morocco a network of interests which were often no more than a pretext for political intervention, and could serve to stake a claim to an eventual colonial operation. The Europeans in Morocco (about 9,000 in 1894, mainly Spaniards) were beginning to extend the field of their activities, and to interest themselves in industrial enterprises, and in agricultural colonization. Sea trade had taken the place of the traditional commercial movements, and produced a demand for new products (tea, sugar, cotton-goods) some of which competed with the products of local artisans. The trade deficit, the indemnities paid out to the Europeans, and the expenses incurred by the modernization of the army, had deprived Morocco of its resources on the eve of the crisis which was to be its downfall.

The organization of Morocco in the last years of the reign of Mawlāy al-Ḥasan, had not developed greatly since Mawlāy 'Abd al-Raḥmān. Absolute monarchs, whose status as *sharīfs* earned them great religious prestige, the sultans had seen their authority consolidated during the nineteenth century, as there had been no crisis in the succession. Even the refractory tribes recited the *khuṭba* in their name, and thus recognized their legitimacy if not their authority. The *Dār al-Makhzan* which surrounded the sultan consisted of a court service (directed by the chamberlain (*ḥājib*) and the *qā'id al-mashwar*) and a state service. The *Makhzan* properly so-called, which was the government of Morocco, remained very rudimentary, in spite of a certain diversification of offices. The *wazīr* fulfilled the function of a prime minister and was in charge of the internal administration. The *wazīr al-baḥr* (minister of the sea) was entrusted with foreign affairs. A *nā'ib al-sulṭān* represented the sovereign at Tangier where the foreign representatives resided. The *'allāf* (paymaster) was a sort of minister of war. The *amīn al-umanā'* (chief commissioner) controlled the finances, which consisted of three sections (receipts, expenditure and accounts), each one being entrusted to an *amīn* (commissioner). Finally the *kātib al-shikāyāt* (clerk of the petitions) was responsible for justice, and received appeals against the decisions of the *Sharī'a* tribunal, complaints against the governors, and so forth. The work of the secretariat was carried out in nine offices (*banīqa*) which corresponded to the ministerial departments. They were large unfurnished rooms, facing on to the interior court of the *Dār al-Makhzan*, in which worked secretaries in varying numbers.

This central administration, which at the beginning of the nineteenth century consisted of a very small staff, increased in number until in about 1900 there were some eighty secretaries. The membership of the *Makhzan* was recruited from among the great families of the *gīsh* and the urban middle class: the legal personnel and the secretaries came from among the '*ulamā*', and the *amīns* were chosen from the merchants. Entry into the governing class was in principle open to all; in fact it became more and more difficult for new recruits to enter, and posts tended to become hereditary. The *Makhzan* became a caste, isolated from the rest of the country, and with a powerful *esprit de corps*. The officials received no salary: they were thus induced to make money out of their positions, and this constituted one of the chief faults of the administrative system.

The main instruments of the *Makhzan*—the army and the financial administration—were only moderately efficient. The modernization of the army had never been completed and the sultan continued to rely on the contingents (*gīsh*) supplied by the four *Makhzan* tribes and the five quasi-*Makhzan* tribes of the south: in all, about 10,000 men, chiefly of use as garrisons in the imperial towns of Marrakesh, Fez, Meknes and Rabat, or as police. To these were added contingents supplied by the non-military tribes and under the command of their *qā'ids*. After the defeat of Isly, the sultans had formed a corps armed and equipped in a modern way. This army, though formed and trained at great expense, was only of mediocre quality, but its arms, and particularly its artillery, gave it a great superiority over the bedouin troops. In any case, when circumstances demanded it, the sultan directed against the refractory tribes *maḥallas* or *ḥarkas*, in which he travelled around the country, accompanied by the contingents of the *Makhzan* tribes, and surrounded by the members of the government.

Another weakness of 'Alawī Morocco was its finances. In addition to the Qur'anic taxes (*zakāt* and '*ushūr*), that of the *nā'iba* from which the *gīsh* tribes were exempt, and the 'gifts' authorized at the times of the three great feasts, the sultan had some difficulty in imposing new taxes, which were considered illegal and were badly received by the population. Hence the importance for the government of the customs revenue, which in 1894 was supplying half of the financial resources. Furthermore these taxes were paid regularly only by the towns and the tribes of the plain, and there were numerous exemptions, including *sharīfs*, *zāwiyas* and *Makhzan* tribes. Finally, although the finance services were relatively well organized under the supervision of the *amīns*, the collection of taxes was chaotic, and extortion was rife, particularly at the level of the *qā'ids*.

The sultan had three *khalīfas*, who in his absence governed Fez and Marrakesh (the two alternative capitals), and the Tafilelt. The administration of the tribes was in the hands of *qā'ids* who were endowed with wide powers: the appointment of shaykhs, the dividing out of taxes, the levying of contingents of troops, and relations with the *Makhzan*. To ensure the docility of the tribes, the *Makhzan* divided them up into very small units, or re-grouped them according to its interests of the moment. For example, Mawlāy al-Ḥasan split the large areas of authority into more than 300 qa'idships. The sultan tried to appoint *qā'ids* who were alien to the tribes that they were to govern, and chosen from the *Makhzan*, but he was not always able to do this. In any case the sultan's authority was truly effective over only a part of his empire, the *bled el-makhzen* who alone paid the taxes and supplied contingents to the army. It consisted essentially of the Gharb and the Ḥawḍ (the communications between these two regions being constantly threatened by the tribes), of the plains of eastern Morocco, of Tafilelt and Sūs. There was moreover no real frontier between the submissive *bled el-makhzen* and the dissident *bled el-siba*: their respective areas varied according to the power of the government, and some tribes lived in an intermediate state between total submission and independence. On the other hand the *bleb el-siba* did recognize the sultan, at least nominally. The *Makhzan* extended its military action only to the border of the *bled el-siba*, in order to maintain as far as possible the state of equilibrium within the country, and it avoided attacking the Berbers in their mountains. It attempted instead to negotiate, using the means available to it (the orthodox Islam of the *'ulamā'* and of the *Sharī'a*, represented by the *qāḍīs* which it appointed, the influence of certain *zāwiyas*, and the support of the *sharīfs*), and fostering the traditional rivalries which existed between and within the tribes. It was ultimately the lack of unity within this huge Berber block which enabled the 'Alawīs to maintain their hold on the other half of Morocco.

The profound opposition which existed between rural Morocco, still medieval in its powerful tribal organization and its backwardness in economic development, and the towns, where society and occupations were infinitely more diversified, was traditional. Nevertheless, European penetration had helped to aggravate these differences by introducing into the coastal towns the seeds of modern activity, and by joining Morocco, with its agricultural economy, to a world-market, from whose fluctuations it was beginning to suffer, while the traditional currents of trade and activities were undergoing profound changes and entering a state of crisis. To a deeply divided and stagnating Morocco, Europe at first brought only additional causes of dissolution.

The Moroccan crisis of the first years of the twentieth century took a double form. The basic elements of the internal crisis, (the lack of organization and weakness of the *Makhzan*, and the Berber problem) had long existed, but it was made more serious by the effects of European penetration, and exploited by the imperialist powers to justify their colonial ambitions. The diplomatic crisis resulted from the rivalry between the various imperialisms: at first it developed simultaneously with the internal upheavals, then independently, so that the Moroccan crisis ended as a mere chapter in European diplomatic history.

Mawlāy 'Abd al-'Azīz (1894–1908), the younger son of Mawlāy al-Ḥasan, was at first prevented from holding any power by the *wazīr* Bā Aḥmad b. Mūsā, whose policy, conforming completely to tradition, aimed at controlling the tribes and warding off European influences. After his death in 1900, the sultan, then about twenty years of age, undertook to rule alone. The young ruler was not without good qualities, but he lacked character, and fell under the influence of European advisors, who exploited his curiosity and his love of novelties, and led him into costly extravagances and innovations which discredited him in the eyes of his subjects. This desire for modernization was not only a childish whim, and the principles which inspired certain changes were not mistaken, but the clumsiness with which they were carried out immediately prejudiced their chance of success.

This was the case with the fiscal reform of September 1901 which was prompted by the double wish to obtain greater revenue for the *Makhzan*, and to introduce into Morocco one simple tax, fixed and applicable to all without privileges or exemptions, the *tartīb*. The simplicity and the fairness of the *tartīb* made it seem attractive, but it was imprudent to abrogate the ancient fiscal system before the new one was established, and dangerous to harm with one single act so many varied traditions and interests. The reform immediately encountered general opposition. The tribes refused to pay the tax, and out of the agitation and anarchy there appeared a pretender to the throne, Jalālī b. Idrīs al-Zarhūnī, (*Bū Ḥmāra*, 'the man with the donkey'). Apart from the discontent provoked by the *tartīb* and hasty and blundering reforms, this revolt was an expression of popular protest against the favour accorded by the sultan to the Europeans, and against the many forms which the foreign penetration took. The occupation of Tuat by France in 1900 and 1901 in particular had made a profound impression on Moroccan public opinion. There is no other explanation for the xenophobic character of the propaganda of certain religious fraternities, and the many attacks made on Europeans. Disorder reigned in Morocco; the progress of Bū Ḥmāra merely made the helplessness of the *Makhzan* more obvious. The way was prepared for the intervention of Europe.

In fact France, which had long aimed at establishing herself in Morocco, had not waited for Moroccan anarchy to pursue on the frontier with Algeria a policy of 'peaceful' penetration which she justified by the necessity for maintaining order. Parallel with this intervention, French diplomacy aimed to neutralize any eventual opposition to its Moroccan policy by concluding a series of agreements based on the principle of bartering recognition of imperial gains with interested powers: Italy (1902), Great Britain and Spain (1904). It seemed that these agreements, and the development of the French commercial and financial enterprises in Morocco (with a loan from a consortium of French banks in 1904) would quickly lead to a French protectorate. It might have begun with the 'plan of reforms' presented at Fez in January 1905. However, France was forced to retreat by the unexpected opposition of Germany, whom the French foreign minister, Delcassé, had imprudently excluded from the Moroccan affair, and who considered that she had political and economic interests to assert. After William II's ostentatious visit to Tangier (31 March 1905), Delcassé had to resign, and Germany insisted on the holding of an international conference, with the connivance of the Moroccan sultan, who hoped thus to be able to avoid the threat of a French protectorate. Regarded as an episode in the diplomatic history of Europe, the Algeciras Conference (16 January–7 April 1906) resulted in a partial failure for Germany. From the point of view of Moroccan affairs, it was a setback for France. It proclaimed the independence of the sultan, the integrity of his empire, and economic equality among the powers; and thus placed Morocco under a sort of international guardianship. Nevertheless special rights were accorded to France and Spain, who were entrusted with the organization of the police, which allowed them wide possibilities of action.

Between 1907 and 1911 Morocco was the theatre of increasing anarchy, for which French intervention, less and less dissimulated, was partly responsible. The progressive nibbling away of Morocco brought the unpopularity of the sultan to its height: the south proclaimed his brother, Mawlāy ʿAbd al-Ḥāfiẓ, who succeeded in getting himself recognized as sultan by Morocco and by the powers (January 1909). After some success (Bū Ḥmāra was captured and put to death in 1909) the situation under the new sultan deteriorated. Obliged to endorse the commitments entered into by his predecessor, reduced to raising new loans to pay the debts, the costs of public works and the indemnities which were exacted from him, and forced to tolerate foreign intrusions into Moroccan affairs, Mawlāy ʿAbd al-Ḥāfiẓ became as unpopular as ʿAbd al-ʿAzīz had been. He had no alternative but to ask for French military support against the revolt of the tribes which besieged him in Fez. While French troops were operating in the neighbourhood of Fez, the Spaniards were beginning in May 1911 to occupy the zone which had been allotted to them in 1904. At this point, Germany, observing the failure of the plans for Franco-German economic co-operation which were worked out in 1909, and fearing that the Moroccan question would be settled without her, provoked a new crisis in July 1911, obliging France to buy her freedom of action in Morocco by consenting to concessions in the Congo by the agreement of 4 November 1911. All that now remained for France to do was to negotiate with the *Makhzan* a treaty of protectorate, largely inspired by that of the Bardo. It was signed on 30 March 1912 at Fez. But the conquest of Morocco which then began was not to be completed until 1934.

ALGERIA TO THE FRENCH CONQUEST (1830)

With the deys there was established in Algiers a monarchy moderated by the insubordination of the Janissary militia, every member of which could aspire to the highest office and for which each revolution was the pretext for substantial gains. Of the twenty-eight deys who succeeded each other from 1671 to 1830, half were assassinated. Only eleven times did the succession take place normally, the revolutions proceeding according to an invariable pattern: the assassination of the dey by a group of Janissaries who occupied the Janīna (the residence of the deys) and its approaches, and proclaimed their candidate who was then officially invested. These violent actions, which had become almost habitual, explain the growth of legends such as that of the 'seven deys' who were said to have been chosen and massacred on the same day, and whose seven tombs were pointed out in early nineteenth-century Algiers.

Nevertheless, the regency of Algiers weathered the crises of the beginning of the eighteenth century to progress towards a more stable form of government, the deys being increasingly chosen from among the dignitaries who shared the power: the treasurer, the commander of the troops, and the receiver of tribute. Between 1724 and 1791, except for a brief period of unrest in 1754, the power was held by only six deys who succeeded each other without violence, the reigning dey often nominating his successor, sometimes even from among his own family. During the same period the western province was, for nearly twenty years (from 1779 to 1796), under the enlightened government of Muḥammad Bey al-Kabīr, the conqueror of Oran; while Constantine experienced, if not quite a 'golden age', at least a restorative period of tranquility and prosperity under the five beys who governed it between 1713 and 1792, and in particular under Ṣāliḥ Bey (1771–92). The long reign of the Dey Bābā Muḥammad b. 'Uthmān (1766–91), who was the contemporary of the two beys mentioned above, was on the whole peaceful, any insubordination of the militia being kept in check by the severity of the dey. The development of trade, which was particularly apparent in the west of the regency, was the sign of real progress in the economic life of the country. From many points of view therefore this last quarter of the eighteenth century can be considered as a period of Algerian renaissance.

In foreign affairs, the situation of the regency appeared equally satisfactory. In order to solve the problems presented to them by Algerian privateering, the European powers, rather than resorting to naval demonstrations, which in any case had little effect, either attempted to conclude treaties with the Regency, which were not always adhered to, or (and this was often the case with the smaller states) submitted themselves to the rather humiliating practice of paying tributes and giving presents. Towards the end of the eighteenth century, the Algerians achieved a series of successes which impressed Europe with a high idea of their power, and convinced them of their own invincibility. In July 1775 a Spanish expeditionary force which arrived off Algiers (344 ships and 22,000 men) was beaten back into the sea. In 1792 Oran was definitively retaken from the Spaniards, and became the capital of the western province. Algerian territory was thus freed from foreign occupation. In its relations with the two neighbouring Muslim countries, the *ojak* of Algiers maintained an almost constant military superiority. After the Algerian troops had three times defeated those of Mawlāy Ismāʿīl there were no further difficulties with Morocco. The deys launched a series of victorious campaigns against Tunisia at the end of the eleventh/seventeenth and beginning of the twelfth/eighteenth century, and they succeeded, after the campaign of 1756, in reducing the regency of Tunis to tributary status.

In the last years of the eighteenth century, however, the stability of Algeria came to an end, and the Regency went through a new period of crisis shortly before its encounter with France. The two fundamental institutions of Algiers, privateering and the militia, were both in danger. The decline of privateering, which in the previous century had been a flourishing occupation in Algiers, and the main source of revenue for the treasury, became marked in the eighteenth century. The fleet was smaller (twenty four ships in 1724, about ten in 1788), the crews of inferior quality, and the raids less profitable. The number of slaves held in Algiers, which in the middle of the seventeenth century had exceeded 25,000, fell a century later to 3,000 and to 1,000 in 1788. The population of the town of Algiers followed the same descending curve as that of the revenues obtained from privateering. At the same time the power of the militia declined. Recruitment became more difficult: between 1800 and 1829, only slightly more than 8,000 recruits were brought from the Levant, and the total number of the effective forces of the militia diminished after the middle of the eighteenth century. These troops no longer possessed their previous quality as fighters, and were concerned chiefly with the advantages which they could obtain from their political role. As the financial difficulties which the deys were experiencing were reflected in some irregularity in the payment of the militia, their insubordination increased.

In order to clear off the deficit, and to satisfy the demands of the militia, the deys were forced to resort to dangerous commercial expedients (monopolies), and to exploit the local population. It was at this time that an intense religious ferment led to the creation or the reformation of many religious fraternities: the order of the Ṭayyibiyya, founded at the beginning of the eighteenth century and very widespread in Oran; the Darqāwa, a branch of the Shādhiliyya which detached itself from them at the beginning of the century; the Tijāniyya, founded by Aḥmad al-Tijānī (1150–1230/1737–1815), with its centre at 'Ayn Māḍī to the west of Laghwat; the Raḥmāniyya, founded by the Kabyle, Muḥammad b. 'Abd al-Raḥmān al-Gushtulī (d. 1208/1793/4). In many cases these fraternities catalysed the discontent of the population and gave a formidable religious interpretation to its anti-Turkish sentiments.

From the end of the century, the power in Algiers was again unstable, affected by the indiscipline of the militia: between 1798 and 1816 seven deys were put into power by revolutions and then perished through them. In 1816, 'Alī Khūja, in order to escape from the domination of the militia, decided to leave the Janīna and to go to live in the Qaṣba with a guard of 2,000 Kabyles. His successor, Ḥusayn Dey (1818–30), followed his example in this. A change was taking place, big with consequences which could have turned the state of Algeria into an hereditary monarchy relying on the non-Turkish elements of the population. Its immediate consequence however, was that the deys deprived themselves of the help of the militia without being able to count on support within the country. The early years of the nineteenth century were marked by continual internal revolts, which were nothing new in Algeria (the Kabyles were in a permanent state of rebellion), but the bitterness of which is perhaps explained by their religious character: the Darqāwī revolt in Kabylia (1803–7) and in Oran; further difficulties with the Kabyles (1810–15); and conflict between the beys of Oran and the Tijāniyya between 1820 and 1828. In the meantime the Regency's position abroad was weakening. In 1807 Tunisia put an end to half a century of Algerian domination. Relations with a rapidly developing Europe were undergoing a marked change. Following a period of renewed privateering activity, which coincided with the Revolutionary and Napoleonic wars, a series of naval operations demonstrated Algeria's true weakness. After an American squadron had forced Algeria to sign a treaty, Lord Exmouth, who had come in 1816 to procure the abolition of slavery, forced the Dey 'Umar to submit to his conditions, following a bombardment which demolished the forts of Algiers. Although Algiers could still on occasion produce an illusion of power, and even believe in it itself, it no longer possessed the means to resist a determined assault.

Although the formalities which implied the position of the deys as vassals of the Ottoman sultan continued to be scrupulously respected, the Regency of Algiers in fact possessed an autonomy which was recognized by the foreign powers who signed treaties with it. The reason why the masters of Algiers could never contemplate breaking the links which united them to the Sublime Porte was that the organization of the state rested on the Janissaries, who could be recruited in the Levant only with the consent of the sultan. Rather than a real monarchy, the Regency continued to be a sort of republic dominated by the Turkish military *élite*. The quasi-colonial antagonism which existed between a minority of foreign masters and the indigenous masses prevented Algeria from becoming a real nation, and was a major weakness in its Turkish government.

Although he held absolute power, the dey was nevertheless only one of the Janissaries (he continued to draw pay and a bread ration), elected from among his equals, and he had difficulty in escaping from the control of the militia, as was proved by the violent disturbances which occurred at the beginning of the century. In addition to his stipend, the dey received very many perquisites, such as fees for the investiture of important dignitaries, tribute from the beys, and presents from consuls, and he had at his command the public treasury. He had his own official house with a *khaznadār* (treasurer), a *turjumān* (interpreter), scribes and ushers. There had gradually grown up around him a sort of government, with five 'powers' (*puissances*) who performed the function of ministers: the *khaznajī*, in charge of the treasury, who was often chosen as the dey's successor; the *agha* of the *sipāhīs* (or of the *maḥalla*) who was in charge of the land forces; the *wakīl al-kharj*, a sort of minister of sea-power; the *bayt al-mālji*, the steward of the dey's household; the *khūjat al-khayl*, who administered the territories of the Regency and received the tribute from the beys. The '*agha* of the two moons', the chief of the militia, held only a secondary and representative role, as did the *Dīvān* of about sixty members, who in principle elected the dey, and from whom the majority of the high officials were chosen. A certain number of clerks (sing., *khūja*) kept the principal registers, and attended to the correspondence.

The militia which dominated and exploited the state was recruited in the Levant, for the most part in Anatolia. On his arrival in Algiers, the Janissary private was entered in the registers of the militia, in which were later recorded his increase in pay and his promotions. The Janissaries were divided into 424 groups of about twenty men, distributed into rooms (sing., *oda*) within eight barracks. Their active service was divided into garrison duty and service in the field. The *yoldash* very often followed a trade, and, with increasing frequency, married Algerian girls; but their children, the *Kul oghlus*, were not admitted to the militia until a later date, and they remained excluded from the highest offices, and from the majority of the prerogatives of the pure Turks. As the *ojak* was renewed by recruitment from outside, it did not in Algeria form a hereditary aristocracy. To these Turkish forces were added Turkish and Arab cavalry *sipahis*, paid Kabylian troops, and contingents of cavalry supplied by the *Makhzan* tribes. Privateering almost disappeared after 1815; the Algerian fleet, destroyed by Exmouth in 1816, and later involved in the Turkish naval disaster at Navarino, consisted in 1827 of no more than about ten ships.

The administration of the country was characterized by a great local variation in administrative usage, and by a wide decentralization, which even extended to a semi-autonomy for the professional, religious or ethnic groups. The Regency was divided into four provinces. That of Algiers (*Dār al-Sulṭān*) came directly under the authority of the dey. The three others were governed by beys: the *beylik* of Titteri (Tīṭarī) with its capital at Medea, the first in rank but the smallest in size, the *beylik* of the West with its successive capitals at Mazouna, Mascara and Oran; and the *beylik* of the East (Constantine). The beys, who were appointed and dismissed by the dey, had around them actual little governments, and had armed forces at their disposal for police operations. They enjoyed wide powers, and some of them were very important persons. Algiers supported them by sending three *maḥallas* (expeditionary forces) a year, in return for which it expected them to send regular tribute, which was brought twice a year by the lieutenant (*khalīfa*) of the bey, and once every three years by the bey himself. The insufficiency of the tribute was a frequent cause of the dismissal of the beys. The provinces were themselves divided into *waṭans* administered by *qā'ids*, who were appointed and usually Turks, and by shaykhs, who were elected. But the actual situations varied greatly between the *Makhzan* tribes, which contributed to the police, supplied military contingents and enjoyed various privileges in return, and the regions which were partially or totally independent, such as Kabylia or the Aurès. Where they were unable to install an effective local administration, the Turkish authorities (whose actual control extended over only a part of Algeria) made use, according to the circumstances and their relative strength at the time, of severity, diplomacy or cunning, for example in taking advantage of the divisions among clans, or ethnic or religious quarrels.

The basic taxes, which weighed especially heavily on the peasants, were traditionally the tithe (*'ushūr*) on the harvests, the *zakāt* on animals, the *lazma*, a sort of poll-tax which replaced the tithe in Kabylia and in the south, and the *kharāj* paid by the *ra'iyya* (subject peoples) in conquered territories. The tribes, who in greater or less degree escaped the government's authority, were made to pay a tax in kind or in money, the *gharāma*. To these taxes, which moreover varied according to the region, were added many other taxes and arbitrary levies. The dey's resources (tributes from the provinces, fees and other perquisites) supplied the budget of the regency. The expenses consisted basically of the pay of the militia, for the officials bought their appointments and afterwards recouped themselves with perquisites, while much of the expenditure on matters of public interest, such as worship and education, was met by private initiative. The dey's treasury seems to have been well filled: it is estimated at 100 million francs in 1830. This system possessed undoubted advantages which were due to its very simplicity: the payments in kind, which were very frequent, were less onerous on the taxpayers, and well adapted to a country lacking in specie, while they provided direct support for the high officials. Nevertheless, because of much waste in the fiscal system and the exactions which were added to the normal levies, the taxation was heavy without in fact contributing very much to the state.

Of the probably three million inhabitants of Algeria in 1830, the rural population represented more than nine-tenths. Because of methods and equipment which in general were rather primitive, and a complex and unsatisfactory system of land-tenure little more than the absolute minimum was produced. It is true that agricultural techniques were well adapted to natural conditions, and that the produce was destined mainly for consumption by a relatively small population: there was much arable soil, which allowed the extensive use of the land by the tribes in the grazing of sheep and goats. Life in the towns seems to have decreased at the end of the period of Turkish rule: there were few real towns apart from Algiers (30,000 inhabitants), Constantine (12,000) and Oran

(9,000). The urban population differed profoundly from the rural population, as much in the diversity of its composition (Turks, Moors and *Kul oghlus* all lived there and sometimes quarrelled; there were also substantial Muslim minorities, Mzabites, Kabyles, and large Jewish communities) as in the variety of its occupations: artisans, traders and '*ulamā*'. The artisans disposed of a relatively restricted internal market, and limited themselves to the processing of agricultural products, and the manufacture of objects of everyday use. They did not contribute to Algerian exports, and internal trade was hampered by the lack of geographical unity of the Regency, the difficulty of communications and the diversity of weights and measures in use. Foreign trade, based on the sale of a few raw materials (wheat, oil, animals) and the purchase of manufactured products (cloth) and some foodstuffs (sugar, coffee) remained rather small in volume. Its profits were concentrated in the hands of some European merchants and a few Andalusian[1] and Jewish families.

The concentration of political power exclusively in the hands of a foreign ruling class, and the often brutal exploitation of the population would to a certain extent justify the description of the Turkish régime in Algeria as 'colonial' if there had not existed between governors and governed strong links, such as the possession of a common religion, culture and social structure, which covered over the antagonism and if, furthermore, any idea of a massive human colonization or of exclusive exploitation of the land had not been completely foreign to the Turkish conquerors. Because of this ambiguity, the revolts of the people against the excesses of the Turkish domination could not assume a truly nationalist character. The Turks had founded the territorial framework of Algeria, but it was French colonization, established on the ruins of Ottoman domination, which was, through the country's reaction, to form the Algerian nation.

The origin of the French expedition of 1830 is found in the very involved affair of the credits held by Jewish merchants in Algiers, for deliveries of grain made to France between 1793 and 1798, partly thanks to the money lent by the dey. Ḥusayn Dey attempted for several years to get his demands heard in Paris, but without success. Finally, tired of the procrastinations of the French government and of the insolent behaviour of the consul Deval, the dey gave the latter the famous 'blow with the fly-whisk', which caused diplomatic relations to be broken off (29 April 1827). There followed three years of blockade of

[1] By 'Andalusian' is meant the descendants of Muslim refugees from Spain.

Algiers with very little result, interspersed with unfruitful negotiations. In August 1829 the French truce ship was fired on by cannon from Algiers, which put an end to the negotiations.

The Polignac government, which had at one time considered using Muḥammad 'Alī Pasha to conquer the Maghrib, then decided to send an expedition against Algiers (31 January 1830). Actually it was less concerned to defeat Algiers than to succeed in a matter of internal politics: it intended by reinforcing the prestige of the monarchy with a success which it hoped would be outstanding, to strangle the opposition, and obtain favourable elections. It was only the business circles of Marseilles which were truly interested in the actual colonization of Algeria. From 14 June 1830, 37,000 men were landed at Sidi Ferruch near Algiers. On the 19 June the Algerian forces attacked the expeditionary force at Staweli, but were defeated. On 29 June the French army resumed its march on Algiers, and on 4 July it occupied the Emperor Fort which commanded the town. Negotiations entered into with some of the important officials ended in the capitulation of the dey, who accepted the conditions of General de Bourmont. On 5 July at 12 o'clock French troops occupied Algiers. This success came too late to save the Restoration monarchy, and France found itself engaged in a colonial enterprise which it had neither really wanted nor seriously prepared.

TUNISIA

Husaynid Tunisia to 1830

The capture of the Bey Ibrāhīm al-Sharīf by the Algerian troops produced a profound reaction in Tunis, where the memory of the two expeditions of 1686 and 1694 was still quite fresh. The unanimity with which the high officials, the officers of the militia and the important citizens of Tunis entrusted the vacant office to the *agha* of the Turkish *sipahis*, Ḥusayn b. 'Alī, considered to be the most capable of saving Tunis, can be regarded as one of the first manifestations of national awareness in Tunisia (Rabī' I 1117/July 1705). Ḥusayn, the son of an Ottoman trooper, born in Candia, who had settled in Tunisia and founded a family there, justified this confidence: before the end of the year 1705, the Algerian troops, abandoned by their allies among the Tunisian tribes, were forced to recross the frontier. Soon afterwards Ḥusayn b. 'Alī thwarted an attempt by the Dey Muḥammad Khūja al-Aṣfar to seize power. The absolute power which the bey held from then on was later to be sanctioned by the Porte, which issued a firman entrusting to him the government of Ifrīqiya (1708). A later attempt by the Porte to re-establish its authority in Tunis failed completely (1127/1715), and after this it contented itself with the demonstrations of submission which reached it from this distant province, without contesting the semi-autonomy which its rulers enjoyed. After the long period of disturbances at the end of the eleventh/seventeenth century, Tunisia first experienced under Ḥusayn b. ʿAlī a period of calm in which to recover. The construction by this bey of very many buildings of public utility (wells, cisterns, reservoirs, bridges), markets and places for worship and education (three *madrasas* in Tunis and several in the towns of the interior), is evidence of this effort at reconstruction. It was particularly active at Qayrawān, which had been destroyed by Murād Bey: the walls were rebuilt and a *madrasa* and two markets erected.

The solidity of the Husaynid monarchy was put seriously to the test during the second quarter of the eighteenth century, during a series of crises which partook of the double character of dynastic struggles and foreign wars. Their origin was the frustrated ambition of Ḥusayn's nephew, ʿAlī Pasha, who had been deprived of the succession to the throne by the late birth of the bey's sons (Muḥammad in 1711 and ʿAlī in 1124/1712). Their seriousness arose from the help which the claimants received in Algiers, where every opportunity was seized to reassert the vassal status of the neighbouring Regency while obtaining profit from it in the form of tribute or of the spoils of war. The failure of the first revolt of ʿAlī Pasha having obliged him to seek refuge in Algiers in 1729, the prince succeeded in persuading Ibrāhīm Bey to support his cause. The Algerian troops marched on Tunis and installed ʿAlī Pasha there (September 1735). Ḥusayn and his sons continued the struggle in the Sahel and at Qayrawān until the town was taken and the bey died (16 Ṣafar 1153/13 May 1740). It was now the turn of his sons to seek refuge and support in Algeria.

A prince of ostentatious tastes (witness his buildings of the Bardo, which had become the habitual residence of the beys) and an enlightened ruler (he was responsible for four *madrasas* in Tunisia), ʿAlī Pasha had to fight in order to impose his authority. The revolt for which he had been responsible resulted in the permanent division of Tunisia into two parties (sing., *ṣaff*), the Ḥusayniyya and the Bāshiyya, whose opposition was in fact based on earlier quarrels. In particular the bey had to subdue powerful tribal confederations on the Algerian frontier in the south of the country. His own son, Yūnus, revolted against him in 1165/1752. Above all he had to face the danger from Algeria which reappeared this time in support of Ḥusayn's sons. The Algerian expedition of 1159/1746 failed, but in 1169/1756 the Algerians seized Tunis, and sacked the town. 'Alī Pasha was put to death, and the Ḥusaynīs were re-established, though not without experiencing some difficulty in ridding themselves of the encumbrance of their protectors. The crises which 'Alī Pasha had had to face (and to which there had been added in 1742 a conflict with France, after the recovery of Ṭabarqa from the Genoese) had obliged him to increase the man-power of the Turkish militia, in spite of the little confidence that he placed in it, especially since the revolt of 1156/1743.

After 1756 the descendants of Ḥusayn b. 'Alī succeeded one another almost without incident: Muḥammad Bey (1169/1756), 'Alī Bey (1172/1759), Ḥammūda Bey (1196/1782), 'Uthmān Bey (1229/1814), Maḥmūd Bey (1230/1814), Ḥusayn Bey (1239/1824), Muṣṭafā Bey (1251/1835). Contrary to the normal order of succession, however (by order of seniority within the family of the bey) 'Alī Bey had his son Ḥammūda (born 1173/1759) as his successor, passing over Maḥmūd, his nephew (born 1170/1757); 'Uthmān, having succeeded his brother Ḥammūda in 1814, was assassinated soon afterwards, and Maḥmūd finally came to the throne after having been twice frustrated.

The Husaynid beys eradicated the traces of the disturbances which Tunisia had suffered. The severe punishment meted out to the turbulent population of the Ousseltia, which was expelled from its *jabal* and dispersed (1759–62), served as an example, and for half a century there was no serious revolt in Tunisia. The second rebuilding of Qayrawān, which had been destroyed by Yūnus, is a positive example of this effort towards internal reconstruction. Under 'Alī and Ḥammūda the country experienced a certain economic prosperity, which was somewhat marred by a series of natural disasters, in particular the epidemics of plague in 1783–5 and 1818–20. During the disturbances of the following century, the reign of Ḥammūda, that 'Tunisian Charlemagne' was often referred to as a golden age. On several occasions the beys affirmed their quasi-autonomy in their relations with the Porte. Ḥammūda did this with a certain amount of *éclat*, first by intervening on his own account in Tripoli, to re-establish the Qaramānlī dynasty there (1794–5), then by his obvious unwillingness to break with France in 1798. This same bey attempted to free Tunis from its humiliating situation as a tributary of

Algiers. Ḥammūda's expedition of 1807 against Constantine was not successful, but the victorious resistance of the Tunisian troops near the frontier (14 July 1807) marked the end of Algerian raids into Tunisia until the definitive peace could be signed, under the auspices of the Ottoman government, in March 1821. In its relations with the European powers, a fair number of which had concluded direct treaties with it (16 in 1816), the Regency also held its own: offering resistance to France in 1770, standing up to the Venetians in 1784–6, pursuing a privateering war against the smaller maritime powers, or exacting from them humiliating tributes or gifts. It was not until September 1819 that the action of the powers taking part in the Congress of Aix-la-Chapelle forced the bey permanently to abolish privateering.

At the beginning of the nineteenth century, the Husaynid beys had become Tunisian princes, Arabic in language and culture, who often allied themselves in marriage with the great families of Tunis. The office of chief minister was filled by Tunisians as well as by *mamlūks*: among them were the shaykh and historian Ibn 'Abd al-'Azīz (under 'Alī Bey and Ḥammūda Pasha), the al-Aṣram, natives of Qayrawān who were hereditary *bāsh kātibs*, or Muḥammad al-'Arabī Zarrūq, under Maḥmūd Bey. The Turkish militia declined rapidly after 1750: in spite of the caution with which Ḥammūda Pasha treated them, it was quite clear that the troops had lost all political influence. It was perhaps an attempt to regain it which led them to revolt in 1811 and 1816. These revolts, and the vigorous repression which followed them, only hastened the decadence of the militia, while the beys naturally tended more and more to have recourse to the local troops. Thus was completed, shortly before the occupation of Algiers, the evolutionary process which had transformed the Regency of Tunis, dominated by the Turkish *ojak*, into a quasi-monarchic national state.

The political and administrative structure of the state of Tunisia immediately before the conquest of Algeria was at the same time very primitive, if we consider the means employed, and very complex, if we take into account the great variety of institutions which had been inherited from the ancient or the more recent past. Whatever may have survived of Ottoman rule, the bey was, at the beginning of the nineteenth century, practically an independent ruler. The hereditary character of the régime was in no way affected by the formality of the double investiture (*bay'a*) which associated the *Dīvān* and the important dignitaries with the enthronment of the ruler, nor by the request for investiture by the sultan, which was granted automatically, carrying with it the title of pasha, and regularly renewed. There were only a few external signs which continued to witness to the fact that in principle the bey was a vassal: it was in the name of the sultan that coins were struck, and that the *khuṭba* was said. The fact was also still expressed in some demonstrations of respect, and in occasional military aid: some Tunisian squadrons joined the Ottoman fleet in 1821 and 1826, which resulted in the destruction of the Tunisian navy at Navarino. Apart from this the bey governed without reference to the Porte. Even the use of Turkish, which had been a symbol of belonging to the Ottoman world, was abandoned in treaties about 1830 and in correspondence with Istanbul in 1838.

Without officially possessing the title of ministers (it was Aḥmad Bey who first appointed *wazīrs*) or exactly their functions, a certain number of high officials surrounding the bey did in fact hold this sort of position: the *ṣāḥib al-ṭābi'* (keeper of the seals), who was often the chief minister; the *khaznadār* (treasurer); the *kāhiya* (commander of the troops); the *kāhiya* of La Goulette, who was also *amīn al-tarsakhāna* (director of the arsenal), in charge of the navy and of foreign affairs. The chief secretary (*bāsh kātib*) also played an important role in the bey's entourage, for he had in his hands all the correspondence of the Regency; he was assisted by Arabic and Turkish secretaries, about ten in number, but enough for the business to be transacted.

To fulfill important political functions and to command the troops, the beys chose *mamlūks*, slaves who were bought in the East and brought up in the palace. In this way they assured themselves of a staff which was relatively competent and generally loyal: the beys gave Husaynid princesses in marriage to the most important of them. The *mamlūks* formed a caste, the highest rank of which was occupied by the Circassians and the Georgians, who had the greatest contempt for their Greek and Italian fellow-slaves (who had become very numerous at the beginning of the nineteenth century), and also for the native Tunisians, whom the exercise of the functions of *kātib* assured of a certain amount of influence over affairs. The Tunisians had also the monopoly of the judicial and religious offices, but the traditional jurisdiction of the *qāḍīs* and of the *majlis shar'ī* (religious court) suffered competition from the justice which was dispensed by the bey and a number of high officials.

The Turkish personnel which had formerly governed the Regency no longer played more than a secondary or honorary role; an example was the dey, who had become a sort of chief of police in Tunis, or the former chief of the militia, the *agha al-kursī*, or the formerly all-powerful *Dīvān*. This decline was reflected in that of the militia, which in about 1830 consisted of scarcely more than 2,500 men. The rulers, who surrounded themselves by a guard of *mamlūks* (four *odas* of twenty-five men) employed mainly native troops (3,000 recruited in Kabylia, four *ojaks* of 500 Arab *sipahis*) and, in case of need, contingents furnished by the *Makhzan* tribes. The regular army, reduced for reasons of economy to about 7,000 men, was of mediocre quality, but nevertheless sufficient to impose order on the tribes, who were even worse armed (and above all lacked cannons) and very poorly disciplined.

To establish his authority in the interior of the country, collect taxes and maintain order, the bey sent two annual columns (sing., *maḥalla*), one in summer to the west, and the second in winter to the south. The local administration was entrusted to governors (sing. *'āmil, qā'id*) who bought their offices and subjected their provinces to an exploitation which was limited only by their concern not to be removed from office and divested of their spoils by the bey. The hold which the government had over the populations, which was exercised through elected shaykhs, varied according to the regions: it was strong in the settled agricultural regions near to the capital and in the Sahel of Sousse, and weak in the mountain areas and in the steppe, which were under the domination of the great tribes.

The calm and stability which the country had enjoyed since 1169/1756 had brought with it a relative economic prosperity which showed itself in various ways: a tendency for the tribes to settle in the high steppes, the formation of new villages, an increase in the cultivation of olive trees in the neighbourhood of Sfax, and an extension of the area of cultivated land (about 750,000 hectares, were under cultivation in about 1840). The country continued to live according to the rhythm of the traditional commercial currents: north-south exchanges between the nomads with their flocks and the growers of wheat and of olives, relations with the Sahara and trade with Algeria and the Levant, in which the local artisan class still played an important part (e.g. the making of 'chechias', woollen caps, which employed 15,000 persons in the eighteenth century, the manufacture of woollen cloth and leather goods).

Foreign trade was expanding and the exports (mainly of oil from the Sahel) definitely exceeded the imports.

At the beginning of the nineteenth century, however, there appeared an increasing number of signs pointing to economic and financial difficulties. The abolition of privateering in 1819 had certainly affected the bey's finances, although its role in Tunis had never been of more than secondary importance. More serious for Tunisia had been epidemics and famines which had impoverished and depopulated it. Following the example of Ḥammūda, the beys attempted to obtain new resources from a policy of monopolies, which hindered trade and was a burden on agriculture. Some efforts were made to improve the system of taxes (which were made heavier by the abuses and the extortions of the *qā'ids*) and, to encourage the peasantry; there was introduced (in November 1819) a tithe (*'ushūr*) on the produce of the olive plantation of Sousse, in place of the fixed *qanūn*, and in 1825 a reform in the system of collection of the tithe on cereals. But the results were not what the beys had hoped. In about 1830, the farmers of the Sahel, overwhelmed by a series of bad harvests, and by the harmful consequences of the commercial monopoly of oil, were on the brink of ruin: the crisis produced the downfall of the minister, and cost the government heavy indemnities to the French merchants. About the same time, monetary difficulties led Ḥusayn Bey to devalue the *riyāl* (piastre) yet a little further. The meagre profit which this operation brought him was largely cancelled out by the aggravation of the monetary and economic troubles: the piastre continued to fall in value, and gold and silver coins became very scarce in the country.

The crisis which was beginning to affect the Regency was in part the effect of European commercial penetration, which was to increase after 1830. Sea trade, which was relatively extensive from Tunisia, took the form of an exploitation of its natural, agricultural resources by the Europeans and their local agents, who had this trade under their control and received all the profit from it. Whereas Tunisia was strengthening most of her commercial relations with Europe (whose merchant navies held a monopoly of the Mediterranean traffic), the traditional outlets towards the Maghrib and the Near East were declining, and with them the economic activity which supplied them, the products of the artisan classes. The break-up of the Ottoman empire in the Mediterranean, beginning with the French conquest of Algiers, was to accelerate the political and economic decline of Tunisia.

Tunisia in the nineteenth century from the reforms to the protectorate

The Algerian expedition was welcomed by the bey of Tunis who at first saw it only as an event which rid him of hated neighbours: he even considered joining with France in the reorganization of the neighbouring Regency. Negotiations led to the project of installing in Constantine and Oran Tunisian princes, tributaries of France. After beginning at Oran, the enterprise was interrupted, the French government having refused to ratify the agreements (1831). In reality a new era was beginning for Tunisia. Isolated, especially from the world to which she had belonged for ten centuries, after the occupation of Constantine in 1837, Tunisia gradually changed into a mere commercial dependency of Europe, to the detriment of its traditional economic equilibrium. Further, the beys tried to counter the political pressure which was exerted directly on them by an attempt at reconstruction and progress which was only to accelerate the process of internal disintegration.

The diplomatic situation of the Regency was immediately and profoundly altered by the conquest of Algiers. In Paris (and still more in Algiers) it was thought that Tunisia was destined to fall sooner or later under French influence, and that it was in France's interest to maintain there a weak and isolated authority: thus French policy tended to break what remained of the links between Tunisia and the Ottoman empire, to consolidate Tunisian autonomy, envisaged as a state of quasi-independence. On the other hand Great Britain, alarmed at the progress of French influence, was led, in order to protect effectively the *status quo* in Tunis, to advocate a *rapprochement* with the Porte, and tried to make the somewhat theoretical dependence of the beys into a reality. At the same time, because of the re-establishment of their authority at Tripoli (1835), the Ottomans were in a favourable position to defend their rights in Tunis, and eventually to try to consolidate their position there. The beys (and in particular Aḥmad Bey), who were truly alarmed by the pressure from France but who were also anxious to stress their autonomy, were forced by circumstances to play a diplomatic game, the subtlety of which was apparent in 1836 and 1837 when French squadrons appeared off Tunis, ostensibly to prevent the Ottomans from repeating there the operation in which they had succeeded at Tripoli. The same situation later recurred almost every year. In the end, as France's ideas on the status of Tunis were more realistic, and above all closer to the wishes of the beys, and as in addition she was in a position to exert an almost irresistible pressure on Tunisia, it was French policy which prevailed. Tunisia continued to detach itself progressively from the Ottoman empire, at the risk, should the British policy change, of finding herself alone face to face with France.

The attempts at reform in Tunis, as in Egypt and Turkey, at first took the form of modernization of the army. In 1830, Ḥusayn Bey had asked for and obtained help in modernizing his troops: thus there were organized the first *Niẓāmī* units, for the creation of which he requested the Porte's approval after the event (1831). This effort was later continued at great expense by the minister, Shākir, an admirer of Muḥammad 'Alī Pasha, and in particular by Aḥmad Bey (1837–55) when he came to power. The formation of a European-style army appealed to his liking for prestige, and was intended to serve his main ambition—to obtain the recognition of the quasi-independence of Tunisia, and to have it respected by the Ottomans. Thus within a few years seven regiments of infantry, two of artillery and one of cavalry were formed, although the quality and the number of these troops did not entirely correspond to the bey's hopes, or to the financial expenditure authorized. Greatly influenced by the example given by Egypt, the bey established a military school in the Bardo (March 1840), and tried, but without much success, to create an industry to support his military effort by a textile mill, a gunpowder factory and a foundry.

However modest this army was (not more than about 10,000 men), it was still disproportionate to the resources of the country: military expenditure ended by absorbing two thirds of the budget. In addition Aḥmad Bey allowed himself to spend money on luxuries, such as the building of a Tunisian 'Versailles' at the Muḥammadiyya near Tunis. He was the victim of European adventurers, or of high officials who pilfered from the treasury. Tunisia thus resorted to financial expedients and seemingly attractive yet disastrous enterprises, such as the creation of a bank and of paper money in 1847, which were to lead to catastrophe. About 1852 it was threatened with bankruptcy: the flight to France of Maḥmūd b. 'Ayyād, the concessionary of the majority of the farms and monopolies, taking with him considerable state funds, and the effort made in 1854 to send some 10,000 men to the aid of the sultan, helped to make the situation even worse.

This rather disorganized attempt at progress was not however entirely without results. It was Aḥmad Bey who by degrees abolished slavery between 1841 and 1846, and who put an end to the humiliating position of the Tunisian Jews. The School of the Bardo produced an *élite* of officers and high officials with modernist ideas, while even the teaching at the great mosque of the Zaytūna was reorganized in 1842. The bey persistently refused to adopt the Ottoman Tanẓimāt because of the diplomatic implications of such a decision; but he did not deny that reform was necessary. The foreign influences to which he opened his country (his visit to Paris in 1846 was from this point of view a particularly spectacular gesture), and the more exact knowledge of the modern world which the Tunisians obtained in the course of many missions to Europe, helped to increase Tunisia's progress.

The period of the real reforms began with Muḥammad Bey (1855–9) who was a traditionalist ruler, but anxious to improve the lot of his subjects. He began his reign by replacing a certain number of taxes by one single tax, the 'subsidy' (*iʿāna* or *majba*) of 36 piastres a year (1856), and by abolishing certain abuses in the collection of the tax in kind. But it required the joint pressure of the French and British consuls which was made possible by the temporary *rapprochement* between France and Great Britain, to force the bey to adopt, on 10 September 1857, the Fundamental Pact (*ʿAhd al-amān*), which was the starting point for actual political reform. Inspired by the Ottoman Tanẓimāt, the text granted to all Tunisians, Muslims and Jews, equal guarantees and rights, and accorded to foreigners the right to hold property in Tunisia. The reformist movement then continued under the impetus of a modernist *élite* (among them the minister Khayr al-Dīn Pasha al-Tūnisī and the historian and minister Ibn Abi'l-Ḍiyāf) and under the vigilant control of the consuls, who expected it to facilitate foreign economic penetration. In 1857 there was established a Commission of Reforms, and in August 1858 a Municipal Council at Tunis. The accession of Muḥammad al-Ṣādiq (1859–82), more definitely modernist than his predecessor, gave new impetus to the movement. After founding the official journal of Tunisia (*al-Rāʾid al-Tūnisī*), and promulgating the law on recruitment (March 1860) and the decrees on the organization of Tunisian ministries (February and April 1860), the bey proclaimed in January 1861 a constitution which established a limited monarchy, the bey sharing his legislative powers with a Grand Council (*al-Majlis al-akbar*) of sixty members; regular tribunals were to be instituted, with legal codes based on European models.

This was an experiment without precedent in the Ottoman world. Some of the foreign powers which had advocated modernization found in practice that an assembly in which the public interest had spokesmen was less malleable than an absolute potentate: the granting of new concessions and privileges encountered serious difficulties. Furthermore the Tunisians, inspired by their attainment of civilization and progress, demanded that foreigners should henceforward come under the jurisdiction of the regular tribunals, a claim which the majority of foreign governments would not accept. While France and Italy opposed the reforms more and more openly, Great Britain was the only country to support the development of the new institutions. She signed in 1863, a convention with the bey which, in exchange for the freedom to trade granted to the British, submitted them to the *lex loci*. Within Tunisia, the reform policy also encountered great difficulties: it disturbed the habits of the peasantry and bedouin (particularly in matters of justice); there was a lack of loyal and competent officials to make the new institutions work: finally the majority of the *'ulamā'* were hostile to these innovations. But it was primarily the financial difficulties, with their international implications, which caused the policy of reform to collapse. The beys aggravated the financial crisis by launching into expenditure of doubtful value, sometimes suggested by untrustworthy European businessmen. In order to obtain the money it required, the government at first borrowed locally at usurious rates of interest. Then it turned to Europe. In 1863 the bey borrowed from the banking house of d'Erlanger in Paris. He actually received a small proportion of the nominal sum, and it was soon dissipated. In need of money once again, the bey decided to double the *majba*. This measure brought the country's discontent to a head: in the spring of 1864, the great tribes of the centre of the country refused to pay the tax, and the revolt became general.

The revolution of 1864 was more than a mere bedouin revolt. The rebels presented a list of precise complaints and chose leaders among themselves. The movement spread to the region of the Sahel, and, in the coastal towns where the European penetration had made itself most felt, it took on an indisputably nationalist character. The revolution failed, however, for lack of unity and clear perspectives. It was nevertheless to have considerable consequences. First of all the bey made it the pretext for bringing the reforms to an end, as he was in any case being encouraged to do by the French consul. The military efforts and then the repression hastened the financial and economic ruin of the country. In 1865 the government contracted a second loan, still more disastrous than the first. The drought, famine and cholera which followed in 1866 and 1867 finally overwhelmed Tunisia. In 1866 the government had to make heavy payments in various annuities and was practically deprived of resources. The bey, faced with bankruptcy, was finally forced to accept the tutelage of an International Financial Commission (5 July 1869). Thus there began the process of internationalization of the Tunisian Question.

This agreement established a sort of triple protectorate of France, Italy and Great Britain over the finances of Tunisia, with France predominating: a French inspector of finances sat on the executive Committee. But the defeat of 1871 forced France to adopt a cautious policy in Tunisia, and the Commission on the Debt finally contributed to halting the Italian efforts at penetration. For several years the superior influence of Great Britain ensured a virtual state of equilibrium at Tunis, the British consul even taking advantage of the circumstances to settle, with the agreement of Khayr al-Dīn, the problem of relations with the Porte: but the firman of 23 October 1871, which reaffirmed the Ottoman sovereignty at Tunis, was to remain a dead letter.

The few years of respite from diplomatic complications which Tunisia experienced after 1871 saw a final attempt to rehabilitate the country. On becoming prime minister in October 1873, Khayr al-Dīn attempted to apply successfully a realistic policy of internal improvements, more fruitful than ambitious but premature constitutional reforms, thus following the principles which he had enunciated in his work *Aqwam al masālik*, published in 1867. Khayr al-Dīn was able to re-establish financial stability, while paying Tunisia's debt. His intense legislative activity contributed greatly to the making of modern Tunisia: it covered the organization of the administration of the 'habous' (*ḥubus*, i.e. *waqf*), the reorganization of justice, the statute concerning share-cropping, the codification of the rules for the corporations, the organization of the teaching at the Zaytūna Mosque, and the foundation of the Ṣādiqiyya College (1875) with a syllabus which was both traditional and modern. Thanks to more favourable harvests, the economic situation improved and trade revived. The experiment, which seemed as if it would succeed, was, however, short-lived. Given less and less support by the powers, who rejected his project of mixed courts, and who were irritated by his resistance to their enterprises of economic penetration, and subjected to contradictory pressures over the Eastern crisis, Khayr al-Dīn was abandoned by the bey, and had to resign (1877).

Henceforward nothing could prevent Tunisia's becoming a protectorate. The decisive step was taken at the time of the Congress of Berlin

(1878) when Great Britain decided, in order to ensure its possession of Cyprus, to place no further obstacles in the way of France's ambitions in Tunisia. Having obtained Germany's support, France had only to overcome the opposition of Italy, and to await a favourable opportunity. In the years 1879 and 1880 there was carried on a bitter struggle between France and Italy, each attempting to develop its influence in Tunisia by means of concessions wrung from a powerless and corrupted Tunisian government. Since April 1880, however, French policy received little support by London, where Granville had replaced Salisbury as foreign secretary. It seemed to be at a standstill in Tunis.

Within a few weeks, however, the French government was to resolve the Tunisian Question to its advantage and according to the wishes of the Quai d'Orsay, the politicians and the business circles in France, where it was considered a matter of urgency to put an end to Italian 'obstruction'. An incursion into Algerian territory (30–31 March 1881) by mountain tribes, who habitually paid very little heed to frontiers, provided the necessary pretext. The president of the Council, Jules Ferry, requested from the Chamber of Deputies, and obtained on 4 April, sums for a punitive expedition to the frontiers, in collaboration with the Tunisian authorities. The operation took quite a different direction however. After three weeks of unopposed advance, the French troops arrived at the gates of Tunis, and the bey was made to sign the Convention of the Bardo (12 May 1881) which tacitly established a French protectorate in Tunisia.

CONCLUSION

Thus the three countries of the Maghrib were led, by different historical evolutions and at different moments in European expansion, towards the same end as colonies. The reasons for this are many: the inability of these states to adapt themselves to the modern world, the backwardness of the economy, stagnation in the social organization and the archaism of their political institutions, the lack of any national cohesion, except in the case of Tunisia, but above all the irresistible force of the European penetration, whether they attempted to canalize it as in Tunisia, or to repel it as in Morocco.

On the whole the destructive effects of the contact with Europe far outweighed any progress that resulted from its influence. In the economic sphere, the expansion achieved seemed in fact to make the local situation still worse. Improvements affected only the system of trade without changing the basic situation, i.e. the methods and means of production, the over-equipment of exploitation contrasting more and more with the under-equipment of production. On the other hand, economic colonization brought with it the alteration of the basic structures of the countries.

In the political sphere, the pressure exerted by the European powers was fundamentally ambiguous. They denounced the abuses and the archaisms of the local administration, and commended 'reform'; but at the same time they hid behind these abuses to obtain the continuance of privileges which prevented reform. Furthermore reform was itself an agent in the dissolution of the countries, and inevitably involved the downfall of precisely those traditional structures which attempts were being made to save. In fact, from a more general viewpoint, the question arises whether in the under-developed countries at the beginning of the twentieth century, 'reform' as it was then envisaged was really possible, and whether the alternative was not between a complete revolution which would have overthrown the whole of the political, economic and social structure, and a semi-protectorate imposing a limited reform.

Algeria had been conquered almost by accident in the first stages of European expansion. Half a century later neither Tunisia nor Morocco was in a position clearly to understand the terms of this dilemma, still less to solve it. Salvation could not come from within: the two countries could have escaped colonization only if the foreign pressures which weighed on them had neutralized each other, as happened in the case of Persia. In a North Africa which was dominated by the presence of France in Algeria, they had no alternative but to succumb.

CHAPTER 4

NORTH AFRICA IN THE PERIOD OF COLONIZATION

ALGERIA (1830–1962)

The occupation of Algiers (1830) led at first to the conquest of Algeria and then to that of the whole of the Maghrib by the French; the conquest was limited until 1834 to a few points on the coast but progressively extended towards the interior in spite of some spectacular reverses. The treaties which were concluded in 1834 and 1837 with the most representative chief of western and central Algeria, the *Amīr* 'Abd al-Qādir, seem to have left the French freedom of action in the east. Thus they occupied Constantine in October 1837. The expedition of the Duc d'Orléans which linked Constantine to Algiers without any armed opposition, far from indicating the pacification of Algeria, as the French government maintained, was the beginning of a period of ruthless conflict. On the one side there was General Bugeaud, governor-general from the end of 1840, who obtained from the government men, supplies, credit, and above all complete freedom of movement; on the other, 'Abd al-Qādir, whose authority was based on his personality, his readiness to use force to reduce opposition, his desire to create, in imitation of Muḥammad 'Alī, if not an Algerian nation at least an Algerian state, and finally his good relations with Mawlāy 'Abd al-Raḥmān of Morocco. The latter gave him substantial help until his defeat at Isly (1844). Bugeaud hounded 'Abd al-Qādir and his partisans. Everywhere where the *amīr* could offer resistance, the general used the methods of total war; devastating the country, and massacring or carrying off women and children. In 1843 the *amīr* lost his own retinue, and was thus deprived of his mobile capital. In 1844 Moroccan help was withdrawn. He failed to gain the *beylik* of Constantine. 'Abd al-Qādir surrendered to the French in 1847, and Bugeaud left Algeria in 1848. From 1852 to 1871 the war continued locally: in Kabylia (1852–64) and the region south of the Sahara (1864–70); in spite of some spectacular reverses French authority spread. The revolt of Muḥammad al-Ḥājj al-Muqrānī (1871) gave the French the opportunity to crush several hundred tribes belonging to Algiers, Constantine, and the south. The last uprisings took place in 1879 and 1880.

The effects of the conquest were twofold. In the first place the war produced destruction and losses in men and in money. The rural economy declined, as did that of the towns, which were totally or partially abandoned as soon as they were occupied by the French. The forced contributions, fines and taxes levied, added to the increase in the traditional taxes, deprived the Algerians of a large part of their financial reserves. But this was nothing beside the irreparable loss of human lives. The population of Algeria fell from about three million in 1830 to 2,600,000 in 1866 and 2,100,000 in 1872; to the losses of the war were added those caused by the destruction of food supplies, by epidemics of cholera or typhus in 1837, 1849–52, and 1866–70, and by famine.

In the second place, the armies were followed by colonization, which produced major changes in the economic life of the country. The European population increased from 3,228 in 1831 to 272,000 in 1870. The colonists settled at first in the towns, then were able to occupy increasing areas of land (they took over 481,000 hectares between 1830 and 1870 and 402,000 hectares between 1871 and 1880), because of the confiscations which resulted from the conquest. A body of legal measures and the policy of 'cantonment' (at first from 1846 to 1848, then from 1856 to 1860), allowed the demands of the concessionaries, whether individuals or companies, to be satisfied, and official or private colonization projects to be carried out. The first efforts met with some serious failures: first, because the concessionaries speculated in land instead of working to improve it; secondly, because the concessions were either too small or too large; thirdly, because the inexperienced colonists lacked basic resources and suffered from economic or climatic crises. Nevertheless, from 1855 their worst trials seem to have been over, and the number of births exceeded that of deaths; even the serious crisis of 1866–70 affected them relatively little. Among the immigrants the majority were Spanish and Italian until 1855, after which the number of French immigrants was greater. All of them lived mainly in the towns, which grew up at an astonishing rate along the coast.

Colonization upset the traditional economy. The price of food rose by an average of 200 to 300 per cent. Financial speculation and the thrusting of the Algerian economy, without protective tariffs, first into the French, and then into the international field of commerce, laid a heavy burden on the peasantry, who perhaps suffered from the hazards of their climate more severely than they had hitherto done. Thus, first in the period from 1845 to 1850 and again from 1866 to 1870, Algeria experienced serious price-rises and famines, which added their effects to those of epidemics. The underground reserves, which normally enabled the peasants to get through the years of drought, had been emptied when grain was fetching a high price (e.g. during the Crimean War), and particularly after the new commercial law of 1851 made it easier for goods to be exported from Algeria. In addition, the *Senatus Consultum* of 1863 broke the links of solidarity among the members of the tribes. Finally, the tribes which depended on the forests for wood, rights of pasturage and cultivated enclaves were, at the end of the Second Empire, partly driven out from these zones. Nor did colonization modify to any extent the agricultural techniques of the peasants or the implements which they used.

In the towns, the *madīnas* (native quarters) were disrupted, and the influx of European immigrants led firstly to increased rents, which resulted in inordinate building and speculation in property, producing an enormous housing crisis in 1848 in Algiers, in Blidah and in Bône. Secondly, it had the effect of changing the basic elements and the emphasis of urban commerce. Thirdly, it gave the Algerians the impression that their normal way of life in their towns was crumbling. Without the support of the *ḥubus*, the traditional centres of education, the *zāwiyas*, *madrasas* and *kuttābs*, were in jeopardy.

The conquest altered the administrative organization of Algeria from top to bottom, especially after 1834. 'The French administration acted exactly as if it believed that the population of Algeria consisted only of an agglomeration of individuals without any common link or any social organization'[1]. In 1833, a parliamentary commission recommended that Algeria should be retained; the royal ordinance of 22 July 1834 therefore announced the decision to entrust the administration of the possessions in North Africa to a governor-general, responsible to the minister of war. A new central administration was installed in Algiers, staffed partly by civilians but consisting chiefly of military personnel. These formed, after the creation of the Arab Bureaux in 1844, a solid administrative framework which included Arab dignitaries, and thus permitted vast territories to be controlled by only a small staff. These territories were divided into circles, the 'Arab territories', within which the tribes lived. The 'civil territories' were defined in 1845 as

[1] Pelissier de Reynaud, *Annales algériennes*, I, 74.

'those in which there exists a European population sufficiently numerous for all the public services to be, or to be capable of being, completely organized'. Finally the 'mixed territories' had a small European and a large Arab population. This demarcation was superimposed on the division of the country into three provinces, Algiers, Oran and Constantine, which in 1848 became three departments.

The brief revolutionary episode of 1848 was followed by the Second Empire. The French in Algeria did not cease to show their opposition to it, and they received support both in Paris and also even from the governors-general. They worked against the Arab Bureaux, and the military government of Algeria which restricted their ambitions and their appetites. Napoleon III and his 'Arabophile' entourage attempted to restrain the movement; but the cause of the colonists who advocated a civil régime was reinforced by the crisis of 1866–70, and by the liberalization of the régime in France. The civil régime triumphed in September 1870. The Empire, however, to a greater extent than the régimes which preceded it, had provided Algeria with the groundwork of a modern range of essential public services.

The Third Republic carried on this progress. The railways increased from 296 kilometres in 1870 to 3,337 kilometres in 1914. All the great French banks established branches in Algeria, and the Bank of Algeria became an issuing house, and above all a central organization and regulator of credit. The value of trade increased from 79 million francs in 1831 to 259 million gold francs in 1870, and reached 1,292 million gold francs in 1913, in spite of the crises of 1846–52, 1865–70, 1875–8 and 1888–95. Imports always exceeded exports, and the major part of Algerian trade was with France; at first because the commercial relations between Algeria and France were based increasingly on reciprocal and absolute freedom from duty, and later because French shipping enjoyed a monopoly. Cereals and livestock, which until 1870 formed the main items of export, were overtaken in 1913 by wine and its by-products, and by iron and phosphates. The chief imports were coal and consumer goods. This change is linked with the economic transformation which took place in Algeria between 1870 and 1914.

The working of the mines, which had begun under the Second Empire, continued actively, particularly in the Constantine area, and the value of mineral products, iron and phosphates in particular, increased from 4,586,000 gold francs in 1872 to 261 million gold francs in 1913. After

1875 the area of vineyards increased regularly. This appeared to be the ideal crop for the colonists; but the freedom with which credit was available, imprudent speculation, and an excessive planting of vineyards produced a serious crisis in Algerian agriculture after 1890. There were various consequences. The small proprietors of vineyards were ruined, and most of the large proprietors were in difficulties, but were on the whole better able to overcome them, and even to buy up abandoned land. The re-establishment of the vineyards demanded much capital and led to a concentration of property in too few hands. Some centres of colonization deteriorated in spite of the many inducements offered by the administration, which provided the country with a medical and public health service, freed the colonists from direct taxes, granted them credit facilities, and equipped the villages at the expense of the native sub-districts, which for this purpose were attached to the colonization centres.

From September 1870 onwards, the colonists had the administration in their power. They were thus able to impose a series of measures; which, in December 1870, gradually transferred all the military territories in which the Arabs lived into civil territory under their authority, and facilitated the sequestration and purchase in 1871, after the revolt of Muqrānī, of Arab personal and tribal holdings of land.

Between 1881 and 1900 the official colonization received from the administration 296,000 hectares. The European population grew considerably, from 272,000 in 1870 to 681,000 in 1911. It was larger in the towns than in the country, forming thirty-three per cent of the total population in 1872, and thirty-five per cent in 1906, and it was feared that still more settlers would abandon the country districts. The towns developed mainly along the coast, and, as they grew more and more enormous, they resembled the Mediterranean towns of European countries. The ratio of French to non-French inhabitants increased as a result of the law of 26 June 1889, which provided that foreign children born in Algeria were automatically naturalized. There arose a new type of person, the Algerian Frenchman, who was different both from the Europeans, whether French or non-French, and from the Algerians. Being French citizens, they were electors, and controlled the whole of the political and administrative life of the country, with the exception of a few high officials who came from France. Thus they were not concerned about French public opinion. The Europeans imposed and maintained the *indigénat*, a discriminatory legal system, which disregarded French common law, and surrounded the native Algerians with a network of restrictions, fines and prison sentences. These were often very severe, and were remitted only at the discretion of the administrative officials, who, in the mixed communes, exercised the powers of judges. This iron régime existed also in the assize courts and the criminal tribunals, where the French magistrates judged without pity, and the juries were entirely French.

Although they had suffered severely during the crisis of 1866–70 and the revolt of 1871, between 1881 and 1891 the Algerian population regained, and even exceeded, its former numbers; although certain observers thought that it would shortly disappear, in 1911 it numbered in fact 4,686,000. Although many Algerians returned to the towns, the majority lived in the country districts. Those in the towns, apart from a few merchants and artisans, formed a class of unskilled workers, which benefited from none of the French social laws. From 1870 to 1913 the peasants lost important areas of land in the north and in the high plains. They were forced back towards the south or towards the mountain regions, and fell into difficulties even more quickly than before. Their economic and social condition deteriorated; the small landowners became hired workers, who, in years of crisis, joined the vagabond army which was a source of anxiety to the colonists and the administration. The problem was all the more serious because the land-legislation from 1863 to 1887 had broken up the tribal system which enabled the poor to survive in times of hardship. The severe crisis which struck them at the end of the nineteenth century led to the sending of a parliamentary commission. Shortly afterwards the administration decided to create native provident societies to succour their members in times of crisis, and to assist them to improve their agricultural equipment (1893). In 1897 it also modified the law of 1887, applying it in a way which was less favourable to the colonists, and made the forest regulations less harsh.

Admiral de Gueydon, who arrived in the spring of 1871 and restored order after the colonists had set up the Commune of Algiers, was the first civilian governor-general. He controlled the whole of the administration of Algeria, which in the departments devolved upon the prefects, in the arrondissements upon the sub-prefects and in the communes upon the mayors. The native Algerians, who were French subjects, were governed in the mixed communes by administrators. From 1881 to 1896 the Algerian administrative services were attached directly to the appropriate ministries in Paris, and the Algerian government was no more than a 'decoration as expensive as it was useless, at the most an inspector of colonization in the palace of an idle king' (J. Ferry). There were delays in settling any matters, even when they were in the hands of the Algerian members of the French parliament, who had now become the real masters of Algeria. This administrative deficiency, added to the crisis in the Algerian economy, gave rise to violent anti-Jewish riots in the towns. Order was restored by the suppression of the attachments, the restoration to the governor-general of real authority over the whole country, the creation of the Financial Delegations representing various economic interests to vote the budget and above all the appointment of an energetic governor-general.

The colonists and the European civilians had imposed on the Algerians a humiliating political situation. They were French subjects, and contributed very substantially to the budget, but the colonists maintained that they were not fitted to occupy seats in the deliberative or consultative assemblies. The *indigénat* and the absence of resources denied the masses any other course than that of resignation, especially after the suppression of the revolts of the Aurès (1879) and of Bū 'Amāma (1880), the conquest of Tunisia, and the British occupation of Egypt. All that the Algerians obtained was the sending, in 1898, to the Financial Delegations of twenty-one delegates who were nominated by the administration (there were forty-eight European delegates) and completely under its power. But pilgrims returning from Mecca brought news from the Middle East of the exile of leaders like Shaykh Muḥammad 'Abduh, and echoes of the Salafiyya reform movement, or of the Young Turk Revolution of 1908. A number of historical or pseudo-historical works sought to 'make known to the descendants the history of their ancestors'. Between 1907 and 1912 political agitation grew; its causes being the project of applying in Algeria the separation of Church and state, compulsory military service, or simply the impression that a Muslim Algerian could no longer live in this country 'accursed by God'. Thus after some affrays in 1907, 1909 and 1911, scores of families fled from Tlemcen to reach Islamic soil, first in Morocco, and later in the Levant. In 1912 certain Algerian newspapers launched a press campaign in which they proposed that Algerians should be able to surrender their rights as French citizens, but without prejudice to personal status, in return for release from compulsory military service. These demands were supported by the Paris newspaper *Le Temps*, but opposed by the Europeans in Algeria.

In spite of promises, the political situations of the Algerians had scarcely changed by 1914.

From 1914 to 1962, Algeria, like the other countries of the Maghrib, and to an even greater extent, went through several phases of tension and of apparent relaxation. From 1914 to 1954, the European population increased, but less rapidly than it had previously done (in 1872–1911 it had increased by 472,000, in 1911–54 by 232,000) because of the losses of the two World Wars and the ageing of the population: in 1911, 435 per 1000 were less than nineteen years of age; in 1953, 350. The Europeans lived mainly in the towns, especially in the ports, which thus grew considerably; the urban population in 1906 was 446,000, and in 1954, 760,000. The creation of colonization centres became very rare, and the villages often lost their European inhabitants entirely; the proportion of non-French decreased still further, from thirty-eight per cent in 1901 to five per cent in 1954, although they occupied 2,700,000 hectares in 1951. The new type of colonist became hardened in a racialism which sometimes took violent forms against the native Algerians. The number of the latter rose spectacularly from 4,686,000 in 1911, to 6,201,000 in 1936, and 8,360,000 in 1954, in spite of the wars, the economic crisis and also the years of partial famine followed by deadly epidemics from 1921 to 1945. It was a very young population (in 1954, 525 per 1,000 were under nineteen years of age) and its rate of growth was high (28 per 1,000 in 1954). It too became increasingly urban, particularly after 1930, and thus formed shanty-towns which became larger and larger.

The Algerian economy suffered from the First World War with its mobilization of men, requisition of goods and property, rise in prices and inflation. The difficulties in obtaining supplies of coal, iron, steel, chemical products and food, resulting from bad sea communications and the difficulty in obtaining credit, weighed heavily on both the colonists and the peasants. 1917 was a year of serious crisis, and by November 1918 Algeria was threatened with economic disaster. From 1919 to 1929 the administration attempted to resume a policy of colonization. It launched vast enterprises (e.g. barrages), and encouraged the colonists to modernize their equipment. For the peasants these years were still difficult.

When the great world economic crisis struck the Maghrib, they suffered more than the colonists, for whom the crisis was mainly one of overproduction and the consequent collapse of prices. Having fallen into debt, the colonists found themselves in an impasse, and began to consider the most violent solutions. The administration attempted to solve the problem by obtaining an increase in credits and improving the quality of the products sold, but only the largest proprietors survived. For the Algerians, the crisis meant the collapse of prices, hence the diminution of resources and financial reserves; and the impossibility of weathering years when the harvest was inadequate. The crisis which forced the colonists, the mines and the various industries to reduce their labour-force meant unemployment for the day-labourers. Algerian workers employed in France returned to Algeria, where they became a liability, whereas they had previously sent back large sums of money. Among the few artisans there was also unemployment; thus every household knew the threat of famine. The administration sought a solution in a very inadequate increase in the credit made available, in measures against excessive interest (1936), and in a guaranteed price for wheat.

The recovery during the years 1936–9 was too short to enable Algeria to face the Second World War without danger. The country was forced to make a tremendous effort, and to send to France and to the Axis powers a large part of its food reserves. After November 1942 sea communications with Europe were broken, and the Allies had too many other tasks to be able to concentrate their attention on the Maghrib alone. These harsh years were characterized chiefly by colossal monetary inflation, general mobilization, and very low levels of agricultural and mining production: 1945 was a year of acute crisis and of epidemics. After 1945 industrial enterprises developed in the areas around the ports, in spite of the resistance of the French industrialists: thus the number of workers increased from about 30,000 in 1914 to 200,000 in 1954, to which should be added the 200,000 who worked in France. In 1954, the banks and almost the whole of the industrial and mining production were in the hands of the Europeans, as was sixty-five per cent of the agricultural production. In 1956 the discovery of petroleum and of gas in the Sahara strengthened the hold of the Europeans on the Algerian economy, in spite of the large-scale participation of the whole of Algeria in the petroleum industry.

The disparity between the growth of the population and that of resources led to an ever-increasing migration of Algerians to Europe, from 21,684 emigrants in 1920 to 148,700 in 1952, which was temporarily stopped only by the crisis and the wars. In an effort partially to solve this problem, the CFLN (*Comité français de libération nationale*) considered a long-term programme dealing with every field; later, in 1959, the Constantine Plan attempted to close this gap which was increasing with the years. In fact all that was achieved was an increase in education, which, from 1950, reduced illiteracy.

Politically, until 1954, the Europeans refused any concessions. They did not recognize the military and financial efforts of the Algerians in the First World War. They reduced as much as possible the already trifling concessions granted by the law of 4 February 1919. The Europeans formed a resolute barrier which intimidated the various French governments. Nevertheless Algerian opinion was influenced by several factors. Among these were external events, such as the struggle being carried on by ʿAbd al-Karīm in Morocco (1923–5), and the Muslim Congress of Jerusalem (1931). Communist, socialist and trade union propaganda was exerted both in Algeria and on the emigrant Algerian workers in France. There was a partial renaissance of Islam, thanks to the *ʿulamāʾ*, who opened Qur'anic schools from 1930, and were anxious to restore to the Algerians the sense of their glorious past. Certain French-educated and liberal Algerians who claimed equal political rights, had the support of some liberal French thinkers. Finally, Messali Hadj demanded the independence of Algeria, from the congress held in 1927 in Brussels by the League against Colonial Oppression.

The administration replied by demonstrating the submissiveness of its supporters, the marabouts and the notables, and attempted to suppress all hostile propaganda. From 1933 Algeria was in a ferment, with both Europeans and Algerians in agitation, and the demonstrations sometimes turned into bloody riots. The Regnier decree (March 1935) and an increase in the police forces did not stop the movement. The governor-general, Le Beau, who was charged with the task of re-establishing contact with the educated *élite* among the native Algerians, and who later had the support of the Blum government, encountered opposition from the majority of the Europeans, who admired the régimes of Mussolini, Hitler and Franco. In response to the demands of the Algerian Muslim Congress (June 1936) the Blum government adopted a certain number of liberal measures, and sought to improve the political situation of some Algerians. The Blum-Viollette project caused the violent expression of opinion among the Europeans. Strikes by mayors, violent press campaigns, riots and incidents involving bloodshed, and interventions in Paris paralysed the will of the government, so that when the war began in 1939 the situation had changed very little for the Algerians since 1919.

After the French defeat in 1940, the majority of the Europeans collaborated with, and admired, the Vichy régime. They applauded the very harsh treatment to which the Algerian Jews were subjected, thinking thus to gain the approval of the native Algerians, nearly all of whom remained very reserved. The Anglo-American landings of November 1942, and the new effort demanded of Algeria, resulted in a renewal of Algerian political demands in a message from the Muslims to the responsible authorities in December 1942, a manifesto of the Algerian people in March 1943, and an addition to the manifesto in June 1943. Without claiming independence, these various documents demanded 'the recognition of the political autonomy of Algeria as a sovereign nation', which went far beyond the views and the minor reforms conceded in 1943 and 1944 by the CFLN. The Algerians' disappointment was all the greater because Muslim public opinion had been rendered sensitive by the fall of France, by the principles of the Atlantic Charter, and by the propaganda emitted variously by the nationalist leaders Messali and Abbas, of the Communists and of the '*ulamā*', all of whom based their teaching on the right of the people to decide their own destiny—a right which was denied by the majority of the Europeans.

This refusal coincided with the departure of the CFLN from Algiers and the culmination of the economic crisis. In May 1945 there was a series of demonstrations which in some regions took a dangerous turn. The assassination of a number of Europeans was followed by bombing, skirmishes, the massacre of several thousands of Algerians, and the arrest and imprisonment of the Algerian leaders. After much discussion the Statute of Algeria was passed in 1947, but all its promises of political evolution were cynically overridden by the administration, by means of an almost universal rigging of elections from 1947 to 1954, to the great satisfaction of the Europeans. Having no means of expressing itself, a part of the Algerian opposition went underground from 1948. The OS (*Organisation spéciale*), which had arisen from the PPA (*Parti populaire algérien*), now the MTLD (*Mouvement pour le triomphe des libertés démocratiques*, led by Messali), attacked and plundered the post office of Oran (1949), and in 1952 organized the escape of the imprisoned nationalists, Ben Bella, Ait Ahmed and Khider. In 1954 it changed into the CRUA (*Comité révolutionnaire d'unité et d'action*) which on 1 November 1954 commenced open warfare.

The French government was then obliged to proceed from police operations to actual war. The 'fellaghas' (revolutionaries) could rely on an inexaustible supply of recruits, on the secret importation of arms from abroad, on the unremitting political and diplomatic action at the United Nations Organization and in the Arab League, of Morocco and Tunisia who were able to help them after 1956, on their intimate knowledge of the country, and on the sympathy (and later on the participation) of the Algerian population. There also worked in their favour the horror at the excesses committed by the French troops, which were publicized by the French and foreign press, and the racialism of the Europeans in Algeria, who refused to allow any political concessions. The latter hardened their position still further as the result of a series of murders; and imposed their intransigence, first on J. Soustelle and then on R. Lacoste, who had become their spokesmen within governments which grew progressively weaker and less and less capable of resisting the pressure of the military leaders. In spite of certain reforms, the rigorous dividing up of towns and country districts, and the transfer of hundreds of thousands of peasants into regroupment centres, the war continued and spread. The French military machine was too cumbersome for this incessant guerilla warfare. The FLN (*Front de libération nationale*) made the following statement of its war aims: 'National independence through (1) the restoration of the sovereign democratic and social State of Algeria within the framework of Islamic principles; (2) respect of all the fundamental liberties without distinction of race or creed'. It organized the action of the FLN and the ALN (*Armée de libération nationale*) at the Congress of Soummam (August 1956) and rallied those who were undecided to its cause. The arrest of some of its leaders in October 1956 did not stop the war, which was a ruthless opposition between the Europeans and the Algerians. The former had the strength, violence and energy of despair; partisans of *l'Algérie française*, they nevertheless accepted the bill (February 1958) which made Algeria an 'integral part of the French Republic'; helped by the army, they had no hesitation in rebelling against their government in order to impose their ideas on the French nation.

The Algerians were convinced that the just cause of independence, which had the support of world opinion, was that of all the Algerian Muslims, they therefore rejected all proposals of negotiation. Convinced that they alone were the legitimate rulers, they set up in Tunis in September 1958 the GPRA (*Gouvernement provisoire de la République Algérienne*), under the leadership of Ferhat Abbas, and formed relations with several states. In the face of the failure of the insurrection of the generals (April 1961), of France's anxiety to end the war in Algeria, and the strengthening of the authority and widening of the following of the GPRA and the FLN, the Europeans, with the help of certain parts of the army, launched, between 1961 and 1962, a campaign which was basically terrorism. Nevertheless the final negotiations were completed at Evian in March 1962, where a political and an economic agreement, signed by France and a delegation of the GPRA, gave Algeria its independence. These agreements were ratified by others concluded between the OAS and the GPRA (June 1962), and in July 1962 the GPRA was installed in Algiers.

TUNISIA (1881–1956)

In spite of the entry of French troops and the Convention of the Bardo (12 May 1881), the first French resident minister in Tunisia, Paul Cambon, realized the weakness of his position. He obtained from the French government a 'treaty establishing the Protectorate, guaranteeing the debt and suppressing the capitulations.'[1] This was the Convention of La Marsa, of 8 June 1883, signed by Cambon and the Bey ʿAlī. This formula allowed 'the continuation of the bey's rule, everything being done in his name and on his responsibility',[2] and the evading of French parliamentary opposition. The ruler retained absolute power, chose his own ministers, and appointed members of the administrative services. The legislative acts and beylical decrees were not valid until his seal had been affixed. The bey chose his prime minister, his minister of the pen, but not his ministers for war, the navy and foreign affairs, who were French generals or admirals, or the resident-general. From the time of the Treaty of the Bardo, and still more from that of La Marsa, the bey reigned but did not rule: he had pledged himself 'in order to assist the French government in accomplishing its protectorate ... to carry out such administrative, judicial and financial reforms as the French government shall consider expedient' (Convention of La Marsa, article 1). In addition, the French government sent to Tunisia a resident minister, who became in 1885 the resident-general, and 'had under his authority all the administrative services concerning both the Europeans

[1] P. Cambon, *Correspondance 1870–1924* (Paris, 1940) T. 1: letter from Cambon to d'Estournelles de Constant, 11 June 1882.

[2] *Ibid.*, letter of 2 March 1882.

and the natives' (decree of 23 June 1885), and without whose endorsement the bey's decrees had no force. From 1883 there were created general administrative departments, and in 1883 there was created a General Secretariat, the holder of which soon came to occupy a very important place, and to fill the role of a minister of the interior and lieutenant to the prime minister, and above all to the resident general, for whom he deputized in the administrative field.

The local administration remained in the hands of the *qā'ids*, who had administrative, judicial and financial powers. They were chosen from old land-owning families, and were assisted by the shaykhs, the *khalīfas* created in 1889, and the *kāhiyas* created in 1912. Between 1881 and 1914 their number decreased. The controllers of civil affairs, first appointed in 1884, supervised the native administration in their district. The number of these controllers of civil affairs grew from three to nineteen. In Tunis itself, the equivalent of the *qā'id* was the *shaykh al-madīna*, but matters of municipal interest were dealt with by a consultative commission. From 1 January 1885 it became possible to appoint municipal councils in the principal districts. In 1892, the chamber of commerce which had been formed in 1885 was divided into two, one for the north and one for the south. The first Chamber of Agriculture, formed in 1892, and representing strictly French interests, was followed by four other such Chambers in 1895 and 1902. Thus the Consultative Conference, created in 1896 to advise on financial problems, had only French delegates.

The Convention of La Marsa ensured the settlement of the Tunisian debt and thus created a healthy financial situation. In 1891, the Tunisian budget, which until then had been in piastres, was drawn up in francs; it retained the taxes which had existed before the protectorate and added taxes and contributions imposed by the new administration, which was thus enabled to launch and support colonization. This, in the form of large societies, had begun before 1881 in some important areas; but until this time all the properties had been subject to Muslim law. Cambon declared that if the country wished to 'attract and retain capital, it is necessary to protect those who acquire land from their ignorance of the language, laws and customs of the country, and to shelter them from unforseen claims; in short to guarantee the facility and the security of the transactions made'. Hence the beylical decree of 1 August 1885 decided that there should be non-compulsory registration of land, and that of 23 May 1886 authorized the transfer of *ḥubus* property against the payment of a perpetual rent. In 1892 the colonists owned 402,000 hectares, and the non-French settlers 27,000. The further acquisition of land for colonization continued, assisted by legislation, in the following years. The Consultative Committee of Colonization, which was created in 1903, and later became the Colonization Commission, played a major economic and political role. In addition the efforts of the colonists were supported by tax concessions and the organization of mutual agricultural credit. By 1913, twenty-five banks were issuing each year short-term loans of more than 12 million gold francs. The societies and the large landowners who possessed most of the land possessed modern implements and equipment. In 1911, 4,088 landowners owned 853,000 hectares, devoted at first to cereals and later to olives, which became from 1892 a spectacularly successful crop in the Sahel and round Sfax.

From 19,000 in 1881 (11,200 Italians, 7,000 Anglo-Maltese, 708 French), the number of Europeans rose in 1911 to 143,000 (88,000 Italians, 46,000 French). The Italians benefited from the proximity of Italy, and the privilege granted by the agreements of 1896. There were few Europeans in the country districts, while the commune of Tunis alone had, in 1911, 69,500 inhabitants (17,800 French and 34,200 Italians). From 1881 France had provided Tunisia with roads, railways and ports, having always only the interests of the Europeans in mind. The discovery of phosphates in 1885, and the granting of the first concessions, encouraged prospecting among the Europeans. The production of phosphates increased from 70,000 metric tons in 1899 to two million metric tons in 1913, that of iron from 98,000 metric tons in 1908 to 590,000 metric tons in 1913, and 59,000 metric tons of lead were produced in 1913.

The customs system as modified in 1898 gave privileged treatment to French products, while avoiding any reduction in the receipts, and any disturbance of the usual commercial relations between Tunisia and purchaser countries. In addition, French shipping had a monopoly of the carrying trade. The volume of trade increased from 37·2 million gold francs in 1880 to 322·9 million in 1913; in the latter year France was Tunisia's chief customer.

European settlement met with very vigorous resistance from the Tunisians. In the field of colonization the opposition showed itself over the seizure of 'waste land' by the Beylical Decree of 1896, and the *ḥubus* property. The political opposition drew its membership from various sources: from Tunisians who had fled to, or were in contact with, the east, from intellectuals from the east who were staying temporarily in the Maghrib, such as Shaykh Muḥammad 'Abduh in 1884–5 and 1903, and who spread information about the Salafiyya reform movement. There were those in Tunisia who wished to restore to the Tunisians the sense of their past. Others criticized French policy openly and vigorously. Some showed conservative tendencies, while others relied on French help for the development of their country. Most of them considered that the best hope for Tunisia's future lay in education. The improvement of education at the Ṣādiqiyya or Zaytūna schools, the spread of French education, the creation of the Khaldūniyya (1896), and the press all played their part in this development. The number of newspapers increased, particularly after 1904, added to those which came from France or abroad; among them was *Le Tunisien*, which had appeared in French in 1907, and in 1909 became *Al-Tūnisī*. At the North African Conference held in Paris in 1908, the Young Tunisians set out their criticisms and their programme.

In 1907 some Tunisian members were admitted to the Consultative Conference, which until then had consisted only of French. In 1910, it was divided into two sections, French and native Tunisian, and a Higher Government Council was formed with a predominantly French membership.

Public opinion, in Tunis particularly, had become so greatly aroused that in 1911 there occurred incidents involving bloodshed. The war between Italy and the Ottoman empire gave the Tunisians the opportunity to demonstrate actively their opposition to the Italians in particular and to the Europeans in general, and their sympathy with the Ottomans. In 1912 further incidents set the administration and the Tunisians against each other, resulting in a state of siege, arrests, and the imprisonment or the banishment of the Tunisian leaders. This unrest in the towns was followed by unrest in the country districts. The Tunisian peasants were driven from their land, though often not without resistance. They also suffered from the long period of depression (1888–1900) which affected Tunisian agriculture. Forced back into areas with an indifferent water supply, they suffered severely during years of drought. In the more fertile areas the rents of the land increased. Their agricultural techniques had scarcely changed. Finally, the peasants, plunged into the currents of French and international trade, were unable to stand up to the fluctuations of a capitalist economy for which they were not equipped. Obliged to settle in one place, and impoverished, they had abandoned their tents, so that they were no longer able to rely on the traditional help from the richer members of the tribes. The former small landowners sometimes became mere agricultural employees without any protection. In 1907 the administration organized native provident societies (later called Tunisian provident societies) to combat excessive interest and help the smaller peasants in times of crisis. In spite of these efforts, the situation of the Tunisian peasantry in 1914 was difficult.

The number of Europeans grew from 146,000 in 1911 to 255,000 in 1956 (180,000 French, 67,000 Italians). This increase in the number of French and decrease in the number of Italians was connected with the law of 20 December 1923, which made it easier to obtain French nationality, and with the defeat of Mussolini's Italy, which enabled the French authorities to denounce the agreements which had given the Italians a privileged position. Thereupon some of them returned to Italy. In 1911, 4,088 Europeans owned 853,000 hectares; in 1949–50, 3,079 European landowners possessed 756,000 hectares, the greater part of it in northern Tunisia. From 1920 to 1929, the Europeans enjoyed wide credit facilities which enabled them to equip themselves with machinery. The number of landowners decreased and production increased. The average harvest of soft and hard wheat from 1910 to 1914 was 320,000 quintals, while that from 1921 to 1925 was 752,000 quintals.

Mining production and commerce also increased between 1913 and 1930: phosphate from 2·044 million metric tons in 1913 to 3·326 in 1930; iron from 0·590 million metric tons in 1913 to 0·978 million metric tons in 1929. Commerce rose from 322·9 million gold francs in 1913 to 678·6 million gold francs in 1929. Trade was largely orientated towards France, especially after the law of 30 March 1928, which gave the latter the advantage of preferential treatment for her imports and of a semi-monopoly of sea transport.

In spite of war, the population of Tunisia seems to have increased. From 1921 to 1931 it increased by 277,575: in 1921 it was 1·938 million. The drift of population from the country to the towns and to the north tended to overcrowd the land and the towns there; after 1930, the north developed still more.

The political demands made by the Young Tunisians were repeated between 1914 and 1919. The reasons for this were the length of the war, the contribution in men and in money demanded from Tunisia by France, the resistance of the Ottoman empire, the German victories and

Islamic propaganda, and the Italian and French withdrawal in southern Tunisia and Libya. Remoter factors included the revolt of the *Sharīf* Ḥusayn of Mecca, the arguments concerning the promises which were said to have been made to him by Great Britain, and President Wilson's Fourteen Points. In 1919, the survivors of the Young Tunisians made further representations to the powers and to France in order to produce a new equilibrium based on the re-establishment of the Constitution ('Destour', i.e. *Dustūr*) of 1861. They founded in 1919 a new party, *al-Ḥizb al-Ḥurr al-Dustūrī al-Tūnisī* (the Destour party), among whose members was 'Abd al-'Azīz al-Tha'libī. *La Tunisie martyre*, ascribed to him,[1] denounced with some exaggeration the evils in Tunisia since 1881, and presented a programme which would transfer the political preponderance to the bey and the Tunisians, within the constitutional framework of a liberal democracy, and would then limit or halt the progress of colonization. The new resident, L. Saint, was faced with the demands of the Destour, supported by the bey; he was a man of liberal ideals, and met with opposition and mistrust from the French in Tunisia. After the failure of the discussions, Saint took measures against the Destour, and intimidated and isolated the bey. While determined to maintain French authority, he introduced certain administrative reforms in 1922. The reforms were accepted by the bey and the reformers, and refused by the Destour. This party had dwindled through the departure of Tha'libī, and the prosecution and imprisonment of its leaders. An attempt to revive political action under cover of trade union action in 1924 failed. The Tunisian opposition appeared to be annihilated for a long time.

The crisis of 1929 was the beginning of a long period of difficulties for Tunisia. The prices of agricultural products fell, in spite of the devaluation of the franc in 1928. The colonists, indebted by their earlier purchases, asked the administration to protect them, which it partly did, through advances on crops, credit facilities, and temporary suspension of the sale of estates. The vine-growing areas decreased from 51,000 hectares in 1934 to 27,000 in 1948, because from 1936 the vines were attacked by phylloxera, and had to be uprooted. Thus colonization suffered setbacks from the crisis and the Second World War, and the ownership of land became concentrated in the hands of a small number of colonists.

[1] A careful reading of *La Tunisie martyre* leads one to believe that, in spite of the generally held opinion, al-Tha'libī is not its author.

The crisis and the Second World War also affected the production of the mines, which did not recover until after 1946. In order to reduce competition between Tunisian, Algerian and Moroccan phosphate production, a depot was set up in 1933 with the task of dividing sales among the three countries. Tunisian trade declined between 1929 and 1947. The balance of trade continued to show a deficit. The chief exports were agricultural and mining products (four-fifths of the total value), and the chief imports manufactured goods, fuel and clothes. Tunisia's principal customer was still France. Industrial and commercial enterprises were almost entirely in French hands; a number of Italian banks which between the wars had attempted some projects were eliminated, to the profit of the French banks.

During the Second World War, inflation, the increases in prices, and the difficulties in obtaining food, accelerated the drift from the land by those Tunisians who had the least resources. The rural population fell from eighty-three per cent in 1931 to seventy-one per cent in 1946, whereas the total population increased from 2,086,000 to 3,441,000. It was a young population, 500 per 1,000 being under nineteen years of age. Tunis grew from 106,800 in 1926 to 272,000 in 1956, and became surrounded by shanty-towns, inhabited by people from the countryside, who had no special skills, and were either partially or completely unemployed.

Nevertheless the majority of Tunisians still lived in the country districts, using traditional methods of cultivation. They produced cereals north of the Dorsal, oil in the Sahel, raised animals in the centre and the south, or grew citrus fruit or market-garden crops on Cape Bon, in the outskirts of the towns, and in the oases. The number of wage-earners increased and the old types of contract-relationship tended to decline. Agricultural workers were driven from the land by mechanization, and suffered more than others the harsh effects of crises or wars.

In the towns the artisans, faced with competition from European products and with the economic crises, were forced to close their shops, the corporations were in jeopardy, and a whole urban society was disintegrating in the same way as the rural society.

The crisis and the Second World War refashioned the political scene in Tunisia, especially as the Ṣādiqiyya College, the Zaytūna and the French educational establishments received many pupils, and as the French trade unions and left-wing parties—both in France and in Tunisia—supported the Tunisians in their claims. The latter, profoundly shocked by the Eucharistic Congress at Carthage (1930), paid much attention to movements in the Islamic world and to newspapers such as *La Voix du Tunisien* and *L'Action Tunisienne*. A group of newcomers, led by a young lawyer Ḥabīb Bourguiba (Bū Ruqayba), formed a new party in 1934, *al-Ḥizb al-Dustūrī al-Jadīd* (the Neo-Destour party) and presented new objectives. These were:

The independence of Tunisia, completed by a treaty of friendship and unity with the great French Republic and guaranteeing to France the safeguarding of the interests of the foreign colony; to turn the French protection into a spontaneous alliance between two free peoples, free from any idea of preponderance or of domination, which should not exist with the great unity of interests of these two peoples, to influence the mass of the Tunisian people.

Peyrouton, the new resident-general, had Bourguiba and his friends put under house-arrest along with a number of militant communists and suppressed the opposition press. His successor, A. Guillon, and the government of the Front Populaire were anxious to inaugurate a new policy, and some liberal measures led to a lessening of tension; but both P. Vienot, who was responsible for Tunisian affairs in the Blum government, and Guillon stated that there was 'no question of France's abandoning her rights as a protecting power'. Furthermore the violent hostility of the colonists to all liberal measures, and the will of the Neo-Destour party, the influence of which was spreading and which sought a further advance, ended in an impasse which resulted in strikes and bloodshed in 1937 and 1938. At Tunis, faced with a gathering, which, when a shot was fired, turned into a riot, the resident announced a state of siege, and it seemed that the arrests and condemnations which followed must hinder any action by the Neo-Destour.

The fall of France in 1940, the accession of the Bey Moncef (Muḥammad al-Munṣif) in 1942, the occupation by German and Italian forces, and the liberation by the Allied armies started up political action again. No sooner was Bourguiba freed than he invited the Tunisians to forget the struggles of the past and to join Fighting France, in spite of the deposition of the bey, who was considered too independent, in May 1945. From 1943 to 1956 the French authorities alternated between reforms and repression, while the Neo-Destour and its supporting organizations continued to seek the independence of Tunisia. The reforms did not prevent the Bey Lamine (Muḥammad al-Amīn) in 1949 from demanding officially 'the introduction of substantial and necessary reforms such as to satisfy the aspirations of all the inhabitants of our kingdom'. The new resident, Perillier, was, in June 1950, 'charged to understand Tunisia, and to lead it towards the full development of its resources and towards independence, which is the final objective for all the territories within the French Union'. At the same time the action of the Neo-Destour spread, through the cells which it had established in the towns and in the country, and also its action at the Arab League and the United Nations.

Strikes and violent clashes clearly illustrated that the local French authorities were willing to yield nothing. The bey might announce in May 1951 'the reorganization of the executive and its method of establishment on the basis of a representation of our people in elected bodies', but the resident and his auxiliaries, supported by the French ministries and the French in Tunisia, refused to yield. On the contrary, the latter aimed at participating equally with the Tunisians in the functioning of the political institutions of the country. The conflict reached its most dramatic phase with the arrival of the new resident, Hautecloque, when there took place police raids, arrests, and summary executions which went unpunished. The strikes and demonstrations, the exile of Bourguiba and the Neo-Destour leaders, the hostility of the bey, who refused to sign the decrees proposed by Hautecloque, the boycott of the municipal elections and armed resistance all showed that the way chosen by the French could not succeed.

The departure of Hautecloque, and the decision of the government under Mendès-France to recognize unconditionally 'the internal autonomy of the Tunisian state', and hence 'internal sovereignty', made discussion easier. The personal action of Bourguiba, and the anxiety of both sides to come to an agreement gave internal autonomy a concrete meaning. On his return to Tunisia in June 1955, Bourguiba announced that this constituted 'an important stage on the way to independence'. Ṣalāḥ b. Yūsuf, who was hostile to Bourguiba and excluded from the party, attempted to launch a movement of armed resistance. This was crushed, and he fled to Cairo. The independence granted to Morocco led Bourguiba to demand the same for Tunisia, and it was conceded on 20 March 1956.

MOROCCO (1912–56)

The Treaty of Fez which was signed between France and the sultan, Mawlāy 'Abd al-Ḥāfiẓ, (1912) permitted France to act officially in the latter's name. Henceforth all Morocco's dealings with other powers were transacted through the French government, which delegated its powers to the resident-general, General Lyautey, who insisted that the ruler should retain all the appearances of power; this was the protectorate in its true sense. Nevertheless, the country was very far from accepting the treaty of Fez, and resisted it vigorously, the more so as Mawlāy 'Abd al-Ḥāfiẓ encouraged this resistance. Lyautey acted quickly: he replaced him by Mawlāy Yūsuf, who was more amenable, in August 1912. This change did not put a stop to the fighting. At the beginning of the First World War the mountain districts were still unsubdued. In order to prevent the recently subdued areas from joining the revolt, Lyautey directed all his military efforts towards the mountain regions. In addition, he applied a policy of carrying out major works, such as would impress foreigners and Moroccans. He thus on the one hand demonstrated France's intention of remaining in Morocco, and on the other maintained bases from which to effect later the submission of the rest of the country. When the war was over, the conquest was continued, and at the same time the administration was organized. The Middle Atlas and the Rif formed the two barriers of resistance led by Abd el Krim ('Abd al-Karīm). After having defeated the Spaniards, the latter was directly threatening Fez and Taza, but he was defeated by a great combined Franco-Spanish military effort (1925), and some years later (1934) further operations suppressed the last pockets of resistance in the High Atlas.

From the first, Lyautey had stated that 'the protectorate must be considered as a permanent régime'. He thus retained the traditional administration (*Makhzan*) with the sultan at its head; but a certain number of services copied from the French model had a controlling function. Some of them with time acquired a dominating political role, others an economic one. At their head, the resident-general was

> the trustee of all the powers of the Republic in the Sharifian Empire; he is the sole intermediary between the sultan and the representatives of foreign powers; he approves and promulgates in the name of the government of the Republic the decrees issued by His Sharifian Majesty; he controls all the administrative services; he has the high command of the army and the disposal of the naval forces (Decree of 11 June 1912, art. 2).

Until 1925 it was Lyautey who impressed on all the administration his very personal style, composed of dynamic efficiency and theatrical ostentation; careful not to repeat the mistakes which had been made in the past, he was anxious to produce an exemplary achievement which would make Morocco the symbol of a successful colony.

This administrative framework did not change greatly. The resident was assisted by a deputy minister at the Residency and by a secretary-general; his acts had no force until sealed by the sultan as 'dahirs' (i.e. *ẓāhirs*), though conversely the dahirs had no effect until the resident had countersigned them. Not until the end of the protectorate was there a disagreement between the sultan and the resident about reforms proposed by the latter. At the local level, the French officials exercised a close control over the Sharifian administration proper, and gave it the necessary impetus and guidance. In practice it was on them that the application of the protectorate rested, and they had all the necessary powers. The country was divided into regions, territories, circles and annexes. The dahir of 8 April 1917 created municipalities in certain towns, but both the French and Moroccan members were appointed by the residency, and merely offered advice. Fez and Casablanca had special régimes of their own. In the tribes, the dahir of 21 November 1916 set up the *Jamā'a*, presided over by the *qā'ids*, and that of 27 April 1919 placed the Moroccan communities under control. The *qā'ids* were the agents of the central power: as judges and tax-collectors, and not very well paid, they were open to corruption. In the towns the place of the *qā'ids* was filled by the pashas.

Lyautey set up advisory chambers of commerce, of industry and of agriculture whose members were at first only French, but later Moroccans also. He also formed a higher agricultural council, then another of commerce and industry. Later he introduced into the governmental council representatives of the colonists, then of the Moroccans, and finally of the French inhabitants who were engaged in neither agriculture nor industry: these representatives of economic interests gave their opinions on the resident's financial projects.

Foreigners had not waited until the Treaty of Fez to gain an economic foothold in Morocco. In 1880 the Convention of Madrid recognized their rights of ownership within certain limits. The Convention of Algeciras increased these facilities, especially in the ports and in some of the towns and their immediate surroundings. In 1913, the Europeans owned more than 100,000 hectares. Between 1913 and 1915, measures introduced the optional registration of land, as a result of which several hundred thousand hectares were transferred to the possession of the French, even though the Moroccans registered vast areas. In spite of the dahir of July 1914, which declared collective tribal land to be inalienable, another of April 1919 allowed the tribes to sell to the state, if land was required for public utilities, or in order to create colonization areas. In 1916 a Colonization Committee was commissioned to distribute the rural estates. In spite of the 1914–18 War and the Rif War, private and official colonization throve. At the end of 1927, 2,044 European colonists, 1,847 of them French, were cultivating 650,000 hectares. Their numbers were few, they were well organized, and enjoyed various advantages: help from the administration, agricultural co-operation, agricultural mutual insurance banks, and above all credit arrangements, to enable them to equip and improve the land. At the same time the phosphate deposits were worked by the Sharifian Office of Phosphates: 8,200 metric tons in 1921, increasing to 1,850,000 metric tons in 1930. From the beginning of the protectorate, and even during the First World War, the French administration provided the country with a network of roads, railways and with a transport system. Casablanca thus arose from nothing. Sheltered by the Convention of Algeciras and by the protectorate, foreign enterprises developed and flourished. The number of Europeans increased from 11,000 in 1911 to 104,700 in 1926; they lived chiefly in the rapidly growing towns.

The Rif War, and above all the crisis of 1929, slowed down colonization and the development of the country. In 1935 private colonization occupied an area of 569,000 hectares divided into 1,754 estates. The area of vineyards increased after 1927 but did not exceed a few thousand hectares. Administrative aid, a more judicious choice of crops (market-garden crops and citrus fruits), an improvement in the trade channels, and the opening of the European markets, facilitated a recovery in 1936, later interrupted by the Second World War. The production of phosphates also decreased between 1930 and 1933, and did not regain its former level until 1945. The exploitation of non-ferrous metals and of iron began immediately before the Second World War, which interrupted it almost completely. The war also resulted in the influx of large numbers of Europeans (who increased from 191,000 in 1936 to 295,000 in 1947), and a spectacular rise in prices.

The Europeans increasingly ignored the country areas inhabited by the Moroccans. These, who numbered perhaps five million between 1912 and 1926, increased by 1947 to more than eight million, including the Jews, who increased from 161,000 in 1936 to 200,000 in 1947, and who lived mainly in the towns. Colonization restricted the area available to some of the tribes, and caused them to become wholly or partially sedentary: it certainly reduced the pasturage in the Atlantic regions, leading to a reduction in the size of the herds. The herds of the nomads in the south or in the steppes also decreased, as their movements from place to place were more strictly controlled. Finally, the traditional methods of transport had to compete with the motor. The agricultural techniques had scarcely changed, nevertheless there was a reduction in the area of unploughed land. To the traditional cereals (hard wheat and barley) were gradually added soft wheat, oats and maize; peas and crops grown for fodder or for industry alternated with beans; forestry and market-gardening spread; but these changes affected only a minority of medium or wealthy landowners.

In spite of the Moroccan provident societies which were formed in 1917 to help the peasants and to protect them from excessive interest-rates, the majority of them lacked means. When difficulties arose, such as the 1930 crisis, the bad harvests of 1945, the inflation of money and the rise in prices between 1940 and 1945, the small farmers sold their land, left it and went to the towns. The old family estates and the rural land owned in common broke up, and gave place to the employment of paid day labourers. The new arrivals, often from the south, filled the native quarters, and overflowed into shanty-towns, which grew up in a disorderly and unplanned fashion. In this way Casablanca spread to enormous proportions: from 20,000 inhabitants in 1900 to 320,000 in 1947. The artisan classes were unable to compete with imported products, and, lacking financial means, were in danger of bankruptcy. Only those with the best resources survived, among them the merchants who were able to force a way into the new channels of trade. Former artisans, unskilled workers, and former peasants who had emigrated to the towns made up the lower proletariat of the new Moroccan industry, which was mainly manufacturing. It was not an organized proletariat, for its members were forbidden to join the French trade unions. The inhabitants of both town and country had to pay increased taxes, linked with the service of debts incurred before the treaty of Fez, with the formation of a more complicated system of administration superimposed upon the *Makhzan*, and with the devaluations of the French franc. The farmers were not able, with the techniques at their disposal, to face the changes in the situation, which were particularly great between 1912 and 1956. Trade appeared to increase: from 221 million gold francs in 1913 to 344 million gold francs in 1947; but the town and country dwellers used more and more imported products, and most of these came from France.

On the death of Mawlāy Yūsuf he was succeeded by Sīdī Muḥammad b. Yūsuf (1927), whose reign saw the beginning and growth of Moroccan political claims. The Berber Dahir of May 1930 aroused Moroccan and Islamic opinion, for it brought under French jurisdiction 'the repression of crimes committed in Berber territory, whatever the status of the person who commits the crime'. It appeared to break the legal unity of the kingdom, and it coincided with other French acts—in Algeria the ostentatious celebration of the centenary of the French occupation, and in Tunisia the Eucharistic Congress at Carthage. The Moroccans saw it as a more or less open attack on Arabism and Islam. The protest took various forms, and drew its forces from the middle-class and the '*ulamā*' of the Qarāwiyyīn mosque. It was manifested at the first royal celebration in 1933, and during the sultan's visit to Fez.

In 1934, the opposition, grouped into the *Comité d'Action Marocaine*, presented to Paris and to Rabat a plan of reform which advocated a number of reforms in administration, justice and education, and presented an economic and social programme. It had the support of certain elements of the French left-wing, but was rejected by the Residency and the French in Morocco. After 1936 (Blum's government being in power), the nationalist leaders extended their action widely throughout the country and carried on negotiations with Vienot, the member of the Blum government in charge of Moroccan affairs. In the spring of 1937 there was a hardening of the French attitude, and the *Comité d'Action Marocaine* split into the Nationalist party and the Popular Movement. Fever was mounting in the country; agitators resorted to violence in the autumn of 1937, and the nationalist leaders, 'Allāl al-Fāsī and al-Wazzānī were arrested and deported. But Franco's victory in Spain and the French defeat in 1940, made Spanish Morocco into a centre of intensive Nazi propaganda and of nationalism until the Anglo-American landings of November 1942.

After 1940 official colonization made little progress, while private colonization continued to increase. The greater part of it was situated in the neighbourhoods of Fez, Meknes, Rabat, Casablanca and the majority of the properties consisted of more than 300 hectares. The colonists concentrated on cereals for export, vines, citrus fruits and vegetables, and their farms were highly mechanized. The influx of foreign capital, the experience of the war-years, and the desire to provide

North Africa with an industrial framework independent of Europe resulted in mining and industrial enterprises, which employed many Moroccan workers controlled by a few European specialists. In spite of its being officially forbidden, the Moroccans joined the French trade unions, and in 1946 the General Union of the Confederated Trade Unions of Morocco was formed with two secretaries—one Moroccan and one French, the latter disappearing in 1951. Removed from their family or tribal background, the workers crowded together in the shanty-towns on the outskirts of the great cities, whence they took part in political and social action.

The Second World War resulted in many difficulties for the peasantry: rises in prices, bad harvests, with famine in 1945, and epidemics. The construction of barrages and the creation of the districts of peasant modernization affected only a very small number. The improvements brought by the Moroccan provident societies could not prevent the land from being increasingly overcrowded by a growing population, and the consequent migration of peasants to the towns.

At the time of the Allied landings, the sultan refused to follow the resident to the interior, and this first gesture of independence was followed by his interview with President Roosevelt who was passing through Morocco in January 1943. Encouraged by this attitude, and realizing that the position was changing, the nationalists led by al-Fāsī and the Popular Movement led by al-Wazzānī united, forming the Istiqlāl party. On 11 January 1944 they presented to the sultan, the resident and the Allies the manifesto of the Istiqlāl party, demanding Moroccan independence and democratic government. Later they stated that they had 'absolutely no intention of realizing their ideal by the use of violence'. The French Committee of National Liberation (CFLN) refused to consider Moroccan independence; it merely granted some minor reforms and, perhaps by means of a conspiracy, deprived the nationalist movement of its leaders. There then began a trial of strength, with street demonstrations and strikes, which were sometimes violent, between, on the one hand the nationalists supported by the Moroccan population and the sultan, and, on the other, the French government and the Residency with the support of a few important Moroccans and the Europeans, who were opposed to any real concession. This state of affairs continued until 1956. By means of its cells planted throughout the country, its action outside Morocco in France, at the United Nations and the Arab League, it support from the Spanish zone, and its unceasing propaganda, the Istiqlāl convinced its audience. The resident attempted to introduce some basic reforms, but they were not welcomed by the French, and did not prevent the sultan from refusing to render homage to France (April 1947). The latent crisis became worse when the sultan, on a visit to France, tried in October 1950 to negotiate with the French government over the head of the resident, Juin, and refused to sign some proposed dahirs. Juin's policy was to ignore the nationalists, excluding them from the assemblies, and threatening to depose the sultan (1950–51). He and his successor, Guillaume, acting independently of Paris, left the field free for a police force and an administration which were favourable to French extremists. The violent strikes of 1952 created an atmosphere of tension, and in August 1953, in the absence of a government, Guillaume took it upon himself to depose the sultan, who was much too intractable. The arrest of the key members of the Istiqlāl, the installation of a new sultan, Muḥammad b. ʿArafa, the departure of Guillaume, and the coming to power of the administration of Mendès-France did not put an end to the struggle, which was carried on from Spanish Morocco, from Algeria and from the secret organization of the resistance, under the guidance of the trade unions and a provisional executive committee of the Istiqlāl. Acts of terrorism continued in the towns, French products were boycotted, and there was activity within the tribes. Between 1953 and 1955 there was built up a Liberation Army which went into action in the autumn of 1955. Further violent action, in the summer of 1955, hastened the solution of the crisis. Negotiations began at Aix-les-Bains. The sultan was recalled from exile in October 1955, to serve as a mediator between the nationalists and the French government. Muḥammad V received a triumphant welcome to Morocco and appointed a government which, on 2 March 1956, procured the independence of Morocco.

CHAPTER 5

THE NILOTIC SUDAN

THE COMING OF THE ARABS

The central axis of the eastern *Bilād al-Sūdān* is constituted by the River Nile. In the north, this is a single stream from the confluence of the Blue and White Niles by the modern town of Khartoum (*al-Kharṭūm*) to the First Cataract above Aswān. Except in certain districts, where rocky cliffs close in on the river, the main Nile is fringed by a narrow strip of irrigable land, which supports numerous villages and a few small towns. The riverain settled area, as far south as the Sabalūqa Cataract, a few miles below the confluence of the Niles, is the historic Nubia (*Bilād al-Nūba*), the seat of the most ancient civilization in what is now Sudanese territory. To its south, around the confluence, on the banks of the Blue and White Niles, and in the peninsula (*al-Jazīra*, the Gezira) lying between them, is another area of settlement, where the greater annual rainfall makes more extensive cultivation possible. In this region, known to the medieval Arabic writers as ʿAlwa, the only ancient urban site lay at Sūba, on the Blue Nile, not far from Khartoum. East and west of the main Nile, the sandy deserts of the north merge imperceptibly into seasonal grasslands further south. This is herdsman's country, and a Hamitic-speaking group of nomad tribes, the Beja (*al-Buja*) have occupied the eastern desert from time immemorial. Their territory (*Bilād al-Buja*) covers the rolling plains, which rise to the arid escarpment of the Red Sea Hills. Below, in the sultry and uninviting coastal plain, are scattered harbours, around four of which in succession, Bādiʿ, ʿAydhāb, Suakin (Sawākin) and Port Sudan, substantial towns have grown up.

The Nubian corridor has, throughout history, been a mingling-place of peoples, but since pharaonic times its culture has been strongly tinctured by the successive phases of civilization in Egypt. At the time of the Muslim conquest of Egypt, Nubia had, within the previous century, been converted to Christianity by missionaries from Egypt. South of Nubia proper, the kingdom of Alodia (i.e. ʿAlwa) had also accepted Christianity. In view of the recent introduction of Christianity, however, one may query whether it had struck very deep roots among the mass of the people. The nomadic Beja remained pagan, except in fringe districts adjoining Nubia or the Red Sea coast, where they were accessible to Christian influences.

The Christian kingdom of Nubia, known to the medieval Arabic writers as al-Muqurra, at first opposed effective resistance to the Muslim Arab conquerors of Egypt on far from unequal terms. The first clashes seem to have been little more than border-raids. A more serious expedition, commanded by the governor of Egypt, ʿAbd Allāh b. Saʿd b. Abī Sarḥ, invaded Nubia and besieged the capital, Dunqula (i.e. Old Dongola). He was unable to win a decisive victory, and withdrew, apparently after concluding an armistice. A Fatimid source gives the text of a treaty alleged to have been concluded between ʿAbd Allāh and the king of Nubia, by which, *inter alia,* the Nubians undertook to pay an annual tribute of 360 slaves to the Muslims. The treaty, almost certainly legendary, represents an attempt to retroject conventions of Muslim-Nubian relations which had developed by the fourth/tenth century. Other evidence indicates that the supply of slaves was an element in the reciprocal trade of Nubia and Egypt.

It is possible, but unlikely, that ʿAbd Allāh b. Saʿd had at first intended to conquer Nubia. His experience, the long and exposed lines of communications, and the difficulties of the terrain, served to discourage any further attempts for centuries.[1] In 568/1172, Tūrān Shāh, the brother of Saladin, led an expedition into Lower Nubia for combined punitive and reconnaissance purposes, but achieved no lasting conquest. Under the Mamluk sultans several further expeditions were made, but although these succeeded in weakening the Nubian kingdom, they did not result in the annexation of Nubia to Egypt.

The submergence of Christian Nubia was really due to the steady pressure of Arab tribes from Upper Egypt. By the middle of the third/ninth century, a frontier society had come into existence east of the First Cataract, composed of Arabs from the tribes of Rabīʿa and Juhayna, who had escaped from the pressure of government, and sought wealth in the gold-mines of the northern Beja territory. Intermarriage with both Beja and Nubians ensued. During the early fifth/eleventh century an arabized and islamized Nubian principality was formed south of the First Cataract. Its princes bore the title of *Kanz al-Dawla*, first conferred by the Fatimid Caliph, al-Ḥākim, in 396/1006, whence they are known as the

[1] It has been suggested (in a private communication) that the Arabs may have found it more convenient to leave Nubia outside the Muslim empire, as a source of slaves and especially eunuchs, since enslavement and mutilation within the frontier were forbidden.

Banū Kanz. The Mamluk expeditions enabled the Banū Kanz to extend their power upstream in the early eighth/fourteenth century, and in the subsequent dark age the Nubian kingdom foundered. A brief reference by Ibn Khaldūn (d. 808/1400) indicates that Nubia had been fragmented into petty states, which suffered the incursions of Juhayna. The ruling dynasties intermarried with the Arabs, to whom authority passed by female succession.

Present-day tribal genealogies show the majority of the Arabic-speaking Sudanese as coming from one or other of two lines of descent. The nomads claim to be Juhayna, while most of the settled clans of the main Nile are regarded as descendants of a certain Ja'al, who is, furthermore, stated to have been an 'Abbasid. Disregarding this assertion (a typical genealogical sophistication), we may reasonably see in these Ja'aliyyūn the descendants of the arabized Nubians of the late Middle Ages. Other groups and tribes claiming to be Ja'aliyyūn (or 'Abbasids) bear witness to a diaspora, which can be traced in recent centuries, but which may well have commenced before the arabization of Nubia.

The fate of 'Alwa is even more obscure than that of Nubia. It was still flourishing in the early seventh/thirteenth century, while a modern Sudanese tradition dates the fall of Sūba, and final subversion of the kingdom, to 910/1504–5. This rests, however, on a false synchronism with the establishment of the Funj capital at Sennar (Sinnār), and Sūba may have fallen at an earlier date. Traditional sources further describe the capture of Sūba by an Arab tribal host under a chief named 'Abd Allāh Jammā', and the flight and dispersion of its inhabitants. The descendants of 'Abd Allāh Jammā', the 'Abdallāb, exercised a hegemony over the nomads who occupied the region around the confluence and the northern Gezira, as well as over the arabized Nubians living north of the Sabalūqa Cataract. Their own residence was on the main Nile.

THE FUNJ SULTANATE

The fall of Sūba represents the final break-through of the nomad Arabs into the grasslands of the Nilotic Sudan. By a curious and fateful coincidence, their southern expansion synchronized with a migration northwards, down the Blue Nile, of cattle-nomads who were neither Arabs nor, at first, Muslims. These people, the Funj, first appear on the Upper Blue Nile at the beginning of the tenth/sixteenth century. Their remoter origins, which are obscure, have given rise to luxuriant speculation. Sennar, which became their dynastic capital, is traditionally stated, with curious precision, to have been founded in 910/1504–5. A nineteenth-century recension of a Sudanese chronicle asserts that the Funj chief, 'Amāra Dūnqas, allied with 'Abd Allāh Jammā' to overthrow Sūba, but the alliance, if it existed, was precarious. A tradition (related by James Bruce) speaks of a battle between the Funj and the 'Abdallāb near Arbajī in the Gezira. Since Arbajī seems to have been the most southerly Arab settlement at that time, the tradition implies a conflict between two groups of nomads for the grazing of the central Gezira. That the immediate victory fell to the Funj is clear from the resulting situation, since the 'Abdallābī chief, although autonomous, was vassal to the Funj king, and bore the non-Arab title of *mānjil* or *mānjilak*.

Lower Nubia, between the First and Third Cataracts, lay outside the area under the Funj-'Abdallābī hegemony. About the middle of the tenth/sixteenth century, this region was annexed to Ottoman Egypt by Özdemir Pasha, a Circassian Mamluk in the service of Sultan Süleymān. It was constituted as a *kashiflik* under the name of Berberistān (i.e. the land of the Berberines), and garrisons of Bosniak troops were installed in the three fortresses of Aswān, Ibrīm and Sāy. The *kashiflik* became hereditary in a clan of Mamluk descent, while the descendants of the Bosniaks also formed a privileged caste.

Özdemir, who, in order to oppose the Portuguese threat to the Red Sea, aimed at the conquest of Abyssinia, also brought under Ottoman rule a strip of the African coast of the Red Sea, including the important ports of Suakin and Massawa (Maṣawwa'). In the earlier Middle Ages, the principal town in this region had been 'Aydhāb, which, at least as early as the third/ninth century, had been a port for pilgrims coming from the Nile Valley. Its commercial importance increased in consequence of the development of Egyptian trade with the Yemen from the fifth/eleventh century. It was destroyed during the first half of the ninth/fifteenth century, and Suakin, which had long existed as a harbour, succeeded to its importance. The development of Pilgrimage and trading-routes between Upper Egypt and the Red Sea contributed to the islamization of the Beja. Their degree of arabization varied: the 'Abābda of the north adopted the Arabic language, while the southern tribes retained their Hamitic speech but acquired Arab genealogies.

The early Funj period witnessed the effective islamization of Nubia and the Gezira. The immigrant Arabs who brought about the dissolution of the Christian kingdoms had, of course, been Muslims, and a dated inscription at Old Dongola shows that the church was converted into a mosque in 717/1317. Nevertheless, there was much scope for Islamic teaching, among the formerly Christian peoples, and among the laxly Muslim nomads and the pagan Funj. This was accomplished by religious teachers, who were also adherents of Ṣūfī orders. The prototype of these *fakīs* (as they are colloquially called) was a Yemeni Arab, Ghulām Allāh b. ʿĀʾid, who settled in Dongola, about the second half of the eighth/fourteenth century. The early Funj period saw a great increase in the number of Muslim teachers. Some of these were aliens, but most were men of local origin. They fall into two main categories: those who were primarily concerned to teach and administer the *Sharīʿa*,[1] and those who were more interested in initiating disciples into Ṣūfī mysticism. A hard and fast division is impossible; the former class never consolidated into an official hierarchy of *ʿulamāʾ*, although there is some evidence of the appointment of *qāḍīs* and cult-officials by the Funj or ʿAbdallābī rulers.

The Ṣūfī teachers enjoyed enormous prestige. Many of them had the reputation of thaumaturges, and they acted as advisers of, and intercessors with, the chiefs. There are, however, some indications of another attitude, that of the dissident *fakīs*, whose mission was to warn and reprove the rulers. In the light of later Sudanese history it is significant that the best known of these, Ḥamad al-Naḥlān (d. 1116/1704–5) proclaimed himself to be the *mahdī*.

The importance of the *fakīs* was enhanced by the grants of land which they received from the Funj or ʿAbdallābī chiefs. There was also a strongly hereditary tendency at work, since a *fakī* transmitted not only his material possessions, his *khalwa*,[2] his books and his land, to his descendants, but also his *baraka*, the mystical power of his holiness. Dynasties of holy men were thus not uncommon.

During the first two centuries of Funj rule, the dynasty at Sennar consolidated its position. Its early conversion to Islam is indicated by the Muslim name (ʿAbd al-Qādir) of a king who died in 965/1557–8. The acquisition (perhaps in the eleventh/seventeenth century) of a genealogy demonstrating the descent of the Funj from the Umayyads

[1] As in the western *Bilād al-Sūdān*, the Mālikī *madhhab* predominated.

[2] A *khalwa* is, primarily, a retreat of Ṣūfī devotees. In the Sudan, it has acquired the meaning of a Qurʾanic school.

symbolized the arabization of the dynasty. Serious clashes between the Funj and the ʿAbdallāb took place in the late tenth/sixteenth and early eleventh/seventeenth centuries, but after a crushing defeat sustained by the ʿAbdallāb in 1016/1607–8, the *status quo* was restored through the intercession of an influential *fakī*. Meanwhile the Funj kings had been expanding their power westwards across the Gezira to the White Nile, where they established a garrison and bridgehead at Alays, among the Shilluk. These were a powerful pagan tribe who raided down the White Nile in canoes: they may have been ethnically connected with the Funj.

Possession of the White Nile bridgehead enabled the Funj king, Bādī II Abū Diqan (1054–91/1644–80), to make an expedition against the Muslim hill-state of Taqalī, lying south of the Kordofan plain. The ruler of Taqalī was made tributary, and the slaves obtained from the pagan Nūba of the hills (not to be confused with the riverain Nūba of Nubia proper) were formed into a slave-guard to protect the Funj ruler and his capital.

While the Funj monarchy was establishing itself in the Nilotic Sudan, another dynasty, further west, was undergoing a similar process of arabization and conversion to Islam. The traditions of the Kayra suggest the marriage of an Arab Muslim into the originally pagan royal clan of Darfur. Sulaymān *Solong* (i.e. in Fūr, 'the Arab'), the first of the historical rulers, probably flourished *c*. 1050/1640. There is little definite information about the dynasty for another hundred years, but it seems to have been connected with the contemporaneous sultanate of Waday[1] (with which it was repeatedly at war), and, more certainly, with the Musabbaʿāt, who established their rule in the Kordofan plain.

During the twelfth/eighteenth century, the Funj-ʿAbdallābī hegemony over the Gezira and Nubia declined. The process had indeed been initiated much earlier, when the Shāyqiyya, a tribal group living on the great bend of the Nile, downstream of the Fourth Cataract, gained their independence of the ʿAbdallāb. The critical battle probably took place in the reign of the Funj king Bādī I Abū Rubāṭ (1020–5/1611–17). The Shāyqiyya appear to be of a different origin from the arabized Nubians who are their neighbours. Although their territory was an important centre of Islamic learning in the early Funj period, the Shāyq-

[1] Waday was the cultural watershed between the eastern and western parts of *Bilād al-Sūdān*.

iyya later became notorious as predatory warriors, forming a confederacy of clans under four chiefs.

As 'Abdallābī power declined, the Sa'dāb Ja'aliyyūn, living to the north of the Sabalūqa Cataract, emerged from obscurity. Their tribal capital, Shandī, became an important centre of trade. At Dāmir, near the confluence of the 'Aṭbarā with the main Nile, was a little tribal theocracy, the home of the Majādhīb clan of hereditary *fakīs*, whose prestige extended to the Red Sea coast. North of the 'Aṭbarā lay the tribal territory of the Mīrafāb, the name of which, Berber (Barbar), probably indicates the late survival in the region of non-Arabic speech. As the bellicosity of the Shāyqiyya increased, during the eighteenth century, their neighbours suffered, notably the ancient Nubian principality of Dongola. This most northerly part of the ancient Funj-'Abdallābī dominions was further harassed when the survivors of the Mamluk grandees, fleeing in 1811 from proscription in Egypt, established their camp[1] where New Dongola now stands, and fought the Shāyqiyya.

While the control of the 'Abdallābī viceroy over the north was thus palpably diminishing, his suzerain, the Funj king, was in no better case. The establishment of a slave-guard by Bādī II, in the late eleventh/seventeenth century, seems to have marked a turning-point, since it created tension between the monarch and the free Funj warriors. They revolted against Bādī III al-Aḥmar (1103–28/1692–1716), who, however, succeeded in overcoming his opponents. The appearance of the *mahdī*, Ḥamad al-Naḥlān, in this region is another indication of unrest. The next king was deposed by the Funj warriors in 1132/1720, and the succession passed to another branch of the royal family, inheriting through the female line.

Tensions soon reappeared. Bādī IV Abū Shulūkh (1136–75/1724–62) antagonized the Funj notables. The former royal clan was proscribed, and the king began to supplant the old ruling group by men of Nūba origin, probably slaves, and Fūr refugees at his court. Following victory over the Abyssinians in 1157/1744, he sent an expedition against the Musabba'at of Kordofan. After initial defeats, this expedition attained success under the generalship of a certain Muḥammad Abū Likaylik in 1160/1747. This man came from the Hamaj, the section of the population which was probably descended from the old inhabitants of 'Alwa, and was thus ethnically distinct from both the Funj and the Arabs.

[1] In Turkish, *ordu*, which has become arabicized as a place-name, *al-'Urḍī*.

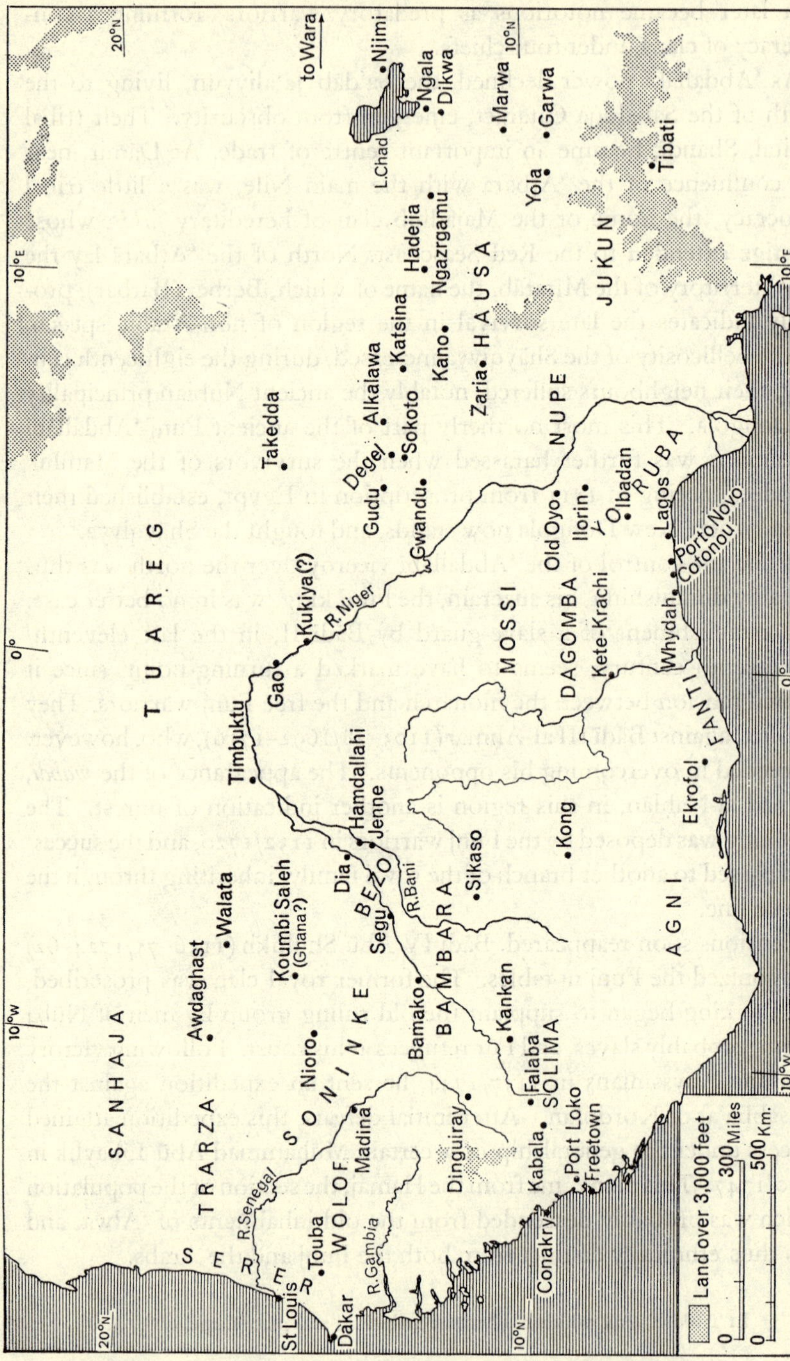

Map 12. Trans-Saharan Africa.

Map 13. Nilotic Sudan and East Africa.

Bādī IV did not himself accompany the expedition to Kordofan, and it may well be that he wished to rid himself of the Funj warriors. Some years after the defeat of the Musabba'at, the king's persecution of their families aroused the Funj chiefs in Kordofan, and, with Abū Likaylik at their head, they marched on Sennar. He was deposed without a struggle in 1175/1769, and the throne passed to his son.

The real power, however, rested with Shaykh Muḥammad Abū Likaylik, who ruled the kingdom of Sennar until his death in 1190/1776–7. He established an hereditary regency which lasted for nearly half a century. The later Funj kings were pawns in the struggle for power, which occupied the last decades of the kingdom. The internecine struggles of the descendants of Abū Likaylik contributed to the decline of the state.

In Darfur, meanwhile, the Kayra sultanate was growing in importance. After the death of Abū Likaylik, the Musabba'at briefly regained power in Kordofan, but the province was conquered by Muḥammad Tayrāb, sultan of Darfur, who died in 1202/1787. A dynastic struggle followed, in which the eunuch, Muḥammad Kurra, procured the accession of 'Abd al-Raḥmān al-Rashīd as sultan. Darfur was at this time becoming better known through trading caravans which went to Egypt by the Khārja Oasis and Asyūṭ along the Forty Days' Road (*Darb al-Arba'īn*), exporting slaves, ivory and ostrich feathers. This commercial activity was in the hands of Nubians of the diaspora. On 'Abd al-Raḥmān's death in 1215/1800–1, Muḥammad Kurra installed the new sultan, Muḥammad Faḍl, but the two became estranged, and Kurra was killed four years later. The long reign of Muḥammad Faḍl—he ruled nearly forty years—saw a decline in the power of Darfur.

THE TURCO-EGYPTIAN PERIOD

The remote and self-contained life of the Nilotic Sudan was brusquely affected by the expedition sent by Muḥammad 'Alī Pasha. The viceroy had various motives: to expel the remnant of the Mamluks from Dongola, where they constituted a potential threat to his rule in Egypt; to restore trade, which had suffered from the growing anarchy in the Nile valley; above all, perhaps, to acquire control of the Sudanese slave trade, which would provide him with military recruits,[1] and the legendary gold of the Sudan.

[1] Russian conquests in the Caucasus had dried up the traditional source of military slaves.

The main expedition advanced up the Nile, and obtained the submission of Berberistān and the riverain states to the south. The last Funj sultan recognized the conqueror in 1821. The only armed opposition came from the Shāyqiyya. A second expedition occupied Kordofan, but failed to annex Darfur. Meanwhile the heavy and unaccustomed taxation imposed on the Nilotic Sudanese provoked a desperate revolt, which was brutally suppressed. Thereafter, for nearly sixty years, there was no general resistance to Turco-Egyptian rule. The Sudanese territories were divided into provinces, administered and garrisoned by Turco-Egyptian officials and troops. A new town, Khartoum, strategically situated at the confluence of the Blue and White Niles, became the residence of the governors-general. Under this régime, the Nilotic Sudan attained a far higher degree of political unity and administrative centralization than it had possessed under the Funj-ʿAbdallābī hegemony.

Towards the end of Muḥammad ʿAlī's reign, a foothold was obtained at Kasala among the Beja tribes. Expansion towards the Red Sea logically entailed possession of the ancient ports of Suakin and Massawa, but although these were briefly leased to Muḥammad ʿAlī, the sultan did not make a permanent cession of them until the time of Khedive Ismāʿīl. The way up the White Nile beyond Alays, the limit of Arab territory, was discovered by three official expeditions under an intrepid Turkish sailor, Selīm Kapudan (Salīm Qabūdān), between 1839 and 1842, and during the decade that followed, the government monopolized the trade of the newly discovered regions. From 1851 onwards, however, European and Ottoman merchants poured into the riverain areas of the Upper Nile, in search of ivory. Their uncontrolled irruption had two evil consequences: the disintegration of tribal society, and the extension of the slave-trade to new areas, and on an increased scale. Similar results followed the rather later penetration of the Baḥr al-Ghazāl, the vast western region, drained by tributaries of the White Nile.

During the reign of Khedive Ismāʿīl (1863–79) the process of expansion was carried further, and a sustained attempt was made to bring the remoter territories under effective control. To achieve this aim, and also to suppress the slave-trade, which had aroused European indignation, Ismāʿīl appointed European and American officials. While the courage and integrity of these aliens temporarily strengthened khedivial rule, their invidious position as Christian servants of a Muslim power, their ignorance of local languages, and their frequent incompatibility with their Egyptian or Sudanese colleagues, all contributed to increase tension.

A prominent figure at this period was the Ja'alī merchant-prince, al-Zubayr Pasha Raḥma Manṣūr. He had made himself the chief operator of the ivory and slave-trade of the western Baḥr al-Ghazāl, where he had enormous political influence. Ismā'īl, having failed to procure his overthrow, recognized him as governor of the Baḥr al-Ghazāl in 1873. A trading-dispute with the Baqqāra or cattle-herding Arabs, through whose territory al-Zubayr's caravans passed, developed into hostilities with their overlord, Sultan Ibrāhīm Muḥammad of Darfur. In 1874, al-Zubayr defeated and killed the sultan, but was prevented by the hasty arrival of a Turco-Egyptian force from carrying out a unilateral occupation of Darfur, which was annexed to the Egyptian Sudan. The vast increase in khedivial territory during Ismā'īl's reign, however, laid an impossible burden on an administration which was renowned neither for its efficiency nor its honesty. The prestige of the khedive, and the energy of the British governor-general, General Gordon, appointed in 1877, postponed the collapse for a few years.

THE MAHDIA

After the deposition of Ismā'īl (1879), which was followed by the resignation of Gordon, the revolutionary situation in the Sudan became apparent. The signal for revolt was given by a widely reverenced *fakī* of Dunqulāwī origin, who dwelt at Abā Island in the White Nile. His name was Muḥammad Aḥmad, and in June 1881 he publicly announced himself to be the Expected Mahdi. His opposition movement was nourished by a variety of resentments: that of the *fakīs* against the hierarchy of orthodox *'ulamā'* introduced by the Turco-Egyptian régime; that of the pious and conservative Sudanese against the administration's westernizing innovations; that of the Nubian diaspora against the repression of the slave-trade; that of local and personal factions against the holders of power and influence in the tribes, the Ṣūfī orders and the provincial towns.

The Mahdia which ensued began as a religious movement for the revival of Islam, primarily in the Sudan, but with universal implications; it developed into a theocratic polity, and this in turn was transformed into a territorial Islamic state.

The Manifestation of the Mahdi in Abā began a period of revolutionary war against the khedivial administration in the Sudan. The Mahdi quickly withdrew from Abā to the distant hill of Qadīr in southern Kordofan, where he recruited tribal forces (mainly Baqqāra) beyond the effective reach of the Turco-Egyptian régime. Emerging from Qadīr he won his first major success with the capture of El Obeid (al-Ubayyiḍ), the provincial capital of Kordofan, in January 1883. A last attempt to mount a large-scale offensive against him was defeated with the annihilation of the Hicks Expedition in the following November. The collapse of the khedivial administration in Darfur and the Baḥr al-Ghazāl followed, while the flame of revolt was carried to the Beja tribes, who dominated the important route from Suakin to the Nile. Gordon, who returned in 1884, ostensibly to carry out the evacuation of the Egyptian garrisons, committed himself to a hopeless resistance in Khartoum. When the city fell, in January 1885, the Mahdia had eaten the heart out of the Egyptian Sudan.

This period saw the elaboration of the characteristic ideology and institutions of the Mahdia. The Mahdi aimed to restore the primitive Islamic *Umma*, and to end the innovations and tyranny of the Turco-Egyptian régime. The strong Ṣūfī tradition of the Sudan imparted to his ideas an eschatological tinge. He envisaged his new *Umma* as a recapitulation of early Islam. He himself was the Successor of the Prophet, as his chief followers were the Successors of the Companions. His letters stress his divine election as Mahdi.

The revolutionary army on which he depended was largely tribal in origin, and consisted of three divisions, under his three chief companions. Pre-eminent among these was *Khalīfat al-Ṣiddīq*, the Successor of Abū Bakr, 'Abd Allāhi b. Muḥammad, a man of Baqqārī origin, who had joined him at Abā before the Manifestation. 'Abd Allāhi commanded the Black Flag division, composed of the levies of the Baqqāra Arabs of Kordofan and Darfur—restless nomads, who found in the Mahdia a release from the growing pressure of the Turco-Egyptian administration.

After the fall of Khartoum, the Mahdi established his residence at Omdurman, where an immense, straggling camp-city grew up. Here he died, in June 1885, to be succeeded as head of the theocratic state by 'Abd Allāhi, who assumed the title of *Khalīfat al-Mahdī*, the Successor of the Mahdi. Once he had secured his position, the Khalifa 'Abd Allāhi pursued a policy of *jihād* against his neighbours. Between 1886 and 1889, there was warfare in three principal areas: the Abyssinian frontier, Darfur and the west, and the Egyptian frontier. Although important temporary successes were gained, the Mahdist state could not make far-reaching conquests. The turning-point came in August 1889, when the long-awaited invasion of Egypt was crushingly defeated at the battle of Ṭūshkī (Toski). The great expanses of the southern Sudan, precariously held by Khedive Ismāʿīl, eluded the Khalifa's grasp. The Baḥr al-Ghazāl had no Mahdist governor after 1886, while the river-line of the Upper Nile was retained only with difficulty.

After Ṭūshkī, the policy of the *jihād* was tacitly abandoned by the Khalifa, who sought instead to strengthen his personal autocracy within his limited territorial state. A rift developed between the Khalifa and the tribesmen belonging to the main Nile and the Nubian diaspora, who filled the cadres of his bureaucracy. The situation was aggravated by the Khalifa's attempt to bring in the Baqqāra, and settle them in Omdurman and the Gezira. Meanwhile, the Khalifa endeavoured to secure his autocracy by appointing his kinsmen and clients to the principal military governorships and key offices of state. Resentment flared out in a revolt, in November 1891, centring around the Mahdi's family. ʿAbd Allāhi temporized, and subsequently destroyed the leaders piecemeal. His former colleague, *Khalīfat al-Karrār* (i.e., the Successor of ʿAlī) Muḥammad Sharīf, a cousin of the Mahdi, who had been the figure-head of the revolt, was tried and imprisoned. There was no other serious internal challenge to the Khalifa during the remainder of his rule.

The Khalifa's sovereignty seems to have gained in popular acceptance, and he began to groom his son for eventual succession. The Mahdist state collapsed only when its conquest was decided upon by the British government. In making the decision, the government was moved by considerations of policy in Europe: the claims and interests of Egypt were a negligible factor: the actual state of affairs in the Sudan had no weight at all.

The reconquest was planned and directed by Sir Herbert (later Lord) Kitchener, then *serdār* of the Egyptian army. Kitchener met with no serious setbacks, and attained his objectives with a notable economy of both lives and money. His success was due to his own administrative and organizing capacity, and to superiority of armament and transport, which depended on railway-construction. The province of Dongola was reconquered in 1896, and the main campaign began in the following year. In September 1898, the Khalifa was decisively defeated at Karārī, near Omdurman. With the fugitive remnants of his followers, he fell in battle in November 1899.

THE ANGLO-EGYPTIAN CONDOMINIUM

Although the Mahdist state ceased to exist in 1898, the work of occupying and pacifying the Sudan still remained. A French attempt to establish a foothold on the Upper Nile, by the Marchand expedition, was prevented by Kitchener's prompt action, but complete control over the tribes was not established for a generation. When the Mahdist state collapsed, the sultanate of Darfur was re-established by 'Alī Dīnār, a member of the Kayra dynasty. Nominally a vassal of the new Sudan Government, he excluded its agents from his territory, until he was overthrown by a military expedition in 1916, when Darfur was re-annexed. Some fringe territories which had recognized the rule of the khedive in 1881 were not regained in 1898; while agreements with France, Abyssinia and the Congo Free State substituted acknowledged frontiers for vague territorial claims.

The status of the reconquered territories was determined by a convention concluded between Britain and Egypt in January 1899. This was drafted by Lord Cromer, as British agent and consul-general, wholly in accordance with British policy. Its principal purpose was to exclude from the Sudan both international institutions, such as the Mixed Courts, and the authority of the Egyptian government. The Sudan was formally a condominium, under joint British and Egyptian rule. In practice, the governor-general, in whom the supreme military and civil command, was vested, was invariably a British subject, as were the chief administrative officials. The Egyptians were restricted to subordinate posts, to which competent Sudanese were also admitted in due course.

Lord Kitchener, the first governor-general, was succeeded in December 1899 by Sir Reginald Wingate. During Wingate's long governor-generalship, ending in 1916, two characteristic institutions of the Sudan government developed: the Sudan Political Service, a corps of civilian administrators, recruited in Britain, who passed the whole of their working careers in the Sudan; and the Governor-General's Council, constituted in 1910, and composed of senior officials, which formed the supreme legislative and executive body. An administration so recruited was naturally paternalist and somewhat parochial in its outlook. But it was efficient and incorruptible, and its members served devotedly the interest of the Sudanese, as they saw it. The country was governed with the utmost economy; even so, revenue did not exceed expenditure until 1913.

Under Wingate and his successor, Sir Lee Stack (1917–24), the economic and educational foundations of the modern Sudan were laid. Kitchener's military railway was expanded to link the provinces of the north. The White Nile, with its regular steamer-services, was the highway to the south. Khartoum rose from its ruins to be, once again, the capital. Omdurman remained the largest Sudanese urban settlement. Suakin and Berber, the old termini of the Red Sea-Nile route, were supplanted by new towns at Port Sudan and Atbara, the railway headquarters. In the Gezira, Wad Medani was not only a provincial capital, but also, after the First World War, the centre of the cotton-producing scheme controlled by the Sudan Plantations Syndicate.

The educational system was at first on a very small scale. It was intended to supply the government with clerks and minor officials, and was not conceived in any spirit of enlightenment. Literacy in Arabic was provided in the elementary schools, while English was taught at the next (intermediate) level. Secondary education was slow to develop: even by the Second World War, there was only one government secondary school. In the southern Sudan, the schools were provided by Christian missionaries, and Arabic was not taught. This religious and educational differentiation, superimposed on underlying geographical and ethnic distinctions, was to promote tensions between north and south.

The golden age of paternalism ended after the First World War. As militant nationalism grew in Egypt, the Condominium in the Sudan was called into question. Inside the Sudan, paternalism no longer satisfied the educated *élite*, and the first signs of Sudanese nationalism appeared in 1921. Then, in November 1924, the assassination of Sir Lee Stack in Cairo was followed by British insistence on the withdrawal of all Egyptian troops from the Sudan. The evacuation was accompanied by a mutiny of Sudanese troops, which was forcibly suppressed. Egyptian civilian officials were subsequently withdrawn, and the share of Egypt in the Condominium diminished to vanishing point.

During the next two decades, paternalism ceased to be an ideal, and turned into an expedient. The Sudan government looked for the future, not to the educated *élite*, but to the traditional tribal leaders, whose authority was extended and codified in pursuance of a policy of 'native administration'. In the southern Sudan, the fostering of native administration was accomplished by the exclusion of northern Sudanese, and a strenuous attempt to combat Islam and Muslim influences. Education was viewed with suspicion, and parsimoniously financed. The great depression of the early 1930s provided retrospective justification for retrenchment.

The Second World War saw the beginning of new political developments. There were two distinct but connected problems. The first was of conciliating the growing nationalist feeling in the Sudan; the second, of reaching agreement with Egypt. The spearhead of Sudanese nationalism was the educated *élite*, most of whom were in government service, and demanded, with varying degrees of moderation, a share in the running of their country. They had organized in 1938 the Graduates' General Congress, and they were able to enlist mass-support, through links with the two chief Muslim religious orders, the Khatmiyya and the *Anṣār*. The head of the Anṣār, ʻAbd al-Raḥmān al-Mahdī, the posthumous son of the Mahdi, was an overtly political figure; while his counterpart in the Khatmiyya, ʻAlī al-Mīrghanī, refused a public political role. The nationalists connected with the *Anṣār* became spokesmen of Sudanese independence, while those with Khatmiyya affiliations advocated union with Egypt.

The problem of the status of the Sudan had been shelved in the Anglo-Egyptian Treaty of 1936. No Egyptian government could abandon the claim that the Nile Valley legitimately formed an indissoluble political unity. On this rock successive negotiations foundered; while, since one Sudanese nationalist group was ostensibly committed to the Egyptian claim, the attempts to associate the Sudanese with the Sudan Government evoked only a partial response.

The first such attempt was made by the inauguration, in 1944, of the Advisory Council of the Northern Sudan. Since its functions were purely advisory, it was not taken seriously by many nationalists, who, moreover, saw in its restriction to the northern provinces, a deliberate attempt to divide the country. In 1948, the Sudan Government set up a Legislative Assembly, representing the Sudan as a whole, and an Executive Council, half Sudanese in composition. These developments took place against the protests of the Egyptians and their Sudanese allies.

In 1943, the rival nationalist groups were organized as political parties. Those under ʻAbd al-Raḥmān's patronage became the *Umma* party—a name which to their opponents had ominous hints of a new Mahdist monarchy—while the pro-Egyptian group, affiliated to the Khatmiyya, were known as the *Ashiqqāʼ*. Their leader, Ismāʻīl al-Azharī, became the most popular and formidable of Sudanese politicians.

While the deadlock between Britain and Egypt over the status of the

Sudan continued, the Sudan government, with British backing, promulgated a Self-Government Statute in April 1952. Three months later, the revolution in Egypt made possible a fresh approach to the problem.

Understanding was reached among the Sudanese nationalist parties, and between the Egyptian and British governments. The Anglo-Egyptian Agreement of 12 February 1953 adopted the Self-Government Statute as the basis for Sudanese constitutional advance. While the Egyptian régime abandoned the demand for the unity of the Nile Valley, and accepted the principle of Sudanese self-determination, the British permitted amendments to the Statute. These set up an international commission to limit the governor-general's powers and another to control the election of the projected Sudanese Parliament.

The new Parliament met in January 1954. Ismā'īl al-Azharī, whose supporters (reorganized in 1951 as the National Unionist party) had won a majority of seats, became prime minister. The sudanization of the army, police and civil service proceeded rapidly. As the British withdrawal proceeded, al-Azharī changed his attitude towards Egypt, in deference to the obvious feeling of Sudanese nationalists. The idea of union was dead: the only issue was by what process, and how soon, the Sudan would become independent. The Anglo-Egyptian Agreement of 1953 had laid down an elaborate procedure, but, under al-Azharī's guidance, the Parliament took more summary measures. These enabled him to proclaim an independent republic, on New Year's Day, 1956.

The republican government succeeded to the entire territory of the former Condominium, but did not command a united people. The split between the nationalists had left a legacy of factionalism in party politics. Al-Azharī handled both his supporters and his opponents astutely, but Sudanese parliamentary democracy was inaugurated in an atmosphere of political opportunism rather than statesmanship, and depended on personalities rather than principles. Still more serious was the rift between north and south, which was demonstrated in August 1955, when a military mutiny led to a breakdown of public security in the southern provinces. Events were to show that the coming of independence was in itself no solution to either of these problems.

CHAPTER 6

THE WESTERN AND CENTRAL SUDAN AND EAST AFRICA

A. THE WESTERN AND CENTRAL SUDAN IN THE EARLY PERIOD

The Sudan (more precisely, *bilād al-Sūdān*, the land of the blacks) is the Arabic name for the trans-continental savannah belt, several hundred miles wide, lying between desert and forest. The Sudan has been the principal theatre for African Islamic history below the northern coast. Only rarely have Saharan movements exercised critical influence—e.g. the Almoravids (fifth/eleventh century) or the Sanūsiyya (nineteenth century). Only recently has Islam taken root in the forest: this is primarily a characteristic of the European colonial period, which checked local wars, opened roads, and encouraged trade and migrant labour—a situation equally true for Muslim penetration south from the savannah, or inland from the East African coast.

The Sahara, with its Berber population, has, however, been of crucial importance as an avenue of approach. The northern Sudan cities, Timbuktu, Gao and others, were ports facing the desert just as the eastern coastal cities faced the Indian Ocean. Gold for export, salt for import, were staples of Saharan trade. Several major routes crossed the Sahara: from Morocco to the goldfields of the upper Senegal and Niger; from Tunisia to the area between the Niger and Lake Chad; from Tripoli to Lake Chad; from Libya to Waday. The eastern Sudan, though closest to the heartlands of Islam, was penetrated last, perhaps because of difficulties of communication along the Nile, and the persistence of Christian states astride the river. Below the northernmost Sudanic strip, called the *Sāḥil* or Coast, another pattern of Muslim mobility developed, chiefly east-west. Here the east coast, lacking any penetrable hinterland, differed fundamentally. The mobility of men and ideas within the Islamic world, across the Sahara or within the Sudan, founded upon trade but stimulated by religious duties, is the most important geographical fact of African Islamic history.

Islam south of the Sahara has followed a threefold development:

first, as represented by foreign Muslim residents; second, commanding some local support but forced to compromise with local custom; and third, able to impose reform at will. The pattern did not begin in all areas at the same time, nor advance at the same rate, so differing stages may exist side by side.

Ghāna

Ghāna is first mentioned by al-Fazārī in the eighth century; al-Bakrī, writing in 460/1067–8, supplies our first detailed description. It is typical of Islam in the first, foreign stage. The capital then included two main quarters, one royal (called *al-Ghāba*, the forest, because of its sacred groves) and one Muslim (presumably mainly for foreign merchants). The Muslim quarter had twelve mosques, including a cathedral mosque, with mosque officials and learned men. The royal quarter had also a mosque, for Muslim ministers constantly attended the king. The king was pagan, hedged with divinity.

The Muslim quarter shows already the mosaic character of Sudan society. Still today many towns have such quarters. So deeply ingrained is the concept that some African traditions, recorded in this century, describe a pagan quarter in Mecca. Muslim separateness was expressed in other ways also. Pagans prostrated themselves and poured dust on their heads before the king; Muslims showed respect by clapping hands, rendering prostration to God alone, and shared with royalty the exclusive right to wear tailored clothes.

Muslim traders were present in other towns as well as the capital; they were respected in some districts when they only passed by. Perhaps their example was already appreciated locally—a woman of Sama, where the inhabitants paid little attention to dress of any kind, asked a passing Muslim for his beard to clothe herself.

This phase of Ghāna history came to an end with the Almoravid conquest (*c.* 468/1076). Almoravid control lasted scarcely a decade. What happened to Ghāna in the twelfth century? It may have been a period of decline; the capital may have revived on the same site; or it may have flourished on a new, riverside site; a Berber dynasty, claiming *sharīfī* origin, may have taken over. All these and other theories have been advanced. It appears that the rulers of Ghāna became Muslim, and that the movement of peoples, particularly Soninke, stimulated by the Almoravid conquest led to the spread of Islam in new areas.

Takrūr

In the fifth/eleventh century, other states already had Muslim rulers. Al-Bakrī records a king of Malal (a Mande state), converted to Islam by the successful prayers for rain of a passing *'ālim*. Later historians said the first Muslim king of Mali was Barmandana, a pilgrim. We do not know if these two were the same. In Malal the commoners remained pagan; but in Takrūr, on the Senegal, we are told that both king and people converted. Takrūr has throughout its Islamic history been inhabited by two main groups, united by a common language: the one nomadic pastoralists, light-coloured, now called Fulani; the other sedentary, of mixed racial origins but mainly Negro, dark, now called Tokolor—that is, people of Takrūr. The Tokolor have been the champions of Islam. Torodbe, a name originally of religious clans, has been virtually another name for Tokolor. Takrūr troops, vainly, helped the Almoravids.

Later writers, in Egypt, began using Takrūr as equivalent for Mali, though Mansa Mūsā (early eighth/fourteenth century) protested that Takrūr was but part of his domains, and scholars knew that to use Takrūr for Mali was a mistake of the commoners. How did this wider, looser Middle Eastern definition arise? Was it pilgrimage usage, as later Java became a collective name for South-East Asian pilgrims? Were there West African communities in Cairo, who popularized the name? Ibn Khaldūn (1332–1406) received information from the *turjumān al-Takrūr*, the interpreter of the Takrūr, in Egypt: was this the head of an immigrant community, perhaps genuine Takrūrīs? Takrūr and *fuqarā'* prayed for the sultan Baybars. Confusion may have arisen from the repeated use, by Arab geographers, of Takrūr as a name linked also with the Gao area. West African Muslims, beginning later to write their own history, adopted this wider sense. Askiya al-Ḥājj Muḥammad was styled *khalīfa* for the land of the Takrūr; Aḥmad Bābā of Timbuktu was called al-Takrūrī; Muḥammad Bello entitled his study of the Fulani *jihād*, 'a study in the history of the country of Takrūr'; and so forth. In the heartlands of Islam, Takrūrī (plural Takārna or Takārīr) came to be applied to every West or Central African visitor. Despite the famous name, Takrūr and Tokolor in the west were of secondary importance until after 1700.

The Almoravids

Early efforts to unite the leading Ṣanhāja clans of the western Sahara were unavailing. Awdaghast, a principal Saharan town, passed under

Ghāna control. In the eleventh century a new Ṣanhāja confederacy was formed under Tarsina, a pilgrim and leader of *jihād*. He was killed, after a short career.

In 1035 or later, Yaḥyā b. Ibrāhīm, son-in-law and successor of Tarsina, left on Pilgrimage with several fellow chiefs. Returning through Qayrawān he heard Abū 'Imrān, from Fez, teaching there. Apparently for the first time, Yaḥyā realized the defects of his Saharan Islam: one of many instances in African Islamic history in which experiences on the way to and from Mecca are at least as important as what is observed in Mecca. Yaḥyā complained about the *'ulamā'* at home, and begged Abū 'Imrān for a missionary. Abū 'Imrān, as impressed with Yaḥyā's intentions as he was dismayed by his ignorance, found none of his students both willing and suitable. He recommended Yaḥyā to another teacher, Wajjāj b. Zalwī, near Sijilmāsa. Among Wajjāj's students a missionary was found, 'Abd Allāh b. Yāsīn, his mother a Jazūlī Berber from the Ghāna borders.

'Abd Allāh b. Yāsīn accompanied Yaḥyā b. Ibrāhīm to the desert. 'Abd Allāh, refusing the milk and meat of his Ṣanhāja hosts, lest their property be legally impure, dissociated himself from unreformed local Islam. Like John the Baptist, he lived on wild food only. He wore the mystic's woollen dress.

'Abd Allāh's witness and preaching won disciples, the *Murābiṭūn*, people of the *ribāṭ*, Almoravids; the word *ribāṭ* seems here to mean 'military service' or perhaps even 'sect'.[1] He attacked reluctant Ṣanhāja, and compelled them to come in. He purified their possessions by annexing one-third, serving financial and religious policy. 'Abd Allāh built a town, Aratnanna, where no house was taller than another. Adultery, lying and drinking were punished with the whip. Anyone entering the *ribāṭ* suffered for past offences. Musical instruments were broken, wine-shops closed.

He enforced the limit of four wives. Keeping within this, he himself married and divorced unceasingly. He never gave more than four *mithqāls* in dowry: his marital life may have made such economy imperative, but low dowries may also be a measure of social reform, such as was enforced for example by the Sudanese Mahdi Muḥammad Aḥmad. Supplementary prayers made up for those omitted in the convert's

[1] Al-Bakrī, our only contemporary observer, does not mention the island *ribāṭ* to which 'Abd Allāh is said to have withdrawn when first training his disciples. Later authorities disagree as to where the *ribāṭ* was, who built it and who went to it.

earlier life. Lateness at prayer, neglect of part of the prayer, even raising one's voice in the mosque, the whip rewarded all.

Dissatisfaction developed. A local *faqīh* and two chiefs overthrew 'Abd Allāh, who fled to Wajjāj. Wajjāj decreed that those who resisted 'Abd Allāh were outside the congregation and outside the law. Dealing death to opponents and wrong-doers alike, 'Abd Allāh fought his way back to power in the Sahara.

With a well-disciplined army, 'Abd Allāh conquered Sijilmāsa and Awdaghast, main terminals of trans-Saharan trade. Both towns had Zanāta colonies or garrisons, Berbers but deadly enemies to the Ṣanhāja. Awdaghast had further offended by acknowledging a Negro governor. When Awdaghast fell (446/1054–5), property was seized, women raped, and a learned pilgrim killed.

Yaḥyā b. Ibrāhīm, a Juddālī, had died; Yaḥyā b. 'Umar, a Lamtūnī, replaced him as temporal *amīr*. Now the Juddāla rebelled. 'Abd Allāh b. Yāsin, called north by trouble in Sijilmāsa, left Yaḥyā b. 'Umar to hold the fort in the Sahara. Yaḥyā, reinforced with Muslim troops from Takrūr—an interesting case of religious alliance across racial frontiers—hazarded battle with the Juddāla (448/1056). He fell, defeated, on Tabfarilla field, haunted afterwards by the crying of ghostly muezzins, so that the dead were left undespoiled. His brother, Abū Bakr b. 'Umar, succeeded him. 'Abd Allāh b. Yāsīn fell fighting in North Africa. Full command passed to Abū Bakr.

Faced with new dissension in the desert, Abū Bakr reconciled the quarrelling parties by leading them against the Negroes. Hitherto, the *jihād* had been against erring or rival Muslims, an ominous precedent. When he tried to return north, his cousin, Yūsuf b. Tāshufīn, to whom he had entrusted Morocco, refused to admit him. Henceforth the movement was split. Yūsuf reduced Morocco, taking Fez in 462/1069, when 3,000 Zanāta are said to have died in the mosques. Muslim Spain was also occupied. Abū Bakr also conquered the capital of Ghāna (*c.* 468/1076). He died soon after; the Almoravid adventure in West Africa concluded.

Mali

The core of Mali was the Mande state of Kangaba, near modern Bamako on the upper Niger; the actual capital moved many times. This southern, agricultural foundation strengthened prosperity, though trade, especially in gold and kola, was important too. In the seventh/

thirteenth century, Sunjata of Mali conquered Ghāna; the Soninke dispersion received another impetus, and the glory of Ghāna finally departed.

The greatest ruler according to written records—that is, from a Muslim point of view, Sunjata dominating oral tradition—was Mansa Mūsā (1312–37 or later). In his time, Mali expanded north to incorporate Walata and Timbuktu; east, to bring in the Songhay of the middle Niger; south and west, to influence Futa Jallon and Takrūr.

In the fifteenth century, as Songhay rose, Mali declined. Tuareg, Wolof, Tokolor and Mossi harassed the frontiers. Mali appealed vainly for Portuguese help. By the seventeenth century, Mali was once again confined to Kangaba, which still exists and is still ruled by the Kayta dynasty, the family of Barmandana.

The rulers of Mali were Muslim, but in the conversation between Islam and the divine kingship, neither side had prevailed. Prostration and dusting before the king were still required. Indeed, while in Ghāna Muslims (probably all foreigners) were exempt, in Mali even pilgrims, even the chief *qāḍī*, had to do this. Such exemption as was granted seems to have been a racial privilege for foreigners, not a religious one for Muslims. Other features of the traditional monarchy also remained: special dress (as in Ghāna, Muslims had a privileged position here), special eating arrangements, rights to the daughters of subjects, etc. '*Ulamā*' depended on royal largesse, distributed particularly in Ramaḍān.

Ibn Baṭṭūṭa visited Mali in 753–4/1352–3. His description of the Muslim festivals, when both the Muslim *khaṭīb* and the pagan poets addressed the kings, shows clearly the intermingling of the two faiths. He complained also about violations of Muslim rules of dress and eating. But the witness to a purer faith survived. In the capital, the cathedral mosque was crowded to overflowing on Fridays, and great stress was laid on youths memorizing the Qur'ān. Even *vis-à-vis* the king, '*ulamā*' maintained a certain detachment. The mosque and the *khaṭīb's* house were sanctuaries in the capital; and outside, Jaba (perhaps the modern Dia) was a religious town, ruled by a *qāḍī*, where the king's writ did not run.

Islam was probably largely upper class and urban, with a strong foreign element. Ibn Baṭṭūṭa stayed in the white quarter at the capital. The white community had two chiefs, one from Egypt, one a Jazūlī Berber from the tribe of Ibn Yāsīn's mother. Ibn Baṭṭūṭa, having trouble with the change of diet, was doctored by another Egyptian. But the chief *qāḍī* was a Negro, and Ibn Baṭṭūṭa was favourably impressed with Negro pilgrims in several villages. His comment that a man with but one shirt would wash it for the Friday prayer suggests that, in the capital at least, Islam had begun to penetrate among poor as well as rich. On the other hand, al-'Umarī reports that, except among persons of rank, no burial was performed, an intolerable procedure for Muslims.

Mali's foreign relations reflect the religious tension. To the south were innumerable pagans. When the imposition of Islam in the gold-producing areas reduced output, the pagan miners were simply placed under tribute, and left undisturbed in their traditional beliefs. Magic was practised in ivory-hunting. When cannibal delegations from the south visited Mali, the *mansa* provided unfortunate victims as a welcome feast. Occasional political incidents suggest that perhaps relations with the south were still closer. At least once the south was a place of exile: Mansa Mūsā sent there a dishonest *qāḍī* from Morocco, who returned after four years, uneaten because 'unripe'. And once (792/1390) a usurper emerged from the south, claiming descent from Sunjata, and seized power.

Relations with North Africa and the Middle East were the counterweight. Embassies passed between Mali and Morocco: Mansa Mūsā sent one (*c.* 1337) to congratulate Abu'l Ḥasan 'Alī, the Marinid sultan, on the capture of Tlemcen. Ibn Baṭṭūṭa attended a memorial dinner in Mali for Abu'l-Ḥasan, at which the Qur'ān was read, and prayers offered for the rulers of Mali and Morocco. Mansa Mūsā's grandson sent another with presents, including a giraffe, which caused great excitement. Once a deposed sultan of Morocco travelled to Mali, where he joined a pilgrim caravan. Barmandana, Sunjata's son and successor Uli, and other Mali kings went on Pilgrimage; that of Mansa Mūsā in the 1320s is the most celebrated in West African history.

Songhay

The Songhay empire was born of the union of river and desert. Traditions recount the early imposition of desert Berbers upon riverain Negroes. Kukiya was the first capital. In the fifth/eleventh century, the capital moved north to Gao, and the *za*, or king, adopted Islam. Early accounts are contradictory; perhaps not all refer to Gao. It seems, despite the *za*'s conversion, that Gao remained two towns, like the Ghāna capital, one for Muslims, one for the king and his people. Elaborate rituals surrounding royal meals show the divine kingship tradition still strong. Kukiya remained a powerful pagan centre, and *zas* resorted thither for part of their inaugural ceremonies. Muslim funeral steles date from 499/1106, if not earlier, in Gao, but do not appear in Kukiya until the fifteenth century.

In the seventh/thirteenth and eighth/fourteenth centuries, Mali exercised intermittent authority over Songhay. The Pilgrimage perhaps provided the Mali rulers with occasion to receive Songhay homage. Mali *'ulamā'* crossed Songhay into Hausaland. By 1400 Songhay had eclipsed Mali. 'Alī, last but one of the *sonnis* (successors of the *zas*), 869–97, 1464/5–1491/2, established Songhay as a great power. His conquests included Jenne and Timbuktu. His main antagonists were Fulani, Tuareg and Mossi.

The Muslim chroniclers, in awe of Sonni 'Alī's military success, abuse him as an impious tyrant. They were apologists for the Askiya dynasty, which deposed Sonni 'Alī's son. They had also genuine grievances, about Sonni 'Alī's lax observance of Islam, his oppression of some *'ulamā'*, particularly those of Timbuktu, and his cultivation of paganism. His words were those of one strong in Islam, as were some of his actions. But in other respects he behaved as an unbeliever. The chroniclers called him a *Khārijī*, here probably used loosely to mean heretic. For the first time, the problem of the 'mixers' was consciously posed.

Sonni 'Alī died; his son, Sonni Baru, replaced him. Askiya Muḥammad, a leading official under Sonni 'Alī, thrice summoned Baru to conversion, the first emissary being a *sharīf*. Baru, already Muslim, probably regarded this summons as a political challenge. He refused. Muḥammad fought and defeated Baru, and ascended the throne in 898/1493, first of the *askiyas*.

Oral tradition affirms Askiya Muḥammad to have been a nephew of Sonni 'Ali—the chronicles make him a Soninke stranger from the west. Oral tradition describes Muḥammad murdering the last *sonni* (apparently 'Alī) as the *sonni* led the festival prayers. The chronicles say Sonni 'Alī died in mystery, at the height of his powers, drowned returning from a campaign—none knows his grave. His death they attribute to the prayers of *'ulamā'* against him.

Whatever Muḥammad's origin, whatever the details of his revolution, his responsibility for the overthrow of the *sonnis* is clear. He at once wooed the Muslim party, paying special regard to *'ulamā'*, *qāḍīs, sharīfs* and pilgrims. Later, when he was firmly established, some of these privileges lapsed. A mysterious passage in the chronicles may relate to

Muḥammad's need for the intercession of religious men. The *qāḍī* of Timbuktu, we are told, later reminded Muḥammad that he had come to the *qāḍī*, beseeching the *qāḍī* to hold him by the hand lest he fall into hell; Muḥammad acknowledged this.

In 902/1496–7, Muḥammad went on Pilgrimage, oral tradition says in penance. Muḥammad was appointed *khalīfa* of Takrūr, probably by the 'Abbasid caliph in Cairo, having first symbolically laid aside his kingly estate. On Pilgrimage, Muḥammad met al-Maghīlī, who later visited Gao, and whose advice greatly helped Muḥammad in justifying the revolution.

The influence of Muḥammad b. 'Abd al-Karīm al-Maghīlī, a Berber *'ālim*, spans four centuries of West African Islam. In Tuat, al-Maghīlī reversed the hitherto tolerant policy towards the numerous Jews of the oasis. The *qāḍī* opposed him. But al-Maghīlī, with supporting opinions from religious authorities elsewhere in North Africa, destroyed (*c.* 897/1492) the synagogue, massacring many Jews and forcing others to wear distinctive dress and badges.

From Tuat, al-Maghīlī visited Takedda, Katsina and Kano, teaching. One of his pupils at Takedda became *qāḍī* of Katsina. In Kano and Katsina, commercial and Islamic centres of Hausa, al-Maghīlī stimulated religious revival.

From Hausa, al-Maghīlī travelled, *c.* 907/1502, to Askiya al-Ḥājj Muḥammad, in Gao. Al-Maghīlī advised the *askiya*, particularly about Sonni 'Alī and his religion and government. Hearing that the Jews had killed his son, and failing to persuade the *askiya* to take vengeance, al-Maghīlī returned to Tuat. He died in 910/1504.

Al-Maghīlī judged both Sonni 'Alī, and his people, as 'mixers'—despite the profession of faith, Ramaḍān, royal largesse in alms, they continued to venerate pagan shrines, and invariably sought the guidance of pagan priests. Against 'mixers', al-Maghīlī decreed, *jihād* is more urgent than against pagans, for 'mixers' lead ignorant Muslims astray.

Sonni 'Alī was also condemned for injustice, but injustice, unlike 'mixing', is only disobedience, not unbelief. What is unbelief is to maintain that injustice is right. Here al-Maghīlī condemned the venal *'ulamā'* (*'ulamā' al-sū'*), who approve whatever the king wishes them to approve. Al-Maghīlī introduced the distinction between good and bad *'ulamā'*, contrasting the *mujaddid*—perhaps the first mention in Sudanese literature of this apocalyptic figure sent each century by God—with the *'ulamā'* of his time. Al-Maghīlī's political recommendation was a centralized *jamāʿa* under a strong *imām*, administering the *Sharīʿa*, using force if need be.

These advices answer the *askiya*'s queries. Did the *askiya* know sometimes what answers to expect? For example, when he asked if he should follow ignorant '*ulamā*', or recompense from state funds those whom Sonni 'Alī had wronged, was he perhaps preparing to consolidate his position by dropping those whose support was no longer essential? We know that his attitude towards the '*ulamā*', at first deferential, later hardened.

On his return from Pilgrimage, Askiya al-Ḥājj Muḥammad launched a *jihād* against the Mossi. This was his only formal *jihād*. His later wars, like those of Sonni 'Alī, were against all neighbours, Muslim and pagan. Expeditions penetrated Mali, Masina, Agades, Hausa, and elsewhere.

Muḥammad, blind and enfeebled, was deposed by his son Mūsā at the *Aḍḥā* festival in 1529. Of all *askiyas* after Muḥammad, only Dā'ūd b. Muḥammad, 956–991/1549–83, enjoyed a long and effective reign. Especially damaging was civil war in the late 1580s. The Muslims backed a rival candidate for *askiya*. They were defeated, and cruelly repressed, as in Sonni 'Alī's time.

Some *askiyas* were good Muslims, but even these were 'mixers' in one way or another. An '*ālim* was astonished to find Dā'ūd observing rituals of the divine kingship; Dā'ūd explained that only so could he control his subjects and protect the Muslims. Dā'ūd used sympathetic magic to kill an opponent. Another *askiya* was a soothsayer. *Askiyas* continued to use the free daughters of their soldiers as concubines.

The position of '*ulamā*' was also ambiguous. They approved measures to enforce Islam, yet sought to preserve a certain religious distance. The chronicles abound in examples of religious defiance and imperial deference. Sometimes '*ulamā*' refused appointment by the *askiyas*, though some were appointed forcibly nonetheless, others taking sanctuary in the mosque. Some '*ulamā*' even cursed the *askiyas*. Timbuktu, proud of its autonomy, championed religious independence, but this autonomy was limited. The *qāḍīs* of Timbuktu itself, drawn from one family, were appointed by the *askiyas*: one *askiya* refused for seventeen months to appoint any *qāḍī* at all in Timbuktu.

Bornu-Kanem

Kanem (whence sprang Bornu) apparently arose through the imposition of Saharan pastoralists, particularly Zaghāwa, upon smaller Negro states, from early in the Muslim era. Only in the sixth/twelfth century was a settled capital established, at Njimi.

Various reports suggest Umayyad influence in early Kanemi Islam, as on the east coast and, to a lesser extent, in Ghāna. The first missionary to Kanem claimed descent from the Caliph 'Uthmān—tradition says the caliphate passed from the Umayyads to Kanem—in the fifth/eleventh century descendants of Umayyad refugees were said to live there.

Links with North Africa and the heartlands of Islam were especially close. The first Muslim king (*mai*), Hume, who lived in the late eleventh century, founder of the Sefawa dynasty, died in Egypt, presumably on Pilgrimage. His son and successor went thrice on Pilgrimage, each time settling slaves in Cairo; finally the Cairenes became suspicious, as in that time of Fatimid disorder they might, and drowned the king. In the seventh/thirteenth century, the reign of Dabalemi, friend of the Tunisian Hafsids, marked the climax of trans-Saharan connexions. Valuable presents from Kanem, again including a giraffe, reached Tunis: Kanem Muslims founded a Mālikī hostel for travellers in Cairo.

Influence abroad but no peace at home. Dabalemi opened the talisman, as in his father's time the sacred snake had been killed; both these acts, sacrilegious in pagan eyes, were perhaps steps towards purer Islam. Dabalemi's father was a black sultan, after a succession of red nomads, so religious reform and racial assimilation may have marched together. Hume was also called 'the son of the black.'

The broken talisman provoked ambition, intrigue, and civil war. Most serious was war with the Bulala, a branch of the royal dynasty. Several Kanemi *mais* were killed. Nomad Arabs moving west joined in. In 794/1391–2, the Mamluk sultan of Egypt received a letter from the *mai* (who claimed Qurashī descent) complaining that Arabs were enslaving Kanemi Muslims. Just afterwards, the *mai*, on the advice of his '*ulamā*', abandoned Kanem and fled southwest to Bornu.

The Bulala ruled in Kanem. Originally perhaps pagan reactionaries, by 1500 they apparently traded with Nile towns, exchanged gifts with Egyptian rulers and merchants, and received with honour learned men and *sharīfs*.

The establishment of the refugee dynasty in Bornu helped to end Hausa isolation. Fulani '*ulamā*', it is said, visited Kanem from Mali about 1300. Now such east-west connexions became closer. One early Bornu *mai* may have had a Hausa mother.

In the late fifteenth and the sixteenth centuries Bornu power waxed.

A new capital, Ngazargamu, was built. Njimi was retaken from the Bulala, but never reoccupied. Idrīs Alawma, *c.* 1580–1610, whose biography by his *imām*, Ibn Fartuwa, survives, is our most detailed example (though perhaps not otherwise the most important) of these Bornu *mais*. He cultivated the north: an embassy went to Tripoli, a large caravan brought horses to Bornu, Alawma went on Pilgrimage and founded a pilgrim hostel. Guns came from the north. Alawma's wars were many and ferocious. Men were killed (save the Bulala, who were Muslims and kinsmen); women and children, usually, saved alive as slaves. Alawma supplemented war with the destruction of crops and trees, enlisting even *'ulamā'* for this, encouraging the work with music and dancers. Sometimes Ramaḍān is singled out as an efficacious time for fighting. Ibn Fartuwa cites the example of Muḥammad's wars. Alawma acted sternly against moral offences; the *Sharī'a* was more generally applied; disputes were referred to *qāḍīs*, no longer to chiefs or the *mai*. Brick mosques replaced thatch. Weights and measures were standardized. People were encouraged to settle and farm.

The eleventh/seventeenth and twelfth/eighteenth centuries were a period of decline. Hausa dominated the Saharan trade. Tuareg pressure increased. The Jukun raided from the south: there are many Jukun stories of Jukun magic pitted against Bornu Islam, the honours always equally divided. The last three rulers before the Fulani *jihād* took refuge in religion and paternity.

Hausa

Hausa, like Kanem, experienced the imposition of nomadic immigration (perhaps associated with the unsuccessful revolt of Abū Yazīd, the Kharijite of the Zanāta, against the Fatimids in the fourth/tenth century) upon an earlier Negro population. Hausa society then developed in relative isolation until the eighth/fourteenth century.

Then the situation altered. The settled city states, characteristic of Hausa from an early date, began to jostle one another. Mali's power was felt in Hausa. And from Mali came Islam: Mandingo immigrants converted the rulers of Kano and Katsina, main trade centres, in the early eighth/fourteenth century.

In Kano, the first Muslims apparently observed prayer, slaughtering regulations, and burial rites. The mosque was built under the sacred tree. Despite this conciliatory gesture, the guardians of the pagan heritage defiled the mosque each night, until struck blind through special prayers of the Muslims.

Yaji, ruler of Kano, perhaps impressed with the punishing power of prayer, enlisted Muslim support in war to the south. The military and political utility of '*ulamā*' to the Hausa rulers (for which rulers sometimes paid handsomely) continues clear until 'Uthmān dan Fodio's conquest. And when Islam seemed ineffectual, the ruler might restore paganism, as Kanajeji b. Yaji did in his war against Zaria. The basic pattern however is not alternation between two extremes, but the judicious counterpoint beloved of the 'mixers.' '*Ulamā*' served also as peace-makers, interceding with invaders to prevent the destruction of cities, or arranging a truce between warring states.

Islam came to Hausa first from Mali. Western religious influence persisted, partly through the Pilgrimage. In the ninth/fifteenth century, for example, Fulani '*ulamā*' brought books on theology and grammar to Kano, and passed on to Bornu. '*Ulamā*' came to Hausa from Bornu-Kanem also, and from North Africa. Political influence was more from the east. By 1400, the Sefawa had moved to Bornu, west of Lake Chad, and Mali was declining. A Bornu prince took refuge in Kano in the ninth/fifteenth century, introducing among other things the first market. Bornu soon brought Kano under tribute, to control the dissident branch of the Bornu dynasty there. Kano, despite occasional wars with Bornu, became the main channel for Bornu influence upon Hausa. Bornu and Songhay struggled to control Hausa. Under Askiya al-Ḥājj Muḥammad, Songhay apparently triumphed, but briefly. The revolt of Kebbi disrupted Songhay communications. Bornu predominance in Hausa revived until the twelfth/eighteenth century.

From Bornu, it seems, Hausa learnt ceremonious despotism. Muḥammad Rumfa, ruler of Kano (late ninth/fifteenth century), first applied Bornu examples wholeheartedly: state councils, eunuchs in high office, a palace, another market, royal regalia, slaving, forced labour and the requisition of property. Subsequent rulers enlarged their prerogatives. In the eleventh/seventeenth century *jangali*, cattle-tax on Fulani, began. In the twelfth/eighteenth, one ruler of Kano taxed '*ulamā*'.

Some of these developments towards centralized authoritarian government were almost certainly associated with Islam. At the same time, several incidents suggest that Hausa shared the continuing, if often impotent, awareness of tension between faith and kingship. 'Umaru b. Kanajeji (early ninth/fifteenth century), once an '*ālim* earnest in prayer, succeeded to the Kano throne. His friend, Abū Bakr, upbraided him, and went to Bornu for some years. 'Umaru ruled well and peacefully. Then Abū Bakr returned, warning of the snares of this world and punishment hereafter. So 'Umaru abdicated, and led a life of penitence. Again, in the tenth/sixteenth century, a deposed ruler of Kano refused to resume the throne even when asked, preferring study among the *'ulamā'*. Again, an eleventh/seventeenth century prince, fearing civil war after his father's death, prayed for his own death, and was heard. Other rulers were so occupied with religious affairs that they were unable to govern effectively. Many, of course, combined faith and rule without qualms.

This awareness seems less vivid east of Hausa. Only here and there do traces appear. A sixth/twelfth century Kanemi *mai* was imprisoned by his mother for executing a thief instead of administering the Qur'anic punishment. He also elaborated royal ceremonial: several Arab writers describe the *mais* screened from public view, their subjects prostrate before them. Alawma's biographer that '...a king's justice quotes the dictum for one day is equal to service of God for sixty years.'[1] For its effectiveness, or its rarity? Might this apparent difference—granting the evidence for it is fragmentary—be associated with the fact that two main groups disseminating Islam in the west, Berbers and Fulani, were in some sense opposition groups, Berbers against Arabs, Fulani against Negroes, while eastwards the example of Middle Eastern Muslim despotism was more pervasive?

Bagirmi and Waday

In the tenth/sixteenth century, states began to emerge in Bagirmi and Waday. The Kenga dynasty in Bagirmi, originally pagan, became Muslim later in the century when 'Abd Allāh ousted his elder brother. 'Abd Allāh's government resembled the Bornu monarchy—he was probably a contemporary of Alawma—but Bagirmi Islam apparently derived from Fulani *'ulamā'* who had entered the country (together with cattlemen) even before the Kenga.

In Waday, the Tunjur dynasty may have been superficially Muslim, but was overthrown in the early eleventh/seventeenth century by 'Abd al-Karīm, perhaps originally of the Nilotic Ja'aliyyūn: he claimed 'Abbasid descent. According to one tradition, 'Abd al-Karīm learnt a

[1] Ahmed ibn Fartua (tr. H. R. Palmer), *History of ... the reign of Mai Idris Alooma of Bornu* (1571–1583) (Lagos, 1926), 9–10.

more ardent faith from the Fulani *'ulamā'* in Bagirmi: according to another, his uncle or father, a pioneer preacher in Waday, inspired him: yet another says that he displaced the leading *'ālim* in Waday (the ancestor of the Kapka Zaghāwa) by removing and reburying a tablet of Qur'anic inscriptions. 'Abd al-Karīm founded the capital, Wara; North African builders may have helped him and his successors.

The political history of Bagirmi and Waday in the eleventh/seventeenth and twelfth/eighteenth centuries centred on resistance to powerful neighbours, Bornu and Darfur. In the later twelfth/eighteenth century, both Bagirmi and Waday succeeded. The ruler of Bagirmi then, Muḥammad al-Amīn, went on Pilgrimage, usually a sign of security. Despite wars, pupils and *'ulamā'* continued to move about. *'Ulamā'* went between Bagirmi and Hausa, perhaps as early as the third quarter of the sixteenth century. Refugee *'ulamā'* from Bornu about 1600 went both to Hausa and Bagirmi. Waday looked east: teachers and traders came there from the Funj kingdom of Sennar, and pupils went to the Nile from Waday.

The Moroccan conquest and the rule of the pashas

Disagreement over the Saharan salt-mines, even fighting, continued between Morocco and Songhay throughout the sixteenth century. It came to a head under the Sa'did Sultan Aḥmad al-Manṣūr (986–1012/1578–1603), son of a Negro concubine. He reopened negotiations with Songhay about the mines, fortified with legal opinions from his *'ulamā'*. In 992/1584 a Moroccan embassy, perhaps a reconnaissance, visited Songhay with rich gifts. In 996/1588, Askiya Isḥāq II ascended the throne. Al-Manṣūr renewed his claims. The *askiya* defied him. Al-Manṣūr, pointing to the wealth of Songhay, and adding that the *askiya*, not being a Qurayshite, had no right to rule, persuaded his notables to support an expeditionary force. In Dhu'l-Ḥijja 998/October 1590, the expedition marched, about 4,000 troops, mostly Spanish musketeers. The muskets were to prove decisive.

Divided counsels ruled in Songhay. A suggestion of the Timbuktu *'ulamā'*, that their city be evacuated south of the Niger, was rejected, since *'ulamā'*, though scholarly, cannot plan war.[1] Jawdhar Pasha, the Spanish renegade commander, advanced on Gao, calling on the *askiya* to

[1] This may reflect a widespread attitude—among Somali, for example, *wadāds* or men of religion have usually only limited influence in political counsels, but are pre-eminent in making peace and reconciling enemies.

acknowledge the sultan, the *Sharīf*, his sovereign. Isḥāq refused. In Jumādā I 999/March 1591 the armies met at Tundibi. During the battle, the *askiya-alfa*, apparently a senior *'ālim* in Isḥāq's service, succeeded after several attempts in persuading the *askiya* to flee. Isḥāq's departure signalled the disintegration of the Songhay army. Only a picked *élite*, who had bound calf to thigh at the beginning, remained and were slaughtered, vainly protesting that they were Muslims. Isḥāq abandoned Gao, leaving only the *khaṭīb* to receive Jawdhar. Jawdhar, finding Gao poor and unhealthy, withdrew to Timbuktu, where he was received quietly by the *qāḍī*, and built a fortress in the Ghadames merchants' quarter.

Some of the Songhay forces abandoned the fleeing Isḥāq, and set up his brother, Muḥammad Gao, as usurper *askiya*. Muḥammad Gao's reign was brief and distracted. His main advisers were the *askiya-alfa*, Bukar, and the *hi-koy* or admiral of the river fleet, Laha Sorkia, representing the older semi-pagan tradition. Time and again, Laha Sorkia counselled resistance, Bukar collaboration. Muḥammad Gao followed Bukar's advice. Finally, the usurper and his colleagues, under safe conduct, were murdered by the Moroccans. Only Bukar went free. The Moroccans set up a third brother as puppet. The *askiya-alfa* seems to have played a traitor's part; perhaps Islam generally, appealing to a literate, urban class, divided the Songhay nation against itself.

In Dhu'l-Ḥijja 999/October 1591, fighting broke out in Timbuktu: the Moroccan garrison lost many killed. What part the Timbuktu *'ulamā'* played is not clear: it is difficult to imagine a general outbreak without at least the tacit approval of 'Umar, the *qāḍī*. This was the opinion of Maḥmūd Zarghūn Pasha, Jawdhar's replacement, and he wrote reproachfully to 'Umar.

Peace was restored, but in 1593 Maḥmūd Zarghūn summoned the *'ulamā'* of Timbuktu to renew their oath of allegiance. Once gathered in the Sankore mosque, they were arrested. In a scuffle outside, some *'ulamā'* were killed. Several others, the *qāḍī* and the celebrated Aḥmad Bābā among them, all apparently of the 'Aqīt family, were exiled to Marrakesh.

Later Aḥmad Bābā was granted an interview with al-Manṣūr. Finding al-Manṣūr concealed behind a curtain, Aḥmad Bābā refused to talk with him, complaining that by speaking without being seen, al-Manṣūr was imitating God. The curtain was removed. Aḥmad Bābā taught in the mosque at Marrakesh, and even gave *fatwās*, but he never accepted appointment as *muftī*. In 1016/1608 he returned to Timbuktu, alone; in 1036/1627 he died. Among his writings is a book on the avoidance of unjust rulers.

Songhay resistance continued downstream, towards Dendi, under Nūḥ, legitimate successor to Isḥāq who was killed. The Moroccans suffered through illness and guerilla warfare in the forests. Maḥmūd was killed. In 1007/1599 Askiya Nūḥ was deposed, and Jawdhar Pasha recalled to Morocco: vigorous campaigning ceased on either side. Northern Songhay remained under the Moroccans; Dendi, divided into several chieftaincies, continued independent.

The usual explanation today of the Moroccan conquest is economic. Certainly al-Manṣūr wanted gold, but the formal justification for conquest, in the letters of al-Manṣūr and Maḥmūd, was religious. When Aḥmad Bābā charged al-Manṣūr with aggression, the sultan replied that he, as a *sharīf*, wished to unit the Islamic world. For a time, the sultan of Morocco controlled his new province directly, making all principal appointments himself. But close supervision across the desert was impossible. Moreover, income from Songhay did not justify the heavy cost in men, money and supplies. The Moroccans had not conquered the gold-fields: even in Timbuktu they had to trade for gold, and trade depended on peaceful conditions. The most interesting item of income, in its religious consequences, was an elephant, whose Negro keepers are said to have introduced tobacco to Morocco, thus igniting the agitated controversy about the legality of smoking.

Morocco gradually lost interest. One of the last acts done at the sultan's order was in 1035/1626, when a senior Moroccan official was tortured to death in Timbuktu. In 1070/1659–60, the *khuṭba* ceased to be recited in the sultan's name. Occasional embassies from Morocco continued. As late as 1893 Timbuktu appealed to these ancient links, for help against the French, but in vain.

The pashalic of Timbuktu quickly became an elective office dependent on the will of the army. By 1750, nearly a hundred pashas had ruled, many several times, as compared with sixteen puppet *askiyas*, and only eleven Timbuktu *qāḍīs* despite an average age of well over fifty on appointment. The pashas collected taxes, but did not interfere with local institutions.

Timbuktu under the *askiyas* had been a religious citadel. *'Ulamā'* continued to serve the pashas, reconciling adversaries, administering an ineffectual oath of peace to a Tuareg chief, and so on. Yet, though it was thought irregular for a pasha directly to appoint a *qāḍī*, it seems that *'ulamā'* did not enjoy much independence of status. Violation of sanctuary at a saint's tomb, but not at the *imām*'s house, was visited by divine vengeance. *'Ulamā'* were faint-hearted in proclaiming the law. Occasional pashas refused alms to *'ulamā'*.

Islam was in some ways strictly observed. Al-Bukhārī was read to the pasha in Ramaḍān. The Prophet's Birthday was especially gaily celebrated. Free women were secluded. One pasha tried to apply *jihād* rules in his wars, but his officials concealed the enemy's acceptance of his appeal to be converted and submit, so that the attack might proceed. Later a rival preached *jihād* against this same pasha.

Relations between conquerors and conquered improved. But vassal revolts and enemy attacks soon restricted effective control by the pashalic to the main centres, Jenne, Gao and Timbuktu. Mali, now once more a chieftaincy only, attacked Jenne in 1007/1599, but was beaten off: the last convulsion of a long overshadowed empire. The Fulani of Masina raided, a portent of their future heritage. In the twelfth/eighteenth century particularly, Tuareg harrassed the pashas, and at last occupied both Gao (1770) and Timbuktu (1787). Nevertheless the Arma (Ar., *al-rumāh*, the shooters), descendants of the Moroccan invaders, are still an influential caste.

The Bambara

Following the Moroccan conquest of Songhay, a new power rose to dominate much of the western Sudan—the Bambara. These are a Mande-speaking people, centred on the upper Niger valley, once subject to Mali, then to Songhay. In the eleventh/seventeenth century, independent but not yet organized in states, they grew in strength. Mamari Kulubali (1712–55) founded the main Bambara state, Segu, while dissidents established Karta. Masina, even Timbuktu paid tribute to Mamari.

It was the essential religious characteristic of the Bambara, sometimes regarded as the champions of paganism, that Islamic elements were absorbed without displacing the pagan. The Bambara are an excellent, if extreme, example of the 'mixers.'

'Ulamā' were active in court life, helping to arbitrate in succession disputes, advising rulers, healing, reconciling officials and kings. Da, king of Segu (1808–27), in whose time arose Shehu Aḥmadu, had been warned by a local *sharīf* not to provoke the Muslims. Rulers themselves became at least superficially Muslim, another branch of their spiritual repertory.

Some, as the Kulubali clan, regarded themselves as Muslim: when al-Ḥājj'Umar called the king of Karta to conversion, he, holding himself already a Muslim, interpreted this as an ultimatum and killed the messenger. But Islam must not compromise clan independence: this was the mistake of Turo-koro Mari, king of Segu (1854–6), for which he paid with his life. Popular religion, observing Muslim festivals as honouring ancestors, employing Muslim and pagan divination, and so forth shows the same pattern. Certain tribal groups within Bambara country, all linked with ancient Soninke Islam, are particularly fervent Muslims.

The Mande dispersion

Dominant among the diverse, widespread, Mande peoples at this time were the Bambara, little influenced by Islam. But a simultaneous Mande dispersion begun long before, west and south to the Atlantic, east across the savannah, was profoundly significant for Islam.

Different Mande groups took part, including pagan cultivators. The traders, however, commonly called *dyula*, were Muslim. So of course were the *'ulamā'*, esteemed by Muslims for whom they provided Qur'anic schools and other services, and by pagans whom they served as diviners, advisers, and so forth. Traders and clerics were complementary. Amulets were an important trade good. Supernatural authority safeguarded the commercial traveller: Owen, an eighteenth-century slave-trader in Sierra Leone called the Mande '. . . wandering pilgrims, who for their holyness is suffer'd to pass and repass, where others would not.'[1] A Mande emigrant (later a great chief under the Bambara king N'golo), intending to trade in Segu, found conditions too unsettled for commerce but did very well with making amulets.

Forms of settlement differed. Jobson, trading on the Gambia in the early seventeenth century, described Muslim towns as carefully separated from the pagan. Muslims married only among themselves. Such towns were staging points for travellers: Mahome, a particular friend of Jobson, '. . . did diverse times lodge and entertain strangers, that came, especially of his own profession. . .'[2] Larger commercial centres grew up in the savannah, as Kankan in upper Guinea, Kong in the Ivory Coast, and further east. Without separation, Muslims might be absorbed utterly by the local environment. Sometimes Mande immigrants became chiefs over local people. Such chiefs might abandon their original

[1] Nicholas Owen, *Journal of a Slave-Dealer* (London, 1930), 56–7.
[2] Richard Jobson, *The Golden Trade* (London, 1932), 93–4.

Islam; elsewhere Muslim chiefs ruled pagan commoners. Trading agents introduced by Europeans, or *'ulamā'* introduced by local chiefs, might become chiefs.

Trade was generally peaceful, but violence occasionally marked the city states. A Mande revolution founded Kong about 1730. Kankan was temporarily destroyed about 1765. Susu (a Mande people) seized Port Loko from the Temne, who regained it (under another Susu leader) about 1816. Mande rivals fought on the Liberian plateau and elsewhere. Refugees fled to new districts: Islam was further diffused.

B. THE WESTERN AND CENTRAL SUDAN IN THE EIGHTEENTH AND NINETEENTH CENTURIES

Introduction

The twelfth/eighteenth century was the birth time of the theocracies, which in a series of revolutions engulfed almost the whole Sudan before European control was imposed. For the most part, the relationships among these, and between them and the wider world of Islam, are obscure. It is tempting to postulate direct Wahhābī influence, but where our knowledge is sufficient to judge this seems unfounded. In 1784 the thirteenth Islamic century began. There was an air of apocalyptic expectancy, but no eminent leader in west or central Sudan emerged as *mahdī*. Two principles underlie reformist doctrine. First, 'mixing' is forbidden. Those who combine pagan and Muslim practices are infidels. And second, as no accommodation between infidel and Muslim practices is permissible, so there can be no association between infidel and Muslim people. An infidel king means an infidel kingdom, and *hijra*, emigration, is obligatory for Muslim citizens of such a kingdom. Between emigrant and stay-at-home Muslims there are no signs of love. The property of stay-at-homes may be confiscated; and, *hijra* should lead to *jihād*. Equally an alliance between an infidel and a Muslim ruler convicts both of infidelity. These two principles, that 'mixers' are infidels and that those who associate with 'mixers' are infidels, are related, whether as cause or effect, to the fact that the *jihāds* were mainly against professing Muslims.

A political revolution complemented the doctrinal. Everywhere the reformers established states, usually incorporating smaller, former states. The Fulani, and the closely related Torodbe, the Tokolor religious class from which both 'Uthmān and al-Ḥājj 'Umar came, were the chief agents. Spreading from the ancient area of Takrūr on the Senegal, they entered Masina perhaps in the fifteenth century, and reached Bagirmi and Adamawa in the 18th. In Futa Toro and Masina, the reformers overthrew existing Fulani dynasties, but certain rules of the game here moderated war among brothers.

The Fulani everywhere were immigrants, sometimes of centuries' standing, sometimes nineteenth-century invaders. Al-Ḥājj 'Umar and al-Kanamī were both foreigners, relying on imported troops. It was an age of Islamic imperialism. Only the later leaders, Samori for example and Lat Dior, appear as nationalists, often in response to European encroachment, and their purely Islamic fervour is in doubt.

Thus the reformed faith, and the revolutionary government, spread over the western and central Sudan, recoiling at the forest beyond Ilorin, at the European presence on the Senegal, at the turbulence of desert nomads around Timbuktu, or where the distance was too great in Bornu and beyond.

Futa Jallon

Militant Islam first revived in Futa Jallon, the highlands where the Senegal and Gambia rivers rise, an area of mixed peoples among whom the Solima were important. In the eleventh/seventeenth century Fulani pastoralists, with *'ulamā'*, began entering Futa Jallon. In 1725, Ibrāhīm Mūsā, a Fulani cleric, took the title *almami* (*al-imām*) and proclaimed against the local rulers *jihād*. About 1776, Ibrāhīm Sori, the Fulani war-leader, himself now *almami*, ended the *jihād*.

Politically, the imamate of Futa Jallon failed. Civil strife was endemic. Finally the descendants of the two Ibrāhīms agreed that the office of *almami* should alternate between them every two years, a precarious arrangement. Yet Futa Jallon had considerable religious influence. The half-century of war encouraged many Muslims, individuals and groups, to move south and west. Pagan tributaries of Futa Jallon learnt of Islam. Most important perhaps, Futa Jallon was a centre of education. The Mandingo king of Forecaria studied there: so also Sulaymān Bal of Futa Toro: a prudent Sierra Leone ruler in 1769 sent one son to learn from the Christians, another to Futa Jallon.

Among some, the sword earned hatred not submission. The Solima, at first allies of the Fulani, their leaders converted to Islam, later broke with Fulani domination. Driven from Futa Jallon, the Solima founded a new capital, Falaba, to the south. Every trace of Islam was abandoned, even Muslim dress, even fashion—Solima women now wore a gold earring in the left ear only, '... in which they will sometimes carry two or even three, in order to show that it is not poverty but purpose, and as a distinction from the women of Fouth Jallon'.[1]

Even here, the power of education held. The king of Falaba in 1822 still cherished the Islam he had learnt in his youth in Futa Jallon, though because of popular feeling he had now to pray secretly. Falaba preserved its independence till crushed by Samori in 1884.

Futa Toro

The Fulani Denyanke dynasty ruled Futa Toro, on the middle Senegal, from the tenth/sixteenth century. At first with strong Mandingo connections, and probably Muslim, the Denyanke later became identified with a pagan Fulani aristocracy, contrasted with the Muslim, more racially mixed, Futa Toro Tokolor. Yet Denyanke princes continued to study under *'ulamā'* in the *Sāḥil*; one *'ālim*, a *sharīf*, healed and converted a Denyanke ruler, father of his pupil.

After the *jihād* began in Futa Jallon, Sulaymān Bal, a Futa Toro *'ālim*, went there to study. He asked his teachers to invoke God against the Denyanke. Once more in Futa Toro, Sulaymān won disciples. He disquieted the Denyanke, but did not attack them. Instead, he fought the Trārza Moors, traditional scourge of the valley.

After seven years' war, he announced that an *almami* should rule Futa Toro. His followers acclaimed him *almami*, but he refused. So did the next popular choice. Finally 'Abd al-Qādir, a Tokolor of reputed Qurashī ancestry, reluctantly accepted, though he was not invested until 1189/1775–6, after Sulaymān had fallen fighting the Trārza.

'Abd al-Qādir continued the Trārza wars, adding civil war and war to the south. In the civil war, aided by a disputed succession, the religious party overthrew the Denyanke. Even so, the Denyanke refrained from murdering 'Abd al-Qādir when they once might, and 'Abd al-Qādir reserved an enclave where a Denyanke *almami* might rule.

In the southern wars, 'Abd al-Qādir fought Futa Bundu, where another *almami* ruled. 'Abd al-Qādir captured and killed him. A Moor, who had come to the Negroes seeking purer religion, returned in disgust at this murder of a Muslim. Attacking the Wolof state of Cayor, 'Abd

[1] A. G. Laing, *Travels ... in western Africa* (London, 1825), 359.

al-Qādir was captured, but was released in respect for his supernatural powers. About 1805, 'Abd al-Qādir faced revolt at home, attacks from abroad. Warned by '*ulamā*' that his salvation was assured only if he was killed on his own soil by his own people, he asked a shaykh to pray for this. 'Abd al-Qādir was killed, some say by the new *almami* of Futa Bundu.

The imamate continued until the French occupation, a religious Tokolor aristocracy supplanting the Denyanke warriors. Elections rivalled the Timbuktu pashas: one *almami* ruled nine or ten times. Al-Ḥājj 'Umar's visits in mid-century increased confusion.

'Uthmān dan Fodio

'Uthmān was born in Gobir in 1167/1754, of a family of scholars. His early life was spent in study, travelling from one teacher to another. One of the most important was Jibrīl b. 'Umar, by oral tradition a Hausa, who initiated him in the Qādiriyya order. Jibrīl had already alarmed the Hausa kings by preaching reform, even attempting *jihād*. About 1775, 'Uthmān began preaching and teaching himself, wandering widely in Kebbi, Zanfara and elsewhere.

'Uthmān's prestige soon attracted the attention of the kings. Oral tradition says he became court tutor under Bawa, king of Gobir. Written records, on the contrary, portray 'Uthmān as very much apart, cautioning his followers not to go to the kings of this world. When Bawa summoned the '*ulamā*' to Magami in the late 1780s, 'Uthmān attended, but he and his party (unlike the other '*ulamā*') refused the royal alms. This meeting may perhaps have been to ask prayers for the forthcoming campaign against Katsina, after which Bawa died of grief at the death of his son. In the contrast between the oral and written reports, the former, reflecting popular conservatism, seems to stress continuity between the old and new régimes, while the latter, reflecting official apologia, favours the 'new broom' interpretation. Both versions may indeed be correct for different stages in 'Uthmān's career.

In the early 1790s, 'Uthmān settled at Degel in Gobir. Tension mounted. 'Uthmān and his brother 'Abd Allāh wrote religious poetry of great popular effect. The Timbuktu Kunta sent a friendly emissary. 'Uthmān instructed his people to begin arming. The Gobir king attempted to curb the growing independence of 'Uthmān's party, the *Jamā'a*, by forbidding emblems such as the turban and the woman's veil. Fighting broke out between the Hausa *'ālim*, 'Abd al-Salām, a partisan of 'Uthmān, and Yunfa king of Gobir. Yunfa threatened Degel. In February 1804, 'Uthmān and the *Jamā'a* emigrated to Gudu, on the Gobir border.

The emigrants began raiding. The kings began persecuting their Muslim subjects. The first main battle was at Kwotto water, 'Abd Allāh defeating the Gobir forces. Hausa and Fulani fought on both sides, Tuareg also aiding Gobir. After this, 'Uthmān established a new base in Zanfara, then friendly because of vivid recollections of recent war with Gobir. Later, violent resistance to 'Uthmān arose in Zanfara. The tribal character of the *jihād* is debated. Official Fulani apologetic may neglect the contribution of Hausa Muslims. Doctrine, seeking general principles, sometimes reinforced tribal distinctions: 'Uthmān ruled that the enslavement of any Fulani was wrong because most Fulani were Muslim; and that all Hausa kings might be overthrown, despite the rare serious Muslim among them. Very rare were Hausa holding military or political office in the *jihād*; a few achieved religious eminence; there may have been some popular support by Hausa Muslim commoners.

The fighting spread. *'Ulamā'* and warriors hurried to 'Uthmān, received banners from him, and returned to lead the *Jamā'a* in their various homes. The fall of the Gobir capital in 1808 meant that the *jihād* was out of danger. Reformed Islam, under Fulani *amīrs*, spread over most of Hausaland and beyond.

The reformed doctrine, sometimes assumed to be Wahhābī, may have had a medieval inspiration.[1] In constitutional theory, the Fulani empire was much more complex than the Medinese *umma*: the sources quoted are often late 'Abbasid. In doctrine, the Fulani respected *ijmā'*; for example, the Fulani attitude towards tomb observances, though puritan, was milder than the Wahhābī. The Fulani were scrupulous about Mālikī orthodoxy: they did not become schismatic. Jibrīl, twice on Pilgrimage, may have been more Wahhābī: 'Uthmān, his son Bello, and 'Abd Allāh were never in Mecca.

The Fulani were deeply concerned with doctrinal precedent. Their writings, largely imitative, were not, however, entirely so. 'Uthmān denied that Muslims through grave disobedience became unbelievers, thus differing, though respectfully, from Jibrīl. Bello affirmed that

[1] M. Hiskett, 'An Islamic tradition of reform . . .', in *BSOAS*, 1962 (3), 577–96.

Muslims helping unbelievers in war against Muslims became unbelievers, 'Abd Allāh denied it. Disputing an opinion of Aḥmad Bābā, 'Uthmān said every scholar decides according to the knowledge of his own time.

The basic argument was not with paganism, but with the 'mixers'. Al-Maghīlī's strictures on Sonni 'Alī were repeatedly cited. 'Abd Allāh argued that the similarity between fifteenth-century Songhay and eighteenth-century Hausa made the *jihād* legal.

Fulani political theory condemned many practices then current. Kings were criticised for abusing the rights of women; but social freedom for women was also reproved. Discipline of women was a favourite point of reformers: a Bornu *'ālim* once objected to women attending 'Uthmān's public preaching. Fines in place of Qur'anic punishments were condemned. Royal titles, royal music, abject reverence to royalty, all came under the ban; customary inheritance and uncanonical taxation likewise. Among the objectionable taxes were the *jangali* or cattle tax, and a tax on meat at the market. Complaints about commandeering livestock, and about penalties for stray animals, confirm a cattle-owning strand among the reformers.

In place of the fractious Hausa kingdoms, 'Uthmān proposed a united polity, the *Jamā'a*, under the *amīr al-mu'minīn*. The *wazīrs* should wake the ruler if he sleeps, make him see if he is blind, remind him if he forgets. Other officials, particularly *qāḍīs*, are specified. All officials should strive for justice and compassion. A good deal of 'Uthmān's political writing attempts the proper regulation of *jihād*.

What happened in practice? After the fall of Alkalawa (1808), 'Uthmān left practical affairs mainly to 'Abd Allāh in the west, and Bello in the east, Gwandu and Sokoto becoming the respective capitals. Was 'Uthmān perhaps already distressed by the materialism of the *jihād*? There is a report that his declining years were haunted by remorse for the many Muslims he had killed. 'Abd Allāh certainly had serious doubts: even while marching on Alkalawa, suddenly filled with revulsion at the selfishness of his colleagues, he started off for Mecca. In fact he went only to Kano. Later, when Bello ousted 'Abd Allāh for the succession to 'Uthmān (d. 1817), 'Abd Allāh overcame in scholarship his disappointment.

Bello's succession signalled widespread Hausa revolts. Indeed, some areas of Hausa resistance continued in arms throughout the century. The Fulani rulers found it politic to compromise with Hausa traditions of government, while they also quarrelled among themselves.

Adamawa

Pastoral Fulani, mainly from Bornu, probably arrived in northern Adamawa in numbers only in the later eighteenth century. Perhaps for this reason, they still speak their own language, and are relatively distinct racially. Few strong, organized societies existed to check their encroachment. Even before the *jihād*, several Fulani lamidates (i.e. amirates) were founded, often peacefully.

Modibbo Adama—he refused out of humility the title *lamido* (i.e. *amīr*)—was born in northern Adamawa, studied in Bornu, and became a teacher. Visiting Sokoto, he received a flag for Adamawa from 'Uthmān, to the chagrin of some who already ruled parts of the country. In 1809, Adama proclaimed *jihād*.

The main early conquests were north of the Benue: important was the Marwa plain, south of Mandara, rich in horses. The sultans of Mandara had been converted early in the eighteenth century, it is said through '*ulamā*' from Fez returning from Mecca. Faith did not save Mandara: Adama occupied the capital. But his troops quickly forgot religion for plunder. Adama, dismayed by their greed, prayed that the Mandarans might regain their city. His prayer was answered. The Fulani were expelled. Mandara was later a buffer between Bornu and Adamawa.

Adama's own campaigns were principally north and east, where Fulani had already penetrated. The plateau country to the south had first to be invaded, then conquered. Begun about 1825, this was speedily accomplished.

Little is known of early Adamawan Islam. Amulets and charms were widespread in Barth's time (1851). Friday and festival prayers were favoured occasions for important announcements—concerning forthcoming expeditions, or the succession—even for capturing an intractable *lamido*.

Adama died in 1848. Four sons succeeded him. Open dissensions among the lamidates appeared. Tibati in particular, defied neighbours and Yola, the capital of Adamawa, alike.

Yola paid tribute to Sokoto, and important questions, often concerning succession, were referred thither. Yola in turn received tribute from lesser lamidates. The Fulani lived in towns and settlements, like colonies; even those with town residences were often absent with herds and flocks. Hausa became increasingly important, exploring new areas through trade, working as artisans, acting as financiers for the *lamidos*.

Kanuri, Shuwa, and some local people closely allied to the Fulani, also shared free Muslim status. Other local people were dependent tributaries. Still others resisted: fighting continued into the twentieth century. There were large slave settlements.

Adamawa was a principal slave reserve. Recaptives far away in Sierra Leone told of Fulani slaving there. Tribute to Sokoto was mainly slaves: often, Sokoto agents came to collect these. Drafts on Yola for slaves were given and honoured. About 1852 a *sharīf*, al-Ḥabīb, came to Sokoto begging. He was given letters for horses in Zaria, and for 200 slaves in Adamawa, which he collected. Later he was involved in Kano politics. Occasionally the demand, external and internal, for slaves so increased that even Fulani, even *'ulamā'*, were enslaved.

Nupe and Yoruba

References to Nupe begin in Hausaland with the eighth/fourteenth century. In the ninth/fifteenth, Nupe exported eunuchs and kola, and imported horses. Later, even guns came from Nupe. Bawa of Gobir exchanged horses and *vedettes* for Nupe slaves and cowries. Bello remarked on the strange and beautiful merchandize of Nupe. Islam probably penetrated with trade, affecting Yoruba as well as Nupe. In the 1580s, an *'ālim* from Nupe is said to have healed a quarrel between king and nobles in Yoruba. A little later, a Katsina *'ālim* wrote in answer to questions from Yoruba *'ulamā'*. The first recorded Muslim ruler (*etsu*) of Nupe is in the twelfth/eighteenth century. With the *jihād*, Islam became more thrusting. Fulani *'ulamā'* and cattlemen had already penetrated Nupe. A court *'ālim*, Mallam Dendo, who became a flag-bearer of 'Uthmān, confirmed Fulani influence by exploiting a disputed succession. The Fulani were few, so Dendo maintained puppet Nupe *etsus*. His son, 'Uthmān Zākī, 1832–59, was the first Fulani *etsu*. Later, disputes among Fulani dynasties led to interventions by Gwandu.

In Yoruba, groups were already splitting from the old Oyo empire, and Dahomey was raiding. About 1817, the Oyo governor of Ilorin, Afonja, revolted, supported by a Yoruba Muslim chief, Alimi a Fulani *'ālim* (whence probably his name), and by Muslim bands, Yoruba, Hausa and Fulani, which were encouraged to come to Ilorin. Traditions differ about Alimi: was he devout, anxious to curb his supporters, refusing a chieftancy; or did he aim at political power? His son, 'Abd al-Salām, who succeeded him in 1833, and whose prayers had formerly helped Afonja against Oyo, did seek power. Afonja fought, but too late. He was killed. Ilorin became the south-western bastion of the Fulani, as Adamawa the south-eastern.

The Yoruba retreated south from old Oyo. The Fulani boasted of dipping the Qur'ān in the Atlantic. Internecine war, fostered by the Fulani, racked Yoruba. Slaving was widespread: in 1852 Muslim traders, mainly in slaves, were in Ibadan, and highly regarded. But 'Abd al-Salām died in 1842; the Fulani were checked in 1843; and Ibadan, triumphant in 1862 over its main Yoruba rival, emerged the scourge of its neighbours and a barricade against the Fulani.

Bornu, Bagirmi and Waday

Eastward 'Uthmān's *jihād* met Muslim resistance. The Fulani, long infiltrating western Bornu, responded to 'Uthmān's inspiration; fighting broke out between them and the *mai*. Twice the Bornu capital, Ngazargamu, fell to Fulani religious warriors; twice the fleeing *mai* appealed to Muḥammad al-Amīn al-Kanamī, a Kanembu *'ālim* recently returned from Mecca; twice al-Kanamī repulsed the Fulani. Al-Kanamī, maintaining a puppet *mai*, founded a new capital, Kukawa, on the spot where he once finished reading the Qur'ān, his habit when travelling.

The *mais* were powerless against their dominating saviour. Al-Kanami's favourite troops were his Kanembu spearsmen. Shuwa and Arabs were among other foreigners whom he encouraged to settle, and in whom he placed chief reliance. Al-Kanamī's sword was not temporal only: a vision called him to war with the Fulani.

The *mais* chafed. In 1817 a conspiracy between the *mai* and Bagirmi, against al-Kanamī, failed. Further fighting followed. In 1824 al-Kanamī, invoking 'Abdal-Qādir, and helped by British cannon, crushed Bagirmi at Ngala. Emboldened, he turned west and marched on Kano. The *amīr* of Bauchi (who before the battle put 200 men to guard his concubines, lest in defeat they disperse and he be thought poor) threw him back in 1826. Thereafter, despite raiding and subversion, spheres of influence were apparently observed between Sokoto and Kukawa.

Al-Kanamī died in 1835 or 1837; his son 'Umar succeeded. 'Umar made peace with Bagirmi, his mother's country. Henceforth the main rivals were Bornu and Waday, often fighting over a prostrate and ravaged Kanem. Bagirmi was a slave reservoir. In 1846 the *mais* made a last attempt to regain authority with help from Waday, but failed. The last Sefawa fell in battle. 'Umar became official, as well as effective, ruler.

In 1856–7 Sharīf al-Dīn, a Fulani ascetic, passed slowly through Bornu towards Mecca. 'Abd al-Qādir, king of Bagirmi, tried to prevent him entering Bagirmi, first by persuasion, then by force. Sharīf al-Dīn, accompanied by many thousands of pilgrims, possessed of such supernatural resource that some called him *mahdī*, defeated and killed 'Abd al-Qādir. Sharīf al-Dīn went on, his following growing, and with it problems of discipline and supply. Some pilgrims turned back: one of 'Abd al-Qādir's sons took vengeance on these, hence his nickname *Abū Sikkīn*, 'father of a knife'. Then Sharīf al-Dīn himself was killed, and his convoy dissolved.

Correspondence survives between al-Kanamī, and 'Uthmān and his colleagues. Fulani apologetic accused Bornu of various offences: injustice, such as bribery and embezzlement; sin, such as free women uncovering their heads; pagan practices, including sacrifices at sacred spots, and river rites; and of aiding the Hausa against the Fulani. Sin and injustice, 'Uthmān admitted, do not constitute unbelief. Al-Kanamī, having lived long in Medina, Cairo and Fez, and having studied history, knew well that no Muslim realm, no Muslim epoch, was free of wrong, yet did not thereby become pagan. Pagan practices, however, 'Uthmān continued, are unbelief: since the *mai* observed these, Bornu was a land of unbelief. The existence of Muslims there made no difference. 'Uthmān urged *hijra* upon al-Kanamī. It was the final charge, of aiding the Hausa, that was the cause of the Fulani attack on Bornu. To aid an unbeliever is to become one. 'Uthmān and al-Kanamī respected each other's learning. Al-Kanamī accused Bello of acting against 'Uthmān's writing. Bello, more sarcastic than 'Uthmān about al-Kanamī, nevertheless disliked such war between religious leaders, and suggested a negotiated peace.

Islam in al-Kanamī's Bornu was quite strict. Al-Kanamī and 'Umar, having like 'Uthmān the title shaykh, renounced dynastic pomp, though Muslim festivals continued occasions of state ritual. The Prophet's Birthday was gay, the women dancing with especial verve. Al-Kanamī severely enforced Ramaḍān, and feminine morality. Once an *'ālim* intervened, successfully, to prevent him hanging two girls for fornication. On another occasion, al-Kanamī overruled a *qāḍī*, and applied the tribal custom of a life for a life. Prayer and food regulations were observed: the *qāḍī* disallowed the oath of a Muslim who had eaten the Christian bread of the first European visitors. Qur'āns copied by Bornu scribes were exported to North Africa.

Bagirmi Islam was not highly regarded. In Waday, the Sanūsiyya made the route through Kufra to Cyrenaica culturally, and perhaps commercially, the most important Saharan crossing in the later nineteenth century. Bornu similarly looked to the Fezzan and Tripoli. The Waday rulers cultivated Sanūsī connexions. The Sanūsiyya probably strengthened Waday, but did not reform Islam there. Dud Murra, the last free king, was enthroned in 1901 with ceremonies combining the divine kingship and Islam. The marriage of these incompatible concepts, against which the Muslims of Ghāna had witnessed in the eleventh century, survived here in the twentieth.

Rābiḥ

Rābiḥ b. Faḍl Allāh had served under al-Zubayr Pasha Raḥma Manṣūr in the Nilotic Sudan. In 1879, to escape growing khedivial authority, Rābiḥ and several hundred rifles vanished into the Baḥr al-Ghazāl. Ten years later he re-emerged, going west. He failed to conquer Waday, but did set up a client state to the south-east. Bagirmi was overrun, and in 1893 Bornu fell. Here Rābiḥ settled; he established his capital at Dikwa, to become a populous, impressive city.

We know little of Rābiḥ's government, or his religion. He was in touch with three main Islamic powers: the Mahdia, the Sanūsiyya, and Sokoto. The Sudanese Mahdi and later the Khalifa 'Abd Allāhi urged Rābiḥ to join them; but Rābiḥ, though he adopted the Mahdist patched *jubba* for his troops, and carried a banner with a Mahdist device, never went. Rābiḥ's relationship with the Sanūsiyya was hampered by his hostility towards Waday. As for Sokoto, Rābiḥ traded west, particularly to Katagum, for ammunition, despite Sokoto efforts to check such trade. And Rābiḥ was once allied with Ḥayātu, a Mahdist, great-grandson of 'Uthmān dan Fodio, from Adamawa, who married Rābiḥ's daughter. One story says Ḥayātu served as Rābiḥ's *imām*, but was later killed by Rābiḥ's son for suspicious contacts with Gombe.

Shehu Aḥmadu

Fulani pastoralists, moving east from Futa Toro from perhaps the eighth/fourteenth century, gained ascendancy in the Masina region. They apparently included '*ulamā*' from an early date. Vassals to Mali, later to Songhay, the Masina Fulani defied the Moroccans in 1598, and sustained their independence. Later Mamari Kulubali (1712–55) of

Segu established suzerainty over Masina. Shehu Aḥmadu was born in 1189/1775–6, in Masina, of a Fulani scholarly family. He combined study and teaching with a shepherd's life. Attracted to Jenne, he quarrelled with the Arma '*ulamā*' there, who banned him from the mosque. Marka and Fulani '*ulamā*' were advised in dreams of Aḥmadu's destiny as leader: a vision, after four months' retreat, confirmed this for Aḥmadu himself. The first bloodshed occurred when Aḥmadu's pupils killed a son of the Fulani *ardo* (ruler) of Masina. Aḥmadu withdrew north to await consequences.

Forces from Fulani Masina and Bambara Segu (still the overlord) attacked Aḥmadu at Noukouma in 1818.[1] The Fulani were not eager to attack, and Aḥmadu defeated the Bambara. Masina was free. Aḥmadu besieged and took Jenne. The Fulani of Kunari, across the Bani, submitted. The leader here, Galadyo, was never a reliable adherent, and at last found refuge eastwards under Sokoto. In Kunari the new capital, Hamdallahi (Ḥamd Allāhi), was built.

Timbuktu was taken. A governor was sent, a new *imām* (a *sharīf*) appointed. But the city's traditional independence was not broken: under Aḥmadu's successors the Kunta established a virtual protectorate, though tributary still to Masina. Even less successful were efforts to control the Tuareg. Raiding continued between Masina and the Bambara. Some Bambara died heroic martyrs for their pagan faith.

The new state, the *dina*, from the Arabic *dīn*, 'religion', was governed by a grand council of forty '*ulamā*' with legislative, executive and judicial authority. Every local capital had a salaried *qāḍī*. There were conciliation councils, censors of public morality (almost spies), clerks, and a sort of advocate. The standard administrative title, from the village upwards, was *amīr*. All main centres had state-supported schools and compulsory education. Aḥmadu himself taught. Ngorori, the only converted *ardo*, enrolled in Aḥmadu's school but showed himself to be more diligent than academically gifted. Students specially qualified in Qur'ān recitation might come to Ḥamd Allāhi for examination by Aḥmadu. State finance was Qur'anic, plus a tax on harvests and a military tax on those not taking direct part in war. Weights and measures were standardized. Society comprised free men, whether of the nobility or of the various castes, and captives. Aḥmadu refused the grand council's request that castes be abolished for the sake of Islamic

[1] Different dates are given for the beginning of the *jihād*; I follow A. H. Ba and J. Daget, *L'Empire peul du Macina* (Paris, 1962).

brotherhood. A touch of mildness concerns free women, who were never struck; judicially decreed beatings were given instead to their huts or possesions.

Many Masina Fulani were nomads. Aḥmadu himself had been a shepherd—the first man to swear allegiance had found him resting on one leg, the Fulani shepherd's habit. At Noukouma horned cattle heads are said to have descended from heaven upon the Bambara: and indeed the Bambara did lose one fight because they were unable to handle cattle. Ngorori was converted sincerely when one stormy night he found Aḥmadu alone, seeking a wild beast among the cattle, and knew him therefore a leader as well as a man of religion. *'Ulamā'* blessed the herds, and the *dina* carefully regulated transhumance. Nevertheless nomads were unmanageable. Aḥmadu encouraged settlement, celebrations at the return of the cattle were banned (apparently ineffectually), and it was known that the shepherds, once beyond Muslim oversight, reverted to pagan rites.

Shehu Aḥmadu died in 1844; his son, Aḥmadu II, ruled 1844–52; his grandson, Aḥmadu III, was killed by al-Ḥajj 'Umar. 'Umar never controlled Masina himself: eventually his cousin, al-Tijānī, mastered the area, and the state survived until the French conquest.

Al-Ḥājj 'Umar

'Umar b. Sa'īd Tal was born in 1793–4,[1] at Halwar village in Futa Toro. He was a Tokolor, of the Torodbe or religious clan. In 1826–7, he left on Pilgrimage, visiting Mecca, Medina and Jerusalem. He formed intimate links with Muḥammad al-Khalīfa al-Ghālī, the Tijānī representative in the Ḥijāz. Returning, 'Umar halted long in Cairo, Bornu and Sokoto. In Sokoto, he participated fully in Bello's court—a severe judge, a mighty man of prayer in war. He married Bello's daughter Maryam, and later took some part in the election of 'Aṭīq, Bello's successor. Slaves and followers from Hausaland were his first and most loyal disciples.

About 1838, passing more quickly through Masina and Segu, he ended his Pilgrimage in Futa Jallon. As his following increased, and his military strength—he was the first *jihād* leader to concentrate systematically on firearms—relations with the Futa Jallon authorities became strained. About 1848, 'Umar made his *hijra* to Dinguiray, just east of Futa Jallon. In 1852, he proclaimed *jihād*.

[1] Many early dates in 'Umar's career are disputed; in such cases the text follows Mohammadou Aliou Tyam, *La vie d'el Hadj Omar* (Paris, 1935).

His first main campaign was northwards, against the Bambara rulers of Karta. Their capital, Nyoro, fell in 1855. 'Umar then proposed to Aḥmadu III of Masina, an alliance against Segu, another Bambara state. Aḥmadu, suspicious perhaps of 'Umar's association with dissident Fulani, sent an army against 'Umar. 'Umar defeated this in 1856. The wounded were tended and returned, in recognition of their faith. 'Umar's wars were often ferocious: once prisoners were killed to observe the Festival of Sacrifices. In 1856 Turo-koro Mari, king of Segu (1854–6), was murdered. He had become so friendly with 'Umar that the Segu people, fearing for the independence of their state, killed him.

Until now, there had been no sign that 'Umar wished either to fight the French, who were increasingly influential in his homeland Futa Toro, or to attack established Islamic states such as Futa Jallon (against which he attempted no victorious return from his *hijra*) or Masina. But his eastern policy had received a double check. Perhaps encouraged by extremist followers, he turned west and attacked Madīna, highest French post on the Senegal, in 1857. He was repulsed.

'Umar might now pursue *jihād*, either westwards against the French, leading probably to defeat, or eastwards against Segu, possibly clashing with Masina. He chose the latter. In 1860, 'Umar agreed with the French a demarcation of spheres, along the upper Senegal and Bafing rivers.

Turning east, 'Umar committed himself to a career of colonization. His visits to Futa Toro, though he could interfere with the imamate there, were not preliminaries to conquest. Rather, he encouraged emigration, so that Muslims might escape European domination, and that his foreign conquests might be secured by settlement. Emigrants, primarily Tokolor, were his most reliable troops. Sometimes 'Umar burnt villages and food stores to force people to follow.

'Umar preached the example of co-operation shown by the *Anṣār* and *Muhājirūn*. The Tijānī bond also helped reconstitute the new communities. Early initiated by a Futa Jallon *'ālim*, he renewed his initiation with al-Ghālī, receiving all the secrets of the order. He became deeply versed in Tijānī doctrine, writing in detail about such concepts as *jihād al-nafs*, the self-conquest which should precede military *jihād*. His command of Tijānī mysteries established his reputation: though not a prophet, he had the habitual gifts of prophets. Time and again, in Hausaland under Bello, or on his own campaigns, he went into *khalwa* (retreat) seeking God's guidance before giving battle. His prayers were effective in finding water or stopping rain. He prayed too to assure his followers and colonists of paradise. This was a lively hope: his troops went into battle confident of conquering here, or of winning Paradise. Rivalry between the Tijāniyya and Qādiriyya *ṭarīqas* spiced 'Umar's conflicts with Masina and Timbuktu.

'Alī, king of Segu (1856–61), sought the aid of Aḥmadu III, given on condition that 'Alī adopt Islam. 'Umar defeated the combined Segu-Masina forces, and in March 1861 entered the capital of Segu. Attempts to negotiate between Aḥmadu III and 'Umar failed. On 15 May 1862 occurred the final battle. Aḥmadu was defeated. 'Umar occupied Hamdallahi. 'Umar's justification for the Masina War followed the Fulani precedent for the Bornu War. As Bornu had supported the Hausa kings against 'Uthmān, so Masina had joined Segu. 'Umar collected the idols which remained in Segu despite 'Alī's conversion, and took these to Masina, to convince the '*ulamā*' there that the alliance had been corrupt.

'Umar's triumph was fleeting. The Kunta, protectors of Timbuktu against the Masina Fulani, now found the Tokolor the main threat, and joined with Balobbo, leader of the Masina resistance. 'Umar was besieged in Hamdallahi. Attempting to escape, he was trapped at Déguembéré, in February 1864, and killed.

Considering the rapidity of 'Umar's conquests—seven years from Nyoro to Hamadallahi—and the disastrous circumstances of his death, it is surprising that anything was salvaged. Yet his successors continued to rule until the French conquest (1890–3). 'Umar himself never settled, or made himself a king: al-Ghālī had warned him against mixing with the rulers of this world. In 1862–3, he confirmed his eldest son, Aḥmadu Seku (born at Sokoto, but not Bello's grandson), as his successor. Aḥmadu Seku, ruling from Segu, faced disaffection from other 'Umarian governors, and from subject peoples. However, the Tokolor regained control of Masina, aided by renewed mistrust between Balobbo and the Kunta. They took vengeance by the execution of 300 Masina '*ulamā*' bound one to another with their turbans. In 1874, Aḥmadu Seku proclaimed himself *amīr al-mu'minīn*.

French policy towards 'Umar was rarely hostile. His first meetings with French officials, in 1846–7, were friendly. Later Faidherbe, governor of Senegal (1854–61, 1863–5), seriously considered extending French influence down the Niger through an alliance with 'Umar.

An embassy arrived in Segu to negotiate this in 1864, but the treaty was never implemented. Later, the French hesitated between posing as liberators of conquered people under the Tokolor yoke, and trying co-operation again. Another embassy brought back another treaty (1880–1); this also was not implemented. British rivalry, and Samori's resistance, turned the French southwards.

The Senegambia and Samori

The European challenge from the coast, the Muslim inspiration from the interior, and the weakening of traditional institutions generally, encouraged the emergence of many Muslim champions in west Africa in the later nineteenth century. On the Gambia, the misnamed 'Soninke-Marabout' wars—'Soninke' here used for pagans and 'mixers', 'Marabout' for stricter Muslims—marked the gradual advance of reformed Islam. Fodi Kabba was a notable marabout: the British twice carried his capital on the lower Gambia by storm in the 1850s, but he was not killed by the French until 1901. Ma Ba, another *'ālim*, in 1862 declared a *jihād* against the rulers of Badibu, and made it for a time the strongest Muslim power on the Gambia. The British had invaded Badibu in 1860–1, but withdrew, perhaps creating a vacuum.

Lat Dior, ruler of Cayor deposed by the French, had adopted Islam as part of the defence of Wolof independence. He took refuge with Ma Ba, and the two worked in concert until Ma Ba's death in 1867. Lat Dior then made peace with the French, and returned to Cayor. Later, when the French decided to build a railway in Cayor, Lat Dior renewed hostilities. He was killed in October 1886, having had the presentiment that he would that day say the evening prayer with Ma Ba. Another religious leader was al-Ḥājj Mamadu Lamin, the Soninke champion whom the French killed in 1887.

These religious wars were fought on three fronts. The war against paganism and degenerate Islam seems clearest on the Gambia: Ma Ba at first invited harmonious relations with the Europeans. The war against European colonialism was chiefly against the French. Finally, there was the war of Muslim against Muslim. Ma Ba was unusually co-operative: he had consulted with al-Ḥājj 'Umar in 1850, and later supported Lat Dior. But Lamin, who had been with Aḥmadu Seku in Segu before going on Pilgrimage in 1874, later found his supporters attacked by Aḥmadu. Defeated himself by the French, Lamin retired to Futa Bondu and fought the *almami* there. In Futa Toro, the *almami* warred with the 'Mahdi of Podor', whose son later resisted the French.

Samori Ture, greatest of the western leaders, was born in a village, south of Kankan, about 1830, of Mandingo parents. His father, once a trader, was a prosperous herdsman, marrying locally, gradually identifying himself with local paganism. Samori broke this pattern. First, he became a trader. As a trader, he practised Islam. Some of his contacts were '*ulamā*', representing the peaceful accommodation of Muslim traders among pagans—the Mande dispersion already described.

About 1851–2, Samori's mother was enslaved by a local warrior chief. Devoted to her, Samori served the chief for several years, raiding and studying the Qur'ān with him until his mother was released. Thus Samori was introduced to militant Islam, already expressed in several chieftaincies in the area. Popular lore today, however, attributes his redoubtable prowess to a liaison with a female *jinn*.

Samori then built up his own state, this first phase of expansion culminating in the capture of Kankan about 1879. Samori was commonly called *almami*. Whether he took also the title *amīr al-mu'minīn* is uncertain: perhaps he did, and later renounced it. For each village, an *imām* was appointed. '*Ulamā*' advised government officials. Samori particularly required that the children of leading families be educated, sometimes examining pupils himself.

In 1882, Samori moving north clashed with the French advancing east against al-Ḥājj 'Umar's successors. This diversion preserved the 'Umarian empire for a decade. In 1886–7, the French signed 'spheres of influence' treaties with Samori.

Samori's most resilient African rival was Tyeba of Sikaso, whose brother and predecessor was a client-convert of Aḥmadu b. al-Ḥājj 'Umar. In 1887–8, Samori besieged Sikaso. The siege failed. Angry that the French had not helped him, Samori renewed his quarrel with them, meanwhile proposing an alliance, which came to nothing, to Aḥmadu. Samori was quickly defeated; and Kankan was occupied in 1891.

Hitherto, Samori had operated in the Mande heartlands. The first of the principal Muslim champions not relying on an immigrant community, he has come to symbolize Mande national resistance to European imperialism. But in the 1890s he had to create a new, eastern empire, in the upper Ivory Coast and beyond. Kong fell in 1895. Refugees, Muslim and pagan, fled in all directions. One, who went south, tells of the wretched, oppressed condition of the dispossessed when they reached French protection—of their gradual establishment, mosques being built, teachers and *'ulamā'* multiplying, until countless animals were slaughtered at the Greater Festival and all wore silk at the Lesser.

European advance, once it reached the Sudan interior, swept the Muslim states like prairie fire. The 'Umarian empire fell to the French (1890–3), Aḥmadu Seku and the irreconcilables fleeing to Hausaland. Samori's sixteen year defiance ended in 1898. Rābiḥ, helped it is said by Bagirmi *'ulamā'*, destroyed the first French force in Bagirmi, but his death in 1900, fighting them in Bornu, established them in both countries. Waday was occupied in 1909. The British Royal Niger Company took Ilorin in 1897; the sultan of Sokoto died resisting the British in 1904. Germans occupied most of Adamawa (1899–1901); the British took Yola, and the Anglo-German boundary decapitated the state.

C. EAST AFRICA

The east coast before the tenth/sixteenth century

Early Islam in Africa south of the Sahara was often a religion of ports. In the western Sudan, the cities which first welcomed Islam were harbours facing the desert ocean of the Sahara. On the eastern coast, the towns looked out upon the Indian Ocean. And, as both the northern and southern littorals of the Sahara shared some degree of common culture, so the East African coast was part of the world of the Indian Ocean. But whereas the western Sudan towns were parts of great states, which could absorb and in some sense use Islam, the eastern coastal towns remained until the nineteenth century disunited, without imperial achievement. It is as if in tropical Africa, Islam, though in its 'mixed' form buttressing existing states, had to wait for the actual creation of states by people for whom Islam was a primary consideration until the theocracies of the eighteenth and nineteenth centuries. The superior protection offered by the Sahara may have contributed, while the east coast was repeatedly distraught by sea-borne interlopers. On the other hand, the east coast became unambiguously a part of the Muslim world much earlier than the western Sudan. Another difference is that the southern Saharan 'ports' backed on to open, savannah country, across which Islam gradually spread, while the eastern ocean ports were pinned to the coast by the forest, a barrier not breached until the nineteenth century. Only the south, where the arrival of the Portuguese in the tenth/sixteenth century perhaps interrupted Islamic penetration on the Zambesi, and the north, where Islam crossed the Horn of Africa and lapped the foothills of Ethiopia, were exceptions.

Even before the Prophet's *Hijra*, some of his Meccan supporters had found refuge in Ethiopia. The East African coast was apparently a frequent sanctuary for the oppressed in the early centuries of Islam. The followers of Zayd, great-grandson of 'Alī, are said to have been the first to flee thither. Later came refugees from al-Aḥsā; these are said to have founded Mogadishu. Still others fled from 'Umān.

Trade continued to be important: ivory, particularly for India; slaves (the Zanj who revolted in 'Irāq in the later third/ninth century were East Africans); perfume, one of the luxuries in which even severe Muslims may indulge; gold; and other things. By the mid-twelfth century, the people of Zanzibar were predominantly Muslim; several Islamic inscriptions survive in Mogadishu from the seventh/thirteenth century. But still the overall character of the coast was pagan.

The most fully documented of the early coastal settlements is Kilwa. Its founding is usually attributed to immigrants from Shīrāz in the fourth/tenth century, but recently it has been argued that *c.* 1200 is a better date, and that the immigrants, though they may have shared some elements of Shīrāzī culture, came from the Banādir coast.[1] The chronicle details, circumstantial and sometimes conflicting, of the founding of Kilwa are perhaps mainly imaginative. The island on which Kilwa was founded was bought from the local people for cloth, suggesting the recurrent link between trade and early Muslim settlement. There were already other immigrant Muslims in the area, and before long fighting broke out between some of them and Kilwa; Kilwa was temporarily conquered, and the Friday prayers were said in the name of a usurper. Then the government returned to the line of the founder, who was, according to one account, the son of an Ethiopian slave woman, and emigrated to Africa because his half-brothers jeered at his descent.

In the early eighth/fourteenth century, benefitting from the gold trade with Sofala, and apparently under a new dynasty, Kilwa prospered. Ibn Baṭṭūṭa visited the town in 731/1331, in the reign of al-Ḥasan b.

[1] N. Chittick, 'The "Shirazi" colonization of east Africa', in *Journal of African History*, vi, no. 3, 1965, 275–94; J. S. Trimingham, *Islam in East Africa* (London, 1964), 10–1.

Sulaymān, surnamed Abu'l-Mawāhib, 'the giver of gifts', for his generosity. Al-Ḥasan is the first of the Kilwa rulers whom we know to have gone on Pilgrimage; on the way, he spent two years in Aden studying. Al-Ḥasan frequently raided the pagan Zanj; these raids were called *jihād*, and a later king killed on such an enterprise was deemed a martyr. Al-Ḥasan divided the booty according to Qur'anic injunction, and *sharīfs* in particular frequented his court, from 'Irāq, the Ḥijāz, and elsewhere. Ibn Baṭṭūṭa visited also Mombasa, Zayla', where many of the people were heretics, (perhaps descendants of earlier refugees), and Mogadishu.

From the mid-eighth/fourteenth century until the coming of the Portuguese at the end of the fifteenth, Kilwa declined politically. During the ninth/fifteenth century, various Islamic offices are mentioned, some of them innovations. The sultans lost control of the great officials, and there was a succession of civil disturbances, depositions, foreign interventions and puppet rulers. But commercial prosperity continued, and on the coast as a whole new powers were rising, first Pate, then Mombasa. In 1498 Vasco da Gama arrived, and within a few years the Portuguese had conquered almost the entire coast.

The Horn of Africa before the tenth/sixteenth century

The towns of the Somali coast, such as Zayla' on the Gulf of Aden, and Mogadishu on the Banādir coast of the Indian Ocean, share to a considerable extent the characteristics of the Swahili culture further south: trading centres, welcoming Arab and other immigrants, evolving distinctive amalgams both of population and of language, witnessing to some form of settled government and to Islam. But, while Swahili culture has throughout been confined to the coast—its very name derives from the Arabic, *sawāḥil*, coasts—the Somali seaboard and hinterland have much in common. Muslim states in the interior were loosely federated with sultanates on the coast, nomadic Somalis shared the townsmen's faith, and all confronted a common challenge in Christian Ethiopia, though in the earliest centuries Ethiopia was exempt from *jihād*.

Perhaps as early as 283/896–7, Arab immigrants established a Muslim state far inland, in Shoa. Late in the seventh/thirteenth century (1280–5) this was absorbed by Ifat, one of seven Muslim kingdoms, all tributary to Christian Ethiopia. Early in the eighth/fourteenth century, Ifat controlled also the port of Zayla'. Students from Zayla' at this time had their own hostel at al-Azhar, and a section of the Umayyad mosque at Damascus. These Muslim territories, sometimes loosely called Adal, were frequently in revolt against their titular overlord. In 1329 the Emperor Amda Seyon undertook a particularly severe campaign against Ifat, indirectly a result of Muslim pressure on Christians in Egypt, and seems to have cleared Ethiopia proper of Muslim influence. Such wars had many religious overtones. Early in the ninth/fifteenth century full-scale war was again being waged. The Emperor Yeshaq (1414–29) killed the ruler of Ifat, Sa'd al-Dīn, in his last stronghold, an island off the Zayla' coast. Sa'd's sons fled to Yemen, but later returned. The *jihād* of the *Imām* Aḥmad Grāñ was the climax of these repeated conflicts.

Ibn Baṭṭūṭa, in Mogadishu in 731/1331, gives us our best description of Muslim society on the Horn at this time. He describes a deeply islamized court, around the ruler or shaykh. Elaborate hierarchy governed precedence. He was lodged in the comfortable students' hostel of the *qāḍī*'s school. The *qāḍī*, the shaykh's secretary, the *wazīrs* and four principal *amīrs* sat as a court, the *qāḍī* dealing with religious law; the shaykh's advice, when necessary, was sought and given in writing. The shaykh could speak Arabic, but this was not his own language. Many details suggest Middle Eastern influence: cloth was exported to Egypt, the *qāḍī* was Egyptian, a eunuch sprinkled Ibn Baṭṭūṭa with rose-water from Damascus, the shaykh wore a cloak of Jerusalem stuff, and so on. A purist might quibble over the golden birds surmounting the royal canopy, an excessive purist over the royal band, but it is clear that here was orthodox Islam.

The Muslim states were threatened not only by their Christian foe, but also by their turbulent nomadic neighbours. It has been widely accepted that the Galla inhabited the Horn at the beginning of the Muslim era, and that they were then gradually expelled by the Somali, who pushed south and west, having perhaps found the Aden Gulf coast overcrowded with Arab settlers. The Somali, steeled by conversion to Islam, were generally victorious. This analysis has recently been questioned, partly on linguistic grounds.[1] It is suggested that Afar (the northern neighbours of the Somali), Somali and Galla all originated in the area of southern Ethiopia. The Afar moved out first, north and east into the Horn, followed by the Somali. The first mention of the name Somali

[1] H. S. Lewis, 'The origins of the Galla and Somali', in *Journal of African History*, vii, no. 1, 1966, 27–46.

is in the time of the Emperor Yeshaq, though a Somali tribe is described near Mogadishu in the seventh/thirteenth, perhaps even in the sixth/twelfth century. In the tenth/sixteenth century, the new interpretation continues, the Galla, expanding into Ethiopia and challenging too the Swahili area as far south as Malindi, also trod on Somali heels towards the Horn: this is the origin of traditions of Galla-Somali conflict, not an earlier expulsion of Galla from the Horn by Somali.

Whichever view is finally accepted, by the tenth/sixteenth century it is clear that the nomadic Somali were a principal Muslim force in the Horn. They are prominent in Grāñ's *jihād*. Somali genealogies insist on an Arab ancestry, preferably within the Prophet's family. Whatever the doubt about the historicity of these claims, they reveal the great importance of Arab immigrants in bringing Islam. Supposed tribal ancestors are revered as saints, and many other Arab missionaries are remembered.

Aḥmad Grāñ

Like two thunder clouds the Portuguese and the Ottoman Turks approached each other in eastern Africa. In 922/1517 the Ottomans took Cairo: in the same year the Portuguese burnt Zaylaʿ. One burst of lightning in this overcharged atmosphere was the *jihād* of Aḥmad Grāñ. In the ninth/fifteenth century, a militant, reforming Muslim movement developed in Adal, under leaders styled *amīrs*, opposed to the traditional Muslim aristocracy. The militants wished to challenge Ethiopia, the traditionalists appreciated peace and commerce. Maḥfūẓ, one dominant *amīr*, proclaimed a *jihād*, but was defeated and killed. For some years no one succeeded in gaining lasting authority in Adal. One ruler enforced piety for three years, but was killed by a rival, Abū Bakr. Finally Aḥmad b. Ibrāhīm (1506–43)—Aḥmad Grāñ—emerged. He was styled *imām*, not *amīr* or sultan. He married the daughter of Maḥfūẓ, and began to challenge Abū Bakr.

The *ʿulamā*' attempted to exercise their traditional role as peacemakers, but failed. Perhaps, since Grāñ was himself an Islamic champion, the *ʿulamā*' did not enjoy the prestige usually derived from the contrast between themselves as men of religion and the warrior leaders.

Grāñ killed Abū Bakr, and replaced him with a puppet. In 1527, with his headquarters at the inland city of Harar, Grāñ began serious fighting with Ethiopia. In 1531, he invaded, and scourged Ethiopia unmercifully for the rest of his life. Churches and monasteries were ravaged, and huge numbers of Ethiopians forced to accept Islam. These wars were *jihād*, but Grāñ was unable to enforce full legal control over the division of booty. The fugitive Ethiopian king cried out for Portuguese aid, and when Portuguese gunmen appeared Grāñ appealed to the Ottomans for help. In 1543 Grāñ was killed, and the invasion collapsed. Grāñ's widow tried to carry on the struggle from Harar; her new husband was made *amīr al-mu'minīn*. He was succeeded by a man of slave origin, 'Uthmān, who pandered to the traditionalists and offended the purists. Civil strife ensued; a final attempt at *jihād* failed.

After the sixteenth century

The Portuguese, and the *jihād* of Grāñ, both weakened the cause of Islamic government in the area. To the south, though the struggle against the Portuguese, a struggle religious as well as economic and military, may have prepared the ground for nineteenth century attempts to unify the coast of Zanzibar, it was not in itself sufficient to bring coastal Muslims together. In the north, the *jihād* led to the final disintegration of Adal, the main sphere of relatively settled Islamic life in the interior. In 1577 the capital was moved from Harar to Aussa, in order to be further from the Ethiopian menace. The dynasty was at last overthrown by the Afar at the end of the seventh century. Earlier in the same century the dynasty of Mogadishu, closely linked with Somali settled on the Shebeli River, collapsed before the challenge of Somali newcomers.

Ironically, and for quite different reasons, the decline of the interior Muslim states was followed by a strengthening of the influence of coastal Muslims. Under the Emperor Susenyos, Roman Catholic missionaries in Ethiopia, inheritors of the soldiers who had fought Grāñ, overplayed their hand. Some Ethiopian chiefs complained that they would prefer Muslim to Portuguese rule. Under Susenyos's son, Fasiladas (1632–67), reaction became policy: he made an agreement with the Ottoman governors of Suakin and Massawa to execute Catholic priests trying to enter Ethiopia. Islam seemed now an ally against the Portuguese, a reversal of the previous position.

While the political power of inland Muslim bases declined—and even at the best of times their authority over the nomads was incomplete—they nevertheless maintained a considerable degree of religious authority. Harar is still regarded by Somalis as a centre of Muslim learning just as Zaylaʿ and Mogadishu. The *ʿulamāʾ* of Aussa were able to intervene to protect their town from an attack by an Arab force. In the early nineteenth century the sultan of Tajura felt obliged to accept their arbitration in a controversy over the marriage of his son. Mukhā Arabs assaulted Harar, encouraged by a disgraced member of the ruling family who represented his countrymen as apostates, but were beaten off.

Two new Muslim powers entered the area. The Ottomans occupied Massawa in 1557, unsuccessfully attacked Ethiopia, and seemed to promise firmer Muslim intervention; but they withdrew in 1633. Apart from stray raids, and two expeditions in the 1580s which were perhaps not officially sanctioned, there was little Ottoman interference further south. Ottoman domination continued in shadowy form—Zaylaʿ and Berbera came under the *sharīfs* of Mukhā in the eleventh/seventeenth century, and were thus nominally within the Ottoman empire. Effective outside Islamic intervention did not come in the south until the mid-seventeenth century, when ʿUmān was invited in by Mombasa Muslims. In 1698 Fort Jesus at Mombasa, the seat of Portuguese government on the coast, fell to them.

In origin, both the Turkish intervention in the north, and the ʿUmānī further south, resulted from appeals by local Muslims for support against a Christian threat. Religion, however, may be more effective in prompting such alliances than in maintaining them. During the twelfth/eighteenth century, there were recurrent suggestions by various coastal rulers that the Portuguese might return, and early in the nineteenth century Mogadishu and Brava sought, unsuccessfully, to exchange ʿUmānī protection for British. Neither Ottoman nor ʿUmānī, the latter with considerably more direct links, was able effectively to control representatives in Africa. Early in the nineteenth century eunuchs held office in Zanzibar, ʿUmān hoping these would be less prone to set up their own principalities.

In the nineteenth century both distant suzerains took a more active interest. In 1840 Sayyid Saʿīd of ʿUmān came and settled in Zanzibar; his authority extended over Mogadishu and the Banādir coast. In the mid-eighteenth century, the first caravans began trading into the interior; these became prominent under Sayyid Saʿīd. But there was still little penetration of Islam beyond the coast. The coast itself, though speaking Swahili (a language with a Bantu grammar but heavily arabicized in vocabulary) and sharing a distinctive Swahili culture, was undeniably part of the *dār al-Islām*. In West and Central Africa, we can visualize Islam as a foreign element introduced into the local African setting, while on the East Coast it is rather African people, through migration, slaving and intermarriage, that are being drawn into an essentially Islamic setting. The persistence too of the eastward orientation of the coast may be seen in Sayyid Saʿīd's encouragement of Indian immigrants, many of them Muslim. All, including Hindus, enjoyed religious freedom. Saʿīd himself was an ʿIbāḍī.

Ottoman claims revived later in the century, through the agency of Egypt, over the coast from Suakin to Berbera and inland to Harar. Despite community of religion, the Egyptians had trouble with the hinterland nomads, and were able to establish their authority partly because the Somali were not united. One Egyptian expedition, intending to penetrate Ethiopia, was annihilated by the sultan of Aussa. Among public works erected during the brief Egyptian period (1870–84) were several mosques.

The Galla

The Galla, perhaps originally from south central Ethiopia, began expanding in the early tenth/sixteenth century, and are today found over nearly half the area of Ethiopia. The Galla expansion was at the expense of Muslim as well as Christian: the Galla devastated Harar (where the ruler, ʿUthmān, attempted the interesting policy of encouraging them to take part in Muslim markets) and attacked Aussa. Some Galla adopted Islam, perhaps through the example of the Muslim residue of Grāñ's invasion. By the early nineteenth century, certain groups were largely Muslim, like the Wallo in the north whom Krapf, travelling among them in 1842, found determined Muslims.[1] He met some on pilgrimage, and at least one chief was entitled *imām*. The Wallo claimed conversion by an Arab called Debelo, for which we may perhaps read Dibuli, traditionally among the first Shīrāzī settlers on the coast.

Among such Galla, Islam affected political and social organization but little. The tribes remained fiercely individualistic and fissiparous. Noticeably out of step with the general Galla pattern, however, were the five despotic Galla kingdoms which emerged in the nineteenth century south-west of the Gibe River—Enarea, Guma, Goma, Gera and Jimma. Perhaps these drew on the local Sidama heritage, or even looked back to

[1] J. L. Krapf, *Travels, researches, and missionary labours* . . . (London, 1860), 82 ff.

pre-sixteenth century Muslim states. Probably trade contributed considerably: revived demand on the Red Sea and in Arabia prompted Ethiopian traders, mostly Muslim, to organize caravans in search of luxury items such as slaves, ivory, gold and civet. A principal route was Massawa-Gondar-Gojam and into the Gibe region. Enarea, under Abba Bagibo, who reigned from about 1825, became the principal resort of merchants trading in the area, and at the same time a centre of Islam. A proposal from Abba Bagibo, for an alliance, was refused by the Christian ruler of Gojam because Abba Bagibo was a Muslim and traded in slaves. But Abba Bagibo's gift of a hundred horns of civet and fifty female slaves was accepted, and firearms together with men skilled in their use were sent in return. Muslim traders are not in themselves adequate explanation why Islam should win local converts: in Kafa, for example, just to the south, they are well regarded, and may perhaps be traced back to the tenth/sixteenth century, but Islam has little local following.

How far Islam was immediately effective is uncertain. Abba Bagibo had twelve official wives. The government of Enarea, even its judicial system, seems in his time to have taken little explicit account of the new faith followed by the ruler, his court, and many of his subjects. Even in the later nineteenth century, though there were several hundred *'ulamā'* at the capital there were virtually no mosques: one hut, called a mosque, near the royal cemetery, was respected as a sanctuary. The common faith did not always unite the new kingdoms: Jimma and Enarea fought for control of the trade-route north; in the later nineteenth century Jimma was pre-eminent. The *jihād*, which in the 1880s a confederacy of four of the Muslim kingdoms declared on their pagan rivals, was perhaps only a continuation of age-old squabbling.

But there is evidence of a recurrent effort after a more effective faith. The dynasty of Goma tried to islamize itself by claiming descent from a Mogadishu shaykh. There was the influence of Sudanese and Egyptian traders, and later of the Mahdists, who allied themselves with Galla Muslims, but were expelled by the Shoans representing central Ethiopian authority. With the Shoan conquest of the Gibe area, begun in 1886, Firissa, heir to the throne of Guma, fled to Massawa. There he joined Shaykh 'Abd al-Raḥmān, a refugee from Goma. The two went frequently on Pilgrimage. In 1899–1900 anti-Shoan agitation arose in Guma: Firissa returned, claimed the throne and proclaimed a *jihād*. He forbade his troops to castrate prisoners (the common Galla custom) or to take prisoners expecting great ransoms, for such profane trophies defiled the *jihād*. Rebuked by *'ulamā'* for observing traditional sacrifices after killing nine enemy horsemen, Firissa gave expiatory alms to the poor. Meanwhile 'Abd al-Raḥmān founded *zāwiyas* of the Mīrghaniyya order in Firissa's domains. An attempt to convert a neighbouring ruler led to Firissa's falling into Shoan hands. He was executed, clasping the Qur'ān. Local Muslims today revere him, last prince of Guma, as a *walī*.

The Gibe Galla story shows again the importance of mobility within Islam: coastal origins are claimed, traders are sometimes effective missionaries, refugees find consolation and friends in the heartlands of Islam and then return. Movements like the Mahdia reach from one area to another, and the orders continue their peaceful penetration: in this century, the Tijāniyya has come from Algeria and the Qādiriyya from the Somalis.

Within Christian Ethiopia, Galla acquired increasing influence at court. 'Alī, a Galla prince (d. 1788), founded a Galla dynasty in Begamder province, and began pilgrimages to the tomb of Grāñ. The internal progress of Islam seemed likely to receive external support. In 1838 Muḥammad 'Alī first attacked Ethiopia, and later the Egyptians thrust in from the coast. Harar, still independent, was captured in 1875, and pagan Galla in the area were forcibly converted. The enlarged challenge brought a more acid response. Ethiopian emperors in the later nineteenth century several times tried to impose Christianity upon their Muslim and pagan subjects. Menelik (1889–1913), the architect of modern Ethiopia, was less ruthless: when Jimma submitted to him, he incorporated the principality bodily, apparently promising not to build churches there.

Arabs in the interior

The earliest caravan traders to the Swahili coast were certain peoples of the interior, as the Nyamwesi and Yao. But throughout the nineteenth century Arabs and Swahili (hereafter in this section called Arabs) gradually moved inland, to Tabora, Ujiji, Nyangwe, to Buganda and Lake Nyasa, to Katanga. At first, the interests of these pioneers were commercial, chiefly in ivory and slaves, but soon, partly through entanglement in local politics, travelling merchants evolved into colonists. During the years 1884–8, throughout East Africa, Arab efforts to build up, or win over, principalities in the interior intensified. The main example was Buganda, discussed below, but similar though lesser instances might be multiplied. A major stimulus was European, particularly German, encroachment on the coast, and many of the Arab political pretensions in the eastern interior were anti-European.

On the coast itself, as the German presence became increasingly felt, Muslim irritation sharpened, and in 1888 Abūshīrī b. Sālim al-Ḥārthī took up arms. Behind this resistance economic motives may have been influential, particularly concern over the slave trade. But the flash-point came in Ramaḍān, over incidents like lowering an Islamic flag, defiling a mosque by bringing dogs in, and interference with festival prayers. A Muslim diviner was called in, and a similar reliance on divination was attributed to German policymakers. The resistance spread: Yao and Kilwa, for example, joined in. But it was crushed, and in 1889 Abūshīrī was hanged.

Further west, in the Congo area, the break did not come until later. The Congo Free State at first found the Arabs of the upper Congo helpful in supplying ivory, finding labour, and as a buffer. Tippu Tib, an outstanding Swahili colonist and slaver, was for a time a Free State official. Had this attempt at indirect rule succeeded, the consequences for Islam in Central Africa might have been far-reaching. But neither Tippu Tib nor the Free State headquarters could control men in the field. In 1892 war broke out—as perhaps it was bound to do at some time, particularly over the slaving question—and within two years Arab power was broken.

The extent to which these events were encouraged from Zanzibar is uncertain. Probably the unrest of the 1880s was so stimulated; but, although Tippu Tib had once been the sultan's agent on the upper Congo, by the 1890s Zanzibar's bolt had been shot. Whatever Zanzibar's part, there was never among the Arabs an authority capable of imposing unity.

The degree of Arab culture established in the interior was sometimes considerable. The Nyangwe area, where Livingstone in 1871 observed most savage slave raiding, was later brought under extensive plantation colonization which maintained a leisured ruling class. A Free State official, European, shortly before 1892, described meetings with Arabs, wearing snowy robes, turbans, and vests of gold and silver braid, drinking coffee from china cups, discussing Napoleon's wars, Turkey's government, and Manchester's cotton. Less is known about the specifically religious aspect: some of the Arabs were devout men, and there were apparently some Wahhābīs among them. There was little or no proselytizing, but considerable imitation, at least among the entourage of the Arabs, of religious practice.

The Yao

The Yao are the only major people south of the Somali to have adopted Islam before the colonial period. Living then midway between Lake Nyasa and the Indian Ocean, the Yao were by the later eighteenth century sending caravans to the coast, part of a trading network stretching from the ocean to Katanga. By the later nineteenth century, with fire-arms they had become a major slave-raiding people. Yao children used to play a game with beans representing traders and slaves going to the coast. The Yao expanded westward into the Nyasa region.

The coast had not only a material effect, demanding slaves and offering guns and other trade goods: it set also a cultural example. Dhows and bedsteads were copied, fashions of dress adopted, mangoes and coconuts planted, all in imitation of the coast. Religion followed. Sixty boys and girls were buried alive at the funeral of one Yao chief, who had traded much to the coast and planted mangoes at his capital. His cousin and successor, summoned home from the coast, was buried in his turn beside the mosque.

The first Yao Muslims went to the coast for initiation; later coastal '*ulamā*' and teachers came to Yaoland; later again Yao '*ulamā*' themselves took the main role. Islam, spreading particularly in the late nineteenth and early twentieth centuries, became a distinguishing feature of Yao nationality. Islamic influence on Yao social life has been curtailed by firm matrilineal traditions, but here and there changes may be seen: Islamic rather than customary marriage, for example, allows a husband to demand that his wife live with him in his village.

Buganda

In East Africa, Buganda is, in its relations with Islam, perhaps the closest parallel to the earlier, greater states of Central and West Africa. It is remarkable how often, in the relatively short story of Buganda Islam, themes already familiar confront us. The faith arrived with trade. The earliest long-distance imports came perhaps in the eighteenth century. In the mid-nineteenth century, under Kabaka Suna, the first Muslims appeared, from Zanzibar and the coast. As the first Muslim visitors to eighth/fourteenth century Kano helped the king in his local wars, so these Arabs marched with the Buganda forces. And, as in Ghāna the immigrant Muslims had held somewhat aloof from the king, so the Buganda Arabs condemned the king's slaughter of his subjects, warning him that the same God who had given him his kingdom had created these his people. The reproof apparently impressed Suna; but later, for reasons now unknown, he expelled the Arabs.

In the 1860s, under Mutesa, Suna's successor, the Arabs returned. Mutesa even more than Suna became interested in Islam. Though never a convert, he adopted the Islamic calendar and Arabic dress, observed Ramaḍān, enforced Muslim greetings, and encouraged mosque building in town and country. But, as in Mali Negro Muslims had not the same privileges as Berber or Arab Muslims in Ghāna, so Mutesa could not grant the same licence to the newly converted Buganda Muslims that Suna had allowed to the Arabs. Tension mounted when Buganda Muslims dressed presumptuously, and refused the royal food as uncleanly slaughtered. A visiting Muslim cautioned the Buganda that Mutesa, despite his interest, was not a full Muslim—he was, for example, uncircumcised—and should not lead the prayers as he had been doing. He was a 'mixer'. In 1875–6 Mutesa struck back. A hundred or more Buganda Muslims were martyred.

No more for Buganda than for Ghāna or Songhay earlier, was Islam a domestic problem only. Mutesa might use Islam in local diplomacy—he sent an unsuccessful mission to convert the ruler of neighbouring Bunyoro, bearing among other gifts shoes suitable for taking off on entering the mosque—but he soon felt the squeeze of larger-scale power politics, particularly Egyptian ambitions. In place of Morocco's Spanish eunuchs, the khedive employed a variety of European officials (one of whom tried, but failed, to build the first brick mosque in Buganda). The khedive was scarcely more likely than Aḥmad al-Manṣūr successfully to administer an empire far to the south. But before annexation could be seriously attempted, the arrival in 1877 of Christian missionaries fundamentally altered the situation.

For a decade, Muslims and Christians, neither possessing political authority, argued their case before the court, but in 1888 Muslims and Christians united to expel Mwanga, Mutesa's successor. He was too much a pagan for either. Within a month, the Arabs, with Buganda Muslim support, had driven out the Christians, and installed almost a puppet *kabaka*, Kalema. As elsewhere in East and Central Africa, Christian European encroachment on the periphery led the Muslim Arabs to attempt political power in the interior. Civil war in Buganda followed. In 1890, the Christians finally triumphed. Very soon after, Buganda passed into the colonial period.

Muḥammad b. ʻAbd Allāh

The Somali leader, Muḥammad b. ʻAbd Allāh (1864–1920/1), found his country distracted on three fronts: Ethiopia, from 1887, expanded east, conquering such Muslim centres as Harar and Aussa, bringing both Galla and Somali under Ethiopian rule; on the opposite side, the pace of British, French and Italian penetration on the coast increased in the 1880s; and the Somali clans were quarrelling among themselves. Ethiopian and European ambitions were fostered by the withdrawal of Egyptian garrisons as a result of the Mahdist rising in the Sudan. The British, taking over from the Egyptians on the coast, met some opposition from Sanūsī and Mahdist agents, who were themselves at odds.

Muḥammad, a precocious Qur'ān scholar, soon embarked on wide-ranging travels for knowledge, visiting Harar, Mogadishu, the Sudan, even Nairobi. While on Pilgrimage, he joined the Ṣāliḥiyya order, a militant and puritan wing of the Aḥmadiyya. He was to apply Shāfiʻī law strictly, with punishments, even mutilation and death, for defaulters at prayer and other such backsliders. The Aḥmadiyya and the Qādiriyya were the main orders in Somaliland. Perhaps because of a ready correspondence between saints venerated by the orders, and ancestors venerated by the clans, to be a Muslim came to involve for almost every Somali membership in an order.

In 1899, from the interior of Somaliland beyond European zones, Muḥammad launched his *jihād*. He was still waging it, often defeated but never captured, when he died some twenty years later. His discipline excelled in severity even that of the Almoravids. He did not, apparently, proclaim himself *mahdī*, as is sometimes said.

His *jihād* challenged four antagonists. First, he fought the other orders. The Qādirīs were his especial enemies. His followers murdered the leading Qādirī shaykh among the southern Somalis in 1909: the Qādirīs asserted it was more meritorious to kill one *darwīsh* heretic than a hundred infidels. Also in 1909 one of Muḥammad's disillusioned supporters secured a letter from the founder of the Ṣāliḥiyya, reprimanding Muḥammad for his excesses.

Second, he fought the British, resisting both foreign and Christian encroachment. Perhaps sensing European rivalries, he was more co-operative with the Italians; they in their turn giving him a small state under their protection in 1905, used him as a buffer between Somali factions. The British occupation of the interior was, however, more the result than the cause of Muḥammad's *jihād*.

Third, he fought the Ethiopians. In 1913, there was a dramatic reversal in Ethiopia. Menelik died, and was succeeded by Lijj Iyasu, son of his daughter and a Galla chief. Iyasu, encouraged by German and Ottoman diplomats, showed great inclination towards Islam. He moved his court to Harar, and adopted many Muslim customs. Among his wives were a niece and a daughter of the Muslim ruler of Jimma. The '*ulamā*' declared him a *sharīf*. In 1916 he proclaimed his conversion and Ethiopia's religious dependence on the Ottoman sultan-caliph, and summoned the Somalis to *jihād*. It was arranged that he should marry a daughter of Muḥammad b. 'Abd Allāh. But the marriage never occurred, for a Christian counter-revolution in 1917 deposed Iyasu, and checked the Galla-Muslim resurgence.

Finally, Muḥammad fought other Somali clans. He applied all the devices of pastoral Somali politics, as of Islam, to build up his following. He was a renowned poet, both in Arabic and the vernacular. Though clan lines broadly demarcated his supporters and opponents, he did have unusual supra-clan appeal, and is revered today as pioneer of a united Somali nationalism.

Muḥammad's career, as that of al-Ḥājj 'Umar, responded to two stimuli. Both moved within an independent Muslim tradition: early study and travel, Pilgrimage leading to special dedication to a particular order and this leading in turn to rivalry with other orders. Both drew inspiration from other reform movements—'Umar from Sokoto, Muḥammad from the Mahdist Sudan. Neither seems to have sought a settled, permanent theocracy for himself, though 'Umar made arrangements for his succession which Muḥammad did not. But both found the Muslim tradition distorted by a second stimulus, that of the European presence. Both tried to keep abreast technically. 'Umar could turn his back on the Europeans; it was too late for Muḥammad to do that. Perhaps because Muḥammad could no longer withdraw, but had to make his stand at home, he seems now, like Samori, a nationalist forerunner.

D. THE MODERN PERIOD

The effects of European colonization

The effect of European colonial control upon the development of Islam in tropical Africa is far from fully analysed. It was in part the effect of a hostile challenge: various Muslim champions fought the Europeans, but often these Muslims felt able to negotiate, and sometimes the Muslim leaders quarrelled among themselves as much as with the Europeans. Some learned Muslims advocated a pacific attitude. Perhaps more important, for the spread and strengthening of Islam, was the association of the faith, in the minds of some, with modern nationalist sentiment. The fact that so many Muslims accommodated themselves to European rule led to new tensions within the Muslim community. In part also, and this was the greater part, the effect of European colonialism was to enlarge Islamic opportunities, in three main ways: indirect rule, direct employment of Muslims, and generally increased mobility.

Indirect rule was clearest in northern Nigeria, where British authority was exercised through the Fulani amirates established by ʿUthmān dan Fodio's *jihād*. Similar systems operated elsewhere, for example in northern Cameroon under Germans and then French. Sometimes Europeans, wishing to organize and simplify, enlarged the realms of the traditional Muslim rulers through whom they chose to govern. Thus the Zaghāwa of Waday were brought under a single sultan by the French in the 1930s; the British confirmed Muslim authority over pagans in Nupe and Ilorin; while in Cameroon the French assignment of certain pagan cantons to Muslim amirates led to such violent resistance that in 1937 one *amīr* was nearly killed and the cantons had to be freed. Indirect rule often implied a complete ban on Christian mission work, as in northern German Cameroon or British Somaliland, or its stringent curtailment, as in northern Nigeria. European authority in indirect rule somewhat limited the operation of Islamic law: some of the more severe punishments for example were forbidden, and slavery was gradually abolished. But *qāḍīs* sometimes found their influence increased by government backing, for instance in turbulent Somalia.

Indirect rule was not confined to traditional Muslim states. The French, at first suspicious of the autocratic control which the leaders of the Ṣūfī orders, especially the Murids, had over their disciples, later found this control another channel for indirect rule, a channel the more important since, with the decline of chiefs, people tended to regroup around religious leaders. Even the short-lived attempt of the Congo Free State to utilize the governing power of Tippu Tib and other Arabs on the upper Congo may be interpreted as an experiment in indirect rule. Indirect rule, while it strengthened traditional forms of Islam, generally hindered new Muslim developments, so that both amirates and Ṣūfī orders seemed increasingly old-fashioned.

European colonialists everywhere relied extensively on the direct employment of the most educated and experienced African groups. These were by no means always Muslim. In Sierra Leone, Christian Creoles were widely employed; in Nyasaland, pagan and Christian Nguru immigrants went more willingly to school and soon outdistanced the Muslim Yao; in Nigeria, the whirlwind sown by Ibo dominance in the Muslim north is still being reaped today. But in some areas, particularly East Africa, and in some callings, particularly the military, Muslims enjoyed considerable influence as the employees of Europeans.

In East Africa, many of the early government officials, foremen on European farms, and so on, were Muslim Swahili from the coast. This was particularly true in German East Africa, where the Germans took over the old Zanzibari pattern of administration, and extended it far into the interior. The fact that the Maji-Maji revolt in German East Africa in 1905 was against Arabs and Swahili as well as Europeans suggests the extent to which the Germans had entrusted power to these subordinates. In East Africa too the early military garrisons were Muslim, Sudanese or Swahili, but this feature was not confined to the east.

The colonial troops of all European powers in Africa were often Muslim. Occasionally such troops were used against other Muslims: Muslim Galla served Italians against Arabs and Turks in North Africa, Hausa served the Free State against the Congo Arabs, Sudanese and Somalis served Germans against Abūshīrī, and more recently Senegalese served the French against the Algerian nationalists. Muḥammad 'Abd Allāh bitterly criticized those who fought for 'the uncircumcised heretic'. The *Union culturelle musulmane* of French West Africa in 1958 condemned sending Muslim troops against Muslims in Algeria. But such troops might also contribute to the spread of Islam. Non-Muslim recruits were often converted.

As for the third opportunity of the colonial period, mobility, this, as indirect rule and direct employment, had some disadvantages. Some underlying patterns were disrupted: the push from Zanzibar into the

Congo was blocked, and links between the western Sudan and North Africa weakened. New boundaries dissected established states: Yola was severed from the rest of Adamawa. Occasionally Muslim trading communities declined, by-passed by new railways and roads.

But in general Muslims were able to take advantage of the new opportunities. Muslims and Europeans shared a common interest in trade. Once colonial rule was established, communications greatly improved. In the earliest days, Europeans sometimes relied on already established Muslim communications: various explorers remarked the relative ease of travel in Muslim areas. Islam spread from town to country. Muslims moved into new areas. Equally, pagans moved into Muslim areas: Bambara infiltrating Fulani regions near Jenne, no longer having to fight the Fulani, ended by becoming Muslim; Mossi were converted when they went to work on Gold Coast cocoa plantations. Even deportations sometimes played a positive part in the pattern of mobility.

Separatists and reformers

The fringes of Africa, north and east, have shared in the major schisms and heresies of the Muslim world. These did not, apparently, penetrate the western or central Sudan to any significant extent. Instead, a new heresy developed there, that of the 'mixers'.

Probably the best known and most important example of modern 'mixing' is the Murids of Senegal, an offshoot of the Qādiriyya. The founder, Aḥmad Bamba, received his call in 1886. Although he was himself in origin part Tokolor, the mass of Murids are Wolof, and the brotherhood has been called the 'Wolofization' of Islam. The founder and his descendants constitute a lineage of saints. Adherents become direct disciples of one leading marabout or another, often a member of the founder's family. The disciple surrenders himself, body and soul, to the teacher. The disciple works for the teacher; the teacher prays in place of the disciple; salvation is assured to both. Manual labour, particularly on the land, is sanctified. Most of the profits go to the teachers, in whose luxurious estate the disciples take vicarious satisfaction. The main festivals of the Islamic calendar are observed at the Murid headquarters, Touba, but more popular than these is the Magal festival, commemorating the return of Aḥmad Bamba from exile.

Although the 'mixing' heresy continued into this century, the arrival of Christianity, of European colonial rule, and of Western civilization, introduced entirely new factors into the African equation. Muslims had to adjust themselves, not only to the local African heritage, but to the Christian and Western challenge also. The Muslim response was twofold: external, a matter of foreign relations between Muslims and the West; and internal, a matter of domestic reform—the adjustments necessary within the Muslim community to enable it to meet the new challenge. As Muslims disagreed among themselves about the proper attitude at both levels, opportunities for divergent, and sometimes heretical, opinions increased. The situation was additionally complicated because heresy, even if defined, could no longer be disciplined as in the old days. Further, most of our information comes from European observers, sometimes inclined to overstate the case. It seems better, therefore, for the modern period to borrow from African Christianity the term 'separatism' for all those Muslim movements which have separated from other Muslims, or from existing Islamic traditions, in order somewhat differently, and perhaps more appropriately, to express the faith.

In the early colonial period, some degree of resistance or aloofness was a mark of orthodoxy, and to co-operate closely with the infidels was a symptom of separatism. Thus the well-known judgment on early heresy in Islam, that the one constant criterion was subversion, was reversed by colonialism. Aḥmad Bamba at first considered *jihād*; he did not put this to the test, but the French were suspicious, and twice exiled him, treatment greatly enhancing his repute. Gradually, however, an unusual degree of co-operation developed. The French, as we have seen, came to use Murid discipline for a form of indirect rule. Economics were important in reconciling Murid marabouts to French rule, and the Murids were soon producing more than half the total groundnut crop, Senegal's main export.

The Murids were in three senses separatist: as 'mixers', as having too close an association with their non-Muslim rulers, and as exploiting their religious organization for economic ends. Tijānī and Qādirī leaders began to imitate the Murids, until what had once been separatist became almost standard. A new separatism arose in reaction, the Hamallists.

Shaykh Ḥamāllāh (Ḥamā Allāh) began preaching in Nioro in the 1920s. He used the shortened prayer, allowed to Muslims in urgent danger, to symbolize the incompatibility of Islam and infidel overrule. He and his followers were repeatedly charged with involvement in violent disturbances. He died in exile in France in 1943. Ḥamāllāh, teaching a reformed Tijānī rite and condemning the temporal comportment of many marabouts, was on angry terms with other Muslims, especially traditionalist Tijānīs.

Neither Murids nor Hamallists proceeded to the second level of Muslim response, that of internal adjustment. One of the earliest examples of this occurs in a variety of separatist episodes, apparently unrelated but much alike, in Freetown, Porto Novo, Cotonou, Lagos, and elsewhere, to which I give the general name 'coastal fever'. Beginning often in the late nineteenth century, it became acute in several places in the 1920s. In Porto Novo, it took the form of tension between Creole Muslims returned from South America, and Nigerian Yoruba and Hausa immigrants. Making allowance for local variations, it is possible to trace certain broad outlines of argument: on the one side a traditionalist party, defending local Islam in its existing form, and on harmonious terms with the colonial authorities; and on the other reformers, wishing to modernize Islamic organization, and to maintain more distance from the colonial régime. The main focus of controversy was the imamate. There were frequently rival *imāms*, and also rival concepts of the imamate, the traditionalists regarding the office as sacred, and succession to it as governed by custom, the reformers regarding it as an elective, representative office. In Lagos, the reformers wished a written constitution for the Muslim community. Both sides showed remarkable willingness to submit to colonialist interference in religious affairs: many reconciliation meetings were sponsored by colonial officials; in Porto Novo twenty-three candidates for the imamate were tested by an official, in Freetown and Lagos ownership of the Friday mosque was thrashed out before colonial courts.

Although the Aḥmadiyya, founded in India by Ghulām Aḥmad late in the nineteenth century, stands partly in the tradition of Shīʿī mystical separatism, it is also perhaps the clearest example of all of response to the Western and Christian challenge, both in external relations and internal adjustment. Ghulām Aḥmad made three major claims: to be the Mahdi waging peaceful *jihād*; to be the Messiah; and to be a prophet. The doctrine of the peaceful Mahdi was rendered suspect in orthodox eyes by the religious romanticism of the Aḥmadīs over the British Empire, regarding it as a step towards a divinely-willed world order, one of the more mysterious ways in which God moves to perform His wonders. As Messiah, Ghulām Aḥmad drew strength from his positive identification with Jesus. The centralized organization of many Christian missions, with professional missionaries, schools, publishing houses, scripture translations, and other modern features, was copied by the Aḥmadiyya. These are to be employed in the struggle against Christianity, for the Aḥmadiyya is more anti-Christian than syncretist. The third claim, that Ghulām Aḥmad was a prophet after Muḥammad, is the ultimate heresy: that he should have ventured this is perhaps a measure of the difficulties which he thought confronted Islam.

The Aḥmadiyya first appeared on the West African coast during the First World War, when several young men in Lagos and Freetown joined by mail. In 1921, the first Indian missionary arrived. Too unorthodox to gain a footing in the Muslim interior, the Aḥmadiyya remains confined principally to southern Nigeria, southern Gold Coast, and Sierra Leone. It strengthened the ranks of those Muslims actively loyal to the British, and it contributed to the modernization of Islamic organization in the area. But its numbers remained small, and its effectiveness was weakened by successive internal schisms. Its chief importance, to be discussed in the next section, has been its pioneering contribution to Muslim-Western education in Africa. It joined the arguments about the nature of the imamate, and the necessity of a constitution; it attempted to regularize finance, forbidding for example extravagant celebrations and thus clashing with the ancient heresy of 'mixing'.

Muslim separatism in Africa is an attempt to maintain a balanced relationship between the faith and the practical circumstances in which the faith exists. If the faith seems too foreign, it will be adapted; if too acclimatized, it will be reformed. In the nineteenth and twentieth centuries, the practical circumstances have included both the African traditional heritage, and the Christian, colonial and Western presences. National independence changes the detail of the practical circumstances somewhat, but in no way removes the tension between them and the ideal faith. Indeed, the demands of nationalism may stimulate new separatisms, whether for or against the state. Another future source of separatism may be the Qur'ān translated. Many leaders of Christian separatism argue their case, partly at least, from the Bible. Such use of the Qur'ān is much less common in Muslim separatism. In Africa hitherto, the standard of reference has been more the Pilgrimage, and the teaching of the '*ulamā*'. The Aḥmadiyya, while still believing that the Qur'ān is essentially untranslatable, has popularized its own English versions, and has encouraged people to think of reading the Qur'ān in their own language, or at least in a language they can readily understand. In East Africa, an Aḥmadiyya Swahili translation appeared in 1953, followed in 1962 by an orthodox version as riposte. It would be surprising if some of the readers of these did not formulate convictions which are at odds with the accepted practices of Muslims round about them.

Education

The European colonial period brought new challenges to African Islamic education, with new subjects and new qualifications needed. The endeavour to adjust education to include the new disciplines without sacrificing the positive Islamic element continues until today. The colonial governments themselves, on a limited scale, embarked on this endeavour before many Muslims took it up. But such European initiatives never really overcame the suspicions of the pious, while students who were committed to Western education preferred the more widely recognized qualifications of fully Western schools.

The French established *madrasas*, advanced schools combining western and Islamic education, in several Muslim centres, using local teachers often trained in North Africa. In the *madrasa* of Timbuktu, set up in 1911, the chief *imām* was one of the teachers. He had led the Timbuktu delegation to Morocco requesting help against the French invaders—last echo of the trans-Saharan ambition of Aḥmad al-Manṣūr in the sixteenth century. He had gone on to Mecca, but later returned home and settled under the French. Arabic, Berber and French languages were taught: one of the Arabic texts was *A Thousand and One Nights*. A similar German school was established at Garwa, in Adamawa, in 1906, to train junior civil servants. This school also offered Arabic, and had compulsory mosque attendance on Fridays. But in 1915, when German rule ended, there were only fifty-four pupils. French officials attempted to regulate traditional Qur'anic schools from as early as 1857. But what the French justified as a means of raising standards, the Muslims condemned as unwarranted governmental interference in religious affairs, and the regulations were only partially effective. The clearest example of Muslim resistance to colonial meddling in education is in British Somaliland. Christian mission schooling had been one of the irritants leading to Muḥammad b. 'Abd Allāh's *jihād*, and from 1910 it was banned. In 1920, British plans to introduce schools financed by a tax on livestock led to a riot in which a district commissioner was killed.

The plans were dropped. In 1936 such proposals were revived, to be blocked by another riot. It was, however, possible for the British government to give grants to a few Qur'anic schools, which taught Arabic and arithmetic, and a few boys went to the Sudan for secondary education. A curiosity among these colonial experiments in Muslim education is the school reported in 1906 from Murzuk, then still a Turkish outpost. The school was maintained and staffed voluntarily by Young Turks, political prisoners banished to the Sahara.

In the long run, the reconciliation of Muslim and Western education depended on African initiative. Edward Blyden (1832–1912), active in various attempts to bring together Muslim and Western, and Muslim and Christian education, in Liberia, Sierra Leone and Nigeria, marks the transition. Though a West Indian and a Christian, he was more identified with local Muslims than European officials could be.

The earliest spontaneous Muslim effort seems to have been the school founded in Ekrofol in southern Gold Coast in 1896, by two Fante Muslims, converts from Methodism. After some years, this school failed. The effective inaugurators of Muslim-Western education in tropical Africa were the Aḥmadīs. Many of the Nigerians and Sierra Leoneans who welcomed the Aḥmadiyya after the First World War, just as many of the Gambians who welcomed it after the Second, were more interested in educational help than doctrinal innovation. When doctrinal innovation was found inherent in the Aḥmadiyya, some African Muslims set up their own, more orthodox, educational groups. The *Anṣār-ud-dīn*, founded in Nigeria in 1923, is now a much larger organization than the Nigerian Aḥmadiyya. The Muslim Brotherhood in Sierra Leone, founded in 1959, is rapidly overtaking the Sierra Leonean Aḥmadīs in educational work. The Brotherhood is heavily backed by the United Arab Republic. This is a great help, since Arabic occupies a prominent place in most modern Muslim school plans. Both the *Anṣār* and the Brotherhood were established by former Aḥmadīs. Similar 'voluntary agency' Muslim educational progress developed later in East Africa, where again Aḥmadīs have contributed, and the Muslim Welfare Association of the Ismā'īlī community.

French-speaking tropical Africa was more influenced by North African developments. The Salafiyya movement, attempting both to reform and to defend Islam, stressed modern Muslim education. The Free Schools of Morocco, flourishing in the 1920s, were a direct result of Salafī teaching. In North Africa, politics often swallowed education;

but in tropical Africa reforming Muslims continued to advocate Salafī ideas until the end of the European period. Reformist schools began about 1950. The principal organization encouraging such work was the *Union culturelle musulmane*, set up in 1953.

Although the French-speaking countries have not had to digest Aḥmadī heresy, the new schools have occasioned considerable controversy and, for example in Bamako, some violence. Three main Muslim viewpoints emerge: the reformist, the purely traditionalist, and that of certain traditional leaders who acknowledge the need for some modernizing and purifying of African Islam. In seeking to purge accretions and reform corruptions, these reformers—and the Aḥmadīs, the *Anṣār*, the Brotherhood, and others—stood in the succession of those who, from the Almoravids onwards, have waged war against 'mixing'. But the class-room has replaced the armed camp; in place of military dedication, these schools offered academic learning. Those, like the reformist schools in French West Africa, or the Brotherhood schools in independent Sierra Leone, with strong North African connexions, could offer also Arabic as an effective, living language.

APPENDIX

South Africa

Slaves and political prisoners, from the Dutch East Indies, were the first Muslims in South Africa, arriving in the late eleventh/seventeenth and early twelfth/eighteenth centuries. Some, such as Shaykh Yūsuf, who had championed Bantam resistance to the Dutch, were men of political and religious stature. Stories of many miracles adorn his memory, and his tomb is still a place of pilgrimage, one of a circle of tombs of early saints, surrounding and guarding the Cape peninsula. In 1767, the Dutch ceased sending political exiles to the Cape.

As for the slaves, their numbers increased during the eighteenth century, and Cape law and customs stiffened against them. Those slaves, for example some from East or West Africa and from Madagascar, who were not already Muslim inclined to the example of their Malay colleagues. A *sharīf*, Sa'id, is said to have come to the Cape after Shaykh Yūsuf's death, and to have taught the slaves, miraculously entering their locked quarters at night to read the Qur'ān and to bring them food. Not until the early nineteenth century were Muslims allowed a regular mosque in Cape Town.

A third wave of Muslim immigration came from 1860 on, when Indian labourers came to the plantations in Natal and Transvaal, followed by Indian traders, especially Bombay Muslims. Muslims from elsewhere in Africa have drifted in too, for instance a few Somalis.

The Cape Malays became skilful artisans; and, in common with various other Muslim groups in Africa, the army was among their vocations. Malay artillerymen distinguished themselves in the defence of the Cape against the British in 1804.

The Cape Malays are frequent pilgrims to Mecca. In the second half of the nineteenth century, ties with Istanbul developed, partly through a controversy among the Cape Malays over the religious respectability of a Malay sword dance—an Asiatic example, perhaps, of the 'mixing' heresy. As in East Africa, Islam in South Africa is represented by several traditional orders; but resistance to novelties, such as the Aḥmadiyya, is keen.

CHAPTER 7

THE IBERIAN PENINSULA AND SICILY

I. ISLAM IN THE IBERIAN PENINSULA

The Muslim conquest

The weakness of the Visigothic monarchy and the apathy of the oppressed Hispano-Roman population offered an easy prey to the Arabs recently established on the other shore of the Straits of Gibraltar. Mūsā b. Nuṣayr, who had just triumphantly overrun Morocco, and his lieutenant, Ṭāriq b. Ziyād, governor of Tangier (Ṭanja), with the complicity of the legendary Count Julian, were the fortunate conquerors of Spain. The first landing of a detachment of 400 men sent to reconnoitre by the Berber, Ṭarīf b. Mallūq, took place in Ramaḍān 91/July 710, and the booty obtained without resistance induced Mūsā to give to his freedman, Ṭāriq, command of the expedition guided by Count Julian which encamped at Calpe (Jabal Ṭāriq, i.e. Gibraltar) and took Cartaja in Rajab 92/spring 711.

King Roderick, who was putting down a Basque revolt, hastened to Cordova, and, after gathering an army together, advanced towards the Algeciras region. Here Ṭāriq awaited him with 12,000 Berbers and a number of partisans of the sons of Witiza, a former king, who were rebels against Roderick. The battle took place on 28 Ramaḍān 92/19 July 711 on the banks of the river Barbate. It is not certain whether Roderick lost his life in the encounter, but, on the dispersal of his troops, Ṭāriq, contrary to the instructions which he had received to return to Africa, or at least to remain where he was until further orders, attacked Écija and took Cordova. Toledo, almost evacuated by its authorities, offered him no resistance, and so he was able to advance with his irresistible cavalcade as far as Guadalajara and Alcalá de Henares. In the face of such extensive conquests, he asked for reinforcements from Mūsā b. Nuṣayr. Mūsā, jealous of the glory acquired by his freedman, and indignant at seeing himself disobeyed, landed at Algeciras with 18,000 men and after taking Medina Sidonia, Carmona, and Alcalá de Guadaira by assault, captured Seville with no great effort. Only before Mérida, where Roderick's chief supporters had assembled, did he have to keep up a siege of six months. Once he had obtained its submission, he made for Toledo, where Ṭāriq, whom he had met and lashed with his scorn at Talavera, handed over to him the treasures of the Visigothic dynasty. He wished to carry on by way of Saragossa to Lérida, but the Umayyad Caliph al-Walīd ordered him to present himself with Ṭāriq at Damascus in order to give an account of his conquests.

Before his departure he completed the subjugation of the sub-Pyrenean region as far as Galicia, and left for Syria at the end of 95/summer 714, handing over the governorship of Andalus to his son ʿAbd al-ʿAzīz, who pacified the whole of south-eastern Spain, and signed a treaty of submission with the Visigothic lord of the Murcia region, Theodomir. He married Roderick's widow. In 97/716 he was assassinated at Seville by order of the Caliph Sulaymān, after a short rule of two years. Before his death, the conquest of the peninsula was for practical purposes finished. It seems that Muslim garrisons had already been established in the chief towns and that a great number of Hispano-Romans had accepted conversion to Islam in order to enjoy full rights of citizenship under the new régime. These converts on becoming the great majority of the population of Andalus, gradually acquired a very original character, for they combined the culture brought by the invaders from the Orient with their native characteristics, which included the preservation of their Romance language, spoken by them as well as by the Mozarabic communities (which continued to be Christian) in the big cities such as Toledo, Cordova, Seville, and Valencia.

The military morale of these invaders, who did not balk at the barrier of the Pyrenees and, disregarding the danger to their line of retreat, invaded Gaul, offers the most vivid contrast with the passive surrender of the native people, who, in spite of their great numerical superiority, their knowledge of the terrain, particularly suited to guerrilla warfare, and their occupation of the strongholds, offered no more than the belated resistance of a few fanatical mystics, who braved Islam and its Prophet only to suffer martyrdom.

The governors dependent on Damascus

The period of roughly forty years, 716–58, which intervened between the murder of ʿAbd al-ʿAzīz and the establishment of the Umayyad amirate in Spain, is characterized by the rivalry and struggles with which the Qaysites and Kalbites revived Arab factionalism in the Iberian peninsula, and by the rapid succession of governors nominated and dismissed by the *wālīs* of Qayrawān, or the caliph in Damascus. Their task was to consolidate the conquest, to put down rebellion, and to launch expeditions against Gaulish territory. These were finally brought to a halt at Poitiers, where Charles Martel defeated and killed the governor of Cordova, 'Abd al-Raḥmān al-Ghāfiqī, in Ramaḍān 114/end of October 732. The fugitives fled to Narbonne, whence another expedition set off in 116/734, invaded Provence, and did not withdraw until four years later. Charles Martel laid siege to Narbonne, and again succeeded in defeating, in 120/737, another column commanded by 'Uqba b. al-Ḥajjāj. Finally his son, Pepin the Short, re-took Narbonne in 133/751, thereby forcing the Muslims definitely to give up the conquest of Gaul. Civil war and the character of the invaders themselves, who were for the most part ignorant soldiers, did not create a propitious climate for the development of culture. Burning with the ardour of their new religion, they needed no more than the Qur'ān, the sole fount of law, to impose their religion without provoking ideological conflicts. During this first period, they contented themselves with the division and organization of the huge patrimony which had fallen into their hands. Not only did they live alongside the vanquished Christians, but they accepted their conversion to Islam; and, as they had crossed over to the peninsula as a military force, and not as immigrant tribes, they suffered from a shortage of women, and so took wives among the vanquished. This fashion was inaugurated by 'Abd al-'Azīz, son of Mūsā b. Nuṣayr, when he married Roderick's widow. It became almost the general rule, especially as the Umayyad *amīrs* themselves, and even the caliph and the *Ḥājib* al-Manṣūr, preferred Basques, Galicians, and Frankish women, although they had women of their own nationality within easy reach.

About 720 a few Visigothic aristocrats and the natives of Asturias began the *Reconquista* with the proclamation of Pelayo and the battle of Covadonga, which later acquired a legendary tinge. When the Berbers evacuated the sub-Pyrenean regions of Galicia and Asturias, this state under Alfonso I succeeded in extending as far as the valley of the Duero. With a patriotism unknown to their Mozarab co-religionists, and with unquenchable valour, these Iberians put a brake on the Islamic advance, and began to recover their ancestral lands. The disproportionate power of their adversaries, with their devastating raids and their assaults on citadels and cities, failed to impose sovereignty on the modest kingdoms of Oviedo, Pamplona, and later León, which were to resist the attacks of the Cordovan power with stoical firmness. Though they may sometimes have acknowledged themselves to be feudatories, they were never to relinquish their sovereignty, and were to show their obvious superiority in battle as soon as the caliphate began to decline.

As regards the law of land-tenure in conquered Andalus, the sources are very scarce and contradictory. The majority state that the division of land was begun by Ibn Nuṣayr, according to law, reserving the 'Fifth' (*al-Khums*) for the state, but Ibn Ḥazm, who betrays the national sentiment of the *muwallads* (native Muslims), assures us that the régime was based on the law of the strongest. The conquerors, arriving from the Maghrib, Ifrīqiya, and Egypt, occupied agricultural properties by force; only to be themselves in their turn, and not much later, evicted by the Syrians brought in to suppress a Berber revolt, without there being in any of these cases any regular and lawful procedure.

The establishment of the Umayyad Amirate of Cordova

The spectacular collapse of the Umayyad Caliphate in Syria, and the accession of the 'Abbasid dynasty, finally loosed the bonds which linked Andalus to Damascus through frequently dismissed governors. 'Abd al-Raḥmān b. Mu'āwiya, grandson of the Caliph Hishām, managed to escape from the extermination of his family, and took refuge in North Africa. Through his faithful *mawlā*, Badr, he made contact with Umayyad clients in Andalus, where he arrived on 1 Rabī' I 138/14 August 755. He entered Seville, and took the road for Cordova, in the neighbourhood of which he achieved a resounding victory, which opened to him the gates of the capital. He was recognized in its mosque as *amīr* of all Andalus.

In the thirty-two years of his reign (138–72/756–88) he showed his great qualities. Surrounded by a court of Umayyad *émigrés*, he devoted himself to the consolidation of his power, and to the energetic suppression of the continual uprisings of his subjects, both Arab and Berber. These bathed almost all his reign in blood, and alternated with the intrigues of his relatives who, though welcomed at his court, attempted repeatedly to dethrone him, and paid for their treachery with their lives.

These internal complications did not allow him to devote all his efforts to the *jihād* on the frontier of the little kingdom of Asturias, with which he kept a truce of twenty years from 150/767 to 169/786. In this interval Charlemagne undertook, in 161/778, his celebrated expedition against Saragossa, which ended in his defeat at Roncesvalles. This disaster showed Charlemagne that uncertain alliances with dissident Muslim chiefs made success against Spanish Islam very doubtful. For this reason he preferred to found the kingdom of Aquitaine to watch and maintain the Pyrenean frontier, and he succeeded, in 169/785, in making the inhabitants of Gerona submit to the Frankish authority.

'Abd al-Raḥmān I preserved and extended the organization which the governors appointed from Damascus had established in the new province. He made Cordova the seat of his government, and refrained from adopting any other title but that of *amīr*. At least at the beginning of his rule, he allowed the *khuṭba* to be recited in the name of the 'Abbasid caliph. About the middle of his reign, he organized an army of mercenaries, Berbers, and *mamlūks* bought in northern Europe. 'Abd al-Raḥmān I died in Cordova on 25 Rabī' II 172/30 September 788 before reaching his sixtieth year. According to the Arabic chronicles, which eulogize him in the warmest terms, he was one of the best rulers of his dynasty. The native population caused 'Abd al-Raḥmān I no anxiety, for both the country people and the town-dwelling proletariat, who had not forgotten Visigothic tyranny, lived on good terms with the central power. Homesickness for his distant homeland caused him to establish a country residence near Cordova, which he called al-Ruṣāfa after the summer palace between Palmyra and the Euphrates, where, as a boy, he had stayed for long periods with his grandfather, Hishām.

From 'Abd al-Raḥmān I onwards, all the history of the Umayyad amirate of Cordova is influenced, not to say dominated, by the instability of the various ethnic groups—Arab, Berber, neo-Muslim, Mozarab, and Jewish—whose passionate rivalries made impossible the pacification of the country until the time of 'Abd al-Raḥmān III. By contrast, the population of the nascent Christian states was much more homogeneous and stable, for the inhabitants of the territory evacuated by the Berbers had once more adopted their old religion, if indeed they had ever abandoned it. Alfonso I and Fruela I would not tolerate Muslim communities within their dominions, and it was not until the beginning of the sixth/twelfth century, when the Reconquest was already far advanced, that Christian rulers allowed nuclei of Moriscos (i.e. Muslims) to remain, in view of the impossibility of peopling the newly conquered territory with their own few subjects.

The successor to 'Abd al-Raḥmān I was not his first-born, Sulaymān, but his second son, Hishām, whose proclamation provoked a dynastic war, in which Sulaymān and another of his brothers, 'Abd Allāh, had to emigrate to North Africa. The reign of Hishām I (172–80/788–96), in contrast with that of his father, was characterized by general internal peace and by the official adoption of the Mālikī *madhhab* in the peninsula. Various Andalusian pilgrims had heard Mālik b. Anas (d. 179/795) expound his chief work, *al-Muwaṭṭa'*. When these disciples returned to Andalus, the information which they gave on the development of Islamic culture in the East interested Hishām I, and contributed to the fact that he, as also his successor, al-Ḥakam I, established the Mālikī *madhhab* on an official basis. The Mālikī teachings soon crystallized into an unchangeable doctrine, opposed to any attempt at innovation, and so made of Andalus a firm stronghold of orthodoxy.

This interlude of peace at home, which Hishām I enjoyed during his brief reign, enabled him to press the religious war against the Asturian kingdom almost every summer. Two armies, one following the Ebro up to Álava, the other marching to the north-west along the Bierzo, won two victories. In 178/791 Álava and Asturias were again the object of a counter-attack, but the column which succeeded in sacking Oviedo was taken by surprise and suffered heavy losses on the way back in a marsh, even though Alfonso II was almost captured on the banks of the Nalón. Hishām died prematurely at the age of forty, after nominating as his successor his second son, al-Ḥakam I (180–206/796–822), whose succession to the throne ushered in a long period of trouble in the country. His two uncles, who had come out against his father, renewed their attacks. The first, Sulaymān, advanced towards Cordova, failed in his attempt to enter the capital, and finally was killed in the Mérida region. The second, 'Abd Allāh, after seeking the support of Charlemagne, whom he visited at Aix-la-Chapelle, was pardoned on condition of residing at Valencia until his death.

Meanwhile uprisings in the three marches of Saragossa, Toledo and Mérida occupied almost all the attention of al-Ḥakam I. Saragossa, where an agitator had declared himself independent, was reconquered, and in order to secure its frontier the fortress of Tudela was established on the right bank of the Ebro. Toledo, always inclined towards dissidence, was brought to heel by terrorism on the famous 'Day of the Ditch' (*Waq'at al-Ḥufra*, 181/797) when the Toledan bourgeoisie was treacherously decimated.

In the Lower March the *amīr* had to struggle for seven years in order to reduce Mérida, and to this series of provincial uprisings was added the plot set on foot to dethrone him, and to put his cousin in his place. The plot was discovered, and savagely repressed. The repression in its turn provoked new disorders, and the excitement of the people boiled over in the revolt of the Arrabal,[1] which came near to costing al-Ḥakam his throne and his life. The vengeance of the *amīr* is vividly remembered

Map 14. The Iberian peninsula and the Maghrib in the late third/ninth century.

in the annals of western Islam. After unheard-of rapine and butchery the survivors of the Arrabal were exiled, and the whole area with its houses was razed, and ploughed, and sown again. Some of the emigrants peopled the quarter of the Andalusians in newly founded Fez, while

[1] I.e. *al-Rabaḍ*, a suburb of Cordova.

others adopted piracy, and were even able to take Alexandria, and found a kingdom in Crete.

Such serious disturbances did not prevent al-Ḥakam from attacking the region which formed the nucleus of Castile, taking Calahorra in the Ebro valley, and raiding the borders of Álava. But even this placed no obstacle in the way of the Christian advance into Muslim territory all over the north, to conquer Lisbon in the north-west, and form the Hispanic March in the east, with the taking of Barcelona by the Franks.

The reign of the cruel al-Ḥakam I coincides paradoxically with the humanization of Andalus, and the first signs of the influence which the ʿAbbasid culture of Baghdād was to exercise on the Iberian peninsula. At the same time, there began to take place a fusion between the Arab aristocracy and the neo-Muslims of Hispanic origin, now that numerous non-Arabs, even Berbers and Slavs, occupied important posts at court and in the administration of the amirate. At the end of his life, after a reign lasting almost a quarter of a century, al-Ḥakam I's outlook grew embittered and his mistrust increased, a fact which the *ʿulamā'* attributed to remorse for his crimes, especially against the people living outside Cordova. He shut himself away in his palace, surrounded by Christian mercenaries, and ignoring his subjects' discontent and his own unpopularity, devoted himself solely to the maintenance of political unity in his kingdom. On 10 Dhu'l-Ḥijja 206/6 May 822, he solemnly proclaimed not only a successor but also the latter's heir presumptive, should his successor die prematurely. Fifteen days later al-Ḥakam I died at the age of fifty-three. On his deathbed, he urged his son to be just and firm.

On succeeding to the throne, ʿAbd al-Raḥman II (206–38/ 822–52) enjoyed thirty years of relative peace in the interior, gained by the harsh energy of his father. In this period of political calm, the intellectual revival flowing from the Orient continued to develop. His paternal great uncle ʿAbd Allāh who, besides being the practically independent governor of Valencia, had designs on the Tudmīr region, died in 208/823–4, and, after putting down at Lorca the unrest provoked by the hostility between Qaysites and Kalbites, ʿAbd al-Raḥmān founded the new city of Murcia.

He left his brother, al-Walīd, to suppress without great difficulty an obscure rebellion which broke out at Toledo, and devoted his activity for the most part to fighting the Christians in the north. In three successive campaigns he attacked the regions of Álava and Old Castile. These campaigns were followed by frequent incursions into Galician territory where Alfonso II reigned. He also launched a number of summer expeditions against Barcelona and Gerona, which he was unable to take; and not until the death of Louis the Pious in 841 did a Muslim army penetrate into France, sacking the Cerdagne, and reaching as far as Narbonne.

Three years later, in 229/844, the Scandinavian pirates reached the Atlantic coast of the peninsula. They disembarked opposite Lisbon, and, after bloody battles, re-embarked to reappear at the mouth of the Guadalquivir, take Cadiz, and attack defenceless Seville, which was sacked, and such inhabitants as did manage to escape, were killed or enslaved. ʿAbd al-Raḥmān II mobilized all his forces and completely defeated the invaders. The demoralized survivors re-embarked, and though in 859 and 866 they repeated their attempts, they were easily repulsed.

The Mozarabs, although subject to severe taxation, were tolerated and no *dhimmī*, as such, was condemned to death until the formation of the party led by the fanatics Eulogio and Álvaro, whose mystic exaltation led them to seek martyrdom in insulting the Prophet, and blaspheming against the Muslim religion. This wave of provocation lasted until 245/859 when, during the amirate of Muḥammad I, Eulogio, its prime mover, was beheaded.

Meanwhile diplomatic relations where instituted between Cordova and Constantinople at the instigation of the Emperor Theophilus, who proposed a treaty of alliance to carry on the struggle against the ʿAbbasids, the natural enemies of the Umayyads as of the Byzantines. The Cordovan *amīr*, however, who sent in his turn an embassy to Theophilus, refused to come to an agreement.

ʿAbd al-Raḥmān II, one of the wealthiest monarchs of the Mediterranean world, was an efficient administrator, who, by generous distributions of wheat, eased the two great famines which desolated Spain in 207/822–3 and 232/846. He perfected the administrative organization and hierarchy in imitation of the ʿAbbasid governmental structure, with monopolies of the mint and of the manufacture of precious fabrics. The army and navy were two of the major preoccupations of this *amīr*, who expanded his fleet, and instituted an arsenal at Seville as a result of the incursions of the Northmen.

He was, moreover, a great builder and, surrounded by unheard-of luxury, encouraged music and art. The Umayyad amirate of Cordova now had no fear of sedition fomented by Baghdād, so 'Abd al-Raḥmān II not only copied the customs of his old enemies, but even decided to imitate their manner of life. His tastes, his refined luxuries, his art, his poets, his musicians, and even his commerce looked towards 'Irāq. This was an orientalization of which the most notable exponent was Ziryāb who, born in Mesopotamia and warmly welcomed at the Cordova court, was the unquestioned arbiter of taste, and able to impose his refinements and his innovations.

At the end of his life the *amīr* made no official choice of an heir among his many sons. A plot aimed at poisoning him failed, but he died within two months. Muḥammad I (238–73/852–86), his son and successor, was proclaimed by various *fatās*[1] of the palace in a *coup d'état*. He followed the same political and administrative lines as his father, and did not compare unfavourably with him in intelligence, loftiness of ambition, and energy in suppressing the almost permanent unrest in the Marches, above all in that of Toledo, which led to the battle of Guadazalete. In Mérida, the capital of the Lower March, 'Abd al-Raḥmān b. Marwān al-Jillīqī (i.e. the Galician) raised a rebellion, and made himself for many years the independent lord of Badajoz. At the same time 'Umar b. Ḥafṣūn fomented a serious insurrection in the districts of Reyo and Tākurunna in the south of Andalusia. Muḥammad I died while trying to clip the wings of Ibn Ḥafṣūn's brigandage, which was extending every day, and al-Mundhir, on succeeding his father, could not master the situation during the two short years which his rule lasted (273–5/886–8). He left no sons.

His brother 'Abd Allāh (275–300/888–912) succeeded him, only to find himself involved in a confusion of family crimes and continuous insurrections, in which the enemies of the Umayyad régime often combined into unstable leagues. The Muslims of Spanish origin (*Muwallads*) had created little independent principalities in the south-west of the peninsula and found themselves in conflict with the Arabs of the province of Elvira, whose internecine struggles were desolating the region. The seamen of the Mediterranean coast between Alicante and Águilas created the semi-independent federation of Pechina, while in Seville Arab patricians and *Muwallads* began a long period of civil strife. This terminated in the creation of a quasi-independent state ruled by the Arab,

[1] The *fatās* were palace officials recruited from the ranks of slaves.

Ibrāhīm b. Ḥajjāj, who later became a relative by marriage of Ibn Ḥafṣūn.

The latter, despite his brilliant but disorganized efforts, was unable to co-ordinate the general dissidence of the country. He was beaten at Poley and then, having forsworn Islam, was further weakened by repeated defeats, and finally succumbed to the pressure of ʿAbd al-Raḥmān III. Just as confused as the situation in the south of Andalusia was that in the Marches, where a mosaic of independent states, subject to a purely formal protectorate, encircled the region of Cordova from Badajoz on the west, to Toledo on the north and Saragossa on the east. By contrast, the kingdom of Asturias, which had shown such activity under Alfonso II against Muḥammad I, launched no attacks of any scope against ʿAbd Allāh, while the Banū Qasī, although weakened by domestic rivalries, kept up the struggle against the Basques of Pamplona. In Catalonia, liberated from Carolingian tutelage, the dynasty of the marquis-counts of Barcelona was founded.

In the first three centuries of the *Hijra* there appeared no philospher among the Spanish Muslims, and it was only contact with the famous Eastern schools which caused Muʿtazilite ideas, considered heretical, to enter Spain, in spite of the rigid official Malikism. With Ibn Masarra these ideas were hidden under a veil of asceticism, and led to the creation of a philosophical and theological system, and finally to Sufism. The most eminent personage of this movement was the Murcian, Muḥyī al-Dīn b. al-ʿArabī, whose pantheistic mysticism spread throughout Andalus, and gained for him in the Orient a reputation as a miracle-worker, almost a prophet.

ʿAbd al-Raḥmān III (300–50/912–61) is the outstanding figure among the Umayyad princes. In a long reign of almost fifty years, he made his country the most flourishing in all Europe, with a prestige rivalled only by that of Constantinople. He succeeded to a toppling throne when he had scarcely attained his majority, and immediately plunged into the struggle against Ibn Ḥafṣūn, inflicting continual defeats on him, until he died hemmed in in his fortress of Bobastro. The four sons of Ibn Ḥafṣūn continued the now hopeless struggle, and at last, in the spring of 316/928, ʿAbd al-Raḥmān III entered the eyrie which had resisted him for so long. With this, Andalus was pacified, and immediately afterwards the Algarve and Levante submitted. Toledo resisted for three years, but finally had to surrender unconditionally. The king of León, Ordoño III, took advantage of the initial difficulties of ʿAbd al-Raḥmān III in putting down these risings, but soon the victory of Valdejunquera and the campaigns of Muez and Pamplona made the Leonese and Navarrese respect him, until the aggressive Ramiro II of León defeated him with great slaughter, and routed him at the Ditch of Simancas (327/939). But with the death of the Leonese king in the winter of 339/950 and the outbreak of discord among León, Castile, and Navarre, 'Abd al-Raḥmān III reached the apogee of his power, and saw the Christian kings hastening to do homage at his court. However, in spite of his overwhelming superiority in men and riches, he did not succeed in annexing any important territory, far less in suppressing any of the Christian principalities with which he had to fight.

In order to counter the danger of a Fatimid invasion of the southern part of his states, the Cordovan ruler intervened in North Africa, occupied Ceuta, and succeeded in making a large part of the north of Morocco, and a considerable area of the central Maghrib, recognize his protectorate.

Towards the end of 316/928 'Abd al-Raḥmān III reached the triumphant culmination of his political career by adopting the caliphal title of *amīr al-mu'minīn*. He took the appellation of *al-Nāṣir li-Dīn Allāh* and founded Madīnat al-Zahrā', where he dazzled the Muslim and Christian embassies who sought audience of him by magnificent receptions. In the course of an unusually long reign he succeeded by his political genius and untiring energy in strengthening authority in his dominions, organizing his administration, and enforcing respect for his frontiers.

The Umayyad state now witnessed a great development of scientific culture, under the influence of the Orient and the personal effort of the heir apparent, al-Ḥakam. Medicine had hardly been studied at all until, from the days of 'Abd al-Raḥmān II onwards, doctors who had received training in 'Irāq, created a school where the works of Galen were studied, and later the *Materia medica* of Dioscorides was translated and utilized. The same was true in the field of history, until Aḥmad al-Rāzī, who had been left in Andalus at the age of three by his father, a native of Persia, codified the rules of historical composition. In the third/ninth century, and even more in the second/eighth, few were the occasional annalists who had gathered together collections of items of anonymous information, contaminated with legends relating especially to the remote period of the conquest. Such as the *Akhbār majmū'a*, a very poor history of little documentary value, as was observed by 'Īsā b. Aḥmad al-Rāzī, who also earned fame as the official chronicler of the dynasty, in the service of the Caliph al-Ḥakam II.

Al-Ḥakam II (350–66/961–76) succeeded his father at forty years of age. His reign was one of the most peaceful and fruitful of the dynasty. He attained his greatest glory through his love of literature and the arts, in assembling an exceedingly rich library, and enlarging and embellishing the incomparable mosque of Cordova.

A landing of Northmen in the region of Lisbon was easily repulsed, and frequent Leonese and Navarrese embassies seemed to affirm the submission of the Christian states of the peninsula. But when León, Castile and Navarre formed an alliance with the counts of Barcelona, al-Ḥakam II was obliged to direct in person an expedition against Castile in the summer of 352/963. The Christian princes had to sign a truce, and for several years new embassies from different regions of the peninsula filed through Cordova along with the envoys of the Holy Roman Emperor Otto II, and the Byzantine Emperor John Tzimisces.

Garci Fernández, count of Castile, taking advantage of a seizure, which kept the caliph inactive for several months in 364/974, with Galician and Basque reinforcements, besieged Gormaz, but was put to flight under its walls by the general Ghālib b. ʿAbd al-Raḥmān. In North Africa, al-Ḥakam II followed the risky policy of his father even though there now remained in his hands only the two citadels of Ceuta and Tangier. When the Fatimid caliph established himself in Egypt, al-Ḥakam was able to subdue the Idrisid princes, who were transferred to Cordova and emigrated to Egypt a little before he died.

On the accession of Hishām II (366–99/976–1009), who was very young and unable to direct the helm of the Cordovan caliphate, the way began to open out for the dictatorship of Muḥammad b. Abī ʿĀmir, who was to be called on account of his victories *al-Manṣūr* (Almanzor, 'the Victorious'). He countered all the plots woven against him, and was dictator of Muslim Spain for twenty years. He annihilated all his old collaborators without pity, and enlisted great Berber contingents in his army. He undertook continental campaigns against the Christians of the north, even as far as Santiago de Compostela and Barcelona, so that a number of counts recognized his sovereignty. It was only in the battle of Peñacervera that he came near to being defeated, after a desperate battle against Count Sancho García, with whom the Leonese and the Basques from Pamplona to Astorga had allied themselves. The sexagenarian al-

Manṣūr died in 392/1002 at Medinaceli on returning from his last expedition against Rioja.

Al-Manṣūr's tireless activity in the peninsula did not prevent him from continuing al-Ḥakam II's North African policy. He tried to conciliate the Zanāta Berber *amīrs* with generous gifts and put an end to the sporadic resistance of the remaining Idrisids. After successive triumphs and defeats in his struggle against the Fatimids he managed to establish a viceroyalty in Fez, which he entrusted to his son 'Abd al-Malik al-Muẓaffar. On succeeding his father, al-Muẓaffar (392–9/1002–8) maintained for six years, until his premature death, the peace at home which was so tragically destined to yield to anarchy and lawlessness. In his campaigns against the peninsular Christians he continued his father's work zealously; he attacked the region of the Spanish Marches, whose count had violated the truce signed but little before, and he defeated the Castilians. However, after suffering some time with a chest complaint, he returned to Cordova to die.

His brother, 'Abd al-Raḥmān, known as Sanchuelo because of his close resemblance to his maternal grandfather, Sancho Garcés II, king of Pamplona, succeeded him in the regency, but after a few months he provoked the tragedy in the history of Muslim Spain, the *fitna* or Andalusian revolution.

Licentious and vain, he demanded that the puppet ruler, Hishām II, name him officially as heir to the caliphate. The Cordovans were outraged and organized a plot to put on the throne an Umayyad pretender, Muḥammad II. Sanchuelo, returning from Toledo, was treacherously taken prisoner and murdered (399/1009), and with this episode there begins the complex and deplorable sequence of nine proclamations, dethronements and reinstatements which in the brief space of thirty years led to the suppression of the caliphate and the sudden collapse of a régime which had imposed its hegemony over the whole peninsula.

Muḥammad II, the victim of a Berber rebellion, was replaced for a moment by Sulaymān, the son of 'Abd al-Raḥmān III, only to be restored and then replaced again by Hishām II, who was killed by Sulaymān, at his new enthronement by the Berbers on their sacking of Cordova (403/1013). Idrisids from Morocco, the Hammudids (Banū Ḥammūd) succeeded Hishām II, with an interregnum by another Umayyad, al-Murtaḍā. Finally in 422/1031, the Cordovans, after fresh but unfruitful attempts at restoration, decided to do away with the caliphate, and formed a council of nobles to administer the reduced territory which was still in their power.

It was only the prestige and the extraordinary ability of 'Abd al-Raḥmān III, al-Ḥakam II, and al-Manṣūr, coupled with the importation of large Berber contingents, which had enabled the Muslims to get the upper hand over the small and divided Christian states. But their victory had not been durable, and no sooner had this sequence of three great leaders come to an end than the superiority of the Christians showed itself as decisively as had that of the Muslims at the invasion. The Arabs of the amirate depending on Damascus had succeeded in rapidly islamizing a great number of Hispano-Romans, but they were unable to annihilate the islets of native resistance in the Pyrenees. Conversely, the reconquerors, who had maintained their resistance heroically, were not successful, despite spectacular territorial advances, in reconverting to Christianity those very neo-Muslims whose ancestors had so easily released themselves from the bonds of the Catholic faith.

The high cultural level attained by the Spanish Muslims during the Umayyad Caliphate, in the confused days of the *fitna*, and the formation of the Party Kingdoms, finds its outstanding exponent in Ibn Ḥayyān in history, and in Ibn Ḥazm in literature and philosophy. Ibn Ḥayyān, the son of Khalaf, the secretary of al-Manṣūr, is the prince of historians of the Umayyad period. His two masterpieces are *al-Matīn*, in sixty volumes, known to us by a few quotations only, and *al-Muqtabis*, in ten volumes, which gives a rich and magnificent panorama of the Cordovan amirate from its beginnings until the time of the author. Three volumes only have been preserved.

Worthy to be associated with him is the famous polygraph Ibn Ḥazm, author of *Tawq al-ḥamāma* ('The Necklace of the dove'), which has been translated into several European languages, and the *Fiṣal*, a history of religions, in which he gives a critical exposition of all the attitudes of the human spirit in the religious sphere. It is an extraordinary work, without predecessor, and was unique of its kind until modern times.

The Party Kingdoms

The state of more or less permanent conspiracy, which disturbed the life of the Muslims of the peninsula until the end of the Umayyad Caliphate, became even more permanent, as a necessary consequence of the *fitna* by the formation of the Party Kingdoms. The slave-troops were largely of Slav origin. Many of them rose to become the most important officers of the caliphal government and of the 'Amirid dictatorship, and made themselves masters of the Levante. Along the Upper Frontier formed by the valley of the Ebro, with Saragossa as its capital, at first, the Tujībīs and later the Hudids (Banū Hūd), took possession. In spite of dynastic rivalries, the Hudids prospered, and allied themselves with the Cid Campeador against the count of Barcelona and the kingdom of Aragon. On the Lower Frontier, formed by the valleys of the Tagus and the Guadiana, two independent kingdoms established themselves with Toledo and Badajoz as capitals. At Toledo the king, al-Ma'mūn (429–67/1037–74) of the Dhu'l-Nunid (Banū Dhī'l-Nūn) dynasty, attached himself to Alfonso VI of Castile and managed to take possession of Cordova and Valencia. The latter city had been ruled by the 'Amirid, 'Abd al-'Azīz, the son of Sanchuelo, and on his death (453/1061) by his son. Al-Ma'mūn's son and successor was the incompetent Yaḥyā al-Qādir, who had to submit, and, abandoning his capital, moved to Valencia under the protection of the Castilians. The Castilians, with the Cid Campeador, finally took possession of Valencia (478/1075), and it remained in their power until it was retaken by the Almoravids. Badajoz was ruled by the Aftasids (Banu'l-Afṭas), a Berber dynasty, which maintained a continual state of war with the 'Abbadids (Banū 'Abbād) of Seville. When Alfonso VI took Coria (471/1079), King 'Umar the Aftasid sought the help of the Almoravids. He was finally beheaded with his two sons for having allied himself again with Alfonso VI against the Almoravids (487/1095).

Seville, governed by the Hispano-Arab dynasty of the 'Abbadids, is the most important and best known of the Party Kingdoms. On expelling the Ḥammudid caliph, the Sevillians formed a republican government under the presidency of the *Qāḍī* Muḥammad b. 'Abbād, who ridded himself of his colleagues and made himself *de facto* king. His son, al-Mu'taḍid (433–61/1042–69), extended his dominions, annexing without scruple the little principalities which had sprung up between Seville and the ocean. But, in spite of his conquests and annexations, he had to pay tribute like the kings of Badajoz, Saragossa, and Toledo to Ferdinand I, who had united León and Castile. Although his son, Muḥammad al-Mu'tamid (461–84/1069–91), took possession of Cordova, he was unable to resist Alfonso VI, and had to ask for the help of the Almoravids. He finally lost his throne, betrayed by the Sevillians, and was exiled to Aghmāt at the foot of the High Atlas, where he died in obscurity. His fame as poet and the pomp of his court won for him the attention and eulogy of Arab *littérateurs*, who made of him an idealized figure with exaggerated virtues.

The Ṣanhāja Berbers, coming from Ifrīqiya, set up a kingdom in Granada when the Umayyad pretender, al-Murtaḍā, was defeated under its walls. Zāwī b. Zīrī, the conqueror, did not believe it possible that his fellow-tribesmen could survive in Andalus, and left the rule to his nephew, Ḥabbūs, whose son, Bādīs, consolidated the Zirid power during a long reign (430–66/1038–73). He repulsed the attacks of the ruler of Seville, al-Muʿtamid, who followed a frankly anti-Berber, Arabo-Andalusian policy. ʿAbd Allāh, Bādīs's grandson and successor, was a coward who was loth to draw his sword, and could not make himself respected within his realm, nor resist the attacks of al-Muʿtamid and the pecuniary demands of Alfonso VI, whose protection he sought after having been present at the battle of Zallāqa and the siege of Aledo (see below). In 483/1000 he was deposed by the Almoravid Yūsuf b. Tāshufīn and exiled to Aghmāt, where he wrote the memoirs of his not very brilliant reign.

The Party Kings inherited, and imitated to the best of their abilities the pomp of the caliphate, and in their little courts, amidst disorder and war, art and culture flourished. This disorder and war prevented them from resisting the Christians in the north, and obliged them to seek help from the Almoravids, who by that time had taken possession of all Morocco and part of Algeria. This extreme measure caused much disquiet and repugnance on the part of these kings and their immediate collaborators, but when the Christian danger became even more grave, they sent ambassadors to Yūsuf to obtain confirmation of his decision to wage Holy War, and to sign the treaty by which the Andalusian kings promised to unite their forces to fight side by side with him. Yūsuf promised to respect their sovereignty and guaranteed not to meddle in their internal affairs; moreover, a term was fixed within which he and his troops undertook to evacuate Andalus.

The era of the Party Kings is characterized by an intellectual liberty considered legitimate by rulers who devoted themselves wholeheartedly to scientific and religious studies. Ṣāʿid (born 420/1029) attributes this renaissance, of which he was a witness, to the cessation of the intolerance imposed by al-Manṣūr, and the dispersal of books and scholars, which the Berber *fitna* provoked at Cordova. These books and scholars created a fertile soil for the 'ancient' studies cultivated by the Greeks and the Romans, i.e. philosophy, mathematics and natural science.

Seville, Badajoz, Almería, Granada and Saragossa were the new intellectual centres born of the decentralization of Cordova.

The Almoravids in Andalus

Yūsuf b. Tāshufīn crossed from Ceuta to Algeciras, which he occupied by force. He reached Seville, whence he proceeded towards Badajoz, accompanied by the Party Kings, in order to face the army of Alfonso VI on Friday, 12 Rajab 479/23 October 1086 at Zallāqa on the right bank of the Guadiana. The defeat of the Christians has a peculiar importance in the medieval history of Spain, not because in itself it was much more than another indecisive battle, but for what it symbolized. It was an unmistakable sign that the interplay of forces and the course of the Reconquest had suffered a change as sudden as it was complete.

Its effects became obvious immediately. The Levante, which had submitted to the protectorate of Alfonso VI, shook off the yoke of Castile, and the Cid Campeador was charged with its recovery. His successes, and incursions from Aledo, provoked repeated calls for help, and al-Mu'tamid succeeded in exacting a promise from Yūsuf b. Tāshufīn to lay siege to Aledo. Yūsuf crossed over to Andalus for the second time and the siege got under way (480/1088). The Muslim camp, however, was a hive of intrigues which prevented a prolonged encirclement, until finally the Almoravid *amīr* lost patience with the Party Kings, who had reopened their treacherous parleying with the Christians, and decided to dethrone them all.

Granada and Málaga were annexed during his third visit to the peninsula; then it was the turn of the king of Seville, al-Mu'tamid, whose capital surrendered in 484/1091, after his son al-Ma'mūn had been killed in an assault on Cordova. Almería and Badajoz yielded to the *Amīr* Sīr, a relative of Yūsuf, but in Levante his advance was blocked by the Cid, who took possession of Valencia in 1094, and defeated the Almoravids in the battle of Cuarte. After the death of the Cid (492/1099) Valencia was taken by the Almoravid *amīr*, Mazdalī; in 503/1110, the Almoravids occupied the kingdom of Saragossa and, in 1115, the Balearic Islands.

Yūsuf died at the beginning of 500/2 September 1106, and his son and successor, 'Alī, continued his offensive policy. The only son of Alfonso VI was defeated and killed on 16 Shawwāl 501/29 May 1108. In the following year 'Alī crossed over to Andalus, and took Talavera de la Reina. His cousin, Mazdalī, made an attack on Oreja and Zorita, only to be defeated and killed in the following year at Mastana. 'Alī arrived in

Andalus for the third time in 511/1117 and besieged Coimbra without result; Alfonso I of Aragon, on the contrary, made clear the premature decadence of the warlike spirit of the Almoravids in his famous year and a half's expedition through the heart of Andalusia, and took Saragossa in 512/1118.

The defeat suffered by 'Alī at Cullera in 522/1129 decided him to send his son Tāshufīn as governor of Granada and Almería, in order to raise morale and reinforce the defences of the frontier against the young and energetic Alfonso VII in Castile, and Alfonso I in Aragon. Tāshufīn showed unfailing courage in a struggle that was as prolonged as it was unequal, until he returned to Morocco, to be nominated hereditary *amīr* on the death of his brother Sīr. In the spring of 533/1139, with his faithful Catalan general Reverter, he undertook the ill-fated military operations which ended in his falling to his death from the cliffs near Oran, in 537/1143.

The Almohads

The collapse of the Almoravid empire brought in a second period of Party Kings, which began in 539/1144, a little before the death of Tāshufīn. Everywhere in Andalusia the new kinglets swarmed. But the resounding triumph of the Almohads in Fez and Marrakesh caused most of these new rulers to send deputations with their recognition to 'Abd al-Mu'min.

Once organized resistance in the Maghrib had ceased an Almohad army crossed over to Andalus, subdued all Algarve, and entered Seville. The new Party Kings, however, seeing the Moroccan rebellion of al-Māssī against 'Abd al-Mu'min, broke their oaths of fidelity, only to submit with the same inconstancy as soon as they learned that 'Abd al-Mu'min had mastered the situation, and was sending more troops to the peninsula.

At the end of 544/spring 1150, 'Abd al-Mu'min undertook the foundation of Rabat. He summoned the turncoat lords of Andalus to Salé and decided to keep them at his court in order that he might be able to carry out with greater security the campaign of 546/1151–2 against Bougie and Constantine. On his return he instituted hereditary rule, and with his customary harshness suppressed the rebellion of the brothers of the Almohad Mahdi, and the tribes of Hargha and Tinmāl.

Seeing his political horizon thus cloudless, he was able from 549/1154 onwards to devote all the resources of his empire to the *jihād* against the kingdoms of Portugal, Castile and Aragon. These had had ten years (539–49/1144–54) in which to reopen their offensive against the feeble Party Kingdoms and against the other territories subject to the almost nominal authority of the Almohads which could offer no serious resistance to the Christian advance. But the picture of this struggle changes completely from 549/1154 onwards. The lost fortresses in the Llano de los Pedroches and in the region of Cordova were retrieved by the Almohads; Portuguese territory was attacked; La Beira was razed to the ground; the castle of Trancoso was attacked. The Almoravids of Granada, impressed by these successes, asked for peace, and offered to hand over the city. This surrender was accepted and ʿAbd al-Muʾmin proceeded immediately to lay siege to Almería, which was taken in the summer of 552/September 1157.

After these triumphs, ʿAbd al-Muʾmin devoted all his efforts for two years, 553–5/1158–60, to his campaign in Ifrīqiya, but his absence had grave consequences for Andalus. Ibn Mardanīsh, the Party King of Murcia, and his father-in-law, Ibn Hamushk, who had allied themselves with the Christians and showed open hostility to the Almohads, laid siege to Cordova, made themselves masters of Jaén, took Granada by surprise, and defeated an army which had come to the help of the city in the Vega; but they were defeated in their turn at the battle of Sabīka, and Granada came again under Almohad occupation.

ʿAbd al-Muʾmin had undertaken great fortification works at Gibraltar, in order to make it a base for his operations. He assembled a large fleet, and recruited the mighty army which was to attack the four kingdoms of Portugal, León, Castile and Aragon, but, at the very moment of preparing this expedition, he fell ill and died at Rabat on Jumādā II 558/May 1163.

His son Abū Yaʿqūb Yūsuf (558–80/1163–84) reconquered Murcia, having defeated Ibn Mardanīsh. He undertook and personally directed several campaigns, but his successes were few, and his reverses extremely serious. The conquest of Murcia was due in great part to the defection of Ibn Hamushk, the lieutenant of Ibn Mardanīsh, and the death of the latter, whose sons accepted Almohad doctrine. Meanwhile Alfonso Enriquez of Portugal and his famous general Giraldo made some spectacular conquests when they assaulted various fortresses in Estremadura. If he failed to take possession of Badajoz, it was only because of the opposition of Ferdinand II of León, who had allied himself with the Almohads.

In order to prove to Yūsuf that they had broken definitely with Castile, the Murcians persuaded him to organize a great offensive against Huete, which was a pitiful failure. Ten years later he undertook a vast campaign against the small but aggressive kingdom of Portugal, choosing as his objective the fortress of Santarem, the base of operations for Portuguese lightning raids. The siege and attack lasted for only five or six days. When the king of León approached to help the besieged, panic seized the Almohad army and made them recross the Tagus in frightful confusion, leaving Yūsuf, almost alone, to be mortally wounded, and withdrawing without fighting toward Seville.

Abū Ya'qūb Yūsuf, although the son of a Zanātī father and a Maṣmūdī mother, and born at Tinmāl in the heart of the High Atlas, was a cultivated monarch, who was well versed in all the subtleties of Arabic literature, and, educated in Seville, surrounded himself with Andalusian literary men, physicians and philosophers. He made Ibn Ṭufayl, the author of the philosophical novel *Ḥayy ibn Yaqẓān*, his medical attendant, and suggested to Ibn Rushd (Averroes) the idea of studying and commenting on the work of Aristotle. These commentaries, translated into Latin and Hebrew, exercised an extraordinary influence on medieval thought. His father had given orders that Cordova should be the capital city of Andalus, but when he died Abū Ya'qūb Yūsuf caused the central administration to return to Seville, and during the years of his residence there as ruler he beautified and enriched it with many buildings.

Abū Yūsuf Ya'qūb al-Manṣūr (580–95/1184–99) was proclaimed on the day following the death of his father, while he was on the road from Évora to Seville. As soon as he arrived at Marrakesh he undertook the foundation of the imperial quarter of Ṣāliḥa as a residence for himself and his successors; but hardly had the work begun, than the ominous news reached him of the landing of the Majorcan Almoravids, the Banū Ghāniya, at Bougie. The very serious consequences of this landing were to disturb the whole of his reign and that of his successor, al-Nāṣir.

With the energy and swiftness which were characteristic of him, Ya'qūb embarked on a large-scale campaign in which, after retaking Bougie, he defeated the Majorcans and obliged them to withdraw into the desert. But the habitual slowness with which the Almohads proceeded, and the necessity for resting his troops after so long and arduous a campaign, gave the Christians time to intensify their attacks in the peninsula. The hardest blow was dealt by the king of Portugal, Alfonso Enriquez, who, in the summer of 585/1189, took Silves with the help of a fleet of Crusaders who were on their way to Palestine.

Ya'qūb crossed over to Andalus, bent upon vengeance. He attacked Torres Novas, to the north of Santarem, but could not take Tomar, which was defended by the Templars. Dysentery and fever played havoc in the Almohad camp, and the caliph himself fell ill. In the summer of the next year, 587/1191, he took Alcacer do Sal, to the south of the Tagus, and regained Silves, a victory which obliged the Christian kings to sign a four-year truce.

On the expiry of the truce Alfonso VIII of Castile made a violent assault on the region of Seville, and Ya'qūb accepted the challenge. At the foot of the citadel of Alarcos on the frontier of Castile the battle took place. The Almohad victory was judged by the Muslim chroniclers to be even more brilliant than that of Zallāqa, and the Christian losses were so heavy that in the campaigns of the two following years, 592–3/1196–7, in which Ya'qūb made such great advances through Estremadura, Toledo and Guadalajara, the Castilian king dared not stand in his way, but signed a truce for ten years.

The caliph returned to his capital sick and exhausted by the fatigues of his long campaigns, and had his son, al-Nāṣir, proclaimed as his heir. His frequent intercourse with Andalusian literary men and philosophers very early made him lose 'Abd al-Mu'min's simple faith in the infallibility and impeccability of the Mahdi. He was a warm admirer of Ibn Ḥazm and his Ẓāhirī doctrine; he declared war on Malikism, which was so well-rooted in the peninsula, and showed the same favour towards Ibn Rushd as had his father, although he found himself obliged for a time to exile him as a result of the intrigues of the jurists. The Arab chroniclers paint the reign of Ya'qūb al-Manṣūr as the culmination of Almohad power. But the fact is that he bequeathed to his son a much less enviable heritage than that which he had received from his father. The struggle on two fronts, which forced him to leave Ifrīqiya in order to hasten to Andalus and vice versa, was the first severe setback, which very soon, with the Castilian victory at Las Navas de Tolosa, the Marinid invasion, and the independence of the Hafsids in Tunisia, was to hasten the downfall of the Almohads and put an end to the dynasty in the midst of continuous strife and subversion.

When al-Nāṣir (595–611/1199–1214) succeeded to the throne at the age of seventeen years, his tutors put a large-scale plan into execution. They took possession of the Balearic islands, suppressed the rebellion of Ibn Ghāniya, and left the government of Ifrīqiya in the hands of the wise and faithful Hafsid, 'Abd al-Wāḥid. Meanwhile the truce signed with

Castile had expired, and Alfonso VIII, burning with desire to avenge the defeat of Alarcos, took the offensive. In the spring of 1212, he and al-Nāṣir, who had now crossed over to the peninsula, led their forces to Las Navas de Tolosa (*al-'Uqāb*), where the battle took place on 14 Ṣafar 609/16 July 1212. This was the most famous battle of the Reconquest. In it disappeared the last Muslim hope of consolidation in Andalus with the support of the great African empires.

With the untimely death of al-Nāṣir and the proclamation of his son, who died without offspring at twenty years of age, civil war became endemic and the caliphs were deposed or assassinated with cold impunity. Al-'Ādil, the son of Ya'qūb al-Manṣūr, rebelled in Murcia, while 'Abd Allāh b. Muḥammad, the great-grandson of 'Abd al-Mu'min, known as al-Bayāsī, proclaimed his independence in Baeza. 'Abd Allāh allied himself with Ferdinand III and handed over to him Martos and Andújar, for which the Cordovans put him to death. At the same time the Almohads in Marrakesh murdered al-'Ādil. Al-'Ādil's brother, al-Ma'mūn, proclaimed himself in Seville in 624/1227, but crossed over to Morocco to fight with his rival Yaḥyā, the son of al-Nāṣir, abandoning Andalus to new Party Kings, who rose against the Almohads, and gave birth to three kingdoms, of which only that of Granada was able to survive for two centuries and a half.

The most ephemeral of these little states was that of Valencia, occupied in 636/1238 by James I of Aragon, who had already made himself master of Majorca. Slightly more durable was the government of Ibn Hūd and his successors in Murcia. Ibn Hūd raised the banner of insurrection in al-Ṣukhūr (Los Peñascales) of the Ricote valley and personified and directed the general insurrection of the Spanish Muslims. When al-Ma'mūn withdrew to Morocco, he was recognized with equal speed and fickleness by almost the whole of Andalus, but when he was defeated at Mérida by León, there rose against him the founder of the Nasrid dynasty of Granada, Muḥammad b. Yūsuf b. Naṣr, and Ibn Hūd, after alternate recognition and rejection, was murdered at Almería in 635/1238.

The union by Ferdinand III of the crowns of León and Castile gave a special impulse to the Reconquest. He proceeded to the conquest of the valley of the lower Guadalquivir, which led to his taking of Seville in 1248. Ibn Hūd was succeeded on his death by his son, al-Wāthiq, who was twice dethroned and restored. The Murcians undertook to pay tribute to Ferdinand III, and handed over their citadel, but finally rose once more, and recognized the king of Granada, so that he might come to their aid. But when this aid proved of no avail, Murcia had to yield.

The Kingdom of Granada under the Nasrids

The rising of Ibn Hūd and the departure of the Caliph al-Ma'mūn for Morocco induced Muḥammad b. Yūsuf b. Naṣr, a member of the Arab family of the Banu'l-Aḥmar, to proclaim himself king in his turn. This he did on 25 Dhu'l-Qa'da 627/5 October 1230 in the little town of Arjona and so founded the dynasty which reigned in Granada until 1492.

Muḥammad I in his kingdom of Granada seemed destined to end as had his rival Ibn Hūd, for the new state had little depth, and its frontiers were eminently vulnerable to Castilian invasion. Ferdinand III took possession of Arjona, devastated the Vega of Granada, and besieged Jaén, whereupon the new king, with an unexpected dramatic gesture, presented himself before Ferdinand, and recognized him as his overlord. He surrendered Jaén, and signed a truce for twenty years in consideration of an annual payment of 150,000 maravedíes. Thus the new Nasrid king won recognition, though he had to contribute to the siege and taking of Seville and to watch passively the submission of the whole of lower Andalusia. His continual and confused struggles with his rival, Ibn Hūd, and the constant threat of the Reconquest, caused him on his deathbed in 671/1273 to recommend his son and successor Muḥammad II, nicknamed *al-Faqīh*, to seek the protection of the Marinids, whose *amīr*, Abū Yūsuf Ya'qūb, in order to rid himself of his rebellious nephews, had made them cross the straits in 660/1261–2 with 3,000 volunteers to wage the Holy War.

Presently Ya'qūb himself landed at Tarifa, which Muḥammad II had ceded to him along with the fortress of Ronda as a base for his operations. He made raids on the regions of Almodóvar, Úbeda and Baeza, and before Écija defeated and killed the *adelantado* of the Frontier, Don Nuño Gonzalez de Lara, who had barred his way with scanty forces. The archbishop of Toledo was also defeated before Martos by the Granadans, who took him prisoner and killed him. Alfonso X of Castile attempted to make good these disasters by laying siege to Algeciras, but the Castilian fleet, which had been watching the straits since 1277, was surprised and scattered almost without struggle by fourteen Marinid galleys. This catastrophe forced Alfonso to lift the siege. The spectacle of these victories, and of Málaga handed over to the Marinid *amīr*, and the fear of being dispossessed by the Africans as the Party Kings had been, made the *amīr* of Granada, negotiate with Alfonso X and with Yaghmurasān, the Zayyanid lord of Tlemcen, against Abū Yūsuf Ya'qūb, though Ya'qūb had been his main support against the Christians. Ya'qūb in his turn received an embassy from Alfonso X, who was asking for his help against his rebel son, Sancho, and seeing himself abandoned by his tributaries, had recourse to his principal enemy. The *amīr* crossed over to the peninsula, and had an interview with Alfonso, who handed over his crown on receiving a loan of 100,000 gold dinars. Together they attacked Cordova, and raided the districts of Toledo and Madrid. Muḥammad II, a victim of endless apprehensions, feared that the two monarchs might decide to dethrone him, so he treated with Alfonso; but then, seeing the Marinids laying siege to Málaga, thought himself lost, and applied to the Moroccan heir apparent to bring about a reconciliation with Abū Yūsuf. The latter then attacked the Cordovan district, passed through Baeza and Úbeda, but did not reach Toledo. He came back laden with booty and returned to Marrakesh at the end of October 682/1283. In the spring of 684/1285, he repeated his raids through lower Andalusia, but with more energy, and such was the devastation caused during the summer, that Sancho IV decided to meet with him near Jerez, and sign a new pact.

In 701/1302 the third king of Granada, Muḥammad III surnamed *al-Makhlū'* ('the Dethroned'), succeeded to the throne but after seven years was deposed in favour of his brother, Abu'l-Juyūsh Naṣr ,who ruled only five years before being replaced by a collateral. Al-Makhlū' recognized Abū Ya'qūb Yūsuf, who was besieging Tlemcen, and took advantage of the minority of Ferdinand IV to take Bezmar and various fortresses, while his troops hurled themselves through Andalusia. But when Ferdinand IV attained his majority, he arranged a three-year truce with Castile, which brought about a breach between Morocco and Granada. The Granadans took possession of Ceuta in 705/May 1306, but lost it in 709/1309, and reconciled themselves with the Marinids.

Meanwhile Castile and Aragon composed their differences in order to continue the Reconquest. Ferdinand IV and James II made a concerted effort to deal a mortal blow to the kingdom of Granada by besieging the Algeciras and Almería respectively. Both failed, although the Castilians won Alcaudete. While this was going on, the confused internal situation in Granada stimulated a new plot by which Abu'l-Walīd Ismā'īl, one of the most capable and energetic of the Nasrid *amīrs*, came to the throne. After twelve years he fell a victim to assassination, after inflicting a bloody defeat on Castilian troops. As a result of this victory Ismāʿīl recovered the fortresses of Huéscar, Orce, Galera, and (in the following years) Martos. Ismāʿīl was succeeded by his son, Muḥammad IV. His reign was disturbed by continual rebellions, and he was obliged to ask for help from the Marinid ruler, with whose assistance he besieged and took Gibraltar. He was murdered, like his father, in 733/1333. He was succeeded by his brother, Abu'l-Ḥajjāj Yūsuf I, who reigned for twenty-three years before he too was assassinated. During his reign he had to face Alfonso XI of Castile, and had to seek assistance from the powerful Marinid *amīr*, Abu'l-Ḥasan, but he and his ally were defeated at the battle of the Salado in 741/1340, and Abu'l-Ḥasan returned hastily to Morocco. The threat of Marinid intervention in the peninsula was now definitely ended. After taking Alcalá la Real, Priego, Rute and other citadels, Alfonso XI contrived to find resources in Castile to undertake successfully the arduous siege of Algeciras and prevent a second crossing by Abu'l-Ḥasan. He died of plague during the siege of Gibraltar, for the loss of which in 1333 he had never been able to console himself, and which he needed as the last base necessary for the conquest of Granada.

The son and successor of Yūsuf I, Muḥammad V, left the government in the hands of the renegade Riḍwān, his father's *wazīr*, and maintained good relations with Castile, whose king, Pedro I, buffeted by many political upheavals, could only intermittently address himself to the Reconquest. Muḥammad V was forced by a plot to abdicate, leaving the throne to his brother Ismāʿīl II, who was assassinated by Muḥammad VI, the ally of Aragon. Pedro seized the opportunity to take possession of Iznájar and other fortresses, penetrating as far as the Vega of Granada. Muḥammad VI, seeing that Málaga was in revolt against him and that Muḥammad V had many partisans, sought an interview with Pedro I, during which he was treacherously stabbed in 763/1362. The second reign of Muḥammad V lasted for thirty years, during which there was a complete reversal of roles between Morocco and Granada, since, through the decadence of the Marinid dynasty, influence and the direction of public affairs at the court of Fez passed into the hands of Muḥammad V. Both kingdoms were the scene once more of family rivalries and civil wars, of which the most outstanding victim was the celebrated *wazīr* and writer Ibn al-Khaṭīb. He was forced to flee from Granada, only to be murdered in Morocco by the henchmen of Muḥammad V.

From this moment onwards, information, and even chronology, become uncertain. The Christian chronicles scarcely pay attention to the Reconquest until its last phase.

With the enthronement of the Catholic Kings, Ferdinand II of Aragon and Isabella of Castile, the distressing death-throes of the Nasrid kingdom begin. In 887/1482 began a long and difficult war which lasted ten years, and might have lasted even longer but for the continual internal struggles, in which Muḥammad XI Abū 'Abd Allāh (Boabdil), his father, 'Alī Abu'l-Ḥasan, and his uncle, Muḥammad XII al-Zaghall, were involved. Abū 'Abd Allāh had come to an agreement with Ferdinand and Isabella by which, when al-Zaghall gave himself up, he should hand over Granada, which was then 'the best fortified city in the world', but he preferred to resist to the end. He tried to provoke an insurrection of the Muslim subjects of the Catholic Kings, and also attacked the fortresses in the hands of the Christians, but very soon the influx of refugees, and the consequent scarcity of provisions forced him to parley. This he did in great secret, but the terms of the capitulation became known, and when a riot put his life in danger, he had to bring forward the date of the handing-over. The Catholic Kings made a solemn entry into Granada on 2 Rabī' I 897/2 January 1492, thus putting an end to the Muslim domination in the Iberian peninsula which had lasted for 780 years.

II. MUSLIM SICILY

At the height of the Middle Ages, when Mu'āwiya succeeded to the caliphate at Damascus, the Arabs, after attacking the islands of Cyprus and Rhodes, launched their first raid against Sicily from the Syrian coast in 32/652. Their forces were small but impetuous, and having spread terror, and encountered no resistance, gathered much booty, and returned to their starting point. The second attack, which also lacked the preparation necessary for a conquest, and had no immediate object beyond that of obtaining loot, was undertaken from Alexandria in 49/669. A landing was made at Syracuse, a great deal of booty was collected in the course of a month, and then the raiders withdrew, in fear of being blockaded by the Byzantine fleet.

Subsequent attacks did not depart from Syria or Egypt, but from the North African coast, where the Arabs had been definitely settled since the foundation of Qayrawān. Pantellaria fell into their hands about 81/700, though meanwhile the Byzantines had concentrated their naval forces in Sicily, and had retaken Barqa in 68/687 and Carthage, for a time, in 78/697. With the arrival of Mūsā b. Nuṣayr as governor of Ifrīqiya, the raids on Sicily became more frequent, but the Byzantines multiplied their coastal defences, and their fleet blocked the way of the African Muslims, and hampered their trade. Moreover, the conquest of Andalus caused a diversion of forces, and the schisms and rebellions which broke out among the Berbers gave a respite of half a century to the oppressed Sicilians, who, though no longer sacked by the Muslim corsairs, were still fleeced by the Byzantine tax-collectors.

The first Aghlabids of Qayrawān maintained diplomatic relations with the patrician who governed the island, and signed a truce, so that the true conquest of Sicily did not begin until 211/827. It was due to the treachery of the Greek governor, Euphemius, who, having been dismissed, revolted in Syracuse, and, in order to avenge himself, crossed the sea, and offered sovereignty over the island to the Aghlabid *amīr*, Ziyādat Allāh. He promised him the co-operation of his numerous partisans, and undertook to pay tribute, on condition of being granted the title and insignia of an emperor.

The *amīr* decided to accept so favourable an offer, once he had put down the rebellions which he had to face in Ifrīqiya. He declared a *jihād*, and sent a fleet and army under the command of the celebrated jurist Asad b. al-Furāt which won a signal victory when it landed at Mazara. Syracuse was on the point of yielding, but the invading general, Asad, died (213/828). The Muslims, seeing their retreat cut off by the Byzantine fleet, gave up the siege, burnt their ships, and, decimated by plague, interned themselves starving in the island. They attacked Mineo and Girgenti, but had to give up the siege of Castrogiovanni. Within two years of the landing at Mazara, the invaders faced the failure of their plan, being reduced to the precarious possession of Mazara and Mineo, while Euphemius had been murdered by the inhabitants of Castrogiovanni.

Although the first steps of the invasion of Andalus and of Sicily were similar, their future course of development was very different. In both cases the morale of the Muslims was greatly superior to that of their enemies, but while the Hispano-Romans gave up without resistance, and embraced Islam, the Greeks and Latins of Sicily offered a tenacious opposition, and, in spite of bloody defeats, neither gave up their cities, nor embraced the invaders' religion so easily.

In the summer of 215/830, Ziyādat Allāh equipped a new fleet with powerful landing forces, and resumed the offensive. The Muslims adopted a new approach from the west, and laid siege to Palermo. Its inhabitants defended themselves heroically for a year until hunger, plague and continuous attacks obliged them to capitulate in the autumn of 216/831, and accept the status of *dhimmīs*. The firm occupation of Palermo, and the great number of African Muslims who hastened to populate it (attracted by the advantages offered by its position, its port, and its fertile countryside), enabled the definite conquest of the island to be begun with the continuous support of the government in Qayrawān. On the death of Ziyādat Allāh, his brother, Abū 'Iqāl, continued to send reinforcements, who pursued the invasion of the island along the coast between Palermo and Messina, and in the interior in the Etna region.

The Greeks could find no better expedient than to transfer the seat of their administration from Syracuse to Castrogiovanni. Although the new governor of Palermo tried to besiege this impregnable fortress, and defeated the Byzantines in the open field, his *coup* against the fortifications failed, and it was not occupied until twenty years later. Meanwhile Muslim domination was being extended, and when it had covered a third of the island, the republic of Naples, without reckoning the gravity of the step, allied itself with the invaders against the Lombards of Benevento. This opened the Italian peninsula to Arab raids during the fifty years for which this alliance lasted.

Its first ill-omened result was the capture of Messina with the co-operation of the Neapolitan fleet. The Byzantines initiated a counter-offensive, which brought about a dreary succession of lootings and alternate local victories and defeats, in which the Muslims, with their bravery and aggressiveness, came off best. The Sicilians, accustomed to the Byzantine yoke and the despotism of the patricians, saw no great difference between paying tribute to the emperor of Constantinople, and to the *amīr* of Palermo, who represented the Aghlabids. In the summer of 239/853 the new governor, al-'Abbās b. Faḍl, after a savage raid which laid waste the whole of the eastern region as far as Catania and Syracuse, forced Butera, after a siege, to give him 6,000 captives. He also took Castrogiovanni by a sudden *coup*.

During this time the Muslim fleet of Palermo, accustomed to sea warfare, and allied with the Neapolitans, had begun to attack the Adriatic coast. In 223/838 it occupied Brindisi and Taranto, beat the Venetian fleet, and extended its advances along the coasts of both the

Adriatic and the Tyrrhenian. On the island itself, after the unsuccessful attempts of 251/865 and 255/869, the Muslims began the final siege of Syracuse in the summer of 264/877. After an heroic defence, having been hemmed in for almost a year by sea and land, and abandoned by Constantinople, (since the Byzantine fleet could not break the blockade and free it from hunger), it was taken by assault and sacked with frightful carnage on Wednesday, 4 Ramaḍān 264/21 May 878.

The serious disturbances which were provoked in Ifrīqiya by the fall of the Aghlabid régime, and the insurrection of Abū Yazīd, 'the man on the donkey', at the head of the Kharijites (332–6/943–7) left Sicily to the mercy of Berber adventurers in the southern part of the island, while many towns which had submitted, declined to pay tribute. This state of affairs persisted until the Fatimid dynasty had become firmly established, and the Kalbī family of the Banū Abī Ḥusayn had gained recognition as the *de facto* independent and hereditary governors of Sicily. Then the war against the eastern part of the island was renewed, and Taormina was besieged and taken within four months at the end of 351/962. In the following year Rameta, the last Greco-Roman *municipium*, where the fugitives from the conquest of Messina and its province had gathered, was besieged. Its inhabitants sought the aid of the Emperor Nicephorus Phocas, but his large fleet and forces suffered a crushing defeat. Nevertheless it resisted until the beginning of 355/966, in which year the city was taken by assault and sacked, its defenders slaughtered, and the women and children taken captive. A further defeat of the Greek navy in the straits of Messina, and raids against the coastal towns of Calabria, which desolated the country and impeded commerce, obliged the Byzantines to sign a peace, and to acknowledge the Muslim right to exact tribute from all the Christians of the island.

The first three Kalbī *amīrs*, had not to resist Byzantine attacks nor civil wars, but frequently intervened by invitation in the struggles of the small and disunited states of southern Italy. Their profitable raids on the mainland enabled them to enrich themselves, and to encourage the development of Muslim culture, which until that time had been limited to the study of the language and Qur'anic exegesis by Mālikī jurists under the influence of the celebrated Saḥnūn. A very clear example of this progress was the collaboration of a Sicilian scholar, 'Abd Allāh, versed in technological and philological matters, in the Arabic translation of Dioscorides's treatise on botany, made for 'Abd al-Raḥmān III, the Umayyad caliph of Cordova.

At the beginning of the eleventh century the Sicilians sacked the cities of Cagliari and Pisa (1002), but the doge of Venice, Orseolo, obliged them to withdraw before Bari in 1003 and the Pisans gained an important naval victory before Reggio. The Sicilians had their revenge in 1009 when they took possession of Cosenza. In 1015 they were besieging Salerno, which was ready to submit to the payment of tribute, when an unexpected episode marked an astonishing turn in the history of Muslim Sicily. A handful of Normans returning from Palestine as Crusaders, outraged at the inactivity of the Christians besieged in Salerno, effected a sudden sally against the besiegers, who, taken by surprise, were put to flight, abandoning their encampment.

It is almost incredible how the morale of the Muslims collapsed when Norman contingents, under the orders of Robert de Hauteville and his brother Roger, intervened, and how easily they allowed themselves to be defeated by a detachment of knights brought together by chance, and with no resources but their personal bravery. Although at first they were so few, almost all being leaders, the Normans managed very soon by their military prestige, their incomparable personal bravery, and their iron discipline, to form a nucleus of French, German, and (above all) Italian adventurers, who, fired by their example, followed them with unusual faithfulness. Even the Muslims themselves, on accepting to be vassals of the Norman dynasty, helped them with intrepidity in their campaign, and contributed in no small fashion towards the establishment of the grand duchy of Apulia, and the new kingdom of Sicily.

Once the principality of Calabria, from which the Byzantines were expelled, had been created, Robert and his brother Roger took advantage of the civil war between the Muslims in Sicily, and crossed the straits. They took possession of Messina, which yielded in terror without resisting, invaded Val Demone, and gained a decisive victory before Castrogiovanni. In the following year, Robert advanced towards Girgenti, and, although the Sicilian Muslims saw a ray of hope when they allied themselves with the Fatimids, he succeeded in defeating them at Cerami. After frustrating an attempt by the Pisan fleet to attack Palermo, the courageous Roger began the difficult siege of this city.

Roger first slowly subdued the little rebel states which had grown up in the interior of the island, and within three years had placed the people of Palermo in so intolerable a situation that they decided to try their luck at the battle of Misilmeri. They were defeated with enormous losses. Five months of rigorous siege, hunger, the defeat of a fleet sent from

Ifrīqiya to render assistance, and the savage assaults of the besiegers, forced the capital of Sicily to yield to the Normans at the beginning of 1072. The conditions concerning personal liberty, respect for property, and the exercise of Islamic law under Muslim judges were relatively humane.

The elder brother, Robert, lord of the Norman territories on the mainland, remained ruler over Palermo, Messina and Val Demone. Roger, with the consent of the whole army, kept the remainder of the territory, already or yet to be conquered. Profiting by the absence of Roger, who was helping his brother in his campaign against the Byzantines and the Holy Roman Emperor Henry IV, the Muslims of Val de Notto staged an armed rebellion, but the tireless Roger attacked Trapani and Taormina, and, after occupying Girgenti, encircled and took Syracuse in 1085, while the Pisans and Genoese were besieging and sacking Mahdiyya on the African coast.

A kinsman of those Hammudids who had occupied the caliphate of Cordova between 1015 and 1027, crossed to Sicily. He was the last, ill-fated *amīr*, who, in cowardly fashion, surrendered the impregnable fortress of Castrogiovanni, and turned Christian, only to end his life in exile in Italy. Butera still offered armed resistance, but when it and Noto surrendered, the whole island passed into Roger's power in 1091. In the same year, in spite of his being sixty years of age, and newly married for the third time, Roger determined personally to undertake the conquest of Malta, which had been captured by the Aghlabids in 869. He met no resistance and liberated many Christian captives, to whom he gave possession of the island.

His military prowess was refined by a political prudence and moderation, by which he kept in balance all the antagonisms of the varied island population. Realizing clearly that the Muslims exceeded the Greeks and Latins in numbers and talents, he treated them in their civil life with a kindness till then hardly heard of. Thus he had at his disposition a social force which hitherto had been wasted. Recognizing his impartiality and moderation, the Muslims obeyed him blindly, and with their support, he was able to impose his will on the other Norman lords, who possessed fiefs to the south of the Tiber. Once the Sicilians were liberated from the continual devastation of war and the consequent unbridled rapine, they could develop their intellectual life, and devote themselves to the cultivation of their literature, poetry, legislation, and the scientific knowledge which they had received from the East. Roger I, though a convinced

Christian, was free from prejudice, and even at the risk of being considered a Muslim, encouraged them to cultivate their gifts. Through the concourse of two mentalities as different as the Greek and the Arab, the works of Plato, Aristotle, Ptolemy, and Dioscorides were translated and studied as they were in Andalus.

Roger II, having reached his majority, succeeded his father in 1105 and transferred his court to Palermo. He declared war on the Zirids of Mahdiyya. This campaign ended in a naval disaster, but, far from discouraging him, it made him determined to renew his attacks against the African coast. He had now been recognized as duke of Apulia, and proclaimed king of Sicily. He attacked the island of Djerba, took Tripoli, and, by the time he had taken possession of Mahdiyya, Sousse and Sfax, it seemed that the conquest of Ifrīqiya by the Normans of Sicily was to be the revenge for the Arab invasion. The arrival of the Almohads frustrated such ambitious plans.

Roger II died on 27 February 1154. He was a worthy successor to his father, from whom he inherited the courage and political skill which allowed him to make of Sicily one of the most powerful and wealthy states of southern Europe, feared equally in southern Italy, on the coasts of Greece, and along the African littoral. The interest which he took in organizing the administration, while preserving the forms of Muslim life, gained for him a fame and a glory only equalled by his celebrity as an open-handed patron. Science and letters flourished in Sicily in the fifth/eleventh and sixth/twelfth centuries on a par with the cultural progress of the Umayyad Caliphate of Cordova, although the court of Palermo did not produce geniuses to be compared with Ibn Ḥayyān in the field of history, or with Ibn Ḥazm in literary and philosophical studies.

Thanks to the close contacts between Muslims and Christians, and the fact of Greek and Arabic both being well understood on the island, it was possible for the *Optics* of Ptolemy to be translated and published. Geography was studied with extraordinary success and is symbolized in the famous *Book of Roger* which was dedicated to Roger II by al-Idrīsī. In his prologue, al-Idrīsī eulogizes Roger's untiring efforts to encourage scientific studies. Philosophical questions were learnedly treated when Frederick II elaborated the *Quaestiones Sicilianae*. The physicians of Palermo contributed to the progress made by the school of Salerno, while mechanical and military arts were made known in Italy by the weapons employed by the Muslim engineers at the sieges of Syracuse and Alexandria.

There could be no greater contrast than that between the tolerance, and scientific and administrative interaction, which the Sicilian Muslims, as subjects, enjoyed, and the conquering rage with which the Norman princes waged war on all the Islamic states in order to subdue them and sack them without pity. When William II married Princess Constantia of Sweden, the new political orientation opened the gates to German domination. This, with the aggressive and warlike spirit created by the Crusades, destroyed the atmosphere in which the Oriental culture of the island, potently fertilized by Latino-Norman activity, had flourished. The conquered people found themselves day by day worse treated; the cultured classes emigrated to Africa, and the rural masses, in revolt so as ultimately to exhaust the patience of their masters, were exiled to the mainland. Soon discredit and finally oblivion overcame the Arabic language and Muslim culture in Sicily.

PART VIII

ISLAMIC SOCIETY AND CIVILIZATION

CHAPTER I

THE GEOGRAPHICAL SETTING

There is a closer relationship between Islam and its geographical setting, than that of any other of the great monotheistic religions. Glance at a general map of the distribution of Muslims throughout the world, and a pattern is revealed which coincides extensively, at least in its principal features, with the arid zone of the Old World. From the Atlantic to Central Asia, Islam found its primary field of expansion in and around the great desert. There is only one, though important, exception: those additional areas, sometimes very densely populated, which spread all round the Indian Ocean, on the eastern shores of Africa, the coasts of south India, and especially in eastern Pakistan and Indonesia. This coincidence of zone and religion is the more remarkable in comparison with the universal spread of Christianity, which was born in an environment, rather of the Mediterranean than of the desert, but not in reality far from that of Islam and in an area which was easily to be submerged in the Muslim torrent. We are brought therefore to ask two sets of questions: (a) How are we to explain such a notable geographical restriction of this religion, in view of its undoubted universal mission, at least from the time of Muḥammad's successors? What factors were at work, what historical, social, and psychological mechanisms? How is the map of Islam to be explained? (b) On the other hand, what effect has this restriction had on Muslim life? How has the face of Islam been modified as a consequence of the geographical setting in which it spread?

THE GEOGRAPHICAL CONDITIONS FOR THE SPREAD OF ISLAM

The geographical setting and the birth of Islam

The Muslim faith drew the essence of its initial drive from the very setting in which it arose. The two characteristic elements in this setting are the sedentary life of the oases and the pastoral nomads, the bedouin. Between the 27th and 24th parallels, the relative subsidence of the elevated edge of the rocky mountains which overlook from the east the rift of the Red Sea, with the interior slope broken up into long tectonic trenches, partially filled with volcanic deposits, created crossroads; in a generally very arid region where the rainfall appears nowhere to exceed 100 millimetres annually, great springs rising from the base of the lava plateaux gave birth to favourable sites for the development of great oases such as Medina. At the time of Muḥammad, the oases of the Ḥijāz were prosperous market towns; these cities were caravan centres which had organized the relations between southern Arabia and the Mediterranean world ever since the decline of the former, towards the end of the fifth Christian century, had permitted them to take up the reins and assume the directing role. Their atmosphere was already that of an active mercantile economy which favoured private enterprise and large profits. The bedouin constituted the other half of the picture and had done ever since the spread of the dromedary in the desert, probably from the beginning of the first millennium B.C. onwards, had secured the gradual expansion and domination of wide-ranging nomads. These bedouin were a basically aggressive people, their life founded on raiding and consequently on tribal solidarity combined with protective structures. Their political structure was highly unstable and subject to continual regroupings with the rise and fall of those outstanding personalities who are at the root of all tribal organization.

Such a situation was not unusual. It was repeated to some extent throughout the arid zone and on its edges, in all the areas of contact between nomadic and sedentary peoples. In such a context there is nothing abnormal about the dynamic power displayed by the new religion. It follows the pattern of other great expansive movements which have set out from arid zones to conquer the areas of cultivation, profiting from the forces available as a constant result of the population surplus. The nomads multiply in the relatively healthy setting of the desert since they are less subject to the epidemics which, until recent years, have limited the progress of sedentary populations. Apart from the remarkable personality of the Prophet, one factor in triggering off the great movement of the Muslim conquest was probably the climatic oscillation, and the series of great droughts occurring between 591 and 640. These made available to the military and religious leaders of the new faith human resources whose aggressive instincts had been strengthened and who were fully prepared to follow them to the promised lands. An expressive couple of lines from Abū Tammām (A.D. 806–47)[1] says:

> 'No, not for Paradise didst thou the nomad life forsake;
> Rather, I believe, it was thy yearning after bread and dates'

[1] Quoted from P. K. Hitti, *History of the Arabs* (London, 1937), 144.

and the Persian general, Rustam, said the same thing to a Muslim envoy in 637: 'I have observed that it is simply poverty and the miserable life you have led which have induced you to undertake so much'.[1]

The singularity of Islam is, however, obvious. In contrast to what has occurred elsewhere, in Islam it is the town-dwellers who were set above the nomads. From this point of view, the turning-point in Muslim history was the battle of Ḥunayn, where, in Shawwāl 8/January 630, victory was won over a tribal coalition led by the Hawāzin, and the nomads were finally brought to follow the flag of the townsmen. The underlying reason for the supremacy of the latter may be found in the actual characteristics of the Near Eastern climate. Central Arabia bears no resemblance to High Central Asia, with its cold winters and rainy summers where sedentary life was literally strangled by the fact that the areas suitable for cultivation were the same as those which offered grazing for the nomads, whether in summer time it was the higher ground suitable for rain-fed agriculture or in winter the irrigable piedmonts. In the Sahara too the routes for commerce across the desert were never sufficiently active, the distances being so immense, to sustain great cities. But central Arabia is situated in the zone of rainy and relatively warm winters and the oases need not necessarily suffer disadvantage from the proximity of the nomads, since these are dispersed in the winter and driven in the summer towards the marginal subdesert regions; furthermore, the desert being restricted in area, and regularly crossed by incense routes in active use, secured the basis for urban development of a size adequate to explain this triumph of the cities.

Whatever the cause, the Muslim conquest, even in its earliest stages, went far beyond the scope of a crisis of expansion among the Arab nomads. The Iranian plateau was largely impenetrable to the bedouin and the conquest of the Maghrib was a purely military and political enterprise in which there was no recourse to them. The nomads in any case were never more than second-rate recruits for Islam, often of indispensable help in the armed struggle as soldiers and warriors but, apart from their military merits, regarded as of bad character and poor religion, uproarious and impious. A celebrated *Ḥadīth* forbids milk in these terms: 'What I fear for my people is milk, where the devil lurks

[1] Balādhurī, *Kitāb futūḥ al-buldān*; cf. trans. P. K. Hitti, *The origins of the Islamic state* (New York, 1916), 411–12.

between the froth and the cream. They will love to drink it and will return to the desert, leaving the places where men pray together.'[1] And the Qur'ān adds: 'The desert Arabs are the most hardened in their impiety and hypocrisy.'[2] The bedouin were merely tools at best. In fact, the politico-religious apparatus of the new faith was incomparably superior in its complexity to the potentialities of the rough bedouin. Islam needs the city to effect its religious and social aims. The creation of a town is a highly praiseworthy act, and pious legends about their foundation are innumerable. Blessings have always been associated with a stay at Medina. Special permission was needed to leave it. Contrariwise, the meritious act *par excellence* was the *hijra*, the departure for Medina, the flight to the town.

The basis of Islam is primarily communal prayer. The most significant is the Friday prayer, that of the whole community (*umma*) assembled together. This demands fixed and permanent mosques where this important assembly can take place. The town is in the first place the site of the great Friday mosque, in opposition to the little mosques for daily prayer which lack the same permanence and fixity. The theologians have discussed at length the exact definition of the places where the Friday prayer can be made, but their subject is really the rigorous description of a city. There are disputes over the importance of the localities meriting this honour, which we should call towns, villages, or large hamlets. The mosque must be fixed and fully built. Certain strict authors consider the Friday prayer null and void if made in a place of worship which is left open momentarily to the sky through a fall from the ceiling. Even apart from the great Friday prayer, the rhythm of Muslim practices is designed for town dwellers. The mosque with its pool for ablutions and the complex installations this demands; the five daily prayers in response to the call of the muezzin; the Ramaḍān fast with its active nights: these are all urban in character. Secondly, town life is not only essential to collective prayer, it is necessary to the dignified life which Islam demands. The *imām* needs to live the life of a townsman. Women should be veiled, which conflicts with the requirements of nomadic, or even rural, existence. This rigorous prudish ideal is that of the austere merchants of the Ḥijāz. There still, Islam resorts to the decorum of the cities rather than the disorder of the fields or the desert. Its social

[1] Quoted from W. Marçais, 'L'Islamisme et la vie urbaine,' *Comptes-rendus de l'Académie des Inscriptions* (1928), 86–100.

[2] Qur'ān 9. 98.

constraints, just as much as its spiritual demands, make Islam an urban religion.

It should also be emphasized that this association of townsfolk and nomads puts agricultural activity in the lowest place in the Muslim ideal of society. In the oases of the Ḥijāz, cultivation of the soil was basically servile, in contrast with the outstandingly noble occupation of commerce. In the Qur'ān the growth of the crops is never seen as the fruit of human labour but as the straightforward expression of the Divine will (e.g. 26. 33–36, or 56. 64–65–God is the real sower) and antagonism against peasants is expressed even more freely in the *Ḥadīths*. The Prophet, seeing a ploughshare, is recorded as saying: 'That never enters the house of the faithful without degradation entering at the same time.' The peasants were the last to be able to assimilate Islam.

PROCESS AND LIMITS OF ISLAMIZATION

Islam is thus a religion which finds its most complete expression in an urban setting, but which, on the other hand, was spread by nomads in the course of vast movements of warlike conquest, while the peasants could hardly be other than strangers to it at the beginning. This threefold description affords the basis for an analysis of the mechanisms at work in its expansion, as well as the limits which that expansion reached.

Bedouinization and peasant resistance

As has already been noted, the Muslim conquests exceeded the compass of the nomadic invasions, and were not necessarily associated with them. But from the viewpoint of world history the most significant feature of the new religion was certainly, even though it was not everywhere simultaneous, the triumph of the nomads and the decline of sedentary life—a general 'bedouinization', the more pregnant with consequences since it affected those countries which had survived the Germanic invasions of the northern shores of the Mediterranean as the greatest centres of urban and civilized life.

It is not difficult to explain from this angle the general line of most of the frontiers of the Muslim world, at least where its realm is continuous. The enlistment of the nomads by Islam facilitated the conquest of all the arid or semi-arid zones of the ancient world and its expansion throughout the climatically marginal zones where rural life was precarious and pastoral life could easily acquire supremacy. Limits were met on the tropical fringe of the arid zone, in the forests which pastoral cultures could not penetrate because of the cattle trypanosomiasis; in contrast, the nomadic Peul were the main impetus for its diffusion in the savannahs of Negro West Africa. The north-west frontier of India is equally typical as a climatic and pastoral frontier, which expresses the military balance between the Islamic shepherds of the arid zone and the dense peasant population of the Indo-Gangetic plain. In the direction of Europe, the boundary, in the final reckoning, was in fact the sea; the sea prevented practically any nomadic penetration into the Iberian peninsula and limited it considerably in the Balkans; the resistance of the peasant societies was thus strengthened, particularly since here, in the temperate zone, they were much more firmly entrenched. On the Russian plain, the forest turned out to be an equally decisive obstacle, north of the steppe covered by the Golden Horde.

This general picture requires some modification in detail. Two very different families of nomadic peoples, the Arabs and the Turks, undertook the diffusion of Islam, and the imprint left on the human landscape differed in each case. The Arab nomads, who in particular poured over the whole Maghrib in the middle of the eleventh century (in the phase known as the Hilālī invasions) were people of the hot deserts, who used as their principal means of transport the dromedary, which has sensitive feet, suffers from the cold and can only be habituated to mountain life with difficulty. The Turkish nomads originated from the coldest part of High Asia, and possessed in the Bactrian camel an animal with a thick pelt, infinitely more hardy and tough, which adapted itself well to a mountain setting even though by origin as much a creature of the sands. The consequences of this contrast were decisive.

Throughout the Arab world the tide of nomads covering the deserts and the steppes lapped at the foot of the mountains without managing to make any serious breach in them. Only the skeletal mountains were open to bedouinization, those reduced to rocky outcrops hardly rising above the wide alluvial valleys, like the Saharan Atlas in Algeria, from the Ksour mountains to those of the Ouled Naïl (and even there traces of a previous way of life are to be found among the Berber mountaineers, with a short pastoral season, using load-carrying oxen, but more or less assimilated to the nomadiç Arabs), or those reduced to broad grassy plateaux, like the Middle Atlas, roamed by Berbers, whose primarily nomadic life developed in the universal insecurity which followed the

Hilālī invasions. In general, the more important ranges rising above the deserts remained untouched, like the ancient massif of the western High Atlas in Morocco, the principal seat of Chleuh settlement, or the Aurès, the only mountain in the Maghrib which has kept unchanged its Classical name (Aurasius mons), itself a speaking witness to the continuity of the occupation of its soil, or, again, the highlands of ʻAsīr and the Yemen in south-eastern Arabia. The ancient way of life, with crops irrigated in terraces in the bottom of the valleys in association with rain-fed agriculture on the higher slopes and with pasturage nearby, has been maintained in such areas without great change. This category also includes the Ethiopian highlands, where the dromedary cannot live; this is undoubtedly one of the main reasons for the failure of the various attempts to establish islamized nomads from the surrounding lowlands on the plateau. Elsewhere, Mediterranean coastal ranges—the Lebanon, the Alawite mountains, the Grande Kabylie—which until the medieval invasions had remained wooded and thinly populated, witnessed an influx of enormous numbers of peoples fleeing from the neighbouring plains. These mountains, whether they remained intact, preserving their ancient pattern of settlement or became refuges, transformed by the upheavals of the Middle Ages, constituted throughout the Arab world decisive obstacles to bedouinization, often to arabization, and even to islamization. We may cite the example of those mountains in the Maghrib where the speech is Berber, the religion is Islam, and the religious setting is pre-Islamic, undoubtedly fairly primitive and never fully converted to Christianity; or, again, the Lebanon or the Ethiopian highlands, which resisted Islam; or the various mountains which have nurtured heresies indicating the inadequacy of any conversion to Islam, like those of the Alawites of the Jabal Anṣāriyya, or the Druzes of the Jabal al-Durūz or the Zaydīs of the Yemen. In these mountainous refuges, Islam found the most stubborn barriers to its triumph.

Nothing similar could occur in the Turkish areas where the nomads had the zoological means to penetrate the mountains. Furthermore, the deep attraction for them of the freshness of summer quarters (*yayla*) drew them irresistibly to the mountains, while the cross-breeding of the Bactrian camel with the dromedary also progressively opened up the low-lying plains to serve them as winter quarters. On all the coastal plains of the Aegean and the Mediterranean, the havoc they brought meant that peasant life practically disappeared, with greater or less speed. The majority of the mountains were bedouinized, either directly, or indirectly by the reversion of their settled inhabitants to nomadic life, extending their previous brief pastoral migrations, as in Kurdistān and Luristān. The only geographically coherent and extended centres of resistance, apart from a few oases and towns, were the coastal forests of Pontus and the Caspian Sea, where the nomads were opposed by insurmountable difficulties in the thick cover of vegetation and the sultry climate, rather than in the sheer slopes. The late survival of the empire of Trebizond (up to 1461) in the first-named area, and the prolonged Iranian resistance to Islam in the Elburz and the heretical communities (particularly Ismā'īlīs) who established themselves there are witness to the exceptional character of these areas, which ensured their escape from the general decay of the deforested highlands and the Mediterranean plains alike, and which produced the great densities of population which mark them out today.

Town-dwellers and merchants: the urban centres of islamization

The essential instruments for the conversion of the countryside to Islam were therefore the nomads rather than the peasants. The towns, as we have seen, were of themselves an especially favourable setting for the new religion to flourish in. We cannot dissociate from this setting the part played by the merchants and traders of every kind, or even the urban artisans, all representatives of those activities which in Muslim eyes ranked highest and deserved most merit. Islam spread along the caravan and sea routes; the web of commercial relations among the towns formed the framework for its progress. It spread throughout the interior of the vanquished countries, where the towns with peculiar speed and intensity made themselves centres for the missionary effort from which Islam spread slowly through the neighbouring countryside. The religion also leapt beyond the border of the continuous territory of Islam, in the pioneering form of colonies of merchants scattered in ports and cities. While the nomadic conquests were limited to the edges of the arid zone, proselytization through commercial expansion was much more widespread and universal. It was responsible for the numerous outgrowths which mark the advance of Islam, far beyond its principal realms. In contrast to the warlike expansion, inseparable from the concept of *jihād* and based on the nomads, this advance was essentially pacific, at least in origin, even if it prepared the way for the organization of Islamic states. This means of progress was to remain active long after the disappearance of the political conditions which permitted conquest by war, and was to function even within those states under Christian rule. It alone is still an active force today.

On a world scale, however, we note at once the distorted pattern of Islam, for which this process is responsible. It had free play only in one direction. The Mediterranean acted like a great moat dug to separate the two religions and reduced to a minimum any human exchange between the two shores. Quite soon Muslim urban life in this area was unable to attract the swiftly progressing Christian world. In the end, the powers of resistance of the Christian peasant communities, supporting a stubborn political reconquest, destroyed, or at least considerably reduced, the Muslim urbanized settlements established by the Islamic powers in the Balkan and Iberian peninsulas.

By contrast, on its Asian and African fronts Islam often appeared in essence as the peaceful bearer of a superior social organization. Throughout Negro West Africa, since the period of colonial pacification, the role of the Muslim states in the propagation of Islam has passed to the traders, Mande-Dioulas in the west and Hausas in the east. Following them, came marabouts and schoolmasters, and so innumerable Muslim groups were diffused right into the true forest zone along the coasts. In central, east and south-east Africa, a region which had hardly ever been touched by Islamic invasion, except in the repellent guise of slave raiding, Islam is expanding dynamically in the same manner along the trade-routes which have carried it with Swahili traders as far as the Congo basin; and it is taking root fast in the recently established detribalized mining centres. In Central Asia too, where religion did not deflect the Turkish expansion from its general pressures towards the West, Islam did not in the main bring the *jihād*; it was the traders and the teachers who spread it along the roads of Turkistān, whence it penetrated into China. Between Buddhist Tibet and Buddhist Mongolia, the Muslim advance into Turkistān represents more than anything else the existence of the transcontinental trade-route to China, along the strings of oases of the Tarim basin; and it is extended by the numerous colonies of Chinese Muslims, composed basically of merchants and carriers.

The most typical successes were to be gained all round the Indian Ocean. The great navigational currents from the Ḥaḍramawt to Indonesia, and from the Deccan to Zanzibar or the northern cape of Madagascar, which put the great rhythm of the monsoons to profit long before Islam, ensured a perpetual flux entirely favourable to cultural interchange. The movement grew by degrees; the Muslim colonies established in the ports of south India sent out their own swarms; and the Indian merchants spread the new religion in this manner throughout the Malay world; meanwhile, the Arabs dominated the east coast of Africa down to Mozambique. This seaborne form of Islam remained basically coastal; only the fairly narrow coastal strips became completely converted, as a general rule. The very intense islamization of certain islands like Zanzibar or the Comoro Islands marks the importance of these landfalls for the seamen, as well as, on occasion, their early capture by trading cultures faced with a massive and hardly penetrable continent. The islamization of the Malay world is similar, though more spectacular numerically. The Malay sultanates were always basically coastal, being located especially at the mouths of the rivers, linked with the favoured sites for settlements which the spits or the sandy alluvial embankments of the rivers offered them above the level of the mudflats and the mangrove swamps, and taking advantage of the opportunities for rice paddies which the major flood-beds offered them lower down. These isolated centres of development, hardly communicating except by sea, produced the Malay synthesis, the result of the superimposition of numerous cultural layers of external origin, crowned by the islamization which the merchant colonies gradually spread among the rulers and which seems the normal product of such a situation. Its expansion into the interior thereafter followed the stages of the progress of the principalities and peoples of the littoral. It was resisted only by the backward and isolated groups in the interior of the large islands—the Batak country in Sumatra and the Dayak country in Borneo. Meanwhile the Hindus took refuge in islands like Bali and gathered together beyond the open sea which acted as a frontier east of Java. The same pattern could not be reproduced in Madagascar, although the north was subject to a very strong influx of Muslim culture, since the political centre of gravity remained fixed in the highlands of the interior. Finally, the islamization of Bengal, exceptional in size and continental sweep, resulted from the coincidence of the presence at the same time of proselyte Muslim merchants and a floating population of outcastes, only loosely attached to Hinduism, who from the middle of the first Christian millennium had gradually settled in the immense forest of the delta of Bengal which the Aryan shepherds had long shunned. Success was rapid in this pioneer fringe, throughout which the habitations were scattered, the markets being the only centres of social flux.

THE HUMAN LANDSCAPE OF ISLAM

Town and country

Muslim cities. The most distinctive feature of the Muslim countries is the appearance of their cities. The place of these towns in the landscape of these Muslim lands is the more important in that the urban ideal of the religion led to the proliferation of urban foundations. Although these countries knew no industrial revolution until very recent times, although the bedouinization of the countryside rendered the bases of regional life very precarious throughout enormous areas, the towns multiplied. Sometimes entrepôt trade and the intermediary function played by these countries in great international commerce, sometimes the organization of caravans on the borders of the arid zone, furnished them with economic support. On occasion the Islamic ideal itself demanded their establishment. So cantonments of the new conquerors, developed at an early date facing the pre-Islamic cities (as Fusṭāṭ, adjoining the later Cairo, faces pre-Islamic Bābilyūn), like an expression of the Muslim personality. So, too, the *ribāṭ* (a kind of fortified convent for soldiers of the Holy War) was scattered in particular all along the sea-frontiers of the eastern and western shores of the Maghrib, and gave rise to many cities. In addition to these, the rulers founded towns which increased in number, both through the instability of the dynasties and, perhaps, through the incompatibility of court life with the austere ideal of the life of a Muslim town-dweller, and, hence, the wish to separate the prince and his courtiers from the mass of the people.

These towns certainly offer a very singular aspect. European towns were early organized in authoritarian fashion by watchful corporations; Indian towns have a structure designed for the juxtaposition of the castes; Chinese towns were carefully planned by the government. But traditional Muslim cities are marked by an apparently disorderly layout, a tangle of blocks hardly ventilated by a labyrinth of winding lanes and dark alleys, low houses, stretching into the distance between closed courtyards with high walls, and the vivacity of a narrowly circumscribed bazaar contrasting with the silence of the residential quarters.

Nevertheless, this apparently confused picture is not lacking in overall plan. The basic elements of its organization are well defined.

The various quarters are disposed concentrically in an ordered arrangement. The central position of the main mosque stems from the primacy of the religious functions of the city. In its immediate neighbourhood stands the commercial quarter, the bazaar; normally this contains the public baths, which Islam finally adopted in view of their usefulness for the major ablutions, in spite of their associations with debauchery. The official quarter with the public buildings lies not far from this central kernel; it is not normal for it to be at the heart of this area, but on its edge, prepared for defence against popular disturbances. The Jewish quarter is often established in the immediate vicinity, under the shadow of the mighty, for protection against the wrath of mobs. Round these public quarters in the centre come the residential districts; then semi-rural areas, still town-like in appearance but inhabited by cultivators, or often sheltering newcomers in improvised dwellings, shacks or straw huts. The whole is enclosed in a grim cincture of graveyards. This outer border is vast, since the family tomb is unknown in Muslim lands; it offers a striking contrast with the churchyards of medieval Christendom.

As well as this regular concentric arrangement, there is also a strict organization of the various elements of trade and craft, and of the residential quarters. The sellers of different goods are rigidly ranked, separated topographically and usually grouped in guilds, following an order which places the noblest of them nearest to the main mosque: first, the candle, incense and perfume merchants, then the booksellers and bookbinders, followed closely by the clothsellers grouped in the *qayṣariyya*, then the tailors, carpet and blanket merchants, jewellers and leather-workers. The purveyors of food, the workers in wood and metal, the blacksmiths and the potters, are set farther away, even at the city gates, where there are usually also to be found the basket-workers and saddlers, who sell mainly to the peasants and the caravans. In the residential quarters, segregation of the different ethnic and religious groups is observed. These are everywhere split up into enclosed units, built up round an axial street which is closed at each end by great gates, from which blind alleys run on each side. The city of the Levant, where the mosaic of cultures and confessions reaches its greatest complexity, has deserved its description as a conglomeration of separate cities, each living under the spectre of massacre. The Muslim town seems cruelly lacking in unity, an assemblage of disparate elements set side by side without any real links.

However, this thoroughly system-ridden framework disappears often enough at first encounter into an inextricable disorder, in which it is extremely difficult to find one's way. Above all in the residential districts the streets are always very tortuous and narrow. Everywhere there are multitudinous projections from the houses, overhangs, *mashrabiyyas*; covered lanes and bridges over the street proliferate; and in many places the roof-tops of opposite houses touch each other. Squares and unappropriated open spaces are correspondingly rare. All this does nothing to assist circulation; Islam has never designed the street for vehicles, but only at most for pack-animals; even they pass each other at times with difficulty. This diminution of the space for public traffic contrasts with the importance of the space devoted to family life. The houses, which are generally low, frequently contain interior courtyards or patios on which life centres. The anarchic maze of streets is left behind, and order and unity are found within the house.

This urban landscape is easily understood in the light of the fundamental ideals of Muslim life. The anarchy in the detailed plan is never the result of design. The Muslim towns generally had an organized plan when they were founded, often of chess-board pattern more or less under the influence of Hellenistic designs, sometimes radial-concentric. But usually this initial plan was quickly obliterated. The Muslim town, in fact, bears the marks of an almost total absence of municipal organization. Whereas the Classical city, like the medieval Western town, is characterized by a lively feeling of solidarity and notable municipal pride, and by various forms of close understanding and co-operation, the Muslim town offers nothing of the kind. It enjoys no exceptional privileges, no particular rights. The price of the supremacy of religious concepts in social organization is the absence of any political interest in the community. Nothing tempers the absolutism of the ruler. The Muslim town boasts no municipal official or magistrate, except the *muḥtasib*, who has hardly any responsibility but the oversight and policing of the markets. In consequence, the communal spaces are devoured rapidly and completely by individual encroachment. Squatters' rights are quickly effective in questions of occupation of the public highway and there is great tolerance in this respect. This point was already well-observed by a seventeenth-century French traveller: 'There is not a single fine street in Cairo, but a mass of little ones turning hither and thither, which clearly demonstrates that all the houses were built without design, each one choosing all those places which pleased him to build on, without considering whether he stop up a street or no.'[1] In the case of ancient towns converted to Islam, the deterioration of the plan had perhaps already begun before the Muslim conquest—in the Byzantine era at Aleppo and Damascus. In Anatolia, it was certainly facilitated by the occurrence of a first period of decadence of urban life, linked with the nomadic conquest, the population dwindling and buildings being abandoned, to be followed by a new disorderly expansion which ignored the previous alignments. Whether their evolution was thus produced in one or two periods, the Muslim towns never experienced the regular reorganizations which constantly remodel Western towns and direct their development.

The rigid segregation by districts, and the cloistered family life, are expressions of the same principle. The unity of the city is replaced by the cohesion of the district or the group, while the aim is to keep the family away from contamination and dispersal, and to keep the authorities away from private life. Even the house itself bears the signs of a similar frame of mind. The avoidance of many-storeyed houses denotes a rejection of luxury and ostentation, since the raising-up of high dwellings seemed a symbol of pride and arrogance. The architecture is further marked by the fragility of its materials, the preponderance of mud and wood, a sign of individualism and the absence of any materialistic group-feeling, while the durable stone house was linked with Mediterranean city-life, and the prospect of centuries before it. At Istanbul, the little wooden houses of the Turks, scattered at random, quickly took the place of the solid brick constructions of the Byzantines, and effaced the network of main roads of the city. The persistence of the pre-Islamic house-plan with a central court, derived from the Greek peristyle house, was furthered in a remarkable way by this simultaneous proscription of tall houses, and use of fragile materials unsuitable for multi-storeyed buildings.

This almost complete absence of any real integration of the diverse elements of city life seems to have had important consequences. The urban ideal of Islam created no forms, no urban structure; its role in the urban landscape was only conservative and negative: conservative in that it preserved the fundamental organs of town life in the same shape which they had received in Classical times, the *sūqs* deriving from the colonnaded avenue, the *qayṣariyya* and the caravanserai from the basilica, the *ḥammām* from the baths, the bazaar from ancient Near Eastern prac-

[1] Thévenot, *Relation d'un voyage fait au Levant* (Paris, 1664), 239.

tices which were no more invented by Islam than segregation into districts; negative in that it replaced the solidarity of a collective community with an anomalous disorganized heap of disparate quarters and elements. Seen on a world scale, it resulted in the persistence over a large area of an outworn pattern of urban life. By a really very remarkable paradox, this religion endowed with the ideal of urban life produced the very negation of urban order.

The traditional exceptions to this general rule were very rare. Some schismatic towns, like the cities of the Kharijites of the Mzab, built with defence needs in mind, pushed out to the edge their economic centre, the market, which had to be accessible to the caravans and the people from outside. The pilgrim towns of Arabia, Jedda and Mecca, are towns without blind alleys, cut everywhere by right-angled crossroads, designed in accordance with the need for space in which large crowds could move about, and dominated by great edifices divided into numerous tiny lodgings and built to function as hostels. Elsewhere serious changes had to await European intervention, by colonization or progressive Westernization.

The traditional urban landscape has been affected by this, but has not in general by any means disappeared. The first signs of evolution hardly appear before the end of the eighteenth and the beginning of the nineteenth century, the main impulse deriving from Muḥammad ʿAlī in Egypt, from the Tanẓīmāt in Turkey, from French colonization in North Africa and, in Persia, delayed until about 1930 under the rule of Riżā Shāh. The phases are well marked. First, the additions to the buildings are attacked, the projections and overhangs of every kind are removed and efforts are made to ease traffic in the old streets by every means possible. Very soon great roads have to be cut through, especially when inter-urban road-traffic develops and demands a way across the built-up areas. This phase was particularly spectacular in Persia, where Riżā Shāh cut open a gigantic chessboard in Tehran, for instance, relegating its traditional aspect to the little side-streets. The third stage is the opening up of the commercial quarters and laying bare the public monuments, frequently concealed until then beneath an undergrowth of private houses. The last stage is that of a change in the style of dwellings, with the very slow modification of the old residential districts. Whereas the first efforts to regularize the pattern are not often characterized by europeanization of the appearance of the city, since the buildings remain traditional in style, there gradually appear thereafter Western-type constructions of greater height. This transformation often remains incomplete and frequently buildings differing greatly in appearance and height stand side by side, and offer a ragged and unfinished impression. The aspect of these towns seems to be caught in the middle of rebuilding operations, paradoxically more like American town-centres, which are quickly rebuilt, than the more uniform and stable appearance of the centre of European cities.

These changes have not been distributed at all equally. Regional types can be distinguished. Algeria is marked by radical alterations, since the European occupation was originally considered to be precarious, and the colonizers establishing themselves in already existing towns thereupon rebuilt them from foundation to roof-tree. Similarly, in the Balkans, the Christian reoccupation came at exactly the same point in time as the beginning of a new era in transport. The most extreme case was Sofia, where the Ottoman town, of 30,000 inhabitants in 1878, was practically razed to the ground. But this is characteristic also of the Pontic regions of Anatolia, and of Istanbul, where the widespread wooden houses constituted excellent fuel for repeated and destructive fires, and equal opportunity for extensive clearances. Thus the areas of Istanbul which were burnt down at the end of the nineteenth and the beginning of the twentieth centuries were rebuilt in a modern style which contrasts strongly with the ancient islands still surviving in the quarters which were spared. On the other hand, Tunisia and Morocco are marked by more modest changes, since there the colonists established themselves beside the older cities and treated them with respect; the same is true almost everywhere in the Arab Near East and in Persia. Beyond the great avenues, the original city centres were generally spared and the introduction of modernity is primarily marked by the development of new towns beside the old. The former centres are gradually abandoned by the middle classes for the newer districts and fall into rapid social devaluation, taking on a proletarian character which radically transforms the social balance of the city. The ethnic and cultural divisions of former days favoured a mingling of the classes and hence a certain harmony in social relations; the new segregation is based on wealth. The previous concentric structure is replaced by bilateral contrasts, as in Tehran, where there is a growing opposition between the comfortable town in the north, near the foot of the mountain, with fresh air and pure water, and the town of the poor which stretches to the south in the dust of the desert. So now principles of internal differentiation make themselves felt in these Muslim cities, while their appearance is remarkably altered. Nevertheless, the heritage of the traditional plan is visible everywhere to a greater or lesser degree.

The rural landscape of Islam. It is much more difficult in the Muslim countryside to distinguish what comes from man and what from nature. The impact of the religion was more limited here.

The dietary regulations of Islam are hardly responsible for more than details. The prohibition of alcoholic beverages, particularly wine, resulted in a displacement of the centre of gravity of wine production from the eastern Mediterranean to the north-western coast. In the Muslim countries the vine, grown primarily for its grapes, became garden rather than field produce; it left the plains, where it had been grown as a dry monoculture, for the hill regions where it persisted, more or less integrated into Mediterranean polyculture. There are rare exceptions, like the Turkish vineyards which were re-established towards the end of the Ottoman period, mainly in Christian villages, under the influence of the Administration of the Public Debt; the Turkish government inherited these at the time of the exchange of populations after the Greco-Turkish War of 1922. The prohibition of pork had more important geographical consequences. It led to the grazing of sheep and goats in the wooded mountains, and certainly accelerated deforestation, which was catastrophic in these arid and semi-arid countries. This factor in the turning of the Muslim countries into deserts should not be underestimated, as may be shown by the significant contrasts in relative areas under timber in the Muslim and Christian sectors on the Balkan frontiers of Islam in Albania. But, equally, its influence should not be exaggerated. The main period of deforestation in the greater part of the Mediterranean and Near Eastern region must considerably antedate Islam, and goes back primarily to the Neolithic or Classical periods of peasant expansion and demographic pressure. In many cases bedouinization, in bringing about a regression of sedentary life, probably encouraged some return to natural vegetation rather than the reverse.

Islam affected the condition of agriculture most through its land-owning structure and laws of real property. The basic principles of these are the state ownership and inalienability of land and the system of pious foundations, *waqf* or *ḥubus*. The origins of this system do not go back to the Prophet, who gave land to his warriors, but traditionally to ʿUmar, who reverted to the old principle of collective tribal property under the form of appropriation to the central authority—the original meaning of the word *waqf* before it took on that of mortmain or religious trust. Although the attitude of the various schools of jurisprudence differs on the status of land acquired by conquest, and the Hanafite in particular permits the *imām* to choose between state ownership and distribution, the land-system in force throughout the Ottoman empire was in fact founded on almost universal state ownership. As in the land policy of ʿUmar, Muslim ideas combined with pre-Islamic traditions—in this case the old traditions of tribal ownership of the Turks of Central Asia. In the last analysis the Muslim preference that land should be owned impersonally is also due to the spread of the religion by nomadic peoples.

The consequences of this were important. The system of state ownership was accompanied by the organization of the land into *iqṭāʿ*, concessions granted to soldier-officials in return for military service. The peculiarity of the *iqṭāʿ* is that the grant is practically detached from the land, which owes no duty in service or labour, but merely a fixed payment determined by the central authority. Thus the possessor has no real interest in the improvement of the working of the soil; the Oriental system of lordship displays hardly any of those personal bonds which constitute the better feature of the Western feudal system, the lord's interest in his vassal, and use of him as a worker and not simply as a payer of taxes. On the other hand, the system of inheritance does not recognize primogeniture, another guarantee against state absolutism. Joint possession by the heirs is the customary usage, frequently pushed to extremes. Although the Muslim law of inheritance therefore is not favourable to the establishment of personal latifundia, its combination with a system of lordship definitely separated from the soil, and with the joint possession of large estates by families, ends in encouraging absentee landlordism. The state ownership of the land, in the form in which the Ottoman Turks pushed it to its most extreme limits, proved disastrous for the shape of rural society, since the progressive influence of great estates run directly by their owners was missing. In the last phase, as the absolute Ottoman system was declining, the developments towards a pattern of great estates, fully appropriated to their owners, of the *chiftlik* type, were certainly of some value, but they came too late, and in a situation of generalized economic disorder which did not favour real progress. The pattern of land-tenure inherited from this system, in which the rights of individuals are always more or less open to question, appears moreover to be everywhere almost impossible to disentangle. In the middle of the nineteenth century, Michaud wrote in his *Correspondance d'Orient*: 'Throughout Turkey the ownership of land is an unknown concept... The village population live in the countryside they till without knowing much about whom the soil that nourishes them belongs to.' In contrast with urban property, ownership of rural land seems burdened with a basic doubt. There is a complete contrast with Western ideas here. While in the West the ploughed field is the image of unfettered property, absolute, virtually eternal, fixed to the soil by demarcation, held down by cadastral survey; in the East, rural land never reaches full individual ownership. The anarchy of the land-system leads inevitably to arbitrary procedures. The true status of a piece of land counts for less than the status of its owner. The imprecise nature of the legal system introduces into the land-market a personal element which has an essential part to play in the development of the system of land ownership.

This is based above all on the large, or even very large, estates which are normally the vast majority (or were so at least before the modern attempts of agrarian reform, still frequently hesitant); this is as much the case in the Levant as in Persia, in eastern Anatolia as in north-western India. It is the result of the joint influence of two factors: the political and social primacy of the cities, and the economic primacy of income from land. The latter is due on the one hand to the lack of industrialization and of opportunities for substantial investment in handicrafts, and on the other to the Qur'anic prohibition of usury, which prevented the establishment of a legal system of return on liquid capital, and meant that it played a restricted part in economic life, so that the acquisition of land was the only normal use for capital. The town-dwellers continually sought to buy up rural properties. They had two principal means of action to hand. The first, in the immediate neighbourhood of the cities, in rich and properly policed areas, was usury, since the religious ban on lending at interest was in fact easily evaded by a notional increase in the sum advanced, so that it had little effect except to render more burdensome the practice it was designed to remove. Secondly, there was the relationship of client and protector in the more distant plains, merging into the great estates of the nomad aristocracy, or of the various powers set up in the anarchic social structure of the mountain ranges; such estates always appeared as a zone of legally defined territorial influence, founded on more or less disguised violence.

The system of exploitation is dominated entirely by its radical dissociation from the principal proprietor. The agrarian system of the Near Eastern countryside has been described with apt brevity: 'The cultivator does not own and the owner does not cultivate.'[1] Here again the basic reasons are to be found in that contempt for land and that flight from agricultural matters characteristic of Islam. The plough brings dishonour. It is a social, almost a moral, victory to free oneself from it. This collective economic renunciation by persons of standing results almost everywhere in the form of exploitation known as share-cropping (*métayage*), by which the farmer pays rent in kind, the owner furnishing stock and seed, which corresponds perfectly to the climate of social subordination. The condemnation in principle which certain *Ḥadiths* bring to bear on contracts for indirect exploitation was quickly evaded and the severity of the *'ulamā'* was most often concentrated on tenant-farming at a fixed rent, which they regarded as too hazardous a contract for the tenant, yet which in the West has been an undeniable factor in capital formation and peasant progress.

Altogether this is a heavy curse weighing on the Muslim lands. In this depressing picture of rural society condemned to mediocrity and sclerosis, only rare sections are lit by a somewhat brighter light. The areas of careful agriculture are really limited in general to the immediate surroundings of the towns, in the suburban zone of gardens and orchards, where property is fragmented and exploitation is intensified in the hands of the working people of the towns. It is there, particularly in the Spanish *huertas*, that are to be found the most positive contributions from Islam to the cultivation of the soil: the exotic trees and plants which it conveyed and introduced into the interior of the Muslim world by means of its far-flung commercial relations; and the irrigation techniques which it perfected, identifying itself with, and spreading, the knowledge of ancient Near Eastern techniques much older than itself. Similarly on its African frontier, Islam has been able at times to appear productive of agricultural progress, in view of the relatively fixed way of life which it recommends instead of the shifting cultivation of burnt clearings typical of the inter-tropical zone; and in view of the influence of agrarian sects like the Murids of Senegal whose collective discipline has worked wonders and has been responsible for great developments, notably in ground-nut growing. But this attraction to the soil is quite exceptional, and specific only to Negro Islam; this preference for agriculture has

[1] Weulersse, *Paysans de Syrie et du Proche-Orient* (Paris, 1946), 121.

only been able to develop to any extent away from orthodox influences.

State and region

Political forms. The very structure of the political forms arises from the economic and moral pre-eminence of the cities which we have already described. The urban state is typical. A Muslim state is first of all a dynasty and a capital, a city where the ruler can have the Friday prayers said on his behalf at the main mosque. Around this capital the authority of his rule extends for a varying distance, normally without interruption, until finally it becomes more and more vague and nominal. Beyond the plain, kept in hand and regularly policed, which serves as a victualling base for the city and the army, one gradually enters the areas of peasant dissidence, especially when control of the country is hampered by hills and mountains. The contrast is perhaps nowhere more striking than in pre-colonial Morocco. In opposition to *bled el-makhzen*, submissive to governmental authority, there stands *bled el-siba* 'the land of insolence', which consists essentially of the Berber mountains. A fragile balance, continually reset, is established between the central power and more or less autonomous tribes. The most extreme case is that of city states by the sea isolated in the middle of an immense tribal hinterland, where their influence is very weak and can only be exercised by full-scale expeditions, such as those which the deys of Algiers mounted annually with their Janissaries to raise taxes in the interior, with the more or less interested complicity of the *Makhzan* tribes. There is nothing comparable here with the Western state which long ago seemed founded, in essence, on territorial possessions, which might often, like those of the House of Austria, be fragmented and discontinuous, but were strictly defined.

A further type of Muslim state should, however, also be noted. Frequently the nomads constituted the main spearhead of advance, and it is here that the ascendancy of a number of dynasties originated, both in early and later times. From the Almoravids of Morocco to the Turkish dynasties of the Near East, 'the land of insolence' produced rulers as frequently as did palace revolutions. The rhythm of Moroccan history is dominated by dynasties, rising in the south, if not in the desert itself, who from time to time come and lay their hands on the rich *Makhzan* plains of the region of Fez. Before the Pahlavī dynasty of the twentieth century, practically all the Persian dynasties were also furnished by Turkish-speaking nomads. These nomad powers even laid the first foundations of certain states, not satisfied with conquering prey already prepared for them. The dynasty which, from the end of the eighteenth century onwards, gradually established the Afghan state, represented the nomadic tribes of Durrānī and Ghilzāy, which achieved the unification of the country for their own benefit, in spite of its being based on mountains mainly inhabited by peasants. Even when the new controlling personalities appear to come from an urban setting, from among scholars or theologians, they can frequently only consolidate their success by reliance on new groupings of nomads. Thus the Safavids in Persia were only able to establish themselves because of the progress of Shīʿī propaganda among the Turcoman tribes of Āẕarbāyjān, although they actually emerged from the urban setting of Ardabīl; and the victory of the Wahhābīs over the urban dynasties of the Ḥijāz can only be explained by the support they received from the nomads.

These nomadic states, more than others, reflect transitory situations. Once raised to the throne, the nomad ruler becomes urbanized, takes up permanent residence in the city, and gradually takes on the mentality of the townspeople who surround him. This change takes place by degrees however and may take a long time in some cases, while in others it occurs quite rapidly. Throughout the nineteenth century the Qājār shahs, true descendants of the great Turkish tribe of that name who wandered in the north, preferred to spend the summer in tents enjoying the fresh air of the Elburz mountains in camps, moving from hunting-ground to hunting-ground, and their ministers had to follow them. Nevertheless, the problems and the methods of political control do not differ fundamentally so much from those common to the states specifically based on cities. The nomad ruler has as much difficulty as the urban prince in extending his influence over the tribes, apart from the actual tribe from which he sprang. And he is subject to the constant threat of intervention by hostile tribes or tribal confederations. The decisive role which the Bakhtiyārīs played in the constitutional crisis of 1907 is well known, when these traditional enemies of the Qājārs marched on Tehran. Nevertheless there is force in the view that the state founded on nomadic power often has a greater facility and greater knack of controlling the 'land of insolence.' It can deploy its supporters more easily than a mercenary army, reluctant to go far from the city gates.

Though the urban state may better fulfil the Muslim ideal, the nomadic state is therefore probably more efficient in the administration of an empire of substantial size. The basic problem in the present-day political life of many Muslim states remains therefore the establishment of effective control and a modern type of administration in many places in their territory. Very often it was not till the colonial period that the 'lands of insolence' were definitely brought under the aegis of the central power. Here the methods of the British and the French colonizers differed profoundly, both in spirit and in manner. The French preferred subjugation, aiming at complete obedience, followed by direct administration; while the British set up military boundaries and then reduced their effective intervention to the minimum by administering indirectly through the medium of the chieftains; but the results of both methods were much the same as far as apparent pacification is concerned. The states which escaped colonization have frequently had to wait until very recent years to attain the same ends, as for instance Persia, in the case of the great Qāshqā'ī confederation in the Zagros mountains. The process of unification has proved relatively easier in those states where urban civilization has long been preponderant, as in Egypt, or Tunisia; it has offered rather more problems for states which, while equally well policed, contain large schismatic or mountain-dwelling minorities and important fringes, like Syria struggling with the 'Alawite problem, or Iraq with the Kurds; for the 'empires', from Afghanistan and Persia to Morocco, it has proved particularly arduous.

Principles of regional organization. The dynamic of regional evolution may be analysed in the light of this political situation. The traditional regional structure of Islam was founded on discontinuity, mainly after the bedouinization which occurred in medieval times. Restricted centres, where a satisfying rural life had been preserved, were separated by immense areas devoted to wandering, decay, and rapine. This preponderance of areas unnaturally turned into deserts prevented the fabrication of those local interconnexions which build up the complex web of regional units, and offer the only basis for any attempt to exploit differing environments on a rational basis. The only kind of regional organization was the urban district, the zone in which a town exercised influence and control over the surrounding countryside, finding its political expression in the urban state. This situation was the natural product of an arid or semi-arid geographical setting, where the intrinsic weakness of rural life, outside the irrigated areas under intensive cultivation, permitted the development of such a state of affairs. It offers a ready explanation for the difficulties found in converting the countryside to Islam beyond the limited range of the cities' influence. The coastal strips converted by the merchants, in a different natural and political setting, were no exception to the rule when set against a hostile hinterland. The great deltaic rice-growing plains, like Bengal or the Javanese plains in monsoon Asia, or like the Nile Delta, belong to the same category. Human organization was only established effectively in a framework of homogeneous natural conditions, though in these cases on a much more considerable scale. The Muslim lands hardly ever produced any regional unity based on the association of areas with complementary economies, such as mountain and plain. It is noteworthy that the sites chosen for towns in Muslim countries are normally linked with the crossroads of long-distance international, or intercontinental routes, or with decisive physical resources at the centre of homogeneous natural units. The towns form the capitals of little isolated basins, or autonomous plains, or oases associated with exceptional water supplies, like Damascus or Fez. The little market-town which acts as a point of contact between differing natural units, along an axis between a mountain and the plain for example, which is so common in Western Europe, is practically unknown in Islam. The rarity of names for districts, which are the most tangible expression of intimacy and intensity in the relationship between men and the land, underlines the inadequacy of regional life in Islam. There used to be a very large number of district-names in Persia, but most of them disappeared from popular speech at the time of the medieval bedouinization.

The diminution of these gaps between centres of intensive occupation is a prerequisite of the progressive development of organized and centralized states. Demographic pressure, which has increased so sharply in contemporary times, since the end of the last century, has been a major influence in this direction by necessitating the utilization of new land. The significant feature of recent developments has therefore been the steady expansion of the ancient centres, and the colonization, or rather the recolonization of the intervening areas. It is the success of this vast movement to conquer new ground which is a precondition of achieving regional balance and satisfying national organization, and which today has become general. Central and eastern Tunisia, where after the Hilālī invasions sedentary life had become confined to the narrow strip of the Sahel—a chain of large villages strung along the coast among their olive groves—has witnessed an astonishing resumption of human occupation of the neighbouring low-lying steppe since the end of the nineteenth century. On the northern border of the Syrian desert, at the foot of the Taurus mountains, in the Jazīra, a cultivable area reserved since the Middle Ages as a kind of winter quarters for the nomads who spent the summer in the highlands, considerable cereal production has been developed from the time of the French mandate onwards. The ʿAlawites, leaving their mountains, are in process of exploiting the Maʿmūra steppe, east of Ḥimṣ and Ḥamāh and south of Aleppo. And in the Mesopotamian plains, where cultivation was confined until recently to narrow irrigated borders beside the rivers, the cultivated area has more than doubled since the middle of the nineteenth century. Everywhere the peasant has become a pioneer.

The human material for this spatial expansion has certainly been supplied to a great extent by the constant demographic surplus of the older centres of population. But a considerable part derives from the settlement of nomads. Their survival in any appreciable numbers is rendered more and more precarious through the progressive colonization of the marginal areas which still offer opportunities for cultivation; this deprives them of their most attractive grazing grounds and pushes them back towards the desert. Settlement is their only recourse, permitting an incomparably higher proportion of human beings to use a given area of land. In this way the settlement of the nomads is an integral part of the process of reconquering the soil. Furthermore, it has been possible for it to figure as a primary goal in the establishment of state control and administration throughout the state territory. It is the most striking manifestation of the revenge of the settled communities against the bedouin which characterizes the present political situation. This attitude is particularly clear in a number of Near Eastern states. Article 158 of the 1950 Syrian constitution laid down the settlement of all the nomads as a fundamental aim to be achieved. Similarly, one of the essential features of Suʿūdī policy has been the settlement of the nomads, and new centres of habitation have been multiplied throughout Arabia, particularly for the *ikhwān*, the companions of the king in battle. Everywhere today the nomadic way of life is retreating rapidly. The sole exception is Afghanistan, where policy is still dominated by the recent nomadic origin of the dynasty, and by the desire to spread Afghan ways through the whole country as quickly as possible. There the state is fostering the spread of those nomads properly called Afghans over the whole of the central arc of mountains, where, if there is not a real bedouinization, the annexation of land by the nomads is making steady progress.

The result of this gigantic movement is a certain change in the economic and social structure of the Muslim countries. The original Islam of towns and nomads is more and more giving way to an Islam of peasants. The old oases are being submerged, and the nomads absorbed by expanding rural societies, swept on in an irresistible movement to conquer the soil, which must be the main activity of these countries where the pace of industrialization remains slow. This acquisition by Islam of a rural character can in itself only be beneficial, and this precisely to the extent to which it destroys the inhibitions imposed by the traditional ideal. The tragedy of the Muslim countries is that this agricultural expansion is being carried out in an unfavourable natural setting, in the marginal areas where rain-fed agriculture is always uncertain. Peasant resistance has generally been concentrated in the mountains and the irrigable districts. The margin for expansion was thus primarily situated in the sub-arid steppes, and the development of irrigated land, even when substantial, cannot follow the rhythm of demographic progress. The economy of these countries is more and more subject to the whims of the weather and the hazards of a particularly variable climate. In these circumstances soil erosion does considerable damage. Gigantic efforts in economic planning and development will be required if this spatial expansion of soil occupation is truly to bring forth stability and progress.

CHAPTER 2

THE SOURCES OF ISLAMIC CIVILIZATION

The spiritual force which suddenly arises as concrete phenomenon before our eyes in unimagined uniqueness cannot be derived from a higher principle. (LEOPOLD VON RANKE)[1]

I

That a civilization should have neatly identifiable sources is a concept of a more limited validity than recent intellectual habituation and customary techniques of scholarship would suggest. It presupposes the notion of developmental units of sufficiently consistent and individual character to be capable of isolation within, though not separable from, the stream of history, and it tends to imply, at least as a metaphor, the idea of a cultural compound resulting from the blending, amalgamation or coalescence of a number of pre-existing historic ingredients. Since obviously these ingredients can be recognized only in retrospect, that is to say, through the analysis of the unit in which they are submerged or active, a teleological outlook is apt to guide the eye of the diagnostician, who also may find it difficult to pry himself loose from the organicism inherent in the image whose persuasiveness only too readily obscures its purely nominalist function as a principle of order.

The concept of sources becomes meaningless in a context in which cultures or civilizations are perceived as essentially changeless, belonging to the world of ideas and withdrawn from historical process which affects or moulds only their surface manifestations. When 'Islamic culture and civilization' are seen to be 'as old as the human race itself', and 'Islamic culture' is defined as 'an interpretation of the will of God as conveyed to humanity through the agency of the prophets starting with Adam and culminating in Muḥammad', it is taken out of history, to which it is not really restored by the statement that 'With Prophet Muḥammad, however, Islamic culture got an extraordinary impetus, attaining to the zenith of its grandeur.'[2]

[1] *Politisches Gespräch* (1836), *Sämmtliche Werke* (Leipzig, 1865–90), 49–50, 325; tr. Th. H. Von Laue, *Leopold Ranke: the formative years* (Princeton, 1950) as *A dialogue on politics* (pp. 152–80), 165.

[2] Abdur Rauf, *Renaissance of Islamic culture and civilization in Pakistan* (Lahore, 1964). Unpublished typescript, 1, 2.

The concept becomes equally devoid of meaning when a civilization is seen if not as all-embracing at least as an absolute without reference to specific historical situations—the component particulars to receive their validation and value (be it positive or negative) from a global verdict of acceptance or rejection. In our period of historicist and post-historicist thinking, this outlook has become rather rare, and it is for this reason that a poem quoted in 1931 as sung by the school children of Baghdād deserves partial mention.

Children of Islam, the world is short of well directed people...Show it your religion for it to follow, that religion of reason and conscience, self-evident as the laws of nature....For us Heaven has lowered itself on to earth when, with the Qur'ān, it has sent down the virtues of the sublime man, star of the earth, Muḥammad, even as every generous aspiration.[1]

Within such an ahistoric perception of cultural environment that implies total acception or rejection, almost like that of the physical reality into which man finds himself thrown, the question of sources, if posed at all, enters consciousness as part either of the sustaining doctrine or of an argument to glorify or deprecate. Thus earliest Islam was rendered aware of preceding revelations and the continuity of God's plan for mankind culminating in the mission of Muḥammad, and soon became alive, owing to circumstances not necessarily connected with the Qur'anic message, to the possibility, even the need, to use the allegation of foreign origin as a tool in its effort at consolidation, be it to substantiate, welcome or to eliminate incongruous patterns of thought and behaviour. Here the 'other' serves but as a means to identify or justify the self and receives its significance solely from its usefulness for self-assertion.

To the historian, whether he arise from within or without that civilization become sure of itself, the temptation is ever-present to unravel results as though they were the inevitable effect of an interplay of vectors, and to reconstruct the development as the successful or miscarried outcome of planning made respectable by the positing of an inner logic which, it is overlooked, is inescapable only in retrospect. There are no doubt intellectual and emotional premisses, as it were, with which the Arabs left the peninsula and which affected their ability to respond to their new environments, and these environments on their

[1] A. Memmi, *La Poésie algérienne de* 1830 *à nos jours* (Paris, 1963), 48; tr. from *al-Balāgh* and *ash-Shihāb* (Algeria), where the poem is recommended as being recited by *les écoliers de Baghdād*.

part were limited in the possibilities and dangers to which they exposed the conquerors. But the interaction of Arab and non-Arab, Muslim and non-Muslim, never was a constant, but oscillated without cease as new concerns unveiled neglected factors that thus turned into 'sources' and newly encountered circumstances disclosed hitherto dormant concerns which again would be activated into 'sources'.

The establishment of Arab Islam in the alien world from Spain to the Oxus marks one of those periods in history when man loses his contact with his ancestors, and when the psychological continuity appears almost, even totally, broken. The new civilization, which represents the means and the goal of recovering lost bearings, creates a common memory constituted by a selection of shared *memorabilia*, largely historical events and judgments on the one hand, human and doctrinal assumptions on the other. That these *memorabilia* were, for the most part, situated in an Arab milieu was to give the new civilization an Arab cachet. There is incessant interaction between the subjective impulses of individual and society, and the objective factors of the cosmic and the social environments. It is certainly true that the Arabs adopted in large measure the civilizations of the conquered, but the formative process of Islamic civilization is to be understood adequately only when it is realized that this civilization is merely the 'dominant average' of many subcultures, and more particularly that associated with the ruling and authoritatively literate groups. More important still, this process may be seen as the clustering about a mobile magnetic centre of particles, large or small, which by design, by accident or by their proper motion, entered its field. Thus the task of the cultural historian becomes the reconciliation of the concept of sources, fundamentally static, with genetic analysis; in other words, of structure with process.

The nature of the power nucleus around which the civilization of Islam was to precipitate is perhaps most graphically described when it is contrasted with comparable power centres that had formed intermittently, not too long before the emergence of the Muslims from the peninsula, on West Roman soil over a period of some three hundred years. The Germanic tribes or agglomerations of tribes which had taken over control in various forms endeavoured without exception to integrate with the *imperium Romanum*. Not only did they allow Roman administration to continue—the Arabs, too, had no thought of dismantling the administrative cadres and only began to modify them in any serious sense more than a generation after the conquest. But the

Germanic nations accepted Christianity as soon as the empire had become *imperium Christianum*, and this acceptance of a new faith, coupled as it was with a network of attitudes and *mores*, was only one aspect of a general readiness to accept the imperial culture. Like the Arabs after them they were but a minority precariously perched on a complex alien substructure, and again like the Arabs, they endeavoured to keep aloof from their subjects, curtailing intermarriage, monopolizing to a large extent military service and remaining content to perpetuate their identity as the exploiting and policy-making stratum. But in sharp contrast to their Germanic predecessors in the West the Arabs had no inclination to exchange their language, however incomplete in terms of their new tasks, for that of the vanquished, and even less did they think of yielding their faith.

The Prophet had imbued them with the certainty of spiritual superiority; victory added the certainty of racial superiority. The depreciation of the intellectual and material achievements of the conquered may have been less pervasive than complacent anecdotes would suggest. In fact, the realization of the existential and practical possibilities that rulership added to the outreach of a Muslim's life occurred early and widely. Yet there never was felt the temptation to yield the Arab, let alone the Muslim identity and to aspire to leadership, in the mode traditional in the Eastern Empire, as the *élite* of a Christian state of Greek tongue. Islam had made the converted Arabs the centre of a universal world-view and hence, when the time came, the centre of a universal state. In contrast to the Germanic peoples who were in need of legitimation and thus of continuing what they displaced, the Muslim Arab had his centre of gravity within himself. His people were chosen and rule belonged as of right to the elect.

Neither his faith nor the law by which he lived needed to be imposed on the subjects. Rather did he feel a certain reluctance to admit the non-Arab to a full share in heaven and earth. A small caste of saved warriors and their kin, possessors of the last word God was to address to humankind and cultivating a spiritual arrogance which, together with their power, fascinated rather than repelled the exploited, the early Muslims had eliminated the hegemony of the christianized world-view of the ancient universe before they had ever realized its implications, not to say its existence. The cutting certainty of the Iraqi student song of 1931 with its artless assertion 'We are the pure, the glorious, the *élite*. Everything good in this world goes back to us alone' could anachronistically be transferred to the sense of collective superiority that propelled the society of the early caliphate.

This interplay of analogy and contrast can be followed further. History was vindicating Islam. In the most literal manner, truth was conquering. Many of the conquered felt relieved from heterodox, alien pressures. Victory and its stabilization in political control sealed for good and all the coalescence of the religious and the political community as it had been forecast by the Prophet's own conceptions and arrangements. The Arab Muslims were an *umma*, unified body, a *jamā'a*, community, and by modern criteria of linguistic and racial identity, they were clearly a nation. Eusebius, too, in the intoxication of the Christian victory under Constantine, saw the Christians as a nation, albeit of transcendental origin. The illusion was cherished in the fourth century that Christianity would bring steady material advance. It took the object lesson of the falling apart of the Western empire to disabuse the enthusiasts of the confusion between a nation and a religious community, and an Augustine to separate, in Western Christian minds, the power of Rome from the growth of Christianity. Islam was spared the political disappointment at the outset only to pay in heartbreak a thousand years later.

Unlike the wandering Germanic peoples, the Muslims had a geographically fixed political centre. Damascus controlled, at least nominally, expansion and rule. Yet for a long time to come there was, strictly speaking, no Muslim state. Where the Frankish king was *rex Francorum* and his territory *regnum Francorum*, the Muslim ruler was *amīr al-mu'minīn* and his territory actually lacked a designation until the lawyers came up with the term of *dār al-Islām*—a concept depending for its meaning on the complementary *dār al-ḥarb*—the lands under and beyond Muslim control. Some one hundred and fifty years after the conquests the great legist and adviser of Hārūn al-Rashīd, Abū Yūsuf (d. 182/798) discusses at length the concept and the role of the ruler without having a word to say of the state.[1] But where in the Germanic states the law of the ruling population was in competition with the more fully developed Roman codes, the revealed character of the fundamentals of Muslim law (and the naïve intransigence of the Muslims) constituted it the *Reichsrecht* that overarched the laws of the subject peoples even as the ruling community overarched those peoples themselves.

The most important analogy, however, lies in the fact that the

[1] Abū Yūsuf Ya'qūb, *Kitāb al-kharāj* (Cairo, 1352), 5–6, 8, 10, 19; tr. E. Fagnan as *Le livre de l'impôt foncier* (Paris, 1921), 5–6, 11, 14, 19–20.

Classical culture which the Germanic intruders of the fifth or sixth, and the Arabs of the seventh and eighth, centuries are supposed to have combated, dislodged or destroyed, had ceased fully to exist before the first invader appeared. Element after element had, as it were, dropped out, sooner perhaps in the West, and neither the intellectual nor the social structure was any more sufficiently rich and compact to offer that resistance or appeal which we, inured to the picture of an earlier phase of ancient civilization, tend to see before us as option and victim of the barbarians. The crumbling was slower in the West; the Germanic yoke was repeatedly shaken off. In the East, the provinces that fell to the Arabs remained Muslim for centuries, if not to the present. The very suddenness of the conquest and the absence of violent reactions on the part of the defeated civilization did, paradoxically enough, preserve relatively more of the ancient institutional heritage under the Arabs than, for instance, under Lombards and Franks. It is merely the language curtain and the selectiveness of the chronicler that tend to conceal this all important fact. Greek certainly receded under Islam, but it practically died out in the West, and the elimination of Latin under Islam is paralleled by an identical, if possibly somewhat slower, decline of Latin in Byzantium. In any event, neither the rapid victory of a rudimentary Islamic civilization nor the failure of maturing Islam to develop certain facets of its potential, e.g., in literature, could be accounted for without the realization that the 'ancient' civilization it encountered had itself already become fragmentary, 'medievalized', and unproductive.

Incontestably, the cultural level and the outreach of experience accessible in the Arabian peninsula at the rise of Islam, were lower and narrower than in the areas that fell to the first Muslim attacks. This differential, however, must not be allowed to blur the fact that Islam strode forth from its homeland with the essential determinations and decisions already made. It had placed itself in the line of the Abrahamic religions, and although at first its distinctiveness went largely unnoticed and unheeded by its Christian subjects, it entered the lands of ancient civilization already marked with that onesidedness which, in the words of Wilhelm von Humboldt, is the goal of any individual, be it person, nation or epoch.[1]

[1] *Ideen über Staatsverfassung* (1791), in *Werke*, ed. A. Leitzmann (*et al.*) (Berlin, 1903–36), I, 81; analysed by F. Meinecke, *Weltbürgertum und Nationalstaat* (Munich, 1962; first published in 1907), 40. For the initial reaction of the subjected Christians cf. C. Cahen, 'Note sur l'accueil des chrétiens d'Orient à l'Islam', *Revue de l'histoire des religions*, CLXVI (1964), 51–8.

Insofar as they conditioned both receptiveness and creativeness in its new environments a certain number of those 'decisions'—as determinants of what elements would enter its orbit as problems and sources—must be specifically identified. (1) Radical monotheism as understood by Muḥammad had laid down irrevocably a dividing line against trinitarian Christianity, and at the same time defined equally irrevocably the nature of the basic kinship of the two faiths. In a parallel manner, the fundamental agreement with Judaism and Christianity on the facts of prophecy and revelation was never to be shaken, while the role assigned to the historic person of Muḥammad b. 'Abd Allāh was to remain an irremovable stumbling-block. Abrahamic monotheism, i.e., monotheism with a personal creator God, revelation and prophecy, carries its distinctive problematics; in the milieu of the Near Eastern tradition, the resolution of this remains linked with a limited choice of intellectual styles, of which the most advanced and most characteristic are the binomial argument by analogy, formally clad as *Ḥadīth* and the Midrashic narrative from which it stems, and the trinomial syllogism of Greek philosophy as naturalized into Christian theology (and philosophy) by the Fathers and thence into Islam.

(2) Although the Qur'anic texts emphasize the specifically Arab mission of the Prophet as much as the oneness of all revealed truth, and although the invading Arabs were less than anxious to share the privilege of their affiliation, there was nothing in the structure of the new religion to block its spread. In fact, the possession of ultimate truth came to be felt by many as an obligation to assist those on the outside in bridging the abyss between unbelief and belief. Where the social organization of power proved recalcitrant, the attraction of power helped to breach it, and although the racial pride of the converts of the first hour left a lasting imprint on religiously sanctioned social regulations and the law—from the privilege reserving the caliphate to Quraysh to the intricate rules of *kafā'a* affecting intermarriage of Arabs and non-Arabs of different status—the attraction of the Muslim faith as such, whatever the supporting motivations, vindicated a universalism which in his last years may have moved close to becoming a factor in the Prophet's self-view and political planning.

The unwelcome influx of non-Arab converts preserved Islam from being submerged by the older faiths or from surviving as the caste-mark of a comparatively small stratum set apart from their surroundings by an ethnically determined, 'private' religion. But what saved Islam undermined the political power of the Arabs, which was soon to decline, in part at least under the impact of the newcomers' discontent at being debarred from an equality within the community which Revelation had assured them. That the disintegration of Arab control furthered rather than impeded the spread of the Arab language, of Islam, and of a civilization identified in its roots with Arab Islam, is even more remarkable than the conscious universalism with which in the ʿAbbasid age Islam came to set itself against provincially confined truths such as that of Zoroastrianism.

The possession of a sacred language proved a source of strength. Zoroastrians and Christians had sacred texts but there was no obstacle to translation, and translation would, in cultural terms, tend to become one important step toward assimilation. Parallelisms of the religious tradition such as the view of Zoroaster as the end of a long line of depositaries of *X^varnah* and the prophetic *charisma*, or the kindred view which placed him in the centre of a chain of prophecy from Gayōmart to Sōshyans, could not but work in favour of Muslim ideology, confirming as they did the basic assumptions of the faith to which both intellectual and political initiative had passed, and which the kindred metahistoric constructions of older religions appeared to legitimize, and in any event consolidated.

The idea of the corruption of Scripture by Jews and Christians put forward in Muḥammad's Medinese period and developed in various ways under the empire proved a strong defensive weapon against corroding influences, and must be counted among the basic armament that permitted the Muslims to face with confidence the older religious learning.

(3) Confidence again was lent to the Muslim by his concept of man. The absolute subjection of creature to Creator, the infinite distance separating man from his God, predisposed some pious circles to contrition and humility as a pervasive attitude, but in the community as a whole the sense of election and collective perfection, at least relative to earlier religious groups, more than balanced the quietism which surrender to a supernatural will might have engendered. Any member of the best community knew himself privileged by nature or destiny over against the heathen from whom he had dissociated himself, and this sentiment was to persist in confrontation with the more advanced communities outside the Arabian peninsula. Obedience to the Lord, fulfilment of His order, justified the individual existence, the more so that no inner

rent called for atonement and redemption—the Muslim was a man without original sin, in need of guidance but not of regeneration. He was used also from time immemorial to see and value himself in the context of a collective, his clan and his tribe; and when in later days the legists proclaimed the infallibility of community consensus, this assertion was little else but an adapted restatement of the inherited self-view in which the nobility or meanness, power or weakness of the group inhered in the individual as a personal quality. But despite this dependence of man on the group, the pagan Arab bequeathed to his Muslim heir an aristocratic self-reliance, bravado and occasional *hubris*, a confident conviction of inalienable excellence grounded in descent and gesture, but most of all in the knowledge of his embodying the norms and expectations of his people. This composite inheritance gave the Muslim conqueror his peculiar invulnerability comparable in kind to that of the Western pioneer in East and South a century ago.

Whatever his defects and however painful his fragility, man was the noblest of existent beings, endowed with command over the other creatures of this earth, beyond whom he had grown and above whom he had been set by the Creator's will.

Built into this attitude and its inevitable adjustment to the restraining values of religion was the seed of the future conflict between two outlooks on man—one putting faith in his excellence, which it would find confirmed in the attunement of the moral law to standards innate in him, and gravitating toward a humanism that would shape and measure the world by his needs and accomplishments; the other, holding to his mediocrity, to the derived character of all his works, his dependence on the supernatural for success and defeat, and looking for protection behind the walls of the community, itself to be enclosed within the walls of the Law.

(4) *'Ilm* and *ma'rifa*, systematic and intuitive, or acquired and vouchsafed, knowledge—to retroject later terminology into the times of the Prophet—were not, as yet, neatly separated. Access to supernatural truth of sorts was conceded to the dreamer, and in a more specialized manner, to the professional soothsayer. An admirably precise observation of the *Lebenswelt* had not led to a clean division between empirical and speculative insights; differently put, it had not resulted in the establishment of criteria to distinguish the possible from the impossible, the material from the spiritual, technique from magic. Truth was concrete and definitive; so was falsehood, both manifest in theoretical

positions as much as in behaviour understood as ancestral custom. In fact, this truth was subject to adaptation in its practical aspect no less than its theoretical formulations; but the collective memory manipulated the past to buttress and harmonize present view and usage. For truth was not self-sustaining, nor was man by his own effort able to sustain it. It rested on authority, and the strength of authority in turn, rested on its age. The personal authority of Muḥammad and the divinity who had chosen him constituted an innovation which the Prophet did everything he could to divest of its unprecedentedness without, however, destroying the sense that a new order had come replacing outmoded truth now become error by new truth and safety everlasting.

The extent is noteworthy to which this concept of truth and its psychological and social function resembled the concept and function of truth as it had come to be accepted 'outside'—in dying Hellenism even more than in a Christianity that was still fighting to define itself. Even the disposition to forgo what we may call a Pelagian concern for free will as the primary motivation for the honour of God in His power and providence, was curiously shared by the Muslims and the tired world they were taking in hand, in which the Platonic idea of philosophy as an unquenchable thirst for comprehension, an indefatigable effort to go further and further, beyond the present limits of the self, in an ever renewing urge to break the deadly grip of acquiescence in an achievement threatening to be accepted as delimitative, was still proclaimed though increasingly introverted. With this expectation of truth goes a readiness to search for mystical experience, for loving absorption into the deity, a longing not yet understood in its dangers for the postulate of divine remoteness. Perhaps it would be more accurate to speak of a search for the mystery rather than of mysticism. In any event, the later development of mystical piety by way of several 'dialogues' with primarily Christian articulations of such experience, would be distorted without recognition of its adumbration in earliest Islam. The vocabulary of mature Muslim mysticism remains to testify to the indelible imprint of certain Qur'anic verses on adepts and advocates.

(5) More than seems to be commonly assumed does the Muslim empire represent an extension of the socio-political concepts prevailing in Arabia among the early community and before. The Arab Muslims as an aristocratic warrior class with weak roots in agriculture and some connexion with commerce continued the part played by a dominant tribe providing protection to weaker groupings. As those weaker

groups retained their own leaders and 'internal autonomy', so the weaker groupings in the conquered territories were under the 'protection' of the Muslim rulers to retain their community organization and their *élite*. The representative of the caliph was to be the military commander on behalf of the 'dominant tribe'.[1] The Muslim community was unstructured as between religious and profane tasks and functions, somewhat like the undifferentiated unity of the family. Divine guidance was always near and unspecialized in regard to the sphere of life which it regulated. Even as membership in a nation will, today, possess the whole person, although it may, in the West at least, leave the individual free to decide and arrange some areas of his existence, so membership in the Islamic 'nation' meant, in principle and increasingly in fact, total submergence, a total 'islamization' of being, thinking and acting.

(6) Less stringently but still noticeably the dominant interests of the Muslim beginnings and of heathendom carried over into Islamic civilization—negatively, an unconcern for architecture and the arts, an almost inevitable concomitant of the physical and social milieu of the peninsula; positively, a passionate dedication to poetry and to the Arabic language altogether. The cult of form coupled with comparative indifference to content variation, an aesthetic of the detail, a sober passion for imagery—these traits were to remain as creative dispositions as well as a specific bequest from pagan times.

Islam thus provided a framework for expansion and integration; it canonized certain limitations of the Arab tradition but deepened and widened the zones of psychological experience and intellectual as much as political activity. The small numbers of the early conquerors guaranteed the continuance of regional differences; the communication problems of the period neutralized the yearning for an all-embracing, uniform Islamic life, and induced the community to ratify a good deal of local custom. The speed of the Muslim expansion, and the speed of the subsequent growth of Islamic civilization, prevented fundamental social changes below the highest level and apart from such arrangements which followed logically from the basic rationale of Muslim community structure. Even when every allowance is made for the contingent character of historical developments, it still remains safe to state that on their exodus from the peninsula the Arab Muslims had made the

[1] Cf. W. M. Watt, 'The Tribal Basis of the Islamic State', *Dalla tribù allo stato* (Rome, 1962), 154–60.

'governing decisions' in regard to what they considered their physical and spiritual ancestry; hence they had, so to speak, predetermined what, on being exposed to a large spectrum of cultural possibilities, was to fit in with their sense of cultural affiliation, and thus, too, the sources on which they might draw to solve problems and fill gaps of which, as yet, they were, for the most part, unaware.

II

What were the intellectual temptations Islam encountered in its new world, and what resources to meet them did this world put at its disposal? The temptations may be described summarily as the availability of, and forced acquaintance with, more fully developed edifices of thought erected with the help of a logical technique of extraordinary subtlety, a rational science, a larger and more varied accumulation of texts to serve as an authoritative basis for deductive reasoning, a wider range of admissible and assimilated experience, and quite generally a higher level of training and sophistication. This sophistication was manifest not least in acute awareness of the implications and problems of a given philosophical or religious position; and it may be argued that the foremost effect of the plunge into the milieux of ancient hellenization was a rise in self-consciousness regarding the meaning of the Muslim postulates, and an inner compulsion of increasing force to think through, articulate and harmonize the accepted religious data. It has frequently and correctly been stated that the dialogue of Christian and Muslim controversialists—which, incidentally, began only some fifty or sixty years after the conquest and remained more often than one is wont to assume in actual fact a monologue addressed to the community of the spokesman—impelled the Muslim intelligentsia to consider and reformulate moot points as they were brought up (and, one may add, as the internal development of the community made such points into critical and always, at least indirectly, political issues). But surpassing by far in ultimate importance the impact of competition and polemical discourse, the mere presence of the Hellenic heritage—in Greek, Syriac and Persian garb—brought about a transformation in the conquerors' outlook without which the civilization of classical Islam with its ambitious and successful outreach into the sciences and into philosophy never could have matured. And it may equally be doubted whether the possibilities of a mystical piety, and again those of building a religious law overarching the total structure of life, would have been realized without the model of the Christian mystics, and the tangible existence of Jewish law as model for the aspiration underlying the *Sharīʿa*, and that of Roman and Syrian ecclesiastical law as partial model of axiomatics and elaboration.

As the thought draws the word, so the word the thought. 'Le mot entraîne l'idée malgré elle.'[1] Systematization of Islamic doctrine would have occurred in any environment of an advanced civilization, but the conceptual apparatus into which the Muslims grew did indeed exercise a decisive influence on the nature of this systematization, and probably also on the problems through the discussion of which systematization was approached. The habituation of the milieu to paired notions such as substance and accident, eternity (pre-existence) and creation in time, the neo-Platonic ideology of mediated descent from the One to the many, the spiritual to the material, together with the redeeming ascent of the striving soul, predetermined in large measure the problems to be faced, and, given the fundamental insights of the Qur'anic revelation and the ratiocinative methods traditionally utilized in the region, the solutions as well. Fear of the inevitable is ever-present, so is the fear of losing what its very fluidity and indistinctness makes appear as unsullied truth. Only rarely does the faithful realize that the naïve directness of unclarified devotion, unless protected by the kind of intellectual armour that is strong enough to withstand the most advanced questioning of the day, is bound to lose its hold on all but the simple; only a theology adequate to the existential and critical needs of a time will maintain alive for the cultured the religious experience it protects; this is true in spite of the fact that to the believer, and often to the theologically schooled believer too, definition and derivation will threaten to chill, not to say kill, spontaneous devotion.

The reaction of many a Muslim *ʿālim* to any movement toward scholasticism could almost be couched in the words of Saint Jerome writing in A.D. 414: 'Unskilled heretics are hard to find... Theirs is not the net of the Apostolic fishermen, but the little chains of dialectic.' The reference is to Aristotelian dialectics—the fear of Aristotle ever paralleled his authority. Al-Tawḥīdī (d. 414/1023) angrily rises against the orthodox and, more particularly, the Hanbalite position, that logic has no right to meddle in law, as little as philosophy has any nexus with

[1] Alfred de Vigny, *Chatterton*, Act III, Scene 1; in *Théâtre*, II (Paris, 1927), 306. The passage is quoted by L. Brunschvicg, *Héritage de mots, héritage d'idées* (2nd ed.; Paris, 1950), 6.

religion or Greek wisdom with the formulation of statutes, *aḥkām*. The tolerance which Revelation and prophetic precedent bespoke for mysticism, that is to say, for the individual seizing his God in a personal intuitive experience, seemingly unmediated by the community or its institutions, made possible a rather rapid growth of Sufism, in part as a reaction to the consolidation of the *Umma* in doctrine and organization. One may wonder how much access the early mystics would have had to Indian practices and theories—despite the conquest of Sind and the presence in ʿIrāq of Indian traders and travellers, effective contacts with Hindu spirituality remained slight down to the days of Maḥmūd of Ghazna and beyond—even if the experience aspired to had been more closely akin to them. With Western mysticism as a whole, early Islamic mysticism, where it went beyond ascetic self-discipline, was most of all a theory of cognition, in other words, an intellectual movement with anti-legalistic and anti-scholastic overtones. This thirst for intuitive knowledge of the divinity, where knowledge implies approach, and vision, unification, as well as the procedures cleansing the seeker in preparation for illuminating grace, were in keeping with Christian endeavours which naturally inspired a major share of the descriptive terminology and, as importantly, of the systematization of the *sālik*'s progress to perfection.

The more sober and, in a measure, community-oriented mysticism of al-Muḥāsibī (d. 243/857), while rejected by many as much for its philosophical implications as for its limited devaluation of the law, found more ready acceptance than the self-centred, pantheizing mysticism of Eastern affinities represented by Bāyazīd al-Bisṭāmī (d. probably in 261/874).

If medieval Islam, despite its leaning on the Hellenic heritage, appears to the modern observer in many important ways estranged from what, to us, are some of the dominant features of this heritage, it must be remembered that our image of Hellenic civilization is a composite one, in which the Periclean Age, the great days of the Hellenistic kingdoms, and selected traits of later antiquity tend to blend; an image moreover that is inseparable from its political forms (especially the *polis*), its outreach into rational science, and its literature. Although a good deal survived of ancient political thinking, the *polis* as a concrete historical phenomenon never did enter the purview of Islam; empirical science had suffered a decline at least from the second Christian century; in fact, the rise to the surface of popular religious ideas had, as early as the first century B.C., begun to sap the drive toward research and a rational critique of natural phenomena, while strengthening the need for authority and the belief in miracles with the comfortable abdication of exploratory effort it implied. What remained as science in areas such as meteorology was little more than crude and arbitrary speculation. Already Lactantius (*c.* 240–*c.* 320) had condemned the natural sciences as 'sacrilegious folly', neo-Platonists like Iamblichus (*c.*250–*c.*330) followed in the same track. When many centuries later, al-Niẓāmī (d. 606/1209) derides the same Iamblichus as an impious philosopher he puts opinions in his mouth which drastically show that the comprehension of the nature of empirical investigation in the natural sciences had long disappeared, in part no doubt because it was felt to be an attack on divine prerogative, an intrusion by an inferior mind into the mysteries of the Lord's government of the world.

The principal centres of Hellenic learning in the countries the Muslims were to overrun in the first wave of conquest were (apart from the Greek schools in Alexandria, Caesarea and Berytos), Edessa, Nisibis and Seleucia near Ctesiphon (Nestorian), and Antioch with Amida (Jacobite) in Syriac-speaking and Gondēshāpūr (Khūzistān, again Nestorian) in Pahlavī-speaking territory. The Syriac institutions, destined to become highly influential in the formation of Muslim civilization, were primarily theological schools. For the most part, profane learning was admitted as an endeavour of secondary importance and limited to grammar and rhetoric, philosophy, medicine, music, mathematics and astronomy. The actual restriction, not to say the loss, of profane learning will not be correctly assessed unless it be realized that philosophy, for example, meant little more than parts of the Aristotelian *Organon*, and medicine, the principal works of Hippocrates and Galen. In Gondēshāpūr, whose Academy goes back to A.D. 530, theoretical instruction was supplemented by practice in a hospital, *bīmāristān*, a method adopted later by the physicians of Baghdad. Through Gondēshāpūr a measure of Indian influence was to reach the Arabs; but it was not to become effective before the 'Abbasid age. It was thus on a depleted ancient heritage that the Arabs had to draw; where they felt the urge to supplement it, the impulse had to come from themselves and those within their orbit who had fallen under the sway and the spell of the *'arabiyya*.

Whether or not the Muslim message was originally intended for the Arabians, or even for the north-western and central Arabians alone, or whether its universalism was at the outset metaphysical rather than political and this-wordly, the empire made Islam, once and for all, a universal faith. Universal versus local, or more precisely, national validity, had long been an issue. The concept of a cultural universalism rendered effective and embodied in a political structure, the world had inherited from the Stoics; the idea of an empire held together by a state religion had become familiar through the Sasanian state, even before the adoption of Christianity as the mortar and the soul of declining Rome and rising Byzantium. Religious universalism had been an issue before the Muslims entered upon the scene. The Christians had followed the Manichaeans in criticizing Zoroastrianism for its restricted validity. The fourth book of the *Dēnkart*, in substance a product of the third/ninth century but incorporating older materials, lists, perhaps in defence, some of the works accepted by Persia from the outside—the *Almagest* as well as rhetorical, astronomical and sociological books of India—all of them reformulated to fit the Persian environment and highly esteemed. More consciously is the defence undertaken in Book Five where the political and civilizing mission of Persia is invoked as assurance that the Zoroastrian message with which Persia is entrusted would be spread throughout the world. In fact, however, the all too narrow link between Sasanian royalty and the *dēn* of the Zoroastrian Church inhibited rather than furthered the acceptance of the Mazdaean faith, even though the concept of the twinship of *dawla* and *dīn*, royalty and religion, was to be taken over by Muslim political thinking, together with a number of other elements of Persian political ethics and wisdom as these had been fixed in the Middle Persian *andarz* works, Books of Council, that were to become highly popular in the form of Mirrors for Princes or as parts of general tracts on *adab* from the second/eighth century onward.

The looseness and early disintegration of the gigantic imperial structure of the caliphate helped rather than harmed the universalism of Islam, enabling it to absorb a healthy localism where the cultural self-consciousness of a region was still alive and creative (as was the case above all in Persian-speaking territory), while safeguarding Arabic as the common language of religion and learning, and therewith, to a considerable extent, a common literature and more particularly a common Arabic prose in the service of religion, the law and the sciences in the widest sense of the word. The universal availability of Islam in its definitive Arabic formulations, together with its wide-meshed permeability for the concerns of local tradition, that could be legitimized and incorporated through the *ijmāʿ* of the local *prudentes*, counteracted the 'nationalistic' reaction of some of the conquered—remarkably strong among the Persians, remarkably weak among the Greek- and Syriac-speaking—who, by and large, aspired not to the displacement of Islam by their ancestral faith but to the acceptance within Islam of the cultural heritage and its moral and intellectual attitudes. It deserves notice that the Zoroastrian reaction of the third/ninth century appeals to the superiority of the Persians, allegedly recognized by their neighbours, in point of beautiful speech (or the beauty of their language) and the cultivation of measure, reflecting, or at any rate recalling, the even more emphatic claims of the Arabs to the perfection of their tongue, and to Islam as the religion of the mean.

On the level of seemingly unconditioned or spontaneous religious reaction, expanding Islam would encounter kindred attitudes that were effective below and behind doctrinal formulations. Thus, for example, the uncertainty which the Qur'ān is wont to attach to assurances of divine reward or human comprehension. 'He admonisheth you, mayhap ye will be reminded' (7. 92).—'Thus doth He perfect His goodness upon you, mayhap ye will become Muslims' (7. 83).—'And this is a Book which We have sent down; [it is] blessed, so follow it and show piety, mayhap mercy will be shown you' (6. 156; it must be appreciated that God is speaking). The uncertainty veils not only the human reaction but also that of the Lord, who is introduced as though wishing to reserve His freedom over against the implied commitment of the command. The same 'absence of "certainty of belief" is typical of Israelite religion' and more particularly of that of the prophets. 'In the relation to Yahweh there was always a *perhaps*. Amos exhorted his people to hate evil and love good. *Perhaps*, he says, Yahweh will be gracious to the descendents of Joseph' (Amos 5:15).[1]

A certain kinship is unmistakable, too, in the Hebrew prophets' shunning of miracle-working and the insistence of Muḥammad on his character as a mere instrument of revelation—both attitudes soon to be overlaid by the popular craving for the wonder as the ultimate testimony to election. On a strictly theological plane, Christianity and Islam maintain the miracle as a witness, or symbol, of the Lord's freedom. God retains unlimited sovereignty and in breaking through the limitations inherent in His creatures and His order, or perhaps merely habitual to

[1] J. Lindblom, *Prophecy in ancient Israel* (Philadelphia, 1962), 340; the italics are Lindblom's.

them, He manifests His redemptive creativeness, and allows man to comprehend that His order subserves His purpose. Wherever possible, early Islam endeavours to remove the miracle from the grasp of man—God uses it to make the unbeliever aware of His messenger's truthfulness, He allows it as testimony of His friends' closeness to Himself, to help and to warn, but like Christianity and, to a somewhat less extent, Judaism, Islam succumbed to the traditional longing to have faith confirmed and made useful by realizations of the impossible, for the most part very modest, at the hand of religious heroes of various sorts. Inevitably, the frame of mind of the elect, supported as it was by a millenary tradition, frayed its way into Muslim thought. The freedom of divine choice provides the precarious justification in Islamic terms of the esoteric pride of the Perfect, who may be classifiable as prophet or saint, and whose overdimensionality comes to be hesitantly accepted in the wake of Gnostic ideas of his cosmic role. The Hellenistic and Gnostic inspiration is audible in the hubristic description of the Perfect Man, who, tenuously integrated in the Islamic experience of God and creation, 'becomes a world unto himself, comparable to the macrocosm, and merits to be called a "microcosm". Thus he becomes Almighty God's vicegerent among His creatures, entering among His particular saints, and standing as a Complete, Absolute Man... At length, between him and his Master no veil intervenes, but he receives the ennoblement of proximity to the Divine Presence.'[1]

Parallelism of approaches in fundamentals not only promoted permeability by newly experienced influences but, in a number of cases, makes it delicate to decide between an organic and a stimulated development. Thus it will have to remain uncertain whether the preponderant concept of reason as an instrument of deduction from authoritatively given premises, rather than for induction with a view to opening new areas of knowledge, a concept which prevailed, though not exclusively, at least as a programme throughout the medieval world, was brought from the peninsula or acquired on settling outside. The inclination to follow authority, be it that of the ancestors or that of the Prophet, was no doubt indigenous to Arab society. But the identification of greater age with greater closeness to truth had been common and commonplace in pagan Greece and Rome and, in fact, had been used as a stock argument in anti-Christian polemics after having played its part in Jewish endeavours to win respectability, not to mention the authority accorded

[1] The Nasirean Ethics by Naṣīr ad-Dīn Ṭūst, tr. G. M. Wickens (London, 1964), 52.

to the Egyptians by the Greeks on the ground of the antiquity of their religion and culture. 'The most ancient cannot be false,' and consequently, 'later invention cannot be held true,' to use the beautifully concise formulations of Ambrosiaster (*c.* 380).[1] Hence the inclination to develop the rules of the Qur'ān first as the *sunna* of the Prophet, supplementing it then by the *sunnat Abī Bakr wa-'Umar* (later designated as *sīra* or *fi'l*), and toward the end of the seventh century, placing the *sunna* of the Prophet as an independent norm by the side of the Qur'ān. Hence also the inclination to view the sequence of generations in history after the appearance of Islam as one of necessary decline—an outlook rather than an empirically substantiated verdict since it proved effective despite the victories of Islam, presumably rationalized on a sense of moral decay, but an outlook, in any case, that had been familiar to the Near Eastern environment at least since the Book of Daniel (cf. 2:31 ff.) and reflected even in Genesis 47:9.

The first generation of Muslims showed a dynamism, will and ability to adjust and to take risks that went well with a vision of the world's course as a drama in which God took an active part, a vision not too far removed from that of the Hebrew prophets. Accompanying perhaps the increasing sense of the distance between God and man, and His abstention from direct and miraculous interference in the details of history, this self-confident dynamism gradually tapered off, and the depreciation of becoming over against being, the dominant attitude of classical antiquity, obtained an ever stronger hold, anchored it seems in the need to safeguard the feeling for Allāh's immutable and monumental majesty as the formative experience of the community. What is subject to change and 'becoming' is necessarily subject to degradation and decay. Rank and value hinge on participation in being, which man cannot increase even for himself. So historical action remains inevitably stained with imperfection; besides, man merely executes while will *stricto sensu* belongs to God alone. If Muslims of today are given to depict the first thirty years of the *Umma* as the ideal period, it is, in the last analysis, its dynamism which they hope to recapture and which had been so soon corroded by, or yielded in response to, an identification of the perfect with the changeless desirable as much within the fundamental religious experience of their faith as within the atmosphere which conquered them as they took over their erstwhile Hellenic provinces.

[1] *Quaestiones* CXIV, 10, and LXXXIV, 3, in *MPL*, XVII, 314, 2 and 145, 15.

The invasion and subsequent integration into Muslim consciousness—not always lastingly nor even briefly effective—of ancient Oriental, Jewish and Christian materials would frequently occur on the level of the popular tale, of which the so-called *Isrā'īliyyāt,* stories attributed to the Children of Israel, are probably the best-known example. Stories of earlier prophets abound: the Muslim concept of numerous prophets and messengers allowing the growth of legendary traditions on the fringes of orthodox doctrine. A good many ideas and customs of the earlier civilizations penetrated more deeply by being formulated as *Ḥadīth*, sayings of or about the Prophet and his Companions, when if accepted they would wield a more significant influence, possibly even entering the sphere of the Law as a precept, its precedent or corroboration. In a sense, the Law must be seen as a symbol of the Muslim identification and hence of Muslim cohesiveness, rather than as a practical tool of everyday legal life—a certain analogy to one of the functions of classical Jewish law is not hard to discover. Both *Ḥadīth* and *qiṣaṣ al-anbiyā'* (tales of the prophets) represent basically arabizations of traditional forms of expression. The Qur'ān, on the other hand, differs notably in many places from religious speech as known and accepted by Muḥammad's contemporaries. It would, however, be erroneous to suspect its style (to the Christian less polished, less varied, occasionally disturbing in the abruptness of its narrative technique and in the limiting topicality of reference) to have been a hindrance to the adoption of Islam. As controversy abundantly shows, knowledge of each others' holy books was confined to an insignificant proportion of Muslims and Christians; the same could be said of Muslims and Jews, and, even more emphatically, of Muslims and Zoroastrians. On the whole, the new Muslim would touch the Qur'ān only after his conversion—the decision to accept Islam preceding its study such as it may have been. It may be useful to remember that the Bible had not been read by the pagan world. Acquaintance at first hand with the Jewish and Christian scriptures, with Jewish and Christian history came, as a rule, only with or after conversion to Judaism or Christianity. One could hardly claim the *apartheid* of Christian and pagan, Christian and early Muslim has lost its validity as *types* for the present-day *apartheid* of members of different faiths in the Near East as elsewhere in the Islamic world.

To see the Arab conquests in their true perspective it must be noted that the invaders did not bring in a superior material or technological equipment. Nor is there any indication of a significant innovation in armament or tactics—speed and mobility were made brilliantly effective but can hardly be thought of as something new—with the possible exception that the early Arab army could be held over in the field as long as required without adding extravagantly to the public expense or without infringement of a customary right to break off the campaign after a certain number of days or months. As it was neither a peasant nor a mercenary army, it represented more of an independent instrument in the hands of the community than medieval armies usually did. The Arab Muslim fought, the conquered sowed and traded; only the dynamism of expansion could bear the cost of the initial establishment.

The separation of populations by religious and ethnic differences was a legal fact in the successor-states of the Western Empire; it was less clearly insisted upon by statute in the East, but nonetheless was generally accepted practice. Community differentiation was stabilized by recognition of community law; the personality of the law, as against its territoriality, congenial as it was to Arab attitudes, must nevertheless be included among the first cluster of foreign elements which the requirements of the situation attached to Arab Muslim cultural and political possessions. Payments in lieu of military service as an impost on the non-Muslim, limited *connubium* between different population groups, graduated blood-wit as between rulers and ruled—all these features, which to later ages no longer alive to the rationale of such discrimination would become disturbing, were anything but unprecedented in the world into which the Arabs came to play their part. Parallel institutions would exist in varying forms throughout the *aikumene*; let it suffice to refer to the Merovingian *hostilitium*, the ban on intermarriage between Romans and Goths, and to the fact that alone among all Germanic conquerors the Visigoths, in 654, introduced a unified territorial law for their Spanish state. The near-monopoly of the 'Roman' population on civil service posts has its parallel in the Muslim state, where the administrative cadres continue both in formerly Byzantine and in formerly Sasanian territory. When in the second generation the government undertakes to arabicize the administration, the personnel itself is less affected than the formal changes would lead one to expect. Where the first echelon was reserved for the Arab, the subordinate ranks continued to be the preserve of the native population—an observation, which must however, be appreciated in the light of the slowly but ceaselessly progressing linguistic amalgamation of old and new settlers.

It is this continuity of the administrative tradition which kept the Muslim state from following its contemporaries in the West all the way in their development from what has been called the 'prohibitive' to the 'repressive' state.[1] Where it is no longer possible—or perhaps not even desired—to maintain the authority of the state as both regular and pervasive by means of a bureaucratic apparatus which, in the long run, will remain effective only by being dependent on the ruler's payments in money, this authority will operate fitfully and, for the most part, only with a view to repressing disorders and to re-establishing itself against disregard or rebellion. Authority is not evenly effective throughout the territory or the communities claimed for it, but tends to assert itself forcefully only in the immediate surroundings of the ruler, who may habitually be moving about his realm, and to thin out toward the fringes or toward such areas as do not command special attention or again, that are, in terms of the logistics of the day, too distant from the power-centre to be kept in consistent dependence. The medieval state in Europe, but not Byzantium, and increasingly, the state of the caliphs exemplify the 'repressive' type with its characteristic restorative and punitive interventions and the loose-meshed network of military and financial controls. The Umayyad state and its 'Abbasid successor in its beginnings accepted the inherited machinery where it still existed. It was governing with its aid that alienated Muʿāwiya from the pious opposition with its apprehension of godless power, and led to the distinction between the *imāma* or *khilāfa* of the first Muslim rulers and the 'kingship', *mulk*, of the new dynasty. Wherever the power of the state exceeded its function to protect and expand the domain of Islam and its believers, and consolidated by means of long-term fiscal and administrative policies, which inevitably threatened to impinge on the group individualism of Arab tradition, tribal sentiment and, more significantly, the scruples of the pious, protested and counteracted.

Fearful of an arbitrariness which they never allowed to be contained by formalizing, under God, the means which the maintenance of the *Umma* imperiously demanded, mistaking also Qur'anic directive for immutable statutory precept, the pious pushed the ruler into permanent

[1] For these concepts cf. L. Hartmann, *Ein Kapital vom spätantiken und frühmittelalterlichen Staate* (Berlin, etc., 1913), 16, who follows A. Wagner, *Handbuch der Staatswissenschaften* (3rd ed.), *s.v.* Staat (in nationalökonomischer Hinsicht). See also H. Aubin, *Vom Altertum zum Mittelalter. Absterben, Fortleben und Erneuerung* (Munich, 1949), 24–5.

illegality by refusing, for example, to enlarge the scope of lawful taxation, and, more generally, to identify themselves with the machinery of government, well knowing that the state would be compelled to exceed the functional limits and hence the application of executive power which they were prepared to read into the revealed texts.

Strictly speaking, for them there existed only the community and its commander; the state as such had no place in their scheme of things. The heritage of Byzantium and the Sasanians would win in large measure *de facto* but scarcely *de jure* recognition. Nor did the concept of the 'juristic person' survive from Roman law. The consequences of this elimination were rather far-reaching. Thus, for example, stealing from the public treasury was not held subject to the *ḥadd* punishment for theft, because the illegal act was not committed against a juristic agent independent of the thief, who was, along with every other Muslim, considered part owner of the *māl Allāh* and thus part owner of what he had stolen. Ultimate authority was with God, who holds sovereignty but does not exercise it; His will, according to the sentiment of a majority of the faithful, permeates the charismatic community, which is apt to split over the legitimacy of institutionalization, with the Kharijites' insistence on personal sanctity and their consequent tendency to divide over the question of a ruler's personal morality, recalling the attitude of the Donatists in North Africa toward the Catholics in the fourth and fifth Christian centuries. In time, the caliph came to embody, as it were, the community not only in its political but also in its religious aspect; in fact, he was to wield rather unrestricted control over the religious 'establishment'; but theory kept him at bay. It would require him to be able to make legal decisions and to act as a judge of no appeal, but it would not allow him to legislate, i.e., to add to, or subtract from the *Sharī'a*. The Byzantine emperor and the Sasanian king were less restrained; hence the distinction between the law of the doctors and the law of the land, which, in proportion to the progress in depth of islamization, was to become ever more characteristic of Muslim territories, existed (or had existed) on their soil only in the shape of special legislation and judicial procedures applicable to clerics—but those exemptive privileges in turn were subject to sanction by the head of the state. Here then is an instance in which a basic 'decision' of early Islam led to rejection of the dominant concept of a political and administrative structure which, in most other facets, was taken over into the mechanism of the Muslim state. The separation of *Umma* and 'state', toward which the community gravitated while simultaneously insisting on the service function of the state *vis-à-vis* the *Umma*, repeats to a remarkable extent the Augustinian vision of the community of believers as the *civitas Dei*, untouchable as it is by the fate of the *civitas terrena* whose ultimate justification yet lies in upholding and defending it. On the other hand, the notion that 'the kingdom of the Divine law and the external order could, presumably, be coterminous',[1] that there can be identity between a particular form of political organization and the kingdom of God, is incompatible with any Christian view of society: this 'standard' Muslim belief about fulfilment in history, with the 'Islamicity' of the state as an enduring characteristic, recurs in Christendom only in marginal millenarianisms as exemplified by the Anabaptists of Münster.

Pious tradition makes the Caliph 'Umar define his function in these words: 'Our duty it is to command you to obey the orders which Allāh has imposed on you, to forbid you such disobedience as God has forbidden you, and to establish the order of Allāh among the people, near and far, without caring on whom the punishment may fall.'[2] A saying is ascribed to the Prophet in which the paradox of the ruler is traced and where he appears as a sacrificial victim as much as a necessary punishment for the community.

> Do not revile the rulers; if they act well, they will be rewarded, and for you it is to be grateful; if they do ill, the burden is theirs, and for you it is to be patient. They are nothing if not a visitation [or 'punishment', *niqma*] which God sends to punish whom He wills; do not accept the visitation of God with rage and fury, accept it with humility and submission.[3]

The limitations which this ambivalent attitude to rulership was to impose on the integration of state and community were not to be overcome, however enticing the available models of other solutions as offered by the traditions of Byzantium, Persia and the ancient Near East.

To protect itself, the state maintained the separation of the non-Muslim communities in so far as feasible, not only from the Muslims but from one another. An alliance of the non-Muslims to shake off Muslim rule

[1] To borrow the formulation of K. Cragg, *Sandals at the mosque* (London, 1965), 124.

[2] Abū Yūsuf, *Kitāb al-kharāj*, 13^{13-15}; Fagnan, *Le livre*, 19–20, translates somewhat differently.

[3] Abū Yūsuf, *Kitāb al-kharāj*, 10^{8-11}; Fagnan, *Le livre*, 14, again has the passage somewhat differently.

was hardly within the ideas of the times, and such isolation as the Muslims sustained or established was no doubt congenial to the spirit of the epoch. In fact, isolation was the best safeguard against encroachments. In spite of occasional endeavours of the rulers not to devalue their privileges by having them shared too widely, conversion to Islam could not and would not be curbed. The institution of *walā'*, or clientship, made integration on the social level possible, not very satisfactorily perhaps, but sufficiently so as to surround the Arab Muslims rapidly with a significant number of 'Arabs' *de seconde zone*, the *mawālī*. In a centre like Baṣra of the early second/eighth century one has already the right to speak of people with 'double nationality',[1] Arab and Muslim, or Persian and Muslim—double community affiliations, double loyalties, a measure of bilingualism, and a sampling of that cultural amalgamation to which Islam owes its susceptibility to Persian ideas and ways.

By the cumulative effect of historical connection with, and the centring of the Umayyad state within, the area of its domination, the elements attracted by the new political-cultural entity were preponderantly of Hellenic or, better, hellenized Near Eastern origin. Down to the disappointments due to the dogged resistance of the Isaurian dynasty and the rise to prominence of the Arabs settled in the eastern provinces together with the Persian and Mesopotamian converts and *mawālī*, the orientation of the leading circles was toward Byzantium, at least in the sense that it was from the Byzantine tradition that architecture and the arts drew inspiration and technicians, that it was a hellenized version of alchemy which, perhaps soon followed by medicine, became the first natural science evoking the concern of a Muslim prince (Khālid b. Yazīd, d. *c.* 85/704) and offered the first material to be translated into Arabic, and that the beginnings of Arab grammar (although as far as we can see owed to natives or residents of the eastern areas and largely Persians by descent) built on concepts and categories that are traceable to the Greek rather than the Indian tradition—an indigenous Persian grammar does not seem to have existed.

This orientation toward the resources of the hellenized provinces—it must be realized that 'hellenization' no longer implies, at this period, the actual use of Greek as a vernacular—will make it at times difficult to decide in individual instances if a parallelism is to be accounted for as a

[1] The expression is C. Pellat's; cf. his *Le Milieu baṣrien et la formation de Ǧāḥiẓ* (Paris, 1953), 34.

newly attracted element or as a trait germane to the literary or intellectual style of the region. Comparisons like that of the generous with the Nile or the ocean, as found, for example in John Chrysostom, are of little significance as *loca probantia*. More problematic is God's oath 'by Me' which is fairly frequent in the *Ḥadīth* and occurs one single time in the Old Testament (Genesis 22:16). Very striking is the coincidence, feature by feature, of the Muslim (or at any rate, of Muḥammad's) idea of a prophet with the portrayal drawn by Philo:

> A prophet does not utter anything whatever of his own, but is only an interpreter, another suggesting to him all he utters; he is enraptured and in an ecstasy; his own reasoning power has departed and has quitted the citadel of his soul, while the divine spirit has entered in and taken up its abode there, playing the instrument of his voice in order to make clear and manifest the prophecies that the prophet is delivering.[1]

The stability of the religious motif is as remarkable as the secular effectiveness which was, at the time, the Muslim contribution to its development. The unsteadying availability of religious ideas in the newly won lands added to the uncertainties of the doctrines of the countless minor conventicles and often abortive sects, whose uncontrolled teeming is characteristic of the first century of the empire. The fluidity of viewpoints is not to be gauged from the systematic or partisan presentation of sources that originated later in a period of considerable intellectual consolidation, and more surely established communal and governmental control. The essential factor in our context is the untrammelled experimentation with every bit of religious thought and mythological imagery which the older faiths and their splinter groups, and the debris of even more ancient systems, put in the way of religiously and politically excited, in many ways uprooted and puzzled people, who found themselves the masters of their superiors in intellectual experience.

The most dramatic achievement of the age, Umayyad art, in mosques and 'desert' castles—actually royal palaces at the centre of domain lands and sedentary settlements, which have long since reverted to the desert in consequence of breakdowns resulting in (or from) the destruction of irrigation—was often combated or passed over by the self-authorized spokesmen for Islam, because they would resent it as anti-Islamic, as an

[1] *De specialibus legibus* iv, 49; paraphrased by Lindblom, *Prophecy in Ancient Israel*, 29. Even more poignant perhaps is the passage *De spec. leg.* i, 65.

excessive yielding to the needs and standards of a profane royalty. It remains true nevertheless, and Muslim consciousness has come to accept this for the Dome of the Rock, that these ambitious buildings were erected, with inherited technical and artistic means, 'to postulate altogether the pre-eminence of the Arab and Muslim aspect of the new state *vis-à-vis* the claims of the older civilizations and especially of the more ancient religions now thought to be superseded by Islam'.[1] The representations of crowns and other imperial jewellery suspended around the rock in the Dome of the Rock are intended to make manifest the defeat of Byzantium and Persia; they are supported by inscriptions proclaiming the new faith and attacking the ancient religions, and in particular, Christian trinitarianism. This technique of propagandistic pronouncement by pictures, half declaratory, half symbolic, has its precedents not merely in Byzantium but in the coinage of the Roman empire, especially its later phases, and before it, in that of the Hellenistic kingdoms. Significantly, the turning away from Byzantium and toward Persia which is by far the most important development of the last decades of Umayyad rule, is adumbrated by a change in style, a partial relinquishing of Byzantine, and fuller utilization of Eastern elements and motifs in the 'declaratory' art of the Caliph Hishām (105–25/724–43).

Less dramatic, but of incalculable consequences, was the move toward full urbanization of the Muslim rulers and the location in urban centres, old and new, adapted and created, of the developments that were leading toward a specifically Islamic civilization—not least the symbiosis of early and later converts, of Arab and non-Arab Muslims, and its corollary, the drifting into *apartheid* of the Muslim and the non-Muslim communities. Islam had been an urban growth from its inception, in spirit as well as in its actual centres of gravity; but this 'inborn' trait had been immeasurably strengthened by the *hijra* into settlement, and the relocation of its political capital into the old culture areas of the Middle East. Soon, Muslim conquest would mean, in peasant or steppe country, the foundation of an urban focus—military and administrative—rapidly to take the cultural lead, and to become the radiating centre of islamization and, on occasion of attempted arabization. Obviously, the Syrian, Mesopotamian or Persian environment called for such concentration, and provided traditions that would facilitate the transition from nomadism to city-dwelling, yet it would be somewhat

[1] R. Ettinghausen, *Arab painting* (Lausanne, 1962), 19.

misleading without serious qualifications to put down the urbanization of Islam to the impact of the milieu and the expediencies of rulership. In later phases of the Islamic development, ruling Muslim groups did endeavour to remain aloof from urbanism, and the Umayyads themselves remained, as persons, astraddle the two ways of life; only the 'Abbasids were entirely committed to an urban mode of living. So once again, an innate tendency, spurred by political and military preferences, finds itself accommodated and encouraged by the prevailing attitudes and habits of the conquered.

To point to a rudimentary habituation to urban life in parts of Arabia is not to deny the fact that Muslim city administration was in many ways patterned after Byzantine, and presumably Persian models, but of the latter we have little tangible evidence. Hippodrome, water conduit and walls which F. Dölger notes as the essential components of the Byzantine town,[1] are replaced in the Muslim view by mosque, market and bath; but the concentration of crafts in one quarter or street, the attachment to the town of a rural district to be exploited by the 'citizens', as well as the office of the *agoranomos* (paralleling and succeeding to the *aedilis curulis*), under the name first of *ṣāḥib al-sūq* and later of *muḥtasib*, testify to continuity, as does, in a more general fashion, the Byzantine origin of the typical square ground-plan of Arab and Berber fortifications. The warring circus parties of the sixth Christian century show a peculiar similarity to the *'ayyārūn* of the Muslim towns, both in function and organizational structure. The Muslim town did not, however, possess a special *Stadtrecht*; but it is doubtful whether the Byzantine town maintained its city statute after Justinian I, in whose reign it is still attested. As it is patterned on a Byzantine model of organization, the creation by the caliphs in the second half of the ninth century of a *ra'īs al-aṭibbā' wa'l-falāsifa*, in imitation of the *archiatros* and *scholarchos*, warrants mention in this context.

III

The victory of the 'Abbasids ushered in the century that brought about that first synthesis of heterogeneous elements, unified in a measure by their purposeful attachment to an Islamic core, which may be called an Islamic civilization. The eastward turn of the period affected state and administration, rulership and *mores*, more than the development of

[1] 'Die frühbyzantinische und byzantinisch beeinflusste Stadt,' *Terzo Congresso internazionale di studi sull'alto medioevo* (Spoleto, 1959), 65–100, at 73–74.

knowledge as a whole, where directly obtained and mediated Greek materials remained the dominant formative factor. The principal aspirations and consequences of the 'Abbasid revolution were the replacement of Syria by 'Irāq as the heartland of the caliphate, the admission of the Persian Muslims on a level of equality with the Arab Muslims to government and social hierarchy, and the implementation of a tendency toward a more profound islamization of institutions, law and life as a whole.

Islam lost much, or most, of its original ethnic connotation; not, however, to the detriment of the Arabic language and the patterns of expression transmitted in it. In fact, the decline of Arab executive power was, curiously enough, accompanied by a consolidation of Arabic as the culture language of Islam, and while islamization had long left behind the range of Arabism it continued to establish an indissoluble tie with it. In theology, philology, the sciences, nothing would be absorbed into the bloodstream of Islamic civilization to the end of the third/ninth century unless it had first received an Arabic formulation. This is true even though Syriac continued the language at Gondēshāpūr into 'Abbasid times, and remained as late as the fourth/tenth century the mother-tongue of many of the scholars who won fame in Baghdād. But translation into Arabic from Greek, Syriac, Sanskrit, and to a more limited extent, Pahlavī, was the order of the day. The philosopher al-Kindī (d. 259/873) professes to labour for *ahl lisāninā*, 'the people of our tongue',[1] and the assimilation of the highest secular thinking to Islam, as far as it went, was throughout accompanied by an almost systematic enrichment of Arab vocabulary, and a gradual increase in the hypotactic possibilities of Arabic syntax.

Under the levelling blanket of the Arabic language, a new scientific terminology and the style and imagery of the Qur'ān (and soon the *Ḥadīth*), the continuity as well as the accretions remain concealed. When it did not directly contravene scriptural ordinance, the Muslim jurists took the substantive heritage of Byzantine or Sasanian law for granted. What needs to be traced is therefore less the substratum of older legal ideas and institutions than the transformations by which they were brought into harmony with the times and theology, with the postulates of Islam itself. The survival of the Zoroastrian *čakar-ẓanīh*, 'Zwischen-

[1] Cf. F. Rosenthal, 'Al-Kindī and Ptolemy', *Studi orientalistici in onore di Giorgio Levi Della Vida* (Rome, 1956), II, 436–56, at 445; also Kindī, *Rasā'il falsafiyya*, ed. M. 'A. Abū Rīda (1369–72/1950–3), I, 260.

ehe', as the *mut'a* marriage of principally Shī'ī Islam is remarkable especially for the place it received within a concept of marriage with which, at first glance, it would appear incompatible. The islamization of commercial law, and the preservation of its applicability to changing economic conditions, in part by 'fictions' or devices, *ḥiyal*, are examples of the same process on a larger and more significant scale. Procedural habits were adopted, presumably without full awareness of the process. Looking backwards from Muslim law, one cannot but note that, from the third Christian century the private law of the Roman empire, and in particular the law of marriage and divorce, had undergone an 'orientalization', and that the position of women had been shifting in the direction which, much more markedly, we rediscover in classical Islam. Similarly, trial by jury had disappeared; the single judge had become the rule. Mutilation, on the other hand, though widely applied as a punishment in late Roman law, would seem to have its Islamic base more directly in Qur'anic regulations.

General principles, too—such as *al-walad li'l-firāsh*—or on the level of *uṣūl*, the use of *al-maṣlaḥa al-'āmma* or *utilitas publica*, persist; so do methods of interpretation which from Roman law had entered the thinking of the rabbis by way of Hellenistic rhetoric, to continue their efficacy in Islam, with 'Irāqī Jewry acting as transmitter. It is, I believe, only our lack of familiarity with Sasanian law which prevents us from uncovering its traces in the *fiqh*. In any event, it was a Persian, only recently converted to Islam, who proposed to the Caliph al-Manṣūr the establishment of a unified, imperial law (or law for the Muslim empire) to displace the regionalism of prevailing laws, in the interest of the firmness of the caliphal state. Some sixty years after Ibn al-Muqaffa' (d. 139/756) and with the same lack of success, Bishop Agobard of Lyons (*c.* 817) addressed to the Emperor Louis the Pious the demand to do away with personal law and to establish a universal Christian law for the universal Christian commonwealth. Neither the caliph nor the emperor would have been in a position to promulgate a unified code; all the caliphs could and would do was to encourage the elaboration of administrative law (e.g., tax law), and to look with favour on such systematizations of the bases of law as came within their purview and seemed to tend towards stabilizing a rationale for, and consolidating, both community and state. The forty years between Ibn al-Muqaffa' and the compilation of Abū Yūsuf's book on taxes witnessed the elaboration of classical Muslim law, more serviceable in the end as the mortar of the community than as the tool of imperial practice for which it must have been intended.

To understand the constant interweaving of problems arising out of the Muslim tradition itself, the built-in challenges of the milieu and the more conscious challenges of religious adversaries, it must be remembered that the period from *c.* 750 to the end of the third/ninth century was a time of great creativity—in some areas against the desire of the most independent minds, who, like Aḥmad b. Ḥanbal, saw their task as the conservation of the conditions and ethos of the early community, and remained blind to the innovatory character of their own resistance to change. The science of *Ḥadīth*, of which the modern, whether indigenous reformer or Western observer, is apt to perceive above all the critical weaknesses and the formalistic results, was actually in its beginnings, a movement toward the expansion of the materials with which a Muslim could in good conscience operate, whether in the field of law, theology or any other area of direct and burning concern to the times. While disclaiming innovation and even tending to erase the suspicion of innovation from ideas and institutions which *Ḥadīth* would justify by the authority of the origins, the *muḥaddith* actually did innovate by creating a firm framework for the Islamic way of thought and life he aspired to, and he was, because of the novelty of his endeavour, the object of attacks by the practitioners of law.

Originality was noted and encouraged in the 'modern' poetry of Abū Tammām (d. 232/846) or al-Buḥturī (d. 284/897); the acceptance of originality in certain circles at least, is accompanied by the realization that progress is cumulative. The translator of Dioscorides, Iṣṭifān b. Basīl, in the days of the Caliph al-Mutawakkil, replaced what Greek terms he knew by Arabic ones; the others he left untranslated 'in the hope God would later send someone who would know them and be able to translate them'.[1] Al-Rāzī (d. 313/925 or 323/935) insists on the continuous progress of the sciences and the consequent superiority of the later scientists. A century later, Abu'l-Faraj 'Abd Allāh b. al-Ṭayyib (d. 435/1043) still professes the same approach and claims that his own observations go beyond what he had gathered from his predecessors. We are in a period of rationalization, which does not necessarily mean that methods of analytical empiricism will dominate, but that the phenomena are to be put into reasoned order, and, more significantly perhaps, that problems are being recognized as such, and explicitly posed, rather

[1] Cf. F. Rosenthal, *Das Fortleben der Antike im Islam* (Zurich and Stuttgart, 1965), 265.

than being answered by myth, rite or revealed citation without being identified as problems, i.e., as fissures in the shell containing and restraining an unruly experience of the universe.

The similarity of the problems of the Christian Logos and the Uncreate Qur'ān has often been noted. Less attention has been paid to other *cruces theologicae* which beset both faiths because potentially germane to them. Whether stimulated by Christian contacts, or whether Christian contacts were merely utilized to develop and solve problems that may be considered inherent in Muslim doctrine itself, will have to be examined from case to case. Thus a theological opinion like Jahm b. Ṣafwān's (executed 128/745–6) denial of the eternity of Paradise and Hell is *qua* problem explicable as Islamic (even though orthodox opinion would reject this on good grounds)—Jahm's starting-point is Qur'ān 57.3, 'He is the first and the last'—it is, however, impossible, to overlook its earlier treatment by Origen (*c.* 185–*c.* 254) and its resumption by Stephen bar Ṣudhailē (*fl.* end of fifth century). A similar statement could be made regarding the distinction between innate and revealed knowledge of God, where Christian antecedents would include St Paul (Romans 1:18–20; 2:15), Clement of Alexandria (*c.* 150–*c.* 215), Tertullian (*c.* 160–*c.* 220) and again Origen, and which *qua* problem was introduced to Islam by Ghaylān b. Marwān (executed in 124/742); the ethical-legal principle of *al-aʿmāl bi'l-niyyāt*; or again the 'determinist' use of *al-qaḍā' wa'l-qadar* in analogy with Syriac precedent.

The early ninth century exhibits an increased interest in the Christian Scriptures, which is almost immediately countered by a movement to avoid such direct contacts with Christian documents, or even discussion with Christian representatives. The political implications of this kind of contacts, as well as of the famed dispute on *qadar*, are too well known to need detailing. Less familiar are influences of Christianity—rejected by the wider community—affecting the concept of God itself. Thus Aḥmad b. Ḥā'it (d. before 232/846) and Faḍl al-Ḥadathī, associates of the Muʿtazilite al-Naẓẓām ascribe divinity to Jesus and arrive at a doctrine of two Lords: Allāh, the uncreated, and Jesus, the created, son of God by adoption, who had been Reason, *logos*, before taking on flesh. In reverse, one may note not only the instructions given by St John of Damascus to his fellow Christians ('When the Saracen says to you such then you will reply...'),[1] but the intrusion of Islamic terms into

[1] M. S. Seale, *Muslim theology* (London, 1964), 2–3; D. B. Macdonald, *Development of Muslim Theology, Jurisprudence and Constitutional Theory* (New York, 1903), 132.

Christian phraseology as in Elia al-Jawharī's identification of the *kāhin* of the Old Testament with the *imām* and his reference to Adam's *khilāfa* of God (cf. Qur'ān 2.28). And one must equally point to a certain affinity between Muslim and Jewish thought as expressed at a much later period in Maimonides's advice to Samuel b. Tibbon to read al-Fārābī: 'all he did is excellent'.[1]

In a different sphere of religious experience we find Ḥunayn b. Isḥāq drawing a parallel between the Muslim way of ornamenting mosques with the pedagogical purpose pursued by Greeks, Jews and Christians in adorning their houses of god with statues and pictures. Where Islam seems to go more determinedly its own way, it is due to the blend of the religious and the political aspects of a theological problem; thus notably in the treatment of the distinction between *islām*, adherence to the Muslim religion, and *īmān*, faith (in the Muslim revelation), and the further distinction between *īmān* and *kufr*, unbelief, or non-belief, in both of which cases the definitions will bear on the individual's affiliation with the *Umma* and hence on his privileged position in this world and the next. There is needed a justification of the elevated rank of the believer, an explanation both legally and metaphysically satisfactory; apart from the criticism of the non-Muslims, an answer must be found to the puzzle why non-believers choose the inferior truth and the inferior rank that goes with it. The elaboration given to a number of Qur'anic verses which show the unbelievers incapable of conversion, and thus fulfilling by their recalcitrance the true will and plan of God, reflects the complex of sentiments and practical problems which were inherent in the symbiosis of Muslims and *dhimmīs*.[2]

In some ways, the Persian components of Islamic civilization are more difficult to separate out than the Hellenic precisely because they are more fully integrated, and have become effective on so many levels. In fact, the Muslim world itself, without necessarily putting this judgment in analytical terms, has long since come to accept Islamic civilization as a 'Perso-Islamic synthesis'. From the third/ninth, and certainly the fourth/tenth, century onwards, the educated assumed the essential 'identity and continuity'[3] of Sasanian and Islamic political institutions—

[1] M. Meyerhof, 'Von Alexandrien nach Bagdad', *Preussische Akad. d. Wiss., Sitzungsberichte* 1930, *philos.-hist. kl.*, 389–429, at 417, quoting S. Munk, *Mélanges de philosophie juive et arabe* (Paris, 1857), 344.

[2] The most important pertinent verses are Qur'ān 2. 7; 10. 88–89; 11. 20; 18. 101; Sūra 101. Cf. R. Brunschvig, 'Devoir et pouvoir', in *Studia Islamica*, XX (1964), 5–46, esp. 8–9.

[3] To use the expression of F. R. C. Bagley, *Ghazālī's Book of counsel for kings* (London, New York, Toronto, 1964), Introduction, ix.

from the 'twinship' of *dīn* and *dawla* to the role in which caliph and *wazīr* were cast,[1] administrative techniques, the style of official documents, the social prejudices imputed to the ruler, and the sententious exchanges between him and his counsellors. The upsurge of Persian self-consciousness, to avoid the phrase 'national feeling', which gave body to the *Shu'ūbiyya* and in the fourth/tenth century to the rise of Persian as one of the great literary languages of Islam and of the world, fostered rather than disrupted the process of integration of Iranian elements. As far as Spain, Persian materials became a habitual part of *adab* literature, as witness the first book of Ibn 'Abd Rabbihi's (d. 328/940) *al-'Iqd al-farīd*, and, in a different sphere, the earlier adoption of Persian manners by the court of Cordova under the impact of the singer-courtier Ziryāb (arrived in Cordova in 207/822).

As the *Shu'ūbiyya*, despite a sympathetic approach to Mazdaism, had striven after a more prominent place within Arab Muslim civilization rather than the establishment of a separatist Persian Islam, so the north Persian Samanids and the north-west Persian Buyids retained Arabic as the language of government. We may recall that in the *Dēnkart* Persia's superiority over India and Rūm is based on the beauty of its language and the appreciation of measure, *patmān*. Almost simultaneously, we find Jāḥiẓ defining beauty as *wazn*, *Ebenmass*, referring to physical beauty as much as to the 'beauty' of a man's behaviour and religion.[2] The interlocking of influences becomes strikingly clear when one sees *patmān*, in the best Aristotelian manner, placed in contrast with *frēhbūtīh*, 'to be too much', and *aβēbūtīh*, 'to be defective'. It is perhaps not sufficiently appreciated that, parallel to the building in Arabic of a philological and theological terminology capable of rendering the concepts of Greek thinking, the world of Mazdaism undertook successfully a labour of comparable scope (if perhaps less completely carried through), in creating a Pahlavī terminology in the areas needed for a restatement, a revitalization of its faith. The outsider is left with the impression that, stylistically at least, the Arab effort was more fully successful; but the 'purity' of enriched Pahlavī remains a remarkable feat. Modern Persian, as it emerges as a literary language under the Samanids, appears more flexible, more clearly structured, less

[1] This is said regardless of the actual origin of the vizier's office; on which cf. D. Sourdel, *Le Vizirat 'abbāside de 749 à 936* (Damascus, 1959–1960), I, 41–61; also S. D. Goitein, 'The origin of the vizierate and its true character', *Studies in Islamic history and institutions* (Leiden, 1966), 168–96.

[2] Jāḥiẓ, *Risālat al-qiyān*, tr. C. Pellat, *Arabica*, X (1963), 121–47, at 135–6.

ambiguous in its pliability to the requirements of hypotactic grouping of thought—Ibn Sīnā himself was sensible to certain advantages, in logical terms, of Persian over Arabic, although Arabic must be judged superior in his time in its ability to cope with abstract strands of ideas.

The dominant concerns of Muslim civilization had originated in the Arab milieu—the style of the law, of *Ḥadīth*, was never persianized: that of *tafsīr*, on the other hand, especially insofar as it confined itself to word-by-word interpretation has its stylistic antecedents almost everywhere in the ancient Near East, from the Accadian dream books to the commentaries of the Avesta and the Jewish tradition. By contrast, the outlook on the outside world was more open to Persian inspiration: the geographical world-view of Islam in the fifth/eleventh century was not only formed by the Sasanian tradition (itself it is true not wholly separable from the Hellenistic) but formulated in Arabic by scholars of Persian background. Remarkably, prosodical forms such as the *Urform* of the metre *mutaqārib* seeped through the language curtain into Arabic; narrative motifs and techniques penetrated the core-stories of the *Thousand and One Nights*; but the epic did not take root, and the lives and legends of the Persian kings came to the Arabs through the Pahlavī prose chronicles, the sources of Firdawsī; neither they nor the Homeric poems in at least partial translation inspired a comparable treatment of the heroic age of Islam. But together with the pre-Islamic tales of the Battle-Days of the Arabs, *ayyām al-ʿArab*, and the Christian *vita* of the *miles Christi*, the Persian *siyar al-mulūk* stimulated historical biography—later to shade off into popular fiction—of which the first and greatest representative is the celebrated *Sīra* of the Prophet by Muḥammad b. Isḥāq (d. 151/768).

Every religion of universal aspiration, and more particularly, a religion which has captured the dominant sectors of society, must sooner or later come to terms with, integrate, explain itself by means of, the highest non-religious thought of the times. The obsolescence of science forms a parallel to the weakening of the specific experience to which a given religion owes its existence; but on the whole, this experience, its adaptations and successors within the organized religious community, remain effective longer than any one phase of scientific thought. The obsolescence of science in late antiquity and most of the Middle Ages was slowed by the prevailing anti-empiricism, and the readiness to accept the conceptual apparatus of Aristotelianism for example, without too much regard for the continued adequacy of the contents which it had been designed to scaffold.

It was the great opportunity of the major religions dominating the first millennium of our era that Aristotelian logic was available as a means of explicit rational self-statement. It was their tragedy that the metaphysics which it undergirded was atheistic in the eyes of the religions concerned, in virtue of its rejection of a personal creator God, the createdness of the world in time, its incompatibility with the doctrine of resurrection, and so forth. Even in the neo-Platonizing form given it by the later commentators, which was to gain undisputed sway over Muslim philosophy since al-Fārābī at the latest, it was a highly uncomfortable bed-fellow for a Qur'anic theology. Nevertheless the wave of Aristotelianism which swept, from *c.* 800, over the thinkers of oriental Judaism and Zoroastrianism as well as those of Islam was not to be arrested. Interestingly enough, the first translator of whom we know seems to have been Muḥammad b. ʿAbd Allāh b. al-Muqaffaʿ, the son of the great writer who more than anybody else represented the Persian tradition in his time. As a result of consistent and long drawn out labours, the Arabs came to have a much richer *corpus* of *Aristotelica* than did the Latins before the thirteenth century. Already before the *Bayt al-ḥikma*, toward the end of al-Ma'mūn's reign, took up the translation of his non-logical works, Aristotle's influence had begun to make itself felt, not only in the capital but in Baṣra where it had reached from Gondēshāpūr. The hunger for facts about the outside world notwithstanding, the logical and the metaphysical writings evoked by far the most intense interest. The peculiar way in which the introduction of Aristotelian concepts affected, or could be utilized in, internal Muslim debates, is well illustrated by the role of 'power' and 'act' (*qudra* and *fiʿl*), in the defining of the complementary ideas of divine omnipotence and human decision. Where, as with the Hanbalites and, in more subtle shadings, the Ashʿarites, *potentia* and *actus* are seen to coincide—man never is potentially capable of doing anything except what he actually does—*potentia* becomes compelling (*mujabbira*): omnipotence is saved in its most rigorous interpretation, but human freedom disappears; on the other hand, where, as with the Muʿtazilites, *potentia* is understood not only as preceding the act but as implying the power to act or not to act or to choose between two different acts or actions, man's freedom is safeguarded but divine omnipotence is self-limited; and this limitation is to be understood as in accordance with divine justice and human reason (*'aql*), implanted in man by his Creator as in harmony with the reason that governs the universe, in other words, with divine Reason itself. Beyond the obvious ethical implications there are almost equally obvious political implications—determinism entails the necessity of governmental actions as well as the necessity of their acceptance by the subjects. The bearing which the understanding of *qudra* (or *istiṭā'a*) and *fi'l* has on the problem of *īmān* and *kufr*, the wider context of which has already been indicated, hardly requires development. Characteristically enough, Maimonides was to identify both Ash'ariyya and Mu'tazila as inspired by the debates, in Greek and Syriac, between the philosophers and their opponents.[1] The Greek philosophers themselves and their Muslim followers had generally to be charged with unbelief; at the same time Greek doctrines were indispensable as the foil against which Islamic doctrine had to be formulated, quite apart from the numerous verities contained side by side with destructive misconceptions. Impregnation with the Classical heritage was facilitated by the temporary breakdown of political and community controls in the fourth/tenth century, when the freedom of the curious to steep themselves in Greek thought was effectively impeded only by inaccessibility of materials. The community might frown, the *'ulamā'* disapprove, but the authorities would bring pressure on the individual solely when his endeavours threatened to entangle him with sectarian revolt or court factions of sectarian recruitment. The limitations lay in the rejection of the literary bequest of the ancients, which was, in a formal sense, complete, in spite of the admission of Greek categories into literary and rhetorical theory, and the favour enjoyed by ancient didactic and biographical writings. For a brief span, when originality was understood as creativeness and prized, and when the multiplicity and relative weakness of power centres functioning as foci of culture protected the intellectual, the beautiful description by Gregory Thaumaturgos (*c.* 213 – *c.* 270) of the atmosphere in which he grew up, would have given an accurate picture of Islamic 'Irāq. 'No subject was forbidden us, nothing hidden or inaccessible. We were allowed to become acquainted with every doctrine, barbarian or Greek, with things spiritual and secular, divine and human, traversing with all confidence (cf. Acts 28:31) and investigating the whole circuit of knowledge, and satisfying ourselves with the full enjoyment of all pleasures of the soul.'[2]

[1] *The Guide of the perplexed* I, 71; tr. S. Pines (Chicago, 1963), 176–9 Ref. in Seale, *Muslim Theology* 129–30.

[2] Trans. M. L. W. Laistner, *Christianity and pagan culture,* 61, from *In Originem oratio panegyrica* xv, 31–33, in *MPL*, X, 1096AB.

Similarity of problems, shared sources and intellectual assumptions, resulted in the adoption of methods of presentation which, regardless of language, link the philosophical-theological and much of the scientific writing of the Latin, the Byzantine and the Arab Middle Ages. Objections are introduced by *qāla* or *qālū*—as practised already by Arnobius *Adversus nationes* (probably 296–7) with his stereotyped *inquit*, *inquiunt*; this minimal formula is developed into *in qāla*...*qultu*, in keeping with the custom of Christian scholastics. More profoundly symptomatic of continuing thought-habits is the recurrence, in the Islamic environment, of the Western medieval propensity towards elaborate classification and towards a full spelling out of even simple syllogisms with no conceivable consequence or implication omitted or left to the imagination, not to say commonplace reasoning on the part of the reader.

The learned men of this science (i.e. scholastic theology) should confine their instruction to men who have the three following traits:...;...the secrets which they (i.e. the favorites of God, al-*muqarrabūn*) do not divulge to the masses may be divided in five categories...;...(the *salaf*) have known that faith is founded upon four pillars each of which involves ten principles.[1]

Classification of the sciences, or the systematic organization of all branches of learning accessible and deemed worth pursuing, become frequent in the fourth/tenth century. That proposed by al-Khuwārizmī (*c.* 366/976) is inserted here because—although not complete, and hence not fully representative of the Islamic scientific effort—it indicates with particular clarity not merely the range but also the origin of the Arab-Muslim sciences and, by implication, suggests the rationale of selecting and ordering the *scibile*.

1. The Sciences of the Religious Law, *'ulūm al-Sharī'a*
    - A. Jurisprudence, *fiqh*
    - B. Dogmatic theology, *kalām* (defined to cover the doctrines of orthodox Islam, the Muslim sects, and non-Muslim religions)
    - C. Grammar, *naḥw*
    - D. The art of the secretary, *kitāba*
    - E. Poetry and prosody, *shi'r* and *'arūḍ*
    - F. History, *al-akhbār*

[1] Ghazālī, *Iḥyā' 'ulūm al-dīn*, Book II, tr. N. A. Faris, *Al-Ghazzālī: the foundations of the faith* (Lahore, 1963), 33, 39, 56.

II. Foreign Sciences, *'ulūm al-'ajam*, equated with philosophy, *falsafa*
  A. Theoretical part, *al-juz' al-nazarī*, including physics (with medicine); zoology; mathematics (with astronomy and music); theology
  B. Practical philosophy, i.e. ethics, domestic economy, politics

Other classifications give logic a prominent place apart.

Measured by its permeability to Hellenistic and Persian elements, the profit drawn by Islamic civilization from India appears slight. This is not to play down the quantity of materials, from the *Pančatantra* to the *Rājanīti*, which, mostly by way of Persia, did enter Arabic literature, nor to deny the kinship of the Indian and Tibetan *mantra* with the Muslim *dhikr* (perhaps a case of 'archetypal' kinship rather than diffusion or derivation), and least of all the significance of Indian astronomy and medicine for the Muslims since the days of al-Manṣūr or of the adoption, under al-Ma'mūn, of the positional system of numbers, and so forth. The statement is rather to suggest that with its 'primary decisions' made before leaving the Arabian peninsula the Islamic world in formation had opted for the Mediterranean and Persian orbit, and cut itself off from even an adequate understanding of, let alone a productive dialogue with, Hindu and Buddhist India. The reaction of Sulaymān al-Manṭiqī to Yaḥyā b. 'Adī's expression of respect for Indian philosophy is typical. 'Ibn 'Adī told me the Indians had accomplished great things in the philosophical sciences, and the thought had occurred to him, science had reached the Greeks from there...I do not know how this notion could have occurred to him.'[1] Travellers to India who have left reports are few and far between, but among them are such notable men as the geographers al-Iṣṭakhrī (*fl. c.* 340/951) and Ibn Ḥawqal (*fl.* 367/977) and the famous geographer-historian al-Mas'ūdī (d. 346/956–7); yet of the three only al-Mas'ūdī shows any real interest in Hindu India; it is also he who has preserved for us the title of the earliest study made in Arabic of Hindu sects. It is true that concern for other cultures was generally weak, and research and exploratory travel but rarely undertaken. Yet the objective importance of India might have induced a different attitude—of contacts with the subcontinent there had been no dearth since the earliest days of Muslim expansion.

[1] Ibn Abī Uṣaybi'a, *'Uyūn al-anbā' fī ṭabaqāt al-aṭibbā'*, ed. A. Müller (Cairo, 1882; Königsberg, 1884), I. 9$^{10ff.}$; cf. Meyerhof, *Von Alexandrien nach Bagdad*, 418.

Although Indian astronomical works were translated into Arabic earlier than Greek ones, and although the *Sindhind* (Brahmagupta's *Siddhānta*) held scholarly attention as far away as Spain into the fifth/eleventh century, the borrowings from that source remained minor. With Sind slipping away from 'Abbasid control (in the third/ninth century), India soon became to the public a remote land of mystery, whose inhabitants were ranked with the Rūm and Chinese among the three or four major civilized peoples outside the Muslim sphere, but whose contribution was only superficially and scantily taken note of, with astronomy, chess, and perfumery figuring prominently in the catalogue of their accomplishments.

Sufism may have absorbed more of Indian mentality than the terminology of its self-statements would indicate. Elements in Bāyazīd al-Bisṭāmī's teachings are at least compatible with the Indian aspiration after self-identification with God; other features in the Ṣūfī movement are reminiscent of Indian ideas, such as the concept of the path and of 'concentration,' which present analogies to the noble path and the *dhyāna* of the Buddhists. Older places of Buddhist worship in Central Asia were islamized as tombs of Muslim saints. In fact, a good many individual parallels in doctrine, disciplinary technique, mystical *Brauchtum*, pantheistic rationalization of the unitive experience can without difficulty be assembled. But behind these formal and verbal parallels there is little resemblance in the spirit that animates the mystical movements in Hinduism or Buddhism and Islam. We can agree with al-Bīrūnī (d. 440/1048) who noticed similarities between certain heterodox Ṣūfīs and Hinduistic ideas, among them metempsychosis; but we must also agree with him, the greatest of the medieval Muslims studying India, when he asserts that 'we (i.e. the Muslims) believe in nothing in which they believe and vice-versa' and 'if ever a custom of theirs resembles one of ours, it has certainly just the opposite meaning'.[1]

Julian had chided the Jews for having done nothing for culture; they as the Christians had been forced to take over Hellenic science. Uttered in a different tone of voice this reproach turns to praise, and may certainly be extended to the Muslims—not that they had 'done nothing' for culture, but rather that they, as their Jewish and Christian predecessors, had gone to the only source which, in the Mediterranean basin and beyond, would yield the tools to cultural ascent. The contact with Hellenism, mediated largely in the form it had assumed in serving

[1] *Alberuni's India*, trans. E. Sachau (London, 1910), i, 19; 179; 62–67.

Christian needs, helped to shape a mentality into a civilization. The blessed origins receded into an inspiring dream which has preserved its potency to this very day.

Know that this [the Muslim state under the first caliphs] was not a state after the fashion of the states of the world, but rather resembling the conditions of the world to come. And the truth concerning it is that its fashion was after the model of the Prophets, and its conduct after the model of the Saints, while its conquests were as those of mighty kings.[1]

But while this state grew, its counterpart in history shrank, to be replaced in its service to Islam by the community and its civilization, that became the greater the more it exceeded its denominational limits. The texture of Revelation and Tradition as woven together by Law was strong enough to permit of joyful enrichment. The meshes were wide enough for a pride to assert itself in the fabric. Where the simple believer and the religious spokesman saw all legitimate strands issue from Revelation, those captivated by an Islamic civilization they had helped to make would jubilantly proclaim their own, often remote, heritage turned contribution.

We are the heirs and offspring of paganism which has spread gloriously over the world. Happy is he who for the sake of paganism bears his burden without growing weary. Who has civilized the world and built its cities, but the chieftains and kings of paganism? Who has made the ports and dug the canals? The glorious pagans have founded all these things. It is they who have discovered the art of healing souls, and they too have made known the art of curing the body and have filled the world with civil institutions and with wisdom which is the greatest of goods. Without paganism the world would be empty and plunged in poverty.[2]

The reference, needless to say, is to the Graeco-Roman, not to the Indian tradition of which Thābit b. Qurra had no knowledge. Sophistication rapidly grew. As early as the fourth/tenth century al-Fārābī obtained that distance between himself and his world which led him to observe that the laws of the victors are not necessarily better than those of the vanquished—a guarded way of casting doubt on the absolute

[1] Ibn al-Ṭiqṭaqā, *Kitāb al-Fakhrī* (written in 1302), ed. H. Dérenbourg (Paris, 1895), p. 102; trans. E. G. Browne, *A Literary History of Persia*, I (London, 1902), 188, slightly adjusted in accordance with C. E. J. Whiting, *Al Fakhri* (London, 1947), 69. For reasons of suggestiveness I have left the somewhat anachronistic 'state' where 'dynasty' would have been more literally correct.

[2] Thābit b. Qurra, a 'Sabian' of Ḥarrān (826–901), quoted by Carra de Vaux, *Les penseurs de l'Islam* (Paris, 1921–6), II, 145–6, from whom L. Dawson, *Making of Europe* (London, 1932), 154, reproduces the reference.

superiority of the Islamic order. And al-Bīrūnī was to comprehend that Islam gathered together the various nations on the basis of mutual understanding. Its mental habit and its scientific tradition range it with the Greeks. But the religion and the state are Arabic. It is the Arab strain that gives the sense of oneness to a pluralistic civilization that has come to express itself in many a language—universalism does not destroy specific character. For 'all life carries its ideal in itself'.[1]

[1] L. von Ranke, *op. cit.*, p. 178.

CHAPTER 3

ECONOMY, SOCIETY, INSTITUTIONS

In the vast empire conquered by the Arabs, it is true that the different regions were later to develop or retain their own more or less pronounced characteristics, but, for all that, they were to be not less deeply marked by the unifying imprint of Islam. However, to appreciate the even greater complexity of Muslim society than of Islam considered as a religion, it is important to understand from the outset that both alike resulted from the increasing symbiosis between the conquerors and the original inhabitants, that they preserved a continuity with the traditions of the latter just as much as with those of the former, and that the coming of the new régime did not bring any real social break with the immediate past. Arab immigration into neighbouring territories to the north of their peninsula had started many centuries before Muḥammad, and the conquest, if it extended this process, did not modify all the basic factors as much as one might be led to believe—far less than the Germanic invasions modified European society. It occurred in two different forms, bedouin immigration and military colonization, certain features of which must be carefully defined.

To understand these correctly, it must be borne in mind that the settlement of immigrants was generally effected on the basis of a distinction between indigenous private properties, the owners of which remained on them to ensure the maintenance of cultivation and which were respected, and domains of the former states, with the addition of private properties whose owners had been killed or had fled, and which were distributed as emphyteutic concessions (*qaṭī'a*; plur., *qaṭā'i'*) to Arab notables who were responsible for their development. This being so, the bedouin at no time received the right to settle on cultivated land, nor did their masters, when they acquired residential estates, do so with a view to threatening agricultural exploitation. In general, the pastoral nomadic economy took possession of the areas which for geographical reasons had necessarily been left vacant between blocks of cultivated land, made possible the utilization of ground which would otherwise have remained unproductive, and enabled mutually beneficial exchanges to be made on the basis of the complementary needs and produce of the stockbreeders and agriculturalists. It is necessary to emphasize this positive aspect of bedouin immigration during the period, because the devastation caused by later nomadic invasions, both in the Near East and in the Maghrib, is liable to give a false impression of the character of the Muslim conquest. In exceptional cases, of course, it did prove harmful to some cultivation closely linked with export to Byzantium, but more often it merely modified the markets that were supplied (for example by diverting to the large garrisons inland and to the Holy Cities of Arabia supplies previously sent from Egypt to Constantinople). Still more generally (as, among other things, the extraordinary stability in the price of Egyptian wheat from the sixth to the ninth century suggests) it can be said that, apart from a temporary crisis in places where the maintenance of cultivation also involved the upkeep of the irrigation canals (which were quickly reconditioned and even extended), agriculture as a whole was not disturbed by the coming of the Arab conquest.

In urban life the changes were possibly somewhat greater, but perhaps not exactly in the way suggested in certain over-simplified accounts. We can agree that the coming of Islam was accompanied by a development of urbanization, as we see, for example, from the founding of Baṣra and Kūfa in ʿIrāq, Fusṭāṭ (Old Cairo) in Egypt, Qayrawān in the Maghrib shortly afterwards, Baghdād rather later. We shall return to this point later, but for the moment we must emphasize that these new cities were not founded in all regions (there were practically none in Syria) and that, where they did occur, it was sometimes a matter of the re-siting of towns nearer to the edge of the desert rather than of any increase in importance, Baṣra and Kūfa replacing the decayed Sasanid capital, Ctesiphon, while Baghdād rose near its ruins, Qayrawān replacing Carthage, Damascus, an ancient city, developing at the expense of Antioch, and so forth. What is incontestable is that, whatever their social provenance in Arabia may have been, the settlement of the Arabs was essentially effected in the form of occupation-garrisons in camps which, with the passing of years, naturally acquired an urban character; the original aim had been to make the military occupation secure and, a necessary condition, to enforce a relative separation between conquerors and conquered. But, of course, it must also not be forgotten that the majority of the towns which were to become Muslim had in fact existed before Islam, nor must we fail to note that the way of life in the Arab towns themselves had become civil rather than military, that natives crowded in, and that consequently a certain affiliation with their own urban traditions came into being.

The Arab immigrants did not at once forget their former tribal structure. Among the bedouin, however, it has remained a reality up to our own time, and, in the Umayyad period, the importance of these issues aggravated the strife that divided them to such an extent that the ʿAbbasid régime rejected the tribesmen. In the towns, on the other hand, elements from different tribes became intermixed and forms of a new way of life were tried out; inevitably, these soon reduced the ancient tribal pattern to a sentimental link which became even further removed from social reality as the natives, whose importance was steadily increasing, did not adhere to it.

It was in fact through the medium of the towns that the two ethnic categories of the population came into contact reasonably quickly. For a considerable period a religious barrier (the social importance of which must not be overestimated, as we shall see) continued indeed to stand between them. But very soon an intermediate group was formed, the *mawālī* (sing., *mawlā*), whose importance during the first two centuries of Islam was considerable. This name was given either to liberated prisoners of war, or else to free non-Arabs who put themselves under the protection of Arab notables; in either case they were native inhabitants living under Muslim patronage. The necessary condition was that they should have adopted the conquerors' religion, into which, however, they could not help bringing, in some measure, the preoccupations derived from their own cultural heritage. Furthermore, the relationship of patronage made it possible to integrate within Arabo-Muslim society men who, knowing nothing of tribal structure, would but for this have been wretched individuals lost in the community of the faithful. In fact, by learning Arabic, by performing for their masters all kinds of services from the humblest to the highest, and bringing them knowledge of every kind, especially in technical or administrative fields which were unknown to the newcomers, the *mawālī*, even when the Arabs looked down on them with a certain racial pride, quickly became a fundamental element of the new social structure at all levels. The unconverted natives were of course able to participate in public life to a certain extent, but more remotely, less completely. It was indeed among the *mawālī* that what later became Muslim thought and Muslim society, during the centuries when the supremacy of the Arab race had disappeared, took shape. The result of the ʿAbbasid revolution was in fact to transform a certain section of them, those who came from Khurāsān, into the military bulwark and source of administrative personnel for the new régime. From that time onwards the two aristocracies, the Arab and that of the *mawālī* natives, were fused together in the towns, with the consequence that, by the third century of the *Hijra*, the term *mawālī* had lost its significance and therefore disappeared.

For the remaining natives who had not been granted patronage or had not adopted the new faith, the principal problems to be faced were of a fiscal nature. Freedom of worship, conditional upon the safeguarding of public order and respect for the conquerors' religion, was guaranteed to them, though subject to the primary requirement of the payment of taxes which symbolized in concrete form their subjection to Islam. The effective regulation of these taxes varied with the traditions of the subject peoples and the conditions of their submission. In a number of cases, particularly in Syria, it seems, tribute was exacted from communities in the form of a lump sum, collected under their own auspices, and paid to the conqueror, without any distinction being made by him between the various sources of payment. But the most usual procedure, especially in Persia and 'Irāq, and, in a different way, in Egypt, was that the subject peoples paid on the one hand a tax on their lands, the *kharāj*, and on the other hand a poll-tax on their persons, the *jizya*. As each local community was entirely responsible for the total amount either of the collective tribute, or at least of the land-tax calculated on its own land, it was in principle laid down that the conversion of certain individuals to Islam, an eventuality not at first envisaged, should not modify it in any way whatsoever. But the attraction of the Arab towns and the desire to escape from this tax did, however, encourage the peasants to flee; in 'Irāq, if not in Egypt, they sought refuge in the chief cities of the various regions and got themselves registered as Muslims. At first, attempts were made to put a stop to these desertions, which were detrimental both to the exploitation of the land and also to the collection of taxes; this also involved resisting conversions to Islam. This paradoxical situation very soon led to a solution which consisted of making a systematic distinction everywhere between the tax on land, which was unaffected by the religious status of the peasants, and the poll-tax, which was waived in the event of conversion (or, more accurately, replaced by the devotional alms, the *zakāt* of the believer). Conversion, which retained the advantage, if not of a clear fiscal gain, at least of placing the converted among the ranks of the dominant faith of society, henceforward took place among the peasants without flight and as in whole communities—with, until modern times, certain zones of resistance, mostly Christian, in Syria-Palestine, the eastern Fertile

Crescent and Egypt. In the towns, where the tax had a more personal character (whether in the case of *zakāt*, *jizya* or the multiple taxes on economic life, which were added to them), conversion, which was accompanied by a more pronounced rise in the social scale, was made individually. The groups remaining faithful to the religion of their fathers *ipso facto* retained their own laws and customs, under the control of their own dignitaries or ecclesiastics, matters of public order and of relations between communities naturally depending upon the Muslim law. To some extent, this was the so-called law of personal status, common in almost all medieval societies in which unfused groups co-existed.

Under the ʻAbbasid Caliphate, through the progressive fusion of the elements enumerated above, a new society thus came into being. As its documentation is less scanty, it is possible to give a rather fuller description of it. Naturally, social hierarchies existed, and disparity of wealth was considerable, but, apart from a limited internal autonomy enjoyed by the whole body of the Prophet's kin, the ʻAlids and ʻAbbasids, the Law did not recognize any legal privilege on the part of any individuals or groups; theoretically, all individuals were equal, and between them and the community as a whole the only body to be interposed was that of the family, as a result of which, by a kind of compensation, there was often a strong though unorganized feeling of solidarity between believers (and, where relevant, between members of the same tribe) which the historian Ibn Khaldūn was to study under the name of *ʻaṣabiyya*.

In the tribe and in the urban aristocracy, the family could easily include two or three generations, but among the poorer classes it was more divided. The law recognized the right of those who were sufficiently rich to have four legitimate wives (and also slave concubines), but these concessions were as a rule not equally operative and clearly the ordinary citizens could not afford them. Polygamy was in conformity with Persian, but not with Christian, tradition, while in Judaism it was unusual but not forbidden; the democratic sects who were accused of wanting to have women in common were apparently protesting against the shortage of wives resulting from the cornering of women by the aristocracy.

If the rich lived surrounded by their dependents, there were few urban families apart from the very poorest who did not have at least one or two slaves. This is not an original feature of Islam, since Christianity itself, at the time of its origin, also retained it, but slavery has had particular importance and has proved particularly enduring in the Muslim countries. But there must be no misunderstanding: although the troops of slaves on the latifundia in the Roman empire were also found on the sugar-plantations of Lower 'Irāq (Negroes imported from Africa by the merchants of Baṣra), until their celebrated revolt (the revolt of the Zanj) in the middle of the third/ninth century, this is an exceptional case. In general slaves were employed exclusively for household duties or urban crafts, not for agricultural labour; being incorporated in their master's family, they in fact enjoyed certain rights and guarantees, and were not necessarily more unhappy than they would have been in the poverty-stricken African, Turkish or Slavonic communities from which they had been taken. Work in the service of the great and of princes was a special case and could even confer power on certain individuals when, like the Turks in the East, they happened to serve in the army or, at a lower level, like the Slavs or Negroes according to the country, acted as eunuchs for harems or as factors for the management of estates. Manumission, especially by testament, was frequent. The female slave generally was, or had been, her master's concubine; but, as the mother of a child, she could no longer be alienated, was set free on the death of her master, and her children by him were free.

The mixed marriages and servile unions explain why, apart from a certain pride taken by the bedouin in the purity of their blood, there was comparatively little racial prejudice in a medieval society in which the caliphs themselves were for the most part the sons of mothers who were slaves from every sort of origin.

In the economic-social structure, the principal distinction to be noted is that between the town and the countryside. In urbanized areas the rural estates were, it is true, in the ownership of town-dwellers, and produce from them supplied the town; but this picture ceases to be accurate when no town was near, and in any case the link holds good in one direction only, the country receiving practically nothing from the town except for tax-collectors and men-at-arms, while trade, when it existed, passed through the countryside without contributing anything to it. This being said, whatever may be the importance of urban crafts and of commerce in the medieval Muslim world, for individuals as for the state the land remained the principal source, in certain zones indeed the almost unique source, of wealth, and it was moreover in land that successful merchants invested a part of their profits.

The medieval Muslim world was situated almost exclusively within the subtropical zone; in general, therefore, it was characterized by the contrast between desert or sub-desert regions which could only support a limited amount of grazing, and, in places where there was water, rich oases or strips of fertile land (for example, along the Nile and Tigris) sometimes capable of producing two harvests a year. The problem of water was naturally vital, and the East had long before developed a vast network of irrigation canals as well as a variety of machines for raising water (particularly wheels with buckets along the water-courses), introduced by the Muslims into their possessions in the West, for instance the gardens (Sp. *huertas*) of Andalusia. Customary law assured the fair distribution of water among users, and the state maintained public works which, even in times of insurrections or wars, were usually respected by the armies.

It is not necessary to repeat what has been said on the question of the economically positive role of nomadism in the waterless zones; we need only make a distinction between large-scale camel-nomadism, found only in the deserts, and nomadism on a smaller scale, especially with sheep; other kinds of animals were bred by settled populations as a subsidiary or complementary part of their cultivation, but less than in Europe. Later, in the East, there was also the nomadism of the Turcomans, whose camels were better adapted to withstand the winters on the cold plateaux of northern Persia and Anatolia than were those of the Arabs. At the end of the Middle Ages, came the Mongol invasions, which disrupted agriculture and led to a diminution of the land under cultivation, in the same way as was to some extent brought about in the Maghrib, from the fifth/eleventh century, by the penetration of the Hilālī Arabs from the Egyptian borders. But the central period of the Middle Ages must not be depicted in the light of this succeeding period.

The agriculture of the Muslim countries has given rise to a special literature, the forerunner of which appeared in ʿIrāq (*c.* 291/904), the 'Nabataean agriculture' (*Kitāb al-filāḥa al-Nabaṭiyya*) of Ibn Waḥshiyya, a mixture of oral traditions and borrowings from ancient treatises. The later study of agronomy was developed chiefly in Spain in a number of works, several of which such as that of Ibn al-ʿAwwām (sixth/twelfth century) were to inspire later Latino-Spanish writings. But we also find works on this subject in Persia, even in the Yemen and elsewhere; an indication of the interest taken by notables and princes in the exploitation of their estates and the laying out of pleasure-gardens. In general, the Muslims did no more than continue the traditions of ancient agriculture;

but they introduced into other regions—this applies particularly to the West—crops or techniques, such as mills and sugar-cane, previously known only in the East; they imported from the remoter parts of Asia certain crops hitherto unknown in the Near East, such as oranges, and, lastly, considerably developed the cultivation of certain products including sugar, flax and cotton. The basic food for human beings was almost everywhere wheat, and for animals barley. In addition to these there appeared, in gardens, a great profusion of vegetables, leguminous and cucurbitaceous plants, and condiments. In the oases, alongside the vegetables, there grew all kinds of Mediterranean fruit-trees and, on the edge of the desert, there were also date-palms, providing the staple food of the poor. Vines yielded grapes and, in localities where there were many Christians, also wine; and olive-trees, planted in arid soil, produced oil, as did sesame. Cane sugar could only be grown on land belonging to the state or to great landowners, on account of the high cost of production. The main industrial crops other than foodstuffs were flax and cotton, which supplemented wool and silk as textile materials, the vast range of flowers used to make scent, and, until the spread of paper brought it to an end in the fourth/tenth century, the papyrus that was exported from Egypt throughout the Mediterranean.

Gardens were cultivated with the spade, fields with the light Mediterranean swing-plough, not the heavy plough of the North. Rotation of crops was known, but this did not prevent land from frequently being left fallow, and the system of annual redistribution of the community's land among the peasants was often practised. Whether or not the management of the land was conducted by a large estate, the method used was generally that of small-scale exploitation. In some places windmills were known, but water-mills were mainly used and in great numbers, on the smallest *wādī*, less for grinding corn, which was a domestic task, than for working oil and sugar presses.

Estates can be roughly divided, in respect of the status of the property, into three categories: land subject to *kharāj*, land subject to tithe (*ʿushr*), and *waqf* or *ḥubus*. As we have seen, all the land of the countries conquered by the Arabs outside Arabia which remained in the hands of the descendants of the owners at the time of the conquest was subject to *kharāj*. The amount of tax that these lands paid varied according to conditions of cultivation, from a half to about a fifth. The lands subject to tithe were, besides the ancient Arab estates in Arabia, those which had been distributed or acknowledged as *qaṭāʾiʿ* from public or abandoned estates, and which, like all categories of wealth among the Muslims, paid a theoretical tax of a tenth. Unlike the first, which were often of modest size and worked by the owners themselves, these were cultivated by peasants, and it was the difference between the dues that they paid and the tax owed by the owner that constituted the latter's income. As for *waqf* or *ḥubus*, which could in general apply, though not everywhere originally, to rural estates as well as to urban sources of income, these consisted of religious foundations set up in principle for the benefit of a group of 'poor men' or of an institution of public interest. Conceived in such a way that the administration of the *waqf*, together with the salary that it involved, was often reserved until the founder's line of descent became extinct, they were often set up as an indirect way of avoiding too strict a division of property under the terms of the law of succession, and of retaining for the male members of the family, and in undivided form, estates which otherwise would have been split up or alienated. The collective character of the right to the income, and the control which the *qāḍī* of the district consequently maintained over the management of the estate, impeded any individual initiative in the exploitation of the land, but it is only in modern times that the inconveniences of the institution in this respect have been clearly revealed.

The relationship between the large and small estates is difficult to define. The only certain factor is that the large estates developed throughout Muslim history, though without succeeding in destroying either the small estates (especially the gardens) owned by townsmen in the vicinity of cities, or those belonging to country gentry (*dihqāns* in Persia), or held jointly by certain rural communities. In all large properties, the land was cultivated by peasants (sing. *fallāḥ*), the majority of whom paid rent in kind and whose tenure of the land was, in theory, based on a contract of *muzāraʿa*. By the terms of this contract, the peasant, who usually had only his labour to offer, paid the owner a proportion of his harvest, generally in its natural state. In the case of fertile land, this could be as much as four-fifths. However, other types of contracts also existed, such as the *musāqāt* which, for land requiring irrigation work and including plantations of trees, divided the proceeds equally between cultivator and owner, and the *mughārasa*, a planting contract, under the terms of which the cultivator had to plant orchards and, when they came into bearing, would receive one-half of the property itself. If one is to take the lawbooks literally, these contracts were said to be concluded for a short term, to avoid any risks; in practice, however, it is certain that in most cases not only were they tacitly renewed, the peasant was in fact by various means bound even more closely to the soil. The hostility of the peasants to the great landowners can be seen in a number of episodes related by the chronicles. However, the point has already been emphasized that labour in the country was in general free from slavery in the strict sense.

It was also in the country—though mostly for the benefit of the towns—that mineral resources were exploited. These were very unevenly distributed and, as a whole, were relatively scarce, though perhaps quantities were sufficient for the needs of the time. Iron was rarer than copper which, apart from the armourers' requirements for which importation had to be relied on, was the basis of metallurgy in the majority of the Muslim countries. Of the other metals, silver was mainly produced in Central Asia and Persia, and gold in Nubia, with monetary consequences to be noted below. Necessary for gold industry, mercury had been produced in Spain since Roman times. Eastern Persia, and India in particular, were rich in precious stones. Quarries supplied the Mediterranean countries with building-stone ('Irāq and Persia used bricks instead), and Egypt had extensive supplies of alum and natron, materials of importance in the manufacture of dyes for textiles and other chemical preparations. It was possible to obtain rock salt, but for the most part salt came from salt-pans along the coast or from inland lakes. From the waters of the Persian Gulf divers collected the celebrated pearls, and coral was also found in the Mediterranean and the Red Sea.

Very little information exists with regard to the techniques used in mining. In regard to status, some mines were the property of the state, and the state (at least in Egypt) held the monopoly of sale of their output; even from private mines and quarries the state exacted a duty of one-fifth, as on all treasure-trove.

The town as such is unknown in Muslim law. It does not possess the individuality either of the ancient city or of the Western commune of the later Middle Ages. However, this distinction must not be misinterpreted, or attributed to Islam. The Muslim town naturally took its place in continuity with the town of late antiquity, which, against the background of empires that became more and more centralized, had lost almost all autonomy; and the European communes came into being in under-organized states, a thing which, by comparison, the medieval Muslim world had never been. Generally speaking, true urban autonomies would have been unthinkable in that world but, as we shall see, it does not follow that the towns formed amorphous and passive communities.

In the first place, and a point of common knowledge, if the town as an individuality was unknown, it is nevertheless true that, in the Muslim world as in the ancient world, but unlike medieval Western Europe, the whole of civilization was found in the town; it was only there that administration, law, religion and culture existed; and from our own point of view, it is consequently from there only that all our records derive. It was pointed out earlier that neither the suddenness nor the extent of Muslim urbanization must be exaggerated; some countries such as Syria were as urbanized before Islam as afterwards, others remained with relatively little urbanization. Nevertheless, the sense of evolution and, still more, the universal dissimilarity of the Muslim world, if not from the Byzantine empire, at least from the Western world before the twelfth and thirteenth Christian centuries, cannot be contested. The majority of the Arabs had become sedentary, and had settled in towns, almost never in the country. And the natives had been attracted to the towns by the courts, business activities and administrative careers. It is quite impossible for us to assess the population of any town; it is no less certain that Baghdād in the third/ninth century and Cairo from the fifth/eleventh were towns which in size could be rivalled only by Constantinople and certain towns in the Far East; and apart from these a multitude of small towns could challenge the largest in the West.

A contrast has also been made between the beautiful orderliness of the Hellenistic-Roman town and the jumble of the medieval Muslim town. This contrast too has been overstressed, since at the time of the conquest many of the towns were vastly different from the theoretical order of the urbanists, while in the Muslim towns municipal dispositions were not entirely lacking. It was not by chance that the various trades and markets were located in relation to the chief mosque, and when necessary to the ramparts; the baths and water-supplies, aids to cleanliness, the maintenance of a certain width in the principal thoroughfares, these and many other matters attest the existence of some form of urban administration. And no doubt many medieval Western towns would have developed features similar to the Eastern ones if they had reached the same dimensions—has it not been said that ancient Rome was already an oriental city? This being said, the medieval Muslim town appears as a conglomeration of a certain number of closed and even hostile quarters separated by undefined stretches of land or by ruins, the one or two principal streets being surrounded by a maze of blind alleys in which the leading citizens mustered their retainers; each was invisible from outside, and the only parts open to the air were the inner courtyards and the roofs, where the nights could be spent in such houses as did not have several storeys. However each trade had its own locality (except, in the large towns, for dealers in foodstuffs who were necessarily represented in all quarters), dealers in textiles, with their central warehouse or *qayṣariyya*, banking and goldsmith's work being nearest to the chief mosque; near the ramparts were located the markets for trade with the nomads, and also the *funduq* or caravanserai for foreign merchants.

In these towns the interrelated rise of commerce and the merchant bourgeoisie was the dominant economico-social factor. However, one must not exaggerate; the officials, the other bourgeois category, in the third/ninth century held an equally important place, while from the fourth/tenth century the soldiers, soon to be joined by the *'ulamā'*, took a more exalted place than the merchant bourgeoisie. The infrequency of direct references to the latter in any kind of literature (in which, for example, as compared with the tens of thousands of biographies of *'ulamā'*, not a single true biography of a merchant has survived), while not expressly proving anything, does nevertheless suggest that it should be given a subordinate place. However, it is still correct to emphasize the rise of commerce for the general repercussions it had on the economy, by comparison with Western Europe at the same time, and even, though to a lesser extent, with the East in late antiquity.

The legitimacy of profit in trade, which, especially at the beginning of the economic decline, some were later to dispute, was never seriously questioned—so long as certain prohibitions were respected—by the founders of Islam, several of whom, starting with the Prophet himself, had been merchants. To the pious souls some writers explained under what conditions one could devote oneself to trade; but for the majority of merchants, considerations of piety remained distinct from professional life. In any case, after a century in which trade sought to adapt itself to the conditions ensuing from the conquest, it is clear that from the beginning of the third/ninth century it was flourishing.

We must make the distinction, here even more systematically than elsewhere, between local small-scale commerce and the commerce organized by powerful merchants (*tājir*; plur., *tujjār*) which not only differs from it, as is obvious, but is indeed essentially distinct from it. All merchandise imported from abroad had to be housed in a *funduq* (cf. shortly afterwards the Italian *fondaco*) where, once duties had been paid to the state, local dealers came to get supplies, the great merchants not being permitted for the most part to make any direct entry into the internal market. It is almost exclusively with this internal market that the legal treatises and summaries of *ḥisba* deal, concerning themselves with day-to-day business, and for the subject of large-scale trade we are reduced to items of information gleaned here and there, in particular from the geographers and from certain descriptions of travels.

In the ʿAbbasid period, the great centre for the whole of the East was Baghdād, to be replaced after the fifth/eleventh century by Cairo, while the distant countries of the Muslim West also had their own activities, though on a smaller scale. From ʿIrāq and Persia, embarking either from Baṣra in the Persian Gulf (or, more accurately, from its port, Ubulla) or from Sīrāf on the Persian coast, and usually with a call at ʿUmān, on the coast of Arabia, their ships sailed to the Yemen and on to East Africa, where they went beyond Zanzibar and the Comoro Islands. Sailing eastwards, they reached India and eventually Malaysia and China (Canton). The Hindus and Chinese, for their part, occasionally visited the Muslim ports or, more often, came to Ceylon or Malaysia to meet merchants from the West. After the disturbances in China which led to the massacre of the merchant colony in Canton at the end of the third/ninth century, these intermediate meeting-places became customary for a time although direct links with China were gradually re-established. Merchandise brought to ʿIrāq was largely absorbed by the court and the wealthy local aristocracy; a certain proportion however was sent on by caravan to the ports of Syria or Egypt, destined for the Christian and Muslim countries of the Mediterranean; some goods were also sent by land or sea from Syria direct to Constantinople, and from there redistributed to eastern Europe and Byzantine Italy. In addition, an overland caravan route led to Muslim Central Asia another centre of international relations from pre-Islamic times; from it, in one direction the traditional Silk Road led to China, in another the Volga lands could be reached. In the fifth/eleventh century the disturbances in the East, Fatimid policy and the rise of Italy led to a re-orientation of the Indian Ocean trade, for which the Yemen became the centre, and the Red Sea the route to the Mediterranean via Egypt. Elsewhere, in the West, relations were maintained with southern Italy and the Nigerian Sudan through the Maghrib, and with the Carolingian countries through Spain.

The goods carried were mostly valuable products of small weight and volume, such as spices (especially pepper) for culinary use, drugs, perfumes, precious stones and pearls, and delicate fabrics such as silks from China. Among the imports, however, certain commodities of greater economic significance were included. From Europe the Muslim countries imported not only hides and furs, but also part of the timber needed for ship-building and the iron for making arms, as well as their indispensable stock of slaves (Slavs, as the word indicates), supplied by merchants, sometimes Jewish, from Verdun, Venice or elsewhere in Italy. Other slaves were brought from black Africa, eastern Europe and Turkish Central Asia; the Indian Ocean also provided the teak and coconut-palm timber that was then indispensable for ship-building. In its turn Europe gradually began to import from the Muslim countries, not only luxury articles and foodstuffs, but also commodities needed for its own manufactures, for example alum from Egypt. Nevertheless, for both parties the basis of the trade resided mainly in speculation on the differences in prices between the countries supplying the goods and those that purchased them, and the question of winning a market never entered the calculations of a merchant, or indeed of a state, in the Middle Ages. The import-export balance which could seldom be achieved purely by merchandise was secured by payments in coin.

The merchants devoting themselves to this trade belonged for the most part to the various creeds to be found in the Muslim East, Muslims, Jews, Christians and Zoroastrians, apparently without any general distinction between them. The Arabs and Persians divided the navigation of the Indian Ocean between themselves, but they carried Jews and Christians coming from beyond the Persian Gulf. Their courage took them among non-Muslim peoples, not to say barbarians in the Sudan and Russia. Nevertheless neither the Muslims nor even the Christians maintained the ancient tradition of relations with the West, which in so far as they existed were kept up, until the fourth/tenth century, either by southern Italians and Venetians or by the problematic Jews from France and Spain known as Radanites whose network of operations extended to the Far East. On the subject of Jewish trade, particularly of North Africa, with the East in the next two centuries, information of great value is being made available by the gradual publication of the treasure of Judaeo-Arabic documents known as the Cairo Geniza. In the time of the Crusades, control of the Mediterranean passed increasingly to the Western Christians; the economic partition of the world left trade with Africa and Asia to the now mainly Muslim East, until the Portuguese discoveries. It was generally in the Egyptian or Syrian ports that the obligatory exchange between Western and Eastern merchants took place, in the same way as at Constantinople in the Byzantine empire. Perhaps Jews used habitually to travel from one end of a trade-route to the other, but we have no evidence that they handled business directly from the Asiatic sphere to the Mediterranean sphere: for this purpose Cairo was always used as the stopping-place.

Whatever their religion, merchants followed the same commercial methods. The capital that they employed for their trade was not theirs alone. Whether they had entered into partnership agreements, or had received goods on *commenda* (*qirāḍ*, *muḍāraba*), they thus combined their own resources with those of others or, conversely, made their own capital multiply in the hands of others, with the object of widening their business activities and spreading the risk. The 'capitalists' whose wealth was used in this way were not other merchants only; just as the merchants invested a part of their profits in land, so all men of substance, from the caliph or sultan downwards, invested part of the income that they drew from their landed properties in trade of this kind, to increase their wealth. Moreover, the merchants often secured the right to farm taxes under conditions that allowed them to use in private business money that in fact belonged to the state. This procedure foreshadows the practice of eminent Italian financiers three or four centuries later.

It has been said that the conditions governing trade compelled merchants to carry hard cash with them. Nevertheless, when they did not go beyond the limits of the Muslim world or the known and established merchant colonies, they took measures to restrict this carrying of money by making agreements with known correspondents. Over sometimes vast distances they thus developed, though they did not entirely invent, the letter of credit (*suftaja*, a Persian word) which allowed someone to have the necessary sum of money advanced to an associate or partner by a third party at some distant place, on a reciprocal basis, a procedure which implied the maintenance of regular accounts and correspondence, which indeed fast couriers often carried. It was of course also possible to contract ordinary loans and make deposits, and private individuals and governments alike made wide use of promissory notes, (*ṣakk*, from which the word cheque may be derived) to be used for payments. Finally, in certain places, in the same way as later at the fairs of Champagne in France, clearing-house procedure was in existence among the bankers; it is known to have been practised in Baṣra in the fifth/eleventh century.

Nevertheless, money naturally played its part. Apart from copper coins, which were only used for local retail trading, there were two others—silver coinage, the unit being the *dirham*, and gold coinage, the unit of which was the *dīnār*. It came to be agreed, in the fourth/tenth century, that their respective legal value was 7/100, corresponding to a ratio by weight of 7 : 10 (or, in metric units, 4 gr. 25 for the *dīnār* and 2 gr. 87 for the *dirham*) and a gold/silver rate of exchange of 10. In reality, neither the market price of precious metals nor the metal content of the coins in circulation regularly corresponded with these definitions. In international markets up to the fifth/eleventh century the *dīnār*, like the Byzantine *solidus* had the prestige now enjoyed by the dollar. But cash payments, made with variable currencies, called for the frequent use of scales. In addition, exchange operations were often necessary, both for the treasury and for trade; they were in the hands of money-changers (sing., *ṣayrafī*) who, as in Europe a little later, formed a special guild; the other operations now performed by bankers were at that time usually carried out by the great merchants themselves. In general, a monometallic system, based on silver, prevailed in the Muslim East until the end of the fourth/tenth century, and also in Spain, while the intermediate countries had a monometallic system based on gold. As a result, the stocks of treasure amassed by the Northmen and discovered on Russian territory and as far as the Baltic are principally of silver. In the fifth/eleventh century silver almost disappeared, and in the seventh/thirteenth gold became a European monopoly, but formerly it was the Muslim currency that was at a premium. The term *mancus* which, in Italy before the Crusades, denoted the principal unit of currency, probably derives from the epithet *manqūsh*, struck, applied to the Muslim *dīnār* as defined by the Caliph ʿAbd al-Malik (65-86/685–705). Certain authors have dwelt on the repercussions of these facts on the European economy, but it would be premature to postulate so unified a market.

In theory, foreign trade was subject to differential tariffs according to the politico-religious status of the merchants, and customs duties were only levied at the frontiers of the Muslim world as a whole. In reality, political and economic requirements resulted, even before the Crusades and still more afterwards, in the conclusion of commercial treaties between Muslim states and others, in which the utility of the merchandise was the prime consideration. The political dismemberment of the Muslim world from the third/ninth century and, even within the principalities then set up, the power of local notables, multiplied the levying of tolls and 'protection' payments. If these did not develop to the same extent as in feudal Europe, the contrast must not be exaggerated. And there was no longer any unity of weights and measures. The relative unity of Law and language, the sense of the community of the faithful had indeed the effect of facilitating exchanges throughout the whole Muslim world; but one must not infer the existence of a single economic market covering the whole world of Islam.

Local trade was not systematically distinguished from industry, many small artisans themselves selling their own products, and the same organization generally including them all. In regard to the character of manufactured goods, the technical contribution of the Muslim world has not been studied sufficiently, and is difficult to define. Its significance seems to have been its unparalleled diffusion, rather than any true inventiveness. No doubt the most important innovation, which was taken from the Chinese in the middle of the second/eighth century, was the making of paper; it quickly spread to the Mediterranean where it superseded the less practical and more costly Egyptian papyrus before reaching Christian Europe. But progress was also made in other fields, though its effectiveness in a slowly developing world is difficult to define; there were advances in metallurgy (the so-called 'damascene' steel, in reality Hindu), in ceramics and glassware, in the textile industry (as is shown by the number of names of fabrics that have passed into the European languages) and the chemical industry (which also has given us its vocabulary), with particular reference to the making of scent and soap, and dyeing.

In industry, a distinction has to be made between the free crafts and the state industries. The dividing line is perhaps not the same everywhere since Egypt, throughout her history, has been more étatist than other countries. Between these two types there were crafts that could be exercised freely, but which were regulated and under compulsion to supply the state. The greater part of the manufacture of arms, the maritime arsenals and even part of the Egyptian merchant fleet were naturally dependent on the state. The same was true of papyrus and paper, and also of certain luxury fabrics, gold brocades intended for princely clothing or gifts, and made in what were known as *ṭirāz* (literally embroidery) workshops. Originally woven according to Byzantine or Sasanid traditions, in the time of ʿAbd al-Malik they were given Muslim inscriptions at the same time as the coinage; there were protests from the foreign clientele, but these did not really restrict their sale. Coinage was naturally a state monopoly, the mints for gold coins being very centralized, while those for silver were more scattered.

The free crafts were extremely numerous and varied. In general, artisans themselves disposed of their products, but there seems to have been a more complex hierarchy in the textile industry in which the powerful merchants (sing., *bazzāz*) employed weavers, spinners and launderers, and, as was the case everywhere during the Middle Ages, represented the merchant aristocracy (sometimes the same men were also *tujjār*). Although naturally there were few collective operations in this work, in the textile industry in particular it was possible for workers to be grouped together in quite large workshops. In the small workshops, artisans worked surrounded by apprentices and slaves; the latter could occupy a shop in their master's name, or indeed even in their own.

As in most medieval towns in all civilizations, and as can still be seen in the traditional quarters of Muslim towns, trades were mostly grouped together, each one in a street or group of streets, (sing., *sūq*) confined to that trade, and often roofed to keep off sun and rain. In addition, there was a corporate organization, the exact nature of which is difficult to specify. What is certain is that in various ways all the artisans of the same trade were organized and grouped, but it is difficult to see whether, as in Byzantium and earlier in Rome, they were set up by state control, or, as in the guilds in the later Middle Ages in Europe, they were spontaneous associations playing an important part in the general lives, both public and private, of their members. The second characteristic is to some extent that of the professional associations which can be studied from the end of the Middle Ages; for the earlier periods, the arguments that have been adduced and that lead to this conclusion rest on analogies which are not proved or have been misinterpreted. It is not possible to confirm the existence of a craft as a collective body except on the ground of the pride that members of a distinguished calling would take in belonging to it, and, more generally, the equivalence that penal law instituted for the definition of rightful claimants to pecuniary compensation, within the tribe, for such of the Arabs as had one, the military administration for soldiers, and the professional collective bodies (sing., *ṣinf*) for those who were neither Arabs nor soldiers. But it is impossible in classical times to ascribe any important role in general life to the truly professional corporate organizations, and those which play that part are not of that character.

An official specially appointed by the police and responsible for trades and local commerce, under the supervision of the *qāḍī*, existed in all towns of any size At first known merely as 'head of the *sūq*', probably a reference to an ancient antecedent, he was later given the more religious title of *muḥtasib*, that is to say, the officer responsible for the *ḥisba*, i.e. the duty to promote good and to repress evil by concerning himself in theory with all questions of public morals, the behaviour of non-Muslims and women, the observance of ritual obligations and the rules of professional ethics. Besides the legal treatises and the *responsa* of the jurisconsults which elaborated these rules during the earliest centuries of Islam, administrative summaries for the special guidance of these *muḥtasibs* also made their appearance in the Arab countries, in both West and East, from the fifth/eleventh or sixth/twelfth century. The regulations which had to be observed were for the most part concerned with honesty in manufacture and selling, protection of the client from fraud, and of the manufacturer from competition, in the same way as in the regulations of the guilds during the late Middle Ages in Europe. On the other hand, apart from basic products in time of famine, and certain objects in which there was a monopoly, the medieval Muslim (but not the Ottoman) state—apparently under the merchants' influence —considered that it did not have the right to fix prices.

If not outside the working population, it was at least outside the framework of the professional system that the only associations which flourished in urban public life existed, namely those which it has become customary to call organizations of *futuwwa*. The references to them in literature are very varied and often obscure, and differ from one period and one country to another, with the result that it is difficult to form any definite idea of their real character. This much is certain, that they always consisted of fairly large solidarity groups, mainly, but not exclusively, recruited from the poorer classes and the young, and of males only. They readily adopted an attitude of hostility to the rich and powerful which resulted, at times when authority was poorly enforced, in violent disorders. One of their principal aims, for the particular purpose of neutralizing repression, was to be enrolled in the police; sometimes they obtained temporary satisfaction of this aim, sometimes powerful leaders recruited henchmen among them, for use in their quarrels, and thus the activities of the *futuwwa* became involved in the general factional strife, which, under various pretexts, sundered many Muslim towns. Entry into the groups of *futuwwa* in the strict sense took place with initiatory rites roughly comparable with those found in other societies, and, in the Muslim world, other associations such as the secret Ismāʿīlī ones; but there seem to be no grounds for concluding that the latter had any specific influence upon the former. Nor is it possible to trace back to the central Middle Ages the influence exercised by the *futuwwa* from the eighth/fourteenth century over trades in the Perso-Turkish countries. Incidentally, the *futuwwa* was always more prominent in the territories of the former Sasanid empire than in the Arab countries, in which we find urban militias of popular *aḥdāth*, without the ritual and ideological developments that characterize the true *futuwwa*. In the Muslim West nothing approaching these *aḥdāth* has as yet been recorded.

From about the fifth/eleventh century certain reciprocal influences came into being between the *futuwwa* associations and the communities of Ṣūfīs. From them resulted a literature of *futuwwa* which, in that it presented only their ritual and mystical aspects, has for a long time prevented us from seeing their real social significance. In a large well-policed town such as Baghdād, this significance might reside in a kind of class opposition to the rich and the rulers, but more generally it appeared as an expression of the latent hostility felt by the whole population of the town towards the usually foreign (or so regarded) governors to whom they were subject. In certain limited cases, by reliance on the strength of the *futuwwa* some notables succeeded in gaining temporary autonomy in a town.

If the subject of government in Muslim society has been left almost until the end, that is because it was never, or almost never, anything other than superimposed; never, or almost never, the emanation or expression of that society. It is in its solidarities at the individual level that the true social coherences and structures of Islam are to be found, not in the princes, their soldiers and their tax-collectors. This was so at least from the time when, in the third/ninth or fourth/tenth century, experience imposed the conclusion that one was obliged to submit to those who were in fact governing, rather than to maintain the idealistic aspirations of the first generations to establish a power expressing in social terms the Islam of the community of believers. This does not alter the fact that, on another level, the political and administrative institutions of the Muslim world are among the most highly developed that had hitherto been known.

The Muslim faith does not distinguish the political from the religious, thereby differing from medieval Christianity with its theory of the Two Powers and even more from Roman tradition or the modern Western world. Consequently, rulers were expected to possess moral and religious qualities, and the religious attitude entailed certain political choices. At the very beginning of Islam the political problem was conceived in terms of a religious problem, indeed the fundamental religious problem.

At the head of the community stood the caliph, that is to say the representative, the successor of the Prophet and, through him, of God. Naturally he had absolute power in principle, absolute however in order that he might apply a Law which was anterior to himself, and for the interpretation of which he had no particular prerogative. The initiatives that he could make must therefore in theory aim only at assuring respect for the Law. The Shīʿa, it is true—and especially the Fatimids in the fourth/tenth century—were to endow their *imām* with more complete authority, in keeping with their belief that in some way God was continuing in him His revelation to the Prophet. But, both before and after the Fatimids, the great majority of Muslims always refused to recognize that the caliph had any claim to interpret the Law outside the consensus of specialists, and that is one of the main lessons of the failure of the Muʿtazilite attempt. This being said, and all true legislation being thus excluded, it nevertheless remains true that, in practice, everyday political activity and the organization of military and financial institutions do in fact imply initiatives which owe nothing to the Law, and that even here, as in every state, there is thus a certain sector which is in effect 'secular'. But the ʿAbbasid Caliphate which sternly rebuked its Umayyad predecessor for having too easily decided in favour of this 'secular' character, itself endeavoured to define its own conduct of government in Muslim terms and consequently, so far as it could do so, to impart a religious orientation to it. We shall see presently how this attempt also finally failed.

In the Umayyad period, the governmental and administrative institutions were still relatively simple. Very broadly speaking, they consisted of an organization of subjects, for the most part governed according to their own traditions and led by agents who came from among themselves—non-Muslim, non-Arab—and, superimposed upon this foundation, the corps of Arab and Muslim rulers whose primary function was to govern the Muslim Arabs, leading them to war, guiding their cultural life and distributing pensions paid for by taxes on non-Muslim subjects. The arabization and islamization which took place from the time of the caliphate of ʿAbd al-Malik were not completed in a day, and did not prevent the institutions from retaining their simple character. In this way of life the caliph, who was easily approached, was no more than *primus inter pares*. In the provinces he left almost all power to the governors whom he appointed, and to whom the local administration was subordinate, with a corresponding limitation of tasks for the central government. Thus, apart from war and religion, the central government hardly needed more than secretary heads of departments who cannot be said to have had any real power.

The evolution which took shape under the Umayyads, and which was accelerated under the ʿAbbasids, was to bring about a profound change in the character of the régime. A considerable effort was made to achieve centralization and control (incidentally, causing uprisings in the provinces in protest), which implies an extensive bureaucracy. In this way, certain traditions of the Romano-Byzantine and Sasanid empires were resumed and developed still further. Offices in which a vast amount of writing was done proliferated and became more complex, with the result that an actual specialized class of officials came into being, the *kuttāb* (literally 'scribes', plur. of *kātib*), mostly arabized and islamized Persians, who also took an influential part in the field of culture and formed a counterpoise to the doctors of the Law. Under the first ʿAbbasids, it was still the caliph alone who co-ordinated the activities of these various departments, and none of the departmental heads had the rank of a real minister. Nevertheless, the caliph gradually gave more and more authority to a personage close to him, the *wazīr*, who originally was no more than a private assistant who helped him to carry his burden—that is the meaning of the word which is Arabic, not Persian as has been stated. The first ʿAbbasids put the *wazīr* in charge of certain departments, and when necessary also made him tutor to their heirs. To the consequent growth of power came reactions, the most famous and spectacular being the fall of the Barmecides, under Hārūn al-Rashīd. But in proportion as the effective power of the caliphate declined, so did that of the wazirate increase and, from the middle of the fifth/eleventh century, the *wazīrs*, who were now recruited from the professional class of the *kuttāb*, were the real heads of the administration, and even played an increasing part in the conduct of purely political activities. Writers were now producing not only biographies of caliphs but also biographies of *wazirs*.

The principal administrative departments were those of the chancery, the exchequer and the army. Justice, which derives from religion, had a different status and a different personnel, with which we need not concern ourselves here. These departments were all denoted by the Persian word *dīwān*, which passed into European languages (*douane, dogana, aduana*, in the sense of customs-house. It was from the chancery (*dīwān al-rasā'il* or *dīwān al-inshā'*) that all political correspondence emanated, for which a formulary, and later an authentic literary style, were, little by little, perfected, with the result that the work could only be performed by the highly literate. The *dīwān al-jaysh* concerned itself with all matters connected with army recruitment, structure, armament and, of course, payment. The department for *'arḍ* held reviews of the troops, checked the identity of the soldiers and the upkeep of arms and animals and, when that was done, distributed the pay, or awarded the concessions that took its place. These, in the form of *iqṭā's* which will be defined shortly, later constituted an independent department. But it was above all upon the exchequer (*dīwān al-māl*) that everything depended. The central organization, with equivalent departments corresponding to it in every province, consisted of offices which established the bases for taxes particularly by checking and upkeep of the cadastral surveys, among which the *dīwān al-kharāj* and the *dīwān al-ḍiyā'* (the latter for estates or *qaṭā'i'* paying the tenth) should be noted; then the *zimām* (later called *istīfā'*, the head of which was the *mustawfī*) which verified the accuracy of the accounts for taxes actually paid; the department for disbursements, which paid out salaries; the treasury (*bayt al-māl*) to which revenues that were not immediately expended on the spot were brought, and with which the shops for valuable clothing, and jewels were associated. Among the officials or agents attached to these departments a special part was played by the *jahbadh*, who was often a merchant by origin and who verified and exchanged the two variable currencies. Taxation was sometimes levied directly, sometimes farmed out to merchants or influential men, sometimes conceded as a *muqāṭa'a*, that is to say left to some important man who simply paid a lump sum for it or undertook responsibility for some military service at his own expense, or sometimes, particularly after the fourth/tenth century, given as *iqṭā'* in return for service and without any payment being made, as the equivalent of army pay. Varying according to the different regions, periods, kinds of cultivation and status of the land, the land-tax was paid in kind, in cash or with a mixture of the two. It was possible to estimate it in advance; extremely accurately in Egypt where all agriculture was governed by the Nile flood, less precisely in other places where estimates were made nevertheless. We still possess actual ʿAbbasid budgets covering the period from the end of the second/eighth century to the beginning of the fourth/tenth. But in these budgets there is no mention of *jizya*, *zakāt* or of local duties on commerce and industry, which were allocated compulsorily for public works in the area where they were collected, or for the salaries (which were regarded as forming part of these) of the police and various agents. This signifies that, at the very time of the rise of the merchant economy, it was less easy for the state to make use of the profits for its own advantage than it was for the merchants to benefit from the public taxes. We shall return in a moment to the consequences of this fact.

The early army was composed of Muslim Arabs fighting in the name of the Holy War, and maintained less by regular pay than by booty. The ending of the conquests dried up this source, and made necessary the establishment of a paid army on the basis of service, not of family and religious standing as at first. The original army had owed its successes to its constant mobility and preparedness, as well as to the disloyalty of the native populations towards the régimes to which they had previously been subjected; but it did not possess the technical aptitude of the old Byzantine and Sasanid armies and in particular lacked any kind of siege weapons. From the last Umayyad days, the need for reform was imperative; the ʿAbbasid revolution achieved this. In the sense that as the new régime relied mainly on its immediate Khurāsānī supporters, for the future it was Persian rather than Arab traditions that prevailed, at least in the East and around the caliph. Henceforward there was a professional army, the only one recorded in the rolls of the *dīwān*—with the exception of the West—to which were attached only light corps of voluntary *ghāzīs* and bedouin Arabs on the frontiers of Anatolia or Central Asia, the latter living on the fruits of their raids, the former benefiting also from pious foundations of believers who were themselves unable to participate in the Holy War and who were anxious at least to win Allāh's mercy for themselves in this way. Besides individual warriors, the army henceforward acquired all that military science then knew in the way of siege engines, Greek fire, and soon afterwards cross-bows. But even this régime did not remain unchanged. Quite soon there came a time when the exclusive guardianship of the Khurāsānīs proved irksome to the caliphs, while at the same time their recruitment became more difficult on account of the increasing concessions of autonomy that had had to be made to the governors of Khurāsān and the surrounding regions. It was thus necessary to summon new populations, such as the semi-islamized Turks of Transoxania, or Daylamites from the south Caspian provinces, the latter as infantrymen, the former as cavalry. But the idea also came to the caliphs, especially to al-Muʿtaṣim (218–27/833–42) that the fidelity of the troops would be more certain if they were recruited from among foreign personal slaves rather than from indigenous freemen who were involved in party conflicts, and that, if acquired while still young, they could also be given technical training more successfully. In fact, the same thing happened that had happened to the Praetorians of Rome. The new soldiers were not slow to see that the caliphate was powerless but for themselves; moreover the leaders whom they really recognized were not the caliphs, who stayed immured in their palaces, but the generals who commanded them. Conflicts occurred between factions, or against the reigning caliph, with the object of bringing to effective power, in the name of a new caliph, a military commander who would show favour to his adherents, and moreover a prince whose first act would be to grant higher pensions to those to whom he owed his power. It was to no advantage, very much the contrary, that such manoeuvres should replace the former ethnic or politico-religious divisions, with which incidentally they were occasionally combined.

The new army was naturally far more costly to maintain than the old one, since the soldiers had to rely entirely on their pay for their maintenance; the arms and instruments being developed entailed additional expenditure, and the commanders being aware of their own strength demanded more; moreover, for some obscure reasons, it appears that the cost of living became generally very much higher during the third/ninth century. The budget therefore became much more heavily burdened, and for that reason the regular disbursements to the army became more difficult to fulfil, while the harshness of taxation and its unpopularity with the populace increased in proportion. Some of the commanders then demanded direct rule over the provinces where they were to maintain their forces; they themselves were so highly esteemed that it was impossible to refuse them, at least in every case. When their *de facto* autonomy merged with the increasing local feeling of the inhabitants, the political dismemberment of the empire soon followed; and what remained of it consequently suffered from yet another increase in taxation since, to save this residue at least, it was essential to avoid cutting down the army. The whole process was a vicious circle which, in the fourth/tenth century, in the very centre of the caliphate, led to the direct seizure of power by the military commanders, and thereafter it was upon them, after their investiture by a caliph, representing and conferring legitimacy, that the whole administration depended, including the *wazīr*, together with all the revenues of the state.

The *de facto* substitution of military commanders—by popular usage, and later, from the fifth/eleventh century, in the official terminology, these were known as sultans—in place of the caliph did not thereby solve the military-financial problem. Some degree of success was reached by the creation of the system of the *iqṭāʿ* (to be distinguished from the early *qaṭīʿa*, which has often been confused with it on account of the common root) which consisted in making a direct allocation to officers of the right to the taxes from a district where the revenue was approximately equivalent to the pay due to the army units—thus in fact removing them from the control of the state administration. The full consequences of this innovation were not immediately revealed, because the officers, being ignorant of the conditions of sound business, at first had their *iqṭāʿs* constantly changed; but later, especially when the system worked for the benefit of the Turks who arrived with the Seljuks in the fifth/eleventh century, they settled on territory which they became accustomed to regard as their own. With the help of protection and commendation, a method that had existed from the beginnings of Islam, if not before, but which now played in their favour, they also acquired an increasing share of the free property. In this way a régime was established in the East which in certain respects resembled Western feudalism. It never acquired the solidity of that system because the law of succession, ignoring the right of primogeniture, divided the inheritances, and because the recruitment of new slaves allowed the princes to fight against former freedmen until such time as one of the invasions which devastated the East temporarily replaced one aristocracy by another. Nevertheless, the inhabitants became accustomed to think that they were ruled by foreign military aristocracies; hence the development of urban discontent which in the long view was inevitably doomed to failure.

The slowing-down of commerce in certain regions and, in others, the fact that the Europeans were henceforward to take their share of profits, effectively reduced the strength of resistance of the merchant class, which was also severely tested by the political troubles. The new masters only asked that their capital should be made to multiply, but in an emergency they did not hesitate to confiscate the merchants' wealth, and in any case it was largely they who disposed of the funds upon which the merchants lived. The result was that the apogee of Muslim trade in the fourth/tenth century was immediately followed by a partial decline, and by what amounts to a form of tutelage exercised by the ruler over the merchants. This requires the historian to be cautious in estimating the social forces at work. Anxiety to protect their descendants from hazards of this sort, as well as to safeguard public foundations, sentiments that no doubt were shared by the new aristocrats, led to the development of the hitherto modest institution of the *waqf* or *ḥubus* which from that time took the form of large foundations for the benefit of mosques, establishments of Ṣūfī devotees, religious schools, and so forth. As a result, a new class of men appeared, living on these foundations, individually of modest wealth but collectively powerful. If they too, in the final analysis, were materially dependent upon the armed forces, the converse was also partly true, in the sense that it was in their interest to support those army leaders who favoured the religious groups to which they belonged against others, and that they possessed great moral influence over the populace of which they themselves formed part. Thus at the end of the so-called Middle Ages, and even more as the bourgeoisie declined, there was to a certain extent a kind of condominium of the army and the religious; this condominium was to be a characteristic feature of the majority of Muslim countries until the dawn of the modern period.

Though necessarily very brief, the foregoing chapter, it is hoped, will nevertheless have shown that Muslim society in its various aspects, from its economy to its political institutions, while displaying certain specific characteristics, continued constantly to evolve, until the time when those who professed to represent the Law stood as guarantors for a régime which in fact no longer owed anything to it. We have been at pains to emphasize this evolution on account of the legendary idea of Oriental conservatism, for which there is no foundation. That Europe in modern times should have accelerated its rhythm and, in so doing, should have retarded that of the very nations whom its competition was overwhelming, does not mean that they too had not earlier developed like others. For this reason it has not been possible to make the present account follow a static pattern, and the reader may thus have found it difficult to assimilate. But if he has absorbed this lesson at least from it, his time will not have been wasted.

CHAPTER 4

LAW AND JUSTICE

The sacred law of Islam, the *Sharī'a*, occupies a central place in Muslim society, and its history runs parallel with the history of Islamic civilization. It has often been said that Islamic law represents the core and kernel of Islam itself and, certainly, religious law is incomparably more important in the religion of Islam than theology. As recently as 1959, the then rector of al-Azhar University, Shaykh Maḥmūd Shaltūt, published a book entitled 'Islam, a faith and a law' (*al-Islām*, *'aqīda wa-sharī'a*), and by far the greater part of its pages is devoted to an exposé of the religious law of Islam, down to some technicalities, whereas the statement of the Islamic faith occupies less than one-tenth of the whole. It seems that in the eyes of this high Islamic dignitary the essential bond that unites the Muslims is not so much a common simple creed as a common way of life, a common ideal of society. The development of all religious sciences, and therefore of a considerable part of intellectual life in Islam, takes its rhythm from the development of religious law. Even in modern times, the main intellectual effort of the Muslims as Muslims is aimed not at proving the truth of Islamic dogma but at justifying the validity of Islamic law as they understand it. It will therefore be indicated for us to survey the development of Islamic law within the framework of Islamic society and civilization, tentative as this survey is bound to be. Islamic law itself is one of our most important sources for the investigation of Islamic society, and explaining Islamic law in terms of Islamic society risks using a circular argument. Besides, the scarcity of expert historical and sociological studies of Islamic law has more often been deplored than it has inspired efforts to fill this gap.

Islamic law had its roots in pre-Islamic Arab society. This society and its law showed both profane and magical features. The law was magical in so far as the rules of investigation and evidence were dominated by sacral procedures, such as divination, oath, and curse; and it was profane in so far as even penal law was reduced to questions of compensation and payment. There are no indications that a sacred law existed among the pagan Arabs; this was an innovation of Islam. The magical element left only faint traces, but Islamic law preserved the profane character of a considerable portion of penal law. It also preserved the essential features of the law of personal status, family, and inheritance as it existed, no doubt with considerable variations of detail, both in the cities and among the bedouin of Arabia. All these subjects were dominated by the ancient Arabian tribal system, combined with a patriarchal structure of the family. Under this system, the individual lacked legal protection outside his tribe, the concept of criminal justice was absent and crimes were reduced to torts, and the tribal group was responsible for the acts of its members. This led to blood feuds, but blood feuds were not an institution of ancient Arab tribal law, they stood outside the law and came under the purview of the law only when they were mitigated by the payment of blood-money, and at this moment the profane character of ancient Arabian law asserted itself again. There was no organized political authority in pre-Islamic Arab society, and also no organized judicial system. However, if disputes arose concerning rights of property, succession, and torts other than homicide, they were not normally decided by self-help but, if negotiation between the parties was unsuccessful, by recourse to an arbitrator. Because one of the essential qualifications of an arbitrator was that he should possess supernatural powers, arbitrators were most frequently chosen from among soothsayers. The decision of the arbitrator was obviously not an enforceable judgment, but a statement of what the customary law was, or ought to be; the function of the arbitrator merged into that of a lawmaker, an authoritative expounder of the normative legal custom or *sunna*. Transposed into an Islamic context, this concept of *sunna* was to become one of the most important agents, if not the most important, in the formation of Islamic law, and the *'ulamā'*, the authoritative expounders of the law, became not in theory but in fact the lawmakers of Islam.

Muḥammad began his public activity in Mecca as a religious reformer, and in Medina he became the ruler and lawgiver of a new society on a religious basis, a society which was meant, and at once began, to replace and supersede Arabian tribal society. Already in Mecca, Muḥammad had had occasion to protest against being regarded as merely another soothsayer by his pagan countrymen, and this brought about, in the early period of Medina, the rejection of arbitration as practised by the pagan Arabs. But when Muḥammad was called upon to decide disputes in his own community, he continued to act as an arbitrator, and the Qur'ān, in a roughly contemporaneous passage, prescribed the appointment of an arbitrator each from the families of husband and wife in the case of marital disputes. In a single verse only, which again is roughly contemporaneous with the preceding passage, the ancient Arab term for arbitration appears side by side with, and is in fact superseded by, a new Islamic one for a judicial decision: 'But no, by thy Lord, they will not (really) believe until they make thee an arbitrator of what is in dispute between them and find within themselves no dislike of that which thou decidest, and submit with (full) submission' (*Sūra* 4. 65). Here the first verb refers to the arbitrating aspect of Muḥammad's activity, and the second, 'to decide', from which the Arabic term *qāḍī* is derived, emphasizes the authoritative character of his decision. This is the first indication of the emergence of a new, Islamic, concept of the administration of justice. Numerous passages in the Qur'ān show that this ideal demand was slow to be fulfilled, but Muḥammad's position as a prophet, backed in the later stages of his career in Medina by a considerable political and military power, gave him a much greater authority than could be claimed by an arbitrator; he became a 'Prophet-Lawgiver'. But he wielded his almost absolute power not within but without the existing legal system; his authority was not legal but, for the believers, religious, and, for the lukewarm, political. He was essentially a townsman, and the bitterest tirades in the Qur'ān are directed against the bedouin.

Muḥammad's legislation, too, was a complete innovation in the law of Arabia. Muḥammad, as a prophet, had little reason to change the existing customary law. His aim was not to establish a new legal order, but to teach men what to do in order to achieve their salvation. This is why Islamic law is a system of duties, of ritual, legal, and moral obligations, all of which are sanctioned by the authority of the same religious command. Thus the Qur'ān commands to arbitrate with justice, to give true evidence, to fulfil one's contracts, and, especially, to return a trust or deposit to its owner. As regards the law of family, which is fairly exhaustively treated in the Qur'ān, the main emphasis is laid on how one should act towards women and children, orphans and relatives, dependants and slaves. In the field of penal law, it is easy to understand that the Qur'ān laid down sanctions for transgressions, but again they are essentially moral and only incidentally penal, so much so that the Qur'ān prohibited wine-drinking but did not enact any penalty, and the penalty was determined only at a later stage of Islamic law. The reasons for Qur'anic legislation on all these matters were, in the first place, the desire to improve the position of women, of orphans and of the weak in general, to restrict the laxity of sexual morals and to strengthen the marriage tie, to restrict private vengeance and retaliation and to eliminate blood feuds altogether; the prohibition of gambling, of drinking wine and of taking interest are directly aimed at ancient Arabian standards of behaviour. The main political aim of the Prophet, the dissolution of the ancient bedouin tribal organization and the creation of an essentially urban community of believers in its stead, gave rise to new problems in family law, in the law of retaliation and in the law of war, and these had to be dealt with. The encouragement of polygamy by the Qur'ān is a case in point. A similar need seems to have called for extensive modifications of the ancient law of inheritance, the broad outlines of which were, however, preserved; here, too, the underlying tendency of the Qur'anic legislation was to favour the underprivileged; it started with enunciating ethical principles which the testators ought to follow, and even in its final stage, when fixed shares in the inheritance were allotted to persons previously excluded from succession, the element of moral exhortation had not disappeared. This feature of Qur'anic legislation was preserved by Islamic law, and the purely legal attitude, which attaches legal consequences to relevant acts, is often superseded by the tendency to impose ethical standards on the believer.

Islamic law as we know it today cannot be said to have existed as yet in the time of Muḥammad; it came gradually into existence during the first century of Islam. It was during this period that nascent Islamic society created its own legal institutions. The ancient Arab system of arbitration, and Arab customary law in general, continued under the first successors of Muḥammad, the caliphs of Medina. In their function as supreme rulers and administrators, the early caliphs acted to a great extent as the lawgivers of the Islamic community; during the whole of this first century the administrative and legislative functions of the Islamic government cannot be separated. But the object of this administrative legislation was not to modify the existing customary law beyond what the Qur'ān had done; it was to organize the newly conquered territories for the benefit of the Arabs, and to assure the viability of the enormously expanded Islamic state. The first caliphs did not, for instance, hesitate to repress severely any manifestation of disloyalty, and even to punish with flogging the authors of satirical poems directed against rival tribes, a recognized form of poetic expression which, however, might have threatened the internal security of the state. This particular decision did not become part of Islamic law, but other enactments of the caliphs of Medina gained official recognition, not as decisions of the caliphs, but because they could be subsumed under one or the other of the official sources of Islamic law which later theory came to recognize. The introduction of stoning to death as a punishment for unchastity under certain conditions is one such enactment. In the theory of Islamic law, its authority derives from alleged commands of the Prophet; there also exists an alleged verse of the Qur'ān to this effect which, however, does not form part of the official text and must be considered spurious. Traditions reporting alleged acts and sayings of the Prophet came into use as proof-texts in law not earlier than the end of the first century of Islam, and the spurious verse of the Qur'ān represents an earlier effort to establish the validity of the penal enactment in question. That the need of this kind of validation was felt at all, shows how exceptional a phenomenon the legislation of Muḥammad had been in the eyes of his contemporaries.

The political schisms which rent the Islamic community when it was still less than forty years old, led to the secession of the two dissident, and later 'heterodox', movements of the Kharijites and of the Shīʿa, but they did not lead to significant new developments in Islamic law; the essentials of a system of religious law did not as yet exist and the political theory of the Shīʿa, which more than anything else might have been expected to lead to the elaboration of quite a different system of law, was developed only later. In fact, those two groups took over Islamic law from the 'orthodox' or Sunnī community as it was being developed there, making only such essentially superficial modifications as were required by their particular political and dogmatic tenets. In one respect, however, the exclusive, and therefore 'sectarian', character of the two secessionist movements influenced not so much the positive contents as the emphasis and presentation of their doctrines of religious law; the law of the Shīʿa is dominated by the concept of *taqiyya*, 'dissimulation' (a practice which, it is true, was forced upon them by the persecutions which they had to suffer), and by the distinction between esoteric and exoteric doctrines in some of their schools of thought; and that of the Kharijites is dominated by the complementary concepts of *walāya*, 'solidarity', and *barā'a*, 'exclusion', 'excommunication'.

At an early period, the ancient Arab idea of *sunna*, precedent or normative custom, reasserted itself in Islam. Whatever was customary was right and proper, whatever their forefathers had done deserved to be imitated, and in the idea of precedent or *sunna* the whole conservatism of

Arabs found expression. This idea presented a formidable obstacle to every innovation, including Islam itself. But once Islam had prevailed, the old conservatism reasserted itself within the new community, and the idea of *sunna* became one of the central concepts of Islamic law.

Sunna in its Islamic context originally had a political rather than a legal connotation. The question whether the administrative acts of the first two caliphs, Abū Bakr and 'Umar, should be regarded as binding precedents, arose probably when a successor to 'Umar had to be appointed in 23/644, and the discontent with the policy of the third caliph, 'Uthmān, which led to his assassination in 35/655, took the form of a charge that he, in his turn, had diverged from the policy of his predecessors and, implicitly, from the Qur'ān. In this connexion, there arose the concept of the '*sunna* of the Prophet', not yet identified with any set of positive rules, but providing a doctrinal link between the '*sunna* of Abū Bakr and 'Umar' and the Qur'ān. The earliest evidence for this use of the term '*sunna* of the Prophet' dates from about 76/695, and we shall see later how it was introduced into the theory of Islamic law.

The thirty years of the caliphs of Medina later appeared, in the picture that the Muslims formed of their own history, as the golden age of Islam. This is far from having been the case. On the contrary, the period of the caliphs of Medina was rather in the nature of a turbulent interval between the first years of Islam under Muḥammad and the Arab kingdom of the Umayyads. Not even the rulings of the Qur'ān were applied without restriction. It can be shown from the development of Islamic legal doctrines that any but the most perfunctory attention given to the Qur'anic norms, and any but the most elementary conclusions drawn from them, belong almost invariably to a secondary and therefore later stage. In several cases the early doctrine of Islamic law is in direct conflict with the clear and explicit wording of the Qur'ān. *Sūra* 5. 6, for instance, says clearly: 'O you who believe, when you rise up for worship, wash your faces and your hands up to the elbows, and wipe over your heads and your feet up to the ankles'; the law nevertheless insists on washing the feet, and this is harmonized with the text by various means. *Sūra* 2. 282 endorsed the current practice of putting contracts, particularly those which provided for performance in the future, into writing, and this practice did in fact persist in Islam. Islamic law, however, emptied the Qur'anic command of all binding force, denied validity to written documents, and insisted on the evidence of eye-witnesses, who in the Qur'anic passage play only a subsidiary part. It is, of course, true that many rules of Islamic law, particularly in the law of family and in the law of inheritance, not to mention worship and ritual, were, in the nature of things, based on the Qur'ān and, we must assume, on the example of Muḥammad from the very beginning. But even here we notice (as far as we are able to draw conclusions on this early period from the somewhat later doctrines of Islamic law) a regression, in so far as pagan and tribal Arab ideas and attitudes succeeded in overriding the intention, if not the wording, of the Qur'anic legislation. This went parallel to, and was indeed caused by, the exacerbation of tribal attitudes in the turbulence created by the Arab wars of conquest and their success. The Qur'ān, in a particular situation, had encouraged polygamy, and this, from being an exception, now became one of the essential features of the Islamic law of marriage. It led to a definite deterioration in the position of married women in society, compared with that which they had enjoyed in pre-Islamic Arabia, and this was only emphasized by the fact that many perfectly respectable sexual relationships of pre-Islamic Arabia had been outlawed by Islam. As against tribal pride and exclusiveness, the Qur'ān had emphasized the fraternity rather than the equality of all Muslims; nevertheless, social discrimination and Arab pride immediately reasserted themselves in Islam. Non-Arab converts to Islam, whatever their previous social standing, were regarded as second-class citizens (*mawālī*) during the first hundred and fifty years of Islam, and all schools of law had to recognize degrees of social rank which did not amount to impediments to marriage but nevertheless, in certain cases, enabled the interested party to demand the dissolution of the marriage by the *qāḍī*. The Qur'ān had taken concubinage for granted, but in the main passage concerning it (*Sūra* 4. 3) concubinage appears as a less expensive alternative to polygamy, a concept far removed from the practice of unlimited concubinage in addition to polygamy which prevailed as early as the first generation after Muḥammad and was sanctioned by all schools of law. Also, the Qur'anic rules concerning repudiation, which had been aimed at safeguarding the interests of the wife, lost much of their value by the way in which they were applied in practice. Early Islamic practice, influenced no doubt by the insecurity which prevailed in the recently founded garrison-cities with their mixed population, extended the seclusion and the veiling of women far beyond what had been envisaged in the Qur'ān, but in doing this it merely applied the clearly formulated intention of the Qur'ān to new conditions. Taking these modifications into account, the pre-Islamic structure of the family survived into Islamic law.

During the greater part of the first/seventh century, Islamic law, in the technical meaning of the term, did not as yet exist. As had been the case in the time of Muḥammad, law as such fell outside the sphere of religion; if no religious or moral objections were involved, the technical aspects of law were a matter of indifference to the Muslims. This accounts for the widespread adoption, or rather survival, of certain legal and administrative institutions and practices of the conquered territories, such as the treatment of the tolerated religions which was closely modelled on the treatment of the Jews in the Byzantine empire, methods of taxation, the institution of *emphyteusis*, and so forth. The principle of the retention of pre-Islamic legal practices under Islam was sometimes openly acknowledged, e.g. by the historian al-Balādhurī (d. 279/892), but generally speaking fictitious Islamic precedents were later invented as a justification.

The acceptance of foreign legal concepts and maxims, extending to methods of reasoning and even to fundamental ideas of legal science, however, demands a more specific explanation. Here the intermediaries were the cultured converts to Islam. During the first two centuries of the *Hijra*, these converts belonged mainly to the higher social classes, they were the only ones to whom admission to Islamic society, even as second-class citizens, promised considerable advantages, and they were the people who (or whose fathers) had enjoyed a liberal education, that is to say, an education in Hellenistic rhetoric, which was the normal one in the countries of the Near East which the Arabs had conquered. This education invariably led to some acquaintance with the rudiments of law. The educated converts brought their familiar ideas with them into their new religion. In fact, the concepts and maxims in question were of that general kind which would be familiar not only to lawyers but to all educated persons. In this way, elements originating from Roman and Byzantine law, from the canon law of the Eastern Churches, from Talmudic and rabbinic law, and from Sasanian law, infiltrated into the nascent religious law of Islam during its period of incubation, to appear in the doctrines of the second/eighth century.

The rule of the caliphs of Medina was supplanted by that of the Umayyads in 41/661. The Umayyads and their governors were responsible for developing a number of the essential features of Islamic worship and ritual. Their main concern, it is true, was not with religion and religious law, but with political administration, and here they represented the centralizing and increasingly bureaucratic tendency of an orderly administration as against bedouin individualism and the anarchy of the Arab way of life. Both Islamic religious ideals and Umayyad administration co-operated in creating a new framework for Arab Muslim society. In many respects Umayyad rule represents the consummation, after the turbulent interval of the caliphate of Medina, of tendencies which were inherent in the nature of the community of Muslims under Muḥammad. It was the period of incubation of Islamic civilization and, within it, of the religious law of Islam.

The administration of the Umayyads concentrated on waging war against the Byzantines and other external enemies, on assuring the internal security of the state, and on collecting revenue from the subject populations and paying subventions in money or in kind to the Arab beneficiaries. We therefore find evidence of Umayyad regulations or administrative law mainly in the fields of the law of war and of fiscal law. All this covered essentially the same ground as the administrative legislation of the caliphs of Medina, but the social background was sensibly different. The Umayyads did not interfere with the working of retaliation as it had been regulated by the Qur'ān, but they tried to prevent the recurrence of Arab tribal feuds and assumed the accountancy for payments of blood-money, which were effected in connexion with the payment of subventions. On the other hand, they supervised the application of the purely Islamic penalties, not always in strict conformity with the rules laid down in the Qur'ān.

The Umayyads, or rather their governors, also took the important step of appointing Islamic judges or *qāḍīs*. The office of *qāḍī* was created in and for the new Islamic society which came into being, under the new conditions resulting from the Arab conquest, in the urban centres of the Arab kingdom. For this new society, the arbitration of pre-Islamic Arabia and of the earliest period of Islam was no longer adequate, and the Arab arbitrator was superseded by the Islamic *qāḍī*. It was only natural for the *qāḍī* to take over the seat and wand of the arbitrator, but, in contrast with the latter, the *qāḍī* was a delegate of the governor. The governor, within the limits set for him by the caliph, had full authority over his province, administrative, legislative, and judicial, without any conscious distinction of functions; and he could, and in fact regularly did, delegate his judicial authority to his 'legal secretary', the *qāḍī*. The governor retained, however, the power of reserving for his own decision any lawsuit he wished, and, of course, of dismissing his *qāḍī* at will. The contemporary Christian author, John of Damascus, refers to these governors and their delegates, the *qāḍīs*, as the lawgivers of Islam. By their decisions, the earliest Islamic *qāḍīs*, did indeed lay the basic foundations of what was to become Islamic law. They gave judgment according to their own discretion or 'sound opinion' (*ra'y*), basing themselves on customary practice which in the nature of things incorporated administrative regulations, and taking the letter and the spirit of the Qur'anic regulations and other recognized Islamic religious norms into account as much as they thought fit. Whereas the legal subject-matter had not as yet been islamized to any great extent beyond the stage reached in the Qur'ān, the office of *qāḍī* itself was an Islamic institution typical of the Umayyad period, in which care for elementary administrative efficiency and the tendency to islamize went hand in hand. The subsequent development of Islamic law, however, brought it about that the part played by the earliest *qāḍīs* in creating it did not achieve recognition in the legal theory which finally prevailed.

A typical example of the way in which the activity of the early *qāḍīs* influenced Islamic law is provided by the law of procedure. The Qur'ān had not only endorsed the use of written documents as evidence; it had also provided for putting the witnesses on oath in certain circumstances (*Sūra* 5. 106–8). Islamic law rejected the first, and neglected the second provision, and had it not been for the early *qāḍīs*, the hard and fast rule that evidence by witnesses, who are not put on oath, has to be produced by the plaintiff, and if no such evidence is produced, the oath in denial has to be taken by the defendant, would have been applied to the letter. The early *qāḍīs*, however, constantly tried to impose safeguards on the exclusive use of the testimony of witnesses as evidence, and this tendency has left more or less extensive traces in several schools of Islamic law.

The jurisdiction of the *qāḍī* extended to Muslims only; the non-Muslim subject populations retained their own traditional legal institutions, including the ecclesiastical and rabbinical tribunals, which in the last few centuries before the Arab conquest had to a great extent duplicated the judicial organization of the Byzantine state. This is the basis of the factual legal autonomy of the non-Muslims which was extensive in the Middle Ages, and has survived in part down to the present generation. The Byzantine magistrates themselves had left the lost provinces at the time of the conquest, but an office of local administration, the functions of which were partly judicial, was adopted by the Muslims: the office of the 'inspector of the market' or agoranome, of which the Arabic designation *'āmil al-suq* or *ṣāḥib al-sūq* is a literal translation. In the last few centuries before the Muslim conquest this office had lost its originally high status, but had remained a popular institution among the settled populations of the Near East. Later, under the early 'Abbasids, it developed into the Islamic office of the *muḥtasib*. Similarly, the Muslims took over the office of the 'clerk of the court' from the Sasanian administration.

The work of the *qāḍīs* became inevitably more and more specialized, and we may take it for granted that from the turn of the first/seventh century onwards appointments as a rule went to specialists, to persons sufficiently interested in the subject to have given it serious thought in their spare time. Their main concern, in the intellectual climate of the late Umayyad period, was naturally to know whether the customary law which they administered conformed to the Qur'anic and generally Islamic norms; in other words, the specialists would be found normally within that group of pious persons who were at the same time working out an Islamic way of life. Once more, the care for efficient administration of justice and the tendency to islamize went hand in hand. Their interest in religion caused them to survey, either individually or in discussion with like-minded friends, all fields of contemporary activities, including the field of law, from an Islamic angle, and to impregnate the sphere of law with religious and ethical ideas. Their reasoning, which in the nature of things expressed their own individual opinion (*ra'y*), represents the beginnings of Islamic jurisprudence. In doing this, they achieved on a much wider scale and in a vastly more detailed manner what Muḥammad had tried to do for the early Islamic community of Medina. As a result, the popular and administrative practice of the late Umayyad period was transformed into the religious law of Islam. But the close personal connexion between the groups of pious persons and the *qāḍīs* notwithstanding, Islamic law did not grow out of the practice, it came into being as the expression of a religious ideal in opposition to it.

The pious specialists on the sacred law were held in respect both by the public and the rulers, and they owed their authority to their single-minded concern with the ideal of a life according to the tenets of Islam. They stood outside the political structure of the Arab kingdom of the Umayyads, and their main function was to give cautelary advice on the correct way of acting to those of their co-religionists who asked for it; in other words, they were the first *muftīs* in Islam. Islamic law has preserved much of this cautelary character over the centuries; it is dominant in the teaching of Mālik in Medina in the second/eighth century, and it recurs in strength in the medieval *ḥiyal* or 'legal devices'. The pious specialists often had occasion to criticize the acts and regulations of the government, just as they had to declare undesirable many popular practices, but they were not in political opposition to the Umayyads and to the established Islamic state; on the contrary, the whole of the Umayyad period was, at a certain distance, viewed as part of the 'good old time'; this idealizing of things past was the first manifestation in Islam of a tendency which, a few decades later, was to lead to one of the most thorough and most successful of literary fictions. The attitude of the pious specialists to the Umayyad government anticipates the attitude of the religious scholars of Islam to any Islamic government.

As the groups of pious specialists grew in numbers and in cohesion, they developed, in the first decades of the second/eighth century, into what may be called the ancient schools of law, a term which implies neither any definite organization, nor a strict uniformity of doctrine within each school, nor any formal teaching, nor even the existence of a body of law in the usual meaning of the term. Their members continued to be private individuals, singled out from the great mass of the Muslims by their special interest, the resultant reverence of the people, and the recognition as kindred spirits which they themselves accorded to one another. It can be said that the division of the Muslims into two classes, the *élite* and the *vulgus*, dates from the emergence of the ancient schools of law. The more important ancient schools of which we have knowledge are those of Kūfa and of Baṣra in 'Irāq, of Medina and of Mecca in the Ḥijāz, and of Syria. The differences between them were caused, in the first place, by geographical factors, such as local variations in social conditions, customary law, and practice, but they were not based on any noticeable disagreement on principles and methods. On principle, the ancient schools were inclined to disturb the practice as little as possible; because of the nature of our documentation, this can be particularly clearly observed in the case of the Medinese and of the Syrians.

The doctrines of the several schools enable us to discern the contrast between the social realities in that ancient Arab land that was the Ḥijāz, and the newly conquered territory of old civilization that was 'Irāq, as well as the various reactions of the ancient lawyers of Islam to them.

The legal integration of the wife into the family of the husband had begun with the Qur'ān, when the wife was guaranteed a share in the inheritance, and the ancient lawyers followed the same tendency by giving the right to inherit to certain female relatives who did not possess it originally. But the school of Kūfa alone went so far as to extend the right to inherit, after the agnates, to a group roughly corresponding to the cognates. The school of Medina rejected this absolutely. On the other hand, the tendency expressed by the school of Kūfa found its consummation only in the doctrine of the Twelver Shī'īs who unite the agnates and the cognates in one single group. The Twelver Shī'īs lay emphasis also on the narrowly defined family, consisting of father, mother and their children and grandchildren, against the broader concept of family, merging into the old Arabian tribal system, which forms the background of the Sunnī law of inheritance. 'Irāq was indeed the intellectual centre of early Shi'ism, and Shī'ī law (and, for that matter, Kharijite law) has occasionally preserved early 'Irāqī doctrines which were later abandoned by the orthodox. The legal position of the unmarried girl and of the wife within the family, and their legal capacity, were decidedly more favourable in 'Irāq than in the Ḥijāz. On the other hand, the marriage bond was more rigid there, in so far as in 'Irāq the wife was inadequately protected even against grave derelictions of duty by the husband, such as failure to provide maintenance, or grave maltreatment; the school of Medina gave her the possibility of suing for divorce in these two cases, a rule which continued, it seems, a practice of Arab customary law which allowed the abandoned or maltreated wife to recover her freedom. As regards the status of the slave, the doctrines of the school of Medina show a certain paternalism which seems to derive from the social conditions in the cities of the Ḥijāz not less than from the civilizing influence of Islam. The Muslim slave, within the patriarchal family, enjoys a status similar to that of a free man; he may conclude a valid marriage by himself, without having secured the previous approval of his master (although the master may subsequently dissolve it); he may marry four wives just as a free man may (in contrast with the general rule which reduces all numbers given in the Qur'ān by half for the slave); he has (notwithstanding certain restrictions) a real right of ownership; if he is authorized to trade, his transactions engage only his stock-in-trade and not his person so that he cannot be sold to pay off a debt; and if he is gravely maltreated he can demand his freedom. None of this is accepted by the school of Kūfa;

in addition, according to the latter, he cannot act as leader of the ritual prayer if it is performed in common, he is not entitled to the Qur'anic procedure of *li'ān* if he suspects his wife of adultery, his blood-money must always be less than that of a free man, and the master is in no case obliged to acknowledge the paternity of children which his female slave has borne. (The rule that children born by a concubine to her master and acknowledged by him as his own are free and in all respects equal to his children by a marriage with a free wife, goes beyond pre-Islamic practice, and is not explicitly laid down in the Qur'ān; it must have asserted itself early in the first century, and it became of great importance in the development of Islamic society.) This hardening shows, no doubt, a more rigid and more differentiated society in which the social classes were more firmly separated, the result, in short, of a certain evolution. On the other hand, the school of Kūfa was more ready to set free certain categories of slaves, to reduce the rigours of penal law for the slave, and to protect his life by making a free man who had murdered him, liable to retaliation. The *'āqila*, the group of persons called upon to pay the blood-money in a case of unintentional killing or wounding, consisted originally, and still consists according to the doctrine of the school of Medina, of the agnates. According to the doctrine of the school of Kūfa, however, it consists of those whose names, as members of the Muslim army, are inscribed in the same army list or pay-roll, alternatively of the members of the same tribe, or alternatively of the fellow-workers in the same craft. This shows most clearly the result of profound social changes. The *qasāma*, the collective oath in criminal procedure when the person of the murderer is unknown, is, in the doctrine of the school of Medina, an affirmative oath by the members of the tribe of the victim which is sufficient to make the accused liable to retaliation. The Umayyad caliphs tried to mitigate its effect. The doctrine of the Kufans, however, recognized only a contradictory oath, not by the members of a tribe but by the inhabitants of the locality in question. Concerning pre-emption, the school of Medina was satisfied with laying down the rule that the co-owner was entitled to it; this was normally sufficient to ensure that strangers did not infiltrate the property owned by members of the same family or clan. In 'Irāq, however, this formula was not found sufficient, and in order to preclude the intrusion of strangers, it was found necessary to extend the right of pre-emption to neighbours, that is to say, owners of adjoining plots even if they were not technically co-owners of the property in question, provided their respective plots were entered by a common gate from a lane or thoroughfare, a kind of settlement common in the new cities of Islam which nevertheless preserved the identity of tribal associations. This provides a vivid picture of the lay-out of building plots in 'Irāq in the second/eighth century. It was only later that the Ḥijāzī and the 'Irāqī doctrines were crystallized into the propositions that the right of pre-emption belonged to any co-owner or to any neighbour, whoever he might be. It is also not by accident that the degrees of social rank which aimed at perpetuating the social superiority of the Arabs over the *mawālī* were elaborated outside Arabia, in 'Irāq, and that the procedure of becoming a *mawlā* by contract was recognized by the school of 'Irāq, where it was of great practical importance, but ignored by that of Medina. The law of property and of obligations, too, as formulated by the schools of Kūfa and of Medina respectively, shows society in 'Irāq more differentiated and more closely controlled by the state than in Medina.

Whereas the ancient schools of law reflected different social realities, their general attitude to popular practice and administrative regulations was essentially the same, and it was certainly not the case, as has often, and recently too, been asserted, that the school of Medina was more traditional in its outlook and the school of 'Irāq more given to individual reasoning. It is true that, apart from differences in social development which are reflected in the doctrine, the doctrines of the school of Medina represent, generally speaking, an earlier stage of development of legal thought. But this means merely that the doctrinal development of the school of Medina often lagged behind that of the school of Kūfa. 'Irāq was the intellectual centre of the first theorizing and systematizing efforts which were to transform Umayyad popular and administrative practice into Islamic law, and the ascendancy of 'Irāq in the development of religious law and jurisprudence continued during the whole of the second/eighth century. This is in keeping with intellectual development generally during the period.

The ancient schools shared not only a common attitude to Umayyad practice and, of course, a considerable body of positive religious law but the essentials of a legal theory, the central concept of which was the 'living tradition of the school'. This idea dominated the development of Islamic law and jurisprudence during the whole of the second/eighth century. Retrospectively it appears as the *sunna* or 'well-established precedent', or 'practice' (*'amal*), or 'ancient practice' (*amr qadīm*). This 'practice' partly reflected the actual custom of the local community of Muslims, but it also contained a theoretical or ideal element, so that it came to mean normative *sunna*, the usage as it ought to be. Already at this early stage, a divergence between theory and practice manifested itself. The ideal practice was found in the unanimous doctrine of the representative religious scholars of each centre. This consensus of the scholars, representing the common denominator of doctrine achieved in each generation, expresses the synchronous aspect of the living tradition of each school. It is significant that the real basis of the doctrine of each school is not the consensus of all Muslims (which also exists) but of the scholars; the function of the class of *'ulamā'* in Islamic society was firmly established in that early period.

The need of creating some kind of theoretical justification for what so far had been an instinctive reliance on the opinions of the majority, led, from the first decades of the second/eighth century onwards, to the living tradition being retrojected, and to its being ascribed to some of the great figures of the past. This process, too, began in Kūfa, where the stage of doctrine achieved in the time of Ḥammād b. Abī Sulaymān (d. 120/738) was attributed to Ibrāhīm al-Nakha'ī (d. 95–6/713–15). The Medinese followed suit and retrojected their own teaching to a number of ancient authorities who had died about the turn of the century, some of whom later became known as the 'seven jurists of Medina'. At the same time as the doctrine of the school of Kūfa was retrospectively attributed to Ibrāhīm al-Nakha'ī, a similar body of doctrine was directly connected with the very beginnings of Islam in Kūfa by being attributed to Ibn Mas'ūd, a Companion of the Prophet who had come to live in that city, and Ibrāhīm al-Nakha'ī became the main transmitter of that body of doctrine, too. In the same way, other Companions of the Prophet became the eponyms of the schools of Medina and of Mecca. One further step in the search for a solid theoretical foundation of the doctrine of the ancient schools was taken in 'Irāq, very early in the second/eighth century, when the term '*sunna* of the Prophet' was transferred from its political and theological into a legal context, and identified with the *sunna*, the ideal practice of the local community and the corresponding doctrine of its scholars. This term, which was taken over by the school of Syria, expressed the axiom that the practice of the Muslims derived from the practice of the Prophet, but it did not as yet imply the existence of positive information in the form of 'Traditions' (*Ḥadīth*), that the Prophet by his words or acts had in fact originated or approved any particular practice. It was not long before these Traditions, too, came into existence, and the persons who put them into circulation were the Traditionists.

The ancient schools of law themselves represented, in one aspect, an Islamic opposition to popular and administrative practice under the later Umayyads, and the opposition group which developed into the Traditionist movement emphasized this tendency. As long as a Companion of the Prophet had been the final authority for the doctrine of a school on a particular point, it was sufficient for a divergent doctrine to be put under the aegis of another Companion of equal or even higher authority, as happened in Kūfa where all kinds of minority opinions were attributed to the Caliph 'Alī, who had made Kūfa his capital. But after the general authority of the Prophet himself had been invoked by identifying the established doctrine with his *sunna*, a more specific reference to him was needed, and there appeared detailed statements or 'Traditions' which claimed to be the reports of ear- or eye-witnesses on the words or acts of the Prophet, handed down orally by an uninterrupted chain of trustworthy persons. Very soon the emphasis shifted from proposing certain opinions in opposition to the ancient schools to disseminating Traditions from the Prophet as such, and the movement of the Traditionists, which was to develop into a separate branch of Islamic religious learning, came into being. It was the main thesis of the Traditionists that formal Traditions from the Prophet superseded the living tradition of the school. The Traditionists existed in all great centres of Islam, where they formed groups in opposition to, but nevertheless in contact with, the local schools of law. Initially the ancient schools offered strong resistance to the disturbing element represented by the Traditions, but they had no real defence against their rising tide; they had to express their own doctrines in Traditions which allegedly went back to the Prophet, and to take increasing notice of the Traditions produced by their opponents. Finally the outlines and many details of Islamic law were cast into the form of Traditions from the Prophet. In this way, one of the greatest and most successful literary fictions came into being.

When the Umayyads were overthrown by the 'Abbasids in 132/750, Islamic law, though still in its formative stage, had acquired its essential features; the need of Arab Muslim society for a new legal system had been filled. The early 'Abbasids continued and reinforced the islamizing trend which had become more and more noticeable under the later Umayyads. For reasons of dynastic policy, and in order to differentiate themselves from their predecessors, the 'Abbasids posed as the protagonists of Islam, attracted specialists in religious law to their court, consulted them on problems within their competence, and set out to translate their doctrines into practice. But this effort was shortlived. The early specialists who had formulated their doctrine not on the basis of, but in a certain opposition to, Umayyad popular and administrative practice, had been ahead of realities, and now the early ʻAbbasids and their religious advisers were unable to carry the whole of society with them. This double-sided effect of the ʻAbbasid revolution shows itself clearly in the development of the office of *qāḍī*. The *qāḍī* was not any more the legal secretary of the governor; he was normally appointed by the caliph, and until relieved of his office, he must apply nothing but the sacred law, without interference from the government. But theoretically independent though they were, the *qāḍīs* had to rely on the political authorities for the execution of their judgments, and being bound by the formal rules of the Islamic law of evidence, their inability to deal with criminal cases became apparent. (Under the Umayyads, they or the governors themselves had exercised whatever criminal justice came within their competence.) Therefore the administration of the greater part of criminal justice was taken over by the police, and it remained outside the sphere of practical application of Islamic law. The centralizing tendency of the early ʻAbbasids also led, perhaps under the influence of a feature of Sasanian administration, to the creation of the office of chief *qāḍī*. It was originally an honorific title given to the *qāḍī* of the capital, but the chief *qāḍī* soon became one of the most important counsellors of the caliph, and the appointment and dismissal of the other *qāḍīs*, under the authority of the caliph, became the main function of his office.

An institution which the early ʻAbbasids, and perhaps already the later Umayyads, borrowed from the administrative tradition of the Sasanian kings was the 'investigation of complaints' concerning miscarriage or denial of justice, or other allegedly unlawful acts of the *qāḍīs*, difficulties in securing the execution of judgments, wrongs committed by government officials or by powerful individuals, and similar matters. Very soon, formal courts of complaints (*al-naẓar fi'l-maẓālim*) were set up, and their jurisdiction became to a great extent concurrent with that of the *qāḍīs*' tribunals. The very existence of these tribunals, which were established ostensibly in order to supplement the deficiencies of the jurisdiction of the *qāḍīs*, shows that their administration of justice had largely broken down at an early period. Since then, there has been a double administration of justice, one religious and the other secular, in practically the whole of the Islamic world.

At the same time, the office of the 'inspector of the market' was islamized. Its holder, in addition to his ancient functions, was now entrusted with discharging the collective obligations of enforcing Islamic morals, and he was given the Islamic title of *muḥtasib*; it was now part of his duties to bring transgressors to justice and to impose summary punishments, which on occasion came to include the flogging of the drunk and the unchaste, and even the amputation of the hands of thieves caught in the act; but the eagerness of the rulers to enforce these provisions commonly made them overlook the fact that the procedure of the *muḥtasib* did not always satisfy the strict demands of the law.

The caliph, too, was given a place in the religious law of Islam. He was endowed with the attributes of a religious scholar and lawyer, bound to the sacred law in the same way as *qāḍīs* were bound to it, and given the same right to the exercise of personal opinion as was admitted by the schools of law. The caliph retained full judicial power, the *qāḍīs* were merely his delegates, but he did not have the right to legislate; he could only make administrative regulations within the limits laid down by the sacred law, and the *qāḍīs* were obliged to follow his instructions within those limits. This doctrine disregarded the fact that what was actually legislation on the part of the caliphs of Medina, and particularly of the Umayyads, had to a great extent entered the fabric of Islamic law. The later caliphs and other secular rulers often enacted new rules; but although this was in fact legislation, the rulers used to call it administration, and they maintained the fiction that their regulations served only to apply, to supplement, and to enforce the sacred law. This ambiguity pervaded the whole of Islamic administration during the Middle Ages and beyond. In practice, the rulers were generally content with making regulations on matters which had escaped the control of the *qāḍīs*, such as police, taxation and criminal justice. The most important examples of this kind of secular law are the *siyāsa* of the Mamluk sultans of Egypt which applied to the military ruling class, and, later, the *qānūn-nāmes* of the Ottoman sultans. Only in the present generation has a secular, modernist legislation, directly aimed at modifying Islamic law in its traditional form, come into being; this became possible only through the reception of Western political ideas. But the postulate that law, as well as other human relationships, must be ruled by religion, has become an essential part of the outlook of the Muslim Arabs, including the modernists among them.

Notwithstanding all this, the office of *qāḍī* in the form which it essentially acquired under the early 'Abbasids, proved to be one of the most vigorous institutions evolved by Islamic society. *Qāḍīs* were often made military commanders, and examples are particularly numerous in Muslim Spain and in the Maghrib in general. They often played important political parts, although it is not always possible to distinguish the purely personal element from the prestige inherent in the office. Particularly in the Ayyubid and in the Mamluk periods, they were appointed to various administrative offices. They even became heads of principalities and founders of small dynasties from the fifth/eleventh century onwards, when the central power had disintegrated; there are especially numerous examples in Muslim Spain in the time of the *Mulūk al-Ṭawā'if* (Party Kings) and others occur in Syria, Anatolia and Central Asia. In the Ottoman system of provincial administration, the *qāḍī* was the main authority in the area of his jurisdiction, and elsewhere, as in medieval Persia, he became the main representative of what is called the religious institution. To some extent the *qāḍīs* (and the other religious scholars, too) were the spokesmen of the people; they played an important part not only in preserving the balance of the state but also in maintaining Islamic civilization, and in times of disorder they constituted an element of stability. Nevertheless, as far as the essence of the *qāḍī*'s office was concerned, a real independence of the judiciary, though recognized in theory, was hardly ever achieved in practice.

Very soon after the 'Abbasid revolution, Islamic Spain broke away and became, under a surviving member of the Umayyad family and his descendants, an independent amirate and later caliphate. It is therefore not surprising that Islamic law and justice as applied in Spain should have diverged in some respects (not very essential ones, it is true) from their counterparts in the East. Whereas the *qāḍī* was always in principle a single judge, it was taken for granted in Spain that he should sit 'in council' (*shūrā*). The 'Abbasid institution of the chief *qāḍī* took a long time to become acclimatized in Spain. Although the adoption of the Sasanian 'investigation of complaints' by Islamic law probably dated from the end of the Umayyad period in the East, it had no real parallel in Spain. The 'inspector of the market' retained his ancient title in Spain for centuries, and the theory of his functions was somewhat different there from what it was in the East.

The first half of the second/eighth century was a period of particularly rapid development for Islamic law, and this is well shown by the memorandum which the secretary of state, Ibn al-Muqaffaʿ, presented to the ʿAbbasid caliph, al-Manṣūr, at some time during the last few years of his life (he was cruelly put to death in 139/756). Written by an intelligent and observant outsider, a Persian convert to Islam, it shows us aspects of the stage reached by Islamic law about 140/757–8 which we should not be able to deduce from more conventional sources. Ibn al-Muqaffaʿ deplored the wide divergencies in the administration of justice which existed between the several great cities and even (a completely unexpected piece of information) between their several quarters, and between the main schools of law. He suggested therefore that the caliph should review the different doctrines, codify and enact his own decisions in the interest of uniformity, and make this code binding on the *qāḍīs*. This code ought to be revised by successive caliphs. The caliph alone had the right to decide at his discretion; he could give binding orders on military and on civil administration, but he must be guided by Qur'ān and *sunna*. This *sunna*, Ibn al-Muqaffaʿ realized, was based to a great extent on administrative regulations of the Umayyads. Therefore, he concluded the caliph was free to determine and codify the *sunna* as he thought fit. The plea of Ibn al-Muqaffaʿ for state control over law (and, incidentally, over religion, too) was in full accord with the tendencies prevailing at the very beginning of the ʿAbbasid era. But this was merely a passing phase, and orthodox Islam refused to be drawn into too close a connexion with the state. The result was that Islamic law grew away from practice, but in the long run gained more in power over the minds than it lost in control over the bodies of the Muslims.

A little later, towards the end of the second/eighth century, al-Shāfiʿī made the essential thesis of the Traditionists prevail in Islamic law. For him, *sunna* was not the idealized practice as recognized by the representative scholars; it was identical with the contents of formal 'Traditions' going back to the Prophet, even if such a Tradition was transmitted by only one person in each generation (a fact which, of course, made it very suspect to the ancient schools). This new concept of *sunna*, the *sunna* of the Prophet embodied in formal Traditions from him, superseded the concept of the living tradition of the ancient schools. According to al-Shāfiʿī, even the Qur'ān had to be interpreted in the light of these Traditions, and not vice versa. The consensus of the scholars, too, became irrelevant for him; he fell back on the thesis that the community of Muslims at large could never agree on an error, a thesis sufficiently vague for his purpose. All this left no room for the discretionary exercise of personal opinion, and human reasoning was restricted, in al-Shāfiʿī's thesis, to making correct inferences and drawing systematic conclusions from Traditions. In accepting the thesis of the Traditionists, al-Shāfiʿī cut himself off from the natural and continuous development of doctrine in the ancient schools, and adopted a principle which, in the long run, could only lead to inflexibility. Also, the positive solutions of problems which he proposed were often, sociologically speaking, less advanced than those advocated by the contemporary ʿIrāqīs and Medinese; his reasoning, dominated as it was by a retrospective point of view, could hardly be productive of progressive solutions. Al-Shāfiʿī's was a personal achievement, and his disciples and followers formed from the very beginning the 'personal' school (*madhhab*) of the Shāfiʿīs. The schools of Kūfa and Medina, too, had seen the formation of groups or circles within each school, and early in the third/ninth century the geographical character of the ancient schools gradually disappeared, and personal allegiance to a master and his doctrine became preponderant.

Whereas the Ḥanafīs and the Mālikīs, who continued the ancient schools of Kūfa and of Medina (their names are derived from Abū Ḥanīfa and from Mālik, respectively), did not change their positive legal doctrines appreciably from what they had been when al-Shāfiʿī appeared, they finally adopted in the course of the third/ninth century, together with the Shāfiʿīs, a legal theory of Traditionist inspiration. This theory differed from al-Shāfiʿī's own thesis in one essential respect, in that it returned to the concept of the consensus of the scholars, which it considered infallible. It endorsed al-Shāfiʿī's identification of the *sunna* with the contents of Traditions from the Prophet, but the legal rules which were to be derived from the Traditions were to be determined by the consensus of the scholars, which left the representatives of each school free to determine them for themselves, by interpretation and so forth. The fact that the Shāfiʿī school itself had to accept this modification of the doctrine of its founder shows the hold which the idea of the consensus of the scholars, embodying the living tradition of the ancient schools, had gained over Islamic law, and, by implication, how strong the position of the class of specialists had become.

Islamic law reached its full development in early ʿAbbasid times, and its institutions reflect the social and economic conditions of Islamic society in that period more than any other. The various social backgrounds of the doctrines of the Medinese and of the 'Irāqīs have already been mentioned. A feature which may, perhaps, reflect conditions proper to the early 'Abbasid period is the detailed treatment of 'usurpation' of the property of another, neither theft nor robbery, but high-handed appropriation. The provisions of Islamic law aim at protecting the rightful owner as much as possible, but at the same time make the frequency of similar acts, and the inability of the *qāḍī* to deal with them, painfully clear. The *waqf* or mortmain, too, found its final regulation at that time. The roots of this institution are various. One, which left only faint traces in Islamic law, and in the Mālikī school more than in the Ḥanafī, can be traced to certain kinds of annuity, to use a modern, roughly approximate term, in use among the ancient Arabs; another, still very important at the beginning of the third/ninth century, though later quite pushed into the background, consisted of contributions to the Holy War, the object of innumerable exhortations in the Qur'ān; a third, particular to Egypt during the first few centuries of Islam, seems to derive from the example of the Byzantine *piae causae*; and a fourth, which expanded enormously, particularly in 'Irāq, in the first half of the third/ninth century, and which was, perhaps, most decisive in shaping the final doctrine of Islamic law concerning *waqf*, arose from the desire of the Muslim middle classes to exclude the daughters and, even more so, the descendants of daughters from the benefits of the Qur'anic law of succession; in other words, to strengthen the old Arab patriarchal family system, and also to provide for the *mawālī* in order to make them reliable dependants of the family of the founder; both aims being in conflict with the purpose of the Qur'anic legislation. The *waqf*, and this may be counted its fifth and last root, also enjoyed a degree of security unknown to any other form of tenure, and its use became popular as a guarantee against confiscation. So was another procedure known to Islamic law, the fictitious sale or *talji'a*. Two things are significant here: confiscation with its concomitant procedure of torture, which had become almost a fixed institution of the Islamic state at the end of the Umayyad and particularly at the beginning of the 'Abbasid period, was not taken into consideration at all by Islamic law; in other words, the pious specialists averted their eyes from procedures which they knew were wrong but which they felt they could not, without material damage to themselves, openly criticize. On the other hand, even the early 'Abbasid caliphs and their highhanded and powerful dignitaries were averse to interfering openly with transactions which on the face of it, were valid under the religious law of Islam. Ibn Qutayba (d. 276/889), Traditionist and man of letters, held that the injustice of rulers and the highhandedness of overweening persons, and even the insistence of a creditor on being paid, justified lies and perjury. At a slightly later period, the poet and philologist Ibn Durayd (d. 321/933) composed a treatise on equivocal expressions for the benefit of people who were forced to take an oath against their will, so as to enable them 'to mean something different from what they appear to say, and to save them from the injustice of the oppressor'.

Another omission of Islamic law is more difficult to explain, that of practically all reference to wholesale trade. The activities of wholesale merchants covered the whole of the Islamic world and extended beyond it, and they have left permanent traces in the merchant law of the early Middle Ages. Islamic law treats in great detail of many commercial transactions, but they are, as a rule, envisaged exclusively as transactions of retail trade, and the background of wholesale trading can only be inferred from occasional remarks and from isolated chapters such as those on the contract of *muḍāraba* or *qirāḍ* (*commenda*, which, incidentally, seems to have come to Western Europe from Islamic law). It is true that Islamic law is in the first place concerned with laying down ethical rules for the behaviour of the individual in a society the composition of which is taken for granted, but it is equally true that the wholesale trader, by the nature of his activities, is exposed, from the point of view of Islamic law, to particular moral hazards, which that law might have been expected to point out and safeguard against with the same interest in details as it does with regard to those involved in a householder sending out a minor to buy a loaf of bread. Generally speaking, Islamic law pays particular attention to transactions involving the middle or the lower-middle class; for instance, it appears clearly from legal terminology that the economic reality underlying the contract of *salam*, the ordering of goods to be delivered later for a price paid in advance, was the financing of the business of a small trader or artisan by his customers. A saying attributed to the Caliph 'Umar, which occurs in Mālik's *Muwaṭṭa'*, is specifically directed against the activities of the rich speculators, who buy up supplies of food, anticipating a rise in prices, but exempts the small importer, who carries merchandise 'on his back in summer and in winter'. Merchants are also forbidden to meet caravans outside the town and to buy up what they bring, and a sedentary ought not to act as a sales agent of a bedouin. On the other hand, the *Ḥamāsa* of al-Buḥturī (d. 284/897) contains numerous extracts from the poetic effusions of bedouin, who boasted of having cheated the merchants from whom they had bought.

We are particularly well-informed concerning relations between neighbours in Mālikī law. As interpreted by this school, Islamic law shows itself more humane than juridical. It puts the interest of certain social groups first; but these groups are, as a rule, neither state nor province nor city; in the last resort it is the family which matters, and this concern is reinforced by an easy-going acceptance of the *fait accompli*. The society envisaged by Islamic law is mainly urban, just as medieval Islam was essentially an urban civilization, but Islamic law did not recognize the city as such, nor did it admit corporate bodies. The doctrine of Islamic law does not attach great importance to differences of social status between free, male Muslims except, to some extent, in the requirement of the bridegroom's rank being equal to that of the bride, and, more important, the disqualification of members of certain low trades as witnesses. The doctrines of the several schools differ in details, and have undergone certain changes in the course of time. In a society in which the most highly respected economic activity was not that of the producer but of the merchant, the moralists tried to enhance the functions of the farmer and of the artisan, without, however, quite succeeding. Trade in cloth is generally regarded as the most honourable of professions, and sometimes trade in spices is associated with it. The professions of money-changer and of grain merchant are generally discredited, the first because it risks transgressing the complicated rules devised against 'usury', and the second because it leads to speculation on rising prices of food. The two 'low trades' *par excellence* were those of cupper and of weaver, and the contempt in which they were held seems to go back, in each case, to pre-Islamic times.

The early 'Abbasid period saw the end of the formative stage of Islamic law, and by the beginning of the fourth/tenth century a point had been reached when the scholars of all schools felt that all essential questions had been thoroughly discussed and finally settled (albeit with a choice of answers provided by the several schools); hence a consensus gradually established itself to the effect that from that time onwards no one could be deemed to have the necessary qualifications for independent reasoning in religious law, and that all future activity would have to be confined to the explanation, application, and, at the most, interpretation of the doctrine as it had been laid down once and for all. This is the 'closing of the gate of *ijtihād*', of independent reasoning in Islamic law. It is only in the present century that the reopening of this gate has been seriously envisaged by a number of '*ulamā*' and by Islamic society at large. The doctrine of the 'closing of the gate of *ijtihād*' was not the cause but a symptom of a state of mind which had been induced by the fear of doctrinal disintegration, a fear which was not far-fetched at a time when orthodox Islam was threatened by the esoteric propaganda of the Bāṭiniyya. When this propaganda had brought the Fatimid caliphs to power, first in Ifrīqiya and then in Egypt, they too felt the need of a doctrine of religious law of their own, and their great lawyer, the *Qāḍī* Nu'mān, provided it for them. It was a learned production which drew largely on the doctrines of the existing orthodox schools of law, rather than the result of organic growth, and it confirms the absence of a genuine Shī'ī (as opposed to the general Islamic) tradition of religious law. Whatever the theory might say on the closing of the gate of *ijtihād*, the activity of the later scholars was no less creative, within the limits set by the very nature of their work, than that of their predecessors. New sets of facts constantly arose in life, and they had to be mastered and moulded with the traditional tools provided by legal science. This activity was carried out by the *muftīs*, specialists on religious law who were qualified to give authoritative opinions on points of doctrine. The earliest specialists on religious law had been essentially religious advisers, *muftīs*, and the later *muftīs* only continued their advisory and cautelary activity. Their function was essentially private, and although *muftīs* could be, and often were, appointed officially, it did not add to their authority. The most important officially appointed *muftī* in later times was the Ottoman *shaykh al-Islām*. The doctrinal development of Islamic law owes much to the activity of the *muftīs*, and their advices, or *fatwās*, show us the most urgent problems which arose from practice in certain places and at certain times. Their decisions, if found acceptable, were generally incorporated into the later handbooks, and, generally speaking, the accretion of new cases and decisions in the interval between two comparable works of Islamic law represents the outcome of the discussion in the meantime.

Whereas Islamic law had been adaptable and growing until the early 'Abbasid period, from then onwards it became increasingly rigid and set in its final mould. A doctrine which had to be derived exclusively from the Qur'ān and, even more important, from a number of detailed Traditions from the Prophet, and became more and more hedged in by the ever growing area of the consensus of the scholars, and by the closing of the gate of *ijtihād*, was unable to keep pace with the changing demands of society and commerce. This essential rigidity of Islamic law helped it to maintain its stability over the centuries which saw the decay of the political institutions of Islam. From the early ʿAbbasid period onwards, we notice an increasing gap between theory and practice. This discordance and mutual interference dominated the history of Islamic law during the whole of the period here under review. This does not mean that Islamic law is entirely utopian. Apart from worship, ritual, and other purely religious duties, where in the nature of things the sacred law was the only possible norm, its hold was strongest on the law of family, of inheritance, and of *waqf*; it was weakest, and in some respects even non-existent, on penal law, taxation, constitutional law and the law of war; the law of contracts and obligations stands in the middle. The law of family and inheritance has always been, in the conscience of the Muslims, more closely connected with religion than other legal matters because the greater part of Qur'anic legislation is concerned with it. But even here, practice has been strong enough to prevail over the spirit, and in certain cases over the letter, of strict religious law. The legal position of women with respect to marriage and inheritance was occasionally improved in practice, but more often it deteriorated by comparison with Islamic law. Also, the institution of *waqf* was used to produce this last result, as has been mentioned above. It is not the most important and essential rules of religious law which are observed most faithfully but rather those which for some reason or other have become part of popular practice, and practice sometimes insists on refinements unknown to Islamic law. The institution of pre-emption in its extended, Ḥanafī form proved extremely popular among the Muslims who followed that school of law, and in India it became part of the matters sanctioned by religion, concerning which the continued validity of Islamic law for Muslims was guaranteed at the beginning of British rule in 1772; but the *Sharīʿa* itself does not attach great importance to it, and the more detailed handbooks describe ways by which it can be avoided. The field of contracts and obligations was ruled by a customary law which respected the main principles and institutions of the *Sharīʿa* but showed a greater flexibility and adaptability and supplemented it in many ways, and the same is true of the special rules concerning real estate, of which only a few rudiments exist in the *Sharīʿa*. The customary commercial law was brought into agreement with the theory of the

Sharīʿa by the *ḥiyal* of 'legal devices' which were often legal fictions, transactions by which the parties might achieve, through legal means, ends which were made desirable by the economic and social conditions of the time, but which could not be achieved directly with the means provided by the *Sharīʿa*. The earliest devices were merely simple evasions of irksome prohibitions by merchants and others, but very soon the specialists in religious law themselves started creating little masterpieces of elaborate juridical constructions and advising interested parties in their use.

Another important area of contact between theory and practice was provided by the continued use of written documents which became the subject of a voluminous and highly technical literature. Islamic jurisprudence ignores custom as an official source of law, however much customs of varied provenance had contributed to forming it. But the Mālikī school in Morocco in the later Middle Ages, where it developed in relative isolation from the rest of the Islamic world, took considerable notice of conditions prevailing in fact, not by changing the ideal doctrine of the law in any respect, but by recognizing that actual conditions did not allow the strict theory to be translated into practice, and that it was better to control the practice as much as possible than to abandon it completely. It therefore upheld the principle that 'judicial practice (*ʿamal*) prevails over the best attested doctrine', and it allowed a number of institutions unknown to strict theory. This Moroccan Mālikī *ʿamal* is not customary law; it is an alternative doctrine valid as long as conditions make it necessary.

We must think of the relationship of theory and practice in Islamic law, not as a clear division of spheres, but as one of interaction and mutual interference. The assimilation of the non-Islamic elements by the Islamic core in the formative period, and the assimilation of the practice by the theory in the Middle Ages, are really stages of one and the same process. This process, seen from outside, appears as a modification of the positive contents of Islamic law; whereas, seen from the inside, it appears as an expansion, a conquest of new fields by the ever dominant influence of Islamic law and jurisprudence. The ideal theory showed a great assimilating power, the power of imposing its spiritual ascendancy, even when it could not control the material conditions. Thus an equilibrium established itself between legal theory and legal practice, an equilibrium delicate in fact but seemingly unshakable in a closed society. As long as the sacred law received formal recognition as a religious ideal, it did not insist on being fully applied in practice. But it could not abandon its claim to exclusive theoretical validity, and acknowledge the existence of an autonomous secular law; its representatives, the *'ulamā'*, were the only qualified interpreters of the religious conscience of the Muslims; and the idea that law must be ruled by religion has remained an essential assumption even of modern Muslims. The works of Islamic law, during the whole of the medieval period, properly interpreted in relation to their place and time, are one of the most important sources for the investigation of Islamic society. The hold which the religious law of Islam had gained over the minds of the Muslims by the fifth/eleventh century can be gauged from the writings of al-Ghazālī (d. 505/1111), who, whilst deploring the ascendancy of legalism which threatened to extinguish religious life, and firmly restricting the subject-matter of the law to matters of this world, nevertheless protested that this did not imply reducing it to a secular subject of knowledge, and was unable to envisage secular rules for what he had insisted were matters which had nothing to do with religion.

The general and normal conditions described in the preceding paragraphs were occasionally disturbed by violent religious reform movements, such as that of the Almoravids in north-west Africa and Spain in the fifth-sixth/eleventh-twelfth centuries, that of the Fulbe in West Africa in the nineteenth century, and that of the Wahhābīs in Arabia in the nineteenth and again in the present century. All these movements made it their aim, in the states which they set up, to enforce Islamic law exclusively, to abolish the double system of administration of justice, and to outlaw administrative and customary law. The effects of these religious reform movements as a rule tended to wear off gradually, until a new equilibrium between theory and practice established itself. Of essentially the same kind, though sensibly different in their effects, were the efforts of established states (later than the early 'Abbasid period) to subject actual practice to the rule of the sacred law. The two most remarkable of these efforts were made in the Ottoman empire and in the Indian empire of the Mughals, whilst the Safavid empire in Persia provides an instructive parallel.

The Ottoman empire in the tenth/sixteenth century is characterized by strenuous efforts on the part of the sultans to translate Islamic law in its Ḥanafī form into actual practice; this was accompanied by the enactment of *qānūn-nāmes* which, though professing merely to supplement Islamic law, in fact superseded it. On the part of the representatives of religious law we find, naturally enough, uncompromising rejection of everything that went against the letter of religious law, but at the same time unquestioning acceptance of the directives of the sultans concerning its administration, and, on the part of the chief *muftīs*, a distinctive eagerness to harmonize the rules of the *Sharī'a* with the administrative practice of the Ottoman state. A parallel effort in the Mughal empire in the seventeenth century was part of the orthodox reaction against the ephemeral religious experiment of the emperor Akbar. In the Persia of the Safavids, the religious institution, including the scholars and *qāḍīs*, was controlled by the *ṣadr*, who exercised control over it on behalf of the political institution, thereby reducing the importance of the *qāḍīs*. The Safavids' supervision of the religious institution was more thorough than had been that of the preceding Sunnī rulers, and by the second half of the eleventh/seventeenth century the subordination of the religious institution to the political was officially recognized. This whole development had already begun under the later Timurids.

CHAPTER 5

RELIGION AND CULTURE

PREFATORY REMARKS

Islam is a religion. It is also, almost inseparably from this, a community, a civilization and a culture. It is true that many of the countries through which the Qur'anic faith spread already possessed ancient and important cultures. Islam absorbed these cultures, and assimilated itself to them in various ways, to a far greater extent than it attempted to supplant them. But in doing this, it provided them with attributes in common, with a common attitude to God, to men and to the world, and thus ensured, through the diversities of language, of history and of race, the complex unity of the *dār al-Islām*, the 'house' or 'world' of Islam.

The history of the Muslim peoples and countries is thus a unique example of a culture with a religious foundation, uniting the spiritual and the temporal, sometimes existing side by side with 'secular' cultures, but most often absorbing them by becoming very closely interlinked with them. It is with the relations between this existing culture and the strictly religious features concerned that we shall try to concern ourselves in this chapter.

Historical landmarks

Between the first/seventh and the ninth/fifteenth centuries, Islamic lands reached great cultural heights. We shall not attempt to outline here all the background of this, still less to draw up an exhaustive catalogue of works and of names. At certain periods the researches, the arguments of the schools and the political repercussions to which they gave rise, the intellectual achievements and the works of art were so abundant that to try to record them in a few pages would be to give an unjust picture of their dynamic qualities. The names which we shall mention therefore will be cited only as examples.

We shall, however, give a few landmarks. The Medinese period and the Umayyad age, particularly the latter, saw the establishment of the first Muslim culture, in which were combined the influences of ancient Arabia and of Byzantium. The Baghdād of the 'Abbasids continually absorbed Persian influences. The greatest advance took place in the third/ninth century when the advent of Greek thought and learning caused the Arabo-Muslim, and soon afterwards the Perso-Muslim, cultures to embrace new methods of thought. The period of the Caliph al-Ma'mūn, the son of Hārūn al-Rashīd and a Persian mother, can be proclaimed as an age of brilliant humanism. More than once Sunnism and Shi'ism overlapped.

The reaction of al-Mutawakkil attempted to re-orientate the 'Abbasid empire, and particularly 'Irāq, towards a deliberately Sunnī domination. The triumph of Sunnism did not take place in a day, and under the Buyid *wazirs* Muslim thought continued, either directly or through the Hellenistic *falsafa* (philosophy), to receive Shī'ī, and more precisely Ismā'īlī, currents. Samanid Khurāsān and its brilliant capital of Nīshāpūr, Hamadān under the Daylamī Buyids, Iṣfahān under the Kakuyid Kurds, were centres of intense cultural influence. Such was the background of Ibn Sīnā (Avicenna). The Aghlabid kingdom of Sicily in the third/ninth century was followed by the appearance, in the next two centuries, of the influence of the Cairo of the neo-Ismā'īlī Fatimids and its al-Azhar university. In the extreme west, Sunnī and Umayyad Cordova of the third/ninth to the fifth/eleventh centuries rivalled 'Abbasid Baghdād in brilliance. The Caliph 'Abd al-Raḥmān III and later the *wazir* al-Manṣūr Muḥammad b. Abī 'Āmir (Almanzor) made the Umayyad court at Cordova into a centre of patronage of letters and arts. To borrow an expression from Sir Hamilton Gibb, it can be said that from the end of the second/eighth to the beginning of the fifth/eleventh century was a truly golden age, in east and west alike, not only of Arabic literature but also of Arabo-Muslim culture considered as a whole.

It is possible to consider the following period, from the fifth/eleventh to the seventh/thirteenth century, as only a silver age, to quote Gibb again. This is true if it is a question only of Arabic literature; but Muslim culture proper, at least Sunnī Muslim culture, established itself during this period with increased vigour. The second half of the fifth/eleventh and the whole of the sixth/twelfth century saw in the east the triumph of Sunnism with the Seljuk Turks and the arrival of the Turcoman tribes. Shi'ism remained active, but firmly supplanted and condemned this time in Baghdād, in Syria, and even in Persia by the Sunnī revival. This was the period when religious teaching was spread by the *madrasas*. The fall of the Fatimids finally took place in 567/1171, while the rigorist

Almoravid and then Almohad dynasties reigned in Morocco and Andalus.

This was the period of Abū Ḥāmid al-Ghazālī, the famous Algazel, 'the reviver of religion', the period also when there were produced vast numbers of encyclopaedias and historical and geographical works. Sufism produced at this time the most noteworthy poetry. In Almohad Spain, where some Ismā'īlī tendencies surreptitiously insinuated themselves, there took place, with Ibn Ṭufayl and Ibn Rushd (Averroes), the last flowering of Hellenistic *falsafa*.

While the point should not be over-stressed, it can be said that the great classical age barely survived the Spanish capture of Seville (646/1248) and the decline of the Almohads in the west, and the capture of Baghdād by the Mongols in the east (656/1258). From the second half of the seventh/thirteenth century and throughout the eighth/fourteenth there were certainly cultural movements of great value but nothing to equal those of Baghdād or Cordova, or the writers patronized by the *wazīrs* and the *amīrs* of the east. This period did not lack great names, however. The Syrian Ḥanbalī jurist, Ibn Taymiyya, who played such an important part in the Muslim revival of this time, the Maghribī social historian Ibn Khaldūn, who has achieved a following in the Western world, and the 'theological' work of 'Aḍud al-Ījī and of al-Taftāzānī all belong to the ninth/fifteenth century. Although there was an increase in the minor genres of annals, commentaries and glosses, it was also an age of syntheses and of wide perspectives.

Within this very broadly outlined historical framework, what were the dominant cultural values? And to what extent were they in accord or in conflict with the fundamental religious ideas?

MUSLIM CULTURE: ITS BACKGROUND AND ITS CONSTITUENTS

The Qur'ān as a religious cultural value

'. . . And this is speech Arabic, manifest.'[1] To the Muslim this is not a simple question of fact. The Qur'anic text emphasizes that God sent down to Muḥammad a revelation, or a preaching in the Arabic language,[2] 'wherein there is no crookedness'.[3] If we consider the veneration in

[1] Qur'ān, 16. 103.

[2] Qur'ān, 41. 3; 42. 7; 43. 3 etc.

[3] Qur'ān, 39. 28. R. Blachère translates this: 'exempte de tortuosité'.

which from the beginning Muslims have held their Book, it is possible to understand that for the devout believer every phenomenon of arabization is of directly religious significance.

In fact this 'preaching in clear language' was the first great Arabic prose text. The respect accorded to it by the Faithful, the incessant repetition of it (*dhikr*), and the recognition of it as the Word of God, were to have a profound influence on ways of thought. At the time of the lightning campaigns of the Umayyads, the Qur'ān was certainly not the only factor of arabization, but it was nevertheless an essential factor. To it the Arabic language owed the distinctively religious cadences which for centuries were to characterize so many expressions and vocables, and to impregnate it down to the primary meaning of the triliteral roots.

It is true that pre-Islamic Arabia, with its poets and its orators and with the whole organization of the life of its tribes, had an inchoate but authentic culture. The state of *Jāhiliyya* (Ignorance), which Islam attributed to it[1] is essentially a religious concept and takes no account of the human riches of this time of heathendom. There is no need to stress the attachment of the first generations of Muslims to their Arab past, to the forms of the ancient poetry, *qaṣīda* and *ghazal*, or to the essentially bedouin virtue of *muruwwa*[2] of which the Umayyad period continually boasted. It is probable that the development and establishment of an Arab culture would have been possible without the appearance of Islam, but it nevertheless remains that Islam gave its own form to the Arab culture which already existed historically. It does not seem that the borderline cases of its poetry and of its secular arts on the one hand, and of its wide acceptance of the foreign sciences on the other, disprove this statement.

It was in fact in an atmosphere which was already made up of Arabo-Muslim culture that the foreign sciences were received; and furthermore a secular literature, some poetic forms and some minor arts could not by themselves have given birth to a culture. If culture is in itself 'the flowering of the earthly city', and 'as such depends upon human effort on earth'[3], yet its development is normally accompanied by an awareness of human destiny, both personal and collective. At other points in

[1] Qur'ān, 33. 33; 48. 26, etc.

[2] Translated by L. Massignon, *Parole donnée* (Paris, 1962), 350, as 'considération, honorabilité mondaine (à l'intérieur du clan)'.

[3] Olivier Lacombe, *Existence de l'homme* (Paris, 1951), 114.

history an Arabo-Christian culture, for example, had been, and would be, possible. It may be that there will arise an Arabic secular de-islamized culture, just as in Europe there has been for several centuries a tendency towards a Western secular de-christianized culture. This is all hypothetical. In fact, and chiefly during the five or six centuries with which we are here concerned, it was in a Muslim atmosphere, or linked to Muslim values, that Arabic culture developed.

For it was the Qur'ān which was the primary vehicle of Arabic culture. Was this accidental? Or does the very expression of the Muslim faith necessarily entail arabization?

Certainly the Muslim faith presents itself as a universal religion. Every man, without distinction of race or language, is called to witness to the Oneness of God and to the mission of Muḥammad by the *Shahāda* sincerely pronounced. Consequently every man is called to adopt the *sha'ā'ir al-Islām* (the marks of Islam): that is, the personal obligations determined by the 'four pillars', prayer, statutory alms-giving, the Ramaḍān fast, the Pilgrimage to Mecca; and those rules concerning food, circumcision, family life, wills, cemeteries etc., with which the life of the believer is surrounded from birth to death. The statement of faith is simple, consisting of the four Qur'anic affirmations: 'The believers believe in God, in His angels, in His books, in His messengers'[1]—these will be explained in *Ḥadīths* which mention the future life, the resurrection, and the Divine decree.

But it was the fact that this *credo* was accepted and lived first by the Arab tribes, and according to the Arabic expression of the Qur'ān and the Traditions, which was to give to the Muslim religion the special direction of its religious culture. There appear to be discernible in it three strands:

1. The cult which surrounded the text of the Qur'ān was to make Arabic the only liturgical language of Islam. It is possible to conceive an arabization which is not also islamization; the existence and the vitality of the Christian groups in the Middle East who adopted Arabic as a cultural language prove this. But all islamization of any depth is accompanied by a greater or less degree of arabization—an arabization which progresses sometimes rapidly and sometimes slowly, and which decreases proportionately as the native language and the past of the peoples to whom the message of the Qur'ān is preached make them less directly accessible to Arab influence. And the language of the Qur'ān,

[1] Qur'ān, 2. 285.

the only language in which prayer is liturgically valid, is nevertheless one of the chief factors in the cohesion of the Muslim world.

2. It would be a patent exaggeration to state either that every religious truth expressed in Arabic must necessarily concern the Muslim faith, or that a Muslim tenet can be expressed only in Arabic; but it is nevertheless once again a question of fact. The Arabic language, centred as it is on the verb, the extreme flexibility of the verbal forms, the frequent involutions of meaning, the correlatives which are simultaneously both complementary and opposite, the contrasting ambivalence of many roots in which opposites are joined, the probative value of allusion or metaphor which becomes a parable; all this combined to form a means of expression dedicated to the service of that relationship of radical discontinuity between the creature and the Creator, who is at the same time both close and remote, which is at the heart of the Muslim religious attitude. Future borrowings from the 'foreign sciences' were certainly to modify and sometimes to enlarge the basic vocabulary. It is none the less true that there is no religious statement in classical Arabic which does not suggest some reference to the Qur'ān.

3. This, then, is why the very early period, that of Medina and the beginning of the Umayyad era, began its religious culture, as it were, in terms of the scriptural text itself. It was not until the second and third centuries of the *Hijra* that there were developed as organized disciplines the readings of the Qur'ān (*qirā'āt*) and commentaries on it (*tafsīr*), and that in 'Irāq the schools of the grammarians of Baṣra and of Kūfa could attempt to pursue free researches and analyses. While the Kūfa school concentrated on exceptions and irregularities, that of Baṣra stressed 'systematization and analogy'.[1] In fact Baṣra, through the school of Gondēshāpūr, was to a certain extent influenced by Aristotelian logic. Khalīl, one of the few grammarians of Arab origin, was to remain the accepted authority on poetics and lexicography, and the grammar of his pupil Sībawayh was to remain a standard work. But whatever the long-term influences may have been, all Muslim reflection originated primarily from the aim to read and to understand the text of the Qur'ān.

The truly cultural ferment which the Qur'ān produced therefore cannot be overemphasized. It was of course the ferment of a religious culture, but of one which, through the semantic values involved, spread to inform all literary expression in its widest sense. Furthermore, the Qur'anic preaching does not deal only with the dogmas of the faith.

[1] R. Blachère, *Le Coran* (*Introduction*) (Paris, 1947), 110.

Great Muslim thinkers, such as al-Ghazālī in the fifth/eleventh century, and Ibn Taymiyya in the eighth/fourteenth century, were to distinguish in the text on the one hand the teaching of the religious truths (*'aqā'id*) and the regulations concerning worship (*'ibādāt*), both of them unalterable; and on the other hand a moral teaching and regulations concerning human actions (*akhlāq*), the application of which may vary according to circumstances; and finally everything connected with 'social relations' (*mu'āmalāt*) which to a certain extent depend on times and places. Although the first concern of non-Arab scholars, who had become arabized with their conversion to Islam, was with grammatical studies, the formulation of juridical rules occupied the attention of the Arabs of Medina as well as of the schools of 'Irāq or Egypt, though the 'Irāqī school of Abū Ḥanīfa and his disciples was chronologically the first. This was a matter of an intellectual application (*fiqh*) in which there was applied to the authoritative argument of the inviolable Text, either the judgment based on opinion (*ra'y*) of the *prudens*, or a reasoning by analogy (*qiyās*). *Qiyās* must be understood here as a mental activity bringing together or separating two terms, like to like or to its opposite, greater to less, less to greater; to which the Ḥanafī school would add the search for the cause (*'illa*), the first attempt to find a universal middle term. One has no hesitation, therefore, in considering the first impetus of Arabo-Muslim culture as being dominated by a style of thought which was indivisibly both juridical and semantic. These two methods of analysis are very typical of the Semitic spirit and the spheres which they cover are very much wider and more diverse than those comprehended by law and grammar in western cultures.

Therefore, although it is possible to speak of a Muslim religious culture, it is not merely a question of religious values which form part of the life of the believer and which may find many different modes of expression (rather as though we were to speak of a Christian culture expressing itself through a whole range of national cultures); it is not even a question of a culture whose first expression borrowed its vocables, adapting them, from the Arabic poetry and rhetoric of the *Jāhiliyya*; it is a question of a culture which was commanded by a text considered as directly dictated by God, and it was to be centuries before any translation of it was to be fully permitted. Or rather: a 'translation' of the Qur'ān can be nothing more than a commentary intended for teaching purposes. A devout Muslim, of whatever race, owes it to himself to approach it in the immutable text of its 'lucid' Arabic language. Furthermore, it was from this Qur'anic foundation that there was to develop in the following centuries the corpus of the religious sciences and their subsidiary sciences, which was to become the main axis of Muslim culture. But in order to assess these sciences, we must first consider according to which dialectic, of integration or of opposition, other Arabic or 'foreign' contributions were added to the Qur'anic basis.

The contributions of Arabic secular poetry and prose

The Qur'ān treats severely poets accused of forgery.[1] Nevertheless the dominant of a religious culture linked to the expansion of the Islamic faith was to welcome the coexistence of a secular Arabic poetry and fairly soon of a secular prose also.

In poetry, until the arrival of the freer forms of the *muwashshaḥ* or the *zajal*, the two forms most used were the *qaṣīda* and the *ghazal*. In the Umayyad period many pre-Islamic customs continued. The lyricism of the ancient *Mu'allaqāt*, the Suspended Poems of the fairs at Mecca, was revived in *qaṣīdas* which combined the praise of bedouin customs and virtues with panegyrics of the reigning caliphs. Nor were there forgotten the great troubadours of the past, above all Imru'l-Qays and Labīd. It was thus that there were produced the *qaṣīdas* of the three great masters, Akhṭal the Monophysite Christian, and Farazdaq and Jarīr the bedouin satirists, or the *ghazals* of Jamīl and of Dhu'l-Rumma. The *Kitāb al-aghānī* ('The book of songs') of Abu'l-Faraj 'Alī, an indispensable source for knowledge of the arts and letters of the first centuries of the *Hijra*, describes an Umayyad army which has left Khurāsān to oppose a Kharijite revolt, but is mainly preoccupied with deciding who is the greater poet: Farazdaq, who mingled satires with bawdy songs, or Jarīr, who sang of bedouin honour, and whose poems show at least some religious impulses.

The beginning of the 'Abbasid period, in which the influence of Persian sensitivity and of the minor arts of Persia was so obvious in the amusements of the court of Hārūn al-Rashīd, was delighted by the chivalrous *ghazals* of 'Abbās b. al-Aḥnaf and by the brilliant satires and bacchic or erotic poems of Abū Nuwās (d. 187/803); while Abu'l-'Atāhiya (d. 211/826), a contemporary of Abū Nuwās, expressed himself in didactic and moral poems in which, perhaps for the first time, there appeared a direct concern with religious values.

[1] Cf. Qur'ān, 26. 224–6; 37. 36; 61. 41.

In the following century, poetry and politics (and very active politics) were to form the two extremes of the career of Abu' l-Ṭayyib, called al-Mutanabbī (d. 354/965), a wandering troubadour when he chose to be, also an agitator and rebel, tainted with Carmathianism (without belonging to the Carmathian movement), and patronized at the end of his life by the *amīr* of Aleppo, the Hamdanid Sayf al-Dawla, becoming his official poet. Al-Mutanabbī's *qaṣīdas*, which are his greatest works, combine with the classical form freer and more personal developments. A century later, they were to influence Abu'l-'Alā' al-Ma'arrī (d. 450/1058), a solitary, even a hermit, and a very great poet, who was hardly at all faithful to the Sunnī teaching and faith. His constant meditations on human destiny and his pessimism show very probable Hindu influences, and he seems to have considered all positive religion as merely a human creation. With Abu'l-'Atāhiya, the great Arabic poetry had changed from secular to religious, or at least it had a religious accent; with al-Mutanabbī it returned to Shī'ī inspiration; with al-Ma'arrī, in spite of certain prudent statements, it reached a vision of men and of the world whose most profound inspiration it would be difficult to call Muslim.

Prose literature was also held in high esteem. Under the Caliph al-Ma'mūn, the great writer al-Jāḥiẓ began a series of prose works in which descriptions, anecdotes, poetic quotations, proverbs, one might say a whole popular humanism, became the occasion for brilliant variations and pungent exercises in style. The master of classical Arabic prose was to be his contemporary Ibn Qutayba (d. 276/889), who belonged to the Kūfa school of grammarians, and whose work, *'Uyūn al-akhbār* ('The fountains of story'), was to be for centuries a source of examples and references. Although in his *Ma'ārif* he was able to combine Persian with Arabic traditions, he nevertheless defended the Arabs and the Arabic language against the claims of the non-Arabs. In the following century, the solitary pessimism of al-Ma'arrī produced *Risālat al-ghufrān* ('The treatise of pardon'). But it is certainly in narrative, either mixed with poetry as in the *qiṣṣa*, or in the form of *saj'*, assonant prose, or in accounts of real or imaginary travels, that Arabic prose reached its highest level. From the fourth/tenth to the sixth/twelfth century there developed the genre of the famous *maqāmāt* (sessions), which very distantly foreshadowed modern short stories or novels. Al-Hamadhānī, and more especially al-Ḥarīrī, excelled in this.

There should also be mentioned works—poetry or prose—of a more flexible and more popular nature: the epic of 'Antar, the love-poem of

Laylā and Majnūn, and the stories of the *Thousand and one Nights*. Although these were much enjoyed, devout believers were always willing to criticize the moral and religious laxity of the poets and prose-writers—particularly the poets. More than once the theologians stirred up opinion against them in the towns; and more than once famous writers owed their freedom of speech to the protection of the rulers alone. The rebellious attitude of al-Mutanabbī, and still more the haughty indifference of al-Maʿarrī, to all established religious values, were censured.

Nevertheless it is not possible to speak of a secular Arabic culture developing in radical opposition to all religious culture. Even the most secular works contained echoes of the Qur'ān. The bedouin poet Jarīr owed the patronage of ʿUmar II to his reputation for piety; and it is said that the bacchic and erotic poet Abū Nuwās adopted asceticism (*zuhd*) in his old age. The prose-writer al-Jāḥiẓ was also a Muʿtazilite theologian. In fifth/eleventh century Andalusia, the very strict Ibn Ḥazm was to add to his Zahirite theology the courtly genre of his 'Necklace of the dove'. In contrast to this, the cult of the Arabic language, the language of the revelation, was to inspire commentators on the Qur'ān or theologians diligently to fathom out the precise meaning of the words, and in order to do this to turn to the famous poets, and especially to the pre-Islamic poets, to provide a verse or couplet as an example.

The way in which the two fields are interdependent may be summarized thus: in any history of Arabic culture, Islamic religious sciences must occupy an important place, while no study of *Muslim* culture as such would be complete without taking into account a certain *marginal* contribution made to it by secular literature.

The arts

The growth in the culture of the Muslim countries would not have been complete if the development of Arabic literature and religious thought had not been accompanied by a flowering of the arts.

In its strict sense Muslim art consists for the one part of the architecture and ornamentation of the mosques and *madrasas*, for the other part of the austere and very beautiful cantillation of the Qur'ān. Strictly speaking, these are the only arts which are fully permitted in Islam.

Religious architecture was affected by many influences—Byzantine, Persian and later Mongol—and there are many different styles of Muslim architecture. Nevertheless the adaptation of the buildings to the liturgical prayer of Islam, and even a certain harmony between the basic pattern of this 'liturgy' and the very flexible use of arcs, vaults and columns, between the affirmation of the One God and the minarets which were necessitated by the call to prayer, created a unity characteristic of its kind, running through the different styles and schools, which can be said in one sense to have reconciled Sunnism and Shi'ism.

The simplicity of the Medina mosque was followed, among others, during the Umayyad period by the Great Mosque at Damascus with its integration of Byzantine influences, or the Dome of the Rock at Jerusalem. In the 'Abbasid era architecture also was subject to Persian influences. The primitive 'Abbasid mosques of Baghdād and Raqqa have unfortunately disappeared, but there is the mosque of 'Amr in Cairo and above all the astonishingly successful mosque of Ibn Ṭūlūn (third/ninth century). Fatimid architecture (in the great mosque of al-Azhar) at one time joined to Persian inspiration influences from Umayyad Andalusia and particularly also from Tulunid art. There should also be mentioned the Turkish art of the Seljuks in the fifth–sixth/eleventh–twelfth centuries; and in the sixth–seventh/twelfth–thirteenth centuries the Mamluk art of Cairo with its many mosques and its City of the Dead or Tombs of the Caliphs.

In Ifrīqiya, the mosques of al-Zaytūna at Tunis, of Sīdī 'Uqba at Qayrawān, and of Sūs were to appear at the same time as the Umayyad art of the east and the beginnings of the 'Abbasid era. And here in the extreme west there appeared the sober harmony of Hispano-Moorish art, with its austere interlacing ornament, which is certainly one of the finest products of Muslim art, and one most characteristic of the spirit which inspires it. Muslim and Christian architects and craftsmen worked on it together. Berber, Byzantine and medieval European influences mingled with Eastern traditions to produce the almost unequalled masterpieces of the mosques of Cordova (second–third/eighth–ninth centuries) and Tlemcen (sixth/twelfth century), of the Kutubiyya at Marrakesh and the Giralda at Seville (sixth/twelfth century) and of the *madrasas* of Fez (eighth/fourteenth century).

The ornamentation of the mosques had to take into account the fact that the Muslim faith forbade any painting, and still more sculpture, which represented the figures of humans or of animals, in order the better to worship the Unique God and not to run the risk of even the smallest representation of idols. Who has not heard the pungent anecdote attributed to the Rightly-guided Caliph 'Umar b. al-Khaṭṭāb?

To a Persian artist who, having become a Muslim, was lamenting the fact that he must renounce his art, 'Umar is said to have replied: 'Come now; you have only to give your figures the shape of a flower and cut off their heads.' Hence the triumph of a decorative art which tended all the time rather to dissolve the floral motifs themselves into a suggestive interlacing of geometrical lines, supported by, and sometimes themselves shaped by the splendid designs of the Arabic letters. In this, as in almost everything, the Maghrib paid more heed to the strict regulations; and it was perhaps this which enabled it to achieve in the interlacing of its bas-reliefs such a degree of perfection that without them there would be a gap in the history of sculpture.

This architectural and decorative art extended from the mosques and other religious buildings to the secular buildings. It is true that the architect of the Umayyad palace at Mshattā did not hesitate to use friezes representing animals and there is also the very beautiful 'Court of the Lions' in the Alhambra at Granada (seventh–ninth/thirteenth–fifteenth century), but the Alhambra as a whole remains as the witness (anticipating, perhaps, Indo-Muslim architecture) of a Muslim view of the world which concerned itself with the palaces of the rulers as well as the places of prayer. The same could be said of the minor arts: ceramics, pottery, metalwork. There were scarcely any beside the Persian miniature painters who refused to cut off the heads of their [human] characters. This miniature-painting, also a minor art, was accepted in eastern Islam so long as there was no question of using it in the decoration of mosques, and so long as the figures reproduced had no volume so as to cast a shadow. But it must be admitted that these minor arts, which included also the weaving of carpets and the ornamentation of rich silks and brocades—although they were forbidden by the strict jurists—went with a way of life which was dominated by the quest for pleasure and luxury.

Qur'anic cantillation (*tajwīd*), linked to the science of the readings (*qirā'āt*) and bound by precise rules, is not music in the true sense of the term, for all music was and still is set apart from liturgical prayer. This led the jurists and devout believers to regard the art of music itself with a kind of suspicion. However, the *samā'*, the 'spiritual oratorio', spread in Ṣūfī circles. In spite of the attacks of the offended traditionalists, al-Ghazālī defended its legality. It is an unaccompanied religious chant, purely modal and devoted to entirely spiritual themes. It is possible to speak of a Muslim religious chant but not of Muslim music.

The same al-Ghazālī in fact considered it a pious action to enter a house where profane music and songs were being performed in order to smash the instruments and scatter the singers. But in spite of this rigorism, the refined atmosphere of the courts of the caliphs was often lulled by the sound of harps, lutes, rebecs and flutes, and they were accompanied by very profane songs. The *Kitāb al-aghānī*, which preserves details of the most famous songs of the third/ninth century, gives much information on the composers and the male and female singers of the period.

Music (*mūsīqī*, or, especially in the Maghrib, *mūsīqā*) moreover was considered as a 'foreign science' in which the Greek tradition of the schools of Pythagoras lent its structure to the Iranian influences. The *faylasūf* (philosopher) al-Fārābī devoted a whole work to this, Ibn Sīnā was careful not to neglect the study of musical rhythms and numbers, and the encyclopaedia of the *Ikhwān al-Ṣafā'* devotes a large section to musical theory. All this contributed to the formation of the two schools, Eastern and Western, of classical Arab music—we no longer refer to Muslim music. Although it made no real use of harmony it devoted itself all the more to the endless ornamentation of variations on the melodic theme. The court at Baghdād in the third *hijrī* century had its own official musicians, the Mawṣilīs. Ziryāb, one of their pupils, fled to the Umayyad court at Cordova under 'Abd al-Raḥmān II, where he became both court musician and *arbiter elegantiarum*. It was this meeting of East and West which produced Andalusian music.

The 'foreign sciences'

An event of primary importance was the penetration of Greek thought into the Baghdād of the early 'Abbasid era. The aptitude of the Arab spirit for absorbing other ideas and its capacity for assimilation here received full scope, and there was a lively enthusiasm for translations of Greek philosophical and scientific works.

Even before the coming of Islam, translations from Greek into Syriac were not unusual, and the arrival of Islam was to give rise to many Arabic translations, either through the intermediary of Syriac or directly from Greek. At Baghdād, there were teams of translators, at first Christians, later Muslims, under the patronage of the caliphs. The most famous is that of the Nestorian Ḥunayn b. Isḥāq, his son Isḥāq, and his nephew Ḥubaysh. There was also the Jacobite Qusṭā b. Lūqā, a little later Abū Bishr Mattā b. Yūnus (a Nestorian), Ibn 'Adī, Yaḥyā b. Biṭrīq, and others. These groups of translators enriched the Arabic language with works translated from Plato and Aristotle—and from Plotinus confused with Aristotle[1]—from Ptolemy, Galen, Hippocrates and many others besides. The libraries multiplied: among them were the *Bayt al-ḥikma* ('House of Wisdom') of the Caliph al-Ma'mūn at Baghdād with its many Greek manuscripts, and the *Dār al-kutub* ('House of Books') at Baṣra, with scholarships which students could hold there. A century later Fatimid Cairo was enriched by the huge Palace Library with 18,000 works of 'foreign sciences', and by the *Dār al-'ilm* ('House of learning') or *Dār al-ḥikma* founded by al-Ḥākim in the fourth/tenth century.

This directly Hellenistic influence, added to the Perso-Greek (and Hindu) contributions of Gondēshāpūr, produced a whole activity of scientific research in the modern meaning of the word: mathematics, astronomy, physics and chemistry, medicine. Although astronomy was still mixed with astrology and chemistry with alchemy, it was in the Arab and Persian Muslim countries that very remarkable progress was made in science at this time, and for several centuries following. Whole chapters and monographs have been written on Arabian science and its riches are still far from having been fully listed.

The sciences continued to be interwoven with philosophy. The impetus thus given encouraged a whole intelligentsia in the exercise of a free thought which took little account of the literal interpretation of the Qur'ān, and which was, moreover, anxious to break out of the entirely semantic and juridical bounds of the earlier culture. In certain milieux, Greek influences existed side by side with dualist Mazdean and Manichaean influences. They are found actively at work within some more or less esoteric circles, even those which were to be denounced as *zanādiqa* (sing. *zindīq*, a term, adapted from Sasanid usage), which can be understood to mean both 'unbelievers' and 'agitators', and hence blameworthy and sometimes condemned by the authorities. One of the best examples of these extremist tendencies was, in the third–fourth/ninth–tenth centuries, Abū Bakr al-Rāzī, the medieval physician Rhazes. His thesis of the Five Eternals (the Creator, the Soul,

[1] It was probably in the sixth Christian century that a Jacobite Christian translated into Syriac some glossed extracts from *Enneads* IV–VI. The Syriac work, translated in its turn into Arabic, was to become the *Theology of Aristotle* (*Uthūlūjiyā Arisṭūṭalis*). It was to have a profound influence on Avicenna, who wrote a commentary on it.

Matter, Time, Space) makes God into nothing more than a demiurge, and his atomistic cosmology is very close to that of Democritus, while his treatise *Fī naqd al-adyān* ('On the refutation [or destruction] of religions') is a protest against all positive religion. The esotericism of the Ismā'īlīs or the Carmathians was influenced by al-Rāzī. He certainly professed a radicalism far more absolute than that professed in the following century by 'the three great *zanādiqa* of Islam', as they were to be called: the philosopher Ibn al-Rāwandī, the gnostic Abū Ḥayyān al-Tawḥīdī and the poet Abu'l-'Alā' al-Ma'arrī.

The jurists and moralists had reproached the court poets and prose-writers for their lack of any sense of religion and for the sensuality of the themes they chose. Secular Arabic literature was criticized by the developing Arabo-Muslim culture. But it cannot be said that there was organized opposition between them. Rather did the massive arrival of the influences of ancient Persia and of classical Greece create, within the same Muslim culture, as it were a state of tension which was constantly being renewed, and which was to govern its future development. The results of this were far from being merely negative. The necessity to defend the beliefs of the faith against doubters and deniers was the origin of all the future philosophico- or theologico-dialectical developments. The whole history of *'ilm al-kalām*, the defensive apologia of Islam, was to be the proof of this.

The influence of Hellenism was the direct source of a discipline, certainly marginal in relation to the 'religious sciences', which the pious and 'people of the *kalām*' continually opposed, but which became one of the finest ornaments of the cultural splendour of the Muslim countries. We have mentioned the *falsafa* (very probably a transcription of *φιλοσοφια*) of al-Kindī, al-Fārābī and Ibn Sīnā in the east, before Ibn Ṭufayl and Ibn Rushd contributed to its fame in the Maghrib. The attitude of the philosophers (*falāsifa*) was by no means one of opposition or of revolt, like that of the earlier *zanādiqa*. They aimed to establish an agreement between the revealed Law (*shar'*) and their philosophy, both one and the other being accepted as a basic datum and as being on the same level of intelligibility. Hence their tendency to treat the text of the Qur'ān according to a method of interpretation (*ta'wīl*) of which another and very similar example is found in the Shī'ī gnosis. While it is easy to understand the mistrust with which the supporters of official Islam regarded the *falāsifa*, the fact remains that the acuteness of the philosophic thought of the greatest of them, linked with the loyalty to Islam which they retained, led them to the most impressive elaborations and syntheses. From the sixth–seventh/twelfth–thirteenth centuries onwards, through the translations from Arabic into Latin of the period, they had a profound influence on the medieval West.

Languages other than Arabic; the quarrel of the Shu'ūbiyya; *the 'sects'*

Falsafa was written mainly in Arabic, though there exist some important works of Ibn Sīnā in Persian. Addressed to rulers of Persian culture and origin, they usually consist of a compendium of the great Arabic treatises, with which are included some new analyses. In fact Muslim or Muslim-inspired culture extended beyond the Arabic-speaking area. We have already emphasized the process of arabization which accompanied the Islamic conquests, but the degree of its completeness depended on the peoples and countries concerned. Apart from the survival (which continues to the present day) of local languages and dialects, there must be mentioned the considerable cultural importance which was retained by Persian. It certainly became arabized, adopting the Arabic script and borrowing from Arabic its poetic forms and the clearest of its religious terms, but whereas there was no *Muslim culture* in the Greek, Syriac, Kurdish, Coptic or Berber languages, there developed very rapidly a great Perso-Muslim culture. The Turco-Muslim culture, both religious and secular, did not begin to assert itself until the seventh–eighth/thirteenth–fourteenth centuries, and was at first to be under Persian influence.

In addition, the use of Persian was regarded from the second–third/eighth–ninth centuries, as an assertion of rights. This was the phenomenon known as the quarrel or revolt of the *Shu'ūbiyya*. *Shu'ūb* originally meant the non-Arab tribes (the Arab tribes being known as *qabā'il*) and this is the meaning which the commentators were to give it when glossing the Qur'anic text, *Sūra* 49. 13: 'We have formed you in confederacies (*shu'ūb*) and tribes (*qabā'il*).' Later, *Shu'ūbiyya* came to mean the 'foreign' peoples who had embraced Islam and who, themselves invoking Muslim principles, protested against the contempt shown to them by the Arabs. At a later time some of them, proud of their own past, considered themselves in their turn to be superior to the Arabs.

In the Umayyad period, those who had newly embraced Islam (and become arabized) became the clients (*mawālī*) of Arab tribes; their political and social claims hastened the coming to power of the 'Abbasids.

The quarrel of the *Shu'ūbiyya* was a kind of repetition, but now on a cultural rather than a political level, of these early claims. Moreover it appeared in very different forms in the west and in the east of the *dār al-Islām*. The *Shu'ūbiyya* of Andalusia were as active as the true Arabs in promoting the Arabic culture and language. They claimed, and in the name of Islam, their integration with the Arabic ethnic group—that integration which the Syrians and the 'Irāqīs, founders of schools of grammar and of law, had formerly so successfully achieved. But the Syrians and 'Irāqīs were very close to the Arabic ethnic group, and their Syriac language was a sister language to Arabic, while the Andalusians were foreigners. In Persia, on the other hand, the movement aimed to restore the authority of the Persian language; it thus took the form of a claim to cultural autonomy.

The preservation of Persian literature and art was certainly not achieved by the *Shu'ūbī* movement alone. It would undoubtedly be an exaggeration to attribute to it that line of court poets which extends from Rūdakī and Kisā'ī in the fourth/tenth century to Kirmānī in the eighth/fourteenth century, and which reached its zenith in the sixth/twelfth century, under the Seljuk Turks, with Anwarī. It is nevertheless true that the *Shu'ūbī* claims helped to arouse a new interest in the Persia of the Great Kings, in its history and its myths. There need be mentioned only, in the last years of the fourth/tenth century, the great epic work of Firdawsī, the *Shāh-nāma*. Although the *Shāh-nāma* was written in a Muslim atmosphere, it remains a major witness to purely Persian culture. It can hardly be classed as a part of Muslim, or even of Perso-Muslim, culture.

It is otherwise with the Shī'ī works in Persian. For one thing, although Shī'ism expressed through the ages a religious phenomenon which was eminently Persian, it was Arab in origin; and secondly, some very great Shī'ī thinkers who were ethnically Persian, such as the Ismā'īlīs, Abū Ḥātim Rāzī and Sijistānī in the fourth/tenth century, or the Imāmīs, Naṣīr al-Dīn Ṭūsī (seventh/thirteenth century) and 'Allāma Ḥillī (seventh–eighth/thirteenth–fourteenth centuries) and many others, were to continue to write in Arabic. In the fifth/eleventh century, the Ismā'īlī, Mu'ayyad Shīrāzī, was to write sometimes in Arabic and sometimes in Persian, and the Ismā'īlī encyclopaedia of the *Ikhwān al-Ṣafā'* is also written in Arabic. Until the reform of al-Mutawakkil, the Arab atmosphere of 'Abbasid Baghdād was, through its Iranian *wazīrs*, as much Shī'ī as Sunnī, and as often Ismā'īlī Shī'ī as Imāmī. The amirates of Hamadān and of Iṣfahān, where Ibn Sīnā lived, were profoundly impregnated with Shi'ism. To ignore these historical facts would be to fail to understand the significance and the value of the writings of al-Fārābī and of Ibn Sīnā and of the whole of the cultural phenomenon of *falsafa*. In Cairo the dominant culture of the brilliant Fatimid empire was also Arab. And there continued to be expressed in Arabic, in the seventh/thirteenth century, the Western (i.e. Yemeni and Egyptian) Isma'ilism which was forced by the Sunnī repression of Saladin to operate clandestinely.

Nevertheless, in the extent to which Imāmī Shi'ism spread among the Persian people, it was to give rise to a whole Persian religious literature; hymns and poems, and especially dramas, resembling mystery-plays, which recount the sorrow of Fāṭima and the martyrdoms of 'Alī and Ḥusayn. They are all the more remarkable in being the only literature in Islam written for theatrical performances. Furthermore, from the time that they had to dissimulate before established authority, Persian Ismā'īlī groups preferred to express themselves in Persian. Among their most notable representatives was Nāṣir-i Khusraw (fifth/eleventh century).

Finally, the seventh/thirteenth century was to produce some great Ṣūfī works in Persian. It is sufficient to mention 'Azīz al-Dīn Nasafī, Farīd al-Dīn 'Aṭṭār and Sa'dī, and above all Jalāl al-Dīn Rūmī, whose *Mathnawī* remains one of the purest literary glories of Persia. But at the end of this century, the rule of the Īl-Khāns (663–736/1265–1337) was a period of decline for Persian culture. Until the age of the Safavids, the only period during which it came to life again was in the second half of the eighth/fourteenth century, under Tīmūr. This was to be the age of the melodious *ghazals* of Ḥāfiẓ and of Sa'dī and then, in the ninth/fifteenth century, of the mystic Jāmī.

It may be useful to summarize briefly the preceding remarks. Concurrently with Arabic culture, the *dār al-Islām* from the second/eighth to the ninth/fifteenth centuries produced a brilliant Persian culture. But whereas Arabic secular literature remained as though attached to Muslim culture, Persian poetry and literature were intentionally a presentation of purely Persian claims. On the other hand, our knowledge of Muslim culture as such would be incomplete if we did not include as part of it many Shī'ī works (and Ismā'īlī Shi'ism in particular) or Ṣūfī works which were written in Persian. But it would be a historical misinterpretation to consider that the only expression of Shi'ism was in Persian. Some very great Shī'ī works are written in Arabic.

It is nevertheless true that Shi'ism, Arab in origin and born of an Arab fidelity to 'Alī and to the 'People of the House', could not have constituted itself in its 'sapiential theosophy' without the contribution of the 'foreign sciences', i.e. of the Greek and Persian traditions. It thus became one of the acting forces of that tension mentioned above, which was to serve as the very mark of the absorption of non-Arab values by the Muslim world. This tension, far from having a destructive effect, was on the contrary to inspire and to universalize the Muslim culture, and especially the Arabo-Muslim culture, of the classical age.

THE ORGANIZATION OF KNOWLEDGE INTO ITS CONSTITUENT DISCIPLINES

Study of the sources of religion, the Qur'ān and *Sunna*, began from the time of Medina. It was the stimulus exerted by the non-Arabs, especially in 'Irāq, which gave rise to the schools of the grammarians. The invasion of the 'foreign sciences' led the doctors and jurists of Islam to defend the dogmas of their faith by rational methods. Sciences, in the modern sense of the word, and literature were cultivated in profusion. There is the well-known *Ḥadīth* which commands: 'Pursue learning (*'ilm*) from the cradle to the grave even as far away as China.' In the eyes of the believer, this learning or knowledge which is to be acquired is that which is related, directly or indirectly, to God, to the things belonging to God and to the Word of God. But the aphorism was frequently applied to all legitimate human knowledge. It is in any case a proof of the respect which Muslim thought was always to have for intellectual research.

Having analysed the constituents of the historical culture of the Islamic countries, we shall now consider in detail the sum of the traditional achievements thus acquired. We must evidently give the most important place to the 'religious sciences'. To these we shall add a mention of the sciences known as 'instrumental', not omitting others which were, it is true, somewhat marginal, but which brought great honour to the cultural climate in which they originated.

The development of the religious sciences

The progressive development of the 'religious sciences' was an innate characteristic of the Muslim mentality. We have mentioned the libraries, plentifully supplied with the works of the 'foreign sciences'.

But there should, nevertheless, be emphasized the importance, from the fourth–fifth/tenth–eleventh centuries onwards, of the colleges (*madrasas*) in which the strictly Muslim disciplines were taught, the role of the great mosque-universities—and the great mosque of Cairo founded by the Fatimids was the first state university—the bookshops in the vicinity of the great mosques, the corporations of students who frequented them, and their influence on the social and even the political life of the cities. To the brilliant life of the palaces and the courts, where often it was secular art and literature which predominated, there corresponded a cultural life of the markets and mosques, centred round the religious sciences and the debates between their various schools. It was often the literate people of the towns who protested against the freedom of thought or the licence in the habits of the great. The triumphs of Sunnism in the fifth/eleventh century, and especially perhaps the Ḥanbalī reaction, were to have their roots in popular movements.

It is possible to enumerate as constituent disciplines five 'religious sciences': that of the 'readings', of Qur'anic commentary, of *Ḥadīth*, of law, and of *kalām* or defensive apologetics. The first four came into being in the Medinese period and the beginning of the century of the Umayyads, the fifth, which arose from the confrontation of Ṣiffīn, was to come to its full development only under the impetus of the 'foreign sciences'. We shall attempt to characterize each briefly.

The Qur'anic sciences

First we have the Quranic science of the 'readings', *'ilm al-qirā'āt*. The first *qurrā'* ('readers' or 'reciters') were devout believers such as Ibn 'Abbās or Anas b. Mālik, Companions of the Prophet. Many 'readers' were also 'bearers' of the Qur'ān, that is to say, they knew it by heart, and meditated on it. After Ṣiffīn, the reading of the Book sometimes became an occupation performed by freed prisoners, who allowed political intrigues to mingle with religion. It was not until the third/ninth century in Baghdād that the readers formed themselves into a corporation and that their function became once again respected.

The influence of the schools of the grammarians was great. Abū 'Amr b. al-'Alā' and Thaqafī at Baṣra, and, a little later, al-Kisā'ī at Kūfa, were both grammarians and 'readers'. It was towards the middle of the second/eighth century that there had been admitted the principle of a plurality of authorized 'readings'. The early Qur'anic recensions of

Ubayy and of Ibn Mas'ūd were sometimes, under the cover of this pluralism, partially reintegrated into the *corpus* of 'Uthmān. The situation, however, still remained somewhat confused during the second half of the second/eighth century. The Shī'īs continued to prefer the 'Irāqī recension of Ibn Mas'ūd, criticizing the vulgate of 'Uthmān for having suppressed texts favourable to the 'Alids. But towards the middle of the third/ninth century there was established a consensus which avoided any divergence from the Qur'anic vulgate, allowing to remain only some variants connected with the vocalizations and with certain consonants. A list was drawn up of seven canonical readings, each of which was referred to a 'reader' of the early generations of Muslims, only two of whom were Arabs.

The science of the Qur'anic commentaries or *tafsīr* ('explanation') is certainly one of the poles of Muslim culture. If it is true that not only a *corpus* but also a *tafsīr* are to be attributed to Ibn 'Abbās, the cousin of the Prophet who died in 68/687–8, then this science began at a very early date. It was to overlap more than once with other disciplines, especially the science of *kalām*, the schools of which were to vary according to their respective tendencies the interpretation (*ta'wīl*) of certain disputed texts. *Falsafa*, and above all Ismā'īlī gnosticism, were to practise largely an allegorical *ta'wīl*. The Sunnīs, who usually favoured the meaning which was clear and evident (*ẓāhir*), were to be in opposition to the *Bāṭiniyya*, or those who upheld the hidden meaning (*bāṭin*).

Two major rules were later to emerge: first, to make the maximum use of lexicography and grammar in order to grasp the exact significance of sentences and words in the Arabic spoken at Mecca in the time of the Prophet; and, secondly, to ascertain precisely, as far as possible, all the circumstances of the revelation, even if this meant using Jewish or Christian sources (*Isrā'īliyyāt* and *Masīḥiyyāt*). But recourse to these sources was treated with suspicion by strict Traditionists.

We shall limit ourselves to citing a few who were to become accepted as authorities: al-Ṭabarī the annalist (d. 310/923), whose commentary reproduces many *Ḥadīths*, and who was not averse to an apologetic and polemical approach; al-Zamakhsharī (d. 539/1143), who was to have a considerable influence, in spite of the accusation of rationalizing *tafsīr* which was brought against him by his enemies; al-Bayḍāwī (d. 685 or 691/1286 or 1291), whose *tafsīr* was to be the type of manual used in teaching and by ordinary literate people. In addition there should be mentioned *al-Tafsīr al-kabīr* ('The great commentary'), called also

Mafātiḥ al-ghayb ('The keys of the mystery'), of Fakhr al-Dīn al-Rāzī (d. 606/1210), the well-known author of *kalām*, who does not hesitate to apply *ta'wīl* to the anthropomorphisms of the Qur'ān, to raise many philosophical and theological problems, and to sketch out some scientific commentaries inspired by the Greek science. As G. C. Anawati says, 'it belongs to the type of commentary which is both philosophical and *bi'l-ra'y* i.e., it does not rely on tradition alone, but on the considered judgment and reflection of the commentator. Into it al-Rāzī put all his philosophical and religious learning.'

The science of Ḥadith

The science of *Ḥadīth* or of Traditions (*riwāyāt*) arose from the devotional attachment of the Muslims to the 'traces' (*āthār*) of the Prophet and his Companions. The collectors of the *Ḥadīths* were numerous. The expression 'people of the *Ḥadīth*' (*ahl al-Ḥadīth*) is used of those who devoted themselves to this task; it refers also to their concern for accuracy and can be used intentionally as a synonym of *ahl al-sunna wa'l-iamā'a* ('people of the tradition and of the community'). They concentrated all their effort not on the criticism of the text (*matn*), but on the establishment of the chains of transmitters (sing., *isnād*), and on their authenticity. It was a matter of ensuring, first, that it was possible for transmitters to have met one another in a direct line, going back to the Prophet, and secondly, that each one of them was completely truthful and trustworthy. This research was the origin of the *ṭabaqāt*, which were collections of biographical notices of the early Muslims, the most famous collection being that of Ibn Sa'd. The genre was extended to cover later generations, and Arabo-Muslim literature was enriched for example by the *Ṭabaqāt* of Ibn al-Farrā' devoted to the Ḥanbalīs, by those of al-Subkī devoted to the Shafi'ites, and by those of Sulamī on the Ṣūfīs.

The science of *Ḥadīth* had as it were two functions in Muslim religious culture: historical research on the lives and the characters of the men who belonged to the very first generations, those of the Companions and of the Followers; and the attribution of a rating to each *isnād*, the value of which it was to determine. This latter normative function should not cause us to forget its historical function. Thus the *Ḥadīth* was pronounced 'sound' or 'good' or 'weak'; according to another view, it was *mutawātir* (with very many chains of transmitters), or simply 'known' or 'uncommon' or 'unique'; or yet again 'well-founded' or 'interrupted', etc. During the second–third/eighth–ninth centuries, six great bodies of *Ḥadīths* were collected and came to be regarded as reliable: those of Bukhārī, Muslim, Abū Dāwūd, Tirmidhī, Nasā'ī and Ibn Māja. The two first, known as the two *Ṣaḥīḥs*, that is to say those which reproduce only authentic *Ḥadīths*, were accorded a preferential authority. To them should be added the famous *Musnad* (i.e. based on uninterrupted *isnāds*) of Ibn Ḥanbal, collected by disciples after their master's death.

Shīʿī Islam also had its collections of traditions (usually called *akhbār*): some of them admitted also by the Sunnīs, others peculiar to Shiʿism, which stressed the ʿAlids and their role in the community. The main Shīʿī collections date from the fourth or fifth/tenth or eleventh century, and were written by Kulīnī, Qummī, Muḥammad al-Ṭūsī, and ʿAlī al-Murtaḍā.

The science of law

The fourth religious discipline is *ʿilm al-fiqh*, the science of the law. From the cultural point of view, with which we are concerned here, we confine ourselves to two observations.

The schools of law are concerned with a much wider area than that which is strictly juridical in the Western sense of the term. In Islam, each of them is the expression, in addition to certain ways of thought, of a certain attitude, which is both practical and intellectual, with regard to the day-to-day behaviour of the devout believer. Many of the speculative quarrels between the schools of *kalām* can be understood in their historical context only by reference to the various schools of *fiqh*: one need only mention the relations between Hanafism and Maturidism, Shafiʿism and Ashʿarism, and the opposition and later the welcome which the last was to encounter in the Malikism of the Maghrib. Finally the Ḥanbalī school, which challenged even the legitimacy of *kalām*, did not hesitate to assume responsibility for the defence of religious beliefs. Ibn Ḥanbal remains the typical figure of the 'Devout Elder', and his six professions of faith (sing., *ʿaqīda*) were the subject of a great deal of meditation and commentary. The Ḥanbalīs, Barbahārī and Ibn Baṭṭa in the third–fourth/ninth–tenth centuries, and the great Ibn Taymiyya in the seventh–eighth/thirteenth–fourteenth centuries, not to mention the Ḥanbalī Ṣūfīs, al-Jīlānī or al-Anṣārī, are among the most important figures in the history of Muslim religious thought and culture.

In the same connexion should be mentioned the cultural importance from the third/ninth to the sixth/twelfth century of the Ẓāhirī school, made famous by Ibn Ḥazm (d. 1064). It was to be conclusively rejected by official Islam. In it all forms of personal judgment or of reasoning were put aside in the process of juridical elaboration, and the emphasis was placed on the literal meaning of the texts in their most obvious sense (*ẓāhir*). The systems of analysis adopted were specifically semantic, according to a very narrow definition of the meaning of 'name' and 'named' (*ism* and *musamma*) and of their connexions. We have here an extreme example of this double method of analysis, both semantic and juridical, which deeply influenced the early directions in which Muslim culture developed.

Finally there should be noted the not inconsiderable influence of the Ibāḍī and Shī'ī schools of *fiqh*. The *Iqtiṣār* of the neo-Ismā'īlī Nu'mān, the chief *qāḍī* of Fatimid Cairo (fourth/tenth century) belongs to the school of Medina (Malikism), but according to the Shī'ī point of view by which the consensus of the doctors (*ijmā'*) was not considered valid without the approval of the *Imām*.

Defensive apologia

The fifth and last religious science, *'ilm al-kalām*, the science of the word (on God, or of God), or *'ilm al-tawḥīd*, the science of the divine Oneness (or of its proclamation), is generally known in the West as theology. We shall dwell on this briefly.

It seems to us more exact, according to the definitions of it given by its doctors, to consider it to mean a defensive apologia, the function of which 'is firmly to establish religious beliefs by producing proofs, and to cast aside doubts'.[1] If we wish to speak of an 'Islamic theology' in the meaning of this word in the Christian West, it is certainly necessary to add to *'ilm al-kalām* many elements which come from *uṣūl al-fiqh* (the sources of the law), and still more widely, many professions of faith or short catechetic treatises grouped under the title of *uṣūl al-dīn* (the sources of religion). It is certain that the great Ḥanbalīs mentioned in the preceding paragraphs would deserve the title of theologians as much as, if not more than, many of the doctors of *kalām*.

'Ilm al-kalām is a specifically Muslim religious discipline. Its origin goes back to the doctrinal ruptures which resulted from Ṣiffīn. However,

[1] Al-Ījī, *Mawāqif* (*apud Sharḥ al-mawāqif* of al-Jurjānī (Cairo, 1325/1907), I, 34–5).

and in contrast to the *tafsīr* for example, for the treatises and the schools to be organized it required an external stimulus: discussions at Damascus with Christian theologians, the influence of Greek science and thought at Baghdād, and the defence of the values of faith against this influence. From this point of view, it is impossible to dissociate from *kalām* the study of the very numerous treatises on heresies which played an important part in the history of Muslim thought.

In the Umayyad period the first debates took place between Murji'ites (who were faithful to the established power and who committed to God the eternal status of the sinful believer), Qadarites, or supporters of human free-will, the Jabarites, who were linked to the strict Traditionists and defenders of the absolute all-powerfulness of God. The ʿAbbasid second–third/eighth–ninth centuries were to see the formation of the Muʿtazilite schools, in their two great traditions of Baṣra and of Baghdād. The solutions given in various quarters to the problems concerning the divine attributes, divine justice, the respective fate of the believer, the sinner and the unbeliever in the next life ('the promise and the threat'), the intermediate state between faith and impiety, the obligation of the community to order the good and forbid the bad—all these solutions could vary among the Muʿtazilites according to tendencies and the subdivisions of the schools. But they were animated by a common spirit: the recognition of the value of reason (*ʿaql*) in the defence of religious values (*ʿaql* even becoming the criterion of the Law), the anxiety to purify the idea of God from all anthropomorphism, the wish to defend the faith and to justify it against the enticements of Greek thought and the attacks of the *zanādiqa* (free thinkers). The Muʿtazilites called themselves 'the people of Justice and Oneness' (of God). Thus it is seen that this is not, as was formerly thought, a matter of rationalism, but of a religious apologia which aimed to use rational methods. It was in this spirit that the school developed one of its central theses, that of the created (*makhlūq*) Qur'ān, in contrast to that of the 'Elders' who considered it to be the eternal and uncreated (*ghayr makhlūq*) Word of God.

Muʿtazilism triumphed for a time and even appeared as official doctrine under the Caliph al-Ma'mūn. It can be said that it belongs to the great humanist age of third/ninth century Baghdād and Baṣra. Among its great writers were Jāḥiẓ (one of the greatest of all Arabic prose-writers), Naẓẓām and ʿAllāf. As it became successful, it began to persecute its opponents, and this was the period of the great *miḥna*, the great 'trial', when the devout elders who defended the uncreated Qur'ān, chief among them being Ibn Ḥanbal, were dragged before the courts, condemned to corporal punishment, imprisoned, and even executed.

This triumph was to be short-lived. The Ḥanbalī influences, which were firmly entrenched in popular circles of 'Irāq, campaigned for the return of 'the old religion' (*al-dīn al-'atīq*). This was the reaction of al-Mutawakkil. The Mu'tazilites in their turn suffered persecutions, condemnations and exile. It is a great loss to the history of ideas that the majority of their works were destroyed, and for centuries were known only through the attacks of their adversaries. It was only recently that some of them were rediscovered and published. However, a direct Mu'tazilite influence was to continue in the Kharijite and Shī'ī sects.

After this, the teaching in the great mosques was to be shared between two great schools of *'ilm al-kalām*: the Ḥanafī-Māturīdī tradition, which arose from al-Māturīdī of Samarqand (d. 333/944), and particularly the Ash'arī school, founded by Abu'l-Ḥasan al-Ash'arī (d. *c.* 330/941), who was a former adherent of Mu'tazilism, and whose treatise on heresies, *Maqālāt al-Islāmiyyīn* ('The opinions of Muslims') remains a documentary source of primary importance. It is possible to distinguish between Māturīdīs and Ash'arīs by emphasizing the intellectualist and also psychological tendencies of the former, and the absolute divine voluntarism of the latter.

The Ash'arī school had to fight continually on three fronts. Against Hanbalism (and at one time against Zahirism), it had to defend the legitimacy of a certain use of reason in matters concerning faith. In his *credo*, al-Ash'arī stated his reverence for the teachings of Ibn Ḥanbal. Nevertheless the Ḥanbalīs were formidable enemies, who, on the day following the death of al-Ash'arī, went so far as to overturn his tombstone in the graveyard at Baghdād. Against Mu'tazilism the school challenged the ontological validity of human free-will and of secondary causes, condemned the theory of the created Qur'ān, and affirmed the separate reality of the divine attributes. Finally, from the fifth/eleventh century, it denounced as tainted with impiety the emanationist theories of the *falāsifa*, their theory of cognition, their tendency to treat allegorically (at least in the cases of al-Fārābī and Ibn Sīnā) beliefs as fundamental as the resurrection of the body.

These arguments were not carried on without borrowing from the *falāsifa* many methods of reasoning or of procedure, and the later

Ash'arīs in their analyses, and even in certain of their conclusions, are sometimes very far removed from their master and founder. They had no hesitation in taking up on their own account the logical, cosmological and ontological problems which *falsafa* had propounded. Nevertheless the philosophies proper to *'ilm al-kalām* could be formulated around either the occasionalist theory of 'atoms' or the conceptualist theory of 'modes', and it is most striking that these two theses, so consonant with the Ash'arī vision of the world, should both be of Mu'tazilī origin.

We should not omit to mention some writers belonging to the Ash'arī school, such as the *qāḍī*, al-Baqillānī (d. 403/1013), his contemporary, al-Baghdādī (d. 429/1037), famous especially for his survey of the sects, and al-Juwaynī (d. 478/1085). The latter was the teacher in *kalām* of the celebrated Abū Ḥāmid al-Ghazālī (450–505/1058–1111), who produced a treatise of *kalām*, the *Iqtiṣād*, and is famous for his *Tahāfut al-falāsifa* ('The incoherence of the philosophers'). In it he refuted al-Fārābī and Ibn Sīnā after having faithfully and objectively set out their principal theses in the *Maqāṣid*.[1] Al-Shahrastānī, his contemporary, was to attack the same adversaries so successfully that he earned the nickname of 'the overthrower of the *falāsifa*'.

One of the last truly original works of the Ash'arī school was to be the *Muḥaṣṣal* of Fakhr al-Dīn al-Rāzī, the only manual of *kalām* studied by Ibn al-'Arabī. Then in the eighth and ninth/fourteenth and fifteenth centuries there appeared the treatises of al-Taftāzānī—perhaps more Māturīdī than Ash'arī—and of al-Ījī with commentary by al-Jurjānī. At this period, and in the following centuries, the Ash'arī school known as 'of the moderns'[2] continually added to its philosophical preambles so as to produce a sort of mixed genre, belonging both to *kalām* and to *falsafa*, which became lost in the endless labyrinths of constantly renewed discussions.

'Instrumental sciences' and related subjects

Many Muslim writers, Sunnīs and Shī'īs, *falāsifa* or people of the *kalām*, or librarians such as Ibn al-Nadīm, have left catalogues of sciences. They frequently mention sciences which may be called 'instrumental', i.e. knowledge which in itself is secular put to the use of the 'religious sciences'. The study of the Arabic language and of its

[1] Whence the contradiction of the Latin Middle Ages which, knowing only the *Maqāṣid*, made 'Algazel' into an Aristotelian.

[2] The expression is Ibn Khaldūn's, in *Muqaddima*, Cairo, 327.

resources is indispensable in order to penetrate the meaning of the texts, and thus is justified the great influence exerted by the grammarians, and even the renown of the poets and prose writers. Astronomy is essential to establish the lunar calendar, the dates of the fast of Ramaḍān and of the Pilgrimage; without recourse to arithmetic, the jurists would not be able to divide legally the shares of an inheritance, and so on.

But these sciences, instrumental though they were, were in fact to develop widely in their own right. We have already mentioned the schools of the grammarians. There should be noted, in the second–third/eighth–ninth centuries, the work of two philologians of Baṣra: the Sunnī al-Aṣmāʿī (d. *c.* 213/828), renowned for his knowledge of poetics, and his rival, the Kharijite Abū ʿUbayda (d. 209/825), who drew attention to the traditions of the pre-Islamic Arab tribes and was one of the authorities cited by the *Shuʿūbiyya*. It should be particularly emphasized that in mathematics, astronomy, chemistry and medicine the Muslim world had no difficulty in continuing the work done by the Indians, the Persians and the Greeks; and that its original contribution was to have an irreplaceable effect on the advancement of science. One need only mention for example Gondēshāpūr, the lively centre of learning at Khūzistān in the second/eighth century, the invention of algebra by al-Khuwārizmī in the third/ninth century, or the works on astronomy by the majority of the *falāsifa*. Yaḥyā al-Khayyāṭ and al-Kindī himself had been preceded by, and prepared by, astrology; algebra had been preceded by gnostic speculations on letters and numbers, such as the famous work attributed to Jaʿfar al-Ṣādiq, the sixth Shīʿī *Imām*; and alchemy was held in much esteem. But distinctions were made. Ibn Sīnā devoted himself to astronomy at the request of ʿAlāʾ al-Dawla, *amīr* of Iṣfahān, adding to it also researches and discoveries in cosmography, geometry and arithmetic. He was able to make progress in chemistry, which, unlike al-Kindī, he clearly distinguished from alchemy, and his great medical work, *al-Qānūn fiʾl-ṭibb*, was still regarded as authoritative by medieval Latin scholars. In the fifth/eleventh century, the mathematician al-Bīrūnī was famous not only for his contribution to the science of numbers and to astronomy, but for his knowledge of Indian culture and his glossed translation of the *yoga-sūtra* of Patanjali. The list of the principal scholars writing in Arabic would be a long one. The apologists freely concede their right to exist in Islam, since the Qurʾān commands to 'reflect on the signs of the universe'[1]; they regard them

[1] Cf. Qurʾān, 2. 164; 3. 190; 6. 99; 13. 2–3; 24. 43–54, etc.

with suspicion only in so far as hypotheses advanced by them contradict the professions of faith.

Finally we must not omit history and geography. The *ṭabaqāt* which we mentioned in connexion with the science of *Ḥadīth* was perhaps the first form of historical narrative in Islam. There were very soon added to it many monographs, which were, however, more annals than history proper, and it was not until the eighth/fourteenth century, with the masterly work of Ibn Khaldūn, thathi story took on the dimension of an explanatory synthesis of the facts. On the other hand, the Muslims, being great travellers, discoverers of countries, organizers of empires and experienced traders, were very early in inaugurating a scientific type of geography. The influence of Greece, of the translations of Ptolemy among others, was decisive. We often find in geography the same names as in astronomy or mathematics: al-Khuwārizmī, al-Bīrūnī and others. In addition we shall confine ourselves to mentioning al-Ya'qūbī (d. 284/897), al-Maqdisī (or al-Muqaddasī) and in particular al-Mas'ūdī (d. 345/956), al-Idrīsī (d. 549/1154), Yāqūt (d. 626/1229), and Ibn Baṭṭūṭa (d. 770/1368–9). This list is by no means exhaustive. Such geographical works as studies on latitudes and longitudes, the science of 'climates' (the Greek *κλίμα*) and the making of maps (it was in Islamic territory that scientific cartography developed) sometimes turned into travel journals in which much space was devoted to the descriptions of the inhabitants of various countries and their customs. These descriptions were mixed with legends and they are still reflected in popular literature, such as the tales of Sinbad the Sailor.

Two 'marginal sciences'

To complete our investigation a brief excursus may be permitted. In fact the traditional classification of knowledge into 'religious sciences', 'instrumental sciences' and 'foreign sciences' is by itself inadequate to express the complexity of the facts.

For example it risks leaving in obscurity that 'marginal' science, which was at times condemned and even brought before the courts, and at times accepted—*'ilm al-taṣawwuf* or Muslim mysticism. We shall not deal with it directly here. It suffices to mention the very great importance of many Ṣūfī works, and even of the life led by the Ṣūfī circles, in the cultural history of the Islamic countries. There are Ṣūfī poems and prose, analyses of spiritual states or gnostic meditations, and even didactic manuals, which are most certainly the highest expression of Arabic or Persian literature. At the time when Sufism was being attacked by established Islam, the second and third/eighth and ninth centuries produced the incomparable testimonies of al-Ḥasan al-Baṣrī, Rābi'a, al-Muḥāsibī, al-Bisṭāmī, al-Ḥallāj and others. The manuals of the following age, and especially the *Iḥyā'* of al-Ghazālī were to procure them acceptance. The sixth–seventh/twelfth–thirteenth centuries produced the masterly work of Ibn al-'Arabī and the very fine poems of 'Umar b. al-Fāriḍ, and we have already mentioned the influence at the same time of Persian Ṣūfī writings. It was no longer a question only of that chiefly formal beauty which characterizes classical poetry and prose; this was a transcription sometimes of personal experiences, sometimes of broadly gnostic evocations, but expressed with such a poetic and literary gift that Arabo-Muslim or Perso-Muslim humanism can be justly proud of it.

Let us reconsider briefly that other 'marginal' discipline, *falsafa*. It belongs so to speak to a fringe-position between the 'religious sciences' and the 'foreign sciences'. Its chief exponents were, as we have seen, both philosophers and scholars, or physicians, and were often involved in the political affairs of their time. The early relations between *falsafa* and *kalām* were far from being hostile. Al-Kindī, the first of the 'philosophers', was often considered as belonging also to the Mu'tazilī *kalām*, and *'ilm al-kalām* has its place in the 'Catalogue of the sciences' (*Iḥṣā' al-'ulūm*) of al-Fārābī. It was after the triumph of Ash'arism in *kalām* that the break between the two disciplines occurred.

It is easy to understand how this rupture came about. Only al-Kindī, but still in a very inchoate fashion, gives us a kind of first outline of what could be called a Muslim philosophy in its true sense. From al-Fārābī onwards, the vision of the world of the *falāsifa* was built on an eternal creation, willed certainly by the First Being (God), but necessarily emanating from Him; and if it is possible to speak of an agreement between the prophetic revelation and the intelligible apprehension of the philosopher, it is,we are told, that the first expresses the second according to the usage of the 'vulgar' (*'awāmm*) in the form of symbols and allegories. It is only the field of worship which specifically belongs to it.

Such an attitude of mind raised no acute problem at the time of the Eastern *falsafa*, from the third/ninth to the beginning of the fifth/eleventh century; but matters were not to continue thus. Eastern *falsafa* in fact existed in an atmosphere profoundly impregnated with Shi'ism; Western *falsafa* in the sixth/twelfth century was under the patronage of the

Almohads, and it was Sultan Abū Ya'qūb Yūsuf who asked Ibn Rushd to produce a commentary on Aristotle. Not only did al-Fārābī and Ibn Sīnā enjoy the patronage of princes, but the milieu in which they lived, accustomed to Ismā'īlī ideas, was not likely to take offence either at their emanationist cosmology, or at the kind of intellectualist mystique which coloured their theory of knowledge, or at their secret preference for an interpretation (*ta'wīl*) which found in the texts of the Qur'ān their own view of the world. On the contrary, the Almohad milieu obliged the Western *falsafa* to present a defence of its Sunnī Muslim faith. Certainly it is true that the philosophy of Ibn Ṭufayl, and in particular that of Ibn Rushd, sometimes opposed some theses of Ibn Sīnā; beyond Ibn Sīnā, he often ended by agreeing with al-Fārābī, though not without affirming his own originality. Also, Ibn Rushd was often faithful to Aristotle, whereas al-Fārābī and Ibn Sīnā were open to neo-Platonic influences and even to influences from ancient Persia. But they all retained essentially the same basic attitude to established religion. The apologia undertaken by Ibn Rushd in his works of self-defence should not be allowed to deceive us over this.

The hundred and fifty years which separate Ibn Sīnā from Ibn Rushd had seen the triumph of Sunnism over Shi'ism, and the launching of the massive attacks of the 'people of the Tradition' or the doctors of *kalām* against *falsafa*. The *Tahāfut* denounced as dangerous seventeen propositions drawn from the works of the eastern *falāsifa* and declared four of their theses to be tainted with impiety (*takfīr*): the double eternity of the world *ante* and *post*, the denial of a true divine knowledge of singular realities, and the denial of the bodily resurrection. The Shī'ī disciple of Ibn Sīna, Naṣīr al-Dīn Ṭūsī, undertook the task of justifying his master. Ibn Rushd, in his *Tahāfut al-tahāfut* and in his *Faṣl al-maqāl* concentrated his efforts on the defence of *falsafa* itself, though not without some criticism of Ibn Sīnā. In the latter work he openly expresses his contempt for the dialectic of the people of the *kalām*, 'sick minds' who do nothing but 'shatter the law of religion in pieces'.[1]

The 'quarrel of the *Tahāfut*' is justly famous, but the rejoinder of the second *Tahāfut* was by no means decisive. In fact the traces of Shī'ī influence, which had marked the beginning of the Almohad reform, had been forced to give way in the face of official severity. The position of the Western *falsafa* was always to be an uncomfortable one, placed as

[1] *Faṣl al-maqāl*, Fr. ed. and trans. by L. Gauthier, (Algiers, 1942), 29; cf. again Ibn Rushd, *Kashf 'an manāhij . . ., apud Falsafat Ibn Rushd* (Cairo A.H. 1313 and 1328), 68.

it was between the intermittent favour of the rulers and the easily offended strict codes of the jurists. Ibn Rushd's self-justification, such an important document in the history of ideas, did nothing at all to disarm the latter. His works were burned in his own lifetime and this Cordovan ended his life in exile at Marrakesh. In short (and unlike al-Fārābī and Ibn Sīnā) Western *falsafa* had scarcely any influence on Muslim thought but was to exert all its influence on medieval Europe.

Broadly speaking, it can be said that the conqueror in the quarrel of the *Tahāfut* was al-Ghazālī, and we should not end this chapter without returning, however briefly, to this interesting figure. Abū Ḥāmid al-Ghazālī is without doubt one of the most famous figures in the history of Muslim culture. His biography is well known: his period of scepticism, then his finding certainty again in first principles, his investigations in *kalām* and *falsafa*, his refutation of the Ismāʿīlī extremists, and finally his conversion to Sufism considered as a personal experience. His great work *Iḥyāʾ ʿulūm al-dīn* ('Revival of the religious sciences') goes beyond the traditional cadres of the 'religious sciences', and concerns them all. The modern Ḥanbalī tendency represented by Ibn Taymiyya was to accuse al-Ghazālī of having watered down Islam first by his broad eclecticism—in which were mingled Christian, Jewish and neo-Platonic influences—and secondly by the affective values which he incorporated in his faith. Some of them even, rather hastily, cast doubts on his sincerity. However, being a Shafiʿite by allegiance, he found among the Shafiʿites passionate supporters, such as al-Subkī, and he was to retain the title of 'Proof of Islam' (*Ḥujjat al-Islām*). It is true that he failed in his task as reformer, and that he failed in the last resort to promote a reasoned understanding of the faith; but after his conversion to Sufism in 488/1095, he produced many pages of spiritual writings on repentance, humility, surrender to God, and the love of God which continue to foster in Islam a genuine piety. They reach beyond the age in which they were written to remain a priceless heritage for men of all time.

CONCLUSION

Thus the cultural movement in the Islamic countries from the first/seventh to the ninth/fifteenth century appears as an extremely rich and complex collection of disciplines. It has its religious field—its 'religious sciences' or learning; it has its field of free philosophical and scientific research, which was at times permitted and protected by the authorities and at times regarded with suspicion by official Islam; and it has its field of the religious and secular arts, and of secular poetry and prose. The question arises whether a distinction should be made between a *Muslim* culture proper, inspired by Islamic values and particularly by the text of the Qur'ān, and a culture which existed *in Muslim territory*, and which either interpreted the religious beliefs of Islam in its own way, or ignored them or even opposed them.

It is certainly true that this distinction has some correspondence with the facts and it can serve as a useful principle for the classification of works and genres, with the proviso however that one should not attribute to it such a sharpness as it would possess, *mutatis mutandis*, in the Christian world. Although the Islam of the jurists and the doctors condemned the licence of the Umayyad or 'Abbasid courts or of the *amīrs* of Syria and Persia, yet the patronage of the princes produced literary and artistic masterpieces, and a way of life which contributed to the brilliance of one of the great civilizations.

Nevertheless the fact is that Islam is, in its deepest sense, *dīn wa-dawla*, 'religion and city', and too rigid a classification into separate sections would not be true to the historic reality. In the Muslim countries neither science nor secular literature or art were separated from religion in the way that certain branches of modern humanism have been in Europe. They were affected by Muslim values. To make again the distinction between *dīn* (religion) and *Islām*, it could be said that they belonged to Islam considered as a community, as a temporal city, without being attached, nevertheless, to the sphere of religion.

Taken as a whole, both religious and secular, Muslim culture of the classical age was always by preference to be Arabic in expression, and even exclusively Arabic in the region from Baghdād to Cordova. There should not be ignored, however, the authentic Persian culture which was contemporary with it. The Turkish culture was not to begin its development until the eighth/fourteenth century; even then it must be remarked that, until the ninth–tenth/fifteenth–sixteenth centuries, in the islamized Turkish countries Arabic was to remain in current use in the field of religion and Persian in that of literature.

Similarly Persian territory should not always be identified with Persian culture. According to the periods and the authors, the chosen language of culture would sometimes be Arabic and sometimes Persian, even within one amirate. In the fourth–fifth/tenth–eleventh centuries, Ibn Sīnā, a native of distant Bukhārā, wrote all his great works in Arabic but adopted Persian for his *Dānesh-nāma* composed at the request of the *amīr* 'Alā' al-Dawla. Firdawsī and al-Ghazālī were born in the same town of Ṭūs. Firdawsī, who wrote of ancient Persia, and only in Persian, seems to have intended to manifest his attachment to the Muslim religion by composing after the *Shāh-nāma* the poem of *Yūsuf u-Zulaykhā*. Nevertheless on his death he was excluded from the Muslim cemetery. Yet a hundred and thirty years later, al-Ghazālī, also a native of Ṭūs, of Shafi'ite and Ash'arite allegiance, was to earn the name of 'Proof of Islam', and his influence was to extend as far as the Almohad reform in the Maghrib.

The third/ninth century saw the development of the basic religious sciences of *tafsīr*, *Ḥadīth* and *fiqh*; the fourth/tenth century produced the great schools of *kalām*, and these two centuries were at the same time the golden age of the freest philosophical and scientific research. In this, Shi'ism, chiefly in its Ismā'īlī branches, played its usual role of catalyst. *Falsafa* cannot be called a Muslim philosophy in the strict meaning of the term: it was rather a Hellenistic philosophy, Arabic or Persian in expression, and with Muslim influences. But it became a vigorous leaven, through its influence, direct or indirect, and through the very refutations which it provoked. The triumph of Sunnism from the fifth/eleventh century onwards is paradoxically a proof of this. Although al-Ghazālī declared himself to be primarily a spiritual writer whose concern was with interior religious experience, yet without *falsafa* his work would have lacked an entire philosophical dimension. In order to oppose *falsafa* effectively, he studied it closely, and carried the debate even into the territory of his adversaries. In this way he had to introduce neo-Platonic elements into the very structure of the traditional problematic. Traces of it are found in the objective summary of the 'religious sciences' to which Ibn Khaldūn devotes several chapters of his *Muqaddima*.

It is probably possible to see in the powerful Ḥanbalī influence one of the most profound and sustained expressions of Sunnī Muslim thought as such. But Ḥanbalī thought was continually enriched by its struggles, sometimes against Shi'ism, and at other times against all trends of *'ilm al-kalām*. A prime example of this is the *Dhamm al-kalām* of the Ḥanbalī Ṣūfī, al-Anṣārī; and even Ibn Taymiyya himself owes many refinements of his analyses to his principal Shī'ī adversaries Ṭūsī and Ḥillī.

The great cultures which came later, the Safavid restoration in Persia and the Mughal civilization in India, were no longer involved in the same way with the *dār al-Islām* in its entirety. It seems, on the contrary, that it was to the combination of its basically Muslim inspiration, to the predominance of the Arabic language, to the patronage accorded (though not always unreservedly) to the arts and literature, and finally to the extensive welcome given to the 'foreign sciences', that the culture of the classical age owed its specific character and influence, and its own complex unity from the Indus to the shores of the Atlantic.

From the ninth/fifteenth century onwards, the 'religious sciences' scarcely developed at all. We cannot consider here the reasons for this. But it is possible to suggest that it was the tension between secular and religious elements which produced the greatness of the Arabo- and Perso-Muslim classicism, and that the presence of both of them was necessary for this. And it may be that a clearer recognition of unity of contrasts will enable Islam as a culture to be accorded its rightful place in the history of universal culture.

CHAPTER 6

MYSTICISM

'Religious mysticism,' wrote W. R. Inge in his classic *Christian mysticism*, 'may be defined as the attempt to realize the presence of the living God in the soul and in nature, or, more generally, as the attempt to realize, in thought and feeling, the immanence of the temporal in the eternal, and of the eternal in the temporal.' Many other definitions of mysticism have been formulated, and some of these have been re-examined with critical acumen by Professor R. C. Zaehner in his *Mysticism sacred and profane.* It is worth recalling that the mystics of Islam were equally at a loss to reach a precise and satisfactory description of the undescribable; Professor R. A. Nicholson once collected a very large list of definitions of Sufism by practising Ṣūfīs.[1] If mysticism in general is beyond accurate and concise definition, the particular variety of mysticism known as Sufism may perhaps be described briefly as the attempt of individual Muslims to realize in their personal experience the living presence of Allāh.

The Christian mystic in his quest for union with God relies first upon the person of Jesus Christ who, being of the Godhead, is Himself both the object of worship, the supreme model, and the goal of attainment. Next he studies the nature of God and His purpose in the world as revealed in the Holy Scriptures. For examples of mystical endeavour he turns to the lives of the saints and the writings of the mystics. Finally he seeks to prepare himself for the gift of Divine grace by observing the sacraments and acts of public worship, by the assiduous practice of self-denial, and by private meditation and other recommended forms of spiritual exercise. The Muslim mystic has no Christ-figure to mediate and intercede between himself and Allāh. The person of Muḥammad, it is true, idealized in time as the Perfect Man, came partly to supply that want; but Muḥammad was never accorded divine honours. For the Ṣūfī, the Logos was God revealed in His speech (the Qur'ān) and His act (the created world); so the Qur'ān was the focus of his faith and meditation, the physical universe the arena in which he observed God in action. Like his Christian brother, he could follow his prescribed discipline of public ritual and private devotion. The early saints of

[1] R. A. Nicholson, 'A Historical Enquiry concerning the Origin and Development of Sufism', in *JRAS* (1906), 303–48.

Islam furnished him with abundant example, the supreme model being the founder of the faith. Later on, many manuals were written for the instruction of the mystic, and convents were founded to promote the communal life of austerity and the service of God.

The formative period of Sufism extended over the first three centuries of the Muslim era. The term *taṣawwuf* (i.e., Sufism) was derived from *ṣūf* (wool); the Ṣūfī by wearing coarse woollen garments, according to some accounts in emulation of Christian practice,[1] proclaimed his renunciation of the world. Asceticism and quietism characterized the first phase of this movement, which was essentially a reaction against the wealth and luxury that, flooding in from the conquered provinces of Byzantium and Persia, threatened to overwhelm Islam and to destroy its primitive simplicity and other-worldliness. An eloquent spokesman of this protest was Ḥasan al-Baṣrī (d. 110/728), a man equally famous in the history of Muslim theology, for he is reputed a founder of the Muʿtazilī school. Enjoying the confidence of the godly ʿUmar II, he set the fashion, followed by later Ṣūfīs to their great personal risk, of blunt preaching against corruption in high places before the caliph himself. Others through the second/eighth century registered their disapproval by going apart from their fellows: in conscious imitation of the Christian anchorites still scattered through the Levant, they took refuge in caves and deserts where they devoted themselves wholly to the life of self-denial. Such were the men described by a woman ascetic of Syria.[2]

Their every purpose is with God united,
  Their high ambitions mount to Him alone;
Their troth is to the Lord and Master plighted—
  O noble quest, for the Eternal One!

They do not quarrel over this world's pleasure—
  Honours, and children, rich and costly gowns,
All greed and appetite! They do not treasure
  The life of ease and joy that dwells in towns.

Facing the far and faint horizon yonder
  They seek the Infinite, with purpose strong;
They ever tread where desert runnels wander,
  And high on towering mountain-tops they throng.

Still others, and they the great majority, sought to solve their personal problem by earning a bare subsistence in honest and lawful toil in the

[1] See A. J. Arberry, *Sufism* (London, 1950), 34–5; L. Massignon, *Essai sur les origines du lexique technique de la mystique musulmane*, (Paris, 1922), 131.

[2] Quoted in al-Kalābādhī, *Kitāb al-Taʿarruf* (Cairo, 1934), 10.

practise of useful crafts, otherwise keeping to their humble apartments and occupying their days and nights with the service of God.

The ascetic movement spread from Medina to Kūfa and Baṣra, to Damascus and newly founded Baghdād, to the distant provinces of Khurāsān and Sind. Presently two principal centres of Sufism developed; in the capital city of Islam, and in north-eastern Persia. A pioneer in the latter region was Ibrāhīm b. Adham, reputed prince of Balkh, who gave up his kingdom in answer to the heavenly challenge, and wandered abroad; he hired himself out as a jobbing gardener in Syria, and achieved the martyr's crown about 160/776 fighting against Byzantium. Contemporary with him were the learned traditionist Sufyān al-Thawrī of Kūfa (d. 161/778) who founded a short-lived school of jurisprudence, and suffered persecution because he refused public office; and the famous woman-saint Rābi'a of Baṣra (d. 185/801), a lifelong virgin by conviction who preached the new doctrine of Divine love.[1]

Two ways I love Thee: selfishly,
And next, as worthy is of Thee.
'Tis selfish love that I do naught
Save think on Thee with every thought.
'Tis purest love when Thou dost raise
The veil to my adoring gaze.
Not mine the praise in that or this:
Thine is the praise in both, I wis.

The transition from simple asceticism to a complex theory of the mystical discipline, and thereafter to a highly developed theosophy, took place during the third/ninth century. The exact course of this transformation cannot now be traced with confidence, since our knowledge of the leading figures in the first phase depends upon secondary sources. Shaqīq of Balkh (d. 194/810), for instance, is said to have been the first to define trust in God (*tawakkul*) as a mystical state (*ḥāl*). This statement rests on a relatively late authority,[2] and presumes that in his time the distinction had already been drawn between station (*maqām*) and state (*ḥāl*). This differentiation, which belongs to a mature and elaborate theory of the mystic's progress towards his goal of passing away in God (*fanā'*), defines 'station' as a degree attained by personal effort, whereas 'state' represents an advance contingent upon grace.

[1] Translation by R. A. Nicholson, *A literary history of the Arabs* (Cambridge, 1941), 234. For another version see D. S. Margoliouth, *The early development of Mohammedanism* (London, 1914), 175.

[2] Sibṭ Ibn al-Jawzī (d. 654/1257), quoted by Massignon, *Essai*, 228.

'The states are gifts, the stations are earnings' is how the classic theorist of Sufism, al-Qushayrī (d. 465/1072) put the matter. In the sayings attributed to Shaqīq the technical term *ma'rifa* also occurs; this word was used by the Ṣūfīs to denote mystical knowledge of God, as distinct from formal knowledge (*'ilm*) derived from revelation and reason and shared by all thoughtful believers; it is generally translated 'gnosis'. Another respectable fifth/eleventh-century source puts this key word already into the mouth of 'Abd Allāh b. al-Mubārak of Merv (d. 181/797), otherwise known as a Traditionist who collected sayings of the Prophet on the theme of self-denial (*zuhd*). Yet the name commonly associated with the introduction into Ṣūfī doctrine of the idea of gnosis is Dhu'l-Nūn al-Miṣrī (d. 246/861), a more substantial figure for all that much legend of alchemy and unriddling of the hieroglyphs and thaumaturgy has gathered around his powerful personality.

In the life of Dhu'l-Nūn, whose grave is still to be seen near the Pyramids, three streams of the Ṣūfī movement ran together. Visited in Egypt by mystics from Persia, he was summoned to Baghdād to answer charges of heresy, and thus had close personal contact with the two principal schools of theosophy. Supposed, after gnostic fashion, to be in possession of the secret of the Greatest Name of God, in his litanies and poems he exhibits a convincing awareness of the presence of God in the world and within the mystic's soul.

> O God, I never hearken to the voices of the beasts or the rustle of the trees, the splashing of waters or the song of the birds, the whistling of the wind or the rumble of thunder, but I sense in them a testimony to Thy unity, and a proof of Thy incomparableness; that Thou art the All-prevailing, the All-knowing, the All-wise, the All-just, the All-true, and that in Thee is neither overthrow nor ignorance nor folly nor injustice nor lying. O God, I acknowledge Thee in the proof of Thy handiwork and the evidence of Thy acts: grant me, O God, to seek Thy satisfaction with my satisfaction, and the delight of a Father in His child, remembering Thee in my love for Thee, with serene tranquillity and firm resolve.

Dhu'l-Nūn's arraignment before the Caliph al-Mutawakkil, relentless champion of strict orthodoxy in its war against the 'rationalizing' Mu'tazila, was symptomatic of the alarm which the growing boldness and popularity of Ṣūfī preaching had awakened in the hearts of professional divines. The Egyptian gnostic was but one of many Ṣūfīs who faced persecution during this period, culminating in the public scandal and cruel execution of al-Ḥallāj (d. 309/922). More shocking to conservative opinion than Dhu'l-Nūn's poetical utterances was the unrestrained language of Abū Yazīd (Bāyazīd) al-Bisṭāmī (d. 261/875), protagonist of the Khurasanian school of 'intoxicated' mysticism. Whether under Indian influence (as Horten and Zaehner have argued) or independently reaching Vedantist conclusions, Abū Yazīd claimed actually to have achieved union with God. '*Subḥānī! mā aʿẓama shaʾnī!*' ('Glory be to me! how great is my majesty!'): this ejaculation of ecstasy, explained away by Ṣūfī apologists as God speaking through the annihilated mystic, sounded to less sympathetic ears very like a claim to divinity. Meditating on the popular story of the Prophet's ascension (*miʿrāj*) to the seventh heaven, Abū Yazīd experienced a like rapture of the spirit and set a precedent which other Ṣūfīs aspired to follow.

When He brought me to the brink of the Divine Unity, I divorced myself and betook myself to my Lord, calling upon Him to succour me. 'Master,' I cried, 'I beseech Thee as one to whom nothing else remains.' When He recognized the sincerity of my prayer, and how I had despaired of myself, the first token that came to me proving that He had answered this prayer was that He caused me to forget myself utterly, and to forget all creatures and all dominions. So I was stripped of all cares, and remained without any care. Then I went on traversing one kingdom after another; whenever I came to them I said to them, 'Stand, and let me pass.' So I would make them stand and I would pass until I reached them all. So He drew me near, appointing for me a way to Him nearer than soul to body. Then He said, 'Abū Yazīd, all of them are My creatures, except thee.' I replied, 'So I am Thou, and Thou art I, and I am Thou.'

The founder of the Baghdād school of speculative mysticism was al-Ḥārith b. Asad al-Muḥāsibī (d. 243/837). Born at Baṣra in 165/781, he moved to the capital early in life and became an accomplished student of Traditions, by then a very flourishing science. His readiness to accept as authentic sayings of the Prophet favourable to Ṣūfī ideas brought upon him the wrath of Aḥmad b. Ḥanbal, formidable inceptor of the conservative Ḥanbalī school of jurisprudence, and for a time he had to flee back to his native city. Presently however he returned to Baghdād, and enlisted a following of disciples to whom he imparted his doctrines in a series of books, most famous of which is *al-Riʿāya li-ḥuqūq Allāh* ('The observance of God's rights'). This work laid the foundations of the 'science' of mysticism; attentively studied, it served as a model for later writers. Al-Muḥāsibī supported his theses with frequent references to the Qur'ān and the Traditions, after the manner of the orthodox lawyer and theologian. In another book, the *Kitāb al-naṣā'iḥ* ('Book of counsels'), he describes his desperate search for the way of salvation out of the seventy-odd sects into which Islam had been split; the 'saved' proved to be the Ṣūfīs, whose company he accordingly joined.

Then the merciful God gave me to know a people in whom I found my godfearing guides, models of piety, that preferred the world to come above this world. They ever counselled patience in hardship and adversity, acquiescence in fate, and gratitude for blessings received; they sought to win men to a love of God, reminding them of His goodness and kindness and urging them to repentance unto Him. These men have elaborated the nature of religious conduct, and have prescribed rules for piety, which are past my power to follow. I therefore knew that religious conduct and true piety are a sea wherein the like of me must needs drown, and which such as I can never explore. Then God opened unto me a knowledge in which both proof was clear and decision shone, and I had hopes that whoever should draw near to this knowledge and adopt it for his own would be saved. I therefore saw that it was necessary for me to adopt this knowledge, and to practise its ordinances; I believed in it in my heart, and embraced it in my mind, and made it the foundation of my faith. Upon this I have built my actions, in it moved in all my doings.

With these words al-Muḥāsibī accepted the challenge flung down by the orthodox, claiming the Ṣūfīs to be the truly orthodox; at the same time he opened the door to that grand reconciliation between theology and mysticism which ensued a century and more after him. He had defended the Ṣūfī cause by using the same weapons as its most rigorous opponents, the powerful coalition of Traditionists and lawyers. His disciple al-Junayd (d. 289/910) resumed the argument and fought it out with the second most influential group, the scholastic theologians. The central problem agitating the minds of the religious learned in this century of decision was to elucidate a comprehensive doctrine of the cardinal dogma of Islam, the Divine Unity (*tawḥīd*). This topic was treated by al-Junayd in a series of subtly-composed epistles (*Rasā'il*) written to or for his fellow-Ṣūfīs, and collected after his death. He summed up his findings in a famous definition which came to be accepted as authoritative by most Ṣūfīs, and commanded the approval of even so strict a Ḥanbalī as Ibn Taymiyya (d. 728/1328): *ifrād al-Qadīm 'an al-muḥdath* ('the separation of the Eternal from what was originated in time'). This formula involved, on the human side, the central point of Ṣūfī theory, that the mystic may hope, by God's grace crowning his own exertions, ultimately to reach a state of self-naughting that he passes away (in *fanā'*) from his human attributes and survives eternally (in *baqā'*) united with God. In this stage 'the servant of God returns to his first state, that he is as he was before he existed'. It has been well pointed out[1] that this idea of a pre-existence of the human soul seems to echo neo-Platonic ideas, specifically as expressed by Plotinus in *Enneads* vi, 4. 14: 'Before we had our becoming here, we existed There, men other than now; we were pure souls . . . Now we are become a dual thing, no longer that which we were at first, dormant, and in a sense no longer present.' If in fact al-Junayd here leaned on what had been already translated of the Greek philosophers, he concealed the borrowing well, citing in proof of his startling theory the celebrated 'Covenant' (*mīthāq*) verse of Qur'ān, 7. 171.

And when thy Lord took from the Children of Adam,
from their loins, their seed, and made them testify
touching themselves, 'Am I not your Lord,'
They said, 'Yes, we testify.'

Al-Junayd gathered around him a large circle of men of like purpose, mostly learned artisans, and the discussions which enlivened those regular meetings for instruction and meditation bore abundant fruit. One of the leading personalities was Abū Sa'īd al-Kharrāz, author of the surviving *Kitāb al-ṣidq* ('Book of truthfulness'), credited by al-Hujwīrī (d. *c.* 467/1075) with the invention of the doctrine of *fanā'* and *baqā'* which loomed so large in his master's teaching. Some of al-Junayd's followers were inspired by what they heard and witnessed to become poets of the mystical life; the handful of their verses saved from the shipwreck of time is a tantalizing reminder of the much more that is lost. Such a one was Abu'l-Ḥusayn al-Nūrī, so named because he saw the Divine Light (*nūr*).

O God, I fear Thee: not because
I dread the wrath to come; for how
Can such affright, when never was
A friend more excellent than Thou?
Thou knowest well the heart's design,
The secret purpose of the mind;
And I adore Thee, Light Divine,
Lest lesser lights should make me blind.

Poetry now became an important element in the discipline as well as the literature of Sufism. One of the exercises found most effective in

[1] Ali Abdel Kader, 'The Doctrine of al-Junayd', in *The Islamic Quarterly*, I (1954), 167–77.

stimulating ecstasy was to listen to the recitation of verses, sometimes to musical accompaniment. The practice of 'audition' (*samā'*) reminiscent of the use of music in Christian liturgies, and even dancing, gave rise to fierce controversy which raged for many centuries; the Ḥanbalīs in particular were loud in condemning so dangerous an innovation. One was dealing not merely with metaphysical poetry, which though strange and novel could hardly be denounced on moral grounds. To al-Junayd himself we owe some verses of this character.

Now I have known, O lord,
What lies within my heart;
In secret, from the world apart,
My tongue has talked with my Adored.

So in a manner we
United are, and One;
Yet otherwise disunion
Is our estate eternally.

Though from my gaze profound
Deep awe has hid Thy face,
In wondrous and ecstatic grace
I feel Thee touch my inmost ground.

In like manner another unknown poet-mystic of the Baghdād circle spoke of the transforming union.

When truth its light doth show,
I lose myself in reverence,
And am as one who never travelled thence
To life below.

When I am absented
From self in Him, and Him attain,
Attainment's self thereafter proveth vain
And self is dead.

In union divine
With Him, Him only I do see;
I dwell alone, and that felicity
No more is mine.

This mystic union
From self hath separated me:
Now witness concentration's mystery
Of two made one.

If the verses recited at Ṣūfī concerts had been confined to such compositions, few would have cavilled. The scandal arose from the use of profane literature—the love-poems of an 'Umar b. Abī Rabī'a, the bacchanalian effusions of an Abū Nuwās—chanted by a handsome youth whose beauty was taken as a focus of concentration, being an example of the handiwork of the Divine Artist. This convention, no doubt innocent enough in its inception, gave rise to suspicion of grave misconduct; it also engendered the rich and fine literature of the Persian *ghazal*.

Whilst the Baghdād circle was thus contributing massively to the development of a metaphysic of mysticism, no less important advances were continuing to be made in Persia. Sahl b. 'Abd Allāh al-Tustarī (d. 283/896), to whom is accredited the first Ṣūfī commentary on the Qur'ān, evolved a doctrine of letters and light which later influenced the Spanish school from Ibn Masarra to Ibn al-'Arabī. Abū 'Abd Allāh al-Tirmidhī (*fl.* 285/898) in a long series of books and pamphlets, many of which are extant, elaborated a kind of mystic psychology which was taken up by al-Ghazālī and incorporated into his system; he also enunciated a novel doctrine of sainthood and prophecy which reappeared in the writings of Ibn al-'Arabī. Meanwhile al-Ḥallāj, born about 244/858 in the province of Fārs, wandered through a large part of the Muslim world, reaching as far as India and the borders of China, preaching a form of union with God which outraged the orthodox, and shocked many of his fellow-Ṣūfīs; condemned as an 'incarnationist' and a blasphemer, he was gibbeted in Baghdād in 309/922.

> If ye do not recognize God, at least recognize His signs. I am that sign, I am the Creative Truth, because through the Truth I am a truth eternally. My friends and teachers are Iblīs and Pharaoh. Iblīs was threatened with Hell-fire, yet he did not recant. Pharaoh was drowned in the sea, yet he did not recant, for he would not acknowledge anything between him and God. And I, though I am killed and crucified, and though my hands and feet are cut off—I do not recant.

The foregoing extract from his *Kitāb al-ṭawāsīn* places in its context the notorious phrase *Ana'l-Ḥaqq* ('I am the Creative Truth') which the adversaries of al-Ḥallāj fastened on as a claim to personal apotheosis. The legend of his death invites comparison with the Christian story of the Crucifixion, which may well have been in his mind as his torturers made ready to slay him.[1]

[1] This and the preceding citation are from versions made by R. A. Nicholson, *The idea of personality in Sufism* (Cambridge, 1923), 32; 'Mysticism', in T. Arnold and A. Guillaume (edd.), *The legacy of Islam* (Oxford, 1931), 217.

When he was brought to be crucified and saw the cross and the nails, he turned to the people and uttered a prayer, ending with the words: 'And these Thy servants who are gathered to slay me, in zeal for Thy religion and in desire to win Thy favour, forgive them, O Lord, and have mercy upon them; for verily if Thou hadst revealed to them that which Thou hast revealed to me, they would not have done what they have done; and if Thou hadst hidden from me that which Thou hast hidden from them, I should not have suffered this tribulation. Glory unto Thee in whatsoever Thou doest, and glory unto Thee in whatsoever Thou willest.'

The brutal martyrdom of al-Ḥallāj startled into circumspection all but the most God-intoxicated Ṣūfīs, who thereafter strove for a way of reconciliation. The mystics of the fourth/tenth century in the main returned to a safer pattern of behaviour and public utterance. The long life of Ibn Khafīf, who died in Shīrāz in 371/982, was a model of scrupulous piety and a careful regard for orthodoxy. A number of scholars now judged the time ripe to sum up the doctrine and practices of the Ṣūfīs as embodied in the school of al-Junayd, and to argue that these were in harmony with the Sunnī code and creed. Abū Naṣr al-Sarrāj (d. 378/988) in his *Kitāb al-luma'* ('Book of flashes'), and Abū Ṭālib al-Makkī (d. 386/996) in his *Qūt al-qulūb* ('Food for the hearts') produced lengthy and learned treatises which in their sedulous advocacy of moderation went far to allay the suspicions of all but the most conservative theologians. In a shorter work, the *Kitāb al-ta'arruf li-madhhab ahl al-taṣawwuf* ('The doctrine of the Ṣūfīs') Abū Bakr al-Kalābādhī (d. *c.* 385/995), who also wrote a commentary on Traditions, prefaced his description of Ṣūfī mystical theory with an account of their theology which corresponds closely to, and even quotes from, a Ḥanbalī creed published in his own lifetime. Then Abū 'Abd al-Raḥmān al-Sulamī (d. 412/1021), a busy author who wrote an extensive Ṣūfī exegesis of the Qur'ān and many lesser works, compiled in his *Ṭabaqāt al-Ṣūfiyya* ('Classes of Ṣūfīs') the first comprehensive register of Muslim mystics. This pioneering book, aimed at proving the right of the Ṣūfīs to be accorded the same serious treatment as Traditionists, theologians, lawyers, poets, grammarians and the rest of 'classified' notables, was followed shortly afterwards by the encyclopaedic *Ḥilyat al-awliyā'* ('Ornament of the saints') put together by that learned biographer Abū Nu'aym al-Iṣfahānī (d. 430/1038) and published in ten large volumes. Then in 437/1045 Abu'l-Qāsim al-Qushayrī (d. 465/1074), who also wrote a Ṣūfī commentary on the Qur'ān and numerous other books, promulgated his famous *Risāla* ('Epistle') which set the seal on the work of rehabilitation and was accepted as the classical exposition of orthodox Sufism. Not many years later Hujwīrī composed his *Kashf al-maḥjūb* ('Uncovering of the veiled'), the first treatise on Sufism in the Persian language. To round off this summary account of the century of consolidation, we may note the names of two of the greatest figures in medieval Islam: the Persians, 'Abd Allāh al-Anṣārī (d. 481/1088) and Abū Ḥāmid al-Ghazālī (d. 505/1111).

By the end of the fifth/eleventh century a broad measure of agreement had been reached on the meaning of Sufism and the details of Ṣūfī experience and theory. Sufism was very far from pretending to be an independent sect of Islam, a separatist movement such as those which had broken to fragments the legendary monolithic communion of the early years of the faith. The great teachers of those times were no Luthers or Wesleys, founding breakaway churches. Islam was in dire need of reform and revival, but the Ṣūfīs elected to reform and revive from within; they even succeeded in overriding the embattled frontiers between *Sunna* and Shī'a. The last obstacle in the path of complete assimilation was swept aside by the gigantic labours of al-Ghazālī, that most eminent theologian and jurist, who demolished the philosophers and philosophizing Ismā'īlīs, and completed a reconciliation between orthodoxy and mysticism which immensely strengthened both to withstand the battery of adverse circumstance soon to be loosed against the very existence of Islam. His masterpiece of irenic propaganda, the *Iḥyā' 'ulūm al-dīn*, proved to be more than what its title claimed, a 'revivification of the religious sciences'; it led to a revival of the religion itself.

As has been stated, the classic description of Sufism, studied as a textbook in the medieval colleges and commented upon by many eminent scholars, was the *Risāla* of al-Qushayrī. Addressed in the form of an epistle general 'to all Ṣūfīs throughout the lands of Islam', the book opens with an eloquent exposition of a familiar theme, lamenting the decay of true religion and calling for a return to true faith and sincere practice. After summarizing the tenets of the Ṣūfīs, with special emphasis on their doctrine of *tawḥīd* (unitarianism), al-Qushayrī lists the leaders of the movement beginning with Ibrāhīm b. Adham and ending with al-Rūdhbārī (d. 369/980). (It is noteworthy that in compiling this catalogue he follows closely the classification established by al-Sulamī; both writers exclude from the register such early figures as Ḥasan al-Baṣrī and Mālik b. Dīnār, admitted to the Ṣūfī canon by Abū Nu'aym and Hujwīrī.)

Next, al-Qushayrī offers to explain the technical terms current amongst the Ṣūfīs; such are *waqt* (mystical moment), *maqām* (station), *ḥāl* (state), *qabḍ* (contraction) and *basṭ* (expansion), *jam'* (concentration) and *farq* (separation), *fanā'* (passing-away) and *baqā'* (continuance), *ghayba* (absence) and *ḥuḍūr* (presence), *ṣaḥw* (sobriety) and *sukr* (intoxication), *qurb* (propinquity) and *bu'd* (remoteness). In defining these terms al-Qushayrī was following in the footsteps of al-Sarrāj, and anticipating the technical dictionaries of al-Kāshānī, al-Jurjānī and al-Tahānawī.

The distinction between *maqām* and *ḥāl*, though not observed with complete rigour by al-Qushayrī, nevertheless enables him to divide the mystic's progress into two parts. The 'stations' come first, being headed by (1) *Tawba* (conversion), as commanded by God in Qur'ān, 24. 31: 'And turn all together to God, O you believers; haply so you will prosper.' (It may be noticed incidentally that this text comes at the end of an exhortation to women to behave with decent propriety.) The primary obligation to repent was stressed by all the Ṣūfī masters; when Farīd al-Dīn 'Aṭṭār came to write his lives of the saints he recounted at the beginning of each biography the circumstances of the mystic's conversion.

Thereafter the mystic progresses through the following stations.

(2) *Mujāhada* (earnest striving), as prescribed in Qur'ān, 29. 69: 'But those who struggle in Our cause, surely We shall guide them in our ways.' The Ṣūfīs liked to quote a Tradition which made the Prophet declare that the 'greater warfare' (*al-jihād al-akbar*) fought against the lusts of the flesh was superior to the 'lesser warfare' (*al-jihād al-aṣghar*) waged in the field against the infidels.

(3) *Khalwa wa-'uzla* (solitariness and withdrawal), the former at the beginning of the neophyte's training and the latter when his initiation is complete, so that he may not be disturbed by his fellows and may be free to attend completely to his inward life with God.

(4) *Taqwā* (the awe of God), for Qur'ān, 49. 13 states: 'Surely the noblest among you in the sight of God is the most godfearing of you.'

(5) *Wara'* (abstention), in the sense meant by the Prophet when he declared, 'One of the signs of a man's excellence as a Muslim is that he abandons what does not concern him.'

(6) *Zuhd* (renunciation), even of permitted indulgences.

(7) *Ṣamt* (silence), as the Prophet said, 'Whoever believes in God and

the Last Day, let him speak good, or else let him be silent.' Silence is both external (the reining of the tongue) and internal (the reining of the heart, so that a man silently accepts God's decree).

(8) *Khawf* (fear). Qur'ān 32. 16 says of true believers that 'their sides shun their couches as they call on their Lord in fear and hope'. The mystic is fearful that God may punish him in the future, whether in this world or the next.

(9) *Rajā'* (hope), the reverse side of the same coin, as Qur'ān, 29. 4 states: 'Whoso hopes to encounter God, God's term is coming.'

(10) *Ḥuzn* (sorrow), for 'God loves every sorrowful heart' that grieves over past sins.

So al-Qushayrī takes us from station to station, until we come to (20) *Riḍā* (satisfaction), according to some Ṣūfīs the last of the 'stations' and the first of the 'states'; they quote in evidence of this Qur'ān, 5. 119, 'God being well-pleased with them and they well-pleased with him' which in its context describes the blessed in Paradise. According to al-Qushayrī, the Khurasanian school held that *riḍā* was a station, being a development out of *tawakkul* (trust in God), whereas the 'Irāqī school maintained that it was a 'stage' since God's good pleasure precedes man's satisfaction; he proposes a compromise, taking the beginning of *riḍā* to be a *maqām* and its conclusion a *ḥāl*.

The transition having been accomplished, the following states then ensue.

(21) *'Ubūdiyya* (servanthood), being constantly aware of God as Lord, as bidden in Qur'ān, 15. 99: 'And serve thy Lord, until the Certain comes to thee.'

(22) *Irāda* (desire), the attitude described in Qur'ān, 6. 52: 'And do not drive away those who call upon their Lord at morning and evening desiring His countenance.'

The last two states enumerated by al-Qushayrī are (44) *Maḥabba* (love) and (45) *Shawq* (yearning), when the imagery of Lover and Beloved is fully applicable. His catalogue is far more extensive than that of al-Sarrāj, who recognized only seven stations and ten states; it differs also substantially from al-Kalābādhī's treatment, and totally from Hujwīrī's. The latter indeed offers a novel classification of the Ṣūfīs into twelve sects, 'of which two are reprobated and ten are approved'. He names these sects, each with its distinctive doctrinal features, as follows.

(1) Muḥāsibīs, the followers of al-Muḥāsibī.

(2) Qaṣṣārīs, the followers of Ḥamdūn al-Qaṣṣār (d. 271/884), named by al-Sulamī as the founder of the heterodox Malāmatī school of those Ṣūfīs who courted blame as a proof of their total detachment from worldly things.

(3) Ṭayfūrīs, the followers of Abū Yazīd al-Bisṭāmī, the 'drunken' school.

(4) Junaydīs, the followers of al-Junayd.

(5) Nūrīs, the followers of Abu'l-Ḥusayn al-Nūrī (d. 295/908).

(6) Sahlīs, the followers of Sahl b. 'Abd Allāh al-Tustarī.

(7) Ḥakīmīs, the followers of Abū 'Abd Allāh al-Tirmidhī.

(8) Kharrāzīs, the followers of Abū Sa'īd al-Kharrāz.

(9) Khafīfīs, the followers of Ibn Khafīf.

(10) Sayyārīs, the followers of Abu'l-'Abbās al-Sayyārī of Merv (d. 342/953). 'His school of Sufism is the only one that has kept its original doctrine unchanged.'

These, according to Hujwīrī, are the ten orthodox Ṣūfī sects. The two 'reprobate' sects, consisting of 'those heretics who have connected themselves with the Ṣūfīs and have adopted Sufiistic phraseology as a means of promulgating their heresy', are lumped together as (11) Ḥulūlīs (Incarnationists), followers of Abū Ḥulmān of Damascus (founder of the Ḥulmāniyya sect, condemned by the Ash'arīs) and of Fāris al-Baghdādī who 'pretends to have derived his doctrine from al-Ḥallāj'.

The pattern of the mystic's progress invented by 'Abd Allāh al-Anṣārī in his celebrated *Manāzil al-sā'irīn* ('Stages of the travellers') is still more formal and elaborate than that of any of his predecessors. Accounted the most eminent Ḥanbalī scholar of his generation, al-Anṣārī published, in the Herati dialect of Persian, biographies of the Ṣūfīs based upon the work of al-Sulamī, and this compilation served in its turn as the foundation of the *Nafaḥāt al-uns* ('Exhalations of intimacy') by the great poet Jāmī. To the classical Persian language he contributed exquisite sentences in rhyming prose in the form of *Munājāt* ('Litanies'), whilst his lectures on the Qur'ān were worked up by a pupil into a massive commentary. Quoting a saying of Abū Bakr al-Kattānī (d. 322/934) that 'between God and the servant there are one thousand stations (*maqām*) of light and darkness', al-Anṣārī announces that in the interest of brevity he will reduce that total drastically. Dividing scholastically the Path into ten sections, he subdivides each section into ten chapters. The following list shows the first and last parts of this methodical and subtle tabulation; each topic is introduced with a quotation from the Qur'ān, further analysed, and supported by appropriate definitions.

I. *Bidāyāt* (Beginnings).

1. *Yaqaẓa* (awaking): Qur'ān, 34. 45: 'Say, "I give you but one admonition, that you stand unto God."'

2. *Tawba* (conversion): Qur'ān, 49. 11: 'And whoso repents not, those—they are the evildoers.'

3. *Muḥāsaba* (self-examination): Qur'ān, 59. 18: 'O believers, fear God. Let every soul consider what it has forwarded for the morrow.'

4. *Ināba* (repentence): Qur'ān, 39. 55: 'Turn unto your Lord.'

5. *Tafakkur* (reflection): Qur'ān, 16. 46: 'And We have sent down to thee the Remembrance that thou mayest make clear to mankind what was sent down to them; and so haply they will reflect.'

6. *Tadhakkur* (recollection): Qur'ān, 40. 13: 'Yet none remembers but he who repents.'

7. *I'tiṣām* (holding fast): Qur'ān, 3. 98: 'And hold you fast to God's bond, together.'

8. *Firār* (fleeing): Qur'ān, 51. 50: 'Therefore flee unto God.'

9. *Riyāḍa* (discipline): Qur'ān, 23. 60: 'And those who give what they give, their hearts quaking.'

10. *Samā'* (listening): Qur'ān, 8. 23: 'If God had known of any good in them He would have made them hear.'

X. *Nihāyāt* (Ends).

91. *Ma'rifa* (gnosis): Qur'ān, 5. 86: 'And when they hear what has been sent down to the Messenger, thou seest their eyes overflow with tears because of the truth they recognize.'

92. *Fanā'* (passing away): Qur'ān, 55. 26: 'All that dwells upon the earth is perishing, yet still abides the Face of thy Lord, majestic, splendid.'

93. *Baqā'* (continuance): Qur'ān, 20. 75: 'God is better, and more abiding.'

94. *Taḥqīq* (verification): Qur'ān, 2. 262: '"Why, dost thou not believe?" "Yes," he said, "but that my heart may be at rest."'

95. *Talbīs* (confusion): Qur'ān, 6. 9: 'And We would have confused for them the thing which they themselves are confusing.'

96. *Wujūd* (discovery): Qur'ān, 4. 110: 'He shall find God is All-forgiving, All-compassionate.'

97. *Tajrīd* (divestiture): Qur'ān, 20. 12: 'Put off thy shoes.'

98. *Tafrīd* (isolation): Qur'ān, 24. 25: 'And they shall know that God is the manifest Truth.'

99. *Jamʿ* (uniting): Qur'ān, 8. 17: 'And when thou threwest, it was not thyself that threw, but God threw.'

100. *Tawḥīd* (unification): Qur'ān, 3. 16: 'God bears witness that there is no god but He.'

In 488/1095 Abū Ḥāmid al-Ghazālī, accounted by many the greatest Ashʿarī theologian since al-Ashʿarī and the greatest Shāfiʿī lawyer since al-Shāfiʿī, at the very height of his powers and fame suddenly resigned from his chair of divinity in the Niẓāmiyya academy in Baghdād and went into retirement. Dissatisfied with the intellectual and legalistic approach to religion, disgusted with the hair-splitting sophistries of the philosophers and the scholastics, he took up the life of a wandering dervish searching for that personal experience of God which alone could resolve his doubts and confusions. He afterwards told the story of his conversion to Sufism in a book, *al-Munqidh min al-ḍalāl* ('Deliverance from error'), which ranks amongst the greatest works of religious literature.[1]

Then I turned my attention to the Way of the Ṣūfīs. I knew that it could not be traversed to the end without both doctrine and practice, and that the gist of the doctrine lies in overcoming the appetites of the flesh and getting rid of its evil dispositions and vile qualities, so that the heart may be cleared of all but God; and the means of clearing it is *dhikr Allah*, i.e. commemoration of God and concentration of every thought upon Him. Now, the doctrine was easier to me than the practice, so I began by learning their doctrine from the books and sayings of their Shaykhs, until I acquired as much of their Way as it is possible to acquire by learning and hearing, and saw plainly that what is most peculiar to them cannot be learned, but can only be reached by immediate experience and ecstasy and inward transformation.... I became convinced that I had now acquired all the knowledge of Ṣūfism that could possibly be obtained by means of study; as for the rest, there was no way of coming to it except by leading the mystical life. I looked on myself as I then was. Worldly interests encompassed me on every side. Even my work as a teacher—the best thing I was engaged in—seemed unimportant and useless in view of the life hereafter. When I considered the intention of my teaching, I perceived that instead of doing it for God's sake alone I had no motive but the desire for glory and reputation. I realized that I stood on the edge of a precipice and would fall into Hell-fire unless I set about to mend my ways.... Conscious of my helplessness and having surrendered my will entirely, I took refuge with God as a man in sore trouble who has no resource left. God answered my prayer and made it easy for me to turn my back on reputation and wealth and wife and children and friends.

[1] The following passage is quoted from R. A. Nicholson, *Idea of personality*, 39–40.

After an interval of self-discipline and meditation al-Ghazālī took up once more his always fluent pen. He applied himself energetically to putting on paper a complete system of belief and practice which embraced all that had been formulated by the moderate Ṣūfīs and incorporated with this the revered teachings of the Fathers of Islam. This great task was accomplished in the *Iḥyā' 'ulūm al-dīn*, later re-presented on a smaller scale for Persian readers in the *Kīmiyā-yi sa'ādat* ('Alchemy of happiness'). These two large works, composed in easy and attractive style, were intended for the edification of the general public. In his last years al-Ghazālī addressed himself to a more select circle of inner initiates, taking into his purview the neo-Platonic doctrine of emanation, thus paving the way for the so-called pantheism of Ibn al-Fāriḍ and Ibn al-'Arabī. The startling conception of the Idea of Muḥammad (*al-ḥaqīqat al-Muḥammadiyya*) as the 'light of lights' (*al-nūr al-Muḥammadī*), present already in the suspect writings of al-Ḥallāj and probably deriving from Shī'ī and ultimately from Gnostic sources, now came into the main stream of Ṣūfī doctrine.

> By ruling that the desire for Lordship, that is, the divine omnipotence, is inherent in man by nature because he is the image of God, Ghazālī smoothed the path for all the pathological excesses that were later to bring Sufism into disrepute . . . It is a matter of regret that Ghazālī should have put the whole weight of his authority in the scale of the monistic brand of Sufism that had invaded the movement in the person of Abū Yazīd; and it is a matter of surprise that a man who, when all is said and done, boasted of an intelligence well above the ordinary, should have shown himself so credulously naïve in his approach to the very questionable practices of the accredited Sufis. After Ghazālī, with but few exceptions, the mystical stream—in Persia at least where little effort was made at systematization—got lost in the sands of religious syncretism in which monism, pantheism, and theism were inextricably mingled; yet this doctrinal confusion, so maddening to the intellect, produced a poetic flowering that has seldom been equalled.'[1]

The sixth/twelfth century saw the beginnings of the full development of an institution which thereafter dominated the Ṣūfī movement and mediated its mass appeal—the *ṭarīqa* or dervish order. Earlier, somewhat ephemeral 'schools' of Ṣūfī teaching had gathered around the leading figures; now the need was felt to perpetuate particular traditions of discipline, the communal life and the shared ritual. Already al-Sulamī had compiled rules of companionship (*ādāb al-ṣuḥba*) which al-Qushayrī and his successors revised. The relationship between spiritual instructor

[1] R. C. Zaehner, *Hindu and Muslim mysticism* (London, 1960), 171, 179–80.

(*shaykh*, *pīr*) and neophyte (*murīd*, *shāgird*) acquired an ecclesiastical aura of authority and infallibility; ceremonies of initiation were devised involving the investiture of a distinguishing robe (*khirqa*) and the bestowal of letters-patent attesting true spiritual descent (*silsila*). Convents (*ribāṭ*, *khānqāh*) to serve as residences and centres of instruction were founded and attracted endowments, much after the pattern of the colleges (*madrasa*, *dār*) of theology and religious jurisprudence.

The oldest of the still surviving orders is the Qādiriyya, so named after its founder ʿAbd al-Qādir al-Jīlānī (471–561/1078–1166). Like al-Anṣārī, ʿAbd al-Qādir was primarily a strict and learned Ḥanbalī and his chief work, *al-Ghunya li-ṭālibī ṭarīq al-ḥaqq* ('Sufficiency for the seekers after the path of truth'), is composed in the form of a regular Ḥanbalī textbook, except that it concludes with a section on the Ṣūfī way of life. The *ribāṭ* in Baghdād in which he taught passed after his death under the control of his sons, and became the centre of a vigorous propaganda which carried the legend of ʿAbd al-Qādir as far afield as Morocco and the East Indies. The saying put into his mouth, 'My foot is on the neck of every saint of God,' was taken to justify his elevation to the rank of a universal mediator with rights of worship not far short of the Divine. To this day his tomb in Baghdād, converted by Sultan Süleymān in 941/1535 into a spectacular shrine, attracts multitudes of pilgrims; its keeper is a direct descendant of the saint.

> The Qādiri order is on the whole amongst the most tolerant and progressive orders, not far removed from orthodoxy, distinguished by philanthropy, piety, and humility, and averse to fanaticism, whether religious or political. It seems unlikely that the founder instituted any rigid system of devotional exercises, and these in fact differ in the various congregations. A typical *dhikr* is the following, to be recited after the daily prayers: 'I ask pardon of the mighty God; Glorified be God; May God bless our Master Mohammed and his household and Companions; There is no God but Allah,' each phrase repeated a hundred times.[1]

Numerous sub-orders developed out of the Qādiriyya, some of which became independent; the most notable is the Rifāʿiyya, founded by ʿAbd al-Qādir's nephew, Aḥmad al-Rifāʿī (d. 578/1183), and widely distributed through Turkey, Syria and Egypt. 'This order was distinguished by a more fanatical outlook and more extreme practices of self-mortification, as well as extravagant thaumaturgical exercises, such as glass-eating, fire-walking, and playing with serpents, which have

[1] H. A. R. Gibb, *Mohammedanism* (London, 1949), 155–6.

been imputed to the influence of primitive Shamanism during the Mongol occupation of 'Irāq in the thirteenth century.[1]

A second order was presently established in Baghdād by Shihāb al-Dīn al-Suhrawardī (539-632/1144-1234), nephew of a Ṣūfī rector of the Niẓāmiyya academy and himself an accomplished Shāfi'ī scholar, a pupil of 'Abd al-Qādir; his best-known work is the *'Awārif al-ma'ārif* ('Benefits of gnoses'), commonly printed on the margins of al-Ghazālī's *Iḥyā'*. The Suhrawardiyya was carried to India by Bahā' al-Dīn al-Mūltānī. Shortly afterwards Nūr al-Dīn al-Shādhilī, born probably near Ceuta in 593/1196 and a pupil of the Maghribī Ṣūfī, Ibn Mashīsh, instituted his own Shādhiliyya community, whose conservative doctrine and orthodox ritual spread rapidly through North Africa, Arabia and Syria. A little later the Mawlawī (Mevlevi) order of Whirling Dervishes sprang up in Konya under the leadership of the great poet Jalāl al-Dīn Rūmī, its characteristic circling dance symbolising the endless quest for the Divine Beloved. Thereafter the orders and sub-orders proliferated with great speed, so that Massignon was able to catalogue no fewer than 175 separate named *ṭarīqas*, many of them having numerous branches.[2]

The lives of three men of exceptional genius spanned the century 560-672/1165-1273, and cast their shadows over the whole world of Islam. The eldest of the trio, Muḥyī al-Dīn b. al-'Arabī, was born at Murcia in southern Spain in 560/1165, studied in Seville and Ceuta, and was initiated into Sufism in Tunis. In 598/1202 he began a long journey eastwards which took him to Mecca, where he resided for a while, through 'Irāq, Anatolia and Syria; he finally settled in Damascus, where he died in 638/1240. One of the most fertile minds and fluent pens in Islam, Ibn al-'Arabī drew upon every available resource—Sunnī, Shī'ī, Ismā'īlī, Ṣūfī, Neoplatonic, Gnostic, Hermetic—to build up a comprehensive system which he expounded in well over three hundred books and pamphlets and a large quantity of poetry. His two chief works are *al-Futūḥāt al-Makkiyya* ('Meccan revelations'), a monument of his Meccan days printed in four huge volumes and running to 560 closely packed sections, and the *Fuṣūṣ al-ḥikam* ('Bezels of wisdom'), a product of his Damascus period. His doctrines have been summarized as follows.[3]

(1) God is absolute Being, and is the sole source of all existence; in Him alone Being and Existence are one and inseparable.

[1] *Ibid.*, 156. [2] The list is printed in *EI*[1], IV, 668-72.

[3] Summarized from A. E. Affifi, *The mystical philosophy of Muhyid Din-ibnul Arabi* (Cambridge, 1939).

(2) The universe possesses relative being, either actual or potential; it is both eternal-existent and temporal-non-existent; eternal-existent as being in God's knowledge, and temporal-non-existent as being external to God.

(3) God is both Transcendent and Immanent, transcendence and immanence being two fundamental aspects of Reality as man knows it.

(4) Being, apart from God, exists by virtue of God's Will, acting in accordance with the laws proper to the things thus existent; His agents are the Divine Names, or universal concepts.

(5) Before coming into existence, things of the phenomenal world were latent in the Mind of God as fixed prototypes (*a'yān thābita*), and were thus one with the Divine Essence and Consciousness; these prototypes are intermediaries between the One as absolute Reality and the phenomenal world.

(6) There is no such thing as union with God in the sense of becoming one with God, but there is the realization of the already existing fact that the mystic *is* one with God.

(7) The creative, animating and rational principle of the universe, or the First Intellect, is the Reality (Idea) of Muḥammad, also called the Reality of Realities (*ḥaqīqat al-ḥaqā'iq*); this principle finds its fullest manifestation in the Perfect Man (*al-insān al-kāmil*).

(8) Each prophet is *a* logos of God; *the* Logos is Muḥammad, the 'head' of the hierarchy of prophets. All these individual logoi are united in the Reality of Muḥammad.

(9) The Perfect Man is a miniature of Reality; he is the microcosm, in whom are reflected all the perfect attributes of the macrocosm. Just as the Reality of Muḥammad was the *creative principle* of the universe, so the Perfect Man was the *cause* of the universe, being the epiphany of God's desire to be known; for only the Perfect Man knows God, loves God, and is loved by God. For Man alone the world was made.

The second of this trio of great mystics, Ibn al-Fāriḍ, was born in Cairo in 586/1181 and died there in 632/1235; his tomb in the Muqaṭṭam hills is a quiet and beautiful shrine. Unlike Ibn al-'Arabī, Ibn al-Fāriḍ was no traveller, his only journey being the Mecca Pilgrimage. For him that rite was a physical counterpart of the spiritual quest, union with the Spirit of Muḥammad, intermediary between God and the world. He expressed this yearning and its ultimate realization in a series of mannered odes, full of the imagery of love and intoxication, culminating in the longest ode in Arabic literature, the *Naẓm al-sulūk* ('Poem of the way').

In a famous passage the poet compares this world of phenomena with the projections of a shadow-play.

And be thou not all heedless of the play:
The sport of playthings is the earnestness
Of a right earnest soul. Beware: turn not
Thy back on every tinselled form or state
Illogical: for in illusion's sleep
The shadow-phantom's spectre brings to thee
That the translucent curtains do reveal.
Thou seest forms of things in every garb
Displayed before thee from behind the veil
Of ambiguity: the opposites
In them united for a purpose wise:
Their shapes appear in each and every guise:
Silent, they utter speech: though still, they move:
Themselves unluminous, they scatter light . . .
Thou seest how the birds among the boughs
Delight thee with their cooing, when they chant
Their mournful notes to win thy sympathy,
And marvellest at their voices and their words
Expressing uninterpretable speech.
Then on the land the tawny camels race
Benighted through the wilderness; at sea
The tossed ships run amid the billows deep.
Thou gazest on twain armies—now on land,
Anon at sea—in huge battalions
Clad all in mail of steel for valour's sake
And fenced about with points of swords and spears.
The troops of the land-army—some are knights
Upon their chargers, some stout infantry;
The heroes of the sea-force—some bestride
The decks of ships, some swarm the lance-like masts.
Some violently smite with gleaming swords,
Some thrust with spears strong, tawny, quivering;
Some 'neath the arrows' volley drown in fire,
Some burn in water of the flaming flares.
This troop thou seest offering their lives
In reckless onslaught, that with broken ranks
Fleeing humiliated in the rout.
And thou beholdest the great catapult
Set up and fired, to smash the fortresses
And stubborn strongholds. Likewise thou mayest gaze
On phantom shapes with disembodied souls
Cowering darkly in their dim domain,
Apparelled in strange forms that disaccord

Most wildly with the homely guise of men;
For none would call the Jinnis homely folk.
And fishermen cast in the stream their nets
With busy hands, and swiftly bring forth fish;
And cunning fowlers spread their gins, that birds
A-hunger may be trapped there by a grain.
Ravening monsters of the ocean wreck
The fragile ships; the jungle-lions seize
Their slinking prey; birds swoop on other birds
Out of the heavens; in a wilderness
Beasts hunt for other beasts. And thou mayest glimpse
Still other shapes that I have overpassed
To mention, not relying save upon
The best exemplars. Take a single time
For thy consideration—no great while—
And thou shalt find all that appears to thee
And whatsoever thou dost contemplate
The act of one alone, but in the veils
Of occultation wrapt: when he removes
The curtain, thou beholdest none but him,
And in the shapes confusion no more reigns.

Jalāl al-Dīn Rūmī, the third of this trinity of mystical giants, was born at Balkh in 604/1207, son of a man who was himself a master Ṣūfī. The father, Bahā' al-Dīn Walad, left a record of his meditations in a book called *Ma'ārif* ('Gnoses') which contains many striking descriptions of occult experiences.

I said, 'God is greater!' I saw that all corrupt thoughts, and every thought but the thought of God, all were put to rout. The idea occurred to me that until a certain form enters the mind, sincerity of worship does not appear; until the word 'God' is uttered, there is no turning from corruption to well-being; until I conceive the image of God's attributes, and gaze upon the attributes of the creature, ecstasy and tenderness and true adoration do not manifest. Then you might say that the Adored is imaged in form; and that God has so created the utterance 'God' and the names of His attributes, that when these are sensibly expressed men at once enter into worship. God, it seems has made the declaration of His unity to be the means of the cutting off of all hesitations, whereas He has made the ascription of partners to Him to be the cause of bewilderment. He has likewise made all words and thoughts to be as it were pivots.

Beholding this I said, 'Come, let me efface from my gaze all that is perishing and vincible, that when I look I may be able to see only the Victor, the Eternal. I desire that, as much as I efface, my gaze may become fixed on God's attributes as Victor and Eternal, and the true perfection of God.' As much as I effaced,

I found myself to be the prisoner of things vincible, things created in time. It was as if God was turning about the things created in time; and in the midst of this I saw that I was upon God's shoulder. I looked again, and saw that not only I, but heaven too, and the skies, earth and the empyrean, all were upon God's shoulder: whither would He cast us?

Bahā' al-Dīn fled westwards when the Mongol hordes stormed into Persia, and after long wanderings finally settled in Konya. There Jalāl al-Dīn Rūmī spent the rest of his life, apart from a visit to Damascus, dying in 672/1273. When he came to write poetry, which he did reluctantly under the overwhelming compulsion of mystical rapture, he poured out his soul in a vast collection of odes and quatrains, naming his *Dīwān* after his beloved mystagogue, the wandering dervish Shams al-Dīn of Tabrīz. He also compiled a famous directory of Ṣūfī discipline and doctrine in the *Mathnawī*, six volumes of didactic verse relieved with brilliantly written illustrative anecdotes. Rūmī freely acknowledged his debt to two poets who had already composed Persian epics on the Ṣūfī way, Sanā'ī and Farīd al-Dīn 'Aṭṭār; the latter he had met as a boy in Nīshāpūr. 'Aṭṭār indeed contributed massively to the exposition of Sufism in a series of long poems, most celebrated of which is the *Manṭiq al-ṭayr*, based upon a brief allegory composed by Abū Ḥāmid al-Ghazālī or his brother Aḥmad, and epitomized by Edward Fitz-Gerald in his *Bird-Parliament*.

The doctrine expounded by Rūmī differs little from that of Ibn al-'Arabī, but their objectives were widely at variance. 'The Andalusian always writes with a fixed *philosophical* purpose, which may be defined as the *logical* development of a single all-embracing concept, and much of his thought expresses itself in a dialectic bristling with technicalities. Rūmī has no such aim. As E. H. Whinfield said, his mysticism is not 'doctrinal' in the Catholic sense but 'experimental'. He appeals to the heart more than to the head, scorns the logic of the schools, and nowhere does he embody in philosophical language even the elements of a system. The words used by Dante in reference to the *Divina Commedia* would serve excellently as a description of the *Mathnawī*: 'the poem belongs to the moral or ethical branch of philosophy, its quality is not speculative but practical, and its ultimate end is to lead into the state of felicity those now enduring the miserable life of man'. The *Mathnawī* for the most part shows Rūmī as the perfect spiritual guide engaged in making others perfect and furnishing novice and adept alike with matter suitable to their needs. Assuming the general monistic theory to be well known to his readers, he gives them a panoramic view of the Ṣūfī gnosis (direct intuition of God) and kindles their enthusiasm by depicting the rapture of those who 'break through to the Oneness' and see all mysteries revealed'.[1]

An illustration of Rūmī's technique is his treatment of the Christian theme of the Annunciation, based upon Qur'ān, 19. 16–18.

> And mention in the Book Mary
> when she withdrew from her people
> to an eastern place,
> and she took a veil apart from them;
> then We sent unto her Our Spirit
> that presented himself to her
> a man without fault.
> She said, 'I take refuge in
> the All-merciful from thee!
> If thou fearest God . . .'

Mary, being privately in her chamber, beheld a life-augmenting, heart-ravishing form: the Trusty Spirit rose up before her from the face of the earth, bright as the moon and the sun. Beauty without a veil rose up from the earth, even like as the sun rising in splendour from the East. Trembling overcame Mary's limbs, for she was naked and feared corruption. Mary became unselfed, and in her selflessness she cried, 'I will leap into the Divine protection.'

For she of the pure bosom was wont to take herself in flight to the Unseen. Seeing this world to be a kingdom without permanence, prudently she made a fortress of the Presence of God, to the end that in the hour of death she might have a stronghold which the Adversary would find no way to assail. No better fortress she saw than the protection of God; she chose a camping-place nigh to that castle.

That Proof of the Divine bounty cried out to her, 'I am the trusty messenger of the Presence. Be not afraid of me. Turn not your head away from the lordly ones of the majesty, do not withdraw yourself from such goodly confidants.'

As he spoke, a candle-wick of pure light spiralled up from his lips straight to the star Arcturus.

'You are fleeing from my being into not-being. In not-being I am king and standard-bearer; verily, my house and home are in not-being, only my graven form is before Our Lady. Mary, look well, for I am a form hard to apprehend; I am both a new moon and a fantasy in the heart. I am of the light of the Lord, like the true dawn, for no night encompasses my day. Daughter of 'Imrān, cry not to God for refuge against me, for I have descended from the refuge of God. The refuge of God has been my origin and sustenance, the light of that refuge which was before ever word was spoken. You are taking refuge from me with God; yet in pre-eternity I am the portrait of that Refuge.

[1] R. A. Nicholson, *Rūmī, poet and mystic* (London), 24–5.

I am the refuge that oft-times has been your deliverance; you are taking refuge, and I myself am that refuge. There is no bane worse than ignorance: you are with the Friend, and know not how to love. You suppose the Friend to be a stranger; you have bestowed the name of sorrow upon joy.

By the end of the seventh/thirteenth century the creative phase of Sufism, as a reconciler of philosophy with theology and of both with personal religion, had been completed. Little remained on the intellectual level but to refine points of doctrine; two names may be singled out, those of ʿAbd al-Karīm al-Jīlī (d. 832/1428) and Jāmī (d. 898/1492. The former, following in the footsteps of Ibn al-ʿArabī, perfected the concept of the Perfect Man in a treatise so entitled (*al-Insān al-kāmil*).[1]

The Perfect Man is the *Quṭb* (axis) on which the spheres of existence revolve from first to last, and since things came into being he is one for ever and ever. He hath various guises and appears in diverse bodily tabernacles: in respect of some of these his name is given to him, while in respect of others it is not given to him. His own original name is Mohammed, his name of honour Abu 'l-Qásim, his description ʿAbdullah, and his title Shamsu'ddín. In every age he bears a name suitable to his guise in that age. I once met him in the form of my Shaykh, Sharafu'ddin Ismáʿíl al-Jabartí, but I did not know that he (the Shaykh) was the Prophet, although I knew that he (the Prophet) was the Shaykh. This was one of the visions in which I beheld him at Zabid in A.H. 796. The real meaning of this matter is that the Prophet has the power of assuming every form. When the adept sees him in that form of Mohammed which he wore during his life, he names him by that name, but when he sees him in another form and knows him to be Mohammed, he names him by the name of the form in which he appears. The name Mohammed is not applied except to the Idea of Mohammed.

The identification of Muḥammad with the Perfect Man encouraged a cult of the Prophet which took shape in such works as the *Dalāʾil al-khayrāt* ('Indications of virtues') of the Moroccan al-Jazūlī (d. 870/1465), a collection of litanies and encomia which became the standard prayer-book and rivalled in popularity the famed *Qaṣīdat al-burda* ('Ode of the mantle') of the Egyptian poet al-Būṣīrī (d. 696/1297); finely calligraphed and illuminated copies of both were prized as much for their *baraka* (magical blessing) as their artistic merit. Meanwhile the trinitarian theme of Lover, Love and Beloved, first given formal treatment by Aḥmad al-Ghazālī (d. 517/1123) and developed by ʿAyn al-Quḍāt Hamadānī (d. 525/1131) and the poet Fakhr al-Dīn ʿIrāqī (d. 688/1289), was taken

[1] R. A. Nicholson, *Studies in Islamic mysticism* (Cambridge, 1921), 105.

up again and given metaphysical form by Jāmī in his *Lawā'iḥ* ('Effulgences').[1]

The Absolute does not exist without the relative, and the relative is not formulated without the Absolute; but the relative stands in need of the Absolute, while the Absolute has no need of the relative. Consequently the necessary connection of the two is mutual, but the need is on one side only, as in the case of the motion of a hand holding a key, and that of the key thus held.

O Thou whose sacred precincts none may see,
Unseen Thou makest all things seen to be;
Thou and we are not separate, yet still
Thou hast no need of us, but we of Thee.

It is in regard to His essence that the Absolute has no need of the relative. In other respects the manifestation of the names of His Divinity and the realization of the relations of His Sovereignty are clearly impossible otherwise than by use of the relative.

In me Thy beauty love and longing wrought:
Did I not seek Thee how could'st Thou be sought?
My love is as a mirror in the which
Thy beauty into evidence is brought.

Nay, what is more, it is the 'Truth' who is Himself at once the lover and the beloved, the seeker and the sought. He is loved and sought in His character of the 'One who is all'; and He is lover and seeker when viewed as the sum of all particulars and plurality.

The following extract from the beginning of the *Lawā'iḥ* of 'Ayn al-Quḍāt further illustrates the meditation on the great mystery of creation, first enunciated in a Tradition beloved of the Ṣūfīs, 'I was a hidden treasure and desired to be known, so I created the creation in order that I might be known.'

Spirit and Love came into existence both at one time, being manifested out of the same Creator. Spirit discovered itself to be intermingled with Love, and Love proved to be in suspense upon Spirit. Inasmuch as it was the property of Spirit to be in suspense upon Love, and Love out of its subtlety was intermingled with Spirit, by virtue of that suspense and intermingling union supervened between them. I do not know whether Love became the attribute and Spirit the essence, or Love became the essence and Spirit the attribute; however the matter may have been, the result was that the two became one.

When the radiance of the beauty of the Beloved first manifested out of the Divine Heart, Love began to converse with Spirit. Inasmuch as the one was related to air and the other to fire, the air kindled the fire while the fire consumed the air, so that the fire became the victor and the air received the vanquished;

[1] E. H. Whinfield (ed. and tr.), *Lawā'iḥ* (London, 1907), 36–7.

and God pronounced over Being the words, *It spares not, neither leaves alone* (Qur'ān, 74. 28). Love, which had been the victor, encountering the rays of the lights of the Beloved became vanquished. For this reason it is impossible to know whether Love conforms more with the Lover or with the Beloved, because Love rules over the Lover, whereas Love is a prisoner in the clutches of the Beloved's omnipotence.

Thy love is now the ruler of my soul,
And helplessly I wait on Thy command;
A prisoner in Thy omnipotent hand,
I do not see what cure may make me whole.

Most Persian poetry (apart from political panegyric) from the fifth/eleventh century onwards was impregnated with the ideas and imagery of Sufism. Jāmī, last of the classical poets, being a convinced Ṣūfī, a member indeed of the Naqshbandī order, in his voluminous writings in prose and verse rehearsed again and again the legends of the mystics and the mystical meaning of the legends. His *Nafaḥāt al-uns* brought hagiography down to his own times and teachers; in his graceful idylls, the *Salamān wa-Absāl*, the *Laylā wa-Majnūn*, the *Yūsuf wa-Zulaykhā*, he interpreted stories religious and profane as variations of the same unchanging theme, the agonizing quest of the Lover for the Beloved. This same topic continued to inspire Persian poets down to the nineteenth century, as in verses ascribed to the Bābī heroine, Qurrat al-'Ayn.[1]

The thralls of yearning love constrain in the bonds of pain and calamity
These broken-hearted lovers of thine to yield their lives in their zeal for Thee.
Though with sword in hand my Darling stand with intent to slay,
though I sinless be,
If it pleases Him, this tyrant's whim, I am well content with his tyranny.

Even into the twentieth century the more intellectual bent of the Arab tradition of Sufism found expression in the writings of an Algerian mystic, Shaykh Aḥmad al-'Alawī (d. 1934).[2]

I am Essentially One, Single, Unencroachable
By the least object. Leave I any crevice,
Any space vacant that to another might go?
For the Inside am I of the Essence in Itself
And the Outside of the Quality, Diffuse Concentration.
'Thither' is there none whither I am not turning.
Doth other than Me exist, empty of My Attribute?
My Essence is the Essence of Being, now,

[1] Translation by E. G. Browne, see *A Persian Anthology*, 70–1.
[2] Martin Lings, *A Moslem saint of the twentieth century* (London, 1961), 203.

Always. My Infinity is not limited by the least
Grain of mustard. Where can the creature
Find room to intrude on the Truth's Infinite?
Where other than It, when All is Full?
Union and separation are thus in Principle the same,
And to behold creation is to behold the Truth,
If creation be interpreted as it truly is.

Indeed, the history of creation from beginning to end was summed up long ago in a couple of stanzas by Rūmī, epitomizing the whole intricate but essentially simple Ṣūfī doctrine.

Happy was I
In the pearl's heart to lie;
Till, lashed by life's hurricane,
Like a tossed wave I ran.

The secret of the sea
I uttered thunderously;
Like a spent cloud on the shore
I slept, and stirred no more.

CHAPTER 7

REVIVAL AND REFORM IN ISLAM

THE TRADITION

The period in which formative developments took place in Islam, and at the end of which Muslim orthodoxy crystallized and emerged, roughly covered a period of two centuries and a half. Since this was the formative period, one cannot strictly speak of either revival or reform in Islam during this time, for both revival and reform can logically occur only after an orthodoxy has been established. Nevertheless, it would be a grave error to overlook the developments that occurred during this period since the very emergence of orthodoxy occurred only after long struggle and conflict in the fields of politics, moral ideas and spiritual motifs. Indeed the germs of all the subsequent major developments in Islam, involving moral and spiritual issues, are traceable to this very early period in the history of the Muslim community after the death of the Prophet. The issues as to whether the Muslims should have a state at all, and, if so, what would be its nature and structure; whether the community should be based on a catholic toleration or exclusivism; what type of economic principles should be generally regarded as Islamic; whether man is free and responsible, or whether his actions are pre-determined; whether the community should decide issues in a collective spirit through *ijmāʿ* or whether it should accept the principle of an infallible *Imām*—all these problems were in some form or another raised, and in some sort answered during the earliest generations of Islam.

These conflicts ultimately resulted by the third/ninth century in the acceptance of certain settled attitudes and opinions which, during the course of these centuries, had been given currency in the form of Traditions (sing., *Ḥadīth*) attributed to the Prophet. The 'people of the Tradition' (*ahl al-Ḥadīth*) were responsible for formulating the content of Sunnism which has continued to constitute orthodoxy since then. In these struggles, one can speak of the Shīʿī group as a protest phenomenon for a period, until Shīʿism developed its own theology and independent system. The protest was essentially social and political, against the suppressive attitude of the ascendant Arabs, particularly during the Umayyad period. But Shi'ism soon ceased to be a phenomenon of reform and protest, and hardened into a sect with its doctrines of the infallible imamate and of *taqiyya*, i.e. dissimulation of belief.

The next reform phenomenon is the Ṣūfī movement which started in the second/eighth century, partly as a reaction against the political situation, and partly as a complementary antithesis to the development of the systems of law and theology in Islam. With the natural and rapid expansion of Muslim administration, the speedy development of Muslim law was inevitable. But since law can regulate only the external behaviour of man, some sensitive spirits reacted sharply to these developments, questioning the validity of law as an exhaustive or, indeed, as an adequate expression of Islam. The Ṣūfī movement gathered momentum, and from its original moral and ascetic phase rapidly developed an ideal of ecstatic communion with God, a doctrine of esoteric knowledge—as opposed to external, rational theology—with a system of moral gymnastics as a means to the realization of its final goal. But Sufism, like Shi'ism, threatened to drift from the social and communal ethos of orthodoxy, both by making the individual the centre of its attention, and by its doctrine of esotericism.

Nevertheless, Sufism has exercised, next to orthodoxy, the greatest influence on the Muslim community because of its insistence on the inner reform of the individual, and has, ever since its birth, posed the biggest challenge to orthodoxy down to the dawn of modern times. Since the fourth/tenth century, when Sufism aligned itself intellectually with liberalizing intellectual trends, and combined with its esotericism the philosophic legacy of neo-Platonism, it has exerted a tremendous attraction on some of the best minds in Islam. Orthodoxy, however, did not and could not yield to the ideal of Sufism, which, being incurably individual, ran counter to the ethos of the community. Finally, in the fifth/eleventh century, al-Ghazālī forged a synthesis of Sufism and orthodoxy which has exercised one of the most durable influences on the subsequent development of the community. The substance of al-Ghazālī's reform lies in adopting a Ṣūfī methodology to realize the orthodox ideal. Sufism for al-Ghazāli is a way whereby the verities of the orthodox creed can be both established, and invested with full meaning. This is, of course, not to say that the Sufism of al-Ghazālī is externally and mechanically attached to the truths of the faith; on the contrary, in his book *al-Munqidh min al-ḍalāl*, he tells us how, after having forsaken traditional faith, and having wandered through philosophic thought and Ismāʿīlī doctrines, he *discovered* the truth in orthodox Islam, which, in the hands of its official exponents, had become a mere shell, a set of formal propositions without inner power.[1] While, however, al-Ghazālī's influence has been of the utmost fecundity in the religious history of Islam, and has produced a broad *via media*, developments occurred soon after him which led Sufism and orthodoxy in different directions. Al-Ghazālī is a great watershed of religious ideas in Islam, and his influence has not altogether been in one direction. Although he himself claimed to rediscover the verities of the orthodox creed through Sufism, and many followed him in this path, there are strong elements in his writings which do not yield easily to this synthetic treatment, and he often gives the appearance of being a pure mystic rather than an orthodox mystic. It is certainly difficult to infer an effective societal ethos from his teachings. During the seventh/thirteenth century, the Spanish Muslim Ibn al-ʿArabī developed Sufism into a full-fledged pantheistic doctrine, and became the apostle of the new theosophic Sufism, around which clustered the majority of heterodox Ṣūfīs in the succeeding centuries. From the sixth/twelfth century onwards, Sufism also became a mass movement in the form of organized brotherhoods (sing., *ṭarīqa*) which invaded the entire Muslim world from east to west. The antinomian tendencies, which had often been latent in Sufism, and erupted sporadically in the form of intellectual and spiritual movements, now became rampant in the Muslim world, through their alliance with local religious milieus. Henceforward, this fact constitutes a permanent challenge and a threat to orthodoxy.

The Ṣūfī movement, in fact, gathered up a multifarious and vast stock of ideas, beliefs and practices; and, indeed, threw its mantle over all those trends which either wanted to soften the rigours of the orthodox structure of ideas, or even rebelled against them, whether openly or covertly. Sufism thus not only afforded a haven to certain primitive practices and beliefs from various regions of the gradually islamized world, such as the worship of saints and veneration of tombs; but, in some of its manifestations, looked like being simply a spiritualized version of Ismāʿīlī esotericism, or a philosophical dissipation of the orthodox position through intellectual or pseudo-intellectual arguments.

[1] That al-Ghazālī's mysticism is a purely external and 'methodological' affair is a thesis put forward by Farid Jabre in his *La notion de la maʿrifa chez al-Ghazālī* (Beirut, 1958); for its criticism, see Fazlur Rahman's review of the same in *BSOAS* xxii/2 (1959), 362–4; also his book *Islam* (London, 1966), Ch. VIII.

Whereas, therefore, Sufism, in its moderate forms, became acceptable to, and was even espoused by, the orthodox, its flanks became the focal points of all those trends of varying degrees of intensity which sought either to reform orthodox Islam, or to dissipate it completely. The concentration of all these under cover of Ṣūfī thought and practice offered a challenge, to meet which henceforth absorbed all the energies of the orthodox *'ulamā'*. We thus see a whole complex of reform and counter-reform.

Just as the 'people of the Tradition' had played a decisive role in the early struggles against the Mu'tazila, the Shī'a and the Kharijites, and had helped to crystallize and formulate Sunnī orthodoxy, so once again the same revivalist and reformist zeal appeared with the remarkable Ibn Taymiyya in the seventh–eighth/thirteenth–fourteenth centuries. Ibn Taymiyya was a professed follower of Aḥmad b. Ḥanbal, and a typical representative of the right wing of orthodoxy. The immediate objects of his fiery criticism were Sufism and its representatives, but he was no less vehement against the pure thought of the philosophers, the esotericism of the Shī'a in general and the Ismā'īlīs in particular. Even the orthodox Ash'arite formulation of the Muslim creed receives its share of Ibn Taymiyya's critique.[1] But although Ibn Taymiyya generally gives the impression of being a rigid conservative, uncompromising with either rationalism or Sufism, this impression is not altogether correct. There is discernible in his writings a positive movement of the mind and spirit which genuinely seeks to go behind all historic formulations of Islam by all Muslim groups, to the Qur'ān itself and to the teaching of the Prophet. There is ample evidence that he did not reject all forms of Sufism, and that he in fact regarded the Ṣūfī 'intuition' as being on a par with the *ijtihād* of orthodox *'ulamā'*, both of which, he demanded, must be judged in the light of the Qur'ān and the *Sunna*.[2] Similarly, his critique of existing orthodoxy on some of the fundamental points of the creed, such as the freedom and the efficacy of the human will, almost tilts the balance in favour of the Mu'tazilites against the entrenched orthodoxy, and shows glaringly his boldness in resenting reigning opinions, even when orthodoxy had thrown its mantle upon them. Ibn Taymiyya, therefore, undoubtedly sought, with a large measure of success, to start afresh from the Qur'ān and the *Sunna*, and to

[1] See Fazlur Rahman's article 'Post-Formative Developments in Islam', in *Islamic Studies*, Karachi, I, 4 (1962), 13.

[2] Cf. Fazlur Rahman, *Islam*, Ch. VI.

assign their due places to the subsequent developments in Islam, both orthodox and heterodox.

Nevertheless, however, salutary and fresh the content of Ibn Taymiyya's attempt at the reconstruction of Islam may have been, it had certain serious limitations, which became conspicuous among his followers. These arose essentially from the fact that rationalism is condemned on principle, and insistence is almost entirely laid on the Tradition in understanding Islam. Ibn Taymiyya had acted as a liberalizing force against the authority of the medieval schools, and this was the reason for the unrelenting opposition of the contemporary orthodox '*ulamā*' who wanted to maintain the medieval structure of beliefs and practices of Islam. Nevertheless the effect of his activity was to make rigid the earliest interpretations of Islam, and to entrench them more thoroughly, because of his summons back to the Qur'ān and the *Sunna*. For the *Sunna* was taken in a literalist sense, since Ibn Taymiyya was opposed on principle to rationalism. Secondly, the *Sunna*, as it appears in the form of *Ḥadīth* literature, is not actually the work of the Prophet, but is largely attributable to the early generations of Muslims. The essentially formal and external canons of criticism of *Ḥadīth*, devised by the classical and medieval Muslim authorities, are inadequate for bringing about a genuine historical evaluation of *Ḥadīth* literature. The net result is that, whenever an invitation is given to the Muslims to go back to the *Sunna* of the Prophet, in actual terms it is an invitation to accept the formulations of the early generations of Muslims.[1]

We have dwelt at some length on Ibn Taymiyya's work because, even though he was opposed by his contemporaries, his teaching has not only had historical consequences, in the form of certain major reform movements in recent centuries, but his spirit of free and fresh thinking and enquiry may be said to be alive in much of Modernist Islam.

THE PRE-MODERNIST REFORM MOVEMENTS

The epitome of Ibn Taymiyya's message may be formulated as follows: Man on earth must discover and implement the will of God. The will of God lies enshrined in the Qur'ān and embodied in the *Sunna* of the

[1] I. Goldziher, *Muhammadanische Studien*, Vol. II; J. Schacht, *The Origins of Muhammadan Jurisprudence* (Oxford, 1959); Fazlur Rahman, 'Sunnah, Ijtihād and Ijmā' in the Early period', in *Islamic Studies*, I,/1, (1962); *idem*, 'Sunnah and Ḥadīth', in *Islamic Studies*, I./2, (1962).

Prophet. This will of God is the *Sharī'a*. A community which consciously sets out to implement the *Sharī'a* is a Muslim community. But in order to implement the *Sharī'a*, the Muslim society must set up certain institutions, the most important of which is the state. No form of the state, therefore, has any inherent sanctity: it possesses sanctity only in so far as it is an effective instrument of the Muslim community.[1] This implementation of the will of God is the *'ibāda* or 'service to God'. It will be seen that this message emphasizes not merely the individual, but the collective being of the community, and, therefore, lays greater stress on social virtues and justice than on mere individual virtues. In so doing, Ibn Taymiyya once again captures the essential spirit of the Qur'ān and of the *Sunna* of Muḥammad, and thus goes beyond the *historic* Muslim community. Now the reform movements which burst upon the Muslim world during the seventeenth, eighteenth and nineteenth centuries exhibit this common characteristic, that they bring into the centre of attention the socio-moral reconstruction of Muslim society, as against Sufism, which had stressed primarily the individual and not the society.

It is common to begin an account of these reform movements with Wahhabism, the puritanical, right-wing reform movement led by Muḥammad b. 'Abd al-Wahhāb (d. 1206/1792) in central Arabia. Already in the first quarter of the seventeenth century, however, the Indian divine, Shaykh Aḥmad of Sirhind, had laid the theoretical basis of a similar reform. Shaykh Aḥmad (d. 1034/1625) reacting specifically against the abuses into which Sufism had fallen both theoretically and at the practical level, and working against the background created by the eclecticism of the Mughal Emperor Akbar under the intellectual sponsorship of the two brothers Abu'l-Fażl and Fayżī, vindicated the claims of the *Sharī'a* with its socio-moral ethos, against the latitudinarianism of the Ṣūfīs, and the vague liberalism of the pure intellectuals. As with Ibn Taymiyya, so with Aḥmad Sirhindī, the activism of classical Islam came into full focus with the re-emphasizing of the *Sharī'a*.[2] But political developments in India, and the rapid decline of Muslim power in the subcontinent, could not provide the necessary conditions for the

[1] This question has been more precisely studied in a forthcoming monograph by Mr Qamaruddin Khan, to be published by the Central Institute of Islamic Research, Karachi; in a general way it has been treated by H. Laoust in his *Les doctrines sociales et politiques d'Ibn Taimiya* (Cairo, 1939).

[2] See Fazlur Rahman *Selected letters of Aḥmad Sirhindī*, to be published by the Historical Society of Pakistan, Introduction.

realization of Sirhindī's objectives. Nevertheless, through his work and that of his followers, a reformed spiritual tradition came into existence which played a prominent role in keeping the threads of the community together in the political and social chaos that followed the decay of Mughal power.

But the Wahhābī revolt in the heart of the Arabian peninsula during the next century was much more radical and uncompromising towards the un-Islamic accretions, and the superstitious cults linked with popular Sufism. The movement of Muḥammad b. ʿAbd al-Wahhāb was directly inspired by the ideas of Ibn Taymiyya, but in some major aspects it departed from Ibn Taymiyya himself. Thus, unlike Ibn Taymiyya, the Wahhābīs rejected all forms of Sufism, even though they termed their system *ṭarīqa Muḥammadiyya*. They also rejected, with much more virulence than Ibn Taymiyya or Aḥmad Sirhindī, the intellectualist trends in Islam, which they looked upon with great distrust. Although they rejected the authority of the medieval schools of law, following Ibn Taymiyya, and, like him, insisted on *ijtihād*, or fresh thinking, they did practically everything in their power to discourage the actual tools of positive fresh thinking by rejecting intellectualism. The untiring emphasis of the Wahhābīs (and kindred groups) on *ijtihād* has hence proved fruitless and *practically* they have become 'followers' (*muqallidūn*) of the sum total of the Islamic legacy of the first two centuries and a half, even though being described as 'followers' is anathema to them. The Wahhābīs, however, have done good work by bringing into relief the principles of Islamic egalitarianism and co-operation, and actually founded co-operative farm-villages.

Reform movements, fundamentally of a puritanical character, and seeking to rid the Muslim society of the causes responsible for its degeneration and corruption, grew up in a large part of the Muslim world in the Indian subcontinent. Shāh Walī Allāh of Delhi (d. 1176/1762), following upon Aḥmad Sirhindī, set to work on broadly similar lines. He saw, however, that the political situation in India had radically changed since Sirhindī's time, and he therefore propounded a system which would be congenial to the spiritual environment of the Indian subcontinent, and at the same time calculated to regenerate Islamic forces. His attitude towards Sufism is not one of rejection, but of assimilation as far as possible. But while interpreting the message of Islam in these terms, Shāh Walī Allāh endeavoured to create a social-political substructure for it. He attacked the social and economic injustices prevailing in society, criticized the heavy taxes to which the peasantry was subjected, and called upon the Muslims to build a territorial state which might be integrated into an international Muslim super-state. The thinking of Shāh Walī Allāh, although fundamentally in agreement with other similar reform movements, so far as the social side is concerned, sharply contrasts with the Wahhābī movement in that it seeks to integrate various elements rather than to reject them. Political conditions were unfavourable to him, and his ideas ultimately generated a purely puritanical type of movement, not unlike that of 'Abd al-Wahhāb. This movement, which swept over northern India during the first half of the nineteenth century, was led by Sayyid Aḥmad Barēlwī of Rāe Barēlī and a grandson of Shāh Walī Allāh, Muḥammad Ismā'īl, both of whom were killed in battle against the Sikhs in 1831. It is doubtful, however, whether Sayyid Aḥmad was directly influenced by the Wahhābīs as is generally believed.[1]

The Sanūsī movement of the nineteenth century in Libya exhibits similar characteristics. Although it had the organized form of a Ṣūfī *ṭarīqa* and included some Ṣūfī practices as well, its objectives were radically different. It was basically a social reform movement, aiming at the purification of society from degenerate beliefs, and particularly from corrupting malpractices. Above all, it sought to promote a sense of moral solidarity based on honesty, egalitarianism and economic justice. In spite of the fact that some of the views of the Sanūsī shaykh were attacked by some of the al-Azhar authorities as being heretical, the sociological bases helped its growth, and subsequently it waged a bitter struggle against the expansionist policies of European colonial powers. On more or less similar, but basically more militant lines, were laid the foundations of the Fulanī *Jihād* movement of 'Uthmān dan Fodio and the Mahdist movement in the Sudan. We may sum up the general characteristics of all these movements as follows.

Although the attitudes of these reform phenomena towards Sufism ranged from an outright rejection to a more or less modified acceptance of it, the purely world-negating attitudes of medieval Sufism were combated by them. Those movements, such as the Indian, which integrated Sufism into their system, developed a much more positive

[1] See Fazlur Rahman, *Islam*, Ch. XII. It is noteworthy, however, that Sayyid Aḥmad also called his movement *Ṭariqa Muḥammadiyya*, cf. Murray Titus, *Indian Islam* (Oxford, 1930, revised edition under the title *Islam in India and Pakistan*, 1960), 181–2.

Sufism, endeavoured to eradicate the socio-moral evils that came in the wake of the spread of Sufism and, on the whole, gave it a more dynamic outlook.

The primary concern of all these movements was with the socio-moral reconstruction and reform of society. Although it would be a bold denial of facts to say that any of these movements gave up or even underplayed the concept of the after-life, yet it is significant to note that the *emphasis* had shifted more towards the positive issues of society, whether in political, moral or spiritual terms. The reason for this is not far to seek. It was the social degeneration of Muslim society that had called forth these movements in the first place. They had not come into existence to rectify or strengthen beliefs about the other world but to reform the socio-moral failures of the Muslim community, through which this society had become petrified.

Because of their very nature, therefore, these movements strengthened, in varying degrees, the activism and the moral dynamism which had been characteristic of pristine Islam. All of these movements were politically active; most of them resorted to *jihād* to realize their ideals. This fact, again, aligns them more directly with pristine Islam rather than with historic Islam.

All of these movements, without exception, emphasized a 'return' to pristine Islam in terms of the Qur'ān and the *Sunna* of the Prophet. In practice, however, as we pointed out in the case of Ibn Taymiyya above, the *Sunna* of the Prophet meant the practice or the doctrines worked out by the earliest generations of Muslims.

For this reason, although all these movements unanimously proclaimed the right of *ijtihād*, and denied final authority to all but the Prophet, they were yet able to make but little headway in the reformulation of the content of Islam. The historical belief that the *Ḥadīth* genuinely contains the *Sunna* of the Prophet, combined with the further belief that the *Sunna* of the Prophet and the Qur'anic rulings on social behaviour have to be more or less *literally* implemented in all ages, stood like a rock in the way of any substantial rethinking of the social content of Islam. When, therefore, the leaders of these movements issued the call 'back to the Qur'ān and the *Sunna*', they literally meant that history should move backwards. For the ideal had already been enacted at a given time in the past, viz. in seventh-century Arabia. We shall subsequently see that this utterly revivalist attitude has undergone a considerable modification under the impact of the Modernist movements in Islam, although what revivalism exactly means still remains unclear to the revivalist himself as we shall see.

MODERN ISLAM

The account given above of the pre-Modernist reform movements which swept over the larger part of the Muslim world during the seventeenth, eighteenth and nineteenth centuries has clearly established that the consciousness of degeneration, and of the corresponding need to remedy social evils and raise moral standards, was generated from the heart of Muslim society itself. This needs to be pointed out emphatically, because there is a common error which leads many observers of present-day Muslim society, and its attempts at rethinking and reconstruction, to regard these as being primarily the result of the impact of the West. There are certain considerations which seem to render such a conclusion plausible. The impact of the modern West upon the Muslim East begins with the political and economic expansionism of the West. In almost every case, the Muslim lands suffered a political and military reverse at the hands of the West, and consequently came under its subjection. Because of this political subjection, and the psychological forces generated by it, the Muslim response to the West on the plane of intellectual and scientific thought, and the religious issues raised by this thought, has not been, in its first phase, as constructive as it would have been if the Muslims had been politically ascendant. An average foreign observer, therefore, tends to look upon the Muslim society as an inert mass suffering from a reaction to the Western impact at all levels, but unable to adopt a positive enough attitude towards it. Worse still, many of the modern educated Muslims themselves have come to believe this. The trouble is that the average modern educated Muslim knows as little about his past heritage as does the average foreign observer. Besides being ignorant of his own cultural background, he is mentally a creature of what is essentially the Western educational system—the projection of the West into the Muslim East. He, therefore, begins to think that in so far as progress is actually being achieved in the Muslim world, or is even conceivably achievable, it will be a mere duplication of the West, and that Islam is either neutral in all this, or is perhaps a positive hindrance.

The reform movements described above naturally owed nothing whatsoever to any foreign influence in their genesis, since to postulate any such influence would be a historical absurdity. From the characteristics common to those movements enumerated at the end of the last section, we must conclude that, in so far as the *fact* and the form of the reformist zeal are concerned, they antedate modern Islam, and that modern Islam is a simple continuation, in these respects, of the pre-Modernist reform movements. Where modern Islam does differ from the legacy of these movements is in its positive content. We have seen above that all these movements laid emphasis on fresh thinking (*ijtihād*), but that they were unable to give any large new content to their thinking, because their actual *intention* was focussed on pristine Islam. What the Modernist Muslim has essentially achieved is the maintenance of pristine Islam as a source of inspiration and motive energy, and to this energy he has sought to attach a Modernist content. The measure of success with which this has been done so far, and the rhythm of this entire movement, are now left for us to describe. But we must once again emphasize the continuity between the pre-Modernist awakening and the Modernist renaissance, inasmuch as both are concerned with society. Even the terrific zest and dynamism displayed by the modern movements of liberation from foreign rule are essentially a continuation of the activism of the pre-Modernist reform movements. It is true that to this early Islamic activism, a new nationalist motif has usually been added; but we shall have to discuss more closely the relationship of the nationalist thrust to the earliest *jihād* motivation in various segments of Muslim society.

Intellectual developments

In the very first reactions of the Muslim leaders towards the West, the political and the intellectual factors have gone hand in hand. Thus, Jamāl al-Dīn al-Afghānī (1839–97) combined both these motives in his powerful appeal to the Muslims to awaken to the current situation, to liberate themselves from Western domination, and to carry out the necessary internal reforms that would make for their regeneration and strength. He not only called upon the Muslims to stand against the West politically, but to establish popular and stable governments at home, and to cultivate modern scientific and philosophical knowledge. Although he was not a thinker of great calibre, his activity has left enduring marks on Muslim Modernism as a whole. Apart from his political agitation, the most salient feature of his spiritual attitude, which he has bequeathed to the Modernist Muslim, is his unbounded humanism. Indeed, there is evidence to the effect that even his appreciation of religion was based upon a humanist *élan*; for religion, including Islam, according to him served human ends. It, therefore, must be concluded that his emphasis on populism was not just a means to an external end, the strengthening of Muslim governments against a foreign enemy, but was possessed of intrinsic value. Indeed al-Afghānī appears to be the sympathetic advocate of the downtrodden and the deprived. This is the reason why al-Afghānī not only stirred up Islamic sentiments to rouse the people to meet the challenge of the West, but even appealed to non-Islamic and pre-Islamic cultural factors for this purpose. In India, Egypt and Turkey, for example, he appealed to past Hindu, Pharaonic and pre-Islamic Turkish greatness, and thereby helped to rouse nationalist side by side with Islamic sentiments.

This brief analysis of al-Afghānī reveals simultaneously the unprecedented challenge faced by the Modernist, the complications latent in the modernist situation, and the magnitude of the intellectual task. Its complications are so great that it looks like a vicious circle; and the breaking of this vicious circle carries with it the inconsistencies and anomalies that are characteristic of Modernist attitudes. We have pointed out that the primary task of the pre-Modernist movements was to reform society. The alliance of the spirit of the modern age with the ethos of the pre-Modernist reformers helped further to weaken the Ṣūfī hold upon the educated classes, and further to accentuate the consciousness of social reform. The criticism of historic Muslim social institutions (like polygamy, unregulated divorce and the status of women in general) by orientalists and Christian missionaries specifies the objectives of social reform for the Modernist. But social reform, on closer examination turns out to be a very complex affair, and begins to assume a purely intellectual aspect, because a mere change in social institutions cannot be carried out without rethinking the social ethic and ideas of social justice. Further, social reform implies legislation, and legislation raises very fundamental issues as to who is to legislate, and by virtue of what authority. The entire philosophy of law becomes involved in this—various theories of *ijtihād* and *ijmāʿ* are put forth. This raises further problems of the political constitution of the state, of representation, and the nature of political authority. But change in political ideas and attitudes not only presupposes legislation but also social change itself. This is what we mean by the vicious circle. For the sake of convenience, however, we shall first outline the intellectual developments in modern Islam, since it is ideas which, when they become objects of conviction, are the most potent moving forces in a society.

The bases of modern reformist thinking are, as we have pointed out above, supplied by the pre-Modernist reform movement. It is, therefore, not an accident that the most important Modernist thinkers of the nineteenth and twentieth centuries come from a purificationist-reformist background. We have quoted the notable example of Jamāl al-Dīn al-Afghānī; similar ones are provided by Muḥammad ʿAbduh (d. 1905) of Egypt and Sayyid Aḥmad Khān (d. 1898) of the Indo-Pakistan subcontinent, even though both of these men propounded somewhat different solutions, as we shall see presently. The purificationist reform-legacy of pre-Modernist days, however, could only have prepared the ground for this Modernist thinking, and in the preceding pages we have brought out its essential limitations. Indeed, in so far as its emphasis was literally on a 'going back' to the Qur'ān and the *Sunna*, it appears a positive hindrance in the way of progressive thinking, and, in fact, most reactionaries or revivalists opposed Modernist thinking on these very grounds. Yet, the unanimous call of all the pre-Modernist reforms to *ijtihād* supplied the requisite inspiration for the Modernist to start his work. The actual purificationist activities of these early movements, and their combined efforts either to reject, or at least to control, the extravagances of Sufism stood the Modernist in good stead. In this connexion too, the objective work of orientalists, which focussed attention on the early centuries of Islam, cannot be denied its value. Even the missionary, with his narrow outlook, did not fail to provoke discussion.

But in spite of continuity with earlier reform phenomena, Modernist thinking had to go far beyond anything achieved by the pre-Modernist reform, both in the nature of the questions raised, and in the content of the answers given. The most fundamental question that was raised in Islam (after a lapse of about nine centuries) was that of the relationship between faith and reason, or of faith and scientific thought. This question had preoccupied the minds of the Western thinkers themselves for centuries, particularly from the beginning of their Renaissance, and one cannot help thinking that, to some extent, they have projected their own preoccupations into Islamic discussions around this particular problem. Nevertheless, this question was not raised in Islam for the first time. The Muʿtazilites and the philosophers had asked the same question, and given their own solutions. But the question as raised in the nineteenth century had acquired a new dimension, because of the fact that the actual or putative conflict was not just between religion and thought, as had been the case previously, but that a new scientific world-view had emerged, or was emerging, which had its own claims for recognition. The answers given to this basic problem, both in their form and content, by Muḥammad ʿAbduh and by Sayyid Aḥmad Khān are highly interesting, and at the same time reveal the different approaches of these two types of Modernist. While both emphasize that there cannot be any conflict between Islamic faith and reason, or the religion of Islam and science, and further maintain that Islam is a positive rational and scientific force in the world, the attitude of Muḥammad ʿAbduh, who was a trained *ʿālim*, is a much more moderate one than that of Sayyid Aḥmad Khān. While Muḥammad ʿAbduh more or less seeks to regenerate the rationalizing spirit of the Muʿtazilite school, Sayyid Aḥmad Khān, on the other hand, espouses the much more radical course of medieval Muslim philosophers, such as Ibn Sīnā and Ibn Rushd. This difference does not stop merely at a general level, but appears in the detailed solutions to specific problems handled by both of them.

While it is the aim of both of these thinkers to encourage belief in the scientific world-view, and consequently to discourage belief in superstitions and miracles, the difference in the formulation of their answers is remarkable. Muḥammad ʿAbduh declares as a general principle that the possibility of miracles is to be accepted, but that every particular miracle claimed may be doubted with impunity, either on rational or historical grounds. Thus, one may reject all the miracles one by one, but one may not reject the possibility of miracles as a principle. Very different is the case with Sayyid Aḥmad Khān. He, first of all, lays down the principle of 'conformity of nature'. Nature he declares to be a closely knit system of causes and effects which allow of no supernatural intervention. Indeed, Sayyid Aḥmad Khān seems to espouse a kind of deism which was fashionable among the nineteenth-century scientific circles of the West, and was also closely related to the spirit and the thinking of the medieval Muslim philosophers. Sayyid Aḥmad Khān, therefore, categorically and on principle, rejects the possibility of miracles. Similarly, in the field of historical criticism, the question of *Ḥadīth* comes under discussion. On this point, again, Muḥammad ʿAbduh maintains that one does not incur infidelity to Islam if one doubts any given *Ḥadīth*, but *Ḥadīth* must be accepted on principle and in general. Sayyid Aḥmad Khān, on the other hand, most probably aided by his colleague, Maulavī Chirāgh 'Alī, rejects all *Ḥadīth*. One may say that the method adopted by Sayyid Aḥmad Khān was more thorough-going and consistent, and its conclusions are more radical than those of Muḥammad 'Abduh. But we must remember that neither of these men was aiming simply at producing scientific thought, but that their basic aim was reformist. Reform imposes its own terms, has its own rhythm; and therefore a reformist may well find that he has to put his conclusions in a way that would be acceptable to a large number, if not the whole, of his community. In this sense, as subsequent developments have shown, Muḥammad 'Abduh's ideas have been more potent, and have taken deeper root in the soil than those of Sayyid Aḥmad Khān, whose educational policies were more acceptable to Muslims than his religious ideas.

Formulation of the principle that Islam not only did not oppose reason and science, but encouraged both, persuaded an ever-increasing number of Muslims to take up the study of modern science. Another attempt made by an Indian Muslim to develop a new rationalist theology was also inspired by the leadership of Sayyid Aḥmad Khān; this was the work of Muḥammad Shiblī Nu'mānī (d. 1914) who is, however, better known as a historian. In his work entitled '*Ilm al-kalām* he described the historical genesis and development of the classical Muslim schools of theology. This was followed by a second work entitled *al-Kalām*, wherein Shiblī endeavoured to restate the theses of classical theology in the light of the general nineteenth-century scientific world-view. In doing so he, like Muḥammad 'Abduh, resurrected the rationalist trends of the Mu'tazilite School. His work was, however, rejected as heretical by the orthodox '*ulamā*' of the Deōband Seminary. Shiblī subsequently left 'Alīgarh School (founded by Sayyid Aḥmad Khān) and joined the *Nadwat al-'Ulamā*' at A'ẓamgarh near Lucknow, where he framed his own syllabus for combining traditional and modern learning. The *Nadwa*, as it is called, however, has not produced any thinker of high calibre, and for all intents and purposes its alumni are indistinguishable from the conservative '*ulamā*'.

An obvious corollary of the principle that Islam encourages scientific and rational enquiry is that Islam is a great civilizing and educative force. The fact that through Islam the Arabs became world conquerors and progenitors of a great civilization, supplies the necessary historical evidence for this. The most effective argument built around this thesis was worked out by the eminent jurist Sayyid Amīr 'Alī (d. 1928), whose main contention was that Islam is inherently a civilizing and progressive force. An inevitable result of this position is that those segments of Muslim history, which represent the decline of the Muslims and their civilization, must be rejected as unrepresentative of *Islamic* history. This is what, in fact, many Islamic historians in the late nineteenth and early twentieth century have done. This procedure has been vehemently criticized by certain Western scholars, who have described it as subjective and betraying a lack of intellectual integrity. Irrespective of this controversy, we may note that the character of the intellectual products of Islamic civilization does exhibit something tangibly different from the ancient period, and we think it undeniable that Muslim thought, especially scientific and philosophic, stands at the threshold of modernity.

As for the charge of selectivity and subjectivity against Amīr ʿAlī and others, we must once again remember that these men were not simply historians but implicitly reformers. This explains why they underline those segments of Muslim history which represent greatness and progress in civilization. These are an implicit invitation to the Muslims to re-create parallel history in the future. We must, therefore, distinguish this from strictly descriptive historiography. If a Muslim sees his faith expressed more adequately in one segment of history rather than another, we cannot see any legitimate objection to it. In any case, the idea that all knowledge and progress is *par excellence* Islamic is part of the stock-in-trade of Muslim Modernism, and an inevitable conclusion from the principle that Islam invites man to search and enquire. This is why Muḥammad Iqbāl (1876–1938), when he speaks approvingly of the rapid movement of the Muslim world towards the West, says that by acquiring knowledge from the West the Muslims are only retrieving their lost heritage which they must once again cultivate and develop.

It is obvious, however, that pure Westernism, i.e., the projection of the West into the Muslim society, could not and cannot succeed unless it creates for itself a moral and cultural basis within Muslim society. This means that there must be a process of integration and assimilation of the new forces, and adaptation of their institutional embodiment to the moral-cultural heritage of Islam and vice versa. This vital function is to be performed by Muslim Modernism. But Muslim Modernism, after its initial launching by thinkers like Muḥammad ʿAbduh, Sayyid Aḥmad Khān and Sayyid Amīr ʿAlī, unfortunately, underwent a rapid transformation, and degenerated, on the one hand, into pure apologetics, and, on the other, developed into a more or less purely secular Westernism. Indeed, the story of the decline of positive Modernist thought, beginning roughly with the second decade of the present century, is both interesting and full of lessons. In the Middle East itself, the synthetic thought-movement of Muḥammad ʿAbduh split itself into three parts. In its main direction, under the leadership of his disciple, Rashīd Riḍā, it developed a fundamentalist character, and, although its reformist zeal remained, it progressively assumed the reactionary features of the original Wahhābī movement. Its reformist programme became really limited to the elimination of differences among the different schools of law; it was essentially a throw-back to eighteenth century pre-Modernist fundamentalism. Secondly, the defensive element in Muḥammad ʿAbduh gave rise to a prolific apologetic literature, particularly at the hands of Farīd Wajdī. On all issues of major reform, this apologetic trend defended the old against the new, and endeavoured to create an effective wall against the influx of modern forces and ideas. From being a defence mechanism, it gradually developed into inhibitionism. When, for example, Qāsim Amīn's book entitled *al-Mar'a al-jadīda* ('The new woman'), arguing for improving the status of women and their emancipation, was published, Farīd Wajdī wrote a reply wherein he defended the traditional place of Muslim women in society; and so on. Thirdly, a more or less unmixed thrust of Westernism developed, among the eminent representatives of which may be counted Dr Ṭāhā Ḥusayn. The truth is that the strength of this pure Westernism is commensurate with the virulence of the resurgent fundamentalism and its defensive arm, the new apologetic; this, in turn, is the full measure of the failure of effective Modernism.

In the Indo-Pakistan subcontinent the same story is repeated. The initial modernism of Sayyid Aḥmad Khān and Sayyid Amīr ʿAlī was subjected to bitter invectives and, in fact, denounced as pure Westernism. Men like Abu'l-Kalām Āzād, and the poet Akbar of Allahabad, attacked uncompromisingly the introduction of new ideas and institutions into Muslim society. While the more learned writings of the former were addressed primarily to the higher classes, the bitter epigrams of Akbar proved very effective at the lower-middle class level. Akbar wrote particularly against the new education, and relentlessly satirized the movement for the emancipation of women. Here is one of his quatrains:

Yesterday, having seen some women without veil,
Akbar sank into the earth out of hurt Islamic pride.
When asked whither their veil had gone, they replied
'The veil has fallen upon men's intelligence'.

The reasons for this vehement reaction, and the submergence and decline of modernist thinking, are manifold, and they can only be briefly indicated here. First, the new ideas brought by modern education needed time to ripen in order to produce mature representatives. The relative immaturity of the representatives of modernity has been a great hindrance to the acceptance of modern ideas, and their consequent assimilation through Modernist thought. Allied to this is the fact that the early exponents of Modernism did not fully grasp the deeper spiritual and moral factors behind the phenomenal flowering of modern Western civilization, and they took mainly into consideration only certain external manifestations of this inner vitality, such as modern democratic institutions, universal education, and the emancipation of women. The deeper fountains of the creative vitality of the West, particularly humanism in its various forms, were not studied properly and given due weight.[1] The result was that an attempt was made to transfer, because of their attractiveness, certain more or less external institutions of the West to a new soil wherein they were not properly adapted to the new conditions. Indeed, the Modernist did not develop traditional Muslim thought from the inside to supply an adequate basis for the new values and institutions. It is perhaps also true that liberalism, as it has grown in the modern West, claims absolute validity for itself, and seeks no compromises or rapprochement with any other system of ideas or values. It is obvious enough that this liberalism, pushed to its logical conclusions, is self-defeating, and that it must impose certain checks upon itself. The early Muslim Modernists, the starting point of whose Modernism lay in Westernism, almost deified liberalism, and sought to impose its categories upon Muslim society. The result was that, when their message penetrated into the interior of the society, it was vehemently rejected.

[1] Muḥammad Iqbāl, in the first chapter of his *Reconstruction of religious thought in Islam*, had warned Muslims against being dazzled by the external glamour of the West and had insisted on a deeper penetration into the spirit that moves the Western civilization. But, despite the fact that Iqbāl himself goes to great lengths to cultivate a humanist spirit at the philosophical level, he rejects it almost uncompromisingly in favour of a pure transcendentalism on the ethical plane. This fact itself demonstrates how difficult it is to change quickly settled habits of thought.

Lastly, Muslim society has had to summon up all its energies and concentrate its force on seeking to liberate itself from the political domination of the West, whether direct or indirect. From approximately the beginning of the Balkan Wars in 1912, the Muslim world became conscious that either it must gain independence of foreign powers, or it must finally go under. In this grim struggle where nationalism and Islam fought hand in hand, unity and solidarity were the overriding dictates. In the history of Islam, whenever unity and solidarity have had to be emphasized, differences of opinion have always been discouraged, since differences of opinion have been seen as creating doubts. Since Modernism involves a strenuous and sustained intellectual effort, and must necessarily breed some difference of opinion (liberalism, in any case, must tolerate difference of opinion and interpretation), intellectualism and Modernism were consequently discouraged, and fundamentalism was proportionately strengthened. It would not be going too far to say that the Muslim community in general has usually tilted the balance in favour of external solidarity at the expense of inner growth. This also explains why the most serious of all intellectuals in modern Islam, Muḥammad Iqbāl, in fact tended to discourage intellectualism by what he wrote. He ceaselessly invited the Muslims to cultivate an unshakable certainty, a firm faith, and derided the claims of the pure intellect. There is little doubt that the genius of Islam is also activist, as we have pointed out earlier in this essay, and Iqbāl largely recaptured that activist spirit; but there is all the difference between saying that knowledge must end in action, and between emphasizing action at the expense of the claims of intellectualism.

Given these trends, it is not surprising that strong groups arose in the Middle East and in the Indo-Pakistan subcontinent which were basically fundamentalist, full of an unbounded zeal for action, and suspicious of both modernity and intellectualism. The Muslim Brotherhood of the Arab Middle East, banned in Egypt in 1956, and the *Jamā'at-i Islāmī* of the Indo-Pakistan subcontinent which became especially powerful in Pakistan, and was banned early in 1964, are similar versions of twentieth-century Muslim revivalism and anti-intellectualist activism. Yet, on closer examination, it appears that the revivalism of these groups is more in spirit than in substance. For whenever the representatives of these movements are pressed on any intellectual issue, it is revealed that their position is characterized not by an actual thought-content from the past, but by hardly any thought at all. They are more suspicious of both Modernism and modernity (making hardly any distinction between these two) than they are committed, in the final analysis, to a literal repetition of any actual segment of past history. What has given them power over the middle (and particularly lower middle) classes is not a systematic and coherent understanding of the past, but their embodiment of a reaction against modernizing trends in the upper strata of society; and the fact that they possess no systematic thinking (despite the fact that they are very vocal), does not count against them, because there is hardly any intellectual Modernism in any case. In terms of thought, therefore, they are not at any real disadvantage *vis-à-vis* the modernized classes.

In the recent past, however, certain important developments have taken place in certain parts of the Muslim world, notably Pakistan and Egypt, where centres for the development of Muslim Modernism have been officially set up. The Council of Islamic Research at al-Azhar is even more recent than the Central Institute of Islamic Research in Pakistan. The extent and depth of impact of these institutions on the intellectual life of the Muslim Society will be revealed only with the passage of time. The real task before the Muslim Modernist intellectual is not so much to integrate any given theory or doctrine of modern science and philosophy, as to create the very postulates under which modern thinking becomes possible. Modern thinking on principle must reject authoritarianism of all kinds and must, therefore, rely upon its own resources, facing its risks and reaping its fruits. Openness to correction and, in this sense, a certain amount of doubt, or rather tentativeness, lie in the very nature of modern thought which is an ever-unfolding process, and always experimental. It is on this crucial point that the very nature of modern knowledge comes into conflict with the mental attitudes inculcated by the modern Muslim revivalist or quasi-revivalist movements. The task is, no doubt, difficult and beset with dangers; but there is no particular reason to be pessimistic about the final result, given the right effort.

Social developments

We have seen above that an adequate Islamic intellectual *milieu* still remains to be created in the Muslim world. Until this is achieved, little can be done to start the necessary debate on socio-moral issues, a debate which must be uninhibited, self-confident, non-controversialist and non-apologetic. Nevertheless, a good deal of writing on social issues has taken place, and much actual social change is taking place in Muslim society. The primary reasons for this are, as we have noted before, first that the actual impact of the modern West on Muslim society has been largely on the socio-political front; and, secondly, that the main criticisms of Islamic society both by Christian missionaries and orientalists have been on these very aspects. The early Westernizing Modernists like Sayyid Aḥmad Khān and Sayyid Amīr 'Alī advocated almost without demur the adoption of modern Western concepts of the family (particularly with regard to the status of women), and equally of modern Western forms of democracy. Indeed, while speaking about Jamāl al-Dīn al-Afghānī, we also said that the democratization of the state was even seen as an internal necessity, in order to build up strong governments based on the popular will.

So far as reforms in family law in particular and the status of women in general are concerned, a very large number of Muslim states have actually enacted legislation, taking up the threads from the early Modernists, and in spite of the strong reaction which was directed against this early Modernism by the revivalists and the conservatives. In Pakistan, for example, although even the most important thinker of this century, Muḥammad Iqbāl, had thrown his weight practically on the side of the conservatives on social issues, the Family Laws Ordinance was promulgated in 1960. The conservative '*ulamā*' and their followers, no doubt, continue to exert pressure for the restoration of the traditional *status quo*, but the Modernist minority in Muslim countries, relatively small but vigorous, is politically influential, and holds the initiative, and it looks as though it is impossible for the conservatives to reverse this movement. There is no doubt that on this question the Modernist's stand is on surer grounds, and is helped by the conviction that the new legislation will tighten up the conditions of family life in Muslim society. The conservative or the revivalist, therefore, despite his ostensible appeal to Islam, feels in his heart of hearts that he is on shaky moral grounds in defending the traditional pattern.

The main problem before the Modernist is, indeed, not primarily whether he will succeed in actually changing society within an Islamic framework. Here the Modernist's attempts are often vitiated by the fact that, instead of facing the problem squarely and on intellectual grounds, he tries to circumvent it and is forced to rely on external patchwork. For example, he may often try to show that the Qur'ān does not *really* allow polygamy at all, and invents explanations for its apparent permission of polygamy which are unfaithful to history, and sometimes violate Arabic linguistic usage. He is on surer grounds when, for example, he contends that the Qur'ān did allow polygamy, but at the same time put conditions upon it which show that monogamy is better than polygamy, and that, therefore, the *drift* of the Qur'anic doctrine is towards monogamy. He would be on still surer grounds if, on all legislation which touches socio-economic life and political institutions, he were frankly to give due importance to the social and historical conditions of the Prophet's time; and, having thus made full allowance for the particular historical context, he were honestly to attempt to enunciate the genuine values of the Qur'ān, and to re-embody these values in present conditions. But, for one thing, he has not yet developed the adequate intellectual equipment for this task—calling as it does for historical criticism, and, for another, one sometimes suspects that even his conviction that society is really changing fails him. This second factor puts him psychologically in an ambivalent state which further impedes the adoption of an honest and bold stand. It is also true that, to a considerable extent, the development of a genuine Muslim Modernism is hampered by the fact that controversy between the Christian West and the Muslim East, which was started by the Christian West, has befogged the intellectual *milieu*, and even the sincere Modernist is sometimes affected by the attitudes of the revivalists. It is necessary to control this controversial spirit, and to concentrate on the genuine issues facing the community itself.

Whereas the development of social modernization has assumed a clear-cut line, on political philosophy the issues are as yet much less clear. There are two main problems. First, the question of the relationship of nationalism to a universal Islamic *Umma* has neither been faced nor answered. We have noted that, during the struggle for political liberation, local nationalisms have played a very prominent role, but that in that context, nationalism has acted in alliance with the Islamic sentiment. In certain countries, Islamic sentiment has played the more prominent role of the two. In Algeria, for example, and in the Maghrib in general, the doctrine of *jihād* as preached by the militant liberationists to the masses, was of decisive importance. In Turkey, on the other hand, the nationalist sentiment became very strong, and, indeed, it is only in Turkey that a secular nationalist state has been officially established. But in Turkey, again, the Turks cherish a lively sentiment for the larger Islamic community, although the issue has not been seriously tackled on the intellectual level. Nor can anybody seriously think that the doctrine of the 'Three Concentric Circles' enunciated by the Egyptian president, Jamāl 'Abd al-Nāṣir, offers the hope of any real solution. What one can safely say is that among the masses throughout the Muslim countries, there exists a very strong sentiment for some form of unity of the Islamic world.

The second question in regard to the nature of the state is the problem of democracy. The contention of the early Modernists that the governments must be based on the popular will through some form of representation is generally accepted; and in fact the Modernist contends, not without plausibility, that since Islam is democratic in its ethos, the adoption of modern democratic institutions cannot be un-Islamic. But the problem does not stop here, and is further complicated by two important factors. First, in all these countries there is a relatively small minority which is educated in the modern sense, and which controls affairs, while the vast majority are illiterate. It is not easy to implement democracy under such circumstances. On major and clear-cut national questions, it is true, even an uneducated person may be able to perceive the issues clearly, but in a democracy not all issues that are debated are so clear-cut. But even more acute than lack of education, although undoubtedly allied to it, is the question of rapid economic development, which is a common problem in the under-developed countries, including all the Muslim countries. The economic problem has many ramifications, including the moral demands for honesty, integrity and a sense of responsibility. The exigency of the situation further demands a very high degree of centralized planning and control of economic development. This is felt to necessitate much stabler and stronger governments than would be the case if democracy were superficially and nominally allowed to work. It is this ubiquitous phenomenon which results in the appearance of strong men to give stability to these countries, primarily in the interests of economic growth. From the Islamic point of view, there can be no harm in this, provided that, at the same time, the spirit of democracy is genuinely and gradually cultivated among the people.

Education

All Muslim countries have adopted modern educational institutions in the form of universities, academies and colleges. This fact itself constitutes one of the most important, probably the most important, fact of social change. It is almost universally true that when these institutions were first adopted by Muslim peoples, they represented modern Western secular education with primary emphasis on its technological aspects. The idea behind this has been that, since the traditional society of Islam had put too much emphasis on spirituality, the balance should be restored by the inculcation of modern technological skills. A combination of modern technology, with its vast potentiality for the production of goods, and the traditional spiritual heritage would, it was thought, regenerate the classical glory and greatness of Muslim society. It is, however, obviously doubtful whether the superficial thesis of a marriage between Eastern spirituality and modern Western technology is meaningful or tenable. Along with the technical and scientific subjects, modern philosophy and thought were also taught, while the seats of traditional learning continued side by side with modern educational institutions. The first problem arising from this phenomenon that has a direct bearing on social change is the education of women. An increasingly large number of modern colleges and universities are co-educational. Although there is still a certain amount of resistance to the large-scale education of women and particularly to co-education, there is little doubt that female education is a *fait accompli*. Its sociological consequences are, of course, far-reaching and will bear fruit in their fullness in a few decades' time.

But the more important educational problem is the integration of the new and the old; or, rather, the assimilation of the ever increasing content of modern knowledge with Islamic culture and its values. It is primarily a lack of integration that has so far resulted in a fundamental dichotomy of the Muslim society. To begin with, it is obvious that the simple borrowing of a foreign system of education, shorn of the spiritual, moral and cultural basis which gave birth to it, is not likely to produce results, unless a new and adequate basis for it is created from Islamic tradition and its values. As pointed out before, even with regard to pure technology, it is more than doubtful whether it will lead to the material creativity envisaged, unless it is made the proper instrument of a system of values adequately adjusted to it. Among the countries of the East, only Japan seems to make great technological headway while keeping its traditional cultural background. But developments in Japan after the Second World War render this view much less acceptable, since during the past two decades, the religio-cultural heritage of Japan has itself been invaded by new ideas on a large scale. To put the matter quite concretely, an engineer may know how to build a bridge; but why he should build one, and with what efficiency and zeal, depend entirely on the values that motivate him. His skill, therefore, must be made part and parcel of a total cultural pattern. But leaving technology aside, the modern humanities of the West themselves are replete with certain moral and cultural values which may be said to belong to the Western tradition, and some, indeed, may be traced back clearly to Christianity. Indeed, it is doubtful whether such a seemingly purely rational system of philosophy as that of Immanuel Kant would have been possible without the Christian tradition. This raises questions of a fundamental order for Muslim society and for its assimilation, modification, or rejection, of the content even of purely Western thought.

But the Muslim world is not intellectually equipped to undertake this task as yet. It is only when the modern and the traditional systems of education are properly combined and adjusted that intellectuals will arise adequate to meet this challenge. At the moment, by and large, the traditional seats of learning continue to function separately from modern universities. So far it is only at al-Azhar in Cairo that certain subjects of modern humanities are taught side by side with traditional subjects, but it is doubtful if their level is very high or their effects are very deep. In Pakistan, the traditional *madrasas* strongly resist any encroachment upon their time-honoured and age-worn curricula, and the teaching of Islam in the modern universities, which has started since Independence, is very limited in its nature and rather ineffective. The teachers, and certainly the trainees, in these 'Departments of Islāmiyyāt', are not even equipped with the primary instruments of Islamic studies—such as the Arabic language. A real, effective renaissance of Islam is not possible until educational developments reach the point of contributing from an Islamic standpoint to the humanities of the world at large.

CHAPTER 8

LITERATURE

ARABIC LITERATURE

Arabic literature in its entirety and in the restricted sense is the enduring monument both of a civilization and of a people. Originally the creation of the pastoral nomads of the Arabian peninsula, it had been in pre-Islamic times the literature of an isolated Semitic community when the Arab conquests in the first/seventh century gave it a new role and a universal significance. Its linguistic medium, the *'arabiyya*, the sacred and administrative language of the Arab Muslim empire, developed into the common literary idiom of the various peoples of that empire, and the literature expressed through this common idiom became the most important cultural constituent in medieval Islamic civilization. This literature stimulated the rise, and influenced the development, of a new literary family, that of Islamic literatures represented by Persian, Turkish and Urdu. Its geographical diffusion in three continents enabled it to leave important traces on several non-Islamic literary traditions; for Europe and the Mediterranean region it became, along with the other two classical literatures, Greek and Latin, an integral part of the medieval complex.

The fortunes of this literature in classical times were closely affected by two external factors. The ruling institution exercised, on the whole, an unsalutary influence on its course, as court patronage restricted the freedom of the literary artist and circumscribed the range of his interests. On the other hand, the religious institution rendered it inestimable services. The doctrine of *i'jāz*, the inimitability of the Qur'ān, ensured interest in Arabic literature and literary criticism as the key to the understanding of that doctrine, but it was indirectly that the religious institution made its more permanent contribution. Its jealous guardianship of High Arabic, the common idiom of the Qur'ān and Arabic literature, contributed decisively towards maintaining the *'arabiyya* as the only standard medium of literary expression. This enabled Arabic literature to be enriched by the talents of non-Arab ethnic groups, and what is more, it ensured its very survival in periods of Arab political eclipse, and preserved the strand of continuity throughout its various literary periods over some fifteen centuries. The very structure of Arabic was a third factor, an internal one, the operation of which may be illustrated by reference to one of the language's most distinctive features, namely, the abundance of rhyming words. This has contributed substantially towards making the structure of Arabic verse atomic rather than organic, while the further exigency of the monorhyme has imposed severe limitations on the composition of long poems.

Shaped by these and other factors, which have stamped it with the genius of Arabic, and imbued it with the spirit of Islam, this literature has acquired an individuality which was heightened by its evolution in relative isolation. No external literary tradition exercised a vital influence on its course until very recent times. This has operated to its disadvantage. The dramatic and epic genres, for instance, remained unknown to medieval Arabic poetry; on the other hand, this isolation has resulted in an intensive internal development of its own 'lyrical' genre to the saturation point.

The pre-Islamic period

The solid foundation of this long literary tradition was laid in the pre-Islamic period, notably in the sixth century A.D., when the shepherds and herdsmen of central and north-eastern Arabia perfected a poetic technique and developed a highly complex metrical system, unique in the literary annals of the Semites and all nomadic societies.

This poetry is important historically, and significant artistically. For the non-literate pre-Islamic Arabs, it has preserved the records of the various aspects of their life and history. For literary art, it has given expression to what might be termed the 'desert scene', with its natural phenomena, its landscapes, its fauna and its flora. It abounds with impressive pictures of *natura maligna*, and with fine descriptions of animals and animal life. It is heavily anthropocentric, even egocentric, but its egocentricity is redeemed by the attractive ideal of *murū'a*, the Arab *vir-tus*, which it blazons, the uplifting tones of heroic encounters, and the chastening notes of chivalrous love.

The atomicity of pre-Islamic verse and the convention of the monorhyme naturally favoured short compositions on single themes. But around A.D. 500, there developed an art-form which represented the supreme effort of the pre-Islamic poet to transcend the confining limits of the short composition towards a more complex and layered artistic structure. The *qaṣīda*, as this new art-form came to be called, is a polythematic ode, the many and diverse motifs of which present a panoramic view of desert life, drawn together and unified by the poet's own personality, as he scans the traces of his mistress's encampment in the elegiac-erotic prelude, then proceeds to describe his mount, the wastelands he has crossed, and other aspects of desert life. The expression of a multiplicity of motifs through a verse system so atomic in structure presented obvious compositional problems for the pre-Islamic poet, and it was given to few poets to master the integrative devices and techniques required by the *qaṣīda*, the tradition of which has dominated the composition of Arabic poetry throughout the ages.

Among the poets of the pre-Islamic period, the foremost position is rightly given to Imru'l-Qays, the vagabond prince of Kinda, whose towering poetic personality clearly divides this period into two parts and whose *floruit* may be assigned to the first quarter of the sixth century A.D. His masterful genius domesticated the metres and rhymes of Arabic verse for the expression of a tempestuous and passionate private and public life. His *qaṣīdas*, with their striking similes, vigorous rhythms and inevitable rhymes, are splendid microcosms of life in sixth-century Arabia, while the poignancy of his lyrical cry *qifā nabki*, '*sunt lacrimae rerum*', has not lost its directness of appeal, even after more than fourteen centuries.

During the second half of the sixth century A.D. a far-reaching change came over the spirit of Arabic poetry. The panegyrical tone already known to it entered the structure of the *qaṣīda* and quickly assumed undue significance as its most important motif; improved economic conditions in sixth-century Arabia drew the poets' attention to the economic benefits which could accrue from composing panegyrics on wealthy chiefs, while the two Arab clients of Persia and Byzantium, the Lakhmids and the Ghassanids, opened spacious opportunities for the Arabian poets to visit their courts, and receive handsome rewards in return for their eulogies. This panegyrical tone which the *qaṣīda* acquired, persisted tenaciously, and affected adversely the course of Arabic poetry in Islamic times.

The Islamic period

It was only natural that the literary achievement of the pre-Islamic Arabs should have been in poetry not in prose. But this imbalance was corrected in the first/seventh century by Muḥammad (d. 11/632), both as the recipient of a divinely revealed Sacred Book, the Qur'ān, and as the composer of many speeches, epistles and convenants. With the authoritative and definitive collection of the Qur'anic revelations during the caliphate of 'Uthmān (23–35/644–55), Arabic literature was endowed with a massive prose work to stimulate the development of its prose literature, and to influence its stylistic varieties in the Islamic period; and indeed, the Qur'ān's influence has been incalculable. It was declared unique and inimitable when it was revealed, and so it has remained throughout the ages, casting its spell over Muslim and non-Muslim alike through a sublimity that grips as its *pluralis majestatis* powerfully transmits to erring humanity the voice of the Deity in measured phrase and confident tone to which all the resources of 'that deep-toned instrument', the '*arabiyya*, are made to contribute. No wonder, then, that poetry was temporarily eclipsed by the new prose during the short period of the Patriarchal Caliphs (11–41/632–61) who, moreover, were opposed to an art from which Muḥammad himself had suffered, and which had been crisply denounced in a Qur'anic revelation.

The Umayyad period (41–132/661–750) witnessed a poetic outburst reminiscent of the pre-Islamic one in sixth-century Arabia. The Umayyads revived the traditions of poetic composition, and for political reasons established a firm relationship between poetry and the caliphal court, which was to persist throughout Islamic times. During this period, Arabic poetry experienced two far-reaching transformations: urbanization and islamization. The literary scene shifted from the deserts of Inner Arabia to the arc which comprises the Fertile Crescent and the Ḥijāz. The poets were mostly city-dwellers or urban in taste, and those who were not, e.g., Dhu'l-Rumma (d. 117/735), were anachronistic. The islamization of Arabic poetry was pervasive, ranging from the superficial employment of Islamic terms and ideas in the poetry of the traditional *qaṣīda*-poets to the expression of deeper religious sentiments in the poetry of the politico-religious parties. Poetry borrowed from Islam three impressive motifs: eschatology, Holy War (*jihād*) and the Pilgrimage. The first two fired the imagination of the Kharijites, whose Islamic *ḥamāsa*, expressed both in prose and in verse, is a vivid and powerful reflection of Islam's militancy and piety of fear, (*taqwā*); while the third, the Pilgrimage, through the rites and place-names associated with it, provided the erotic poets of the period with a new context for setting their plots and dialogues, and a host of entirely new associations, through which they restated and refreshed the old themes of love.

The major poets of the period are a triad, al-Akhtal (d. ?92/710), al-Farazdaq (d. ?110/728), and Jarīr (d. ?114/732) who composed for the Umayyad caliphs and their governors in the Fertile Crescent. The closest to the caliphs was al-Akhtal, who was also the last great Christian poet of classical times. The three wasted their prodigious talents as they divided most of their time between the composition of splendid panegyrics and indulgence in unsavoury invectives, with which they entertained Umayyad society.

Far more interesting were the developments in the Arabian peninsula. A new type of poetry came into being and it is the most attractive of all Umayyad poetry. The erotic motif of the old polythematic ode was disengaged from it, and was now developed independently as a love-lyric. The *ghazal*, as this new love-lyric came to be called, was of two kinds. The first was urban, sensuous and gay; it grew in the two cities of the Ḥijāz, Mecca and Medina, stimulated by music and song, and nourished by the affluence and the luxury wholeheartedly granted by the Umayyads to the unfriendly Ḥijāz. It was simple lexically and metrically, almost conversational, and its master was the somewhat narcissistic Qurayshite, the Meccan ʿUmar b. Abī Rabīʿa (d. ? 101/719). The second was bedouin, and it spread in the *bādiyas* of Najd and the Ḥijāz. It was chaste, hopeless and languishing, and was known as ʿUdhrite, after the tribe of ʿUdhra, which produced its most outstanding representative, Jamīl (d. 82/701). But it was the half-legendary Qays from the tribe of ʿĀmir, whose love for his inamorata, Layla, cost him his reason and earned him the sobriquet *al-Majnūn*, that has exercised the greatest influence on later Arabic, Persian and Turkish romancers.

The literary art of the Umayyad period was predominantly poetic. Nevertheless, it enriched Arabic with what is undoubtedly its finest oratorical prose, for which a fertile ground was provided by the intense political conflicts and religious passions of the times. Towards the end of the period, ʿAbd al-Ḥamīd b. Yaḥyā (d. 132/750), the secretary of the last Umayyad caliph, Marwān II, emerged as the first major *kātib* and preluded the contributions of even more illustrious secretaries to the development of Arabic prose literature in the riper age of the ʿAbbasids.

The revolution which brought to power a new dynasty, the ʿAbbasids, also opened for Arabic literature its golden age (132–447/750–1055).

New factors began to operate, and literature developed new features and characteristics. Baghdād centralized literary life as Umayyad Damascus had never done, and its prestige persisted even after its fall to the Buyids in 334/945. Through the rise of provincial centres, Arabic literature was no longer restricted to the Semitic homeland in western Asia, but spread east and west to Central Asia and the farthest shores of the Mediterranean. The contributors to this literature were no longer predominantly Arabs, as they had been in Umayyad times, but belonged to various ethnic groups, of whom the Persians were the most important, both by virtue of their numbers and by their mediation and transmission of foreign influences, e.g., Sasanid court-literature and Indian fables. The rapid development of an Islamic civilization under the ʿAbbasids, cosmopolitan in its facets but nevertheless Qur'ano-centric, 'matured' that literature as it passed on to it, through the common idiom of High Arabic, some of its terms and concepts. The growth and development of Arabic literary criticism evidences this maturity, but unfortunately criticism exercised no salutary influence on literature, as it remained microscopic in its outlook and preoccupations, perhaps answering to the atomic structure of Arabic verse and artistic prose, and thus only confirmed the involvement of literature with pure form and verbal perfection.

Although the ʿAbbasid period is the golden age for both Arabic prose and Arabic poetry, it is the development of the first that is arresting. After being the language of a simple Arab culture in Umayyad times, the *ʿarabiyya* became the language of a complex Islamic civilization. The various specialized disciplines which constituted that civilization developed their own terminologies and modes of expression, but all this redounded to the benefit of Arabic prose—the confluence of many currents from these tributary disciplines. A variety of styles were brought to maturity, and they fall into three main categories: the *muṭlaq* or *mursal*, the free unadorned style of the second/eighth century represented by Ibn al-Muqaffaʿ; the *muzdawij* or *mutawāzin*, the assonantal style of the third/ninth century represented by al-Jāḥiẓ; and the *musajjaʿ*, the rhyming style of the fourth/tenth century represented by Badīʿ al-Zamān. The tendency towards ornateness as prose style progressed from the *muṭlaq* to the *muzdawij* and the *musajjaʿ* was irresistible, encouraged by the very genius of Arabic, by the model of verbal and formal perfection presented by the rival poetic art, and by the views of the literary critics and theorists. It was not so much the *sajʿ*, which can be effective when judiciously used, but the *badī'*, the new style with its ornamental devices and artifices, and particularly one of them, *jinās*, homophony, that deprived Arabic prose of the vigour and functionalism which had characterized it in early 'Abbasid times.

The first group of writers to contribute to the growth of 'Abbasid prose literature were the *kuttāb*, the chancery secretaries, a well-defined group who, as state officials, endured in the service of Arabic literature as long as rulers needed secretaries, and who counted among their numbers in later times Ibn al-'Amīd (d. 360/970), the famous *wazīr* of the Buyids, and al-Qāḍī al-Fāḍil (d. 596/1200), Saladin's secretary. Their most important representative, however, was Ibn al-Muqaffa' (d. *c.* 139/757), who holds a central position not only in the history of Arabic literature, but also in the history of Arabic culture. His *Kalīla wa-Dimna*, an adaptation of the Indian fables of Bidpai from a Pahlavī version, is an Arabic classic which has had a fateful history. The second group of writers were the humanists of the third/ninth century, to whom Arabic prose style, prose literature, and Arabic culture are deeply indebted. They are represented by Jāḥiẓ (d. 255/868) and Ibn Qutayba (d. 276/889). The first is the larger literary personality, a veritable genius who wrote on a wide range of subjects, e.g., 'The book of animals', 'The book of misers'; his Mu'tazilite tastes are reflected even in the intellectual accent of his prose, which ultimately betrays the Hellenic current in the mainstream of his cultural consciousness. To the same group may be added the late figure of al-Tawḥīdī, (d. 414/1023). These humanists enriched the concept of *adab* and enlarged it from the narrow 'secretarial' connotation of 'manners' with its emphasis on the Sasanid tradition, to a wider and fuller one, signifying 'letters', the core of which was the Arabic-Islamic tradition. In so doing, they gave the indigenous Arabic literary tradition a privileged position in the concept of *adab* as it emerged in medieval Islamic times; but they were too much preoccupied with the cultural crisis of their time and with their war against the *Shu'ūbiyya*, and consequently much of their work was educational and didactic.

It was the generation that followed them in the fourth/tenth century, which may be termed the belletrists, that rarefied further the concept of literature—not necessarily to its advantage—and turned it into pure literary art, as is evident from the two prose genres which enjoyed a wide vogue in the fourth/tenth century, namely the *maqāmāt*, 'assemblies' and the *rasā'il*, 'epistles'. The unsurpassed master of the *maqāmāt*,

Badīʿ al-Zamān, '*stupor mundi*' (d. 398/1007) was also its originator. His 'assemblies' are vignettes of a vagabond who lives on his wit and wits but they are also valuable documents of social life in the medieval Islamic city. The *rasāʾil* are literary essays in highly ornamental prose which treat a wide variety of subjects. They have many masters, including Badīʿ al-Zamān and his contemporary Abū Bakr al-Khuwārizmī (d. 383/1002). The most celebrated of all these *rasāʾil*, however, is the substantial *Risālat al-ghufrān* ('Epistle of Pardon') of Abu'l-ʿAlāʾ al-Maʿarrī (d. 339/1058) which describes the journey of a philologist to interview the poets of Heaven and Hell. But its audacity and brilliance of conception are vitiated by the frequent alternation of pedantry and obscurity with which its blind author has, perhaps deliberately, encumbered it.

Unlike prose, Arabic poetry in this, its golden age, presents what might possibly be termed a case of arrested development, as the explosion of intellectual and cultural life touched it peripherally and superficially. It lost the social function it had before, and increased its unwholesome dependence on court patronage. Unable to break away from its atomic structure and unvitalized by any external influence, it ruminated on its own resources and on its pre-ʿAbbasid heritage. Soon enough it became involved in *badīʿ* to which the old *qaṣīda* was married; but the marriage was inconvenient as *badīʿ* encouraged artificiality and tended to drown the fresh impulses and wholesome stirrings which were reaching Arabic poetry from some facets of Islamic civilization, notably philosophy and mysticism.

Bashshār, (d. 167/783) a Persian, heralded the advent of ʿAbbasid poetry, just as it was another Persian, Ibn al-Muqaffaʿ, who opened the history of ʿAbbasid prose. He and his younger contemporary, Abū Nuwās (d. ?195/810) outraged their age and posterity by their unorthodoxy and profligacy, as much as they fascinated it by their versatility and mastery of all forms of Arabic poetry, old and new; but it is their love-lyrics and their wine-songs that have the most enduring interest, both as literary artefacts, and as documents for the movement towards the 'debedouinization' of Arabic poetry. The third/ninth century is dominated by a trio. The first, Abū Tammām (d. 231/846), is the representative of ʿAbbasid neo-classicism, a great poet who strained his poetry by over-intellectualization and a hankering after *badīʿ*. His famous ode on the conquest of Amorium in 223/838 by the Caliph al-Muʿtaṣim reveals equally well the excellencies and failings of his style and technique. A sweeter bard is his disciple and admirer, al-Buḥturī (d. 284/897), a verbal alchemist who avoids the lexical and conceptual difficulties of the master. In him, ʿAbbasid palaces and establishments found an eloquent panegyrist, although his most celebrated ode was composed on the Sasanid Īwān Kisrā (the Arch of Ctesiphon). The third, Ibn al-Rūmī (d. 283/896) is a highly introspective and hyper-sensitive poet who excels in the elaboration of single themes at great length, as in the ode on the songstress Waḥīd. But the greatest of all ʿAbbasid poets was yet to come. Al-Mutanabbī (d. 354/965), 'the would-be prophet' as the poet was nicknamed, was the master of almost all the traditional themes of classical poetry, and his firm artistic will imposed on the *qaṣīda* a certain organic unity. But what distinguishes his poetry is a series of splendid epinician odes which may be termed the *Rūmiyyāt*. The Arab conquests of the first/seventh century found no poet to do justice to their epic sweep and heroic character, and it was left to this scion of the old tribe of Kinda, three centuries later, to compose for Arabic its finest heroic poetry. In fiery and sonorous verse, the 'would-be prophet' sang the exploits of his patron, Sayf al-Dawla, the Hamdanid warrior-prince (*reg.* 333–56/944–67) who was fighting a valiant but hopeless war against Byzantium. The belated figure of Abu'l-ʿAlā' al-Maʿarrī closes this golden age. His *Luzūmiyyāt* with their gratuitously complex rhymes are the philosophical *dīwān* of Arabic literature, where poetry alternates with rhymed philosophy, and where even a highly intellectual man of letters succumbs to the temptations of the meretricious *badīʿ*.

The political decentralization of the Arab empire in the fourth/tenth century, and the reduction of Baghdād itself in 334/945 to a provincial capital by the Buyids, inevitably affected the course of a literature whose fortunes were closely tied up with court patronage. The linguistic and cultural division of the Islamic empire into a Persian-speaking East and an Arab-speaking West began to tell. Arabic poetry lost its Persian contributors, but Arabic prose, partly owing to the prestige of the hieratic *ʿarabiyya*, continued to count many Persians among its brightest stars, e.g., Badīʿ al-Zamān and Ibn al-ʿAmīd. However, it was becoming amply clear that the future of Arabic literature lay in the western half of the empire, Arabic-speaking and for some time ruled by Arab dynasties, such as the Hamdanids of Syria (at whose court a brilliant circle was formed around Sayf al-Dawla), and the Fatimids of Egypt (358–565/

969–1171) who had their *muqaddam al-shu'arā'*, 'the foremost of the poets' and who gave poetry an important propagandist function. But more important was the Far West, consisting of the African mainland and the two transmarine colonies, Sicily and Spain. It is the last, al-Andalus, a slice of Islam on a highly christianized and romanized substrate, which merits most attention on account of its nature poetry and its exploration of new verse forms.

The moods of *natura benigna* already known to early 'Abbasid poetry, were reflected in a new type of nature poetry which was developed later by the Syrian school represented by al-Ṣanawbarī, 'he of the pine tree', who belonged to the circle of Sayf al-Dawla. The poets of the Muslim Occident were even more susceptible to these moods: Ibn Ḥamdīs, 'the Arabic Wordsworth' (d. 533/1138), caught them in Sicily, but it was an Andalusian, Ibn Khafāja (d. 533/1138), who became the Occident's most dedicated nature poet. The new forms developed in al-Andalus were the *muwashshaḥ* and the *zajal*, whose connexions with music and song were intimate and whose themes were erotic. The appearance of the *muwashshaḥ*, 'the girdled', towards the end of the third/ninth century is associated with the opaque figure of a certain Muqaddam b. Mu'āfā. It was a novelty in its strophic scheme of composition and it refreshed Arabic poetry by relieving it of the exigency of the monorhyme; but it also encumbered it with verbal arabesque. The *zajal*, 'melody', another form of strophic composition represented by Ibn Quzmān (d. 555/1159) was a more basic innovation, since by its employment of the popular speech it challenged the hitherto unquestioned claims of High Arabic as the sole medium of literary expression. It is not impossible that the spread of vernacular poetry in medieval Romance literature may have been due to the Arabic *zajal*. The two main figures of Andalusian literature are Ibn Zaydūn (d. 463/1070) and Ibn al-Khaṭīb (d. 776/1374). Both were masters of Arabic prose and verse, and composers of some beautiful strophic odes, *mukhammas* and *muwashshaḥ*, respectively. Like much of Andalusian poetry, their art is nostalgic, wistful, and anxious, reflecting the uncertainties and instabilities of Andalusia's political life.

In 447/1055 the Seljuk Turks occupied Baghdād, and ushered in the period of Turkish domination which lasted for almost a millennium, as the Seljuks were followed by the Mamluks and the Mamluks by the Ottomans. Although their services to Islam and the *dār al-Islām* were undoubtedly great, the influence of the Turks on the course of Arabic literature was not salutary. To be sure, religious literature and encyclopaedic compilations abounded during this period, but secular and original composition progressively dried up. This was natural, as the interest of Turkish-speaking dynasts in a literature composed in Arabic was understandably minimal.

The Seljuk period is illumined by three major figures who justify its being called the silver age. In 'Irāq, al-Ḥarīrī (d. 516/1122) composed his famous *maqāmāt* in which he carried the tradition of *badī'* to its farthest limits; in Syria, al-Qāḍī al-Fāḍil (d. 596/1200) continued the tradition of the *kuttāb*, and his association with Saladin ensured an enduring interest for his highly ornate prose; in Egypt, Ibn al-Fāriḍ (d. 632/1235) bestowed on Arabic verse the glitters and whispers of its best mystic poesy. Vastly different in temperament as these three masters were, they were all slaves to *badī'* and its conventions.

The fall of Baghdād to the Mongols in 656/1258, was another fateful date for Arabic literature and history alike. Egypt supplanted 'Irāq as the centre of the Arabic-speaking Muslim West, and its central position under the Mamluks was further accentuated by the fall of Granada in 897/1492. But the Mamluk sultans (648–922/1250–1517) were Turkish- or Circassian-speaking rulers and their courts were no market for Arabic literature, which consequently withered. The scene of literary activity shifted from the sultans' courts to the streets and coffee-houses of Cairo, where professional reciters entertained enchanted audiences with their stories and romances. Ironically enough, it was one of these story-cycles, the famed *Thousand and One Nights*—an earlier version of which had been characterized in 377/988 by the understandably supercilious Ibn al-Nadīm as 'a vulgar and insipid book'—that later, and in translation, was to be the contribution of the Arabs to the World Fair of International Literature.

The defeat of the Mamluks by Sultan Selīm in 922/1516 opened the third and last period of Turkish domination, the Ottoman period which lasted until the First World War. During this period, even more adverse factors operated to the disadvantage of Arabic literature; Egypt, its centre, was reduced to provincial status; Cairo was superseded as capital by Istanbul; and the Ottoman sultans were neither Arabic-speaking, nor even like the Mamluks, resident in Arab lands. This was the golden age of a new Islamic literature, Turkish, just as the preceding period of the Seljuks and the Mongols was the golden age of another

Islamic literature, Persian. The vitality of the Arabic literary tradition was transferred to younger and more vigorous Islamic literatures, whose growth it had directly or indirectly stimulated, namely, Persian, Turkish and Urdu. It was during this period, when the ruling institution was not patronizing Arabic literature, that the religious establishment rendered its greatest service by performing a custodial function which made possible the very survival of the traditions of High Arabic. The significance of the Fatimid foundation, the collegiate mosque of al-Azhar, emerges clearly in this long Ottoman winter which set in on the Arab lands. And once suitable conditions in the nineteenth and twentieth centuries obtained, al-Azhar participated in its own way and through its reformers in the modern Arab renaissance.

The modern period

Modern Arabic literature is but one manifestation of the general Arab awakening for which the stage was set by Bonaparte's dramatic invasion of Egypt in 1798. The decisive factor in its evolution has been that highly complex phenomenon known as the 'impact of the West'. The two processes of democratization and secularization, the operation of which has set modern Arabic literature apart from its classical parent, are part of this phenomenon; the first severed its relations with the ruling institution, the second relaxed its ties with the religious establishment. Among the instruments of these two processes of democratization and secularization, the printing press and the Western-style university have played a major role. The printing press has encouraged the translation of foreign works, and has facilitated the rise of journalism (which has been a most potent force in the development of a straightforward functional prose), and the cultivation of the modern literary essay; furthermore, it has established a relationship between the writer and the reading public which has affected the writer's conception of himself, given him an important social function, and relieved him of the inconvenience of court patronage. The university, as an institution of higher learning, has become the centre of organized literary studies, whence new literary traditions and new critical theories are systematically disseminated; consequently, the university has succeeded in relieving the religious institutions, e.g., al-Azhar in Egypt, of their sole custodianship of Arabic. As a result, literature has lost much of the Islamic tinge which coloured it in classical times, and this tendency towards secularization has been accelerated by one of the most powerful factors in the making of modern Arab history, namely, nationalism. Perhaps nothing is better illustrative of this tendency than the emergence of the Christian Arabs as active contributors to Arabic literature, and the rise of Christian Lebanon as a major literary province, whose enterprising emigrants gave impetus to the Egyptian renaissance in the nineteenth century, and carried the Arabic literary tradition to its farthest geographical limits in the New World. In addition to secularization and democratization, the most significant result of the 'impact' has been the opening of the Arab literary mind to the direct influence of Western literary art and literary theory, a chapter long overdue in the history of cultural encounters between the Arabs and the West. A new conception of literature has arisen which emphasizes experience. New literary genres have been added to both prose and poetry, while the fruitful dialogue between artist and critic, often united in one person, has kept the former conscious of the aesthetic foundations of his literary endeavours. But this modern literature has its problems; e.g. the *ʿarabiyya* itself, with the classical associations and modes of expression of which the poet has to wrestle, while the divorce between the spoken and the written language presents a problem, not an insoluble one, to the novelist and the dramatist in the composition of dialogue.

For Arabic prose it is the introduction of new literary genres that has been the West's most valuable gift. The short story, the novel and the drama, have all found competent practitioners in various parts of the Arab world. Among the earliest pioneers was a Lebanese immigrant to the United States, Kahlil Gibran (Jubrān Khalīl Jubrān) (d. 1931) whose essays, parables and short stories reveal the complex personality of a poet, painter and mystic. He profoundly influenced the literary taste and fashion of his generation, although he wrote his best known work, *The Prophet*, in English. His contemporary and friend, the prolific Mikhā'īl Naimy (Nuʿayma) (b. 1889) is the other major figure in this Arabo-American School—a master essayist, short story writer and critic, whose *Gibran* is the classic of all Arabic biographical literature. It is, however, in Egypt that prose literature has had its foremost authors, where Ṭāhā Ḥusayn (b. 1889) the doyen of Arabic letters has dominated the literary scene for the last half-century. A versatile genius, blind from early childhood, he has functioned indefatigably as a literary critic, a cultural catalyst, a prose stylist and a creative writer. For Arabic he has fashioned a new prose style possessed of great expressiveness, flexibility and elegance, in which he wrote his autobiographical masterpiece, *al-Ayyām*. In the field of dramatic literature, the short story and the novel, three other Egyptian writers, Tawfīq al-Ḥakīm (b. 1898) Maḥmūd Taymūr (b. 1894) and Najīb Maḥfūẓ (b. 1912) respectively, have distinguished themselves as masters of these literary genres. Farther to the west, the Arab Occident has produced an author, the Tunisian Maḥmūd al-Mas'adī (b. 1900), who has attained celebrity for his existentialist dramatic composition, *al-Sudd*.

Modern Arabic poetry, too, has felt the full impact of the West. It has explored new prosodical dimensions in order to emancipate itself from its bondage to rhyme and to a constricting metrical system, and it has plumbed the depths of poetic experience in its attempt to win free from the embrace of traditional verbal craftsmanship. This new creative outburst was made possible by a school of Revivalist poets who successfully rejuvenated Arabic poetry from within by exploiting its inner resources and drawing on the best elements in its classical tradition. They were heralded by the heroic figure of the soldier-poet, Maḥmūd Sāmī al-Bārūdī (d. 1904), and it was another Egyptian, Aḥmad Shawqī (d. 1932), who incontestably became Revivalism's most brilliant representative, and in a sense the greatest Arab poet of modern times. Shawqī succeeded in adding a new genre to Arabic poetry, although his dramas, e.g. *Majnūn Laylā*, are more remarkable for their lyric power than for their dramatic effect. In his *dīwān*, *al-Shawqiyyāt*, poetry often alternates with verse but the accent of great poetry is always audible. There is nothing better than his best, and he is at his best when he remembers contemporary events which have touched his sensibilities, or 'recollects in tranquillity' the historic past which has moved him as a Muslim, an Ottoman, an Egyptian or an Arab, e.g. the fall of Adrianople, 'Andalusia's sister', the extinction of the Caliphate, the valley of the Nile, the Alcázar of Granada and the sunset glow of Moorish Spain. Having performed its restorative and rejuvenating function, the poetry of the Revivalists began to recede before the new waves which were breaking upon Arabic poetry from the West. The most powerful was that of Romanticism, which in the thirties swept over the whole of the Arab world, both in its traditional centres in the East and in such newly revived and emergent literary provinces as Tunisia and the Sudan which produced Abu'l-Qāsim al-Shābbī (1909–34) and al-Tījānī Bashīr (1912–37). But it was the representative of Symbolism who has been the most strikingly original among the poets of these new literary movements—Lebanon's Sa'īd 'Aql, a consummate literary artist with a lustrous poetic style who has cut for the treasury of modern Arabic verse some of its most precious stones. All these poets, however, composed in the classical idiom of Arabic metrical prosody, and it was left to the youngest of the new schools, the school of Free Verse, to bring about the most revolutionary change in the history of Arabic poetry since pre-Islamic times. A new prosodical form has been evolved; not necessarily a substitute for the traditionally measured and mono-rhymed verse but an alternative or a complement which has endowed the atomically constituted Arabic poem with an organic structure and a subtler internal cadence. With the advent of Free Verse a new dawn may be said to have broken for Arabic poetry, and this has been Iraq's great achievement where a Pleiad whose bright stars include 'Abd al-Wahhāb al-Bayātī (b. 1926) and Nāzik al-Malā'ika (b. 1923) have successfully established Free Verse as a legitimate prosodical idiom and in so doing have probably determined the future course of Arabic poetry.

As a result of two World Wars, a new Arab world has risen from the ashes of the old, extending from the Persian Gulf to the Atlantic Ocean. New literary provinces have come into existence such as Jordan, the Sudan and Libya, while old ones have been resuscitated into new life, as Arabia itself, the birthplace of Arabic poetry which has been rather silent since Umayyad times when Arabic literature was still the literature of a people. And it is as such that it has re-emerged in the twentieth century, after it had been the literature of a multi-racial society in medieval Islamic times.

PERSIAN LITERATURE

Of the countries falling completely under Arab rule in the early days of Islam, Persia was the only one which succeeded in preserving her national language, thereby maintaining a separate identity within the Islamic world. The language of the country, however, did not remain static, but gradually adjusted itself to the profound changes which the advent of Islam caused in Persian society. When after two hundred years of Arab rule Persian emerged again as a literary medium, it had assumed a fresh colouring, distinct from that of the Middle Persian of the Sasanian era. It had adopted a simpler morphology and had shed most of the words with Zoroastrian connotations, acquiring instead a considerable Arabic vocabulary.

In imperial Persia secular literature had been of a courtly character, and both its form and content reflected the tastes and interests of the kings and nobles who were its chief patrons. The destruction of Sasanian power brought to an end this system of patronage, and in the subsequent period of disruption, change and readjustment, Muslim Persians began to apply their talents to the enrichment of Arabic writing. Their contributions did much to develop Arabic literature into a diverse and truly living structure.

In the third/ninth century, however, with the weakening of the central power of the caliphs in Baghdād and the establishment of autonomous dynasties on Persian soil, the way was once again open for the emergence of a national literature. Now, once again 'the lively and graceful fancy, elegance of diction, depth and tenderness of feeling and a rich store of ideas' which, in the words of R. A. Nicholson,[1] had characterized the contributions made by the Persians to Arabic literature, could be devoted to the development of their own national literature, destined to become 'one of the great literatures of mankind'.[2]

This renaissance of Persian literature owes much to the encouragement of the enlightened princes of the Samanid dynasty, who brought a period of relative peace and stability to their kingdom in eastern and north-eastern Persia and championed the cause of Persian cultural rebirth. They revived or encouraged many old Persian customs and gave expression to the widespread, if not always vocal, desire of many Persians for a distinct national identity. They devised an adminstrative system and revived cultural patterns, largely based on the Sasanian model, and these survived with little change until the Mongol invasion, and even after. Their learned *wazīrs* and secretaries were the predecessors of a brilliant host of Persian statesmen and administrators who helped to maintain Samanid traditions in later periods.

It was under Samanid patronage that the blind bard Rūdakī (d. 330/940), rightly considered the father of Persian poetry, composed his poems. It was under the Samanids that Abū 'Alī Bal'amī, the erudite *wazīr* of Manṣūr I (350/961–366/976) gave the fledgling Persian prose literature his adaptation of the famous universal history in Arabic by his fellow-countryman al-Ṭabarī. Again it was under the Samanids that Firdawsī (d. *c.* 411/1020), the pre-eminent poet of Persia, composed the bulk of his *Shāh-nāma*, the monumental work which was to become the national epic of Persia.

[1] *A literary history of the Arabs* (Cambridge, 1956), 290.
[2] A. J. Arberry (ed.), *The Legacy of Persia* (Oxford, 1953), 200.

Having made their first strides under the auspices of the Samanids, poetry and prose soon expanded into an impressive literature, which flourished not only in Persia, but in other areas influenced by Persian culture, notably in Turkey, but above all in India, which under the Great Mughals became the second home of Persian literature.

Poetry

The first feature of this literature to attract our attention is the preponderance of poetry. Poetry is the great art of Persia, and it is in poetry that we must seek the most intimate and refined expressions of Persian thought and sentiment. It is only natural, therefore, that in a discussion of Persian literature, poetry should be given pride of place.

Whereas the spirit and the content of poetry in Muslim Persia clearly bear national marks, its formal pattern takes its imprint from Arabic. Over the years, however, within the framework of Arabic metres, the Persians developed forms better suited to their literary temperament. Of these one is the *mathnawī*, based on the rhyming couplet, which, though originally adapted from Arabic, was moulded into a distinctively Persian form, employed mainly for longer poems of a narrative or didactic nature. Another is the *ghazal*, a short poem of some seven to fifteen lines, all having the same rhyme, the last line normally including the signature of the poet. This form, which in some ways resembles the sonnet, is generally used for lyric poetry. Yet another example is the *rubāʿī*, or quatrain, a Persian invention, best exemplified by those of ʿUmar Khayyām and employed mostly for epigrammatic expressions of amorous and mystical sentiments and philosophical thought. The *du baytī* is a more homely version of the *rubāʿī*. It is native to the land, and though occurring mainly in folk-lyrics, it is occasionally elevated to the level of high poetry. The *qiṭʿa* is a monorhyme, normally of three to twenty lines, employed mostly for casual subjects, satire, and ethical or moralizing themes.

The *qaṣīda*, the basic form of Arabic poetry, consisting of a long monorhyme, was also adopted. It remained the most favoured form for court poetry, and many poets who flocked to the courts of kings and others wrote poems of praise, congratulation, condolence or of satire in this form. The *qaṣīda* was generally written in the grand style, value being placed above all else on eloquence, polished diction, ingenious expression and resounding phrases. In the course of time excessive embellishment and exaggerated rhetorics led to florid and pedantic panegyrics which afford little pleasure to the reader.

The formal *qaṣīdas* of professional court poets, however, tell us little of the true range and depth of Persian poetry or of its distinctive features. Discussing such features, particularly in relation to those of Arabic poetry, J. Rypka concludes that

> the Arabs, in complete contrast to the Persians, have no sense for the epic. Only in the hand of the Persian poet do the *disjecta membra* of the tales of Laylī and Majnūn become a really unified work of art. The immense number of epics of a narrative nature in Persian literature also leads to the same conclusion. Likewise, Sufism failed to find the same fertile ground in Arab lands as it found in Persia, where the poetry is to a large extent plainly saturated with it, even though at times only superficially or apparently. Whereas the true expression of the Arab spirit is the *qaṣīda* in the broadest sense of the word (and not only in the panegyric sense), the lyrical way of thinking of Persia finds its true form in the *ghazal*.[1]

It is indeed to epic, lyrical, and mystical poetry that we must turn for a true appreciation of Persian literary genius. Before Islamic times several massive compilations in Sasanian Persian dealt not only with the histories and legends of Persian kings and heroes but were concerned also with the institutions of the empire, the orders of its aristocracy, rules of conduct and good government, and the arts and skills cherished by the nobility. Their illustrated folios were the ancestors of Persian miniatures.

The Arab conquest and conversion to Islam failed to suppress the memory of a proud past. The nostalgic perspective of the past gave impetus to a series of attempts to collect, translate or recompose the national history. Ibn al-Muqaffaʿ (d. between 139/757 and 142/759–60), one of the founders of Arabic prose literature, translated into Arabic the *Khwatāynāma* ('Book of kings'), compiled towards the end of Sasanian times.

This work, or Persian editions of it, also attracted the attention of Persian poets. Of several attempts made by the early poets at its versification, that of Firdawsī resulted in the birth of an epic of extraordinary power and dignity. The exploits of Rustam, the invincible Persian Hercules and the indomitable defender of the Persian kingdom, dominate the tales told by the poet. With rare poetic gift Firdawsī creates a heroic atmosphere where his characters move as formidable giants and

[1] *Iranische Literaturgeschichte* (Leipzig, 1959), 109.

their deeds assume cosmic proportions. His pure and lofty language, his vigorous diction and virile tones are eminently suited to the treatment of his heroic theme. His genius as a poet is such that one is often apt to forget that he was bound to a prose text which considerably limited the freedom of his imagination. When the episodes are well constructed in the original and suitable for epic treatment, they are moulded in the hands of Firdawsī into supreme examples of epic art. Such is the case with the episode of Rustam and Suhrāb in which the great hero inadvertently kills his brilliant son, a tragedy which inspired Matthew Arnold's poem 'Sohrab and Rustum'.

Although the *Shāh-nāma* is primarily conceived as a heroic epic, concerning itself mainly with the exploits of warrior heroes, it is by no means devoid of the moralizing comments and philosophical and contemplative asides so characteristic of the main stream of Persian literature. In fact early Persian poetry, if somewhat archaic in its simplicity, exhibits remarkable maturity in thought; for although Persian poetry was young, the Persian people were old, and had a long and eventful history behind them.

The *Shāh-nāma* was written in an era when historical events, particularly in eastern Persia, encouraged a hopeful and spirited mood. The pervasive melancholy and mystical detachment which characterize much of late classical Persian poetry are barely perceptible in the poetry of the fourth/tenth and fifth/eleventh centuries. Persian poetry of this period displays a youthful spirit, with unmistakable delight in nature and its beauties. Love shines in a carefree manner and, more often than not, the songs of the poet display the joys of satisfaction rather than the sorrows of frustration.

As the years go by, poetry gradually progresses from youth to maturity, gaining in depth of sentiment and tenderness of feeling. Mystical views begin to affect the poet's themes and a certain detachment mellows the tone of his meditative lines. The animation of Rūdakī (d. 330/940) and Farrukhī (d. 429/1037) gives way to the tenderness of Sanā'ī (d. 536/1141) and Niẓāmī (d. 613/1217). With 'Aṭṭār (d. 627/1230) and 'Irāqī (d. 688/1289) the tone becomes considerably more passionate and moving. The song of love is now set to a minor key and often reveals a lover with an acute sense of tragedy. He rejoices even in the suffering that love brings. The virile tone, the rigorous diction, and the syncopated rhythms of the earlier poets are now mellowed into suaver songs.

The esteem in which wine, the age-old comfort of all Persian poets, is held, grows, and the poet finds the company of the *sāqī* (the cup-bearer) and the ruby rim of the cup a remedy for the afflictions of love and reverses of fortune. To enjoy the moment and forget what the perfidious world may hold in store, is the advice most frequently given.

As lyric poetry develops, a set of conventions with regard to both theme and imagery begin to emerge. The beloved is idealized as the supreme epitome of beauty, ruthless in inflicting the pains of love without much concern for the wretched state of the lover. The lover, passionate and humble on the other hand, is ready to renounce both worlds if the beloved will but deign him a single glance of favour. The interminable hours of separation are a continual motif in his laments. In the sad songs of the nightingale, poured forth to the inconstant rose, he sees a reflection of his own fate; in the perishing of the moth in the consuming flame of the candle, to which it is drawn, he discovers a parallel to his own plight. Wine is his greatest comfort. It frees his mind from the shackles of an inexorable passion and the cares of a perverse world.

With the development of the wine-cult in Persian lyrics, there develops a further set of conventions closely related to social satire. In a world blighted by hypocrisy and pretension, wine-drinkers, with their typical abandon and their lack of concern for the approval of the world, come to symbolize the very idea of sincerity and serenity so dear to the poet's heart. The tavern rather than the mosque is the place in which to gain wisdom. Presently the devoted and daring lover, the carefree drunkard and the honest *qalandar* emerge as the characters admired in the lyrics. In contrast, the preacher, the *muftī*, the Ṣūfī and their like become the frequent targets of subtle, if biting, satire. The poet's unremitting praise is not for those who prescribe the sterile arguments of reason; but for those who answer the call of the heart and follow the path of love.

In its continued criticism of bigotry, fanaticism and misuse or misinterpretation of religious dogma, the *ghazal* embodies the most consistent, concise and delicate form of social satire to be found in Persian poetry. It is particularly this satire, often cloaked in the form of irony, that gives Persian lyrics their surprisingly liberal atmosphere.

If the strict forms of Persian poetry and its often conventionalized imagery limit the poet's freedom of expression—a fact that makes his achievements all the more worthy of admiration—he enjoys almost complete freedom in the arrangement of his themes. Each line of a *ghazal* is generally self-contained, expressing a complete idea, and very tenuously connected—if at all—with the next line. The poet is at liberty to jump from one idea to another, now marvelling at the beauty of the beloved, now singing the praise of wine; in one line bewailing his lot, in the next satirizing the pretence of the false preacher, and in the third invoking a metaphor to illustrate the ways of the world. This may appear disparate and lacking in unity and coherence, but a *ghazal* is held together first, as regards form, by its single rhyme and metre; secondly, by the prevailing mood of the *ghazal* which helps to throw an imperceptible bridge over the lines; and thirdly, and most effectively, by the larger context of Persian lyric poetry with its conventional and immediately recognizable themes, concepts and metaphors, related to each other after their own logic, and from among which the poet chooses those which happen to suit his purpose in a given *ghazal*.

One of the main traits of the Persian lyric, and in fact of Persian poetry as a whole, is its abstract character—this despite the predominantly romantic outlook of the Persian poet. We are not allowed to identify any character or gain an intimate knowledge of the circumstances, time, or place of any particular event. It is hardly ever possible to know which particular preacher or *muftī* the poet is satirizing, or how the beloved of Sa'dī (d. 691/1292) differed from that of Rūmī (d. 671/1273) or Majmar (d. 1225/1810). It is equally well-nigh impossible to distinguish the patron praised by Unṣurī (d. between 431/1040 and 441/1050) from that of Qā'ānī (d. 1271/1853).

The characters that a poet treats, are in fact idealized and abstract entities who appear on the stage of poetry with the mask of a type and not with the face of an individual. Even in works of fiction, the treatment is generally that of an allegory. But the types are brought to life by the acute and passionate feelings of individual experience. The combination of abstraction and intense emotion imparts to Persian lyrics a universality and at the same time a moving effect peculiar to themselves.

It is in this genre that the three giants of Persian lyric poetry, Sa'dī, Rūmī and Ḥāfiẓ (d. 792/1390), wrote their best.

Sa'dī, a versatile poet and writer of extraordinary verve and finish, matches wit and humour with a deep sense of humanity. His lyric poetry surpasses all that was written before him in felicity of phrase, ease of diction, melodious rhythm and a sustained level of lively imagination.

It is in the hands of Ḥāfiẓ, however, that lyric poetry reaches the heights of the sublime. He cloaks the creation of his sensitive imagination, his delicate sentiments, his lofty thoughts and his subtle satire in a brocade of words so aesthetically designed and so masterfully woven that his art has proved the joy and despair of the host of poets who have attempted to imitate him. His widespread popularity and the unlimited belief felt in his genius, make him the national poet of Persia, and yet he remains a poet's poet.

Rūmī (d. 671/1273), a contemporary of Sa'dī, is in a class of his own. Although his reputation rests mainly on his discursive mystical poem, the *Mathnawī*, his claim as a great lyric poet must rest on his *ghazals*. He was an impassioned lover and mystic, the burning intensity of whose love knew no respite. His rhapsodical *ghazals* derive much of their moving quality from the sheer intensity of their feeling and the potent music of their words. His genius, like the touch of a magician, is able to turn everything that comes his way into poetry, and let cosmic elements become humble tools to his devouring and restless imagination. In his rapture he often stretches the possibility of words and images to the utmost limit, occasionally approaching a ravishing unintelligibility. At his best, Rūmī surpasses perhaps all Persian poets in the width and breadth of his imagination, the forcible rhythm of his words, depth of emotions and tenderness of feelings. But his work, unlike that of Ḥāfiẓ, Sa'dī and Firdawsī, is not even, and he is too absorbed in his all-consuming passion to care for refinement and polish.

As a mystic poet, Rūmī provides a perfect example of that blending of mystical sentiment and amorous feelings characteristic of so much of Persian literature. The Ṣūfī way of life, which advocated intense love and devotion as the means of attaining truth, found a considerable following in Persia, and Ṣūfī convents grew increasingly popular after the fourth/tenth century. Persian mystics often were men of outstanding sensitivity and employed poetry or poetical diction to express their thoughts and to move their fellow men. It was only natural for a school of thought which distrusted 'reason' and relied on the inspiration of the 'heart', to adopt the language of lyrics and to employ the symbolism of sensuous love.

The spread of certain Ṣūfī doctrines which tended to see in the human form a revelation of the Divine Being, further blurred in a great many Persian lyrics the distinction between mystical and erotic love. The symbol and the idea merged and what had been in earlier periods a rather mundane love poetry, limited in its application, assumed with 'Aṭṭār, Rūmī, and 'Irāqī mystical depth and significance, and was now capable of being interpreted on a spiritual plane and of inspiring devotional feelings. After Ḥāfiẓ, a master of equivocal expressions in this sense, this mystical vein itself became a convention to be followed by a host of poets in Persia, India and Turkey, even though not all of them based their mystical utterances on personal experience.

The *ghazal*, which has been discussed at some length already, is the form that embodies the essence of Persian poetry; it is intimate, intense and concise, and owes very little to courtly patronage. It is not, however, because of its structure, suitable for narrative and coherent discourse. The form employed for this purpose is the *mathnawī* or couplet form, and it is in this that Persian poetry displays its fullest range.

With Firdawsī's *Shāh-nāma* the supreme example had been set up for all subsequent heroic poetry. A little later, Gurgānī (d. 442/1050) gave us an exquisite romance based on a legend of pre-Islamic origins. Next, Niẓāmī (d. 613/1217) composed no less than four epics of a predominantly romantic nature, thus setting the model for a plethora of similar compositions, among which those of Amīr Khusraw of Delhi (d. 726/1325), Jāmī (d. 895/1490) and Vaḥshī (d. 991/1583) attained renown. The celebrated *Mathnawī* of Rūmī gave the Islamic world its greatest monument of mystical thought, while Sa'dī's *Būstān* provided it with a masterpiece of great charm and delight. The latter strings together a series of moralizing and philosophical poems written in a uniformly exquisite, mellow and intimate style, illustrated by anecdotes and stories. An immense number of poems in the *mathnawī* form were written in India under the patronage of the Muslim courts, particularly those of the Mughal emperors.

The style of Persian narrative and discoursive poetry reflects the Persian distaste for constructions which are too rigid and too closely controlled. Such poetry is like the natural meanders of a free-flowing river rather than the controlled flow of a canal. Reading a Persian narrative poem is frequently like taking a stroll through a garden which has been laid out with taste and with great care for detail, but not along strict lines. At intervals the poet makes a halt to reflect on the transcendent significance of views and events, and to contemplate and moralize on what can be seen beyond the immediate aspect of physical forms, but only to return once again with renewed enthusiasm to the sensuous world of shape and colour.

This flexible treatment of themes and tendency to meandering, which in some poems lead to an almost 'centrifugal' style of composition, as is the case of Rūmī's *Mathnawī*, is not confined to works of poetry, but may be seen also in prose fiction and in works of a didactic or moralizing nature.

Prose

Turning to prose literature, it is true that prose was used in Persia predominantly for scholarly writing, but *belles-lettres* were by no means neglected. Much has perished in the course of a turbulent history; what remains in prose, however, is rich and diversified. It is only in comparison with Persian poetry that it loses some of its brilliance.

In the field of fiction there exists, first of all, a whole tradition of tales, stories, and popular epics, many of which have their origin in pre-Islamic Persia. The *Hazār afsāna*, the precursor of the *Arabian nights*, is now lost, but works of a similar character such as the *Sindbād-nāma* (556/1160–61) and *Bakhtyār-nāma*, are still extant. Tales of adventure enjoyed a considerable vogue in Persia, a fact attested by such works as the *Samak-i ʿayyār*, the *Dārāb-nāma* and several versions of the *Iskandar-nāma* ('The tale of Alexander') as well as the more recent *Amīr Arsalān*, belonging to the nineteenth century. To the category of fiction there belongs also a series of fable collections with a strong moral tenor, the most remarkable of which is the *Kalīla va-Dimna* (*c.* 538/1144) of Naṣr Allāh, which goes back to an Indian origin.

Story telling, which was always a popular art in Persia, has found its way into many works which are not primarily concerned with stories; thus a large number of Persian works on practical ethics and rules of government, commentaries on the Qur'ān, literary essays, mystical writings and romances are generously illustrated by anecdotes, stories and parables, and they owe much of their readability to such stories.

The crowning achievement of Persian prose is generally considered to be the *Gulistān* of Saʿdī, a volume of practical wisdom, wit and humour written in elegant rhyming prose, and largely consisting of a series of anecdotes and maxims. It is typical of Persian literary taste in its moralizing, its concern for refinement of form and embellishment of phrase, its play on words, as well as in its frequent recourse to citations of poetic fragments and supporting dicta. To the modern taste, however, many a less elegant work of simpler prose and tenderer feeling might well be more attractive.

The works of many Persian mystics belong to this class of writing, notably 'Aṭṭār's *Tadhkirat al-awliyā'* ('Memorial of the saints'), as well as some commentaries on the Qur'ān which reflect mystical sentiments. Among the latter one may mention Maybudī's copious *Kashf al-asrār* (belonging to the sixth/twelfth century), which has considerable literary merit.

There has always existed in Persia an acute sense of style. For this reason, learned writing, particularly in the humanities (*adab*), generally exhibits a high degree of literary skill, emphasizing, at times excessively, the importance of style. It is not always easy, therefore, to make a clear distinction between works of *belles-lettres* and the works of *adab* in general. This is particularly true of Persian histories which are remarkable for their style, be it straightforward, precise and effective like that of the *Tārīkh-i Bal'amī* (fourth/tenth century) and the *Tārīkh-i Bayhaqī* (fifth/eleventh century), more rhetorical as in Rashīd al-Dīn's *Jāmi' al-tawārīkh* (eighth/fourteenth century), or utterly florid and bombastic as in the *Durra-i Nādirī* (twelfth/eighteenth century).

Of works of literary merit in other fields of the humanities one may mention the *Qābūs-nāma* (fifth/eleventh century), truly a 'mirror for princes', by the sagacious prince Kay Kāvūs; the *Siyāsat-nāma*, a very readable manual of the rules of good government by the able *wazīr* Niẓām al-Mulk; and the *Kīmiyā-yi sa'ādat* ('The elixir of happiness'), a treatise of ethics and philosophy by the outstanding theologian al-Ghazālī (d. 505/1111).

Prose, however, was no more immune than poetry from the inevitable decline whose approach could be sensed in excessive refinement, exaggerated embellishment and turgid amplification. The decline in Persian letters may be said to begin after the holocaust wrought by a succession of Mongol and Tatar invasions of the country beginning in the seventh/thirteenth century. Persian poetry, although still written in abundance, lost its freshness, turning out repetitious configurations of the same old themes in ever more languid tones. Occasionally a bright star like the subtle poet Ṣā'ib (d. 1080/1670) appeared in the sky of Persian letters, but its glow was hardly sufficient to illuminate the once brilliant course of Persian literature.

During the period of the Safavids the main centre of Persian literature was tranferred to India, where it received generous patronage at the courts of the Mughal emperors. A large number of works in both prose and poetry was written in all the familiar old forms, and a tradition was established on Indian soil which continued into our own time and gave to Persian poetry a significant lyric writer in the person of Iqbāl of Lahore (d. 1938).

A new era in Persian literature began in the nineteenth century when a reaction against the stilted and uninspiring style of the previous century brought about a return to the simplicity and vigour of earlier Persian poetry. This literary renaissance produced poems which were both rigorous and delicate, but it was soon to give way to methods and styles which reflected the impact of the West. The modern period of Persian letters which belongs to the present century, has seen the development of fiction in the Western sense, has brought about a healthy, balanced and cultivated style of prose, and has given rise to a lively poetry which at its best is imaginative, original and refined, and can hold its own in comparison with the classical poetry.

TURKISH LITERATURE

Following the general trend and development of Turkish cultural history, it is possible to divide Turkish literature into four main periods:

(1) The literature of the Turks before they accepted Islam (from the origins to the eleventh century).
(2) Islamic Turkish literature (from the eleventh century to the middle of the nineteenth century).
(3) Turkish literature under Western influence (1850–1910).
(4) National and local literature (since 1910).

The first products of the old Turkish literature have not reached our times. We only have Chinese translations of the first examples of epics and lyrics. The extant products of the earliest written literature fall into two main groups. One of these consists of the inscriptions in north-east Asia. The most representative of these which are written in an alphabet developed from Aramaic through Sogdian, not deciphered until the end of the nineteenth century, are the Orhon inscriptions. They are known by this name because they were discovered near the Orhon river, a branch of the Selenga which flows into Lake Baykal. They were erected for Prince Kül (or Köl) and Bilge Khan (d. 731 and 734 respectively) of the Kök-Türk dynasty which flourished between the sixth and eighth Christian centuries. They relate the history of the Kök-Türks, their surrender to the Chinese and liberation under the guidance of Bilge Khan. The Turkish of the inscriptions gives the impression of a mature language and its lively style has in various places an exciting and epic atmosphere.

The second group of writings, largely of a religious nature, was developed in the Uigur territory in eastern Turkistān (present Sinkiang) between the ninth and twelfth Christian centuries, by Turks belonging to various religions. These Turks used the same written language but in different alphabets according to the religions to which they belonged. The Uigur alphabet, which was used by the Buddhist Turks who were in the majority, was developed from Sogdian. This alphabet was later adopted by the Mongols, and continued to be used by the eastern Turks to a limited extent after Islam.

Dīvān lughāt al-Turk, written by Maḥmūd Kāshgharī in 468/1074 when Islam had begun to spread among the Turks, and a struggle between Muslim and non-Muslim Turks had commenced, contains examples of passages pertaining to this transitory stage. Many forms of poetry—epic, romantic, pastoral, elegiac—are represented, if briefly, in this work, giving a good idea of the literary tradition of the pre-Islamic period. We can judge from these examples that there was an original and rich literature, much of which is no longer extant.

Islam came to the Turks through Persia. From the fifth/eleventh century, general Islamic culture was adopted by the Turks in a rather Persian form, and the new Persian literature became the source of inspiration for Turkish writers. Persian prosody was accepted in place of the Turkish syllabic metre, as well as Islamic verse-forms such as the *qaṣīda*, *ghazal* and *mathnawī* (*mesnevī*). Islamic culture derived from sources such as the Qur'ān, *Ḥadīth*, stories of the prophets, legends of the saints and mysticism began to dominate Islamic Turkish literature, which was also inspired by the *Shāh-nāma* of Firdawsī.

The Turks spread to many countries of Central and western Asia, the Near East and eastern Europe. Within this wide geographical area, various dialects of the Turkish language were spoken, and a rich oral literature also developed. The written literature developed mainly in two major dialects: Eastern Turkish, which can be considered as the continuation of one kind of Uigur; and Western Turkish, which comprises the Ottoman and Āẕarbāyjānī dialects developed from Oghuz.

Eastern Turkish

Eastern Turkish was used as the literary language from the eleventh century until the end of the nineteenth century in all the countries where Turkish was spoken or where Turks ruled except the Ottoman empire, western Persia and southern Crimea. Later on it was replaced by written languages that developed from local spoken languages. Eastern Turkish has gone through three periods of development.

In the Kara-Khanid period, the language, also called *Hakaniye* and Middle Turkish, developed in the fifth–sixth/eleventh–twelfth centuries from the Uigur language in eastern and western Turkistān, Kashghar being the centre, and became the first literary dialect of the Muslim Turks. Their first known work is the *Kutadgu bilig* ('Knowledge that gives happiness') written in 462/1069–70. Its author, Yūsuf of Balāsāghūn, presented his work to Tapgach Bughra Kara-Khan, sultan of Kashghar, and was made first chamberlain as a reward. Research on the content and the language of this important allegorical-didactic poem which comprises more than 6,000 couplets in the *mutaqārib* metre and in the *mes̱nevī* style, is yet at a beginning. This work by Yūsuf, who is striving after an ethical and religious ideal, is mainly formed by conversations between the Ruler, the *Vez̤īr*, the *Vez̤īr*'s son and his friend. As the government and also relations between rulers and subjects are discussed at length, this work has the nature of a political essay. Even though the general principles of Islamic literature have been adopted in respect to the verse-form and philosophy of life, pre-Islamic traditions appear both in the quatrains scattered in it and in many of the ideas concerning government.

Another work of the fifth/twelfth century is the *'Aybat al-ḥaqā'iq* written by Adīb Aḥmed of Yüknek. This little book in verse records the general moral rules of the Islamic world. It is interesting from the linguistic viewpoint, rather than as literature. The Qur'ān was translated into Turkish in this period. Though all the extant copies are quite late, the linguistic characteristics of one (Istanbul, Türk-Islam Eserleri Müzesi, Number 73) shows that it was made in the sixth/twelfth century.

The second stage in Eastern Turkish literature is the Khwārazm-Golden Horde period. In the seventh/thirteenth century a written language which was the continuation of Kara-Khanid Turkish was developed in Khwārazm in the Sir Darya (Jaxartes) delta, and from here it passed on to the Golden Horde. Unlike Kara-Khanid, this written language was also mixed with Oghuz and Kipchak elements.

Among the abundant products of religious literature of this period *Qiṣaṣ al-anbiyā'* (710/1310) by Rabghūzī and *Nahj al-Farādīs* (761/1360) by Maḥmūd of Kerder are especially worth mentioning. The first one of these belongs to the category of works recording the lives of prophets, and the second belongs to the genre of the Forty *Ḥadīths*. Both these works, which were written in the popular language and with a lively style, were widely read and loved until the end of the last century.

In this period parallels to the works of classical Persian literature for the *élite* also began to be written. Quṭb of Khwārazm wrote *Khusrū u-Shīrīn* (741/1341) for the ruler of the Golden Horde, in parallel to Niẓāmī's well-known *mathnawī*. Its content of much material from local culture and its considerable closeness to the language of the people commands attention. It seems that the *mes̱nevī* named *Maḥabbet-nāme* in *hazaj* metre, completed by Khwārazmī on the banks of the Sir Darya in 754/1353, was inspired by the *Vīs u-Rāmīn* of Gurgānī.

The third stage in the development of Eastern Turkish literature is the Chaghatay period. This literature which began during the Timurid period in Central Asia in the ninth/fifteenth century, developed in cultural centres such as Samarqand, Herat, Bukhārā, Khīva, Farghānā and Kashghar, and spread to the whole eastern Turkish world and India. Sakkārī, the poet who lived at Ulugh Beg's court in Samarqand during the second half of the century, and later on other poets, especially Luṭfī of Herat (d. 867/1462–3), who worked up this literary dialect in their *dīvāns*, *mes̱nevīs* and disputations, prepared for the appearance of 'Alī Shīr Navā'ī. In the second half of the fifteenth century, Chaghatay literature enjoyed its golden era at Herat. The sultan of Herat, Ḥusayn Baykara (d. 912/1506), was himself a poet. His court became a sort of academy to which poets, scholars, and artists gathered. 'Alī Shīr Navā'ī (844–906/1441–1501), one of the greatest poets of Eastern Turkish literature and one of the most able in Turkish literature as a whole, was nurtured there. Navā'ī was extremely original and fertile in poetry a worthy scholar and an able statesman. His great service to Chaghatay literature has resulted in this dialect often being called Navā'ī.

In recent times Navā'ī has been regarded both as one of the greatest poets of the world, and as a mere follower of the Persian classics. The truth lies between these two extremes. Like all Turkish classical poets, he was inspired by the great poets of Persian literature, such as Niẓāmī, but more often by Amīr Khusraw of Delhi, who was close to his period, and by Jāmī, his contemporary. However, using the common Islamic themes, the common forms and motives, he developed a very personal and original style. He brought out the ingenuity of the Turkish language with all its fineness and expressiveness. In these respects, together with Yūnus Emre, Fużūlī and Nedīm, he is one of the four great poets of classical Turkish literature, but he is the most fertile of them all. Because the majority of his *ghazals* were woven around the same theme they are different from the common tradition. His *mesnevīs* also vary in many instances from the common themes and display individuality.

Navā'ī also wrote many works on other subjects. Among these *Majālis al-nafā'is* (897/1491) is the first collection of biographies of poets in Turkish and moreover, even though brief, it is illustrative of its period. *Mīzan al-awzān* (898/1493) is an essay that he wrote about metre. It also contains some information about the kinds of poetry peculiar to Eastern Turkish. Although actually taking over Jāmī's *Nafaḥāt al-uns* in his *Nasā'im al-maḥabba min shamā'im al-futuwwa*, Navā'ī enlarged it with appendices and also made use of other sources. It is an excellent source for the biographies of the mystics of Turkistān. In his work named *Muḥākamat al-lughatayn* (905/1499) he makes a comparison of Turkish and Persian, the two competing languages and cultures of the time in Central Asia, and he tries to prove the superiority of the Turkish language.

After Navā'ī there are two great names in eastern Turkish literature, both of rulers. The first one of these, Ẓahīr al-Dīn Muḥammad Bābur, the founder of the Mughal empire in India, is known especially for his memoirs, which represent the prose of Eastern Turkish, as well as for his poems, which are equal to Navā'ī's. In his memoirs, which are probably incomplete, Bābur records his most active and interesting life with a frankness and honesty which is rarely found in this sort of work. Here we find Bābur, not only as a ruler and commander, but also as an artist of quality and as a man not hiding his weaknesses or boasting about his merits. His *Bābur-nāme*, which was translated first into Persian and then into the main Western languages, is a valuable source about his family, his circle and his contemporaries in all kinds of professions. The last notable representative of Eastern Turkish literature, Abu'l-Ghāzī Bahādur Khān, was the ruler of Khīva (1054–74/1644–63) and belonged to the Shaybānī Özbeg dynasty. Before he became khan he visited Turkish countries and collected Turkish, Persian and Mongolian sources of Turkish history. In addition to documents, he also made a collection of stories and legends. Besides these he studied the history of the Shaybānī dynasty. The two works that he wrote as a result of his enquiries, *Shejere-i Terākime* (1070/1659) and *Shajarat al-Atrāk* (left unfinished at his death and completed by his son, in 1076/1665), contain much historical information; but are especially important as examples of Chaghatay prose which are close to the popular language and far from ornamentation or artificiality. The second of these works has been translated into various European languages.

Sufficient study has not yet been made on Chaghatay literature after the eleventh/seventeenth century. It is generally accepted that no more than a mere superficial imitation of the old works was achieved, and the literature eventually began to decline. However, the results of some recent research show that writers of considerable importance lived in this period, but their work could not reach beyond a limited circle. Hence it is too early yet to judge the late Chaghatay period. However towards the end of the nineteenth century this common written language was eventually abandoned, and local dialects became literary languages.

Western Turkish

Even though the Eastern Turks in Central Asia had adopted Islamic literature in the fifth/eleventh century, the formation of a written literature was delayed for about two centuries among the Oghuz (Seljuk) Turks who had settled in Anatolia in continuous waves after the fourth/tenth century, and who eventually turkicized and islamized the area. In fact we see the first examples of written Turkish literature in Anatolia during the time of the principalities (*beyliks*) in Anatolia between the Seljuk and Ottoman periods. The main reason for this is the fact that the Seljuk Turks used Persian as the official language and Arabic for learned works until the very end. The expansion of the Turkish language as the official language in Anatolia starts at the time of Karamanoghlu Meḥmed Bey (660–77/1261–78). The emergence of a written literature with a two centuries time-lag between the Eastern and Western Turks, and in geographical areas far distant from each other, affected the orthography of Eastern and Western Turkish. When the Eastern Turks became Muslim and adopted the Arabic script, they developed a many-vowelled orthography following the Uigur tradition, and this system continued in the Kara-Khanid, Khwārazm and Chaghatay periods. Since Eastern Turkish literature was not brought into Anatolia as a whole, Arabic texts with vowel-points were taken as models for the Turkish written in Anatolia in the seventh/thirteenth century, and a spelling system largely marked with vowel-points but generally few vowels was developed in the period in the succeeding two centuries.

Western Turkish literature, comprising the Āẕarī and Ottoman areas, developed in three separate branches: the *dīvān* literature that followed Persian models, intended for an *élite* with a classical *medrese* or palace-school education; mystical folk-literature or *tekke*-literature that developed as a result of the expansion of mysticism among the people and the increased impact of the religious orders; and secular folk-literature.

The *dīvān* literature meant for the higher social classes took Persian literature as a pattern from the thirteenth to the middle of the nineteenth century, and adopted some local elements. The trend of this literature, especially in language and style, until the mid-ninth/fifteenth century (or to be more exact until the period of Meḥmed the Conqueror) and its development after this date, shows an important difference. In the seventh/thirteenth and eighth/fourteenth centuries the capitals of the principalities in Anatolia, e.g. Kütahya, Kastamonu and Aydın, were centres of culture. Although the literary and artistic life was concentrated around the prince's residence, poets and writers in these small towns joined in the daily lives of the people. They were in contact with them in their homes, in the market-place, in the bazaar or in the mosque. Therefore even though they had accepted the Persian type of forms and content of the common Islamic literature, the language they used was not widely different from the spoken language of the people. To some extent the same thing can be said for the first century and a half of the Ottoman empire. The first capital, Bursa, and the second capital, Edirne, were both medium-sized provincial towns, and the courts of the first Ottoman sultans could not completely divorce the poets and the writers they patronized from the people. But all this changed after the conquest of Istanbul and the establishment of this metropolitan city as the capital of the empire. During Meḥmed the Conqueror's period, the poets of the court eventually became divorced from the people, and Arabic or Persian terms superceded Turkish, even for common and frequently used words.

In Western Turkish, the *élite* literature that began in Anatolia followed especially classical Persian verse, and worked upon the same common themes and motives. We see the products of the *mesnevī* form after the seventh/thirteenth century. These *mesnevīs* took as a subject well-known legendary love-stories, or the principles of mysticism in a symbolic way, or moral ideas, of which sometimes five were written by the same author to form a *khamsa*.

Hundreds of poets whose names are mentioned in the Ottoman biographies of poets have worked upon the same limited *mesnevī* subjects. The most favoured theme in western Turkish literature is the story of Yūsuf and Zulaykhā, which is actually taken from the Qur'ān and from the classical commentaries depending on midrashic material. Some of these *mesnevīs* are based on the simple Qur'anic story, but the majority of them have been worked upon in detail, from those in Persian literature. The theme of Laylā and Majnūn was used by some thirty poets, but the presentation by Fużūlī (d. 963/1556) much surpassed others before and after him, except Navā'ī's, and in Turkish literature this theme has become inseparable from Fużūlī's name. Husrev u-Shīrīn (or Ferhād u-Shīrīn) is one of the most popular *mesnevī* themes in Turkish. The most beautiful example of this theme was by Sheykhī at the beginning of the ninth/fifteenth century. Other themes have also been employed. A special characteristic of the *Iskender-nāme* written by Aḥmedī (d. 815/1413) is that it contains a chronicle of the earlier periods of Ottoman history.

Besides the common subjects of the classical tradition, hundreds of *mesnevīs* were written on religious, mystical, ethical, didactic and other subjects. Two religious *mesnevīs* which are read by great numbers of people up to the present day are the *Mevlit* (*Mawlid*) (812/1409) by Süleymān Chelebi of Bursa, which is about the life of the Prophet and is still read on special occasions, and the mystical *Muḥammediye* (853/1449) of Yazıjıoghlu Meḥmed Bijan.

The *dīvān* poetry employed all the forms of Persian literature, with the *qaṣīda* and the *ghazal* having prime importance. Even after a new literature started to develop under Western influence, there have still been groups and individuals who carried on the taste for *dīvān* poetry.

In *dīvān* poetry where common themes, limited motives, certain forms and clichés are dominant, great poets could only show their personalities by means of characteristics of style and the innovations they could contribute to the common material. Among these poets the most outstanding are: Nesīmī (d. 821/1418), who wrote with a great and sincere mystical emotion and was distinct from his contemporaries by his fluent style and his competence in prosody; Nejatī (d. 914/1509) who was near to the language of the people and who brought a new spirit to *dīvān* poetry; Fużūlī (d. 964/1556) who employed the concept of mystical love in a very original way, though showing loyalty to the conventions of his time, and with a deep sincerity in style and expression, a personality that grasps the reader, and the description of pain and sorrow in a most human form; Bāqī (d. 1008/1600) whose poetry was influenced by the welfare and splendour of the period of Süleymān the Magnificent and who wrote the best elegy for this sultan; Nef'ī (d. 1045/1635) the greatest representative of the eleventh/seventeenth-century Ottoman *dīvān* literature, which was influenced by the new Indo-Persian style, known as the *sabk-i Hindī*, who most successfully reconciled fine images with flowery expressions; Nābī (d. 1124/1712). who became distinguished in the symbolism of wisdom, and Nedīm (d. 1143/1730) who wished to make a real reform in *dīvān* poetry. However neither the environment in which he lived, nor the social and cultural conditions, were convenient for a radical change. In spite of this, Nedīm made many great innovations, without touching the traditional forms and clichés. He tried to change *dīvān* poetry from being abstract by putting his own environment and his period into it. Without reading Nedīm we cannot have a complete idea of the life, traditions, costumes, entertainment and personalities of the time of Aḥmed III. He put the spoken language of Istanbul into his poetry, though among it some old clichés can be found. Besides all this, he was a great poet. But the last great master of *dīvān* poetry, Ghālib Dede (d. 1214/1799), a Mevlevī leader, took a contrary direction as a result of his personal taste, tendencies, education, training and environment, though he was influenced by Nedīm in certain respects. Ghālib did not favour the language of the people, and by combining the *sabk-i Hindī* style of the eleventh/seventeenth century and especially the manner of Nā'ilī (d. 1077/1666) with his own sophistic tendencies, he preferred a style which only a very limited group of people could understand. Thus he brought the *dīvān* literature into a dead-end, despite his power as a great poet, and in a way he prepared the decline that took place in the nineteenth century.

Parallel to the *dīvān* literature, two other movements in poetry developed. One of these, popular mystical poetry, or *tekke* poetry, originated from poetry written in the popular language and in the old Turkish syllabic metre by leaders or members of religious orders propagating Sufism among the people, partly in order to gain sympathy and recognition for this movement. The second of these movements, folk-poetry or *ashık* literature, originated from poems generally also written in syllabic metre and in the popular language by illiterate or little-educated poets who came from the masses of the common people.

One of the greatest poets of all Turkish literature, according to some the greatest of all, Yūnus Emre (d. 720/1320), united these three tendencies and created a poetry in the popular language inspired by local Turkish, by mystical and by Persian classical sources; he generally used the syllabic metre. Yūnus Emre was an ardent, deeply inspired, sincere poet of genius whose life-story became woven into legends and myths. His works are preserved in comparatively late manuscripts, but many of his poems have become confused with the productions of his admirers, who took the name of Yūnus after him. He used the themes of life, religion, mysticism and death in a most effective way and had the finest command of the Turkish language. No poet of a calibre to continue his work has followed him. For many centuries Yūnus was held in veneration all over Turkey. His hymns were sung in ecstasies, and he was the greatest source of inspiration for the young poets during the period of literary revival at the beginning of the twentieth century. However after Yūnus Emre, Turkish poetry developed into the three separate branches which have already been mentioned; that is *dīvān*, *tekke* and folk-poetry.

In *tekke* poetry, Kaygusuz Abdal and Pīr Sulṭān Abdal (both of the ninth/fifteenth century) are names worth mentioning because of their great personalities and originality. Research about the lives and works of these poets is as yet only beginning.

Folk-poetry has many representatives in every century up to our time. These poets generally used the popular language and syllabic metre, but they were rarely original. Mostly they developed into formalization and clichés, and some of them even attempted to imitate the *dīvān* poets within the forms of folk-poetry. The greatest poet of this branch, Karajaoghlan (tenth/sixteenth century), is worth mentioning as one of the distinguished exceptions. His poetry, written in a lively, active, colourful style and a fluent language, describes the life of the Anatolian in his village and in the plateau, the mountains, the rivers, the country, the lakes, with all their animals, birds and trees. His works have greater literary value than any other of their kind. In folk-poetry there are also some successful examples of the epic, pastoral, elegiac, humorous and satirical kinds. Generally, these poems are recited with a musical composition written for them. Dadaloghlu (d. ? 1868), who came from the nomadic tribes living on the Taurus mountains, is the last great name to continue the tradition that came from Karajaoghlan, mainly in the epic field.

In Western Turkish literature classical prose has a very different characteristic from poetry. Though Persian examples fundamentally dominated the poetry, they exerted a very limited effect on Turkish prose, which could therefore develop as the most native and original branch of the literature. Until recent times what was meant by prose was the *inshā'* form where the aesthetics of the *dīvān* poetry and many of its arts were used. Prose other than *inshā'* started to be considered as literature only after the Tanẓīmāt, and even then only to a limited extent. Apart from this, the opinion of the literary Reformers that 'Turkish prose which was formerly pure, became gradually elaborate after the fifteenth century and did not tend towards purity before the nineteenth century' has lasted down to our times, though it is not correct. Actually, this prose developed in three parallel categories, from the beginning to the Tanẓīmāt period.

The first is pure prose based on the popular spoken language; although *inshā'* affected this kind of prose in various degrees. After the seventh/thirteenth century, it included commentaries on the Qur'ān enlarged with popular stories, *Ḥadīth* and Islamic legend. The Dede Korkut stories are believed to have been written down in the ninth/fifteenth century in the present form, but are considered to be remains of the lost Oghuz epics, and form the most original example of Turkish epic literature. Popular religious epics, inspired by the legends of the period of conquest and islamization of Anatolia, accounts of Ottoman campaigns written in an epic way, histories of the House of 'Os̲mān, some anonymous, and books on ethics and politics, were also written in this pure prose. One may also mention in this category *Mir'āt al-mamālik* by Seayyidī 'Alī Re'īs, which relates his travels; ten volumes of *Seyāhat-nāme*, an endless treasury of information, written in a colourful style by Evliya Chelebi, the greatest traveller of the eleventh/seventeenth century; an Ottoman history known as *Fez̲leke* by Kātib Chelebi, a scholar of a very progressive mind for his time, together with his various essays on current controversial problems or containing his proposals for reform within the empire; the histories of Pechevi (1059/1649) and Silaḥdār Meḥmed (1136/1723) which describe their own times, written realistically and with very vivid scenes; and finally, hundreds of works in this prose style ending with short stories by Giritli 'Alī 'Azīz (d. 1798) making a bridge between the old popular stories and the modern novel.

The second category is ornamented prose (*inshā'*). This is where a word from the Arabic or Persian vocabularies was taken at random and used according to the grammatical rules of either language, with Turkish words given an unimportant place; many of the verbal tricks of *dīvān* literature were adopted, and rhymed prose regarded as fundamental. Although literature in prose was in general unaffected by the divorce from popular speech which affected poetry, in some small circles *inshā'* still continued as an artificial prose language with the purpose of differentiating it completely from the popular language and showing off the writers' skill. Mainly the *Tevārīkh-i Āl-i ʿOsmān* by Kemāl Pasha-zāde (941/1531), the well-known *shaykh al-Islām* of Selīm I and also a great scholar and historian, the *Tājal-Tevārīkh*, by Saʿd al-Dīn, a leading *shaykh al-Islām* at the end of the tenth/sixteenth century, also some biographies of poets and some official and private collections of letters have followed this ornamented style of prose. Two classical representatives of this artificial prose carried it to an extreme, Veysī (d. 1037/1628), who wrote a biography of the Prophet and Nergisī (d. 1045/1635), who wrote the only prose *khamsa*. The work of Sinān Pasha, the great prose-writer of the ninth/fifteenth century, is generally classified as *inshā'*, although it actually only resembles this form because of its rhymed prose and symmetry. Otherwise its language is generally pure.

The third category is middle prose, where the popular spoken language was left far behind, but, the desire to show off the writer's skill by mere verbal tricks was not the goal, since he was mainly concerned with what he wanted to relate. The ratio of foreign and compound words varies from one writer to another, and some even show an interest in rhymed prose. In all forms of the old literature, this middle prose preponderates. It includes many of the histories, for instance those of Selānīkī (d. 1009/1600), Gelibolulu ʿAlī (d. 1009/1600), and Naʿīmā (d. 1129/1716), the last a masterful compilation and one of the most vivid in Ottoman prose, an important source for the eleventh/seventeenth century although the original of the book is lost. A large part of the official correspondence and journals, memorials of reform presented to the sultan, reports of ambassadors, the most colourful and interesting of which is the *Sefāret-nāme* of Yirmisekiz Meḥmed Chelebi, who died in 1145/1732, and some books on ethics and politics, were all written in middle prose.

The political and administrative reform movement known as the Tanẓīmāt, which begin in 1839, had also some effect on literature after

1850. The leader of this movement, called the Tanẓīmāt literature, was Ibrāhīm Shināsī (1821–71), who was educated in Paris. On his return to Turkey he brought back a completely new literary understanding. He made translations of poems from a Western language, French, for the first time. He introduced new concepts in the poems, which he wrote in the old style. He discussed the fatherland, the country, the people and the state, instead of the age-old clichés. He established the first private newspaper. He wrote the first Turkish play, and influenced his environment by his articles and speeches. The modernist spirit that he established with Namıq Kemāl (1840–88) and Żiyā Pasha (1825–80) developed a literature under the influence of the eighteenth-century French writers and the nineteenth-century Romantic poets, who were close to the public and opposed to despotism. After ʿAbd ül-Ḥaqq Ḥāmid (1852–1937) joined this group, the taste for *dīvān* literature was almost completely eliminated, in spite of intense resistance and the forms of Western literature were gradually applied to Turkish. The literary movement started by the *S̱ervet-i Fünūn* journal run by Tevfīq Fikret (1867–1915), Jenāb Shihāb al-Dīn (1870–1934) and Khālid Żiyā Uşaklıgil (1866–1945), who came together at the end of the century, saved the Turkish literature from the effects of Persian culture and created a fully Western (French) literature, although it delayed the formation of a native Turkish literature in Western forms and concepts, which was the real ultimate goal. The three leaders, of which the first was a poet, the second a poet and a prose-writer, and the third a novelist believed in the principle of art for art's sake. They preferred to be read and understood by a very small number of intellectuals rather than come down to the public. By carrying out a complete reaction in the language they created a sort of literary jargon consisting of rarely used words from Arabic and Persian. The literature that had been saved from the influence of Persian culture became a perfect imitation of French literature, again in a language which the public did not understand. Writers such as Aḥmed Midḥat (1844–1912) Aḥmed Rāsim (1864–1932), Ḥüseyin Raḥmī (1864–1944), and poets like Meḥmed Emīn (1869–1944) and Riżā Tevfīq (1869–1949), whose subjects as well as language were close to and addressed to the public, preferred to stay outside the *S̱ervet-i Fünun* movement. Though these writers and poets were underrated by their contemporaries, they established the foundations of a truly native Turkish literature which started in 1910 and obtained its full form and direction after 1930.

URDU LITERATURE

Urdu is the language spoken by the Muslims and by certain non-Muslim elements in the urban areas of West Pakistan and north-western India. It is the chief literary language of the Muslims of the subcontinent. The name 'Urdu' is of Turkish origin, familiarized in Persian by the Il-Khanid historians, and adopted in India by the Sayyid ruler Khiżr Khān (817–24/1414–21) for his army and court under Timurid influence. During the reign of the Great Mughals in India it came to be applied generally to the imperial camp, and during the late eleventh/seventeenth century to the language the camp spoke.

The language itself and its earlier regional literatures are much older than its present name. From the thirteenth to the eighteenth century it was referred to as 'Hindawī' or 'Hindī' or given dialectal names, 'Dakhanī' and 'Gujarātī'. This is rather confusing as its philological and literary growth remained quite distinct from the languages known today as Hindī or Gujarātī.

It is descended from one or more dialects of the Indo-Aryan Śawraseni Prākrit. It was evolved by the Indian Muslims for communication with Hindu fellow-citizens in town and country, and for use in the harems in which were Hindu women as wives, concubines or domestics.

The origins of Urdu date back to the period of Ghaznavid rule in the Panjāb in the sixth/twelfth century. The Muslims wrote it in Persian script. While they retained much of its grammatical structure and essential verbs, adjectives and adverbs, unrestrained borrowings from Persian, and through Persian from Arabic and to some extent Turkish, gave it a pronounced Muslim linguistic and literary character.

Its centre of gravity shifted to Delhi in the seventh/thirteenth century with the establishment of the Sultanate. Under the Khaljīs it was carried by Muslim armies to the Deccan and Gujarāt, where it developed a literary character earlier than in northern India. But it is quite possible that the first experimental literary use of the new language was made in the Ghaznavid Panjāb.

In Delhi from the seventh/thirteenth to the tenth/sixteenth century its literary use appears to have been whimsical and half-serious. Most of the pre-Urdu (Hindawī) work attributed to Amīr Khusraw (651–725/1253–1325) has now been demonstrated to be of apocryphal origin, written much later, possibly in the eleventh/seventeenth century.[1]

[1] Maḥmūd Shērānī, *Punjāb men Urdū* (Lahore, 1928), 128–43.

The only Urdu verses which can be attributed to Khusraw with any certainty are the few he has himself quoted in the introduction to one of his Persian *dīwāns*. These are couplets, half-Persian, half in a 'double' language which could be read either as Persian or Urdu, with a *double entendre*, serving as bantering *jeux d'esprit* written for the amusement of his friends. In this tradition a single bilingual couplet, a quarter Turkish, three-quarters Urdu, is also found in the *Dīwān* of Bābur, reflecting throughout these centuries the arrested growth of Urdu's potentialities as a literary language in the north.

The breakthrough towards the development of Urdu for literary purposes was made during these very centuries, away from the northern court, in the Ṣūfī hospices of outlying provinces. The Ṣūfī shaykhs, engaged in the dual task of converting the non-Muslims around them, and of evolving a technique of religious communication with their ill-educated disciples, used an early form of Urdu for their popular writings, reserving the use of Persian more and more for learned dialectics. The treatise *Mi'rāj al-'āshiqīn* of Sayyid Muḥammad 'Gēsūdarāz' (*c.* 750/1350) is generally considered to be the first prose work in Urdu. Mīrāñjī Shams al-'Ushshāq established Urdu as a recognized medium of Ṣūfī narrative verse. These Ṣūfīs freely transplanted Persian and Arabic religious vocabulary and forms of thought and experience into Urdu.

In the courts of Golkondā and Bījāpur in the Deccan, secular literature developed in the Dakhanī (southern) dialect. Sultan Muḥammad Qulī Quṭb Shāh (989–1020/1581–1611) of Golkondā, founder of the city of Ḥaydarābād, was himself a refined poet who grafted local Dravadian and Hindī loan words on the persianized texture of his Urdu verses with a spontaneous and instinctive artistry. He is one of the rare exceptions among Urdu poets, who chose to write intensely of Indian life and love. Among the luminaries of the Golkondā court was Mullā Wajhī, whose prose allegory *Sab ras* (1635) was a free rendering of Fattāḥī's (d. 852/1448) Persian poem *Dastūr-i 'ushshāq*, an allegory of love which contains interesting parallelisms with the *Roman de la rose*. In the court of Bījāpur, Nuṣratī (*c.* 1060/1650) bestowed a classical maturity upon the Urdu *ghazal*, and gave to the *mathnawī* a remarkable resilience as the vehicle of fabled story or contemporary epic.

In choice of material, as in the cultivation of a poetic diction, the literature of these courts showed an uninhibited exuberance, a momentum of development, and a freedom from the obligations of established tradition. Without fear of the loss of cultural identity, elements were borrowed from Hindu *milieux* and diction;[1] a process which seems to have been halted with Awrangzēb's occupation of these southern Muslim states in the second half of the eleventh/seventeenth century, and with the impact of the highly persianized and islamized *Urdū-i muʿallā*, the 'exalted' (Urdu) language of the imperial camp, on the poet and the intellectual of the Deccan. But the 'exalted' Urdu brought by the Mughal army from the north was only a spoken medium. Its refinements were conversational and social. Inhibited in the north by the undisputed sway of Persian, it had not yet bloomed into literary creativity. With Awrangzēb's conquest of the Deccan the two dialectal growths of Urdu, the literary but demotic southern, and the polished but uncreative northern, interfused. The south accepted the northern norms of persianized sophistication; the north was quickened by the precedent and example of the southern literary genius.

This cultural exchange[2] took place towards the close of the eleventh/seventeenth and the beginning of the twelfth/eighteenth century at Awrangābād, Awrangzēb's secondary capital in the Deccan. Walī (1668–1744), the chief representative of this new school, has two styles, an earlier southern and a later northern. He visited Delhi twice, in 1700 and in 1722, where by then the tradition of Indo-Persian poetry had lost most of its creative activity, as the arrival of fresh talent from Persia had ceased after the embitterment of Mughal-Safavid relations during the reign of Awrangzēb. In this inspirational vacuum, Walī's example almost overnight switched the northern desire for poetic expression from Persian to Urdu. But the north preserved its centuries-old Persian heritage almost intact in Urdu.

The School of Delhi rose in the early twelfth/eighteenth century under very inhospitable circumstances. The Mughal capital was sacked many times by invaders from outside, such as Nādir Shāh and Aḥmad Shāh Durrānī, and by the barbaric indigenous hordes of Jāts and Marāthās. This school shows all the sensitivity of individual and social suffering, and all the fortitude of an almost other-worldly composure. Two of its early representatives, Mīrzā Maẓhar Jān-i Jānān and Khwāja Mīr Dard (1720–84), were venerated Ṣūfīs who impregnated Urdu verse with the sublimation of pained love and resignation. The social disorganization of Delhi and the disintegration of human personality contributed to mould the delicately sensitive and intensely poetic

[1] Rām Bābū Saksena, *A history of Urdu literature* (Allahabad, 1940), 32–44.
[2] Aziz Ahmad, *Studies in Islamic culture in the Indian environment*, 251–2.

genius of Mīr Taqī Mir (1724–1808). His contemporary Mirzā Rafī Sawdā (1717–80) reacted to the surrounding chaos and the general decadence of men and morals with fierce invective in his satires.

These two poets, and several others, migrated from insecure Delhi to Lucknow where the nawabs of Awadh (Oudh) patronized a brilliantly degenerate court. Here the foundations of the School of Lucknow were laid.

The decadence of the Court of Lucknow was not uncreative. A comparative security under the indirect protection of the East India Company gave its social life a semblance of stability, and its *élite* the leisure to cultivate a taste for music, and for the witty, the droll and the banal in poetry, and to appreciate conceit, word play and verbal jugglery. Emigrés from Delhi, like Inshā' (1757–1817), soon fell under the spell of Lucknow; though his contemporary Muṣḥafī (1750–1824) maintained a sedate sensitiveness with a strain of asceticism. Inshā' and one of his friends, Rangīn, experimented in the invention of *Rīkhtī*, a frivolous, but linguistically most valuable genre of verse which used the segregated colloquial vocabulary of women of pleasure. *Rīkhtī* reached its culmination in the effeminate work of Jān Sāḥib (d. 1897).

The School of Lucknow had its redeeming features. Nāsikh (d. 1838) effectively 'purified' the Urdu poetic diction; and presumably as a reaction to the influx of demotic and effeminate expressions in Urdu verse, standardized the idiom and vocabulary of poetry by a ruthless and unimaginative process of linguistic elimination which deprived it of much of its indigenous heritage. His contemporary, Ātish (1778–1846), occasionally rose to heights of true inspiration from a morass of conventional bathos. In the last years of the Shī'ī state of Awadh a great school of martyrological verse arose, and bloomed in the passionate fervour of Anīs.

In 1765 Shāh 'Ālam, the nominal Mughal emperor of Delhi, appointed the British East India Company his revenue collector. In practice he thus became a pensioner of the Company, his effective régime confined to the four walls of the Red Fort. But this gave the much-tormented Delhi some respite. Here, under him and his successors, the second School of Delhi achieved a dignified style in the panegyrics of Ẕawq (1789–1854) and in the crystal-clear subjective lyricism of Mū'min (1800–51). In this milieu wrote Asad Allāh Khān Ghālib (1796–1869), the greatest of Urdu poets, moulding emotional verities into concrete image-symbols, balancing the magnitude of his structural intellectuality with tantalizing wit, adding nuance to nuance in externalizing the emotionally intricate, giving the inner content of his verse an unprecedented dimension by a fusion of fancy and feeling. He made any further use of conventional verse seem absurd, and pointed the way to the new intellectual styles which were ushered in by the deadly impact of the events of 1857.

Until the beginning of the nineteenth century, Urdu prose had consisted either of theological literature with an arabicized syntax or of ornate magical romances. The administration of the East India Company was, on the other hand, in pressing need of a simpler vernacular for use at the lower levels of administration. This policy was implemented by John Gilchrist at the Fort William College (founded in 1800) at Calcutta. There he guided his literary employees towards evolving a direct, fluent, almost utilitarian, prose style.

The need for a simpler style was being generally felt and there were other experiments in that direction, chiefly Ghālib's colloquially eloquent letters. Finally, all these elements converged on the genius of Sayyid Aḥmad Khān (1817–98), who elevated Urdu prose to the point of scientific precision of expression, and used it as a vehicle for historical and theological scholarship and for advanced journalism. He and his associates of the ʿAlīgarh Movement raised Urdu in expression and richness of content to a rank equal to other great Islamic languages. In acceptance and transmission of Western ideas Urdu outpaced them. Shiblī Nuʿmānī (1857–1914) shares with Zakā Allāh (d. 1910) the credit of forging a methodology of historiography which was to some extent a synthesis of the Islamic and Western disciplines. Shiblī is also the author of a monumental history of Persian literature, the *Shiʿr al-ʿAjam*, which grafts modern chronological method on the classical *tazkira* technique. Naẓīr Aḥmad developed the didactic *qiṣṣa* (story) to the artistic level of the modern novel. Alṭāf Ḥusayn Ḥālī (1837–1914), as great a prose-writer as he was a poet, established norms of intellectual criticism in his literary biographies and his Prolegomena on poetry. Muḥammad Ḥusayn Āzād (1834–1910), the only great prose-writer of the age who was almost entirely unconnected with Sayyid Aḥmad Khān's movement, was stylistically, though not as a theorist of poetry, the antithesis of Ḥālī, and wrote in an ornately beautiful style with a fascinating gift for telling an anecdote.

The Mutiny of 1857, its failure, and the liquidation of Muslim supremacy in Delhi, mark a sudden revolution in Urdu poetry. So far the

Urdu *ghazal* had blinded itself to its own geographical and ethical environment. Like its model, Persian, it had used a mathematics of imagery and convention, occasionally corresponding to the nuance of an individual emotional experience, but more often multiplying into infinite combinations of verbal arabesques, symbols of Persian heritage, that were accepted and manipulated, but not actually experienced. As Ḥālī, under the inspiration of Sayyid Aḥmad Khān, broke away from this classical pattern, he made a novel use of much of its familiar didacticism and its wealth of phrase and image in the construction of his forceful and profoundly stirring poem of Islamic revivalism, the *Musaddas*, which marks the rise of the political poem in Urdu as a powerful weapon of religio-political agitation.

Ḥālī thus paved the way for the emergence of Muḥammad Iqbāl (1873–1938), by far the most influential of Urdu poets and the most dynamic intellectual personality in the recent history of Islam in the sub-continent. His popularity began with his early nationalist poems written before 1905; during his pan-Islamic phase which followed he achieved poetic greatness. But for the formulation of his philosophical ideas and for their dissemination more widely in the *dār al-Islām* he turned to Persian. It is principally in his Persian poems that he formulated his doctrine of Self, its relation to society, and the ideal role of both the individual and society in a process of creative evolution, through the values of power and movement, in the ultimate quest of a co-existent association with the Infinite Reality that is God. In 1933 he returned to Urdu again and developed a new style, less lyrical, but of unprecedented intellectual forcefulness. To this period belong some of his finest poetic achievements such as the explosively resplendent imagery of his *Masjid-i Qurṭuba* ('Mosque of Cordova') in which he outlines the metaphysical eternity of artistic creation.

Since Iqbāl, Urdu poetry has produced some lesser luminaries, sensitive writers of the *ghazal* like Ḥasrat and Jigar, exuberantly demotic revolutionaries like Josh, and among younger poets Fayż Aḥmad Fayż, who won the Lenin Prize in 1962. Fayż has evolved for himself a technique of cryptic impregnation of the familiar image with a newer significance occasionally producing a highly artistic political *double entendre* which evades all censorship.

The development of Urdu prose since Ḥālī has been extensive rather than intensive. It has continued to borrow fresh vocabulary from English and Arabic; it has translated concepts and popularized them; it has tried to be the vehicle of modern sciences; it is the source of expression and of momentum to extensive journalistic venture.

Urdu fiction had begun in the later eighteenth century with the *dāstāns* of the Amīr Ḥamza cycle. These were voluminous, labyrinthine magical romances peopled with heroes, *'ayyārs* (*tricheurs*) and demons making and breaking enchanted cities in monotonously identical exploits. At Fort William College Mīr Amman dissolved this technique and *métier* to the simpler preternatural story of the familiar Arabian Nights type in his *Bāgh u-bahār*. European influences came to be established in the didactic novel of Naẕīr Aḥmad in the later nineteenth century. The Hindu mind, more expert in visualizing a three-dimensional human character than the iconoclastic Muslim mind, made a significant contribution to the growth of the Urdu novel in the works of Sarshār and Prem Chand, who placed it firmly in the many-faced Indian milieu. The Muslim historical novel in the hands of 'Abd al-Ḥalīm Sharar romanticized the Muslim past in stereotyped colour and imagery and rather cheap sentimentality. It was in the vindication of the 'noble courtesan' that the Muslim Urdu novel showed a certain lyrical realism in the work of Mirzā Ruswā and Qāżī 'Abd al-Ghaffār. From 1935 the leftist 'Progressive Movement' ushered in the down-to-earth naturalistic short story of exquisite realism. Compared to the short story, the contemporary Urdu novel has so far been of a secondary stature.

Since the partition of the subcontinent in 1947, the emphasis of Muslim writing in Pakistan as well as in India has been overwhelmingly religious. In Pakistan, Abu'l-'Alā' Mawdūdī has a lucid and torrentially eloquent style. The style of Ghulām Aḥmad Parwīz has an element of intellectual persuasion. In Pakistan as in India hagiology is being welded into recent Indo-Muslim history, though with a different distribution of emphasis from divergent political angles. In Abu'l-Kalām Āzād's highly arabicized style, and in his intellectual proximity to Egyptian Islamic modernism, a beginning was made towards a closer understanding of Islamic thought in other parts of the Muslim world. This movement has gathered a certain momentum in Pakistan. Publishers' catalogues in Pakistan reflect a wide fluctuation in the book market, and a growing demand for classical and contemporary Islamic literature at the expense of fiction and *belles lettres*.

CHAPTER 9

ART AND ARCHITECTURE

PRIMITIVE ISLAM

The proper usage of the collective name 'Islamic art' has been seriously questioned by a number of scholars during the past two or three decades. As alternatives 'Arab art', 'Persian art', 'Turkish art' have been suggested. Others have even gone as far as denying any common ground or characteristics in this art, and claimed that it should be simply named after the respective country where the monuments stand or where particular art objects were produced. It seems desirable, therefore, before describing the achievements of Islamic art, to answer these critics; to define, as far as is possible, the common characteristics of Islamic art, to reveal its sources and to throw some light upon the foreign influences which contributed to its evolution.

It is a well-known and accepted fact that the Arabs had hardly anything which could be called art when they set out to invade the territories in the north. There was a highly developed architecture in southern Arabia well before the advent of Islam, but that had hardly anything to do with those primitive tribesmen who were united under Islam, and who constituted the backbone of its victorious army. Neither had the Prophet any intention of giving an impetus to a religious art. Indeed, we cannot talk about Islamic art in a religious sense, as we can talk about Christian or Buddhist art.

It was the helping hand of highly skilled craftsmen and artists of the conquered territories which provided the resources needed to erect and adorn the earliest religious and secular buildings of Islam. The effect of these cultures—Byzantine, Coptic, Sasanian and later on Central Asian—can be clearly recognized and distinguished in the early period. Thus we cannot speak of an Islamic style during the first one or two centuries of the *Hijra*. From the amalgamation of these foreign elements, which can be regarded as the sources of this new type of art, was born a new style which made its imprint on art and architecture throughout the Islamic world. The late Sir Thomas Arnold formulated the concept of Islamic art—or, as he called it, 'Muhammadan art'—in the following way: 'By the term "Muhammadan art" is meant those works of art which were produced under Muhammadan patronage and in Muhammadan countries; the artists themselves were of diverse nationalities and were not always adherents of the faith of Islam'.[1]

No monument has survived from the earliest period of Islam. The earliest mosques, such as the Prophet's mosque at Medina, or those of Kūfa and Baṣra, were primitive structures, erected of perishable material. The Prophet, it seems, had no intention of erecting temples for daily prayer. Yet his house in Medina soon became a public building, a gathering place for Muslims and later a *masjid*, a mosque. A detailed description of his house is preserved by Ibn Sa'd. It was a primitive structure with a central court surrounded by mud-brick walls. It had a roofed portico on the north side, the roof being supported by palm trunks. There were also small huts attached to it on the east side which served as dwelling places for the Prophet's wives.

In the first two years of the *Hijra* the *qibla* or direction of prayer was on the north side of the building, that is towards Jerusalem; but after a sudden revelation the Prophet changed it towards the Ka'ba in Mecca. Orientation of prayer or *qibla* was an accepted custom in many religions, but was particularly important among the Semitic people. In Islam the *qibla* is marked by the *miḥrāb*, which is usually a niche placed in the centre of the *qibla* wall. The *miḥrāb* in niche form was first erected in Medina, when they rebuilt the Prophet's mosque in 88/706–7. Before that it was indicated by a strip of paint on the *qibla* wall or a block of stone placed in the centre.

There was also a simple pulpit or *minbar* in Medina, which was later on generally accepted in Islam. Another important feature of the sanctuary, introduced by the first Umayyad caliph, Mu'āwiya, was the *maqṣūra*, a place reserved for the caliph and surrounded by a wooden screen.

Three more mosques had been erected during the reign of the Patriarchal Caliphs. The first was at Baṣra in 14/635 and the second at Kūfa in 17/638. The third mosque was built by 'Amr b. al-'Āṣ, the conqueror of Egypt, at Fusṭāṭ in 21–2/641–2. Historians also gave account of an early mosque in Jerusalem, built by the Caliph 'Umar in 16/637. All these mosques were again primitive buildings, following generally the plan of the Prophet's mosque at Medina.

THE UMAYYAD PERIOD

It was under the Umayyad Caliph 'Abd al-Malik (65–86/685–705) that the first surviving monument of Islam was erected. It is the Qubbat

[1] *Painting in Islam* (Oxford, 1928), n. 1.

al-Ṣakhra, the Dome of the Rock in Jerusalem. It was built above the Holy Rock where David's altar stood and from where, according to legend, the Prophet made his famous night journey to heaven.

The building is an octagonal structure surrounding the rock. Above there is a huge wooden dome resting on a high drum supported by four piers and twelve columns. Between this colonnade and the outer walls is an intermediate octagon supporting the sloping roof of the building. The outer walls are decorated by eight large bays on each side. Five of these bays have been pierced by windows. The upper part of the walls was coated by faience tiles in the early tenth/sixteenth century. There are four doors in the building facing the four cardinal points. Below the rock there is a small chamber with two small *miḥrābs*.

The decoration inside the arcades and of the drum consists of beautiful glass mosaics, most of which are original. These mosaics display fruits, vine and acanthus scrolls and trees, some of them adorned with jewels. They also include a Kufic inscription giving the date of completion as 72/691. The mosaics reveal both Byzantine and Sasanian influences. They were most likely made by Syrian mosaicists, as there was a famous school in Syria in pre-Islamic times.

'Abd al-Malik had a number of reasons, mainly political, for erecting such a splendid mosque for Islam. First of all the new faith had to compete with the beauty of Christian churches in Jerusalem, such as the Holy Sepulchre, which it seemed to imitate. Also he had a rival caliph, Ibn al-Zubayr in Mecca. For this reason he wanted to prevent pilgrims from visiting Mecca. That would explain the unusual plan of the building which makes possible a circumambulation of the holy rock, just as Muslims circumambulate the Ka'ba.

Ibn Taghrī-Birdī mentions that 'Abd al-Malik even had the intention of turning the *qibla* back from Mecca to Jerusalem.[1] Al-Ḥajjāj's contemporary mosque at Wāsiṭ certainly supports that surmise. Archaeologists, when searching for his mosque and palace, found four different mosques one above the other. The upper three buildings were properly oriented towards Mecca, but the lowest mosque with al-Ḥajjāj's palace attached to it, had a deviation of 34 degrees towards the west. A second mosque, that of Isqaf Banī Junayd, a little north of Baghdād, also attributed to al-Ḥajjāj, had almost the same deviation.[2]

Another important mosque, the Great or Umayyad Mosque in

[1] Ibn Taghrī-Birdī, *al-Nujūm al-ẓāhira*, I, 71.

[2] Verbal information given by my Iraqi colleague, Dr 'Abdul 'Azīz Ḥamīd.

I (*a*) Damascus, the Great or Umayyad Mosque, the so-called '*Baradā*' mosaic panel under the western portico.

(*b*) The Umayyad palace of Mshattā: audience hall with the triple apse.

2 (*a*) Quṣayr ʻAmra, view from the north.

(*b*) Quṣayr ʻAmra, painting of the enthroned monarch in the alcove.

3 (*a*) Jericho, Khirbat al-Mafjar, mosaic floor in the bath.

(*b*) Ewer of the Umayyad Caliph Marwān II,
Persian, second/eighth century.

4 (*a*) Ukhayḍir, the eastern gateway, looking from the north.

(*b*) Sāmarrā, the Jawsaq al-Khāqānī palace, the Bāb al-ʿĀmma 221/836).

(*b*) Sāmarrā, Jawsaq al-Khāqānī palace, wall fresco representing dancing girls from the harem.

5 (*a*) Sāmarrā, stucco panel from a recently excavated private house.

(*c*) Sāmarrā, the Great Mosque with the Malwiyya.

6 (*a*) Beaker, splashed and mottled ware, Mesopotamia, third/ninth century.

(*b*) Large dish, tin-glazed cobalt blue painted ware, Mesopotamia, third/ninth century.

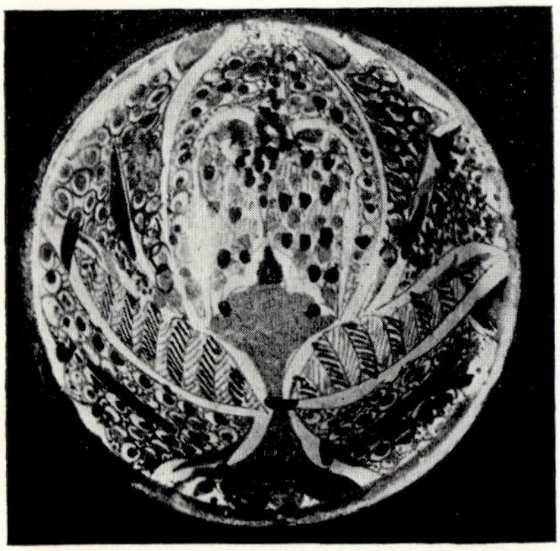

(*c*) Small bowl painted in polychrome lustre, Mesopotamia, third/ninth century.

(*d*) Large bowl, slip-painted ware, Nīshāpū fourth/tenth century.

7 (*a*) Cairo, mosque of Aḥmad b. Ṭūlūn, 263-5/876-9.

b) Cairo, mosque of Aḥmad b. Ṭūlūn, view of the sanctuary with two stucco flat *miḥrābs* on two pillars in the foreground.

8 (a) Cordova, the Great Mosque, the *miḥrāb*, 354/965.

(b) Bukhārā, the mausoleum of Ismāʿīl the Samanid, 295/907.

9 (*a*) Tim, Üzbekistan, mausoleum of ʿArab Ata, 367/977-8, zone of transition.

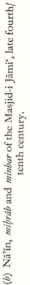

(*b*) Nāʾīn, *miḥrāb* and *minbar* of the Masjid-i Jāmiʿ, late fourth/tenth century.

10 (*a*) Cairo, mosque of al-Azhar, dome over court end of sanctuary with stucco decorations and window grilles, *c*. 545/1150.

(*b*) Kharaqān, a recently discovered Seljuk tomb-tower, 486/1095.

11 Cairo, mosque of al-Juyūshī, the stucco *miḥrāb*, 478/1085.

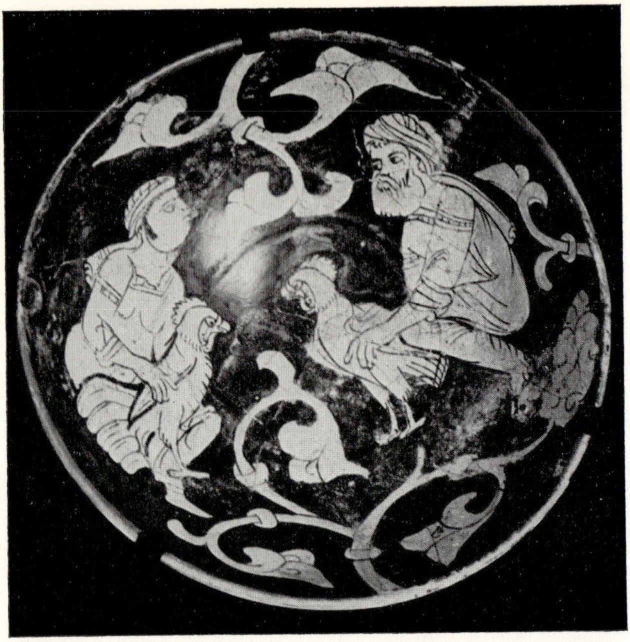

12 (*a*) Large dish, lustre painted, Egypt, fifth/eleventh century.

(*b*) Fatimid painting: siege of a fortress, Egypt, sixth/twelfth century.

13 Damāvand, a recently discovered Seljuk tomb-tower late fifth/eleventh century.

14 (*a*) Ardistān, Masjid-i Jāmi', 553-5/1158-60, zone of transition.

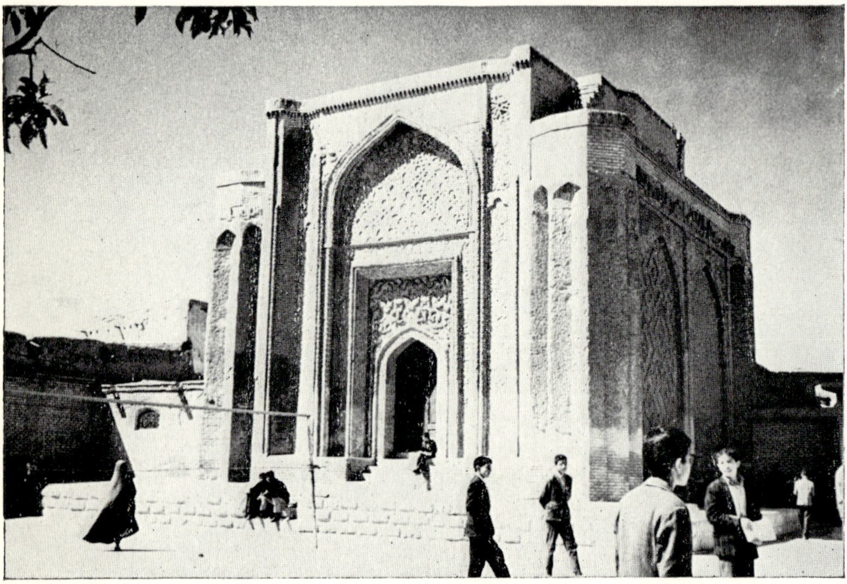

(*b*) Hamadān, Gunbad-i 'Alawiyyān, sixth/twelfth century.

15 (*a*) Naṭanz, Masjid-i Kūchī Mīr, stucco *miḥrāb*, sixth/twelfth century.

(*b*) Mosul, the Great Mosque, 543/1148, the minaret.

16 (*a*) Divrighi, Ulu Jāmiʿ, detail of the main entrance, 626/1229.

(*b*) Ankara, Arslankhāne Jāmiʿ, faience *miḥrāb*, 688–9/1289–90.

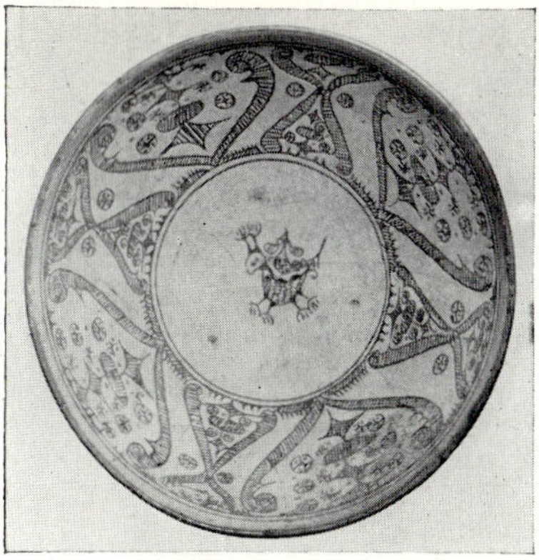

17 (*a*) Bowl, decoration in *sgraffiato* technique; Persian, Āmul, late fourth/tenth or early fifth/eleventh century.

(*b*) Jug, so-called 'Seljuk white ware'; Persian, Rayy or Kāshān, late sixth/twelfth century.

) Large dish, lustre-painted; Persian, ayy, late sixth/twelfth or early seventh/ thirteenth century.

(*d*) Bowl, overglaze, so-called *mīnā'ī* painted; Persian, Rayy, late sixth/twelfth or early seventh/thirteenth century.

18 (*a*) Bucket, inlaid with silver, made in Herat, signed and dated: 559/1163.

(*b*) Ewer, brass, inlaid with silver, signed by Shujāʿ b. Manaʿ, dated: 629/1232.

19 (*a*) Miniature painting: the Pharmacy, from Dioscorides's *Materia medica*, Baghdād, 681/1224.

(*b*) Miniature painting: Abū Zayd before the governor of Merv. From the *Maqāmāt* of al-Ḥarīrī, Baghdād, *c*. 622-33/1225-35.

20 (*a*) Islamic calligraphy: (i) simple Kufic, (ii) foliated Kufic, (iii) floriated Kufic, (iv) *Naskhi*, (v) *Thuluth* ,(vi) *Nasta'līq*.

(*b*) Seljuk carpet from Anatolia, seventh/thirteenth century.

21 (*a*) Aleppo, gateway to the citadel, sixth/twelfth century.

(*b*) Cairo, the mausoleum of the *Imām* al-Shāfiʿī, woodcarvings of the cenotaph, 608/1211.

22 (*a*) Detail of an inlaid bronze canteen, early seventh/thirteenth century.

(*b*) Rabat, minaret of Mosque of Ḥasan.

23 (*a*) Granada, the Alhambra, eighth/fourteenth century.

(*b*) Naṭanz, the minaret of the Masjid-i Jāmiʿ 704-9/1304-9, and the dome of the tomb of Abū Ṣamad, 707/1307.

24 (*a*) Samarqand, Gūr-i Mīr mausoleum, general view, 807/1404.

(*b*) Samarqand, Shāh-i Zinda, detail of portal of Tughluk Tekin's mausoleum, 774/1372.

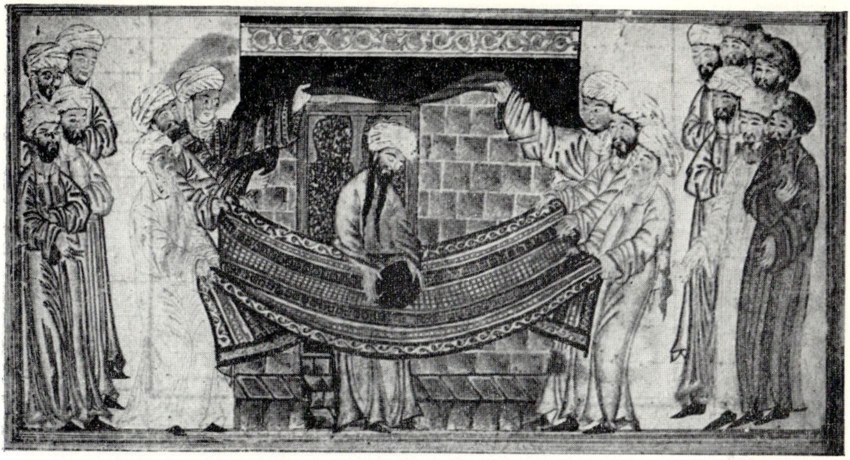

25 (*a*) Miniature painting from the *Jāmiʿ al-tawārīkh* of Rashīd al-Dīn, 714/1314: Muḥammad replacing the Black Stone in the Kaʿba.

(*b*) Miniature painting from the *Shāh-nāma*: Bahrām Gūr hunting and the death of his mistress, Āzāda; Shīrāz school, early eighth/fourteenth century.

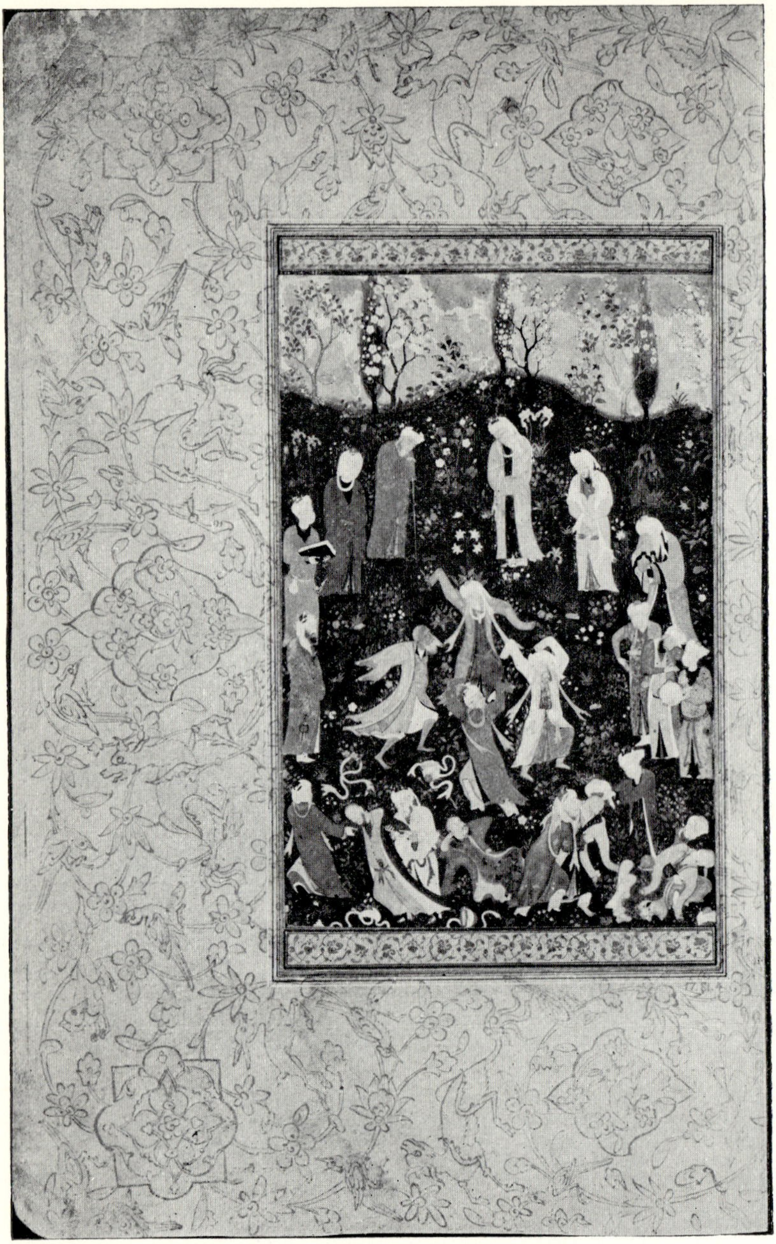

26 Miniature painting from the *Dīwān* of Ḥāfiẓ: Dance of the dervishes; Herat, Bihzād's school, late ninth/fifteenth century.

27 (*a*) Cairo, façade of the mausoleum of Qalawun 683-4/1284-5.

(*b*) Mamluk carpet, Egypt, ninth/fifteenth century.

28 (*a*) Iṣfahān, the ʿAlī Qapu palace, early eleventh/seventeenth century.

(*b*) Edirne, Selīmiye Jāmiʿ, built by Sinān Pasha, 977-83/1569-75.

29 (*a*) Dish, Iznik pottery, third period, early eleventh/seventeenth century. Crown copyright.

(*b*) Turkish embroidery, twelfth/eighteenth century.

30 Iṣfahān, minaret of the Masjid-i Shāh, 1020-48/1612-38.

31 (*a*) The so-called 'Polish rug', silk pile: Persian, eleventh/seventeenth century.

b) Safavid metalwork: covered bowl, dated: 1089/1678. Crown copyright.

32 (*a*) Large dish, so-called 'Kubachi' ware, north-western Persia, eleventh/seventeenth century. Crown copyright.

(*b*) Persian white, so-called 'Gombroon', ware, ewer, late eleventh/seventeenth century. Crown copyright.

Damascus, was erected by the Caliph al-Walīd, son of 'Abd al-Malik. This huge rectangular building was originally a pagan temple, dedicated to Jupiter. Later it was converted to a Christian church. After the Arab conquest of Damascus the building was jointly used by Muslims and Christians. When Damascus became the capital of the Umayyad empire, and the number of Muslims greatly increased in the city, the entire building was taken over from the Christians. That was in 86/705 when al-Walīd succeeded his father as caliph.

Al-Walīd ordered a complete reconstruction of the building. They demolished the inside walls but left the enclosure walls intact, except that the three main entrances on the south side were walled up and new ones were opened on the north. The original building had a tower at each corner; these were also left untouched and served as the first minarets in Islam. Of these four minarets only one, over the south-west corner, survives today. The minaret over the northern entrance is much later, probably as late as the sixth/twelfth century.

Internally, the courtyard (*ṣaḥn*), is surrounded by porticoes on three sides and by the impressive façade of the sanctuary on the south side. The sanctuary has three aisles running parallel to the *qibla* wall, with a trancept in the centre. There are four semicircular *miḥrābs* in the *qibla* wall. One of them, in the centre of the eastern half of this wall, is known as 'the *miḥrāb* of the Companions of the Prophet'; it is the second concave *miḥrāb* in Islam. The other three are later in date.

The walls of the mosque were decorated with mosaics, parts of which are still preserved. These mosaics, in contrast to those of the Dome of the Rock, display not only floral designs, but mainly architectural elements. The walls of the western portico, which were whitewashed at a later date, revealed the most beautiful mosaic panel, known to scholars as the 'Baradā panel' after the river which flows through Damascus. It represents contemporary Damascus with its palaces and houses and the villages of the Green Valley [pl. 1(*a*)].

Umayyad architecture, however, was not confined to religious buildings. The Umayyad caliphs longed for the open spaces of the desert, and therefore erected richly decorated palaces and baths in the Jordanian and Syrian steppe. Several of these buildings have been discovered and excavated during the last sixty years. One of the most impressive, and probably the earliest of them all, is Mshattā, some forty miles south of 'Ammān. For a long time it was considered a pre-Islamic building. Its Umayyad origin, however, has now been firmly established: a semicircular *miḥrāb* was found in the southern part of the building, and a few years later, during the course of excavations by the Jordanian Department of Antiquities, Kufic inscriptions and an Umayyad coin were found.

Mshattā is a square walled enclosure (473 feet, 144 metres) with semicircular intermediate towers on each side and two octagonal ones flanking the gateway on the south side. Internally the enclosure is divided into three tracts, the central ones being somewhat wider than the outer ones. Work was never completed in Mshattā, with the exception of the northern, or palace part of the central tract. Here there was a large hall ending in three apsidal recesses and probably covered by a dome [pl. 1(*b*)].

The outer face of the enclosure wall on the south was richly carved. The design is mainly based on vine and acanthus scrolls enclosing birds and lions. Most of this decorated façade is now in the East Berlin Museum.

The small bath of Quṣayr ʿAmra, about fifty miles east of ʿAmmān, was attributed to the Caliph al-Walīd [pl. 2(*a*)]. Recent research, however, points to a somewhat later date. The building is composed of a large audience hall with an entrance on its northern side, and a small alcove opposite. The alcove is flanked by two small apsidal rooms on either side. There are two more small rooms attached to the audience hall on the eastern side, continued by a third, domed room which has apsidal recesses.

The building is particularly famous for its frescoes. The frescoes were unfortunately damaged during the last fifty years, but they were copied by an Austrian painter at the beginning of this century.[1] There are in particular, two frescoes which assist us in dating this structure. The first painting is that of an enthroned monarch on the back wall of the little alcove [pl. 2(*b*)]. It has a Kufic inscription which refers to a prince, probably the owner of the building. The second painting represents six kings with four inscriptions underneath in Arabic and Greek. The inscriptions identify the first four figures as those of the Byzantine emperor, the Visigothic king of Spain, the emperor of Persia and the negus of Abyssinia.

The largest and probably the most beautiful Umayyad palace is Khirbat al-Mafjar in Jericho. The vast enclosure includes a number of buildings. The palace areas surround the square courtyard with a monumental entrance on its eastern side. The decoration consisted of richly

[1] *Kuṣejr ʿAmra*, Kaiserliche Akademie der Wissenschaften (Vienna, 1907), 2 vols.

carved stones and stuccoes, but fragments of fresco paintings were also discovered. North of the palace, the excavators discovered a huge bath which was covered with a dome. The floors were covered with mosaics, revealing some unusual designs [pl. 3(*a*)]. Recent excavations by the Department of Antiquities behind the bath uncovered workshops and storerooms, which may prove that Khirbat al-Mafjar was not only a palace, but an Umayyad town, just as 'Anjarr in Lebanon.

There are two great palaces in the Syrian desert, both attributed to the Caliph Hishām (105–25/724–43), Qaṣr al-Ḥayr al-Sharqī, north-east, and Qaṣr al-Ḥayr al-Gharbī, south-west of Palmyra. In the latter building two frescoes were discovered by the excavators, one of them revealing western, the other Sasanian influences. Excavation in Qaṣr al-Ḥayr al-Sharqī is in progress.

The Caliph Marwān II (127–32/744–50) moved his capital from Damascus to Ḥarrān in northern Mesopotamia (today in southern Turkey). Very little is known about his buildings in Ḥarrān, but the minaret of the Great Mosque may date from that period.

Finally, a small marble *miḥrāb* should be mentioned, which is at present in the Archaeological Museum in Baghdād. It is called the 'Khāṣṣakī *miḥrāb*', because it was found in a mosque bearing that name. Until quite recently it was considered to be an early 'Abbasid work. The *repertoire* of its decoration, however, rather suggests an Umayyad date and a Syrian origin.

Very little is known about the decorative arts of the Umayyad period. Potteries which were found in the Umayyad palaces were either plain coarse kitchen utensils, or reddish-brown painted unglazed wares. No glazed pottery is known from that period. A metal object, a ewer, should be mentioned here as it is connected with the name of the Caliph Marwān II [pl. 3(*b*)]. It was found with other metal objects near Marwān's tomb in the Fayyūm area in Egypt. The ewer has a globular body with a high tubular neck ending in a pierced decoration, and has a spout in the form of a cock and an elaborate handle. The body has engraved decoration consisting of a row of arches with rosettes and animals. The ewer was definitely made in Persia, and like all other early Islamic metalwork reveals a strong Sasanian influence.

EARLY 'ABBASIDS AND TULUNIDS

The Umayyad dynasty was otherthrown by the 'Abbasids in the year 132/750. The second 'Abbasid caliph, al-Manṣūr (136–58/754–75) founded the new capital, Baghdād, on the River Tigris. Nothing has survived of al-Manṣūr's city, as it was destroyed by the Mongols in 656/1258, and modern Baghdād was built upon the ruins. For this reason, excavations are hardly possible. However, we have quite a considerable amount of information from contemporary sources of its ground plan.

It was a round city, enclosed by two parallel walls made of mud bricks. There were four gateways in the walls, roughly facing the four cardinal points: the Baṣra Gate on the south, the Kūfa Gate on the west, the Syrian Gate on the north and the Khurāsān Gate on the east. In the centre of the city stood the caliph's palace, called the Palace of the Green Dome. The Great Mosque was attached to the palace on the south side. It was a simple structure. Later it was enlarged and decorated by Hārūn al-Rashīd (170–93/786–809) and al-Mu'taḍid (279–89/892–902). The construction of the city was completed by 149/766.

Some 120 miles south-west of Baghdād and roughly thirty miles from Karbalā' lies the fortified rectangular enclosure of Ukhayḍir [pl. 4(*a*)]. It has a gateway on all four sides and ten intermediate half-round towers. In the northern half of the enclosure is the palace area connected with the main entrance. In the centre is the court of honour, flanked by living quarters on each side. There is a small mosque in the western part of the enclosure, which has a small rectangular *miḥrāb*. In the corners of the enclosure are staircases leading up to the gallery on the second floor, which runs right round. The exact date of the building is not yet known, but it is believed to be of the third quarter of the eighth Christian century.

From about the same period dates the earliest surviving mosque of Persia, the Tārī Khāna in Dāmghān. Because of its ground-plan and exceptionally large bricks it was formerly considered to be a Sasanian building. The plan is quite simple: a rectangular enclosure surrounded by a single arcade on three sides and a sanctuary three aisles deep on the fourth. The original *miḥrāb* had a rectangular form, as *miḥrābs* usually have in Persia. At present it has an oblique form, since it had to be stilted so as to correct the *qibla* direction. There is no sign of any decoration in the building. A trial excavation which was made in the middle of the courtyard proved that the building is entirely a Muslim construction.[1]

[1] Erich F. Schmidt, *Excavations at Tepe Hissar, Damghan* (Philadelphia, 1937), 12–16.

During al-Mu'taṣim's caliphate (218–27/833–42) the riots of the Turkish troops caused so many disturbances in Baghdād that the caliph ordered the erection of a new capital, Sāmarrā, further up the Tigris. Immense palaces and mosques were built there by al-Mu'taṣim and by his successors. The Jawsaq al-Khāqānī palace, erected by al-Mu'taṣim, had a triple-arched entrance, the so-called Bāb al-'Āmma [pl. 4(*b*)]. The throne-room was built in a cross-shaped form, the centre of which was originally covered by a dome. The excavators recovered marble and stucco fragments which originally must have ornamented the walls. The harem was decorated with wall paintings showing dancing figures, birds and large garlands [pl. 5(*b*)].

The Great Mosque of Sāmarrā, built by al-Mutawakkil (232–47/847–61), is the largest mosque in Islam. Only the enclosure walls have survived, along with its helicoid minaret [pl. 5(*c*)]. In the mosque the excavations again revealed stucco fragments and glass mosaics. The Sāmarrā excavations, which were conducted by Ernst Herzfeld and Friedrich Sarre before the First World War, uncovered a second, the Balkuwārā palace, at the southern part of the city. The vast rectangular enclosure included a palace complex and two small mosques richly decorated with stucco and mosaics. This palace is also attributed to al-Mutawakkil.

The same caliph was responsible for the construction of the Ja'fariyya district somewhat north of Sāmarrā. It was here that the second great mosque of the city was erected. That was the mosque of Abū Dulaf, which is better preserved than the Great Mosque. The courtyard is surrounded by arcades, two aisles deep on the north. The sanctuary is divided into seventeen aisles running perpendicular to the *qibla* wall. The *miḥrāb*, for some unknown reason, was doubled. The minaret is similar in form to that of the Great Mosque. Recent excavations by the Iraqi Department of Antiquities uncovered a palace behind the sanctuary.

During the reign of al-Mu'tamid (256–79/870–92), Sāmarrā was abandoned, probably in the year 270/883. Thus its building activities are confined to only forty-seven years, which allows a nearly accurate dating. The great importance of Sāmarrā lies in two facts: first, that the stucco decorations reveal three distinct styles, clearly indicating the main sources of Islamic art [pl. 5(*a*)]; secondly, that it is here that, for the first time, artistic Islamic pottery was found.

Herzfeld recognized the three Sāmarrā styles, and called them the First, Second and Third styles. Professor Creswell, however, realized that the earliest style was Herzfeld's 'Third Style'. He therefore changed the order, the Third Style becoming 'Style A', the Second 'Style B' and the First 'Style C'. In 'Style A' the ornaments are based mainly on floral and plant patterns (vine scrolls, pine-cones, palmettes, etc.), arranged within geometrical compartments. In 'Style B' the patterns are again taken from the plant motives but appear in an abstract form. These first two styles are related to each other, but are totally different from 'Style C'. The latter style displays for the first time Central Asian elements, obviously introduced to Mesopotamia by Turkish artists. Certain elements in this style even reveal Far Eastern motives as well.

Far Eastern influence is, however, more evident in the pottery which has been exposed from the palaces and houses of Sāmarrā. From the excavated material four types of pottery can be distinguished: (1) the unglazed wares with incised or relief decorations; (2) lead-glazed mottled wares [pl. 6(*a*)]; (3) a great variety of tin-glazed vessels which were painted in cobalt blue, yellow or green, sometimes displaying abstract designs [pl. 6(*b*)]; (4) the celebrated lustre technique, which at the beginning started in polychrome [pl 6(*c*)]. No figural subject appears in polychrome lustre, except cocks on some wall-tiles and a peacock on a bowl which is in the Ashmolean Museum, Oxford. By the beginning of the fourth/tenth century lustre became monochrome and vessels from that period display primitively drawn human figures and animals. The production of fine pottery apparently started under Chinese influence, by imitation of the imported T'ang pottery and porcelain. That particularly applies to the mottled and tin-glazed wares. The lustre technique was entirely a Near Eastern invention.

Aḥmad b. Ṭūlūn, who became the governor of Egypt in 254/868 and founded an autonomous dynasty there, built a new city north of Fusṭāṭ. It was here that he erected a congregational mosque which was called after him. Its plan, a rectangular courtyard surrounded by porticoes, two aisles deep on three sides and five aisles on the *qibla* side, the stucco decorations and the form of the minaret, reveal strong stylistic connexion with Sāmarrā [pls. 7(*a*) and (*b*)].

SPAIN AND NORTH AFRICA

The famous mosque of Cordova was erected by 'Abd al-Raḥmān I in 168-9/784-6. In the following century it was enlarged (218/833) and the decoration of the west door was completed in 241–2/855–6. During the fourth/tenth century a new minaret was built, further enlargements were carried out and the decoration of the *miḥrāb* was completed. The mosque is a vast rectangle with a deep covered sanctuary which is divided into nineteen aisles by eighteen arcades. The beauty of the mosque is in the construction of these arcades which have double-tier horse-shoe arches, and in the colourful decoration of its *miḥrāb* [pl. 8(*a*)]. Marble and gold mosaics were used for its lining. The niche itself is seven-sided and is very spacious. The upper part of the niche is decorated by seven trefoil arches. This *miḥrāb* served as a model for other *miḥrābs* in North Africa and Spain.

One of the earliest mosques in North Africa was built at Qayrawān in Tunisia. The original mosque was built in the Umayyad era, but it was demolished, rebuilt and enlarged several times, until Ziyādat Allāh I in 221–2/836 rebuilt the whole structure. It has been preserved in that form up to the present day. It is a great irregular enclosure with eight doorways and a minaret in the middle of the north side. The sanctuary is a deep covered hall of seventeen aisles. The *miḥrāb* has a horseshoe form and, like that of Cordova, is richly decorated. The walls around the niche are coated with polychromed lustre tiles imported from Mesopotamia, while the niche itself is lined by pierced marble panels and the semi-dome has wooden panelling. There is a richly carved wooden *minbar* in the mosque which also dates from the third/ninth century.

THE PRE-SELJUK PERIOD OF PERSIA AND CENTRAL ASIA

During the third/ninth century the power of the ʿAbbasid caliphs started to decline rapidly. Petty dynasties sprang up all over the empire. In the east the most significant among these dynasties were the Samanids (261–389/874–999), who ruled over Transoxania and eastern Persia. They became patrons of the arts. Their capital was at Bukhārā, where one of their earliest surviving monuments was erected: the mausoleum of Ismāʿīl, completed in 295/907.

The mausoleum is a square structure covered by a hemispherical dome. It is as beautiful and perfect as a jewel-box. It was built and decorated entirely of fired bricks, thus being the earliest known building where the decorative brick technique, called *hazārbāf* in Persian, was applied. The mausoleum actually owes its plan to Sasanian architecture. Sasanian fire-altars with their square structures and hemispherical domes served as a model for domed mausoleums of the Islamic period. The plan presented an architectural problem; the transition from square to circle. The earliest successful solution to this problem is known from the fire-altar of Ribāṭ-i Safīd (third Christian century). The problem was solved by the introduction of a series of squinches in the zone of transition.

In the Samanid mausoleum at Bukhārā the zone of transition appears in an elaborated and decorated form [pl. 8(*b*)]. A more complicated zone of transition appears in the recently discovered mausoleum of ʿArab Ata at Tim in Soviet Uzbekistan. The building, which is again square and has a decorated façade, is dated to 367/977–8. In the zone of transition the square squinches were applied in a trefoil form [pl. 9(*a*)]. Previously the earliest of such trefoil squinches were known from the Davāzdah Imām at Yazd, dating from 429/1037.

Excavations by Soviet archaeologists in Samarqand and Afrāsiyāb, and by the Metropolitan Museum at Nīshāpūr, exposed an interesting type of pottery. First it was called Samanid slip-painted ware, or East Persian ware. The decoration is painted with coloured slip under transparent glazes. The body is usually red and has a white, creamy or brownish ground slip. The colours used for decoration were mainly manganese-purple, yellow, tomato-red and green. Kufic inscriptions, stylized birds and floral patterns appear on these vessels, which can be dated to the tenth and early eleventh Christian centuries [pl. 6(*d*)].

There is an early mosque in central Persia, the Masjid-i Jāmiʿ of Nāʾīn, which deserves special attention. The date of the building is not known, but on stylistic ground it is considered to be the second half of the fourth/tenth century. The mosque has a rectangular courtyard surrounded by porticoes, which are deeper on the sanctuary side. There is a small, tapering minaret in one corner. The *miḥrāb* and the surrounding area are coated with richly carved stucco [pl. 9(*b*)], displaying, according to Upham Pope, 'the implicit theme of the age-old concept of fertility'.[1]

In north-east Persia, not far from the Caspian Sea, is the small village of Gunbad-i Qābūs, where, previous to the Mongol invasion, there stood the town of Jurjān. It was here that the earliest Islamic tomb-tower was erected by Qābūs b. Wushmgīr in 347/1006–7. It is a high, cylindrical, slightly tapering tower, capped with a conical top, built

[1] A. U. Pope, *Persian architecture* (London, 1965), 86.

entirely of fired bricks. The sole decoration of the tower is the Kufic inscription which runs around the building above the entrance and below the roof.

A few caravanserais have survived from that period in eastern Persia and Central Asia. The earliest known, that at Āhuwān, near Simnān, dates from 420–41/1029–49. These caravanserais have strong enclosure walls, usually strengthened by buttresses. Inside there are four great *īwāns*[1] opening on to a central court. This cruciform plan with the four *īwāns* goes back to Parthian times, where it first appeared in the palace at Assur (first Christian century).

Meanwhile another dynasty appeared further east, in present-day Afghanistan, the Ghaznavids (351–582/962–1186). The greatest ruler of the dynasty, Maḥmūd (388–421/998–1030), had his capital, Ghazna, near the Indian frontier. Only two polygonal towers survive from this capital. Further south-west, at Lashkar-i Bāzār, palaces and mosques were excavated by the French Archaeological Mission, exposing frescoes, stuccoes and similar slip-painted pottery which were already known from the Samanid period.

The minaret of Jām, in northern Afghanistan, should also be mentioned here, though it is somewhat later in date. It was erected by the Ghurid Ghiyāth al-Dīn Muḥammad between 548/1153 and 599/1203. The minaret has a very fine decoration in stucco, containing Qur'anic and historical inscriptions. The minaret, which was discovered only in 1957, clearly shows its connexion with the Quṭb Mīnār in Delhi, erected in the seventh/thirteenth century.

THE FATIMID PERIOD

The Fatimids came to power in Tunisia and founded their capital Mahdiyya with its Great Mosque. This mosque has the first example of a monumental entrance, recalling in appearance some of the Roman triumphal arches. Later on, in 356/969 the Fatimids conquered Egypt and founded Cairo. Their adherence to Shi'ism marked their religious and political differences with the 'Abbasid caliphs of Baghdād.

The Fatimids erected several buildings in Cairo, among which the mosque of al-Azhar is the most outstanding example. The original mosque was nearly square in plan, with five aisles in the sanctuary

[1] *Īwān* in Islamic architecture means a portal or a hall, which is usually enclosed on three sides and is roofed by a barrel vault.

running parallel to the *qibla* wall. There were three domes, one in front of the *miḥrāb*, and two more at either end of the *qibla* wall. Later on there were several additions and alterations made in the mosque, and today it looks like a labyrinth. Some of the original stucco decorations in the sanctuary, and a number of window grilles have survived up to the present day [pl. 10(*a*)].

Another Fatimid mosque in Cairo is that of al-Ḥākim, erected between 380/990 and 394/1003. Later on it became the Friday Mosque of the city. It is an immense square building, recalling the mosque of Ibn Ṭūlūn with its arcades supported by brick piers. It also resembles the mosque of al-Azhar with its three domes in the sanctuary. There are two minarets at the corners of the main façade. The decoration of the sanctuary contains a band of beautiful floriated Kufic inscription running the length of the arcades.

Badr al-Jamālī, the commander-in-chief and *wazīr* (466–87/1074–94), rebuilt the walls of the city by replacing the former mud-brick walls with excellent stone masonry, and strengthened them with towers. He also built three monumental gateways: Bāb al-Naṣr which has two great square towers and a beautiful semicircular arch; Bāb al-Futūḥ, where the archway is again flanked by two solid towers; and Bāb Zuwayla, very similar to that of Bāb al-Futūḥ. All three gateways reveal the strong North African influence which is obvious throughout the Fatimid period. This period also witnessed the introduction of a new kind of structure, the *zāwiya* or domed mausoleum with three bays.

The little covered mosque of al-Juyūshī dates from the end of the fifth/eleventh century. It has a remarkable *miḥrāb*, one of the finest stucco works in Egypt [pl. 11]. The mosque of al-Aqmar was built in 519/1125. Its façade is very impressive, with two niches flanking the entrance. The niche-heads are decorated with stalactites or *muqarnas*.

Nothing has survived of Fatimid secular buildings. It is known, however, from literary sources that the Fatimids erected a palace in Cairo. A number of wooden panels from this palace are preserved in the Museum of Islamic Art in Cairo. They show human figures: musicians, dancers, animals and birds against a dense scroll background. In the same Museum there are also a few wooden *miḥrābs* demonstrating the great skill of Fatimid artists in this field.

The potter's art flourished throughout the period, and lustre wares in particular are worth mentioning. At the beginning the same naïvely drawn human figures and animals were represented, like those on Mesopotamian forerunners in the early fourth/tenth century. Later examples, however, reveal great progress in rendering the figures and also in their selection of subjects. Episodes from everyday life appear frequently on dishes and bowls [pl. 12(*a*)]. A number of vessels are signed by the potters, and among them the name of Sa'd appears very often. This potter seems to have been very active at the end of the fifth/eleventh and beginning of the sixth/twelfth century.

Apart from lustre wares, splashed and monochrome, glazed vessels were also produced, probably in Fusṭāṭ and the Fayyūm.

Very little is known of Fatimid metalwork. A small number of engraved vessels, zoomorphic aquamaniles and incense-burners, are attributed with more or less certainty to the period. These are in the Museum of Islamic art in Cairo and in the Benaki Museum of Athens.

The earliest known Islamic paintings on papyri were found at Fusṭāṭ and in the Fayyūm region of Egypt, dating from the fifth/eleventh and sixth/twelfth centuries. Apparently a lively school of painting functioned in the Fayyūm under the Fatimids, as is mentioned by a later Egyptian writer.[1] Very few of these paintings have survived, and these are mostly in Cairo. There is one such painting in the British Museum showing the siege of a fortress, most likely representing a fight between Muslims and Crusaders [pl. 12(*b*)]. It probably dates from the second half of the sixth/twelfth century.

Fatimid painting can be observed on the ceiling of the Capella Palatina of Palermo which was executed by Egyptian painters around 535/1140. The enthroned monarch, musicians, dancers, slave girls and fantastic animals painted on the ceiling clearly resemble the decorations of the lustre-painted vessels or wall frescoes of Sāmarrā, which in turn can be traced back to Central Asia.

The earliest known Islamic textiles are the so-called *ṭirāz* bands which contain inscriptions in beautiful Kufic. These were produced in Egypt, where Tinnis (near Port Said), Damietta and Alexandria were the main centres in the Tulunid and Fatimid era. There are also *ṭirāz* bands decorated in polychrome wool, and lined or embroidered in silk. The Fatimid era produced the finest silk and linen the decoration of which continued the scheme of earlier examples: a broad inscription band followed by narrow fields of animal figures and arabesques.

[1] Al-Maqrīzī, *Khiṭaṭ*, I, 486–7; II, 318. Al-Maqrīzī also wrote a book on the history of painters, which has unfortunately not survived.

THE SELJUKS IN PERSIA, ʿIRĀQ AND ANATOLIA

The Seljuk period is frequently called the 'Persian Renaissance'. Architecture and decorative arts certainly reached a very high apex in their development, but this does not apply only to Persia. The Seljuks, who extended their domination over ʿIrāq and parts of Anatolia, greatly affected the development of arts in these two regions as well. In architecture the period witnessed the perfection of decoration in brick technique. Several ways of brick bondings were invented or further developed.

The earliest monuments of the period, like the recently discovered tomb-tower in Damāvand, express both the power and grace of the brick technique. The Damāvand tomb-tower [pl. 13], which can be dated to the third quarter of the eleventh Christian century, reveals a great variety of designs, all executed in brick. There is an early sixth/twelfth century tomb-tower at Melik Ghāzī, east of Kayseri in Turkey, the decoration of which, but particularly the herringbone patterns of the dome, comes very close to the Damāvand tomb-tower.

Two more tomb-towers were also discovered recently in Persia, not far from the Qazvīn–Hamadān road. Both of these are octagonal buildings capped by double domes [pl. 10 (*b*)]. They reveal the finest brick decoration of the period. According to their inscriptions, they were erected in 460/1067–8 and 486/1093 respectively.

In mosque architecture, a great number of surviving monuments bear witness to Seljuk activity. In Persia the dome over the northern *īwān* in the Masjid-i Jāmiʿ of Iṣfahān, which dates from 480/1088 should be mentioned. The zone of transition here again has trefoil squinches. The Masjid-i Jāmiʿ of Iṣfahān is actually a four-*īwān* building. Other Seljuk mosques in Persia were erected in the same style. In Ardistān, the zone of transition below the dome in the *jāmiʿ* indicates a further development. Within the trefoil squinch appear four niches with pointed arches resting on engaged columns [pl. 14(*a*)]. That trend had actually begun in Iṣfahān in the Masjid-i Jāmiʿ, a hundred years earlier.

Decoration in stucco also reached its apex under the Seljuks. Entire wall surfaces were coated with carved stucco, revealing not only a variety of patterns, but also ingenious application of the design in a number of superimposed layers. In this respect first of all two Seljuk monuments should be referred to: the Madrasa Ḥaydariyya in Qazvīn, and the Gunbad-i 'Alawiyyān in Hamadān [pl. 14(*b*)]. In both buildings the *miḥrāb* and the surrounding areas, the cornice and the zone of transition in part, are decorated in very dense stucco. The richness of the design reminds us of the exaggerations and wildness of the rococo. In Hamadān the façade is also coated with carved stucco, and there is an inscription which runs round the square building.

The Masjid-i Kūchī Mīr in Naṭanz has an entirely different ground-plan. Instead of the cruciform plan with four *īwāns*, it is completely roofed with a small dome in front of the *miḥrāb*. It is one of the earliest known completely roofed mosques in Persia. The actual date of the mosque is not known, but it is considered to be of the sixth/twelfth century. While the building is quite simple and unadorned, its *miḥrāb* [pl. 15(*a*)] is coated with carved stucco. Two small rectangular recesses are set in a rectangular frame. The columns, capitals, spandrels and the back panel of the inner or lower recess are decorated in the Seljuk style.

A great number of Seljuk minarets survive in Persia. All these are tall, round, tapering towers decorated in brick technique. On rare occasions, glazed brick or tiles were used for the decoration of inscriptions or other horizontal patterns. Such a minaret exists in Nigār, south of Kirmān.

Very little is known of Seljuk secular architecture in Persia. So far no palace has been found. There is a Seljuk bath in Nigār, but even that has been drastically altered on several occasions. A few caravanserais are known from the period, among them the most interesting is Ribāṭ-i Malik in eastern Persia, dating from 471/1078. The enclosure walls are of massive bricks, strengthened one side by a row of cylindrical piers which are connected to each other by arches above. Another caravanserai, again in eastern Persia, close to the Afghan frontier, is the Ribāṭ-i Sharīf built by Sultan Sanjar in 447/1055. Inside it has an extensive stucco decoration, including a stucco *miḥrāb* within the mosque.

Seljuk building activity in the Fertile Crescent was associated with the name of Nūr al-Dīn (541–69/1146–73). He ordered the erection of a number of *madrasas*, and was also responsible for the Great Mosque in Mosul. It is better known as the Jāmi' al-Nūrī. Only the sanctuary and the minaret have survived in their original form. The cylindrical minaret has a cubical base [pl. 15(*b*)], and the cylindrical part is divided into seven equal horizontal fields all of which are decorated in different brick designs.

Though the Seljuk empire began to decline in the middle of the sixth/twelfth century, and a number of petty dynasties shared its realm, the vigorous and lively trend and style in art and architecture continued in Persia up to the Mongol invasion in the early seventh/thirteenth century, while in Anatolia it continued until about 700/1300. A great number of Seljuk monuments have survived in Anatolia, particularly in Konya and Kayseri.

Seljuk mosques in Anatolia are different from those of Persia or Mesopotamia. Since they had to be suited to a more severe climate, they were completely roofed. Thus the courtyard disappeared, and was replaced by a large central dome with a fountain beneath. One of the earliest of these Seljuk mosques in Anatolia was erected in Silvan (ancient Mayyāfāriqīn, east of Diyār Bakr), dating from the fourth/eleventh century. Here the zone of transition was formed by stalactites.

The basic element of the stalactite is a quarter dome, unsupported above and applied in several rows. Its origin is still ambiguous, but as far as is known today, the earliest examples are found in Central Asia, dating from the third/ninth and fourth/tenth centuries. From the fifth/eleventh century onwards they were widely used nearly everywhere in Islamic architecture.

Another early Seljuk mosque is in Kızıltepe (ancient Dunaysir, west of Mardin). It is in a ruinous state, and the dome collapsed some time ago. The mosque has a richly carved stone *miḥrāb*. It should be noted here that in Anatolia the building material was stone, while bricks, both fired and unfired, were used in Persia.

The most beautiful of the Seljuk monuments is the Ulu Jāmiʿ and annexed hospital in Divrighi, in central Anatolia. It is without any doubt the masterpiece of Seljuk workmanship. Whatever beauty was achieved in stucco in Persia, appeared in stone at Divrighi. The main entrance of the building [pl. 16(*a*)] displays a great variety of Seljuk patterns, appearing as if it were in a number of superimposed layers.

Another richly carved portal is that of the Inje Minäre in Konya, which was built in 657/1258. It is actually a *medrese*. *Medreses* in Anatolia are different from those of Persia. There are in fact two different types. The first type has an open court with a large *īwān* opposite the entrance. Sometimes even four *īwāns* appear, just as in Persia. The second type is similar to Anatolian Seljuk mosques, that is a small covered building with a central dome and a fountain placed below. *Medreses* in general had minarets, richly decorated either in bricks, or, as an addition, glazed bricks and tiles, which were used for horizontal panels and inscriptions.

The technique of covering large surfaces with glazed tiles was actually a Seljuk innovation. It first appeared on mausoleums at Marāgha in western Persia. In Seljuk Anatolia they were frequently used, particularly for decorating *miḥrābs*. The earliest known examples of these faience *miḥrābs* are in Konya in the 'Alā' al-Dīn Jāmi' (618/1221), Sirjeli Medrese (640/1242), and Laranda Jāmi' and Ṣaḥib Ata Jāmi', both dating from 656/1258. Among the later examples are those of the 'Alaja Jāmi' at Kharput (672/1273), in the Eshrefoghlu Jāmi' at Beyshehir (697–8/1297–8), and probably the most colourful faience *miḥrāb* is in the Arslankhāne Jāmi' of Ankara [pl. 16(*b*)] dating from 688–9/1289–90.

Mausoleums in Anatolia followed the Persian tradition. These were built mainly in stone. Their ground plan varied from octagonal, polygonal to square. One Anatolian mausoleum with a square form, has already been mentioned; that of Melik Ghāzī, on the Kayseri–Malaṭya road. A number of mausoleums survived in Kayseri, among which the Döner Gümbet (675/1276) is probably the most decorative.

The Seljuks built up an entire network of caravanserais. The number of surviving Seljuk caravanserais in Anatolia is even greater than in Persia. Their ground-plan closely follows the Persian models, but here the building material was stone, and they were more richly decorated. The earliest examples are around Konya, such as the Altınapa (598/1201), and the Kızılören khans (601/1204) on the Konya-Beyshehir road. The most famous caravanserai is probably Sulṭān Khān on the Kayseri–Sivas road, dating from 634/1236.

A number of bridges are also known from the period. These were sometimes used for frontier customs or tolls. The finest example of a Seljuk bridge is the Shahristān bridge in Persia which spanned the Zāyanda Rūd river near Iṣfahān. In Anatoliā, the bridge over the Kızılırmak, near Kirshehir, is a monument to the ingenuity of Seljuk engineers.

The Seljuk period was a golden age for decorative arts, particularly for pottery. Previous to the Seljuk invasion, about the beginning of the fifth/eleventh century, new pottery centres sprang up in the northern and north-western mountainous parts of Persia, in the Caspian borderland, in Āẕarbāyjān and Kurdistān. The significance of these kilns in these parts is outstanding, since their products greatly differed from other

Islamic wares. They reveal a strong Sasanian influence. Though the Arabs conquered the Sasanian empire, Sasanian traditions and Zoroastrianism nevertheless lingered, particularly in more remote areas of the country. One of the strongholds of Sasanian and Zoroastrian traditions centred around Ṭabaristān, which was long ruled by native princes.

It was in this part of Persia that pottery making was taken up soon after the decline in Samarqand and Nīshāpūr. These local potters developed special wares of the incised so-called *sgraffiato* technique. It was actually the pottery equivalent of the engraving in metalwork, frequently used in Sasanian metalwork. Even some of the designs were borrowed from Sasanian metalwork, such as the stylized bird in a bowl, which is in the Ashmolean Museum, Oxford [pl. 17(*a*)]. There are three different types of *sgraffiato* wares, which are dated to the fifth–seventh/eleventh–thirteenth centuries.

The coming of the Seljuks brought about great changes in Islamic pottery. First of all, a new white composite material was introduced, and was henceforward used in all parts of the Near and Middle East. Secondly there was a gradual evolution in the methods of decorating the white material by carving, staining the glaze, painting under the glaze, and painting in lustre and polychrome over the glaze.

The wide range of Seljuk pottery starts with monochrome-glazed wares. The glaze might be white, or coloured in different shades of green, turquoise blue, aubergine, purple and brown. The body was very fine and thin. Actually this was an attempt to imitate Chinese porcelains and celadon. Muslim potters of Persia, ʿIrāq and Anatolia produced a variety of finely executed bowls, jugs, ewers, vases and tankards. Occasionally these vessels are so thin that they seem translucent, an impression which is further enhanced by working pierced openwork into them. The jug shown in pl. 17(*b*) was executed in the same way. The field around the moulded inscription was pierced, and the small holes were filled with the glaze which then produced tiny windows giving the impression of glass.

The decoration of these monochromed wares consisted of floral patterns, inscriptions in *naskhī* script or human figures, which had been carved, moulded or incised into the body before the glazing took place. The date of these fine Seljuk wares is considered to be sixth–seventh/twelfth–thirteenth centuries. The main production centres in Persia were Rayy and Kāshān; in Syria, Raqqa and Ruṣāfa. The same types were also produced in several parts of Anatolia.

A further development in the decoration of pottery was the painting in blue, black and turquoise, under a clear glaze of transparent turquoise or deep blue. Underglaze-painting was again a practice which was introduced under the Seljuks but was quickly accepted all over the Middle East.

Lustre painting was also introduced into Persia. Its appearance coincides with the fall of the Fatimids in Egypt. The greatest change in these medieval lustre wares from those of the early period is that while on the earlier examples the decoration was painted in lustres, it is now the background which is lustred in deep brownish or yellow, thus leaving the space open for the decoration. A number of important centres are known to have been producing lustre wares during the second half of the sixth/twelfth century and during the seventh/thirteenth century. Among them Rayy, Kāshān, Sāva and Raqqa should be mentioned. A beautiful large dish (diameter 18½ inches) comes from Rayy, and probably dates from the sixth/twelfth or early seventh/thirteenth century [pl. 17(*c*)]. Human and animal figures, depicted on a floral background, are the favourite subjects.

The last phase of development in pottery decorations was that of painting in polychrome over the glaze. Two kinds of techniques were used: *mīnā'ī* and *lajvardina*. The so-called *mīnā'ī*, meaning enamel, denotes a technique in which the colours are usually blue, green, brown, black, dull red, white and gold, and are painted over an opaque white ground under transparent colourless or turquoise glaze. There was a close connexion between *mīnā'ī* wares and miniature painting, and most likely the decorations were executed by painters. The designs display court-scenes or scenes from Persian legends. A *mīnā'ī* bowl here depicts the meeting of two horsemen under a tree. An inscription outside gives the date of the vessel as 583/1187. It was probably made in Rayy [pl. 17(*d*)].

The other overglaze painted technique, the *lajvardina*, took its name from the cobalt-blue glaze on which the decoration was painted in red and white, and leaf gilding was added. The production of *lajvardina* wares is considered to have taken place in the Sulṭānābād region of Persia.

In metalwork the Seljuk period also brought about a considerable change. Previously, metal vessels in Persia, which was the cradle of Islamic metalwork, appeared as a straight continuation of Sasanian metalwork. Silver dishes, bowls and ewers displayed the same ornaments for another three or four hundred years. On some specimens, however, Kufic inscriptions were added. On ewers the decoration was engraved. As a general trend necks and spouts, or even whole vessels, followed the form of birds or animals. Aquamaniles and incense-burners in zoomorphic forms, are known from the third/ninth to the sixth/twelfth century.

A new technique, inlaying in bronze or brass with silver, copper or gold, was introduced during the sixth/twelfth century. The earliest piece of inlaid metalwork known today is a pen-box made in Herat by 'Umar b. al-Fażl and dated 542/1148. The next inlaid object in chronological order is a large bucket made of bronze and inlaid in silver and copper [pl. 18(*a*)] also made at Herat and signed by the caster, Muḥammad b. 'Abd al-Wāḥid, and by the inlayer, Mas'ūd b. Aḥmad, and dated 559/1163. Both objects are in the Hermitage Museum of Leningrad.

The elaborate inlaid decorations of the bucket are disposed in five registers, out of which three contain inscriptions, while the other two present festive court and hunting scenes. The Kufic inscription deserves special attention. The vertical strokes of the letters end in human and animal heads. This is known as 'animated inscription', common in Islamic metalwork from the end of the seventh/thirteenth century.

There are a great number of ewers, candlesticks, boxes, incense-burners and buckets preserved in public and private collections, dating from the late sixth/twelfth century or early seventh/thirteenth century, decorated in the inlay technique and most likely originating from Khurāsān and Herat.

The approach of the Mongols uprooted these craftsmen, and some of them set up their workshops in Mosul in Mesopotamia. Not long ago, all fine inlaid metalwork was designated as a product of Mosul. But in fact there are only a few specimens which can be attributed to Mosul without any doubt. Among them is a very fine brass ewer signed by a certain Shujā' b. Mana' of Mosul, dated 629/1232 [pl. 18(*b*)]. The medallions depict scenes from Persian legends. The T-fret and swastika patterns among the polylobed medallions and the elaborate star rosettes are characteristic of the new Mosul style.

There was a school of miniature painters in Mesopotamia and Syria during the seventh/thirteenth century. In Mesopotamia, these schools were probably in Baghdād and in Mosul. A number of illuminated manuscripts are preserved from that period, among them the Arabic translation of Dioscorides's *Materia medica*, dating from 621/1224. The paintings of the manuscript reveal the powerful influence of Byzantine art [pl. 19(*a*)].

Among the earliest manuscripts is the *Kalīla wa-Dimna*, a collection of fables about animals. More important, however, are the copies of the *Maqāmāt* of al-Ḥarīrī, which recall the adventures of Abū Zayd. The illustrations give us glimpses of contemporary Arab life. They are not related to Byzantine paintings, figures and all elements being presented in a true Arabic manner [pl. 19(*b*)].

In connexion with painting, calligraphy should be mentioned, as it played an important role in Islamic art. There were two main styles in calligraphy: the angular Kufic and the cursive *naskhī*. Kufic [pl. 20(*a*) (i)], which is alleged to have been invented at Kūfa, was used during the first four or five centuries of Islam. It appears in architecture, tombstones, early Qur'āns, on pottery and in textiles. Foliated Kufic [pl. 20(*a*) (ii)] was a more advanced form, decorating the endings of vertical strokes in lobed leaves or half-palmettes. The floriated Kufic [pl. 20(*a*) (iii)] developed in Egypt and reached its apex under the Fatimids.

Naskhī [pl. 20(*a*) (iv)] was developed in Baghdād, and from the fifth/eleventh century onwards gradually replaced Kufic. In Persia and Anatolia several cursive styles were developed in subsequent centuries, among which *thuluth* [pl. 20(*a*) (v)] should be mentioned. In this style, certain elements, such as the vertical strokes and horizontal lines, are exaggerated. From the second half of the fourteenth century the elegant *nasta'līq* becomes the predominant style in Persian calligraphy [pl. 20(*a*) (vi)].

Carpet weaving was also practised during the Seljuk period, as is attested by a few carpets discovered in the 'Alā al-Dīn Jāmi' of Konya and in the Eshrefoghlu Jāmi' of Beyshehir. Later on more carpet fragments turned up in Fusṭāṭ which betray a close relationship with their Anatolian counterparts. These Seljuk carpets, which are coloured in two shades of blue, green, red and yellow, reveal geometric designs in their central parts and mostly Kufic characters in the borders [pl. 20(*b*)]. The origin of carpet-making must be sought in Central Asia, where they were woven by Turkish nomads who then brought the technique with them to the Middle East.

THE AYYUBID PERIOD

Though the Ayyubids were preoccupied with military campaigns against the Crusaders, they made an important contribution to Islamic architecture and the decorative arts. In architecture, solid stone buildings, expressing strength and durability, are the most characteristic. A unique example is the citadel of Aleppo. Its history goes back to pre-Islamic times, [pl. 21(*a*)]. Saladin, the first Ayyubid ruler, further strengthened the walls of Cairo and erected the citadel on the Muqaṭṭam. He was responsible for the erection of a number of *madrasas* in Damascus and for their introduction into Egypt. These *madrasas* are, however, different from Persian examples, as they have only two *īwāns* instead of the usual four. The most famous *madrasa* in Cairo is that of the Sultan al-Ṣāliḥ Ayyūb built between 640–2/1242–4. It has four *īwāns*, but they are arranged in two separate blocks connected by the archway of the entrance, which at the same time carries a beautiful minaret.

A large number of mausoleums (Arabic sing., *qubba*) were also erected in Damascus and in Cairo, of which quite a number have survived. In Cairo two should be particularly mentioned: that of Shajar al-Durr (648/1250), and the mausoleum and mosque of the *Imām* al-Shāfiʿī, erected in 608/1211. Stucco played an important role in the decoration of Ayyubid mausoleums as is attested by the richly carved stucco *miḥrāb* of the mausoleum of Shajar al-Durr.

The marble decoration of the mosque and mausoleum of the *Imām* al-Shāfiʿī dates from the Mamluk period, but its wooden cenotaph is a very fine example of Ayyubid woodwork. It is decorated with finely carved scrolls and inscriptions placed on a dense scroll background [pl. 21(*b*)].

In metalwork the inlaid tradition of Mosul continued with slight alterations in the style. This was of course due to the migration of Mosul artists to Syria and Egypt. Candlesticks, large basins and incense-burners are known from this period, some of them decorated with Christian scenes. A bronze canteen in the Freer Gallery of Art in Washington is a unique piece of work of a Syrian artist or artists. Among the Christian scenes one represents Christ's entry into Jerusalem [pl. 22(*a*)]. Obviously the scene was borrowed from contemporary miniature paintings. It also seems very probable that most of these objects with Christian scenes were made for Christians, or even that some of the artists themselves must have been Christians.

In pottery, partly Fatimid, partly Persian Seljuk types, were followed. Lustre was produced in Syria. Wares which were underglaze-painted in polychrome, copying Persian *mīnā'ī* ware, decorated with human and animal figures, were made in Ruṣāfa and Damascus. Painted tiles have survived from the period in some of the Damascus mosques. Their decoration is in blue, black and green under a transparent colourless glaze. Ivory and bone carving was also practised both in Egypt and Syria, and reached a very high standard.

SPAIN AND NORTH AFRICA IN MEDIEVAL TIMES

The golden age of Muslim rule in Spain came in the reign of ʿAbd al-Raḥmān III (300–50/912–951), who founded the new capital, Madīnat al-Zahrāʾ near Cordova. A great variety of limestone and marble fragments disclose the strong connexion which still existed between Spanish Umayyad architecture and that of the second/eighth and third/ninth centuries in the eastern half of the Islamic world.

In the first half of the sixth/twelfth century the Almoravid ʿAlī b. Yūsuf ordered the enlargement of the mosque of the Qarawiyyīn at Fez, and the decoration of the Great Mosque at Tlemcen. The Almohads, who succeeded the Almoravids in North Africa, founded a new capital, Tinmāl, in the High Atlas in southern Morocco, and erected there a congregational mosque in 548/1153. This is now in ruins, but its *miḥrāb* is still preserved in good condition. The Kutubiyya mosque at Marrakesh, particularly its *miḥrāb*, resembles that of Tinmāl. The minaret is square, like all minarets in North Africa and Spain. The second largest mosque in Islam, the Mosque of Ḥasan (the Great Mosque of Sāmarrā being the first) was erected in Rabat. It also has a square minaret, opposite the sanctuary [pl. 22(*b*)]. The building is in ruins now. Only the minaret, bases of columns and the enclosure-walls survive. In Spain the Great Mosque of Seville is an Almohad building. Its minaret, the famous Giralda, was completed in 591/1195.

The best-known Islamic structure in the Western countries of the Islamic world is of course the celebrated Alhambra at Granada, erected by the Nasrid, Muḥammad b. Yūsuf. It was completed in its present form in the early eighth/fourteenth century. The palace, which is in the citadel, comprises two complexes, each surrounding a central court [pl. 23(*a*)].

Qalʿat Banī Ḥammād in Algeria was the capital of the Hammadid dynasty for nearly one hundred and fifty years. It was founded in 398/1007–8, and destroyed by the Almohads in 547/1152. Excavations there have revealed a number of palaces. There is also a mosque with a surviving square minaret. Glass and pottery kilns were also uncovered in the course of the recent excavations.

North African and Spanish architecture differs from that of the rest of the Islamic world, yet it seems to be a direct descendant of the earlier Umayyad art in Syria. The horseshoe arch, which originated in Syria, played an important role. After the early second/eighth century it disappeared from Syria and reappeared in the Maghrib, and also at the other extreme of the Islamic world, in Afghanistan. In stucco carvings, the minute and accurate workmanship and the extensive use of the stalactite reached a very high standard.

Pottery is known to have been produced in Spain from early Islamic times. The earliest specimens were excavated in Cordova and at Madīnat al-Zahrā'. Much more is known about later Hispano-Moresque pottery, dating from the ninth/fifteenth and tenth/sixteenth centuries. Potters, even after the Christian reconquest of Spain, continued to decorate their vessels in Moorish style. The pottery centres of Paterna, Málaga and Manisa produced golden and ruby lustre vessels, large dishes, bowls and vases, sometimes adding blue to the decoration. Kufic letters, arabesques and scrolls were the favourite designs. By the late sixteenth century the Moorish style had gradually disappeared and pottery-making had gradually slipped into the hands of Christian artists.

Textiles made in Muslim Spain are also worth mentioning. Almería, Granada, Málaga, Murcia and Seville were the main textile-producing centres, making tapestry-woven bands, silks and golden brocades displaying human figures and animals, usually placed in round medallions. Textile designs were similar to those of ivory carvings. Ivory carving played an important role in Andalusian art and reached a very high standard under the Umayyad rulers. A large number of ivory boxes have survived and can be seen in various public and private collections. The Victoria and Albert Museum possesses a few Moorish ivory carvings which are decorated with vine scrolls, palmettes, human and animal figures and Kufic inscriptions.

Moorish metalwork greatly resembles that of the eastern Islamic world, and uses the same techniques. A great number of engraved and inlaid vessels are preserved in Spanish collections, mostly dating from the tenth to the fourteenth centuries.

Very little is known of Maghribī and Andalusian paintings. A famous seventh/thirteenth-century manuscript, containing the love story of

Bayād and Riyādh was illustrated in Ceuta in Morocco. Though the actual story takes place in 'Irāq, the architectural elements depict Maghribī forms. In calligraphy the Maghribī style was quite distinct from the rest of the Islamic world by reason of the round forms of the letters and the placing of the dot under the *fā'*.

PERSIA AFTER THE MONGOL INVASION: ĪL-KHĀNS AND TIMURIDS

The Seljuk period was a golden age for art and architecture in Persia. It was followed by a brief rule of the Khwārazm-Shāhs and by the disaster caused by the successive Mongol invasions during the first half of the seventh/thirteenth century. Recovery from the Mongol devastation was very slow. Some cities, such as Rayy, a former centre of pottery and textile industry, never regained their previous vitality. But the recovery was initiated by a Mongol dynasty, the Īl-Khāns, who later embraced Islam. From their capital at Tabrīz they encouraged artisans and builders to heal the severe wounds caused by their predecessors.

It was Hülegü, the captor and destroyer of Baghdād, who made Tabrīz his capital, and was also responsible for the erection of an observatory in Marāgha. His architect was al-'Urdī, an engineer and astronomer. The real recovery and building activity, however, started under Ghāzān Khān, who became the ruler of the Il-Khanid empire in 694/1295. After his death in 703/1304 his brother, Öljeitü, continued his work. Rashīd al-Dīn, the famous historian, was their contemporary and their minister.

Öljeitü ordered the erection of a new capital, Sulṭāniyya, south of Tabrīz, in 706/1306. Mosques, palaces and a citadel were erected there. The only surviving building today is his own mausoleum. It is an octagonal building partially coated with faience bricks inside and outside. The platform outside carries the huge dome and eight small minarets above each corner. The building today is partially ruined.

Öljeitü was also responsible for the erection of a very fine stucco *miḥrāb* in a prayer-hall in the Masjid-i Jāmi' of Iṣfahān. According to the inscription it was completed in 710/1310. The stucco decoration is arranged in several layers above each other, just as those of the Seljuk period. The details of the design, however, differ from those earlier examples.

The Masjid-i Jāmi' of Tabrīz, better known as the Masjid-i 'Alī

Shāh, with its massive walls, looks rather like a fortress or a citadel. It was erected by Tāj al-Dīn ʿAlī Shāh, Öljeitü's *wazīr*, and the rival of Rashīd al-Dīn, between 710/1310 and 720/1320. The building is in ruins to-day. The existing ruins are parts of the *qibla īwān*. There is no sign of any decoration today, but contemporary sources mention a faience-tiled lustre *miḥrāb*.

The most interesting and probably the best preserved monument of the Il-Khanid period is the Masjid-i Jāmiʿ complex in Naṭanz, in central Persia, east of Iṣfahān. It was built between 704/1304 and 725/1325. The mosque is of the four-*īwān* type with an octagonal dome and a tall slender minaret, partly decorated with enamelled bricks [pl. 23(*b*)]. The building has a faience-tiled portal. The original *miḥrāb* was of faience-lustred tiles. Parts of this are now in the Victoria and Albert Museum.

Faience-tiled lustre *miḥrābs* were made in Kāshān during the second half of the seventh/thirteenth and at the beginning of the eighth/fourteenth centuries. While pottery production came to a halt in Rayy after the Mongol destruction, Kāshān, it seems, quickly recovered. Underglaze-painted and lustre-painted wares were produced there until the end of the eighth/fourteenth century.

New pottery centres emerged in the Sulṭānābād region. Here the main type was the underglaze-painted ware, using grey as the main colour for the background, reserving the designs in white or blue, sometimes in relief. Far Eastern elements are apparent in Sulṭānābād wares.

Large dishes and bowls are known from the eighth/fourteenth and ninth/fifteenth centuries painted in heavy green or purple lines, frequently with cross-hatchings. These are considered as rustic wares. Their actual provenance has not yet been identified.

A more important group of the period is the Persian blue and white, which was produced in Kirmān and Mashhad. It was previously thought that blue and whites were first made in China. Recent research, however, has established that their origin should be sought in Persia. In fact the cobalt ore which was used for the decoration of Chinese blue and whites was imported from Persia. Very little is known of early Persian blue and whites, and no piece can be confidently dated to the eighth/fourteenth century. From the ninth/fifteenth century a number of small bowls are known. Their shapes resemble those of Chinese rice-bowls. The designs are confined to scrolls and palmettes. In one instance a flying crane is depicted. Later Chinese influence becomes more and more apparent, and from the eighteenth century onwards designs are outlined in black.

In 737/1336 the last Il-Khaṇid ruler died. The Il-Khanid empire disintegrated and was divided among a number of petty dynasties. Then in the late eighth/fourteenth century a new and ruthless leader emerged in the east: Tīmūr. He sacked and plundered a number of cities in Māzandarān in the north, and some also in Fārs and Kirmān in the south. Nevertheless, he had great respect for beautiful and sacred monuments. He also systematically collected artists in his capital, Samarqand, to beautify it. Tīmūr's work, the patronage of arts, was continued by his sons and successors, who later on moved the capital to Herat. There was then a new renaissance in Persia. Beautiful buildings were erected, painting, calligraphy and bookbinding, and all the other arts, flourished.

In architecture the most outstandings building can be found in Samarqand. The finest among them are the mausoleum-complex of the Shāh-i Zinda. Some of the buildings date from pre-Timurid times. The buildings are richly decorated with faience mosaics and painted tiles. Dense stalactite semidomes hang over the portals. Openwork is frequently apparent [pl. 24(*b*)].

To the Shāh-i Zinda complex is attached Tīmūr's own mausoleum, the Gūr-i Mīr, which was completed in 807/1404. The building is dominated by a huge bulbous dome, covered with enamelled tiles. Walls and portals are similarly decorated [pl. 24(*a*)].

Other religious buildings in Samarqand, Bukhārā, Herat or in Persia proper, are similarly decorated. Of these the *muṣallā* of Gawhar Shād in Herat, the four-*īwān madrasa* in Khargird and the Masjid-i Gawhar Shād in Mashhad should be mentioned. In western Persia the Blue Mosque of Tabrīz deserves special attention. It is one of the very few completely roofed mosques of Persia. Its inner walls were decorated with cobalt-blue faience tiles. The rectangular building was crowned with a central dome surrounded by smaller ones over the sanctuary and the galleries. The mosque was completed in 869/1465.

Islamic architecture in Persia reached its highest quality during the Timurid period, and this was never surpassed in refinement and elegance. The importance of the period for the history of Islamic art, however, is not due to architecture alone. Great progress was made in the art of painting, development of which had already started under the Il-Khanids. Rashīd al-Dīn compiled his universal history, *Jāmi' al-*

tawārīkh, between 707/1307 and 714/1314. One of the manuscripts, which is divided between Edinburgh University Library and the Royal Asiatic Society, has a number of illustrations. These miniatures clearly reveal the new, Far Eastern elements, which are, however, fully incorporated into the pictures. Landscapes, particularly rocks, trees and clouds, appear in Chinese style [pl. 25(*a*)]. The manuscript was executed in Tabrīz, the home of one of the most important schools of painters during the Il-Khanid and Timurid periods. Copies of the *Kalīla wa-Dimna* are also attributed to Tabrīz.

One of the most famous illuminated manuscripts of Tabrīz is the so-called Demotte *Shāh-nāma* of Firdawsī. The manuscript is dated 730/1330. Far Eastern elements are still evident, but Persian features appear somewhat stronger than in the illustrations of the *Jāmiʿ al-tawārīkh*.

A second school of painting existed in Shīrāz. It was a prosperous city during the Il-Khanid period and was the home of great poets like Saʿdī and Ḥāfiẓ. Four *Shāh-nāma* manuscripts are known to have been illustrated in Shīrāz during the first half of the eighth/fourteenth century [pl. 25(*b*)]; as well as a copy of the *Kalīla wa-Dimna*, dating from 733/1333. The pictures are rather naïvely drawn, in comparison with those of Tabrīz. The backgrounds are painted in red, yellow or blue. Architectural elements are represented by a few small features such as arches. Pictures are small and fully incorporated into the text.

During the Timurid period the centre of painting shifted to Herat, where Shāh-Rukh (807–50/1404–47) became the great patron of artists. Several *Shāh-nāma* and *Kalīla wa-Dimna* manuscripts illustrated in Herat during the middle of the ninth/fifteenth century have survived. The great importance of Herat in painting, however, started under the patronage of ʿAlī Shīr Navāʾī, a politician, painter and poet. He patronized Bihzād, the greatest painter in Islamic art.

Bihzād was active from the late ninth/fifteenth century until his death in Tabrīz in *c.* 942/1535–6. He excelled in battle scenes, but was equally outstanding in depicting architectural elements or in the very fine drawing of human figures. Very few signed miniatures are known today. Four of such works illustrate the *Bustān* of Saʿdī. The finest miniatures by Bihzād are, however, in two copies of the *Khamsa* of Niẓāmī in the British Museum. Bihzād had a number of pupils who continued to paint in his style (pl. 26).

In 913/1507 Herat was occupied by the Özbegs and three years later by Shāh Ismāʿīl, the founder of the Safavid dynasty. He made Tabrīz his capital and as a consequence most of the artists, among them Bihzād, followed the new ruler there.

In parallel with book illuminations, bookbinding also reached a very high standard. In Persia, Timurid bookbindings are the finest specimens. Leather was used, the decorations being stamped and incised, and then painted in red, green or blue and gilt. In a number of instances, birds appear against scroll backgrounds.

In calligraphy also great progress was made in Herat. The best calligraphers of the time were working there. The *nasta'līq* script developed in Herat during the Timurid period, as did the *dīwānī* and *dashtī*.

THE MAMLUK PERIOD OF SYRIA AND EGYPT

During the Mamluk period (648–922/1250–1517), Muslim traditions in arts and architecture continued and flourished without any interruption. The Mongols were halted and defeated by the Mamluks. The Mamluk sultans of Egypt and Syria erected a number of significant buildings. A great number of *madrasas*, mausoleums and mosques were built in Cairo. Most of these have survived up to the present day in more or less satisfactory condition.

Among the religious buildings the mosque and *madrasa* of Sultan Baybars I al-Bunduqdārī, erected between 660/1262 and 668/1269, should be mentioned. Here, unfortunately, only the outer enclosure-walls have survived. The complex of Sultan Qalawun (built in 683/1284–85) comprises a *madrasa*, a mausoleum and a hospital. It is one of the most significant buildings of the Mamluk period, because of its monumental façade with the double windows, the beautiful crenellations and the rich stucco carvings [pl. 27(*a*)]. Inside, the stone and marble coatings and the woodcarvings mark the apex of the Mamluk art.

The mosque of al-Azhar was enlarged and altered a number of times by the addition of the Ṭaybarsiyya *madrasa* in 709–10/1309–10, the Aqbuqāwiyya in 741/1340, and the Jawhariyya *madrasa* in 844/1440.

The mausoleums are mostly domed square buildings with usually a stucco *miḥrāb* and a stucco decorative panel running round the inside of the building. The mausoleum of Aḥmad b. Sulaymān al-Rifā'ī is unique with its glass mosaic decorated *miḥrāb*, dating from 689/1290.

Of secular architecture not much has survived. Some Mamluk

alterations and additions in the citadels of Cairo, Aleppo and in Ḥarrān are still visible. The palace of Dār Bashtāk in Cairo, dating from 742/1341, and a few caravanserais in Egypt and Syria are still standing. In private houses and palaces the *mashrabiyyas* or wooden lattices were generally introduced.

Arabesques played a more important role in Mamluk woodcarvings, of which a great number of *minbars* and *miḥrābs* are preserved in Cairo. The decorations of these are divided into small compartments filled either by arabesques or by geometrical patterns. By the end of the period wood-carving started to decline.

Glass-making reached a high standard during the Mamluk period. A number of mosque-lamps decorated with enamel and gilt are known. The decorations are arranged in horizontal bands containing inscriptions, giving the names and titles of sultans, *amīrs* and high officials for whom the particular object was made. Their heraldic blazons are illustrated in round medallions. Leading glass centres were in Damascus. The making of fine enamel and gilt glass came to an end by the end of the eighth/fourteenth or at the beginning of the ninth/fifteenth century.

In pottery, Mamluk artists followed the examples of the Ayyubid period. The main type of pottery was the lead-glazed *sgraffiato* ware. The glaze is usually transparent brownish-yellow. Large inscriptions appear sometimes on a floral background. Official blazons, so common in Mamluk glass and in metalwork, are also frequently depicted. The production of lustre ware was discontinued in Egypt. Polychrome underglaze-painted wares presenting human and animal figures were still produced.

The production of fine metalwork greatly increased, particularly in three towns: Cairo, Damascus and Aleppo. At that time the inlay technique reached its highest quality. Human figures rarely appear; the main decorative theme is the *naskhī* inscription and heraldic blazons. Some new motives were also apparent, resembling Chinese elements. The best pieces were made under the reign of al-Nāṣir Muḥammad b. Qalawun (693–741/1293–1340), and these were mainly bowls, large basins and candlesticks.

It was about at that time or somewhat later, during the fifteenth and sixteenth Christian centuries, that fine metalwork was produced in Venice in the old Islamic style by craftsmen from Syria and Egypt. Overcrowding, the extensive use of silver and the curious round form of vessels are the characteristic and distinguishing features of the Venetian metalwork. The majority of them date from the sixteenth century.

One of the greatest achievements of the period was the weaving of geometrical carpets, which seems to have developed during the ninth/fifteenth century, and continued right up to the tenth/sixteenth century. The design, as its name indicates, is confined to geometrical forms: octagons, stars, triangles, etc. The ground colour is red and the decorations are in golden-yellow, blue and in green [pl. 27(*b*)].

THE OTTOMAN PERIOD

The Ottomans made Bursa their first capital in 727/1326, and the earliest monuments of the period can be found there and at Iznik. Some forty years later the capital was moved to the European territories, to Edirne, the former city of Adrianople, and after the conquest of Constantinople in 857/1453, it became the seat of the new empire.

The earliest Ottoman buildings were modelled on Seljuk architecture, as can clearly be seen in the Ulu Jāmiʿ of Bursa, erected between 799/1396 and 803/1400. This is a rectangular building divided into twenty equal parts by arcades resting on twelve piers. Each part is roofed by a dome. The ground-plan of the Eski Jāmiʿ of Edirne (807–17/1404–14), or that of the Zinjirli Kuyu Jāmiʿ of Istanbul (end of the ninth/fifteenth century) follow the same principle.

These mosques are not characteristic of the period. Ottoman mosques, as a principle, are square buildings, covered by a large central dome. To this main part a number of smaller parts can then be added which are then roofed by smaller domes or semi-domes. Minarets played an important part. These are slender, tall, round or polygonal towers with a balcony on the upper part for the muezzin.

Medreses largely follow the traditional Anatolian types, the cells of students and lecture rooms being connected by an arcade and surrounding the rectangular courtyard. *Türbes* or mausoleums are square or polygonal and are covered by the traditional conical or pyramidal roof.

The inner decoration of religious buildings deserves special attention. Large surfaces were covered by painted faience tiles or faience mosaics, which were mainly produced at Iznik. The earliest known faience *miḥrāb* of the period is in the Green Mosque of Bursa (824/1421), which was signed by a Tabrīzī artist. The building itself is the work of a Turkish architect.

The finest Ottoman religious buildings were erected by Sinān Pasha, one of the greatest Turkish architects (896–997/1490–1588). Some three hundred and fifty buildings are attributed to him, of which the Süleymāniye mosque in Istanbul (965/1557), and the Selīmiye Jāmiʿ of Edirne (977–83/1569–75) [pl. 28(*b*)] are the best known. The mosque of Sultan Aḥmed, or Blue Mosque (so called because of its inner tile decoration), is the last among the great Ottoman mosques (1018–26/1609–17).

In secular architecture the Ottoman caravanserais, which differed somewhat from previous Seljuk models, should be mentioned. Arranged around a central rectangular courtyard the buildings were provided with two floors, the ground floor providing accommodation for shops, workshops and stables, and the upper one rooms for travellers merchants and craftsmen.

Ḥammāms or baths followed the traditional line. These were covered by a number of small domes. Great numbers of Ottoman *ḥammāms* are preserved in Anatolia and in other parts of the former Ottoman empire.

Covered bazaars roughly followed the ground-plan and arrangement of the caravanserais but without the central courtyard. Public fountains were decorated with richly carved stones of Iznik faience tiles. Among the palaces the Topḳapî Sarayî complex in Istanbul should be mentioned. Later palaces, like the Dolmabaghche, Beylerbeyi and many others, were erected in European styles. From the eighteenth century onwards, Turkish architecture, both religious and secular, follows the contemporary European styles, such as baroque and rococo.

In pottery a distinct type was discovered during an excavation some forty years ago by the late Friedrich Sarre at Miletus. Thus the name 'Miletus ware' was wrongly given to them. They are of red clay and are painted on a ground white slip under a clear glaze in blue, green and black. The decorations are presented in a naturalistic style. Rosettes, scrolls, flowers or birds appear on the small bowls, which are the commonest type of this 'Miletus ware'. Excavations by Professor Oktay Aslanapa at Iznik have established that the 'Miletus ware' was produced at Iznik and can be dated to the eighth/fourteenth and ninth/fifteenth centuries.

Later Iznik pottery can be divided into three main groups. The first period, which was previously called the 'Abraham of Kütahya' group, is generally considered to date from 896/1490 to 932/1525. The body in all three groups is white and soft. During the first period vessels like large dishes, mosque-lamps, jars, ewers, and standing-bowls, were painted in cobalt-blue on a white ground. The designation of 'Abraham of Kütahya' derives from a signed piece.

The decorations of the second period specimens were painted, in addition to cobalt-blue, in turquoise-green and sometimes also in purple. They date from 932/1525 until about 963/1555. An outstanding example of this period, a mosque-lamp, which was made for the Dome of the Rock in Jerusalem in 956/1549, is in the British Museum.

In the third period (*c.* 964–1113/1555–1700) a lively red is added to the colour scheme. Wall-tiles belonging to this group are preserved in a number of mosques in Istanbul and in the Selīmiye Jāmiʿ of Edirne. Carnations, tulips, and roses appear in dishes, and jars. Ships, human and animal figures, and birds are also depicted [pl. 29(*a*)].

After the decline of pottery-making in Iznik, a new pottery centre emerged at Kütahya, producing vessels mainly for the Armenian communities of Anatolia. Kütahya wares are of white earthenware and decorations are painted in yellow, blue, grey and green on a white ground under a clear glaze. Many signed and dated pieces are known from the eighteenth and nineteenth centuries.

Another pottery centre of less importance was at Chanakkale on the Dardanelles. Porcelain was also manufactured in Turkey, but the cheap imported mass-produced European porcelain seems to have put an end to these experiments.

Great progress was made in calligraphy and miniature painting under the Ottomans. There was a school of calligraphists and painters in the palace of Istanbul under the patronage of the sultans. Among them Sultan Meḥmed the Conqueror had the greatest name for supporting the arts. He invited Italian painters to Istanbul and sent Turkish artists to study in Italy. Naqqāsh Sinān Bey also studied in Italy and on his return to Turkey painted, among many other things, the portrait of Sultan Meḥmed.

Turkish calligraphists and illuminators developed a new style and their great achievement and merit was in the fact that they recorded the important historical events of their time. Matraqji, the celebrated geographer and historian, for example narrated the Persian campaign of Sultan Süleymān the Magnificent. 'O̲smān, in his *Hüner-nāme* (dated

957–68/1550–60), recorded the history of the Ottoman sultans in two volumes. In the accounts of the Szigetvár campaign written by Ferīdūn Pasha in 976/1568, events of the campaign and Sultan Süleymān's death are described, and are illustrated by a number of miniatures.

There are about 10,000 or even more illuminated Turkish manuscripts in the Topkapi Sarayi Müzesi in Istanbul, recording historical events and topography of cities or depicting the portraits of sultans and high officials. Other manuscripts, quite contrary to Islamic tradition, depict scenes from the Prophet Muḥammad's life and of the greatest events of Islamic history.

One of the last great Ottoman painters was Levnī, who lived in the eighteenth century. His greatest work represents the festivities organized for the wedding of Sultan Aḥmed II's daughter. Levnī was already working under the strong influence of European painting, which eventually completely destroyed the real character of Ottoman painting.

Apart from painting it was in the field of textiles and carpets that great progress was made under the Ottomans. The Turks, who had already excelled in carpet making for many centuries, developed many new types during that period. One of the earliest types was the so-called 'animal carpet', which can be dated to the eighth/fourteenth and ninth/fifteenth centuries. The so-called 'Holbein rugs' with arabesque patterns in the field and Kufic characters on the border, are known from Dutch and Italian paintings of the sixteenth and seventeenth centuries.

Several types were produced and developed in Ushak. Among them the medallion and star Ushak and the so-called 'Transylvanian carpets' should be mentioned. Prayer rugs representing *miḥrāb* niches are known to have been made in Ghiordes, Kula, Ladik, Bergama and at Mujur. Rugs made in the Caucasus have distinct geometrical designs. Persian influence on them is apparent. They mostly date from the nineteenth century.

Brocades, velvets and embroideries were made in Bursa, in the neighbourhood of Edirne, and at a number of places along the Aegean coast. On brocades and velvets some Italian influence can be observed. Embroideries are very colourful, sometimes so fine that they give the impression of painting [pl. 29(*b*)]. These are embroidered on linen or silk. They are reversible, and generally represent beautiful flowers and cypress-trees. They mostly date from the eighteenth and nineteenth centuries.

THE SAFAVID PERIOD IN PERSIA

Shāh Ismāʿīl (907–30/1502–24), the founder of the Safavid dynasty, occupied Herat in 913/1507, and took a great number of artists with him to his capital in Tabrīz. No monuments survive of his or his immediate successors' time. His palace at Kwuy, north-west of Tabrīz, is known only from the description of European travellers. Later on the capital was moved to Qazvīn, where Shāh Ṭahmāsp (930–84/1524–76) erected the royal mosque and his palace, parts of which can still be seen today.

Great building activity did not really start until the accession to the throne of Shāh ʿAbbās I (985–1038/1587–1629). He once again moved the capital to Iṣfahān, and was responsible for the planning and erection of the royal square, the Maydān-i Shāh. The Maydān-i Shāh is surrounded by the royal mosque, the Masjid-i Shāh on the south, the Masjid-i Shaykh Luṭf Allāh on the east, the Qayṣariyya Bazaar on the north and the ʿAlī Qapu palace on the west.

The Masjid-i Shāh, one of the greatest achievements of Safavid architecture, is a large four-*īwān* mosque, the walls of which are covered by faience tiles and mosaics. The monumental portal is flanked by two slender minarets with balconies on their top (pl. 30), then the axis of the whole mosque is turned around the entrance hall for the correction of the *qibla* towards the south-west. There is a large dome over the *qibla īwān*, decorated inside and outside with faience mosaics, recalling the ornaments of carpets. The building, which was erected between 999/1590 and 1025/1616, bears the signature of the architect, Ustād Abu'l-Qāsim and a number of calligraphers.

The Masjid-i Shaykh Luṭf Allāh is a small covered mosque, again turned behind the entrance hall in order to correct the orientation of the *qibla*. It has a huge dome similarly decorated to that of the Masjid-i Shāh. The building was completed in 1028/1618.

The ʿAlī Qapu palace was the seat of Shāh ʿAbbās's government, and his official residence. The ground floor provided rooms for offices and for the guards, while on the first floor was a large audience hall and a gallery, a *tālār*, opening into the royal square [pl. 28(*a*)]. There are two more floors, the rooms of which were decorated with mural paintings, openwork and niches for glass and pottery.

The shah's private residence was in the Chihil Sutūn or 'Palace of the forty columns'. There is a large pool in front of the building in which the columns of the gallery, the *tālār*, are reflected. From there opens the audience hall, the walls of which were originally decorated with mural paintings representing hunting scenes and landscapes. The palace originally had a number of lacquer painted doors, which are now scattered in a number of European and American museums. The building was partially destroyed by fire in the eighteenth century.

The Safavids contributed a great deal to the decoration and enlargement of the complex of the *Imām* Riżā's shrine in Mashhad. Work began there under Shāh 'Abbās I in 1010/1601. Oratories, *madrasas*, and libraries were added and richly decorated in faience mosaic and glass.

The last great contribution to Persian architecture was the erection of the Madrasa Mādar-i Shāh in Iṣfahān, at the beginning of the eighteenth century. It is built in the traditional style, having four *īwāns* opening on to a central courtyard. The *qibla īwān* has a dome and a minaret. Walls are covered all over with painted faience tiles. Decorations of later buildings, such as the Vakīl Madrasa in Shīrāz (twelfth/eighteenth century), or the shrines at Karbalā' and Sāmarrā, and the Sipahsālār Mosque in Tehran (nineteenth century), never reach the heights of previous architecture.

In miniature painting, Herat remained the centre only for a few years after Shāh Ismā'īl's occupation of the city. Artists, like Bihzād and many of his pupils, moved to the new capital, Tabrīz. Thus Tabrīz became once more a centre of Persian painting. Another new centre emerged in Bukhārā, which was very active during the tenth/sixteenth and early eleventh/seventeenth centuries. Illumination of manuscripts of the *Shāh-nāma* and *Khamsa* of Niẓāmī continued. Bihzād's style was followed for quite a long time. Upon the moving of the capital to Iṣfahān under Shāh 'Abbās I, a new school of painters was founded there which excelled not only in miniature painting, but also in the production of bookbindings and in lacquer-works as well.

Carpets of the Safavid period were greatly influenced by contemporary miniature-painting and bookbinding. Under Shāh Ismā'īl and Shāh Ṭahmāsp, Tabrīz became an important centre of carpet-weaving, but places like Kāshān, Iṣfahān, Yazd and Kirmān also produced a number of types. Animal and hunting carpets are known from the tenth/sixteenth and eleventh/seventeenth centuries. Large medallion carpets were made in the tenth/sixteenth century. The finest example of that type is the Ardabīl carpet in the Victoria and Albert Museum. It dates from 946/1539. The vase rugs, it seems, were made in north-western Persia in the tenth/sixteenth and eleventh/seventeenth centuries, while the 'garden carpets' may have been the products of south and south-eastern Persia, possibly of the Kirmān region.

Rugs with Chinese cloud-patterns and extensive floral designs came from Khurāsān and Herat, and may date from the tenth/sixteenth and eleventh/seventeenth centuries. Some floral and animal rugs were made in silk in the tenth/sixteenth century. The so-called 'Polish rugs', the name derived from the eagle on them, believed for a long time to be the Polish eagle, were actually made in Persia and sent out as gifts by Shāh 'Abbās I. They were probably manufactured in Kāshān and Iṣfahān [pl. 31(*a*)]. Tapestry-woven silk rugs, *kilims*, of the same period were made in medallion, floral, vase and in animal designs. Carpet-making still flourishes in Persia in the Tabrīz, Hamadān, Kāshān, Iṣfahān and Kirmān regions.

Safavid brocades, velvets and embroideries were influenced by miniature painting just as carpets were. Designs frequently depicted scenes from the *Shāh-nāma* and the *Khamsa* of Niẓāmī. These brocades and velvets were exported to Europe, and a number were presented by Shāh 'Abbās I to European rulers. He supported the weaving-centres, which apparently were located in Kāshān and Iṣfahān.

Metalwork in the Safavid period was still flourishing, and a number of dated and signed pieces are preserved in museums and private collections. Inlaying was not so much favoured, and was used on copper or brasswork. It more often appears on iron and steel vessels, or zoomorphic figures are weapons. These were inlaid in gold and silver, but gold inlay is more characteristic of the period. Brass vessels are engraved or in relief decoration; backgrounds are frequently filled with niello [pl. 31(*b*)]. Metalwork centres were in Tabrīz, Iṣfahān and in Kirmān. Tabrīz was and still is famous for its fine silverware, decorated with minutely drawn engraved designs.

Several new types of pottery appeared during the Safavid period. Among them the earliest and probably the finest was the so-called 'Kubachi ware'. These were most likely made in north-western Persia in the Tabrīz region. Decorations, which often present human figures, animals and birds, are painted in blue, yellow, green and dull brownish-red under a clear glaze on a white ground [pl. 32(*a*)]. There seems to be a connection with or influence by Iznik pottery. The finest specimens date from the tenth/sixteenth century.

During the eleventh/seventeenth century, lustre painting was re-introduced, using brownish or ruby lustre on a very hard, white earthen-ware. The place of production is not yet known. Fine white wares, similar to those of the Seljuk period, decorated with incised lines, in openwork, or painted in black and blue, appeared again in the eleventh/seventeenth century [pl. 32(*b*)]. These wares are known as 'Gombroon wares', after the harbour (modern Bandar 'Abbās) in the Persian Gulf, whence they were shipped and exported to Europe.

Kirmān seemed to have been responsible for the production of a number of monochrome-glazed wares, mainly of celadon, brown or blue colours. Sometimes these were painted in white, or the design was incised right down to the white body. Underglaze-painted polychrome wares were also made in Kirmān during the eleventh/seventeenth and twelfth/eighteenth century.

In later times, Iṣfahān and Tehran produced underglaze-painted vessels and tiles. Decorations often appeared in relief. Figures were naïvely drawn, and the quality was far inferior to those of the earlier types. Import of mass-produced European and Far Eastern porcelain caused the final decline of the industry in Persia.

CHAPTER 10

SCIENCE

'Say, shall those who have knowledge and those who have it not be deemed equal?' (Qur'ān 39.12). 'Seek knowledge, in China if necessary.' 'The search after knowledge is obligatory for every Muslim.' 'The ink of the scholars is worth more than the blood of the martyrs'. It would be possible to quote many such texts from the Qur'ān and many from the Tradition (*Ḥadīth*) in which knowledge is extolled, in terse phrases, in the sight of the faithful.

Actually, the knowledge here envisaged is preeminently religious knowledge, which enables man to have a better understanding of the Book of God and the teaching of His Prophet. And it may be maintained, without paradox, that, with the possible exception of its poetry and its proverbs, all Muslim intellectual activity in the widest sense had its starting-point in the Qur'ān: grammar was created by non-Arabs so that they might be able to read the sacred text correctly, rhetoric for the emphasizing of its beauties, the Tradition assembled in order to explain it and supply its omissions, jurisprudence drawn up as a system of principles for moral and social life, and finally theology to defend against sceptics, or even to demonstrate, the truths taught by the Book.

It would have been surprising if this taste for knowledge had not been extended to the 'profane sciences' when the Muslims came into contact with those peoples who had inherited them. Even if there were, here and there and at certain periods, theologians of a narrow and defensive orthodoxy who forbade them, it must be said that Muslims in general, led by their caliphs and princes, showed a great thirst for instruction and were eager to assimilate the treasures of ancient science when it came within their reach. The original religious fervour still remained, for Muslim scientists, whether astronomers, mathematicians or physicians, were not seeking any the less to work for the glory of God and the service of religion when they devoted themselves to the sciences derived from Greece, from Persia or from India.

The actual course of Arab conquests was from the beginning a conducive factor. Leaving a 'canton isolated from the world', to use Pascal's phrase, the Arabs at once found themselves in contact with Syria and its Byzantine culture, with Egypt, heir to the ancient world of the Pharaohs, with the Persia of the Sasanids, with India and before long with North Africa and Spain. Various peoples (Persians, Turks, Berbers, Andalusians, Egyptians, etc.) embraced Islam; other elements, 'the People of the Book' (Christians, Jews and Sabaeans), remained in the midst of the Muslim community, second-class citizens but protected by the law and taking an active part in cultural life. All contributed to the development of the sciences in Islam, and all or nearly all of them wrote their works in Arabic, so that for medieval Western Europe 'Arab' was synonymous with 'Muslim.' It should cause no surprise if both terms are used indiscriminately in the present account when dealing with ancient Islam; in this context it seems hardly likely that national susceptibilities will take it amiss.

The importance of this 'Muslim' or 'Arab' science to the general progress of culture is beyond question, and much evidence of it can be adduced. In the first place, numerous Arabic words have passed into some of the Western languages, especially terms used in chemistry, navigation and astronomy. 'Arabic' figures, which came from India, were transmitted to Europe by the Muslims. An even more significant fact is that in his monumental *Introduction to the history of science* Sarton has given the name of a Muslim scientist to seven chapters of the second volume, deeming that the period under consideration can be designated by him. Finally, the visitor entering the chapel of Princeton University may be somewhat surprised to find there a window representing an outlandish personage: clad in a long eastern robe and a majestic turban, he holds in his hand an unrolled parchment on which can be read in Arabic *Kitāb al-ḥāwī*. That those who inspired or endowed this chapel should have deemed al-Rāzī (Rhazes), the author of the book, worthy to be represented in a place of Christian worship among the great figures of mankind, is a sufficient indication of the position occupied by Muslim science in the history of culture. Its importance has moreover become more apparent as a result of studies accomplished during the past half-century. Thanks to the work of researchers, many unpublished texts have been made available to readers. It may be added that Oriental scientists have also made interesting contributions to the history of science among the Arabs.

The subject under consideration is immense and it is not possible within the narrow limits assigned to deal with more than the essentials. In the first place mention should be made of the interest taken by many Muslim thinkers or historians in classifying the various sciences of their time. This was the treatment accorded to the subject by Ibn al-Nadīm in his *Fihrist*, by al-Fārābī in the *Iḥṣā' al-'ulūm*, in the dissertations of the *Ikhwān al-Ṣafā'*, in the 'Keys of the sciences' of al-Khwārizmī, by al-Ghazālī in several of his writings, by Ibn Khaldūn in his famous 'Prolegomena,' by Tashköprüzādeh in his *Miftāḥ al-sa'āda*, and later by al-Tahānawī in his *Kashshāf*.

From all these classifications it emerges that two kinds of science must be distinguished: (a) the religious sciences, which form to some extent the spinal column of Muslim thought: Qur'anic exegesis, Tradition (*Ḥadīth*), jurisprudence and all the propaedeutic disciplines which enable its depths to be explored; and (b) the 'foreign' or rational sciences, also called the 'sciences of the ancients', which were introduced into Islam as a result of contact with various peoples. The former lie outside the scope of the present chapter; it remains to consider the latter.

The first Muslim thinker to have given an overall picture of the sciences in his time is al-Fārābī (d. 339/950), whose 'Catalogue of Sciences' (*Iḥṣā' al-'ulūm*) known in the Latin Middle Ages by the name of *De Scientiis*, sets out to be an analytical review of all the sciences of his time with their subdivisions. He enumerates them as follows:

1. The linguistic sciences.
2. Logic (containing the eight books of the *Organon* of Aristotle).
3. Mathematics (comprising arithmetic, geometry, optics, astronomy, music, statics, mechanics).
4. Physics, reproducing the Aristotelian divisions.
5. Metaphysics.
6. Politics.
7. Jurisprudence.
8. Theology.

It will be observed that the Muslim sciences take their place beside all the other sciences which form the hierarchy within the framework, enlarged by tradition, of the Aristotelian classification.

Another philosopher, Ibn Sīnā (Avicenna, d. 428/1037), a disciple of al-Fārābī, was to extend the classification further. Confining himself to the rational sciences (*al-'ulūm al-'aqliyya*), he divided them into (a) speculative sciences (seeking after truth), and (b) practical sciences (aimed at wellbeing). Into the former class he relegated physics (eight basic sciences drawn from the works of Aristotle and seven derivative sciences as follows: medicine, astrology, physiognomy, interpretation of dreams, talismans, charms, alchemy); mathematics, including arithmetic, geometry, astronomy and music, with some ten derivative sciences; and metaphysics, which comprised the five great divisions of the *Metaphysics* of Aristotle and two derivatives—prophetic inspiration and eschatology.

Practical science was composed of personal morality, domestic morality and politics, to which Ibn Sīnā also appended prophetology. It is clear that philosophy was the queen of the sciences, and it was indeed by philosophy that they were governed.

In opposition to this philosophical view of the sciences, a mystical theologian like al-Ghazālī was more concerned with the religious aspect. What chiefly interested him was the relationship of these sciences to the ultimate happiness of man and the religious usefulness to be derived from them by the community of believers. It was accordingly this criterion which he was to apply in judging the value of the 'rational sciences'. At the beginning of his great work, *Iḥyā' 'ulūm al-dīn*, he divides the 'science which directs our progress towards the future life' into two main parts: (1) the science of relationship with God and with one's neighbour, and (2) sciences of the 'revelation'. The second category had pure knowledge as its sole object, while the first combined action with knowledge.

In the third chapter of his first volume, al-Ghazālī gives a detailed classification of the sciences from the standpoint of legal obligation: certain sciences are compulsory for each individual (*farḍ 'ayn*) while others are compulsory only for the community (*farḍ kifāya*). The former class concerns only the sciences of relationships; with regard to the communal obligation, al-Ghazālī distinguishes two kinds of sciences, those which are of a juridico-religious nature (*al-'ulūm al-shar'iyya*) and those which are not. The first are those which are communicated by the prophets and cannot be acquired by reasoning (like arithmetic), or by experiment (like medicine), or by ear (like language).

The non-religious sciences may be recommended, culpable or merely permitted. The recommended sciences are those which are closely connected with wordly affairs, like medicine and calculation, and are of two kinds. Some ought to be undertaken by the community (communal obligation): in this category are the sciences without which life in a community becomes impossible, such as medicine and calculation; the others have an optional character and are supererogatory, but devotion to them is laudable since to acquire them increases competence. An example is the pursuit of calculation or medical studies beyond the point required by practical utility. The culpable sciences are such as magic, the science of talismans, and prestidigitation, while the sciences which are merely tolerated are poetry—provided that it is not immoral—and history. The juridico-religious sciences are all recommended and are obligatory only for the community.

In the 'Prolegomena', Ibn Khaldūn, the celebrated historian and sociologist of the eighth/fourteenth century, has given a clear account of the whole field of the sciences as they appeared in his time. The principle of classification is based on the part played by reason or tradition in their acquisition. He distinguishes (a) the sciences which are 'natural' to man, in the sense that he can acquire them by his own reflections; these are the philosophical sciences; and (b) those which are only attainable through 'tradition'; these are the positive sciences of the tradition, all of which are derived from the lawgiver who first established them. He means, of course, the religious sciences, whose sources are to be found in the Qur'ān and the *Sunna*. They are characteristic—and a monopoly—of Islam, as opposed to the rational philosophical sciences which can be found elsewhere, and which, moreover, have always existed, being the natural product of human reason. The latter are called 'philosophy' or 'wisdom' and comprise the four main classical divisions of the Aristotelian tradition. The complete plan of this classification is as follows:

Classification of the Sciences according to the 'Prolegomena' of Ibn Khaldūn[1]

A. *Traditional religious sciences*

1. Exegesis of the Qur'ān.
2. Qur'anic readings.
3. Science of Tradition.
4. Science of the principles of jurisprudence including:
   (a) the science of controversial questions,
   (b) dialectics
5. Science of jurisprudence, which includes the science of the law of inheritance.
6. Speculative theology (*kalām*).
7. Mysticism (*taṣawwuf*).

[1] Ibn Khaldūn, *al-Muqaddima*, Cairo edn., 305 ff.; tr. de Slane, II, 450 ff., III, 1 ff.; tr. Rosenthal, II, 436 ff., III, 1 ff.

8. Interpretation of dreams.

Under provisional heading:

Philological sciences.

B. *Philosophical sciences*

1. Logic (the eight books of the *Organon* of Aristotle).
2. Physics, including:
   - (a) Medicine.
   - (b) Agriculture.
   - (c) Magic.
   - (d) Talismans.
   - (e) Prestidigitation.
   - (f) Alchemy.
3. Metaphysics.
4. Mathematics, comprising:
   - (a) the numerical sciences:
     - (i) arithmetic,
     - (ii) calculation,
     - (iii) algebra,
     - (iv) commercial transactions,
     - (v) partition of inheritances.
   - (b) the geometrical sciences:
     - (i) spherical and conical geometry,
     - (ii) surveying,
     - (iii) optics.
   - (c) astronomy, which also includes:
     - (i) astronomical tables,
     - (ii) judicial astrology
   - (d) music.

Subsequent Muslim authors were not to add anything essential to this classification, though some of them, like Tashköprüzādeh, adopted a different criterion as their starting-point, distinguishing between four kinds of existence: in writing, in speech, in the mind and in external reality, and in this last category differentiating between the speculative and the practical viewpoints, within each of which, finally, that which appertained to religious Law was separated from that which was philosophical. Hence seven major off-shoots were obtained, each containing many sub-sections. Eventually the author reached the point of classifying 316 'sciences', some of which were merely simple techniques, such as phlebotomy, preparation of inks and construction of apparatus.

It would be wrong to regard the work of Muslim scientists simply as an appropriation of the ancient legacy. The Muslims welcomed the great works of Greece, and some from India, with avidity, with love and with infinite respect, and, instigated by powerful patrons, a succession of translators rendered into Arabic the works of Plato and Aristotle, Hippocrates and Galen, Ptolemy, Euclid and Archimedes, Apollonius and Theon, Menelaus and Aristarchus, Hero of Alexandria, Philo of Byzantium and many others. The admirable flexibility of the Arabic language made it possible for them to coin an exact philosophical and scientific vocabulary, capable of expressing the most complicated scientific and technical terms. On this subject it is rewarding to read the penetrating studies of Louis Massignon, who has shown how helpful the Arabic language is to the internal exploration of thought, and for this reason it is 'particularly suitable for the expression of the exact sciences and for their development along the lines of the historical progress of mathematics: the transition from an arithmetic and a geometry which were intuitive and almost contemplative...to a science of algebraic constructions in which arithmetic and geometry were ultimately united.'[1]

From being enthusiastic and industrious disciples, the Muslims proceeded to the second stage of becoming masters, enamoured of research and experiment, exploring not only the books of the ancients, but also nature itself. Islam was soon to produce original scientists in various branches of study, such as astronomy, mathematics and medicine, who were the equals of the greatest known in history. To illustrate this scientific activity, which was at the same time assimilating inherited science, and inclined towards the perfecting of the old and the discovery of the new, mention may be made of three institutions or factors which appear to be characteristic of this medieval Muslim science: the libraries and translation centres, the hospitals, and finally the instruments for observation, especially the astronomical observatories.

With regard to the 'books' (which means, of course, the manuscripts) of Muslim civilization; it is enough to know that there exist at the present day, in spite of many losses by destruction, nearly a quarter of a million manuscripts in the various libraries of the Muslim world, and in the great libraries of Europe and America. A large part of this wealth deals with scientific subjects, and includes both Arabic translations of

[1] L. Massignon and R. Arnaldez, *La science antique et médiévale* (Paris, 1957), 450.

ancient Greek works, and original works written by Muslim scholars themselves.

The history of these libraries is well known. At first religious instruction was given in the mosques; then, very generously, the mosques were put at the disposal of scholars, who were able to teach there not only religious sciences but also related disciplines, and even the profane sciences of the ancients. Gradually the libraries bequeathed by scholars came to be housed in buildings specially intended for the purpose, and soon the scholars themselves were lodged in dwellings reserved for their use.

In 218/833 al-Ma'mūn founded the famous 'House of Wisdom' (*Bayt al-ḥikma*), which was bound to have an important influence on the transmission of ancient learning to the Islamic world, and to stimulate a burst of intellectual activity. This academy was reminiscent of the one which had existed at Gondēshāpūr. It contained an important library and was soon enriched with numerous translations (see below). A later 'Abbasid caliph, al-Mu'taḍid (d. 290/902) installed in his new palace lodgings and rooms for all branches of science, and professors were paid salaries for teaching there. Private individuals followed the example of the caliphs, among them 'Alī b. Yaḥyā known as *al-Munajjim* (d. 275/888) who possessed a palace and a library called *Khizānat al-ḥikma* which he placed at the disposal of scholars, the study of astronomy being especially favoured there. In Mosul there existed a *Dār al-'ilm* with a library, where students were not only able to work without payment, but were even supplied with paper. At Shīrāz a great *Khizānat al-kutub* was administered by a director and his assistant. Yāqūt recounts in his *Mu'jam al-udabā'* that at Rayy a *Bayt al-kutub* contained more than four hundred camel-loads of books, catalogued in a *Fihrist* of ten volumes.

It was in Cairo, however, under the Fatimids that the richest libraries of Islam were established. Al-Maqrīzī describes in his *Khiṭaṭ* a *Khizānat al-kutub* directed by the minister of the Caliph al-Mu'izz. It consisted of forty store-rooms containing books on all branches of science, 18,000 of which dealt with the 'sciences of the ancients'. But the library which surpassed all others was the *Dār al-ḥikma* founded by the Caliph al-Ḥākim in 396/1005, which contained a reading-room and halls of courses of study; efficient service was secured by means of paid librarians, and scholars were given pensions to enable them to pursue their studies. All the sciences were represented there. Other similar institutions were founded at Fusṭāṭ. In the year 435/1043 a traveller saw a library in Cairo containing 6,500 books on astronomy, geometry and philosophy.

It should not, however, be inferred from this extraordinary abundance of written documents that Muslim science was purely a matter of books. It borrowed a great deal from the ancients, but it also applied itself to the direct observation of nature and to experiment, as is demonstrated both by the institution of hospitals, and by the instruments for observation and experimental apparatus.

Like the mosques, tombs, cupolas and sanctuaries, hospitals in Islam were institutions inspired by charity for pious purposes, but they made it possible for medical science to develop experimentally. These hospitals, called by the Persian name of *bīmāristān*, were designed both to care for the sick and to provide theoretical and practical medical training. Special buildings were erected, and considerable funds were assigned to them in *waqf*. Four of the largest of these hospitals are especially well known: al-ʿAḍudī in Baghdād, al-Kabīr al-Nūrī in Damascus (both of which bear the names of their founders) and the two in Cairo, al-ʿAtīq founded by Saladin and, in particular, al-Manṣūrī, founded by Sultan Qalawun with its imposing building which can still be admired in Cairo today.

Each hospital contained one section for men and another for women. Each section contained several wards: one for internal diseases, a second for surgery, a third for opthalmology and finally a fourth for orthopaedics. In addition the ward for internal diseases was divided into subsidiary wards, for fevers, for maniacs, for melancholics, for mental derangement, and for diarrhoea. In every hospital there was a pharmacy under the direction of a head-pharmacist which made up the prescriptions of the doctors. The director of the hospital was assisted by the heads of sections, each a specialist in his own branch. Servants of both sexes watched over the sick, under the supervision of nurses and administrative staff who received fixed salaries paid out of endowments.

The physician had complete freedom for his experiments there, and was able to advocate new treatments. He wrote up the results of his experiments in special reports, which could be consulted by members of the public. Physicians gave courses of instruction to their pupils, and, on the completion of teaching and practical work confirmed by an examination, granted them the *ijāza* which allowed them to practise medicine. Several hospitals had libraries, and students used to travel in pursuit of instruction from celebrated teachers. Spanish sources mention that a physician of Cadiz established a botanical garden in the park of the governor, where he cultivated the rare medical plants which he had brought back from his travels. Some hospitals, or at least infirmaries, were mobile, and were designed specifically to care for casualties of war.

Ultimately the Muslim scientists surpassed their masters in powers of observation and care in verification. When studying the *Materia medica* of Dioscorides, for example, they succeeded in identifying, from observation of nature, the botanical terms which the original translation had left obscure. In the mathematical sciences they checked calculations and measurements, twice measuring afresh, for example, the arc of the terrestrial meridian instead of being satisfied with the figure left by Eratosthenes. From his clinical observations, al-Rāzī succeeded in distinguishing smallpox from measles; the laboratory apparatus which he used for his chemical experiments was unknown to the ancients. Geographers and travellers noted and described the wonders of nature, the riches of the soil, types of agriculture, techniques of craftsmanship. Al-Bīrūnī succeeded in determining specific gravities with an exactitude quite remarkable for his time. Moreover the observatories founded by caliphs and princes were provided with important collections of instruments. Al-Battānī, for example, made use of astrolabes, tubes, a gnomon divided into twelve parts, a celestial sphere with five rings, of which he was perhaps the inventor, parallactic rules, a mural quadrant, horizontal and vertical solar quadrants. These instruments were of considerable size—in fact the Arabs enlarged their instruments as much as possible in order to reduce the margin of error; they then began to make special instruments for certain measurements.

The foregoing account has put into perspective the state of the various sciences in Islam and their relationship with the whole field of learning and has described both their debt to ancient science and the spirit which inspired them. The exact sciences, mathematics and astronomy will now first be discussed and after them, in the second part, the natural sciences.

Arithmetic

Arithmetic (*al-ḥisāb*) was, as Ibn Khaldūn observed in his 'Prolegomena,' the first of the mathematical sciences to be used by the

Muslims, being indeed a means of solving such material problems which present themselves in daily life as assessment of taxes, reckoning of legal compensation, and division of inheritances according to Qur'anic law.

Arabic manuals of arithmetic divide numbers into whole numbers, fractions, and non-rational. Basic principles and definitions are taken from the Greeks. The definitions of certain progressions are mentioned, and the authors give methods for calculating sums, for example the the aggregate of equal numbers, and of certain unequal numbers, but without explaining these in general terms. Al-Karajī (d. 420/1029) nevertheless offers a neat solution of the problem of summing the third powers of the progression $1 + 2 + 3 \ldots + n$, and later al-Kāshī (d. 841/1437) a mathematician, physician and astronomer, was to give the sum of the fourth powers.

Muslim arithmeticians practised exponentiation, and the extraction of square and cube roots, sometimes using the formulae of root approximation borrowed from the Byzantines, although equivalent processes of root-extraction may be found, for example, in Hero's works. The knew the fundamental rules of numerical manipulation: identity, permutation, associativity, combination and distributivity, for example, the laws $am + bm = (a + b)m$; $\sqrt{a} \times \sqrt{b} = \sqrt{ab}$.

They noted that numbers which ended in 2, 3, 7, 8 or in an odd number of noughts were not perfect squares. They constructed abaci to make calculation easier. Without explicitly giving the formula of the rule of three they applied it by means of ratios. The discovery of the proof by casting out nines is sometimes attributed to them, and the procedure known by the name of 'the rule of double false', which is found again among European arithmeticians from Pacioli (1494) onwards.

Being ingenious and spontaneously inquisitive, they studied the properties of the 'amical' numbers, and Thābit b. Qurra (d. 289/901), a Sabaean, discovered their remarkable characteristics. 'Amical' numbers are those in which the sum of the proportional parts of one is equal to the other and *vice versa*. For example, taking the numbers 220 and 284: $220 = 1 + 2 + 4 + 71 + 142$, the parts of 284, and likewise $284 = 1 + 2 + 4 + 5 + 10 + 11 + 20 + 22 + 44 + 55 + 110$, the parts of 220.

Lastly, Muslim authors showed a predilection for the composition of magic squares (called in Arabic *wafq*, pl., *awfāq*), which gave in figures the value of the Divine Names and were used in talismans (cf. the *Shams al-maʿārif* of al-Būnī).[1]

Geometry

Arabic geometry was founded on a deep knowledge of prior Greek works, particularly those of Euclid, Archimedes and Apollonius, and it was also influenced by the Indian *Siddhānta*. In constructing the regular polygons which were included in the design of certain arabesques, they made use of intersecting conic sections. Thus to construct a regular nine-sided polygon, Abu'l-Layth used the meet of a hyperbola and a parabola. Profiting by the researches of Ibn al-Haytham on a theorem not proved by Archimedes in his *On the sphere and the cylinder*, 6–7, al-Kūhī constructed a segment of a sphere equal in volume to the segment of a given sphere and in its surface area to another segment of the same sphere. He resolved the problem very ingeniously with the help of two auxiliary cones and the intersection of two auxiliary conic sections—a hyperbola and a parabola—and then discussed limit cases.

For these problems of the construction of interrelated figures, the Banū Mūsā in particular showed outstanding talent. Another aspect of geometry of especial interest to Arab authors was its use in making calculations. Also to be noted are the works of Ibrāhīm b. Sinān on the quadrature of the parabola; of Abu'l-Wafā' (d. *c*. 387/997) on the construction of regular polygons which led to equations of the third degree; of Abū Kāmil (third/ninth century) on the construction of the pentagon and the decagon, also by means of equations. The commentary of ʿUmar Khayyām (d. 526/1131) on Euclid is an important precursor of non-Euclidean geometry, which may also have been inspired by Naṣīr al-Dīn al-Ṭūsī.

Certain problems gave rise to discussions bordering on natural philosophy, such as the nature of the mathematical point, line, and angle or of space, which was conceived of sometimes as a container or a support (cf. the Aristotelian definition), sometimes as a receptacle (Plato and Abu'l-Barakāt [d. 547/1152]).

[1] With regard to arithmetical notation, the Arab mathematicians used sexagesimals, and after al-Kāshī's time decimals, in their large-scale computations: this was an immense advance upon the standard Greek 'literal' number scale with which even Archimedes had to cope. To point this, there is a world of difference between Archimedes's best inequality $3\frac{1}{7} > \pi > 3\frac{10}{71}$ (which yields π correct only to two decimal places) and al-Kāshī's computation of π correct to 16 decimal places. Without the facilities afforded by the ease of manipulation of sexagesimal (and later decimal) fractions, it is probable that Arab computational astronomy (and perhaps practical optics too) would have been significantly retarded.

Applications of geometry were numerous: problems of surveying, studies of mechanical tools in 'Irāq and in Persia in the fourth/tenth century, the construction of improved mills, of *norias* (from Arabic sing., *nā'ūra*, wheels with scoops for the continuous drawing of water from a watercourse), mangonels (stone-throwing machines), tractors etc.

Algebra

Algebra, as the form of the name indicates, is an Arabic word: *al-jabr*, which signifies the restoration of something broken, the amplifying of something incomplete. The word *jabr* is sometimes associated with the word *ḥaṭṭ*, descent; it expresses the diminution of a number so as to make it equal to another given number. More often *jabr* is associated with *muqābala*, the balancing of the two sides of an equation. In the equation $12x^2 - 6x + 9 = 6x^2 + 18$ for example, it is possible to obtain by *al-jabr*:

$$12x^2 + 9 = 6x^2 + 6x + 18$$

by *al-ḥaṭṭ*:

$$4x^2 + 3 = 2x^2 + 2x + 6$$

by *muqābala*:

$$2x^2 = 2x + 3$$

Muḥammad b. Mūsā al-Khuwārizmī (third/ninth century), the latinized distortion of whose name has produced the word 'algorithm', was chiefly responsible for laying the foundations of Islamic algebra. He began his treatise on the subject with a clear if long-winded exposition of equations of the second degree, after which he discussed algebraic multiplication and division, then the numerical measurement of surfaces, the division of estates and other legal questions. Such problems were always presented in the form of numerical examples.

Perhaps following Diophantus, al-Khuwārizmī distinguished sixty pes of the general quadratic:
$ax^2 = bx; ax^2 = c; bx = c; ax^2 + bx = c; ax^2 + c = bx; bx + c = ax^2$.
Having laid down rules for solving them by verbal means, algebraic notation not yet having been invented, he then proved these rules geometrically in Euclidean style.

With 'Umar Khayyām algebra made considerable progress. In a work which bears this title he classified the equations of third degree into twenty-five categories according to the number and the nature of the terms on each side of the equation, and then attempted to solve them, giving numerical solutions for equations of the first and second degrees and geometrical solutions (by means of conic intersections) for those of third degree. Although he had no knowledge of negative and imaginary solutions, the results which he obtained are noteworthy.

Trigonometry

The Arabs were, according to Carra de Vaux, unquestionably the inventors of plane and spherical trigonometry, which did not, strictly speaking, exist among the Greeks. In fact, Hipparchus had calculated a table of chords, and Ptolemy gave a more elaborate one in Book I of his *Syntax* (ch. 9) for arcs at intervals of half a degree. Computation of this was made in effect, by first calculating the length of the side of a regular polygon with angles of 18°. With the Arabs, the trigonometrical functions of sine, tangent, cosine and cotangent became explicit. They adopted for 'sine' the name *jayb* which signifies an opening, bay, curve of a garment, specifically the opening of an angle. The Latin term 'sinus' is a mere translation of the Arabic *jayb*. It appears in the twelfth Christian century in the translation of *De motu stellarum* of al-Battānī, (d. 317/929), the Albategnius of the Latins. The definition of the cotangent expressed as a function of the sine and of the cosine appears there for the first time, and in ch. III trigonometry begins to assume the appearance of a distinct and independent science.

In spherical trigonometry also al-Battānī presented an important formula (uniting the three sides and one angle of a spherical triangle) which has no equivalent in Ptolemy:

$$\cos a = \cos b \cos c - \sin b \sin c \cos A$$

A further advance was made with Abu'l-Wafā', and he was probably the first to demonstrate the sine theorem for the general spherical triangle. He proposed a new technique for the construction of sine tables, the value of sin 30′ thus computed being correct to the eighth decimal place. He also knew the identities which are, in modern form,

$$\sin (a \pm b) = \sin a \cos b - \cos a \sin b$$

$$2 \sin^2 \frac{a}{2} = 1 - \cos a \qquad \sin a = 2 \sin \frac{a}{2} \times \cos \frac{a}{2}$$

Making a special study of the tangent, he tabulated its values, and introduced the secant and the cosecant; he knew the simple relationships between these six basic trigonometric functions, which are often used even today to define them. Indeed, Carra de Vaux has demonstrated, following Moritz Cantor, that it was Abu'l-Wafā' and not Copernicus who invented the secant; he called it the 'diameter of the shadow' and set out explicitly the ratio (in modern form)

$$\frac{\tan a}{\sec a} = \frac{\sin a}{1}$$

Optics

The application of the principles of geometry to light made possible the construction of mirrors and lenses. A remarkable practitioner of this science among the Arabs is to be found in the person of al-Ḥasan b. al-Haytham (d. *c.* 431/1039), well known to the West under the name of Alhazen. A native of Baṣra, he came to Cairo, and entered the service of the Caliph al-Ḥākim, who set him to find a means of regulating the annual inundation of the Nile. His failure to do so nearly cost him his life, for the Fatimid caliph, who was known for his eccentricities, was prone to dangerous outbursts of anger. It, however, cast no doubt on al-Haytham's scientific ability in the field of optics, and his book *Kitāb al-manāẓir* ('On optics') exercised an important influence in the Middle Ages, prompting the studies of Roger Bacon and of Witelo. Ibn al-Haytham discussed the nature of light, declaring that light emanated from the object. He treated the eye as a dioptric system, by applying the geometry of refraction to it. He had some knowledge of reflection and refraction and brilliantly investigated the phenomenon of atmospheric refraction, calculating the height of the atmosphere (ten English miles). He made a study of lenses, experimenting with different mirrors—flat, spherical, parabolic and cylindrical, concave and convex. He also described experiments which he made on starlight, the rainbow and colours, and observed the semi-lunar form of the sun's image cast during eclipses on a wall set opposite a screen with a tiny hole in it: this is the first known instance of the camera obscura. His catoptrics included the problem known by his name: given object and image by reflection in a spherical mirror, to find the reflection point. Ibn al-Haytham's solution of this is wholly geometrical: the algebraic solution was a discovery of Huygens and Sluse in the mid-seventeenth century.

One of his successors, Kamāl al-Dīn al-Fārisī (d. *c.* 720/1320), repeated and improved the accuracy of the experiments of Ibn al-Haytham on the camera obscura, and also observed the path of the rays in the interior of a glass sphere, hoping to determine the refraction of solar light through raindrops. His findings enabled him to give an explanation of the formation of the primary and secondary rainbows.

Mechanics, hydraulics and technology

The demands of Muslim civilization, which extended from one ocean to the other, obliged rulers to make the maximum use of the resources of the countries which they conquered. Science was required to make its contribution, and technical arts were rapidly developed in the most varied fields: the construction of irrigation works, of canals for the provision of water, of ways of communication, and the erection of hydraulic machines. The first textbook of mechanics dates from 246/860 and is the *Book of Artifices* of the Banū Mūsā, the mathematicians Muḥammad, Aḥmad and Ḥasan, sons of Mūsā b. Shākir, who were all both scientists and enlightened patrons of learning. The work in question contains about a hundred technical constructions, some twenty of which are of practical value: apparatus for hot and cold water, wells of a fixed depth, the lifting of weights by machinery, a whole series of the scientific and automatic toys so much beloved by the courts of princes in the Middle Ages.

In the seventh/thirteenth century al-Jazarī, a native of ʿIrāq, wrote a *Kitāb fī maʿrifat al-ḥiyal al-handasiyya*, 'a great book on mechanics and clocks, the best extant in the Islamic world'.[1] An engineer, Qayṣar, who died in Damascus in 649/1251, constructed irrigation wheels on the Orontes, as well as fortifications, for the prince of Ḥamāh. It was he who set up the celestial globe which is today in the National Museum at Naples. Generally speaking, the mechanical devices encountered in the countries of the Orient were improved and perfected during the Crusades or in Spain.

With regard to measuring devices, al-Khāzinī (*c.* 494/1100), making use of the works of the ancients (he quotes Archimedes, Aristotle, Euclid, Menelaus, Pappus and especially his co-religionist al-Bīrūnī), expounded a detailed theory of balance in his book entitled 'The balance of wisdom' (*Mīzān al-ḥikma*) in which he defined the centre of gravity of a body and conditions for various types of equilibrium. Al-Bīrūnī (d. 442/1050) one of the greatest scientists of Islam, ascer-

[1] M. Meyerhof, 'Science and medicine', in T. Arnold and A. Guillaume (ed.), *The legacy of Islam* (Oxford, 1931), at p. 342.

tained experimentally a certain number of specific gravities, by means of a 'conical instrument' which may be regarded as the earliest pycnometer. Al-Khāzinī, in dealing with liquids, used a hydrometer similar to those used by the Alexandrians. The results obtained by these two scientists 'constituted one of the finest achievements attained by the Arabs in the realm of experimental physics.'[1]

In addition to the balance (*mīzān*), the Muslims were also familiar with the steelyard (*qaristūn*) inherited from antiquity, which they employed both for the measurement of time (by a weight in perpetual equilibrium with an hour-glass), and theoretically to illustrate certain equations, for example those arising in inverse proportions. Likewise al-Bīrūnī used the balance to demonstrate the rules of *jabr* and *muqābala*.

Certain mechanical concepts, such as the nature of time, of the force of movement, were discussed in philosophical terms. Arab atomists revived the theory of rectilinear movement, and envisaged circular motion as an infinite sequence of indefinitely small displacements from the straight line, but this theory was not defined explicitly in scientific terms.

Astronomy

It has been seen above that Muslim authors following the Greeks classified astronomy among the mathematical sciences; it was called *'ilm al-hay'a* (the science of the aspect of the universe) or *'ilm al-aflāk* (the science of the celestial spheres). For the Arabs as for the Greeks, this science had as its sole object the study of the apparent movements in the heavens, and their representation in mathematical terms. It consisted of what we call spherical astronomy, together with the calculation of planetary orbits, with applications to the composition of astronomical tables and the theory of instruments. On the other hand, the study of meteors, of comets, shooting-stars, etc., that is of what might be called elementary celestial physics (origin of celestial movements, nature of the spheres, light of the stars, etc.), was regarded as a part of physics and of metaphysics.

A special branch of the subject called the 'science of fixed moments' (*'ilm al-miqāt*) determined, by calculation and instrumentally, the hours of the day and night in order to establish the times of the five canonical prayers; a fact which serves to emphasize the close connexion of as-

[1] A. Mieli, *La science arabe* (Paris, 1938), 101.

tronomy with prescribed religious practices. Indeed in the *Jāhiliyya*, the Arabs, as they travelled by night over their peninsula, had had the opportunity of observing the heavens, of noting the names and positions of certain constellations, the rising and setting of the bright stars, from which they were able to tell how many hours of the night had elapsed. They had defined twenty-eight successive groups of stars called 'stations' or 'lunar stages' (*manāzil al-qamar*) and the position of the moon in relation to these groups made it possible to determine the season of the year. The agricultural seasons, the meterological prognostications were linked with the annual rising of certain stars or with the cosmic setting (*naw'*) of the lunar stations.

The new religion borrowed certain elements from this pre-Islamic heritage in order to fix the hours for prayer, in particular that of the night, which had to be carefully determined to comply with the religious law; it was also necessary to ascertain the direction of Mecca for the *qibla*, and the beginning and the end of the month of Ramaḍān by the exact definition of the time of the new moon (from observation, not calculation). Moreover certain ritual prayers were prescribed on the occasion of an eclipse of the sun or moon; for these it was necessary to prepare, and therefore to be able to predict them. In this way religion stimulated research, and when the Muslims came into contact with other civilizations, they did not fail to take immediate advantage of the latter's astronomical knowledge, the more so because it is stated in the Qur'ān that the stars were created for the benefit of man, whom they invite to contemplation. For this reason it is hardly surprising to find astronomy as a kind of science allied to religion, subject, at least ostensibly, to the condition that none of its theories should clash with the assertions of the Sacred Book.

When and how did the study of astronomy as a science begin among the Arabs? Ibn Ṣā'id relates in his *Ṭabaqāt al-umam* that 'the Caliph al-Manṣūr received in audience a native of India who had a thorough knowledge of the calculation called *Sindhind* concerning the movements of the stars'. This occurred in Baghdād in 155/771. From this astronomical treatise, called in fact the *Siddhānta*, Ibrāhīm b. Ḥabīb al-Fazārī extracted the elements and methods of calculation for the astronomical tables (*zīj*, pl. *azyāj*) which he adapted to the Muslim lunar year. At about the same period Ya'qūb b. Ṭāriq composed a similar book, making use both of the Indian *Siddhānta*, and other sources provided by a second mission from that country, while Abu'l-Ḥasan al-Ahwāzī communicated to the Arabs the information concerning the planetary movements which is expounded in the treatise of *al-Argiabhad*. These Indian works, particularly the *Sindhind*, had many imitations in the Muslim world up to the first half of the fifth/eleventh century.

Very shortly after the introduction of the Indian sources and before the end of the second/eighth century, an Arabic translation was made of a Pahlavī work, the 'Astronomical table of the king' (*Zīj al-shāh*), which had been produced in the last years of the Sasanids. The Arab version had a great success among the Muslims. Mā Shā' Allāh (Messahala), an astrologer and astronomer at the beginning of the third/ninth century, used it for his calculations, and in the first half of the third/ninth century Muḥammad b. Mūsā al-Khuwārizmī extracted from it his account of the periodicities of planetary movements. Abū Ma'shar (Abumasar d. 273/886), also availed himself of the *Zīj al-shāh* for his astronomical tables, but after the third/ninth century it came to be referred to less and less in the Orient. In Spain, on the other hand, it remained in use until about half way through the fifth/eleventh century.

The most important sources of all, however, although they became available later than those described above, were the classical Greek authors. At the end of the second/eighth century and the beginning of the third/ninth the Barmecide Yaḥyā b. Khālid, a great patron and protector of scholars and men of letters, caused to be translated into Arabic for the first time the μεγάλη σύνταξις μαθηματική of Ptolemy which, under the contracted and arabized title *al-Majisṭī* (*Almagest*), had a tremendous success in the Orient in the Middle Ages. It was especially after the production of two new and more accurate versions (notably the later rendering of Ḥunayn b. Isḥāq as revised by Thābit b. Qurra) that its influence superseded that of the works of Indian or Persian origin. Other works of Ptolemy which came to enrich the Muslim heritage were the *Geography*, the *Tabulae manuales*, the *Hypotheses planetarum*, the *Apparitiones stellarum fixarum* and the *Planispherium*.[1] Contributions from other Greek authors included the *Tabulae manuales* of Theon of Alexandria, the book of Aristarchus, *On the size and distances*

[1] While it must be agreed that everything significant in technical Arab astronomy falls within the shadow of Ptolemy's *Almagest* and his minor works, the *Hypotheses* particularly, its originality should also be stressed. For example the Ptolemaic models for the orbits of Mercury and the Moon were particularly inadequate representations of reality, and ingenious improvements were suggested by al-Ṭūsī, al-Shīrāzī and al-Shāṭir in the seventh/thirteenth century. Some of al-Shāṭir's planetary models, in particular, are very close to Copernican models, except that the centre of motion is kept centred on the earth. See E. S. Kennedy, 'Later medieval planetary theory' in *Isis*, 57 (1966), 365–78.

of the sun and of the moon, the *Isagoge* of Geminus, two small works of Autolycus, three of Theodosius, the short study of Hypsicles on ascents and finally the astronomical tables of Ammonius.

The Muslim astronomers in their turn composed treatises in imitation of those which reached them from the outer world: general elementary introductions, such as the compendia of Thābit b. Qurra (d. 289/901), and of al-Farghānī (Alfraganus) who died after 247/861, systematic treatises corresponding to the *Almagest*, treatises of spherical astronomy for use of the calculators and observers, consisting essentially of calculation tables, and finally specialized treatises, such as catalogues of the stars, dissertations on instruments, etc.

What are the characteristics of the Muslim science of astronomy? Speaking generally, it may be said that the only system professed was geocentrism, for a variety of reasons: firstly, out of deference to the authority of the philosophy of the great master Aristotle; then, in astronomy, by reason of the authority of Ptolemy; finally, and somewhat surprisingly, because of the demands of astrology, which was almost unanimously accepted as a true science in the Middle Ages, and which was based on a strict geocentrism. In any case heliocentrism could not be demonstrated irrefutably, nor, in the absence of the telescope, could it be of any use in practical astronomy. The same planets were known to the Arabs as to the Greeks, and also their movements. Moreover the method of representing them was necessarily similar, being eccentric and epicyclic. Only those authors who were more philosophers than astronomers, like Ibn Ṭufayl or al-Biṭrūjī (Alpetragius), tried to substitute an original (although not heliocentric) theory, but one which did not affect the strictly circular movement of the celestial bodies.

Some details may be given of this classical Muslim astronomy. The number of the spheres, which in the medieval West were sometimes called the heavens, amounted in Aristotle and Ptolemy to eight (seven for planets and one for fixed stars), a number which was to be retained by the first Arab astronomers such as al-Farghānī and al-Battānī. Some would have liked to reduce them to seven in order to conform with the Qur'ān (2. 27), but this figure was never accepted by the astronomers. When Ibn al-Haytham introduced into his teaching Aristotle's doctrine of the solid spheres, it was necessary to add a ninth without 'stars', imparting the daily movement to the other spheres, and this was not the first appearance of this doctrine. This ninth sphere, which was subsequently accepted by all astronomers, was called the universal sphere, the greatest sphere, the sphere of spheres, the united sphere (*al falak al-aṭlas*), etc. In general the *falāsifa*, such as Ibn Sīnā and Ibn Ṭufayl, accepted the nine spheres, but Ibn Rushd was not willing to go beyond eight.

Ptolemy's order for the planets was retained, although, like the Hellenic astronomers, Muslims recognized that there was no empirical justification for the relative positions of Mercury and Venus in regard to the sun. Astrological requirements likewise guaranteed the continuing sway of the Ptolemaic system. The following were the Arabic names of the seven planets in the traditional order: *Zuḥal* (Saturn), *al-Mushtarī* (Jupiter), *al-Mirrīkh* (Mars), *al-Shams* (the Sun), *al-Zuhara* (Venus), *'Uṭārid* (Mercury), *al-Qamar* (the Moon).

The obliquity of the ecliptic in relation to the terrestial equator, one of the basic parameters of astronomical calculation, necessarily presented a problem to Muslim astronomers. The Greeks, from the time of Eratosthenes (230 B.C.) on making calculation had found the result 23° 51′ 20″, a figure which they assumed to be constant. Great was the surprise of the Arab astronomers when they subsequently arrived at a lower figure: al-Battānī, for example, made it 23° 35′. Hence the question arose, whether there might have been some diminution in its obliquity or whether the ancient observations had been inaccurate. Al-Battānī supported his own figure, correctly alleging the latter hypothesis, but there were others who, relying in addition on the precession of the equinoxes, conceived the illusory theory of 'trepidation' (or 'libration') of the constant angle which was accepted by Ibn Qurra and, in a slightly different form, by al-Zarqālī. But repeated observations led to the widespread conviction that there was in fact a slight diminution, which was admitted by all the astronomers of the seventh/thirteenth century. Whether its change was continuous or intermittent, and within what limits, was a question Muslim astronomers were unable to decide. On the other hand the astronomers of al-Ma'mūn did discover that the motion of the solar apogee was tied to the movement of the fixed stars and to that of the apogees of the planets, i.e. to the displacement in longitude caused by the gradual precession of the equinoxes.

The general Ptolemaic theory, accepted by nearly all Muslim astronomers, met with opposition only in Spain, where Ibn Bājja, Ibn Ṭufayl and Ibn Rushd rejected, in the name of Aristotle, the Ptolemaic account of the movements of the heavenly bodies. Al-Biṭrūjī (d. *c.* 601/1204), went further, and denied all motion of heavenly bodies from west to east. These theories of the Spanish philosophers did not, however, command any wide credence among contemporary astronomers.

Like Ptolemy, the ancient Muslim astronomers refrained from defining the nature of the celestial sphere, a problem which belonged to physics and metaphysics rather than to astronomy. For their part they were interested only in its mathematical aspect. The Aristotelian theory of solid spheres was introduced to Islam by Ibn al-Haytham, and Muslim authors accordingly came to consider spheres and celestial bodies as composed of a single substance, the fifth element, differing essentially from the four sublunary elements. The solidity of the spheres secured the permanence of the stars, which by their rotation they drew after them.

Complementary to astronomy is geography, the science of lands and their resources. Here too the Muslims were indebted to India and above all to Greece, especially the works of Ptolemy and of Marinos of Tyre. In the third/ninth century, thanks to the labours of such astronomer-geographers as al-Khuwārizmī, al-Farghānī and al-Battānī, geography, which had hitherto been merely a literary subject, was able to develop in the direction of a cosmography. At the same time travellers were making journeys about the vast Muslim empire and bringing back personal observations, and reports of strange and marvellous facts.

This geographical activity in the widest sense may be summarized in the following periods and categories: (a) literary geography, which flourished in the third-fourth/ninth-tenth centuries and consisted of compendiums for the use of secretaries (cf. the books of Ibn Khurradādhbih, Ibn Rusta, Qudāma) and of popular works; (b) the second period, fourth–sixth/tenth–twelfth centuries, saw the expansion of these original types in different directions, either in the form of travellers' reports (Ibn Faḍlān, Buzurg b. Shahriyār) or descriptions of cities and of the high roads connecting them. Works of this kind (al-Ya'qūbī, al-Balkhī, al-Iṣṭakhrī, Ibn Ḥawqal, al-Muqaddasī, al-Bakrī, al-Idrīsī) have, in part, been published in the *Bibliotheca Geographorum Araborum*, and there was a popularization of geography through such works as the *Murūj al-dhahab* ('Fields of gold') of al-Mas'ūdī and the *Qanūn al-Mas'ūdī* of al-Bīrūnī. Finally (c) a third period from the sixth/twelfth century onwards included geographical dictionaries (al-Bakrī, Yāqūt), works on cosmography and universal geography (al-Qazwīnī, Abu'l-Fidā'), the historico-geographical encyclopaedias (al-'Umarī) and detailed and picturesque accounts of travels like those of Ibn Jubayr

(d. 614/1217) and of Ibn Baṭṭūṭa (d. 779/1377). Note must also be taken of maps, some of which, in colour, illustrate several of these works.[1]

Since mention has been made of al-Bīrūnī, it should be added that this first-class scholar was one of the most remarkable personalities of the Muslim world. His 'Chronology' (*al-Āthār al-bāqiya*) is a work devoted to an examination of the calendars of various peoples—Persians, Greeks, Jews, Melkite Christians, Nestorian Christians, Sebaeans, Arabs both pagan and Muslim—and within it are to be found numerous details concerning historical facts and traditions. Besides this treatise, which is equally important for the history of religion, al-Bīrūnī wrote on the astrolabe, the planisphere and the armillary sphere; he also composed tables for Sultan Mas'ūd. His knowledge of Sanskrit allowed him to draw information at first-hand from the sources themselves, which enhances his work on India inestimably; indeed it is still useful today. He also wrote a work on precious stones.

Astrology

After the science of astronomy, the scientific character of which was never questioned in any of the classifications, a few words must be said in respect of a pseudo-science which was very popular in the Middle Ages but which encountered lively opposition among most philosophers and among theologians and was eventually condemned by religious thinkers as being incompatible with itself—the subject of astrology.

It is difficult for people at the present day to understand the important place occupied by such a science in the Middle Ages, after it had, moreover, occupied a similar position in antiquity. In order to comprehend its scope, it is necessary to remember the fundamental principle on which it rested, that the universe is a single whole and that the sublunary world is subject to the movements of the stars, whether by the direct influence of the latter or because there is a certain correspondence, an 'analogy', between changes on earth and the movements of the stars; the latter may, thus, provide signs and indications.

Henceforth the observation of the stars was to permit those who knew how to read these indications to ascertain present or future events, which were taking place, or would take place, in the world below. The astrologer had therefore to make use of a certain number of these 'signs in the sky' and this 'astrological apparatus' was derived essentially

[1] Cf. the articles DJUGHRĀFIYĀ in Supplement to *EI*[1] and in *EI*[2], II.

from the following elements. In the first place the stars themselves and their positions in relation to the earth and to one another, which would give rise to five combinations: conjunction and the five 'aspects' or 'dispositions'. Next, the signs of the zodiac, considered either in isolation or grouped in threes. It was possible to carry the division of the zodiac further, and to imagine a special character for each degree; it would then be possible to distinguish the masculine or feminine signs, the shining ones, the dark, the coloured, the nebulous, those which increased happiness, etc. Certain parts of the zodiac had a particular importance in relation to the sun, to the moon and to the five planets, for they were their 'limits', 'domiciles' and 'detriments', their 'exaltations' and their 'downfalls'.

The horizon and the meridian also played a considerable part; their points of intersection with the ecliptic were called the four pivots: the ascendant (*al-ṭāliʿ*), which was the point of the ecliptic rising to the horizon, the pivot of the earth, the descendant and the point of culmination. The ecliptic was thus divided into twelve sections, called the twelve celestial mansions (*buyūt*), which were the basis of every astrological exercise. Lastly, since each geographical region was subject to a particular influence, it was necessary also to take account of them.

The combination of these various factors, exactly noted, would enable the astrologer to devote himself to three kinds of exercises, based on different principles. Thus (1) he could, in the first place, reply to 'interrogations' (*masāʾil*, *questiones*)—how some absent person fares, who was responsible for a theft, where would a lost object be found, etc.; (2) he could calculate the propitious moment for undertaking some important course of action or other (*ikhtiyārāt, electiones*). For example, al-Yaʿqūbī when writing about the foundation of Baghdād, recounted that the Caliph al-Manṣūr laid the foundations 'at the time appointed by the astrologers Nawbakht and Mā Shāʾ Allāh'.

Finally (3) he could foresee the future, the genethialogical system making it possible, with the help of data concerning the birth of an individual or the beginning of a reign, of a sect or of a religion, to 'foresee' what would happen to them in the future. This last system, which was different from the two previously mentioned, was based on the principle that at the moment of the birth of a human being or the occurrence of an event the configuration of the celestial sphere fixed irrevocably the destiny of the newly-born or the consequences of the event.

This determinism which regarded man as the mere instrument of cosmic forces was not slow to arouse the censure of religious teachers. Many philosophers likewise attacked its basic principles, particularly al-Fārābī, Ibn Sīnā and Ibn Rushd. Some, however, like al-Kindī, the *Ikhwān al-Ṣafā'*, and theologians like Fakhr al-Dīn al-Rāzī, held it in esteem. One thing is certain, that in spite of all condemnation, astrology remained very popular in daily life. It was only in the modern period, following on the Copernican revolution which undermined its foundations, and the introduction of Western civilization, that astrology lost practically all credence among serious people. A few journals alone draw up horoscopes, perhaps in imitation of those in the West.

What must be mentioned, however, is the superiority of Arab astrology over that of its sources. These sources were, for astrology as for astronomy, Indian, Persian and above all Greek, including especially the works of Ptolemy (*Tetrabiblos*), of Dorotheos Sidonius, Antiochus, Vettius Valens, Teucros and others. But the immense progress achieved in astronomical observation itself, the use of mathematical methods for the calculation of the 'astronomical apparatus' mentioned above, gave to Muslim astrology a 'scientific' turn, especially in the preparatory stages of establishing 'data'. Besides, all these preliminary operations were based on astronomy properly so called and were demonstrated with all the exactitude to be desired in treatises of astronomy, alongside problems of trigonometry.

Natural sciences

According to the classification of the sciences previously considered, it has been seen that the field of the 'natural sciences' includes physics properly so called, in the Aristotelian sense of the word, and a certain number of related sciences. Physics in this sense is based on philosophy and will not be discussed here; only the two sciences which were especially studied by Muslim scholars, medicine and alchemy, will be examined in detail.

Medicine

When the Muslims appeared on the world scene, medicine had already covered a long period of its history, with Hippocrates, Galen and Dioscorides and the doctors of the school of Alexandria, finally becoming concentrated, during the sixth century, in the city of Gondēshāpūr.

This city of south-western Persia had in fact been accepting a succession of refugees—the Nestorians of Edessa when their school was closed in 489, followed by the Neoplatonic philosophers of the school of Athens, when in turn this latter school was closed by Justinian in 529.

The Nestorians brought with them to Gondēshāpūr the Syriac translation which they had already had in Edessa. The city soon became aware of a remarkable intellectual fermentation, and under the reign of Chosroes Anūshirwān, the Kisrā of the Arab chronicles, the school reached the zenith of its activity. Greeks, Jews, Christians, Syrians, Hindus and Persians lived side by side in a splendid atmosphere of toleration, united by the same love of science. Gondēshāpūr became a medical centre of first importance: hospitals were established there where, in addition to the care of the sick, facilities were assured for the theoretical and practical teaching of medicine.

In 17/638 the city was taken by the Arabs. In view of its nearness to the Arab city of Ḥīra it is probable that Arabic was spoken there even before the conquest. At all events doctors must have been speaking the language very soon afterwards, since Ibn Abī Uṣaybiʿa, the famous historian of Arab medicine, recounts that on the occasion of the visit of the physician Jurjīs b. Jibrīl of Gondēshāpūr to the Caliph al-Manṣūr, Jūrjīs addressed the caliph in Arabic. In this city there were actual dynasties of medical families, who handed down their scientific knowledge, enriched by personal experience, from father to son. And it was the physicians of Gondēshāpūr who became the teachers of the Muslims in medicine.

Until 132/750, that is to say before the coming of the ʿAbbasids and the foundation of Baghdād, this influence was chiefly indirect, inasmuch as there were Arabs who arrived in Gondēshāpūr for the purpose of being initiated into the science of medicine. It is said that the first of the Arabs to have earned the title of physician, Ḥārith b. Kalada, was born at Ṭā'if towards the middle of the sixth Christian century. After being admitted to the court of Chosroes, he had a conversation with him which has been preserved. The basis of his system of hygiene was moderation in eating. What was most harmful, he said, was to introduce food on top of food, that is to say to eat when one was already satisfied. He forbade the taking of baths after meals and sexual relations in a state of drunkenness, and he advocated bed-coverings at night, the drinking of water for preference and the total avoidance of undiluted wine. Meat which was salted or dried, or which came from young animals, he regarded as undesirable. Fruit might be eaten when it first came into season and at the proper stage of ripeness. With regard to the use of medicine, he replied to Chosroes in the following terms: 'So long as your health lasts, leave medicines alone, but, if illness comes, check it by all the means available before it can take root.' He also prescribed methods of combating every ailment individually and recommended the use of enemas. Cupping-glasses should be applied when the moon was waning, in calm weather and when the body was in an active state. He was on close terms with Muḥammad, who sent sick people to him, and his son, al-Nadr, inherited his medical knowledge.

Ibn Abī Uṣaybi'a quotes, according to al-Nadr, a certain Ibn Abī Ramtha of the tribe of Tamīm who practised surgery. When he was with Muḥammad one day he saw that he had between his shoulders the excrescence (*al-khātim*) which was regarded as the attribute of prophets and proposed to remove it by surgery. Muḥammad refused his offer.

Apart from the various physicians mentioned by Ibn Abī Uṣaybi'a, tradition relates a certain number of medical aphorisms attributed to Muḥammad himself which have been collected and annotated in books entitled 'The medicine of the Prophet' (*al-Ṭibb al-nabawī*). These collections embody Traditions of the Prophet in a systematic medical treatise, with notes and additions.

It was, however, in the second/eighth century in Baghdad that the science of medicine began to make rapid progress among the Muslims. The Caliph al-Manṣūr was ill, and demanded that the best physician in his empire should be brought to him. Jurjīs b. Jibrīl, the leading physician in Gondēshāpūr, was recommended, and he at once sent messengers in search of him. From that time these Christian physicians, and particularly the family of the Bukhtīshū', were in firm favour with the ruling princes and in consequence Jibrīl b. Bukhtīshū' remained in the service of Hārūn al-Rashīd for twenty-three years, after which he was successively the physician of al-Amīn and of al-Ma'mūn.

These physicians had free entry into the palace, being consulted constantly by the caliphs on what they should eat or what they should avoid. Many anecdotes are recounted by the historians showing to what extent the caliphs accepted, for the sake of their health, the recommendations, sometimes severe, of their Christian doctors.

The virtual monopoly which the Christians exercised over the medical profession could not fail, after a certain time when the numbers of practitioners had increased, to make life somewhat difficult for non-

Christian physicians. An echo of it is perceptible in a curious anecdote narrated by al-Jāḥiẓ in his 'Book of misers' (*Kitāb al-bukhalā'*). The privileged position of the Christians was not, however, to last indefinitely, and indeed under the powerful influence of the Caliph al-Ma'mūn there was a concentrated attempt to translate scientific and philosophical works inherited from antiquity, which constitutes, from the point of view of the history of thought, one of the most important landmarks in culture.

For the realization of his desires in this field, al Ma'mūn employed a man of genius. Born of a Christian tribe in the neighbourhood of Ḥīra, Ḥunayn b. Isḥāq (d. 260/873) by dint of hard work succeeded in mastering perfectly the four languages of the cultivated world of his age: Arabic, Persian, Greek and Syriac. He also studied medicine under the guidance of the Christian teachers of the day. No one could have been better prepared for the immense work of translation which al-Ma'mūn entrusted to him. After accompanying the mission which was sent to Byzantium in search of good manuscripts, he gathered around him an excellent team of translators, and the task was begun. Ḥunayn's own activity as a translator exceeds imagination. Not only did he translate or revise the works of Plato, Aristotle, Autolycus, Menelaus, Apollonius of Tyana, Alexander of Aphrodisias and Artemidorus, but also the greater part of the three authors who provided the basis of all Greek medical science and who performed the same service for Arab medicine: Hippocrates, Galen and Dioscorides. These works became the reference books of all those who wanted to study medicine, and summaries, commentaries and extracts were made. Enriched by the personal experience of the Arab physicians, they laid the foundations for the great treatises subsequently produced. Ḥunayn, not content with translating a large number of works, also wrote a hundred or so himself, the major part of this output being concerned with medicine. The book which made him famous in the Latin Middle Ages was his *Ars parva Galeni*, also known under the title of *Isagoge Johannitii*.

Those of his books which had the most influence in the Orient were three in number: 'Medical questions,' a general introduction to medicine in the form of questions and answers, which was a favourite method with writers of this period, and two ophthalmological works, 'Ten dissertations on the eye' and 'Questions on the eye.' The 'Ten dissertations' is the most ancient systematic manual of ophthalmology. In the series of ten dissertations, which follow Galen closely, Ḥunayn explains the anatomy of the eye, describes the brain and the optic nerve, examines nosology, aetiology and symptomatology, the diseases of the eye and the properties of useful medicaments. Mention must also be made of the diagrams which accompany the book: they are the first known on the anatomy of the eye, and they are much superior to similar works produced during the Middle Ages in the West.

This intense activity in translation, combined with the application of the principles transmitted by the Greeks, and supplemented by medical traditions derived from Persia and India, was not slow to bear fruit. The art of medicine became more extensive; precious manuscripts were distributed over the vast territories of the Muslim empire and commentaries were made in all the important centres, in Spain, North Africa, Egypt and Syria. Soon there appeared Muslim physicians, who lost no time in attaining the fame of their Christian and Jewish predecessors. Hospitals were built, as was mentioned earlier, and celebrated physicians appointed by the caliphs to direct them. The government even had to supervise the control of medical practice, a function which was exercised under the *ḥisba*. Handbooks of *ḥisba*, drawn up with the object of enabling officials to fulfil their responsibilities conscientiously, contained lists of all the occupations of the time. The medical and para-medical professions had, of course, their special chapters: pharmacists and druggists, perfumers, makers of syrups, veterinary surgeons, phlebotomists and cuppers, finally oculists, surgeons and orthopaedists. These books outlined the questions which should be put to these different experts, and the instruments which they ought to possess.

One of the most eminent physicians, perhaps the greatest clinical doctor of Islam, was without question Abū Bakr al-Rāzī (d. 313/925), the Rhazes of the medieval Latins. Like so many great men, he has become surrounded by legend. It was maintained by some that, when he was attempting to perform certain experiments in alchemy before al-Manṣūr which were not successful, the caliph flew into a passion and hit him on the head, and that as a result of this ill-treatment he lost his sight. Others, however, and especially al-Bīrūnī, who dedicated a short treatise especially to him, declared that it was his own excessive reading which had caused his blindness. Moreover, he did not wish to undergo an operation, and questioned the oculist who proposed to operate on him about the anatomy of the eye, asking him the number of membranes of which it was composed. The answer was not satisfactory and he sent his friend away, adding: 'In any case, I have seen enough of the world and have no desire to see it further.'

In medicine al-Rāzī was the least dogmatic of the Muslim physicians, as is shown by his clinical day-book, which he kept carefully, describing the progress of each malady and the results of treatment. The literary output of al-Rāzī, like that of most of the great authors of the Middle Ages, was enormous and encyclopaedic. The list given by al-Bīrūnī named fifty-six medical treatises, thirty-three dealing with natural sciences, eight on logic, ten on mathematics, seventeen on philosophy, six on metaphysics, fourteen on theology, twenty-two on chemistry, ten on miscellaneous subjects. The three principal medical works will be discussed here; his important work on chemistry will be considered later.

The most famous of the medical works is that which deals with smallpox and measles, known in the medieval Latin translations as *De variolis et morbilis* or sometimes *Liber de pestilentia*. This book is not simply an outline of Hippocrates or of Galen, but is truly original. It is based on al-Rāzī's personal observations, patient and detailed, from which his clinical genius made its deductions, and it is the first treatise in existence on infectious diseases. Al-Rāzī distinguished two kinds, true smallpox and measles, describing them with care and basing their respective diagnoses on signs and symptoms. In examining the course of a disease, al-Rāzī advised paying great attention to heart, pulse, breathing and excrements. He observed that a high temperature helped to bring out the rash, and he enjoined precautions for protecting the eyes, face and mouth and for the avoidance of pockmarks.

The second important book of al-Rāzī is the *Kitāb al-ṭibb al-Manṣūrī*, called in the Latin translations *Liber medicinalis ad al-Mansorem*. It is an encyclopaedia of practical medicine composed of two treatises, derived almost entirely from Greek sources: anatomy, constitution, hygiene, skin diseases, simple medicaments, diet for travellers, surgery, poisons, treatment of various complaints and finally fevers.

Under the title of *Opera parva Abubetri* several minor works of al-Rāzī were printed together with his *al-Manṣūrī*, consisting of: divisions, antidotes, diseases of the joints, children's diseases, aphorisms, prognosis, experimental data, medical observations, diet, the discourses of Hippocrates, who should be a physician, a formulary, prophylactic calculations, cauteries and cuppings, properties, animals.

Finally al-Rāzī's most important work is his celebrated *Kitāb al-ḥāwī fi'l-ṭibb* which in Latin became the *Continens*, that is to say a work containing the whole of medicine.

Before speaking of Ibn Sīnā (Avicenna, d. 429/1037) some mention may be made of medical and pharmacological science in northern Africa and Spain.

A contemporary of al-Rāzī was the Jewish physician, Isḥāq b. Sulaymān al-Isrā'īlī, known to the Latins by the name of Isaac Judaeus. He practised medicine in Qayrawān in Tunisia, and was particularly famous as an oculist. His books on the elements, fevers and on urine were translated into Latin in the Middle Ages by Constantine the African. Another of his works, the 'Physician's guide,' of which the Arabic original is lost, has been preserved in the Hebrew translation. His treatise 'Peculiarities of diet,' printed in Latin at Padua in 1487, is the first printed treatise on dietetics.

The best pupil of Isaac Judaeus was the Muslim, Ibn al-Jazzār, also called Algazirah, a native of Tunisia who died in 1009. His *Zād al-musāfir* was also translated by Constantine the African under the title *Viaticum peregrinantis* and later in Sicily there was a Greek translation with the title *Ephodia*.

In Muslim Spain also there was a ready supply of physicians, pharmacologists and botanists. Under Arab domination numerous useful plants were introduced: date-palms, sugar-cane, rice, cotton, orange trees, etc.; in southern Spain they cultivated a number of medicinal plants which were very successful.

Cordova was pre-eminently the seat of culture and of science, and among the great figures who were illustrious in medicine, three were later than Ibn Sīnā, namely Ibn Zuhr (Avenzoar d. 557/1162), Ibn Rushd (Averroes, d. 595/1198) and Maimonides (d. 601/1204), while Abu'l-Qāsim al-Zahrāwī (Abulcasis d. *c.* 404/1013), was earlier than Ibn Sīnā. He is the leading representative of Arab surgery and his work *al-Taṣrīf* had the same authority in surgery as the *Canon* of Ibn Sīnā had in medicine. The thirtieth dissertation of this work was devoted to surgery; it was produced separately and was the first medical work to contain diagrams of surgical instruments.

The *Taṣrīf* contained three books, the first of which was concerned with cauterization, used generously in Arab medicine since being recommended by the Prophet. Al-Zahrāwī advised it for various surgical disorders, and also for apoplexy, epilepsy and dislocation of the shoulder.

For arterial haemorrhage, he recommended compression with the fingers, followed by cauterization. The second book described operations performed with the scalpel and also ocular and dental surgery, operation for stone, obstetrics, extraction of arrows, etc. It advocated the use of artificial teeth made of bull's bones, and also described methods of treating wounds, and the numerous sutures employed as well as instruments. In conclusion the third book dealt with fractures and dislocations, and mentioned paralysis resulting from fracture of the spine. It also dealt with the gynaecological position known as 'Kalcher's position', with a note on gynaecological dressings.

With Ibn Sīnā, Muslim medicine reached the peak of its achievement. While less of a clinical physician than al-Rāzī, he was more philosophical, more systematic; he tried to rationalize the immense accumulations of medical science which had been inherited from antiquity and enriched by his predecessors. He left behind him a lively autobiography, from which it emerged that he had been a precocious genius, who by the age of sixteen had already mastered the medical science of his time. In spite of a disturbed social and political career, he succeeded in pursuing his studies, writing all the time on his travels, in the evenings after his day's work, and even in prison when the troubled turn of events had brought him there. Since Ibn Sīnā was more of a philosopher than a physician, his biography and his great philosophical work, *al-Shifā'*, which had such a resounding effect on Christian thinkers of the Middle Ages, are discussed in the chapter on Philosophy. Here it will be enough to examine his great medical work, the *Canon of medicine* (*al-Qānūn fi'l-ṭibb*), the Arabic replica in the Middle Ages of the great works of Hippocrates and Galen.

The work consisted of five books, of which the first, *Kitāb al-kulliyāt* (the Latin name being the distorted form *Colliget*), contained generalities of medical science: (1) the elements and fluids, the limbs, muscles, nerves, veins, in a word anatomy; (2) diseases and their causes regarded from a general viewpoint, pulse, digestion; (3) hygiene; (4) general rules for treatment—purges, baths, etc. The second book was devoted to simple medicaments. It was the most complete dissertation of its time, and comprised eight hundred paragraphs describing medicaments of animal, vegetable and mineral origin. The treatises of Galen and of Dioscorides on the subject were systematically reproduced, and a number of new medicaments were included. The third book had as its subject the disorders particularly affecting each limb, both internally and externally. They were classified from head to foot in descending order. The fourth volume dealt with maladies which were not peculiar to any particular members, such as fevers. There was also some discussion of tumours and pustules, poisons, fractured limbs and also of beauty treatment. The fifth and final book was devoted to compounded medicaments—theriacs, electuaries, crushed medicaments, powders and dry drugs, potions, syrups, etc. At the end of this book there was inserted a short fragment on balances and an instrument for measuring taken from Ibn Serapion.

Ibn Sīnā was not satisfied with completing the work of his predecessors: he knew how to supplement it from his own experience. Thus he distinguished between mediastinitis and pleurisy, recognized the contagious nature of tuberculosis, the transmission of epidemics by land and water, and noted that he had tested the efficacy of garlic against snakebite, etc.

The *Canon* of Ibn Sīnā was studied enthusiastically and lavishly annotated over the centuries by Muslim physicians, who also made summaries of it. One of the most celebrated, *al-Mūjaz*, was that of the seventh/thirteenth-century physician Ibn al-Nafīs, a native of Damascus who practised in Cairo, was appointed leading physician in Egypt and died there in 687/1288. In 1924, Dr Tatawi, a young Egyptian doctor at the University of Freiburg, who was working on the unpublished text of the commentary of Ibn al-Nafīs on the anatomy of Ibn Sīnā, demonstrated in his medical thesis that the Damascus physician took the opposite standpoint to that of Galen and Avicenna, and that he had given an almost exact description of the small or pulmonary circulation nearly three centuries before its discovery by Michael Servetus (1556) and Rinaldo Colombo (1559).

Closely connected with the medical sciences, pharmacology became very fashionable among Muslim authors. In addition to the names of physicians given above, it is necessary to mention in this connexion the book, *Kitāb al-saydala fi'l-ṭibb* ('The science of drugs') by al-Bīrūnī (d. 432/1050), and the important work of Ibn al-Bayṭār, a native of Malaga, the vast *Jāmiʿ al-mufradāt* ('Collection of simples').

In the field of pharmacology, Muslim physicians enriched the *materia medica* inherited from Greece. They also added valuable remedies, such as camphor, senna, tamarind, the purgative cassia, myrobalans, nutmeg, ergot, rhubarb, galanga root and a host of other drugs which are now obsolete. It is known, moreover, that it was the Arabs who introduced into the West sugar, lemon and other varieties of citrus fruit, mangoes, jasmine, pepper, etc., and that they prepared numerous colorants, including tannins.

If it were not for the strict limitations of space, it might have been possible to discuss here other branches of Muslim achievement connected with the medical sciences, such as hygiene and dietetics, dentistry, ophthalmology, gynaecology, toxicology, physiognomy, as well as other natural sciences such as zoology (the works of al-Jāḥiẓ, al-Damīrī, and al-Qazwīnī), agriculture (cf. 'Nabataean agriculture' of Ibn Waḥshiyya, the *Kitāb al-filāḥa* of Ibn al-'Awwām), botany, horticulture, the veterinary art, hippiatry, falconry, etc. and to demonstrate the part played by Muslims in each of these sciences. Discussion must, however, be confined to a science which was of considerable importance in the Middle Ages and to which Muslim scholars made a decisive contribution—namely alchemy.

According to the *Fihrist* of Ibn al-Nadīm, the first of the Arabs to concern himself with it was the Umayyad prince, Khālid b. Yazīd, who died in 85/704. Enamoured of science in general, he was particularly interested in alchemy, and, adds Ibn al-Nadīm, it was the first time under Islam that the work of translation was begun.

Khālid must have learned alchemy at Alexandria under the guidance of a certain Marianos, who had himself been the disciple of the Alexandrian alchemist Stephanos. According to the Ottoman historiographer Ḥājjī Khalīfa the most celebrated treatise on alchemy attributed to Khālid was the 'Paradise of wisdom,' composed of 2,315 verses. Contrary to Ruska, who is sceptical concerning this attribution, Holmyard regards it as probable.

With Jābir b. Ḥayyān the ground becomes firmer. Jābir, who was born in about 103/721 at Ṭūs in Persia (whence his by-name of al-Ṭūsī), was also called *al-Ṣūfī*, 'the mystic'. Bereaved of his father, he was sent to Arabia, where he studied the Qur'ān, mathematics and other disciplines, then returned to live at Kūfa. He emerges as a personality after being established as alchemist at the court of Hārūn al-Rashīd, and becoming the personal friend of the sixth Shī'ī *Imām*, Ja'far al-Ṣādiq (d. 148/755) whom he regarded as his master. He also was in favour with the celebrated ministers, the Barmecides, one of whom, Ja'far, brought him into contact with the caliph. For him he wrote 'The book of the flower', describing chemical experiments in an elegant style. He had a laboratory at Kūfa, which was rediscovered two centuries after his death, in the quarter near the Damascus gate. A golden mortar was found there, weighing two and a half pounds. In 188/803, with the collapse of the Barmecides, Jābir fell into disgrace. He returned to Kūfa and spent the rest of his life there. According to some, he may have died at Ṭūs in 200/815, with the manuscript of his 'Book of mercy' under his pillow.

There exists an immense corpus of material connected with Jābir which has been closely studied by Paul Kraus; he has shown that a large part of this corpus was written later (?*c.* 900) by a group of Ismā'īlīs, and it is difficult to distinguish what actually belongs to the master.

Jābir's alchemical theory was based on the Aristotelian theory of matter being composed of earth, water, air and fire, but developed it along different lines. There existed in the first place four elemental qualities or 'natures', heat, cold, aridity and humidity. When these were united with a substance, they formed compounds of the first degree, i.e. the hot, the cold, the dry, the wet. The union of two of these properties give:

hot	+	dry	+	substance	=	fire
hot	+	wet	+	,,	=	air
cold	+	wet	+	,,	=	water
cold	+	dry	+	,,	=	earth

In metals, two of these 'natures' were external and two internal. For example, lead was cold and dry externally, hot and wet internally. Gold was hot and wet externally, cold and dry internally.

The sources of these 'natures' were sulphur and mercury—not ordinary sulphur and mercury, but hypothetical substances of which sulphur and mercury represented the nearest equivalents. Sulphur provided the hot and dry 'natures'; mercury the cold and wet 'natures'. Under the influence of the planets, metals were formed in the heart of the earth by the union of sulphur and sugar. This theory was to become general until the appearance of the phlogiston theory of combustion in the seventeenth century.

When sulphur and mercury were completely pure, and were blended together in perfect balance, they produced the most perfect of all metals, gold. Flaws in the purity and especially in the proportions resulted in the production of other metals: silver, lead, tin, iron, copper. Since the elements were the same, however, it was possible to try to remove this impurity and to regain the equilibrium which was characteristic of gold and silver. This process was achieved by means of elixirs. To avoid considerable loss of time in attempting these experiments, Jābir worked out his 'theory of balance', based on the fact that everything in nature contained weight and dimension: it was a question of establishing not equality of mass or of weight, but an equilibrium of 'natures'. According to Jābir, there existed various elixirs for specific conversions, and also a 'master elixir', capable of effecting all conversions.

Jābir was not merely a theorist, but was above all an excellent practitioner, who gave very clear directions for the preparation of certain products. He divided minerals into three groups: (a) spirits, which became volatile when heated (sulphur, arsenic (realgar), mercury, camphor, sal ammoniac); (b) metals, which were fusible, malleable, resonant, lustrous substances (gold, silver, lead, tin, copper, iron and *kharsini*); and finally (c) non-malleable substances, which could be reduced to powder, subdivided into eight groups.

Jābir left some interesting observations. In his *Kitāb ṣundūq al-ḥikma* ('Chest of wisdom') he mentioned nitric acid. Elsewhere he pointed out that copper coloured flame green; he indicated methods of producing steel, of refining other metals, of dyeing clothes and leather, manufacturing a varnish which made clothing waterproof, keeping iron free from rust, dyeing cloth with alum, and of making phosphorescent ink from gilded marcasite instead of from gold, which was too costly. He referred to the use of manganese dioxide in the manufacture of glass, and knew how to concentrate acetic acid in distilling vinegar. In some of his works he gave an exact description of processes such as calcination, crystallization, solution, sublimation and reduction.

With al-Rāzī, who has already been discussed in relation to the medical sciences, alchemy was to take on a more scientific aspect and the descriptions of apparatus and experiments were to be more precise. Like Jābir he accepted the four elements as being at the base of all substances, but did not accept his complicated theory of the 'balance'. For him the object of alchemy was twofold: it taught on the one hand how to transform non-precious metals into silver or gold, on the other hand how to convert quartz or even ordinary glass into precious stones, emeralds, sapphires, rubies, etc. by means of the appropriate elixir. It is remarkable that al-Rāzī never called these elixirs 'the philosopher's stone', but he accepted the theory of Jābir that metals were composed of sulphur and mercury, sometimes adding to them a third element of a saline nature.

The interest of al-Rāzī, however, lies particularly in his practical chemistry. His *Sirr al-asrār* (*Secretum secretorum*) gave for the first time a lucid classification of chemical substances, and he preferred the positive work of the laboratory to unfounded theoretical lucubration. His descriptions of apparatus make it probable that his laboratory was well equipped, since he mentions (1) instruments used for melting substances: fireplace, bellows, crucible, the *botus barbatus* of the medieval chemists, ladle, tongs, scissors, hammer, file; (2) instruments for the preparation of drugs: cucurbit and alembic with evacuation tube, 'blind' alembic (without evacuation tube), receiving mattress, aludel, beakers, flasks, flasks of rose-water, cauldron, pots with covers glazed on the inside, water-bath and sand-bath, furnace, small cylindrical stove for heating the aludel, funnels, sieves, filters, etc.

With regard to chemical processes, al-Rāzī mentions distillation, calcination, solution, evaporation, crystallization, sublimation, filtration, amalgamation, ceration (this last process being the conversion of a substance into a doughy mass or into a fusible solid).

Finally al-Rāzī gives a systematic classification of the products of the three realms of nature employed in alchemy, which really belongs to true chemistry. Thus, for example, mineral substances are divided into six groups: (1) spirits (mercury, sal ammoniac, sulphur of arsenic [orpiment and realgar], sulphur); (2) substances (gold, silver, copper, iron, lead, tin, *kharsini*); (3) stones (pyrites, iron oxide, zinc oxide, azurite, malachite, turquoise, haematite, oxide of arsenic, lead sulphur, mica and asbestos, gypsum, glass); (4) vitriols: (black, alums, white, green, yellow, red); (5) boraxes; (6) salts.

To the 'natural' substances mentioned above, al-Rāzī adds a certain number of substances which are obtained artificially: litharge, oxide of lead, verdigris, oxide of copper, oxide of zinc, cinnabar, caustic soda, polysulphurs of calcium, various alloys.

His great merit was that he rejected magical and astrological practices, while adhering to what could be proved by experiment. Al-Rāzī's insistence on promoting research work in the laboratory did not fail to bear fruit in pharmacology, and Abu'l-Manṣūr Muwaffaq, a Persian of the fourth/tenth century, mentions chemical details about certain medicaments which show real progress in this field. Facts observed with so much care demonstrate, as Holmyard says, 'that a by-product of alchemy was a steadily increasing body of reliable chemical knowledge, a trend which Razi did most to establish and for which he deserves the gratitude of succeeding generations.'

To make a study of the sciences in Islam reasonably complete, it would be necessary to be able to discuss their application to the various techniques in arts and crafts as well as in industry: textiles, cloth, carpets, dyeing, enamels, ceramics, manufacture of various kinds of paper, perfumes, preparation of leather, tempering of steel, extraction of metals, jewellery, embossing, etc.—fields in which the ingenuity of the craftsman profits from the experiments and discoveries of the scientist. The present survey, however, must be terminated here.

In it an attempt has been made to throw into relief the magnificent scientific achievements which distinguished the Muslim Middle Ages but which virtually ceased in the ninth/fifteenth century, and in conclusion it is necessary to face the questions: what were the reasons for what George Sarton was pleased to call 'the Arab miracle', and what were the reasons for its decline? It is indeed a very complex problem, which it is neither easy nor wise to try to dispose of in a few words.

One thing which can be stated with certainty, apparently, is that in the first place questions of race or nationality do not play an essential part. Indeed the emergence has been witnessed, in Baghdād, Cairo, Cordova and Samarqand, of the Persian and the Arab, the Turk and the Andalusian, the Berber and the Sabaean. There appears to be a constant supply of cultural entities, independent of race or nationality, which develop or decline and die according to whether they find a soil which is favourable to them or an environment which destroys them.

Secondly, Islam, of itself, did not offer any kind of opposition to scientific research, in fact quite the contrary. Reference was made at the outset to the stimulus provided by the Qur'ān since God was glorified by wonder at His creation. So long as the interpretation of religious data remains broad enough to enable different theological and philosophical doctrines to confront each other in complete freedom, and, so to speak, on terms of equality, the scientist is living under conditions which are favourable for bringing his researches to a successful conclusion, and for expounding his hypotheses. When the time comes, however, for the triumph of a narrow and defensive theology, which, in the name of official orthodoxy, puts fetters on free research, persecutes the scientists and confines them, then science is not slow to disappear.

In the Middle Ages, Muslim scientists were indisputably at the peak of their progress, scientific curiosity and research. In order to do full justice to the importance of their work, contemporary Western scientists must put into their historical context those who were, in former times, the teachers of their ancestors. In recent years, on the other hand, the movement of the *Nahḍa*, of the Arab renaissance in the Middle East from the middle of the nineteenth century, and, more generally, the awakening of *élites* in all the Muslim countries, has not failed to produce achievements in the scientific field. Modern universities and research institutes have been founded in the great capitals of the Islamic world. There can be nothing but rejoicing at a revival which thus links the present with the glorious past.

CHAPTER II

PHILOSOPHY

Islamic philosophic thought presents a rather greater diversity than medieval Christian philosophy, and the range of the differences of opinion is perhaps wider. For the purposes of the present survey, a division into two main classes may conveniently be adopted. One of these classes comprises the *falāsifa* (this Arabic word for philosophers being used as a technical term) and philosophical theologians whose scheme of reference is provided—whether they acknowledge this fact or not—by the Aristotelian, the Platonic or the neo-Platonic systems of thought. The second main class will comprise the *mutakallimūn* and various other thinkers whose opinions are related to theirs or derived from them. Some of these thinkers profess to be hostile to *kalām*. In contradistinction to the philosophers and the philosophical theologians, the *mutakallimūn* and the other thinkers belonging to this class do not as a rule use the concepts of the Aristotelian, Platonic or neo-Platonic systems as their scheme of reference, though in many cases an influence of these dominant currents of antique philosophy as well as other Greek schools of thought may be discerned. The sociologist and historian Ibn Khaldūn does not belong to either of these two classes. The Ismāʿīlī theologians constitute a border case.

FIRST PERIOD: LATER SECOND/EIGHTH TO EARLY FOURTH/TENTH CENTURY

(a) *The translators and the* Falāsifa

The fact that the Arab invasion did not wholly destroy in the conquered countries the continuity of the administrative and economic life has often been remarked upon. Early Islam took over in a certain measure the social fabric of the provinces which were incorporated in the caliphate. It did not seek to operate in a vacuum. A similar explanation might be adduced to account for the adoption of Greek science and philosophy in Islam, and the case for it could be strengthened by a reference to the fact that the Islamic empire included one of the main centres of Greek philosophical and scientific tradition, namely Egypt, and strongly hellenized regions such as Syria. Nevertheless this explanation does not constitute more than a half-truth. For the development of philosophy in Islam, centred at the beginning in provinces which before the Arab conquest belonged either to the Syrian or the Iranian cultural domain, differs considerably in degree and in kind from the philosophical activities which existed in these regions before the rise of Islam.

One of the most noteworthy examples of the cultural continuity which this explanation presupposes is provided by the history of the so-called Alexandrian academy. According to information which may be substantially correct, this institution of Greek philosophical and scientific learning was transferred some time after the beginning of the Islamic era to Antioch, where it was active for a considerable period. Finally, however, the academy dwindled away, and only one professor was left. Its two students left Antioch and in their turn engaged in teaching. In the second half of the third/ninth century, the great Muslim philosopher al-Fārābī, from whom this information derives, received part of his philosophical training from a pupil of one of these two scholars, while the somewhat older Abū Bishr Mattā b. Yūnus, an outstanding Christian translator and commentator of Greek texts, studied in Baghdād with another pupil of the same scholar.

This story admirably illustrates how a small group which, in spite of various political and religious transformations and a change of the linguistic *milieu*, succeeded in maintaining itself for many generations, was able to transmit a knowledge of Greek philosophy to certain select individuals. In a similar way Ibn Sīnā (Avicenna) of Bukhārā got a first notion of philosophy from the teaching of al-Nātilī, a philosopher who took up his abode in the remote far east of the Muslim empire, where Ibn Sīnā grew up.

However, the story of Islamic philosophy is by no means only that of the contacts of isolated individuals; it has also a social and political aspect, which in its beginnings is made evident in the activity of the translators, sponsored and maintained by the caliphs and numerous other powerful and rich patrons, the pillars of society. It was with their help and protection that the great and sustained work of a number of schools of translators was accomplished. Most of the translations, though not all of them, were carried out within a period of roughly two hundred years, ranging from the first half of the third/ninth to the first half of the fifth/eleventh century. In that space of time Arabic versions of a very considerable part of the Greek philosophical and scientific literature were provided. All the principal works of Aristotle were translated (with the possible exception of his *Politics* or of a part of that work) and also many of his less important treatises as well as numerous Greek commentaries on Aristotle, some of which have not come down to us in the original. Arabic translations were also made of paraphrases of many of Plato's dialogues (and perhaps also of the complete text of some dialogues), and of various texts of Plotinus, or deriving from him (these texts being generally attributed by the Arabs to other authors). A sizeable portion of Proclus's writings and certain other neo-Platonic texts were also made known to the Arab intellectuals. In the same period a considerable portion of Greek scientific literature, including mathematical, astronomical, astrological, medical, alchemical and technological texts not preserved in the original, was also translated. On the other hand, Greek poetry and *belles lettres* remained virtually unknown and an object of indifference to the Muslim *élite*, who were keenly interested in the translations referred to above.

In fact the Arabic translations seem to represent the earliest large-scale attempt known in history[1] to take over from an alien civilization its sciences and techniques regarded as universally valid, while other manifestations of that civilization, which were supposed to lack this kind of validity, were more or less neglected. The contrast which this attitude presents to the reception of Greek culture, including the arts in their religious contexts, by the Roman *élite* is instructive, but the point cannot be elaborated here. The fact that philosophy and the sciences, in the form in which they were taken over and developed by the Muslims, had generally speaking no special tie to any particular religion, facilitated their acceptance in Christian Western Europe.

It may be added that the translators created in a remarkably short time a serviceable philosophical vocabulary which was previously totally lacking in Arabic. This vocabulary was enriched and made more accurate, but not essentially altered, by the philosophers who used the translations. This philosophical terminology is to a considerable extent modelled upon the Syriac. There are some Greek loan-words, for which generally an Arabic equivalent is available. A few Persian words, for instance *jawhar*, substance, have also been adopted in the philosophical vocabulary in the strict sense of the term. Words of Persian origin form a a considerable part of the nomenclature of the sciences.

[1] There have been many since, among them that made by the Christian medieval scholars when they became acquainted with the Arabic translations from the Greek.

What was the impulse at work in the translations? As it has already been suggested, they may have continued cultural processes which can be discerned already before the rise of Islam in the countries in which the translations were carried on. Under the auspices of certain monasteries, Greek philosophical and scientific works were being translated into Syriac long before the Arab conquest. Many of the translators who were employed in the incomparably more numerous translations undertaken in the Muslim period were Syriac-speaking Christians, who used in the novel task the traditional technique worked out in turning Greek texts into their native language which, being Semitic, has a certain affinity with Arabic. In fact, these specialists sometimes seem to have found it easier to provide, as a first stage, a Syriac version of a Greek text, and then to translate this version into Arabic, than to attempt a direct translation from Greek to Arabic. This technique seems to have been widely practised in the school of Ḥunayn b. Isḥāq, a Syriac-speaking Christian, who was perhaps the most celebrated of the translators. However, the pre-Islamic monastic Syriac translations appear to have been undertaken mainly to integrate for apologetic purposes certain parts of philosophy, and perhaps also of the sciences, into a syllabus dominated by theology. In fact great prudence was exercised in this integration; for instance, certain portions of Aristotelian logic were judged dangerous to faith, and banned.

In Islam the story is quite different. The translations, which for many successive generations were brought in an unceasing flow to the knowledge of a not inconsiderable public of intellectuals, were clearly not undertaken or patronized for the benefit of Islamic apologetics. Nor were they carried out under the auspices of a traditionalist hierarchy of Sunnī Islam. By contrast, during a long period, zealous religious dignitaries in the main cultural centres had no power to interfere with a relatively free circulation of this dangerous knowledge. Thus, while a certain continuity exists between the Syriac translations carried out under ecclesiastical auspices and the Arabic ones, the impulse behind the latter is quite different. It appears to have been of a purely secular nature.

In this respect a certain analogy may exist between the university of Gondēshāpūr founded in Sasanid Persia and the House of Wisdom (*Bayt al-ḥikma*), the central institute for translations set up by the 'Abbasid Caliph al-Ma'mūn. It is not beyond the bounds of possibility that the latter sought to revive the cultural tradition of pre-Islamic Persia.[1] In the present context, however, it may be more significant to note that—as far as our very incomplete information goes—both the professors of the university of Gondēshāpūr and the early Arabic translators were concerned with the propagation of the practically useful sciences at least as much as, and perhaps more than, with the diffusion of purely theoretical knowledge. Not only Greek philosophy, in Syriac and perhaps also Pahlavī translations, but also Greek (possibly also Indian) medicine seems to have been taught as a main subject at Gondēshāpūr.

It is also certain that treatises dealing with the three practical sciences, astrology, alchemy and medicine constitute a very considerable part of the early Arabic translations.[2] It may accordingly be presumed that the hope to enjoy the advantage of a knowledge of the future, or to possess unlimited wealth and the power over man and nature promised by the alchemists, as well as the wish for scientific medical care, may have been a prime factor in the patronage accorded to the Greek sciences. On this view the reception of the theoretical sciences was favoured because of their close connexion with the practical disciplines.[3] In point of fact, very few Islamic philosophers had any use for alchemy, and belief in astrology was prevalent among those thinkers who may be said to belong to the main stream of philosophical thought only in the first period, i.e. during the third/ninth century. Virtually all philosophers, however, as distinct from the *mutakallimūn*, up to the end of the sixth/twelfth century, and perhaps even later, were practising physicians. Medicine was regarded as a characteristic way in which philosophers earned their living.

This phenomenon and this conception (which is foreign to Christian medieval Europe and also generally speaking to classical antiquity) may be explained by the lack of universities or other officially recognized institutions in which philosophy was studied. Al-Ma'mūn's House of

[1] For that matter, it is not impossible that he may have wished to found an institution rivalling the imperial university of Constantinople or some other Byzantine seat of learning. Some evidence points this way.

[2] Arabic translations of treatises on astrology and medicine were made already before al-Ma'mūn's reign. There is also some, perhaps not quite reliable, evidence that treatises on alchemy had been translated or adapted into Arabic already in the Umayyad period.

[3] Al-Bīrūnī practised astrology, but seems inclined to regard it as largely a pseudo-science. He suggests that it was invented as a protective device by the theoretical astronomers, who wished to be allowed to devote themselves in peace to the pursuit of their science, which was abhorrent to the common run of men. The latter could be brought to accept this theoretical avocation only because of their interest in astrology, which is bound up with scientific astronomy.

Wisdom was not a durable institution, and the religious universities which were founded at certain periods taught as a rule, as far as Sunnī Islam is concerned, the theology of whatever *kalām* school was favoured by the government, and were interested in philosophy only as an object of polemics.

Owing to the absence of such institutions as the ecclesiastically controlled universities of Christian Western Europe, which integrated Greek philosophy into the doctrine approved by the Catholic hierarchy, and ensured its continued study (but required the philosophers to conform to theological doctrine), the philosopher *qua* philosopher had no recognized social function. The hallmark of respectability which he often had was due not to his being a university professor teaching philosophy, but to his practising medicine or some similar avocation. The fact that philosophers as such did not belong to an ecclesiastical or governmental establishment had, of course, from their point of view an advantage. For a long time they could, with some equivocation, escape from tailoring their thoughts to the requirements of a dominant theology. On the other hand, the ambiguity of the position of the philosophers in society may have exacerbated for some of them the preoccupation with the problem of the true political and social function of the philosopher, and of the duties incumbent on him in this field of action, if circumstances permit. This is the main topic of philosophical discussion from the time of al-Fārābī in the first half of the fourth/tenth century till the end of the sixth/twelfth. We have no evidence indicating that this problem engaged the attention of al-Kindī, the main philosophical author of the first period of Islamic thought.

Abū Yūsuf Ya'qūb al-Kindī, a philosopher and author of pure Arab origin, who died probably some years after the middle of the ninth Christian century,[1] was a rich patron of the translators, and sometimes revised their work. As a philosophical author, he is first and foremost a product of the intellectual climate which their activity had created. He is often described as the first Islamic philosopher, and this designation has some justification, provided that it is not understood to mean that he was an original thinker. No such claim can be made for him, if we may judge by his extant treatises, although it is true that they form a very small part of his immense literary output. As far as Greek learning is concerned, his foremost function seems to have consisted in expound-

[1] The exact date is unknown but surmises have been made on the basis of indirect evidence.

ing or adapting texts which the translators had rendered accessible to the Arabic reading public.

As his treatises show, he had a good grasp of the various physical doctrines of Aristotle, and of the concept of mechanical causality on which some of them are based. On the other hand, a probably authentic treatise attributed to him, which as far as is known is extant only in a Latin translation, sets forth a theory of universal radiation, which is foreign to the Greek philosophy. In a treatise on the soul purporting to give the opinion of Plato, Aristotle and other ancient philosophers, he asserts that the soul is immortal, that it is a substance deriving from the substance of the Creator, and, when separated from the body and purged of the latter's dross, omniscient. God as conceived by al-Kindī is principally described by negatives, but his is a moderate form of negative theology. Contrary to what has been sometimes asserted, there is no clear evidence for a strong influence of Muʿtazilite *kalām* on al-Kindī, though his method of interpreting the Qurʾān has some resemblance to that of the Muʿtazila. It is true that he speaks of one God who created the world out of nothing, but this was not only a religious, but also a philosophical doctrine. It was professed by late Greek neo-Platonists, who were mostly Christians. He attributes to the prophets an intuitive immediate knowledge, which contrasts with the knowledge of other men which is acquired step by step. This view, which is also held by later philosophers such as Ibn Sīnā, is by no means characteristic of the Muʿtazila, who generally tend to minimize the difference between the Prophet and other men.

Al-Kindī, who was the author of numerous medical works, seems to have rejected alchemy, but believed in astrology, and composed a certain number of writings dealing with questions pertaining to this science. It is worth noting that one of these treatises deals with a politically explosive subject: it purports to determine by astrological methods the duration of Islamic rule, which at a certain time will come to an end. Obviously al-Kindī did not apply to the claims of astrology the kind of critique which led to the rejection of that science by later Islamic Aristotelians. His largely uncritical acceptance of the heritage of antique civilization that was known to him appears to have led him to see in a favourable light the religion of the *Ṣābiʾa* (Sabians). This was a designation of a baptizing sect named in the Qurʾān as one of the three protected religions together with Judaism and Christianity. It came to be applied to a Syriac-speaking pagan community which survived in

Ḥarrān and practised a cult which is reported to have been impregnated with philosophical elements. It is at all events certain that this community included a number of persons acquainted with Greek philosophy. One of its leaders, Thābit b. Qurra, who belongs to the generation after al-Kindī, was a distinguished philosopher and translator of Greek texts. Finally *Ṣābi'a* became a blanket designation for pagan religion, which in Christian polemics was regarded as a single entity including all the various cults, and was called *Hellenismos*. The term 'Sabian religion' was used as an equivalent of the religion of the Hellenes, and had an even wider extension, being applied for instance to Buddhism. For evident reasons it was, however, often associated with the Greek philosophers; at least in one Arabic text it is said to be the religion they professed. It is perhaps on these grounds that al-Kindī in a survey of Sabian beliefs and customs (preserved in a work of his pupil Aḥmad b. Ṭayyib al-Sarakhsī, of which an extract has come down to us) gives an account of the fundamental dogmas, which was clearly calculated to dispel Muslim suspicions; the Sabian dogmas being shown to be virtually identical with the Muslim ones.

Al-Kindī influenced in the course of the third/ninth and fourth/tenth centuries certain Muslim and Jewish writers of compilations, such as the authors of the encyclopedia of the *Ikhwān al-Ṣafā* and Isaac Judaeus. As far as I can see, no strong influence of his can be discerned in the writings of al-Fārābī, who started a new philosophical tradition.

In conclusion of this account of the first period of Islamic *Falsafa*, a brief reference may be made to the Sabian ,Thābit b. Qurra, who appears to have had epistolary relations with al-Sarakhsī. In his philosophical writings, composed in Arabic, he affirmed in opposition to Aristotle the existence of an actual infinite. He also wrote in Syriac a work in which he extolled the cultural achievement of paganism.

(b) *The* Mutakallimūn

The various theological doctrines and schools of thought to which the general appellation *kalām* (literally: speech) is applied developed in close connexion with other manifestations of Islamic civilization. The early attempts to meditate upon and to understand the theological meaning implicit in the text of the Qur'ān and to discover the correct Islamic solution for such problems as the relation between God's decree and human actions certainly contributed to the formation of the *kalām* as well as to the origination of Ṣūfī mysticism, which in its inchoate period did not manifest the sharp antagonism to the *kalām* theology which later on often characterized it. Indeed it may be argued, with a certain show of reason, that the Mu'tazilite *kalām* and a dominant Ṣūfī tradition stem from the same school, that of Ḥasan al-Baṣrī (d. 110/728). There is also a close relation between *kalām* in its early period and the Muslim legal science (*fiqh*). To quote but one example, it is more than probable that the Mu'tazilite conception of the role of reason owes a great deal to parallel notions expounded by certain jurists. The impact of various political positions and options on the origin and evolution of the different schools is even more evident.

However, since Islamic civilization, even before its full exposure to the influence of Greek philosophy and science, was by no means self-contained, *kalām* cannot be understood without an inquiry into the relations of its exponents with other religions and theologies, and into the possibly non-Islamic origins of some tenets of its main schools. It is certain that *kalām* is greatly indebted to Christian theology, both because some concepts were taken over from the latter, and because the polemics against the Christians helped to crystallize Islamic theology. Islamic apologetic literature directed against the Manicheans, or perhaps in certain cases against the Zoroastrians, played an analogous, though probably a less important role.

The first beginnings of *kalām* in the proper sense of the word go back at the latest to the end of the Umayyad period, i.e. the first part of the second/eighth century; that being the time when the Mu'tazilite and a great number of other sects appear as separate entities. There are no *kalām* texts dating from this period. Later Mu'tazilite texts however and the accounts of Islamic heresiographers, some of whom are reliable, enable us to have a fair idea of the common doctrines of this sect, and of the formulations of, and variations upon, these doctrines found in the teachings of such outstanding ninth-century Mu'tazilite theologians as Abu'l-Hudhayl 'Allāf (d. 226/841 or 235/849), Ibrāhīm al-Naẓẓām (d. between 220–30/835–45), al-Mu'ammar and others, some of whom seem to have propounded coherent systems of thought.

Wāṣil b. 'Atā' and 'Amr b. 'Ubayd, who, according to tradition, founded the Mu'tazila in the second/eighth century are much more shadowy figures, and so are the founders and chiefs of other early *kalām* sects or schools, such as Jahm b. Ṣafwān, al-Najjār and many others. Seen in historical perspective, the importance of these sects is incomparably less than that of the Muʿtazila; but their members played a certain part in the lively controversies which are characteristic of the history of *kalām* in the third/ninth century and probably also earlier, and which continue in a changed theological atmosphere in the fourth/tenth century.

None of the incipient *kalām* sects of the Umayyad period seems to have whole-heartedly accepted the dynasty and the régime. Their attitudes seem to have greatly varied, running the whole gamut from the toleration shown by the Murji'a, to active hostility. The Muʿtazila do not form an exception to this rule. Indeed it has been maintained that the Muʿtazila contributed to the success of the ʿAbbasid insurrection.[1] However that may be, the accession of the ʿAbbasids ushered in what was perhaps the intellectually most lively and most uninhibited period in the history of *kalām*. Moreover, the Muʿtazilite doctrine was declared by al-Ma'mūn to be the official theology of the caliphate. Al-Ma'mūn's immediate successors followed suit. It was not until approximately 235/849 that al-Mutawakkil reversed this policy, putting an end to the privileged position of the Muʿtazilite theologians and taking various measures against them. As the heresiographer al-Shahrastānī puts it: 'As for the splendour of *kalām*, it begins with the ʿAbbasid Caliphs Hārūn al-Rashīd, al-Ma'mūn, al-Muʿtaṣim, al-Wāthiq and al-Mutawakkil.'[2] In this sentence al-Shahrastānī seem to equate—perhaps justifiably, as far as the early period is concerned—*kalām* with Muʿtazilism. The latter's preponderance among the *kalām* schools was jeopardized only with the rise of the Ashʿariyya in the fourth/tenth century.

[1] The appellation Muʿtazila has been interpreted as meaning those who do not take sides either for the Caliph ʿAlī or for his adverseries. Nyberg argues that this attitude of the Muʿtazila facilitated their adoption of the ʿAbbasid claims, to which, as he thinks, they gave whole-hearted support. It may be noted that Abū Muslim, the military leader of the ʿAbbasid insurrection, seems to have used men known as *mutakallimūn* as some kind of field-preachers or missionaries. An anonymous Arabic historian, whose work contains abundant and apparently reliable information on the ʿAbbasid revolt states: '[Abū Muslim] ordered the *mutakallimūn* among his partisans to go to Merv to spread information about their opinions (*amrahum*: literally "method") and to describe their position (*mā hum ʿalayhi*), in so far as it consists in following the religious tradition (*al-sunna*) and in doing what is right (*al-ʿamal bi' l-ḥaqq*).' (*Nubdha min kitāb al-ta'rīkh li'l-mu'allif al-majhūl min al-qarn al-ḥādī ʿashar*, ed P. A. Griaznevich (Moscow, 1960), 269b of the Arabic facsimile, 110 of the Russian translation) No further particulars are given about the *mutakallimūn* in question, but the passage rather suggests that, *mutatis mutandis*, they played in Abū Muslim's insurrection, which had a religious side to it, an analogous role to that played later by the missionaries (*duʿāt*) of another revolutionary movement, that of the Ismāʿīlīs. It is at least arguable that the *mutakallimūn* referred to in this passage may have been some sort of proto-Muʿtazila, or at least close to the sect.

[2] *Kitāb al-milal wa'l-niḥal* (Cairo, 1948), I, 39.

As we have seen, al-Ma'mūn favoured both Greek philosophy and the Mu'tazilite *kalām*. It may be maintained that there is a certain affinity between the two schools of thought; for both accord a preeminent value to reason or to the intellect (both English terms being possible translations of the Arabic word *'aql*). And to a certain limited extent, this contention may be justified. However, the Mu'tazilite conception of reason is very different from that of the Aristotelian philosophers. One aspect of this difference may become clear if one considers the doctrines involved in the principle of justice (*'adl*). This is one of the five main principles (with two of which we shall be concerned here) which were used by the Mu'tazila with a view to a classification of their theological teachings.

Dealing with problems related to this principle, the Mu'tazila assert that it is a primary function of reason to distinguish between good and evil, justice and injustice; these being in their opinion objectively existing qualities inherent in actions. The discernment of what is right and wrong can claim the same degree of universal validity as the perception of a colour. Regarded from the point of view of the Islamic Aristotelians, this doctrine would seem to imply a thesis wholly unacceptable to them, namely that practical reason has the same kind of truth-content, the same universal validity and the same dignity as theoretical reason. The Mu'tazilite view has some affinity with the Stoic idea of natural law and with the cognate Christian conceptions, and may in the last analysis derive from the one or from the other, or from both. But it is very different from either, one reason being that the Mu'tazilites could not have used the expression 'natural law', as it seems to imply the existence of a stable cosmic order, which they denied.

Furthermore certain particularities of their conception may have also been due to the fact that they flouted the popular Muslim idea of the omnipotence of God. To some extent this position was determined by the Mu'tazilite belief that good and evil were independent of God's will, and that human actions could be judged to be right or wrong without any reference to the divine commandments. This doctrine concerning the objective existence of the quality of goodness led them to the belief that God has the same kind of knowledge as men with regard to the distinction between good and evil. As a corollary, He could not be supposed to do evil; all His actions being *sub ratione boni*, which means that a restriction was imposed on His freedom of action. As far as God's dealings with men and, even according to certain theologians, with brute animals are concerned, this means that all suffering is either merited, being a punishment for a transgression, or must entail for the innocent victim a compensation in the other world. All good actions must be rewarded; God cannot act otherwise. This view can of course be derived from Jewish and Christian conceptions, and perhaps also in part from the Qur'ān, but there exists in addition the possibility that the central position held by it in the Mu'tazilite doctrine may be partly due to the necessity of combating Manichean and Zoroastrian dualistic conceptions, which maintain that, in view of the prevalence of evil in the world, an omnipotent God cannot be considered as just.

The fact that men (i.e. as it would appear, all men of sound mind) are held by the Mu'tazilites to have a spontaneous and immediate knowledge of what is good implies that, at least in this important respect, there are no essential differences between human beings. This egalitarian tendency of the Mu'tazilites is clearly opposed to the Shī'ī conception of a strict hierarchy, with, at the top, the prophets and *imāms*. In point of fact the Mu'tazilites are, as has already been stated, generally inclined to reduce to a minimum the differences between the prophets and ordinary people; the former and the latter having one supremely important thing in common; namely the fact that both are endowed with reason. The radicalization of the Mu'tazilite doctrine by such heretics as Ibn al-Rāwandī sets in at this point.

The principle of unification (*tawḥīd*) was as characteristic of the Mu'tazila as the principle of justice. They were currently designated as 'the people of justice and of unification' (*ahl al-'adl wa'l-tawḥīd*). The unification which is referred to is that of God. The principle in question appears to be concerned both with the relation of God to the world, and with God considered in Himself. According to the Mu'tazilite view, which was adopted also by their adversaries the Ash'arites, the existence of God is not, as far as man is concerned, an object of immediate and evident knowledge. It has to be deduced from a consideration of the world, which, being obviously created in time, calls for the conclusion that an eternal Creator must exist. It can also be proved that there is only one Creator. The Mu'tazilites contended that the unity of God would be impaired if there existed divine attributes superadded to God's essence. They accordingly maintained—using various formulations—that such attributes as God's will, God's wisdom and so on are identical with the divine essence. This thesis, the adoption of which may have been facilitated by polemics against the Christian dogma of the

Trinity, was one of the points which provoked the most vehement attacks against the Mu'tazilites on the part of the Ash'arites and others. The Mu'tazilite belief that the Qur'ān was created in time likewise pertains to the principle of unification. This belief too caused them to be stigmatized as heretics.

Most of the Mu'tazila were atomists.[1] This meant that they rejected the Aristotelian idea of an orderly cosmos, and believed in a world which called for incessant direct intervention on the part of God. They posited the existence of indivisible corporeal atoms, a minimum number of which was needed to form a body, of atoms of time and space, of atoms of motion and of atoms of the various categories of accidents, such as of colour. According to them there were atoms of life, and even atoms of belief. In motion a corporeal atom passed in an atom of time from one atom of space to another; the differences in the speed of various motions were due to the lesser or greater number of atoms of rest which were interspersed in the atoms of motion. It is a discontinuous universe and an impermanent one. After having taught that the duration of the existence of the atoms of accidents did not exceed one atom of time, and that at every instant God created new atoms of accidents to replace those which had existed in the instant which had just come to an end, the Mu'tazilites in a later phase of the doctrine extended this conception to the corporeal atom. With every atom of time the world was created anew.

They were consistent in denying as a general rule causality, which appears to be hardly admissible in a discontinuous universe. Using an argumentation which bears a certain resemblance to Hume's, they denied that a causal relation may be proved from the fact that one phenomenon usually follows upon another. Cotton put close to fire generally burns. But this should be regarded merely as a habit. It does not mean that it pertains to the nature of fire to produce this effect. They did not extend this theory to human actions, which, according to them, had within certain limits a causal effect. A man who throws a stone and kills another man was in their opinion the cause of the death. In this case the Mu'tazilite principle of divine justice prevails over the doctrine of discontinuity. This principle posits on one hand that murder is punished by God, and on the other, that such punishment would be unjust if the murderer were not the cause of the victim's death. Thus

[1] The one great exception is Ibrāhīm al-Naẓẓām who believed, like Anaxagoras and the Stoics, that bodies resulted from a total mixture of infinitely small particles of various substances. Al-Naẓẓām's physical theories may have been influenced by the Manicheans.

the principle of justice made it necessary to attribute to man a certain freedom and independent power of action. Owing to their atomism not being consistent the whole way through, God was not the sole agent. Because of the ascription to man of God's prerogative of action, a saying attributed to Muḥammad charges the Muʿtazila with being the Magians (i.e. the dualists) of Islam. It is by no means impossible that the disputations with the Iranian dualists may have contributed to the crystallization of this Muʿtazilite doctrine. On the other hand, the possibility of a Christian influence should also be taken into account. The Oriental Christians with whom the Muslims came into contact appear to have believed in man's freedom of action.

The question of the origin of *kalām* atomism is even harder to answer. The Muʿtazilite theory is very different from all the Greek atomistic doctrines known to us. However, our information as to these doctrines is incomplete. The possibility of one of them bearing a greater resemblance than now seems likely to the *kalām* conception cannot be entirely ruled out. It also seems clear that the *mutakallimūn* are indebted to the Greek atomists for at least some of their views. There exists on the other hand an undeniable similarity between various important points of the *kalām* doctrine and the Indian (Nyāya-Vaishēshika and Buddhist) atomistic doctrines. It is not beyond the bounds of possibility that the *mutakallimūn* may have adopted some Indian concepts, which may have been transmitted to them directly from Indian sources, or through some Iranian intermediary.

The *mutakallimūn*, apparently including the Muʿtazila, were accused by the philosophers from al-Fārābī onwards of putting the power of ratiocination, such as it was, at the service of religion; they were supposed to be wholly indifferent to truth, being exclusively concerned with apologetics. This charge may have been true in some measure with regard to many *mutakallimūn*, both Ashʿarites and Muʿtazilites, posterior to al-Fārābī; but it seems a gross misrepresentation, not only of numerous earlier Muʿtazilites, but also of the fourth/tenth century doctors of the sect, al-Jubbā'ī and his son Abū Hāshim, who certainly had genuine theoretical interests not connected with religion. In fact, from the religious point of view, reason as conceived by the Muʿtazila (however superficial it might, rightly or wrongly, appear to the Aristotelian) was a two-edged weapon. It was sometimes used with telling effect against Islam. The most famous case is that of a renegade Muʿtazilite, Ibn al-Rāwandī, who probably died around 250/864.

In a lost work, known only from quotations, Ibn al-Rāwandī put into the mouth of mythical Brahmans, whom he chose to be his spokesmen, arguments in all likelihood suggested by the Mu'tazilite position, which sets up reason as a judge of religion, and distinguishes between the rational and non-rational religious commandments. According to Ibn al-Rāwandī's Brahmans, God, who is assumed to be wise, cannot be supposed to have imposed upon man obligations not legitimated by reason. What the prophets say is either in accordance with reason, in which case no prophets are needed (the common run of men being endowed with the power of reasoning), or it does not conform to reason; in that case it has to be rejected. Ibn al-Rāwandī specifically mentions a number of religious commandments which are not in conformity with reason. All this obviously involves on his part a critique of the current assumption regarding prophetic inspiration, and this critique goes hand in hand with the belief in miracles attributed to Muḥammad. This ex-Mu'tazilite was one of the earliest free-thinkers of Islam and a veritable precursor of the Platonist, Abū Bakr al-Rāzī.

SECOND PERIOD: FOURTH/TENTH TO MID-SIXTH/TWELFTH CENTURY

(a) *The philosophers and the philosophical theologians*

(i) *Al-Fārābī.* Muḥammad b. Muḥammad b. Tarkhān al-Fārābī, a descendant of a Central Asian Turkish family, died, apparently in ripe old age, in 339/950. He is said to have lived for some time in Damascus. The last period of his life was spent in Aleppo, at the pro-Ismā'īlī court of Sayf al-Dawla, a fact which may be significant. Al-Fārābī was not only a product of what Massignon has called the Ismā'īlī century of Islam, which can be said to have begun some time before 287/900; he also appears to have helped to mould its political ideology. In a larger context, he may be said to be the earliest outstanding Islam-minded philosopher (if the term is interpreted as excluding the *mutakallimūn*). I do not of course refer to his reportedly having been an observant Muslim. The statements labouring this point may be correct, but they are irrelevant. His genuine position can only be discovered in his writings.

In these one point stands out clearly: al-Fārābī's preoccupation with a certain category of problems connected with the beliefs, the political institutions, the law and the apologetics of Islam and of other religions set in the same pattern accounts for some of the most important themes of several capital works of his, such as *Ārā' ahl al-Madīna al-Fāḍila* ('The opinions of the people of the Virtuous City'), *al-Siyāsāt al-madaniyya* ('Political régimes'), and others. As has been indicated, this seems to have been a new departure among the Islamic philosophers; it was the religion of the pagans that appears to have engaged al-Kindī's particular interest.

It is, however, clear that al-Fārābī's attitude is a purely philosophical and not a religious one. He is alive to the capital importance of Islam and the other monotheistic prophetic religions as a subject-matter for philosophical study; they have to abide the philosopher's judgment. In al-Fārābī's case this integration of the science dealing with the prophetic religion, complete with its political aspect, into the general system of philosophy was rendered possible by his Platonism, proved by all his political treatises.[1] The reasons he gives for the creation of political societies and for man's need for them derive from those found in Plato's *Republic*. Al-Fārābī points out that in order to subsist and to develop a useful activity, men must co-operate, division of labour being necessary. He does not profess the theory, which seems already to have been current in his time, that unless men's natural instincts were curbed by the authority of religious legislation and of a state founded by a prophet, the human species would run the risk of being destroyed, all men being naturally animals.

A look at the various categories of thought posited by al-Fārābī in the two works mentioned above may give some idea of the complexity of his political thought and of the way he amalgamates, apparently in accordance with a reasoned plan, philosophical (mainly Platonic) and Islamic elements. These categories are: the Virtuous City (*al-Madīna al-Fāḍila*), the existence of which is a philosophical postulate—which may or may not be equated with an actually existent state, e.g. the Islamic. The term is clearly philosophical. It does not belong to the specifically Islamic vocabulary. Opposed to the Virtuous City are the various categories of inferior states which have as their scheme of reference the Virtuous City and may be defined by their particular kind of difference or deviation from it. Differences and deviations from an orthodox conduct of the state can of course be defined by means of terms used in Muslim law, in the Qur'ān or in Islamic tradition, and this is done by al-Fārābī.

[1] He composed a paraphrase of Plato's *Laws*, part of which is pure al-Fārābī.

The categories of the inferior states are: (1) the Ignorant (*al-Jāhiliyya*), (2) the Transgressing (*al-Fāsiqa*), (3) the Falsifying (*al-Mubaddila*), and (4) the Erring (*al-Ḍālla*). All of these are Islamic terms: *al-Jāhiliyya* designates the pagan Arabs before Islam. In al-Fārābī's terminology, the term applies to states which have never been 'virtuous', whereas the other categories enumerated above are indicative of deviations from and corruptions of the Virtuous State. *Al-Fāsiqa* is a legal term, supposedly used by Wāṣil b. 'Atā', the founder of Mu'tazilism, to designate the perpetrators of actions contrary to the religious law, which, according to al-Fārābī's scheme of reference, is that of the Virtuous State. *Al-Mubaddila*, refers in Islamic terminology to such communities as the Jewish, which are said to have falsified the prophetic books. *Al-Ḍālla*, can signify in this vocabulary people holding wrong beliefs which are a distortion of the correct ones; this being the meaning which al-Fārābī proposes for this appellation. Al-Fārābī also enumerates the categories into which the Ignorant or Pagan State can be subdivided. These subdivisions correspond in the main to the variety of imperfect states described in Plato's *Republic*: the state providing for the bare necessities of life only, the states whose inhabitants are solely preoccupied with the pursuit of wealth, or with pleasure, or with honours; the democratic state concerned with freedom; and the tyrannical state, the goal of whose inhabitants is power and domination. The Virtuous State, which is opposed to all the others, is characterized by the fact that its inhabitants co-operate with a view to achieving true happiness, the Greek *eudaimonia*.

What is the relation between this more or less ideal state conceived by al-Fārābī and the Islamic commonwealth? The answer to this question hinges to some extent on al-Fārābī's characteristic of the founder of the state, designated by him as the First Chief, the *Imām* (meaning religious leader, the word is not used in this context in the pregnant Shī'ī sense) and the principal Limb; the community being compared to a living organism. This founder, who is the first cause of this state—in this connexion al-Fārābī draws a parallel between this chief and God, the state being analogous to the world[1]—is also a prophet, according to 'The opinions of the people of the Virtuous City,' or at least, may be one.

This treatise discusses the intellectual illumination which comes from an entity called the Active Intellect, this being the last of the incorporeal

[1] Al-Fārābī is a partisan of the world state. This state is, according to him, the most perfect, being more self-sufficient than all the others. According to him, the First Chief is at the head of the whole habitable earth.

Separate Intellects, which in a way are intermediaries between God and the created universe. This illumination actualizes the potentiality for intellection existing in man; and this brings about the production in human beings of the forms of actualized intellect that are called the intellect in act, and the acquired intellect. An intellect belonging to this last category is close to the active Intellect. Man can, however, go beyond this and achieve union with the Active Intellect.[1] If this involves the theoretical and practical rational faculty and also the imagination, the man in question is said to have received a revelation[2] from God through the intermediary of the Active Intellect. Such a man may be called with respect to his intellectual capacity a philosopher and a sage; with respect to his imaginative power (by means of which he is able to have veridical dreams, to see visions and to perceive events in the present and in the future) he may be called a prophet.

The connexion between al-Fārābī's First Chief and Plato's Philosopher-King is quite evident; in fact, al-Fārābī attributes to the former a number of qualities obviously taken over from a description of the rulers of the ideal city in Plato's *Republic*. On the other hand, the fact that the First Chief must be, or at least in many cases is (a passage in 'The opinions of the people of the Virtuous City' seems to imply that there is no necessity about it[3]), endowed with a powerful imagination, enabling him to see visions and to foretell the future, makes it possible to identify him with such prophetic lawgivers as Muḥammad. This would of course imply that the latter was a philosopher.

The First Chief is an originator of religious legislation. The second, who follows him, and the successors of the second, are guardians and students of this tradition. This and other characteristics of theirs enumerated by al-Fārābī seem to have been taken over from an exposition of the qualifications of a caliph set forth in a Sunnī (rather than a Shīʿī) legal treatise, for al-Fārābī does not ascribe to the Second Chief superhuman qualities, such as were attributed to ʿAlī and the *Imāms* by all but the most moderate Shīʿa.

From a certain point of view, the inhabitants of the Virtuous State possess a common system of belief. There are, however, essential

[1] The verb *ḥalla* is used to describe the descent of the Active Intellect upon the man in question. This verb is applied by theologians to the incarnation of the Deity in Christ, as conceived by the Christians.

[2] As a rule the term is used exclusively of prophetic revelation.

[3] Al-Fārābī's parallel treatise entitled 'Political régimes' does not mention the imaginative faculty of the First Chief, who is described there at some length.

differences between them. The philosophers (*ḥukamā'*, literally, sages) know through the exercise of their intellectual powers the naked, undisguised truth regarding God, the Separate Intellects, the heavenly and terrestrial bodies, the processes of generation and corruption, and finally man, the faculties of his soul, his intelligence, the First Chief, prophecy, the Virtuous State and the other states, and so on. Another category of persons does not profess the truth concerning these matters because of their own capacity for knowledge, but because of their belief in the philosophers. All the other categories have access to these truths only through the parables 'imitating' them. Some of these parables come closer to the undisguised truth than others, but all of them indicate the same truth, and all of them point to one and the same happiness.

In other words, the core of all religions is identical in all of them; whereas the outward manifestations, i.e. myths and stories, vary from one religion to another. It follows from al-Fārābī's definitions that divergences between the religions are not a matter of primary importance, because they do not entail, as far as the philosophers who profess these faiths are concerned, any disagreement as to the scientific and philosophical truths which are the kernel of all religion. Obviously, this system of doctrines gives a philosophical legitimation to the beliefs and institutions of Islam and the other prophetic religions. It also consecrates the principle of the essential inequality of human beings; the prophets, who are also philosophers, and the philosophers, who lack the imaginative power of the prophets, being at the top of the pyramid.

Many elements of these theories, (for instance to some extent what may be called the psychological explanation of prophecy), could be found in philosophical doctrines which antedated al-Fārābī. However, the latter manifested indubitable originality in his interpretation of the primordial facts of the society in which he lived; he used both the concepts of Islamic law and, at least in a certain measure, Plato's political science for his own philosophical purposes.

What are the truths which are known without disguise to the philosophers and may be discovered in the parables of the prophetic religions? The concepts in question are concerned with physics, with metaphysics and with anthropology in general, in particular with politics; i.e. with the human sciences as they are thought of by al-Fārābī, whose more or less Platonic views on some of the problems posed in these sciences have been referred to above.

Al-Fārābī's physical doctrine is Aristotelian. The origin of his metaphysics, on the other hand, cannot be defined with comparable certainty. According to al-Fārābī, who on this point follows Aristotle, God is a pure intellect. In formulae which smack of Mu'tazilite *kalām*, the existence of attributes superadded to the divine essence is denied. On the other hand, the appellation 'The First' (*al-Awwal*) applied to God is of neo-Platonic provenance. It is used in the same sense by Proclus.

All that is not-God emanates from God; this doctrine of al-Fārābī appears to be likewise influenced by neo-Platonism. In expounding this doctrine al-Fārābī stresses the point that there is no difference between being as it is in the substance of God, and being as it is in the emanated things. All being is essentially one. This conception, which in its latter elaborate forms was known as the doctrine of the 'unity of being' (*waḥdat al-wujūd*) was to have a considerable influence on Islamic philosophical and mystic thought.

The first emanations, as far as the order of being is concerned (for the priority is not of a temporal nature, the entities in question as well as the cosmos being eternal) are ten incorporeal intellects, each of which, except the last, produces two emanations: one of them being the intellect which immediately follows in the series, and the other a celestial sphere. The tenth and last of these Intellects was, doubtless, already identified by al-Fārābī with the Active Intellect (see above) which illuminates man's reason.

These Intellects have much in common with Aristotle's prime movers. These are also Intellects, and each sphere has one of them as its mover. This kind of connexion between the Intellects and the spheres is also propounded by the Arab Aristotelians. The main differences are that al-Fārābī restricted the number of the incorporeal Intellects to ten, whereas Aristotle mentioned much greater numbers; and that Aristotle did not speak of the emanation of the Intellects from God. On the other hand, the neo-Platonists referred to emanations, but they did not have the conception of a series of incorporeal Intellects. Al-Fārābī's doctrine is an amalgam of these two elements.

In several passages of his works, al-Fārābī appears to expound the Aristotelian view that there is nothing superior to the achievement of philosophical knowledge. However, he sometimes expresses a somewhat different opinion. Thus, in his treatise *Taḥṣīl al-sa'āda* ('The achievement of happiness') he refers to the false (*bāṭil*) philosopher who has theoretical knowledge, but not the power to engender it in other people. The true philosopher has this power and is for this reason identified by al-Fārābī with the true lawgiver, the true king and the true *imām*. In other words, al-Fārābī considers that the supreme activity of the highest type of man has an educational purpose and is of a political nature. This conception has obvious Platonic overtones—it may also have revolutionary implications. It certainly fits in with the programme of the philosophically minded among the sympathisers and propagandists of the Ismā'īlī movement in the fourth/tenth century.

With regard to the destiny of the soul after death, self-contradictions of al-Fārābī were noted by the Spanish Muslim philosopher Ibn Ṭufayl; one of his opinions, incompatible with the others, being that the soul is annihilated by death. He is also reported to have denied (in a work which is no longer extant) the possibility—which he affirms elsewhere—of man's union with the Active Intellect. We do not know whether these inconsistencies indicate some kind of evolution in al-Fārābī's thought. It might be argued that some of them might be due to considerations of prudence. But this is not certain, though al-Fārābī was certainly not unaware of the necessity of being cautious. In fact, the seemingly deliberate abstractness, which occasionally calls to mind Spinoza's way of expressing himself, may have been meant to mask his intentions and the content of his reflections, many of which must have been unacceptable to even a very tolerant religious and political orthodoxy.

Al-Fārābī disbelieves in astrology. He apparently considers that the prophets, the true philosophers and the *imāms* rule, or should rule, not through recourse to one of the 'practical' natural sciences, but by virtue of personal superiority, which enables them to acquire theoretical knowledge, to transmit it in the most suitable form to the various classes into which the inferiors are divided, and to rule the people as a whole. This was a question which had at that time some measure of actuality. The extremist Shī'a, of which the Ismā'īlī propagandists were in the fourth/tenth and fifth/eleventh centuries the most prominent, but by no means the only representatives, were preoccupied with the promise of personal and political power held out by the sciences of alchemy, astrology and magic.

Al-Fārābī, 'the Second Teacher' after Aristotle, was considered as the greatest Muslim philosopher up to the advent of Ibn Sīnā, who was decisively influenced by him, but who superseded him in the Islamic East as 'the Master of those who know.' In Spain and the Maghrib, al-Fārābī's prestige remained among Aristotelians superior to that of Ibn

Sīnā. There is no doubt that the distinctive Islamic Aristotelianism, which is to some extent Platonism, is in a great measure his personal creation.

(ii) *Al-Rāzī*. The celebrated physician Abū Bakr Muḥammad b. Zakariyā al-Rāzī (i.e. a native of Rayy, near Tehran) who died in the early fourth/tenth century, and was consequently a near-contemporary of al-Fārābī was, as far as his philosophical position is concerned, in many ways the latter's direct opposite. It is true that he too was a Platonist of sorts, but his Platonism derives from the *Timaeus*, and not the *Republic* or the *Laws*, and he was emphatically not an Aristotelian. Of his main philosophical works only two ethical treatises and the partly philosophical, as yet unpublished, *Shukūk 'alā Jālīnus* ('Doubts concerning Galen') have been preserved. But the polemics which are directed, first and foremost by Ismā'īlī authors, against other writings of his, notably against his *al-'Ilm al-ilāhī* ('Divine science'), are of great help in reconstituting his doctrine.

Al-Rāzī is totally opposed to the principle of authority, and is an egalitarian, believing that ordinary people are endowed with the capacity to handle their own affairs, in a reasonable way, and they are even able, with the help of a sort of rational inspiration accorded to everybody, to perceive in an immediate way scientific truths. This view has an obvious resemblance to Ibn al-Rāwandī's conception of reason, but al-Rāzī's theory seems to have been more elaborate and, contrary to his predecessor, he had a profound knowledge of the Greek sciences.

According to al-Rāzī, no authority in philosophy, which includes the sciences, should be beyond the reach of criticism. He considers himself entitled to attack the views of Galen, whom he professes to revere, because having come after him, and being versed in Galen's writings, he can see further than the Greek physician. For al-Rāzī believes in the progress of the sciences through the accretion of knowledge, which occurs in all periods. He is even more opposed to the religious authorities. In his opinion, the Qur'ān and the scriptures of the other religions are a tissue of absurd and inconsistent fables; the miracles of the prophets are based on trickery or the stories regarding them are lies. The people who gather around the religious leaders are either feeble-minded, or they are women and adolescents. Religion stifles truth and fosters enmity. If a book in itself can constitute a demonstration that it is a true revelation, the treatises of geometry, astronomy, medicine and logic can justify such a claim much better than the Qur'ān, the transcendent literary beauty of which, denied by al-Rāzī, was thought by orthodox Muslims to prove the truth of Muḥammad's mission.

Al-Rāzī's extant writings contain no reference to a positive political function of the prophets and of religion. He was obviously not particularly interested in political science; but it is also clear that he considered that human beings did not need to be coerced by the prophets and the religious law into behaving in a manner compatible with the existence of an orderly community. In his only extant, and rather sketchy, *exposé* of the origin of human society, he sets forth the economic reason, i.e. the utility of the division of labour.

Since, in al-Rāzī's opinion, the existence of mankind and the avoidance of anarchy do not depend on respect for religious authority, he does not consider the disclosure of truths that tend to undermine this authority as dangerous—as most Aristotelians believed it to be. Unlike them, he has no use for esotericism.

In physics, he totally rejects the Aristotelian doctrine, professing an atomism which is very different from that of *kalām* and has, in spite of important divergences, some similarity with the doctrines of Democritus and Epicurus. According to al-Rāzī, all bodies are composed of corporeal atoms, which as far as we know he considered to be all alike, and of empty spaces. The qualities of all substances can be accounted for on a quantitative basis; they reflect the proportion in that substance of one of these components to the other.

Contrary to Aristotle, al-Rāzī considers that space (or place) exists independently of the bodies which are in it, and that time is not a function of motion. In arguing against the Peripatetic conceptions, al-Rāzī appeals to the immediate certainties of common people. Their testimony, in accordance with his egalitarian tendencies, he regards as more trustworthy than that of the scholars, who, in the opinion of the Aristotelians, alone have access to philosophic and scientific truths. An ordinary person would in al-Rāzī's view be perfectly clear that outside the world there exists an empty three-dimensional space, and that if the world were to disappear, time would continue to flow. Infinite three-dimensional space is designated by him as absolute space, and infinite time as absolute time; to these he opposes relative space and limited time. There is, *mutatis mutandis*, a curious similarity between his use of these two pairs of antithetical terms and Newton's distinction between absolute and relative time and space.

According to agnostic myth, which al-Rāzī adopted at some stage in the evolution of his thought, there existed before the creation of the world five eternal entities; God, the Soul, Matter, Time and Space. The ignorant Soul having desired Matter, God, in order to ease her misery, created the world conjoining her with matter, but also sent to her the Intellect to teach her that she would be finally delivered from her sufferings only by putting an end to her union with Matter. When the Soul grasps this, the world will be dissolved. This view of the role of matter might appear to entail a rigorous asceticism. Yet one of the ethical treatises of al-Rāzī, perhaps written at a time when he did not profess this myth, is devoted to inculcating moderation in this respect.

Believing as he did that the sciences progressed from generation to generation, and that, consequently, one had to keep an open mind, al-Rāzī was interested in alleged facts, which the Aristotelians, because they could not fit them into the framework of their theories, considered as dubious or untrue. Because of his empirical approach, he wrote a treatise on the sometimes apparently inexplicable properties ascribed to various substances, which, as he admitted, were not always verified. He was a noted alchemist.

(iii) *The Ismā'īlī theologians and 'The Brethren of Purity'*. Al-Rāzī's bitter opponents, the Ismā'īlī missionaries, developed a theory affirming the natural inequality of man. In addition, the doctrine that prophets are needed because the spontaneous impulses of human beings would, if they were left unrestrained, prevent the establishment of a viable society, was currently held, and not only in Shi'i circles.

In the course of the fourth/tenth century, the Ismā'īlī doctors, many of whom were active propagandists for the Fatimid dynasty, adopted a theology which derives from a perhaps christianized neo-Platonism. Later in the fifth/eleventh century, some of the theologians adopted a doctrine which seems to have been influenced by al-Fārābī's and Ibn Sīnā's theory of the Incorporeal Intellects. Part of their appeal to the intellectuals or the would-be intellectuals, was due to their being popularizers of a predigested science. They were accordingly alive to shifts in philosophical fashions.

These philosophical Ismā'īlī theologies teach the existence of two parallel hierarchies; the spiritual, constituted by cosmic entities (such as the Universal Intellect and the Universal Soul or the separate Incorporeal Intellects), and the corporeal, constituted by the dignitaries of the sect, from the *Imām* downwards. The Ismā'īlīs did not submit to the tendency found in the Shī'a from the earliest times to regard human beings, to the exclusion of cosmic entities, as the only intermediaries between God and men, and indeed sometimes as God incarnate.

In the second half of the fourth/tenth century, a small group of Ismā'īlī sympathizers or propagandists composed the so-called *Rasā'il Ikhwān al-Ṣafā*, ('Epistles of the Brethren of Purity'), the 'Brethren of Purity' being supposed to be a ubiquitous hierarchical society. These epistles are, in the main, an encyclopaedia of the Greek sciences, with the notable exception of Aristotelian metaphysics. The last epistle deals with the science of magic. This is probably the earliest encyclopaedia composed, like that of Pierre Bayle or that of the eighteenth-century *Encyclopédistes*, with a view to undermining the existing political and religious order. Propaganda for an *imām*, who is not named, occurs frequently in its pages.

The authors of this encyclopaedia drew heavily upon the philosophical literature with which they were acquainted, and incorporated various passages of earlier writers, one of them being al-Fārābī, by whose political doctrines they were manifestly influenced. They quote, without mentioning his name, his list of the qualities which the First Chief (to use al-Fārābī's term) is required to have.

A fable in this encyclopaedia, which was translated or adapted into several languages, tells of an animal rebellion against human domination, and the speeches of their spokesmen and those of their opponents, the human beings, before the arbiter, who is a king of the Jinn. In spite of the telling arguments of the animals, the final verdict affirms the legitimacy of human rule, which will be abolished only after certain periods of time have passed. It may be mentioned in this connection that the authors of these epistles believed in the transmigration of souls. It is, I believe, certain that this verdict is intended to set forth the legitimacy of human social inequality and of authoritarian hierarchical rule.

The authors of the encyclopaedia look forward to an eschatological future which, *inter alia*, holds out the promise of deliverance from religious commandments and from tyrannical rulers.

(iv) *Ibn Sīnā* (*Avicenna*). Abū 'Alī ibn Sīnā, known in Christian medieval Europe as Avicenna, who is said to have been born thirty years after the death of al-Fārābī and died in ?429/1036, acknowledges the great debt he owes to al-Fārābī's writings, and refers to the respect he felt for that philosopher. And yet, partly at least because of Ibn Sīnā, and also in consequence of a shift in the political and social situation, the specific doctrines of al-Fārābī concerning political science, did not, from the time of Ibn Sīnā onwards, arouse any interest at least in the countries of the Muslim East, as opposed to the Maghrib and Spain. In the thirteenth century, the Spanish Muslim philosopher, Ibn Sab'īn, mentions Ibn Sīnā's Platonism, and, at the time of the Renaissance, Pico della Mirandola makes a similar remark. This characteristic certainly fits an important aspect of Ibn Sīnā's philosophy, but, on the other hand, contrary to Plato and to al-Fārābī, he apparently did not consider that, circumstances permitting, it was the duty of the philosopher to become a ruler or an adviser of rulers. Ibn Sīnā played a certain role in practical politics, but there is no evidence for supposing that in this activity he was impelled by theoretical reasons.

Ibn Sīnā was a native of Bukhārā and familiar with both Persian and Arabic. He mentions in his autobiography that his father and brother had Ismā'īlī sympathies, and this may have aroused his interest in philosophy, which he began to study systematically under the tuition of al-Nātilī, who sojourned at that time in Central Asia. This story seems to be typical of the way in which interest in philosophy was acquired in remote regions of the Islamic world. Ibn Sīnā is said to have become possessed of all his immense book-learning before attaining the age of eighteen, having had in his early youth the run of a great library.

As an adult, he had a position of some eminence at the court of certain sultans in Persia proper, and displayed some political activity. He was a renowned physician and wrote one of the standard medical works of the Middle Ages, namely *al-Qānūn*, which was studied in both Islamic and Christian lands. This work contains a set of rules for experiments to determine the efficacy of medicaments, which seem to be an advance on anything to be found in earlier Greek or Arabic texts.

As a philosopher, he had a number of disciples, who played a certain part in the explanation and propagation of his doctrine, and many adversaries. In particular, he was an antagonist of the Baghdādī, mostly Christian, interpreters of Aristotle. In relation to Ibn Sīnā, who was a native of Bukhārā and lived in Persia, these were Westerners. This is a significant point in view of the fact that Ibn Sīnā opposes to the Greek philosophical tradition an Oriental (*mashriqī*) one, which according to him, is of immemorial antiquity. However, there is not the slightest indication that Ibn Sīnā used, or indeed had a modicum of knowledge of, any ancient Oriental sacred or profane tradition. The evidence tends to show that in speaking of the antique 'Oriental wisdom' or 'philosophy', he had in mind his own contemporary personal philosophy, with which he confronts the Western one, namely the Baghdādī philosophy and perhaps also that of the Greek commentators of Aristotle.

The growing strength of Persian national sentiment, which led in Ibn Sīnā's lifetime, to Persian partly replacing Arabic as the administrative language in Maḥmūd of Ghazna's empire, and which may have been to a certain extent responsible for Ibn Sīnā's composing some philosophical and scientific treatises in Persian, may have been one of the factors which suggested this mystification. As we shall see, the notion of 'Oriental wisdom' (*al-ḥikma al-mashriqiyya*) appealed to later Islamic thinkers, and may have inspired in al-Suhrawardī a new departure in philosophy.

Ibn Sīnā's enormous literary output includes the following major works:

(1) *Kitāb shifā' al-nafs*, ('The book of the healing of the soul'), known in medieval Europe under the title of *Sufficientia*. This voluminous work gives detailed expositions of the Greek sciences, those treatises which are included in the *Corpus Aristotelicum* and some others. Ibn Sīnā's intention in composing this work was to set forth the Peripatetic system, but, as he states in his preface, he himself was no Aristotelian, and the book often expresses his personal view. Its sheer size turns it into the earliest specimen of the new genre of philosophical texts. Neither the extant Greek nor the Arabic writings prior to Ibn Sīnā provide an example, other than the *Corpus Aristotelicum* taken together with its commentaries, of an all-inclusive work of this kind, in which the problems of the various sciences are exhaustively discussed. The fact that *Kitāb shifā' al-nafs* is not a commentary and does not have to refer to the letter of the Aristotelian text is in this connexion of great historical importance. As a direct consequence, this work and other writings of Ibn Sīnā largely superseded in the Muslim East as philosophical textbooks the *Corpus Aristotelicum* and also the treatises of al-Fārābī and other relatively early Islamic authors.

(2) *Kitāb najāt al-nafs* ('The book of the salvation of the soul'), appears to consist of extracts from *Kitāb shifā' al-nafs*.

(3) *Kitāb al-ishārāt wa'l-tanbīhāt* ('The book of indications and hints') composed in the last period of Ibn Sīnā's life, was meant to be

an esoteric work, written for the chosen few. It labours much less than *Kitāb shifā' al-nafs* at demonstration, striving rather (at least this is the impression it makes) to bring about intellectual illumination. Certain parts of the Aristotelian doctrine, which Ibn Sīnā found unconvincing are omitted in this work, and his personal contributions to philosophy are much more in evidence than in the earlier work.

(4) *Kitāb al-mubāḥathāt* is a chaotic mass of notes, made known to the public after the death of Ibn Sīnā, and giving invaluable insight into the philosopher's hesitancy and changes of mind, as he endeavours to fit his novel conception into the rigid framework of medieval Arab Aristotelianism.

A point on which Ibn Sīnā may have been opposed to the Baghdādī Aristotelians of his time, and which he appears to have claimed to be part of the tradition of 'Oriental philosophy', concerns the immortality of the individual soul. This was denied by the post-Avicennian orthodox Aristotelians of Spain and the Maghrib, who probably followed an interpretation of Aristotle adopted in such earlier centres of Muslim philosophy as 'Irāq. From the Aristotelian point of view, an individual soul could not continue to exist after its separation from the body, because it is matter, which is only present in the corporeal substance, that is the principle of individuality. Consequently only the intellect, which has no individuality (an intellectual act performed by Peter being strictly identical with the same intellectual act performed by Paul) can survive death. Ibn Sīnā gets around the difficulty by supposing that the individual soul, which, in his opinion, is created at the same time as his body, acquires through its association with the latter, an individuality which it originally does not possess. This individuality is preserved after death. The details, or even the whole of Ibn Sīnā's solution, may be to some extent a novel contribution to the debate, but the thesis itself is clearly not a new one. The immortality of the individual soul was maintained by al-Kindī, not to speak of the Greek Platonists, Pythagoreans and so forth. However, other conceptions of Ibn Sīnā manifest a marked originality. They struck out new roads for Islamic philosophy, and two of them have exerted a lasting influence on European philosophy by providing it with two of its main themes.

One of these themes, which stems from a conception of Ibn Sīnā, is concerned with the radical division between essence and existence, or being. According to the Muslim philosopher, this duality is to be found in all things except God; existence being superadded in them to the essence. By themselves, the essences are neutral with regard to existence. The domain of essence is in some respects reminiscent of that of the Platonic Idea; but the latter, contrary to the essences of Ibn Sīnā, possesses being. As Ibn Sīnā puts it, existence is an accident that happens to the essences. However, it does not happen by chance, but by necessity; everything that exists, including the activity of God, being subject to a strict determinism. The things that are contingent *per se*, i.e. all things that are composed of essence and of existence, or in other words, all things that are not God, are necessary if referred to Him. This determinism does not derive from Aristotle, according to whom random happenings may occur in the sublunar world.

The second Avicennian theme which became an intrinsic part of European (as well as of the Eastern Islamic) philosophy, derives from what may be described as Ibn Sīnā's discovery of the ego and of man's self-awareness. According to Ibn Sīnā, a man suddenly created in full possession of his faculties would, if he were floating in the air, with no previous knowledge of, and no opportunity to perceive, the external world, and with no possibility to sense his own limbs, yet be fully aware of his personal existence. This immediate certainty as to one's ego is Ibn Sīnā's favourite proof for the existence of the soul; he prefers it to the Aristotelian arguments which cite as evidence the motions of animals. Obviously, this proof tends to imply the identification of the soul with the ego and to attribute paramount importance to consciousness and its immediate certainties. In this approach, Ibn Sīnā may have been influenced by some unknown Greek neo-Platonist. He was certainly unaquainted with Augustine, some of whose conceptions have a certain kinship with his. The impact of this philosophy of the ego and of self-awareness both on Islamic and on medieval Christian philosophy, which influenced Descartes on this point, was immense.

However, Ibn Sīnā would not abandon the Aristotelian distinction between the soul and the actual intellect, which, as his doubts and changes of mind on crucial points of the doctrine indicate, was incompatible with this new insight. Some of the more radical conclusions which seemed to be called for were drawn by Abu'l-Barakāt al-Baghdādī.

As far as we know, no notice was taken by the earlier Aristotelian philosophers of the great Ṣūfī mystics. Accordingly Ibn Sīnā seems to have struck out new ground when he recognized in the last section of *Kitāb al-ishārāt wa'l-tanbīhāt* that their experiences were a valid subject for philosophical study; he integrated the varieties of religious experience into his philosophical system. He also seems to consider that the illuminations of the mystics may be on a par with the cognitions of the philosophers.

Occasionally, he englobes the mystics and the prophets in one category. Thus the mystic experience which the Ṣūfīs attempt to express can be made available for the study of the psychology of the prophets. The persons belonging to the category in question can in Ibn Sīnā's opinion have natural powers which enable them to perform actions called miracles, though they are in conformity with the natural order. For the rest, he assigns to the prophets a political role, in accordance with the current idea that men, because of their natural instincts of domination and aggression, cannot establish a viable society unless they are disciplined by a superior authority which they cannot but obey. According to Ibn Sīnā, the prophets are devices of nature with a view to the preservation of the human species. He shows no trace of the interest manifested by al-Fārābī in the various kinds of pagan or monotheistic communities.

A literary form employed by Ibn Sīnā in three of his smaller works may be noted, because it gave rise to a genre which has some importance in the history of Islamic philosophy. I refer to what Ibn Sīnā himself calls parables, i.e. allegorical tales which are meant to express philosophical truths. The composition of such tales clearly requires both philosophical insight and a recourse to imagination. It is not clear whether Ibn Sīnā paid attention to the fact that these are exactly the requirements, as formulated by the philosophers, needed for prophetic visions and revelations. At all events, he showed by his example that a philosopher could fittingly permit his imagination to help his intellect in communicating abstract concepts. Imagination thus became a useful part of a philosopher's equipment. This lesson was not lost upon some of Ibn Sīnā's successors, in particular the Ishrāqī philosophers.

Within a generation or two of Ibn Sīnā's death, or even before that, his doctrine was dominant among the philosophers of the Muslim East, as is proven by the fact that it was the object of the criticism which Abu'l-Barakāt al-Baghdādī and al-Ghazālī directed against the prevalent philosophical views.

(v) *Abu'l Barakāt al-Baghdādī*. Abu'l-Barakāt Hibat Allāh al-Baghdādī (who died as an octogenarian or nonagenerian in 547/1152) was a physician, and lived most of his life in or near Baghdād. Of Jewish origin, he was converted in old age to Islam. The Jews living in Muslim countries used Arabic as their language of philosophical and scientific writing, and Abu'l-Barakāt was no exception. His *magnum opus, Kitāb al-mu'tabar,* a title, which according to his explanation means 'The book of that which has been established by personal reflection' and all his other works were written in that language. *Kitāb al-mu'tabar* had a great influence on later Islamic philosophy and belongs to its history.

As Abu'l-Barakāt lets us know, this work was composed from a collection of jottings in which he had noted his observations upon, and criticism of, the philosophical texts he read. As has already been stated, he apparently referred, in the first place, to texts by Ibn Sīnā. His work has sections dealing with most Greek sciences except mathematics. In view of its genesis, it is not surprising that *Kitāb al-mu'tabar* does not propound a wholly coherent philosophical doctrine. Sometimes Abu'l-Barakāt takes over without any alteration Avicennian theories which do not fit in with his personal view. However, on some essential points, he perceives and eliminates the inconsistencies in Ibn Sīnā's views. Moreover, as regards certain fundamental questions of physics he seems to follow a quite different tradition, which at least in some details clearly derives from Plato's *Timaeus*. There is a certain kinship between some of Abu'l-Barakāt's physical opinions and those of the professed Platonist, Abū Bakr al-Razī. Like the latter, Abu'l-Barakāt rejects the Aristotelian formulations according to which place (or space, one term is used for both concepts) is a limit, i.e. should be identified with a certain relation between two bodies, and that time is a function of motion. Again, like al-Rāzī, Abu'l-Barakāt considers that space is independent of the existence of bodies and is three-dimensional and infinite. However, he differs from al-Rāzī in his view of time, which he defines as the measure of being; a formulation which is similar to that of the Greek neo-Platonist, Damascius.

Ibn Sīnā's teaching concerning the ego and self-awareness presented an unresolved contradiction. For while it was based on a recourse to the primal certainty of self-awareness, which proves the existence of the ego, Ibn Sīnā, in deference to the Aristotelian separation of the intellect from the soul, differentiates—perhaps only in the last period of his life—between self-awareness accompanying an act of intellection (which alone has the characteristics which he generally attributes to self-awareness *tout court*), and the inferior self-awareness accompanying an act of imagination or any other not strictly intellectual human (and also animal) activity. Abu'l-Barakāt sweeps away this distinction, taking his stand on the fact of one's being certain through self-awareness that all the acts which one performs, whether they be intellectual, imaginative, volitional or sensual, are accomplished by one and the same subject, the ego. This appeal to the self-evident character of one's self-awareness disproves, according to Abu'l-Barakāt, the Aristotelian theory elaborated by Ibn Sīnā as to the multiplicity of the psychic faculties. According to Abu'l-Barakāt, there are no distinct faculties; nor is there a distinction between the intellect and the soul.

God is conceived by Abu'l-Barakāt to some extent after the analogy of the human 'I'. He is not, and obviously cannot be, the pure intellect of the Aristotelians, or the divinity of negative theology, but has pre-eminently the characteristics and the capacity for various activities which are found in a lesser degree in human beings.

Events in our world are determined by causality or by chance, which, as Abu'l-Barakāt defines it, results from the encounter of two independent lines of causation. For instance, a man impelled by certain causes sets out to cross the road, and so does a scorpion impelled by another set of causes. In such a case, their meeting and the fact that the man is stung by the scorpion is an effect of chance. However, God, who *inter alia* has the power to will, sometimes—by no means always—directly intervenes in terrestrial affairs.

(b) *Kalām*

From the point of view of *kalām*, this period is marked by the emergence of the Ash'arite school. This does not mean that with the coming of the fourth/tenth century the Mu'tazilites had lost their intellectual vigour. Abū Hāshim, who was the son of the noted Mu'tazilite al-Jubbā'ī and died in 321/933, i.e. at the beginning of the period we are dealing with, continues the Mu'tazilite tradition of almost uninhibited enquiry into a great variety of such acts. Later on, this kind of intellectual curiosity may have weakened among the Mu'tazilites. Such authors as Abū Rashīd al-Nīshāpūrī (d. after 415/1024) and especially 'Abd al-Jabbār al-Hamadhānī (d. 415/1025), the greatest name among these later Mu'tazilites, seemed to be engaged in taking stock of the idea and discussions of their school; 'Abd al-Jabbār's enormous encyclopaedia of Mu'tazilite opinions is the kind of work which often marks the waning of a movement. It should be recognized that his was a very difficult position. Sunnī Islam, with which he fully identified himself, was not only overwhelmingly anti-Mu'tazilite. It was also, as he believed, in the beginning of the fifth/eleventh century, in desperate straits because of the combined effects of the Byzantine victories and of the subversive activities of the Fatimids and other extremist Shi'ites.

(i) *Al-Ash'arī.* Abu'l-Ḥasan 'Alī b. Ismā'īl al-Ash'arī (d. 324/935 or thereabouts) who is said to have been for forty years a companion of the famous Mu'tazilite al-Jubbā'ī, had, perhaps in 300/912–13, a change of heart, brought about, as one of the stories goes, by three dreams in which the Prophet Muḥammad laid his commands upon him. One of these ordered al-Ash'arī not to give up *kalām*—of which he had an exhaustive knowledge attested by his great doxographical work *Maqālāt al-Islāmiyyīn* ('The views of the Muslims')—but to adapt *kalām* to what was regarded as the orthodox Islamic doctrine. In point of fact, the Ash'arites set a considerable value upon 'knowledge' and rational argument, but they implemented them with a view to the defence of religion. This was the veritable function of *kalām*, as al-Fārābī defined it. But the Mu'tazilites seem occasionally to have pursued knowledge with no reference to religion, whereas the Ash'arites, by and large, lived up to al-Fārābī's definition. They met the need for an official theology which was felt at a certain period by the rulers of Sunnī Islam, who had to oppose the propaganda of the hierarchic Ismā'īlī organization with its several elaborate systems of theology. Al-Ash'arī rejects the Mu'tazilite view on the divine attributes, which he considers as not identical with God's essence, and thus, denies the Mu'tazilite conception of God's unity. He also believes that the Qur'ān, regarded as God's speech, was not created in time.

Al-Ash'arī considers that the agent who produces human actions is not man, but God, and thus lays himself open to the objections stemming from the Mu'tazilite principle of justice. However, the Mu'tazilite arguments are founded upon the idea that good and evil have an objective existence independent of God, and that He is obliged to recognize the difference between them and to do good, whereas according to the Ash'arite view what is good and what is evil is determined by God's will.

While man does not perform his own actions, he can 'acquire' them (*kasb* or *iktisāb*, terms which may be derived from the Qur'ān but which, rather curiously, call to mind a somewhat similar doctrine of 'acquisition', *arj*, of action occurring in the Indian Sāmkhya philosophical system). The *kalām* use of the Arabic terms predates al-Ash'arī. The latter is careful practically to annul the minimal concession to man's freedom implied in the doctrine of acquisition, which may refer to man's acquiescence in the actions he is obliged to do, by affirming that the 'acquisition' of an act can only be brought about in every particular case through a power of acquisition specially created by God in the man in question.

The Ash'arites, and there is every reason to suppose their master before them, took over atomism from the Mu'tazila. Like the latter, they disbelieved in causality as far as natural causes were concerned, and indeed were more consistent than the earlier sect with respect to this doctrine. For they did not believe, as did the Mu'tazilites, that human actions produced a series of causes and effects. The Ash'arites had no need of this doctrine. They were not called upon to justify God for punishing a man for a crime of which the latter was not the author; the reason being that, as we have seen, in their opinion, man does not perform even the actions which proceed from him; and that God is in no need of justification, His Will being the sole criterion of right and wrong.

Al-Ash'arī's doctrine was elaborated by Abū Bakr Muḥammad al-Bāqillānī (d. 403/1013) and by Abu'l-Ma'ālī al-Juwaynī *Imām al-Ḥaramayn*, 'the *Imām* of the Two Sanctuaries', (d. 478/1085), who was al-Ghazālī's teacher.

(ii) *Al-Ghazālī*. Abū Ḥāmid Muḥammad al-Ghazālī (450/1058–505–1111) transcends *kalām*. As his account of the evolution of his ideas shows, his crisis of doubt, a time of anguish, during which he lost faith even in the so-called self-evident truths, was a stage in his spiritual progress towards Ṣūfī mysticism, which gave him, according to his own words, lasting peace.

However, he was also an eminent *mutakallim*, the first who was able to expose from a *kalām* point of view, but with a profound knowledge of the doctrine of his opponents, the heresy and weaknesses of what paased for Aristotelian philosophy. In reality, he attacked the system of Ibn Sīnā, with which he was familiar. In fact, he was the author of an excellent, widely read account of it entitled *Maqāṣid al-falāsifa*, ('The intentions of the philosophers'). It is because of such versatility that Ibn Rushd and others accused al-Ghazālī of wishing to be all things to all men.

His critique of philosophy is set forth in *Tahāfut al-falāsifa* a much-debated title which can be translated as 'The incoherence of the philosophers.' This relatively early work (finished in ?488/1095) starts by pointing out that the partisans of philosophy adopt its doctrines because of a blind belief in authority, and goes on to attack some of these doctrines, starting with the conception of the eternity of the world. Al-Ghazālī uses some of the arguments of John Philoponus, the Greek Christian philosopher of the sixth century, showing that this conception must lead to the absurd conclusion that an infinite number is less than another infinite number. For the number of the revolutions of the sun which have occurred up to the present, must, on the hypothesis of the eternity of the world, be infinite, and the same applies to the revolutions of Saturn, and yet the former number must be greater than the latter, since the sun accomplishes its revolutions in one year, whereas Saturn's period is thirty years. At the end of the work, al-Ghazālī formulates the three points on which the conceptions of the philosophers are radically opposed to the Islamic religion. These are, the belief in the eternity of the world, the denial of God's knowledge of particulars, the denial of resurrection.

'The incoherence of the philosophers' had a considerable impact. It has been occasionally maintained that it brought about the decline or the end of philosophy in the Islamic East. This is a pure legend—the fact being that some of the most interesting philosophers of that region come after al-Ghazālī. It is true that not all of them conformed to the pattern of thought which had been attacked by him, but their deviations are not to be laid at his door. It may be mentioned that some of al-Ghazālī's own late works, belonging to his Ṣūfī period, have strong neo-Platonic elements.

PHILOSOPHY IN SPAIN AND THE MAGHRIB

(a) *The Spanish Aristotelians*

The history of Aristotelian philosophy (to use this convenient, though not in all cases quite accurate, term) in Arab Spain is a short one. It begins and it ends in the sixth/twelfth century, or as near as makes no difference. Yet it produced among the Muslims three outstanding philosophers, and had an immense influence on the history of thought in Christendom and Judaism. This impact can be partly explained by the political division of Spain, and by the presence in that country of a considerable Jewish community. Spain was half-Muslim and half-Christian, and this facilitated intellectual contacts, notably the translation by the Latins (often with the co-operation of Jews) of Arabic texts or Arabic versions of Greek texts, into Latin. During the lifetime of Ibn Rushd (Averroes), Arabic texts were being translated into Latin in Toledo. The famous Muslim philosophers of Spain who lived in that period, were, for obvious reasons, better known to the Latin translators and to their patrons, and consequently more likely to be translated than the equally famous philosophers of the same period who lived in the Muslim East.

Thus the accident of biographical proximity accounts for the fact, which had incalculable repercussions, that many of Ibn Rushd's commentaries were translated into Latin and Hebrew. In the last analysis, this accident is also responsible for an optical error which often causes, even at present, the later philosophers of the Muslim East, who were not known in medieval Europe, to be undervalued when compared to the Muslim philosophers of Spain. It may be added in this connexion that Maimonides, the greatest Jewish Aristotelian of the Middle Ages, was a product of the Aristotelian school of Islamic Spain, and occasionally stressed this fact.

Before the sixth/twelfth century, intellectual life in Islamic Spain had been influenced by offshoots of neo-Platonic philosophy, i.e. a philosophy centred on the theory of emanation, and on the formulation of the various planes of being. The theologian Ibn Ḥazm (d. 456/1064), a many-faceted personality, may also be mentioned. While his most popular work is a treatise on love, his *magnum opus, Kitāb al-fiṣal*, is concerned with heresiography and contains bitter attacks both on the Ashʿarites and on the Muʿtazila.

At the end of the fifth/eleventh century, Muslim Spain was annexed by the fanatical Almoravids, whose armies came over from Africa and defeated the Christians in 479/1086. In their turn, the Almoravids were defeated in 541/1147 and the territories they ruled taken over by the Almohads, an even more intolerant sect, which, contrary to the Almoravids, had adopted *kalām* doctrines, influenced by al-Ghazālī. The first in the outstanding trio of Spanish Aristotelians, Ibn Bājja, lived under the rule of the Almoravids, the other two, Ibn Ṭufayl and Ibn Rushd, under that of the Almohads. These biographical details may account for a certain resigned awareness on the part of all the three of the practical impossibility of philosophy effecting a change in the state of society, an attitude which contrasts with that of al-Fārābī. In the case of Ibn Rushd, the political situation may account for his profound conviction that the *mutakallimūn* do great harm.

(i) *Ibn Bājja (Avempace) and* (ii) *Ibn Ṭufayl.* This attitude of resignation is perhaps most clearly expressed by Abū Bakr b. Bājja (d. 533/1138), in his work entitled *Tadbīr al-mutawaḥḥid* ('The governance of the solitary'). His thesis is that in the imperfect and diseased states and societies of his time, as well as in the great majority of those of the past of which we have report, the men dedicated to the pursuit of wisdom, and capable of achieving this aim, 'the happy ones' as he calls them, have, and should have, nothing in common with the ordinary population, except in so far as such communications are required for the necessaries of life. They should regard themselves as solitary strangers. This opinion can only be held on the supposition that man's highest end is not of a political nature. In fact, Ibn Bājja considers that this end consists in union with the Active Intellect. He also holds (contrary to Ibn Sīnā) that the individual soul dies with the death of the body. The intellect which survives it has no individual quality. Only what is universal in man survives.

Abū Bakr Muḥammad b. Ṭufayl (d. 581/1185), a *wazīr* and physician of the Almohad rulers, is known as the author of the philosophical novel *Ḥayy ibn Yaqẓān*, a title taken from one of the philosophical tales of Ibn Sīnā, and meaning 'The Living son of the Waking One'. This refers to the Soul, principle of life, which is supposed to be engendered by the Unsleeping Intellect. The fact that Ibn Ṭufayl borrowed the name from Ibn Sīnā is no accident. He is the only one among the three Spanish Aristotelian philosophers referred to above who professes to be a disciple of the philosopher from Bukhārā. As he makes it clear, he is most interested in the 'Oriental philosophy', which seems to hold out the promise of esoteric lore. Like Ibn Sīnā, he believes that the individual soul is an immaterial substance, which survives the death of the body.

Ḥayy ibn Yaqẓān, the principal character in Ibn Ṭufayl's novel is a solitary who, unlike the philosophers for whom Ibn Bājja prescribes isolation, is not exposed to the vexations and dangers of life in an imperfect society. From his birth onwards he lives alone on a desert island and, after having gradually learned the skills necessary for the preservation and comfort of life, he acquires, without the aid of books or teachers, knowledge of the philosophical sciences and finally achieves a mystic unitive ecstasy. In the last part of the work, Ḥayy receives information about a community of people, living on a neighbouring island and obeying a religious law promulgated by a prophet. He admires the hidden allusions contained in the law, which being interpreted refer to the truths he knows, and wishes to explain to the people of this community the true significance of the prophetic revelation. However, these people are refractory to his teaching. This failure makes him grasp the difference existing between the different kinds of men, most of whom are comparable to animals, being devoid of the faculty of philosophic understanding. He recommends that their minds should not be confused by interpretations of the law that are beyond their intellectual capacity; they should confine themselves to obeying the commandments and honouring the religious tradition. Thereupon he returns to his island. In Ibn Ṭufayl's tale, the solitary, of whom Ibn Bājja spoke, recognizes at least one social duty: he must not disturb the religious way of life of ordinary people.

(iii) *Ibn Rushd* (*Averroes*). This was also the opinion of Ibn Rushd, whom Ibn Ṭufayl protected at the beginning of his career. According to this younger philosopher, there are three categories of people: first, the great multitude of common folk, whose simple religious beliefs should not be disturbed by allegorical interpretations of the prophetic revelation, which, with these unsophisticated people, might lead to the abandonment of religion; secondly, the philosophers who, being capable of grasping the truth, have a twofold legal duty: they must devote themselves to the pursuit of philosophy, and they must take care not to divulge the truth to people who are unfit to understand it; thirdly, the dialecticians, to use Ibd Rushd's term, i.e. the *mutakallimūn*, who on the one hand do not attain truth by the sole correct way of philosophical demonstration, and on the other hand, propagate, with dangerous results, frequently false interpretations of the Qur'ān among the ignorant masses of the first category. Moreover, these semi-intellectuals tend to be intolerant. This is an undisguised attack on the oppressive régime instituted or inspired by the *mutakallimūn*, who had formulated the dogmas of the Almohad movement.

Abu'l-Walīd Muḥammad b. Aḥmad b. Rushd (520–95/1126–98), who was known in medieval Christian Europe under the name of

Averroes, was a practising jurist; it is as such that he was able to answer in the affirmative the question as to whether the study of philosophy by those who have the capacity for it is an obligation imposed by the religious law. For some years he was *qāḍī* in Seville, having received this appointment from an Almohad ruler interested in philosophy. Later he became chief *qāḍī* in his birthplace, Cordova, and in 578/1182 he succeeded Ibn Ṭufayl as the royal physician in the capital, Marrakesh. A few years before his death he fell into disgrace, and was ordered to live in a small town, while many of his books were burnt. However, after a period of one or two years, he was allowed to return to the capital, where he died. Under the Almohads, the pursuit of philosophy entailed certain risks, but it could also procure the favour of the ruler.

It is as a commentator that Ibn Rushd is best known. He wrote three sorts of 'commentaries': a Great, an Intermediate and a Paraphrase, dealing in this way with nearly all the principal works of Aristotle: the most notable omission being that of the *Politics*. As he could not find a manuscript of the Arabic translation of this treatise (although, according to his information, such a translation was available in the Muslim East), he wrote a paraphrase of Plato's *Republic*, which he used as a substitute for Aristotle's *Politics*. In these commentaries, he attempts to set forth Aristotle's authentic opinion, eliminating neo-Platonic and various other accretions, which are found in the writings of earlier Muslim philosophers.

Ibn Rushd's often proclaimed belief in Aristotle's intellectual supremacy naturally provoked rather facile jibes. Thus Ibn Rushd's countryman, Ibn Sab'īn, observes that the commentator would have agreed with Aristotle even if he had heard him saying that one can be sitting and standing at the same time. In fact, however, Ibn Rushd is characterized by considerable originality of thought, which he sometimes manifests as it were unintentionally, while endeavouring to discover Aristotle's true meaning.

His much-debated thesis concerning the unity of the hylic intellect is a case in point. Intending to clarify a section of Aristotle's *De Anima,* Ibn Rushd puts forward the view that the faculty of intellection, called the hylic or material intellect, is one and the same for the whole of mankind, participated in by the individual human being. This faculty is permanently actualized, which means that the existence of philosophy in every generation is part of the nature of things. The fact that in a given period there seem to be no philosophers at all, is not a decisive objection, for there may be some in the unknown southern part of the habitable earth.

In his paraphrase of Plato's *Republic*, Ibn Rushd indicates the possibility that Plato's ideal state may come into being through the action of a succession of enlightened rulers, who may gradually bring about a transformation of the conduct and the beliefs of their subjects. In spite of the resignation which he sometimes manifests, there is no reason to suppose that he excluded the possibility that this kind of good fortune might befall the Almohad state in which he lived.

A considerable portion of Ibn Rushd's commentaries were translated into Latin, either directly from the Arabic, or from a Hebrew version. Their impact on Christian (and also on Jewish) philosophy, can hardly be overestimated. This influence may have been due in the first place to the knowledge and understanding of Aristotle's thought that could be gained from them. Soon, however, intellectual controversy was centred upon some of Ibn Rushd's own theses, as distinct from those of his master. Latin Averroism became, notwithstanding the opposition of the ecclesiastical authorities, a vigorous philosophical school, the derivation of which from Ibn Rushd is, in spite of many deviations, unmistakable.

Ibn Rushd's thought had incomparably less influence in Islam. The political conditions in the West—in the first place the progressive deterioration of the position of the Muslims in Spain—may perhaps account for the fact that he did not found a lasting school in the countries in which he lived. In the East, people interested in philosophy were mostly partisans of the system of Ibn Sīnā or of that of al-Suhrawardī, or of some amalgam of the two.

(b) *The Ṣūfī current in Spanish philosophy*

Muḥyī al-Dīn b. al-ʿArabī, a native of Murcia (d. 638/1240), who is one of the most influential thinkers of Islam, was first and foremost a Ṣūfī. He believed in the primordial unity of all being.

Abū Muḥammad ibn Sabʿīn, who, according to report, committed suicide in Mecca (in 669/1270) because he wished to achieve union with God, seems to have been greatly influenced by neo-Platonic works currently attributed to Aristotle (such as the *Theology of Aristotle*, deriving from Plotinus's *Enneads*, and *Kitāb al-khayr al-maḥḍ* ('The book of absolute good', known in Europe as *Liber de causis*) which derives from Proclus's *Elements of theology*), and by the unitive experience of the Ṣūfīs. He lays stress on the philosophical doctrines which imply God's immanence in the world. For instance he states that God is the form of every existent thing. His theory of emanation is different from that adopted by al-Fārābī and Ibn Sīnā.

(c) *Ibn Khaldūn*

Abū Zayd 'Abd al-Raḥmān Ibn Khaldūn (733–809/1332–1406), is primarily an historian and a sociologist rather than a philosopher. But the great work which he entitled *al-Muqaddima* ('The introduction', *sc.* to a universal history) may fittingly receive a brief mention in the present chapter, because, from a certain point of view, it draws a line under the history of philosophy in Spain and the Maghrib. It should be noted that Ibn Khaldūn was a descendant of Muslims who had left Spain, a country in which he himself sojourned for two years, and that his personal political and sociological experience was mainly drawn from north-western Africa. He came to live in Egypt in 784/1382 at the age of fifty, when the *Muqaddima*, or a first draft of it, was already written, though he continued working upon it when in Egypt.

Ibn Khaldūn correctly claimed that he had created a new science—which approximates both to sociology and to a sort of philosophy of history. This science is in the last analysis based upon the recognition of the law, established by Ibn Khaldūn, that societies and civilizations are by nature mortal, and that in the course of their existence they go through parallel phases. In the first 'bedouin' phase, life is hard, simple and savage; in order not to perish, people are obliged to be brave and to feel intense loyalty to their family and tribe. This life, which is especially characteristic for a desert habitat, develops the military virtues. In due course the bedouin overrun the civilized countries. This way of life also prepared people, especially the Arabs, to accept the religious truth and the guidance of a prophet.

The second 'sedentary' phase, which is in store for the savage conquerors, is marked by an increase in the comforts and luxuries of life and by the growth of the crafts, arts and sciences. As life becomes easier, the old loyalties and the warlike qualities of the population tend to disappear. The community loses its power of resistance against aggression. It is in its turn ripe for conquest by whatever vigorous uncivilized barbarians yet remain.

Some of the characteristics of the two phases, especially of the first, conform to the schema, found in Greek political philosophy, of the transformation of the natural simple healthy community into a diseased community hankering after luxury.

Ibn Khaldūn applied the philosophical theory of these two phases to the history of the Arab, or the bedouin, people and to the destiny of various Islamic dynasties and régimes. As a result, the description of the two phases had to be somewhat modified in order to make them fit Arab or Islamic history. On the other hand, Arab history was used to illustrate the unchanging historical laws and thus became a paradigm for the course of history in the various kinds of states and communities, some of which have already gone through one or both phases, while others will have this experience in the future.

This historical or sociological approach entails a shift of attention. The problem which concerns Ibn Khaldūn first and foremost is not the truth or falsehood of a particular religion, but its place in the historical process which leads societies from primitive barbarism to civilized effeteness. The arts and the philosophic and other sciences are also regarded from the historic point of view. Their appearance in the second phase is a symptom of the ripeness and approaching senility of a given society. As has sometimes happened in Western civilization, historicity is seen to be an essential element of all theoretical and practical sciences.

ISLAMIC THOUGHT IN THE EAST AFTER THE MID-SIXTH/TWELFTH CENTURY

In the history of Islamic thought in the East, the second half of the sixth/twelfth century is marked by the appearance of a new system of thought, namely the Ishrāqī philosophy (*ḥikmat al-ishrāq*). Its author, Shihāb al-Dīn Yaḥyā al-Suhrawardī (often called *al-Maqtūl*, 'the Slain', because in 578/1191, at the age of thirty-six, he was executed as a heretic in Aleppo), has influenced the evolution of Islamic philosophy in the later period nearly as much as Ibn Sīnā himself.

Al-Suhrawardī himself adapted for his own purposes elements of Ibn Sīnā's thought and vocabulary. There is, for instance, little doubt that the appellation *ḥikmat al-ishrāq* ('The philosophy of [the sun] putting forth its rays') is at least in part meant to be a counterpart to Ibn Sīnā's oriental (*mashriqiyya*) philosophy. Al-Suhrawardī showed that he had a greater interest in, and knowledge of, Eastern wisdom than Ibn Sīnā, to whom he frequently makes disparaging references. While Ibn Sīnā makes no attempt to substantiate his claim that the Oriental philosophy derives from an ancient eastern philosophical tradition, al-Suhrawardī, who was of Persian origin, and some of whose works are written in Persian, incorporates into his own system many Zoroastrian terms and concepts.

As far as philosophical tradition is concerned, he is first and foremost a Platonist, hostile to the Peripatetics (whom he follows in some of his earlier writings), though not to Aristotle himself, and full of respect for the Hermetic writings, which, in his opinion, antedated Plato. He adopts the doctrine of Platonic ideas considered as existent, and not as neutral with respect to existence like Ibn Sīna's essences. These ideas form a part of an elaborate system of incorporeal entities.

Fakhr al-Dīn al-Rāzī (d. 606/1209), a contemporary of al-Suhrawardī, was a philosopher, a *mutakallim* and a commentator on the Qur'ān. Some of his most important works are decisively influenced by Abu'l-Barakāt al-Baghdādī. Fakhr al-Dīn wrote a very critical commentary on Ibn Sīnā's *Kitāb al-ishārāt wa'l-tanbīhāt*. This was countered by another commentary on the same work written by Naṣīr al-Dīn al-Ṭūsī (d. 672/1273), a faithful disciple of Ibn Sīnā. The debate thus inaugurated had many repercussions in Islamic philosophic literature.

As far as philosophy is concerned, the Avicennian and the Ishrāqī doctrines show the greatest vigour in the three centuries that follow upon Naṣīr al-Dīn al-Ṭūsī. The numerous philosophical texts of this period have not yet been sufficiently studied. Nor has the *kalām* literature of the period after 1150, which had several eminent representatives, for instance Hāfiẓ al-Dīn al-Nasafī (d.710/1310), and Mas'ūd al-Taftazānī (d. 792/1390). The Shī'ī theologian, Zayn al-Din al-'Āmilī (d. 966/1558), may also be mentioned in this connexion.

There are grounds for thinking that the most original attack upon philosophical thought made in Islam, perhaps not even excluding al-Ghazālī's, was not made by a professed *mutakallim* but by a Ḥanbalī Taqī al-Dīn b. Taymiyya (d. 729/1328), who from his strictly Traditionalist standpoint opposes *kalām*, the pantheism of the mystics and that inherent in Ibn Sīnā's doctrine. In his great work, *Kitāb al-radd 'ala'l-manṭiqiyyīn* ('The book of the refutation of the logicians') Ibn Taymiyya criticizes Aristotelian logic. He points out the very limited utility of definitions in giving knowledge of the thing defined and the uselessness of logical 'demonstration' in so far as it refers to existent things, for demonstration only concerns universals, which possess reality solely in thought and not in the external world.

The composition of *kalām* texts, and of Ḥanbalī treatises concerned with anti-philosophical polemics or with theology, was not confined in the period with which we are dealing to any one region of the Islamic East. They were written both in the Arab and in the Persian countries, and also in other parts of the Muslim world.

In contrast, a living tradition of philosophical writing can only be discovered during this period, apart from a few exceptions, in the Persian-speaking countries. In Persia this tradition had a last flowering in the Safavid period, in which a great name, Ṣadr al-Dīn al-Shīrāzī (d. 1058/1648) stands out. His 'Four books', *al-Asfār al-arba'a*, written in Arabic, which continued to be, to an incomparably greater extent than Persian, the linguistic medium of the philosophers, is a sort of *summa* of the philosophical doctrines of the schools of Ibn Sīnā and of al-Suhrawardī, who, with a touch of Persian patriotism, is called by al-Shīrāzī 'the Reviver of the Traces of the Pahlavī Sages.' This tradition survived to an even later period. It seems not to have been entirely moribund when, in the nineteenth century, Western orientalists began to take a scholarly interest in Islamic philosophy.

CHAPTER 12

WARFARE

The Arabs, within the two decades which followed the death of the Prophet Muḥammad (11/632), won for themselves a large empire embracing Syria, Egypt, 'Irāq, Persia and much of Arabia itself. The battles at Ajnadayn (13/634), on the river Yarmuk (15/636) and at 'Ayn Shams, i.e. Heliopolis (19/640), foreshadowed for the Byzantines the definitive loss of Syria and Egypt; the battles of al-Qādisiyya and Jalūlā' (16/637) and at Nihāvand (20/641) marked crucial moments in the reduction of Sasanid 'Irāq and Sasanid Persia to Muslim control. It was a conquest at once rapid, astonishing and durable.

The success of the Arabs must be ascribed in no small measure to the circumstances prevailing at that time in the conquered territories. Byzantium and Persia, a little before the Arab assault, had come to the end of a protracted conflict, extending over almost a hundred years and destructive of their resources—neither of these states was in a condition to meet a new and formidable threat from outside. Grievances political, religious and financial made the rule of Byzantium unwelcome to the populations of Syria and Egypt—populations which, being Semitic in origin, were more akin to the Arabs than to their masters at Constantinople. In 'Irāq, too, there was a population of Semitic descent, also with grievances of a similar nature and little inclined to favour the alien domination of Persia. Throughout the lands constituting the Fertile Crescent the Arabs fought, therefore, with the mass of the local people passive towards their intrusion or, more often, sympathetic towards the Muslim cause.

Of great importance in the campaigns of conquest were the physical toughness of the Arab warriors born and reared in a desert milieu, the high morale deriving from their identification with Islam and the confidence bred of continuing and remarkable success in the field. The tribesmen living adjacent to Syria had acquired no doubt some degree of acquaintance with the art of war practised in Byzantium. Moreover, the tribes located on the western fringes of 'Irāq must have been familiar to some extent with the methods of warfare used in Persia. None the less, even with due allowance made for these factors of refinement, it remains true that the practice of war common to the mass of the Arab warriors was of an unsophisticated kind: no elaborate organization for warfare, no developed system of tactics and no armament equal to the weapons used in the Byzantine and Sasanid armies. Swift and fluid in movement, mounted on camels but fighting at need on foot, the Arabs excelled in the arts of sudden manoeuvre and of the harassment of their foe. On the field of battle the various tribal elements fought as distinct units arranged often in lines; the usual mode of procedure was an alternation of frontal assault, of withdrawal and of renewed advance, the javelin and the lance being prominent at first, with the sword to follow as the main weapon at close quarters. The campaigns of conquest represented in fact the *Kleinkrieg* of the desert raised to abnormal proportions and carried out with forces of unwonted size—for the Muslim régime at Mecca and Medina acted as a mechanism of concentration, bringing together the Arab tribesmen in numbers far transcending the small bands characteristic of nomad warfare in Arabia.

The warriors who, under the banner of Islam, came out of Najd to win a new empire found themselves perforce separated from their former habitat. With success once gained, the Muslim armies became in effect forces of occupation within the conquered territories—forces located in cantonments which soon developed into large garrison cities, e.g., Kūfa and Baṣra in ʿIrāq or Fusṭāṭ in Egypt. Here the Arabs, now constituting a dominant warrior caste in the Muslim empire, lived with their households, enjoying the prestige and profit accruing to them from their imperial role.

Their means of subsistence were, in general, twofold: plunder taken in war (*ghanīma*—a rich reward, as long as the tide of conquest flowed without abatement) and also allowances (*ʿaṭā*ʾ) paid to active soldiers, Muslim in faith and Arab in descent, from the revenues of the the state. Most of these soldiers received *ʿaṭā*ʾ amounting perhaps to 500 or even 1,000 dirhams per annum in the time of the Umayyad régime (41–132/661–750), although the higher ranks no doubt obtained much more. As to the average strength of the Arab forces serving in the first hundred years of Muslim rule, no clear estimate is available. A total of 50,000 has been suggested for the reign of the Caliph ʿUmar I (13–23/634–644) and of 100,000 for the golden age of the Umayyad state (*c*. 81/700). The value of these figures is, of course, no more than approximate, but even at such a modest level of calculation the payment of *ʿaṭā*ʾ would have been a serious burden on the finances of the central government.

The burden tended to become heavier as the tide of conquest slowed down and the spoils of war diminished in amount. Warfare itself, more complex than before and waged now on distant frontiers, rose in cost. Of urgent importance, too, was the growing movement of conversion to Islam among the subject peoples of the empire. Of the new converts a large number, known as *mawālī*, stood in a relation of clienthood to the Arab tribal elements constituting the armies of Islam and fought at their side as auxiliaries, but for rates of remuneration and a share in the plunder of war less than the Arabs enjoyed. The *mawālī*, as Muslims, aspired to an equal status with the Arabs—and this on a financial and economic, as on a religious and social, level. A claim of this magnitude, if realized in practice, would perforce undermine the domination of the Arab warrior caste within the empire.

The role, in the armies of Islam, of soldiers Muslim through conversion and non-Arab in ethnic origin grew in importance during the years of Umayyad rule. Of great significance for the Umayyad state was Khurāsān, a vast region embracing north-eastern Persia and much of Turkistān. Here a warlike frontier population, long accustomed to defend itself against the nomads inhabiting the western steppe lands of Central Asia, had come over in large numbers to Islam and, as *mawālī*, had taken service with the Arab armies located in that area. The men of Khurāsān and also of other regions in Persia, conscious of their Iranian origin, of their imperial past and of their cultural pre-eminence over the Arabs, soon become impatient, to an ever increasing degree, of the inferior status which the Arab warriors sought to enforce on them. Also important for the future was the fact that the recrudescence of tribal feuds, so marked within the Arab warrior caste during the later years of Umayyad rule, made itself felt with peculiar violence in Khurāsān. A combination of *mawālī* grievances and Arab feuds offered to the subversive elements ranged against the Umayyads a fertile ground for the dissemination of their propaganda—and it was indeed from Khurāsān that the armies came which, in the great revolution of 132/750, overthrew the house of Umayya and raised to the caliphate the house of al-ʿAbbās.

The events of 132/750 did not at once eliminate the Arabs as a factor of importance in the armies of Islam—indeed, the troops from Khurāsān responsible for the fall of the Umayyads included numerous soldiers of Arab as well as of Iranian origin. It is true, however, that the succeeding hundred years saw the gradual diminution in number of the

Arabs serving in the forces of the 'Abbasid régime and, at the same time, the progressive limitation—not least for financial reasons—of the *'aṭ ā'* payments.

After 132/750 the Khurāsānīs constituted for some two generations the hard core of the 'Abbasid armies, having the status of regular and, as it were, professional troops in receipt of pay and maintenance from the central government. It was their fate to be severed from their former *milieu* in Khurāsān and assimilated more and more to their new environment in 'Irāq—in short, to become identified above all, in outlook and allegiance, with the capital of the empire, Baghdād.

This condition of affairs was altered in the time of the civil war between the sons of the 'Abbasid Caliph Hārūn al-Rashīd (170–93/786–809)—i.e. between the Caliph al-Amīn (193–8/809–13) and the future Caliph al-Ma'mūn (198–218/813–33). Al-Ma'mūn, victorious over his brother, recruited in Khurāsān and the neighbouring lands the forces which raised him to the throne. The civil war was in fact a conflict of the 'new Khurāsānīs' under al-Ma'mūn against the 'old Khurāsānīs' of 132/750, or rather their descendants, long established at Baghdād as the *élite* troops of the 'Abbasid régime. Of Arab elements in the armies of al-Ma'mūn there is little mention in the sources—their number was indeed to diminish in the course of his reign and to decline still further in the time of his successor, al-Mu'taṣim (218–27/833–42). Only rarely in the future would Arab warriors assume once more a role of major importance in military affairs and then only within a restricted sphere, as, for example, in Syria and al-Jazīra, where the local Hamdanid and Mirdasid dynasties, both of Arab origin, flourished during the fourth/tenth and fifth/eleventh centuries.

As the 'Abbasid caliphate fell into decline, new régimes began to make their appearance in the Muslim empire, each of them maintaining its own separate establishment for war. The composition of the various Muslim armies, in respect of race, was now becoming more diversified than it had been before. A good example can be seen in the Fatimid caliphate of Egypt (356–567/969–1171). The Fatimids had in their service Berber tribesmen from the Maghrib, but also regiments of Turks, black troops from the Sudan and, in addition, though to a lesser degree, contingents of Slavs from the Balkan lands and of Armenians from Asia Minor. An element of serious danger existed in the recruitment of mixed armies, for differences of ethnic origin, of language and of technical competence in war led often to bitter conflict along ethnic lines—a phenomenon well exemplified in the 'time of troubles' which beset Egypt during the years 452–70/1060–77, when the rivalries of the Turks and the Sudanese reduced the land to a state of confusion.

Of all the peoples represented in the armies of Islam none would surpass in importance the Turks, destined to become the warrior race *par excellence* of the Muslim world. There was some recruitment of Turks—though still, no doubt, on a small scale—in the time of the first 'Abbasid caliphs and perhaps even earlier. The 'new Khurāsānīs' of al-Ma'mūn included soldiers described as Farāghina (men from Farghānā), also as Bukhārīs and Khwārazmīs (men from the regions of Bukhārā and Khwārazm)—troops, in short, drawn from the eastern areas of Khurāsān and from Transoxania. Amongst the 'new Khurāsānīs' are numbered, too, the *Atrāk*, i.e. the Turks. The reign of al-Mu'taṣim, the brother of al-Ma'mūn, was to see a large increase in the recruitment of Turkish soldiers. This inflow of Turks must have come at first from districts close to the north-eastern frontiers of the empire. Soon, however, with the gradual consolidation of Muslim influence in Transoxania, it became possible to draw recruits from the steppe lands beyond the border zones—i.e. Turkish children acquired, through war and trade, as slave material, made Muslim, trained as slave soldiers (*mamlūks*) and then manumitted to become the regular, professional troops of the caliphate and of the local dynasties now emerging within the 'Abbasid territories, e.g. the Tulunids in Egypt and Syria (254–92/868–905) or the Samanids in Persia and Transoxania (261–389/874–999). Henceforward the fame and pre-eminence of the Turks as soldiers would be universal in the lands of Islam.

The pattern of warfare which had brought the Arabs success in the time of the great conquests was soon overlaid, as it were, with procedures drawn from the traditions of Byzantium and Persia. It was to be altered still further through the changes of recruitment occurring in the first two centuries of Muslim rule. The Arab warriors had as their main arms the javelin (*ḥarba*) and the lance (*rumḥ*), with the sword (*sayf*) as their chief weapon for close combat. The bow (*qaws*) was also known to them. A superior skill in the use of this arm did not become common, however, in the Muslim world until contact had been made with the Persians and, above all, with the Turks, who excelled as archers, being able to let loose a hail of light arrows while riding their horses at speed. The cross-bow, too, was employed in the armies of the 'Abbasid caliphate. As to means of defence, mention can be made here of the shield (*daraqa*), the cuirass (*tarīka*), the coat of mail (*dir'*) and the helmet (*khūdha*).

To the general in charge of a campaign was given the title of *amīr*—later, under the 'Abbasids, the expression *amīr al-umarā'* came into use with the sense of head of the *amirs*. The troops sent into the field might constitute a number of separate corps reflecting various lines of division, e.g., tribal allegiance or ethnic origin, dependence on a particular general or technical function in war. It was usual for each corps to have its own flags (sing., *rāya*) and sometimes a distinctive mode of dress also. The general in command had a special banner (*liwā'*) located near his tent. On the march the arrangement of the troops (*ta'biyya*) was into a fivefold order known as *khamīs*, i.e. into a vanguard (*muqaddama*), a centre (*qalb*), a right wing (*maymana*), a left wing (*maysara*) and a rearguard (*sāqa*). The *khamīs* was an ideal, a theoretical arrangement which often had to be modified in order to meet the demands of the moment—e.g. to overcome the difficulties of the terrain or to counter the operations of the foe.

The march itself tended to be slow, since the rate of progress was dependent on the speed of the foot-soldiers, of the flocks and herds carried along as food supplies, and of the camels, asses and mules laden with the tents, baggage and munitions of war. Great care was taken to choose suitable encampments in the field, the defensive possibilities of each site and the nearness to water and pasturage being of particular importance. Should the halt be a long one, the camp would be surrounded with a trench (*khandaq*). The fivefold order was often maintained inside the camp, with broad avenues separating the different corps and with the general stationed at the centre. The normal covering for the troops in summer consisted of tents (sing., *khayma*); in winter more solid accommodation was sometimes built of wood.

As to the order of battle, the vanguard and the rearguard might now be combined with the main forces, the actual line of battle comprising a firm centre and two wings. At times the troops would be aligned in small squadrons or companies (sing., *kardūs*). An alternative method was to fight in ranks, often three in number, one behind the other. Of these ranks the first might contain archers and cross-bowmen; the second would be of infantry armed with lances, swords and shields; and the third might consist of the heavy cavalry. At the centre of the battle formation was the standard of the general. The battle itself was in essence a cavalry charge repeated at need several times. To the bowmen fell the task of disrupting the enemy assault at long range; the role of the infantry was to repulse that assault in close combat, should need arise. The cavalry, if successful in breaking through on one sector of the battle front and if well-led and disciplined, would then turn with effect against the flank and rear of the foe.

A manoeuvre sometimes attempted was to ambush the hostile forces along their line of march, or with the battle once engaged, to lure them into terrain subject to attack from positions prepared in advance. Of great advantage here would be not so much the tactics of the Arab horsemen, often wont to charge in line formation, but the tactics of the Turks, i.e. the sudden onset, the feigned flight, the infiltration to the flanks, the arrow bombardment from all sides and the swift renewal of the assault.

The pre-eminence in such warfare rested with the cavalry. Now and again, however, it was the infantry which came to the fore. A good example can be found in the men of Daylam, a mountainous region south of the Caspian Sea. The Daylamīs attained a notable reputation as foot-soldiers. Their expansion southward from Daylam in the third/ninth and fourth/tenth centuries led to the establishment of the Buyid régime in Persia and 'Irāq, but Daylamī warriors also served as mercenaries in the armies of other Muslim states. A mountain race inured to stress and privation, the Daylamīs fought on foot and exhibited great skill in the use of their own particular weapons, above all the *zhupīn*, a short, two-pronged javelin for thrusting or throwing, and the battleaxe. On ground which allowed them some freedom of manoeuvre their frequent mode of fighting was to link together their tall, painted shields in the form of a wall and then to join combat at close quarters. Often the Daylamīs, seeking to achieve in some degree the mobility characteristic of horsemen, came to the field of battle on camels and mules—a practice also in use among the palace infantry of the sultans of Ghazna in the fourth/tenth and fifth/eleventh centuries.

The Arabs who conquered a great empire for Islam had little acquaintance with the techniques of siege warfare. It was not long, however, before the Muslims took over the methods practised in Byzantium and in Sasanid Persia. Their command of the relevant techniques became, in due course, more refined and elaborate, reaching its highest level of development—at least in the world of medieval Islam—during the time of the Crusades, when siege warfare assumed a decisive importance in the long conflict between Muslim and Christian. None the less, with allowance made for some measure of advance in respect of the siege instruments themselves, it remains true that the siege warfare of the Muslims—as indeed of the Christians also—was still, with no fundamental change, the siege warfare of the Ancient World.

The armies of Islam made much use of the *manjanīq* or mangonel, a machine which involved the swinging of a beam or the movement of a counterpoise to strike and propel a missile with great force; also of the *'arrāda*, a ballista which hurled projectiles through the torsion of ropes. The *qaws al-ziyār*, a large cross-bow machine shooting great arrows and requiring several men to operate it, became known to the Muslims perhaps a little before 597/1200. Of frequent use, too, were the wooden tower (*burj*, *dabbāba*) and the battering ram (*kabsh*). The sources refer, in addition, to multiple-shooting bows, which the Mongols introduced into the Muslim world. A special corps of troops (*naffāṭ*) existed for the employment in siege warfare of naphtha (*nafṭ*), emitted from copper tubes (sing., *naffāṭa*) or thrown in pots (sing., *qārūra*). The art of mining (*naqb*) attained a high standard of excellence in the sixth/twelfth and seventh/thirteenth centuries. Tunnels would be excavated towards a fortress wall, the foundations of which were then hollowed out, wooden beams being inserted to support the stone-work. Once the beams had been set alight, the wall, in due course, would collapse of its own weight.

The period of the 'Abbasid decline (third–seventh/ninth–thirteenth centuries) saw a large increase in the use of *mamlūks* recruited as slaves, trained in the practice of war and freed to serve as professional troops—i.e. as horsemen bearing into combat a considerable weight of armament, but still mobile and far less burdened than the feudal knights of Western Europe who met them in battle during the time of the Crusades. The lands of Islam, in general, bred horses excellent for speed and endurance, but in no wise comparable for size and strength with the horses of Christendom. This factor was of great importance, since it limited the weight of armour that a Muslim soldier might wear in battle.

With the gradual disintegration of the Great Seljuk Sultanate after 485/1092, a number of small states made their appearance, notably in 'Irāq, al-Jazīra (Mesopotamia) and Syria, each having its own *'askar* or establishment of *mamlūk* soldiers. To maintain an effective *'askar*—and above all to maintain it at the highest level of professional excellence—was an expensive business. The state had to make regular payments to its *'askar* and also various donatives granted on special occasions, e.g. after a great success in the field or on the accession of a prince to the throne. It was the state, too, which in large measure bore the cost of the equipment and supplies distributed to the *mamlūks* at the beginning of a campaign. The manufacture of siege machines, the purchase of transport animals, the gathering of provisions—all meant additional expenditure, and on a lavish scale. Finding the expense of its armies more and more difficult to sustain, the central government of the caliphate, long before the rise of the Seljuks, had to abandon the system of cash payments and to replace them with assignments on the taxation due from a given area. The caliphs, failing to meet the cost of the imperial forces, began to make over even whole provinces to individual *amīrs*, on condition that the *amīrs*, and not the state, should maintain the troops essential for the defence of a particular region—a procedure which favoured greatly the emergence of local autonomies within the empire. At the same time it became not uncommon to see grants of taxation allotted to the rank and file amongst the *mamlūks*. This device underwent a long evolution which gave it at length the character of a grant (*iqṭā*ʿ). To each *mamlūk*, after the completion of his training as a slave soldier and his subsequent manumission, was accorded a definite assignment of revenue per annum based on an estimate (*ʿibra*) which was calculated in a fictitious unit of account. The actual revenue, comprising payments in kind as well as in cash, came to the *mamlūk* from specific lands ascribed to him—i.e. from the local population cultivating those lands and owing taxation to the state. A grant of *iqṭā*ʿ involved no right of ownership in the estates constituting the grant. The *mamlūk* soldier enjoyed only the unsufruct of the land, the right to receive certain defined revenues from it. He was obliged, from the yield of the fief, to provide for the equipment that he needed to maintain himself as an efficient soldier (tents, arms, beasts of burden, etc.) and also for a personal retinue which would go with him to war. It was advantageous for the *mamlūk* to be at home during harvest-time in order to ensure that he obtained the revenue in cash and in kind due to him from his grant. This recurring need meant that it was almost impossible to keep a *mamlūk* force in the field from one campaign season to the next or even, at times, to bring them to war over a consecutive number of years. It was a signal evidence of the esteem accorded to the great Ayyubid Sultan Saladin (564-89/1168–93) that he was able to sustain unbroken for nearly two years (August 1189–July 1191) his operations against the Christians at ʿAkkā (Acre) in Palestine.

The *iqṭā*ʿ system was reaching its full development in the sixth/

twelfth and seventh/thirteenth centuries. Of the troops endowed with these grants two characteristics deserve to be underlined here: their ethnic origin, which was in general Turkish, and their function in war, which was to serve above all as mounted archers. The bow was the dominant weapon in use amongst them, but with the lance, sword, mace and shield (a small round target) also constituting a normal part of their equipment. Their tactics in the field offered little that was new—unless perhaps in their formidable excellence—over the practice of earlier centuries. Combat at a distance with missile weapons, notably the bow, also feigned retreat leading into ambush, pressure on the flank and rear of the opposing forces, and harassment of the foe, while his columns were still on the march—manoeuvres of this sort find ample illustration in the campaigns, for example, of the armies which served Saladin. It was a warfare marked by the indubitable pre-eminence of the cavalry and of the bow, distinguished, too, by mobility, by superb horsemanship and by a skill no less superb in the individual management of arms. A classic expression, as it were, and embodiment of this warfare can be seen in the famous régime known as the Mamluk Sultanate of Syria and Egypt (648–922/1250–1517), a régime composed at first of Turks drawn from the Kıpchak steppe adjacent to the Caspian and Aral Seas, but later of Cherkes (Circassians) recruited from the Caucasus. Here, indeed, was a splendid example of a warrior caste sustaining itself through a continuing inflow of slave material destined to be trained in the arts of war and then manumitted to assume the full status and privileges of a *mamlūk* soldier.

The Mamluks stood at the end of a long evolution already in 648/1250 more than six centuries old. There had been, during that time, notable changes in the composition of the armies of Islam (e.g. the growing importance of the Turks) and in the institutions which sustained those armies (e.g., the rise of the *mamlūk* element or the emergence of the *iqṭāʿ*). On the tactical side, too, there were changes of note. The tactics of nomad warriors—at first of the Arabs and later of the Turks—had been combined with modes of procedure characteristic of more complex societies like Byzantium and Persia to form a Muslim pattern of warfare. One major line of evolution was towards the undeniable dominance of horsemen in war, above all of mounted archers swift and fluid in manoeuvre, adept in the use of the bow. The degree of change was much less marked on the technological front. Here the personal weapons of the Muslim warrior, such as the lance, the sword and the mace, differed little from the weapons familiar, at an earlier date, to the Byzantine or the Sasanid soldier. If there was a change of genuine importance in respect of armament, it is to be found in the gradual rise to pre-eminence of the bow—and also of the tactics appropriate to its efficient use in battle. As to siege operations, the instruments and techniques employed in the armies of Islam were still, in general, the instruments and techniques known to the armies of Byzantium and of Sasanid Persia. A revolution of a technological kind would soon begin, however, to alter in radical fashion the character of warfare. Of this revolution the basic cause was the introduction of gunpowder, cannon and firearms.

No exact date can be given to mark the first use of cannon in the lands of Islam. A broad perspective can be obtained, none the less, from the evidence available in the sources. The Arabic authors al-Qalqashandī and Ibn Khaldūn, describing events which occurred in the time of the Mamluk Sultanate, afford some reason to believe that cannon (sing., *midfa*ʿ, *mukḥula*) existed at Alexandria and Cairo in the years *c.* 767–78/1365–76. There was, however, no serious attempt amongst the Mamluks to exploit the possibilities of the new weapon on a large scale, until conflict with the Portuguese in the Indian Ocean after 1498 and with the Ottoman Turks in 890–7/1485–91 and again in 922–3/1516–17 forced them into such a course. The arquebus (*al-bunduq al-raṣāṣ*, *bunduqiyya*) did not make its appearance in Egypt, it would seem, until as late as 895/1489–90 in the reign of the Mamluk Sultan al-Ashraf Qā'it Bāy.

As to the Ottoman empire, a register for Albania, dating from the year 1431, indicates that cannon (*top*) had been introduced at least in the time of Sultan Meḥmed I (816–24/1413–21) and perhaps even somewhat earlier. There are references to the Ottoman use of cannon, e.g. against Constantinople in 825/1422, at Adalia in 827/1424 and against the Hexamilion on the isthmus of Corinth in 849/1446. It is, moreover, well known that Meḥmed II (855–86/1451–81) brought a number of large cannon to the siege of Constantinople in 857/1453. The Ottomans would seem to have used cannon for the first time on a battle-field at Kosova in 852/1448. The arquebus (*tüfenk*) found acceptance amongst them *c.* 1440, i.e. in the course of the Hungarian campaigns fought during the reign of Sultan Murād II (824–55/1421–51).

The employment of cannon and of the arquebus, at least on an appreciable scale, tended to occur a little later in time elsewhere in the Muslim world. Persia came into contact with the new instruments of war during the reign of Uzun Ḥasan (d. 883/1478), the head of the Ak-Koyunlu Turcomans. A number of references bear witness to the use *c.* 1506–8, of cannon (*tūp*) and of the arquebus (*tufang*) in the first years of the Safavid régime in Persia. Guns would appear to have been well known in northern India under the Lodī sultans (855–930/1451–1526). There is evidence, too, of their employment in the Deccan states before 1500. Cannon had also a considerable role at the battle of Pānīpat (932/1526), which marked the establishment of the Mughal empire in northern India. As to the far western reaches of the Muslim world, guns and firearms, although noted in connexion with events of an earlier date, did not come into more general use in Morocco until the rise of the Saʿdid régime (960–1065/1553–1654).

The adoption of the cannon and the arquebus was nowhere more earnest and intensive than in the Ottoman empire. A major role in the transmission of these arms and of the techniques associated with them fell to the peoples of Serbia and Bosnia. Troops skilled in the employment of guns and firearms and recruited in these lands are known to have served under Meḥmed II. No less important was the continuing flow of specialists from Europe, most of them German and Italian at first, but with experts from France, England and Holland becoming more numerous in later times. A specialist of Hungarian origin, by name Urban, cast some of the great cannon that the Ottomans brought to the siege of Constantinople in 857/1453. Artillerists of European descent, Italian, Dutch and English, served the Ottoman guns in 1048/1638, when Sultan Murād IV besieged and retook Baghdād from Shāh Ṣafī of Persia. French officers came to Istanbul on a number of occasions in the late eleventh/seventeenth and twelfth/eighteenth centuries in order to advise the Ottomans on the techniques of warfare then current in Europe. Experts of Christian origin constituted, indeed, a permanent and indispensable element in the technical corps of the Ottoman army—i.e. amongst the armourers (*jebejiler*), the artillerists (*topjular*), the transport corps handling guns and munitions of war (*top ʿarabajilari*), the bombardiers (*khumbarajılar*) and the sappers (*laghım ıılar*).

Even the names which the Ottomans gave to their cannon derived, to some extent at least, from Europe—e.g. *bajalushka* (cf. Italian *basilisco*), *balyemez* (perhaps from the German *Faule Metze*) and *kolonborna* (cf. Italian *colubrina*—i.e. culverin). The sources also contain expressions of non-European origin, such as the name *ḍarbzāna* indicating (in

Ottoman usage) a falconet type of cannon. *Ḍarbzan* is found, too, as the name employed for a particular kind of gun in the armies of Safavid Persia. How strong, in the field of war, the Ottoman influence was in the lands to the east of Anatolia and 'Irāq can be seen from the fact that words current in Ottoman Turkish like *bajalushka*, *ḍarbzan*, and *tabanja* found acceptance in the armies of Mughal India. It is well known that artillery experts from the Ottoman empire often took service and rose to high rank in the armies of various Indian states: a Muṣṭafā Rūmī was active under Bābur and a Rūmī Khān under the sultan of Gujarāt. Even the battle order adopted in these armies is said to have been arranged at times in accordance with the custom of Rūm, i.e. of the Ottoman empire.

The dissemination of firearms was often a slow and gradual affair. To the Mamluks, for example, proud of their status, yet also exhibiting the indurated mentality of a cavalry *élite* bred in a tradition now old and over-rigid, skill in horsemanship and in the management of the bow, the lance and the sword was central to their whole lives. The new firearms, if taken over, would involve the relinquishment, at least in no small degree, of their familiar weapons and in addition the need to fight dismounted, since the arquebus was too cumbersome to be used on horseback. The arquebus, indeed, was to them the instrument of a craven and treacherous foe, a device unchivalrous and undignified, against which no warrior could demonstrate with success his valour and his pre-eminence in the art of personal combat. The danger threatening from the Portuguese in the Indian Ocean and also from the Ottomans forced the Mamluks, at a late hour, to countenance the introduction of guns and firearms—not for their own use, but for special corps recruited, however, from elements regarded as of inferior status, e.g. black slaves (*'abīd*), Turcomans and Maghāriba (men from the Maghrib). At the same time, care was taken to ensure that these special troops did not become too strong. Their unrestricted growth would have undermined the dominance of the Mamluk *élite*, which was itself of no great numerical strength.

Amongst the Ottomans, too, there was resistance to the adoption of firearms. The mounted regiments of the imperial household, also the *sipahis*, i.e. the horsemen endowed with fiefs in the provinces of the empire, and, in addition, the retinues of the high officials and dignitaries, all constituted a cavalry *élite* not less proud than the Mamluks of their skill in horsemanship and in arms, nor less identified with the older methods of warfare. Ogier Ghiselin de Busbecq, the ambassador of the Emperor Ferdinand I at Istanbul, relates how the Ottoman grand *vezīr*, Rustem Pasha, sought to accustom some of his retinue to the use of firearms, only to see them become engrimed with gunpowder and subjected to the laughter and scorn of the other soldiers, a humiliation which led them to ask—and to receive—from their master permission to end the distasteful experiment. The same author tells also of an Ottoman *deli*, a member of a special corps of horsemen, who, explaining the reasons for a reverse that he and his comrades had undergone, ascribed the misfortune not to the valour of the foe, but to his employment of firearms, adding that the result would have been quite different, with success going to the Ottomans, had the conflict been fought *vera virtute*, i.e. with true courage involving physical prowess and personal skill in the conduct of arms. With the gradual appearance of lighter and more manageable types of hand-gun the reluctance of the Ottoman cavalry to adopt firearms was broken down, although the process was in fact a slow one. Venetian sources relating to the Hungarian War of 1001–15/1593–1606 between Austria and the Ottoman empire note that the *spahi di paga*, i.e. the mounted regiments belonging to the household of the sultan, had begun to arm themselves with the *terzarollo*, a short-barrelled arquebus, but that as yet the pistol was not in use amongst the Ottomans. Paul Rycaut, describing the situation which existed in the time of the first two Köprülü *vezīrs* (1066–87/1656–76), was still able to state that the cavalry of the imperial household, though now armed with carbines and pistols, yet had no great love for the new weapons. A hundred years later soldiers and authors of European origin would confirm this judgment, attributing to the horsemen of the sultan a marked preference for *l'arme blanche* and underlining their incomparable adroitness in this form of warfare.

The arquebus found a much readier acceptance amongst the infantry than amongst the cavalry of the Ottoman sultan. It became well established in the corps of Janissaries during the reign of Meḥmed II. The more general extension of its use, both inside and outside the corps, was, however, a long and gradual affair. The changing pressures of warfare, above all in the Caucasus (986–98/1578–90) and along the Danube (1593–1606), enforced on the Ottomans a rapid increase in the number of foot-soldiers serving the sultan. The increase was achieved through the recruitment, notably from Anatolia, of Muslim-born soldiers into the troops of the imperial household and also as 'irregular' levies known under such names as *levend, sarija* or *sekban*. These levies served, too, in the retinues of the provincial governors and of other high officials—retinues much larger now than in earlier times. Of the new forces, the main weapon—with the sword and the pistol—would be the arquebus and later the musket.

The fame of the Janissaries as a corps of foot-soldiers expert in the use of firearms extended far and wide throughout the lands of Islam. It is not surprising that other Muslim states should seek to imitate the splendid model set before them. The Safavid régime in Persia had been the creation of Shāh Ismā'īl I (d. 630/1524). Its military strength consisted primarily of warriors drawn from the Turkish tribes long resident in Anatolia. These warriors retained in Persia their tribal identities; their chieftains became governors of provinces under the shah; the young men of the tribes continued to form the mass of the Safavid armies. At the same time there were feuds amongst them and indiscipline arising from tribal enmities and from the conflict for domination centred around the throne; a serious threat, in short, to the well-being of the state. Shāh 'Abbās I (995–1038/1587–1629), the ablest of the Safavids, strove to fashion a counterpoise to the influence of the tribal warriors, a concentration of armed strength under his immediate control. To achieve this aim he established three corps: of arquebusiers, of artillerists, and of horsemen equipped with firearms, all of them recruited from the Circassian and Georgian peoples of the Caucasus. A further example can be found in Morocco. Here the *Sharīfs* of the Sa'did line, moving out of the southern Atlas, employed the tribal forces at their command to subdue almost the whole of Morocco. As a means of defence against enemies at home and abroad the Sa'dids maintained a corps of arquebusiers (*rumāt*) embracing various ethnic elements, e.g. men of Rūmī descent (i.e. from the Ottoman lands) and also renegades from Christendom, often Spanish in origin.

The arquebus of the Ottomans, like that of North Africa, tended to be longer in the barrel than the Christian model and of a calibre enabling it to fire heavier bullets. Its range is not often indicated in the sources, but there is mention of distances as great as five and six hundred paces. The skill of the Ottoman arquebusiers at the siege of Malta in 972–3/1565, even when firing by moonlight, earned special praise in some Christian accounts of the event. As improved versions of the hand-gun made their appearance, the technical expressions used in Turkish reflected the change, e.g. *mushkat tüfenkleri* (muskets), *karabina* (carbine) and *tabanja* (pistol: cf. also *chifte tabanjalı tüfenk*—a double-barrelled pistol). Words and phrases of this kind underline the continuing influence of Europe on the Ottoman practice of war.

The transition in siege warfare from the machines employed in earlier times, such as the *manjanīq* and the *ʿarrāda*, to the cannon and gunpowder was not abrupt. Old instruments and techniques had still a role in the Ottoman sieges of the ninth/fifteenth and tenth/sixteenth centuries: mantlets, for example, at Otranto in 885/1480 and at Nicosia in 978/1570, also wooden towers at Malta in 972–3/1565. Moreover, the Ottomans—as at Rhodes in 928–9/1522—found it advantageous to continue the ancient method for bringing down the walls of a fortress, i.e. excavation under the walls and the insertion of wooden beams later to be set on fire, so that the stonework would collapse, once the flames had burnt through the supporting timber.

It was in siege warfare, however, that cannon first came into their own. The methods employed to cast guns were still crude, the finished products incapable of a performance at once accurate and predictable over a sustained sequence of firing. As to the procedure for aiming the cannon, it consisted of little more at first than the use of wooden baulks and wedges under the barrel to fix the elevation of the gun and around the loading chamber to control the recoil. Cannon, during the earlier phases of their development, had no great effect, therefore, on objects in motion. The ideal target was something large and immoveable—for example, a fortress which could be bombarded at leisure. The conviction was strong that the bigger the gun and the heavier the projectile that it hurled, then the more devastating its performance would be. It was a belief which, given the primitive character of the metallurgical and ballistic techniques then available, contained some measure of truth; massive cannon-balls did cause much damage on striking their target. Of the large cannon used in siege warfare an excellent example can be found in the *bajalushka* of the Ottomans. One of these guns, present at the siege of Malta, is said to have weighed 180 quintals and to have thrown iron shot one quintal in weight.

A Spanish artillerist, Collado, describes the Ottoman cannon as ill-proportioned and defective, but of sound metal. Chemical analysis of an Ottoman gun made in 1464 and now located at the Tower of London has shown it to be fashioned out of good bronze, although the smelting process was imperfect. The Ottomans often carried supplies of metal into the field, rather than whole cannon, ponderous and difficult to haul. The metal would be cast into guns before the actual fortress under attack and, once the siege was over, might be broken into pieces for convenience of transportation and for re-use on a subsequent occasion.

On the rate of fire the sources offer only scattered information. At Scutari (Ishkodra) in 883/1478–9 the Ottomans, using eleven great guns, fired *per diem* at different times 178, 187, 183, 168, 178, 182, 194, 131, 193 and 173 shots against the town. The extreme range of such cannon is difficult to assess. Some of the Ottoman batteries, however, at Malta began their bombardment from a distance of a thousand paces and more. The technique of the Ottoman gunners was a reflection of the methods current in Europe, e.g. a concentrated fire of batteries at one section of a fortress wall: medium cannon of the *kolonborna* (culverin) type would be used to achieve deep penetration into the stonework along transverse and vertical lines, the large *bajalushka* guns being employed thereafter in salvo to smash down the enfeebled wall with the violent surface impact of their shot.

Of much importance in siege warfare were devices other than cannon, yet depending on the use of gunpowder. Amongst them can be numbered the mortar (*havān*) throwing great shot of stone or metal; the bomb (*khumbara*) filled with explosives and fragmented material, e.g. pieces of iron or glass, and projected from the *havān*; the hand grenade (*el khumbarası*) made of bronze, glass or even earthenware and containing combustible and explosive matter; *sacchi di polvere* provided with a fuse and intended to be thrown at close quarters; also inflammable mixtures used as smoke-screens to cover the digging of trenches or as fire-balls to give illumination at night. Of all the instruments of siege warfare none was more potent, however, than the mine (*laghım*). The Ottomans excelled in this branch of siege-craft, not least because of their command over large resources of human labour, e.g. troops like the *ʿazab* soldiers, levies from the population of a given area, and also the skilled mining communities of the empire. Montecuccoli, in describing the siege technique of the Ottomans, refers to 'des mines simples, doubles et triples l'une sur l'autre...très profondes...de 120 et de 150 barils de poudre et davantage'.[1] The subterranean mines excavated beneath a fortress often consisted of several galleries each with a terminal chamber holding large amounts of gunpowder.

[1] *Mémoires de Montecuculi* (Paris, 1746), 345.

Although guns soon achieved a dominant role in sieges, their effectiveness was far less marked in battle. It was to be long indeed—in Europe as in the lands of Islam—before a true field artillery came into being as a result of continuing technological advance. The Muslim sources for the ninth/fifteenth and tenth/sixteenth centuries mention several kinds of light cannon, such as the *zanbūrak* used in Persia and in Mughal India, also the Ottoman *chakaloz* (or *shakaloz*: cf. Hungarian *szakállas*) and *pranghi* (or *pranki*: perhaps from the Italian *petriere a braga*). There are numerous references to the *ḍarbzan* or *ḍarbūzan* noted earlier—a light to medium gun, much more mobile than heavier cannon like the *bajalushka*, the *balyemez* and the *kolonborna*. It would seem to have been in the time of Bāyezīd II (886–918/1481–1512), or perhaps a little earlier, that the Ottomans began to make a more extensive use of the lighter types of gun. The Arabic historian Ibn Zunbul, writing about the campaigns of Selīm I (918–26/1512–20) against Syria and Egypt, refers to small Ottoman cannon which he calls *ḍarbzānāt* and which he describes as protected with covers of red felt and travelling in waggons, each having a team of four horses. The ammunition boxes for the guns hung suspended from the underside of the waggons and contained shot large enough to fill the palm of a hand. How effective such cannon were on the field of battle is difficult to see with exactitude. Ibn Zunbul declares that the Ottomans owed to their guns and firearms the victories of Marj Dābiq (922/1516) and Raydāniyya (922/1517) over the Mamluks. At Mohács (932/1526) the cannon massed in the centre of the Ottoman battle line drove back the Hungarian cavalry, but their fire was delivered, it would seem, at almost point-blank range.

The Ottomans sought, in respect of their field guns, to assimilate the advances made in Europe—and not without some degree of success. New words and phrases, or new meanings for old ones, came into use: e.g. *sachma toplar*, cannon firing a form of grape-shot or langrage; *alay topları*, 'regimental' guns, light and mobile; and also *balyemez*, employed now not so much to designate a particular type of cannon, but with the sense of the European *canon de batterie*. The process of standardization which was being carried out in Europe had some effect in the Ottoman empire, but the rate of advance was slow, at least before 1700. To read, for example, the lists of guns taken by the Christians from the Ottomans in the long war of 1094–1110/1683–99 is to encounter still a wide range of different calibres, weights and dimensions—although even here a qualification is advisable: the lists tend to be somewhat misleading, since the Ottomans, in order to make good rapidly the severe losses of cannon sustained by them, during this war, on the field of battle, at times pressed into service guns of ancient type, often well over a hundred years old, and relegated long before to the defence of fortresses far from the frontiers of the empire. Montecuccoli noted that the Ottoman artillery, though effective when it could be brought into action, was cumbersome to handle and transport, and consumed, moreover, large quantities of munitions.[1]

The rapid development of cannon and firearms extended greatly the logistic side of warfare. To prepare now a major campaign was to undertake in effect a full-scale industrial enterprise. The range of material needed was wide and varied: it would of course include guns, muskets, bombs and grenades, but also such items as powder-horns, leather sacks (for gunpowder), saltpetre, quick-match and lead (for bullets); picks, mattocks, shovels, axes, crow-bars, scythes and sickles (to gather forage); carts, axle-trees of iron, waggon-wheels, grease and tallow; cables, ropes, nails, horseshoes, anvils and bellows; and, in addition, pitch, resin, sulphur, tar, petroleum, wool and cotton. A list of this kind reflects in miniature the economic resources of a given state—in this case, of the Ottoman empire. And yet it can, and should, be amplified further. To a great campaign the Ottomans brought transport animals in large numbers: draught horses from Wallachia and Moldavia; oxen from state 'ranches', e.g. in the region of Cilicia; buffaloes from Thrace, Bulgaria and Greece; camels from the desert areas adjacent to Syria and 'Irāq; and mules, above all from Anatolia. The mineral wealth of the empire would also serve the needs of the war machine—lead from the silver mines of Bosnia and Serbia; iron from Bulgaria; copper from Anatolia; and tin, much of this metal coming from sources outside the direct control of the sultan. Of the constituents of gunpowder, sulphur was available in Anatolia, while rich supplies of saltpetre existed in Egypt, Syria and 'Irāq.

An important source of *matériel de guerre* was the contraband traffic flowing from Christendom to the Muslim world. It had long been illicit, under the canon law of the Catholic Church, for Christians to export to the infidel materials useful in war. The Church indeed had tried time and again, though without much success, to prevent the sale, to the Muslims, of horses, arms, iron, copper, tin, sulphur, saltpetre,

[1] *Mémoires*, 280.

timber and the like. At various times this contraband trade assumed a special importance, as it did for the Ottomans during their great wars against Persia (1578–90) and Austria (1593–1606). It was now that the English carried into the Levant numerous cargoes containing tin, lead, copper, saltpetre, sulphur, swords and arquebuses, also broken bells and broken images (i.e. bronze taken from the churches despoiled in England during the course of the Reformation). There is mention, too, in the Ottoman chronicles, of *Ṭalyan tüfenkler*, muskets of Italian origin, produced no doubt in such famous centres as Brescia.

After their conquest of the Mamluk Sultanate in 922–3/1516–17 the Ottomans ruled over most of the central lands of Islam, together with much of North Africa and a large proportion of the Balkan territories. Of other Muslim states strong enough to fill a role of the first importance there remained no more than two, Persia and Mughal India, neither of which could equal the Ottoman empire in extent and resources. Muslim warfare, during this, the last distinctive phase of its development, was to find perhaps its most splendid formulation in the Ottoman procedures of war, and nowhere with more richness of detail than in the spectacle of the Ottomans marching to a great campaign. Much care was taken to render the advance as smooth as possible. Orders went out for the repair of roads and bridges to facilitate the movement of guns and waggons. Piles of stones and wooden stakes might be used to indicate the actual line of march. The crossing of rivers like the Euphrates and the Danube demanded the construction of large pontoon bridges. Often the Ottomans took with them into the field prefabricated parts of the structure, together with quantities of timber, cables and nails. The order of march included an advance screen of light horsemen (Tatars from the Crimea or Turcomans from Anatolia), a vanguard of picked cavalry, a main force embracing the troops of the imperial household (the Janissaries, the mounted regiments of the sultan and the specialist corps, e.g. the artillerists and armourers), two wings of 'feudal' *sipahis*, one on each flank, and a rearguard covering the baggage and supplies.

The day's march began during the small hours of the morning and continued until about noon, when the site of the next encampment would be at hand. Access to water and pasture was of prime importance in the choice of a site. At the centre of the camp stood the sultan, the Janissaries and the other household troops, and here, too, the high dignitaries had their station, with their personal retinues in attendance on them; beyond this nucleus would lie the 'feudal' *sipahis*, a separate quarter being assigned to each provincial contingent. Water-carriers moved through the camp, providing refreshment for all; artisans and craftsmen from the guilds at Istanbul—saddlers, smiths, butchers, bakers, etc.—awaited the frequent call for their services, working in small huts, over each of which floated a pennant indicating the trade practised there. A special enclosure held strayed animals until their owners came to collect them. Herds of cattle and flocks of sheep accompanied the Ottomans to war as sustenance for the troops in the field. The life of the Ottoman soldier on campaign was sober and frugal, dried beef, mutton and rice, onions, bread or biscuit, and water constituting the main ingredients of his diet. To the Christians who saw these great encampments nothing was more remarkable than the wonderful silence prevailing in them and the high level of personal and public hygiene maintained amongst the troops.

A word must here be said about the composition of the Ottoman armies. Of notable importance were the soldiers belonging to the central régime—i.e. the Janissaries, a corps of infantry equipped with firearms and numbering some 12–15,000 men in the time of Süleymān the Magnificent (926–74/1520–66); the six mounted regiments of the imperial household, expert with the bow, the lance and the sword and, at least in later times, trained also in the use of the lighter forms of hand-gun, e.g., the pistol and the carbine; and, in addition, the various technical services—the armourers, the artillerists, the transport corps, the bombardiers and the sappers. Also at the command of the sultan were the *sipahis*, who held grants of small (*timar*) or of large (*ẓiʿāmet*) yield per annum. No right of ownership was granted to them in the lands constituting their grants; as in the *iqṭāʿ* system of earlier times, the soldier holding the grant also enjoyed only the usufruct of the lands assigned to him, i.e. the right to certain revenues in cash and in kind from the population dwelling within the limits of his grant. Out of the annual yield accruing to him the *sipahi* had to maintain himself as an efficient warrior and also, when summoned to war, to bring with him on campaign a retinue, the personnel of which increased in number with the value of his *timar* or *ẓiʿāmet*, as promotion came to him, and the cost of which, in respect of arms, tents, supplies and transport, he himself was obliged to meet from the revenues allotted to him.

The excellence of the Janissaries as infantry made a deep impression on the Christian world of the fifteenth and sixteenth centuries—to such an extent, indeed, that their role in Ottoman warfare, and that of the various technical corps, has tended to receive an emphasis stronger than their undoubted importance perhaps warranted. No force of 12–15,000 men, however formidable their skill, is numerous enough to be the decisive element in the armed forces of a vast empire. The main weight of the Ottoman armies was to be found in the *sipahis*, who far out-numbered the troops of the central régime. This fact determined in large degree the battle order and the field tactics of the Ottomans. Their order of battle, reduced to its essentials, consisted of a firm centre and two wings of *sipahi* cavalry. The centre, embracing the Janissaries and the other corps of the imperial household, was defended with trenches, waggons and with guns placed at intervals along its front—in short, a kind of *Wagenburg* formation. Here was the solid nucleus designed to break the onset of the foe. On either side of this centre stood the powerful formations of the *sipahis*, seeking the moment to infiltrate along the flanks and to the rear of the opposing forces and, if all should go well, to over-run them in a relentless assault and pursuit. The tactics natural to these horsemen differed little from the methods used in the armies of earlier Muslim states. Of the Ottoman cavalry engaged in the war of 1182–88/1768–74 against Russia one Christian author gives a vivid and informative account:

...these are light troops of the best kind. They attack in lively fashion, without order, without co-ordination, without a plan devised in relation to the terrain or the position of the enemy: they surround him and fall upon him from all sides. Numerous banners are in the first rank and in front of them to heighten their courage. Their officers set an example by fighting at the head of their troop. One body of horsemen is repulsed; another takes over from it, without more success. They carry away in their flight the horsemen who are hastening up behind them. Cavalry and infantry become inter-mingled. Their attacks weaken; the confusion becomes general and leads to a retreat almost as lively as the first shock of battle.

An assault so confused is of little danger to an army war-hardened and disciplined; but a force which allowed its ranks to be broken by these troops would be lost. Not a man would escape, because of the swiftness of their horses, managed by riders who rarely deliver a blow without effect. To be avoided with them are the skirmishes that they try ceaselessly to induce, small detachments, open ground, and affairs of outposts. In these latter, above all when they are on the defensive, their courage, patience and stubbornness are extreme...[1]

[1] L. F. Guinement de Kéralio, *Histoire de la dernière guerre entre les Russes et les Turcs* (Paris, 1777), I, 113–14.

As to the role of the Ottoman infantry, e.g. the Janissaries, their mode of procedure on the battle-field is well illustrated in yet another Christian source dating from the eighteenth century:

...in flat country they rush in large groups on the foe, with the *enfans perdus* at their head: and, since they keep no order, only the foremost amongst them can use their fire-arms. They hold a sabre or a knife in the right hand, with their musket in the left, before the head, in order to ward off the bayonet and sword thrusts delivered against them. The rearmost of them as a rule carry their musket slung over the shoulder. Some of them also take up in their teeth the hem of their jacket and breeches, which are very ample, and fall like bulls, head down, on the enemy, crying with all their might Alla, Alla: God, God...[1]

There were occasions, however, when the tactics of the Ottoman infantry assumed a different form, and here, with the Janissaries, can be included the troops known as *levend, sarija* or *sekban* and also the Albanian levies, i.e. troops equipped with firearms, fighting as infantry and serving often under a contract for a given period of time. The Albanians, in particular, gained a high reputation as soldiers in the seventeenth and eighteenth centuries. One Christian source observes of them that

...the Albanians are a militia from Bosnia, Albania and Macedonia, most of them on foot; they are counted amongst the volunteers. They serve by contract...they are recruited in this fashion: a Turkish officer proposes to raise a corps of eight to ten thousand men, whom he will arm and maintain in consideration of ten crowns [*écus*] per month for each man; and this contract is normally for one campaign or five months. If there is further need of these troops, the contract is renewed...[2]

Amongst the Albanians, and also amongst the *sekban* and the Janissaries, there were excellent marksmen, employed frequently to cover the flanks of the Ottoman armies and to harass the foe. Troops of this kind, advancing in open formation through irregular or broken terrain and using independent fire from the protection of trees and the like, fought sometimes with decisive effect as at Grocka in 1739, where their long muskets drove back the Austrian columns in confusion.

The same general pattern of development can be discerned elsewhere than in the Ottoman empire. It is visible in the Persian armies of this time, the main strength of which consisted of horsemen. The

[1] De Warnery, *Remarques sur le militaire des Turcs* (Leipzig and Dresden, 1770), 24.
[2] De Warnery, *op. cit.*, 30.

continuing importance of the mounted soldier is reflected in the career of an able captain like Nādir Shāh (d. 1160/1747), whose military reputation derives largely from his great skill as a cavalry general. He also had at his command, however, a corps of *jazāyirjīs*, i.e. of infantry armed with the long musket known as *jazāyir*, which often did excellent service in the course of his campaigns. Nādir Shāh was less successful in siege warfare, notably because of deficiencies in the amount and quality of his artillery, the difficulties attendant on the transport of guns over arduous terrain, and the relative inexperience of his military engineers.

The manner of warfare which can be described, in a meaningful sense, as Muslim was now entering into the last phase of its evolution. It was becoming in fact out of date. The process of obsolescence can best be understood once more in the context of the Ottoman empire, and this for the simple reason that the Ottomans, standing in close contact with states like Austria and Russia, felt the impact, immediate and sustained, of the innovations wrought in the European practice of war. Even in respect of sieges, a field of endeavour which had seen some of their greatest triumphs, as at Constantinople (857/1453), Rhodes (928–9/1522) and Candia (1078–80/1667–9), the general trend of development was unfavourable to the Ottomans. The art of fortification had been raised to new levels of excellence through the efforts of men like Rimpler and Vauban. Now, although the mines and mortars of the Ottomans and their lavish employment of human labour in siege operations continued to earn the approval of the Europeans, the prospect that the old methods would remain viable was doubtful indeed. As to the defensive side of siege warfare, the technological advance in the casting of guns, especially during the later years of the War of the Austrian Succession (1740–8) in Europe, called into question even the achievements of a Vauban. The great soldier, Maurice de Saxe, was to declare of fortresses in general that the old ones had no value and that the modern were hardly of more worth.

On the field of battle the prospect before the Ottomans was still less reassuring. To keep abreast of developments in Europe, if only to an approximate degree, had never been a simple task for the Ottomans. Already in 1596 a Muslim from Bosnia was lamenting that the Christians, using the latest types of firearm, held a distinct advantage in battle. The European practice of war had begun in fact to take a new and, for the Ottomans, a fateful orientation—one which led at length to the repeated victories of Austria and Russia over the armies of the sultan in the seventeenth and eighteenth centuries.

Of the technical improvements made in Europe at this time none was more notable than the creation of light and mobile cannon built to a few standardized calibres. A soldier of great judgment like the Maréchal Duc de Villars attributed the success of the Austrians in the war of 1683–99 against the Ottomans to their possession of an excellent field artillery. On the Ottoman guns, however, the comment of the Christians was almost unanimous—they were far too cumbersome, difficult to transport, wasteful in their consumption of gunpowder and only rarely effective in the open field. And indeed, time and again in their wars with Austria and Russia, the Ottomans would suffer defeat in battle and lose at once all the cannon and all the equipment gathered together for the campaign.

Important, too, were the developments occurring in Europe with regard to the hand-gun. The arquebus yielded place to the musket, the carbine and the pistol came into more extended use—arms, in short, more manageable than the arquebus, lighter and quicker to load and discharge. All these new weapons made their appearance in due course amongst the Ottomans. In general, however, the Ottoman *tüfenk* or musket was longer in the barrel and heavier, carried farther and gave a more accurate fire than the types common in Europe, but at the same time it was much slower to prepare and use.

An effective combination of all arms was difficult to achieve, while the rates of fire for the cannon and the hand-gun remained low. Technological advances leading to the development of the light field gun and of the musket made possible the elaboration of a tactical system efficient enough to realize in battle the potentialities of firearms. The end result was the square or rectangle, each side composed of alternating groups of horse and foot, with *chevaux de frise* in front of them, the cannon being located at the corners, and the reserve troops and the baggage at the centre of the formation. Changes introduced in the course of time involved a diminution in the size of the squares and an increase in their number, with a view to greater mobility, and also the elimination of the pikemen and the strengthening of the musketeers, in order to ensure a maximum of fire-power. It was Raimondo Montecuccoli who, on the tactical basis of the square, formulated the principles of action which brought Austria and Russia such remarkable success in their wars against the Ottoman empire. Emphasizing that the best means to overcome the

Muslim foe was to force him into a major battle, Montecuccoli urged that the Ottomans, foot and horse alike, be subjected to a continuing bombardment, from the square, with field guns and all available fire-arms; that intensive musket-fire should be used to drive back the *sipahis*; and that cuirassiers be employed to rout the Janissaries, once the cannon had disrupted their advance. Here indeed—though often modified to suit the terrain of a given encounter—was a blueprint for war which, in the hands of able soldiers like Louis of Baden and Prince Eugene for Austria and Münnich, Rumyantsev and Suvorov for Russia, led to a long series of Christian victories over the armies of the Sultan, and which laid bare the fact that the old Muslim pattern of warfare, even in its most developed and elaborate, i.e. its Ottoman exemplification, had become inadequate to meet the demands of the modern age.

It was not that the Ottoman empire lacked the strength, human and material, for war; its wealth and resources were as abundant in the era of defeat as in the golden age of success. Nor, in relation to new elements of warfare from Europe, was the power to assimilate visible in the reign of Sultan Süleymān less evident in the time, for example, of the first Köprülü *vezīrs*. The great change was in the nature of the elements now demanding assimilation. As long as technological developments in Europe connected with cannon and firearms remained below the level at which tactical evolution of a major kind became possible, the Ottomans did not find it difficult to take over the latest advances in equipment and technique. The capture of guns on the battle-field or in a fortress, converse with prisoners of war, the services of renegade experts, these and other means of contact enabled the Ottomans to learn about the new types of cannon or hand-gun and the most recent devices employing gunpowder. And at this 'simple' level of assimilation such borrowings continued to be made during the fifteenth and the sixteenth, but also in the seventeenth and the eighteenth centuries, as the introduction of new terms into Ottoman usage, e.g. *aghaj top* (petard) and *mushkat* (musket), bear witness.

The case was quite different, when the technological progress achieved in Europe called forth tactical systems involving the use, in close interdependence, of cannon and muskets, of infantry and cavalry. The Ottomans might, with ease, borrow from Europe a new instrument of war—but not a new complex of ideas embodied in a tactical formation. The weapon would fit into a pre-existing context, where it would not be out of place; the tactical system had no such context of absorption awaiting it. To attempt the assimilation of the enlarged modes of warfare now developing in Europe meant, for the Ottomans, to recast the whole practice, and indeed the structure itself, of their armies, and even the fabric of their governmental machine. Not until the impact of continuing defeat in battle against Austria and Russia had become unendurable was the need for radical reform at last accepted amongst them. The movement of reform in imitation of European procedure began in earnest with the accession to the Ottoman throne of Selīm III (1789–1807), gathered momentum under Maḥmūd II (1808–39) and found its full expression in the era of the Tanẓīmāt (1839–76). This movement was not confined to the Ottoman empire. It was extended in the course of the nineteenth and twentieth centuries to the other lands of Islam. The Muslim practice of war now lost those features which had given it hitherto a distinctive character—more and more it became identified with the general course of technical advance and performance attained in Europe. With the advent of radical reform *à l'européenne* Islamic warfare had reached in fact the verge of dissolution. A last comment—almost a formal valediction—can be left to Maurice de Saxe: writing of the Ottomans and their traditional mode of war, he was to declare that neither courage, nor number, nor wealth was lacking to them, but order, discipline and 'la manière de combattre'.[1]

[1] Maurice Comte de Saxe, *Mes rêveries*, ed. Pérau (Amsterdam and Leipzig, 1757), I, 87.

CHAPTER 13

THE TRANSMISSION OF LEARNING AND LITERARY INFLUENCES TO WESTERN EUROPE

THE TRANSMISSION OF LEARNING

In the early days the Latin West knew the Arabs only as conquerors and marauders. From the seventh to the ninth Christian century, Muslim invasions and raids in the Mediterranean basin (to which, rightly or wrongly, Pirenne attributes the function of breaking up its old economic and cultural unity), brought Christendom face to face with the warlike and destructive aspect of Islam. It was not until the second phase, when the Arab onslaught had passed its zenith, and these two religious and political worlds began to have contacts other than those of war, that the West became aware of the high level of culture and learning achieved by the 'Saracens' in their own domains. Envoys and individuals travelling for business reasons or as pilgrims were the first to bring news to Europe of the existence of Muslim culture and science. But above all it was the collective contact between Arab Islamic and Christian communities in the areas of mixed population on the borders between the two worlds that revealed to Christendom the wealth of cultural attainments of which the Arabs were now the depositaries, the promoters and the transmitters. A famous and much-quoted passage from the works of Alvaro of Cordova bears witness to the interest felt by Mozarabic circles in ninth-century Spain for Arab literature, including its poetry, ornate prose and epistolography; but from our point of view this is merely an isolated phenomenon. What impressed the West in the intellectual achievements of the Arabs was the role of mediators of Greek philosophy and science which they had assumed, and the impulse they had imparted to the various branches of learning. The attitude of the Latin West towards the ancient heritage, and in particular to Greece, was much the same as that of the Islamic East—indifference to the artistic element, but keen interest and admiration for the philosophic and scientific aspects, direct contact with which, however, was generally precluded by ignorance of the language. Now it was discovered that these barbarian infidels had translated into their own tongue the wisdom of the ancients, the lofty concepts of Plato and Aristotle, the medical lore of Hippocrates and Galen, the astronomical and mathematical teachings of Ptolemy; and in all these fields they had enriched the inheritance with their own speculations and experiments. This twofold aspect, Greek and Arab, of the knowledge which from the eleventh century onwards the Christian West had been eagerly striving to acquire, is clear; clear, too, is the awareness of its hybrid character on the part of the West. This second contact between East and West in the cultural field was a repetition, in Europe after the year 1000, of that which had taken place in Mesopotamia and 'Irāq between Greek and Islamic culture during the third/ninth and fourth/tenth centuries.

Muslim and Mozarabic Spain, before its reconquest by the Christians, was the theatre and the most important centre of this new contact. Contacts between the West and Graeco-Arab culture in other Mediterranean areas such as Sicily and Italy were of secondary importance compared with the intensity and significance of the work accomplished in Spain; and the influence of the Crusades, to which at one time it was customary to attribute a considerable share in these scientific and cultural exchanges, now appears to have been very slight. In reality, so far we know only of one or two cases of Arab texts reaching the West from the *milieu* of the Crusades, and as a result of them. Less negligible, though not so great as might have been expected, was the part played in the translation and transmission of scientific knowledge by southern Italy and Sicily, despite the fact that the latter was under Arab domination for centuries, while the mainland had often been the goal of Arab raids. In this field much is obscure, and will probably remain so, but the little we know brings us back, so far as southern Italy is concerned, to the school of Salerno, where the only clearly identifiable figure of interest to us in this connexion is Constantine the African (d. 1087), a Tunisian Muslim converted to Christianity, a great traveller and translator into barbaric Latin of Graeco-Arab medical works, which he often passed off as his own, such as writings of Hippocrates and Galen, the *Kāmil al-ṣināʿa al-ṭibbiyya* by 'Alī b. 'Abbās al-Majūsī, also known as the *Liber regius,* the *Zād al-musāfir* and other works by Isḥāq al-Isrā'īlī (Isaac Judaeus). Constantine, who ended his life as a monk at Montecassino, was on the whole a mediocre figure, lacking the high ethical standards of a Gerard of Cremona, but so far as we know he was the first in chronological order to produce in Italy Latin translations and adaptations of Arab works. To a much later age, after the efflorescence of these studies in Spain during the twelfth century, belongs the work of Christian and Jewish translators at the courts of Frederick II, Manfred and the first Angevins: Michael Scot (d. 1235), who had previously worked in Spain, the translator for Frederick II of Aristotelian works on natural history with the commentaries of Ibn Rushd and Ibn Sīnā; the astrologer Theodore, the Sicilians John and Moses of Palermo, who all belonged to Frederick's circle; the Jew of Agrigento, Faraj b. Sālim, who for Charles of Anjou translated *al-Ḥāwī* or *Continens,* al-Rāzī's great medical encyclopaedia; the Provençal Jew, Kalonymos ben Kalonymos, translator during the reign of King Robert of the *Tahāfut al-tahāfut* of Ibn Rushd—the polemical defence of Peripatetic philosophy against al-Ghazālī. With these few names and titles we have exhausted the list of what was accomplished in Italy and Sicily in the field of direct translations from Arabic of scientific works, whether it was a matter of purely Arab science and technics or of Greek science—a meagre result when we remember the close political and cultural ties between that part of Italy and the Arab world, from the conquest of Sicily in the ninth century down to the end of the Saracen colony in Lucera in 1300. It is a result which appears even more meagre when we compare it with the superb harvest reaped at the same time in Spain.

Here the cultural contact between Islam and Christendom, which began in the days of the Cordova amirate, was carried on intensively by the Mozarabic and Jewish elements throughout the period of Arab domination, and it yielded its best fruits at the time when this domination was declining. We know that translations from Arabic into Latin were made in Catalonia from the tenth century onwards, and during the first half of the twelfth century Barcelona was the abode of the first translator of those days whose identity can be established—Plato of Tivoli Between 1116 and 1138, with the help of an Andalusian Jew, Abraham bar Ḥiyyā, called Savasorda (*Ṣāḥib al-shurṭa*), Plato of Tivoli translated Jewish and Arab works on astrology and astronomy, including the astronomical tables of al-Battānī. About this time the centre of such activities shifted to Toledo, which had been restored to Christendom a few decades before, and had become a beacon of Graeco-Arab-Hebraic culture for the whole of the Latin West. The praiseworthy activities of the learned men who flocked thither from every part of Europe, in order to study the treasures of Graeco-Arab philosophy and science, were a striking feature of a great part of the twelfth century. In reality we know very little of the part played in the promotion and guidance of this movement by the archbishop of Toledo, Raymund (1125–52), or of the organization of the work and the relations between the various translators. This does not alter the fact that the name of Raymund has become almost a symbol of this noble undertaking, and the term 'Toledo school', applied to this group of translators, expresses the spirit by which they were animated, even if it does not imply institutional organization. In most cases they probably knew no Arabic at all when they arrived in Toledo, and certainly not enough to enable them to understand the original text of the difficult works on philosophy, medicine, mathematics, astronomy, astrology and matural science which they were eager to study. Consequently, most of them availed themselves of the services of Jewish or Mozarabic scholars living in Toledo, who translated the Arabic text literally into Spanish, which they then turned into Latin. It was, however, only natural that after spending some time in this polylingual *milieu* they acquired in the course of their work a knowledge of Arabic sufficient to enable them to read the originals of their beloved texts without outside assistance, and their work thus became more and more personal and independent. This was certainly the case with the leading members of the group, for example Dominicus Gundisalvi, archdeacon of Segovia, and Gerard of Cremona. Nevertheless, collaboration between these Latin scholars and their teachers and advisers on oriental matters—Savasorda in the case of Plato of Tivoli, the Mozarab Galippus (Ghālib) in Gerard's case, and the converted Jew Avendeath (Ibn Dāwūd), better known under the name of Johannes Hispanus, in the case of Gundisalvi—remains a characteristic feature of those times. Johannes Hispanus, whose long collaboration with Gundisalvi made these two a typical example of this method of working, also produced a number of translations on his own account, such as the *Differentia spiritus et animae* of Qusṭā b. Lūqā, the *Fons Vitae* of Ibn Gabirol, several works of Avicenna, and the *Liber de causis*. Nowadays it is customary to separate the work of this Johannes, who died in 1166, from that of the almost homonymous Johannes Hispalensis or John of Seville (d. 1157), who was also a translator, not of philosophical texts, but of works on astrology by Mā Shā' Allāh, al-Farghānī, Abū Ma'shar and al-Zarqālī.[1] The partner of Johannes Hispanus, Dominicus Gundisalvi (d. 1181) was also the principal or sole translator of great Arabic philosophers such as al-Fārābī's *Liber de*

[1] M. Alonso, *Juan Sevillano, sus obras propias y sus traducciones*, in *al-Andalus*, XVIII (1953), 17–50.

scientiis, De intellectu and *Tanbīh 'alā sabīl al-sa'āda,* al-Kindī's *De intellectu,* al-Ghazālī's *Maqāṣid al-falāsifa,* Ibn Sīnā's *Metaphysics, Physics, De coelo et mundo,* and others.

To these indigenous members of the Toledan group must be added the foreigners, drawn thither by their thirst for knowledge. They include two Englishmen, Adelard of Bath (translator of Euclid, Abū Ma'shar and al-Khuwārizmī) and Robert of Chester, who produced the first Latin version of the Qur'ān, and, independently of Plato of Tivoli, also translated al-Battānī; a Slav, Herman the Dalmatian, who concerned himself with apologetic, astronomical and astrological works; and above all the Lombard Gerard of Cremona (1114–87), whose mighty figure dominates the whole group, not only on account of the extent of his work, but also because of his lofty moral character. A testimony to both is provided by the bio-bibliographical note compiled shortly after his death by his colleagues and pupils in the Toledan circle and inserted in the manuscripts of several of his translations. From this note we learn that Gerard, scorning the worldly riches which he possessed, led an austere life entirely devoted to science, for love of which he learned Arabic and translated from that language more than seventy works, a list of these being given in the note. Prominent among them are the *Almagest,* the search for which appears to have been the reason for his first coming to Spain, and which he finished translating in 1175, perhaps from the version of al-Ḥajjāj b. Yūsuf; Ibn Sīnā's *Canon of medicine,* which with this translation by Gerard began its triumphal progress throughout the Western Mediterranean lands; works of Euclid, Aristotle, Hippocrates, Galen, Alexander of Aphrodisias, Menelaus, Themistius; and, among the Arab writers, Thābit b. Qurra, al-Kindī, al-Fārābī, al-Qabīṣī, al-Khuwārizmī, al-Nayrīzī, al-Rāzī, al-Zahrāwī and al-Zarqālī. In short, the whole range of Hellenistic-Arab science which had inspired the 'Abbasid culture of the ninth and tenth centuries and later, in the twelfth century, the international circle in the Toledo of Archbishop Raymond, seems to have been included in the vast *opus* of this indefatigable scholar, who, after devoting most of his life to this work of mediation, returned to his Lombard home to die, leaving behind him an imperishable fame in the history of knowledge.

This first great Toledan period, personified in the names of Archbishop Raymund, Gundisalvi and Gerard, was followed in the thirteenth century by a second efflorescence of translations, centring around the figure of another archbishop of Toledo, Rodrigo Jiménez de Rada

(1170–1247), in whose time appeared the second translation of the Qur'ān, by Marcus of Toledo, and Michael Scot translated al-Biṭrūjī, while Herman the German, translator of Aristotle, al-Fārābī and Ibn Rushd, was active a little later. The work of this second group was continued at Seville in the propitious atmosphere of the court of Alfonso the Wise. Here in 1256 Egidio de Tebaldis of Parma and Pietro da Reggio translated the astrological works of Ibn Abi'l-Rijāl and Ptolemy's *Quadripartitum,* while Castilian or Latin translations were also made of works on magic like the *Picatrix* of the pseudo-Majrīṭī, or of literary works in the old Eastern tradition such as the *Kalīla wa-Dimna* and the *Book of the seven wise men*; of the eschatological *Liber scalae* we shall speak below (pp. 879–80). The last famous Spanish translator was Arnald of Villanova (d. 1312), who specialized in medical works, among them those of Ibn Sīnā and Galen. During this later period interest in the Arabic language spread from the purely scientific and philosophical field, as parts of the ancient heritage, to the Muslim religion, the intention being either apologetic or missionary, as is proved by the part played by the Dominican and Franciscan orders in the teaching of Arabic and the works of great apologists like Ramón Martín and Raymund Lull. But this sector of the study of Arabic in Spain and in the rest of Europe is outside the scope of our subject.

Each of these branches of learning was transmitted by this group of translators and commentators in a manner which on the whole was reasonably faithful, if we bear in mind the *gravitas materiae* (which Plato of Tivoli invoked at the beginning of his translation of al-Battānī as an excuse for any obscurities or difficulties of interpretation) and the often mediocre knowledge these Latin interpreters had of the technical terms they found in the Arabic originals. A typical example in philosophical and theological texts is the frequent use of *loquentes* as a translation of *mutakallimūn,* thus using a generic word to express the specialized sense of the Arabic term denoting the speculative Muslim theologians; while even the great Gerard, when translating one of al-Farghānī's astronomical works, *Jawāmi' 'ilm al-nujūm,* called it *De aggregationibus scientiae stellarum* instead of 'elementary notions of astronomy', because he failed to understand the technical meaning of *jawāmi'*. Despite these and other shortcomings, very natural if we remember how little was known of the Arabic language at that time, it can be said that the Latin approach to Graeco-Arab thought through these medieval translators was on the same level as the Arab approach to the heritage of antiquity three centuries earlier. In one respect it may even be said to have surpassed it, owing to a certain affinity of spirit even when technical adequacy was lacking, since both the Arab philosophers and scholars of the 'Abbasid era and their Latin interpreters were men of the Middle Ages, with a mental outlook which on the whole was more closely akin than that of the Arabs to the thinkers and scientists of pagan Antiquity, particularly of the Classical period. This intellectual affinity helped them to bridge the gap created by the unfamiliarity of the language and the different technical level, so that in our opinion it would be wrong to describe what the West received as a sheer travesty of the Graeco-Arab heritage, a term which is frequently applied to the transmission of the antique originals to the medieval East.

THE INFLUENCE OF THE ARAB HERITAGE

Let us now see to what extent this Arab heritage influenced the medieval West and the Renaissance, how much the West came to know of Arab-Islamic thought and through it of Greek thought, and what effect this contact had on the subsequent evolution of Western thinking. The theme is so vast that here we shall have to limit ourselves to a few brief notes on the various branches of philosophy, theology and science.

In the field of philosophy it is generally maintained that what the West knew of Greek thought, and in particular of Aristotle, was transmitted to it by the Arabs. Such a statement needs qualification and a more precise formulation, but on the whole it remains valid. In reality, the direct channel of transmission through Byzantium was never completely closed to the West, and during the twelfth and thirteenth centuries works of Plato and Aristotle were translated directly from Greek into Latin (the *Meno* and the *Phaedo* in Sicily by Enrico Aristippo (d. 1162); the *Metaphysics,* the *Nicomachean ethics,* the *Physics* and the *De anima* during the first half of the thirteenth century). Of some works the medieval Latins received two translations almost at the same time, one from the original Greek and the other from Arabic. Yet, at the end of the thirteenth century, in one of his most famous passages, Roger Bacon could affirm that the knowledge of Aristotelian philosophy had remained hidden from the West since the days of Boethius and had been revived in his own time thanks to Arab mediation, and above all to Ibn Sīnā. And it is a fact that during the late Middle Ages and the Renaissance, Greek philosophy was studied in the West on the basis of Arab re-elaborations, rather than through direct transmission and translation. The logic, physics and metaphysics of Aristotle were studied either in re-translations from Arabic or in the works of Ibn Sīnā. The latter's great encyclopaedia of philosophy, *Kitāb al-shifā'*, was in substance a recapituiation of Aristotelian thought, though with many interpolations, either deliberate or unconscious, of neo-Platonist ideas. It was in this somewhat hybrid form that the Peripatetic doctrines reached the Latins for the first time. With them, amidst misunderstandings and misinterpretations, came the quarrel that had flared up in the East as to the validity of these Aristotelian-Avicennian doctrines and the possibility of reconciling them with Islamic orthodoxy. The two greatest Muslim thinkers after Ibn Sīnā—al-Ghazālī (d. 505/1111) and Ibn Rushd (d. 595/1198)—encountered each other on this field. The former's attack on Peripatetic philosophy, which he had learned through Ibn Sīnā, was formulated in his *Maqāṣid al-falāsifa* (which in reality contained only an exposition of the doctrines he was fighting against, mistaken in the West for his own ideas) and in the *Tahāfut al-falāsifa,* both of which were translated into Latin. Ibn Rushd defended Aristotle in his polemical *Tahāfut al-tahāfut,* and most of the works he wrote in his attempt to give a more faithful picture and interpretation of Aristotelianism were also translated and studied, in fact many of them have survived only in the Latin translations. Consequently, the figure of the philosopher of Cordova soon became the focal point of the attention of the Latin world, as an interpreter of Aristotle and also as an original thinker, more or less faithfully interpreted.

Contrary to historical truth, which has been re-established only as a result of more recent study of the works of Ibn Rushd, the West assigned to this philosopher an attitude of pure rationalism, averse to any form of revelation, and he was made a symbol of impious unbelief—the feeling against him found expression even in the visual arts, in a painting by Traini in Pisa showing Averroes vanquished by St Thomas Aquinas. In reality, as has been shown by Asín Palacios, the positions of Ibn Rushd and Aquinas regarding the substantial accord between reason and faith were identical, and Ibn Rushd explained his own attitude in the little treatise entitled *Faṣl al-maqāl,* which Aquinas may well have got to know through Maimonides and Ramón Martín. For Ibn Rushd, instead of a 'twofold truth' there was only one truth, on which, on different planes and through different channels, philosophical speculation and revelation converge, the former by means of purely rational arguments and the latter with the occasional aid of symbols and images, which can be interpreted allegorically if necessary, but are not for that reason any less cogent or respectable, and moreover are more easily understood by the masses. It is thus legitimate to speak of the existence in Aquinas of a veritable 'theological Averroism', as Asín Palacios calls it; an Averroism which must, of course, be distinguished from the conceptions that spread in the West under that name, had their most illustrious exponent in Siger of Brabant, and were carried on in France, in England and in Italy (at Padua down to the eighteenth century), with clearly defined aspects of antidogmatism and anticlericalism. To this Latin Averroism are due the theories of the twofold truth (a hint of which can be found, on the Islamic side, in the works of Ibn al-'Arabī, who died in 638/1240), of the denial of the immortality of the individual soul and of a future life. The first of these, as we have said, was extraneous, and even directly opposed, to the authentic ideas of Ibn Rushd, while the others are two corollaries (not unjustified, it is true, but which the Muslim philosopher never intended, or had the courage, to deal with explicitly himself) of the principle propounded by Ibn Rushd of the unity of human minds and the generic Aristotelian concept of the eternity of the world.

Such, in brief, is the story of the transmission of Aristotelianism to the West through Arabic mediation. Apart from this general trend, we must not forget the other factor, to a certain extent bound up with it but in other respects opposed to it, of Platonism, or rather neo-Platonism, of which, as we have seen, al-Fārābī was the leading exponent and interpreter in the East. In its Arab form it had already penetrated to the West through Muslim and Jewish thinkers in Spain, like Ibn Masarra (d. 319/931) and Ibn Gabirol (Avicebron, d. *c.* 450/1058). The original text of the former's work has been lost, but it has been reconstructed by Asín Palacios and can be distinguished from Eastern neo-Platonism by the introduction into its emanationist system of a 'prime element' or 'prime matter', purely spiritual and symbolized by the throne of God, considered as having been the prime aim of divine creation. But a far more direct influence on Christian philosophy and theology was exercised by Avicebron, whose *Fons vitae* translated by Gundisalvi and Avendeath was a favourite textbook of the Franciscan school of William of Auvergne, Alexander of Hales and others, whereas it was opposed by the Dominicans under the influence of Aquinas. Nor, in addition to these purely intellectual influences, must we forget that which earlier Muslim writers had exercised in the field of mysticism on the corresponding Christian evolution, a typical example being the one brought to light by Asín Palacios, who in the figure of Ibn 'Abbād of Ronda (d. 792/1389), in his speculations and even in his vocabulary, identified an Arab precursor of St John of the Cross.

In this way, far from being merely the transmitters of the philosophical ideas of antiquity, the Arabs, and the Muslims in general, became the teachers and inspirers, or else the controverted and confuted adversaries, of the West. The chief factors in the transmission of philosophy and the controversies that followed, regarding questions such as the reconciliation of reason with faith, were in reality extraneous to genuine Classical philosophy, or were at least barely touched upon, since the relationship between these two elements had been completely different in Antiquity. But from its distant cousin, Islam, Christianity inherited the ideal formulation and the dramatic tension of the problem. The Muslim element was reflected in scholasticism, in medieval apologetics and even, elaborated and perhaps adulterated or misunderstood, in the philosophy of the Renaissance and the Enlightenment—we need only mention the success achieved at that time by Ibn Ṭufayl's *Ḥayy ibn Yaqẓān*, originally starting from a standpoint of accord between reason and faith in perfect harmony with that of the authentic Ibn Rushd. Hence the function of Islam as regards this legacy to the West, far from being merely extrinsic and passive, became dynamic and fruitful.

The nexus between philosophy and the sciences, which dates from the origins of Greek thought and can be followed throughout Antiquity, was bequeathed to the Arabs as part of the ancient heritage and was by them transmitted to the Western world. Just as Ḥunayn b. Isḥāq and his successors turned their attention to Greek science, in particular to medicine and mathematics, so did the Latin translators devote themselves to Arab and Greek works of pure theoretical speculation (Aristotle and pseudo-Aristotelian logic and metaphysics, Plato, and their great Muslim commentators) and at the same time to the patrimony of antique science or pseudo-science that Muslim culture had greeted so eagerly and which it had so much enriched. Our own differential specialization tends to make us break down this nexus, and deal separately with each single branch of thought and knowledge, but in the sphere of medieval civilization, whether Eastern or Western, this unity of conception must never be overlooked. The particularly close connexion between philosophy and medicine (of which there is a reflection in the ambiguity of the Arabic word *ḥakīm,* often used indifferently to denote either 'philosopher' or 'physician'), is revealed in the works of the greatest Islamic thinkers, such as al-Rāzī, Ibn Sīnā and Ibn Rushd, whom the Middle Ages ranked as physicians and at the same time philosophers (the first-named essentially as a physician). The importance of Arab medicine, which was not merely an echo of the Greek, but was fortified by its own experiments and conquests, was clearly recognized by the West, and led to the translation not only of Arabic versions of Greek texts, but also of the original works of great Muslim writers, regarded as classics of the art of medicine.

The first great figure in Arabian medicine to achieve canonical status in the West was al-Rāzī, the Rhazes of Latin translations, whose chief work, the *Continens,* as we have seen, appeared in translation, by order of Charles of Anjou, in the thirteenth century, but whose other books and minor writings such as the *Liber Almansoris,* the *De morbis infantium* on smallpox and measles, and the *Aphorisms* had already been turned into Latin during the preceding century by Gerard of Cremona and other anonymous translators. The next in chronological order was 'Alī b. 'Abbās al-Majūsī (d. 384/994), whose *Kāmil al-ṣinā 'a* was one of the first medical works made known to the West through the translation of Constantine the African, while under the other title of *Kitāb malikī* or *Liber regius* it appeared in 1127 in a new and better translation by Stephen of Antioch—one of those rare cases of a translation being known to the Latin East from the *milieu* of the Crusades. For the medieval Latins, another important Arab authority on medicine was Abulcasis (Abu'l-Qāsim al-Zahrāwī, d. 404/1013), the great physician of Umayyad Spain, whose great encyclopaedia of medicine, *al-Taṣrīf,* unlike al-Rāzī's *al-Ḥāwī*, was never translated in its entirety, but only in parts, the most important being the section on surgery, translated by Gerard, which enjoyed a great reputation throughout the Middle Ages. Other Arabic writers on medicine well known to the West were the Maghribīs Isḥāq al-Isrā'īlī, or Isaac Judaeus (d. *c.* 320/932), and Ibn al-Jazzār (d. 395/1004), both of whom were translated by Constantine the African; 'Alī b. Riḍwān, or Haly Rodoam, of Cairo (d. 459/1067) and his contemporary and adversary Ibn Buṭlān of Baghdād (d. after 455/1063), the former being the author of a commentary on Galen translated by Gerard, and the latter of the *Taqwīm al-siḥḥa* (*Tacuinum sanitatis*), translated by an anonymous scribe; the Spaniards, Avenzoar or Ibn Zuhr (d. 557/1162), whose *Taysīr* was translated at Venice in 1280 by Paravicius, and Ibn Rushd, whose *Kulliyyāt fi'l-ṭibb* ('General principles of medicine') was translated in 1255 by the Paduan Jew Bonacossa under the title of *Colliget*. But in the eyes of posterity the names of all these illustrious writers were overshadowed by the fame of Ibn Sīnā.

The *Canon* (*al-Qānūn fi'l-ṭibb*) of the great scholar from Bukhārā was in fact destined to be the bible of the physicians of both East and West for several centuries. In the East, where the native scientific traditions still survive, it is studied and used even to this day; in the West it remained a classic throughout the Middle Ages until the advent of modern medicine with Paracelsus and Vesalius. Translated about the middle of the twelfth century by the omnipresent Gerard, whose version was revised and corrected in the sixteenth century by the Venetian Andrea Alpago, the *Canon* was printed in Latin in more than thirty editions from the beginning of the sixteenth century onwards, while a printed edition of the original Arabic text appeared in Rome in 1593. This remarkable success was due not so much to any special scientific originality in Avicenna's work, but rather, in the words of one competent to judge, to 'the unrivalled methodicalness with which the author welded into an organic whole all the material of the medical traditions of the Greeks and of Islam' (Plessner). The section of the *Canon* dealing with opthalmology has been the subject of special study on the part of modern medicine, which reminds us that this branch of medical science had an illustrious tradition in the East, and was likewise transmitted through the Arab-Latin channel to the medieval West; in fact the *De oculis* of Constantine the African, whom we have already had occasion to mention several times, is nothing but a re-hash of Ḥunayn's *Kitāb al-ʿashr maqālāt fi'l-ʿayn*, the fruits of that great translator's personal experience as a doctor.

Arab medicine, culminating in Ibn Sīnā, thus remained until the closing years of the Renaissance the most authoritative source of Western theory and praxis. But while, as regards the transmission of the old philosophical doctrines, Arab mediation was relegated to second place after the re-establishment of direct contact with classical tradition, a new phase in the history of medical science was inaugurated by the experimental method, which rapidly outstripped both Greeks and Arabs and set medicine on the path of its great modern progress.

Pharmacology may be considered a kind of appendix to medicine and it was assiduously cultivated by Muslim followers of Dioscorides. Here, since we are dealing only with transmission, we will confine ourselves to mentioning the names of Māsawayh or Mesue of Baghdād

(d. 405/1015),[1] whose *De simplicibus* was translated in the sixteenth century by J. Dubois (Jacobus Sylvius), though his other work, *De medicinis universalibus et particularibus,* had been known since medieval days, and the Spaniard, Ibn Wāfid (d. 466/1074), the Abenguefit of Gerard, who translated his *De medicamentis simplicibus*.

Muslim civilization acted as teacher to medieval Europe of other branches of knowledge as well as philosophy and medicine, these being mathematics, astronomy and astrology. Here too the legacy of Classical and Hellenistic Antiquity was presented to the West enriched with the further studies, comments and experience of Islamic science, one proof of this being the number of technical words that passed from Arabic into Latin and the other languages of Western Europe, e.g., algebra, algorithm, zenith, nadir, azimuth and cipher. The work of the great Arab mathematicians, astronomers and astrologers (it is not always easy to distinguish the three activities) was among the features of Islamic science that appealed to the translators of Toledo or at the court of Alfonso X the Wise of Castile and León, and in general everywhere during the twelfth and thirteenth centuries. Here we can only give a brief list, in chronological order, of the authors who were most widely known and studied in the West. We begin with the great al-Khuwārizmī, whose name, as is well known, as a result of medieval Latin distortions, gave rise to the term *algorithm*; his little treatise on algebra, the earliest of its kind in Arabic, was translated into Latin twice during the twelfth century, by Gerard, who retained the Arabic title, *De jebra et almucabala,* and by Robert of Chester, who gave an exact Latin rendering of it, *Liber restaurationis et oppositionis numeri,* while al-Khuwārizmī's astronomical tables, as rearranged about the year 1000 by Maslama al-Majrīṭī, were translated by Adelard of Bath. With a contemporary of al-Khuwārizmī, Abū Ma'shar (the Albumasar of the Latins, d. 272/886) we pass from pure mathematics to astronomy and astrology; his great introduction to astrology, *al-Madkhal al-kabīr,* was translated by Johannes Hispalensis under the title of *Introductorium maius,* and in abridged form by Herman the Dalmatian; his *Dalālāt al-ashkhāṣ al-'ulwiyya* was also translated by John of Seville under the title *De magnis coniunctionibus et annorum revolutionibus*. Both these works had a great influence on Western astrology, one reflection of them being the representation of the ten degrees of the zodiac as described by Abū Ma'shar on the frieze

[1] This means Mesue 'the younger', often confused, even in the attribution of works, with the ninth-century doctor and translator of the same name.

in the Palazzo Schifanoia at Ferrara. No less famous in medieval times (and mentioned by Dante, among others) was the other great astronomer al-Farghānī or Alfraganus (d. after 247/861), whose compendium *Fī jawāmiʿ ʿilm al-nujūm* was translated by John of Seville and again by Gerard of Cremona. Arabic works on geometry and trigonometry were known to the Latins through translation of the *Liber trium fratrum* (on the measurement of plane and spherical surfaces) written by the three Banū Mūsā, the brothers Aḥmad, Ḥasan and Muḥammad b. Mūsā b. Shākir, whose joint scientific work was one of the glories of the caliphate of al-Ma'mūn (d. 218/833). The two great Sabian scientists of the ninth century, Thābit b. Qurra and al-Battānī, were likewise well known to the medieval West, thanks to the labours of Gerard, John of Seville and Plato of Tivoli. Of the writings of Thābit, Gerard translated the *Liber carastonis* on the mathematical theory of the steelyard, the *De figura sectore* on the theorem of Menelaus, fundamental for the study of spherical trigonometry, and the *De motu accessus et recessus,* which elaborates the theory of the twinkling and oscillation of the fixed stars, and attempts to bring the data given by Greek astronomers into harmony with the observations of the Arabians. On the other hand, John of Seville devoted himself mainly to the astrological works of Thābit, such as the *Liber iudiciorum astrorum*. The chief work of al-Battānī or Albategnius (d. 317/929), the celebrated astronomical tables known as the *Zīj al-Ṣābi'*, was translated several times, either in part or in its entirety, during the Christian Middle Ages: once by Plato of Tivoli in the first half of the twelfth century, once at the court of Alfonso the Wise in Seville (latter half of thirteenth century), and in the early years of the twelfth century by Robert of Chester.

Another medieval astrological classic of Arab origin was the *Introductio in astrologiam,* of al-Qabīṣī (Alcabitius), the fourth/tenth-century astrologer who compiled his manual for the Hamdanid prince of Aleppo, Sayf al-Dawla; in Europe it became known thanks to the translation by John of Seville, to which was added the little treatise entitled *De coniunctionibus planetarum,* and for centuries, together with the *Tetrabiblos* or the *Centiloquium* of Ptolemy (both likewise translated several times from Arabic versions), it constituted an authoritative and handy introduction to the science of astrology. Alhazen, the physicist and mathematician Ibn al-Haytham (d. 430/1039), was made famous in the West by Gerard's translation of his little booklet on astronomy, *De crepusculis et nubium ascensionibus,* and by his great treatise on physico-mathematical optics, *De optica* (translated and revised by a certain Witelo in the thirteenth century from an Arabic original which seems to have disappeared), which in the opinion of competent judges was one of the major glories of the Muslim Middle Ages. On the other hand, the versatile and brilliant al-Bīrūnī (d. 440/1048), nowadays regarded as the leading figure in medieval Muslim science, was practically unknown to the West at that time, even if he can be identified with a certain 'Rinuby', author of a few astronomical writings preserved in Latin translations.

The last effervescence of Arab mathematics and astronomy passed on to the West includes the works of the Spanish scholars al-Zarqālī (Azarquiel), Jābir b. Aflaḥ al-Ishbīlī and al-Biṭrūjī, all of the twelfth century, and almost contemporaries of the great translation period in Toledo and Seville. Al-Zarqālī's treatise explaining the modified form of astrolabe he had invented was translated into Latin by Gerard, and into Castilian by order of Alfonso the Wise. Gerard also translated Jābir's compendium of the *Almagest,* together with the important treatise on trigonometry prefixed to it by the author of the Arabic original, *Gebri filii Affla Hispalensis de Astronomia libri novem.* Lastly, al-Biṭrūjī (Alpetragius, d. 600/1204) with his treatise on astronomy of anti-Ptolemaic tendency evolved a cosmographical system more consonant with pure Aristotelian principles and was for this reason studied and translated by Michael Scot; the work was later translated into Hebrew and in the sixteenth century from Hebrew again into Latin.

It was by such means that Arab knowledge of mathematics, astronomy and astrology gave a helping hand to the early days of scientific activity in the West. In those same early years of the thirteenth century, Leonard of Pisa compiled his *Liber Abbaci,* strongly imbued with Arab algebra, which was a landmark in European mathematics, and introduced the system of 'Arabic' numerals, in reality Indian, which were adapted but used only in part by the Arabs themselves. Arab astronomy and astrology remained in vogue throughout Europe until well on into the Renaissance, down to the days of Regiomontanus and the Copernican revolution.

No less profound was the influence of Islamic culture and science in the field of alchemy and magic, which throughout the Middle Ages and until the eve of the modern era formed a conspicuous part of the intellectual patrimony of mankind. This was derived also from the Hellenistic and late antique legacy, singularly congenial, because of the Eastern elements it already contained, to Muslim culture of the 'Abbasid period, during which it was also cultivated by non-Arab and heterodox circles.

The Latin Middle Ages greeted these speculations and researches with equal enthusiasm, and important Arabic texts on magic and alchemy have come down to us in numerous Latin translations of which the original versions have been lost. For example, the text that might be called the Magna Carta of the earliest Arab alchemy, said to have been found by Apollonius of Tyana in a cave, engraved on a tablet of emerald, is included in a treatise on hermetic cosmology, *Sirr al-khalīqa,* better known by the Latin title of *Tabula smaragdina,* under which it enjoyed wide circulation in the West in early times. Scanty fragments of an Arabic original also exist of another celebrated work on alchemy, very popular in the Middle Ages, of which several versions of an anonymous translation have come down to us. This is the *Turba philosophorum,* the original of which was apparently written about the year 900, containing the description of a conference presided over by a certain Arisleus (Aristeus or Archelaos ?), with numerous speeches by Greek philosophers on subjects connected with alchemy and natural philosophy, the latter being considered as a premiss of alchemy. From such purely theoretical speculations, Arab alchemy passed to praxis with the corpus of writings going under the name of Geber (Jābir b. Ḥayyān); the pseudographical character of these writings has been shown, and the compilation of them, going back to Ismāʿīlī circles, is nowadays attributed to a number of authors of the ninth and tenth centuries. Here we are interested only in the Latin Geber, who soon became classed as an Arab authority, thanks mainly to Gerard of Cremona, who translated at least the first of a group of seventy little treatises attributed to Jābir (*Liber divinitatis de septuaginta*), and later through a whole series of anonymous translations (*Liber adabesi, De arte alchemiae, Flos naturarum, Summa perfectionis metallorum,* etc.), which gave added authority to the mythical Arab alchemist, or rather to the writings passing under his name, and created a vogue for them in the Latin West. Such was the fame of this 'Geber' that works on alchemy of later date and of undoubted Latin origin were attributed to him. The works of the great physician and philosopher al-Rāzī (d. *c.* 320/932), who knew at least the earlier writings of the Geber corpus and gave a vigorous impulse to the experimental side of such researches, were also translated into Latin (*Liber secretorum, Liber experimentorum*) and as a result this original and profound thinker was looked upon as an authority even in this field lying halfway between science and fantasy, which was destined to engage the energies of so many generations to come.

Alchemy as a science soon became chemistry and eventually the most rigorous form of modern research, but originally its extravagant aberrations and its conception of nature brought it closer to magic. Since the days of late Antiquity, magic, concentrating on the production of talismans and amulets, which were supposed to counteract the forces of nature and the whims of fortune, had undergone extensive development. Its high priest and grand master was, in Eastern tradition, Apollonius of Tyana (in Arabic, Bālīnās or Bālīnūs), to whose theurgic figure every sort of prodigy was attributed. In the West, Bālīnās became Belenus, and to him were ascribed various writings on alchemy, astrology and magic current in Latin translations at that time. But the most comprehensive Arab manual of magic that the West knew was the *Picatrix* (perhaps a corruption of Hippocrates, the name of a suppositious Greek author), the Arabic original of which was entitled *Ghāyat al-ḥakīm* ('The philosopher's aim'), attributed to a tenth-century mathematician living in Spain, Maslama al-Majrīṭī, whereas in reality it would appear to have been compiled about a century later. The Latin version of this encyclopaedia of magic, based on a mixture of astrology and neo-Platonism, but with the fundamental practical aim of producing natural phenomena and invoking spirits at the request of the initiate, was made by order of Alfonso the Wise during the latter half of the thirteenth century, and its influence in the Middle Ages and the Renaissance was prolonged and tenacious. The survival of this most irrational and extravagant sector of late antique culture transmitted by the Arabs to Europe, down to the beginning of the modern era, is exemplified in a most significant way in this curious treatise on talismans and magic exhalations; here we touch the lowest level of that cultural heritage which at its apex had the philosophy of Aristotle and Plato, the science of Ptolemy and Galen. Gold and dross were studied and transmitted by Islam in equal parts.

To complete this brief review, we must mention a few Arabic texts on technical subjects, the results of observations and experiments made by Muslims independently of ancient tradition, which eventually reached the West. Among them are treatises on falconry and hunting with dogs, a genre well represented in Arab technical literature. Two authors, 'Moamin' and Ghaṭrīf, are known to us through translations, and it would appear that at least part of the original texts has recently been discovered.[1] 'Moamin' is known to have been a falconer in the service of Frederick II, who had his work translated into Latin by his interpreter,

[1] E. Viré, in *Arabica*, VIII (1961), 273.

Theodore, and certainly made use of it in his own treatise, *De arte venandi cum avibus*. We do not know whether this Latin translation has survived, but what has been preserved and recently published is a Romance translation, in Franco-Italian, of both 'Moamin' and his possible contemporary, Ghaṭrīf, a rare example in its genre, since such works were normally translated only into Latin.

THE TRANSMISSION OF LITERARY INFLUENCES

In the scientific field, the chief function of Islam was the transmission to the West of a goodly portion of the ancient heritage, though it is true that it made certain contributions of its own. In the spheres of literature and art, however, it transmitted far more of its own stock. By saying this we do not mean to imply that in these fields no Classical elements reached the West as a result of Islamic mediation (for example, through the *Thousand and one nights*), but it is nevertheless a fact that apart from such sporadic cases, Eastern influence on Western literature and art presupposes the existence in Islamic civilization of a clearly defined spiritual patrimony evolved in the East in a spirit and in forms peculiar to it, and constituting a counterpart to Classical culture and the continuation of that culture after its transformation in the Romance lands. Here the East acted not only as mediator and elaborator, but also as a creator on its own account; and the West—almost unwittingly during the Middle Ages, but more consciously and systematically in the modern era—received from these contacts and sought in them cultural elements completely extraneous to its own tradition, making experiments in grafting them which were more or less successful, the very fact that they were made being a testimony to the vitality of the Islamic heritage and the contribution it made in this way to the common heritage of all mankind.

There would seem to be no doubt that throughout the Middle Ages and the Renaissance, down to the threshold of the modern era, only Arabic literature need be taken into account when we are dealing with literary contacts with, and influence upon, the Christian world. It was not until the second phase, the spiritual rediscovery of the East by the Enlightenment and European Romanticism, that Persian, and to a lesser degree Turkish and the other minor literatures, took their places by the side of Arabic literature. Differing in language, in their areas of diffusion, in the volume and complexity of their output, all these literatures had nevertheless one common denominator, which was precisely that conferred upon them by Islam, of which they are the expression.[1] The spirit of Islam permeates them all, just as Arabic, the language of the Qur'ān, gave them its vocabulary and its script. But this plurality of Islamic languages and literatures was, we repeat, a phenomenon affecting only the modern phase of the contacts between East and West. During the first thousand years of its existence, Islam was revealed and expressed to Europe almost exclusively through Arabic literature, and in the West, for obvious geographical and historical reasons, 'Arabic' and 'Saracen' were synonyms. Throughout the Middle Ages, the literary position of the two worlds, Islam and Latin Christendom, was thus as follows. On the one side was a supranational language and literature, Arabic, which from being the language of one nation had become the vehicle of culture for a whole civilization. The use of different dialects in the spoken language, of considerable importance for certain aspects of our theme, never led to the formation of autonomous literary languages, and this is true even today. On the other side was a language, medieval Latin, also international, but out of which, by contrast with what happened with Arabic, the Romance vernaculars gradually evolved, each with a thriving literature of its own.

Since we are dealing here only with the influence of Arabic literature on the West, we shall mention only a few of its general characteristics which can be used for purposes of comparison with medieval Latin literature. First and foremost there was poetry, and then prose, carefully cultivated, stylized and codified. From the very beginning the poetry was completely autochthonous, going back in origin to the dim past of pre-Islamic civilization, and remaining for a very long time free from foreign influence—a poetry that soon became a canonical model, little tolerant of new development. The prose, after a first unique and inimitable monument in the shape of the Sacred Book, flourished exceedingly during the Islamic era; it too at first immune from foreign influences, as the language not only of religion, philosophy and science but also of history and jurisprudence, of culture and art. Throughout their evolution, Arabic poetry and prose retained that learned and intellectual character which made them the prerogative of the cultured classes, with an ever-widening gap between them and the life of the people. These characteristics of the Islamic East's major literature have

[1] Cf. F. Gabrieli, 'Literary Tendencies', in the volume *Unity and Variety in Muslim Civilization* (ed. G. E. von Grunebaum) (Chicago, 1955).

a certain affinity with those of medieval Latin and Graeco-Byzantine literature, giving, one might say, a common physiognomy to the literary output of the early Middle Ages in both East and West. But whereas in the West, after the year 1000, the spirit of each of the individual nations made itself more and more felt in literary activity, as a result of the birth of new languages, new forms and new ideas—some of which, as we shall see, were fertilized by contacts with the East—Oriental literature clung tenaciously to its aristocratic character and in the end became fossilized. Between lofty, refined literature and formless, genuinely popular expression there was, in Islam, a gap that was never filled; and so, while medieval literature in the international Latin language gave birth—not only in the linguistic sense—to neo-Latin offshoots, Arabic literature knew no such new development. It paid for this by contracting sclerosis and by centuries of decadent sterility, until the advent of the modern revival, when the trend of influence was reversed and Arabic literature was fertilized and invigorated by the West. But during its golden age, which lasted until the Renaissance, it gave much to the West, and received nothing in return.

The Middle Ages

Until quite recently we were in the dark as to how much literary influence, if any, the Islamic East had on the West in medieval times, when relations between East and West were those of war and commerce, with little opportunity for cultural exchanges. Here too an exception—and at the same time an anticipation—is provided by Spain, where the Arab-Islamic and Latin-Christian elements soon learned to live together in a fruitful symbiosis. Alvaro of Cordova's celebrated testimony shows that as early as the ninth century, only a hundred years after the conquest, his Christian contemporaries were assiduously cultivating Arabic literature. He laments the fact that, instead of poring over the Holy Scriptures, they were reading the poems, the epistles and the stories of their infidel conquerors, vying with one another in imitating them, spending vast sums in acquiring libraries of Arabic books and, though ignorant of Latin, using Arabic with a fluency equal to that of the Arabs themselves. Nothing has survived of this ancient Mozarabic literature, and very few of the originals by which it was inspired, if we except a few fragments of poetry dating from the days of the Cordovan amirate. It should, however, be noted that at that time, and even during the golden century of the Cordovan caliphate, Arab culture in Spain still retained a definitely oriental stamp, and did not until later assume an Andalusian character of its own. In any case, the cultural supremacy of Arabic among the Christian community in Spain in those distant days would seem to be well documented, while traces of translations from Latin into Arabic (for example, of the historical works of Orosius) confirm that there was cultural contact between the two worlds. The most recent and sensational novelty in this field was the discovery of the Romance-Arabic *kharjas,* the early history of which leads us back to this same remote period of Muslim–Christian Spain. But this discovery was only the last chapter in the thorny problem of Arabic poetry and European poetry, which first came to the fore at a much later date and is now the focal point of every controversy on literary influences and the relationship between East and West in medieval times.

The theory that the Arabs had a pre-eminent influence on medieval Romance culture, and in particular on its poetry, was first advanced in the sixteenth century by Barbieri, and then by Andrés in his erudite work on the history of literature written in the days of the Enlightenment, when there was much curiosity concerning the East.[1] As regards poetry, they identified the classical Arabic poets, the only category then known, as the inventors and transmitters to the neo-Latin world of rhyme. Nineteenth-century Romanticism, with Sismondi and Fauriel, shifted the stress from the field of form to that of content, and considered the Arabs as precursors and inspirers of the concept of courtly love elaborated by the troubadours. In this way they laid the double foundation of that 'Arab theory' on the origins of Romance lyric verse—a theory which, though combated and almost shelved by the positivists, was destined to have a vigorous revival in our own century and to become the apple of discord between students of oriental and Romance literatures, giving rise to a violent controversy which is still going on.

We have just spoken of a double foundation, but it would perhaps be better to speak of two threads, often rightly or wrongly intertwined and entangled. One is the question of the influence on metre, of rhyme and later of the strophe, which from Andalusia might have crossed the Pyrenees and entered Provençal, Old French and Italian poetry, while in the Iberian peninsula they might have been adopted by the nascent Gallego-Portuguese and Castilian poetry. The other problem, which

[1] G. Andrés, *Origine, progresso e stato attuale di ogni letteratura,* (Parma, 1782–99); G. M. Barbieri, *Dell'origine della poesia rimata* (ed. by Tiraboschi, 1790).

can be considered as either bound up with the question of metre or else distinct from it, concerns the spiritual background of the sentiments, concepts and images expressed by Romance lyric poets and above all by the troubadours, the real or supposed oriental precedents of which are being sought for and identified. Before Ribera and the more recent studies and discoveries, this latter element of a migration across the Pyrenees to the Romance world of a conception of love and of woman unknown to the Classical world was the most assiduously pursued and asserted. The conception of love as humble service and chaste adoration was rediscovered in the ʿUdhrite poets of the desert, and among city-dwellers in ʿAbbās b. al-Aḥnaf, of the early ʿAbbasid period. It was easy to follow its passage from the East to Arab Spain in the works of poets like Ibn Zaydūn (d. 463/1071) or in treatises on love like those of Ibn Ḥazm (d. 456/1064), whose pleasing little book on the phenomenology and case-histories of love, *Ṭawq al-ḥamāma*, owed most of its success in the West to the fact that it was supposed to be a pre-troubadour manual of courtly love against a Muslim background. The undeniable analogies between the basic concepts and certain stock situations and figures in Arabic and troubadour lyrics (the jealous lover, the *raqīb/guadador,* the *wāshī/lauzenjaire,* etc.) were so striking as inevitably to encourage the idea that the Arab-Andalusian world must have exercised a direct influence on Romance poetry. Borne on the waves of intercourse—diplomatic and commercial, religious and cultural (through pilgrimages), social and even military, since wars also promote contacts—Moorish mentality and literary conventions were believed to have fertilized the nascent poetry in *langue d'oc*, despite the diversity of language, faith and culture. The language difficulty was actually the knottiest problem for these champions of a migration across the Pyrenees of concepts and themes—a stumbling-block which the opponents of the 'Arab theory' did not fail to point out.

In the early years of the present century the whole problem entered upon a new phase, thanks to the Arabic and Hispanic scholar J. Ribera. On the one hand he threw light on the Arabic-Romance bilingualism prevalent in the social life of Muslim Spain and its consequences in the literary field, which subsequent studies were to confirm and extend. On the other hand, by his study of the works of the twelfth-century poet Ibn Quzmān, he opened a new chapter in the history of Arabic literature and its relations with the Romance world. The *dīwān* of Ibn Quzmān was found to have been composed, not in classical Arabic, but in the Arab-

Hispanic vernacular, not in the classical metre of the monorhyme quantitative *qaṣīda,* but in the popular form of the *zajal*—syllabic strophes (though sometimes showing traces of quantitative schemes, or adapted to them) with various combinations of rhymes. Some of these 'zejelesque' strophic forms seemed to Ribera to be almost identical with those of the earliest Provençal troubadours, e.g. William of Poitiers, Cercamon and Marcabru (for example, the simplest and most typical form rhyming *aaab, cccb, dddb,* etc., preceded, like the strophes of the Arabic *zajal,* by a prelude-refrain *bb* and ending with a finale repeating the same rhyme—the famous *kharja*). This identity, however, was not confined to the Provençal poets. Ribera was able to show that the 'zejelesque' strophe in its various combinations is to be found in the early lyrics of other Romance languages—in Galician in the Alfonsine *Cantigas,* in Castilian *villancicos,* in Franco-Provençal popular poetry and in the *laudi* of Jacopone da Todi and of the Franciscans in general. The old and unproven assertion of former scholars that rhyme was introduced into the Romance world by the Arabs, found an unexpected confirmation of a concrete kind in this popular type of poetry, in which the debt of Romance poetry to the Arabs seemed to be supported by chronological data that could not be ignored. According to Arab tradition the inventor of Arabic-Andalusian strophic poetry (the *muwashshaḥa* in classical language, the *zajal* of Ibn Quzmān and other poets being merely a variant in the vernacular) was Muqaddam or Muḥammad of Cabra, who flourished about the year 900. Ibn Quzmān (*c.* 1080–1160) and William of Poitiers (1071–1126) were contemporaries, but the Cordovan poet was only the most illustrious representative of Arabic 'zejelesque' poetry whose work has come down to us, and we have ample documentary evidence of the existence in Arab Spain during the tenth and eleventh centuries of this form as well as of the metrically equivalent *muwashshaḥa.* Even if we exclude—as we should—the possibility of Ibn Quzmān having had any direct influence on the earliest Provençal troubadour, it would seem to be beyond all doubt that the Arab strophic form existed before the days of the troubadours and Romance poetry in general.

As regards form and metre, Ribera's studies certainly gave valid support to the 'Arab theory', but it cannot be said that he contributed anything new to the question of content and concept. In reality, Ibn Quzmān was anything but a singer of courtly love, and his carefree cynicism could be better compared with analogous realistic traits which we find side by side with the prevalent idealistic trend in certain Provençal poets. In any case, Ribera's new formulation of the metrical problem was developed by Arabic scholars like Nykl (editor and first translator of Ibn Quzmān), Tallgren-Tuulio, García Gómez, and above all by that great authority on Romance literature, R. Menéndez Pidal. The last named, in a classic paper, made a profound study of 'zejelesque' metre in Romance poetry and finally accepted the 'Arab theory' when he found that the identity of strophic schemes extended to all seven variants of the original Arabic and corresponding Romance forms, remarking that this Arabic-neo-Latin type of strophic verse constitutes 'a family group that cannot be confused with any other tristich, or with any other strophe having a refrain'. With this precise formulation he took his stand against the tenacious attempts of adversaries of the 'Arab theory' to ascribe the origin of the Romance strophe to the Latin monorhyme tristichs with a *volta,* the only possible alternative to the theory that it was due to the passage of Arabic influence across the Pyrenees. Such tristichs exist, but those which can be dated were not written until after the days of William of Poitiers and cannot therefore constitute a profound substratum of tradition such as the Arabic forms can boast in the country of their origin, as A. Roncaglia, the most recent and most conscientious student of Romance literature to tackle the problem, has to admit. Nevertheless, the reasoned and instinctive objections of the Romance camp have not yet been entirely confuted, and scholars like Spanke and Le Gentil still prefer to resort to an agnostic 'not proven', or to maintain that any analogies are purely casual and extrinsic, instead of bowing to what would now seem to have been convincingly established.[1]

While he is obliged to accept, almost by force of circumstances, the Arabic origin of Romance rhythmics, Roncaglia rightly insists on antedating the actual fertilizing influence to a period before the end of the eleventh century or the early years of the twelfth, to which that typical pair, Ibn Quzmān and William, would otherwise bring us. Between a 'pre-troubadour melic tradition', which might have had a Romance background, and the Arab *milieu* in Spain, one would have to presuppose contacts some time before the year 1000, during a protoliterary phase concerning which we have only very fragmentary documentary

[1] S. M. Stern has recently made a strong case against the theory of the borrowing of rhyme in Western Europe from Arab models. See *L'Occidente e l'Islam nell'Alto Medioevo,* Centro di studi di Spoleto, XII, 1965, II, 639-66.

evidence, but which would provide a better explanation for the slow osmosis of these rhythmical elements, and also of certain *topoi* of Eastern origin in the nascent Romance lyric poetry. This reconstruction and backdating of the process are based in their turn on the most recent phase in the study of Arabic-Andalusian verse, that is to say on the discovery of the existence in the latter of the Romance *kharja,* which has opened up new perspectives in the whole field and raised new problems.

The presence of isolated Romance words in Ibn Quzmān's *zajal* written in colloquial Arabic had already been noticed by Ribera. But since 1948, thanks mainly to S. M. Stern and E. García Gómez, some fifty *kharjas* have been studied and published, taken from *muwashshaḥāt* written in Hebrew (a simple imitation of the Arabic forms) and in Arabic, in which the classical Arabic strophic group ends with a finale that can only be explained as due to a commingling of Arabic and Romance, and sometimes seems to be pure Romance. Most of them are love poems (distant precursors of the *Cantigas de amigo*), in which a girl gives vent to her feelings, her passions and her reproaches; but there are also *kharjas* of a laudatory or descriptive kind, all more or less closely connected with the subject-matter of the *muwashshaḥa* containing them. Ribera's theory of Arabic-Hispanic bilingualism even in the field of popular or would-be popular literature—a theory which also finds support in certain passages in Arabic anthologies and treatises, for example those of Ibn Bassām and Ibn Sanā' al-Mulk—could not have a more striking confirmation. Quite apart from the exceptional importance of such documents dating from the earliest phase of the Iberian vernacular (these *muwashshaḥāt* were written by poets of the tenth, eleventh and twelfth centuries even if the anthologies containing them are of later date), here we seem to have a reversal of the trend of give and take between the Arab and the Romance worlds. We find, namely, the Arabs using and inserting in their poems a very old Mozarabic tradition; perhaps because, as some scholars maintain, such Romance *kharjas* existed before the various *muwashshaḥāt* and were extracted ready-made from their Romance background, or else because the Arab poet composed them himself with all the gusto of a virtuoso for pastiches, deriving them, however, from some familiar tradition of his own milieu. In either case, one thing is now certain. Starting from the type of poetry in rigorously classical language and quantitative metre, which in Spain preserved the Eastern spirit and forms, we arrive at this other type of strophic structure (likewise not without Eastern precedents, but receiving its own characteristic form and development in Spain, whence it later returned to the East), and find a polylingual foundation wherein Arab tradition and the Romance spirit are closely interwoven, so much so that we are left in doubt to which branch individual features are to be attributed. And whereas during the purely literary phase (the only phase we knew until quite recently) there was very probably an Arab influence on the Romance world on both sides of the Pyrenees, its slow maturing in Andalusia reveals a participation of Romance elements the extent of which it is still difficult to estimate. This would be the only exception to the maxim we laid down above, namely that in the literary field during the Middle Ages the East gave everything to the West and received nothing in exchange. But it is certainly difficult to continue to apply the term 'East' to that very remarkable crucible of races and cultures which Muslim Spain, in the light of the most recent discoveries, would more and more appear to have been, down to the centuries of the reconquest.

To conclude our remarks on this fascinating theme, still the subject of study and controversy, we should like to say that to us the 'Arab theory', on a somewhat broader basis, seems to be firmly established, that is to say in so far as concerns form, rhythmic structure and rhyme, transmitted by the Arabs in their 'zejelesque' shape to the Romance lands on either side of the Pyrenees. Likewise undeniable, though with certain limitations and reservations, is the transmission through Arab tradition to the courtly lyric poetry in *langue d'oc* of certain motifs and thematic notions, in an atmosphere, however, of spiritual autonomy, which should be rightly claimed as a counterpoise to the strict adherence to the actual metrical schemes. In other words, the Arabs gave the Romance world the form of the strophe and rhyme, through their happy innovations on Andalusian soil; while the Romance world filled this form with a spirit which, though it too may have been in part of Arab origin, with its complexity, variety and creative originality, opened up new paths for the West.

The great argument, still in progress, about 'Arab poetry and European poetry' has tended to distract attention from the other fields in which Spain, and in general all the medieval West, received Oriental matter from the Arabs and developed it. In the field of literature, we must first of all consider didactic and gnomic works, and then narrative, often connected with them. Interest in, and translation of, such works seems to have awakened in Christian Spain rather later than was the case with works of philosophy and science, and was mainly thanks to the influence of Alfonso X the Wise (1252–84). For example, from Alfonso's time and milieu we have the translation, under the title *Bocados de oro,* of an anthology of maxims of the ancient sages compiled in Egypt during the eleventh century by Mubashshir b. Fātik. The same may be said of the translation from Arabic into Castilian of the *Kalīla wa-Dimna,* probably made by order of Alfonso in 1251, and of the *Book of Sindibād* (the *Syntipas* or *Dolopathos* or *Book of the seven wise men,* to quote the titles of other Western translations), translated about the same time at the behest of Alfonso's brother under the title *Libros de los engannos et los asayamientos de las mujeres.* In all these cases the subject-matter was not specifically Arabic but part of the earliest Hellenistic and Oriental tradition, going back to Persia and India but known to the West through Arabic versions, the earliest originals of many of them, like that of the *Sindibād,* having been lost. The West absorbed all this material eagerly and it had a far wider circle of readers than the works of philosophy and science, which explains the preference in this field for translations into the vernacular. But apart from translations in the strict sense of the term, Arabic didactic works and narrative poured into Spain during the late Middle Ages and the Renaissance in the form of adaptations, re-elaborations and imitations, the Oriental models of which can sometimes be conjectured and often definitely identified. First we have the *Disciplina clericalis* by Petrus Alfonsi, a converted Jew (early twelfth century), which may originally have been written in Arabic, and even in the Latin version shows clear traces of derivation from the *Kalīla,* the *Sindibād* and the *Thousand and one nights,* one of the most popular works in Muslim Spain. Next we have the *Conde Lucanor* by Don Juan Manuel (1282–1349), many of whose stories are drawn from the same sources, and the Catalan *Disputa del ase* by Fra Anselmo of Turmeda (d. 1420 at Tunis, after conversion to Islam), which goes back to an apologue of the Arabic philosophical encyclopaedia of the *Ikhwān al-Ṣafā'.* Lastly there is the *Patrañuelo* by Timoneda (*c.* 1520–*c.* 1583), the curious vicissitudes of which were noted by Cerulli, who points out that the Arabic subject-matter passed from medieval Spain into the Italian *novella,* and later returned to Spain thanks to this Renaissance story-teller. The Arabic element, often transmitted via the narrative traditions of the Moriscos, characterizes all Spanish literature, even that of the classical period, from Cervantes to Gracián (1601–58), whose *Criticón,* as has been shown by García Gómez, refers in its prologue to a Morisco tale, the common source of this seventeenth-century Jesuit and of the twelfth-century Muslim, Ibn

Ṭufayl, author of *Ḥayy ibn Yaqẓān,* which enjoyed such popularity at the time of the Enlightenment.

The fortunes of this Arabic didactic-narrative material as it spread from Spain throughout medieval and Renaissance Europe have hitherto been followed in single threads which it would be premature to try to draw together. The Arabic, or to speak more generically, Eastern, origin of many *fabliaux,* and of old French romances like *Floire et Blanchefleur* and *Aucassin et Nicolette* (in which the first name is the Arabic al-Qāsim) is now generally admitted. In Italy, no adequate study has yet appeared on the more or less direct Arab sources of the *Novellino,* of Fiorenzuola and Doni—all names which remind us of the transmission, nearly always by way of Spain, of Oriental narrative to Italian culture between the thirteenth and the sixteenth centuries. Outside the field of narrative, other points of contact between the Islamic East and the medieval West have been suggested rather than established for literary forms such as the *tenson* and the *contrasto,* for which some scholars, in addition to a more probable derivation from Middle Latin *altercationes,* have thought of a possible influence of the Arabic and Persian *munāẓarāt,*[1] perhaps through Hebrew mediation. During the last few decades, all these matters of purely historical and literary interest have been overshadowed by another question, important for the history of religion as well. This is the problem of the knowledge and interpretation in the West of Arab-Islamic ideas, images and works relating to the other world, which brings Islamic eschatology into touch with the loftiest medieval expression of poetry and spirituality, the great poem of Dante.

The search for Oriental, and in particular Islamic, sources of Dante's vision was, as is well known, a thorough one, and the results were presented in 1919 by M. Asín Palacios in his book *La escatología musulmana en la Divina Comedia*. After establishing a not altogether convincing, but on the whole impressive, series of analogies in structure, concept and details between Dante's portrayal of the other world and certain Arab-Islamic eschatological sources, Asín Palacios reached the conclusion that, while the poetical genius of Dante as creator of the poem remains intact, the subject-matter was to a considerable extent drawn more or less directly from these Islamic sources. Among the texts which he analysed most minutely, and collated with the *Divine Comedy,* were the

[1] Cf. E. Wagner, *Die arabische Rangstreitdichtung und ihre Einordnung in die allgemeine Literaturgeschichte,* Akademie der Wissenschaften und Literatur, Abhandlungen der Geistes- und Sozialwissenschaftlichen Klasse (1962), No. 8.

Risālat al-ghufrān by Abu'l-'Alā' al-Ma'arrī (d. 449/1057), a half-fantastic, half-satirical description of a journey to the other world, and the works of the Spanish mystic Ibn al-'Arabī (d. 638/1240), especially *al-Futūḥāt al-Makkiyya,* abounding in eschatological descriptions accompanied by graphic illustrations. There was, however, and still is, no trace of any medieval translations into a Western language of these literary and religious texts, the interpretation of which is by no means easy even for modern Arabic scholars, and this linguistic barrier made it extremely unlikely that Dante could have had the precise, detailed knowledge of them that Asín Palacios's theory postulated. In addition to Abu'l-'Alā' and Ibn al-'Arabī, the Spanish scholar also mentioned more generally a number of other Islamic eschatological sources in both learned and popular literature, but here the same objection of the language difficulty could be raised, as well as the problem of the cultural *milieu* in which Dante could have got to know them. The spirited opposition to the theory on the part of Romance philologists and students of Dante was based not only on arguments such as the intrinsic improbability of the whole story, and on doubts as to the validity of some of the alleged analogies, but also on the lack of any vehicle through which these Islamic descriptions of the other world could have been transmitted to Europe and Italy in Dante's time.

Round about 1950, however, the discovery of the Romance *kharjas* threw an unsuspected light on the cultural contacts between the Arabs and the Romance lands through Spain, and at the very same time there came to light what seemed to be the missing link, in the transmission of Islamic eschatology to the West. This was the *Liber scalae Machometi* or *Livre de l'eschiele Mahomet,* to give it the titles of the two versions so far discovered, one in Latin and the other in Old French, published independently and simultaneously, in Spain by Muñoz, and in Italy by Cerulli. Both these translations were made by an Italian, Bonaventura da Siena, from a lost Castilian version of an Arabic *Mi'rāj*—a popular religious text describing the journey of Muḥammad to the other world—which Alfonso X had caused to be translated into Castilian, and then into the two languages of the surviving versions. Cerulli's exhaustive researches, published as part of his edition of this text, have thrown light on its fortunes and provide documentary proofs that it was known (and by this we mean more or less directly and completely) in fourteenth-century Italy, and even by followers and imitators of Dante—the *Liber scalae* is mentioned expressly under the Italian title *Libro della scala* by the

Tuscan poet Fazio degli Uberti in his *Dittamondo* and under the Arabic title *Helmaerich* (= *al-Miʿrāj*) by a fifteenth-century Franciscan preacher. With the discovery of this text and of its migration across the Pyrenees and the Alps, the obstacle of the missing link was removed, and we can now disregard the authors of learned works like Abu'l-ʿAlā' and Ibn al-ʿArabī and concentrate our attention on this vein of popular Muslim piety, which Asín Palacios mentioned, though he was unable to produce any evidence of a contact between it and the age and background of Dante. It would now seem to be at least possible, if not probable, that Dante may have known the *Liber scalae* and have taken from it certain images and concepts of Muslim eschatology, thus providing confirmation of Asín Palacios's bold theory. But the function which this presumed knowledge played in the conception and execution of his poem, the manner of his absorption and utilization of these Muslim elements, and their share in the prevailing spirit and tone of his masterpiece, are a very different matter.

In this very delicate field of research, which has to be conducted with due regard for what we know from other sources of Dante's notions of Islamic religion, science and culture, the conclusions drawn by Cerulli and others who accept the new factual elements provided by the *Liber scalae* are extremely cautious. Any data which the poet may have culled through this channel from Muslim eschatological beliefs constitute only one element, a limited portion of his intellectual and cultural preparation, and are of secondary importance compared with the essential elements he drew from the Classical world and the Christian Bible. Moreover, these Islamic elements were inserted and interpreted in his poem in a spirit very different from that of their source—in the spirit of medieval Christendom. Such conclusions, very different from those reached by Asín Palacios in his eagerness to prove his case, and stressed even more forcibly by some of his followers after the discovery of the *Liber scalae,* are curiously close to those of the more discreet supporters of the 'Arab theory' regarding the influence of Islam on Romance lyric verse. In both cases there would seem to have been a utilization of motifs, notions and concepts of Arab-Islamic origin, but these, in the case of Romance poetry, were interpreted by a whole nascent civilization and culture, and in Dante's, by the great individual soul of one poet, in a different spirit and in harmony with a new and different tradition.

To sum up, Dante, notwithstanding the episode of the *Liber scalae,* cannot have known any more about Islam, its literature and civilization, than the average Italian of his day. Did Petrarch, that other great Tuscan who left his mark on the poetry and doctrines of the fourteenth century, know more? A minor nineteenth-century Italian Arabist, P. Valerga, also believed that he could establish some sort of connexion—of ideas, if not of imitation—between the poems of Petrarch and certain aspects of Arabic love-lyrics.[1] But the Arabic poems which he compared with the *Canzoniere* were not songs of earthly love, like those of the poet Jamīl al-'Udhrī or of 'Abbās b. al-Aḥnaf, the 'minstrel of Baghdād', but those of 'Umar b. al-Fāriḍ (d. 633/1235), the leading exponent of mystical poetry in Arabic, in which the poetical form clothes and gives allegorical expression to experiences and passions of divine love. Although, from the strictly aesthetic point of view, even an allegorical poem ought to be judged by the perfection and efficacy of its form, it is obvious that no opinion can be formed nor comparisons made on a cultural and historical basis without having at least some knowledge that one of the two objects compared had an allegorical significance. Valerga knew nothing of this essential characteristic in Ibn al-Fāriḍ and consequently ignored it, so that the parallels he draws between the Arab and the Italian fall to the ground. The former was in reality a religious soul burning with mystical zeal, while the latter was bound to this earth and to mundane emotions, the conflict between these and the call of Heaven being one of the most moving aspects of his poetry.

Another thing that Valerga did not know was that the first person to be astonished and aggrieved by these gratuitous comparisons with the Arabs would have been Petrarch himself. It would seem that he, unlike Dante, really knew something about Arabic poetry, which, if we are to believe what he says in a curious passage in one of his epistles, he did not like at all.[2] Writing to a friend who was a physician, he says: 'Arabes vero quales medici, tu scis. Quales autem poetae, scio ego: nihil blandius, nihil mollius, nihil enervatius, nihil denique turpius. Vix mihi persuadebitur ab Arabia posse aliquid boni esse.' Since Petrarch could not have read the originals, we must suppose that he had seen some samples of Arabic verse translated for his benefit into Latin or Italian by some returned traveller or missionary who knew the language. In the same way, though for a very different reason, Petrarch tried to learn

[1] P. Valerga, *Il Divano di Omar ben al-Fared tradotto e paragonato al canzoniere del Petrarca* (Florence, 1874). It should be noted that Valerga confined his study to the minor odes of Ibn al-Fāriḍ and did not include the great *Tā'iyya*.

[2] *Epistole Senili*, XII, 2.

something of the poetry of Homer through translations. But to what category of Arabic poets was he referring? We are bound to think that it was either Ibn al-Fāriḍ himself (whose personal qualities as an artist, in defiance of general opinion, we do not rate very high) or some late Syrian or Egyptian poet of the Ayyubid or Mamluk period, for example Bahā' al-Dīn Zuhayr or Ibn Sanā' al-Mulk, with their re-hashes of old motifs. Ignorance of the language would have made it impossible for him to judge the form, and in this case the author of the *Canzoniere* can only have been acquainted with Latin or Italian renderings of images which to him must have seemed clumsy and grotesque—images of languishing bedouin love or laudatory baroque hyperbole. Consequently, while some influence of Arabic poetry on the origins of Italian vernacular verse, at least as regards form, could, as we have seen, have existed, this fleeting contact between the Arabic muse and one of the greatest figures of the Tuscan Parnassus remained completely sterile—a case of disappointed curiosity.

The Renaissance and afterwards

At the time of the Renaissance, Islam was a political and religious factor, not a literary problem. The revival in Europe of the cult of Classical Antiquity and the drying up about the same time of the creative genius of Islamic civilization helped to make the period from the fifteenth to the seventeenth century one of the poorest as regards literary contacts between East and West. Ciriaco of Ancona toured the Levant with his eyes fixed only on relics of antiquity, and even Pietro Della Valle, who took such a keen interest in the contemporary Islamic East which he visited, seems to have been hardly aware of its high level of literary culture in Arabic, Persian and Turkish. Not until the advent in the eighteenth century of the Enlightenment and cosmopolitanism did Europe show in the world of Islam an interest not merely political and religious, but also spiritual, sentimental and aesthetic. In the early years of the eighteenth century, almost as a symbol of this new attitude, the *Thousand and one nights,* in Galland's French translation, made their triumphal entry into European culture.

The history of this famous collection of tales reflects in its formation and fortunes an almost stratigraphic succession of cultures in both East and West. Late medieval Egypt had given a more or less definite form to this corpus of narrative, containing, as is known, ingredients of

Indian, Persian and Arab origin, from ʿAbbasid ʿIrāq and from the Egypt of the Mamluks. Muslim Spain also made its contribution (the story of the slave-girl Tawaddud, who in Spanish became the learned damsel Teodor) and transmitted individual themes and incidents from the *Arabian nights* to Castilian literature. But in Galland's incomplete translation, based on material of Oriental origin, this composite medley of stories and folklore of the East with its Arab-Islamic patina acquired full citizenship in the Europe of the Enlightenment. In the course of the same century, Galland's pioneer efforts were continued and imitated, e.g. in the *Mille et un jours* by Pétis de la Croix, and the *Veillées du Sultan Chahriyar* by Chavis and Cazotte; and the early nineteenth century, with the English translation by Edward Lane and the German version by Hammer-Purgstall and Weil, was able to present readers, whether cultured or not, with the whole corpus of the by then famous collection of stories, which for several generations was their chief, or only, introduction to the East.

But even during the latter half of the eighteenth century, the more cultured classes of Europe were offered a broader view of the Muslim East. In addition to the Arab world, which for the medieval West had been the sole representative of Islam, and that of Ottoman Turkey, which had found its way in during the Renaissance, Persia was discovered towards the end of the eighteenth century as a source of literature and culture. As early as the seventeenth century, Olearius had made the *Gulistān* of Saʿdī known to the Germans. In the following century and the early years of the nineteenth, Anquetil Duperron revealed the religion and the sacred texts of the *Avesta,* while Ḥāfiẓ, Firdawsī and the other great poets of Islamic Persia began to be known and appreciated in Europe. To the Europe of the Enlightenment and Romanticism, Persia thus displayed the double aspect of its ancient national religion and civilization and its Islamic phase, in which many scholars have tried to discern the survival of characteristics peculiar to Aryan Iran. To the colourful and fabulous, but in reality shallow and at times puerile, world of the *Thousand and one nights,* which for many, together with the newly accessible Qur'ān (Sale's English translation appeared in 1734), represented the sum of Arabic literature, there were thus added the exquisite flowers of the lyrical, epic and gnomic poetry of Muslim Persia, till then unknown to the West. This new literary harvest from Persia was soon to be supplemented by the discovery of the poetry and wisdom of India. The ethnic and linguistic links between India and

Persia had already been perceived at that time, but were overrated, to the detriment of the historical and religious differences. All these new Eastern literatures joined the choir of the 'voices of the nations' re-echoed by Herder, in the garland of that *Weltliteratur* which was Goethe's dream. Such was this 'Oriental Renaissance', as Schwab calls it, which is one of the most complex and fascinating features in European culture from the late eighteenth to the twentieth century.

Goethe's *West-Östlicher Divan* (first published in 1819), the most illustrious fruit of this new European attitude of curiosity and sympathy for the East, and in particular the Muslim world, was a phase in his versatile experience and gave the German language and German culture the leading place in this field, a place which Germany was destined to retain throughout the nineteenth century. The East in which Goethe sought refuge, with the aid of translations, but above all on the wings of fancy and wisdom, was the East of the Arab-Persian Middle Ages, in which the literary and gnomic Persian element played a leading part. Of the Arab world, in which the figure of the Prophet himself had already attracted Goethe—and to this we owe the magnificent lyric *Mahomet's Gesang,* a fragment of a projected drama—there are but few traces in the *Divan,* but there are more in the accompanying *Noten und Abhandlungen,* among them a forceful translation of Ta'abbaṭa Sharran's 'song of vengeance'. Pride of place is given to the Persia of Ḥāfiẓ and Sa'dī, of sultans and dervishes, of Suleika-Willemer and Hatem-Goethe, because, it is hardly necessary to say, the poetry of the *Divan* is not an antiquary's evocation, but a continuation in an orientalized form of that great autobiographical *Bekenntnis* which the whole of Goethe's work represents. What interests us here is the Oriental dress, a striking testimony to the poet's widespread intellectual interests and to a whole trend in European science and culture. In those same years during which the aged Goethe was assimilating and remoulding the lyrico-gnomic world of medieval Islam, a young man who died at an early age, Wilhelm Hauff (1802–27), was absorbing the Muslim art of storytelling and imitating it in his *Märchen,* which, inspired by the world of the Arabian Nights, are the most colourful echo of them produced by the Romantic movement, and from the artistic point of view are often superior to their models. The fame of Goethe and the fortunes of Hauff marked the entry of the Muslim East into German literature, and though Hauff knew no Arabic or Persian and Goethe contented himself with a superficial attempt—little more than a game—to learn these languages, other poets interested in the

East, like Platen and Rückert, with the inspiration and virtuosity of artists, based their *Nachdichtungen* on a direct acquaintance with the originals—Platen in his *Abbasiden* and the exquisite *Ghaselen* and likewise Rückert in his *Östliche Rosen*, his translations from the *Ḥamāsa*, from al-Ḥarīrī and Firdawsī, and above all his *Morgenländische Sagen und Geschichten*, do not merely re-echo Eastern motifs, but reveal a direct knowledge of the original texts in which they sought inspiration. The Muslim East thus remained a favourite motif in German literature throughout the nineteenth century—from genuine poets like Heine (*Der Asra, Firdusi, Almanzor*) to pleasing rhymesters like Bodenstedt (*Die Lieder des Mirza Schaffy*) and gifted dilettanti like A. von Schack, who used his literary talent to further the cause of Oriental poetry (*Poesie und Kunst der Araber in Spanien und Sizilien*). During the last decades of the nineteenth century, scholarship gradually suffocated this form of poetical evocation, and, as the world of Islam became in Germany the subject of ever more thorough scientific study by Nöldeke, Wellhausen, Goldziher, Brockelmann and others, the roses of this artistic *Nachdichtung* withered. In the troubled days of the twentieth century, Semitic philology, Iranistics and *Islamkunde* have blocked the way to any approach to the East which is not of a strictly scientific, political or journalistic nature.

Literary France, like Germany, had its Oriental phase during the nineteenth century. Heralded by the interest of men of the Enlightenment, such as Boulainvilliers and Voltaire, in Islam and its founder, by the success of the translations of the Arabian Nights published by Galland and his followers, and by the great scientific work of a scholar like Sylvestre de Sacy, the Arab-Persian-Turkish world was appropriated as an integral part of the patrimony of Romanticism. The French pendant to the *West-Östlicher Divan* was Victor Hugo's *Les Orientales* (1829), published just after the Greek rising and on the eve of the Algerian expedition. But unlike Goethe's *Divan,* which is a poetical meditation on mankind and the universe based on Oriental notions, and on what one might almost call 'pretexts', Victor Hugo's little book was more than anything else a colourful fresco of the Levant and the Maghrib of those days, of the splendours and horrors of the tottering Ottoman empire, and of that African colouring which a few years later was to inspire the brush of Delacroix. Interesting, for the light they throw on the author's tastes and his knowledge of Eastern matters, are the notes, a reflection, filtered through Hugo's sensibility, of opinions on Islamic poetry and history current in France during the early nineteenth century. Islamic motifs are also to be found in *La Légende des Siècles* (*L'an neuf de l'Hégire*, *Mahomet*, *Les trônes d'Orient*), and again in that Parnassian 'légende des siècles', the *Poèmes* of Leconte de Lisle (*L'apothéose de Mouça-al-Kébyr*, *Le suaire d'al-Mançour*), but between the youthful Hugo and Leconte de Lisle lies the whole generation of the Romantics, who sought, in a more or less conventionalized East, sensations, experiences and colouring —from the Chateaubriand of the *Itinéraire* and the *Abencérages* to Lamartine, the revealer of the story of 'Antar and of the beauties of Lebanon, to the Flaubert of the letters from the East and the Gobineau of the *Nouvelles asiatiques*, whose aesthetic admiration for the East was coupled with an ideological contempt for its civilizations. Notwithstanding the scientific pretensions of this theoretician of the *Inégalité des races humaines*, the link between Oriental scholarship and literature seems to have been less close in France than it was in Germany, and none of the poets and men of letters we have just mentioned, or of the many others who could be added to the list, can be said to have been himself an orientalist. But thanks to that more rapid circulation of knowledge which is so characteristic of France, these literary roses were nourished by the contemporary labours of the specialists and by their talent for vulgarization. For this reason, the gap, in this field too, between science, art and general knowledge, was narrower in France than elsewhere. The end of the nineteenth century and the early years of the twentieth witnessed an increase in the output of exotic literature and books on travel, e.g. by Pierre Loti, Maurice Barrès, as well as a revival of the vogue for the East, thanks to the translation of the *Thousand and one nights* published by J. C. Mardrus (1899–1904)—fair and faithless indeed, since in conformity with the decadent taste of the time it presented the Muslim East under a refined and precious guise reminiscent of theatrical scenery and the ballet (Bakst's *Scheherazade*) or of Dulac's illustrations.

In Britain, which, like Holland, had had a pioneer role in the modern study of the Arab-Islamic world (we need only recall the names of Pococke, Ockley and Sale), criticism of the old Arabic poetry was inaugurated by William Jones (1746–94), author of the first translation of the *Mu'allaqāt*, which Goethe, among others, found useful. But side by side with this serious approach to real Arabism, English poetry and narrative were swamped by conventionalized travesties of Islamic civilization like Beckford's fantastic but very successful *Vathek* (1786) and, during the Romantic period, certain works of Byron (*The Giaour*, 1813) and Thomas Moore (*Lalla Rookh*, 1817). The *Thousand and one nights*—that barometer of interest in the East in every European country—was translated into English three times in the course of the nineteenth century, by Lane (1839–42), Payne (1882–4) and Burton (1885), the last-named version being the most famous of all on account of its literary quality and abundance of notes. But the most fertile encounter between English literature and the Islamic East was in Persian rather than in Arabic, since the higher aesthetic values of Persian literature had the same fascination for Anglo-Saxons that they had for German culture. That mysterious Asia which as early as 1816 had inspired Coleridge's *Kubla Khan* was revealed by Firdawsī's great epic to Matthew Arnold (*Sohrab and Rustum*, 1853), and by Jāmī, 'Aṭṭār and above all 'Umar Khayyām to Edward Fitzgerald. Every student of English literature knows the extraordinary vicissitudes of this Persian scholar-poet of the eleventh-twelfth centuries, who enjoyed what was practically a second life in Britain and America after the publication in 1859 of the Victorian poet's exquisite and artistic re-interpretation. Ever since that time there has been controversy as to the truthfulness of Fitzgerald's rendering of 'Umar Khayyām. Here we must confine ourselves to the statement that the Persian *Rubā'iyyāt* attributed with more or less certainty to 'Umar provided inspiration in the nineteenth century for a great English poem in the same metrical form—a phenomenon which was not repeated to the same degree in any subsequent translation of 'Umar in the various European languages. To this we would like to add that, according to the most competent judges in Oriental matters—whose opinion we share—Fitzgerald managed to grasp and transmit in a substantially faithful manner one essential aspect of the ambiguous original—that pessimistic and at the same time hedonistic mood which is the most characteristic feature in 'Umar's physiognomy, even if he gave to his interpretation a coherence lacking in the original. This contact with the Eastern world established by Fitzgerald in a work of pure literature was developed during the nineteenth and twentieth centuries in a series of brilliant works by British Oriental scholars and travellers, such as E. G. Browne, R. A. Nicholson, A. J. Arberry and Gertrude Bell, some of whom also turned their attention to Arabic, for example Nicholson, who among other things studied the 'Arab Khayyām', Abu'l-'Alā' al-Ma'arrī. The Arab world attracted the British to an equal degree with its past and present problems, as can be seen in classics of travel like Kinglake's *Eothen*, Doughty's *Travels in Arabia Deserta*, books on customs (Lane's *Manners and customs of the modern Egyptians* or politics and war (T. E. Lawrence's *Revolt in the desert* and *Seven pillars of wisdom*).

The scarcity of material and our own shortcomings prevent us from adding more than an even briefer summary regarding other countries and literatures. In Spain, the scholarly study of Islamic civilization and its influence on literature was naturally bound up with that of Arabism, as a basic factor of national history and culture in the Iberian peninsula. In more recent times, and in our own, it would perhaps be more correct to speak of an increasing interest in the 'Arab problem' in historiography and journalism; above all of the different values assigned to the old Islamic factor in the sociological and historical fields by students of *hispanidad*, e.g. A. Castro, Cl. Sanchez Albornoz. In another Latin country, Italy, which was also for a time partially occupied and frequently raided by the Arabs, we find, on a smaller scale, the same problem. In so far as this problem concerns Sicily, it has already been dealt with in the historical writings of Michele Amari (1806–88), while from the standpoint of literary history and linguistics there is today a revival of interest among Arabic and Romance scholars. But when we pass from this well-defined historical field to the general influence of the Muslim East on Italian literature and modern Italian thought, there seem to be few signs of interest, despite, or perhaps because of, the rigorously scientific tradition of Italian Arabic scholarship. By this we mean that, contrary to what has been the case in other countries, in Italy the scientific study of Islam, of its literary history and civilization, has been the jealously guarded preserve of a small group of scholars. It has hardly ever penetrated into the living literature and culture of the country, this being in contrast to what has happened in other fields of orientalism such as Indology. An exception is to be found in the work of the Iranist Italo Pizzi (1849–1920), translator of the *Shāh-nāma,* who with an enthusiasm more laudable than his talent as an artist tried to popularize in Italy the 'flowers of the East', to quote the title of one of his anthologies. In our own days Pizzi's example has been followed with a more delicate feeling for literary values and a keener historical sense by the living Iranist, A. Bausani.

Before concluding this brief review of the literary impact of Islam on the modern West, there is one general observation which concerns the whole trend of these influences exchanged between the two worlds, for long enemies but each complementary to the other. Whereas during the Middle Ages the trend was almost entirely from East to West, in modern times the direction of influence has been reversed. Europe still continues to seek inspiration and ideas in the East, but these are almost invariably confined to the spheres of landscape and customs (in so far as the East still has customs of its own that can be contrasted with those of Europe), or to the spiritual heritage of the past, when Islam acted as the teacher of the West. Now that this active role of Islam has been eliminated by the paralysis that began in the Middle Ages, the Muslim East, which renewed its contacts with Europe in the nineteenth century, no longer has original elements to transmit; on the contrary, it is the East which now absorbs the myths, the political ideologies and the literary theories of the West.

THE UMAYYADS OF SPAIN

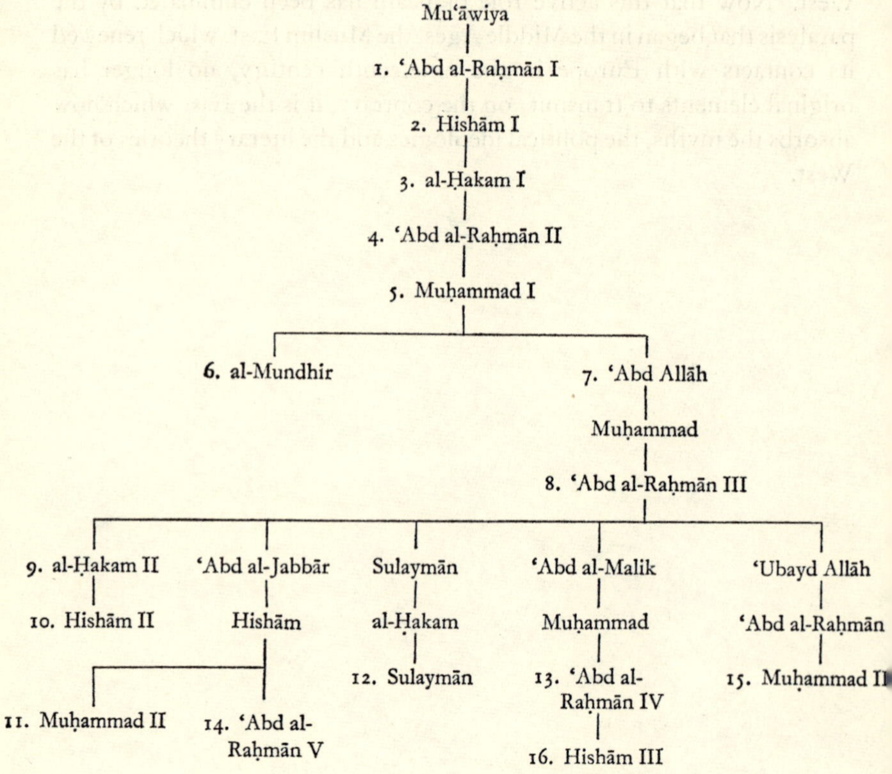
Mu'āwiya
1. 'Abd al-Raḥmān I
2. Hishām I
3. al-Ḥakam I
4. 'Abd al-Raḥmān II
5. Muḥammad I
6. al-Mundhir
7. 'Abd Allāh
Muḥammad
8. 'Abd al-Raḥmān III
9. al-Ḥakam II
'Abd al-Jabbār
Sulaymān
'Abd al-Malik
'Ubayd Allāh
10. Hishām II
Hishām
al-Ḥakam
Muḥammad
'Abd al-Raḥmān
12. Sulaymān
13. 'Abd al-Raḥmān IV
15. Muḥammad II
11. Muḥammad II
14. 'Abd al-Raḥmān V
16. Hishām III

BIBLIOGRAPHY

The following book-lists are intended as a guide to further reading, and consist almost entirely of secondary sources in the principal European languages. Articles in learned journals, *Festschriften* and other collective works of the kind are not normally included; a comprehensive and systematic guide to such materials is provided by:

Pearson, J. D. *Index Islamicus 1906–55*, with its two *Supplements* for 1956–60 and 1961–5 respectively. Cambridge, 1958, 1962, 1966.

An indispensable work of reference on the bibliography of Islamic studies is:

Sauvaget, J. *Introduction à l'histoire de l'orient musulman.* 2nd edn. revised by Cahen, Cl. Paris, 1961.

An English version of this, incorporating some revision and expansion, has appeared as:

Jean Sauvaget's Introduction to the History of the Muslim East. Berkeley and Los Angeles, 1965.

A general introduction to Islamic studies is offered by:

Pareja, F. M. *Islamologia.* Rome, 1951. French edn., *Islamologie,* Beirut, 1957–63.

Numerous articles on Islamic history will be found in:

The Encyclopaedia of Islam. 1st edn. Leiden, 1913–42. 2nd edn. Leiden and London, 1960– (in progress).

There are also relevant chapters in *The New Cambridge Modern History, The Cambridge Medieval History, The Cambridge History of India,* and *The Cambridge History of Iran.*

A survey of the historiography of the Muslim Middle East is provided by:

Lewis, B. and Holt, P. M. *Historians of the Middle East.* London, 1962.

The historiography of Islam in other areas is dealt with in chapters in:

Philips, C. H. (ed.). *Historians of India, Pakistan and Ceylon.* London, 1961.
Hall, D. G. E. (ed.). *Historians of South East Asia.* London, 1962.

Amongst aids to the student, the following atlases will be found useful:

Hazard, H. W. *Atlas of Islamic History.* 3rd edn. Princeton, 1954.
Roolvink, R. *Historical Atlas of the Muslim Peoples.* Amsterdam, 1957.
Atlas of the Arab World amd the Middle East. Macmillan; London, 1960.
Oxford Regional Economic Atlas: The Middle East and North Africa. Oxford University Press; London, 1960.

Genealogical and dynastic lists and tables are given by:

Lane-Poole, S. *The Mohammadan Dynasties.* Paris, 1925.
Zambaur, E. de. *Manuel de généalogie et de chronologie pour l'histoire de l'Islam.* Hanover, 1927.

The following works are of basic importance to the student of Islamic history, society and institutions. They have in different ways contributed to the corpus of knowledge about Islam, to its interpretation and understanding, and to the development of methods of research and investigation.

Becker, C. H. *Islamstudien.* Leipzig, 1924–32.

Gibb, H. A. R. *Modern Trends in Islam.* Chicago, 1947.
—— *Mohammedanism: An Historical Survey.* London, 1949.
—— *Studies in the Civilization of Islam.* Ed. Shaw, S. J. and Polk, W. R. Chicago, 1962.
Goitein, S. D. *A Mediterranean Society.* Vol. I. Berkeley and Los Angeles, 1967.
Goldziher, I. *Muhammedanische Studien.* Halle, 1889–90; Hildesheim 1961. Eng. tr. of Vol. I, ed. S. M. Stern, *Muslim Studies.* London, 1967.
—— *Vorlesungen über den Islam.* 1st edn. Heidelberg, 1910. (French tr. by Arin, F. *Le dogme et la loi de l'Islam.* Paris, 1920.)
Grunebaum, G. E. von. *Medieval Islam: A Study in Cultural Orientation.* 2nd. edn. Chicago, 1953.
—— *Islam: Essays in the Nature and Growth of a Cultural Tradition.* London, 1955.
Hurgronje, C. S. *Verspreide geschriften.* Bonn, Leipzig, Leiden, 1923–7.
—— *Selected Works.* Ed. Bousquet, G.-H. and Schacht, J. Leiden, 1957.
Macdonald, D. B. *Development of Muslim Theology, Jurisprudence and Constitutional Theory.* New York, 1903; Beirut, 1964.
—— *The Religious Attitude and Life in Islam.* Chicago, 1906; repr. Beirut, 1965.
Schacht, J. *The Origins of Muhammadan Jurisprudence.* Oxford, 1950.
Wellhausen, J. *Skizzen und Vorarbeiten.* Berlin, 1884–99.

The Indian Sub-continent

A History of the Freedom Movement. Karachi, 1957–61.
Aga Khan. *The Memoirs of Aga Khan.* London, 1954.
Ahmad, A. *Studies in Islamic Culture in the Indian Environment.* Oxford, 1964.
Ahmed, Jamil-ud-Din. *Speeches and Writings of Mr. Jinnah.* Lahore, 1960.
Ali, M. (ed. Iqbal, A.). *My Life: A Fragment.* Lahore, 1946.
—— (ed. Iqbal, A.). *Select Writings and Speeches of Maulana Mohamed Ali.* Lahore, 1944.
Ambedkar, B. R. *Pakistan, or the Partition of India.* Bombay, 1946.
Ayub Khan, M. *Friends Not Masters.* London, 1967.
Azad, A. K. *India Wins Freedom.* Calcutta, 1959.
Baljon, J. M. S. *The Reforms and Religious Ideas of Sir Sayyid Aḥmad Khān.* Leiden, 1949.
Bazaz, P. N. *A History of Struggle for Freedom in Kashmir.* Delhi, 1954.
Bolitho, H. *Jinnah, Creator of Pakistan.* London, 1954.
Brown, P. *Indian Painting under the Mughals.* Oxford, 1924.
Callard, K. *Pakistan; A Political Study.* London, 1957.
Chand, T. *Influence of Islam on Indian Culture.* Allahabad, 1943–6.
Chandra, S. *Parties and Politics at the Mughal Court, 1707–1740.* Aligarh, 1959.
Chandra, T. *Society and State in the Mughal Period.* Delhi, 1961.
Coupland, R. *The Indian Problem 1833–1935.* Oxford, 1942–3.
Das, M. N. *Indian under Morley and Minto.* London, 1964.
Edwardes, M. *British India, 1772–1947.* London, 1967.
Erskine, W. *A History of India Under the First Two Sovereigns of the House of Taimur.* London, 1854.

Faruqi, Z. H. *The Deoband School and the Demand for Pakistan*. Bombay, 1963.
Feldman, H. *Revolution in Pakistan*. London, 1967.
Gopal, R. *Indian Muslims. A Political History, 1858–1947*. Bombay, 1959.
Gopal, S. *British Policy in India, 1858–1905*. Cambridge, 1965.
Graham, G. F. I. *The Life and Work of Sir Syed Ahmed Khan*. London, 1885.
Gwyer, M. and Appadorai, A. *Speeches and Documents on the Indian Constitution, 1921–47*. Bombay, 1957.
Habib, I. *The Agrarian System of Mughal India, 1556–1707*. London, 1963.
Hodivala, S. H. *Studies in Indo-Muslim History*. Bombay, 1939, 1957.
Hunter, W. W. *The Indian Musalmans*. London, 1871.
Husain, S. A. *The Destiny of Indian Muslims*. London, 1965.
Husain, Y. *Medieval Indian Culture*. Bombay, 1957.
Ibn Hasan. *Central Structure of the Mughal Empire*. London, 1936.
Ikram, S. M. *History of Muslim Civilization in India and Pakistan*. Lahore, 1961.
—— *Modern Muslim India and the Birth of Pakistan, 1858–1951*. 2nd edn. Lahore, 1965.
—— and Spear, P. *The cultural heritage of Pakistan*. Karachi, 1955.
Kabir, H. *Muslim politics, 1906–1942*. Calcutta, 1944.
Khan, M. A. *History of the Fara'idi Movement in Bengal*. Karachi, 1965.
Korbel, J. *Danger in Kashmir*. Princeton, 1954.
Majumdar, R. C. (ed.). *The Delhi Sultanate*. Bombay, 1960.
Mallick, A. R. *British Policy and the Muslims in Bengal, 1757–1856*. Dacca, 1961.
Menon, V. P. *The Transfer of Power in India*. Bombay, 1957.
Misra, B. B. *The Indian Middle Classes*. London, 1961.
Moreland, W. H. *The Agrarian System of Moslem India*. Cambridge, 1929.
Mosley, L. *Last Days of the British Raj*. London, 1961.
Mujeeb, M. *The Indian Muslims*. London, 1967.
Palmer, J. A. B. *The Mutiny Outbreak at Meerut in 1857*. Cambridge, 1966.
Philips, C. H. *India*. London, 1949–8.
—— (ed.). *The evolution of India and Pakistan, 1858 to 1947*. London, 1962.
—— (ed.). *Politics and Society in India*. London, 1963.
Prasad, B. *History of Jahangir*. 5th edn. Allahabad, 1962.
Prasad, I. *The Life and Times of Humayun*. Bombay, 1955.
Prasad, R. *India Divided*. Bombay, 1947.
Qureshi, I. H. *The Administration of the Sultanate of Dehlī*. 4th edn. Karachi, 1958.
—— *The Muslim Community of the Indo-Pakistan Subcontinent, 610–1947*. The Hague, 1962.
—— *The Struggle for Pakistan*. Karachi, 1965.
Rizvi, S. A. A. *Muslim Revivalist Movements in Northern India in the Sixteenth and Seventeenth Centuries*. Agra, 1965.
—— and Bhargava, M. L. (ed.). *Freedom Struggle in Uttar Pradesh: source material*. Lucknow, 1957–61.
Saksena, B. P. *History of Shahjehan of Dihli*. Allahabad, 1932.
Sarkar, J. N. *History of Aurangzib*. Calcutta, 1912–24.
—— *Shivaji and His Times*. 2nd edn. London, 1920.

Sarkar, J. N. *Fall of the Mughal Empire*. Calcutta, 1932–4.
Sayeed, K. B. *Pakistan the Formative Phase*. Karachi, 1960.
Sharma, S. R. *Mughal Government and Administration*. Bombay, 1951.
Smith, D. E. *India as a Secular State*. Princeton, 1963.
Smith, V. A. *Akbar, the Great Mogul, 1542–1605*, 2nd edn. Oxford, 1927.
Smith, W. C. *Modern Islam in India*. London, 1946.
Stephens, I. *Pakistan*. London, 1963.
Symonds, R. *The Making of Pakistan*. London, 1950.
Tinker, H. R. *India and Pakistan: A Political Analysis*. 2nd edn. London, 1967.
Tripathi, R. P. *Some Aspects of Muslim Administration*. Allahabad, 1936.
Williams, L. F. R. *The State of Pakistan*. 2nd edn. London, 1966.

South-East Asia

Al-Attas, Sayyid Naguib. *Some Aspects of Sufism as Understood and Practised among the Malays*. Singapore, 1963.
Arnold, T. W. *The Preaching of Islam*. 2nd edn. London, 1913.
Benda, H. J. *The Crescent and the Rising Sun: Indonesian Islam Under the Japanese Occupation, 1942–1945*. The Hague and Bandung, 1958.
Berg, L. W. C. van den. *Le Hadhramout et les colonies arabes dans l'Archipel indien*. Batavia, 1886.
Bousquet, G.-H. *La politique musulmane et coloniale des Pays-Bas*. Paris, 1938.
Burger, D. H. *Structural Changes in Javanese Society: The Supra-village Sphere*. Ithaca, N.Y., 1956.
Drews, G. W. J. 'Indonesia: mysticism and activism', in Grunebaum, G. E. von. (ed.). *Unity and variety in Muslim civilization*. Chicago, 1955.
Geertz, C. *The Religion of Java*. Glencoe, Ill., 1960.
Gullick, J. M. *Indigenous Political Systems of Western Malaya*. London, 1958.
Hurgronje, C. S. *The Achehnese*. Leiden, 1906.
—— *Verspreide geschriften*. Vol. IV, Parts 1, 2. Bonn, Leipzig and Leiden, 1924–6.
—— *Mekka in the Latter Part of the 19th Century*. Leiden and London, 1931.
Itagaki, Y. 'Some aspects of the Japanese policy for Malaya under the occupation, with special reference to nationalism', in Tregonning, K. G. (ed.). *Papers on Malayan History*. Singapore, 1962.
Jay, R. R. *Religion and Politics in Rural Central Java*. New Haven, 1963.
Niel, R. van. *The Emergence of the Modern Indonesian elite*. The Hague and Bandung, 1960.
Nieuwenhuijze, C. A. O. van. *Aspects of Islam in Post-Colonial Indonesia*. The Hague and Bandung, 1958.
Pijper, G. F. *Islam and the Netherlands*. Leiden, 1957.
Roff, W. R. 'Kaum Muda—Kaum Tua: innovation and reaction amongst the Malays, 1900–1941', in Tregonning, K. G. (ed.). *Papers on Malayan History*. Singapore, 1962.
—— *The Origins of Malay Nationalism*. London and New Haven, 1967.
Schrieke, B. J. O. *Indonesian Sociological Studies: Selected Writings of B. Schrieke*. The Hague and Bandung, 1955.

Wertheim, W. F. *Indonesian Society in Transition: A Study of Social Change.* 2nd edn. The Hague and Bandung, 1959.
Wilkinson, R. J. *Malay Beliefs.* London and Leiden, 1906. (Republished as 'Malay customs and beliefs', in *Journal of the Royal Asiatic Society, Malayan Branch,* xxx, 1957).
—— and Winstedt, R. O. *Papers on Malay Subjects: Malay Literature.* Kuala Lumpur, 1907.
—— and Rigby, W. J. *Papers on Malay Subjects: Malay Law.* Kuala Lumpur, 1908.
Winstedt, R. O. *The Malays, a Cultural History.* 6th ed. London, 1961.
Zoetmulder, P. 'L'Islam', in Stöhr, W. and Zoetmulder, P. *Les religions d'Indonesia.* Paris, 1968.

North Africa

Ageron, C. R. *Histoire de l'Algérie contemporaine, 1830–1956,* Paris, 1966.
Ashford, D. E. *Political Change in Morocco.* Princeton, 1961.
Aubin, E. *Le Maroc d'aujourdhui.* Paris, 1904.
Ayache, A. *Le Maroc: bilan d' une colonisation.* Paris, 1956.
Barbour, N. (ed.). *A Survey of North West Africa.* London, 1959.
Behr, E. *The Algerian Problem.* London, 1961.
Bel, A. *Les Benou Ghânya.* Paris, 1903.
—— *La religion musulmane en Berbérie.* Paris, 1938.
Bernard, A. *Le Maroc.* 7th edn. Paris, 1931.
Berque, J. *Le Maghreb entre deux guerres.* Paris, 1962.
—— *Structures sociales du Haut-Atlas.* Paris, 1955.
Boyer, P. *La vie quotidienne à Alger à la veille de l' intervention française.* Paris, 1964.
Braudel, F. *La Méditerranée et le monde méditerranéen à l'époque ce Philippe II.* Paris, 1949.
Brunschvig, R. *La Berbérie orientale sous les Hafsides des origines à la fin du XVe siècle.* Paris, 1940, 1947.
Catroux, G. *Lyautey, le marocain.* Paris, 1952.
Colombe, M. 'L'Algerie turque', *Initiation à l'Algérie.* Paris, 1957.
Corbett, J. S. *England in the Mediterranean (1603–1713).* London, 1917.
Cour, A. *L'établissement des dynasties des Chérifs au Maroc.* Paris, 1904.
—— *La dynastie marocaine des Beni Wattâs (1420–1554).* Constantine, 1920.
Debbasch, Y. *La nation française en Tunisie, 1577–1835.* Paris, 1957.
Delmas de Grammont, H. *Histoire d'Alger sous la domination turque (1515–1830).* Paris, 1887.
Depont, O. and Coppolani, X. *Les confréries religieuses musulmanes.* Algiers, 1897.
Despois, J. *La Tunisie orientale. Sahel et basse steppe.* 2nd edn. Paris, 1955.
—— *La Tunisie: ses régions.* Paris, 1961.
—— *L'Afrique du Nord.* 3rd edn. Paris, 1964.
Deverdun, G. *Marrakech des origines à 1912.* Vol. I. Rabat, 1959.

Drague, G. *Esquisse d'histoire religieuse de Maroc*. Paris, 1951.
Emerit, M. *L'Algérie à l'époque d'Abd-el-Kader*. Paris, 1951.
Evans-Pritchard, E. E. *The Sanusi of Cyrenaica*. Oxford, 1949.
Favrod, C. H. *Le F.L.N. et l'Algérie*. Paris, 1962.
Fisher, G. *Barbary legend*. Oxford, 1957.
Fitoussie and Benazet, A. *L'état tunisien et le protectorat français*. Paris, 1931.
Fournel, H. *Les Berbères. Etude sur la conquête de l'Afrique par les Arabes d'après les textes arabes imprimés*. Paris, 1875–81.
Ganiage, J. *Les origines du protectorat français en Tunisie, 1861–1881*. Paris, 1959.
Gautier, É.-F. *Le passé de l'Afrique du Nord. Les siècles obscurs*. Paris, 1937.
Golvin, L. *Le Magrib central à l'époque des Zirides*. Paris, 1957.
Grandchamp, P. *La France en Tunisie de la fin du XVIe siècle à 1705*. Tunis, 1920–33.
Hahn, L. *North Africa: Nationalism to Nationhood*. Washington, D.C., 1960.
Huici Miranda, A. *Historia política del imperio almohade*. Tetuan, 1956–7.
Idris, H. R. *La Berbérie orientale sous les Zīrides (Xe–XIIe siècle)*. Paris, 1959.
Julien, C.-A. *Histoire de l'Afrique du Nord (Tunisie, Algérie, Maroc). De la conquête arabe à 1830*. 2nd edn. Paris, 1956.
—— *Histoire de l'Algérie contemporaine I: La conquête et les débuts de la colonization (1827–1871)*. Paris, 1964.
Lacoste, Y., Nouschi, A., Prenant, A. *L'Algérie passé et présent*. Paris, 1960.
Lane-Poole, S. *The Barbary Corsairs*. London, 1890.
Le Coz, J. *Le Rharb, fellahs et colons*. Rabat, 1964.
Leduc, G. and others. *Industrialization de l'Afrique du Nord*. Paris, 1952.
Le Tourneau, R. *Fès avant le protectorat*. Casablanca, 1949.
—— *Fez in the age of the Marinides*. Norman, Oklahoma, 1961.
—— *Évolution politique de l'Afrique du Nord musulmane 1920–1961*. Paris, 1962.
Lévi-Provençal, É. *Les historiens des Chorfa*. Paris, 1922.
Mandouze, A. *La révolution algérienne par les textes*. Paris, 1962.
Marçais, G. *La Berberie musulmane et l'orient au moyen âge*. Paris, 1946.
—— *Les Arabes en Berbérie du XIe au XIVe siècle*. Constantine and Paris, 1913.
—— *Tlemcen*. Paris, 1950.
—— *L'architecture musulmane d'occident. Tunisie, Algérie, Maroc, Espagne, et Sicile*. Paris, 1954.
Marçais, W. 'Comment l'Afrique du Nord a été arabisée', *Articles et conférences*. Paris, 1961.
Massignon, L. *Le Maroc dans les premières années du XVIe siècle*. Algiers, 1906.
Masson, P. *Histoire des établissements et du commerce français dans l'Afrique barbaresque*. Paris, 1903.
Miège, J. L. *Le Maroc et l'Europe, 1830–1894*. Paris, 1961–64.
Monchicourt, Ch. *L'expédition espagnole contre l'île de Djerba*. Paris, 1913.
Montagne, R. *Les Berbères et le Makhzen dans le sud de Maroc*. Paris, 1930.
—— (ed.). *Naissance du prolétariat marocain*. Paris, 1951.

Nouschi, A. *Enquête sur le niveau de vie des populations rurales constantinoises de la conquête jusqu'en 1919*. Paris, 1961.

—— *La naissance du nationalisme algérien*. Paris, 1962.

Pignon, J. 'La Tunisie turque et husséinite', in Basset, A. and others. *Initiation à la Tunisie*. Paris, 1950.

Playfair, R. L. *The Scourge of Christendom: Annals of British Relations with Algiers Prior to the French Conquest*. London, 1884.

Poncet, J. *La colonization et l'agriculture européennes en Tunisie depuis 1881*. Paris, 1962.

Raymond, A. *La Tunisie*. Paris, 1961.

Rézette, R. *Les partis politiques marocains*. Paris, 1955.

Ricard, R. *Études sur l'histoire des Portugais au Maroc*. Coimbra, 1955.

Rinn, L. *Marabouts et Khouan*. Algiers, 1884.

—— *Le royaume d'Alger sous le dernier dey*. Algiers, 1900.

Rossi, E. *Storia di Tripoli e della Tripolitania dalla conquista araba a 1911*. Rome, 1968.

Rousseau, A. *Annales tunisiennes ou aperçu historique de la Régence de Tunis*. Paris-Algiers, 1864.

Sebag, P. *La Tunisie*. Paris, 1951.

Talbi, M. *L'émirat aghlabide 184–296/800–909. Histoire politique*. Paris, 1966.

Terrasse, H. *L'art hispano-mauresque des origines au XIIIe siècle*. Paris, 1932.

—— *Histoire du Maroc des origines à l'établissement du protectorat français*. Casablanca, 1949–50.

Venture de Paradis, J. M. de. *Alger au XVIIIème siècle*. Algiers, 1898.

Vonderheyden, M. *La Berbérie orientale sous la dynastie des Benoû'l-Arlab, 800–909*. Paris, 1927.

Weir, T. H. *The Shaikhs of Morocco in the XVIth Century*. Edinburgh, 1904.

Yacono, X. *Les Bureaux arabes et l'évolution des genres de vie indigènes dans l'ouest du Tell algérois*. Paris, 1953.

—— *La colonization des plaines du Chelif*. Algiers, 1955–6.

Ziadeh, N.A. *Sanūsīyah*. Leiden, 1958.

Trans-Saharan Africa

Abbas, M. *The Sudan Question*. London, 1952.

Abun-Nasr, J. M. *The Tijaniyya*. London, 1965.

Allen, B. M. *Gordon and the Sudan*. London, 1931.

Anderson, J. N. D. *Islamic Law in Africa*. London, 1954.

Ba, A. H. and Daget, J. *L'empire peul du Macina*. Paris, 1962.

Balewa, A. T. *Shaihu Umar*. London, 1967.

Bovill, E. W. *The Golden Trade of the Moors*. 2nd edn. London, 1968.

Collins, R. O. *The Southern Sudan, 1883–1898*. New Haven and London, 1962.

Crawford, O. G. S. *The Fung Kingdom of Sennar*. Gloucester, 1951.

Evans-Pritchard, E. E. *The Sanusi of Cyrenaica*. Oxford, 1949.

Fisher, H. J. *Ahmadiyyah. A Study in Contemporary Islam on the West African Coast*. London, 1963.

Froelich, J.-C. *Les Musulmans d'Afrique noire*. Paris, 1962.
Gray, J. R. *A History of the Southern Sudan, 1839–1889*. London, 1961.
Hasan, Y. F. *The Arabs and the Sudan*. Edinburgh, 1967.
Henderson, K. D. D. *The Making of the Modern Sudan*. London, 1953.
Hill, R. L. *A Biographical Dictionary of the* [*Anglo-Egyptian*] *Sudan*. 2nd edn. London, 1967.
—— *Egypt in the Sudan, 1820–1881*. London, 1959.
Hogben, S. J. and Kirk-Greene, A. H. M. *The Emirates of Northern Nigeria*. London, 1966.
Holt, P. M. *The Mahdist State in the Sudan, 1881/1898*. Oxford, 1958.
—— *A Modern History of the Sudan*. 2nd edn. London, 1963.
Klein, M. A. *Islam and Imperialism in Senegal: Sine-Saloum 1847–1914*. Stanford, 1968.
Kritzeck, J. and Lewis, W. H. *Islam in Africa*. Princeton, 1968.
Last, M. *The Sokoto Caliphate*. London, 1967.
Levtzion, N. *Muslims and Chiefs in West Africa: A Study of Islam in the Middle Volta Basin in the Pre-colonial Period*. Oxford, 1968.
Lewis, I. M. *A Pastoral Democracy*. London, 1961.
—— *The Modern History of Somaliland*. London, 1965.
—— (ed.). *Islam in Tropical Africa*. London, 1966.
MacMichael, H. A. *A History of the Arabs in the Sudan*. Cambridge, 1922.
Monteil, V. *L'Islam noir*. Paris, 1964.
Sanderson, G. N. *England, Europe and the Upper Nile, 1882–1899*. Edinburgh, 1965.
Smith, M. F. *Baba of Karo: A Woman of the Muslim Hausa*. London, 1954.
Smith, M. G. *Government in Zazzau, 1800–1950*. London, 1960.
Shibeika, M. *British Policy in the Sudan, 1882–1902*. London, 1952.
Theobald, A. B. *'Alī Dīnār, last sultan of Darfur*. London, 1965.
Trimingham, J. S. *Islam in the Sudan*. London, 1949.
—— *Islam in Ethiopia*. London, 1952.
—— *Islam in West Africa*. Oxford, 1959.
—— *The Influence of Islam upon Africa*. London, 1968.

The Iberian Peninsula and Sicily

Amari, M. *Storia dei Musulmani di Sicilia*. Florence, 1854–72. Revised edn. Catania, 1930–9.
Bosch Vilá, J. *Los Almorávides*. Tetuan, 1956.
Cágigas, I. de las. *Los Mozárabes*. Madrid, 1947–48.
Codera y Zaidin, F. *Decadéncia y disparición de los Almorávides en España*. Saragossa, 1899.
—— *Estudios críticos de historia árabe española*. Saragossa-Madrid, 1903–17.
Dozy, R. P. A. *Histoire des musulmans d'Espagne*. 2nd edn. revised by Lévi-Provençal, E. Leiden, 1932.
—— *Recherches sur l'histoire et la littérature des Arabes d'Espagne pendant le moyen âge*. 3rd edn. Leiden, 1881.

Famin, C. *Histoire des invasions des Sarrazins en Italie du VIIe au XIe siècle.* Paris, 1843.
Gabrieli, F. *Aspetti della civiltà arabo-islamica.* Turin, 1956.
Gaspar Remiro, M. *Historia de Murcia musulmana.* Saragossa, 1905.
González Palencia, A. *Historia de la España musulmana.* 4th edn. 1951.
Huici Miranda, A. *Historia política del imperio almohade.* Tetuan, 1956.
—— *Las grandes batallas de la reconquista durante las invasiones africanas. Almorávides, Almohades y Benimerines.* Madrid, 1956.
—— *Estudios de la Edad Media de la corona de Aragón.* 1962.
Lévi-Provençal, E. *L'Espagne musulmane au Xème siècle.* Paris, 1932.
—— *Histoire de l'Espagne musulmane.* 2nd edn. Paris and Leiden, 1950–3.
Menéndez Pidal, R. *La España del Cid.* Madrid, 1956.
Perez de Urbel, J. *Historia del condado de Castilla.* Madrid, 1948.
Pons Boigues, F. *Historiadores y geógrafos arabico-españoles.* Madrid, 1898.
Prieto y Vives, A. *Los reyes de taifas, estúdio histórico-numismatico.* Madrid, 1926.
Primaudie, E. de la. *Arabes et Normands.*
Saavedra, E. *Estudio sobre la invasión de los Árabes en España.* Madrid, 1892.
Watt, W. M. *History of Islamic Spain.* Edinburgh, 1965.

The Geographical Setting

Capot-Rey, R. *Le Sahara français.* Paris, 1953.
Coon, C. S. *Caravan. The Story of the Middle East.* London, 1952.
Despois, J. *L'Afrique du Nord.* 3rd edn. Paris, 1964.
Fisher, W. B. *The Middle East.* 4th edn. London, 1961.
Hogarth, D. G. *The Nearer East.* London, 1902.
Humlum, J. *La géographie de l'Afghanistan.* Copenhagen, 1959.
Montagne, R. *La civilization du désert.* Paris, 1947.
Planhol, X. de. *Le monde islamique: essai de géographie religieuse.* Paris, 1957. Eng. tr. *The World of Islam.* Ithaca, N.Y., 1959.
—— *Les fondements géographiques de l'histoire de l'Islam.* Paris, 1968.
Robequain, C. *Le monde malais.* Paris, 1946.
Spate, O. H. K. *India and Pakistan.* 3rd edn. London, 1967.
Weulersse, J. *Paysans de Syrie et du Proche-Orient.* Paris, 1946.

The Sources of Islamic Civilization

Aubin, H. *Vom Altertum zum Mittelalter. Absterben, Fortleben und Erneuerung.* Munich, 1949.
Bark, W. C. *Origins of the Medieval World.* Stanford, 1958.
Baumstark, A. *Geschichte der syrischen Literatur.* Bonn, 1922.
Bloch, M. 'Pour une histoire comparée des sociétés européennes (1928)', *Mélanges historiques.* Vol. I. Paris, 1963.
Brunschvig, R. and Grunebaum, G. E. von. (ed.). *Classicisme et déclin culturel dans l'histoire de l'Islam.* Paris, 1957.
Carra de Vaux, B. *Les penseurs de l'Islam.* Paris, 1921–26.

Dawson, G. *The Making of Europe*. London, 1932.
Dubler, C. E. 'Das Weiterleben der Antike im Islam', in Wehrli, F. (ed.). *Das Erbe der Antike*. Zurich and Stuttgart, 1963.
Durand, G. *Les structures anthropologiques de l'imaginaire*. Paris, 1963.
Grunebaum, G. E. von. *Kritik und Dichtkunst*. Wiesbaden, 1955.
—— 'Muslim world view and Muslim science', in *Islam: Essays in the Nature and Growth of a Cultural Tradition*. 2nd edn. London, 1961.
—— *Der Islam in Mittelalter*. Zurich and Stuttgart, 1963.
—— *Islam: Experience of the Holy and Concept of Man*. Los Angeles [1965].
Hartmann, L. *Ein Kapitel vom spätantiken und frühmittelalterlichen Staate*. Berlin, 1913.
Laistner, M. L. W. *Christianity and Pagan Culture*. Ithaca and New York, 1957.
Lot, F. *La fin du monde antique et le début du moyen âge*. 2nd edn. Paris, 1951.
Madkour, I. B. *L'Organon d'Aristote dans le monde musulman*. Paris, 1934.
Makdisi, G. *Ibn 'Aqīl et la résurgence de l'Islam traditionaliste au XIe siècle, Ve siècle de l'Hégire*. Damascus, 1963.
Menasce, J. P. de. *Une encyclopédie mazdéenne: le Dēnkart*. Paris, 1958.
Meyerhof, M. *Von Alexandrien nach Bagdad*. Berlin, 1930.
Misch, G. *Geschichte der Autobiographie*. 3rd edn. Vol. II, Part 1. Frankfurt, 1955. Vol. III, Part 2. Frankfurt, 1962.
Momigliano, A. D. (ed.). *The Conflict between Paganism and Christianity in the Fourth Century*. Oxford, 1963.
Moreno, M. M. *Mistica musulmana e mistica indiana*. Vatican City, 1946.
Pellat, C. *Le milieu baṣrien et la formation de Ǧāḥiẓ*. Paris, 1953.
Rahman, Fazlur. *Islamic Methodology in History*. Karachi, 1965.
Rosenthal, F. *Das Fortleben der Antike im Islam*. Zurich and Stuttgart, 1965.
Stein, E. and Palanque, J.-R. *Histoire du Bas-Empire*. Vol. I. Paris, 1959.
Stroheker, K. F. *Germanentum und Spätantike*. Zurich and Stuttgart, 1965.
Tavadia, J. C. *Die mittelpersische Sprache und Literatur der Zarathustrier*. Leipzig, 1956.
Watt, W. M. 'The tribal basis of the Islamic state', in *Dalla tribù allo stato*. Rome, 1962.
Widengren, G. *Mani and Manichaeism*. London, 1965.

Social, Economic and Institutional History

Arnold, T. W. *The Caliphate*. Oxford, 1924.
Ayalon, D. *L'esclavage du mamelouk*. Jerusalem, 1951.
—— *Gunpowder and Firearms in the Mamluk Kingdom*. London, 1956.
Baron, S. W. *A Social and Religious History of the Jews*. Vols. III, IV. New York, 1957.
Coulson, N. J. *A History of Islamic Law*. Edinburgh, 1964.
Dennett, D. C. *Conversion and the Poll-tax in Early Islam*. Cambridge, Mass., 1950.

Fattal, A. *Le statut légal des non-musulmans en pays d'Islam*. Beirut, 1958.
Fries, J. N. *Das Heereswesen der Araber zur Zeit der Omaijaden nach Tabarî*. Tübingen, 1921.
Gardet, L. *La cité musulmane*. 2nd edn. Paris, 1961.
Gaudefroy-Demombynes, M. *Muslim Institutions*. London, 1950.
Gibb, H. A. R. 'The armies of Saladin', in Shaw, S. J. and Polk, W. J. (edd.). *Studies on the civilization of Islam*. Boston, Mass., 1962.
Goitein, S. D. *Studies in Islamic History and Institutions*. Leiden, 1966.
—— *A Mediterranean Society*. Vol. I. Berkeley and Los Angeles, 1967.
Heyd, W. *Histoire du commerce du Levant au moyen-âge*. Paris, 1885; Leipzig, 1923.
Horn, P. *Das Heer- und Kriegswesen des Grossmoghuls*. Leiden, 1894.
Hourani, G. F. *Arab Seafaring in the Indian Ocean in Ancient and Early Medieval Times*. Princeton, 1951.
Irvine, W. *The Army of the Indian Moghuls*. London, 1903; New Delhi, 1962.
Juynboll, T. *Handbuch des islamischen Gesetzes*. Leiden, Leipzig, 1910.
Khadduri, M. *War and Peace in the Law of Islam*. Baltimore, 1955.
Kremer, A. von. *Culturgeschichte des Orients unter den Chalifen*. Vienna, 1875–77. Partial English tr. in Bukhsh, S.K. *The Orient Under the Caliphs*. Calcutta, 1920; *Studies, Indian and Islamic*. London, 1927.
Lambton, A. K. S. *Landlord and Peasant in Persia*. London, 1953.
Lapidus, I. M. *Muslim Cities in the Later Middle Ages*. Cambridge, Mass., 1967.
Le Tourneau, R. *Fès avant le protectorat*. Casablanca, 1949.
Levy, R. *The Social Structure of Islam*. Cambridge, 1957.
Lewis, A. R. *Naval Power and Trade in the Mediterranean* A.D. *500–1100*. Princeton, 1951.
Løkkegaard, F. *Islamic Taxation in the Classic Period with Special Reference to Circumstances in Iraq*. Copenhagen, 1950.
Mez, A. *The Renaissance of Islam*. London, 1937 (tr. from German).
Rodinson, M. *Islam et capitalisme*. Paris, 1966.
Sachau, C. E. *Muhammedanisches Recht*. Stuttgart, Berlin, 1897.
Santillana, D. 'Law and society', in Arnold, T. W. and Guillaume, A. (ed.). *The Legacy of Islam*. Oxford, 1931.
—— *Istituzioni di diritto musulmano malichita*. Rome, 1925–38.
Sauvaget, J. *Alep*. Paris, 1941.
—— *La poste aux chevaux dans l'empire des Mamelouks*. Paris, 1941.
Schacht, J. *An Introduction to Islamic Law*. Oxford, 1964.
—— (ed.). *G. Bergsträsser's Grundzüge des islamischen Rechts*. Berlin and Leipzig, 1935.
——*Origins of Muhammadan Jurisprudence*. 4th edn. London, 1968.
Sourdel, D. *Le vizirat 'abbaside de 749 à 936*. Damascus, 1959–60.
Tyan, É. *Institutions du droit public musulman*. Paris, 1954–7.
—— *Histoire de l'organisation judiciaire en pays d'Islam*. 2nd. edn. Leiden, 1960.

Religion

Abdel-Kader, A. H. *The Life, Personality and Writings of al-Junayd.* London, 1962.

Adams, C. C. *Islam and Modernism in Egypt.* London, 1933.

Affifi, A. E. *The Mystical Philosophy of Muḥyid Din-Ibnul Arabi.* Cambridge, 1939.

Ahmad, A. *Islamic Modernism in India and Pakistan, 1857–1964.* London, 1967.

Arberry, A. J. *Introduction to the History of Ṣūfism.* London, 1942.

—— *Sufism: An Account of the Mystics of Islam.* London, 1950.

—— *Revelation and Reason in Islam.* London, 1957.

Baljon, J. M. S. *Modern Muslim Koran Interpretation, 1880–1960.* Leiden, 1961.

Bausani, A. *Persia Religiosa.* Milan, 1959.

Corbin, H. *L'imagination créatrice dans la Soufisme d'Ibn ʿArabi.* Paris, 1958.

Dar, B. A. *Religious Thought of Sayyid Aḥmad Khān.* Lahore, 1957.

Depont, O. and Coppolani, X. *Les confréries religieuses musulmanes.* Algiers, 1897.

Fyzee, A. A. A. *A Modern Approach to Islam.* Bombay, 1963.

Gardet, L. and Anawati, G.-C. *Introduction à la théologie musulmane.* Paris, 1948.

Gibb, H. A. R. *Modern Trends in Islam.* Chicago, 1946.

—— *Mohammedanism.* London, 1949.

—— 'The structure of religious thought in Islam', in Shaw, S. J. and Polk, W. J. (ed.). *Studies on the Civilization of Islam.* Boston, Mass., 1962.

Goldziher, I. *Le dogme et la loi de l'Islam.* Paris, 1958.

Keddie, N. R. *An Islamic Response to Imperialism.* Berkeley and Los Angeles, 1968.

Kedourie, E. *Afghani and ʿAbduh.* London, 1966.

Laoust, H. *Essai sur les doctrines sociales et politiques d'Ibn Taimiyah.* Cairo, 1939.

—— *Les schismes dans l'Islam.* Paris, 1965.

Lings, M. *A Moslem saint of the twentieth century.* London, 1961.

Macdonald, D. B. *Development of Muslim Theology, Jurisprudence and Constitutional Theory.* New York, 1903.

—— *The Religious Attitude and Life in Islam.* Chicago, 1912. Repr. Beirut, 1965.

—— *Aspects of Islam.* New York, 1911.

Massignon, L. *La passion d'al-Ḥallāj, martyr mystique de l'Islam.* Paris, 1922

—— *Essai sur les origines du lexique technique de la mystique musulmane.* Paris, 1922.

Nicholson, R. A. *The Mystics of Islam.* London, 1914.

—— *Studies in Islamic Mysticism.* Cambridge, 1921.

—— *The Idea of Personality in Ṣúfism.* Cambridge, 1923.

Rahman, Fazlur. *Islam.* London, 1966.

Seale, M. S. *Muslim Theology: A Study of Origins with Reference to the Church Fathers.* London, 1964.

Smith, M. *Studies in Early Mysticism in the Near and Middle East.* London, 1931.

—— *An Early Mystic of Baghdad.* London, 1935.

—— *Readings from the Mystics of Islām.* London, 1950.

Smith, W. C. *Modern Islām in India*. Revised edn. London, 1946.
—— *Islam in Modern History*. Princeton, 1957.
Wensinck, A. J. *La pensée de Ghazzālī*. Paris, 1940.
—— *The Muslim Creed, its Genesis and Historical Development*. Cambridge, 1932.
Zaehner, R. C. *Mysticism Sacred and Profane*. Oxford, 1957.
—— *Hindu and Muslim Mysticism*. London, 1960.

Architecture, Art and Literature

Ahmad, Aziz. 'Urdu literature', in Ikram, S. M. and Spear, P. *The Cultural Heritage of Pakistan*. Karachi, 1955.
Anthologie de la littérature arabe contemporaine. Paris, 1964–7.
Arberry, A. J. 'Persian literature', in Arberry, A. J. *The Legacy of Persia*. Oxford, 1953.
Arnold, T. W. *Painting in Islam*. 2nd edn. Oxford, 1965.
Bailey, T. G. *A History of Urdu Literature*. Calcutta, 1932.
Barrett, D. *Islamic Metalwork in the British Museum*. London, 1949.
Bausani, A. *Storia della letterature del Pakistan*. Milan, 1958.
Bombaci, A. *La letteratura turca*. Rev. ed. Milan, 1969.
Browne, E. G. *A Literary History of Persia*. Cambridge, 1928.
Cresswell, K. A. C. *Early Muslim Architecture*. Oxford, 1932–40.
—— *A Short Account of Early Muslim Architecture*. London, 1958.
—— *The Muslim Architecture of Egypt*. Oxford, 1952, 1959.
—— *A Bibliography of the Architecture, Arts and Crafts of Islam*. Cairo, 1961.
Dimand, M. S. *A Handbook of Muhammadan Art*. 3rd edn. New York, 1958.
Ettinghausen, R. *Arab Painting*. Lausanne, 1962.
Gabrieli, F. *Storia della letteratura araba*. Milan, 1962.
Gibb, E. J. W. *A History of Ottoman Poetry*. London, 1900–9.
Gibb, H. A. R. *Arabic Literature*. 2nd edn. Oxford, 1963.
Gray, B. *Persian Painting*. Lausanne, 1961.
Hill, D. and Grabar, O. *Islamic Architecture and its Decoration*. London, 1964.
Lane, A. *Early Islamic Pottery*. London, 1947.
—— *Later Islamic Pottery*. London, 1957.
Levy, R. *An introduction to Persian Literature*. Repr. New York, 1969.
Nicholson, R. A. *A Literary History of the Arabs*. Cambridge, 1907, etc.
Pagliaro, A. and Bausani, A. *Storia della letteratura persiana*. Milan, 1960.
Pellat, Ch. *Langue et littérature arabes*. Paris, 1952.
Pope, A. U. *Persian Architecture*. London, 1965.
Rypka, J. *History of Iranian Literature*. Dordrecht, 1968.
Sadiq, Muhammad. *A History of Urdu Literature*. London, 1964.
Saksena, R. B. *A History of Urdu Literature*. Allahabad, 1940.
Sarre, F. *Die Ausgrabungen von Samarra II: Die Keramik von Samarra*. Berlin, 1925.
Survey of Persian Art. Oxford, 1939.

Science and Philosophy

Boer, T. J. de. *The History of Philosophy in Islam*. London, 1903.

Bouyges, M. *Essai de chronologie des oeuvres de al-Ghazali, Algazel*. Beirut, 1959.
Carra de Vaux, B. *Les penseurs de l'Islam*. Paris, 1921–26.
—— 'Astronomy and mathematics', in Arnold, T. W. and Guillaume, A. *The Legacy of Islam*. Oxford, 1931.
Corbin, H. *Avicenna and the Visionary Recital*. London, 1960.
—— *Histoire de la philosophie islamique I: Des origines jusqu'à la mort d'Averroës*. Paris, 1964.
Gardet, L. *La pensée religieuse d'Avicenne*. Paris, 1951.
Gardner, W. R. W. *Al-Ghazālī*. Madras, 1919.
Gauthier, L. *Ibn Thofaïl, sa vie, ses oeuvres*. Paris, 1909.
—— *La théorie d'Ibn Rochd (Averroès) sur les rapports de la religion et de la philosophie*. Paris, 1909.
—— *Ibn Rochd, Averroès*. Paris, 1948.
Goichon, A. M. *La distinction de l'essence et de l'existence d'après Ibn Sīnā (Avicenne)*. Paris, 1937.
Kraus, P. *Jābir et la science grecque*. Cairo. 1942.
McCarthy, R. J. *The Theology of al-Ashʿarī*. Beirut, 1953.
Madkour, I. *La place d'al-Fârâbî dans l'école philosophique musulmane*. Paris, 1934.
Mahdi, M. *Ibn Khaldûn's Philosophy of history*. London, 1957.
Massignon, L. and Arnaldez, R. *La science antique et médiévale*. Paris, 1957.
Meyerhof, M. 'Science and medicine', in Arnold, T. W. and Guillaume, A. *The Legacy of Islam*. Oxford, 1931.
Mieli, A. *La science arabe et son rôle dans l'évolution scientifique mondiale*. Leiden, 1938.
Nader, A. N. *La système philosophique des Muʿtazila*. Beirut, 1956.
Nasr, S. H. *Science and Civilization in Islam*. Cambridge, Mass., 1968.
Pines, S. *Beiträge zur islamischen Atomenlehre*. Berlin, 1936.
Plessner, M. 'Storia delle scienze nell'Islam', in *La civiltà dell'oriente*. Vol. III. Rome, 1958.
Sarton, G. *Introduction to the History of Science*. Vols. I-III. Baltimore, 1931–47.
Steinschneider, M. *Die arabischen Übersetzungen aus dem Grieschischen*. Leipzig, 1889–96; Graz, 1960.
Walzer, R. *Greek into Arabic*. Oxford, 1962.
Watt, W. M. *Free Will and Predestination in early Islam*. London, 1948.
Wensinck, A. J. *La pensée de Ghazzālī*. Paris, 1940.
Yuschkevich, A. P. *Mathematik im Mittelalter*. Leipzig. 1964.

The Transmission of Learning and Literary Influences

Arnold, T. and Guillaume, A. (ed.). *The Legacy of Islam*. Oxford, 1931.
Cerulli, E. *Il Libro della Scala e la questione delle fonti arabo-spagnole della Divina Commedia*. Vatican City, 1949.
Daniel, N. *Islam and the West: The Making of an Image*. Edinburgh, 1960.
Fück, J. *Die arabischen Studien in Europa bis in den Anfang des 20. Jahrhunderts*. Leipzig, 1955.

Gabrieli, F. 'La poesia araba e le letterature occidentali'. *Storia e civiltà musulmana*. Naples, 1947.

Menéndez Pidal, R. *Poesía araba e poesía europea*. Madrid, 1941.

Monneret de Villard, U. *Lo studio dell'Islām in Europa nel XII e XIII secolo*. Vatican City, 1944.

Schaeder, H. H. *Goethes Erlebnis des Ostens*. Leipzig, 1938.

Schwab, R. *La renaissance orientale*. Paris, 1950.

Southern, R. W. *Western views of Islam in the Middle Ages*. Cambridge, Mass., 1962.

Steinschneider, M. *Die europäischen Übersetzungen aus dem Arabischen bis Mitte des 17. Jahrhunderts*. Repr. Graz, 1956.

Stern, S. M. *Les chansons mozarabes*. Oxford, 1964.

GLOSSARY

‘ĀLIM (pl., *‘ulamā’*). A scholar in the Islamic sciences relating to the Qur’ān, theology and jurisprudence.

BID‘A. An innovation in Muslim belief or practice; the converse of *sunna,* the alleged practice of the Prophet. *Bid‘a* thus tends to be regarded as blameworthy by Muslims.

DĀR AL-ḤARB. ‘The abode of war’, i.e. territory not under Muslim sovereignty, against which warfare for the propagation of the faith is licit; cf. *Jihād*. It is the converse of *Dār al-Islām,* ‘the abode of Islam’.

DHIMMĪ. An adherent of a revealed religion (especially Judaism or Christianity) living under Muslim sovereignty, under the protection of the *Sharī‘a* (q.v.).

DIHQĀN (Persian). A member of the lesser feudal nobility in the Sasanian empire. The *dihqāns* largely retained their positions after the Arab conquest, but declined in status from the fifth/eleventh century.

FATWĀ. A formal statement of authoritative opinion on a point of *Sharī‘a* (q.v.) by a jurisconsult known as a *muftī*.

FERMĀN (Turkish, from Persian, *farmān*). An order or edict emanating from an Ottoman sultan.

GHĀZĪ. A frontier-warrior, taking part in raids (sing. *ghazā*) in the Holy War (*Jihād,* q.v.) against the infidel. The term was used as a title of honour, e.g. by Ottoman rulers.

ḤADĪTH (pl., *aḥādīth*). A Tradition of an alleged saying or practice of the Prophet. A *Ḥadīth* consists of a chain of oral transmitters (*isnād*) and the text transmitted (*matn*).

ḤAJJ. The Pilgrimage to the Holy Places of Mecca, which is a legal obligation upon individual Muslims. The rites of the *Ḥajj* take place between 8 and 12 Dhu’l-Ḥijja, the last month of the Muslim year. The ‘Lesser Pilgrimage’ (*‘Umra*) may be performed at any time.

‘ĪD AL-AḌḤĀ. ‘The Feast of Sacrifices’, or *al-‘Īd al-Kabīr* (the Great Feast), held on 10 Dhu’l-Ḥijja, to coincide with the sacrifice which is one of the rites of the *Ḥajj* (q.v.).

‘ĪD AL-FIṬR. ‘The Feast of the Breaking of the Fast’ or *al-‘Īd al-Ṣaghīr* (the Small Feast), held after the end of Ramaḍān, the month of fasting.

ILTIZĀM. A farm of taxes of state-lands. The tax-farmer was known as a *multazim*.

IMĀM. The leader of a group of Muslims in ritual prayer (*ṣalāt*); more specifically, the head of the Islamic community (*Umma*). The title was particularly used by the Shī‘ī claimants to the headship of the community.

IQṬĀʿ. A grant of state-lands or revenues by a Muslim ruler to an individual usually in recompense for service.

JIHĀD. The Holy War against infidels, which in some cirumstances is an obligation under the *Sharīʿa* for Muslims. See also *Ghāzī*.
JIZYA. Poll-tax paid to a Muslim government by the male members of protected non-Muslim communities (see *Dhimmī*).

KHUṬBA. The sermon delivered at the Friday congregational prayer in the mosque. Since it includes a prayer for the ruler, mention in the *khuṭba* is a mark of sovereignty in Islam.

MADHHAB. Sometimes translated 'rite' or 'school', a *madhhab* is one of the four legal systems recognized as orthodox by Sunnī (q.v.) Muslims. They are named after their founders—the Ḥanafī, Ḥanbalī, Mālikī and Shāfiʿī *madhhab*.
MADRASA. A school for teaching the Islamic sciences, frequently connected with a mosque.
MAMLŪK. A slave, usually white-skinned (especially of Turkish, Circassian or Georgian origin) and trained as a soldier.
MAWLĀ (pl., *mawālī*). A client of an Arab tribe; more especially a non-Arab convert during the first century of Islam, who acquired status by attachment to an Arab tribal group.
MIḤRĀB. A recess in the wall of a mosque to indicate the *qibla,* i.e. the direction of Mecca, for the correct orientation of ritual prayer.
MILLET (Turkish, from Arabic *milla*). A religious community in the Ottoman empire, usually used of the non Muslim (*dhimmī,* q.v.) communities, which had some measure of internal autonomy.
MINBAR. The pulpit in a mosque, from which the *khuṭba* (q.v.) is delivered.
MUJTAHID. A Shīʿi *ʿālim* (q.v.), exercising the functions of a jurisconsult.
MULLĀ (modern Turkish, *molla*, from Arabic, *mawlā*). A member of the *ʿulamā'*.
MURĪD. A disciple of a Ṣūfī (q.v.) teacher.

PĪR (Persian). The Persian equivalent of the Arabic term *shaykh,* in the sense of a Ṣūfī (q.v.) teacher.

QĀḌĪ. A judge in a *Sharīʿa* (q.v.) court.
QĀNŪN. A statement of administrative regulations in the Ottoman empire.

SAYYID. Literally, 'lord'. Used to signify a descendant of the Prophet, more specifically through al-Ḥusayn b. ʿAlī. See also *Sharīf*.
SHARĪʿA. The revealed Holy Law of Islam, derived in theory from the Qur'ān, *Ḥadīth* (q.v.), the consensus (*ijmāʿ*) of the *ʿulamā'*, and analogical reasoning (*qiyās*).

SHARĪF. Literally 'noble'. Used to signify a descendant of the Prophet, more specifically through al-Ḥasan b. 'Alī. See also *Sayyid*.
SHĪ'A. Literally 'party'. Originally the supporters of 'Alī's claims to the caliphate, the Shī'a evolved into the principal minority religious group of Muslims, with numerous branches including the Twelver Shī'a and the Ismā'īlīs.
SHĪ'Ī. A member of the Shī'a.
SIPAHI (Turkish, from Persian). In Persian a soldier. In the Ottoman state, a cavalryman, maintained by the grant of a *timar* (q.v.). From this term in Indian and North African usage are derived the English 'sepoy' and the French 'spahi'.
ṢŪFĪ. A Muslim mystic, more especially a member of a religious order (*ṭarīqa*), which has special liturgical and other practices as a means to mystical ecstasy.
SUNNĪ. A member of the majority group of Muslims (in contradistinction to the Shī'a), belonging to one of the four *madhhabs* (q.v.), which claim the authority of the *sunna* of the Prophet as transmitted in the *Ḥadīths* (q.v.).

TIMAR. The Turkish equivalent to *iqṭā'* (q.v.): in particular, the smallest type of Ottoman land-grant. See also *Sipahi*.

VILAYET. A province of the Ottoman empire.

WAQF (pl., *awqāf*). An endowment (usually of landed property) established for pious purposes (*waqf khayrī*), or for the benefit of the donor's family (*waqf ahlī*). In North Africa the equivalent term is *ḥubus*.

ZĀWIYA. A Ṣūfī convent.

INDEX

Note. al—: names *beginning* thus are indexed under the capital letter immediately following. Figures in bold indicate a main entry.

al-Mustanṣir, Hafsid ruler recognized as Caliph, 230
al-Muʿtaḍid, ʿAbbasid Caliph, 708, 748
al-Muʿtaḍid, of Seville, 421, 422, 423
mutakallimūn, **787–94**, 816, 817, 856; *see also* *kalām* theology
al-Muʿtamid, ʿAbbasid Caliph, 709
al-Muʿtamid, of Seville, 421, 423
al-Mutanabbī (Abu'l-Ṭayyib), 577, 578, 665
al-Muʿtaṣim, ʿAbbasid Caliph, 644, 709
al-Mutawakkil, ʿAbbasid Caliph, 499, 709
  reacts towards Sunnism, 570, 585
  as champion of orthodoxy, 594, 607, 789
al-Mutawakkil, of Morocco, 243
Muʿtazilites
  school of *kalām* of, 593–4, **788–94**, 811, 812
  in Spain, 416
  Ḥasan al-Baṣrī as founder of, 605, 788
  members of: al-Naẓẓām, 500; al-Jāḥiẓ, 578
  war of orthodoxy against, 607, 635
  rationalizing spirit of, 644, 645
  al-Kindī and, 786
  attacked by Ibn Ḥazm, 815
  also: 500, 504, 505, 531
Mutesa, Buganda ruler, 393
mutilation, as legal punishment, 498, 557
Muwallads (Muslims of Spanish origin), 409, 415
muwashshaḥ form of poetry, 666, 873, 875
al-Muẓaffar, *see* ʿAbd al-Malik al-Muẓaffar
Muẓaffar Khān, of Gujarāt, 26
Muẓaffar Shāh, of Malacca, 126
muzāraʿa (share-cropping contract), 519
Mwanga, Buganda ruler, 393
Mysore, India, 79
mysticism, 478, 480, 482, 597–8, **604–31**
  Javanese, 153, 156
  of Turkistān, 686
  Ibn Sīnā on, 808–9
  see also Sufism
Mzab, Kharijite towns of, 457
Mzabites, Muslim minority, 284

Nābī, 690
Nadhīr Aḥmad, 87
Nādir Shāh, 697, 847
Nadiyā, Bengal, 5
al-Nadr, 767
Nadwat al-ʿUlamā' (organization to bring old and new Islamic learning together), 88
Nagarkōt, 3
Nahdatul Ulama, Javanese reformist association, 194, 195, 202
Nā'ilī, 690
Naʿīmā, 693
Naimy, Mikhā'il (Nuʿayma), 669
Nā'īn, Persia, mosque at, 712, Pl. 9(b)
Nairobi, East Africa, 394
Najīb al-Dawla, Afghan chief, 70
Najīb Maḥfūẓ, 670
al-Najjār, 788
Nakodo Ragam, *see* Bulkiah
Namıq Kemāl, 694
Nānā Ṣāḥib, 80
Nānak, 61
naphtha, in siege warfare, 831
Naples, 434
Napoleon III, of France, 302
Napollon, Sanson, 257, 261
Naqqāsh Sinān Bey, 735
Naqshbandiyya order of Ṣūfīs, 630
  in India, 34
  Mujaddidiyya branch of, 63, 71
  in South-East Asia, 153, 173, 176
Nardin, battle of (1192), 5
Nasā'ī, collector of *Ḥadīths*, 591
Nāsikh, 698
al-Nāṣir, Almohad ruler, 427–8
Nāṣir al-Dīn, of West Bengal, 13, 24
Naṣīr al-Dīn al-Ṭūsī, *see* al-Ṭūsī
Nāṣir al-Dīn Maḥmūd, of Delhi, 6, 7, 24
Naṣīr Khān, of Khāndēsh, 27
al-Nāṣir Muḥammad b. Qalawun, Mamluk Sultan, 732
Nāṣir-i Khusraw, 586
naskhī style of calligraphy, 723, Pl. 20(a)
Naṣrallāh, 680
Nasrid dynasty, Granada, 428, 429–32, 725
nastaʿlīq style of calligraphy, 723, Pl. 20(a)
Naṭanz, Persia, mosque at 717, 728, Pls. 13(a), 23(b)
al-Nātilī, 781, 805
nation, definition of, 106
  confusion between religious community and, 473
National Mohammedan Association (Calcutta), 81
nationalism, 642, 643, 650, 653, 669
Navā'ī, *see* ʿAlī Shīr Navā'ī
Navarino, naval battle of (1827), 282, 289
Navarre, 417, 418
Navarro, Pedro, 249, 261
navies
  of Muslims, 27; Cordovan, 414; Aglabid, 433; Marinid, 429; Ottoman, 253; Algerian, 282; Tunisian, 289
  Castilian, 429
  Portuguese, 27
  Byzantine, 432–3, 435
  European, in Mediterranean, 253, 256
  American, 280

slaves (*cont.*)
trade in, 524; trans-Saharan, 236; Nubian, 336, 337; from Adamawa, 371; in Ibadan, 372; East African, 382, 389 391
Slavs
in Fatimid armies, 827
at Cordova, 413
as slaves to Muslims, 420–1, 516, 524
Sloot, Jan Albert, Dutch commander in Java, 150
Snouck Hurgronje, Christiaan, adviser to government of Dutch East Indies, 172, 173, 180–1, 187
social status, occupation and, 563
society
concern of reform movements with, 640, 642
origin of (al-Rāzī), 802
Soewardi Soerianingrat, *see* Dewantoro
Sofala, East Africa, 382
Sofia, 458
Sokoto, West Africa, 371, 372, 374, 386
British and, 381
soldiers, in Muslim cities, 522; *see also* armies
Solima people, Futa Jallon, 365
Somali coast, 383–5
Somali people, 359n, 384–5, 386, 394–5
as soldiers for Germans, 397
British attempts to provide schools for, 402–3
Somnāth, India, 3
Songhay people, middle Niger, 350, 351–4, 359–60
'Soninke Marabout' wars, 379
Soninke people, 346, 350, 352, 363
Sonni 'Alī, of Songhay, 352, 353, 354, 369
Sonni Baru, of Songhay, 352
soothsayers, as arbitrators in ancient Arabian law, 540
souls
doctrine of transmigration of, 508, 804
doctrine of immortality of, 807, 814, 816, 859
Ibn Sīnā's proof of existence of, 808
distinction between intellect and, 808, 810, 811
Sousse, North Africa, 438
South Africa, 404–5
South-East Asia, Islam in
to 18th century, 123–54
in 19th century, 154–81
in 20th century, 182–207
Spain
Muslims consider attack on, 214; Muslims invade, 406–9
Umayyad amirate and caliphate in, 409–20
Party Kingdoms in, 420–3, 428
Almoravids in, 223, 224, 349, 422, 423–4
Almohads in, 225, 424–9
kingdom of Granada in, 428, 429–32
Muslim trade through, 524
Islamic law in, 558
art and architecture in, 579, 710–11
Shu'ūbiyya in, 585
Arabic literature in, 666, 870–8
medicine in, 771–3
philosophy in, 814–21
contact between West and Muslim culture in, 852
Christian reconquest of, 408, 410, 428, 432
translations from Arabic into Latin in, 852–7
Spaniards
in the Philippines, 128, 129–30
in North Africa, 236, 238, 239, 242, 243, 268, 300, 320
specific gravity, determination of, 750, 757
Speelman, Admiral Cornelis, 139
Spice Islands (Moluccas), 133, 135–9
spice trade, 138, 524, 563
in pepper, from Acheh, 127, 178; from Bantam, 144
in cloves, from Ternate, 135, and Ambon, 136
Stack, Sir Lee, 342
stalactite in architecture, 718, 726, 729
state
Muslim, typically urban, sometimes nomadic, 463–5
development from prohibitive to repressive, 490
separation of *Umma* and, 491–2
Ibn Taymiyya on, 637
democratization of, 652
virtuous, of al-Fārābī, 796–8
Stephen of Antioch, 861
Stephen bar Ṣudhailē, 500
Stern, S. M., 875
Stoakes, Admiral John, 264
Stoics, 484
stucco
buildings ornamented with, 709, 713, 716–17, 724, 726, 731, Pls. 5(a), 7(b), 10(a)
miḥrābs of, 712, 714, 717, 727, Pls. 7(b), 9(b), 11, 15(a)
Suakin (Sawākin), Red Sea port, 327, 330, 342
Egyptians and, 337, 386
Sūba, Blue Nile, 327, 329, 330
al-Subkī, 590

Tokolor people, 347, 364, 366, 367, 377,
  under French, 305
  mosque at, 579, 725
tobacco, cultivation of, 361
Todar Mall, *dīwān* under Akbar, 56